FH

INDIVIDUAL
FAM
HIST

796459042

CORNISH HERITAGE

Map of Cornwall 1630 described by the travels of John Norden, augmented and published by I. Speed

CORNISH
HERITAGE

KEITH SKUES

WERNER SHAW • LONDON

To Janice for her patience, love and affection,
but not necessarily in that order.

ISBN 0 907961 00 2
© Keith Skues, 1983

First published 1983

Main text set in 10 on 12 pt Baskerville by
Universal Studio, 14-16, Hennessy Road,
Hong Kong.
Printed and bound in Hong Kong for Werner
Shaw Limited, Suite 34, 26, Charing Cross Road,
London WC2H 0HY by
Bright Sun Printing Press Co. Ltd.

BIRTHS

MARRIAGES

DEATHS

ILLUSTRATIONS

I am most grateful to the many members of the Skewes, Skewis, Skews, Skues and Skuse families for kindly loaning me portrait photographs from their own private collections for inclusion in *Cornish Heritage*. I should also like to acknowledge the following for allowing me to reproduce old prints and photographs:

The front cover is Porkellis Mine, Wendron. Reproduced by kind permission of Poldark Mining Company, Wendron, Cornwall.

Army Public Relations	542
Kenneth Bright	664
J.C. Burrow	112
Jill Carmichael	312, 576
City of Ballarat Municipal Libraries	253, 256
Gladys Clark	312, 546, 547
College of Arms	356-358
Cornwall County Council	351
Cornwall Local Studies Library, Redruth	144, 191, 202, 204, 210, 288
Roy Darlington	454
Duchy of Cornwall Office	351
Carol Jenkin	184
William John Kimble	664
Library of Congress	275
Oswald Pryor and Rigby Publishers	262
Registrar General	50, 64, 81
Royal Institution of Cornwall	103, 121, 152, 154, 232, 247
South Australian Archives	572
Peta-Anne Tenney	562
J.M.W. Turner	119

All other unacknowledged photographs (other than family portraits) where identification is not known have been taken by the author on location in England, Mexico, Australia, Canada and the United States of America.

Contents

Foreword
How It All Began

Let me say from the very beginning this is not a book about the history of Cornwall. Simply it is about a group of Cornish people who bore the same surname as myself and who farmed and mined in the county for generations. During the tin mining depression in the mid 1800's many migrated and emigrated, but wherever they lived they were justly proud of their Cornish background.

Thirty years ago I began our "family tree". To be perfectly honest I had no intention of making a book out of my findings. Genealogy had not really caught the imagination of the general public. I suppose Alex Haley must take a lot of credit with his book *Roots*. Since then the pastime has given so many more people an interest in their family background.

"What made you trace your family tree?" This has been the first question people have asked me from a genealogical point of view during the many years I have been compiling *Cornish Heritage*. "What a fascinating subject. You know, I have often wanted to write about our family, but it must take a very long time."

Yes indeed, it does take a very long time, and moreover a great deal of patience is required on the part of the researcher. Even more so, one has to have a genuine interest to delve into the past. I have spent many hours searching through ancient deeds and documents with no noticeable success. But let us go back to the beginning and the very first step which, in turn, resulted in the long chase to track down the various members of the family.

It all started in 1951 when I first attended the County Grammar School, Altrincham, Cheshire. Masters and fellow students insistently asked me as to the derivation of my unusual surname. Some thought it was German, others believed it had its origins in Scandinavia. At that time I had to admit I did not know.

On a visit to Manchester a year or so later, I happened by chance to call in at one of the city's large bookshops. And there to my surprise, indeed bewilderment, I noticed a book on the subject of angling. Nothing surprising in this, you may say? But the title of this book was *The Way of a Trout With A Fly*, written by G.E.M. Skues.

As soon as I arrived home in the evening I told my father of the "find." He, too, appeared a little surprised but remarked that during the Second World War a "Professor Skues" broadcast from the BBC (sound radio those days!) on angling. My father presumed the Skues — he did not recall his Christian name — to be a long distant relation as there were literally only a handful of people with our surname, and they were "few and far between."

This was one of the deciding factors in trying to find out a little more about our surname. Weeks after my encounter with the angling literature, I came across *Skuse's Complete Confectioner*, which added to the excitement. Yet another variation in the spelling appeared each week in the *Radio Times*. This was Dennis Scuse who was at the German end of "Two Way Family Favourites" from 1955 to 1958 and broadcasting to a weekly audience of 18,000,000 listeners. As well as being the "presenter", he was also Station Director of the British Forces Network in Germany. It was indeed coincidence that I should follow him to BFN in Cologne in 1959. He eventually joined the BBC and later Trident Television — as did I.

But we're jumping ahead. Let us go back to one Saturday morning during the summer of 1953 when I went along to the Central Reference Library in Manchester to look up the derivation of SKUES. In *Patronymica Cornu-Britannica* (Etymology of Cornish Surnames) — Charnock 1870, SKUES and SKUSE were referred to SKEWES.

From SKEWES (formerly SKEWIS in Crowan) or SKEWES (formerly SKEWYS in Cury) these names signify a shady place. From SKEZ, a shade or shadow. JOHN SKEWYS was Sheriff of the County of Cornwall in the 12th year of the reign of Henry VIII (1521).

For the time being I was happy. I could tell my colleagues at school from whence the name originated. Naturally the first move after gleaning this information was to personally visit Cornwall and find out even more. However, through one setback and another, this was not accomplished until four years later — in the summer of 1957. During these four years time was not wasted, as I came into correspondence with numerous people, including relations. Every telephone directory for this country and overseas was searched, along with hundreds of town guides. All entries of SKUES were noted.

A clue from a relation, the late Charles Ayre Mackenzie Skues said that the family originated from Helston, Cornwall, many generations ago. As all his records were lost during the last war he could give no further information as to who his ancestors were. Many more hours were spent searching through hundreds of pages of Phillimore's *Cornwall Parish Registers*, a copy of which was kept in Manchester Central Library, and I made a note of all variations in the spelling. Over 500 entries were logged which, in the main, date from 1538 to 1812. All these names, together with hundreds more transcribed from various parish registers in Cornwall, appear in Chapter Five.

Due to the pressure of studying (I was still at school) and moreover preparing to sit for the General Certificate of Education, the Skues affairs had to be temporarily shelved. When I left school in 1956 and started work in Manchester many of my lunch hours were spent in the Central Library looking through scores of reference books on the subject of genealogy and heraldry, and in particular history books relating to the county of Cornwall.

As one will appreciate, Manchester only has a limited amount of material dealing with Cornwall. Their speciality is Lancashire. The main books to do with Cornwall are kept in either libraries, museums or the County Record Office in Cornwall.

Time on the family history was again cut down towards the end of 1956, for in September that year I was elected secretary of a Cheshire youth club, and two months later became editor of *Youth Fellowship Times*. The latter took up most of my spare time.

During the summer of 1957 one of my wishes was to come true — a visit to Cornwall. I spent a fortnight in and around Helston, and this undoubtedly helped to sort out many outstanding problems to do with the family history.

A large percentage of the material which follows has been compiled from the original notes made in Cornwall visiting libraries, museums, town halls, County Record Office and churches. Many ancient deeds and documents were transcribed, as indeed a number of parish registers. True, this is not everyone's idea of a holiday — but it was mine!

Time had not been on my side since the days I commenced tracking down the Skues family, but there were to be more delays on the way. In 1958 I received my call-up papers for military service, so the family history came to another standstill. Whilst serving in the Royal Air Force I had entered into correspondence with some Skues' who were living in Australia. I had found their names in a Melbourne telephone directory. In American directories I had noted two families with our surname and had written to them.

Towards the end of 1958 I was posted to 229 Operational Conversional Unit at RAF Chivenor in North Devon. During my stay there I managed to pay a weekend visit to Helston and witnessed the famous Furry Dance.

In 1959 I was posted to Germany and attached to the British Forces Network in Cologne as an announcer — still serving in the RAF. There was no chance to further my family history studies.

Two years later I returned to Britain to visit the headquarters of the British Forces Network (now called British Forces Broadcasting Service) and also the Ministry of Defence where I secured a civilian commission as a staff announcer. During my brief stay in London I paid my first ever visit to the Public Record Office, the British Museum and Somerset House. As regards the latter, time did not allow me to search the entire registers (births, marriages and deaths) from their inauguration in 1837 to approximately nine months prior to my visit. But I did make a thorough search for all SKUES' registered at birth. Over a period of twenty years I have managed to collate all names and variations — SKEWES, SKEWIS, SKEWS, SKUES etc — all of which can be found in Chapter Four.

Whilst in London I purchased a tube of SKUSE's toothpaste. Sadly this brand now appears to have disappeared from the counters of chemists and supermarkets.

Shortly after my visit to BFN headquarters I was sent out to the desert of Kuwait in the Persian Gulf during a spot of trouble with Iraq in 1961. My job was to send programmes to Cyprus, Germany, Singapore, Aden, Kenya and other countries from where British troops had come, as well as linking into "Two Way Family Favourites". This was for a period of three months. I was then sent to British Forces Broadcasting Service in Nairobi, Kenya — even further away from Cornwall!

In 1963 I came back to Britain for a BBC course lasting three months at Broadcasting House, London. It was during this occasion in London that I obtained a reader's ticket for the Public Record Office and searched the Census Returns for the years 1841 and 1851. (See Chapter Thirteen).

I returned to Nairobi in time for Christmas, 1963 a few days after Independence. By March, 1964 the Ministry of Defence decided that they should close down the forces radio station in Nairobi, and I was transferred to Aden where I remained until July, 1964. I did not take too kindly to the political climate so I decided to resign from BFN as they could not offer me an alternative posting. So I returned to England to try my luck.

I did not have to look around very long, for "within minutes" of arriving in London I was offered a job as a disc jockey aboard Radio Caroline, which operated from a ship moored off the Essex coast. We worked two weeks on board, followed by a week's holiday. It was then that my research on the Skues family took on a new lease of life. On average I spent four of my seven days' break scanning the Census Returns for 1861 and rechecking my searches through 1841 and 1851 at the Public Record Office in London. All these returns were handwritten and arranged by areas — not in alphabetical order. There was no name index.

In 1964 I became a member of the Society of Genealogists who have their headquarters at 37, Harrington Gardens, London SW7 4JX. The Society was founded in 1911 and originally operated out of the Strand, but now it occupies three floors of a house of character near to Gloucester Road.

Reference has been made earlier to correspondence I had with some Skues' from Australia. In 1964 I was fortunate in meeting up with a Miss Margaret Skues from Melbourne, Australia. Margaret, who had the same Christian name as my late sister, was on a working holiday from Australia. Lots of useful information was exchanged, like the coincidence of names. A similarity arose between "their side" and "our side" — for example our mothers both had the Christian name Doris, and close relations were John, Florence and Jack.

Margaret Skues of England (left) meets Margaret Skues of Australia. Looking on: Keith Skues

Just as everything was going along fine, delays were just around the corner. In October, 1964 I was involved in an accident whilst on board Radio Caroline when a metal stake broke loose during a force 10 gale and somehow managed to splinter into my right eye. This put me out of action for three months. After a spell in hospital in Harwich and Colchester, Essex I eventually returned to work in 1965, but even up to one year after the accident I found my eye particularly weak. I certainly could not read small print, so writing was kept to a minimum.

In January, 1966 I joined Radio Luxembourg as a disc jockey where I had my own show, and throughout 1966 I sorted out thousands of sheets of paper relating to the family history, many of which had become duplicated over the years. Eventually a filing system was instigated, together with a card index for names. To say the least it was confusing to find 240 people called John Skewes!

It was during 1966 that I read a book by Nevil Shute called *No Highway*. Imagine my surprise when I came across a Mr SKUES appearing in the text. In Chapter Four the particular part of the story takes place at Gander Airport in Newfoundland when a Mr Dobson talks to a Mr Symes about odd people they had encountered:

> My Symes grunted: 'You get some funny sort of people coming from those places. Remember SKUES in the Air Worthiness at Farnborough, back in 1928 or so? No — before your time. He always used to take his Siamese cat with him, in the offices, or into conferences — everywhere he went he took this blessed cat . . .'

I appreciate *No Highway* is a novel and that all characters are fictitious, but an interesting point is that not too far away from Gander Airport George Edward Mackenzie Skues was born in 1856 and four years later Mary Isabella Mackenzie Skues, son and daughter of Brigade Surgeon and Mrs William Mackenzie Skues who were married in Newfoundland in 1857.

In 1967 I joined the BBC in London as an announcer, and in my off-duty hours was able to spend many happy days at the Society of Genealogists which, in turn, gave me the opportunity of adding a section dealing with "Boyd's Marriage Index" (Chapter Eleven).

Since then I have annually taken my holidays in Cornwall and been able to keep up to date with the comings and goings of people in the various branches of the family. I have not just confined my research to the SKUES branches, although initially I traced all people with that spelling. But as the years rolled by I accounted for thousands of SKEWES, SKEWIS and SKEWS. I would also have dearly liked to have traced the families of SCUSE, SKUCE and SKUSE.

Over the years I have been compiling this book I have learned not only a great deal about my own particular surname, but about all Cornish names. History becomes far more interesting when we read and learn about our long lost ancestors and the part they played in the making of it.

By 1974 when I had moved to Sheffield, South Yorkshire as Director of Programmes for Radio Hallam, I had struck up correspondence with members of the family as a whole all over the world, and my intention was to try and trace as many of their ancestors back to Cornwall as was possible.

In the summer of 1979 I visited Mexico, Canada and the United States of America. Of all the Skewes' (and all variations in spelling) I had the great pleasure of meeting, *all* had descended from Cornish families. The majority had emigrated from Cornwall during the tin mining depression in the mid-1800's either to become farmers in the Mid-west of America, or miners in California and Mexico. George Owen Skewes of Escondido, California gave me many facts and figures as well as photographs of his particular branch from Mexico.

Had I commenced my research some twenty years later my job would have been made much easier, for the Church of Latter Day Saints in Salt Lake City have documented family records from all over the world. Salt Lake City was outlawed in 1890, when some 25,000 Mormons were believed to be practising polygamy. Now nearly a century later the city boasts the best genealogical centre in the world with 130,000 volumes of family tress, 900,000 catalogued rolls of microfilmed documents and 7 million family group records. And that's not all. There is a consultation service, a research survey service, church records, a computer file index and instructional aids. Within 20 seconds I was shown 500 Skewes' from Cornwall — information which I had in my records, but which had taken me many years to collate.

The Americans and Mexicans went to so much trouble to make my job of research that much easier. They produced old diaries and photographs and in some cases letters dating back over a century. To list all the families who made me very welcome would fill another twenty pages, but worthy of mention are: Dorothy Skewis of Iowa, USA; Alice Eve Kennington (née Skewes) of Maryland, USA; Alice Ruth Skewes Ford of Lexington, Kentucky, USA; Frank Skewis, Jack Skewes and Jim Skewes of Seattle, Washington, USA; John B. Skewes of Salt Lake City, USA; Arthur Russel Skewes of Lexington, Kentucky, USA; Guillermo Skewes and his many cousins in Mexico; Hetty Louise Davies (née Skewes) of Toronto, Canada; the numerous Skewes' of Hamilton, Ontario, Canada and Ann Marie Skewes of Toronto, Canada.

In January, 1981 I spent a stimulating three weeks in Australia and began to tackle an almost impossible mission in meeting up with 500 or so Skewes' and Skues'. I had been in correspondence with a handful of the family, but there was no real enthusiasm until I arrived in the country. Their hospitality was overwhelming.

Within minutes of my arrival I appeared on 6PM news in Perth, Western Australia. Norman and Marge Campbell bore the brunt of taking phone calls concerning the Skewes family and I thank them, as indeed the Chubb family, Colin Nicol, Edith Mary Blair, Cath Grosvenor and the numerous Skewes' I had the pleasure of meeting in Western Australia.

From there to New South Wales and Sydney, Tamworth and Watsons Creek. Thanks here go out to Veronica and Noel Skewes for organising a Skewes reunion when no less than 92 members of the family turned up to greet me. I was very flattered. Watsons Creek is a very small hamlet miles from anywhere, but people travelled hundreds of miles to say "good day." Thence to Uralla, the home of William and Elizabeth Skewes, who had come out from Cornwall and married in Sydney in August, 1856. Some of their descendants still live in Uralla and it was a pleasure to meet Mesdames Couchman, Bullen, Nelson and Barnden (all née Skewes) and their families.

In Sydney Jill and Kevin Carmichael went to great trouble to see that I had plenty of information about the Skewes' of Watsons Creek and Tamworth. Likewise June Dally Watkins.

Melbourne, Victoria was an impressive city where I enjoyed meeting Doctor Kenneth Frederick Skues and his family. Also Jack and Doris Skues, Mervyn Leigh Skues and his brother John Leslie Skues. It was also in Melbourne that three variations in spelling of our surname came together — Clarence George Skewes, Eric Skuse and the writer, Richard Keith Skues.

Left to right: Keith Skues, Eric Skuse and George Skewes at Mitcham, Victoria, Australia, January 1981

In Ballarat, Victoria, famed for its gold, Doctor David Buick Skewes and his family were hospitable, as were Glenleigh Bertie William Skewes and his sizeable family in Sebastopol. Glen was kind enough to let me copy out extracts from a fascinating diary he kept whilst a prisoner-of-war in Thailand, which can be found in the Appendix.

In 1980 a Geoff Skewes arrived in Britain from Australia. News soon reached me through the music business and we met up and exchanged notes. So it was good to see Geoff on his home ground "down under", together with his wife Donna Louise and son Grayson Paul.

Dot and Garfield Skewes of Adelaide herded together many of the Skewes' who descended from Moonta, Kadina and Wallaroo, three mining towns on the Yorke Peninsula in South Australia. They were very generous in devoting a lot of time to drive me hundreds of miles to meet many different Skewes' as well as visiting the old copper mines where their ancestors used to work.

Warren Skewes contacted the media whilst I was in Tamworth, New South Wales. To be absolutely honest I was staggered by the reception I was given right across Australia by the media and I thank all those television, radio and newspaper journalists who were kind enough to give me air time and columns in their journals.

I should like to thank most sincerely everyone who has kindly been of assistance during the last 30 years. It is impossible to mention them all by name. Many have now sadly passed on. I should, however, like to thank all those members of the Skewes/Skewis/Skews/Skues and Skuse families all over the world for supplying me with such valuable information. I can only hope that I have done them justice.

The "thanks department" takes in a wide variety of people ranging from the Post Office, for letting me look through their old telephone directories, to the editors of newspapers who have allowed me to freely reproduce facts.

I am grateful to the many young ladies over the years who have typed letters and other information — Barbara, Margaret, Carole, Rachel, Maureen, April, Dianne and Vicky, although I have to admit I had to type the manuscript of *Cornish Heritage*, which seemed to take forever; especially the regular updating. Much of the work was done at the Lugger Hotel, Portloe, Cornwall between 1974 and 1981 when I took my annual holidays, and I owe the Powell family a few pints for allowing me the use of an office so that I could thump away at the keys until the early hours of the morning without annoying other paying guests.

Portloe, Cornwall

It has been a difficult job in tracing old photographs and prints and I am indebted to the many people who have brought out amazing material from their bottom drawers. I should also like to acknowledge the talents of Christopher Seaman, well-known Sheffield photographer, who has shown considerable expertise in copying a wide selection of old prints.

Much help came from the County Record Office, Truro, The Royal Institution of Cornwall, The British Library, The General Registry, Somerset House, Public Record Office, clergy and library staff of towns and villages in Cornwall, and further afield. To the owners of the various SKEWES and TRESKEWES farms who have let me trample over their property to take photographs. To anyone else who has contributed in any way to make this book possible — a very big "thank you." Certainly the staff of Radio Hallam, Sheffield who have allowed me to take annual leave to faraway countries in pursuit of long lost ancestors.

Carol Currie, Stuart Beresford, Barry Shaw, Ros and Fred Boulden, Jim Kelly, Leo Leung and colleagues at the *Morning Telegraph*, Sheffield have been most encouraging to ensure I did not have too many idle moments in the designing and layout of the book.

I am pleased to say that genealogy has never been a more popular pastime, with more and more families writing books and compiling their family histories. Long may it continue.

Had time allowed I should have liked to describe in more detail how one actually encounters problems, but more important how those problems are eventually solved, whether it be obtaining permission to look through a parish register or making an application for a reader's ticket to the Public Record Office.

I well remember writing to one family in Britain who, unbeknown to me, had had a recent bereavement. All photographs and family documents had been given to the refuse collector less than a week previously...

Or the family who thought I was a tax collector and refused to let me chat or ask questions and told me to write. This I did enclosing a stamped-addressed envelope. The letter was written in 1969 with a reminder the following year, and guess what? I am still awaiting a reply...

Or trying to communicate with the Skewes' of Chile and Mexico, who spoke little or no English, and I spoke no Mexican or Spanish. Initially my letters in English received no attention. But thanks to Ann Garlick of Sheffield for translating letters into Mexican and Chilean Spanish and for getting the ball rolling...

Or of almost completing a family tree dating back 250 years, but not being given information concerning today's children. This happened time and time again in overseas countries where families did not answer letters and reminders...

Or of the considerable number of Skewes'/Skues' who were in no way co-operative and said they had more important things to worry about than from where their surname came. "It's no good going back in history as you'll only find skeletons!" or "We don't want our dirty washing hung out in public."

I have been disappointed in the people who have denied who they are. On more than a dozen occasions I can recollect writing to people and asking them to confirm a particular date of birth or marriage. Came back the reply "You must have got the wrong person. I never married so and so..." or "Those were not my parents' names and I was not born on such a date." Of course nowadays it is quite easy to track down whether or not they are telling fibs. A certificate from the General Register Office in London will reveal all! On a few occasions I have been threatened with court action if I print certain information relating to a family. Of course I respect people's wishes... if they play ball with me. However, if one is compiling a factual history of a family or families, names cannot be left out, although personal information can be if requested. Wherever possible I have tried to oblige the person who has specifically asked that certain personal details be omitted.

Just as this book was being completed I received a phone call from an auctioneer in Doncaster to say that a 19th century medical box was being put under the hammer in June, 1981. It was inscribed W.M. Skues, M.D. It had belonged to William Mackenzie Skues, a Brigade Surgeon and was dated 1855. I went along to the auction and was fortunate in "buying it back" into the family. It was in remarkable condition, made of mahogany with brass surrounds. The medical instruments have now

A good 'buy' at a Doncaster auction

been replaced by family heirlooms all neatly stored in a valuable depository within the medical box.

In a book of this nature the index is as valuable as the general text. People researching family histories always check an index first to see if the information they are seeking is referred to in the book. This index is long and detailed.

I began way back in 1978 with a simple card index which grew at such an alarming rate that I almost had to move out of my flat as the cards were taking up so much space.

But we live in a technological age. I began to think of the vehicle licensing people at Swansea who had computerised millions of driving and vehicle licences. Could 10,000 Skewes' be done in a similar way?

I spoke with a colleague, who is also chief engineer at Radio Hallam in Sheffield — Derrick Connolly, a knowledgable gent who has written a number of different programmes for his computer. "Yes", he replied and emerged two weeks later with a suitable programme. He even lent me his "kit" and during the five weeks which followed I fed thousands of names and places into the computer. To say this was the most boring part of 30 years' work would be an understatement. However, the end product was worth the effort. My thanks to Derrick for giving me an insight into the world of computers.

This book is not a novel. It is fact. No poetic licence has been issued. My critics may say that certain sections of this book are dull and uninteresting, even boring. I make no apologies. Lists of names may appear boring, but they are important to a family history. On showing the "Parish Registers" chapter to an acquaintance he remarked "You should have called your book 'Not so much a story, but what a cast'!"

A book of this nature is out of date from the very second it is published. New information comes through the post daily. Only this month I have received much information concerning a branch of the family of Skews from Liskeard who emigrated to New Zealand and another branch who emigrated to Queensland, Australia.

As I write this Foreword news has reached me of a Ted Skuse, solicitor from Alice Springs, Australia who, in his job, was defending a client in a courtroom when a gunman ran in and shot him with a .22 pistol. Fortunately he survived the attack, but he had also experienced bad luck the previous year when he witnessed his house totally destroyed as Cyclone Tracy demolished the property around his ears.

I learned of a property up for sale called Skewes in Nansladron, Cornwall (a branch of the family had lived there from 1750 to 1850). Deeds and documents shown to me by the owners would have been of interest to the chapter "In a Skewes Manor".

A new international darts champion received much publicity towards the end of 1982 — Tony Skuse, although many papers spelt his name Skues.

St. Austell's newest estate agent came into the news in October, 1982 — Derek Skuse. All this information was too late to include in the main text of *Cornish Heritage*.

Whether I had decided to put a deadline on the text in 1960 or 1980, new information would always come to light.

More delays happened in the summer of 1982 when the manuscript of *Cornish Heritage* was stolen from my car. Fortunately the master copy was held in Hong Kong, but it did take a while to obtain a duplicate set and a further three months to check the proofs. It's simply amazing how many rogue printing errors creep in when your back is turned.

But all dramas were not confined to the United Kingdom. The book was printed in Hong Kong. Little could happen there — or could it? In this exotic centre in the Far East work is progressing on the Mass Transit underground railway, with tunnelling in operation between Hong Kong Central and Causeway Bay. As 1983 dawned much of Hennessy Road collapsed and disappeared downwards for 20 feet or more. This enormous hole (yes, police were looking into it!) was some 30 feet long and right outside the building where the master copy of *Cornish Heritage* was under lock and key. All adjacent buildings were evacuated. Fortunately no damage was done to the artwork, but it gave me a few more grey hairs.

The main purpose of this book has been to collate information regarding a family from the Middle Ages up to 1980. When someone comes to compile the Skewes family history in 100 years time, I hope that much of this material will prove useful.

I will naturally maintain updated files on the family throughout the world.

The family as a whole may not have produced any kings, queens, prime ministers, statesmen or internationally known figures. It is a typical middle/working class family whose members have expressed joy with the arrival of a new born baby, celebrated a wedding, mourned a loss in the family or gone through the painful time of divorce, or faced tragic circumstances when a son or daughter has taken his or her own life or been killed in an accident. Others have suffered through two world wars.

It has been a fascinating 30 years tracing the roots one Cornish family. A hobby, which, incidentally, has cost thousands of pounds over the years. But with a hobby cost is not important. What really matters at the end of the day is job satisfaction, and I have certainly had my fair share of that. It has also given me the opportunity of visiting countries in which otherwise I would not have set foot... the United States of America... Hong Kong... Canada... South Africa... Mexico and Australia. It has given me the great joy of meeting so many hundreds of Cornishmen and women and their descendants scattered throughout the world, but all of whom are proud to learn of their "Cornish Heritage."

To rearrange a well known phrase or saying, "It's the game of the name."

KEITH SKUES
April, 1983

SHEFFIELD
South Yorkshire,
England.

1 An Introduction to Surnames

THE STORY of our surnames is of extraordinary convincible charm, for we all have a genuine interest in knowing who our ancestors were, and tracing them back as far as possible. It is only human nature to feel delighted at being descended from a long line of distinguished and noble gentry. However, it is still no less a matter of interest to trace a family history if the ancestors were members of the more humble walks of life, and were not in the least distinguished at all. To delve into the past and chase through musty records, deeds, documents, old diaries, wills, ancient letters and more recently photographs and press cuttings is, to a large number of people, far from a waste of time and energy. In fact it can lend itself to a most fascinating hobby and pastime.

From the study of surnames we learn a great deal about the Middle Ages, which would otherwise remain hidden and indistinct. History is actually turned through its revealing light. It divulges the personal and intimate affairs of our grandfathers in bygone centuries; it discloses their loves and hates; their fears and superstitions; their habits and occupations.

To really appreciate how our surnames came into being we must remember the circumstances that were dominant in England after the Norman Conquest which lasted from 1066 to 1072. From all parts of the world, especially France, Scandinavia and the Low Countries, priests, traders and those seeking adventure simply flocked into this country in their thousands. Every boat which pulled into our ports brought more and more people who wanted a new life. The feudal system which had been brought into force in England by William the Conqueror changed conditions both economically and socially. Feudalism lay in the two ideas that every man had certain rights over his social inferiors and certain duties towards his superiors, and that those rights and duties were determined in every case by the position he held on the land.

The men of the district banded themselves together to protect each other against invaders under the leadership of the principal land-owner of the district, who became their lord, and they became his vassals. These lords banded themselves together in the same way and became vassals of more powerful lords who, in turn, were vassals of the King, who was ultimately responsible for justice.

Form the King all land was held directly or indirectly, and the head vassals (or tenants-in-chief) were granted large areas of land. These were usually Barons and Earls, and under the tenants-in-chief were mesne-tenants (sub tenants & knights) who held land from some lord other than the King. These mesne-tenants were usually lords of manors. Below them were various classes who were not free men, the best known being villeins (meaning a villager), who had to perform certain military duties.

There was a complicated system of feudal dues and of forced labour. For the privilege of working on his own particular strips of land, the villein had to farm on his lord's land on certain days of the week. This was known as demesne. In turn, each vassal had to render to his own lord as much military service as he held knights fees. A "family tree" of feudalism can be drawn up as follows: —

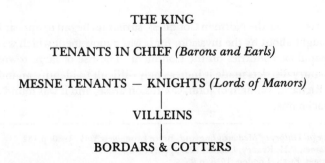

THE KING
|
TENANTS IN CHIEF *(Barons and Earls)*
|
MESNE TENANTS — KNIGHTS *(Lords of Manors)*
|
VILLEINS
|
BORDARS & COTTERS

Feudalism was based upon the assumption that every man and woman had a place to which he or she belonged, and generally speaking it proved quite a strong defence in the time of war.

Vassals were expected to work in their fields at their own cost for forty days a year.

When a vassal died his fief did not automatically descend to his son through performance of homage. The son had to pay a kind of inheritance tax, styled relief.

Should a vassal fail in his feudal obligations, the lord confiscated his fief. Should he die without a male heir the fief reverted to the lord, who could dispose of it as he wished.

When a vassal died leaving a young son, the lord acted as the guardian of this minor, until he was old enough to become a knight and fulfill his feudal obligations.

During a vassal's life, or after his death, the lord's permission had to be obtained for marriage. If a vassal died, the lord became guardian and married the heiress off to the most suitable man with the highest bid.[1]

The development of the feudal system made it essential that the king should know exactly what service each knight owed. Payments to and by the exchequer required that debtors and creditors should be particularised. The lawyers saw to it that the parties to transfers of land or those concerned in criminal proceedings could be definitely identified. Monasteries drew up surveys and extents with details of tenants of all classes and their services and later the net was thrown wider in the long lists of those assessed in the Subsidy Rolls. It was the official who required exact identification of the individual. His early efforts often consisted of long-winded descriptions attached to a personal name. Any description which definitely identified the man was satisfactory — his father's name, the name of his land or a nickname known to be his. The upper classes — mostly illiterate — were those with whom the officials were chiefly concerned, and among them surnames first became numerous and hereditary.[2]

Feudal tenures were abolished by statute in this country in 1660, although from 1495 they had been practically inoperative.

In France the system remained in existence until the revolution in 1789. There was a feudal system in Japan as late as 1871. But back to our family names...

English speech was represented by many dialects, chief of which was northern, southern and midlands. Though these dialects had a great deal in common they were yet so different that a Wessex man found it very difficult to make himself understood by a Northumbrian person. In the 13th century there were six languages spoken in the British Isles — English, Cornish, Gaelic, Welsh, Irish and French besides a little Hebrew, Manx and Norse. For use in legal records Latin was the recognised language.

The sources from which early surnames may be obtained include manuscript records, although these (and even some contemporary ones) are not always true, due to incorrect spelling which is not always preserved. For that difficulty there is little or no remedy, unless other examples of the name can be found, or the words forming it be identified. This want of standard orthography combined with misreadings on the part of copyists (not at all unusual) has led to many strange and curious variants being handed down in the list of names.

Originally all names were words, and exactly in the same way we can express a given statement by more than one combination of words, so formerly the identification of a person by alternative designations, the meaning remaining the same, was a common practice calling for little or no comment.[3]

Almost immediately after the Norman Conquest, surnames began to appear in this country, and this was not only brought about by the invasion, for it was a movement which was already spreading through the more populous countries on the Continent. The rise of large towns, and the growing population in the country districts made it increasingly difficult to identify an individual who bore a Christian name like Richard, William or John. Confusion arose, and it was found more convenient to confer upon him a nickname.

---

[1] *A Constitutional and Legal History of Medieval England*, Bryce Lyon, New York, 1980, p.132.

[2] *Origin of English Surnames*, P.H. Reaney; London 1967, pp.314-315.

[3] *Origin of British Surnames*, Ewan, London, 1938, p.85.

The unsettled state of surnames during these early days makes it quite a difficult problem to trace a pedigree of any family beyond the 13th century.

In England, family names were first introduced by the Norman barons. The practice became fashionable and gradually spread to the lords of smaller manors. The system was found useful by officials and lawyers who gradually extended it to men who held no land, naming them by reference to their father, by a nickname or from their place of residence, often varying the description, until in time the combined influence of fashion and convenience provided all men with a fixed surname.

Throughout this long period the process continued at different rates not only in separate parts of the country but also among varying classes.

From the 12th century there is steady increase in the growth of family names among the land-holders, at the same time with considerable variation of name. Up to the year 1200 the peasant had no fixed surnames, but there are signs of their development from about 1225 and they become steadily more common as the century advanced and were in fairly general use about 100 years later. The north was less advanced than the south, and here many surnames, even amongst the landed gentry, did not become hereditary until about 1380, some not until after 1400.[4]

The people in outlying districts still clung to the old habit of using baptismal names centuries after surnames had been in use. A great many of these baptismal names are the surnames of today such as Andrew-s, William-s, Richard-s, Roger-s, Peter-s, Matthew-s, Mark-s, Frank-s, Stephen-s and Robert-s. Others did not incorporate the "s" at all, for example George, Henry, Arthur, Bernard, Bertram, Floyd, Howard and Jeffery.

One of the most important documents listing names in the 11th century is the Domesday Book compiled by William the Conqueror (William I) in the year 1086. Throughout the many pages of this invaluable record, it tells us who were the landowners under Edward the Confessor in 1066 right up to the date it was prepared. Its contents have proved a "gold mine" to investigators, and has enabled them to solve many difficult problems that would otherwise have defied solutions.

Domesday Book contains the names of thousands of persons, and the places where they lived, all of which have been written down phonetically in Norman French. The names of the people mentioned in the book were, in the main, Normans or foreigners whom William the Conqueror had brought into England, and only a minority of people living today have ever traced their descent from any of these Domesday tenants. In the Exeter section of Domesday Book the nearest resemblance to Skewes is ESCEUUIT. The author of an article on Cornish surnames writing in the *West Briton* (26 November 1959) associated this name with the Skewes family.

Compiled two centuries later than the Domesday Book, *The Hundred Rolls* is a record of a similar kind and equally as valuable. It appeared in 1323 when Angevin kings ruled the greater part of France as well as England, and the French had displaced the Norman dialect as the language of the court and ruling classes.

Other records of interest are *State Rolls, Pipe Rolls, Patent Rolls, Charter Rolls, Fine Rolls, Writs of Parliament* and *Inquisitions Post Mortem*. There are many more minor records, all of which cover a period of about 250 years from the middle of the 12th century. Entries of Skewes, Skywys, Skewis etc taken from these various "rolls" can be found in the Appendix.

Many people today are under the impression that genealogy, topography and heraldry is a new and fascinating encounter. There are more books available on family history than ever before, and during the 1970's genealogy became one of the most popular hobbies for a family in which to become actively involved.

But genealogy is nothing new. Proof enough is the written word, and what better example than the Bible. We find a "family tree" in the first book of the Old Testament — Genesis, Chapter 5 verses 1-32:

> This is the book of the generations of Adam. In the day that God created man, in the likeness of God made he him;
> Male and female created he them; and blessed them, and called their name Adam, in the day when they were created.

---

[4]*Origin of English Surnames*, P.H. Reaney; London 1967; p.315

And Adam lived an hundred and thirty years, and begat a son in his own likeness, after his image; and called his name Seth.

And the days of Adam after he had begotten Seth were eight hundred years; and he begat sons and daughters.

And all the days that Adam lived were nine hundred and thirty years: and he died.

And Seth lived an hundred and five years, and begat Enos:

And Seth lived after he begat Enos eight hundred and seven years, and begat sons and daughters.

And all the days of Seth were nine hundred and twelve years: and he died.

And Enos lived ninety years, and begat Cainan:

And Enos lived after he begat Cainan eight hundred and fifteen years, and begat sons and daughters.

And all the days of Enos were nine hundred and fifteen years: and he died.

And Cainan lived seventy years and begat Mahalaleel:

And Cainan lived after he begat Mahalaleel eight hundred and forty years, and begat sons and daughters.

And the days of Cainan were nine hundred and ten years: and he died.

And Mahalaleel lived sixty and five years and begat Jared:

And Mahalaleel lived after he begat Jared eight hundred and thirty years, and begat sons and daughters: And all the days of Mahalaleel were eight hundred ninety and five years: and he died.

And Jared lived an hundred sixty and two years, and he begat Enoch:

And Jared lived after he begat Enoch eight hundred years, and begat sons and daughters.

And all the days of Jared were nine hundred sixty and two years: and he died.

And Enoch lived sixty and five years and begat Methuselah:

And Enoch walked with God after he begat Methuselah three hundred years, and begat sons and daughters.

And all the days of Enoch were three hundred sixty and five years.

And Enoch walked with God: and he was not; for God took him.

And Methuselah lived an hundred eighty and seven years, and begat Lamech.

And Methuselah lived after he begat Lamech seven hundred eighty and two years, and begat sons and daughters.

And all the days of Methuselah were nine hundred sixty and nine years: and he died.

And Lamech lived an hundred eighty and two years, and begat a son:

And he called his name Noah, saying This same shall comfort us concerning our work and toil of our hands because of the ground which the LORD hath cursed.

And Lamech lived after he begat Noah five hundred ninety and five years, and begat sons and daughters.

And all the days of Lamech were seven hundred and seven years; and he died.

And Noah was five hundred years old: and Noah begat Shem, Ham and Japheth.

Here we have eleven generations; one has to admit there were cases of longevity and certainly not to be seen in modern "pedigrees."

Although the spelling of the English language has been made uniform, no attempt has been made to normalise the spelling of surnames.

The modern form of very many of our surnames is due to the spelling of some 16th or 17th century parson or clerk, or even to one of a later date. It is not a matter of illiteracy in our sense of the word. These parsons who kept the parish registers were men of some education. Their ability to read cannot be questioned, but they had no guide as to the spelling of names. Of the many generations of people who lived and died in Great Britain, only an infinitely small proportion have ever had their names recorded in print. The short and simple annals of the poor were limited to entries of birth, marriage and death.

Their names were given to the clerk orally and he put them into writing as best he could. They would be written down phonetically, using his own system of spelling, sometimes spelling the same name in different ways at different times, and it is this variation in spelling which often gives us the clue to the real origin and meaning of the surname.[5]

Forty to fifty per cent of our surnames were derived from place names and topographical features. According to the Census of 1881, there were approximately 16,000 parishes, townships and hamlets in England, and each of these must have covered a number of localities, like fields and buildings known by distinct names, any of which might have served to describe a person working or dwelling in or about the same. The possible sources for names of the local class therefore will run well into a million or so.[6]

---

[5] *Origin of English Surnames*, P.H. Reaney (1967, London), p.25.
[6] *Origin of British Surnames*, Ewan, ibid.

The names of towns, villages and estates all add to the long list which must include craft and trade names, baptismal names, official names, pageant names, nicknames and surnames taken from the Bible. We find surnames taken from flowers, birds, animals, fishes, mountains, streams, as well as the wood, the dale and every other feature of the countryside.

In Cornwall there are more local surnames proportionately than in any other part of the country, and in general they are most distinctive, although owing to corrupt orthography, the signification is not very easily determined with certainty.

If one were researching Cornish surnames perhaps a first guide would be to the rhyming couplet:
"By TRE, ROS, CAR, LAN, POL and PEN
You will know all Cornishmen."

>   TRE — denotes home, village, farm or town.
>   ROS — moor, heath, peninsula.
>   CAR — enclosed space, fort.
>   LAN — enclosure, monastic cell, church.
>   POL — pool, anchorage.
>   PEN — headland, top.

But that list, although a basic guide, is far from complete. Here are some popular Cornish surnames without any of the abovementioned prefixes.

ANGOVE, BECKERLEG, BLAMEY, BOLITHO, CHEGWIDDEN, CRAGO, CURNOW, EDDY, FOXWELL, GEACH, GOLDSWORTHY, GRYLLS, GUNDRY, HENDY, HOCKING, HOSKING, IVEY, JASPER, JEWELL, JOSE, KEAST, KNEEBONE, LAITY, LIDDICOAT, LORY, LUGG, MOYLE, NANCE, OATES, ODGERS, OPIE, PASCOE, PEARN, PRISK, PROUSE, RETALLACK, ROWSE, RULE, SPARGO, UREN, VENNING and YELLAND.

Throughout the coming chapters we follow another Cornish surname, SKEWES, and its variations.

2 Origin of SKEWES

THE NAME SKEWES/SKEWIS/SKEWS/SKUES derives from the county of Cornwall and was very popular in the Camborne, Redruth and Helston districts which are situated in the western part of the county. However, there was a family by that name residing in the parish of St Wenn near Bodmin in the 14th and 15th centuries.

From time immemorial the SKEWES' have held and been proud of their respectable name. During the 18th and 19th centuries it was rated as one of the more popular Cornish surnames.

Sir Thomas Cox, solicitor and J.P. adopted the name SKEWES alongside his own surname in 1874 and descendants of his family are still known as SKEWES-COX.

Of the many thousands of SKEWES' the author has come across either in print or in person only two in Great Britain have changed their name by authority.

WHITEHALL, 12 March 1827.

"The King has been pleased to give and grant unto RICHARD SKUES of Devonport, in the county of Devon, Deputy Steward in his Majesty's Coinages in Cornwall and Devon, and unto Susannah Maria Martha his wife, only surviving child of John Scott of Saltash, in the county of Cornwall, Esq., sometime a Principal Officer in His Majesty's Dockyard at Devonport, aforesaid, deceased, His Royal licence and authority, that they may henceforth, in order to testify their grateful respect to the aforementioned John Scott, instead of that of SKUES, and that the said RICHARD SKUES may also bear the arms of Scott only; such arms being first duly exemplified according to the laws of arms, and recorded in the Herald's Office, otherwise the said licence and permission to be void and of none effect. And also to command that the Royal concession and declaration be registered in His Majesty's College of Arms."

Notice is hereby given that MARION SKUSE of 8, Exley Bank, Salterhebble, Halifax, in the county of York, Spinster and British Subject, resident of the United Kingdom assume the name of Stewart. Dated 13 January 1945. [1]

An unofficial name change was that of WILLIAM JOHN SKEWES of Helston (born 26 May 1850) who married Louisa Emma Jarvis of Bangor and changed the family name to Williams, and moved north to Sheffield, South Yorkshire.

In the United States of America EDWARD SKEWIS, son of JAMES EDWARD SKEWIS legally changed his name to Brown early this century. JOHN MARTIN SKEWES of America changed his name to James Patterson in 1920.

It is now well and truly understood, especially among genealogists, that no one family can go on forever. It seems a sort of legal maxim that eventually the direct male line will "die out." Although the Skewes family was at its peak, as far as actual numbers are concerned, from 1750 to 1900, there is every chance that the SKUES spelling may become extinct with the next hundred years. Since 1900 the majority of Skues' who have been born were females, and not unnaturally married, thus losing the name SKUES. By 1980 the number of males left to "carry on the line" could be counted on one hand. However, this is not the case of SKEWES, SKEWIS, SKEWS and SKUSE.

The name SKEWES, originally spelt SKEWYS and SKYWYS, is taken from the Cornish word Skez or Skeu meaning "a shade or shadow" — "a sheltered place."

Says Barber's *British Family Names* — "It's a local name from Cornwall or Dutch Schüss, a personal name."

Bannister's *History of Cornish Names* lists the name as follows: "SKEWES, SKEWISH, SKEWS — a shady place. (Sces, scod; a shade.)"

---

[1] London Gazette, 1827 and 1945.

In *Patronymica-Cornu-Britannica* (Etymology of Cornish Surnames) by Richard Stephen Charnock (1870) we find "SKEWES, SKEWIS, SKEWYS — from SKEWES (formerly SKEWIS in Crowan) or SKEWES (formerly SKEWYS in Cury). These names signify a shady place. From Skez, a shade or shadow. John Skewys was the Sheriff of the county of Cornwall in the 12th year of the reign of Henry VIII. Hence also the names SKEWISH, SKUSE and SKUES."

Richard Blewett writing in the *West Briton* newspaper in November, 1959 found that 130 SKEWES (including variations in spelling) lived in 29 West Cornwall towns and villages apportioned as follows: —

GRADE RUAN 3; ST. HILARY 3; ST. KEVERNE 4; LUDGVAN 2; MARAZION 3; MAWGAN-IN-MENEAGE 2; MULLION 7; PERRANUTHNOE 10; CAMBORNE 16; ILLOGAN 16; REDRUTH 8; LANNER 3; CROWAN 3; FALMOUTH 5; MABE 2; ST. AGNES 3; MITHIAN 2; ST. AUSTELL 6; TYWARDREATH 2; ST. DENNIS 2; PERRANPORTH 3; TRURO 5; CALLINGTON 5; CALSTOCK 2; ST. IVES 8; LANDRAKE 2; LISKEARD 2; ST. KEW 2 and NEWQUAY 1.

It is interesting to note that where Blewett listed the families, the majority of towns and villages coincided with the Census Returns taken over a hundred years ago. In most cases descendants of families still live in towns like Camborne, Illogan and Redruth, but this is not the case where no returns were made by Blewett. It is known that a large number of the SKUES/SKEWES family (Helston branch) moved to Plymouth in the early 1800's and later north to Yorkshire. Others went to Scotland. Although Blewett did not record any families called SKEWES living in Helston the author did find eleven families listed in the 1969 Voters Register for the town.

Through the ages the spelling of SKUES has changed considerably, and the following are a few variations of the surname found in text books and documents relating to Devon and Cornwall.

1086	ESCHEUUIT	— Exeter Domesday Book
1086	SCHEWIT	— Domesday Book
1284	SKEWYT	— In St Wenn Parish
1302	SKEWES	— In Crowan Parish
1327	SKYNES	— In Cury Parish
1350	SKEWYS, John de	— In St Wenn Parish
1357	SKUYS, John	— In St Wenn Parish
1408	SKEWES	— In Cury Parish
1524	TRESKEWES	— In Stithians Parish
1524	TRESKYWIS	— In Stithians Parish
1619	SCUIS	— In Camborne Parish
1664	SCUES	— In Camborne Parish
1680	SKUES, William	— In Redruth Parish
1689	SKUIES, Mary	— In Redruth Parish
1692	SKEUES	— In Camborne Parish
1693	SKUES	— In Camborne Parish
1698	SKUESS, Joan	— In Redruth Parish
1757	SKUES	— In Helston Parish

The first appearance of the SKUES spelling is in Redruth in 1680; Wendron 1688; Camborne 1692; Kenwyn 1700; Sancreed 1734; Helston 1757 and Mylor 1802. In Devonshire, Ottery St Mary shows the present spelling in 1634 whereas 1718 is the first mention of the name in Bristol. London (Stebonheath) records 1672 — Poole, Dorset, 1676. All entries however spelt and listed in Cornwall Parish Registers can be found throughout Chapter Five.

The founder of the SKEWES line is reputed to have been an ancestor who went on one of the Crusades to the Holy Land and was injured while saving the life of a Bishop at sea. On return to this country the ancestor was rewarded for his gallant act by the Bishop who granted him a Manor at GREAT SKYWYS in the parish of St. Wenn, Cornwall.

Just over a hundred years ago this Manor House was gutted by fire. Today, still on the original ground, there is a farmstead which goes under the same name — GREAT SKEWES. LITTLE SKEWES is adjacent. SKEWES, St. Wenn is still shown on Ordnance Survey maps.

At a period so early as the Crusades it was custom for only the more notable persons to distinguish themselves with surnames. These people were usually lords of manors or wealthy land owners. The ancestor who was granted the manor became known as JOHN de SKYWYS (John of the Manor House called SKYWYS). In time the "de" (of) was dropped and through the ages the spelling changed. In 1386 we find JOHN SKEWYS, Lord of SKEWYS.

There are large farm houses to this day standing at Nancegollan in the parish of Crowan (SKEWIS); Cury (SKEWES) and as mentioned earlier St. Wenn (GREAT SKEWES and LITTLE SKEWES). In Crowan and Cury there are separate buildings listed as SKEWES COTTAGE. In the parishes of St. Keverne and Stithians there are farmsteads called TRESKEWES.

In Canada there is a SKUCE LAKE and SKUCE CREEK in Osler Township, Nipissing, Ontario.

There is a SKUSE PARK in Rochester, New York and SKEWES PARK, Ives Grove, Wisconsin, USA.

There are SKEWES STREETS in Elizabeth, Adelaide, South Australia; Mount Isa, Queensland, Australia; and Watcham, Victoria, Australia. There is a SKEWIS STREET in Inwood. Iowa, USA.

Cornwall and the Channel Islands have a great deal in common and have been in touch with each other for centuries. Several Jersey families have Cornish surnames. On the western side of the island is a considerable area called the "Quennvais" which has through the ages become overwhelmed by sand. In this area there is shown on old maps (even in older Ordnance Survey Sheets) a small strip of water marked "SKEWES CANAL". Today the canal has vanished.

To close this chapter on a note of coincidence, SKEWES CANAL lies for the most part in the parish of St. Ouen which the people of Jersey pronounce St. Wenn. In Cornwall St Wenn was the area where the Skewes family first "took root."

Skewis Street, Iowa, USA

3 Records, Records, Records

THE FIRST STEP

The first step in the preparation of a family tree is to start with the latest known generation (usually the present line) and work backwards. It would be unwise to begin one's search with someone with the same name either in Roman or Saxon times as the chances are the name would have been spelt in a different manner from today.[1]

Although one might be a complete novice to genealogy one will probably know the name of his mother and father, brothers and sisters, uncles and aunts and possibly his grandparents. Therefore personal knowledge comes first. Information gleaned from older members of the family will prove invaluable, as they usually manage to relate fascinating stories of their childhood days and those of their relations. The writer has found that in collecting information from relations about ninety-nine per cent of the facts have been correct, but one or two senior citizens have tended to slip up on actual dates.

DRAWING YOUR OWN CONCLUSIONS (THE CHART DEPARTMENT)

The normal and recognised way of designing a pedigree is to work on a large sheet of paper (the actual size of the family will determine how large the sheet should be), listing the names, dates of birth, marriage and death, if known.

Useful information like professions and qualifications add a certain colour to the family pedigree.

JOHN SKUES = Mary Hockin

Born 8 June, 1744,
Helston, Cornwall.
Profession: Borough
Mason at Helston.
Married 28 March, 1769
at Helston Parish Church.
Died 20 September, 1801,
aged 57 years.

Born 1746
Died 20 August, 1799,
aged 53 years.

WILLIAM SKUES

Born 22 December, 1776
Died 24 November, 1842
aged 66 years.

RICHARD SKUES

Born 24 October, 1784
Died 21 December, 1794
aged 10 years

CHARLES SKUES

Born 26 March, 1786
Married Mary Bennett
5 January, 1815 at
Helston Parish Church.
Died: Date not known.

You will notice that John and Mary's children were also shown — William, Richard and Charles. From these names one will work down the generations listing their children and in turn their grandchildren. The "tree" soon "branches out."

The "branch" of JOHN SKUES is not the earliest known generation of the SKUES family. The names, although quite genuine, were only given as an example.

---

[1] *Genealogy for Beginners*, A.J. Willis. London, 1955; p.15.

FAMILY BIBLE

A Family Bible is the ideal source of information. These Bibles were probably most popular in the 18th and 19th centuries, and the information contained on the fly-leaves is always of great importance. As far as the writer is concerned no such Bible exists in his direct line. However, on the MACKENZIE SKUES side of the family there was a Bible. Prior to his death in 1958 Charles Ayre Mackenzie Skues was good enough to copy some of the information which can be found in the Appendix of this book.

There are a number of Family Bibles in the possession of Skewes' and Skews' of Australia and the United States of America.

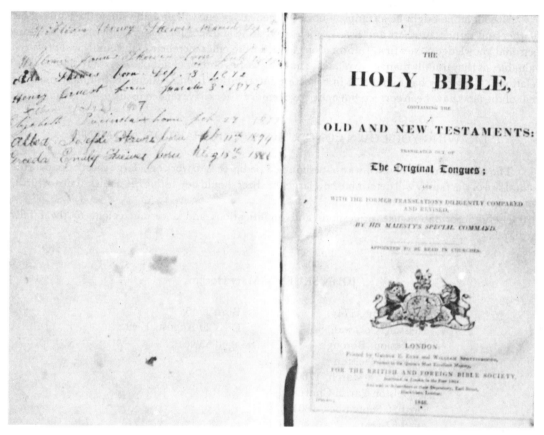

Family Bible of Henry Skewes purchased in Cornwall, now in the possession of George Skewes of Mitcham, Victoria, Australia. Entries go back to 1827

WILLS

Wills are probably the next most important set of documents likely to be found in family archives. In England, wills have been in existence since Saxon times. Wills have proved to be invaluable sources of information, for in the majority of cases the father who makes the will refers to his wife and children by name. Sometimes nieces and nephews come in for a mention. However, it is not always that a wife will find her name in print. On occasions she may die before her husband, but in other cases she is not worthy of mention, which was not uncommon in the 18th century. Mention or no mention, all available wills should be examined and transcribed wherever possible. The information may come in useful at a later date. The writer clearly remembers copying an old Cornish will of DEGORY SKEWES, a miner from Kea, who died in 1824 and which was kept at the County Record Office in Truro. The copy was made in 1957, and twelve years later it proved invaluable in solving a query from an interested descendant now living in the United States of America.

Old wills can make very interesting reading, and indeed some are even amusing. But I am sure that some relations did not think so when they were told of their particular share in a will by their solicitor. It was common practice in the 19th century to leave a married daughter the sum of "one shilling". The writer was told of a will left by a person in Yorkshire. Part of the contents read "I Give, Bequeath and Demise to my dearly beloved son my kind regards." From this extract one can only presume that the father was by no means in the best possible financial position at the time of the execution of the will. On the other hand one must be grateful for small mercies!

Chapter Fifteen is devoted entirely to SKEWES/SKEWIS/SKEWS/SKUES wills and administrations, some held at the County Record Office, Truro, Cornwall and others at Somerset House, London.

GRAVESTONES

Useful evidence is sometimes exhibited on gravestones in churchyards and cemeteries. On visits to a number of Devon & Cornwall churches the author searched for Skewes' on headstones. In certain places he was disappointed. For example, in Helston where there were some thirty burials, according to the parish register, he could not find one gravestone or any evidence of the burials.

The following are names taken from headstones in various Devon and Cornwall churchyards:

BERE ALSTON, DEVON

In Loving Remembrance of JANE devoted wife of SAMUEL D. SKEWES (of Bere Alston) who through Faith entered into rest 24 Apl 1881, aged 54 years.

Also of FLORENCE ROSALIE, youngest daughter of the above who fell asleep 13 April 1874, aged 6 years.

Also of MARY ANNIE COURTIS, eldest daughter of the above who passed away 5 February 1881 (at Brisbane), aged 22 years.

So he giveth his beloved sleep.

Also of SAMUEL D. SKEWES, husband of the above who died 15 August 1903, aged 71 years.

In Loving Memory of EMMA SKEWES who died 2 February 1922, aged 75 years. Rest in peace.

Also ERNEST SKEWES, 364th Infantry US Army, killed in France, 28 September 1918, aged 30 years.

Also EDITH, sister of the above, who died 17 March 1916, aged 26 yrs.

BEER FERRIS, DEVON

MARY ANN SKEWES, wife of Daniel Skewes of this parish who died 18 January 1863, aged 67 years.

Also DANIEL SKEWES, husband of the above who died 20 Dec 1863, aged 57 years. "For if we believe that Jesus died and rose again even so they also which sleep in Jesus will God bring with him".

CONSTANTINE

"Life is a shadow that departeth."
Sacred to the Memory of JOSIAH SKEWES of Bosawsack in the parish of Constantine, who died 2 June 1878, aged 58 years. "Live close to God."
Also five children who died in their infancy.
Also FANNY, his beloved wife, who died 18 June 1895, aged 68 years.

CROWAN

HETTY SKEWES, wife of Rev. HERBERT SKEWES.
Born 31 December 1889. Died 2 April 1942.

CURY

At the entrance to Cury Churchyard there are four gravestones set in neat turf. Two are SKEWES'.

JAMES SKEWES died 7 February 1877, aged 27 years.
"For me to live in Christ, and to die is gain."

JAMES SKEWES of Treloskan in this parish.
Died 19 October 1856, aged 59 years.
"The Memory of the Just is Blessed."

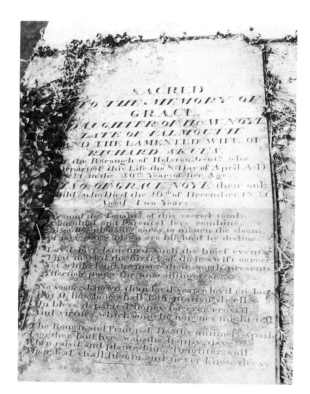

Left: *Mawnan gravestone of Grace and Grace Noye Skues*

Below left: *Cury gravestone of James Skewes*

Below right: *Gravestones of Samuel Dawe Skewes (1833-1903) and his family in Bere Alston Church cemetery, Devon*

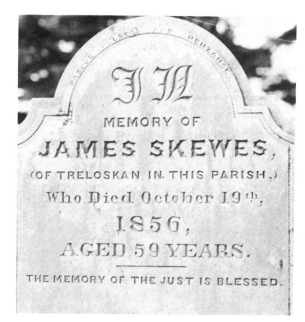

About one hundred yards away there is an extension to the churchyard with about 100 graves of which three are SKEWES'.

JOHN SKEWES died 7 April 1922, aged 71 years, and of his beloved wife THIRZA who died 11 February 1941, aged 87 years.

EDWARD SKEWES who departed this life at Poleskan in this parish 20 February 1878, aged 64 years. Also of JULIA his wife who departed this life 13 August 1910, aged 85 years. "Peace Perfect Peace."
And EDITH their daughter who died 21 April 1938, aged 75 years.
"Sweet is the Memory of the Departed."

In Loving Memory of HENRY SKEWES.
Born 31 January 1857. Died 12 September 1926.
"Rock of Ages Cleft For Me."
Also of EDWARD SKEWES. Died 14 August 1952, aged 86 years. "At Rest."

GWENNAP
Sacred to the Memory of ANN, beloved wife of COLLAN SKEWES who departed this life in Lanner in this parish 15 July 1859, aged 60 yrs.
"I cannot lay thee in the tomb without a falling tear,
Nor repress the thought that I shall soon be numbered here."
Also RICHARD, their son, who fell asleep at Wareham, Dorset, 8 December 1867, aged 43 years.

OLD KEA
The Church of St Kea became dilapidated and was demolished in 1802, except for the 15th century tower which still stands. The present parish church of Kea is three miles west of Old Kea and was consecrated in 1896. There are only three headstones visible in Old Kea churchyard which is now very overgrown: One reads:

In Memory of HENRY SKEWES who died 17 June 1791, aged 77 years.
"Blessed are the dead which believe of the Lord."

KENWYN
Sacred to the Memory of HENRY SKEWES, the beloved son of JAMES and ANN SKEWES, who died 4 March 1841, aged 6 years.
"Jesus said suffer the little children to come unto me for such is the Kingdom of Heaven."

Sacred to the Memory of MARGARET, wife of HENRY SKEWES, who died 17 August 1847, aged 78 years.

Also MARY, daughter of the above, who died 25 March 1868, aged 73 years.

Also LAVINIA, their daughter, who died 10 July 1868, aged 61 years.
"Their end was peace."

ST KEVERNE
Sacred to the Memory of MARGARET, daughter of HENRY and JANE SKEWES, who died 12 May 1798, aged 4½ years.
Also of MARGARET HARRIS her sister who died 13 February 1834, aged 3½ years.

MAWNAN
In Loving Memory of EDWARD SKEWES.
Born 22 August 1845. Died 24 January 1942.
"The Day Thou Gavest Lord is Ended."

In Memory of JAMES SKEWES
Born 24 June 1815. Died 30 July 1899.
Fifty years clerk to this parish.

Resting in Hope
HESTER A. SKEWES.
Born 11 June 1847. Died 9 October 1932.

Also JAMES LUGG, brother of the above
Born 25 December 1860. Died 20 February 1878.
"Thy will be done."

In Loving Memory of FRANCES, wife of JAMES SKEWES of this parish.
Born 29 November 1824. Died 10 May 1907.
"Her children rise up and call her Blessed."

Sacred to the Memory of MARY R. SKEWES, beloved wife of EDWARD SKEWES who died 25 February 1867, aged 46 years.

MAWNAN continued
>In Memory of CHRISTIAN SKEWES who died 11 November 1865, aged 70 years. "Blessed are the Dead which Die in the Lord."

>In Memory of EDWARD SKEWES who died 22 June 1870, aged 51 years.
>Erected by his wife MARY ELLEN SKEWES.

>In Memory of WILLIAM SKEWES who died 10 August 1861, aged 66 years.
>"Man dieth and wasteth away.
>Yea, man giveth up the ghost and where is he?"

>A Table Tomb
>Sacred to the Memory of GRACE, daughter of H & W Noye, late of Falmouth and late lamented wife of RICHARD SKUES, of the Borough of Helston, Gentleman, who departed this life 8 April 1821 in the 20th year of her age.

>Also of GRACE NOYE their only child who died 26 December 1821, aged 2 years.

RUAN MAJOR CHURCH Now derelict. Churchyard only accessible with difficulty.
>Sacred to the Memory of HENRY SKEWES.
>Died 20th day of October 1831, aged 77 years.
>"The days of man are but grass, as flowers of the field, so he flourisheth.
>For as soon as the wind goeth over it, it is gone.
>And the place thereof shall know it no more."

>Also JANE SKEWES, his wife, who died 2 February 1853, aged 84 years.

The discovery of diamonds in South Africa occurred at the same time the Cornish tin mines were being depleted, and this situation forced many thousands of Cornishmen and women to emigrate. Some went to South Africa, others to the United States of America and Canada and a large number to Mexico and Australia. In time we came to discover monumental inscriptions outside Great Britain.

AUSTRALIA — CHURCH OF ENGLAND, ST THOMAS, SYDNEY
>WILLIAM SKEWES late of Manchester, England died 6 October 1900, aged 41 years.

AUSTRALIA — BENDIGO
>LILY SKEWES, wife of GEORGE H. SKEWES died 31 December 1918, aged 51 years.

AUSTRALIA — GORE HILL CEMETERY
>JANE SKEWES died 1 February 1917, aged 70 years.

SOUTH AFRICA[2] — BOSBURG CEMETERY
>FRANK SKEWS Born Illogan, Redruth 1868. Died 17 October 1922.

SOUTH AFRICA — BRIXTON CEMETERY
>EDWIN SKEWES Born Redruth 1856. Died 27 September 1935.

SOUTH AFRICA — BRIXTON CEMETERY
>ELIZABETH SKEWES Born Redruth 1854. Died 28 May 1917.

Headstone of Christian Skewes, buried in Mawnan churchyard

[2] South Africa entries taken from Roll of British Settlers in South Africa, A.A. Balkema, 1971.

UNITED STATES OF AMERICA

JACKSON CEMETERY, MINERAL POINT, WISCONSIN

SKEWS CLARA J.	1860-1950
SKEWS JOHN	1855-1945
SKEWS ALICE J.	Born 31 July 1861. Died 4 July 1896.
SKEWS HARVEY	son of William and A.J. Skews. Born 19 July 1883. Died 7 Sept 1898.
SKEWS THOMAS	son of William and A.J. Skews. Died 1882, infant.
SKEWS GAYLE M.	1909-1927.
SKEWS THOMAS	Died 11 September 1874, aged 46 years 10 months and 3 days.
SKEWS WILLIAM	Born 2 December 1856. Died 13 May 1925.
SKEWS MARY JANE	Born 8 January 1880. Died 15 Feb. 1928.
SKEWS THOMAS H.	son of William and A.J. Skews. Died 25 March 1879 aged 11 months 15 days.

SHULLSBURG CEMETERY, WISCONSIN

In Loving Memory of EDWARD SKEWIS who fell asleep in Jesus 28 January 1872, aged 77 years.

ELIZABETH, daughter of Edward and Mary SKEWIS. Born 15 August 1819. Died 10 January 1852.

MARY, wife of Edward SKEWIS. Born 17 December 1793. Died June 1858. "Here I lay my burden down. Change the Cross into the Crown."

JANE T. SKEWIS wife of A. Skewis. Born 9 March 1828. Died 14 November 1866, aged 39 years. "Asleep in Jesus."

ABSALOM SKEWIS. Born Camborne, England 4 November 1825. Died 14 April 1880.

HENRY SKEWIS died 25 February 1859, aged 28 years.
MARY, his wife, died 16 October 1860, aged 26 years.

JAMES SKEWIS. Born 13 June 1863. Died 28 October 1948.
EDWARD SKEWIS. Born 22 December 1824. Died 28 January 1899.
"Rest for the toiling hand. Rest for the anxious brow. Rest for the weary way. Sore feet. Rest from all labour now."
KITTY M., his wife, born 16 May 1831. Died 3 September 1911.

WILLIAM H. SKEWIS. Born 15 January 1865. Died 25 July 1934.

EMMA SKEWIS. Born 29 October 1857. Died 25 February 1928.

MARY SKEWIS WINN. Born 2 May 1861. Died 10 December 1930.

SKEWIS CLARENCE G. Born 25 March 1878. Died 5 February 1953.

SKEWIS MARY LEHR. Born 7 October 1876. Died 7 May 1971.

MOUNT OLIVET CEMETERY, SALT LAKE CITY, UTAH

SKEWES WILLIAM	1826-1891
SKEWES WILLIAM Jnr	1857-1892
SKEWES ROBERT B.	1859-1908
SKEWES CLARA F. HEATH	1869-1905
SKEWES DORIS	1881-1967

MEXICO — PACHUCA CEMETERY (All written in Spanish)

Mrs JUAN BRITO de SKEWES (wife of James Henry Skewes). Died 25 July 1947.

LUIS SKEWES BRITO died 27 August 1974. In memory from his wife and sons. "Father this grave keeps your body. God keeps your soul and we keep your memory."

ENRIQUE SKEWES. Died 8 December 1915. In memory from his wife and children.

FRANSISCO SKEWES BRITO. Died 28 December 1943. In memory from his mother, wife and son. For ever.

ROSA MARES, widow of SKEWES. Died 23 March 1977. In memory from her sons and grandsons.

Headstones on graves in different countries. Above left: *Pachuca, Mexico.* Above right: *Shullsburg, Wisconsin, USA.* Below left: *Mineral Point, USA:* Below right: *Kadina, South Australia*

MEXICO — REAL DEL MONTE CEMETERY

Sacred to the memory of THOMAS SKEWES who departed this life 1 November 1873, aged 33 years.

Affectionate memory of MARY, dearly beloved wife of RICHARD SKEWES. Born 16 April 1848. Died at Pachuca 11 May 1896, aged 48 years. "Wash me and I shall be whiter than snow."

In memory of GEORGE H. SKEWES beloved son of P. and E. SKEWES. Born 29 March 1871. Died 13 December 1884. "We shall gather the lambs with his arms and carry him in his bosom."

PETER SKEWES died 21 May 1891, aged 48 years.

Sacred to the memory of PETER, son of RICHARD and LOUIE. Died 31 December 1895.

In Loving memory of RICHARD H. SKEWES, husband of LOUIE SKEWES who died in Real del Monte, 4 March 1899, aged 28 years. "Why do we mourn departing friends or shake at death's alarm. Tis but the voice that Jesus sends to call them to his arms."

In Loving memory of NAZARIO SKEWES. Born 28 July 1867. Died 14 February 1922.

In Loving memory of JOHN SKEWES who died at Rosario Mine, Pachuca, Hidalgo 30 November 1903, aged 65 years. "Should not the judge of all earth do right."

RICARDO RICHARDS SKEWES born 19 March 1891. Died June 1942. In memory from his wife, sons and grandson.

ELSA SKEWES M. Born 2 December 1900. Died 11 September 1962.

MARIA SKEWES Died 12 November 1963, aged 92 years.

TOMAS SKEWES Died 4 April 1964, aged 94 years.

CAROLA FEDERICO SKEWES RAMIREZ — no dates.

PARISH REGISTERS

Parish Registers most certainly play a very large part in the tracing of one's family history, and Chapter 5 is devoted to registers transcribed from Devon and Cornwall parishes. It is interesting to note there were a number of inter-marriages:

For example in Cury, Cornwall ANTHONY SKEWES married ELEANOR SKEWES on 11 December 1760, and at Falmouth, Cornwall on 26 September 1794 ALICE SKEWES married WILLIAM SKEWES of Cury. And it was at this popular village in Cury that MARY SKEWES married WILLIAM SKEWES on 3 November 1834.

On 9 September 1818 JOHN SKEWES of Chacewater married NANCY SKEWES of Twelveheads. In Kea on 11 June 1832 JANE SKEWES married THOMAS SKEWES. At Constantine, Cornwall JAMES SKEWES of Cury married GRACE SKEWES of Brill, Constantine on 8 April 1834.

NON PAROCHIAL REGISTERS

Copies of many Cornish Non Parochial Registers, now retained at the Public Record Office in London, have been searched. Where entries were noted they were transcribed and can be found indexed by parish in Chapter 5.

TITHE APPORTIONMENT SURVEYS

These were carried out in the county of Cornwall between 1838 and 1842 listing landowners, lessees and occupiers. A number of SKEWES' were landowners and details can be found in the Appendix. INQUISITIONS POST MORTEM, COURT ROLLS, CHARTER ROLLS, FINE ROLLS, BRIEFS IN CHANCERY, CHANCERY PROCEEDINGS, PATENT ROLLS, CLOSE ROLLS, PIPE ROLLS, PLEA ROLLS, HEARTH TAX and EARLY MUSTER ROLLS.

Where written evidence has been taken down from the various documents which are all kept at the Public Record Office in London, transcripts may be found in the Appendix.

STREET AND TRADE DIRECTORIES

Many old directories list members of the family. But the searcher has to know the whereabouts of that family. As the Skewes family originated in Cornwall, it was fair to expect entries in an old Cornish directory. The 1856 Kelly's Directory for Cornwall listed the following SKEWES'.

Mine Agents
SKEWES H.   Tuckingmill, Camborne
SKEWES W.   Mitchell, Grampound

Beer Retailers
SKEWES J.   Chacewater, Kenwyn, Truro
SKEWES M.   Chacewater, Kenwyn, Truro

Builders
SKEWES THOMAS   Daniel Street, Truro

Carpenters and Joiners
SKEWES H.   Lizard Helston

Farmers
SKEWES A.   Ruan Major, Helston
SKEWES J.   Cargenwen, Crowan, Camborne
SKEWES J.   Treloskin, Cury, Helston
SKEWES W.   Bolitha, Crowan, Camborne
SKEWIS J.   Mawnan, Falmouth
SKEWIS J.   Roscroggan, Illogan, Redruth

Grocers
SKEWES THOMAS   Daniel Street, Truro

Milliners and Dress Makers
SKEWES M.A. (Mrs)   St. Day, Redruth

Hotels — Publicans
"General Wolfe" SKEWS JOHN   Bodmin Road, St. Austell
"Golden Lion" SKEWES LAVINIA (Miss)   Calenick Street, Truro
"Three Tuns" SKEWES H. etc.   Lizard, Helston

Shopkeepers
SKEWES L.   Ruan Minor, Helston
SKEWES R.   Lanner, Gwennap, Redruth
SKEWIS J.   Mawnansmith, Mawnan, Falmouth

Smiths and Blacksmiths
SKEWIS E.   Mawnansmith, Mawnan, Falmouth

Wheelwrights
SKEWES H.   Lizard, Helston

As one branch of the Skewes family lived in Bere Alston, Devon, an 1856/1857 Kelly's Directory of Devon was checked and the following entry found: —

SKEWES DANIEL — Shopkeeper and Mine Agent, living in Pepper Street, Bere Alston.

An 1878 Directory for Devon mentioned SAMUEL DAWE SKEWES, grocer and druggist.

From family relations the writer learned that his great grandfather RICHARD SKUES moved to Halifax from Plymouth (date not known) so various old directories for the county of Yorkshire were searched. Names listed included:

Directory of Halifax (1866)
SKUES RICHARD, Printer   13 New Bond Street, Halifax

Directory of Halifax (1890-1)
SKUES and WILSON, Milliners   22 Crown Street, Halifax
SKUES RICHARD, Mr.   3 Heath Mount, Savile Park, Halifax

Halifax County Borough Directory (1905-6)
SKUES Mrs ADA, Milliner   23 Boothtown Road, Halifax
SKUES RICHARD   41 Moorfield Villas, Savile Park, Halifax
SKUES RICHARD   Oriental Cafe, 4 Princess Street, Halifax
SKUES RICHARD J.   31 York Crescent, Rochdale Road, King Cross, Halifax

Halifax County Borough Directory (1936)
SKUES FLORENCE M. (Miss)   38 Hough Shaw Road, Halifax
SKUES FREDERICK   4 Atlanta Terrace, Halifax
SKUES RICHARD J.   5 Kingston Drive, Halifax

During various other searches the writer learned that a number of SKUESES lived in London, and another branch resided at Dartford, Kent. So spot checks were as follows:

Directory for Dartford, Kent (1952)
SKUES LESLIE J.   119 Great Queen Street, Dartford
SKUES NORAH E.   46 Barnham Road, Dartford
SKUES EDWIN T.   54 Lansbury Crescent, Dartford

Post Office Directory for London (1827)
SKUES CHARLES, Tailor   18 Lower Queen Street, Westminster

Post Office Directory for London (1868)
SKUES Mrs. W. MACKENZIE   4 Alfred Road, St. Johns Road N.

Post Office Directory for London (1886-1887)
SKUES GEORGE HENRY   Tailor, 6 Little Chapel Street, Soho, W.

Post Office Directory for London (1888)
SKUES JAMES   Greengrocer, 77 Webber Street, Blackfriars Road, London S.E.
SKUES GEORGE HENRY   Tailor, 6 Little Chapel Street, London, W.
SKUES G.E.M.   Solicitor, 34 Essex Street, Strand, London, W.C.

Post Office Directory for London (1890)
SKUES G.E.M.   Solicitor, 34, Essex Street, Strand, London, W.C.
SKUES GEORGE HENRY   Dairyman, 14, Sale Street, Paddington, London, W.
SKUES GEORGE HENRY   Tailor, 6 Little Chapel Street, Soho, London, W.
SKUES FREDERICK   15, Oval Road, Gloucester Gate, London, N.W.

Post Office Directory for London (1894)
SKUES GEORGINA MARY (Miss), 33 Hastings Road, Ealing, London, W.
SKUES FREDERICK MACKENZIE, Deputy Surgeon General, 21, Linden Grove, Peckham, S.E.
SKUES GEORGE EDWARD MACKENZIE, Solicitor, Hyrst View, Campden Road, South Croydon and 34, Essex Street, Strand, W.C.

Post Office Directory for London (1895)
SKUES GEORGE EDWARD MACKENZIE, Solicitor, 34, Essex Street, Strand.
SKUES GEORGE HENRY, Dairyman, 14, Sale Street, Paddington, London, W.

Post Office Directory for London (1908)
SKUES CHARLES AYRE MACKENZIE, Surveyor with Smallpiece, Allen & Company.
SKUES GEORGE EDWARD MACKENZIE, Solicitor with Powell and Skues.
SKUES HENRY, Confectioner, 24, Oakley Street, Lambeth, S.E.

Post Office Directory for London (1912)
SKUES GEORGE EDWARD MACKENZIE, Solicitor, 34, Essex Street, Strand, W.C.
SKUES WALTER EDWARD, Chandlers Shop, 88, Shaftsbury Street, Hoxton, N.

Post Office Directory for London (1914)
SKUES GEORGE EDWARD MACKENZIE, Solicitor, 34, Essex Street, Strand, W.C. and 5, Campden Road, South Croydon.
SKUES WALTER EDWARD, Chandlers Shop, 88, Shaftsbury Street, Hoxton, N.

Post Office Directory for London (1920)
SKUES GEORGE EDWARD MACKENZIE, Solicitor, 34, Essex Street, Strand, W.C. and 5, Campden Road, South Croydon.
SKUES CHARLES AYRE MACKENZIE, Architect, 45, Lincoln's Inn Fields, W.C. 2.

Post Office Directory for London (1922)
SKUES GEORGE EDWARD MACKENZIE, Solicitor, 34, Essex Street, Strand, W.C., with Powell and Skues. Telephone number — CEN 6098.
SKUES CHARLES AYRE MACKENZIE, Architect, 45, Lincoln's Inn Fields, W.C. 2. Telephone number HOL 1367.

Post Office Directory for London (1930)
SKUES CHARLES AYRE MACKENZIE, F.S.I., Architect, 45, Lincoln's Inn Fields, W.C. 2.
SKUES GEORGE EDWARD MACKENZIE, Solicitor with Powell and Skues and Graham Smith, 34, Essex Street, Strand W.C.
SKUES CLAUDE, Gold and Silver Mounter, 21, John's Square, London, E.C.1.
SKUES PHILIP ERNEST, Fishmonger, 79, Rodney Road, S.E. 17.

Post Office Directory for London (1951)
SKUES CHARLES AYRE MACKENZIE, FRICS, Architect, 16, Tooks Court, E.C.4.

ARMY LISTS

These lists were printed from the latter end of the 18th century, and all those who were commissioned indexed each year. Searches from 1740 to 1900 were undertaken and entries were as follows.

1797   SKUES RICHARD Lieutenant, Volunteers, Helston, 25th May, 1796
1797   SKUES WILLIAM Ensign, Volunteers, Helston, 17th November, 1796
1803   SKUES RICHARD Captain, Volunteers Infantry, Meneage Loyal
        (From 1810 the writer only listed entries every ten years)
1820   SKUES GEORGE 2nd Lieutenant (Royal Marines)
1830   SKUES GEORGE 2nd Lieutenant on half pay
1840   SKUES GEORGE 2nd Lieutenant on half pay
1850   SKUES GEORGE 2nd Lieutenant on half pay
1860   SKUES GEORGE 2nd Lieutenant on half pay
1860   SKUES EDWARD WALKER, M.D. Commissioned into the Army 11 June, 1852. Date of last appointment to the staff — 11 June, 1852. Assistant Surgeon, Medical Department
1860   SKUES FRED MACKENZIE — 1st West Indian Regiment of the Foot. Assistant Surgeon 28th February, 1855. (In 1866 Army List FMS listed as being in the Gold Coast. In 1867 he was posted to Sierra Leone.)
1860   SKUES RICHARD ALEXANDER, Lieutenant, 69th (South Lincolnshire) Regiment of the Foot: "Java", "Bourbon", "India", "Waterloo". Rank in Regiment 30 April, 1858. Rank in Army 14 May, 1857
1860   SKUES WILLIAM MACKENZIE, M.D., Royal Newfoundland Companies. Assistant Surgeon. Rank in Regiment 2 November, 1855. Rank in Army 29 July, 1853. (In 1865 Army List WMS referred to as being with 109th Foot.)
1870   SKUES GEORGE 2nd Lieutenant on half pay
1870   SKUES FREDERICK MACKENZIE, 26th Cameronian (Infantry Surgeon 14th October, 1868)
1870   SKUES RICHARD ALEXANDER, Lieutenant (details as in 1860)
1870   SKUES WILLIAM MACKENZIE, M.D. Surgeon 8 July, 1862, Malta (details as in 1860)
1880   SKUES FREDERICK MACKENZIE, Medical Department. Brigade Surgeon (Ranking with Lieutenant Colonel) 28 July, 1880, Bengal
1880   SKUES WILLIAM MACKENZIE, M.D. Surgeon 8 July, 1862. Surgeon Major 29 July, 1873
1900   SKUES FREDERICK MACKENZIE. Date of first appointment 28 February, 1855. Date of retirement 16 December, 1882. Brigade Surgeon

The majority of the Skues family were commissioned into the Medical Branch of the Army. There is published a "Roll of Commissioned Officers in the Medical Service of the British Army (20-23 June, 1898) in which the following are named:

SKUES EDWARD WALKER

Assistant Surgeon to the Forces	11 June	1852
Surgeon to the Forces	11 September	1860
Born in Aberdeen	17 July	1830
Died in Calcutta	15 March	1862
M.B. Maris College, Aberdeen		1852
Was appointed acting Assistant Surgeon to the Forces	25 May	1852

SKUES FREDERICK MACKENZIE

Assistant Surgeon to the Forces	28 February	1855
First West Indian Regiment Staff	11 September	1860
Surgeon to the Forces	14 October	1862
26th Regiment of the Foot	1 April	1870
Army Medical Department — Surgeon Major	14 October	1868
Brigade Surgeon	28 July	1880
Retired with Honorary Rank of Deputy Surgeon General	16 December	1882
Born in Aberdeen	21 October	1833
Died at Streatham, Surrey	13 August	1910
M.B. Maris College, Aberdeen		1885
Was appointed Acting Assistant Surgeon	28 February	1885

SKUES WILLIAM MACKENZIE

Assistant Surgeon to the Forces	29 July	1853
Royal Newfoundland Companies	2 November	1855
Staff	21 September	1860
Surgeon to the Forces	8 July	1862
109th Regiment of the Foot	28 June	1864
Staff	23 July	1870
Army Medical Department: Surgeon Major	8 July	1862
Retired with Honorary Rank of Brigade Surgeon	2 December	1881

Born Aberdeen	15 March	1828
Died	10 June	1892
M.B. Maris College, Aberdeen		1853
M.D.		1860

(M.B. is Bachelor of Medicine; M.D. is Doctor of Medicine)

Looking at the Army Lists for the years 1797 to 1803 there were entries for Captain RICHARD SKUES and Ensign WILLIAM SKUES, listed as Volunteers of the Meneage (Loyal) Infantry. Between the years 1794 and 1802 some 400,000 Volunteers of all kinds had been enrolled in Great Britain and Ireland. Shortly after the Treaty of Amiens in March, 1802, however, the greater part of the Voluntary Corps and Associations had been disbanded.

Various minor acts of legislation had sufficed to keep the framework of Volunteering alive during the latter part of 1802 and into the succeeding year. In late March, 1803, a circular from the Horse Guards expressed to Lords-Lieutenant the desirability of effecting preliminary preparations for a full revival of the Volunteer Force. War with France broke out on 18th May, 1803, and in June a new Defence Act permitted the reconstruction of Volunteer Corps and Troops of Yeomanry. By December, 1803 some 463,000 persons had enlisted in the various arms of the Volunteer Force.[3]

During the period 1794-1802 there were some 49 military units which sprang up all over the county of Cornwall known as Volunteers — Artillery Volunteers, Yeomanry Cavalry and Infantry Volunteers.

It was the Volunteers of the Infantry that members of the Skues family tended to become associated with. These Infantry Volunteers were small units — usually a single company — and ranged in strength anything from thirty to fifty men. They would have a captain, a lieutenant, an ensign, three sergeants, two corporals, two drummers and the remainder of the company made up from private men. Normally a major commanded the Company of Volunteers.

The Helston Volunteers were formed in June, 1794. On 3rd September, 1798 RICHARD SKUES was promoted from Lieutenant to Captain with the First Helston Volunteers then under the command of Major William Johns. On the same date Ensign WILLIAM SKUES was promoted to Lieutenant. Also in the same company there was another WILLIAM SKUES — a private.

All this information came from "Muster Rolls" for Cornish Volunteers kept at the Public Record Office in London.[4] Other names which came to light during the search were:

Private	RICHARD SKUES	with the Company of Germoe Volunteers commanded by Captain William Esdale.
Private	JOSEPH SKUES	with Breage Volunteers (1798-1801). He quite the Volunteers 25th April, 1801.
Drummer	WILLIAM SKEWES	with the Volunteer Corps of Helston (1797-1798)
Private	WILLIAM SKEWIS	with Camborne Volunteers (1798-1799). William, whose spelling changed to SKEWES in "Muster Rolls" (1799) was discharged on 27th December, 1799.
Private	JOHN SKEWIS	with Camborne Volunteers (1798-1800). John, whose spelling changed to SKEWES in "Muster Rolls" (1799 and 1800) was discharged on 16th March, 1800.

The payment per day to soldiers was as follows: major 14/1d; captain 9/5d; lieutenant 4/4d; ensign 3/5d; sergeant 1/0¾d; corporal 1/-d and private 1/-d.

Follows now a list of the service with payments made to members of the Skues/Skewes family.

Monthly pay list and Return of Company of Germoe Volunteers commanded by Captain William Esdale from *25th December, 1799 to 24th December, 1800.*

Private RICHARD SKUES　　　　　　　　*49 days* exercise at one shilling per day.　　£2 9 0d

He was sick on 2nd and 9th November

---

[3] Charles Thomas *Devon & Cornwall Notes & Queries*, April, 1959.
[4] P.R.O. London W.O. 13-3980-4233.

Private RICHARD SKUES   *79 days*   *£3 19 0d*
25th December, 1800 to 24th December 1801
He was sick 20th September, 4th October and 18th November
1801

From 25th December 1801 to 24th April, 1802 RICHARD SKUES completed 35 days Exercises and was paid £1 15
0d. In the Germoe Volunteers there was a captain, a lieutenant, an ensign, three sergeants, two corporals, two
drummers and fifty privates.

Monthly Pay list of Helston Company of Volunteers commanded by Major William Johns.

25th July, 1798 to 24th August, 1798
Ensign WILLIAM SKUES   9 days   £1 10 9d
Private WILLIAM SKUES   7 days   7 0d
Lieutenant RICHARD SKUES   9 days   £1 19 0d

25th August, 1798 to 24th September, 1798
Ensign WILLIAM SKUES was promoted
    to Lieutenant 3 September   7 days   £1 7 7d
Private WILLIAM SKUES   8 days   8 0d
(Was sick on 3rd September)

25th August, 1798 to 24th September, 1798
Captain RICHARD SKUES.
Was promoted from Lieutenant
3rd September, 1798   9 days   £3 9 6d

General State of 30 weeks Pay for the non-commissioned officers and privates of the Volunteer Corps
raised for the defence of the town of Helston in Cornwall from the 25th day of December, 1797 to the
24th day of July, 1798, both days inclusive.

Drummer WILLIAM SKEWES   60 days   £3 0 0d

General State of 30 weeks Pay for the Commissioned Officers of the Volunteer Corps raised for the
defence of the town of Helston in Cornwall from the 25th day of December, 1797 to the 24th day of
July, 1798, both days inclusive.

Captain RICHARD SKUES   60 days   £13 0 0d
Ensign WILLIAM SKUES   60 days   £10 5 0d

Monthly pay list of Helston Company of Volunteers commanded by Major John Trevener.
25th October, 1798 to 24th November, 1798
Captain RICHARD SKUES   9 days   £4 4 9d
Lieutenant WILLIAM SKUES   3 days   13 0d
Was sick on October 7th, 10th,
14th, 17th, 21st and 24th
Private WILLIAM SKUES   8 days   8 0d

25th November, 1798 to 24th December, 1798
Captain RICHARD SKUES   8 days   £3 15 4d
Lieutenant WILLIAM SKUES was
sick for the whole time.
Sick claim for £1 14 8 d

Yearly Return of Captain SKUES's Company of First Helston Volunteers, commanded by Major William Johns,
25th December, 1798 to 24th December, 1799.
Captain RICHARD SKUES   104 days   £48 19 4d
Lieutenant WILLIAM SKUES   101 days   £21 17 0d
Private WILLIAM SKUES   96 days   £4 16 0d

Yearly Return of Captain SKUES's Company of First Helston Volunteers, commanded by Major William Johns,
25th December, 1799 to 24th December, 1800.
Captain RICHARD SKUES   105 days   £49 8 9d
Lieutenant WILLIAM SKUES   53 days   £11 9 8d
(He died 18th August, 1800)
Private WILLIAM SKUES   60 days   £3 0 0d
(He quit on 29th September, 1800)

Lieutenant William SKUES was sick five times from December, 1799 to January, 1800 and claimed
for £1 1 8d sick pay. From January to February he was sick nine times and claimed for £1 19 0d sick

pay. He was sick eight times in March, nine times in April, eight times in May, nine times in June, and nine times in July. He finally died on 18th August, 1800.

Private WILLIAM SKUES was on duty at Penryn four times guarding 102 French prisoners by order of the Mayor of Helston, directing the prisoners "to remain in our charge until General Simcoe's pleasure is known." Skues was sick once in August, 1800 and six times in September. He quit the Volunteers on 29th September, 1800.

In the Breage Volunteers Private JOSEPH SKUES collected £2 10 0d for 50 days exercises from December, 1798 to December, 1799 and a further £2 12 0d for 52 days of Exercises from December, 1799 to December, 1800. SKUES remained with the Breage Volunteers until 25th April, 1801. From December, 1800 through to April, 1801 he worked 16 days and collected 16/-d.

In the Camborne Volunteers Private WILLIAM SKEWIS and Private JOHN SKEWIS worked under Captain William Harris from 25th December, 1798 to 24th December, 1799. From 25th December, 1799 onwards their spelling changed from SKEWIS to SKEWES. Private WILLIAM SKEWES was discharged from the Volunteers on 27th December, 1799 and Private JOHN SKEWES was discharged on 16th March, 1800.

For the years 1804, 1805 and 1807 we find listed in *The Officers of the Gentlemen and Yeomanry Cavalry—Voluntary Infantry of the United Kingdom* (Cornwall—Meneage Loyal), Captain RICHARD SKUES and Surgeon RICHARD SKUES.

In *Returns presented to the House of Commons of the Volunteer Corps of Cavalry, Infantry and Artillery in Great Britain*, (printed 1806) the Loyal Meneage Company was commanded by Lieut. Colonel Jonathan Papingham. Listed as Captain was RICHARD SKEWES. The Company was inspected at Helston 21st February, 1805 by Lieut. Colonel John Enys who said "The Loyal Meneage Volunteers Infantry is a most excellent Corps and are able to act in any way you wish them to do, either as Infantry or Light Infantry. Their arms are very good and well kept, and their clothing good."

For the year 1825 Cornet RICHARD SKUES is found in *The Extract of War Office Lists of Officers of the Militia Yeomanry and Volunteers* (Cornwall Hussars).

The Loyal Meneage Yeomanry Corps was three troops strong, with an establishment of 129 all ranks. The first was the Helston Yeomanry Cavalry which appears in the 1803 *Army List* and names RICHARD SKUES as Captain of the Volunteer Infantry. A second troop was added in 1804 from the Trelowarren area and the two were amalgamated with a small corps, the Penryn Cavalry.

A List of the Uncommissioned Officers and Privates, enrolled and serving in the Loyal Meneage Gentlemen and Yeomanry, Cornwall, commanded by Vyell Vyvyan, Esquire, Major Commandant, 24th June, 1806 includes Private WILLIAM SKUES.

Return of persons actually serving in the Penwith Yeomanry Cavalry commanded by the Right Honourable Lord de Dunstanville and Bassett, Major Commandant, 24th June, 1806, in Captain Hamilton's Troop — Private HENRY SKEWIS.

Pay list of Captain Michell's Troop of Cornwall Yeomanry Cavalry whilst assembled for permanent duty at Helston.

Private EDWARD SKEWES	8 days	£2 0 0d
22nd July, 1818 to 30th July, 1818, both days inclusive		
Private EDWARD SKEWES	8 days	£2 0 0d
14th September, 1819 to 21st September, 1819, both days inclusive		
Private EDWARD SKEWES	8 days	£2 0 0d
3rd October, 1821 to 10 October, 1821, both days inclusive		
Private EDWARD SKEWES	8 days	£2 0 0d
15th September 1822 to 22 September, 1822, both days inclusive		

Pay list of Captain Hoskin's Troop of the Second Cornwall Yeomanry Cavalry whilst assembled for permanent duty at Penzance from 13th June, 1820 to 21st June, 1820, both days inclusive.

Private STEPHEN SKEWIS	9 days	£2 5 0d
Private JAMES SKEWIS	9 days	£2 5 0d

Pay list of Captain Vyvyan's Troop of the Cornwall Yeomanry Cavalry whilst assembled for permanent duty at Helston from 26th July, 1820 to 2nd August, 1820, both days inclusive.
Private EDWARD SKUES   8 days   £2 0 0d
24th July, 1822 to 31 July, 1822, both days inclusive

Pay list of Captain Howell's Troop of the Second Cornwall Yeomanry Cavalry whilst assembled for permanent duty at Penzance from 11th September, 1822 to 19th September, 1822, both days inclusive
Private JAMES SKEWIS   9 days   £2 5 0d

Pay list of Captain Pender's Troop of Cornwall Yeomanry Cavalry whilst assembled for permanent duty at Helston from 24th July, 1822 to 31st July, both days inclusive.
Private WILLIAM SKUES   8 days   £2 0 0d

Whilst dealing with the military a look now at some other publications:
THE MILITARY GENERAL SERVICE MEDAL (1793-1814) compiled by Colonel K.O.N. Foster.

A list of 26,240 Officers and Men of the British Army who fought in the Peninsular and elsewhere, together with the Battles in which they took part and who survived until 1847 when they eventually received their medal.
5th Foot. Other Ranks: WILLIAM SKEWS, Corporal. Two Clasps representing Battles in Salamanga and Vittoria.

WATERLOO ROLL CALL is a book which lists Quartermaster JOHN SKUCE as joining the 3rd Regiment of the Foot Guards (2nd Battalion) and who left the Regiment in May, 1819. The Battle of Waterloo was 18th June, 1815.

NATIONAL ROLL CALL OF THE GREAT WAR (1914-1918) names Rifleman G. SKUSE with the 9th London Regiment (Queen's Victoria Rifles) and a home address of 194, Kilburn Lane, North Kensington, London, W.10.

INDEX OF MARINE OFFICERS says 2nd Lieutenant GEORGE SKUES was reduced to half pay on 1st September, 1814.

COMMISSIONED SEA OFFICERS OF THE ROYAL NAVY (1660-1815) lists Lieutenant THOMAS SKUES (1685).

LIST OF PURSERS, BOATSWAINS, GUNNERS and CARPENTERS of HIS MAJESTY's FLEET says that WILLIAM QUARME SKEWES received his first Warrant from Admiralty Office, London on 20th April, 1810.

SCHOOLS, COLLEGES and UNIVERSITIES

Many schools, colleges and universities printed lists and registers of pupils and teachers and the following have been noted by the writer.
UNIVERSITY OF WASHINGTON, AMERICA ALUMNI (Published 1941)

SKEWES JAMES M.: BA in E and B, 1939. Address 4210 Brooklyn, Seattle, Washington
SKEWES THOMAS JOHN Junior: BSc in Chemistry, 1938. Address: 1337 4th Avenue, Seattle, Washington
SKEWIS FRANCIS JAMES: LLB, 1914. Address: Greenville, Iowa
SKEWIS MARY: BM, 1924 (teacher). Address: Longview, Washington
SKEWIS SHIRLEY MARTIN: B.A., 1919. Address: Tacomba, Washington

DULWICH COLLEGE REGISTER 1619-1926
SKUES, CHARLES AYRE MACKENZIE born 2nd October, 1875, youngest son of Brigade Surgeon WILLIAM MACKENZIE SKUES, M.D., of 17 Linden Grove, Nunhead; brother-in-law of Herbert Everett Gaute; Rugby Football Fifteen 1894; Architect and Surveyor; Fellow of Surveyors Institution; Great War, Captain, Royal Garrison Artillery (Special Reserve); married 12th August, 1903 Lillie, youngest daughter of Edward Everett Gaute. Address: 45 Lincoln's Inn Fields, London, W.C. 2.

REGISTER OF ALL HALLOWS (ROUSDON) SCHOOL, 1852-1952
SKEWES, IAN ROBERT MORRISON born 8th May, 1927. House Prefect in 1944; Football Fifteen, 1943; Hockey Eleven, 1942-1944; Triple Colour; proceeded to Bristol Academy of Art.

REGISTER OF WINCHESTER COLLEGE, 1836-1906
SKUES, GEORGE EDWARD MACKENZIE born 13th August, 1858 at St Johns, Newfoundland, eldest
son of Brigade Surgeon WILLIAM MACKENZIE SKUES, M.D., A.M.D., and Margaret his wife,
daughter of Christopher Ayre, Esq., Clerk of Parliament, Newfoundland. Left July, 1877; at Victoria
College, Jersey, 1877-1878; articled to Mr James Powell, January, 1879; Solicitor, 1884, practising at 34
Essex Street, Strand, London WC and at Croydon (Messrs Powell and Skues) since 1895 in partnership with
Mr Powell; author of an article on trout fly-dressing in the *Encyclopaedia of Sport*; books: *Minor Tactics of
the Chalk Stream* (1910); and *The Way of a Trout With a Fly* (1921). Address: 5 Campden Road, South
Croydon, Surrey.

REGISTER OF ADMISSION TO KING'S COLLEGE, CAMBRIDGE, 1919-1958
SKUSE, REGINALD ALLEN son of Robert Skuse; born 25th January, 1938 in Ilford, Essex; educated at
Leyton County High School for Boys. King's College Basketball Captain 1959-1961; Degree — BA in 1961.
Post Grad Student in Education, King's College, London. Married July, 1958, Christine Margaret Judd.
Address: 26, St Leonard's Road, East Sheen, Barnes, London, S.W. 14.

ADMISSION TO KING'S COLLEGE, 1797-1925
SKEWES, STANLEY son of Henry Skewes. School — South African College School; afterwards at
University in Capetown. BSc., 1920. MA 1922; Admitted 10th October, 1923. Second Class Mathematical
Tripos, Pt II, 1925. Degree BA, 1925. Now a lecturer in Mathematics at Capetown University. Married
1926 Vera Florence Rothkugel. Address: Chetwynd, Links Drive, Pinelands, Capetown, South Africa.

REGISTER OF NEWNHAM COLLEGE 1871-1950 (Published 1963)
SKUES, MINNIE MACKENZIE Born 27th December, 1870 at Sliema, Malta daughter of WILLIAM
MACKENZIE SKUES, Army Medical Officer and Margaret Ayre. Education — private tuition
Haberdashers' Aske's Girls School, Hatcham (latterly as a pupil teacher); Newnham 1892-1895; Drapers
Scholar, 1893; Nat. Sci. Trip. Pt.1. C.1., 1895; Oxford Educ. Diploma 1905 MA (TCD); Assistant Mistress
at Pendelton High School, 1895-1897; at St. Leonard's School, St Andrews, 1897-1899; at Bradford Girls
Grammar School, 1899-1904; Headmistress of Newark High School, 1905-1916; of Rugby High School,
1919-1926; Assistant Mistress in temporary posts 1918-1919; at Queen's College, Barbados, 1926-1929.
Died 21st June, 1962.

REGISTER OF THE ALUMNI OF TRINITY COLLEGE, DUBLIN (published 1937)
SKUES, MINNIE MACKENZIE proceeded to a degree in the University of Dublin from the University of
Cambridge (1906) M.A. Address: The Corner, Bexted, Sussex.
SKUSE, Rev. WILLIAM (1909) BA. Address: Grean Rectory, Pallasgreen, Co. Limerick.

UNIVERSITY OF LEEDS CALENDAR (1939-1940)
SKUES, ERIC: B.A. (1922)

ALUMNI OXONIENSIS (1500-1714)
SKEWISH (SKUISH), JOHN. A Cornishman educated at Oxford, a member of Cardinal Wolsey's Cabinet
Council.

COMMERS OF EXETER COLLEGE, OXFORD (by Rev. Charles William Boase, 1894)
SKEWYS, JOHN son of John, by Joan, daughter of Richard Tomyowe; at Exeter College; agent for Wolsey;
had privilege of wearing his hat in the King's presence. Married Catherine, daughter of John Trethurfe.
Died 23rd May, 1544.

MEMBERS OF THE UNIVERSITY OF OXFORD, 1715-1886
SKEWES, JOHN third son of William Skewes of Bolitho, Cornwall, Gent. Non Coll, matric 23rd April,
1870, aged 24 years. B.A. 1873; M.A. 1876.

UNIVERSITY OF CAMBRIDGE LIST, 1957-1958
SKUES, J.A. Queen's College. B.A. 1952; M.A. 1956.
SKUES, A.E. Downing College. B.A. 1954.

A look now at other printed books and documents.

From *Who's Who in Australia* we find:

SKUES, KENNETH FREDERICK, O.B.E. (1967); D.D.Sc., Melbourne. Principal Dental Officer Repat
H.Q. since 1956. Chairman Melbourne University Grad. Union 1967, 1968. Vice President Melbourne
Dental Hospital since 1966. Consulting Dentist Royal Melbourne Hospital since 1965; Senior Dental
Surgeon 1950-1965. Son of F.H. SKUES, Bendigo, Victoria. Born 17th March, 1905 in Bendigo.
Educated at Bendigo; Queen's College and University of Melbourne. Hon. Dentist, Royal Melbourne
Hospital since 1928. Member of the Committee, Melbourne Dental Hospital since 1933.
Is author of *Development of Dental Enamel in Marsupials*, published 1932. Married 1st August, 1942,
Katherine P., daughter of Major H. Turner Shaw, O.B.E. One son and one daughter. Recreations — golf
and tennis. Clubs: Melbourne Naval and Military. Royal Melbourne Golf. V.R.C. M.C.C. Address: 407,
Beach Road, Beaumaris, Victoria, Australia. Tel. Victoria 393.

ERNEST SKUES is listed in "The Register of Pharmaceutical Chemists". He was registered on 10th July, 1909 (17634), his address being 3 Broadwater Road, London, S.W.17. He worked as Superintendent of Barker's Chemist (Croydon) Limited of 105, Church Street, Croydon, Surrey. Date of registration 6th September, 1951 — Director.

Ernest Skues was apprenticed to H.C. Brierly of Halifax, Yorkshire and gained experience in the West End of London before joining Reynolds and Branson of Leeds for eight years. He qualified in 1909 and started business on his own in South West London in 1913. He has served as President of the Proprietary Articles Trade Association, The Photographic Dealer's Association, the London Pharmaceutical Association and has been on the Board of Directors of Unichem which celebrated its 21st birthday in May, 1960.

CHARLES AYRE MACKENZIE SKUES (3425) is named in "The Royal Institution of Chartered Surveyors list of Members, 1957". He became a Fellow of the Royal Institution of Chartered Surveyors in 1901 and a Professional Associate of the Royal Institution of Chartered Surveyors.

Crockfords Clerical Directory (1967/1968) lists five members of the family who have been ordained:

SKUCE, FRANCIS JOHN LEONARD — Trinity College, Dublin. B.A. 1948. Deacon 1950; priest, 1951. Dromore College of Warrenpoint with Clonallan 1950-1953; Incumbent of Innishmacsaint, Diocese of Clogher from 1953. Address: Rectory, Derrygonnelly, Enniskillen, County Fermanagh, Northern Ireland.

SKUES, ERIC — University of Leeds. B.A. 1922. College of Resurrection, Mirfield, 1919. Deacon, 1924 Sheffield for Shantung. Priest, 1926. Mission at Yenchow 1924/1928; Furlough 1928/1929 and 1934/1935; Pingyin, 1929/1934; Shantung Chaplain Missionary at Weighaiwei 1935/1940; Tsing-Tao 1940/1945; Furlough, 1946. Society for the Propagation of the Gospel (S.P.G.) Area Secretary, Diocese of Coventry 1947/1953; Diocese of Gloucester and Worcester 1947/1965; Diocese of Hereford 1953/1965; United Society for the Propagation of the Gospel, Diocese of Hereford and Worcester from 1965; Permission to officiate Diocese of Coventry 1947/1953; Diocese of Gloucester 1947/1965; Diocese of Hereford from 1953; Licence to officiate Diocese of Worcester from 1947. Address; Rosedale, Park Road, West Malvern, Worcester. Telephone number Malvern 3915.

SKUES, JOHN — Queen's College, Cambridge. B.A. 1952. M.A. 1956. College of Resurrection, Mirfield, 1952. Deacon 1955, Lincolnshire; Priest Grimsby for Canterbury, 1956; Curate of Boston 1955/1958; Stroud 1958/1959; Cirencester with Watermoor 1959/1962; Chaplain to the Forces from 1960. Hospital Chaplain to St. Thomas's Hospital, London from 1962. Address: 23 St Thomas Mansions, Stangate, London, S.E. 1. Telephone number WAT 4059.

SKUSE, FRANK RICHARD — Trinity College, Dublin. B.A. 1942. Deacon, 1942; Priest 1943, Clogher; Curate of Monaghan 1942/1945; Drumcondra with North Stroud 1945/1950; Curate in charge Clonaslee and Rosenallis Union 1950/1954; Incumbent of Kinneigh with Ballymoney, Diocese of Cork from 1954. Address: Rectory, Ballineen, Cork, Eire. Telephone number Brandon 47143.

SKUSE, WILLIAM — Trinity College, Dublin. B.A. 1909. Deacon, 1910; Priest, 1911; Limerick county of Kenmare with Templence and Tuosist 1910/1912; Ematris with Rockcorry 1912/1915; Dingle with Ventry 1915/1916; Chaplain of Villiershewn and Curate of Cappoquin 1916/1919; Incumbent of Kilfynn with Ratot 1922/1032; Incumbent of Grean with Caherconlish 1932/1951; Domestic Chaplain to the Bishop of Cash 1949/1955; Diocesan Curate of Cash and Emly 1951/1956. Address: Woodcoate, Roundhill, Bandon, County Cork, Eire.

ELECTORAL ROLL REGISTERS

The registers can be most useful and date back in the main to the turn of the last century. If the exact street is not known a great deal of time can be spent searching the lists as they are not normally indexed by the person's name, but rather by streets. The writer searched through the entire county of Cornwall in the Electoral Roll Registers, copies of which are kept at the British Museum (now called the British Library) in London. Follows now a selection from spot checks.

VOTERS LIST FOR CAMBORNE, REDRUTH AND GWINEAR DIVISION OF CORNWALL, 1885/1886.

SKEWES HENRY	Adelaide Street, Camborne (House & Shop)
SKEWIS EDWARD	Newton, Camborne
SKEWIS JOHN	Bolenowe Crofts, Camborne
SKEWIS JAMES	Bolitho, Crowan
SKEWIS WILLIAM	Bolitho, Crowan
SKEWES JOHN	Cargenwen, Crowan
SKEWES-TEAGUE RICHARD	Highway, Redruth
SKEWIS HENRY	Lamin, Gwinear
SKEWES WILLIAM	Treloweth, Illogan
SKUES JOHN	Hodders Row, Redruth
SKEWES SAMUEL	Fords Row, Redruth

At SKEWIS, Crowan, Edwin Trevenen resided. Samuel Reynolds resided at SKEWIS COOSE, Crowan.

VOTERS LIST FOR CAMBORNE & REDRUTH, CORNWALL, 1897

SKEWES HENRY	Adelaide Street, Camborne
SKEWIS HENRY O.	College Street, Camborne
SKEWIS MATTHEW	Carnarthen Street, Camborne
SKEWIS JOHN	Condurrow, Camborne
SKEWES JAMES	Bolitho, Crowan
SKEWES EDWARD	Tuckingmill, Illogan
SKEWIS WILLIAM	Treskillard, Illogan
SKEWES GRACE	Barncoose Terrace, Illogan
SKEWES MATTHEW	Rose Row, Redruth
SKEWES-TEAGUE RICHARD	Highway, Redruth
SKEWES ELIZABETH	Bassett Street, Redruth

At SKEWIS, Crowan resided John Trevenen. The resident at SKEWIS COOSE was James Charles Mewton. Edward Charles Harvey lived at KUS SKEWIS, Crowan as did George Ward. Fortescue William Millett resided at SKEWIS-KERS-SKEWIS.

VOTERS LIST FOR CAMBORNE & REDRUTH, 1906

SKEWIS HENRY	Adelaide Street, Camborne
SKEWIS HENRY O.	Moor Street, Camborne
SKEWIS JOHN	Condurrow, Camborne
SKEWES ALFRED JOHN	Tuckingmill, Illogan
SKEWES EDWARD	Tuckingmill, Illogan
SKEWES FREDERICK TRESIZE	Carnkie, Illogan
SKEWES JAMES	Bosleake, Illogan
SKEWES JAMES	Treskillard, Illogan
SKEWES MATTHEW	Illogan Highway
SKEWES WILLIAM	Treskillard, Illogan
SKEWES GRACE	Barncoose Terrace, Illogan
SKEWES LEWIS	Bellview, Redruth
SKEWES MATTHEW	Rose Row, Redruth
SKEWES MARY	Buller Terrace, Redruth
SKEWES ELIZABETH ANN	Higher Fore Street, Redruth

At SKEWIS, Crowan resided Alfred Rowe who also let a room (1st floor bedroom) to another Alfred Rowe for 5 shillings a week. Also living at Skewis were John Trevenen and Kate Trevenen. William J. Nicholls resided at KUS SKEWIS as did James Merton and Elizabeth Symons.

VOTERS LIST FOR CAMBORNE & REDRUTH, 1922

SKEWES HENRY OSWALD	Moor Street, Camborne
SKEWES EMILY ANNE	
SKEWIS LOUISA JANE	2, College Street, Camborne
SKEWES WILLIAM HENRY	Brea, Illogan, Camborne
SKEWES WALTER NICHOLAS	Pendarves Street, Beacon
SKEWES EDWARD	Condurrow, Camborne
SKEWES WILLIAM JOHN	
SKEWES HERBERT JOHN	Salem House, Chacewater, Kenwyn
SKEWES HENRIETTA	
SKEWES RICHARD	Unity, St Day, Gwennap
SKEWES MINNIE	
SKEWES THOMAS WILLIAM	Carnmarth Cove, Gwennap
SKEWES ELIZA EMMA	
SKEWES WILLIAM JOHN	Carnmarth North, Gwennap
SKEWES EDITH MARY	
SKEWES ALFRED JOHN	Pengelly's Row, Illogan
SKEWES MATILDA	
SKEWES SAMUEL FRANCIS	Barncoose Terrace, Illogan
SKEWES THOMAS HENRY	Carnkie, Illogan
SKEWES CHARLES	Whitecross Hill, Illogan
SKEWES ADA JANE	
SKEWES MAUDE ANNIE	Packsaddle, Mabe
SKEWES HENRY	
SKEWES LIONEL JAMES	
SKEWES FREDERICK	South Carn, Brea, Illogan
SKEWES ADA	
SKEWES FREDERICK TRESIZE	Bowling Green, Illogan
SKEWES ANNIE MAUD	
SKEWES JAMES	Bosleake Row, Illogan
SKEWES EDITH	

SKEWES JOHN	Plain-an-Gwarry, Redruth
SKEWS SARAH	
SKEWS MARTIN	12, Bellview, Redruth
SKEWS ETHEL	
SKEWS MARY JANE	3, Bellview, Redruth
SKEWES RICHARD ERNEST	18, Adelaide Road, Redruth
SKEWES MINNIE	
SKEWES ELIZABETH ANN	79, Higher Fore Street, Redruth
SKEWES WILLIAM HEDLEY	Dopp's Terrace, Redruth
SKEWES NELLIE	
SKEWES ETHEL	23, Trefusis Road, Redruth
SKUES JAMES FREDERICK	16, Trefusis Road, Redruth
SKUES ADA	
SKEWES THOMAS HENRY	Redruth Coombe, Redruth
SKEWES ANNIE MAUD	

Residing at SKEWIS, Crowan were Alfred and Alice Rowe and John and Joanna Trevenen. At KUS SKEWIS were William Giels and Bessie Nichols and George & Mary Jane Warn. At HIGHER SKEWIS resided Kate, Mary and Madeline Trevenen.

VOTERS LIST FOR CAMBORNE, REDRUTH, GWENNAP and PERRANZABULOE 1932

SKEWES CHARLES	Helstonwater, Perranwell Station,
SKEWES BESSIE ANNIE	Kea
SKEWIS LOUISA JANE	70, College Street, Camborne
SKEWES HENRY OSWALD	4, Centenary Street, Camborne
SKEWES EMILY ANN	
SKEWES VERONICA MAY	
SKEWES DORIS MURIEL	
SKEWES GEORGE	
SKEWES ADA	37, Dolcoath Avenue, Camborne
SKEWES MINNIE	Unity, St Day, Gwennap
SKEWES GEORGE HOLDSWORTH	Coswinsawen, Gwinear
SKEWES THOMAS WILLIAM	Trevarth Road, Carharrack, Gwennap
SKEWES ELIZABETH	Barncoose Road, Illogan Highway
SKEWES ARTHUR	Lower Pumpfield Row, Pool, Illogan
SKEWES ETHEL WINIFRED	
SKEWES HENRY	Packsaddle, Mabe
SKEWES MAUDE ANNA	
SKEWES LIONEL JAMES	
SKEWES BERTRAM	Mithian, St Agnes
SKEWES ELIZA	
SKEWES ALFRED JOHN	Mayne's Row, Tuckingmill, Camborne
SKEWES MATILDA	
SKEWES JAMES HENRY OSWALD	7, Moor Street, Camborne
SKEWES JESSIE VICTORIA	

Maynes Row, Tuckingmill

SKEWES WILLIAM JOHN	Condurrow Farm, Beacon, Camborne
SKEWES LILLIAN MAY	
SKEWES ADA	10, Condurrow Road, Beacon, Camborne
SKEWES MARY MARJORIE	
SKEWES WALTER NICHOLAS	51, Pendarves Street, Beacon, Camborne
SKEWES KATIE	
SKEWES FRED TRESIZE	Loscombe Lane, Four Lanes, Redruth
SKEWES JAMES	Carnarthen Moor, Carn Brea, Illogan
SKEWES HILDA	
SKEWES JOHN HENRY	Carnarthen Villas, Carn Brea, Illogan
SKEWES EVELYN MAY	
SKEWES JOHN HENRY	Four Lanes, Illogan
SKEWES ELIZA JANE	
SKEWES DORIS	
SKEWES WILLIAM HENRY	Brea, Camborne
SKEWES GLADYS	
SKEWES THOMAS HENRY	Higher Carnkie, Illogan
SKEWES ANNIE MAUDE	
SKEWES WILLIAM JOHN	West Carnarthen Farm, Brea, Adit
SKEWES EDITH MARY	
SKEWES JAMES HENRY	Golla, Callestick, Perranzabuloe
SKEWES MAUD MARY	
SKEWES LILIA	
SKEWES HARRY	
SKEWES WILLIAM FRANK	Lovely Value, Mithian, St Agnes
SKEWES ANNIE DORIS	
SKEWES HERBERT JOHN	Crowan Vicarage, Crowan
SKEWES HENRIETTA	
SKEWES MARTIN	3, Bellview, Redruth
SKEWES ETHEL	
SKEWES WILLIAM HEDLEY	61, East End, Redruth
SKEWES NELLIE	
SKEWES RICHARD ERNEST	18, Adelaide Road, Redruth
SKEWES MINNIE	
SKUES JAMES FREDERICK	16, Trefusis Terrace, Redruth
SKUES ADA	
SKUES JAMES FREDERICK	
SKUES PHYLLIS	

Residing at SKEWIS, Crowan were Alice James and Kathleen Rowe; also Alfred Ernest, Olive and Alice May Rowe. At KUS SKEWIS were Frederick and Mary Harvey.

VOTERS LIST FOR CAMBORNE & REDRUTH, 1949

SKEWES EMMA	Trevarth Vean, Lanner, Redruth
SKEWES WILLIAM	
SKEWES ENID	Buckingham Place, St Day, Redruth
SKEWES HARRY	27, Cardew Close, Redruth
SKEWES ETHEL	
SKUES JAMES FREDERICK	16, Trefusis Terrace, Redruth
SKUES ERNEST	
SKUES LEWIS	
SKEWES RICHARD ERNEST	36, Adelaide Road, Redruth
SKEWES MINNIE	
SKEWES ANNIE	Palmleigh, Four Lanes, Redruth
SKEWES THOMAS H.	Four Lanes, Redruth
SKEWES JOHN H.	Western Froggeries, Peace,
SKEWES FLORENCE	Carnkie, Redruth
SKEWES CHARLES	Penpol, Chariot Road, Illogan Highway
SKEWES MATILDA	Barncoose Hospital, Illogan Highway
SKEWES DORIEL	1, Penhallick, Carn Brea, Illogan
SKEWES EDITH	
SKEWES MURIEL	
SKEWES ALFRED JOHN	Bartles Row, Tuckingmill, Camborne
SKEWES EDWARD	
SKEWES MATILDA	
SKEWES GEORGE	12, Lower Pumpfield, Pool, Redruth
SKEWES JOYCE	
SKEWES GEORGE	32, Wellington Road, Camborne
SKEWES PHYLLIS	

SKEWES LESLIE	15, Newton Road, Troon, Camborne
SKEWES LILIAN	
SKEWES VIOLET	3, Laity Road, Troon, Camborne
SKEWES CECIL	51, Pendarves Street, Beacon, Camborne
SKEWES WALTER	42a, Fore Street, Beacon, Camborne
SKEWES CATHERINE	
SKEWES ADA	10 Condurrow Road, Beacon, Camborne
SKEWES WILLIAM	Lower Condurrow, Condurrow, Camborne
SKEWES LILIAN	
SKEWES ANNIE	Lower Pengegon, Pengegon, Camborne
SKEWES JAMES	12, Atlantic Terrace, Camborne
SKEWES JESSIE	
SKEWES DORIS	35, North Parade, Camborne
SKEWES HORACE	6, Roskear Road, Camborne
SKEWES IRIS	

Residing at SKEWIS FARM, Crowan were Joseph and Clarinda Jenkin; at SKEWIS COTTAGE, Edwin and Carol Jenkin; The Pascoe Family lived at LITTLE KUS SKEWIS and Daisy & John C. Rowe resided at KUS SKEWIS.

VOTERS LIST FOR THE COUNTY OF CORNWALL, 1980

SKEWS ENID	11 Bogara Way, Liskeard
SKEWS KENNETH W.	
SKEWS STEPHEN K.	
SKUES ELSIE M.	**Trebron, The Downs, West Looe**
SKEWS DEREK T.	4 Moonsfield, Callington
SKEWS LINDA	
SKEWS COURTENAY J.G.	35 Sunnybanks, Hatt, Saltash
SKEWS SYLVIA I.	
SKEWS ANDREW I.	19 Fairfield Estate, St Germans
SKEWS PAMELA E.L.	
SKUSE DOROTHY J.	Anos-I-Bey, The Quay, St Germans
SKUSE BERNARD E.	Tideford Lodge, St Germans
SKUSE JEAN M.P.	
SKEWS WILFRED G.	1, Albert Cottages, St Ive
SKEWS ELIZABETH J.	Leyspring, Jubilee Road, St Ive
SKEWS MAUREEN J.	
SKEWS STANLEY G.	
SKEWS ALBERT P.	3, Princess Terrace, St Ive
SKEWS MARY	
SKEWS HARRY	Mount View, Quarry Road, Pensilva
SKEWS JEAN	
SKEWS MARTIN REX	14 Kernick Road, Penryn, Falmouth
SKEWES SAMUEL P.	Manor Farm, Trequite, St Kew
SKEWES HILDA	
SKEWES CONSTANCE	
SKEWES GWENDOLINE	Trengrouse House, Helston
SKEWES CHRISTOPHER J.	7 Lady Street, Helston
SKEWES HAZEL J.	
SKEWES ANNIE D.	30 Glebe Place, Ruan Minor
SKEWES JOHN T.	
SKEWES WILLIAM F.	
SKEWES MAVIS E.	Seagulls Cry, Cadgwith
SKEWES NICOLA	
SKEWES JOHN R.	
SKEWES ARTHUR R.	
SKEWES LEONNIE P.	The Jolly Tinners, Churchtown, St Hilary
SKEWES RICHARD J.	
SKEWES HARRY	6 Bowling Green Terrace, St Ives
SKEWES JOSEPHINE	
SKEWES ARTHUR R.	White Close, Trevalsoe, St Keverne
SKEWES MARGARET B.	
SKEWES JUNE	White Rocks, Porthallow
SKEWES DENNIS I.J.	
SKEWES EDITH	2 Carn Villas, Ludgvan
SKEWES ANNIE	Trewince Farm, St Martin in Meneage
SKEWES MATTHEW H.	
SKEWES WILLIAM C.	
SKEWES JOHN O.	Gweal Mor, Newtown, St Martin in Meneage
SKEWES PATRICIA A.	

SKEWES GILBERT J.	Trelaminney, St Martin in Meneage
SKEWES JANET M.	
SKEWES JOHN C.	
SKEWES KATHLEEN J.	
SKEWES SANDRA	
SKEWES CELIA	Trezemper Farm, Goonhilly Downs, Garras, Helston
SKEWES OSWALD C.	
SKEWES SUSAN	
SKEWES ANGELA	Restormal, Nansmellyon Road, Mullion, Helston
SKEWES JEFFREY L.	
SKEWES MAURICE	Laflouder, Laflouder Lane, Mullion, Helston
SKEWES THELMA	11 Chiverton Way, Rosudgeon, Penzance
SKEWES WILLIAM R.	
SKEWES DOROTHY B.	Chiverton Farm, Rosudgeon, Penzance
SKEWES LAURA	
SKEWES ANITA E.	Ridge Mount, Trebarvah Lane, Rosudgeon, Penzance
SKEWES DONALD J.	
SKEWES EDITH	Trebarvah Farm, Rosudgeon, Penzance
SKEWES WILLIAM R.	
SKEWS PAMELA E.	9 Railway Cottages, Falmouth
SKEWES LOTTIE D.	10 Loscombe Road, Illogan South
SKEWES COLIN	Colvreath Cottage, Colvreath, Roche
SKEWES EDWINA A.	
SKEWES ELIZABETH	7 Chegwyn Gardens, St Agnes
SKEWES JAMES H.	Woodlands, Mithian, St Agnes
SKEWES RONALD	25 Trevanion Road, St Austell
SKEWES NATALIE E.	
SKEWES JACK P.O.	12 Atlantic Terrace, Camborne
SKEWES HORACE	49 Dolcoath Avenue, Camborne
SKEWES IRIS V.	
SKEWES CARL	33 Roskear Road, Camborne
SKEWES DOREEN	
SKEWES ALFRED J.	8 Scowbuds, Tuckingmill
SKEWES LILY	
SKEWES CECIL	51 Pendarves Street, Beacon, Camborne
SKEWES DOLORES	
SKEWES JAMES F.	1 Ford's Row, Redruth
SKEWES VIOLET M	46 Laity Road, Troon, Camborne
SKEWES KENNETH ROY	
SKEWES GEORGE H.	53 Tehidy Road, Camborne
SKEWES PHYLLIS	
SKEWES LESLIE	44 Weeth Lane, Camborne
SKEWES LILIAN	
SKEWES GEORGE	Roskeith, 140 Agar Road, Illogan Highway
SKEWES JOYCE	
SKEWES ANNIE M.	Fernside, Carn Lane, Carnkie, Redruth
SKEWES PRISCILLA	
SKEWES FLORENCE	27 Tresavean Estate, Lanner, Redruth
SKEWES LEWIS	90 Tresaderns Road, Redruth
SKEWES WILLIAM J.	27 Beacon Parc, Helston
SKEWES WENDY V.	
SKEWES PETER N.	
SKEWES WILLIAM J.	78 Wheal Rose, Porthlevan, Helston
SKEWES NORA	
SKEWES GWENDOLINE	4 Kynance Terrace, Landewednack, The Lizard

Residing at GREAT SKEWES, St Wenn were James and Daisy Hawkey; at LITTLE SKEWES — Lavinia and Clive A. Rowse; at SKEWES FARM, Cury — Antony and Sandra Boaden; SKEWES FARM COTTAGE, Cury — Alec C. and Phyllis M. Tucker; Clara Keverne lived at TRESKEWES FARM COTTAGE, St. Keverne; at TRESKEWES FARM, St Keverne — Mary L. and Phyllis M.P. James; Edwin T. Rowe was at TRESKEWIS FARM, Stithians and Carol and Leslie Jenkin lived at SKEWIS FARM, Crowan.

TELEPHONE DIRECTORIES

Directories for the London area date back to 1880 (later in the provinces) and are retained at the headquarters of the London Telecommunications Centre situated near Old Street tube station, London. By 1883 some 2500 persons had their phones connected to the General Post Office Exchange and paid an annual rental of £20.

The first entry for a SKEWES was THOMAS SKEWES-COX of 15, Red Lion Square, London WC (Telephone number 2798) which appeared in 1887. Six years later the name was extended to SKEWES-COX, Nash and Company moving to 8, Lancaster Place, London, W.C., but retaining the same telephone number. There was also an extra entry for SKEWES-COX, solicitor, based at 40, George Street, Richmond (telephone number Richmond 126). In 1908 THOMAS SKEWES-COX was knighted and appeared in the directory as Sir T. SKEWES-COX, solicitor, working from 40, George Street, Richmond, and living at The Manor House, Petersham (telephone number P.O. Richmond 734). He died in 1912 and Lady Skewes-Cox took over the "billing". She remained at the same address retaining the same telephone number until 1930 when she died. A Miss S.P. SKEWES-COX appeared in the 1941 directory at 411, Nell Gwynne House, Sloane Avenue, London, S.W.3. (telephone number Kensington 1521).

JOHN KEMPTHORNE SKEWES appeared in the 1902/1903 London telephone directory. He was a milliner, draper and outfitter of 31, Broadway, Wimbledon (telephone number Wimbledon 84).

Meanwhile the Bristol 1902/1903 directory listed SKEWES Brothers, Tailors, of 21, Clare Street (telephone number Fishponds 125X). It is interesting to note that in the late 1950's there were some 80 entries for SKUSE in Bristol although the number had dropped by 1975. There was not one entry for SKUSE in 1902/1903.

In Plymouth the first entry for SKEWES was in 1904/1905 with J. SKEWES of 41, Old Town Street. (telephone number Plymouth 10YL).

The first SKUSE was E. SKUSE, a specialist in confectionary at 1, Ashmore Road, London W. (telephone number Paddington 1372). This entry is from the 1904/5 telephone directory.

The first SKEWIS was EDWIN SKEWIS, surveyor and auctioneer of 29, Park Place, London W. (telephone number Paddington 4252) — 1904/5 directory.

The first SKUES was CHARLES AYRE MACKENZIE SKUES, architect and surveyor of 45, Lincoln's Inn Fields, London WC (telephone number Holborn 2591) who appeared in the London directory from 1914 to 1917 and later moved to 16, Tooks Court, London WC.

A search through the 1979/1980 telephone directories for England, Scotland, Wales and Northern Ireland brought these results:

LONDON

SKEWES	D.G.	Doctor. 27 Riverview Grove, London W.4.	01 994 6846
SKEWES	JAS. E.	Opthalmic Optician. 240 Earl's Court Road, London SW5	01 370 4912
SKEWES-COX	F.	28 Chaldron Road, London SW6.	01 385 5185
SKEWS	G.J.	8 Chewton Road, London E. 17.	01 520 7603
SKUES	J.J.G.	178 Maxey Road, London SE 18.	01 854 0060
SKUES	S.T.	55b Compton Road, London N 21.	01 360 9567

OUTER LONDON S.W. ESSEX

SKEWS	D.G.	60 Valentines Way, Dagenham	01 592 5974
SKEWS	M.E.	2 Bedford House, Petersfield Avenue, Romford, Essex	04023 70174

SOUTH HERTS and NORTH MIDDLESEX and WEST MIDDLESEX

SKEWS	H.G.	Captain. 107 Bulstrode Avenue, Hounslow	01 572 3041
SKEWS	H.M.	23 Cole Park Road, Twickenham	01 892 4927
SKUES	ERNEST J.	13 Blundell Road, Edgware	01 959 0582

NORTH WEST KENT

SKEWS	D.M.	26 Embassy Court, Lansdowne Road, Sidcup, Kent	01 300 4355
SKUES	D.J.	85 James Road, Dartford	0322 70539
SKUES	L.A.	97 Kingswood Road, Shortlands	01 460 9169

CAMBRIDGE
SKEWS   J.H.   14 Chepstow Road, Bury St Edmunds   0284 63564
SKEWS   D.A.   619a Newmarket Road, Cambridge   02205 3521

SOUTHEND-ON-SEA
SKEWS   W.   40 Little Wakering Road, Great Wakering   0702 217267
SKUES   S.V.   Rena, Branksome Avenue, Wickford   03744 4304
SKUES   T.F.   87 High Mead, Rayleigh   0268 776343

BIRMINGHAM
SKEWES   S.L.   60 Burnside Way, Birmingham 31   021 477 3914
SKUES   G.E.   31 Eastern Road, Sutton Coldfield   021 355 3492

COLCHESTER
SKEWS   C.R.   9 Friends Field, Bures   0787 227885
SKEWS   F.   5 The Willows, Colchester   0206 43865
SKUES OF WALTON   The Builders, St. John's Yard, Skelmersdale Road, Clacton-on-Sea   0255 28252
SKUES   V.   6a New Gate Road, Walton-on-Naze   02556 5611
SKUES   V.   General Shop, The Cabin, Connaught Avenue, Walton-on-Naze   02556 71806

COVENTRY
SKUES   J.A.   Rev. 8 Shirley Road, Coventry   0203 614193

LEICESTER
SKUES   A.   32 Blaby Road, South Wigston   05378 6985

PETERBOROUCH
SKEWIS   J.A.   7 Ivatt Court, Grantham   0476 72879
SKEWS   J.G.   28 South Street, Crowland   0733 210352

LINCOLN
SKEWS   L.   53 Dar Beck Road, Scotter   0724 762959

NEWCASTLE UPON TYNE
SKEWS   F.C.   23 South Hetton Road, Easington Lane, Hetton-le-Hole   0783 264768
SKEWS   JOHN H.   St Nicholas House, Hetton-le-Hole   0783 262331
SKEWS   KIRTLEY   29 Wordsworth Avenue East, Houghton-le-Spring   0783 843338

LEEDS
SKEWES   J.H.   5 Station Fields, Garforth   0532 862440
SKEWES   JOHN HORNBY & Co Ltd.   Salem House, Main Street, Garforth   0532 865381

NORTH EAST SURREY
SKEWES   E.M.   49 Addiscombe Road, Croydon   01 688 3925
SKEWES   P.B.   1 Marlowe Court, Parkleys, Richmond   01 546 9439
SKUES   A.   36 Well House, Woodmanstone Lane, Banstead   07373 52403
SKUES   R.A.   42 Poplar Crescent, West Ewell   01 397 8434

MANCHESTER
SKEWES   E.   31 Curzon Gardens, Offerton   061 483 2427
SKEWES   E.T.   11 Eastway, Sale   061 973 2722
SKEWES   J.F.   12 Walnut Walk, Stretford   061 865 5748
SKEWES   J.H.   48 Petersfield Drive, Manchester, 23   061 969 5822
SKEWS   D.   15 Eydal Close, Bury   061 761 1341
SKEWS   R.D.   65 Ullswater, Macclesfield   0625 20587

PRESTON
SKUES   E.   Vinclyn, Dawson Lane, Whittle-le-Woods   02572 3192

GLASGOW
SKEWIES   A.F.   4 Douglas Drive, Glasgow   0698 852268
SKEWIS DAVID   9 Drumry Place, Glasgow, 15   041 944 1426
SKEWIS   G.   42 Kaystone Road, Glasgow, 15   041 944 2034
SKEWIS   H.M.   8/5, 19 Pinkston Drive, Glasgow, 21   041 557 0139

STOKE-ON-TRENT
SKEWS   P.J.   12 David Street, Shelton   0782 271204

SOUTH WEST SCOTLAND
SKEWIES   ANITA G.   66 Cameron Crescent, Hamilton   0698 423383

SKEWIES	JAS.	Hall Road, Nemphlar, Lanark	0555 61402
SKEWIS	JOHN J.	16 Ridge Park Drive, Lanark	0555 3894
SKEWIS	JOHN	17 Springwood Bank, Kelso	05732 2546

SWANSEA

| SKEWS | T.W. | 9 Waun Road, Upper Loughor, Gorseinon | 0972 896280 |

BRIGHTON

SKEWS	R.W.	1 Meadow Way, Littlehampton	09064 5849
SKUES	R.T.	16 Lower Drive, Seaford	0323 894436
SKUES	S.M.	1 Rydal Mount, St John's Road, Eastbourne	0323 26897

CANTERBURY

SKEWIS	T.	24b Old Park Avenue, Canterbury	0227 51672
SKEWS	R.E.	73 James Street, Gillingham	0634 572101
SKUES	B.R.	Chene, Stumble Lane, Kingsnorth	0233 34895
SKUES	M.	Tamboo, Chalksole Garden, Alkham	03047 4118
SKUES	R.A.T.	7 Rylands Road, Bybrook	0233 23057

BOURNEMOUTH

| SKUES | R. | 26 Pine Park Mansions, Wilderton Road, Branksome Park, Poole | 0202 760786 |

BRADFORD

SKEWES	C.W.	9 Croft Rise, Menston	0943 73051
SKUES	E.	11 Bell Hall Terrace, Savile Park, Halifax	0422 58604
SKUES	F.	14 Second Avenue, Halifax	0422 60720

EXETER

| SKEWES | C.L. | 80 Wellington Road, Exeter | 0392 74543 |
| SKEWES-COX (Colonel) | | Uphill House, Ponsworthy, Ashburton | 03643 386 |

GLOUCESTER

| SKEWS | A.E. | 52 South View Avenue, Swindon | 0793 29884 |

TAUNTON

| SKEWES | G.M. | Farmer. Barford Farm, Spaxton | 027867 266 |

PLYMOUTH

SKEWES	A.R.	Kittiwake, Churchtown, Mullion	0326 240727
SKEWES	C.	Colvreath Cottage, Colvreath	07253 474
SKEWES	D.I.L.	Cellar Gar., Porthallow	03266 214
SKEWES	D.J.	Ridgemount, Trebarvah, Perranuthnoe	0736 710042
SKEWES	G.	18 Agar Crescent, Illogan Highway	0209 215334
SKEWES	G.H.	53 Tehidy Road, Camborne	0209 713518
SKEWES	H.	Boskewys, Burthallen Lane, St Ives	0736 797896
SKEWES	J.	Manor Farm, Panwartha	087257 3604
SKEWES	JOHN H.	10 Rose Cottages, Camborne	0209 712571
SKWEWS	J.L.	Restormal, Nansmellyon Road, Mullion	0326 240143
SKEWES	J.P.	Trecarne, Atlantic Terrace, Camborne	0209 712422
SKEWES	L.	44 Weeth Lane, Camborne	0209 714629
SKEWES	L.D.	10 Loscombe Road, Four Lanes	0209 214696
SKEWES	M.	Electrical Contractors. Chy-an-Coth, Laflouder Lane, Mullion	0326 240707
SKEWES	M.	6 Roseland Park, Camborne	0209 714566
SKEWES	M.H.	Potato Merchant. Trewince, St Martin	032623 304
SKEWES	O.C.	Trezemper Farm, Goonhilly Downs	0326 22607
SKEWES	RONALD	14 Trevear Close, St Austell	0726 3171
SKEWES	R. JOHN	The Jolly Tinners, St Hilary	0736 710144
SKEWES	W.	Farmer. Chiverton	0736 710412
SKEWES	W.J.	27 Beacon Parc, Helston	0326 4722
SKEWES	W.J.	87 Wheal Rose, Porthlevan	0326 62344
SKEWES	W.R.	Market gardener. Trebarvah Farm, Perranuthnoe	0736 710430
SKEWES	W. ROGER	Market gardener. Chiverton Way, Rosudgeon	0736 763344
SKEWIS	ARTHUR & EFFIE	31 Agar Road, Illogan Highway	0209 216576
SKEWS	A.J.	19 Fairfield Estate, St Germans	05033 557
SKEWS	C.J.C.	35 Sunnybanks, Hatt, Saltash	07555 4760
SKEWS	C.R.	53 Eastcliffe Road, Par	072681 405
SKEWS	D.M.	The Mount, Central Treviscoe, St Stephen	0726 822263
SKEWS	HARRY	Mount View, Quarry Road, Pensilva	0579 62733
SKEWS	J.W.	2 Urban Terrace, Callington	05793 2789
SKEWS	M.	20 Saunders Walk, Southway	0752 778904
SKEWS	M.R.	14 Kernick Road, Penryn	0326 72419

SKEWS	N.G.	72 Conway Road, Penryn	0326 72648
SKEWS	P.	Iona, Princess Road, Pensilva	0579 62872
SKUES	R.P.	Trebron, The Downs, West Looe	05036 2739
SOUTHAMPTON			
SKUES	C.H.V.	Sylcombe Hunt Lodge, Petersfield Road, Ropley	096277 3463
CARDIFF			
SKEWES	ALARINA	West End Stop, Caldicot	0291 420214
SHREWSBURY			
SKEWS	E.	3 Featherbed Lane, Shrewsbury	0743 51969
NORTHAMPTON			
SKEWIS	J.	95 Greenhill Rise, Corby	05366 65957
HULL			
SKEWIS	DAVID	10 Devon Street, Gipsyville	0482 501627
SKEWIS	M.I.	3 Woodhall Street, Stoneferry Rd	0482 217770
SKEWS	S.	161 James Reckitt Avenue	0482 798492
SHEFFIELD & ROTHERHAM			
SKEWS	D.	11 Woodland View, Wombwell	0226 753530
SKEWS	J.	67 Wood Walk, Wombwell	0226 755053

PRESS CUTTINGS

These are an extremely useful source of information and many newspapers dating back to 1800 have been retained in the Newspaper Library at Colindale, North London — a branch of the British Library.

The two leading newspapers for the county of Cornwall from the middle of the last century were *Royal Cornwall Gazette* and *West Briton*. A great deal of time was spent searching through "Births, Marriages and Deaths" in each edition. A few unusual entries (not connected with the Skues family) caught the writer's eye:

RCG — 13 March, 1813 "Marriages-Captain James Baryunanna of Gwennap to Miss Jane Teague of Redruth, an amiable young lady with a large fortune!"

RCG 12 March, 1814 "The death at Penzance of Thomas Hugh, aged 81, for many years Sexton of this parish, and famous for his eccentricities. Complaining of the badness of the times he declared in support of his argument he had "not buried one *living* soul for upwards of a month."

RCG 28 May, 1814 "Married last week J. May of Ham House in this county aged 42 years to Miss Dixon, aged only 13 years and ten months."

RCG 4 February, 1815 "Died at Gwithian, the Rev. Rowland Veale who had for ten years nearly been a lunatic."

RCG 21 December, 1816 "Married last week after a courtship of 18 years, Lieut John Arnall, R.N. of the Borough of Camelford to Miss Toy of Penryn."

RCG 21 December, 1817 "Died in the Barracks, Truro on Monday morning of a Dropsy in the chest, Mrs Herd, wife of Sergeant Major Herd of the 15th Hussars."

RCG 20 March, 1820 "Died at St Austell on Friday last, while engaged in conversation in the Market Place, Matthew Rosewear of Luxillian. Also Sampson Vivian, of this parish, on his road, from his field to his house. Also Richard Julian, Esq., our much lamented Mayor — awful instances of the frail and uncertain tenure of human life — the persons whose names are recorded having been one moment in possession of perfect health, and the next suddenly expired."

RCG 4 April, 1835 "Married at Steynton Church, Mr J.T. Mason of Milford to Mrs Elizabeth Stephens of the former place. The Bridegroom has attained the patriachal age of 101 years, and is possession of considerable property. The blooming Bride is about 33 years, and ten months ago consigned her former spouse to the silent tomb."

Now follows a list of Skues/Skewes who found themselves in print. All extracts from the *Royal Cornwall Gazette* or *West Briton*, except where stated:

RCG 27 April, 1811 "Died on Saturday after an illness of seven years which she bore with distinguished fortitude and Christian recognition, Mrs Mitchell, wife of Mr Mitchell of Truro, and daughter of Mr SKEWES of Helston."

Journal 1810, No 46 (Edited by Christopher Wallis), 17 November, 1811 "This day died at Helston, Mr RICHARD SKUES, Surgeon and Apothecary, aged 45 years. He has left a widow (formerly Mary Richards) and four children. Buried at Helston 20 November, 1811. He had the care of Sithney poor."

RCG 23 November, 1811 "Died on Sunday at Helston, esteemed and regretted, Mr SKUES, Surgeon and Apothecary, aged 45 years."

RCG 7 January, 1815 "Married on Thursday last Mr CHARLES SKUES to Miss Mary Bennett at Helston."

RCG 1 March, 1817 "Died suddenly at Helston on Saturday last at the advanced age of 82, much lamented by a very numerous aquaintance WILLIAM SKUES who faithfully filled the office of the Tin Coinage for Cornwall and Devon, under the Duke of Cornwall, upwards of 50 years. He is succeeded in his office by his grandson RICHARD SKUES."

RCG 21 June, 1817 "Married at Camborne on Monday last Edward Tippett to Miss SKEWES, daughter of Mr HENRY SKEWES of Rosewear, in Gwinear."

RCG 12 September, 1818 "Married on Wednesday at Kenwyn, Mr JOHN SKEWS of Chacewater to Miss NANCY SKEWS of Twelveheads."

RCG 6 November, 1819 "The birth lately at Helston, the lady of RICHARD SKUES, Esq., of Helston, of a daughter."

RCG 17th and 24 March, 1821 JOHN SKEWES a freeholder, HENRY SKEWES an inhabitant of Meneage and JOHN SKEWS, inhabitant of Illogan lent their name to "The Declaration" which approved the conduct of the High Sheriff of Cornwall in refusing to call a county meeting to consider the propriety of petitioning the House of Commons for the insertion of the Queen's name in a liturgy.

RCG 14 April, 1821 "Died at Trenarth last Sunday, the Lady of RICHARD SKUES, Esq., of Helston."

RCG 5 January, 1822 "Died last week at Trenarth, the seat of Henry Noy, Esq., at the early age of two years and two months, of water on the chest, Miss GRACE NOY SKUES, only child of RICHARD SKUES of Helston."

RCG 24 August, 1824 "Married at Helston on Wednesday last, Mr. W. Radford, Methodist Minister at Ashburton, Devon to GRACE, eldest daughter of the late RICHARD SKUES of Helston."

RCG 14 July, 1827 "Died at Carharrack, Gwennap, on Tuesday, Mr R. SKEWES, age 28 years."

RCG 26 January, 1828 "Married at Crowan on Thursday, Mr Paull of Camborne to Miss Trevenen, eldest daughter of Mr Trevenen of SKUES, Crowan."

RCG 13 September, 1828 "Birth at Carharrack, to Mrs SKEWES, a daughter."

RCG 3 June, 1829 "The Roman Catholic Question."
"We the undersigned Gentry, Clergy, Shopkeepers and Owners or Occupiers of land in the Hundred of Kerrier being firmly attached to our Protestant constitution as by law, established, have considered it necessary to make a Declaration of our adherence to its principals, and to express our unfeigned hope, that persons professing the Roman Catholic Faith, and acknowledging the spiritual supremacy of a foreign Priest, may never become members of the legislative or executive government of Great Britain. The Protestants of this district should have the opportunity of declaring their sentiments publicly, and we hereby invite them to meet us in Helston, on Wednesday 7th January at 12 o'clock, there and then to take into consideration the necessity of petitioning Parliament against the concession of political power to Roman Catholics."
(There were some 200 names listed and included among them were ALEXANDER SKEWES of East Kerrier and WILLIAM SKUES of Meneage)

RCG 17 July, 1830. At the Cornwall Sessions in Bodmin. "ANN SKEWES, aged 34, was charged with stealing printed cotton belonging to Joseph and John Tynell in consquence of informality in the indictment, was acquitted."
Had Ann Skewes been found guilty of stealing she could have received a very serious sentence — which was not at all uncommon during that period in history. People had received the death sentence of stealing.

RCG 5 November, 1831 "Death at Ruan Major last week after a lingering affliction, aged 82, Mr HENRY SKUES, a respectable farmer of that parish."

RCG 24 March, 1832 "Birth at Holmbush near Charlestown, last week Mrs DANIEL SKEWES, of a son."

RCG 31 March, 1832, JAMES SKEWES of Fairmantle Street, Truro was a principal witness in a murder case which was heard at Cornwall Lent Assizes in Launceston on 28th March, 1832. Full story in the "Appendix".

RCG 7 April, 1832. At the Cornwall Lent Assizes (Quarter Sessions)
"John William was indicted for obtaining under false pretences the sum of five shillings from HENRY SKEWS, innkeeper of Helston. 'Guilty' and sentenced to six months imprisonment and hard labour".

RCG 10 November, 1832 "Married at Gwennap on 27th October, Mr A. Bray of Minglers, to JOHANNA, third daughter of ALEXANDER SKEWES, Esq., of Chenhall House."

RCG 3 May, 1834 "Married at Constantine last week Mr JAMES SKUES of Cury to Miss SKUES of Brill, Constantine."

RCG 21 March, 1835 "Died at Camborne on Saturday, ANN SKEWES aged 32 years. She went to bed apparently in good health, was taken ill and died before morning."

RCG 21 March, 1835 "Died at Camborne, on Sunday morning, having retired to bed in good health ANN SKEWES, aged 40 years. She was a consistent member of the Wesleyan Society for 13 years, and walked worthy of her profession."[5]

RCG 16 October, 1835 "Married at Constantine on the 8th October, Mr T. Medlin to Miss SKUES."

RCG 9 February, 1838 "Death at Helston on Monday last Miss A. SKEWES aged 63 years. Also on Tuesday last of her sister-in-law Mrs SKEWES, wife of Mr W. SKEWES, carpenter, aged 55 years."
A similar article appeared in the *West Briton*, but spelt the name SKUES and was more specific with the "W" of Mr W. SKEWES, and the "A" of Miss A. SKEWES.
"Death at Helston on Monday last of Miss ANN SKUES, aged 63 years. Also on Tuesday Mrs SKUES, wife of WILLIAM SKUES, carpenter (sister-in-law of the above), aged 55 years."

RCG 10 August, 1838 "Marriage at St Hilary on Monday last, Mr HENRY SKEWES to Miss Courtis."
West Briton and Cornwall Advertiser, 25 October, 1838. "Born at Helston on 22nd October to the wife of Mr H. SKUES, schoolmaster, a son."

RCG 14 December, 1838 "Married at Helston on Tuesday last, Mr William Pearce to Miss ANN SKEWES, both of that place."

RCG 5 February, 1841 "Death in London of Mr CHARLES SKEWES who formerly carried on business in Helston as a tailor and druggist." (*West Briton* also carried the death notice but spelt the name SKUES.)

RCG 9 July, 1841 "Cornwall Midsummer Sessions."
At the Cornwall Midsummer Sessions held in Bodmin on 30th June, BENJAMIN SKEWES was accused of stealing in the parish of Budock, a quantity of old copper, the property of James Ball.
Mr Bennallack for the prisoner moved the Court, and contended that the indictment was in many ways very incorrect, which was agreed, and the prisoner acquitted.

WB 10 September, 1841 "Important to Retail Brewers."
"On Tuesday last, Mr JOHN SKEWES, of Carthew in the parish of St Austell, retail brewer, was summoned before the bench of magistrates at St Austell for allowing spirits to be consumed on his premises. The complaint was grounded on the 4th and 5th William c85, s16, which enacts that if any person licenced to sell beer or cider, shall permit or suffer any wine or spirits, sweet or made wines, mead or metheglin, to be brought into his house or premises to be drunk or consumed there, by any persons whomsoever, such person shall, over and above any excise penalty, forfeit £20. The facts of the case were as follows:
Mr Elias Martin, of St. Austell, gave a dinner party to the numerous persons employed at his clay works, on the 24th August, and used the rooms of Mr SKEWES's house, of which Mr Martin is the proprietor for the purpose. Mr Martin gave after the dinner a glass of spirits; two bowls of punch were also made. It was therefore contended to SKEWES that he was not liable to the penalty, in as much as he had not knowingly permitted the spirit to be consumed, and the bench coinciding in this view, dismissed the case."

W.B. 21 January, 1842 "To Sir Charles Lemon, B.T. We the undersigned Electors of the Western Division of Cornwall, gratefully recollecting your unremitting and able attention to the business of this county — your intimate knowledge of its various interests, and the valuable services you were thereby enabled to render, and feeling that your independent and enlightened conduct through four successive Parliaments is the best guarantee for the future, are induced earnestly to request that you will permit yourself to be placed in nomination as a Candidate for this Division, at the approaching Election."
Dated 10th January, 1842 and signed by WILLIAM SKEWES, JOHN SKEWES, HENRY SKEWES, JAMES SKEWES, HENRY SKEWES, ALEXANDER SKEWES, SAMUEL SKEWES, ANTHONY SKEWES and JAMES SKEWES and 1700 other Electors.
(In the following week's paper Charles Lemon replied from Carclew, dated 15th January, 1842 saying that he was overwhelmed by the signatures on the Requisition and this had induced him to stand again for Parliament.)

W.B. 22 July, 1842
"Wedding at the Registrar's Office in Helston on Wednesday last of Mr FRANCIS SKEWES of Mullion to Mrs Catherine Chirgwin of Cury."

W.B. 25 November, 1842
"Death at Helston on Saturday last of Mr WILLIAM SKEWES for many years collector of the market tolls of that Borough."

---

[5]These entries have been copied exactly from the newspapers which list Ann Skewes with two different ages.

W.B. 21 July, 1843
"Death on Sunday last at Pengigan, in the parish of Camborne, ANN, wife of HENRY SKEWES, aged 23 years."

W.B. 18 August, 1843
"Married at Kea Church on Monday last Mr Thomas Williams, late of Truro, Excise Officer, to Miss THOMASINE SKEWES of Kea."

W.B. 11 August, 1844
"Died at Killivoase, in Camborne, on 4th instant the wife of Mr JAMES SKEWES."

W.B. 4 October, 1844
"Marriage at Kenwyn of Mr William Scoble to Miss MARY SKEWES."

W.B. 21 February, 1845
"Marriage at the Registrar's Office in Helston on the 13th instant, Mr EDWARD SKEWES to Miss Julia Roberts, both of Cury."

W.B. 22 August, 1845
"To Francis Rodd, Esq., High Sheriff of Cornwall.
We the undersigned request you to convene a County Meeting for the purpose of taking into consideration the most effectual means of insuring for this County, and its various important interests, the most direct and available Railway Communication between Penzance, Falmouth and Exeter.".
Signed by WILLIAM SKEWES and JOSIAH SKEWES and 1000 other names. The High Sheriff arranged a meeting which was held at the Shire Hall in Bodmin on Tuesday 19th August, 1845

W.B. 17 October, 1845
"Death at Cury on the 8th instant of Mr JAMES SKEWES, aged 59 years."

W.B. 23 January, 1846
"Birth at Camborne, on Friday last, the wife of Mr JAMES SKEWES, of a son."

W.B. 12 February, 1847
"Death at East Stonehouse, on Monday last, ANN relict of the late RICHARD SKUES, Esq., Surgeon, formerly of Helston, aged 83 years."
Plymouth, Devonport & Stonehouse Herald, 13 February, 1847 "Death at Durnford Street, East Stonehouse on the 8th instant at the residence of her son-in-law Richard Rodd, Esq., Solicitor, Mrs ANN SKUES, widow of RICHARD SKUES, Esq., Surgeon, formerly of Helston in the county of Cornwall, aged 83 years.
(Identical article in the *Plymouth & Devonport Weekly Journal*)

W.B. 11 December, 1847
Death at Truro on Tuesday last, MARGARET wife of Mr HENRY SKEWES of the New Inn, aged 78 years."

W.B. 10 March, 1848
Death at East Stonehouse on 29th February, MARY, wife of Richard Rodd, Esq., and daughter of RICHARD SKUES, Esq., Surgeon, formerly of Helston, aged 47 years."

W.B. 29 December, 1848
"Marriage at Breage last week of Mr William Pearce to Miss SKUES, both of Helston."

W.B. 8 June, 1849
The Cornwall Agricultural Association awarded numerous prizes including a £5 prize for bringing up the largest family in a parish without any parochial relief. Winner was JOHN SKEWES of Kea who brought up fifteen children.

W.B. 2 November, 1849
"Death at Camborne on Monday last at the house of his son-in-law, Mr Edward Tippett, Mr HENRY SKEWES, late of Truro, and formerly of Roseworthy in the parish of Gwinear, Yeoman, aged 78 years."

W.B. 7 December, 1849
"Marriage at Kenwyn, on Monday last, Mr JOHN SKEWES, cabinet maker, to Mary Brown only daughter of the late James Wendon, shipwright of Padstow."

W.B. 8 February, 1850
"Birth at Truro, on Tuesday last, the wife of Mr JOHN SKEWES, cabinet maker, a daughter."

Articles and extracts from the various West Country newspapers do not end in 1850. In the Appendix there is a complete list of extracts from 1851 to 1980, arranged chronologically.

The search through every edition of the *Royal Cornwall Gazette* and *West Briton* took many years, but a tremendous amount of useful information was collected. It was known that certain members of the family moved to Plymouth, Abergavenny, Durham, London, Halifax, Dartford and Salford.

When a town is known searches through local newspapers can prove beneficial. For example this notice appeared in the *Stockport Advertiser* (Cheshire) in April, 1945.

DEATH OF Mr ERNEST SKUES
The funeral took place from the home of his daughter, 1, Ashburn Grove, Heaton Norris, Stockport, at Cheadle Cemetery Wednesday of Mr ERNEST SKUES, who died on 29th March at the age of 76. Mr Skues was well-known in business circles at Manchester and Stockport. He was connected with the multiple firm of Messrs Goodsons and later Ryans of Stockport. He retired ten years ago and was a well-known figure of the Lancashire and Yorkshire grounds, where for twelve years he and his son Mr RICHARD SKUES, a former well-known cricketer, and contributor to the *Advertiser* never missed a match. Mr and Mrs SKUES celebrated their Golden Wedding in February. He leaves a widow, three sons and a daughter. Prior to the interment, the service was conducted at the home by Rev. W.P. Bates. There were present Mrs SKUES (wife), Mr VINCENT SKUES and Mr RICHARD SKUES (sons), Mrs F. Coulthurst (daughter), Mrs VINCENT SKUES, Mrs RICHARD SKUES, Mrs JACK SKUES, Miss J. SKUES, Miss M. SKUES, Mrs A. Roberts, Mrs W. Frayne, Mr & Mrs Glazebrook. Wreaths were sent by Mrs. E. SKUES (wife), Mr & Mrs VINCENT SKUES; Mr and Mrs RICHARD SKUES; Mr and Mrs JACK SKUES; Mr & Mrs Harold Coulthurst; JOAN & MURIEL SKUES; KEITH SKUES & Anne Coulthurst; JOY, JENNIFER & PAT SKUES; Florence Dick & Nellie; Mrs Roberts & Family; Bert; Nellie and Mary; Ted Allan & Sadie; Mr and Mrs Davies & Pat; Mr & Mrs Hughes & Family; Mr & Mrs Bennett & Family; Mr & Mrs Cowie, Janet & Margaret; Mr & Mrs Salter & Babs; Mr & Mrs Cooper & Family; Mr & Mrs Harden & Marjorie; Mr & Mrs Williams, Stella & Billy; Mr & Mrs Lambert & Family. Funeral arrangements were in the care of Messrs George Meredith.

The *London Gazette* published daily (first edition 1663) also gives useful items of genealogical interest like service promotions and legal affairs of both individuals and families. Some of the "advertisements" do not exactly boost the morale of a family when one reads of a "bankruptcy" or a company going into "voluntary liquidation." A search through *London Gazette* from 1900 to 1976 brought the following entries: —

LG 3 November, 1903
SKEWES SAMUEL DAW, deceased late of Bere Alston, Devon; grocer; died 15 August, 1903. Solicitors Page & Thompson, 2, Bristol Chambers, Nicholas Street, Bristol.

LG 17 July, 1917
SKEWES ANNIE, deceased, late of The Anchorage, Holmbush, St Austell, Cornwall; died 7 December, 1916; widow. Solicitors: John T. Phoenix, Gresham Chambers, Kingsway, Cardiff.

LG 30 November, 1917
SKEWES JAMES, deceased, late of 5, Mutley Park Villas, Plymouth, formerly of 29, Cecil Street, Plymouth, who died on 24 September, 1917. Solicitors Skelly & Johns, Princess House, Princess Square, Plymouth, Devon.

LG 8 April, 1932
SKEWES WILLIAM, deceased, formerly of the parish of Landewednack, Lizard, Cornwall; retired civil servant; died 2 October, 1930; John Antrom Thomas is named as the lawful Attorney of GUILLERMO ENRIQUE SKEWES. Solicitors: Randle, Thomas & Thomas, Helston, Cornwall.

LG 15 December, 1933
SKUES EDWARD GEORGE, deceased, late of Quiet Street, Claremont, Wynberg, Cape Colony in South Africa; died there 30 June, 1933. Solicitors: Bristows Cooke and Carpmeal, 1, Copthall Buildings, London, E.C. 2.

LG 24 May, 1935
SKEWS MATTHEW, deceased, formerly of 17, Best View Terrace, Chester Road, Shiney Row, Durham; miner; died 17 December, 1934. Solicitors: Cooper & Jackson, 18, Market Street, Newcastle Upon Tyne: Executrix — AMELIA SKEWES.

LG 14 June, 1942
SKEWES EDWARD — All persons having claim against the estate of EDWARD SKEWES, late of West Close, Mawnan, Cornwall; farmer; died 24 January, 1942, and whose will was proved in the Bodmin District Probate Registry 8 May, 1942 to contact solicitors Reginald Rogers and Son, Falmouth, Cornwall.

LG 18 May, 1943
SKEWES MARY ANNA, late of 1, Penmere Hill, Falmouth, Cornwall; widow; died 8 April, 1943. Executor & Trustee: Lloyd's Bank Limited, Ewhurst, Guildford, Surrey.

LG 9 March, 1943
The King has been graciously pleased to give orders for the appointment and the following award "The Distinguished Service Medal" for bravery and coolness in action whilst serving defensively equipped Merchant Shipping during operations in North Africa: Temporary Acting Leading Seaman CHARLES GILBERT SKUES (C/JX 179863).

LG 16 January, 1945
Notice is hereby given that MARION SKUSE of 8, Exley Bank, Salterhebble, Halifax in the county of York, spinster and British Subject resident in the United Kingdom assume the name of Stewart. Date 13 January, 1945.

LG 5 October, 1945
SKEWES HOWARD late of Berry Down Farm, Gidleigh, Chagford, formerly of the Old Rectory, Gidleigh, aforesaid, and afterwards of Chapple House, Gidleigh, Devon; farmer (retired); died 11 May, 1945. Solicitors: Page & Co., 2, Bristol Chambers, Nicholas Street, Bristol.

LG 20 December, 1946
SKEWES MARY late of West Close, Mawnan, Cornwall; spinster; died 20 February, 1946. Solicitors: John Percival Rogers (Reginald Rogers & Son), Falmouth, Cornwall.

LG 19 October, 1948
SKUES ELIZABETH late of 22, Tintern Road, Lordship Lane, Wood Green, Middlesex (formerly of 24, Tintern Road); widow; died 4 December, 1946. Claims to be given to VICTOR CLAUDE SKUES and Bertha Elizabeth Humphrey. Solicitors: W.J. Pitman & Sons, 12 City Road, Finsbury Square, London, E.C.1.

LG 22 August, 1952
SKEWES EDWARD Winsford, Ashton, Helston, Cornwall (formerly of Wood View, Gweek, Cornwall); retired farmer; died 14 August, 1952. Solicitors: Randle Thomas & Thomas, 2, Wendron Street, Helston.

LG 10 October, 1952
SKEWES ELIZABETH formerly of 15, Hooton Road, Rusholme, Manchester; spinster; died 23 June, 1952. Solicitor: George Davies, 81, Fountain Street, Manchester, 2.

LG (Volume 2, page 3164), 1957
Territorial Army. Reserve of Officers. Lieutenant A.E. SKUES (414396) from Active List (Unattached) to be Lieutenant 1st March, 1957 retaining his present seniority.

LG (Volume 3, page 5319), 1958
SKUES CHARLES AYRE MACKENZIE of Yew Tree House, Stafford Road, Market Drayton, Shropshire (formerly of 20, Copers Cope Road, Beckenham, Kent); retired Architect & Chartered Surveyor. Died 12 April, 1958. Solicitors: Powell, Skues & Graham Smith, 34, Essex Street, Strand, London, W.C.2.

LG 9 January, 1959
SKUES CHARLES HENRY of "Mawgan", 11, Priory Road, Chalfort St. Peter, Bucks; retired office accountant. Died 28 December, 1958. Solicitors: Tillson, Philips & Co., Lex House, 61a South Road, Southall, M/sex.

LG 19 May, 1959
SKEWES ALFRED JOHN of Kenwyn Vicarage, Truro; retired mining engineer; died 25 April, 1959. Claims given to ALFRED JOHN SKEWES, Salisbury House, Mullion; EDWARD MORLEY SKEWES, Bartles Row, Tuckingmill, Camborne, Cornwall. Solicitors: Peter Bray and Harris, Belmont, Green Lane, Redruth, Cornwall.

LG 4 August, 1959
SKEWES JOHN HENRY (otherwise JOHN H.) of 415a Hill Street, Laguna Beach, California, U.S.A; Tailor; died 18 February, 1959. Solicitors: Bartlett West & McLoughlin, 15, Old Square, Lincoln's Inn Fields, London, W.C.2.

LG 18 March, 1960
Royal Army Chaplain's Department, Regular Army. Reserve of Officers. Rev. J.A. SKUES, M.A. (464570) to be Chaplain to the Forces (C or E) 10 February, 1960.

LG (1962) page 5468
SKUES MINNIE MACKENZIE, Yew Tree House, Stafford Street, Market Drayton, Shropshire; spinster; died 21 June, 1962. Solicitors: Morrish Strode & Fougler Robinson, 10, Great James Street, Bedford Row, London, W.C.1.

LG 9 November, 1962
W.R.A.C. Territorial Army Reserve of Officers.
Lieutenant P.B. SKEWES (456174) from Active List to be Lieutenant. 30 September, 1962.

LG 3 December, 1965
Bankruptcy Act — Receiving Orders.
SKUES PETER PERCIVAL of 38, The Parade, Walton-on-Naze, in the country of Essex, unemployed, formerly trading and carrying on business at 32, Newgate Street, Walton-on-Naze as a carpenter and lately trading and carrying on business with another under the style and name of "Walton Portable Buildings" at Mill Lane, Walton-on-Naze, aforesaid, as Shed Builders.
Court-Colchester. Date of filing petition 26 November, 1965. Number of matter: 29 of 1965
Date of Receiving Order: 26 November, 1965
Number of Receiving Order: 26
Whether Debtor's or Creditor's Petition — Debtor's

LG 14 December, 1965
SKUES PETER PERCIVAL (as above, and then)
Date of First Meeting — 14 December, 1965 at 10.30am.
Place: Room 1, Nos 3-5 Northgate Street, Ipswich, Suffolk.
Date of Public Examination: 3 February, 1966 — 10.30am
Place: The Law Courts, Town Hall, Colchester, Essex

LG 2 August, 1966
SKUES PETER PERCIVAL (as above 3rd and 14th December, 1965) with the heading "Bankruptcy Act
— Release of Trustees", and then Northgate Street, Ipswich, Suffolk.
Date of release: 22 July, 1966.

LG 1 January, 1967
The Queen has been graciously pleased, on the advice of her Australian Ministers to give orders for the
appointment to be Ordinary Officers of the Civil Division of the Most Excellent Order of the British Empire (O.B.E.)
SKUES, KENNETH FREDERICK, Esq., Dental Consultant, Repatriation Department, Victoria.

LG 30 October, 1972
SKEWES, ERNESTINE MARY late of Gilmore House, Crowan, Praze, Camborne, Cornwall. Retired
Civil Clerk (County Police). Died 8 October, 1972. Claims to Barclays Bank Trust Company Ltd., 3,
Pydar Street, Truro, Cornwall by 31st January, 1973.

LG 3 September, 1973
J. SKEWES LIMITED.
At an Extraordinary General Meeting of the above named Company duly convened and held at 419,
Watford Way, Hendon, London, NW4 on 16th August, 1973 the subjoined Extraordinary Resolution
was duly passed:
"That the Company be wound up voluntarily and that Walter Frederick Hague, FCA of Marcol House,
289/293, Regent Street, London, W.1., be and is hereby appointed Liquidator for the purposes of such
winding up." J.E. SKEWES, Chairman

Appointment of Liquidators

Name of Company	J. SKEWES Limited
Nature of Business	Manufacturing Opticians
Address of Regd Office	212, Ballards Lane, London, N.3.
Liquidators name and	Walter Frederick Hague, Marcol House,
address	289/293, Regent Street, London W.1.
Date of Appointment	16 August, 1973
By Whom Appointed	Members

LG 1 July, 1975
King's Division, Regular Army.
Lt. Col. M.L.D. SKEWES-COX (95614) Q.L.R. retires on retired pay 30 June, 1975.

LG 22 April, 1976
Bankruptcy Acts 1914 & 1926 — Applications for Discharge SKUES, PETER PERCIVAL of 38, The
Parade, Walton-on-Naze, in the county of Essex, unemployed, formerly trading and carrying on
business at 32, Newgate Street, Walton-on-Naze, Essex, as a carpenter, and lately trading and carrying
on business with another under the style and name of "Walton Portable Buildings", at Mill Lane,
Walton-on-Naze, Essex, as "shed builders."
Court: Colchester & Clacton. No. of matter — 29 of 1965
Date fixed for hearing — 9 June, 1976. 11.15am. Place — The Town Hall, Colchester, Essex.

LG 30 July, 1976
Order made on Application for Discharge
SKUES, PETER PERCIVAL of 38, The Parade, Walton-on-Naze, in the county of Essex, unemployed,
formerly trading and carrying on business at 32, Newgate Street, Walton-on-Naze, Essex, as a
carpenter, and lately trading and carrying on business with another under the style and name of "Walton
Portable Buildings," at Mill Lane, Walton-on-Naze, Essex, as "shed builders".
Court: Colchester & Clacton. No of matter — 29 of 1965
Date of Order — 9 June, 1976. Nature of Order made — Bankrupt's discharge suspended one month
and that he be discharged as from 9 July, 1976. Grounds named in Order for refusing an absolute
discharge — proof of facts mentioned in section 26 sub section 3 (a & b), Bankruptcy Act 1914 as amend-
ed by Section 1 of the Bankruptcy (Amendment) Act, 1926.

LG 2 November, 1976
Meeting of the Creditors — J. SKEWES Limited
Notice is hereby given, in pursuance of Sections 290 and 341 (1) (b) of the Companies Act, 1948, that a
General Meeting of the above named Company will be held at Marcol House, 289/293, Regent Street,
London WIR 8BB, on Thursday 16th December, 1976, at 10 o'clock in the morning, for the purpose of
having an account laid before the members showing the manner in which the winding up has been con-
ducted and the property of the Company disposed of, and of hearing any explanation that may be given
by the Liquidator, and also of determining by Extraordinary Resolution the manner in which the books,

accounts and documents of the Company and of the Liquidator shall be disposed of. A member entitled to attend and vote at the above Meeting may appoint a proxy or proxies to attend and vote instead of him. A proxy need not be a Member of the Company. Dated 28 October, 1976.

As well as British papers such as the aforementioned *London Gazette*, the writer searched overseas press like *New York Times*.

NYT 7 May, 1958
DEATHS: JAMES H. SKEWES
JAMES H. SKEWES, Editor and Publisher of the *Meridian Star*, Mississippi died today after a long illness. He was 70. Mr SKEWES headed the Sunshine Press which owned the newspapers in Las Cruces and Artesia, N.M., and other newspapers in the South. He moved here as Editor and Publisher of the *Star* in 1922. A native of Cornwall, England, Mr SKEWES came to the United States of America with his parents in 1891. He was educated in Racine, Wis., and at Milwaukee State Normal College. During his career he was a reporter for the *Milwaukee Journal* and *The Milwaukee Daily News, The Kansas City Star* and the *Racine Daily News*.
He published the *Danville Press* from 1918 to 1922. Survivors include his widow, the former Grace Buckingham, and a son JAMES B. SKEWES.

NYT 9 March, 1948
TWO AMERICAN WOMEN SLAIN NEAR SAIGON
Bodies of State Department Employees found with their buried jeep in Indo-China. Saigon, Indo-China, 8 March, 1948.

Two American women employed by the United States State Department were shot to death near Saigon last night. Their attackers were believed to be anti-French guerillas.
The women's jeep, found twisted and burned out west of Saigon airport, was flying an American flag. Victims of the shooting were JEANNE R. SKEWES, 32 of Evanston, Ill., and Miss Lidia Ruth James, 30, of Hillside, Ind. They were the first American civilians killed in Indo-China fighting since VJ day. It is believed the women left home together about 5pm and were returning home after a pleasure drive, just at dusk when attacked. The body of Mrs SKEWES, in the driver's seat was badly burned. Miss James's body had several bullet wounds in the head.
American Consul General said Mrs SKEWES was a Librarian in Saigon for the U.S. Information Service. She was a wartime employee of the Office of War and Information in San Francisco. Her parents, Mr and Mrs E.H. Workman, live in Phoenix, Arizona. Miss James was a secretary in the Consulate and her parents Mr and Mrs Otto James live in Hillside.

NYT 7 June, 1934
DEATH OF THOMAS J. SKUSE
THOMAS J. SKUSE Assistant Controller of Customs at the Port of New York died suddenly yesterday afternoon of a heart attack which overcame him while he was in Room 219 of the Custom House, the Office of Collector of the Port, Harry M. Downing. Stricken shortly before four o'clock he was dead when a doctor arrived soon afterwards from the Broad Street Hospital.
Mr SKUSE who was 65 years of age resided at 337 Senator Street, Brooklyn with his wife, Anna M. SKUSE his only near surviving relative. He had been connected with the Customs Service in New York for 46 years. He passed through the civil service grades to that of Controller, the highest in that Office.

The SKEWES/SKUSE family appear to have received more publicity in *New York Times* as compared with our very own *The Times*. However, there was a "Letter to the Editor" worthy of mention which appeared on 14th February, 1939.

Dear Sir,
I read with considerable interest the points from a letter of Mr T.N. Hugh-Davies. On making enquiries I discovered, however, that the Overseas League cannot undertake to send 50 cigarettes duty free to an individual of the B.E.F. During the last war one half pound of tobacco or 200 cigarettes could be sent to those serving in France, and I see no reason why such a small concession should not be allowed to relatives of our fighting men of today.

Mr. A. SKUES, 157, Regent Road,
London, W.1.

Here is an extract from *The Field* magazine dated 1st May, 1958, page 788.
YOUNG SKUES
Although CHARLES AYRE MACKENZIE SKUES had not been seen at Whitehall Court for some months, his death at his Market Drayton home has left a considerable gap in the ranks of the Flyfishers' Club. He was still affectionately known as "Young Skues" to distinguish him from his better known elder brother GEORGE EDWARD MACKENZIE SKUES. Like his brother, Skues was an expert fly-fisher and fly tier. He was also a surveyor, and many a trout came to grief as a result of his applying a professional eye to a water.
John Eastwood was only one who was glad of his friendship and support. He had it in full in the formation of the Anglers' Co-operative Association of which Skues was a vice-president.

NIMROD

Other snippets from newspapers include the following:

News of the World — Sunday, 1 August, 1956
A. SKUES and family of Leigh Road, Highbury, London were among some 200 winners in a competition that asked readers to place in order of importance six features which would help to make a cruise on the Queen Mary the thrill of a lifetime for an ordinary family. The prize? A six day cruise to the Canary Islands during Christmas, 1956.

A not so happy event was reported in the *Beckenham Journal* on 26th January, 1957.

OPEN VERDICT ON LOCAL WOMAN FOUND ON LINE
A 52 year-old Beckenham woman found dead on the line at Bickley Station on 13 January was said at a Bromley inquest on Wednesday to have several times previously opened carriage doors on the wrong side and to have realised her mistake only at the last moment.
An open verdict was returned by the jury on Miss JOAN MACKENZIE SKUES of 20, Copers Cope Road, Beckenham, who was said by witnesses to have been extremely religious, but at times alarmingly depressed. Her body was found by a porter, Mr Albert Sargent of 13, Waldo Road, Bromley at 11am. He said it was lying beside the rail furthest from the platform. A handbag was lying on the platform some distance back from the edge. Mr Sargent said there were very few people about, and nobody had seen what had happened.
Doctor David Winstanley, Pathologist, said he thought the cause of death was multiple injuries, but it was possible Miss Skues could have previously been electrocuted.
Doctor William Penny of 21, Wickhams Way, Beckenham, said Miss Skues became his patient in 1946, after returning from India, where she had been depressed. She improved, but in 1954 became "alarmingly depressed" at times, and entered a hospital voluntarily. She returned there several times, her last discharge being in September, 1956, although after that she was still under the care of the outpatients department which she attended up to 8th January. She suffered from blindness in her left eye.
Mr Charles Ayre Mackenzie Skues said his daughter, who lived with him, told him recently of an occasion when she opened the door on the wrong side of the train, under the impression that she was travelling from the London direction. A similar incident three years ago was recalled by Miss Skues's sister Miss Sheila Mackenzie Skues.
Police Inspector Albert Neale of Bromley, said he found in Miss Skues's handbag on the platform half a ticket from Holborn Viaduct to Bickley, stamped 13th January.

KEEPING WRITING IN THE FAMILY

Many of the Skues/Skewes family were authors. The earliest known gentleman was JOHN SKEWYS who, in the sixteenth century, wrote *Brevyat of a Cronacle made by Matthew Paris of the Conquests of Duke William of Normandy uppon his Realme*. He also wrote a treatise *De Bello Trojano*, *Chronicorum Epitome*, *Abbreviationes Chronicorum* and *The Black Book of Merthen*.

In recent times the most famous author has been GEORGE EDWARD MACKENZIE SKUES who was an authority on trout and fly fishing. His books are *Minor Tactics of the Chalk Stream* (1910: reprinted 1974), *The Way of a Trout With A Fly* (1921: reprinted 1961), *Side Lines Side Lights and Reflections* (1932: reprinted 1976 with *Chalk Stream Angler*) and *Nymph Fishing For Chalk Stream Trout* (1939: reprinted 1974). Two further books were published after Skues's death in 1949: *Silk, Fur and Feathers* and *Itchen Memories*.

C.F. Walker edited *Angling Letters of G.E.M. SKUES* which was published by Adam & Charles Black (publishers of all Skues's previous books) in 1957. In 1977 Donald Overfield wrote *G.E.M. SKUES — The Way of a Man With A Trout*, published by Ernest Benn.

George Edward Mackenzie Skues also wrote for the *Encyclopaedia of Sport* and magazines such as *The Field*, *Fishing Gazette*, *The Salmon and Trout Magazine*, *The Bulletin of the Anglers' Club of New York* and *The Journal of the Fly Fishers Club*. Sometimes he wrote under pseudonyms! Articles containing statistical information would have the pen name E.O.E. and those of a humorous nature would be signed "B. Hinde" or "I. Caunter Fordham." In *The Field* he wrote under the pseudonym "Val Conson" — the legal abbreviation for Valuable Consideration.

The writer's great-grandfather RICHARD SKUES had a crack at the journalistic whip as well! He published midweekly the *Halifax Free Press* from 18, Barum Top, Halifax, Yorkshire which was sold for one halfpenny. The news was liberal and it devoted itself exclusively to local and district news, making a special feature of athletic jottings. The paper, which circulated in Halifax and throughout the surrounding villages was a strong supporter of the labour classes. The first edition of the *Halifax*

Free Press was published on 26th March, 1890. It appeared to be running smoothly until it was involved in a libel action which went heavily against the paper which ceased publication in 1894. The editor was RICHARD SKUES and publisher FREDERICK GORDON SKUES.

But all was not lost, for according to the *Halifax Daily Courier* dated 15 April, 1916 Mr RICHARD SKUES was held in high esteem!

DEATH OF Mr RICHARD SKUES
LENGTHY ASSOCIATION WITH THE "COURIER"
The death occurred on Monday at 10 Norfolk Place, of Mr RICHARD SKUES, for many years in the employ of the *Halifax Courier* as overseer in the composing department. He was 83 years of age, and had been failing in health for some time. He came from Plymouth to join the staff of the *Courier* in May, 1853, four months after the paper commenced and remained in its employ until March, 1890. Mr Skues was one of six men who came from Plymouth, all under a three year agreement. Obstacles were put in the way of Mr Skues coming here, his employers at Plymouth being desirous of retaining his services there. Instead of being here for the production of the first paper on 8th January, 1853, he did not arrive until Easter. His manager told him he was going to an uncivilised part of the country; that they were barbarous in Yorkshire and that he would be starved to death.
Mr Skues in later years recalled his first impression of Halifax... "a wretched hole, with but a dozen or so lamp posts about... and those only lit in winter, and many shops were lighted with candles or lamps." In the early days the *Courier* had a struggle for its existence, and at one time funds were so short that Mr Skues could not get the full amount of his wages. He went back to Plymouth, but after six weeks his arrears were sent on, and he returned to Halifax. He often told with pride that, with the exception of those six weeks, he never missed being present at the publication of every issue during his 27 years association with the paper.
For a period of 40 years he never had a day in bed through illness, the long record being broken about nine years ago. Soon after the advent of Mr J.T. Hutchinson and Mr Thomas Birtwistle on to the paper in 1856, Mr Skues had his first promotion, being made the manager of the composing and publishing departments. Later, he succeeded Mr Henry Wilson as collector and advertisement canvasser, and for a long time he reported theatres and concerts.
On his retirement from the paper he was presented with a marble clock and side ornaments: "Presented to Mr RICHARD SKUES by the proprietors and employees of the *Halifax Courier* on his retirement after 37 years service. March 18th, 1890."
After leaving the service of this journal he took over as editor of the *Halifax Free Press,* a weekly which did not have a long existence. Later, he commenced a cafe business, and this is still continued.
The interment took place on Thursday at All Saints Cemetery. The Rev. Hugh Bright conducted the service, one being held in St. Paul's Church.
The private mourners were Mr and Mrs RICHARD SKUES (son and daughter-in-law), Mr and Mrs ERNEST SKUES (son and daughter-in-law), Miss SKUES, Mrs FRED SKUES (daughter-in-law), Cecil, Lucy, Eric and Fred (grandchildren), Mr A. Furness (Sheffield), Mr H. Spencer, Mr R.G. Pearson and Mr Appleyard.
The coffin of pitch pine with brass mounting had a cross inscribed "RICHARD SKUES — AT REST — 3 April, 1916. R.I.P."

ITCH TO WRITE

RICHARD SKUES'S grandson, the Rev. ERIC SKUES was the author of a booklet *Shensi — China's Mission to the Chinese* (with plates) 22 pages. SPG, SPCK (London) 1935: Price Threepence.

Another grandson, RICHARD SKUES wrote educational articles on the game of cricket for the *Stockport Advertiser* from 1927 to 1930. He was a well-known cricketer in his day playing for Sir Julian Cahn's XI.

In turn the "itch to write" passed to the present writer, who edited *Youth Fellowship Times* (1958-1959) and wrote articles for *Altrincham & Bowdon Guardian*. From 1961 to 1964 he wrote articles on "pop music" and "show business" for a daily paper in Kenya, *Daily Nation*, and also *The Sunday Post* when he was in East Africa with the British Forces Broadcasting Service. He has also written various historical items for papers and magazines including *Devon & Cornwall Notes and Queries* and the *North Devon Journal*, in addition to compiling parish histories of Frodsham, Cheshire and Heanton Punchardon, North Devon. In 1968 his book *Radio Onederland* (The Story of BBC Radio One) was published by Landmark press of Suffolk (hardback £1.00p — softback 50pence), 224 pages with 50 photographs. He edited the booklet *This Is Hallamland* (The Story of Radio Hallam, Sheffield) 36 pages, illustrated. Price 15 pence (1975).

Other members of the Skues/Skewes/Skewis/Skews/Skuse family who have written books and booklets are:

SKEWES, EDWARD, miner. He wrote an essay on the Gwinear Mining District. Rep. RCP Soc. 1875; 32 pages.

SKEWES Rev JOSEPH HENRY, M.A. wrote *A Complete Digest of the Polity of Methodism* (London — Elliot Stock; 1869); *The Pulpit Palladium of Christendom* (Lectures on the fundamental essentials of man's personal salvation) — London, S.W. Partridge, 1891; *A Complete and Classified Index of the Journals of Rev. John Wesley, M.A.* (London, Elliot Stock, 1874) and *Sir John Franklin — The Secret Discovery of his Fate* (London, Bembrose and Sons, 1889).

Three times before his ordination to the full work of the Ministry JOSEPH HENRY SKEWES was taken from his regular work to superintend three extensive county circuits. It was in this capacity that he had a wide area for personal and close observation as to the knowledge of the working of Methodism possessed by large numbers of people in rural districts. In his book *A Complete Digest of the Polity of Methodism* each subject is arranged in alphabetical order. On publication Skewes said: *I have no wish to parade this, my maiden effort, before the public as a paragon of perfection.*

SKEWES EDUARDO wrote *Estudios de las venas superficials, del antebrazo en los chilenos.* 1944, Mexico.

SKEWES ALICIA BEZIES wrote *El Hospital de Pachuca.* El frotis citologico como metodo de diagnostico en ginecologia. Mexico, 1952. Thesis, University of Mexico.

SKEWES GEORGE T. (joint author with Donald H. Painter) *General Science for High School*; Chicago, Mentzer, Bush, 1955.

SKEWES HELEN J. *Mineral Resources in Illinois in 1911, 1912, 1913 and 1914.* (In Illinois, Geological Survey Bulletin No 23, pp 25 — 44; No 30 pp 23 — 49; Urbana, 1917).

SKEWES JOHN B. *Report to the State Road Commission of Utah on contract administration 1 January, 1970 to 31 December, 1970.* Salt Lake City, 1971.

SKEWIES A.F. *The Analysis of Uranium-Ziroconium Alloys* (1953). H.M.S.O. 2/6d.

SKEWES-COX, BENNET *United Nations Charter and World Federalism*, Washington, 1947. Thesis, M.A. Georgetown University.

SKEWIS DOROTHY D. *Handwriting in the United States*, a study of the American copy books in the Rickett's collection. Detroit. Wayne University, 1943. (Typewritten). Also wrote *Neoferkephtah and the Book of Troth.* Chicago, 1925. Compiled from a collection of old Egyptian legends and designed, set and printed with an illustration cut in wood by Dorothy D. Skewis.

SKEWS DORIS MAY *Letter Writing for General and Commercial Courses* (1935). Oxford University Press, price 4/6d; and *Principals of Precis*, London University Press, 1961.

SKEWS B. *Profiles of Diffracting Shockwaves*, Johannesburg, University of Witwatersrand, 1966.

SKUCE WALTER C. *Management Controls in Industry*, Washington, 1956; and *War production in future energencies and reconversion to a peacetime economy.* Washington, 1958. United States Industrial College of the Armed Forces.

From books published in Norway we find *SKUESPILLERINDE.* Breve fra og til en Skuespillerinde legwe af Nemo. HJO Benhaven, 1868, 12850. a.a.a. 29. Also listed as SKUESPILLERFORBUND, Norsk Kirkeg 34, Oslo, Norway. SKUESPILLER means "actor", SKUESPILLERINDE, "actress" and SKUESPILLERKUNST "dramatic art."

In Australia Doctor KENNETH SKUES, O.B.E., D.D. Sc., Melbourne wrote *Developments of Dental Enamel in Marsupials*, published in 1932.

SKUSE ALLEN (joint author) *Government intervention and Industrial Policy*, London, Heinemann, 1970.

SKUSE E. *Skuse's Complete Confectioner.* Thirteen editions have been published.

SKUSE F.A.A. *British Stalk Eyed Crustaceans and Spiders.* An extract from Australian Encyclopaedia, Volume III relates:

"The study of Diptera in Australia was started by F.A.A. SKUSE (1888-1896) working on the Nematocera".

SKUSE MARGARET *Okinawa Briefs.* Text and illustrations by Margaret Skuse. Rutland, Vt., America. C.E. Tuttle, 1954.

SKUSE W.W. *Entire Engineering of two reinforced concrete bridges.* Thesis, Washington State University, Pullman.

SKUSE HARLAND G. *Basic electricity, theory and practise.* New Brunswick, 1956.

SKEWS WILLIAM IAIN *Highlands and Islands* (1962)

SKEWES SISTER AGNES *Life Comes to Newness.* To be published in Australia in 1982.

In addition to the above who wrote specific articles or books there is ELIZABETH MARY (BETTY) SKEWES of Croydon, Surrey who was Home Feature Editor of *Poultry World* from 1947 to 1967.

In America JAMES HENRY SKEWES was editor and publisher of *Meridian Star*, Mississippi, USA from 1922 to 1958. He was succeeded by his son JAMES BUCKINGHAM SKEWES who is the current editor and publisher.

So the SKEWES/SKEWIS/SKEWS/SKUCE/SKUES/SKUSE family has contributed to the world of journalism, and one interesting fact is that no two members of the family have had identical interests, whether they be writing about *De Bello Trojano* or the study of fly fishing; cricket or the media; dentistry or cooking; transport or engineering; uranium-zirconium alloys or crustaceans and spiders; the interests of China's mission to the Chinese or studying management countrols in industry — all have added a little to the literary world.

4 Births, Marriages and Deaths

MANY PEOPLE are under the impression that if they went along to Somerset House in London officials there would trace a family history if requested to do so. This is not exactly true, for the records only go back as far as 1 July, 1837. Furthermore, the various registers — Births, Marriages and Deaths — only give the name of the individual, and not his or her entire pedigree.

At the end of 1973 it was decided to move the indexes of Births, Marriages and Deaths across the road from Somerset House to St Catherine's House, known as the General Register Office. This chapter has taken the longest to compile — in all twenty years — involving countless visits to Somerset House, and more recently St Catherine's House. Somerset House overlooks the Strand to the north and the River Thames to the south. It was built in 1775 and now contains audit, inland revenue, Registrar General's offices and the probate registry where wills are retained. The east wing is occupied by King's College. Somerset House is built on the site of a palace designed for the Duke of Somerset who was Lord Protector during the reign of Edward VI. He offended land owners by his attempts to check on their affairs. Whereas he was charitable towards the poor, he was arrogant and overbearing to the rich and powerful. However, in 1549 he was overthrown and finally brought to the block and beheaded on 22 January 1552.

St Catherine's House has no history to relate and is a modern block. There is much overcrowding with members of the public trying to make use of the indexes. There is no seating. Generally speaking the General Register Office is very reliable, although there have been omissions reported. Also at St Catherine's House are Registers of Adoptions; Marine Register Book covering births and deaths since 1 July 1837; Army returns of births and marriages and dating back to 1790. R.A.F. returns begin in 1920.

There are Overseas registrations of births, marriages and deaths from 1849.

Early in 1981 the index of deaths was transferred to Alexandra House, Kingsway, London.

The entries which appear on the following pages represent names from 1 July 1837 to December 1978. One has to wait for a year before the most recent indexes of births, marriages and deaths appear on the shelves.

These indexes list all the persons registered for birth, marriage or death for England and Wales. They are truly invaluable as prior to 1837 only parish registers provide as much information.

There are talks currently going on to decide whether or not to move to the Public Record Office all records of births, marriages and deaths more than a hundred years old. These would be available for inspection by members of the public and would be a great step forward for researchers and genealogists.

Due to the many variations in the spelling of the surname, only SKUES, SKEWES, SKEWIS and SKEWS entries have been made. As will be seen in later pages all these families are interlinked whereas the writer has seen no connection with families spelling their name SCUSE, SKUCE and SKUSE who appear to have resided around the Bristol area. Perhaps if and when time allows all variations in spelling appearing in the General Register Office will be published, but that would probably take another twenty years to compile.

Incorrect spellings of the surname do unfortunately exist, and in earlier times it varied a great deal. However, by 1900 the majority of the family spelling their name SKEWES kept it that way, as indeed did SKUES, SKEWIS and SKEWS. But as recently as 1958 the writer found in the index of deaths at General Register Office CHARLES AYRE MACKENZIE SKUES entered as SKUSE.

Glancing through the names to be found in the next few pages one comes across many unusual Christian names as well as names in everyday use. All spelling has been copied from the Registers as it appeared.

The first section will deal with births, followed by marriages and finally deaths.

The writer is most grateful to the Registrar-General for his kind permission to allow the re-printing of names for this chapter.

Births 1837 — 1978

1837	SKEWIS	JOSEPH	Merthyr Tydfil
1837	SKUES	LAVINIA	Truro
1838	SKEWES	WILLIAM	Truro
1838	SKEWES	WILLIAM HENRY	Helston
1838	SKEWES	GRACE TERESA	Truro
1838	SKEWES	EMMA	Helston
1838	SKEWES	MARY	Abergavenny
1838	SKEWES	JOHN	Truro
1838	SKEWES	HANNIBAL	Helston
1838	SKEWES	EDWARD	Helston
1838	SKEWES	RICHARD LORY	Helston
1838	SKEWES	STEPHEN	Redruth
1838	SKEWES	LOUISA JANE	Falmouth
1838	SKEWES	MARY ANN LIPSOM	Tavistock
1838	SKEWES	SUSAN	Redruth
1838	SKEWIS	JOSEPH	Redruth
1838	SKEWIS	MARY SAMPSON	Penzance
1838	SKEWIS	CHRISTIAN	Falmouth
1838	SKEWIS	BLANCHE	Penzance
1838	SKEWS	THOMAS	Truro
1838	SKEWS	GRACE	Truro
1838	SKEWS	SAMUEL	Truro
1838	SKEWSE	FANNY	Malmsbury
1838	SKUES	PETER	Patrington

(Many other entries for Patrington listed as SKU*SE*)

1839	SKEWES	ELIZABETH ANN	Redruth
1839	SKEWES	MARY	Redruth
1839	SKEWES	MARY ODGERS	Redruth
1839	SKEWES	JOHN	Truro
1839	SKEWIS	SAMUEL	Falmouth
1839	SKEWIS	EMILIA	Merthyr Tydfil
1839	SKEUES	CHARLOTTE	Portsea
1839	SKEWS	CATHERINE ELIZABETH MARY	Derby
1839	SKEWS	SAMUEL	Truro
1839	SKEWS	ELIZA	North Aylesford
1839	SKUES	JAMES	St. Geo. East
1839	SKUES	MARY EMILY	Truro
1840	SKEWES	ELIZABETH STEVENS	Truro
1840	SKEWES	ELIZABETH JANE	Helston
1840	SKEWES	EMILY	Helston
1840	SKEWES	GEORGE EMANUEL	Helston
1840	SKEWES	JAMES HENRY	Helston
1840	SKEWES	JANE	Helston
1840	SKEWES	RICHARD	Redruth
1840	SKEWES	MARY	Redruth
1840	SKEWIS	SAMUEL	Abergavenny
1840	SKEWS	HENRY GEORGE	Bloomsbury
1840	SKEWS	LOUIS	Redruth
1840	SKEWS	PETER	Truro
1840	SKEWS	WILLIAM FRANCIS DENNIS	Truro
1840	SKEWS	THOMAS	Truro
1840	SKEWS	MARY	Truro
1840	SKUES	WILLIAM	Bath
1841	SKEWES	GEORGE	Tiverton
1841	SKEWES	BETSY	Helston
1841	SKEWES	GRACE	Helston
1841	SKEWES	CHRISTIAN	Helston
1841	SKEWES	PHILIP JAMES	Redruth
1841	SKEWES	PHILIPPA	Falmouth
1841	SKEWES	SARAH ANN	Helston
1841	SKEWES	LOVEDAY HENDY	Helston
1841	SKEWES	EMMA	Truro
1841	SKEWES	GEORGE BENNETTS	Truro
1841	SKEWES	MARY	St. Austell
1841	SKEWES	THOMAS ALBERT JEFFREY	Truro
1841	SKEWIS	JANE	Abergavenny
1841	SKEWIS	JAMES	Penzance
1841	SKEWIS	HENRY	Penzance
1841	SKEWS	EMMA	East London
1841	SKEWS	JOHN	Redruth
1841	SKEWS	WALTER TREZIZE	Truro
1841	SKEWS	ELIZABETH JANE	Truro
1841	SKUES	GEORGE HENRY	St. Geo. East
1841	SKUES	MARY	Truro
1842	SKEWES	EMMA STEPHENS	Truro
1842	SKEWES	JAMES FEARGUS O'CONNOR	Redruth
1842	SKEWES	SAMUEL	Helston
1842	SKEWES	MARY	Helston
1842	SKEWES	JAMES	Helston
1842	SKEWES	MARY	Redruth
1842	SKEWES	PETER	Truro
1842	SKEWIS	JAMES	Merthyr Tydfil
1842	SKEWS	ELIZABETH JANE	Truro
1842	SKEWS	MARY	Truro
1842	SKEWS	WILLIAM	Truro
1842	SKUES	HONORA HARRIET	Malmsbury
1842	SKUES	WILLIAM	Tonbridge
1843	SKEWES	MARTHA	Helston
1843	SKEWES	HENRY CHARLES	Truro
1843	SKEWES	MATTHEW	Redruth
1843	SKEWES	MARY	Redruth
1843	SKEWES	JOANNA	Truro
1843	SKEWIS	EMMA	Crickhowell
1843	SKEWIS	JOHN JAMES SQUIRES	Falmouth
1843	SKEWIS	(Female)	Redruth
1843	SKEWIS	JANE	Abergavenny
1843	SKEWS	ELLEN	Truro
1843	SKUES	ALFRED	Bath
1843	SKUES	CHARLES JOHN	St. Geo. East

On checking with the Registrar for Births, Marriages and Deaths in Helston there are entries for the following two persons between 1840 and 1844 inclusive:

	SKEWES	SUSANNAH JANE	St Keverne
	SKEWES	CATHERINE	St Keverne
1844	SKEWES	ELIZABETH MARY	Helston
1844	SKEWES	ELIZA	Helston
1844	SKEWES	ELIZA	Helston
1844	SKEWES	JAMES	Helston
1844	SKEWES	LAVINIA	Truro
1844	SKEWIS	SARAH ANN	Penzance
1844	SKEWIS	JANE TUBB	Redruth
1844	SKEWIS	JOHANNA	Redruth
1844	SKEWS	EDWIN NATHANIEL	Medway
1844	SKEWS	MARY AGNES ELIZABETH DANIEL	Redruth
1844	SKEWS	RICHARD NATHANIEL EDWARD	Gravesend
1844	SKEWS	WILLIAM TREZISE	Truro
1844	SKEWS	EMMA	North Aylesford
1844	SKEWS	EMILY	Truro
1844	SKEWS	GRACE	Truro
1844	SKUES	LOVELIA	Lambeth
1845	SKEWES	ELIZABETH ANN LANYON	Redruth
1845	SKEWES	GRACE	Truro
1845	SKEWES	SAMUEL HENRY	Helston
1845	SKEWES	BLANCH	Helston
1845	SKEWES	ELLEN	Truro
1845	SKEWES	SIMON DAVEY	Redruth
1845	SKEWES	SARAH ANN	Helston
1845	SKEWES	SUSANNAH JANE	Helston
1845	SKEWS	JOHN	Truro
1845	SKEWS	MARY AGNES ELIZABETH DENNIS	Truro

Year	Surname	Name	Place
1845	SKEWIS	ROBERT	Abergavenny
1845	SKEWIS	ANNE	Penzance
1845	SKEWIS	HENRY JAMES	Redruth
1845	SKEWIS	JOHN SAMUEL	Redruth
1845	SKUES	GRACE	Truro
1846	SKEWES	THOMAS JOHN	Redruth
1846	SKEWES	MARY	Helston
1846	SKEWES	ELIZA GRACE	Helston
1846	SKEWES	HENRY	Helston
1846	SKEWES	HESTER ANN	Falmouth
1846	SKEWES	JOHN WILLIAM	Redruth
1846	SKEWES	WILLIAM HENRY	Redruth
1846	SKEWES	WILLIAM HENRY	Redruth
1846	SKEWIS	JOHN	Helston
1846	SKEWIS	JOSEPH	Abergavenny
1846	SKEWIS	JOSEPH RICHARD	Tynemouth
1846	SKEWIS	NANNY	Redruth
1846	SKEWIS	CHARLES	Redruth
1846	SKEWIS	ROBERT	Abergavenny
1846	SKEWS	MARY	Neath
1846	SKUES	AMELIA MARY ANN	Medway
1846	SKUES	GEORGE ALFRED	Gravesend
1846	SKUES	WILLIAM HENRY	St. Geo. East.
1847	SKEWES	CHARLOTTE MARY	Redruth
1847	SKEWES	CHARLOTTE MARY JANE	Redruth
1847	SKEWES	ELIZA ANN	Helston
1847	SKEWES	ELLEN	Truro
1847	SKEWES	MARIA	Truro
1847	SKEWES	MARY JANE	Redruth
1847	SKEWES	RICHARD	Helston
1847	SKEWES	SAMUEL LAITY	Helston
1847	SKEWES	ELIZA	Helston
1847	SKEWES	ELIZABETH EMMA	Redruth
1847	SKEWES	JOSIAH	Redruth
1847	SKEWES	SAMUEL	Helston
1847	SKEWS	JOHN HENRY	Truro
1847	SKEWS	SARAH ANN	North Aylesford
1848	SKEWES	ELIZABETH	Helston
1848	SKEWES	RICHARD	Truro
1848	SKEWES	ELIZABETH	Helston
1848	SKEWES	JAMES HENRY	Helston
1848	SKEWIS	JANE BAWDEN	Redruth
1848	SKEWIS	FRANCES MARIA	Falmouth
1848	SKEWIS	STEPHEN JOHN	Redruth
1848	SKEWS	TERESA HERMINNA AMELIA	Redruth
1848	SKEWS	JOHN GREGORY	Launceston
1848	SKEWS	ELIZABETH CHARLOTTE	Isle of Thanet
1848	SKEWS	MARIA	Liskeard
1848	SKEWS	RICHARD	Neath
1848	SKUES	ELIZABETH	Bath
1849	SKEWES	ELLEN	Helston
1849	SKEWES	ELIZABETH	Abergavenny
1849	SKEWES	JAMES	Redruth
1849	SKEWES	EDWARD	Falmouth
1849	SKEWES	ISABELLA REYNOLDS	Redruth
1849	SKEWES	JOHN	Helston
1849	SKEWES	WILLIAM JOHN BILLING	Redruth
1849	SKEWES	ELIZA	Truro
1849	SKEWIS	ANN BAWDEN	Liskeard
1849	SKEWIS	HENRY	Redruth
1849	SKEWS	ELIZABETH	Truro
1849	SKEWS	EDWARD	North Aylesford
1849	SKUES	MARY GARRETT	St. James
1849	SKUES	ELIZA	Medway
1850	SKEWES	ALEXANDER	Redruth
1850	SKEWES	ELIZABETH JANE	Truro
1850	SKEWES	MARY ANN	Truro
1850	SKEWES	WILLIAM JAMES	Helston
1850	SKEWES	WILLIAM JOHN	Helston
1850	SKEWES	JAMES	Helston
1850	SKEWES	JAMES ROBERTS	Helston
1850	SKEWES	MARY JANE	Redruth
1850	SKEWIS	EDWIN	Abergavenny
1850	SKEWS	MATTHEW HENRY	Redruth
1850	SKEWS	ELIZA JANE	Liskeard
1850	SKEWS	JOSEPH	Liskeard
1850	SKUES	ELIZA SUSANNAH	St. Geo. East
1851	SKEWES	JOHN	Helston
1851	SKEWES	JOHN	Redruth
1851	SKEWES	THOMAS	Redruth
1851	SKEWES	WILLIAM HENRY	Falmouth
1851	SKEWES	EDWARD	Redruth
1851	SKEWES	ELIZABETH MARY	Redruth
1851	SKEWES	ELIZABETH MARGARET EDWARDS	Swansea
1851	SKEWES	SAMUEL	Truro
1851	SKEWS	ELIZABETH JANE	Launceston
1851	SKEWS	LAVINIA	Launceston
1851	SKEWS	WILLIAM	East Stonehouse
1851	SKEWS	ANN	Liskeard
1851	SKEWS	MARY WILKINS	Truro
1851	SKEWS	MATTHEW WARNE	Truro
1851	SKUES	ISABELLA	St. James
1852	SKEWES	NANNY	Redruth
1852	SKEWES	THOMAS JAMES	Truro
1852	SKEWES	THOMAS WILLIAM	Helston
1852	SKEWES	JOHN FREDERICK	Helston
1852	SKEWIS	MARY	Redruth
1852	SKEWIS	SARAH	Cricklewood
1852	SKEWIS	ELIZABETH	Abergavenny
1852	SKEWIS	JOHN	Liskeard
1852	SKEWIS	SARAH ANN	Penzance
1852	SKEWS	SAMUEL	Liskeard
1852	SKEWS	JAMES	North Aylesford
1852	SKEWS	SARAH	Redruth
1852	SKEWS	ALFRED	Redruth
1852	SKEWS	JESSIE	Abergavenny
1853	SKEWES	EDWARD	Helston
1853	SKEWES	JAMES HARRIS	Redruth
1853	SKEWES	WILLIAM	Helston
1853	SKEWES	JOHN	Redruth
1853	SKEWES	ESTHER ANN	Penzance
1853	SKEWES	LAVINIA	Truro
1853	SKEWES	MARY FANNY SOPHIA	Wareham
1853	SKEWES	(Female)	Falmouth
1853	SKEWES	EMILY KEMPTHORNE	Falmouth
1853	SKEWIS	JAMES HARRIS	Redruth
1853	SKEWIS	EDWIN	Liskeard
1853	SKEWIS	ELIZABETH ELLEN	Redruth
1853	SKEWS	WILLIAM HOOLIER	Bodmin
1853	SKEWS	JOHN GREGORY	Launceston
1853	SKEWS	AMELIA	Liskeard
1853	SKUES	AMELIA	St. James
1853	SKUES	MARK	Malmsbury
1853	SKUES	SARAH	Redruth
1854	SKEWES	ELIZABETH MARY	Helston
1854	SKEWES	JOHN HENRY	Helston
1854	SKEWES	ORELIA	Truro
1854	SKEWES	MARY ANN MANDER	Helston
1854	SKEWES	HENRIETTA MARIA	Truro
1854	SKEWES	HENRY	Helston
1854	SKEWES	LAURA	Falmouth
1854	SKEWES	SARAH	Redruth
1854	SKEWES	WILLIAM ALEXANDER	Swansea
1854	SKEWIS	WILLIAM	Penzance
1854	SKEWS	JOHN	Redruth
1854	SKEWS	JOHN WILLIAM HENRY	Plymouth
1854	SKUES	JAMES	Medway
1854	SKUES	CHARLOTTE	St. James
1854	SKUES	HANNIBAL	Helston
1854	SKUES	THOMAS JOHN	Truro
1855	SKEWES	ANNIE	Wareham
1855	SKEWES	JAMES LUGG	Falmouth
1855	SKEWIS	FANNY	Abergavenny
1855	SKEWIS	WILLIAM BAWDEN	Redruth
1855	SKEWS	JOHN	Bodmin
1855	SKEWS	JOHN GREGORY	Launceston
1855	SKEWS	EMMA	Liskeard
1855	SKEWS	THOMAS PROUSE	Plymouth
1856	SKEWES	THOMAS HENRY	Helston
1856	SKEWES	CHARLES COLLAN	Wareham
1856	SKEWES	JOHN	Truro

1856	SKEWIS	ANN AMELIA	Penzance
1856	SKEWIS	ELIZABETH	Redruth
1856	SKEWIS	ANN	Redruth
1856	SKEWIS	THOMAS HENRY	Penzance
1856	SKEWS	EDWIN	Redruth
1856	SKEWS	JOHN	Liskeard
1856	SKEWS	SAMUEL GREGORY	Launceston
1856	SKEWS	SARAH ANNE	Redruth
1856	SKEWS	WILLIAM	Truro
1856	SKEWS	WILLIAM	Lewisham
1856	SKEWS	FANNY GREGORY	Launceston
1857	SKEWES	CHARLES	Falmouth
1857	SKEWES	JAMES	Falmouth
1857	SKEWES	HENRY	Helston
1857	SKEWES	ALMA JANE	Falmouth
1857	SKEWES	FREDERICK TRESIZE	Helston
1857	SKEWES	GEORGE ALLWORTH	Helston
1857	SKEWIS	WILLIAM JAMES	Helston
1857	SKEWS	EMMA	Launceston
1857	SKEWS	GEORGE	Mevagissey
1857	SKEWS	MARY GRACE	Liskeard
1857	SKEWSES	THOMAS GEORGE	Penzance
1857	SKUES	THOMAS GILBERT	St James
1858	SKEWES	THOMAS WILLIAM	Truro
1858	SKEWES	ALEXANDER RICHARD	Wareham
1858	SKEWES	MARY ANNA COURTIS	Tavistock
1858	SKEWES	(Male)	Truro
1858	SKEWIS	HENRY	Penzance
1858	SKEWIS	MARY JANE	Redruth
1858	SKEWS	SARAH FRANCES	Blean
1858	SKEWS	ELIZABETH MARY	Liskeard
1858	SKEWS	MATTHEW	Liskeard
1858	SKEWS	WILLIAM HENRY PERREN	Plymouth
1858	SKEWS	WILLIAM HENRY	Launceston
1858	SKUES	EDWARD FRANCIS	Strand
1859	SKEWES	ANN	Helston
1859	SKEWES	JAMES LUGG	Falmouth
1859	SKEWES	SUSAN ANN	Redruth
1859	SKEWES	ELIZABETH MARIA HICKS	Helston
1859	SKEWES	EMILY	Wareham
1859	SKEWIS	MARY ANN	Redruth
1859	SKEWS	JOHN	Penzance
1859	SKEWS	JOHN WILLIAMS	Launceston
1859	SKEWS	SARAH	Redruth
1859	SKEWS	ELIZABETH	Abergavenny

On checking with the Registrar for Births, Marriages and Deaths in Helston there is an entry for the following birth which does not appear at Somerset House. Birth took place between September, 1858 and November, 1860.

	SKEWES	MARY ANN	Breage
1860	SKEWES	EDWIN SCOTT WARNE	Truro
1860	SKEWES	RICHARD	Helston
1860	SKEWES	WILLIAM JOHN	Falmouth
1860	SKEWES	(Male)	Falmouth
1860	SKEWES	JOHN WESLEY	Helston
1860	SKEWES	JANE	Tavistock
1860	SKEWES	MARY ANN	Redruth
1860	SKEWES	ELIZABETH ELLEN	Redruth
1860	SKEWES	HENRIETTA MARIA	Truro
1860	SKEWES	MARY	Falmouth
1860	SKEWES	MARY	Redruth
1860	SKEWS	HARRIET MARY	Marylebone
1860	SKEWS	SAMUEL	Liskeard
1860	SKEWS	ALFRED	Launceston
1860	SKEWS	ANNIE	Stoke D.
1860	SKEWS	JOHN GREGORY	Liskeard
1860	SKEWS	MARY	Penzance
1860	SKEWS	SARAH ANN	Plymouth
1860	SKUES	ELIZABETH	Redruth
1860	SKUES	FREDERICK GORDON	Halifax
1860	SKUES	ELIZABETH ANN	St James
1861	SKEWES	WILLIAM HICKS	Helston
1861	SKEWES	ROBERT BILLING	Redruth
1861	SKEWES	THOMAS JOHN	Truro
1861	SKEWES	(Female)	Helston
1861	SKEWES	EDWARD JAMES	Redruth
1861	SKEWES	WILLIAM JAMES	Redruth
1861	SKEWES	GEORGE	Falmouth
1861	SKEWES	WILLIAM	Newton Abbot
1861	SKEWES	MARY ELLEN	Newton Abbot
1861	SKEWES	EMMA MAUD	Truro
1861	SKEWIS	WILLIAM JOHN	Redruth
1861	SKEWIS	GRACE ANNE	Redruth
1861	SKUES	EMMA	Bath
1862	SKEWES	ALICE KATE	Tavistock
1862	SKEWES	AMELIA	Penzance
1862	SKEWES	ELIZABETH ELLEN	Redruth
1862	SKEWES	MARIA	Redruth
1862	SKEWES	EMILY JANE	Redruth

Birth certificate of Frederick Gordon Skues

CERTIFIED COPY OF AN ENTRY OF BIRTH

The statutory fee for this certificate is 3s. 9d.
Where a search is necessary to find the entry,
a search fee is payable in addition.

GIVEN AT THE GENERAL REGISTER OFFICE,
SOMERSET HOUSE, LONDON

Application Number ....738538....

REGISTRATION DISTRICT *Halifax*

1860.   BIRTH in the Sub-district of *Halifax*   in the *county of York*

No.	When and where born	Name, if any	Sex	Name, and surname of father	Name, surname and maiden surname of mother	Occupation of father	Signature, description, and residence of informant	When registered	Signature of registrar	Name entered after registration
Columns:—	1	2	3	4	5	6	7	8	9	10*
125	Tenth April 1860 4 Colour Street Halifax	Frederick Gordon	Boy	Richard Skues	Lucy Skues formerly Pickard	compositor	Richard Skues father 4 Colour Street Halifax	Twentieth May 1860	J. Ledley registrar	

CERTIFIED to be a true copy of an entry in the certified copy of a Register of Births in the District above mentioned.

Given at the GENERAL REGISTER OFFICE, SOMERSET HOUSE, LONDON, under the Seal of the said Office, the ___ day of ___ 19__.

*See note overleaf

BC 229406

This certificate is issued in pursuance of the Births and Deaths Registration Act, 1953 (1 & 2 Eliz. 2, c. 20).
Section 34 provides that any certified copy of an entry purporting to be sealed or stamped with the seal of the General Register Office shall be received as evidence of the birth or death to which it relates without any further or other proof of the entry, and no certified copy purporting to be given in the said Office shall be of any force or effect unless it is sealed or stamped as aforesaid.
CAUTION.—Any person who (1) falsifies any of the particulars on this certificate, or (2) uses a falsified certificate as true, knowing it to be false, is liable to prosecution.

Year	Surname	Name	Place	Year	Surname	Name	Place
1862	SKEWES	WILLIAM	Redruth	1866	SKEWES	ELLEN	Falmouth
1862	SKEWES	EDITH	Helston	1866	SKEWES	ELLEN M.	Tavistock
1862	SKEWES	ELIZA	Falmouth	1866	SKEWES	(Female)	Wareham
1862	SKEWES	JOHN THOMAS	Penzance	1866	SKEWS	ANN E.	North Aylesford
1862	SKEWIS	ANNE JANE	Helston	1866	SKEWS	JAMES	Truro
1862	SKEWS	CAROLINE ANNE	North Aylesford	1866	SKEWS	HARRIET	Liskeard
1862	SKEWS	EMMA	Launceston	1866	SKEWS	PETER	Truro
1862	SKEWS	WILLIAM JOHN	St. Columb	1866	SKEWS	CHARLES	Launceston
1862	SKEWS	MARTIN	Redruth	1866	SKEWS	JANE	Redruth
1862	SKEWS	ALFRED	Liskeard	1866	SKEWS	WILLIAM J.	Farnham
1862	SKUES	JAMES	Redruth	1866	SKUES	EMMA	Bath
1862	SKUES	LUCY SOPHIA	St. James	1866	SKUES	FREDERICK MACKENZIE	Islington
1862	SKUES	RICHARD JAMES	Halifax	1866	SKUES	ISAAC	Chester-le-Street
1863	SKEWES	ALBERT HENRY	Wareham				
1863	SKEWES	MARY	Redruth	1866	SKUES	WILLIAM	Halifax
1863	SKEWES	CHARLES STEPHEN	Redruth	1867	SKEWES	EDWARD ALBERT	Redruth
1863	SKEWES	DANIEL	Truro	1867	SKEWES	EDWARD	Redruth
1863	SKEWES	JAMES	Redruth	1867	SKEWES	JOHN TROUNSON	Helston
1863	SKEWES	MARY ANN PETERS	Truro	1867	SKEWES	ARTHUR	Helston
1863	SKEWES	WALTER	Truro	1867	SKEWES	MINNIE	Redruth
1863	SKEWES	FREDERICK AUGUSTUS	Truro	1867	SKEWIS	EMMA JANE	Chorlton
1863	SKEWES	HENRIETTA	Newton Abbot	1867	SKEWIS	HENRY	Penzance
1863	SKEWES	KATE	Falmouth	1867	SKEWS	EMMA	Redruth
1863	SKEWES	RICHARD	Penzance	1867	SKEWS	EDMUND	Liskeard
1863	SKEWES	WILLIAM HENRY	Redruth	1867	SKEWS	THOMAS	Truro
1863	SKEWES	THOMAS JAMES	Truro	1867	SKUES	PHILIP HENRY	Lambeth
1863	SKEWIS	MARY JANE	Penzance	1867	SKUES	FREDERICK WILLIAM MACKENZIE	Islington
1863	SKEWIS	SARAH	Chorlton				
1863	SKEWIS	RICHARD	Redruth	1867	SKUES	GEORGE HENRY	St. James
1863	SKEWS	ELIZABETH ANN	Truro	1867	SKUES	MARIA	Bath
1863	SKEWS	JOHN EDWIN	Falmouth	1868	SKEWES	JULIANA	Helston
1863	SKEWS	ALFRED	Launceston	1868	SKEWES	HENRY	Falmouth
1863	SKUES	ROSINA	Bath	1868	SKEWES	EDWARD ERNEST	Falmouth
1863	SKUES	AMELIA	Bath	1868	SKEWES	ELIZABETH JANE	Truro
1864	SKEWES	JOHN	Truro	1868	SKEWES	EMMA	Newton Abbot
1864	SKEWES	JOHN COURTIS	Tavistock	1868	SKEWES	FLORENCE ROSALIE	Tavistock
1864	SKEWES	JOHN HENRY	Helston	1868	SKEWS	MARY	Launceston
1864	SKEWES	LAURA	Helston	1868	SKEWS	ANNIE	Redruth
1864	SKEWES	WILLIAM	Redruth	1868	SKEWS	MARY JANE	Liskeard
1864	SKEWES	ARTHUR	Helston	1868	SKEWS	SAMUEL FRANCIS	Redruth
1864	SKEWES	DANIEL	Newton Abbot	1868	SKUES	CHARLES WILLIAM	Westminster
1864	SKEWES	ELLEN LOUISA	Redruth	1868	SKUES	ERNEST	Halifax
1864	SKEWES	HARRY	Redruth	1868	SKUES	GEORGE CHARLES	Marylebone
1864	SKEWES	JOHNNY	Redruth	1869	SKEWES	SIDNEY HOPE	Aylesbury
1864	SKEWS	MARY ANN PERREN	Plymouth	1869	SKEWES	DANIEL	Newton Abbot
1864	SKEWS	AMOS	Launceston	1869	SKEWES	WILLIAM JOHN	Helston
1864	SKEWS	RICHARD	Liskeard	1869	SKEWES	JOHN	Falmouth
1864	SKEWS	MATTHEW	Truro	1869	SKEWES	ALFRED JOHN	Redruth
1864	SKUES	JOHN WALTER WILLIAMS	St. James	1869	SKEWS	WILLIAM	Liskeard
1864	SKUES	CHARLES PICKARD	Halifax	1869	SKEWS	SAMUEL GREGORY	Liskeard
1864	SKUES	MARGARET GEORGINA SARAH	Axbridge	1869	SKEWS	ALBERT WILLIAM	North Aylesford
				1869	SKEWS	GEORGE WILLIAMS	Guisbro'
1864	SKUES	ROSINA	Bath	1869	SKUES	THOMAS EDWARD	Lambeth
1865	SKEWES	ELIZABETH ANN	Truro	1869	SKUES	EDWARD GEORGE	Islington
1865	SKEWES	ELIZABETH MARY TREZIZE	Helston				
1865	SKEWES	HERBERT	Truro				
1865	SKEWES	ADELAIDE	Truro				
1865	SKEWES	CHARLES	Helston		SKEWES	JOHN TROMSON	Helston
1865	SKEWES	CHARLES HENRY	Redruth	1870	SKEWES	FLORENCE CECILIA	Truro
1865	SKEWES	JOSEPH JOHN	Penzance	1870	SKEWES	CATHERINE	Redruth
1865	SKEWES	ALFRED	Redruth	1870	SKEWES	JANE	Helston
1865	SKEWES	JOSIAH	Falmouth	1870	SKEWES	SARAH ANN	Helston
1865	SKEWES	SARAH JANE	Redruth	1870	SKEWES	MARY AGNES	Helston
1865	SKEWIS	ELIZABETH	Chorlton	1870	SKEWS	FREDERICK	Truro
1865	SKEWS	THOMAS GEORGE	Liskeard	1870	SKEWS	HENRY	Launceston
1865	SKEWS	WILLIAM HENRY	Redruth	1870	SKEWS	JANE ROGERS	Redruth
1865	SKEWS	ALICE MATILDA	North Aylesford	1870	SKEWS	MARY ANN E.	Portsea
1865	SKUES	EMMA	Strand	1871	SKEWES	ELIZA JANE	Redruth
1865	SKUES	JOHN GILBERT	St. James	1871	SKEWES	HOWARD	Tavistock
1866	SKEWES	LAURA ANNE	Helston	1871	SKEWES	RICHARD HENRY	Truro
1866	SKEWES	PHILIPPA M.	Redruth	1871	SKEWES	JOHN	Redruth
1866	SKEWES	WILLIAM L.	Truro	1871	SKEWES	LAURA HUNT	Truro
1866	SKEWES	ANNIE	Redruth	1871	SKEWS	MARY JANE	Helston
1866	SKEWES	EDWARD	Helston	1871	SKEWS	WILLIAM WHITE	Helston
1866	SKEWES	JOSEPH V.	Redruth				
1866	SKEWES	CLARA A.	Newton Abbot				

On checking with the Registrar for Births, Marriages and Deaths in Helston District there is an entry for the following which does not appear at Somerset House. Birth took place between 16th July, 1869 and 18th July, 1870.

1871	SKEWIS	SUSAN JANE	Penzance	1876	SKEWS	EMILY	St. Austell
1871	SKEWS	FREDERICK JOHN	North Aylesford	1876	SKEWS	JAMES HENRY	Gravesend
1871	SKEWS	ALFRED DAVID R.	Holborn	1876	SKEWS	MINNIE SARAH	Gravesend
1871	SKEWS	DAVID	Launceston	1876	SKUES	ANNIE FRANCES	Devizes
1871	SKEWS	MARY JANE	Guisbro'	1876	SKUES	ALEXANDER JAMES	Westminster
1871	SKUES	ELEANOR LUCY L.	Marylebone	1877	SKEWES	JAMES	Redruth
1871	SKUES	EMILY CONSTANCE	Westminster	1877	SKEWES	EDITH JANE	St. Austell
1871	SKUES	ELIZABETH HARRIET	Lambeth	1877	SKEWES	ALFRED JOHN	Redruth
1871	SKUES	EMILY JANE	Pancras	1877	SKEWES	WILLIAM HENRY	Totnes
1871	SKUES	ALICE	Bath	1877	SKEWES	ELLEN JANE	Helston
1872	SKEWES	HARRIET JANE	Helston	1877	SKEWES	JOHN HENRY	Redruth
1872	SKEWES	HENRY	Redruth	1877	SKEWES	CLARA	Redruth
1872	SKEWES	JAMES HENRY	Helston	1877	SKEWIS	EMMA NORTHCOTT	Newton Abbot
1872	SKEWES	MARY ELLEN	Redruth	1877	SKEWIS	HENRY PERCY	Wellington,
1872	SKEWES	WILLIAM RICHARD	Newton Abbot				Somerset
1872	SKEWES	ROSA MARIA	Truro	1877	SKEWS	FLORENCE	Truro
1872	SKEWS	HARRY	Liskeard	1877	SKEWS	JOANNA	Liskeard
1872	SKEWS	JAMES JOHN	Neath	1877	SKEWS	WILLIAM THOMAS	Bethnal Green
1872	SKEWS	THOMAS	Liskeard	1877	SKEWS	ELLEN ANNIE	Liskeard
1872	SKEWS	GEORGE FRANCIS W.	Holborn	1877	SKEWS	FREDERICK WILLIAM	Dartford
1872	SKEWS	JOHN	Redruth	1877	SKEWS	WILLIAM	Redruth
1872	SKEWS	MATILDA	Liskeard	1877	SKUES	CHARLES HENRY	Marylebone
1873	SKEWES	ARTHUR DAW	Tavistock	1877	SKUES	ETHEL EMMA	Bath
1873	SKEWES	HENRY	Helston	1877	SKUES	MAUD CHARLOTTE	Eton
1873	SKEWES	JULIA ANNIE	Helston	1877	SKUES	NOAH JAMES	Tonbridge
1873	SKEWES	MARY	Redruth	1878	SKEWES	HEDLEY JAMES	Redruth
1873	SKEWES	EDITH	Redruth	1878	SKEWES	JOHN	Redruth
1873	SKEWES	LAURA MARY	Helston	1878	SKEWES	MARY LOUISA T.	East Stonehouse
1873	SKEWIS	RICHARD HENRY	Penzance	1878	SKEWES	ANNIE MARY	Redruth
1873	SKEWIS	EDWIN GEORGE	Sheffield	1878	SKEWES	SENERETTA ELIZABETH	Helston
1873	SKEWS	EDWARD GEORGE	Dartford	1878	SKEWES	RICHARD CHARLES	Redruth
1873	SKEWS	FLORENCE KATE	Redruth	1878	SKEWES	ROSINA	Redruth
1873	SKEWS	HARRY	Launceston	1878	SKEWIS	ALBERT	Sheffield
1873	SKEWS	SAMUEL JOHN	Liskeard	1878	SKEWIS	GERTRUDE ALICE	Wellington,
1873	SKEWS	EMMA FRANCES	North Aylesford				Somerset
1873	SKUES	WALTER EDWARD	Westminster	1878	SKEWIS	JOHN	Bedwellty
1873	SKUES	ELIZA HELEN	Marylebone	1878	SKEWS	TOM	Redruth
1873	SKUES	HENRY ERNEST	Lambeth	1878	SKEWS	ALICE ANNIE	Bethnal Green
1874	SKEWES	FREDERICK	Truro	1878	SKEWS	GRACE	Neath
1874	SKEWES	JOHN	Redruth	1878	SKEWS	PERCY LOUIS	Dartford
1874	SKEWES	MARY	Redruth	1878	SKEWS	LOUISA	North Aylesford
1874	SKEWES	WILLIAM ERNEST	Helston	1878	SKEWS	MATTHEW	Easington
1874	SKEWIS	EVA LOUISE	Sheffield	1878	SKEWS	MARY ANN	Liskeard
1874	SKEWIS	JOHN WOODLEY W.	Newton Abbot	1878	SKUES	EVELYN ROSE	Westminster
1874	SKEWS	RICHARD ERNEST	Redruth	1878	SKUES	JOHN WILLIAM	Lambeth
1874	SKEWS	MARY	Neath	1879	SKEWES	GEORGE	Totnes
1874	SKEWS	NATHANIEL EDWARD R.	Bethnal Green	1879	SKEWES	MARY ELLEN	Redruth
1874	SKEWS	PETER	St. Austell	1879	SKEWES	EMILY	Redruth
1874	SKEWS	EMILY JANE	Liskeard	1879	SKEWES	SUSAN	Helston
1874	SKEWS	LUCY ELIZABETH	Islington	1879	SKEWES	WILLIAM HEDLEY	Penzance
1875	SKEW	WILLIAM GEORGE	Lymington	1879	SKEWS	MATILDA SARAH	Bethnal Green
1875	SKEWES	ALFRED JOHN	Helston	1879	SKEWS	FLORA LEE	Redruth
1875	SKEWES	ESTHER	Helston	1879	SKEWS	LILY	Truro
1875	SKEWES	GEORGE HARRIS	Truro	1879	SKEWS	EMILY LOUISA	North Aylesford
1875	SKEWES	MARY	Redruth	1879	SKUES	JAMES FREDERICK	St. Austell
1875	SKEWES	ELIZABETH MAY	Helston	1879	SKUES	EDITH	Thetford
1875	SKEWES	SYDNEY JAMES	Helston	1880	SKEWES	ETHEL WOODMAN	East Stonehouse
1875	SKEWIS	ROBERT MORGAN	Bedwellty	1880	SKEWES	RICHARD CHARLES	Bethnal Green
1875	SKEWIS	EMMA	Newton Abbot	1880	SKEWES	ADELINE HARRIET R.	Helston
1875	SKEWS	MATTHEW	Liskeard	1880	SKEWES	STEPHEN JAMES	Redruth
1875	SKEWS	WILLIAM	Truro	1880	SKEWES	CLARA CAROLINE S.	Penzance
1875	SKEWS	ARTHUR JAMES	Dartford	1880	SKEWIS	ADA	Sheffield
1875	SKUES	FLORENCE MARY	Halifax	1880	SKEWS	HENRY JAMES	Bethnal Green
1875	SKUES	ADA JOHANNA	Lambeth	1880	SKEWS	LAURA	Truro
1875	SKUES	BESSIE ANNIE	Marylebone	1880	SKEWS	ROSE SELINA	North Aylesford
1875	SKUES	CHARLES AYRE		1880	SKEWS	THOMAS	Neath
		MACKENZIE	Islington	1880	SKEWS	BEATRICE	Redruth
1875	SKUES	FREDERICK JOHN	St. Geo. Hann	1880	SKEWS	ELIZABETH JANE	Newton Abbot
			Square	1880	SKEWS	JOHN HENRY	Stoke D.
1876	SKEWES	CLARA CAROLINE	Redruth	1880	SKEWS	ALBERT JOHN	Dartford
1876	SKEWES	JAMES	Redruth	1880	SKEWS	DAVID CHARLES	Bethnal Green
1876	SKEWIS	MARY EMMA	Sheffield	1880	SKUES	BLANCHE LOUISA	Redbrook
1876	SKEWIS	ELIZABETH	Williton	1880	SKUES	WILLIAM GEORGE	Eton
1876	SKEWS	HARRIET	Neath	1881	SKEWES	ERNEST JOHN	St. Geo.
1876	SKEWS	ELIZABETH ANN	Totnes				Han Square
1876	SKEWS	FLORENCE ELIZABETH	Edmonton	1881	SKEWES	JOHN WILLIAM	Penzance
1876	SKEWS	MARY JANE	Redruth	1881	SKEWES	AMY	Helston

1881	SKEWES	EDWIN	Redruth	1885	SKEWES-	EVELYN MARY	Richmond
1881	SKEWES	JOHN HERBERT	Truro		COX		South
1881	SKEWES	CATHERINE ANN S.	Redruth	1885	SKEWIS	ADA	Redruth
1881	SKEWES	CHARLES	Truro	1885	SKEWS	FREDERICK	Easington
1881	SKEWES	JANE	Totnes	1885	SKEWS	BERNARD	Dartford
1881	SKEWES	HERBERT	Ulverston	1885	SKEWS	JAMES ARTHUR	Bethnal Green
1881	SKUES	WILLIAM JOHN	Fulham	1885	SKUES	ERNEST	Halifax
1881	SKUES	(Female)	Bath	1886	SKEWES	BESSIE EDITH A.	St. Columb
1881	SKUES	CHARLES JOHN	St. Austell	1886	SKEWES	DORCAS	Penzance
1882	SKEWES	ANNIE	Penzance	1886	SKEWES	JAMES HENRY	Helston
1882	SKEWES	BESSIE	Helston	1886	SKEWES	MABEL	Redruth
1882	SKEWES	JESSIE	Truro	1886	SKEWES	MARY ELIZA	Redruth
1882	SKEWES	MAY MARGARET	Redruth	1886	SKEWES	ELIZABETH	Salford
1882	SKEWES	WILLIAM ARTHUR	Redruth	1886	SKEWES	ELLA	Helston
1882	SKEWES	CLARINDA JANE	Helston	1886	SKEWES	THOMAS EDGAR	Truro
1882	SKEWES	EDWARD FREDERICK	Helston	1886	SKEWES	ANNIE	Penzance
1882	SKEWES	HILDA LAURA W.	Truro	1886	SKEWES	FREDERICK	Truro
1882	SKEWES	CATHERINE MARY	Helston	1886	SKEWS	AMELIA	Redruth
1882	SKEWIS	GRACE MARIA M.	Ulverston	1886	SKEWES	GERTRUDE	Penzance
1882	SKEWS	ELIZABETH EMILY	Bethnal Green	1886	SKEWES	JOHN EDWARD	Chorlton
1882	SKEWS	JAMES EDWARD	Gravesend	1886	SKEWES	MABEL JANE	Redruth
1882	SKEWS	RICHARD	Neath	1886	SKEWES-COX	VERNON	Richmond
1882	SKEWS	MATTHEW HENRY	Redruth				South
1882	SKEWS	EDITH FLORENCE	Stoke D.	1886	SKEWIS	MAUD RAY	Islington
1882	SKUES	HAROLD FREDERICK		1886	SKEWIS	THOMAS HAROLD	Sheffield
		CLAUDE	Westminster	1886	SKEWS	MARTIN	Redruth
1882	SKUES	EDITH MARY	Eton	1886	SKEWS	MARY ANN	Stepney
1882	SKUES	FRANCIS ALBERT	Chelsea	1886	SKEWS	ANNIE EDITH	East Ashford
1883	SKEWES	BESSIE ELLEN	Redruth	1886	SKEWS	ELIZABETH MAUD	Bethnal Green
1883	SKEWES	ETHEL MAY	Helston	1886	SKEWS	THOMAS	Ecclesall
1883	SKEWES	RICHARD CHARLES	Redruth	1886	SKEWS	EDWARD	Easington
1883	SKEWES	MYRA	Redruth	1886	SKUES	FLORENCE AUGUSTA	Eton
1883	SKEWES	CHARLES FREDERICK	Falmouth	1886	SKUES	REGINALD PENROSE	Fulham
1883	SKEWES	ELIZABETH ELLEN R.	Redruth	1887	SKEWES	CERETA	Truro
1883	SKEWES	GRACE ELIZABETH	Truro	1887	SKEWES	JESSIE	Manchester
1883	SKEWES	JAMES	Penzance	1887	SKEWES	THIRZA	Helston
1883	SKEWES	WILLIAM	Salford	1887	SKEWES	WILLIAM HENRY R.	Redruth
1883	SKEWIS	EDWIN	Newton Abbot	1887	SKEWES	TOM	Penzance
1883	SKEWIS	HARRIET	Totnes	1887	SKEWES	BARRINGTON	Helston
1883	SKEWS	CHARLOTTE REBECCA	Bethnal Green	1887	SKEWES	MARY CAMPBELL	Penzance
1883	SKEWS	ALBAN EDGAR	Dartford	1887	SKEWES-COX	MARGARET	Richmond
1883	SKEWS	CLARA	Houghton				South
1883	SKUES	ELIZA	Whitechapel	1887	SKEWIS	ALFRED	Woodbridge
1883	SKUES	ETHEL JANE	Eton	1887	SKEWIS	WILLIAM	Newton Abbot
1884	SKEWES	EMMA	Penzance	1887	SKEWIS	MARGARET JANE	Barnet
1884	SKEWES	MARY	Helston	1887	SKEWS	ALICE GERTRUDE	Preston
1884	SKEWES	PRISCILLA	Redruth	1887	SKEWS	LILIAN MARGARET	Bethnal Green
1884	SKEWES	WILLIAM MUNDY	Helston	1887	SKEWS	ROBERT ALBERT	Bethnal Green
1884	SKEWES	AMELIA	Penzance	1887	SKUES	FLORENCE EMILY	Tonbridge
1884	SKEWES	GWENDOLINE	St. Thomas	1887	SKUES	JOSEPH PEARN	Redruth
1884	SKEWES	JOHN	Helston	1887	SKUES	GEORGE	Halifax
1884	SKEWES-COX	THOMAS EDMUND	Richmond	1888	SKEWES	ERNEST	Tavistock
			South	1888	SKEWES	LILIAN MAUD	Redruth
1884	SKEWIS	WILLIAM HENRY	Newton Abbot	1888	SKEWES	WILLIAM JOHN	Redruth
1884	SKEWIS	JOHN JAMES	Ulverston	1888	SKEWES	RICHARD HENRY	Penzance
1884	SKEWS	FLORENCE EMMA	Liskeard	1888	SKEWES	GRACE	Helston
1884	SKEWS	ABSALOM	Neath	1888	SKEWES	BLANCH	Truro
1884	SKEWS	EDWIN ARTHUR	Bethnal Green	1888	SKEWES	WALTER JAMES	Redruth
1884	SKUES	ALBERT VICTOR	Westminster	1888	SKEWIS	CAROLINE	Redruth
1884	SKUES	WINIFRED VIOLET Twins		1888	SKEWS	EMILY GERTRUDE	Preston
1885	SKEWES	ALICE EMILY	Redruth	1888	SKEWS	ELIZABETH MARTHA	St. Olave
1885	SKEWES	FLORENCE ANNIE	Redruth	1888	SKEWS	ESTHER ISABEL U.	Plymouth
1885	SKEWES	FREDERICK	Salford	1888	SKEWS	ETHEL MARY	Dartford
1885	SKEWES	LOUISA JANE	Truro	1888	SKUES	EDGAR CLAUDIUS	Edmonton
1885	SKEWES	WILLIAM	Penzance	1888	SKUES	HAROLD SEARLE	Eton
1885	SKEWES	(Female)	Helston	1889	SKEWES	BEATRICE ANNIE	Redruth
1885	SKEWES	KATIE BEATRICE	Truro	1889	SKEWES	ELIZABETH MILDRED	Redruth
1885	SKEWES	LEWIS LLEWELLYN	Redruth	1889	SKEWES	LOUISA	Manchester
1885	SKEWES	WILFRED	Redruth	1889	SKEWES	ERNEST JOSEPH	Bethnal Green
1885	SKEWES	ELLA GWENDOLINE	Helston	1889	SKEWES	ROSENA	Easington
1885	SKEWES	HERBERT JOHN	Truro	1889	SKEWES	CHARLES	Chorlton
1885	SKEWES	JANE MITCHELL	Helston	1889	SKEWES	CLARINDA	Redruth
1885	SKEWES	WILLIAM FRANCIS	Helston	1889	SKEWES	EDITH	Tavistock
1885	SKEWES	WILLIAM HENRY	Redruth	1889	SKEWES	JOHN	Penzance
1885	SKEWES	WILLIAM HENRY	Helston	1889	SKEWES	WILLIAM	Penzance
1885	SKEWES	RICHARD JOHN	St. Columb	1889	SKEWES	CHARLES	Salford
1885	SKEWES	WILLIAM JAMES	Redruth	1889	SKEWIS	ELIZABETH GERTRUDE	Sheffield

Year	Surname	Name	Place
1889	SKEWIS	WILLIAM HENRY	Hendon
1889	SKEWS	SARAH ANNIE	Redruth
1889	SKEWS	MINNIE	Barnsley
1889	SKEWS	DAISY EMILY	Bethnal Green
1889	SKEWS	MARY LOUISA	Preston
1889	SKUES	ADA ALICE	Tonbridge
1890	SKEWES	ARTHUR ERNEST	Helston
1890	SKEWES	EDWARD JAMES	Redruth
1890	SKEWES	JOSEPH JOHN	Penzance
1890	SKEWES	THOMAS	Penzance
1890	SKEWES	JAMES ARTHUR	Redruth
1890	SKEWES	WILLIAM TREVENA	Penzance
1890	SKEWES	HENRIETTA	Truro
1890	SKEWES	JESSIE MARGARETTA	Redruth
1890	SKEWIS	FEODORA	Helston
1890	SKEWS	EDITH JANE	Easington
1890	SKEWS	ALFRED WILLIAM	St. Olave
1890	SKEWS	JOHN HENRY	Stoke D.
1890	SKEWS	WILLIAM JOHN	Easington
1890	SKUES	SIDNEY ST. JOHN	Edmonton
1891	SKEWES	FREDERICK HENRY	St. Thomas
1891	SKEWES	SARAH	Penzance
1891	SKEWES	LILIAN GREENLAW	Helston
1891	SKEWES	RINA MARY	Wareham
1891	SKEWES	WILLIAM JOHN	Redruth
1891	SKEWES	LAURA	Penzance
1891	SKEWES	WILLIAM RICHARDS	Redruth
1891	SKEWIS	ELIZA ELLEN	Redruth
1891	SKEWIS	WILLIAM STRATHEWAY	Ulverston
1891	SKEWS	GERTRUDE MARY	Plymouth
1891	SKEWS	LOUISA	Barnsley
1891	SKEWS	CLARENCE	Liskeard
1891	SKEWS	MARY LILIAN	Bethnal Green
1891	SKUES	JOHN PHILIP W.	Lambeth
1891	SKUES	ARTHUR	Halifax
1892	SKEWES	ARTHUR WEATHERBY	Helston
1892	SKEWES	CHARLES	Redruth
1892	SKEWES	LILIE	Helston
1892	SKEWES	HAROLD	Salford
1892	SKEWES	LILIAN LINDA M.	Penzance
1892	SKEWS	NELSON	Dartford
1892	SKEWS	ANNIE	Liskeard
1892	SKEWS	BESSIE HARRIET	Preston
1892	SKEWS	ELIZABETH ETHEL G.	Stoke D.
1892	SKEWS	GEORGE JOHN A.	Bethnal Green
1892	SKEWS	BETSY	Barnsley
1893	SKEWES	HAROLD COURTIS	Windsor
1893	SKEWES	HARRY STANLEY	Helston
1893	SKEWES	LILIAN MAY	Redruth
1893	SKEWES	NORMAN	Redruth
1893	SKEWES	THOMAS HENRY	Redruth
1893	SKEWES	ERNEST	Penzance
1893	SKEWES	HILDA JANE	Helston
1893	SKEWES-COX	ST JOHN	Richmond South
1893	SKEWIS	GEORGE	Penzance
1893	SKEWIS	EDWARD	Redruth
1893	SKEWS	JAMES HENRY	Liskeard
1893	SKEWS	MABEL	Barnsley
1893	SKEWS	SAMUEL JOHN	Launceston
1893	SKEWS	WILLIAM GEORGE	St. Olave
1893	SKUES	PERCIVAL WALTER	Islington
1893	SKUES	VICTOR CLAUDE	Edmonton
1893	SKUES	ALBERT EDWARD	St. Saviour
1893	SKUES	WINIFRED ROSE	Pancras
1894	SKEWES	WILLIAM	Redruth
1894	SKEWES	WILLIAM HENRY	Redruth
1894	SKEWES	GEORGE ERNEST	Salford
1894	SKEWES	WILLIAM FREDERICK	Chorlton
1894	SKEWES	JAMES HENRY OSWALD	Redruth
1894	SKEWES	LILIAN	Redruth
1894	SKEWS	THOMAS PROWSE P.	Preston
1894	SKEWS	VICTOR GEORGE	Dartford
1894	SKEWS	JOHN	Liskeard
1894	SKEWS	NELLIE	Bethnal Green
1894	SKEWS	FLORENCE BEATRICE	Liskeard
1894	SKEWS	ALBERT EDWARD	Stoke D.
1894	SKEWS	WILLIAM GEORGE A.	Bethnal Green
1894	SKEWS	THOMAS HENRY J.	St. Saviour
1894	SKUES	WALTER EDWARD	Islington
1894	SKUES	THOMAS GEORGE	Paddington
1895	SKEWES	DOROTHY GWENDOLINE	Newton Abbot
1895	SKEWES	SYDONIA	Salford
1895	SKEWES	JOHN EDGAR	Windsor
1895	SKEWES	CLARENDA	Redruth
1895	SKEWES	SAMUEL	Penzance
1895	SKEWES	HETTY LOUISE	Penzance
1895	SKEWS	ROSE PEARL	Launceston
1895	SKEWS	ERNEST	Barnsley
1895	SKEWS	ELIZA MAY	Bethnal Green
1895	SKEWS	GLADYS VIOLET	Liskeard
1895	SKEWS	MARY ANN	Houghton
1895	SKEWS	EMILY ANNIE	St. Olave
1895	SKEWS	LUCY ELIZABETH	Bethnal Green
1895	SKUES	BERTHA ELIZABETH	Edmonton
1896	SKEWES	ARTHUR COURTIS	Barton R.
1896	SKEWES	EDWARD	Redruth
1896	SKEWS	CHARLES WILLIAM	Liskeard
1896	SKEWS	CLARENCE	Liskeard
1896	SKEWS	GERTRUDE ALBERTA	St. Austell
1896	SKEWS	FREDERICK CHARLES	Stoke D.
1896	SKUES	ARTHUR LEONARD	St. Saviour
1896	SKUES	ATLANTA VIOLET	Edmonton
1897	SKEWES	ARTHUR GEORGE	Chorlton
1897	SKEWES	CATHARINE	Redruth
1897	SKEWES	CHARLEY	Penzance
1897	SKEWES	LIONAL JAMES	Falmouth
1897	SKEWS	HENRY FREDERICK	St. Olave
1897	SKEWS	LIZZIE	Plymouth
1897	SKEWS	GEORGE	Barnsley
1897	SKEWS	MARY	Bethnal Green
1897	SKEWS	ISABELLA	Plympton
1897	SKEWS	JOHN GEORGE	Shoreditch
1897	SKUES	CECIL	Nottingham
1898	SKEWES	FREDERICK CECIL	Helston
1898	SKEWES	JONATHAN BRADDON	Penzance
1898	SKEWES	EDITH	Redruth
1898	SKEWES	HENRY	Salford
1898	SKEWS	DORIS MAY	Redruth
1898	SKEWS	RICHARD CHARLES	Bethnal Green
1898	SKEWS	ALICE MARTHA R.	Bethnal Green
1898	SKEWS	MAUD	Stoke D.
1898	SKEWS	WILLIAM JOHN	Houghton
1898	SKEWS	WILLIAM HEDLEY	St. Austell
1898	SKEWS	WINIFRED MARY	Liskeard
1898	SKUES	CHARLES GILBERT	Edmonton
1898	SKUES	FREDERICK HAROLD	Edmonton
1898	SKUES	LUCY	Halifax
1899	SKEWES	MARY VERONICA	Redruth
1899	SKEWES	ADA	Redruth
1899	SKEWES	GERTRUDE ANNIE	Redruth
1899	SKEWES	EDITH	Penzance
1899	SKEWES	WILLIAM FREDERICK	Wigan
1899	SKEWES	WINNIE	Truro
1899	SKEWIS	EDWIN HENRY	Rochford
1899	SKEWS	DAVID GEORGE	Bethnal Green
1899	SKEWS	GEORGE THOMAS	St. Olave
1899	SKEWS	SAMUEL JOHN	Devonport
1899	SKEWS	ALFRED GEORGE W.	Hackney
1899	SKEWS	MATTHEW THOMAS	Redruth
1899	SKUES	CLAUDE WILLIAM	Shoreditch
1899	SKUES	DOROTHY KATHLEEN	Edmonton
1899	SKUES	VINCENT	Nottingham
1899	SKUES	ERIC	Halifax
1899	SKUES	FREDERICK	Rochford
1899	SKUES	PHILIP ERNEST	St. Saviour
1900	SKEWES	WILLIAM JOHN	Helston
1900	SKEWES	MABEL	Helston
1900	SKEWES	VIOLET GWENDOLINE D.	Penzance
1900	SKEWES	EDITH	Redruth
1900	SKEWES	EMILY ROSAMUND	Redruth
1900	SKEWES	LILIAN	Helston
1900	SKEWIS	ERNEST RONALD	Marylebone
1900	SKEWIS	OLIVE MAY	Totnes

1900	SKEWS	ELIZABETH	Barnsley
1900	SKEWS	FRANCIS	Shoreditch
1900	SKEWS	HARRY	Liskeard
1900	SKEWS	EDITH SARAH	Bethnal Green
1900	SKEWS	LILIAN MAY	Devonport
1900	SKEWS	ELIZABETH GRACE	Devonport
1900	SKUES	FREDERICK	Halifax
1901	SKEWES	ARTHUR	Helston
1901	SKEWES	CATHARINE	Redruth
1901	SKEWES	DORIS MURIEL	Redruth
1901	SKEWES	LILIAN MAY	Redruth
1901	SKEWES	EDWARD JOHN R.	Redruth
1901	SKEWES	LAURIE ANNIE	Wigan
1901	SKEWIS	HILDA MAUD	Redruth
1901	SKEWS	EDITH JANE	Liskeard
1901	SKEWS	GEORGE CHARLES	Bethnal Green
1901	SKEWS	GEORGE WEALE	Plymouth
1901	SKEWS	JOSEPH	Barnsley
1901	SKEWS	MARTHA MARGARET	St. Olave
1901	SKUES	LUCY DOROTHY	Shoreditch
1901	SKUES	NINA MAY	Edmonton
1902	SKEWES	ELIZABETH JOANNA	Redruth
1902	SKEWES	AGNES CORONA	Penzance
1902	SKEWES	BERTRAM	Helston
1902	SKEWIS	FRANK	Tonbridge
1902	SKEWIS	FEARNLEY JOHN	Totnes
1902	SKEWS	CAROLINE CHARLOTTE	Bethnal Green
1902	SKEWS	FLORENCE JANE	Devonport
1902	SKEWS	ALBERT EDWARD	Edmonton
1902	SKEWS	ELIZABETH ANNIE	Liskeard
1902	SKEWS	MABEL MILLICENT	St. Austell
1902	SKEWS	NATHANIEL R.H.	Bethnal Green
1902	SKEWS	PERCIVAL	Truro
1902	SKEWS	REGINALD ERNEST	Devonport
1902	SKUES	EVELYN	Halifax
1902	SKUES	JOHN CHARLES	Redruth
1903	SKEWES	FLORENCE MAY	Redruth
1903	SKEWES	SAMUEL JOHN	Redruth
1903	SKEWES	HENRY ERNEST	Falmouth
1903	SKEWS	LILLIE	Swindon
1903	SKEWS	ALBERT EDWARD	Strood
1903	SKEWS	WILLIAM JOHN	St. Austell
1903	SKEWS	HARRY	Devonport
1903	SKEWS	SAMUEL	Barnsley
1903	SKUES	GWENDOLINE	Redruth
1903	SKUES	LILY MARIE	Shoreditch
1904	SKEWES	BEATRICE MARY	Redruth
1904	SKEWES	JAMES ELDRED	Islington
1904	SKEWES	WILLIAM FRANK	Helston
1904	SKEWES	FREDERICK	Redruth
1904	SKEWES	JACK PATTISON	Redruth
1904	SKEWES	EDWARD	Salford
1904	SKEWES	GEORGINA MIRIAM	Bideford
1904	SKEWIS	GEORGE	Paddington
1904	SKEWS	ELIZABETH	Bethnal Green
1904	SKEWS	ERNEST EDGAR	Bromley
1904	SKEWS	PERCY VICTOR	Dartford
1904	SKEWS	ELIZABETH JANE	St. Austell
1904	SKUES	RICHARD	Brentford
1904	SKUES	FLORENCE RUBY	Shoreditch
1904	SKUES	JAMES FREDERICK M.	Redruth
1904	SKUES	JOAN MACKENZIE } Twins	Lambeth
1904	SKUES	SHEILA MACKENZIE	Lambeth
1905	SKEWES	ARTHUR	Redruth
1905	SKEWES	BELLA CLARK	Plymouth
1905	SKEWES	OLIVE IRENE	Helston
1905	SKEWES	WILLIAM FREDERICK C.	Truro
1905	SKEWIS	RONALD	Totnes
1905	SKEWS	ALBERT EDWARD	Swindon
1905	SKEWS	EDGAR	Barnsley
1905	SKEWS	RUBY IRENE	Devonport
1905	SKEWS	GEORGE FRANCIS	Edmonton
1905	SKEWS	HERBERT JAMES S.	Bethnal Green
1905	SKUES	LEONARD	Edmonton
1905	SKUES	ADA MAY	Redruth
1905	SKUES	FLORENCE MURIEL	Halifax
1905	SKUES	SAMUEL WILLIAM	Chippenham

1906	SKEWES	GORDON	Penzance
1906	SKEWES	MONA DAVIE	Penzance
1906	SKEWES	RICHARD CHARLES	Redruth
1906	SKEWS	ALICE ELIZABETH	Strood
1906	SKEWS	PETER	St. Austell
1906	SKUES	CLORINDA DORIS	Southwark
1906	SKUES	JOSEPH CHARLES	Redruth
1906	SKUES	DOROTHY MARGARET	Shoreditch
1906	SKUES	FLORENCE LILIAN	Redruth
1907	SKEWES	ALFRED JOHN	Redruth
1907	SKEWES	JAMES HENRY	Helston
1907	SKEWES	MARY MARJORIE	Redruth
1907	SKEWIS	JOHN	Totnes
1907	SKEWS	WILLIAM DAVID	Hackney
1907	SKEWS	FERNLEY WALTER	Liskeard
1907	SKEWS	HILDA BLANCH	Devonport
1907	SKEWS	MAUD	Strood
1907	SKUES	DORA BEATRICE	Shoreditch
1907	SKUES	JAMES ALBERT	Redruth
1908	SKEWES	ELIZABETH MARY	Helston
1908	SKEWES	GEORGE HENNESSY	Redruth
1908	SKEWIS	VIDA	Totnes
1908	SKEWIS	WILFRED ROY	Tonbridge
1908	SKEWIS	ELIZABETH MARY	Helston
1908	SKEWS	RICHARD	St. Austell
1908	SKEWS	VIOLET ALICE	Bethnal Green
1908	SKEWS	CHARLES	Bethnal Green
1908	SKUES	ENID ELIZABETH	Dartford
1908	SKUES	GRACE JOAN	Greenwich
1908	SKUES	PHYLLIS	Redruth
1909	SKEWES	SAMUEL PERCY	Helston
1909	SKEWIS	ETTIE	Totnes
1909	SKEWIS	LESLIE	Tonbridge
1909	SKUES	IVY MARGARETTA	Southwark
1909	SKUES	IVY MAUD	Edmonton
1909	SKUES	MAUD EVELYN	Shoreditch
1909	SKUES	JAMES FREDERICK	Redruth
1909	SKUES	FRANCIS HENRY	Dartford
1910	SKEWES	CAROLINE LOUISE	Truro
1910	SKEWES	LILIA	Helston
1910	SKEWES	NELLY	Salford
1910	SKEWES	JOHN HENRY	Redruth
1910	SKEWES	JOHN H.	Redruth
1910	SKEWIS	ELSIE	Helston
1910	SKEWS	FREDERICK C.	Dartford
1910	SKEWS	MATTHEW JOHN	Redruth
1910	SKUES	HUGH WILLIAM	Greenwich
1910	SKUES	OLIVE EMILY	Shoreditch

Towards the latter end of the year 1911 Somerset House Registers listed the maiden name of the mother.

1911	SKEWES	MARY ELIZABETH Vallantine	Plymouth
1911	SKEWES	FREDERICK C. Smith	Houghton
1911	SKEWES	WILLIAM JOHN Gilbert	Helston
1911	SKEWIS	CLARENCE J.	Totnes
1911	SKEWS	ERNEST W.	West Ham
1911	SKEWS	HENRY G.	West Ham
1911	SKEWS	ERNEST	Bethnal Green
1911	SKEWS	ERNESTINE MARY Skews	St. Olave
1911	SKEWS	ADA I. Bradley	Barnsley
1911	SKEWS	ARTHUR G. Davis	Strood
1911	SKUES	JACK Roberts	Barnsley
1912	SKEWES	WILLIAM C.M. Marsh	Croydon
1912	SKEWIS	DOROTHY M. Shute	Totnes
1912	SKEWS	MARGARET Jarvis	St. Geo. East
1912	SKEWS	ALICE D. Fawcett	Edmonton

Year	Surname	Given Name	(Mother)	Place
1912	SKUES	EDWIN THOMAS	Jeffery	Dartford
1912	SKUES	ERNEST JOHN	Bond	Shoreditch
1912	SKUES	LEWIS	Tregonning	Redruth
1912	SKUES	VIVIAN WILLIAM	Garvey	Watford
1913	SKEWES	WILLIAM RICHARD	Roberts	Penzance
1913	SKEWES	ALBERT J.	Ford	Redruth
1913	SKEWES	HORACE	Truran	Redruth
1913	SKEWIS	DELILAH C.	Hughes	Haverfordwest
1913	SKEWS	ROY	Bradley	Barnsley
1913	SKEWS	VIOLET IRENE	Rickard	St. Austell
1913	SKUES	LESLIE JAMES	Jeffery	Dartford
1914	SKEWES	DORIS M.	Lally	Chorlton
1914	SKEWES	KATHLEEN MURIEL	Marsh	Croydon
1914	SKEWES	WILLIAM DOUGLAS	Teague	Truro
1914	SKEWES	ARTHUR S.A.	Jarvis	St. Geo. East
1914	SKEWES	SARAH E.E.	Smith	Brentford
1914	SKEWES	FLORENCE	Allcock	Salford
1914	SKEWIS	MILDRED E.	Waters	Haverfordwest
1914	SKEWS	FREDERICK	Hilliard	West Ham
1914	SKUES	ALFRED EDGAR	Bond	Shoreditch
1914	SKUES	DORIS A.	Brissendon	Lewisham
1915	SKEWES	EDWARD	Gichero	Chorlton
1915	SKEWES	HARRY	Pollard	Redruth
1915	SKEWES	SUSAN	Richards	Helston
1915	SKEWES	Female — Jory } Twins		Redruth
1915	SKEWES	Female		
1915	SKEWES	DOREEN M.	Ford	Redruth
1915	SKEWES	LILY	Lally	Chorlton
1915	SKEWES	MARY A.	Boyd	Fulham
1915	SKEWES	OSWALD	Gilbert	Helston
1915	SKEWS	ALFRED J.	Skews	Whitechapel
1915	SKEWS	IRENE	Smith	Houghton
1915	SKEWS	KATHLEEN	Bradley	Barnsley
1915	SKEWS	WINIFRED A.	Whiting	Bodmin
1915	SKUES	HARRY	Bond	Shoreditch
1915	SKUES	HERBERT W.	Jeffery	Dartford
1916	SKEWES	FREDERICK JOHN C.	Teague	Truro
1916	SKEWES	CECIL	Ford	Redruth
1916	SKEWES	IRIS M.	Jory	Redruth
1916	SKEWES	ROY	Truran	Redruth
1916	SKEWES	SYLVIA DOREEN	Hill	Redruth
1916	SKEWES-COX	SUSETTE P.	Struben	Newton Abbot
1916	SKEWIS	ALFRED W. St. E.	Hughes	Haverfordwest
1916	SKEWS	KATHLEEN P.H.	Smith	Brentford
1916	SKEWS	RICHARD N.E.	Jarvis	St. Geo. East
1916	SKEWS	CHARLES R.	Rickard	St. Austell
1916	SKEWS	LESLIE	Smith	Houghton
1917	SKEWES	GLADYS C.	Gurney	Truro
1917	SKEWS	ELSIE	Childs	Bethnal Green
1917	SKEWS	MARY K.	Barrett	Plymouth
1917	SKEWS	MABEL	Bradley	Barnsley
1917	SKUES	CYRIL A.J.	Bremer	Camberwell
1917	SKUES	CHRISTOPHER H.V.	Harris	Shoreditch
1918	SKEWES	JOHN HOWARD	Richards	Helston
1918	SKEWES	VIOLET MAY	Jenkins	Penzance
1918	SKEWES	MATILDA JOAN	Hill	Redruth
1918	SKEWES	PHYLLIS	Harris	Redruth
1918	SKEWES	BELINDA O.M.	Webber	Devonport
1918	SKEWES	JOSEPH F.	Lally	Chorlton
1919	SKEWES	GWENLLIAN F.	Phelps	Pontypridd
1919	SKEWES	JAMES	Pollard	Redruth
1919	SKEWES	HENRY R.	Revell	Marylebone
1919	SKEWES	JOHN H.	Lally	Chorlton
1919	SKEWES	VERA	Harris	Redruth
1919	SKEWES	LEONARD	Roberts	Penzance
1919	SKEWS	MARTIN REX	Nancecarrow	Redruth
1919	SKEWS	AGNES	Jarvis	Stepney
1919	SKEWS	JOHN	Jarvis	Stepney
1919	SKEWS	THOMAS F.	Bradley	Barnsley
1919	SKEWS	EDWIN ARTHUR	Smith	Brentford
1919	SKEWS	ELLEN M.	Waite	Poplar
1919	SKEWS	MORLEY D.J.	Mallet	Liskeard
1919	SKEWS	STANLEY	Hilliard	West Ham
1919	SKEWS	THOMAS HENRY	Rickard	St. Austell
1919	SKUES	BERNARD E.	Jeffery	Dartford
1919	SKUES	ARTHUR E.W.	Harris	Shoreditch
1920	SKEWES	EDITH	Skewes	Penzance
1920	SKEWES	LESLIE	Ford	Redruth
1920	SKEWES	EDWARD MORLEY	Hill	Redruth
1920	SKEWES	WINIFRED JEAN	Vallantine	Plympton
1920	SKEWES	ERNEST LLOYD	Teague	Falmouth
1920	SKEWES	THOMAS G.	Phelps	Pontypridd

Year	Surname	Name	District
1920	SKEWES	ENID Jory	Redruth
1920	SKEWES-COX	Male Struban	Farnsham
1920	SKEWIS	SAMUEL LESLIE Waters	Haverfordwest
1920	SKEWS	DORIS Childs	Hackney
1920	SKEWS	LILY Smith	Houghton
1920	SKEWS	MABEL Smith	Houghton
1920	SKEWS	MURIEL Rump	Houghton
1920	SKEWS	WILLIAM A. Childs	Hackney
1920	SKEWS	EILEEN Jarvis	Stepney
1920	SKEWS	BEATRICE M.I., Jane	Liskeard
1920	SKEWS	CONSTANCE M. Mallet	Liskeard
1921	SKEWES	MARION JOYCE Drew	Truro
1921	SKEWES	WILLIAM HENRY Harris	Redruth
1921	SKEWES	GEORGE Jory	Redruth
1921	SKEWS	ELIZABETH H. Skews	Devonport
1921	SKEWS	MURIEL A. Gallacher	Devonport
1921	SKEWS	MABEL I. White	Kettering
1921	SKEWS	MABEL J. Rickard	St. Austell
1921	SKEWS	GEORGE Randerson	Barnsley
1921	SKUES	SIDNEY THOMAS Harris	Shoreditch
1922	SKEWES	IESTYN J. Phelps	Pontypridd
1922	SKEWES	EDNA Barrett	Halifax
1922	SKEWES	HARRY Skewes	Penzance
1922	SKEWS	COURTENEY J.G. Jane	Liskeard
1922	SKEWS	STANLEY R.E. Dyer	Poplar
1922	SKUES	ERIC E.A. Meades	Tonbridge
1922	SKUES	RAYMOND J. Jeffery	Dartford
1922	SKUES	PHILIP ERNEST Bremer	Camberwell
1923	SKEWES	EDNA M. Lally	Chorlton
1923	SKEWES	JACK PATTERSON O. Cockram	Axbridge
1923	SKEWES	MATTHEW HENRY Allen	Penzance
1923	SKEWS	ERIC Randerson	Barnsley
1923	SKEWS	MARGARET B. Gosnell	Southwark
1923	SKEWS	ALBERT EDWARD V. Weston	E. Stonehouse
1923	SKEWS	JOHN G.P. White	Kettering
1923	SKEWS	JOSEPH M.M. Jane	Liskeard
1923	SKEWS	KIRTLEY Rump	Houghton
1923	SKUES	CLORINDA A. Pinto	Lambeth
1923	SKUES	ERNEST Tregonning	Redruth
1924	SKEWES	WILLIAM ARTHUR Rosevear	Helston
1924	SKEWES	CERETA BETTY Drew	Truro
1924	SKEWIS	BRENDA G.S. Hughes	Haverfordwest
1924	SKEWS	GORDON H.L. Webber	Totnes
1924	SKEWS	BARON S. Randerson	Barnsley
1924	SKEWS	MARION R. Mallet	Liskeard
1924	SKEWS	DAVID G. Lampey	Whitechapel
1924	SKEWS	STANLEY Rickard	St. Austell
1924	SKUES	BETTY I. Meades	Tonbridge
1924	SKUES	GEORGE ERNEST Thompson	St. Geo. East
1924	SKUES	VERA JOAN Rowland	Blackburn
1924	SKUES	ELSIE F.R. Harris	Shoreditch
1924	SKUES	MARGARET PAMELA March	Epsom
1925	SKEWES	MURIEL Truran	Redruth
1925	SKEWES	ARTHUR J. Morrison	Bristol
1925	SKEWS	WILFRED G. Jane	Liskeard
1925	SKEWS	WILLIAM C. Rump	Houghton
1925	SKEWS	LILIAN L. Charles	Hackney
1925	SKEWS	MARJORIE E. Waite	Poplar
1925	SKUES	SIDNEY V. Ingney	Edmonton
1926	SKEWES	ROZE PEARL Whiting	Launceston
1926	SKEWES	DOROTHY BARBARA Allen	Penzance
1926	SKEWES	DORRIEL Truran	Redruth
1926	SKEWES	ELIZABETH MARY Marsh	Croydon
1926	SKEWS	ARTHUR S. Randerson	Barnsley
1926	SKEWS	JOAN L. Dyer	Stepney
1926	SKEWS	COLIN Parden	Barnsley
1926	SKEWS	FREDERICK T. Jane	Liskeard
1926	SKUES	MURIEL M. Rowland	Liverpool
1926	SKUES	JOHN JOSEPH G. Bremer	Camberwell
1926	SKUES	GLADYS M. Clemmans	Wandsworth
1927	SKEWES	WILLIAM JOHN Curnow	Helston
1927	SKEWES	ANNIE M. Caddy	Pontypridd
1927	SKEWES	IAN R.M. Morrison	Bristol
1927	SKEWES	FRANK R. Hacking	Manchester S.
1927	SKEWS	EUNICE D. Atkinson	Dartford
1927	SKEWS	EILEEN S. Childs	Hackney
1927	SKUES	BERYL I. Lamont } Twins	Barrow in F.
1927	SKUES	DOREEN M. Lamont } Twins	Barrow in F.
1928	SKEWS	WILLIAM Jarvis	Romford
1928	SKEWS	JANET A. Rump	Houghton
1928	SKEWS	WILLIAM A. Lampey	Stepney

Year	Variant	Name	Place	Year	Variant	Name	Place
1928	SKUES	EILEEN Cullingham	Camberwell	1934	SKEWES	THIRZA A.J. Morrison	Bristol
1928	SKUES	AUDREY F. Bremer	Camberwell	1934	SKEWES	DENNIS I.J. Rashleigh	Helston
1928	SKUES	ROY A.T. Clemmans	Wandsworth	1934	SKEWES	BARBARA JOAN Thomas	Helston
1929	SKEWES	GLADYS MARY Allen	Penzance	1934	SKEWIS	GRETTA Hughes	Haverfordwest
1929	SKEWES	LILIAN GLADYS Williams	Truro	1934	SKEWS	DOROTHY J. Harding	Edmonton
1929	SKEWES	RONALD Curnow	Helston	1934	SKEWS	DOROTHY T.E. Webber	Totnes
1929	SKEWS	RITA Lumb	Barnsley	1934	SKEWS	YVONNE M. Parsons	Birmingham
1929	SKEWS	OLIVE D. Dyer	Bethnal Green	1934	SKEWS	BRIAN A.A. Atkinson	Dartford
1929	SKEWS	STANLEY G. Jane	Liskeard	1934	SKEWS	GORDON Addy	Barnsley
1929	SKEWS	DORA N.J. Charles	Totnes	1934	SKEWS	JEAN Q. Holgate	Lexden
1929	SKUES	DONALD Rowland	Leeds South	1934	SKUES	PETER PERCIVAL Merton	Romford
1929	SKUES	RAYMOND A. Pinto	Southwark	1935	SKEWES	JOHN TREVOR Williams	Truro
1929	SKUES	ROYDEN T. Meades	Tonbridge	1935	SKEWES	MARGARETTE Cork	Redruth
1929	SKUES	SYLVIA G. Wyatt	Edmonton	1935	SKEWS	JOAN Eddy	East Stonehouse
1930	SKEWES	VERONICA J. Jory	Redruth	1935	SKUES	JEAN M. Franklin	Finsbury
1930	SKEWES	BARBARA Lally	Manchester S.	1936	SKEWES	ALBERT E. Skewes	Salford
1930	SKEWES	ELIZABETH Caddy	Cardiff	1936	SKEWS	RENEE Thompson	Houghton
1930	SKEWS	JOAN L.D. Lampey	Romford	1937	SKEWES	GILBERT JAMES Thomas	Kerrier
1930	SKEWS	DESMOND Lumb	Thorne	1937	SKEWES	BRIAN C. Millett	Redruth
1930	SKUES	GENE M. Woodyer	Edmonton	1937	SKEWES	MAUREEN Gory	Redruth
1930	SKUES	ALBERT E. Cullingham	Bromley	1937	SKEWS	PATRICIA Joyce	Pancras
1931	SKEWES	ROSEMARY Jory	Redruth	1937	SKUES	MIRIAM M. Pinto	Southwark
1931	SKEWES	WILLIAM A.R. Williams	Helston	1937	SKUES	JOY CHRISTINE Bruckshaw	Stockport
1931	SKEWES	ELIZABETH J. Peters	Redruth	1938	SKEWES	ELIZABETH MARLENE Prowse	Truro
1931	SKEWIS	BARBARA M. Baker	Sheppey	1938	SKEWES	PRISCILLA Reynolds	Kerrier
1931	SKEWS	GEORGE D. Rump	Houghton	1938	SKEWES	KENNETH ROY Trengove	Redruth
1931	SKEWS	MONICA E. Parsons	Cannock	1938	SKEWES	WILLIAM ROGER Moon	Penzance
1931	SKEWS	RAYMOND Lumb	Barnsley	1938	SKEWIS	CHRISTINE J. Gilbert	Tonbridge
1932	SKEWES	DONALD JAMES Allen	Penzance	1938	SKEWS	BETTY F. Snowshill	Paddington
1932	SKEWES	BARBARA ANN Hornby	Doncaster	1938	SKEWS	MONICA O. Skews	Totnes
1932	SKEWES	PAMELA J. Prowse	Truro	1938	SKEWS	EVELYN M. Falconer	Croydon
1932	SKEWS	REGINALD E. Weston	East Stonehouse	1938	SKEWS	MARION Duke	St. Germans
1932	SKEWS	ALBERT P. Jane	Liskeard	1938	SKEWS	ROLAND G. Rump	Houghton
1933	SKEWES	MAURICE Curnow	Helston	1939	SKEWES	SHIRLEY A. Millett	Redruth
1933	SKEWES	ANTHONY RONALD Thomas	Helston	1939	SKEWES	GILLIAN A. Pearce	Truro
1933	SKEWES	JOHN HORNBY Hornby	Doncaster	1939	SKEWES	DOROTHY M.M. Cork	Redruth
1933	SKEWS	KENNETH D. Parden	Barnsley	1939	SKEWS	JOHN W. Wilcocks	Plymouth
1933	SKEWS	BRENDA Lumb	Barnsley	1939	SKEWS	IRENE M. Falconer	Hackney
1933	SKEWS	IRIS D. Lampey	Shoreditch	1939	SKEWS	MARION Skews	Portsmouth
1933	SKEWS	JOHN H. Rump	Houghton	1939	SKUES	RICHARD KEITH , Hughes	Bucklow
1933	SKUES	DEREK A. Bremer	Camberwell	1939	SKUES	JENNIFER Bruckshaw	Stockport

Year	Surname	Name / Mother	District
1940	SKEWES	ROSALIE SUSAN / Thomas	Kerrier
1940	SKEWES	CARL / Jose	Redruth
1940	SKEWES	CHRISTINA A. / Lundell	Edmonton
1940	SKEWS	LAWRENCE / Thompson	Durham North
1940	SKEWS	CHRISTOPHER J. / Berryman	Brentford
1940	SKEWS	LESLIE / Wakefield	Durham North
1941	SKEWES	PETER M. / Williams	Kerrier
1941	SKEWIS	EILEEN M. / Wyatt	Totnes
1941	SKEWS	ROBERT W. / Falconer	Essex S.W.
1941	SKUES	SHIRLEY C.J. / Brassett	Islington
1942	SKEWES	MAXWELL / Body	Penzance
1942	SKEWES	EILEEN / Hacking	N.E. Cheshire
1942	SKEWES	KEVIN P. / Wynne	Bucklow
1942	SKEWIS	TREVOR / Baker	Thanet
1942	SKEWS	HARRY / Jane	Liskeard
1942	SKUES	CAROL C.A. / Kethro	Bristol
1942	SKUES	EDWIN MICHAEL / Hawkins	Dartford
1943	SKEWES	CONSTANCE / Tremayne	Kerrier
1943	SKEWES	WILLIAM JOHN / Little	Truro
1943	SKEWES	RICHARD JOHN / Moon	Penzance
1943	SKEWES	LILIAN S. / Foster	Hastings
1943	SKEWS	DAVID / Boynton	Wortley
1943	SKEWS	BARRY S. / Barnson	Staincross
1943	SKUES	PATRICIA MARY / Bruckshaw	Stockport
1944	SKEWES	DIANE M. / Wynne	Manchester
1944	SKEWES	ANNE M. / Ambrose	Reading
1944	SKEWES	BEVERLEY D. / Foster	Hastings
1944	SKEWES	MARGARET ROSEMARY / Little	Truro
1944	SKEWS	VALERIE B. / Joyce	Hammersmith
1944	SKEWS	PATRICIA / Stroud	Wrexham
1944	SKUES	SANDRA J. / Pinto	Surrey Mid E.
1944	SKUES	DAVID J. / Norris	Wellingboro
1945	SKEWES	JOHN OSBORNE / Thomas	Kerrier
1945	SKEWES	JUDITH M. / Lundell	Edmonton
1945	SKEWS	MARGARET / Boynton	Wortley
1945	SKEWS	PETER B. / Harris	St. Austell
1945	SKUES	CHRISTINE EVELYN / Hawkins	Dartford
1946	SKEWES	DAWN / Woolcock	Truro
1946	SKEWES	CAROL / Morgan	Redruth
1946	SKEWES	JEFFREY LIONEL / Thomas	Kerrier
1946	SKEWS	SANDRA / Littledike	Sheffield
1946	SKEWS	WENDY L. / Hardcastle	Hull
1946	SKEWS	CHRISTOPHER R. / Falconer	Essex S.W.
1946	SKEWS	NIGEL G. / Martin	Redruth
1946	SKEWS	ROGER D. / Lewis	Reading
1946	SKEWS	BRIAN J. / Lumb	Wortley
1946	SKEWS	SANDRA / Batchelor	St. Austell
1947	SKEWES	CAROL W. / Williams	Redruth
1947	SKEWES	COLIN / Moon)Twins	Penzance
1947	SKEWES	ELIZABETH A. / Moon)Twins	Penzance
1947	SKEWES	LINDA R. / Ambrose	Croydon
1947	SKEWES	PATRICIA ANNE / Penhaligon	Truro
1947	SKEWES	ANNETTE / Skewes	Redruth
1947	SKEWIS	MICHAEL I. / Fox	Hull
1947	SKEWS	ANGELA / Rosburn	Bradford
1947	SKEWS	WENDY A. / Soady	Redruth
1947	SKUES	MARGARET ELAINE / Hughes	Stockport
1947	SKUES	TERENCE F. / Brassett	Islington
1948	SKEWES	IRENE / Woolcock	Truro
1948	SKEWES	PAUL / Thomas	Kerrier
1948	SKEWIS	JAMES / Fox	Hull
1948	SKEWS	GWENDOLINE D. / Parrott	Ilford
1948	SKEWS	LINDA J. / Soady	St. Austell
1948	SKEWS	MICHAEL R. / Martin	Eton
1948	SKEWS	JOHN / Brayford	Sheffield
1944	SKUES	JEFFREY F. / Hart	Dartford
1948	SKUES	KENNETH P. / Jackson	London C.
1949	SKEWES	CHRISTOPHER JOHN / Williams	Redruth
1949	SKEWES	SUSAN BARBARA / Morgan	Penzance
1949	SKEWES	MICHAEL J. / Williams	Redruth
1949	SKEWS	JACQUELINE A. / Harris	St. Austell
1949	SKEWS	ELIZABETH A. / Stroud	Stepney
1949	SKEWS	JANE M. / Martin	Eton
1949	SKUES	CHRISTOPHER RAYMOND / Hughes	Manchester
1950	SKEWES	PETER NEIL / Williams	Kerrier
1950	SKEWES	MARGARET H. / Trengove	Redruth
1950	SKEWES	GEOFFREY KEITH / Hawken	Redruth
1950	SKEWES	CARLTON B. / Blenes	Redruth
1950	SKEWES	JAMES A. / Keast	Truro
1950	SKEWIS	DAVID / Fox	Hull
1950	SKEWS	PATRICIA E. / Lewis	New Forest
1950	SKEWS	TERENCE W. / Leach	Bury
1950	SKEWS	LYNN / Rosburn	Staincross

Year	Surname	Name	Mother's maiden	Place
1950	SKEWS	MICHAEL J.	Soady	St. Austell
1950	SKEWS	STEPHEN J.	Boyland	Peterborough
1950	SKEWS	ANDREW J.	Arnold	St. Germans
1950	SKUES	STEPHEN J.	Parnell	Hackney
1951	SKEWES	DEREK T.	Adam	Plymouth
1951	SKEWES	JACK	Thomas	Kerrier
1951	SKEWES	RAYMOND V.	Williams	Redruth
1951	SKEWS	PAMELA J.	Soady	St. Austell
1951	SKEWS	MICHAEL	Skews	Birmingham
1952	SKEWES	LINDA L.	Williams	Redruth
1952	SKEWS	SUSAN	Batchelor	St. Austell
1952	SKEWS	MELVYN	Thompson	Durham North
1952	SKEWS	DAVID A.H.	Boyland	Peterborough
1952	SKUES	ALAN J.	Lucchesi	Tonbridge
1953	SKEWES	JILL ALEXANDRA	Morgan	Penzance
1953	SKEWES	MARTIN	Wynne	Manchester
1953	SKEWES-COX	JULIAN H.L.	Macmullen	Marylebone
1953	SKEWIS	SADIE	Fox	Hull
1953	SKEWS	BARBARA K.	Hardcastle	Hull
1953	SKEWS	DAVID P.	Soady	St. Austell
1953	SKEWS	TREVOR	Rosburn	Staincross
1953	SKEWS	KEVIN R.	Morrell	Sunderland
1953	SKUES	IAN KEITH	Cox	Brentwood
1954	SKEWES	ANTHONY	Skewes	Truro
1954	SKEWES	LINDA ROSEMARY	Penhaligon	Truro
1954	SKEWES	WILLIAM CLIVE	Morgan	Penzance
1954	SKEWS	CHRISTOPHER	Boyland	Bourne
1954	SKEWS	CATHERINE	Brayford	Staincross
1954	SKUES	BARRY R.	Causton	Wandsworth
1954	SKUES	RICHARD ANTHONY	Littlewood	Rugby
1954	SKUES	GILLIAN	Parnell	Hackney
1955	SKEWES	LINDA MARION	Freeman	Leeds
1955	SKEWES	SALLY	Thomas	Kerrier
1955	SKEWS	BARRY J.	Harris	St. Austell
1955	SKUES	ANDREW P.	Cox	Brentwood
1956	SKEWES	KEVIN } Twins	Bray	Redruth
1956	SKEWES	PAUL		
1956	SKEWES	NICOLA	Rogers	Kerrier
1956	SKEWS	PAUL	Rosburn	Staincross
1956	SKEWS	ANDREW P.	Soady	St. Austell
1956	SKUES	ANDREW J.	Parnell	Hackney
1956	SKUES	ANTHONY) Twins	Whincop	Woolwich
1956	SKUES	PAUL		
1957	SKEWES	PAUL	Williams	Redruth
1957	SKEWES	JONATHAN ROSS	Hawken	Redruth
1957	SKEWIS	PHILIP E.	Fox	Hull
1957	SKEWS	TRUDY M.	Soady	Redruth
1957	SKEWS	JANE	Cadmore	Worcester
1957	SKEWS	MICHAEL D.	Leach	Bury
1957	SKEWS	NICHOLAS	Barson	Halifax
1957	SKEWS	ROBERT W.	King	Thurrock
1957	SKEWS	GERALD N.	Boyland	Bourne
1957	SKUES	MARK ALASTAIR	Littlewood	Rugby
1957	SKUES	JUDITH ANN	Bamber	Boston
1958	SKEWES	JANET MAY	Dennis	Kerrier
1958	SKEWES	DIANA ROSE	Curtis	Redruth
1958	SKEWES	KAREN ELIZABETH	Freeman	Leeds
1958	SKEWS	ALAN D.	Sylvester	Liskeard
1958	SKEWS	MARTIN C.	Soady	St. Austell
1958	SKEWS	DAVID	Pascoe	Plymouth
1958	SKEWS	SHARON	Lunn	Barnsley
1958	SKUES	MARTIN	Whincop	Woolwich
1958	SKUES	DAVID A.	Cox	Brentwood
1959	SKEWES	ANTHONY R.	Taylor	N.E. Cheshire
1959	SKEWES	JOHN CHARLES	Dennis	Kerrier
1959	SKEWES	SUSAN	Holbrook	Redruth
1959	SKEWS	HEATHER J.	King	Thurrock
1959	SKEWS	LYNN	Thirwell	Sunderland
1959	SKEWS	TINA P.	Alldis	Dartford
1959	SKEWS	BEVERLEY J.	Lord	Worth Valley
1959	SKEWS	MARTYN R.	Lowe	Plymouth
1959	SKEWS	MAUREEN J.	Fishleigh	Liskeard
1959	SKEWS	SONIA	Batchelor	St. Austell
1959	SKUES	BRIDGET MARY	Bamber	Stroud
1959	SKUES	JOHN M.	Causton	Ashford
1960	SKEWES	ALISON E.	Isaac	Barton
1960	SKEWES	JOHN R.	Rogers	Redruth
1960	SKEWES	SANDRA	Dennis	Redruth
1960	SKEWS	NIGEL	Sylvester	Liskeard
1960	SKEWS	DAVID G.	Fishleigh	Liskeard
1960	SKUES	CLIVE P.	Lucchesi	Sidcup
1961	SKEWES	ROGER T.	Rogers	Redruth

Year	Surname	Name	District
1961	SKEWES	JANE Taylor	Bucklow
1961	SKEWES	MELANIE A. Isaac	Barton
1961	SKEWES	NICHOLAS MARK Curtis	Redruth
1961	SKEWS	DIANA Alldis	Dartford
1961	SKEWS	BOBBIE Rosburn	Barnsley
1961	SKEWS	NIGEL S. Lord	Worth Valley
1962	SKEWES	BARRY Williams	Redruth
1962	SKEWES	DAVID Dennis	Kerrier
1962	SKEWS	MARK H.V. Lowe	Plymouth
1962	SKEWS	DAVID Thirwell	Sunderland
1962	SKEWS	KAREN D. Soady	St. Austell
1963	SKEWES	PETER Dennis	Kerrier
1963	SKEWES	JOHN Holbrook	Redruth
1963	SKEWES	PENELOPE Richards	Penzance
1963	SKEWS	JANE Skews	Sheffield
1963	SKEWS	DEBBIE Rosburn	Sheffield
1963	SKEWS	RICHARD T. King	Rochford
1964	SKEWES	PAUL ANDREW Williams	Redruth
1964	SKEWES	TONY Williams	Redruth
1964	SKEWES	TONY S. Williams	Redruth
1964	SKEWIS	WILLIAM S. Lyons	Kettering
1965	SKEWES	CAROLE MARY Dennis	Kerrier
1965	SKEWIS	MARK Hanslip	Canterbury
1965	SKEWIS	COLIN Lyons	Kettering
1965	SKEWS	KIRTLEY R. Greaves	Aldershot
1965	SKEWS	DAVID J. Duff	Birmingham
1965	SKUES	JONATHAN PAUL Cockerell	Lambeth
1965	SKUES	CHRISTOPHER A.J. Falk	Hammersmith
1966	SKEWES	IAN Clackworthy	Redruth
1966	SKEWIS	DEBBIE Kilpatrick	Kettering
1966	SKEWIS	ANDREA DAWN Humphries	Hull
1966	SKEWS	KEVIN Skews	Sheffield
1966	SKEWS	NICOLA LOUISE Soady	Plymouth
1966	SKEWS	JOHN MICHAEL Lunn	Staincross
1966	SKEWS	OLWYNNE Thirwell	Sunderland
1966	SKEWS	STEPHEN JOHN Greaves	Aldershot
1967	SKEWES	JOHN ANTHONY Letcher	Penzance
1967	SKEWES	KEEFE MITCHELL Skewes	Paddington
1967	SKEWS	ASHLEY JANE Brown	Sunderland
1967	SKEWS	MICHELLE JAYNE Blight	St. Austell
1968	SKEWES	SUSAN Clackworthy	Redruth
1968	SKEWIS	RICHARD Lyons	Kettering
1968	SKEWIS	KAREN JAYNE Bratton	Holderness
1968	SKEWS	MARIA Walls	Falmouth
1968	SKUES	PAULA MARIE Collie	Surrey Mid. E.
1969	SKEWES	JOANNA MARY Payne	Penzance
1969	SKEWES	PETER Clackworthy	Redruth
1969	SKEWES	FIONA Wills	Truro
1969	SKEWS	HELEN DOROTHY Newby	Enfield
1969	SKEWS	JOHN ANTHONY Skews	St. Austell
1970	SKEWES	ANTHONY JOHN Payne	Kerrier
1970	SKEWES	JILL KATHRYN Isaac	Barton
1970	SKEWS	HAYLEY LISA Blight	St. Austell
1970	SKUES	JANE LOUISE Moore	Newham
1971	SKEWES	RICHARD ANDREW Letcher	Truro
1971	SKEWES	KATHERINE Berryman	Truro
1971	SKEWS	JASON MARK Skews	Truro
1971	SKEWS	SALLY JEAN Hooper	Truro
1971	SKUES	CAROLYN LOUISE Cooke	Eastbourne
1971	SKUES	ALICIA ANN Weighill	Dartford
1971	SKUES	CLAIR Moore	Barking
1972	SKEWES	CHARLOTTE LOUISE Jordan	St. Austell
1972	SKEWES	JASON PETER Wathing	Truro
1972	SKEWES	MARIE LESLEY Hall	Truro
1972	SKEWES	RICHARD TERRY Hall	Truro
1972	SKEWES	MICHAEL JAMES Williams	Redruth
1972	SKEWES	RAYMOND VERNON Williams	Redruth
1972	SKEWS	RICHARD JOHN Agates	Barking
1972	SKEWS	DAVID FALCONER Kempson	Redbridge
1972	SKUES	MICHAEL DAVID E. Cooke	Eastbourne
1973	SKEWES	DARREN VERNON Hall	Truro
1973	SKEWS	THERESA JANE Newby	Enfield
1973	SKUES	TERENCE JAMES Moore	Barking
1973	SKUES	TERRY STEVEN Skues	Chelmsford
1973	SKUES	ANDREW JOHN Weighill	Dartford
1974	SKEWES	EDWARD SIMON Hall	Truro
1974	SKEWES	EMILY CLAIRE Jordan	Truro
1974	SKEWES	SARAH JANE Hooper	Truro
1974	SKEWIS	SANDRA Lyons	Kettering
1974	SKEWIS	ZQUIN JAMES B. Bratton	Hull
1974	SKEWS	LISA JAYNE Clifft	Truro

1975	SKEWES	JULIE ANN Lissemore	Southend
1975	SKEWIS	ANNA MARIE Smart	Hull
1975	SKEWS	NICOLA JANE Kempson	Sudbury
1975	SKEWS	VICTORIA ANNE Searle	Plymouth
1975	SKEWS	EMMA JANE Ackroyd	Barnsley
1975	SKEWS	PHILIP ADRIAN Binnersley	Macclesfield
1975	SKEWS	THADDEUS JOHN Claridge	Peterborough
1976	SKEWS	ZOWIE Searle	Plymouth
1976	SKEWES	REBECCA PHYLLIS Jordan	St. Austell
1976	SKEWIS	DARREN ANDREW Gibson	Hull
1976	SKEWS	JONATHAN MICHAEL Perry	Stoke on Trent
1976	SKEWS	ALISTAIR DEREK McManaman	Plymouth
1977	SKEWES	VICTORIA CLARE Thomas	Truro
1977	SKEWES	WILLIAM JOHN P. Hall	Truro
1977	SKEWES	AMANDA ELIZABETH Williams	Truro
1977	SKEWS	DONNA MARIE Whitfield	St. Austell
1977	SKEWS	MICHELLE DEBORAH Daniels	St. Austell
1977	SKEWS	REBECCA MARIE Claridge	Peterborough
1977	SKEWS	DANIEL RICHARD Clifft	Truro
1977	SKEWS	KAREN EMMA Walters	Swansea
1977	SKEWS	STEPHEN TREVOR Guirey	Barnsley
1978	SKEWES	MARK CHRISTOPHER Williams	Truro
1978	SKEWES	PAUL DAVID Easton	Nottingham
1978	SKEWIS	CLAIRE CATHERINE Park	Kettering
1978	SKEWS	KATHERINE REBECCA Snowden	Newham
1978	SKUES	EMMA CATHERINE Epps	Ashford

Marriages 1837 — 1978

1837	SKEWES	MARY	Falmouth
1837	SKEWES	EDWARD	Helston
1837	SKEWES	MARGARET	Redruth
1837	SKEWES	JOHN	Redruth
1837	SKUES	JOHN	Redruth
1838	SKEWES	THOMAS	Truro
1838	SKEWES	HENRY	Penzance
1838	SKEWS	WILLIAM	Liverpool
1838	SKUES	ANN	Helston
1839	SKEWES	MARY	St. Austell
1839	SKEWES	WILLIAM	Truro
1839	SKEWES	JANE	Truro
1839	SKEWES	JAMES	Falmouth
1839	SKUES	MARY	Redruth
1840	SKEWES	RICHARD	Truro
1840	SKEWS	WILLIAM	Truro
1840	SKUES	GEORGE	St. Martin
1840	SKUES	WILLIAM TRUSCOTT	St. Austell
1840	SKUSE	ISAAC	Bath
1841	SKEWES	JEMIMA	Truro
1841	SKEWES	SAMUEL	Helston
1841	SKEWES	GEORGE	Truro
1841	SKEWES	ELIZABETH	Truro
1841	SKEWES	JAMES	Penzance
1841	SKEWES	WILLIAM	Helston
1841	SKUES	ELIZA	Truro
1842	SKEWES	THOMAS	Swansea
1842	SKEWES	CAROLINE	Redruth
1842	SKEWES	ELIZABETH	Truro
1842	SKEWES	HARRIET	Penzance
1842	SKEWES	SAMUEL	Helston
1842	SKEWES	ELIZABETH	Truro
1842	SKEWES	GRACE	Truro
1842	SKEWES	ELIZABETH	Penzance
1842	SKEWIS	FRANCIS	Helston
1842	SKEWIS	HENRY	Redruth
1842	SKEWIS	JANE	Redruth
1842	SKEWS	MARY	Truro
1842	SKUES	MARY ANN	Plymouth
1843	SKEWES	JOHN	Truro
1843	SKEWES	MARY	Falmouth
1843	SKEWES	THOMASINE	Truro
1843	SKEWES	MARY	Redruth
1843	SKEWES	JANE	Redruth
1843	SKEWS	GEORGE	Aylesford
1843	SKEWS	SARAH	Plymouth
1844	SKEWES	ANN	Redruth
1844	SKEWES	MARY WILLIAMS	Truro
1844	SKEWES	EDWARD	Helston
1844	SKEWIS	JAMES	Redruth
1844	SKEWS	JENNIFER	Truro
1844	SKEWS	JAMES	Truro
1844	SKEWS	MARY	Truro
1844	SKUES	JAMES	Redruth
1845	SKEWES	EDWARD	Helston
1845	SKEWES	HENRY	Helston
1845	SKEWES	JOHN	Redruth
1845	SKEWES	HENRY	Redruth
1845	SKEWES	WILLIAM	Plymouth
1845	SKEWES	JAMES	Falmouth
1845	SKEWIS	JOHN	Helston
1845	SKEWS	ANN	Plymouth
1845	SKEWS	ELIZABETH	Liskeard
1845	SKUES	JAMES	Marlborough
1846	SKEWES	NANNY	St. Germans
1846	SKEWES	ANN	Liskeard
1846	SKEWES	ELIZA JANE	Truro
1846	SKEWES	ELIZABETH	Falmouth
1846	SKEWES	SUSANNAH	Redruth
1846	SKEWES	JOSIAH	Helston
1846	SKEWES	THOMAS JENKIN	Bristol
1846	SKUES	JOHN HOSKIN	Redruth
1847	SKEWES	SAMUEL	Newton Abbot
1847	SKEWES	HENRY	Helston
1847	SKEWES	ANN	Falmouth
1847	SKEWIS	WILLIAM	Redruth
1847	SKEWS	JOHN	London E
1848	SKEWES	FANNY	Falmouth
1848	SKEWES	ANN ENYES	Truro
1848	SKEWES	WILLIAM	Redruth
1848	SKEWIS	ELIZABETH	Penzance
1848	SKEWIS	JAMES	Helston
1848	SKEWS	JOHN	Launceston
1848	SKUES	GEORGE GILBERT	Strand
1848	SKUES	ELIZABETH	Helston
1849	SKEWES	ANNE	Redruth
1849	SKEWES	CAROLINE	Falmouth
1849	SKEWES	ELLEN	Truro
1849	SKEWES	JOSEPH	Liskeard
1849	SKEWES	THOMAS	St. Columb
1849	SKEWES	JOHN	Truro
1849	SKEWIS	HENRY	Redruth
1849	SKEWIS	MARY	Falmouth
1849	SKEWS	JOHN	Launceston
1850	SKEWES	HENRY	Falmouth
1850	SKEWES	JANE	Truro
1850	SKEWES	WILLIAM	Falmouth
1850	SKEWS	JANE	Truro
1850	SKEWS	JOHN	Liskeard
1851	SKEWES	CAROLINE	Plymouth
1851	SKEWES	JOHN	Truro
1851	SKEWES	RICHARD	Truro
1851	SKEWES	ELIZABETH JANE	Truro
1851	SKEWES	ANN	Helston
1851	SKEWES	FRANCIS THOMAS	Helston
1851	SKEWES	HENRIETTA	Truro
1851	SKEWES	JULYA	Truro
1851	SKEWS	MARTIN	Truro
1851	SKEWS	HARRIET	Neath
1851	SKEWS	SOPHIA	Liskeard
1852	SKEWES	RICHARD	Truro
1852	SKEWES	THOMAS LEAN	Lewisham
1852	SKEWES	DANIEL	Newton Abbot
1852	SKEWES	ELIZA	Falmouth
1852	SKEWES	JOSIAH	Falmouth
1852	SKEWES	MATTHEW	Truro
1852	SKEWIS	HANNAH	Helston
1852	SKEWS	SARAH	Truro
1852	SKEWS	MARY ELLEN	East Stonehouse
1852	SKUES	MARY ANN	Shoreditch
1853	SKEWES	ELIZABETH	Bedford
1853	SKEWES	ELIZABETH	Truro
1853	SKEWES	JANE	Truro
1853	SKEWES	JANE	Helston
1853	SKEWES	MARY ANN	Truro
1853	SKEWES	WILLIAM	Redruth
1853	SKEWES	JOHN	Helston
1853	SKEWS	ROBERT HENRY	Plymouth
1854	SKEWES	EMMA	Truro
1854	SKEWES	WILLIAM	Penzance
1854	SKEWES	AMELIA	Truro
1854	SKEWES	JOHN	Redruth
1854	SKEWES	JULIA	Redruth
1854	SKEWS	JOHN	Plymouth
1854	SKEWS	WILLIAM	Westminster
1855	SKEWES	ANN	Falmouth
1855	SKEWES	THOMAS	Plymouth
1855	SKEWES	GRACE	Falmouth
1855	SKEWIS	JAMES	Redruth
1855	SKEWS	PETER	Launceston
1855	SKEWS	ELIZABETH	West Stonehouse
1856	SKEWES	SAMUEL DAW	Tavistock
1856	SKEWES	CHARITY	Redruth
1856	SKEWES	DIGORY	Liskeard
1856	SKEWES	MATTHEW	Liskeard
1856	SKEWES	WILLIAM	Redruth
1856	SKEWIS	MARY	Helston
1856	SKEWIS	MARY	Abergavenny

1856	SKUES	SARAH	Stepney	1862	SKEWS	SUSAN JANE	Truro
1857	SKEWES	MARY	Redruth	1862	SKEWS	JOHN	Falmouth
1857	SKEWES	CHARLES	Falmouth	1862	SKEWS	MARY ANN	Falmouth
1857	SKEWES	EMMA JANE	Truro	1862	SKEWS	WILLIAM TREZIZE	Redruth
1857	SKEWES	JOANNA TRUSCOTT	Tavistock	1862	SKEWS	MARY	St. Columb
1857	SKEWES	SUSAN	Redruth	1862	SKEWS	PETER	Truro
1857	SKEWIS	LAVINIA	Redruth	1862	SKUES	GEORGE	Pancras
1857	SKEWS	ELIZABETH	Merthyr Tydfil	1863	SKEWES	MARY ANN LIPSOM	Tavistock
1858	SKEWES	ELIZABETH	Truro	1863	SKEWES	CATHERINE	Helston
1858	SKEWES	EMILY	Truro	1863	SKEWES	MARY JANE	Redruth
1858	SKEWES	MARGARET ANN	Mile End	1863	SKEWES	DANIEL HODGE	Tavistock
1858	SKEWES	ANN	Redruth	1863	SKEWES	ELIZABETH JANE	Redruth
1858	SKEWES	SUSAN JANE	Redruth	1863	SKEWS	ELIZA	Lambeth
1858	SKEWES	PHILIPPA	Truro	1863	SKUES	SARAH	Dursley
1858	SKEWES	JAMES	Redruth	1864	SKEWES	EDWARD HENRY	Penzance
1858	SKEWES	RICHARD	Truro	1864	SKEWES	WILLIAM RICHARD FRANCIS DENNIS	Redruth
1858	SKUES	WILLIAM JAMES GORDON	Plymouth				
1859	SKEWES	BENJAMIN HELLINGS	Falmouth	1864	SKEWES	PHILIPPA JANE	Truro
1859	SKEWES	JOHN	Helston	1864	SKEWES	EMILY	Helston
1859	SKEWES	MARY EMILY	Redruth	1864	SKEWES	GRACE	Truro
1859	SKEWES	MARY AGNES	Redruth	1864	SKEWES	JOSEPH	Helston
1859	SKEWS	WILLIAM	Newington	1864	SKEWES	LOVEDAY HENDY	Helston
1859	SKUES	RICHARD	Halifax	1864	SKEWES	MARTHA ELIZABETH	Helston
1859	SKUES	JOHN	Penzance	1864	SKEWIS	JANE	Bedwellty
1860	SKEWES	ELIZABETH ANN	Truro	1864	SKEWIS	MARY	Redruth
1860	SKEWES	MARY	Truro	1864	SKEWIS	SAMUEL	Chorlton
1860	SKEWES	THOMAS	Truro	1864	SKEWS	WILLIAM	Truro
1860	SKUES	WILLIAM	Bath	1864	SKUES	JANE	Redruth
1861	SKEWES	ELIZABETH	Bodmin	1865	SKEWES	JAMES HENRY	Redruth
1861	SKEWES	EDWARD	Redruth	1865	SKEWES	THOMAS	Redruth
1861	SKEWES	PHILIP	Redruth	1865	SKEWES	WILLIAM	Portsea
1861	SKEWS	LOUISA	Gravesend	1865	SKEWS	MARY	Truro
1861	SKEWS	MARY	St. Austell	1865	SKEWS	SAMUEL	Redruth
1861	SKEWS	MATTHEW	St. Columb	1865	SKUES	ELLEN EMMA	Halifax
1861	SKEWS	ALICE	Redruth	1865	SKUES	CHARLES	Pancras
1861	SKEWS	JOHN	Helston	1865	SKUES	EMMA ELIZABETH	St. Martin
1861	SKEWS	WALTER TREZISE	Truro	1866	SKEWES	JULIANA	Helston
1862	SKEW	JANE	Truro	1866	SKEWES	RICHARD	Redruth
1862	SKEWES	JOHN	Redruth	1866	SKEWES	JOSEPH H.	Leeds
1862	SKEWES	JANE FRANCES	Liskeard	1866	SKEWES	WILLIAM	Redruth
1862	SKEWES	SAMUEL	Helston	1866	SKEWES	ELIZA G.	Helston
1862	SKEWIS	GEORGE	Chorlton	1866	SKEWIS	ELIZABETH	Crickhowell
1862	SKEWIS	EMMA	Manchester	1866	SKEWS	JOHN	Kensington

Marriage certificate of Richard Skues to Lucy Pickard in 1859

CERTIFIED COPY OF AN ENTRY OF MARRIAGE
The statutory fee for this certificate is 3s. 9d.
Where a search is necessary to find the entry,
a search fee is payable in addition.

Given at the **GENERAL REGISTER OFFICE,**
SOMERSET HOUSE, LONDON.

Application Number 270187

| | REGISTRATION DISTRICT | HALIFAX |

1859. Marriage solemnized at ----- in the Parish of Halifax in the County of York

No.	When married. (1)	Name and surname. (2)	Age. (3)	Condition. (4)	Rank or profession. (5)	Residence at the time of marriage. (6)	Father's name and surname. (7)	Rank or profession of father. (8)
120	July 9	Richard Skues	26	Bachr.	Compositor	Halifax	Richard Skues	Surgeon
		Lucy Pickard	23	Spinr.	-----	Halifax	Samuel Pickard	Saddler

Married in the Parish Church according to the Rites and Ceremonies of the Established Church by Certificate by me

This marriage was solemnized between us, { Richard Skues / Lucy Pickard } in the presence of us, { Joshua Spooner Furness / Ellen Skues }   Alexander Taylor

CERTIFIED to be a true copy of an entry in the certified copy of a Register of Marriages in the District above mentioned.
Given at the GENERAL REGISTER OFFICE, SOMERSET HOUSE, LONDON, under the Seal of the said Office, the 14th day of July 1958

MA 455063

1866	SKUES	HONORA H.	Marlborough

Note: There are a large number of entries for SKUSE in Marlborough around this time.

1867	SKEWES	EDWARD	Falmouth
1867	SKEWES	ELIZA ANN	Helston
1867	SKUES	MARY GARRETT	St. James
1867	SKUES	MARY ANN	Medway
1868	SKEWES	ELIZA	Helston
1868	SKEWES	ELIZABETH	Helston
1868	SKEWES	MARY	Helston
1868	SKEWES	RICHARD	Truro
1868	SKEWES	EMMA	Truro
1868	SKEWES	JAMES FEARGUS	Bristol
1868	SKEWES	JESSIE	Bedwellty
1869	SKEWES	JAMES	Redruth
1869	SKEWES	JOHN	Helston
1869	SKEWES	JAMES	Helston
1869	SKEWES	WILLIAM JAMES	Helston
1869	SKEWES	EDWARD WILLIAM	Redruth
1869	SKEWES	JAMES HENRY	Helston
1869	SKEWIS	MARY	Kensington
1869	SKEWS	EMMA	Brentford
1869	SKUES	CHARLES PENROSE	Marylebone
1870	SKEWES	EMILY	Truro
1870	SKEWES	SAMUEL	Helston
1870	SKEWES	RICHARD	Neath
1870	SKEWES	CHRISTIAN KATE	Helston
1870	SKEWS	CAROLINE	Lambeth
1870	SKEWS	GEORGE ALFRED	Strand
1870	SKUES	ISABELLA	St. James
1871	SKEWES	MARY ANN	Plymouth
1871	SKEWES	ELIZABETH MARY	Helston
1871	SKEWES	MARY JANE	Redruth
1871	SKUES	HENRY	Cricklade
1871	SKUES	JANE	Chippenham
1872	SKEWES	RICHARD	St. Austell
1872	SKEWES	JOHN	Helston
1872	SKEWES	ELLEN	Redruth
1872	SKEWS	AMELIA	Liskeard
1872	SKEWS	ELIZABETH JANE	Launceston
1872	SKEWS	SAMUEL	Liskeard
1872	SKEWS	EDWARD	Chelsea
1872	SKEWS	MARY ANN	Kensington
1873	SKEWES	JAMES	Helston
1873	SKEWES	MATTHEW	Redruth
1873	SKEWES	GRACE	Helston
1873	SKEWES	MARY ANN	St. Thomas
1873	SKEWES	MARIA	Helston
1873	SKEWIS	ELIZABETH	Sheffield
1873	SKEWS	RICHARD NATHANIEL	Islington
1873	SKEWS	ELIZABETH MARY J.	Clifton
1873	SKUES	CHARLES	Sheffield
1874	SKEWES	THOMAS WILLIAM	Helston
1874	SKEWES	HERMINNA	Redruth
1874	SKEWES	GRACE	Truro
1874	SKEWES	MARY	Redruth
1874	SKEWES	ANNIE	Redruth
1874	SKEWES	WILLIAM	Redruth
1874	SKEWES	ELIZABETH L.	Truro
1874	SKEWES	MATILDA	Redruth
1874	SKEWES	ELIZA ELLEN	Redruth
1874	SKEWES	ELIZABETH	Penzance
1874	SKEWES	JOHN JAMES	Plymouth
1874	SKUES	THOMAS	St. Geo. Han. Square
1875	SKEWES	GRACE	Helston
1875	SKEWES	JAMES	Helston
1875	SKEWES	ANN	Helston
1875	SKEWIS	EDWIN	Bedwellty
1875	SKEWS	WILLIAM	Totnes
1875	SKUE	EMILY	Croydon
1875	SKUES	JOSEPH	Chippenham
1876	SKEWES	EDWARD	Redruth
1876	SKEWES	HENRY	Redruth
1876	SKEWES	MARIA	Truro

1876	SKEWES	ANN	Redruth
1876	SKEWES	ESTHER	Ulverston
1876	SKEWIS	FANNY	Newport M.
1876	SKEWS	JAMES	Farnham
1876	SKEWS	MARY ANN M.	Plymouth
1876	SKUES	FREDERICK	Thetford
1876	SKUES	CHARLOTTE SOPHIA	Westminster
1876	SKUES	MATILDA JANE	Chippenham

Note: This last name is also listed as SKUSE. There are a number of SKUSE in Chippenham.

1877	SKEWES	LEWIS	St. Austell
1877	SKEWES	SARAH	Penzance
1877	SKEWES	ELIZABETH MARY	Lambeth
1877	SKEWIS	DANIEL	St. Thomas
1877	SKEWIS	MARY	Newton Abbot
1877	SKEWS	ELIZABETH	Plymouth
1877	SKEWS	JOHN WILLIAM HENRY	Plymouth
1877	SKUES	MORRIS	Doncaster
1878	SKEWS	FRANCES	Plymouth
1878	SKEWS	MATTHEW LEE	Redruth
1878	SKEWS	EDWIN	Redruth
1879	SKEWES	ANNIE	Helston
1879	SKEWES	FRANCES MARIA	Falmouth
1879	SKEWES	ELIZABETH JANE	Truro
1879	SKEWES	ELIZABETH MARY	Helston
1879	SKUES	JESSIE	Pontypridd
1880	SKEWES	JOHN	Truro
1880	SKEWES	MARY GRACE	Lewes
1880	SKEWES	ANNIE	Pancras
1880	SKEWES	FREDERICK TRESIZE	Helston
1880	SKEWES	THOMAS GEORGE	Penzance
1880	SKEWES	JOHN BROWNE	St. Geo. Han. Square
1880	SKEWIS	JOHN	Ulverston
1880	SKEWS	ELIZABETH	Bedwellty
1880	SKEWS	JOHN	Plymouth
1881	SKEWES	THOMAS HENRY	Penzance
1881	SKEWES	THOMAS HENRY	Falmouth
1881	SKEWES	JOSIAH	Helston
1881	SKEWES	WILLIAM	Salford
1881	SKEWES	WILLIAM JOHN	Helston
1881	SKEWS	HARRIET	Bethnal Green
1882	SKEWES	JOHN	Chorlton
1882	SKEWES	LAURA	Helston
1882	SKEWES	EMILY KEMPTHORNE	Falmouth
1882	SKEWES	MARY JANE	Redruth
1882	SKEWES	ANNIE AMELIA	Redruth
1882	SKEWES	LAURA	Falmouth
1882	SKEWS	EMMA	Plymouth
1883	SKEWES	CHARLES	Chorlton
1883	SKEWES	EMMA LAITY	Helston
1883	SKEWES	JAMES	Redruth
1883	SKEWES	WILLIAM	Redruth
1883	SKEWES	AMELIA	Lambeth
1883	SKEWES	EDWARD JAMES	Redruth
1884	SKEWES	EMILY JANE	Redruth
1884	SKEWES	MARIA	Redruth
1884	SKEWES	WILLIAM	Redruth
1884	SKEWES	HENRIETTA MARIA	West Ham
1884	SKEWES	RICHARD	Truro
1884	SKEWES	ANNIE	E. Stonehouse
1884	SKEWES	RICHARD	Redruth
1884	SKEWES	WILLIAM HENRY	Redruth
1884	SKEWES	GRACE ANNIE	Redruth
1884	SKEWS	EDWIN	Islington
1884	SKUES	FREDERICK GORDON	Halifax
1885	SKEWES	WILLIAM	Redruth
1885	SKEWES	EDWARD	Chorlton
1885	SKEWES	SAMUEL	Penzance
1885	SKEWIS	ANNIE JANE	Helston
1885	SKEWS	ALFRED	St. Olave
1885	SKUES	MOSES	Bristol
1886	SKEWES	JOHN WESLEY	Helston
1886	SKEWES	RICHARD	Penzance
1886	SKEWIS	WILLIAM BAWDEN	Tavistock

Year	Surname	First Name	Place
1886	SKEWIS	HENRIETTA	Totnes
1886	SKEWIS	WILLIAM	Newton Abbot
1886	SKEWS	THOMAS	Ecclesall
1887	SKEWES	SARAH ANN	Redruth
1887	SKEWIS	MINNIE	Redruth
1887	SKEWS	MARY ANN P.P.	Plymouth
1887	SKEWS	ELIZABETH	Pancras
1887	SKEWS	SARAH	Redruth
1887	SKUES	JOHN GILBERT	Westminster
1888	SKEWES	EDWARD JAMES	Redruth
1888	SKEWES	MARY FLETCHER	Derby
1888	SKEWES	MARY ELLEN	Newton Abbot
1888	SKEWES	MARY JANE	St. Austell
1888	SKEWES	SAMUEL DAW	Newton Abbot
1888	SKEWES	JANE	Plymouth
1888	SKEWES	KATE	Falmouth
1888	SKEWS	ALICE	Dartford
1888	SKEWS	ANN ELIZABETH	Dartford
1888	SKEWS	ELIZABETH ANN	St. Austell
1888	SKUES	GEORGE HENRY	Pancras
1888	SKUES	LUCY SOPHIA	Pancras
1889	SKEWES	ELIZA JANE	Redruth
1889	SKEWES	JAMES	Penzance
1889	SKEWIS	CLARA ANN	Newton Abbot
1889	SKEWS	GEORGE	Easington
1889	SKEWS	SARAH ANN	Dartford
1890	SKEWES	THOMAS LEAN	Barnstaple
1890	SKEWES	ALBERT EDWARD	Wareham
1890	SKEWES	BESSIE	Helston
1890	SKEWES	ELLEN	Falmouth
1890	SKEWES	HANNIBAL	Helston
1890	SKEWES	FLORENCE CECILIA	Truro
1890	SKEWES	JOHN	Liskeard
1890	SKEWS	AMOS	Stoke D.
1890	SKUES	PHILIP HENRY	St. Saviour
1891	SKEWES	ADA LOUISA	Helston
1891	SKEWES	EMMA	Redruth
1891	SKEWES	HENRY	Penzance
1891	SKEWES	MARY ANN P.	Truro
1892	SKEWES	JOSEPH JOHN	Lambeth
1892	SKEWES	REBECCA ANNIE	Falmouth
1892	SKEWES	ALICE KATE	Tavistock
1892	SKEWES	ELIZABETH JANE	Truro
1892	SKEWES	HARRY OSWALD	Redruth
1892	SKEWES	SARAH ANN	Helston
1892	SKEWES	JOHN COURTIS	Exeter
1892	SKEWIS	EDWARD	Redruth
1892	SKEWS	GEORGE WILLIAM	Bethnal Green
1892	SKEWS	EDMUND	Liskeard
1892	SKEWS	MARY JANE	Redruth
1893	SKEWES	HENRY	Redruth
1893	SKEWES	HERBERT	Newton Abbot
1893	SKEWES	MARY JANE	Helston
1893	SKEWS	EMMA FRANCES	Bromley
1893	SKUES	WALTER EDWARD	Westminster
1894	SKEWES	ELLEN MAUD	Plymouth
1894	SKEWES	GEORGE	Salford
1894	SKEWES	JANIE	Redruth
1894	SKEWES	JANE	Redruth
1894	SKEWES	PHILIPPA MARY	Truro
1894	SKEWES	FREDERICK	Salford
1894	SKEWES	JULIA HANNAH	Helston
1894	SKEWES	THOMAS JAMES	St. Columb
1894	SKEWS	WILLIAM JOHN	Sunderland
1894	SKUES	GERTRUDE ELIZA M.	Croydon
1895	SKEWS	FLORENCE ELIZABETH	Bethnal Green
1895	SKEWS	WILLIAM	St. Austell
1895	SKEWS	MATTHEW	Redruth
1895	SKUES	ELEANOR LUCAS	Marylebone
1896	SKEWES	LAURA	West Ham
1896	SKEWES	EDITH	Redruth
1896	SKEWES	EMILY	Bideford
1896	SKEWES	HENRY	Falmouth
1896	SKEWS	JOHN EDWIN	Highworth
1896	SKEWS	MINNIE	Bromley
1896	SKEWS	CHARLES	St. Austell
1896	SKEWS	JANIE	Bedminster
1897	SKEWES	BELITA	Redruth
1897	SKEWES	HENRY	Redruth
1897	SKEWES	ELLEN	Helston
1897	SKEWES	JULIA ANNIE	Helston
1897	SKEWES	MARY	Redruth
1897	SKEWS	HENRY	Holyhead
1897	SKEWS	ELLEN	Liskeard
1897	SKUES	ERNEST	Nottingham
1897	SKUES	RICHARD JAMES	Kendal
1898	SKEWES	JAMES HENRY	Helston
1898	SKEWES	KATE	Redruth
1898	SKEWES	CHARLES	Salford
1898	SKEWIS	WILLIAM RICHARD	Totnes
1898	SKEWS	ALFRED DAVID R.	Shoreditch
1898	SKEWS	MATTHEW	Redruth
1898	SKEWS	LOUISA	Bromley
1898	SKEWS	MARY JANE	Redruth
1898	SKUES	EVELYN ROSE	Westminster
1899	SKEWES	JAMES	Redruth
1899	SKEWES	ELIZABETH	Truro
1899	SKEWS	SAMUEL GREGORY	Liskeard
1899	SKUES	ELIZABETH HARRIET	Rochford
1900	SKEWES	ALFRED JOHN	Redruth
1900	SKEWES	LOUISA JANE	Chorlton
1900	SKEWES	SUSAN ANNIE	Penzance
1900	SKEWES	MARY LOUISA T.	Brentford
1900	SKEWES	ELIZABETH	Truro
1900	SKEWES	ARTHUR	Helston
1900	SKEWIS	JAMES	Redruth
1900	SKUES	THOMAS EDWARD	Lambeth
1901	SKEWES	ALFRED JOHN	Holyhead
1901	SKEWES	EDWARD	Chorlton
1901	SKEWES	CATHERINE	Redruth
1901	SKEWS	MERCY	Milton
1901	SKEWS	PETER	St. Austell
1902	SKEWES	ARTHUR DAW	Plymouth
1902	SKEWES	CLARA	Redruth
1902	SKEWES	RICHARD	Falmouth
1902	SKEWES	MARY AGNES	Helston
1902	SKEWIS	MARGARET	Haverfordwest
1902	SKUES	JOHN CHARLES	Redruth
1903	SKEWES	ADELINE HARRIET R.	Helston
1903	SKEWES	ELIZABETH MARY	Helston
1903	SKEWES	JOSIAH	Hampstead
1903	SKEWIS	ANNIE	Haverfordwest
1903	SKEWS	ROSINA	Redruth
1903	SKEWS	ALBERT JOHN	Strood
1903	SKUES	CHARLES AYRE MACKENZIE	Camberwell
1903	SKUES	HAROLD FREDERICK CLAUDE	Shoreditch
1903	SKUES	ELSIE MACKENZIE	Croydon
1904	SKEWES	ALFRED JOHN	Bideford
1904	SKEWES	FLORENCE	Truro
1904	SKEWES	JOHN HENRY	Helston
1904	SKEWS	ALICE ANNIE	Bethnal Green
1905	SKEWES	WILFRED	Falmouth
1905	SKEWES	EDITH JANE	Redruth
1905	SKEWES	CHARLES	Truro
1905	SKEWES	SUSAN	Midhurst
1905	SKEWES-COX	EVELYN MARY	Richmond S.
1905	SKEWIS	GEORGE	Totnes
1905	SKEWS	MARY ANN	Witham
1905	SKEWS	ELIZABETH EMILY	Bethnal Green
1905	SKEWS	FLORENCE EMMA	Liskeard
1905	SKEWS	PERCY LOUIS	Strood
1905	SKUES	JAMES FREDERICK	Redruth
1905	SKUES	BLANCHE LOUISA	Tonbridge
1906	SKEWES	ELIZA JANE	Helston
1906	SKEWES	EDWARD JAMES	Redruth
1906	SKEWS	JOHN HENRY	Totnes
1906	SKEWS	ELLEN JANE	Redruth
1906	SKEWS	RICHARD ERNEST	Redruth
1906	SKUES	JOSEPH PEARN	Redruth
1907	SKEUSE	AMELIA KATE	Bath
1907	SKEWIS	CHARLES	Truro
1907	SKEWES	JOHN	Helston

1907	SKEWES	LOUISA JANE	Hereford
1907	SKEWES	RICHARD CHARLES	Redruth
1907	SKEWES	THIRZA	Helston
1907	SKEWES	WILLIAM HEDLEY	Shoreditch
1907	SKEWES	ADA	Truro
1907	SKEWES	MARION	Barnstaple
1907	SKEWES	ELIZABETH JOANNA	Redruth
1907	SKEWIS	HOWARD	Bristol
1907	SKEWIS	EDWIN	London C.
1907	SKEWS	ETHEL MARY	Strood
1907	SKEWS	EMILY	Redruth
1907	SKEWS	EDITH FLORENCE	Plymouth
1907	SKUES	ETHEL JANE	Eton
1907	SKUES	NOAH JAMES	Southwark
1907	SKUES	ETHEL	Chippenham
1907	SKUES	FRANCIS ALBERT	Dartford

Note: 1907 is the year which proved most popular for marriages registered at Somerset House from 1837—1978 inclusive. Nineteen took place.

1908	SKEWES	AMELIA	Redruth
1908	SKEWES	HERBERT JOHN	Truro
1908	SKEWES	WILFRED HAWKINS	Totnes
1908	SKEWES	RICHARD	Redruth
1908	SKEWES	CARRIE	Redruth
1908	SKEWES	ELIZABETH ELLEN R.	Redruth
1908	SKEWES	ELLEN JANE	Helston
1908	SKEWES	ETHEL MAY	Helston
1908	SKEWES	FLORENCE ANNIE	Redruth
1908	SKEWS	ROSINA	Southampton
1909	SKEWES	AMY	Helston
1909	SKEWES	JAMES	Truro
1909	SKEWES	LILIAN MAUD	Abergavenny
1909	SKEWES	MARY ELIZA	Redruth
1909	SKEWES	RICHARD HENRY	Kensington
1909	SKEWES	BESSIE	Helston
1909	SKEWES	ALICE EMILY	Redruth
1909	SKEWES	ANNIE	Penzance
1909	SKEWES	FREDERICK	Ashton
1909	SKEWES	RICHARD HENRY	Helston
1909	SKEWIS	FREDERICK	Houghton
		(Also listed as SKEWS)	
1909	SKEWS	NATHANIEL EDWARD R.	West Ham
1909	SKUES	ADA ALICE	Tonbridge
1909	SKUES	ELLEN	Amersham
1910	SKEWES	FLORENCE BLANCHE	Truro
1910	SKEWES	WILLIAM JOHN	Redruth
1910	SKEWES	WILLIAM	Hackney
1910	SKEWES	ELIZABETH A.	Barnstaple
1910	SKEWES	WILLIAM	Penzance
1910	SKEWES	GERTRUDE A.	Kensington
1910	SKEWS	HENRY JAMES	Bethnal Green
1910	SKEWS	JAMES A.	Stepney
1910	SKEWS	CHARLOTTE REBECCA	Bethnal Green
1910	SKEWS	ANNIE	Swindon
1911	SKEUES	ELIZABETH M.	Bath
1911	SKEWES	STEPHEN J.	Redruth
1911	SKEWES	CERETA	Truro
1911	SKEWS	MATTHEW	Houghton
1911	SKEWS	MINNIE	Barnsley
1911	SKEWS	THOMAS	Barnsley
1911	SKEWS	BETSY	Easington
1911	SKEWSE	SARAH	Easington
1911	SKUES	WILLIAM JOHN	Amersham
1911	SKUISE	WILLIAM S.H.	Lambeth

Note: As from 1912 Somerset House Marriage Registers listed the surname of the person they married.

1912	SKEWES	HAROLD	Chorlton
		Lally	
1912	SKEWES	RINA MARY	Christchurch
		Angold	
1912	SKEWES	EMMA E.	Devonport
		Bowdon	
1912	SKEWIS	WILLIAM B.	Sheppey
		Solomon	
1912	SKEWS	MATILDA S.	Bethnal Green
		Rolph	
1912	SKEWS	LOUISA	Barnsley
		Briggs	
1912	SKEWS	ELIZABETH MARTHA	St. Olave
		Hewitt	
1912	SKEWS	DAISY EMILY	Bethnal Green
		Deway	
1912	SKEWS	EDWIN ARTHUR	Bethnal Green
		Smith	
1913	SKEWES	WALTER NICHOLAS	Redruth
		Ford	
1913	SKEWIS	ALFRED	Haverfordwest
		Hughes	
1913	SKEWIS	EMMA NORTHCOTT	Totnes
		Pethybridge	
1913	SKEWIS	SAMUEL	Haverfordwest
		Waters	
1913	SKEWS	ADA	Barnsley
		Dolan	
1913	SKEWS	MARY L.	Poplar
		Sutton	
1913*	SKUES	FLORENCE	Chelsea
		Marjoram	
1914	SKEWES	MARY M.	Redruth
		Bird	
1914	SKEWES	CHARLES	Chorlton
		Gichero	
1914	SKEWES	ELLA	Helston
		Johns	
1914	SKEWES	JOHN E.	Chorlton
		Gleave	
1914	SKEWES	MARY	Falmouth
		Pedler	
1914	SKEWES	SARAH ANNIE	Redruth
		Jeffrey	
1915	SKEWES	CLARINDA JANE	Falmouth
		Thomas	
1915	SKEWES	SAMUEL JOHN	Bodmin
		Whiting	
1915	SKEWES	THOMAS H.	Redruth
		Jory	
1915	SKEWES	SARAH	Penzance
		Symons	
1915	SKEWES	WILLIAM TREVENA	Penzance
		Jenkin	
1915	SKEWS	ALBAN EDGAR	Gravesend
		Crowhurst	
1915	SKEWS	ERNEST	Yarmouth
		Gilbert	
1915	SKEWS	JAMES E.	Bromley
		Allridge	
1915	SKEWS	MARTIN	Redruth
		Nancarrow	
1915	SKEWS	MARYLL	Preston
		Thomas	
1915	SKEWS	NELLIE	Aston
		Meredith	
1915	SKEWS	WILLIAM	Bethnal Green
		Childs	
1915	SKUES	THOMAS MACKENZIE	Marylebone
		Kretschmann	
1915	SKUES	JOHN P.W.	Camberwell
		Bremer	
1915	SKUES	MARGARET	Redruth
		Drew	
1916	SKEWES	WILLIAM	Falmouth
		Gosling	
1916	SKEWS	ELIZA MAY	Mile End
		Hawkes	
1916	SKEWS	BERNARD	Dartford
		Murphy	
1916	SKEWS	GERTRUDE MARY	Plymouth
		Axon	
1916	SKUES	WALTER E.	Islington
		Bundy	
1917	SKEWES	WILLIAM HENRY	Redruth
		Harris	

Year	Surname	Name		Location
1917	SKEWS	ELIZABETH	Fletcher	Barnsley
1917	SKEWS	FREDERICK C.	Charles	Totnes
1917	SKEWS	MABEL	Hunt	Barnsley
1917	SKUES	NOAH JAMES	Manning	Greenwich
1918	SKEWES	GRACE ELIZABETH	Moses	Truro
1918	SKEWES	JAMES A.	Cooke	Bristol
1918	SKEWES	GEORGE	Phelps	Pontypridd
1918	SKEWES	WILLIAM R.	Wills	South Shields
1918	SKEWS	JOHN H.	Gallacher	Devonport
1918	SKEWS	ROBERT ALBERT	Waite	Bethnal Green
1918	SKEWS	JOHN	Mallet	Liskeard
1918	SKEWS	NELLIE	Waite	Bethnal Green
1919	SKEWES	RICHARD H.	Revell	Marylebone
1919	SKEWIS	ARTHUR J.	Mahiew	Cardiff
1919	SKEWS	REGINALD PENROSE	Eadon	Ecclesall
1919	SKEWS	WILLIAM J.	Rump	Houghton
1919	SKUES	WINIFRED ROSE	Carey	Newton Abbot
1919	SKUES	REGINALD A.	Quede	St. Geo. Han. Square
1919	SKUES	ERNEST	Marsh	Camberwell
1919	SKUES	BERTHA E.	Jenkins	Edmonton

Note: The REGINALD SKEWS/SKUES/SKUSE seem popular. In 1919 a REGINALD SKUSE married in Thornbury. But above REGINALD PENROSE SKEWS who married Eadon in Ecclesall should have been listed in Somerset House as SKUES.

Year	Surname	Name		Location
1920	SKEWES	ELIZABETH E.H.	Spencer	Wakefield
1920	SKEWES	CLARINDA	Mayne	Redruth
1920	SKEWES	FREDERICK HENRY	Lithiby	St. Thomas
1920	SKEWES	JAMES H.O.	Cockram	Axbridge
1920	SKEWES	FREDERICK WILLIAM	Denton	Chorlton
1920	SKEWES	SENERETTA ELIZABETH	Mitchell	Helston
1920	SKEWS	JOHN G.	White	Northampton
1920	SKEWS	HENRY JAMES	Morgan	West Ham
1920	SKEWS	MATTHEW	Taylor	Sunderland
1920	SKUES	EDWARD A.	Meades	Tonbridge
1921	SKEWES	HARRY STANLEY	Rosevear	Helston
1921	SKEWES	LILIE	Williams	Helston
1921	SKEWES	WILLIAM JOHN	Drew	Truro
1921	SKEWES	HARRY	Barrett	Halifax
1921	SKEWES	SYDONIA	Wilson	Salford E.
1921	SKEWES	WILLIAM	Allen	Penzance

Year	Surname	Name		Location
1921	SKEWS	MARGARET	Easom	Southwark
1921	SKEWS	ELIZA	Midson	Gravesend
1921	SKEWS	JOSEPH	Randerson	Barnsley
1921	SKEWS	HENRIETTA	West	Truro
1921	SKEWS	ALBERT E.	Weston	E. Stonehouse
1921	SKUES	ATLANTA VIOLET	Bignell	Islington
1922	SKEWES	BESSIE E.A.	Allen	Redruth
1922	SKEWES	GRACE	Nicholls	Helston
1922	SKEWES	HENRY	Matthews	Falmouth
1922	SKEWES	LILY MAY	Bray	Redruth
1922	SKEWS	CAROLINE C.	Askew	Kettering
1922	SKEWS	HENRY FREDERICK	Gosnell	Southwark
1922	SKUES	ARTHUR	Thompson	Downham
1922	SKUES	LUCY D.	Dawson	Islington
1922	SKUES	PHILIP ERNEST	Pinto	St. Geo. Han. Sq.
1922	SKUES	VINCENT	Rowland	Blackburn
1923	SKEWES	LILIAN G.	Stevens	Helston
1923	SKEWES	MABEL	Rogers	Helston
1923	SKEWES	HILDA JANE	Carter	Helston
1923	SKEWS	DAVID GEORGE	Lampey	Bethnal Green
1923	SKEWS	FLORENCE A.	Powell	Maidenhead
1924	SKEWES	JOHN EDGAR	Morrison	Chelsea
1924	SKEWES	BEATRICE MARY	Harvey	Redruth
1924	SKEWS	MARY	Tapson	St. Columb
1924	SKEWS	WINNIE	Oliver	Redruth
1924	SKUES	DOROTHY KATHLEEN	Abbott	Edmonton
1924	SKUES	VICTOR CLAUDE	Ingrey	Edmonton
1924	SKUES	ERIC	Brearley	Halifax
1925	SKEWES	GEORGE	Caddy	Pontypridd
1925	SKEWES	LILIAN	Ivey	Helston
1925	SKEWES	GEORGE ERNEST	Ashton	Salford
1925	SKEWES	WILLIAM J.	Curnow	Helston
1925	SKEWS	ALBERT E.	Atkinson	Dartford
1925	SKEWS	ALICE E.	Law	Gravesend
1925	SKEWS	EDITH S.	Frost	E. Preston
1925	SKUES	ARTHUR LEONARD PETER	Lamont	Barrow-in-F.
1926	SKEWES	ARTHUR	Rashleigh	Helston
1926	SKEWES	LIZZIE M.	Vercoe	Truro
1926	SKEWES	EMILY ROSAMUND	George	Redruth

Year	Surname	Given Name / Other	District
1926	SKEWES	LAURA ANNIE Danvers	Lincoln
1926	SKEWS	SAMUEL Parden	Barnsley
1926	SKEWS	LILIAN MAY Wells	Devonport
1926	SKUES	THOMAS H.J. Clemmans	Southwark
1926	SKUES	ALBERT EDWARD Cullingham	Southwark
1927	SKEWES	ARTHUR GEORGE Hacking	Manchester N.
1927	SKEWS	ALFRED G.W. Snowshill	Edmonton
1927	SKEWS	ELIZABETH A. Drew	Liskeard
1927	SKEWS	EDITH Kenny	Devonport
1927	SKUES	NINA MAY Hale	Edmonton
1928	SKEWES	WILLIAM F. Williams	Helston
1928	SKEWIS	MARGARET J. Wass	Brighton
1928	SKEWS	LUCY ELIZABETH Williams	Bethnal Green
1928	SKEWS	JANE Braidwood	West Derby
1928	SKEWS	JOSEPH Lumb	Barnsley
1928	SKEWS	LILLIE Gardner	Swindon
1928	SKUES	CHARLES GILBERT Wyatt	Edmonton
1928	SKUES	BERTHA ELIZABETH Humphrey	Edmonton
1928	SKUES	WALTER EDWARD Mertons	Hackney
1929	SKEWES	FLORENCE MAY Vincent	Redruth
1929	SKEWES	WILLIAM F.C. Hornby	Doncaster
1929	SKEWES	DORIS Peters	Redruth
1929	SKEWS	MARY Luxton	Redruth
1929	SKEWS	GEORGE Addy	Barnsley
1929	SKUES	LEONARD Woodyer	Pancras
1929	SKUES	FREDERICK Kaye	Halifax
1930	SKEWES	CATHERINE Philips	Redruth
1930	SKEWES	CONSTANCE J. Cannicot	Helston
1930	SKEWES	BERTRAM Prowse	Truro
1930	SKEWES	ELIZABETH MARY Eustice	Helston
1930	SKEWES	JOHN HENRY Cork	Redruth
1930	SKEWIS	ARTHUR Peters	Redruth
1930	SKEWIS	FRANK Baker	Canterbury
1930	SKUES	IVY MAUD Dawson	Edmonton
1931	SKEWS	EDGAR Royston	Barnsley
1931	SKEWS	WINIFRED MARY Kelly	Plymouth
1931	SKUES	ENID ELIZABETH Bayes	Dartford
1931	SKUES	THOMAS GEORGE Taylor	Hampstead
1932	SKEWIS	HILDA MAUD Carter	Redruth
1932	SKEWS	HILDA BLANCHE Wilson	Devonport
1932	SKEWS	LILY Searle	Islington
1932	SKEWS	ALBERT E. Harding	Edmonton
1932	SKEWS	ELIZABETH Eaton	Bethnal Green
1932	SKEWS	ADA I. Hesketh	Barnsley
1933	SKEWES	JESSIE M. Hunt	Chepstow
1933	SKEWES	JAMES ELDRED Schwersee	Hampstead
1933	SKEWES	WILLIAM J. Thomas	Helston
1933	SKEWES	DORIS McKenna	Manchester S.
1933	SKEWS	HENRY G. Holgate	Maldon
1933	SKEWS	MATTHEW JOHN Thomas	Truro
1933	SKEWS	RUBY IRENE Blewett	Devonport
1933	SKUES	IVY MARGARETTA White	Camberwell
1934	SKEWES	DORIS MURIEL Rogers	Redruth
1934	SKEWES	ALFRED J. Matthews	Helston
1934	SKEWES	LILIA Cleave	Truro
1934	SKEWES	MARY ELIZABETH Polkinghorn	Plymouth
1934	SKEWES	JAMES HARRY Pearce	Truro
1934	SKEWIS	RONALD Wyatt	Totnes
1934	SKEWIS	DELILAH C. Gough	Haverfordwest
1934	SKEWS	MAUD Browne	Devonport
1934	SKEWS	WILLIAM DAVID Groves	Hackney
1934	SKEWS	OLIVE M. John	Totnes
1934	SKUES	PHYLLIS Waters	Redruth
1935	SKEWES	STANLEY Allen	Cambridge
1935	SKEWES	MONA DAVIE Mayrick	Penzance
1935	SKEWES	DOREEN M. Foster	Redruth
1935	SKEWES	LIONAL J. Symons	Redruth
1935	SKEWS	MABEL MILLICENT Rosevear	St. Austell
1935	SKEWS	GEORGE Cudgeon	Edmonton
1935	SKUES	ERNEST J. Franklin	Shoreditch
1935	SKUES	JACK Bruckshaw	Stockport
1936	SKEWES	GLADYS C. Lappin	St. Thomas
1936	SKEWES	PHYLLIS Williams	Redruth
1936	SKEWES	WILLIAM HENRY Reynolds	Redruth
1936	SKEWES	WILLIAM R. Moon	Penzance
1936	SKEWIS	WILLIAMINA A. McKechnie	Pancras
1936	SKEWS	BESSIE H. Thomas	Amounderness
1936	SKEWS	FREDERICK C. Thompson	Easington

Year	Surname	Name	Place		Year	Surname	Name	Place
1936	SKEWS	FREDERICK Joyce	Islington		1940	SKEWS	BEATRICE M.I. Congdon	Liskeard
1936	SKEWS	GEORGE W. Hill	Stourbridge		1940	SKEWS	ELLEN M. Gowers	Stepney
1936	SKUES	ADA MAY Pearce	Redruth		1940	SKEWS	MARTIN R. Martin	Falmouth
1937	SKEWES	LILY Taylor	Manchester S.		1940	SKEWS	ARTHUR S. Stroud	Romford
1937	SKEWES	CECIL Millett	Redruth		1940	SKEWS	KATHLEEN Cooke	Staincross
1937	SKEWES	VERA Risden	Penzance		1940	SKEWS	LESLIE Wakefield	Durham N.
1937	SKEWES	SYLVIA D. Tredinnick	Redruth		1940	SKUES	ALFRED E. Brassett	Finsbury
1937	SKEWIS	GEORGE Crook	Tonbridge		1940	SKUES	CYRIL A.J. Norris	Woolwich
1937	SKEWS	ERNEST W. Falconer	Croydon		1940	SKUES	EDWIN THOMAS Hawkins	Dartford
1937	SKEWS	CLARENCE Duke	St. Germans		1940	SKUES	ARTHUR E.W. Jackson	Islington
1937	SKEWS	SARAH E.E. Marker	Hammersmith		1941	SKEWES	JOHN H. Wynne	Manchester
1937	SKEWS	WINIFRED Lawry	St. Germans		1941	SKEWES	LESLIE Body	Kerrier
1938	SKEWES	ROY Trengove	Redruth		1941	SKEWES	MILLICENT M. Phillips	Truro
1938	SKEWES	MARY VERONICA Cockram	Redruth		1941	SKEWES	VIOLET MAY Tresize	Penzance
1938	SKEWS	FERNLEY WALTER Wilcocks	St. Germans		1941	SKEWS	MABEL Thewlis	Barnsley
1938	SKEWS	KATHLEEN P.H. Painter	Hammersmith		1941	SKUES	CHRISTOPHER H.V. Kethro	Bristol
1938	SKUES	GRACE JOAN Goodwin	Stoke N'ton		1942	SKEWES	ADA Whitford	Redruth
1938	SKUES	RICHARD Hughes	Runcorn		1942	SKEWS	THOMAS E. Brayford	Staincross
1938	SKUES	FLORENCE MURIEL Coulthurst	Stockport		1942	SKEWS	VIOLET IRENE Pearce	St. Austell
1938	SKUES	RUBY F. Barrett	Romford		1942	SKEWS	ELIZABETH H. Clements	Plymouth
1938	SKUES	MAUD EVELYN Wackett	Romford		1942	SKEWS	CONSTANCE M. Hurst	Plymouth
1938	SKUES	OLIVE EMILY Sharp	Essex S.W.		1942	SKEWES-COX	PAMELA S. Tritton	Westminster
1939	SKEWES	CYRIL WILLIAM Ambrose	Croydon		1943	SKEWES	ROBERT A. Foster	Hendon
1939	SKEWES	JOYCE M. Whitburn	Truro		1943	SKEWES	EDNA M. Booth	Manchester
1939	SKEWES	HORACE Jose	Redruth		1943	SKEWES	JAMES HARRY Woolcock	Truro
1939	SKEWES	IRIS M. Prisk	Redruth		1943	SKEWS	BARON S. Barson	Staincross
1939	SKEWES	MARY A. Wright	Battersea		1943	SKEWS	EDWIN A. Lewis	Camarthen
1939	SKEWES	DAVID B. Brunsdon	Pancras		1943	SKEWS	ELIZABETH Townsend	Staincross
1939	SKEWES	JOHN H. Lundell	Edmonton		1943	SKEWS	MABEL I. Footer	Kettering
1939	SKEWES	WILLIAM DOUGLAS Little	Truro		1943	SKEWS	THOMAS HENRY Harris	St. Austell
1939	SKEWES	RICHARD N. Stonebridge	Lewisham		1944	SKEWES	MARY Faust	Stockport
1939	SKEWS	ROY Boynton	Knaresborough		1944	SKEWES	EDITH Milton	Penzance
1939	SKEWS	EILEEN Dickerson	Romford		1944	SKEWS	ETHEL Harris	Plymouth
1940	SKEWES	MATHILDA JOAN Polkinghorne	Redruth		1944	SKEWS	STANLEY Hardcastle	Hull
1940	SKEWES	BELINDA O.M. Rossitter	Portsmouth		1944	SKEWS	GEORGE Littledike	Barnsley
1940	SKEWES	MARY M. Nile	Redruth		1944	SKEWS	SUSAN S. Boyson	St. Germans
1940	SKEWES	SAMUEL P. Tremayne	Kerrier		1945	SKEWES	WILLIAM H. Pollard	Redruth
1940	SKEWIS	MILDRED E. Hawkins	Haverfordwest		1945	SKEWES	MATTHEW HARRY Morgan	Woolwich
1940	SKEWS	JOHN Cox	Plymouth		1945	SKEWIS	BRENDA G.S. Parsons	Haverfordwest

Year	Surname	Name	Place
1945	SKEWS	MARGARET B. Hirst	Camberwell
1945	SKEWS	ERIC Rasburn	Staincross
1945	SKUES	MARGARET PAMELA Pawlak	Surrey Mid E.
1946	SKEWES	HARRY S. Hockin	Kerrier
1946	SKEWES	EDNA Waller	Halifax
1946	SKEWES	GEORGE H. Capel	Redruth
1946	SKEWES	ERNEST L. Penhaligon	Truro
1946	SKEWES	WILLIAM J. Williams	Kerrier
1946	SKEWS	AMELIA E. Burgess	Essex S.W.
1946	SKEWS	JOHN G.P. Boyland	Peterborough
1946	SKEWS	MARIAN R. Pollard	Plymouth
1946	SKEWS	MARY A. Usher	Watford
1946	SKEWS	OLIVE D. Wilkinson	Don Valley
1946	SKUES	BETTY J. Bishop	Tonbridge
1946	SKUES	FRANCIS HENRY Henson	Dartford
1946	SKUES	VIVIAN W. Macdonald	Truro
1947	SKEWES	OLIVE IRENE Lawrance	Kerrier
1947	SKEWIES	ANDREW F. Holt-Kentwell	Oxford
1947	SKEWIS	CLARENCE J. Maddick	Totnes
1947	SKEWIS	MILDRED E. Morrow	Wellington
1947	SKEWS	DAVID G. Parrott	Ilford
1947	SKEWS	FREDERICK E. Meadows	Leeds
1947	SKEWS	LEWIS P. Cadmore	Birmingham
1947	SKEWS	STANLEY Soady	St. Austell
1947	SKUES	MURIEL M. Hesketh	Chorley
1947	SKUES	ELSIE F.R. Martin	Islington
1948	SKEWES	CERITA B. Gosling	Truro
1948	SKEWES	GEORGE Hawken	Redruth
1948	SKEWES-COX	MILES L.D. Macmullen	Westminster
1948	SKEWS	MARY K. Trodd	Gloucester C.
1948	SKUES	GEORGE Ashcroft (Note: Also listed as SKUSE)	Ince
1948	SKUES	SYDNEY THOMAS Parnell	Edmonton
1948	SKUES	ERNEST Hiscock	Southampton
1948	SKUES	FREDERICK MACKENZIE Arnold	Manchester
1949	SKEWES	FLORENCE Phillips	Salford
1949	SKEWES	JOHN H. Beenes	Redruth
1949	SKEWIS	SAMUEL LESLIE Holdsworth	Chatham
1949	SKEWIS	WINIFRED K. Morgan	Bridge
1949	SKEWS	EUNICE D. Phillips	Dartford
1949	SKEWS	WILLIAM C. Morrell	Durham N.
1949	SKEWS	WILLIAM A. Leach	Ilford
1949	SKUES	GEORGE ERNEST Littlewood	Melton Mowbray
1949	SKUES	GLADYS M. Goulston	Wandsworth
1949	SKUES	PHILIP E. Lucchesi	Woolwich
1949	SKUES	AUDREY F. Johnson	Woolwich
1949	SKUES	SIDNEY V. Cox	Brentwood
1950	SKEWES	JOHN H. Keast	Truro
1950	SKEWES	WILLIAM F.C. Corbett	Doncaster
1950	SKEWS	COURTNEY J.G. Arnold	St. Germans
1950	SKEWS	DORA N. Hickman	Wednesbury
1950	SKEWS	MONICA E. Phillips	Birmingham
1951	SKEWES	ROSEMARY Thomas	Redruth
1951	SKEWES	EVELYN M. Pustelnyk	Truro
1951	SKEWS	KENNETH W.W. Pascoe	Liskeard
1951	SKEWS	DAISY Dean	Dartford
1951	SKEWS	MABEL J. Lander	St. Austell
1951	SKUES	SYLVIA G. Slatter	Edmonton
1952	SKEWES	EMILY R. Lawry	Redruth
1952	SKEWES	ENID Curnow	Redruth
1952	SKEWES	WILLIAM H. Hill	Kerrier
1952	SKEWES	CECIL Williams	Redruth
1952	SKEWES	IAN R. MORRISON Brampton	Bristol
1952	SKEWES	LILIAN GLADYS Johnson	Kerrier
1952	SKEWIS	ELIZABETH J. Brown	Falmouth
1952	SKEWS	DORIS Cocks	Kerrier
1952	SKEWS	BARON S. Cielemecka	Calder
1952	SKEWS	ALBERT EDWARD Henley	Swindon
1952	SKEWS	IRIS D. Houchell	Ilford
1952	SKEWS	JANET A. Brown	Durham N.
1952	SKEWS	JOHN H. Duff	Birmingham
1952	SKUES or KETHRO	WINIFRED C. Morgan	Bristol
1953	SKEWES	PAMELA J. Roberts	Truro
1953	SKEWS	WILLIAM King	Rochford
1953	SKUES	ROY A.T. Causton	Ilford
1953	SKUES	GENE M. Gola	St. Albans
1954	SKEWES	WILLIAM A. Bray	Redruth
1954	SKEWES	RONALD Curtis	Redruth
1954	SKEWS	DESMOND Lunn	Staincross

Year	Surname	Name	Place	Year	Surname	Name	Place
1954	SKEWS	YVONNE M. Chapman	Birmingham	1959	SKEWES	ELIZABETH M. Ball	Truro
1954	SKUES	JEAN D. Boothman	Gloucester	1959	SKEWS	KIRTLEY Tubmen	Durham N.
1955	SKEWES	JOHN HORNBY Freeman	Leeds	1959	SKUES	JENNIFER Reeves	Blackpool
1955	SKEWES	BARBARA M. Logue	Manchester	1960	SKEWES	GEORGE Gilbert	Redruth
1955	SKEWES	ARTHUR R. Rogers	Kerrier	1960	SKEWES	PEGGY M. Trenear	Redruth
1955	SKEWES	ROZE PEARL Tancock	Launceston	1960	SKEWS	MONICA O. Goring	Chesterfield
1955	SKEWS	JEAN Q. Hodges	Ealing	1960	SKUES	CAROL C.A. Cox	Weston
1955	SKUES	DOREEN M. Paterson	Barrow-in-F.	1960	SKUES	RAYMOND A. Collie	Surrey Mid. E.
1955	SKUES	BERYL E. Houlden	Barrow-in-F.	1961	SKEWES	DORIEL Harfoot	Redruth
1955	SKUES	JOHN J.G. Davies	Woolwich	1961	SKEWS	RENEE Hackett	Durham E.
1956	SKEWES	ELSIE Laity	Penzance	1961	SKEWS	MARY H.W. Blench	Durham N.
1956	SKEWES	JOHN HENRY Trenear	Redruth	1961	SKUES	ERNEST J. Porter	Islington
1956	SKEWES	MURIEL Bodilly	Truro	1961	SKUES	JENNIE E. Chandler	Hackney
1956	SKEWES	CARYL I. Muntz	Kensington	1962	SKEWIS	CHRISTINE J. Harrison	Tonbridge
1956	SKEWES	FRANK R. Taylor	Macclesfield	1962	SKEWS	JOHN H. Lennox	Durham N.
1956	SKEWES	MARGARETTE J. Pearson	Willesdon	1962	SKEWS	SALLY J. Pettet	Middlesex S.
1956	SKUES	JEAN M. Davies	Hackney	1962	SKEWS	EVELYN M. Genovese	Essex S.W.
1956	SKUES	JOHN P.W. Rawson	Woolwich	1963	SKEWES	DIANE M. Guest	Manchester
1956	SKUES	JOHN ANTHONY Bamber	Malvern	1963	SKEWES	JUDITH M. Lane	Bromley
1957	SKEWES	DOROTHY M.M. Phillips	Truro	1963	SKUES	JOHN ANTHONY Cockerell	Lambeth
1957	SKEWES	BARBARA J. Johnson	Kerrier	1964	SKEWES	DENNIS I.J. Letcher	Redruth
1957	SKEWES	GILBERT J. Dennis	Kerrier	1964	SKEWES	EDWARD Ingleby	Stockport
1957	SKEWES	JILLIAN A. Bone	Truro	1964	SKEWES	THOMAS HENRY Williams	Redruth
1957	SKEWES	VERONICA J. Hawkin	Redruth	1964	SKEWES	LIONEL Jones	Aled
1957	SKEWS	BETTY F. Archer	Edmonton	1964	SKEWIS	EILEEN M. Drennan	Totnes
1957	SKEWS	GEORGE D. Thirlwell	Durham E.	1964	SKEWS	DAVID Ackroyd	Staincross
1957	SKEWS	KENNETH D. Lord	Staincliffe	1964	SKEWS	JOHN W. Hill	St. Germans
1957	SKUES	JOY CHRISTINE Cooper	Blackpool	1964	SKEWS	PATRICIA Webb	Devon C.
1958	SKEWES	BARBARA ANN Pickering	Holderness	1964	SKEWS	ROLAND G. Greaves	Durham N.
1958	SKEWES	SHIRLEY A. Rumdan	Redruth	1964	SKEWS	VALERIE B. O'Brien	Hammersmith
1958	SKEWS	ALBERT E.V. Lowe	Plymouth	1965	SKEWES	RICHARD JOHN Hall	Penzance
1958	SKEWS	BRIAN A.A. Alldis	Shoreditch	1965	SKEWES	CARL Clackworthy	Penzance
1958	SKEWS	STANLEY G. Fishleigh	St. Germans	1965	SKEWIS	TREVOR Hanslip	Bridge
1958	SKEWS	JOSEPH F. Isaac	Barton	1965	SKEWS	BRIAN A.E. Newby	Edmonton
1958	SKEWS	MAUREEN Thomas	Redruth	1965	SKEWS	CHRISTINE Simcock	Calder
1958	SKEWS	OSWALD Holbrook	Kerrier	1965	SKEWS	WENDY LYNNE Coulman	Hull
1958	SKEWS	ALBERT E. Wills	Plymouth	1965	SKEWS	GEORGE Proudly	Barnsley
1958	SKEWS	DOROTHY I. Harvey	Edmonton	1965	SKEWS	LILIAN Hucalak	Halifax
1958	SKEWS	PATRICIA E. Dale	Hammersmith	1965	SKEWS	SANDRA Cordingly	Bradford
1959	SKEWES	ROSALIE Peters	Kerrier	1965	SKUES	SHIRLEY C.J. Everton	St. Pancras
1959	SKEWES	WILLIAM R. Richards	Penzance	1966	SKEWES	MAXWELL Wills	Penzance

Year	Surname	Name	District
1966	SKEWES	MAURICE Payne	Hatfield
1966	SKEWES	EILEEN M. Cooper	Newton Abbot
1966	SKEWES	ANNIE M. Skinner	Redruth
1966	SKEWES	DAWN Trevethan	Truro
1966	SKEWES	ELIZABETH A. Hatham	Penzance
1966	SKEWIS	MICHAEL I. Humphries	Hull
1966	SKEWS	WENDY A. Sturtridge	St. Austell
1966	SKEWS	LAWRENCE Brown	Durham N.E.
1967	SKEWIS	DAVID Brattan	Hull
1967	SKEWS	MARGARET Lawson	Staincross
1967	SKEWS	SANDRA Brown	Birmingham
1967	SKEWS	ANGELA Binney	Staincross
1967	SKEWS	ELIZABETH A. Drew	Exeter
1967	SKEWS	EVA Mirza	Huddersfield
1967	SKEWS	PETER B. Blight	St. Austell
1967	SKEWS	ROBERT W. Agates	Islington
1967	SKEWS	BARON S. Ramsden	Calder
1967	SKEWS	NIGEL G. Walls	Falmouth
1967	SKUES	DAVID J. Weighill	Dartford
1968	SKEWES	MARGARET R. Pitt	Truro
1968	SKEWES	ROBERT J. Nairne	Bexley
1968	SKEWES	PATRICIA A. Purkis	Truro
1968	SKEWS	CHRISTOPHER R. Kempson	Waltham Forest
1968	SKEWS	LINDA J. Westley	St. Austell
1968	SKUES	NORAH E. King	Bexley
1968	SKUES	TERENCE F. Moore	Barking
1968	SKUES	DOREEN Bushnell	Manchester
1969	SKEWES	IRENE Keast	Truro
1969	SKEWES	ANTHONY RONALD Coward	Kerrier
1969	SKEWIS	RONALD Tape	Newton Abbot
1969	SKEWIS	JAMES Rode	Holderness
1969	SKEWS	GWENDOLINE D. Cooper	Barking
1969	SKEWS	LYNN Atkinson	Staincross
1969	SKEWS	ALICE Slade	Staincross
1969	SKEWS	IRENE M. Andrews	Waltham Forest
1969	SKEWS	JOHN G. Mills	Peterborough
1969	SKUES	ROYDON T. Cooke	Eastbourne
1970	SKEWES	JAMES A. Hooper	Truro
1970	SKEWES	CAROL W. Treleor	Kerrier
1970	SKEWES	JOHN OSBORN Williams	Kerrier
1970	SKEWES	SHIRLEY E. James	Redruth
1970	SKEWES	LINDA ROSEMARY Fussey	Cambridge
1970	SKEWES	COLIN Jordan	Penzance
1970	SKEWIS	JAMES A. Fox	Hull
1970	SKEWIS	JAMES A. Wilson	Hull
1970	SKEWS	PAMELA J. Osborne	St. Austell
1970	SKEWS	ROGER D. Binnersley	Shrewsbury
1970	SKEWS	JANE M. Collins	St. Pancras
1971	SKEWES	JOHN Easton	Nottingham
1971	SKEWES	CARL Berryman	Redruth
1971	SKEWIS	SADIE A. Ducker	Hull
1971	SKEWS	SUSAN Guy	St. Austell
1972	SKEWES	CAROL A. Lawrence	Kerrier
1972	SKEWES	RAYMOND V. Hall	Redruth
1972	SKEWS	TREVOR Guirey	Staincross
1972	SKEWS	BRIAN J. Wharam	Barnsley
1972	SKEWS	DEREK Gould	Worth Valley
1972	SKUES	CHRISTINE EVELYN Bourne	Chanctonbury
1972	SKUES	EDWIN MICHAEL Brothwell	Dover
1973	SKEWES	IAN R.M. Grimes	Kensington
1973	SKEWES	GLADYS M. Rosewarne	Penzance
1973	SKEWES	JEFFREY L. Caddy	Kerrier
1973	SKEWES	WILLIAM J. Pope	St. Austell
1973	SKEWIS	DAVID Gibson	Holderness
1973	SKEWIS	JEAN S.O. Dobson	Kettering
1973	SKEWS	BARON S. Sherburn	Calder
1973	SKEWS	BETTY J. Proctor	Chichester
1973	SKEWS	MELVYN Snowden	Durham E.
1973	SKEWS	BARBARA KATHLEEN Smith	Hull
1973	SKEWS	JAQUELINE A. Truman	St. Austell
1973	SKEWS	TERENCE W. Walters	W. Glamorgan
1973	SKUES	ALAN J. Buck	Barking
1974	SKEWES	HARRY Short	Southwark
1974	SKEWES	SYLVIA A. Mahon	Truro
1974	SKEWIS	ELIZABETH I. Short	Grantham
1974	SKEWIS	JACK Robertson	Surrey S.E.
1974	SKEWIS	CHRISTINE Dalee	Hull
1974	SKEWS	MICHAEL J. Clifft	St. Austell
1974	SKEWS	ANDREW J. Searle	St. Germans
1974	SKEWS	DAVID P. Reseigh	Truro
1974	SKEWS	SANDRA King	St. Austell
1974	SKEWS	TRUDY M. Stephens	St. Austell

1975	SKEWES	SALLY	Kerrier
		Marsh	
1975	SKEWES-		
	COX	NICOLA A.	Westminster
		Gladstone	
1975	SKEWIS	CAROL B.	Corby
		Gray	
1975	SKEWIS	MOIRA E.	Beverley
		May	
1975	SKEWIS	JAMES	Hull
		Smart	
1975	SKEWS	BARRY S.	Halifax
		Campbell	
1975	SKEWS	PAUL J.	Stoke on Trent
		Perry	
1975	SKEWS	STEPHEN J.	Peterborough
		Claridge	
1976	SKEWES	CHRISTOPHER JOHN	Kerrier
		Williams	
1976	SKEWES	DONALD JAMES	Penzance
		Thomas	
1976	SKEWES	SUSAN B.	Kerrier
		Dowland	
1976	SKEWES	LINDA MARION	Leeds
		Walmsley	
1976	SKEWES	DIANA R.	St. Austell
		Foster	
1976	SKEWES	KENNETH R.	Camborne
		Trengove	
1976	SKEWES	JOHN G.P.	Peterborough
		Growns	
1976	SKEWIS	JOHN C.	Corby
		Eady	
1976	SKEWS	MARY	Waltham Forest
		Fallan	
1976	SKEWS	MARTIN C.	St. Austell
		Daniels	
1976	SKUES	BARRY R.	Canterbury
		Epps	
1976	SKUES	KATHLEEN	Croydon
		Ring	
1976	SKUES	STEPHEN J.	Islington
		Wosket	
1977	SKEWES	JILL ALEXANDRA	Kerrier
		Jenkin	
1977	SKEWS	PAUL	Barnsley
		Taylor	
1977	SKEWS	JANE	Waveney
		Lockwood	
1977	SKEWS	SHARON	Barnsley
		Knowles	
1977	SKEWS	THOMAS H,	Evesham
		Gould	
1977	SKEWS	LYNN	Sunderland
		Arkley	
1978	SKEWES	NICOLA	Kerrier
		Jose	
1978	SKEWES	MICHAEL J.	Camborne
		Shore	
1978	SKEWES-		
	COX	MILES L.D.	Westminster
		Hirsch	
1978	SKUES	RICHARD ANTHONY	Glyndwr
		Johns	
1978	SKEWS	CATHERINE	Barnsley
		Lowe	
1978	SKUES	JOAN M.	Worthing
		English	
1978	SKUES	ALAN J.	Canterbury
		Vesma	

Deaths 1837 — 1978

Year	Surname	Name	Place	Year	Surname	Name	Place
1837	SKEWES	HENRY	Redruth	1845	SKEWS	EMMA	E. London
1837	SKUES	ANN	Helston	1845	SKUES	EDWARD	Helston
1837	SKUES	MARY	Helston	1846	SKEWES	WILLIAM	Falmouth
1838	SKEWES	MATTHEW	Truro	1846	SKEWES	LAVINIA	Truro
1838	SKEWES	JANE	Redruth	1846	SKEWES	MARY	Helston
1838	SKEWES	THOMAS	St. Austell	1846	SKEWES	ANN	Redruth
1838	SKEWES	WILLIAM	Truro	1846	SKEWIS	CATHERINE	Redruth
1838	SKEWES	PHILIPPA	Redruth	1846	SKEWS	ELIZABETH	E. London
1838	SKEWIS	JAMES	Merthyr Tydfil	1847	SKEWES	ELIZABETH	Truro
1838	SKEWS	JAMES	St. Austell	1847	SKEWES	MARGARET	Truro
1839	SKEWES	JOHN	Truro	1847	SKEWES	SARAH	Plymouth
1839	SKEWES	JOHN	Redruth	1847	SKEWIS	ANN	Falmouth
1839	SKEWIS	EMMA	Abergavenny	1847	SKEWIS	GRACE	Redruth
1839	SKEWS	JOHN	Greenwich	1847	SKEWS	HENRY	St. Austell
1839	SKEWS	ELIZABETH	Plymouth	1847	SKEWS	AMELIA	Liskeard
1839	SKUES	JOHN	St. Geo. East	1847	SKEWS	THOMAS	St. Austell
1840	SKEWES	FRANCES	Chippenham	1847	SKUES	ANN	East Stonehouse
1840	SKEWES	GRACE	Truro	1847	SKUES	ISABELLA	Penzance
1840	SKEWES	MARY	St. Austell	1848	SKEWES	SUSANNAH	Redruth
1840	SKEWIS	JOHN	Redruth	1848	SKEWES	ELIZABETH JANE	Helston
1840	SKEWIS	ELIZABETH STEPHENS	Truro	1848	SKEWES	WILLIAM	Stoke D.
1840	SKEWS	CATHERINE		1848	SKEWES	ANN HENDY	Helston
		ELIZABETH MARY	Derby	1848	SKEWES	CAROLINE	Stoke Dam.
1840	SKUES	WILLIAM	St. Austell	1848	SKEWES	WILLIAM	Helston
1841	SKEWIS	PHILIPPA	Falmouth	1848	SKEWES	GRACE	Truro
1841	SKEWIS	HENRY	Truro	1848	SKEWS	JOHN GREGORY	Launceston
1841	SKEWIS	JANE	Abergavenny	1848	SKEWS	LUCY	St. Giles
1841	SKEWS	JANE	Truro	1849	SKEWES	WILLIAM	Helston
1841	SKUES	CHARLES	Strand	1849	SKEWES	JAMES	Truro
1842	SKEWES	CHRISTIAN	Helston	1849	SKEWES	AVIS	Helston
1842	SKEWES	ELIZABETH	Redruth	1849	SKEWES	HENRY	Redruth
1842	SKEWES	EMMA	Helston	1849	SKEWS	MARIANNE	Launceston
1842	SKEWES	GEORGE EMMANUEL	Helston	1849	SKEWS	JAMES	Neath
1842	SKEWES	JANE	Redruth	1849	SKEWS	GRACE	Neath
1842	SKEWES	ELIZABETH ANN	Redruth	1849	SKUES	WILLIAM HENRY	St. Geo. East
1842	SKEWES	MARY	Helston	1849	SKUES	GEORGE HENRY	St. Geo. East
1842	SKEWES	MARY	Redruth	1850	SKEWES	EDWARD TIPPET	Falmouth
1842	SKEWES	SIMON DAVEY	Redruth	1850	SKEWES	HENRY	Helston
1842	SKEWES	THOMAS	Redruth	1850	SKEWES	SARAH ANN	Helston
1842	SKEWES	WILLIAM	Helston	1850	SKEWES	MARY ANN	Truro
1842	SKEWS	NANCY	St. Austell	1850	SKEWS	ANN	Truro
1842	SKEWS	ALEXANDER	Redruth	1850	SKEWS	ELIZABETH CHARLOTTE	Bethnal Green
1842	SKEWS	THOMAS	Malmsbury	1851	SKEWES	ELIZABETH	Helston
1842	SKUES	JAMES	St. Geo East	1851	SKEWES	JOSEPH	Abergavenny
1842	SKUES	ELIZABETH	Helston	1851	SKEWIS	THOMAS	Abergavenny
1842	SKUES	ELIZA	St. Geo. East	1851	SKEWS	ANN BAWDEN	Liskeard
1843	SKEWES	MATTHEW	Redruth	1851	SKEWS	WILLIAM	E. Stonehouse
1843	SKEWES	GRACE THERESA	Truro	1852	SKEWES	ALFRED	Redruth
1843	SKEWES	MARTHA	Helston	1852	SKEWES	ELIZABETH MARGARET	
1843	SKEWES	SELINA	Truro			EDWARDS	Swansea
1843	SKEWIS	ELIZA	Truro	1852	SKEWES	LAVINIA	St. Columb
1843	SKEWIS	– Female –	Redruth	1852	SKEWES	JAMES	Redruth
1843	SKEWIS	ANN	Redruth	1852	SKEWES	HENRY	Redruth
1843	SKUES	ROSE	Truro	1852	SKEWES	JANE BAWDEN	Redruth
1844	SKEWES	HENRY CHARLES	Truro	1852	SKEWES	ALFRED	Redruth
1844	SKEWES	HENRY	Falmouth	1852	SKEWS	JOHN RULE	Liskeard
1844	SKEWES	MARY	Redruth	1852	SKEWS	JOHN	Helston
1844	SKEWIS	MARY AGNES ELIZABETH	Redruth	1852	SKEWS	JOHN	Liskeard
1844	SKEWIS	WILLIAM	Redruth	1852	SKEWS	RICHARD MARTIN	Redruth
1844	SKEWIS	JOANNA	Redruth	1852	SKEWS	SARAH	Redruth
1844	SKEWIS	JOSEPH	Merthyr Tydfil	1852	SKEWSE	JAMES	Greenwich
1844	SKUES	LOVELIA	Lambeth	1853	SKEWES	JANE	Helston
1845	SKEWES	ELIZA	Helston	1853	SKEWES	MARY	Truro
1845	SKEWES	JANE	Helston	1853	SKEWES	– Female –	Falmouth
1845	SKEWES	SUSAN JANE	Helston	1853	SKEWES	ELLEN	Truro
1845	SKEWES	ELLEN	Truro	1853	SKEWES	LAVINIA	Truro
1845	SKEWES	JAMES	Helston	1853	SKEWS	JOHN GREGORY	Launceston
1845	SKEWES	MARY ANN	Tavistock	1853	SKUES	AMELIA	St. James
1845	SKEWIS	JOHANNA	Redruth	1853	SKUES	SARAH	Redruth
1845	SKEWIS	ROBERT	Abergavenny	1853	SKUES	SARAH	Redruth
1845	SKEWIS	HENRY JAMES	Redruth				different entries
1845	SKEWIS	WILLIAM	Redruth	1854	SKEWES	ELIZABETH MARY	Helston
1845	SKEWS	LOVELIA	St. Germans	1854	SKEWES	ELIZA	Rochford
1845	SKEWS	ELIZABETH	Bodmin	1854	SKEWS	ELIZABETH	Truro

Year	Surname	Name	Place
1854	SKEWS	WILLIAM HOOPER	Bodmin
1854	SKEWS	WILLIAM	Plymouth
1854	SKEWS	MARY	Truro
1854	SKEWS	RICHARD	Truro
1854	SKUES	WILLIAM HENRY	St. Geo. East
1855	SKEWES	JOHN	Redruth
1855	SKEWES	ELIZABETH	Truro
1855	SKEWES	JAMES	Redruth
1855	SKEWES	ELIZABETH	Redruth
1855	SKEWES	MARY	Helston
1855	SKEWIS	ROBERT	Abergavenny
1855	SKEWS	JOHN GREGORY	Launceston
1856	SKEWES	ANN	Redruth
1856	SKEWES	ANN	Redruth / different entries
1856	SKEWES	ANN	Redruth
1856	SKEWES	JAMED LUGG	Falmouth
1856	SKEWES	WILLIAM	Redruth
1856	SKEWES	CHARLES COLLAN	Wareham
1856	SKEWES	HENRY	Helston
1856	SKEWES	JAMES	Redruth
1856	SKEWES	MATTHEW	Truro
1856	SKEWS	THOMAS JOHN	Liskeard
1856	SKEWS	JANE	St. Austell
1857	SKEWES	HENRIETTA MARIA	Truro
1857	SKEWES	THOMAS JAMES	Truro
1857	SKEWES	EDWARD	Helston
1857	SKEWES	GRACE	Truro
1857	SKEWS	GEORGE	Abergavenny
1857	SKEWS	MATTHEW	Liskeard
1857	SKUES	THOMAS GILBERT	St. James
1858	SKEWES	JOHN	Helston
1858	SKEWES	CHARITY	Redruth
1858	SKEWES	WILLIAM HENRY	Helston
1858	SKEWES	JOHN	Truro
1858	SKEWES	ALEXANDER RICHARD	Wareham
1858	SKEWES	ELIZABETH	Redruth
1858	SKEWS	STEPHEN	Liskeard
1858	SKEWS	JOHN	St. Austell
1858	SKEWS	MARY	Stepney
1859	SKEWES	NANCY	Truro
1859	SKEWES	STEPHEN	Falmouth
1859	SKEWES	ANN	Redruth
1859	SKEWES	ANN	Redruth / different entries
1859	SKEWS	MARIA HICKS	Helston
1859	SKEWS	DIGORY	Liskeard
1859	SKEWS	JOHN	Penzance
1860	SKEWES	JOHN	Helston
1860	SKEWES	— Male —	Falmouth
1860	SKEWES	MARY	Redruth
1860	SKEWES	JULIA	Helston
1860	SKEWES	WILLIAM	Bideford
1860	SKEWES	WILLIAM JAMES	Helston
1860	SKEWIS	MARY ANN	Redruth
1860	SKEWS	ELIZABETH	Abergavenny
1860	SKEWS	ELIZABETH	Bodmin
1860	SKEWS	AGNES	Truro
1861	SKEWES	EDWARD	Helston
1861	SKEWES	CORDELGER	Bideford
1861	SKEWES	ANNE	Redruth
1861	SKEWES	MARY	Truro
1861	SKEWES	SUSAN JANE	Helston
1861	SKEWES	ANN	Redruth
1861	SKEWES	WILLIAM	Falmouth
1861	SKEWES	WILLIAM	Falmouth / different entries
1861	SKEWS	MARY	Penzance
1861	SKEWS	NANCY	Plymouth
1861	SKEWS	JOSEPH	Liskeard
1861	SKUES	GEORGE GILBERT	Marylebone
1862	SKEWES	ELIZABETH ELLEN	Redruth
1862	SKEWES	JOHN	Truro
1862	SKEWES	THOMAS JOHN	Truro
1862	SKEWES	RICHARD LORY	Helston
1862	SKEWES	ALEXANDER	Redruth
1862	SKEWES	ALFRED	Liskeard
1862	SKEWES	BLANCH	Redruth
1862	SKEWES	ELIZA	Falmouth
1862	SKEWES	WILLIAM	Redruth
1862	SKEWES	ALFRED	Launceston
1862	SKEWS	ANN	Greenwich
1862	SKEWS	JOHN	Liskeard
1862	SKEWS	CATHERINE	Greenwich
1863	SKEWES	MARY ANN	Tavistock
1863	SKEWES	DANIEL HODGE	Tavistock
1863	SKEWIS	JOHN THOMAS	Penzance
1863	SKEWS	MARY	Plymouth
1863	SKEWS	WILLIAM	Aylesford
1863	SKEWS	EMMA	Launceston
1864	SKEWES	JAMES	Redruth
1864	SKEWES	SOPHIA	Liskeard
1864	SKEWES	CHARLES	Redruth
1864	SKEWES	PETER	Truro
1864	SKEWIS	WILLIAM	Redruth
1864	SKEWS	ALFRED	Launceston
1864	SKEWS	MARTHA	Kensington
1864	SKEWS	ANN	N. Aylesford
1864	SKEWS	MARY	Truro
1864	SKUES	JOHN WALKER WILLIAMS	St. James
1864	SKUES	ELIZABETH ANN	St. James
1864	SKUES	JAMES	Redruth
1864	SKUES	JOANNA	St. Austell
1864	SKUES	ROSINA	Bath
1864	SKUES	— Female —	Strand
1865	SKEWES	JULIA	Redruth
1865	SKEWES	ADELAIDE	Truro
1865	SKEWES	AVIS	Bodmin
1865	SKEWES	CHARLES	Helston
1865	SKEWES	ELLEN LOUISA	Redruth
1865	SKEWES	SUSAN	Falmouth
1865	SKEWES	CHRISTIAN	Falmouth
1865	SKEWS	PETER	Truro
1865	SKEWS	MARY	Redruth
1865	SKUES	CHARLES PICKARD	Halifax

Monumental inscription on grave of Ann Skewes of Gwennap who died 1859.

As from the year 1866 the age of the deceased was included in the Somerset House Register and for easy reference the writer has calculated the actual year of birth, whilst double checking with the birth entries.

1866	SKEWES	ELIZABETH A.	37	1829	Truro
1866	SKEWES	ELIZABETH J.	24	1842	Redruth
1866	SKEWES	MARY TREZIZE	0	1866	Helston
1866	SKEWES	FREDERICK AUGUSTUS	2	1864	Helston
1866	SKEWES	JAMES	14	1852	Redruth
1866	SKEWES	SIMONETTA	67	1799	Redruth
1866	SKEWES	— Female —	0	1866	Wareham
1866	SKEWES	EDWARD	70	1796	Helston
1866	SKEWIS	HENRY	47	1819	Helston
1866	SKEWS	THOMAS	0	1866	Launceston
1866	SKEWS	WILLIAM J.	0	1866	Farnham
1866	SKEWS	SELINA G.	24	1842	Tavistock
1867	SKEWES	MARY	46	1821	Falmouth
1867	SKEWES	ROSETTA	33	1834	Kensington
1867	SKEWES	RICHARD	43	1824	Wareham
1867	SKEWESS	ANN	61	1806	Truro
1867	SKEWS	PETER	64	1803	Truro
1867	SKEWS	ANNIE	6	1861	Redruth
1867	SKEWS	PETER	1	1866	Liskeard
1867	SKEWS	MARY	68	1799	Truro
1867	SKEWS	RICHARD	84	1783	Truro
1867	SKEWS	WILLIAM	34	1833	Westminster
1868	SKEWES	MARY	73	1795	Truro
1868	SKEWES	REBECCA	67	1801	Redruth
1868	SKEWES	EMMA	0	1868	Newton Abbot
1868	SKEWES	ALICE	77	1791	Helston
1868	SKEWES	LAVINIA	60	1808	Truro
1868	SKEWES	THOMAS	69	1799	Truro
1868	SKEWES	EDWARD HENRY	32	1836	Helston
1868	SKEWES	MARY	79	1789	Newton Abbot
1868	SKEWIS	DIGORY	43	1825	Penzance
1868	SKEWS	HARRIET	1	1867	Liskeard
1868	SKEWS	LUCRETIA	70	1798	St. Austell
1868	SKEWS	MARY	0	1868	Launceston
1869	SKEWES	CAROLINE	43	1826	Redruth
1869	SKEWES	THOMAS	62	1807	Helston
1869	SKEWES	EDWARD ALBERT	1	1867	Redruth
1869	SKEWES	ELIZABETH ANN	18	1851	Truro
1869	SKEWES	EDWARD ERNEST	1	1868	Falmouth
1869	SKEWES	ALFRED JOHN	0	1869	Redruth
1869	SKEWES	HENRY	66	1803	Redruth
1869	SKEWES	WILLIAM HENRY	18	1851	Falmouth
1869	SKEWS	JOHN	70	1799	Plymouth
1869	SKEWS	ANN	74	1795	Plymouth
1869	SKUES	MARY BENNETT	48	1821	Westbury
1870	SKEWES	WILLIAM JOHN	0	1869	Helston
1870	SKEWES	EDWARD	51	1819	Falmouth
1870	SKEWES	ELIZABETH MARY	21	1849	Helston
1870	SKEWES	ALMA	13	1857	Falmouth
1870	SKEWES	ANN	72	1798	Falmouth
1870	SKUES	JAMES	73	1797	Medway
1871	SKEWES	BLANCHE	83	1788	Helston
1871	SKEWES	GRACE	60	1811	Falmouth

1871	SKEWES	JOHN	0	1870	Redruth
1871	SKEWES	THOMAS	77	1794	Falmouth
1871	SKEWES	JAMES	78	1793	Redruth
1871	SKEWS	DAVID	0	1871	Launceston
1871	SKEWS	HENRY	1	1870	Launceston
1871	SKEWS	MARY ANNE E.	0	1870	Portsea
1871	SKUES	CHARLES WILLIAM	2	1868	Westminster
1871	SKUES	ALICE	0	1871	Bath
1872	SKEWES	PHILIP	75	1797	St. Austell
1872	SKEWES	MARY ELLEN	0	1872	Redruth
1872	SKEWS	THOMAS	0	1872	St. Austell
1872	SKEWS	HENRY	0	1872	Liskeard
1872	SKUES	GEORGE	74	1798	Islington
1873	SKEWES	ANTHONY	63	1810	Helston
1873	SKEWES	HARRIET JANE	1	1872	Helston
1873	SKEWES	RICHARD	54	1819	Truro
1873	SKEWES	ROSA MARIA	0	1872	Truro
1873	SKEWES	SAMUEL JOHN	0	1873	Liskeard
1873	SKEWS	MATTHEW	8	1865	Guisbro'
1873	SKUES	EMILY CONSTANCE	2	1871	Westminster
1874	SKEWES	ANN	73	1801	Helston
1874	SKEWES	ELIZABETH	75	1799	St. Austell
1874	SKEWES	PRISCILLA	43	1831	Redruth
1874	SKEWES	JAMES	13	1861	Redruth
1874	SKEWES	FLORENCE ROSALIE	6	1868	Tavistock
1874	SKEWIS	ELIZABETH	37	1837	Redruth
1874	SKEWS	MARY	0	1874	Redruth
1875	SKEWES	FREDERICK	0	1874	Truro
1875	SKEWES	JAMES	85	1790	Redruth
1875	SKEWES	THOMAS	83	1792	Truro
1875	SKEWES	JECOLIAH	35	1840	Redruth
1875	SKEWES	JAMES	73	1802	St. Austell
1875	SKEWIS	ELIZABETH	42	1833	Newton Abbot
1875	SKEWIS	EMMA	0	1875	Newton Abbot
1875	SKEWIS	ROBERT MORGAN	0	1875	**Bedwellty**
1875	SKEWS	ELIZABETH ANN	0	1875	Houghton
1875	SKEWS	WILLIAM HENRY	17	1858	Plymouth
1875	SKEWS	FREDERICK	5	1870	Truro
1876	SKEWES	WILLIAM ERNEST	1	1874	Helston
1876	SKEWES	EDWARD	64	1810	Helston
1876	SKEWES	SYDNEY JAMES	0	1875	Helston
1876	SKEWS	EMILY	0	1876	St. Austell
1876	SKEWS	SUSAN	55	1821	Truro
1876	SKUES	WILLIAM	64	1812	Lambeth
1877	SKEWES	CLARA CAROLINE	1	1876	Redruth
1877	SKEWES	JAMES	27	1850	Redruth
1877	SKEWES	JOHN	48	1829	Helston
1877	SKEWES	ELIZABETH	66	1811	Redruth
1877	SKEWES	RICHARD	56	1821	Penzance
1877	SKEWES	WILLIAM	68	1809	Helston
1877	SKEWES	MARY	66	1811	Redruth
1877	SKEWES	SARAH	82	1795	Helston
1877	SKEWS	JAMES	54	1823	Truro
1877	SKEWS	FREDERICK	0	1877	Dartford
1877	SKUES	ALEXANDER JAMES	0	1876	Westminster

1878	SKEWES	EDWARD	64	1814	Helston
1878	SKEWES	JOSIAH	58	1820	Falmouth
1878	SKEWES	HEDLEY JAMES	0	1878	Penzance
1878	SKEWES	JANE	88	1790	Redruth
1878	SKEWES	RICHARD CHARLES	0	1878	Redruth
1878	SKEWIS	JOHN	0	1878	**Bedwellty**
1878	SKUES	CHARLES JOHN	35	1843	Holborn
1879	SKEWES	ANNA MARIA M.	50	1829	Wareham
1879	SKEWES	ELIZABETH	65	1814	Helston
1879	SKEWES	JAMES	66	1813	Redruth
1879	SKEWES	MARY FANNY SOPHIA	26	1853	Wareham
1879	SKEWS	JOSEPH JORDAN	52	1827	Liskeard
1879	SKUES	EDITH	0	1879	Thetford
1880	SKEWES	JOHN	8	1871	Redruth
1880	SKEWES	ELEANOR	65	1815	Helston
1880	SKEWES	ETHEL WOODMAN	0	1880	East Stonehouse
1880	SKEWES	MARY ANN	31	1849	Helston
1880	SKEWS	SUSAN	24	1856	Helston
1880	SKEWS	ELIZABETH JANE	0	1880	Newton Abbot
1880	SKEWS	EMILY LOUISA	0	1879	N. Aylesford
1880	SKUES	JOHN WILLIAM	2	1878	Lambeth
1881	SKEWES	JANE	53	1828	Tavistock
1881	SKEWES	CLARA CAROLINE	0	1880	Penzance
1881	SKEWES	HENRY	69	1812	Redruth
1881	SKEWS	JOHN	58	1823	Launceston
1881	SKUES	WILLIAM GEORGE	0	1880	Eton
1881	SKUES	— Female —	0	1881	Bath
1881	SKUES	MARY GIBBS	85	1796	Brentford
1882	SKEWES	ELIZABETH	74	1808	Helston
1882	SKEWES	JESSIE	0	1882	Truro
1882	SKEWES	LAURA	2	1880	Truro
1882	SKEWES	LILY	3	1879	Truro
1882	SKUES	MARGARET	46	1836	Plymouth
1883	SKEWES	PHILIPPA	78	1805	Helston
1883	SKEWES	RICHARD CHARLES	0	1883	Redruth
1883	SKEWES	WILLIAM	0	1883	Salford
1883	SKEWIS	EDWIN	0	1883	Newton Abbot
1883	SKEWIS	THOMAS	70	1813	W. Derby
1883	SKEWS	EDWIN	1	1882	Redruth
1883	SKUES	ELIZA	0	1883	Whitechapel
1883	SKUES	ELIZA	28	1855	Whitechapel
1883	SKUES	EDITH MARY	1	1882	Eton
1884	SKEWES	JOHN	80	1804	Redruth
1884	SKEWES	MYRA	0	1883	Redruth
1884	SKEWES	MARGARET	67	1817	Penzance
1884	SKEWES	MARY ELLEN	20	1864	Redruth
1884	SKEWIS	WILLIAM HENRY	0	1884	Newton Abbot
1884	SKEWS	HARRIET	0	1883	Totnes
1884	SKEWS	LILIAN	11	1873	Highworth
1884	SKEWS	CLARA	1	1883	Easington
1884	SKUES	ALBERT VICTOR	0	1884	Westminster
1885	SKEWES	EMMA	1	1884	Penzance
1885	SKEWES	FREDERICK	0	1885	Salford
1885	SKEWES	RICHARD	25	1860	Helston
1885	SKEWES	— Female —	0	1885	Helston

1885	SKEWES	ESTHER	10	1875	Redruth
1885	SKEWES	JANE MITCHELL	0	1885	Helston
1885	SKEWS	ELIZABETH ANN	33	1852	Redruth
1885	SKUES	WINIFRED VIOLET M.	1	1884	Westminster
1886	SKEWES	JAMES	72	1814	Penzance
1886	SKEWES	JANE	80	1806	Helston
1886	SKEWES	WILLIAM	0	1885	Helston
1886	SKEWES	DORCAS	0	1886	Penzance
1886	SKEWES	ELLA GWENDOLINE	0	1885	Helston
1886	SKEWES	JOHN	74	1812	Helston
1886	SKEWES	MABEL	0	1886	Redruth
1886	SKEWES	WILLIAM	1	1885	Penzance
1886	SKEWES	WILLIAM HENRY	0	1885	Helston
1886	SKEWES	KATIE BEATRICE	1	1885	Truro
1886	SKEWES	WILLIAM JAMES	0	1885	Redruth
1886	SKEWES	WILLIAM HENRY	80	1806	Helston
1886	SKEWES	WILLIAM HENRY	1	1885	Redruth
1886	SKEWS	WILLIAM	69	1817	Redruth
1886	SKEWS	ELIZABETH	0	1886	Bethnal Green
1886	SKEWS	— Male —	0	1886	Redruth
1887	SKEWES	ANN	77	1810	Truro
1887	SKEWES	CHRISTIAN	73	1814	Helston
1887	SKEWES	THOMAS EDGAR	0	1886	Truro
1887	SKEWES	MARY ANN	70	1817	Truro
1887	SKEWES	MARGARET ANN	53	1834	Penzance
1887	SKEWES	SUSAN	64	1823	Redruth
1887	SKEWES-COX	MARGARET	0	1887	Richmond
1887	SKEWIS	ELIZABETH	67	1820	Williton
1887	SKEWIS	SAMUEL	65	1822	Newton Abbot
1887	SKEWS	LILIAN MARGARET	0	1887	Bethnal Green
1887	SKUES	WILLIAM	45	1842	Lambeth
1888	SKEWES	HARRIET	65	1823	Helston
1888	SKEWES	WILLIAM HENRY H.	1	1887	Redruth
1888	SKEWES	ANNIE	81	1807	Redruth
1888	SKEWS	EDWARD	1	1887	Easington
1888	SKEWS	ALICE GERTRUDE	1	1887	Preston
1888	SKUES	GEORGE	1	1887	Halifax
1888	SKUES	MARGARET CAROLINE M.	27	1861	Camberwell
1889	SKEWES	WILLIAM	72	1816	Helston
1889	SKEWES	BEATRICE ANNIE	0	1889	Edmonton
1889	SKEWES	CATHERINE	34	1854	Truro
1889	SKEWES	THOMAS	60	1829	Plymouth
1889	SKEWES	JANE	90	1799	Truro
1889	SKEWES	WILLIAM	54	1834	Falmouth
1889	SKEWIS	WILLIAM HENRY	0	1889	Hendon
1889	SKEWIS	HENRY	69	1820	Williton
1889	SKUES	EDGAR CLAUDIUS	0	1888	Edmonton
1890	SKEWES	THEODORA	0	1890	Helston
1890	SKEWES	JOHN	0	1889	Penzance
1890	SKEWES	LOVEDAY	81	1809	Helston
1890	SKEWES	MARIA	53	1837	Liverpool
1890	SKEWES	WILLIAM WHITE	17	1872	Redruth
1890	SKEWES	JOHN	75	1815	Redruth
1890	SKEWIS	GRACE	64	1826	Ulverston
1890	SKEWS	EDITH JANE	0	1890	Easington
1890	SKEWS	ROSINA	1	1889	Easington
1890	SKEWS	WILLIAM JOHN	0	1890	Easington
1890	SKUES	MARGARET	54	1836	Christchurch
1890	SKUES	WILLIAM	24	1866	Halifax

1891	SKEWES	JAMES ARTHUR	0	1890	Redruth
1891	SKEWES	WILLIAM	30	1861	Redruth
1891	SKEWES	MARTHA	74	1817	Helston
1892	SKEWES	ELIZABETH	62	1830	Salford
1892	SKEWES	CHARLES	0	1892	Redruth
1892	SKEWES	WILLIAM JAMES G.	55	1837	Plymouth
1892	SKEWES	GRACE	83	1809	Helston
1892	SKEWS	ANN JANE	65	1827	Plymouth
1892	SKEWS	CLARENCE	0	1891	Liskeard
1892	SKEWS	REBECCA	33	1859	Easington
1892	SKEWS	ANNIE	0	1892	Liskeard
1892	SKUES	WILLIAM MACKENZIE	64	1828	Camberwell
1893	SKEWES	EDWARD	25	1868	Helston
1893	SKEWES	ELEANOR HENDY	66	1827	Helston
1893	SKEWES	ELIZA ELLEN	2	1891	Redruth
1893	SKEWES	EDWARD	0	1893	Redruth
1893	SKEWES	HAROLD COURTIS	0	1893	Windsor
1893	SKEWES	NORMAN	0	1893	Redruth
1893	SKEWES	EDWARD FREDERICK	11	1882	Redruth
1893	SKEWES	HESTHER ANN	46	1846	Falmouth
1893	SKEWIS	WILLIAM	71	1822	Tavistock
1893	SKEWIS	SUSAN	68	1825	Newton Abbot
1893	SKUES	GEORGE CHARLES	25	1868	Kensington
1894	SKEWES	JOSIAH	69	1825	Helston
1894	SKEWES	THOMAS	59	1835	St. Olave
1894	SKEWES	JANE	64	1830	Truro
1894	SKEWS	THOMAS GEORGE A.	1	1893	Bethnal Green
1894	SKEWS	LUCY ELIZABETH	18	1876	Shoreditch
1894	SKEWS	ROBERT HENRY	70	1824	Birmingham
1894	SKEWS	ALBERT WILLIAM	24	1869	Dartford
1894	SKEWS	FLORENCE BEATRICE	0	1894	Manchester
1895	SKEWES	CHARLES	5	1889	Salford
1895	SKEWES	ELIZABETH	78	1817	Helston
1895	SKEWES	FANNY	68	1827	Falmouth

Death certificate of George Henry Skues, 1897

CERTIFIED COPY OF AN ENTRY OF DEATH

Given at the **GENERAL REGISTER OFFICE,**
SOMERSET HOUSE, LONDON.

The statutory fee for this certificate is 3s. 9d.
Where a search is necessary to find the entry,
a search fee is payable in addition.

Application Number ....384793........

	REGISTRATION DISTRICT		PADDINGTON					
1897. DEATH in the Sub-district of	Saint John		in the	County of London				
Columns :—	(1)	(2)	(3)	(4)	(5)	(6)	(7)	(8)	(9)
No.	When and where died	Name and surname	Sex	Age	Occupation	Cause of death	Signature, description, and residence of informant	When registered	Signature of registrar
318	Twentythird April 1897 14 Sale Street	George Henry Skues	Male	30 years	Dairyman	Influenza 5 days Double Pneumonia 4 days Certified by H.J. Capon M.D.	Thomas Sebright Father in law present at the death 14 Sale Street	Twentysixth April 1897	M.B. Cranstone Registrar

CERTIFIED to be a true copy of an entry in the certified copy of a Register of Deaths in the District above mentioned.

Given at the GENERAL REGISTER OFFICE, SOMERSET HOUSE, LONDON, under the Seal of the said Office, the   20th   day of   August   19 64

DA 463711

1895	SKEWES	WILLIAM	1	1894	Redruth
1895	SKEWES	JOHN	77	1818	Helston
1895	SKEWES	THOMAS	39	1856	Preston
1895	SKEWS	BETSY	53	1842	Redruth
1895	SKEWS	THOMAS PROWSE S.	0	1894	Preston
1895	SKEWSE	ANNIE	19	1876	Totnes
1895	SKUES	FREDERICK GORDON	35	1860	Hartlepool
1896	SKEWES	ANN BUCKLAND	85	1811	Truro
1896	SKEWES	GRACE	89	1808	Truro
1896	SKEWES	ANNA	82	1814	Redruth
1896	SKEWS	FANNY	37	1859	Bristol
1896	SKEWS	EMILY ANNIE	1	1895	St. Olave
1896	SKEWS	WILLIAM	58	1838	Strood
1896	SKUES	JOHN PENROSE	81	1815	Redruth
1897	SKEWES	EDWARD JAMES	7	1890	Redruth
1897	SKEWIS	JOHN WOODLEY W.	24	1874	Newton Abbot
1897	SKEWS	LIZZIE	0	1897	Plymouth
1897	SKEWS	ELIZABETH	64	1833	Liskeard
1897	SKEWS	MARY	0	1897	Bethnal Green
1897	SKEWS	MARY ANN	77	1820	Fulham
1897	SKEWS	TOM	19	1878	Highworth
1897	SKUES	GEORGE HENRY	30	1867	Paddington
1897	SKUES	HANNAH	96	1801	Wheatenhurst
1898	SKEWES	JOSEPH HENRY	61	1837	W. Derby
1898	SKEWES	MATTHEW	55	1843	Truro
1898	SKEWES	EMILY	54	1844	Redruth
1898	SKEWES	FREDERICK CECIL	0	1898	Helston
1898	SKEWES	DORIS MAY	0	1898	Redruth
1898	SKEWES	ANN	49	1849	Redruth
1898	SKUES	FREDERICK HAROLD	0	1898	Shoreditch
1899	SKEWES	ADA	0	1899	Redruth
1899	SKEWES	EDWARD	35	1864	Chorlton
1899	SKEWES	JOHN BEARE	68	1831	Truro
1899	SKEWES	FRENETTA	31	1868	Penzance
1899	SKEWES	JAMES	84	1815	Falmouth
1899	SKEWES	BARRINGTON	12	1887	Helston
1899	SKEWES	HARRIET	80	1819	Truro
1899	SKEWS	GEORGE THOMAS	0	1899	St. Olave
1899	SKEWS	SAMUEL JOHN	0	1899	Devonport
1899	SKUES	SIDNEY ST. JOHN	9	1890	Edmonton
1899	SKUES	EDWARD FRANCIS	41	1858	Pancras
1900	SKEWES	EDITH	1	1898	Redruth
1900	SKEWES	SUSAN	55	1845	Truro
1900	SKEWES	ELIZABETH JANE	55	1845	Brentford
1900	SKEWS	EMILY GERTRUDE	11	1889	Preston
1900	SKEWS	ELIZABETH	58	1842	Fulham
1900	SKEWS	ELIZABETH GRACE	0	1900	Devonport
1900	SKEWS	ISABELLA	3	1897	Devonport
1900	SKUES	ELIZABETH	75	1825	Bethnal Green
1900	SKUES	FLORENCE AUGUSTA	14	1886	Eton
1900	SKUES	CLAUDE WILLIAM	1	1899	Hackney
1901	SKEWES	CATHERINE	0	1901	Redruth
1901	SKEWES	LOUISA JANE	63	1838	Lambeth
1901	SKEWES	AMELIA	33	1868	Redruth
1901	SKEWES	GEORGINA FRANCES	24	1877	Holyhead
1901	SKEWIS	JANE	19	1881	Totnes
1901	SKEWIS	WILLIAM HENRY	24	1877	Totnes
1901	SKEWS	JOHN	84	1817	Fulham
1902	SKEWES	EDWARD JOHN R.	0	1902	Redruth
1902	SKEWES	ELIZABETH JOANNA	0	1902	Redruth
1902	SKEWES	WILLIAM	37	1864	Redruth
1902	SKEWES	FANNY	75	1827	Penzance

1902	SKEWES	ELIZA JANE	58	1844	Redruth
1902	SKEWES	HENRY JOHN	30	1872	Pancras
1902	SKEWES	SUSAN	52	1850	Helston
1902	SKEWS	ALFRED	39	1863	St. Olave
1902	SKEWS	ETHEL	13	1889	Plymouth
1902	SKEWS	FLORENCE JANE	0	1902	Devonport
1902	SKEWS	CHARLOTTE	82	1820	Chelsea
1903	SKEWES	THOMAS LEAN	75	1828	Bideford
1903	SKEWES	CAROLINE	78	1825	Penzance
1903	SKEWES	SAMUEL DAW	70	1833	Bristol
1903	SKEWES	JANE	76	1827	Redruth
1903	SKEWES	JOHN JAMES	60	1843	Brentford
1903	SKEWIS	FEARNLEY JOHN	1	1902	Totnes
1903	SKUES	ELIZABETH	74	1829	Redruth
1903	SKUES	MARY ELIZABETH	74	1829	Lewisham
1903	SKUES	GEORGINA MARY	63	1840	Brentford
1904	SKEWES	HENRY ERNEST	0	1903	Falmouth
1904	SKEWES	JAMES	62	1842	Battle
1904	SKEWES	JACK PATTISON	0	1904	Redruth
1904	SKEWES	SAMUEL JOHN	1	1903	Redruth
1904	SKEWES	THOMAS HENRY	48	1856	Helston
1904	SKEWES	CHARLES	24	1880	Redruth
1904	SKEWS	LUCY CAROLINE	58	1846	Bethnal Green
1904	SKEWS	MARY ANN	73	1831	Redruth
1904	SKEWS	EMMA	46	1858	Sedgefield
1904	SKEWS	WILLIAM	34	1869	St. Austell
1904	SKUES	EVA	29	1875	St. Olave
1905	SKEWES	ARTHUR ERNEST	15	1890	Helston
1905	SKEWES	FREDERICK	0	1904	Redruth
1905	SKEWES	ELIZA	51	1854	Devonport
1905	SKEWES	ELIZABETH	92	1813	Swansea
1905	SKEWS	ELIZABETH JANE	0	1904	St. Austell
1905	SKEWS	GEORGE ALFRED	4	1901	Bethnal Green
1906	SKEWES	EDWARD	1	1904	Salford
1906	SKEWES	RICHARD CHARLES	0	1906	Redruth
1906	SKEWS	HERBERT JAMES S.	0	1905	Bethnal Green
1906	SKUES	LILY MARIE	3	1903	Hackney
1906	SKUES	DOROTHY MARGARET	0	1906	Holborn
1907	SKEWES	JOHN	56	1851	Truro
1907	SKEWES	ALICE	34	1873	Salford
1907	SKEWES	FRANCES	82	1824	Falmouth
1907	SKEWES	AMELIA	80	1827	Helston
1907	SKEWES	NORMAN	3	1904	Redruth
1907	SKEWES	RICHARD	75	1833	Truro
1907	SKEWS	JANE GRACE	66	1841	Redruth
1907	SKEWS	GEORGE	38	1869	Easington
1907	SKUES	HARRIET	69	1838	Lambeth
1908	SKEWES	MARY	53	1855	Tavistock
1908	SKEWES	JAMES FEARGUS	66	1842	Truro
1908	SKEWES	MARY JANE	73	1835	Truro
1908	SKEWES	JOHN	70	1838	Redruth
1908	SKEWES	JAMES	62	1846	Penzance
1908	SKEWS	MARTHA	33	1875	Hackney
1908	SKEWS	VIOLET ALICE	0	1908	Bethnal Green
1908	SKEWS	HARRIET	60	1848	Gravesend
1908	SKUES	LEWIS	68	1840	Redruth
1908	SKUES	ELLEN	72	1836	Islington
1908	SKUES	ISABELLA	84	1824	St. Giles
1908	SKUES	THOMAS	55	1853	Tonbridge
1909	SKEWES	CAROLINE	79	1830	Truro
1909	SKEWES	EDWARD	70	1839	Redruth
1909	SKEWIS	JOHN	2	1907	Totnes

1909	SKEWIS	EDWIN	56	1853	Tonbridge
1909	SKEWIS	PEGGY	86	1823	Tavistock
1909	SKEWS	CHARLES	0	1908	Whitechapel
1909	SKEWS	WILLIAM GEORGE	16	1893	Camberwell
1909	SKUES	SARAH	73	1836	Medway
1909	SKUES	MARY SOPHIA	66	1843	Edmonton
1909	SKUES	SAMUEL WILLIAM	4	1905	Chippenham
1910	SKEWES	ELIZABETH	61	1849	Helston
1910	SKEWES	NELLIE	0	1910	Salford
1910	SKEWES	JULIA	85	1825	Helston
1910	SKEWIS	VIDA	3	1908	Totnes
1910	SKEWIS	ETTIE	1	1909	Totnes
1910	SKEWIS	ANNIE E.	59	1851	Rhayader
1910	SKUES	FREDERICK MACKENZIE	76	1833	Wandsworth
1910	SKUES	CHARLES	66	1843	Grimsby
1911	SKEWES	EDWARD J.	47	1864	Redruth
1911	SKEWES	CHARLES	73	1838	Salford
1911	SKEWES	ELIZABETH M.	22	1889	Redruth
1911	SKEWES	LOUISA	65	1846	Helston
1911	SKEWES	WILLIAM	77	1834	Redruth
1911	SKEWS	THOMAS	43	1867	Barnsley
1911	SKEWS	ERNEST	0	1911	Bethnal Green
1911	SKUES	LUCY	74	1837	Halifax
1912	SKEWES-COX	THOMAS	63	1849	Richmond S.
1912	SKEWIS	MARY LANGMEAD	73	1839	Totnes
1912	SKEWS	EDWIN	67	1845	Fulham
1912	SKEWS	PETER	**84**	**1828**	Liskeard
1912	SKEWS	EDWARD	63	1849	Dartford
1913	SKEWES	ANNIE	56	1857	Salford
1913	SKEWES	BENJAMIN HELLINGS	91	**1822**	Truro
1913	SKEWES	JOHN	62	1851	Yarmouth
1913	SKEWES	ALBERT J.	0	1913	Redruth
1913	SKEWES	MARY	75	1838	Redruth
1913	SKEWIS	DOROTHY M.	1	1912	Totnes
1913	SKEWS	JANE	74	1839	St. Columb
1913	SKEWS	JOHN WILLIAM HENRY	58	1854	Plymouth
1914	SKEWES	MARY	82	1832	Truro
1914	SKEWES	CAROLINE LOUISE	4	1910	Truro
1914	SKEWES	EMILY ANN	64	1850	Helston
1914	SKEWS	WILLIAM	74	1840	St. Columb
1914	SKEWS	MARGARET E.M.	2	1912	St. Geo East
1914	SKUES	JAMES	48	1866	Lambeth
1914	SKUES	SARAH A.M.	31	1883	Lewisham
1914	SKUES	FLORENCE LILIAN	8	1906	Redruth
1914	SKUES	DORIS A.	0	1914	Lewisham
1915	SKEWES	— Male —	0	1915	Redruth
1915	SKEWES	EDWARD	63	1851	Huddersfield
1915	SKEWES	— Female —	0	1915	Dartford } different
1915	SKEWES	— Female —	0	1915	Dartford } entries
1915	SKEWS	ELIZA	52	1863	Chorlton
1915	SKEWS	JAMES	63	1851	Dartford
1915	SKEWS	ALFRED J.	0	1915	Bethnal Green
1915	SKEWS	IRENE	0	1915	Houghton
1915	SKEWS	SARAH E.	77	1838	Portsmouth
1915	SKUES	SARAH A.	82	1833	Grimsby
1915	SKUES	ATLANTA E.	43	1872	Shoreditch
1915	SKUES	ELIZA E.	68	1847	Amersham
1915	SKUES	HARRY	0	1915	Shoreditch
1916	SKEWES	EDITH	26	1889	Tavistock
1916	SKEWES	CATHERINE M.	75	1841	Falmouth
1916	SKEWES	ELIZABETH	78	1838	Bolton
1916	SKEWES	ANNIE	63	1853	St. Austell

1916	SKEWIS	ALFRED W. St. E.	0	1916	Haverfordwest
1916	SKEWS	NATHANIEL EDWARD R.	42	1874	Epsom
1916	SKUES	RICHARD	83	1833	Halifax
1917	SKEWES	BLANCH	55	1862	Truro
1917	SKEWES	JAMES	60	1857	Plympton
1917	SKEWS	MAUD	9	1907	Strood
1917	SKUES	JOHN	74	1843	Lambeth
1917	SKUES	JOSEPH	69	1848	Eton
1918	SKEWES	FREDERICK J.C.	1	1916	Truro
1918	SKEWS	GEORGE A.	72	1846	Bethnal Green
1918	SKEWS	MARY A.	38	1880	Strood
1918	SKUES	HERBERT W.	3	1915	Dartford
1919	SKEWES	ADA ELIZABETH	47	1872	Falmouth
1919	SKEWES	ELIZABETH	89	1830	Liskeard
1919	SKEWES	LEONARD	0	1919	Penzance
1919	SKEWES	GWENLLIAN E.	0	1919	Pontypridd
1919	SKEWES	MARY	68	1851	St. Columb
1919	SKEWS	AGNES	0	1919	Stepney
1919	SKEWS	JOHN	0	1919	Stepney
1920	SKEWES	ANNIE	76	1844	Penzance
1920	SKEWS	ALLEN E.	35	1885	Romford
1920	SKEWS	WILLIAM A.	0	1920	Hackney
1920	SKEWS	ARTHUR G.	8	1911	Strood
1920	SKEWS	DORIS	0	1920	Bethnal Green
1920	SKEWS	ELIZABETH	30	1890	West Ham
1920	SKEWS	HARRIET A.	59	1861	Liskeard
1921	SKEWES	EMILY J.	55	1866	Redruth
1921	SKEWES	WILLIAM	67	1854	Totnes
1921	SKEWES	ELIZABETH M.	32	1889	Penzance
1921	SKEWES	STEPHEN JAMES	41	1880	Redruth
1921	SKEWIS	HARRIET	68	1853	Totnes
1921	SKEWS	MATTHEW HENRY	70	1850	Redruth
1921	SKEWS	LILY	1	1920	Houghton
1921	SKUES	BERNARD E.	1	1919	Dartford
1922	SKEWES	CLARINDA	64	1858	Penzance
1922	SKEWES	ELIZABETH J.	82	1840	Redruth
1922	SKEWES	EMMA	75	1847	Plympton
1922	SKEWES	JOHN	71	1851	Helston
1922	SKEWES	MARGARET	25	1897	Pontypridd
1922	SKEWES	HENRY	74	1848	Redruth
1922	SKEWIS	MARY J.	58	1864	Penzance
1922	SKEWS	CHARLES	77	1845	Poplar
1922	SKEWS	MABEL	1	1921	Houghton
1923	SKEWES	THOMAS JAMES	59	1863	St. Columb
1923	SKEWS	JANE	74	1847	Dartford
1923	SKEWS	PERCY VICTOR	18	1904	Maidstone
1924	SKEWES	RICHARD	76	1848	Penzance
1924	SKEWS	MURIEL	3	1920	Houghton
1924	SKEWS	REGINALD ERNEST	21	1902	Devonport
1924	SKEWS	ELIZABETH A.	64	1860	Redruth
1924	SKUES	WINIFRED R.	59	1865	Willesden
1924	SKUES	GEORGE HENRY	82	1842	Edmonton
1925	SKEWES	MARY E.	83	1842	Brentford
1925	SKEWES	RICHARD	67	1858	Redruth
1825	SKEWES	THOMAS G.	4	1920	Pontypridd
1925	SKEWES	EDITH L.	47	1878	Redruth
1925	SKEWES	WILLIAM R.	32	1893	South Shields
1925	SKEWS	JOSEPH M.M.	2	1923	Liskeard
1925	SKEWS	LILIAN L.	0	1925	Bethnal Green
1925	SKEWS	ALICE D.	13	1912	Edmonton

1925	SKEWS	AMOS	60	1864	Devonport
1925	SKEWS	PETER	85	1840	St. Austell
1925	SKEWS	BERNARD	40	1885	Dartford
1925	SKUES	ELIZABETH	81	1844	Axminster
1925	SKUES	ELIZABETH	72	1853	Cuckfield
1926	SKEWES	AURELIA	71	1855	Truro
1926	SKEWES	EMMA STEPHENS	85	1842	Truro
1926	SKEWES	ARTHUR J.	0	1925	Bristol
1926	SKEWES	WILLIAM JAMES	76	1850	Helston
1926	SKEWES	ALICE ANN	89	1837	Helston
1926	SKEWES	HENRY	69	1857	Redruth
1926	SKEWS	EMMA	51	1875	Stepney
1926	SKEWS	NELLIE	26	1900	Barnsley
1926	SKEWS	NATHANIEL R.H.	24	1902	Weymouth
1926	SKUES	NOAH JAMES	49	1877	Greenwich
1927	SKEWS	WILLIAM JOHN	24	1903	St. Austell
1928	SKEWES	GWENDOLINE	43	1885	Exeter
1928	SKEWES	HANNIBAL	73	1854	Helston
1928	SKEWES	ELIZABETH	72	1856	St. Thomas
1928	SKEWES	SAMUEL	33	1895	Penzance
1928	SKEWES	ELIZA E.	78	1850	Redruth
1928	SKEWS	EDMUND	61	1867	Plymouth
1928	SKEWS	KATHLEEN	55	1873	Gravesend
1928	SKEWS	EMMA G.	71	1857	Bournemouth
1929	SKEWES	JANE	72	1857	Croydon
1929	SKEWS	RITA	0	1929	Barnsley
1929	SKEWS	JOHN	54	1874	Redruth
1929	SKEWS	PETER	23	1906	St. Austell
1929	SKEWS	MARY J.	79	1850	Redruth
1930	SKEWES	ADA	74	1856	Redruth
1930	SKEWES	RICHARD CHARLES	50	1880	Redruth
1930	SKEWES	JANIE	15	1915	Redruth
1930	SKEWES	ELIZABETH	0	1930	Pontypridd
1930	SKEWES	WILLIAM	77	1853	Helston
1930	SKEWES-COX	JESSIE	68	1862	Richmond
1930	SKEWS	COLIN	3	1926	Sheffield
1930	SKEWS	RICHARD	23	1908	St. Austell
1930	SKUES	PHILIP HENRY	63	1867	Lambeth
1931	SKEWES	FRANCES ANN	76	1855	Helston
1931	SKEWS	RAYMOND	0	1931	Barnsley
1932	SKEWES	AGNES	68	1864	Huddersfield
1932	SKEWES	WILLIAM	64	1868	Falmouth
1932	SKEWS	JOAN L.	1	1930	Romford
1932	SKEWS	MARY A.	66	1866	Houghton
1932	SKEWS	RICHARD NATHANIEL EDWARD	88	1844	Bethnal Green
1932	SKEWS	JOHN GREGORY	72	1860	Liskeard
1933	SKEWES	GLADYS MARY	38	1895	Redruth
1933	SKEWS	BRENDA	0	1933	Barnsley
1933	SKEWS	ELLEN	80	1853	Dartford
1933	SKUES	DEREK A.	0	1933	St. Olave
1934	SKEWS	ELIZABETH SARAH	76	1858	Plymouth
1934	SKEWS	GORDON	0	1934	Barnsley
1934	SKEWS	MATTHEW	76	1858	Houghton
1935	SKEWES	LIZZIE MARION	62	1873	St. Columb
1935	SKEWES	FREDERICK TRESIZE	78	1857	Helston
1935	SKEWIS	WILLIAM BAWDEN	81	1855	Truro
1835	SKEWS	AMELIA	79	1856	Houghton
1935	SKEWS	WILLIAM JOHN	73	1862	Houghton
1935	SKUES	JOHN GILBERT	71	1865	Edmonton

1936	SKEWES	LOUISA J.	69	1867	Redruth
1936	SKEWES	RICHARD HENRY	65	1871	Battersea
1936	SKEWES	JOHN COURTIS	72	1864	Crediton
1936	SKEWES	GEORGE ALLWORTH	80	1857	Penzance
1936	SKEWIS	EMILY	62	1874	Tonbridge
1936	SKEWS	ALBERT JOHN	55	1880	Dartford
1936	SKEWS	JOHN	72	1864	St. Austell
1936	SKEWS	SARAH	83	1853	Bethnal Green
1936	SKUES	DONALD	7	1929	Blackburn
1937	SKEWES	MINNIE	69	1868	Barnet
1937	SKEWES	SUSANNA	89	1848	Penzance
1937	SKEWES	WILLIAM	48	1889	Penzance
1937	SKEWS	EDWARD	64	1873	Dartford
1937	SKEWS	MARGARET M.	72	1865	Southwark
1938	SKEWES	EDITH	75	1863	Kerrier
1938	SKEWES	FREDERICK JOHN	66	1871	N. Aylesford
1938	SKEWES	THOMAS HENRY	82	1856	Penzance
1938	SKEWES	NELLIE	54	1884	Redruth
1938	SKEWS	SAMUEL GREGORY	68	1869	Liskeard
1938	SKUES	MAUD C.	59	1879	Honiton
1939	SKEWES	JAMES	62	1877	Redruth
1939	SKEWES	MARY ELLEN	83	1856	Rochford
1939	SKEWES	ALFRED JOHN	64	1875	**Bridgwater**
1939	SKEWES	GEORGE	79	1861	Salford
1939	SKEWES	HENRY	71	1868	Falmouth
1939	SKEWIS	HELEN THOMASINE	68	1871	Penzance
1939	SKUES	CHARLES PENROSE	92	1847	Amersham
1940	SKEWES	JAMES	21	1919	Bodmin
1940	SKEWES	JOHN HENRY	61	1877	Redruth
1940	SKEWES	HARRY OSWALD	74	1866	Penzance
1940	SKEWES	JOHN KEMPTHORNE	70	1870	Plymouth
1940	SKEWES	EMILY ANN	69	1871	Redruth
1940	SKEWIS	ELIZABETH	63	1877	Hull
1940	SKUES	HANNAH	66	1874	Colchester
1940	SKUES	FREDERICK WM. MACKENZIE	72	1867	Croydon
1940	SKUES	CLORINDA A.	16	1923	Southwark
1940	SKUES	MARGARET GEORGINA SARAH	76	1864	Exeter
1941	SKEWES	ANN	79	1862	Devon Central
1941	SKEWES	JOHN B.	84	1857	Exeter
1941	SKEWES	THIRZA	87	1854	Kerrier
1941	SKEWES	CHARLES	83	1857	Manchester
1941	SKEWES	WILLIAM B.	84	1857	Truro
1941	SKEWS	REGINALD E.	8	1932	Plymouth
1941	SKEWS	VIOLET V.	40	1901	Plymouth
1941	SKUES	JAMES FREDERICK	61	1879	Redruth
1942	SKEWES	EDWARD	92	1849	Falmouth
1942	SKEWES	HETTY C.	52	1889	Kerrier
1942	SKEWES	ROY	25	1916	Redruth
1942	SKEWS	DORIS	32	1909	Truro
1942	SKEWS	MARTIN	56	1886	Redruth
1942	SKEWS	EDITH	81	1861	Amounderness
1942	SKEWS	ELIZA	77	1865	Swindon
1943	SKEWES	MAUD ANNA	71	1872	Falmouth
1943	SKEWES	EVA	65	1878	Plymouth
1943	SKEWES	CHARLES	54	1889	Manchester
1943	SKEWES	LILIAN S.	0	1943	Hastings
1943	SKEWES	THOMAS WILLIAM	91	1852	Redruth
1943	SKEWS	WILLIAM	84	1859	Liskeard
1943	SKEWS	FREDERICK T.	17	1926	Liskeard
1943	SKEWS	WILLIAM THOMAS	66	1877	Bethnal Green
1944	SKEWES	WILLIAM FREDERICK	49	1894	Manchester

1944	SKEWS	ANNIE	75	1869	St. Germans
1944	SKEWS	HENRY JAMES	64	1880	Essex S.W.
1944	SKUES	MARY THERESA	83	1860	Tiverton
1945	SKEWES	CLARA	83	1861	Penzance
1945	SKEWES	GERTRUDE M.	65	1880	Surrey N.E.
1945	SKEWES	HOWARD	74	1871	Newton Abbot
1945	SKEWES	BEATRICE A.	54	1891	Kerrier
1945	SKEWS	EMILY S.	63	1882	Hendon
1945	SKUES	ERNEST	76	1868	Stockport
1945	SKUES	ADA	84	1861	Wandsworth
1945	SKUES	DORIS GAMBLE	56	1889	Surrey Mid E.
1945	SKUES	FLORENCE MARY	70	1875	Halifax
1945	SKUES	THOMAS EDWARD	76	1869	Pancras
1945	SKUES	VERA JOAN	21	1924	Chorley
1946	SKEWES	ANN	95	1851	Manchester
1946	SKEWES	MARY	85	1861	Falmouth
1946	SKEWES	MAUD MARY	70	1876	Truro
1946	SKEWS	ALBERT EDWARD	43	1903	Dartford
1946	SKEWS	JOHN HENRY	66	1880	Plymouth
1946	SKEWS	JAMES HENRY	53	1893	Birmingham
1946	SKUES	ADA	60	1886	Redruth
1946	SKUES	ELIZABETH	83	1863	Edmonton
1947	SKEWES	DOROTHY MARION	49	1898	Doncaster
1947	SKEWS	JOHN EDWIN	83	1863	Swindon
1947	SKUES	MARY ISABELLA MACKENZIE	87	1860	Surrey Mid E.
1947	SKUES	ALBERT EDWARD	54	1893	London C.
1947	SKUES	HENRY ERNEST	74	1873	Lambeth
1948	SKEWES	JOSIAH	83	1865	Hendon
1948	SKEWES	MARY S.	84	1864	Kerrier
1948	SKEWES	MAGGIE ISABELLA SIMPSON	62	1886	Sunderland
1948	SKEWS	GEORGE FRANCIS	43	1905	Edmonton
1948	SKEWS	ALICE	77	1871	Edmonton
1948	SKUES	ELIZABETH	87	1861	Redruth
1948	SKUES	RICHARD JAMES	85	1862	Halifax
1948	SKUES	EDWARD ALBERT	55	1893	Tonbridge
1949	SKEWES	ROSE	59	1890	Truro
1949	SKEWES	WILLIAM JOHN	58	1891	Redruth
1949	SKEWIS	FRANK	47	1902	Canterbury
1949	SKEWIS	LAVINIA	71	1878	Totnes
1949	SKEWS	PETER	75	1874	St. Austell
1949	SKUES	GEORGE EDWARD MACKENZIE	92	1856	Bromley
1949	SKUES	CLORINDA EMMA	78	1871	Wandsworth
1950	SKEWES	HARRY STANLEY	57	1893	Kerrier
1950	SKEWES	MARGARET H.	0	1950	Truro
1950	SKEWES	ANNIE	55	1895	Redruth
1950	SKEWES	MARY A.	76	1874	Salford
1950	SKEWS	ALFRED DAVID RICHARD	78	1871	Edmonton
1950	SKUES	CHRISTOPHER RAYMOND	0	1950	Bucklow
1950	SKUES	FRANCIS HENRY	40	1909	Dartford
1950	SKUES	HAROLD FREDERICK CLAUDE	68	1882	Pancras
1951	SKEWES	BEATRICE MARY	48	1903	Kerrier
1951	SKEWES	JOHN WESLEY	89	1862	Penzance
1951	SKEWES	ALBERT EDWARD	89	1863	Poole
1951	SKEWES	ALARINA I.	89	1862	Chepstow
1951	SKEWES	SUSAN JANE	63	1888	Kerrier
1951	SKEWS	VICTOR GEORGE	57	1894	Chatham
1951	SKEWS	ROBERT ALBERT	63	1887	Poplar
1951	SKUES	ELIZABETH	75	1876	Bromley
1951	SKUES	JANE EMILY	78	1873	Amersham
1951	SKUES	BESSIE ANNIE	76	1875	Amersham
1952	SKEWES	ELIZABETH	66	1886	Manchester

1952	SKEWES	LILIAN L.M.	60	1892	Penzance
1952	SKEWES	EDWARD	86	1866	Kerrier
1952	SKEWS	THOMAS	66	1886	Sheffield
1953	SKEWES	WILLIAM TREVENA	63	1890	Penzance
1953	SKEWES	GEORGE ERNEST	59	1894	N.E. Cheshire
1953	SKEWES	WILLIAM FREDERICK CHARLES	54	1899	Doncaster
1953	SKEWS	ERNEST J.	63	1889	Ilford
1954	SKEWES	JAMES HENRY OSWALD	59	1894	Redruth
1954	SKEWES	ELIZABETH J.	62	1892	Bodmin
1954	SKEWES	SAMUEL JOHN	61	1893	St. Germans
1954	SKEWES-COX	JULIAN H.L.	1	1953	St. Albans
1954	SKEWS	BERTHA	83	1871	St. Austell
1954	SKEWS	JOHN HENRY	63	1890	Plymouth
1954	SKUES	FRANCIS ALBERT	72	1882	Dartford
1955	SKEWS	WILLIAM JOHN	56	1898	Durham N.
1955	SKEWS	FREDERICK	70	1885	Durham N.
1955	SKEWS	MARIA	87	1868	Plymouth
1955	SKUES	FLORENCE M.	65	1890	Woolwich
1955	SKUES	ERNEST	32	1923	Truro
1956	SKEWES	KEVIN	0	1956	Redruth
1956	SKEWES	PAUL	0	1956	Redruth
1956	SKEWES	EDITH MARY	65	1891	Redruth
1956	SKEWES	WILLIAM HENRY	61	1894	Penzance
1956	SKEWS	MATTHEW HENRY	74	1882	Durham N.E.
1956	SKEWS	RICHARD ERNEST	81	1874	Redruth
1956	SKEWS	FRANCES	74	1882	Durham N.
1957	SKEWES	WILLIAM VERDAYNE	81	1876	Croydon
1957	SKEWES	ANN MARIA	77	1880	Bridgwater
1957	SKEWES	FLORENCE LUCY	77	1880	Exeter
1957	SKEWES	HARRY	59	1898	Halifax
1957	SKEWIS	LAURA	67	1890	Haverfordwest
1957	SKEWIS	WILLIAM RICHARD	84	1872	Newton Abbot
1957	SKUES	JOAN MACKENZIE	52	1904	Bromley
1958	SKEWES	FREDERICK	86	1872	Salford
1958	SKEWES	MATILDA	78	1880	Redruth
1958	SKEWES	FREDERICK C.	74	1884	Redruth
1958	SKEWES	HERBERT JOHN	73	1885	Redruth
1958	SKEWES	WALTER JAMES	69	1888	Redruth
1958	SKEWIS	SAMUEL	71	1887	Haverfordwest
1958	SKEWS	DAVID	0	1958	Plymouth
1958	SKUES	LILY	64	1894	Malvern
1958	SKUES	ANNIE FRANCES	82	1876	Exeter
1958	SKUES	CHARLES HENRY	81	1877	Maidenhead
1958	SKUES	WALTER EDWARD	85	1873	Hackney
1958	SKUSE	CHARLES AYRE MACKENZIE	82	1875	Whitchurch

(This last entry should have been listed in register as SKUES)

1959	SKEWES	ELIZA J.	77	1882	Redruth
1959	SKEWES	ALFRED JOHN	81	1877	Truro
1959	SKEWES	RICHARD HENRY	85	1873	Penzance
1959	SKEWS	ETHEL	74	1885	Durham E.
1959	SKEWS	GEORGE W. FRANCIS	86	1872	Leicester
1960	SKEWES	OLIVE MAY	57	1903	Falmouth
1960	SKEWES	ARTHUR DAW	87	1874	Truro
1960	SKEWES	JANIE	86	1874	Falmouth
1960	SKEWES	SARAH A.	68	1892	Manchester
1960	SKEWS	SARAH E.	76	1884	Bournemouth
1960	SKUES	ELEANOR	88	1872	Halifax
1960	SKUES	ROSEMARY M.	29	1931	Cheltenham
1961	SKEWES	WILLIAM JOHN	73	1888	Redruth
1961	SKEWES	CHARLOTTE	70	1891	St. Germans

1961	SKEWS	AMY EVA	68	1893	Plymouth
1961	SKEWS	GEORGE WEALE	59	1901	Stepney
1961	SKEWS	CAROLINE	89	1872	Kettering
1961	SKUES	CLARA	86	1875	N.E. Cheshire
1961	SKUES	MARGARET E.	77	1884	Wood Green
1961	SKUES	AUGUSTA	74	1888	Marylebone
1962	SKEWES	ANNIE MAUD	68	1894	Redruth
1962	SKEWES	ELIZABETH M.	82	1880	Penzance
1962	SKEWS	MAUD M.	81	1881	St. Austell
1962	SKEWS	ELSIE	36	1926	Wharfendale
1962	SKEWS	EDWIN ARTHUR	79	1884	Bournemouth
1962	SKUES	MINNIE MACKENZIE	91	1871	Whitchurch
1963	SKEWES	ETHEL J.	81	1882	Redruth
1963	SKEWES	MINNIE	94	1869	Redruth
1963	SKEWES	WILLIAM J.	71	1892	Redruth
1963	SKEWS	ALICE ELIZABETH	80	1883	Dartford
1963	SKEWS	ETHEL J.	73	1890	Croydon
1963	SKEWS	GERTRUDE ALBERTA	66	1896	St. Austell
1963	SKEWS	JOSEPH	61	1901	Barkston Ash
1963	SKEWS	MABEL COOPER	68	1895	Lewes
1964	SKEWES	WILLIAM HEDLEY	85	1879	Redruth
1964	SKEWS	ANNIE EDITH	79	1885	Amounderness
1964	SKEWS	BEATRICE	84	1880	Bodmin
1964	SKEWS	SUSAN	73	1891	Hackney
1964	SKUES	THOMAS GEORGE	69	1895	Willesdon
1965	SKEWES	BELLA CLARK	59	1905	Plympton
1965	SKEWES	ELIZABETH	82	1883	Croydon
1965	SKEWES	GEORGE	85	1880	Plymouth
1965	SKEWES	JAMES HENRY	92	1872	Truro
1965	SKEWES	LIONAL JAMES	67	1897	Redruth
1965	SKEWES	CHARLES	67	1897	Penzance
1965	SKEWES	ROSA M.	78	1887	Dover
1965	SKEWIS	LILIAN M.	56	1909	Totnes
1965	SKEWS	ELIZABETH E.G.	73	1892	Plymouth
1965	SKEWS	EVA MARY	84	1881	Bexley
1965	SKEWS	MINNIE	87	1879	Redruth
1965	SKUES	ELSIE K.	69	1896	Edmonton
1966	SKEWES	JAMES M.S.	84	1882	Wycombe
1966	SKEWES	JACK	15	1951	Kerrier
1966	SKEWES	RACHEL CARDWELL	77	1889	Christchurch
1966	SKEWS	HILDA	65	1901	Liskeard
1966	SKEWS	SARAH	90	1876	Penzance
1966	SKUES	REGINALD PENROSE	80	1886	Liskeard
1966	SKUES	EVA	77	1889	Truro
1966	SKUES	PHILIP ERNEST	68	1899	Sutton
1967	SKEWES	EDWARD MORLEY	47	1920	Redruth
1968	SKEWES	ERNEST JOHN	87	1881	Exeter
1968	SKEWES	HAROLD	76	1892	Manchester
1968	SKEWIS	IRENE	42	1926	Hull
1968	SKUES	MARGARET ELAINE	21	1947	Ormskirk
1968	SKUES	WALTER EDWARD	74	1894	Braintree
1968	SKUES	ADA J.	91	1877	Lambeth
1969	SKEWES	ANNIE	87	1882	Kerrier
1969	SKEWES	FREDERICK HENRY	78	1891	Exeter
1969	SKEWS	ALBERT EDWARD	75	1894	Newton Abbot
1969	SKEWS	ANNIE LOUISA	69	1900	Colchester
1969	SKEWS	RICHARD CHARLES	71	1898	Hounslow
1969	SKUES	JAMES FREDERICK	59	1909	Redruth

Note: As from 1970 Somerset House Records listed the exact birthdate in the register

1970	SKEWS	JAMES ARTHUR	85	Born 26/10/1885	Southend
1970	SKEWS	MARGARET	81	28/ 1/1889	Southend
1970	SKEWS	ALBERT EDWARD VICTOR	47	22/ 7/1923	Plymouth
1970	SKEWS	WILLIAM GEORGE A.	76	29/ 7/1894	Hackney
1970	SKEWS	WILLIAM DAVID	63	30/ 3/1907	Worthing
1970	SKEWS	EDWIN ARTHUR	51	20/11/1919	Shrewsbury
1970	SKUES	FLORENCE		(birthdate unknown)	St. Pancras
1970	SKUES	LESLIE JAMES	57	18/ 8/1913	Dartford
1970	SKUES	VINCENT	71	7/ 5/1899	Amounderness
1971	SKEWES	BESSIE SARAH	90	10/10/1881	Bodmin
1971	SKEWES	EMMA	78	10/ 2/1893	Redruth
1971	SKEWES	JOHN EDWARD	88	19/ 9/1886	Bournemouth
1971	SKEWES	CATHERINE	82	23/ 1/1889	Redruth
1971	SKEWES	IDA MARY	69	24/ 9/1902	Ealing
1971	SKEWES	GEORGE	78	23/ 8/1893	Penzance
1971	SKEWES	THOMAS HENRY JAMES	77	12/ 8/1894	Redruth
1971	SKEWIS	AGNES FORBES	77	27/ 7/1894	Kettering
1971	SKEWIS	SAMUEL LESLIE	51	9/ 3/1920	Chatham
1971	SKEWS	MINNIE	86	17/ 7/1884	Birmingham
1971	SKEWES-COX	THOMAS EDMUND	87	5/ 1/1884	Lothingland
1971	SKUES	ARTHUR LEONARD PETER	75	28/ 6/1896	Barrow-in-F.
1971	SKUES	MADGE IRENE	78	3/11/1893	Tonbridge
1971	SKUES	THOMAS HENRY J.	77	21/ 6/1894	Bridge
1972	SKEWES	VIOLET	69	14/ 7/1903	Kerrier
1972	SKEWES	RUTH	69	19/ 8/1903	Torbay
1972	SKEWES	ERNESTINE MARY	61	13/ 6/1911	Truro
1973	SKEWES	SYDNEY ARTHUR	72	12/ 2/1901	Truro
1973	SKEWS	MATTHEW JOHN	63	7/ 8/1910	St. Austell
1973	SKEWS	GEORGE	76	20/ 6/1897	Rother Valley
1973	SKEWS	WILLIAM HEDLEY	75	17/ 6/1898	St. Austell
1973	SKEWS	ESME ETHEL	69	23/ 9/1904	Spalding
1973	SKEWS	HARRY	73	10/ 1/1900	Plymouth
1973	SKUES	CARMELLA	71	16/ 6/1901	Surrey Mid E.
1973	SKUES	HELEN MARY	27	24/12/1946	Dover
1973	SKUES	RHODA SARAH	80	25/10/1893	Greenwich
1974	SKEWES	DOLORES ELIZABETH	52	28/ 7/1922	Camborne
1974	SKEWES	FANNY	80	16/ 6/1894	Manchester
1974	SKUES	DORIS EILEEN	61	8/ 3/1913	Poole
1974	SKUES	EDWIN THOMAS	63	13/12/1911	Cuckfield
1975	SKEWES	AVIS MAY	63	15/ 8/1912	Camborne
1975	SKEWES	HARRY	53	5/12/1922	Scilly
1975	SKEWES	JOHN	91	4/ 5/1884	Kerrier
1975	SKEWIS	EDITH ALICE	82	5/11/1893	Haverfordwest
1975	SKEWIS	ELSIE ALICE J.	81	30/10/1894	Newton Abbot
1975	SKEWS	CONSTANCE PATRICIA	52	15/ 6/1923	Truro
1975	SKEWS	DAVID GEORGE	76	3/ 3/1899	Barking
1975	SKUES	VICTOR CLAUDE	82	6/ 4/1893	Colchester
1975	SKUES	ANNIE MARIE	80	28/ 2/1895	Brentwood
1975	SKUES	KATHLEEN ELIZABETH N.	59	1/12/1916	Islington
1976	SKEWES	MARIA	97	8/ 8/1879	Penzance
1976	SKEWES	ADA JANE	94	4/ 2/1882	Camborne
1976	SKEWES	HENRY FREDERICK	78	4/ 1/1898	Lambeth
1976	SKEWES	LILIAN MAY	83	20/ 2/1893	Bodmin
1976	SKEWES	BERTRAM	74	29/ 4/1902	Truro
1976	SKEWES-COX	GILLIAN	48	5/11/1928	Newton Abbot
1976	SKEWS	FREDERICK CHARLES	79	About 1897	Plymouth
1976	SKEWS	MARJORIE ELIZth M.	56	27/ 3/1920	Peterborough
1976	SKEWS	JOHN HENRY	48	30/11/1928	Walsall
1976	SKUES	ARTHUR	85	6/ 9/1891	Leicester
1976	SKUES	WILLIAM JOHN	96	2/ 2/1880	Truro

1977	SKEWES	WILLIAM JOHN	77	29/10/1900	Truro
1977	SKEWES	FLORENCE WILLIAMS	64	3/ 7/1913	Truro
1977	SKEWES	JESSIE VICTORIA	80	About 1897	Truro
1977	SKEWS	CONSTANCE MARY	76	18/ 7/1901	Barnsley
1977	SKEWS	JOYCE	51	24/ 4/1926	Sunderland
1977	SKEWS	CLARENCE	81	28/ 2/1896	Plymouth
1977	SKUES	JOHN PHILIP W.	86	28/ 3/1891	Greenwich
1977	SKUES	ERNEST	92	8/ 7/1885	Sutton
1978	SKEWES	JAMES HENRY	71	21/ 7/1907	Truro
1978	SKEWES	ARTHUR GEORGE	81	15/ 4/1897	Torbay
1978	SKEWES-COX	FLORENCE LILIAN	85	12/ 4/1894	Waveney
1978	SKEWIS	JOSEPH RICHARD	48	3/ 9/1930	Kettering
1978	SKEWS	JANE	85	24/ 3/1893	Barnsley

PUBLIC INDEX TO ADOPTED CHILDREN REGISTER, 1927—1980, GENERAL REGISTER OFFICE.

1927 — 1950	No Entry	
1951	SKEWS PAUL JAMES	Born 1951
1952 — 1959	No Entry	
1960	SKEWS STEPHEN KENNETH	1959
1961 — 1967	No Entry	
1968	SKEWS TERRY	1963
1969 — 1970	No Entry	
1971	SKUES RICHARD JOHN	1971
1972	No Entry	
1973	SKUES DAVID DANIEL	1972
1974	No Entry	
1975	SKEWES ANN TRACEY	1967
	SKEWES ANTHONY MARK	1967
	SKEWES IAN	1966
	SKEWES SUSAN	1968
	SKEWS MICHELE ROSEMARY	1970
	SKUSE EMMA JUDITH	1974
	SKUSE MICHAEL DAVID	1974
1976	No Entry	
1977	No Entry	
1978	No Entry	
1979	No Entry	
1979	SKUSE IAN RICHARD	1968
1979	SKUSE JACQUELINE	1967
1979	SKUSE JOANNE LOUISE	1978
1979	SKUSE PAUL DAVID	1979
1980	SKEWS ZOE REBECCA	1976
1980	SKUSE JEANNINE WILLIAMS	1963

EXTRA INFORMATION OBTAINED FROM GENERAL REGISTER OFFICE, LONDON. INDEX TO CONSULAR BIRTHS 1849 — 1965

SKEWES	ROBERT MONTAGUE	Caldera District, Chile	Approx 1880
SKEWES	WILLIAM HENRY	Caldera District, Chile	Approx 1880
SKUES	JOHN ANTHONY	Station Tsinan	Between 1926/30
SKUES	JOYCE	Station Tsinan	Between 1926/30
SKEWS	ANDREW J.	Hanover, West Germany	Between 1961/65

REGIMENTAL REGISTERS 1761 — 1924 (BIRTHS)

| SKEWS | ALICE E. | Limerick (52nd Regiment) | 1868 |
| SKEWS | WILLIAM J. | Aldershot (52nd Regiment) | 1866 |

MARRIAGES ABROAD 1849 — 1854

| SKEWS | MATTHEW | Aporto, Portugal | Between 1849/54 |

WAR DEATHS OTHER RANKS ARMY 1914 — 1921

SKEWS	ALFRED	Lance Corporal	1915	R.F. London
SKEWS	ERNEST	Driver	1918	R.F.A.
SKEWS	NELSON	Private	1919	R.W.K.R.
SKUES	CECIL	Rifleman	1917	K.R.R.C.

| SKUES | HAROLD S. | Corporal | 1916 | O.B.L.I. |
| SKUES | PERCY W. | Lance Corporal | 1917 | London R.B. (19th W) |

WAR DEATHS OFFICERS, ARMY 1914 — 1918

| SKEWES | ARTHUR COURTIS | Temp 2nd Lieut. | 1916 | Devon & Gloucester |

WAR DEATHS OTHER RANKS ARMY 1939 — 1945

| SKUES | HUGH WILLIAM | Gunner | 1945 | R.A. |
| SKUES | JAMES D. | Private | 1943 | R. Norfolk |

MARINE DEATHS 1837 — 1965

SKEWS	ALBAN E	aged 35	1920	Aboard Vessel "Unity"
SKEWIS	EDWIN H.	unknown	1917	H.M.S. Wellington from Mignonette
SKEWES	JAMES L.	aged 17	1875	Aboard "Webfoot"

ROYAL AIR FORCE DEATHS ALL RANKS 1939 — 1945

| SKEWES | WILLIAM H. | Flt/Sgt 1384994 | 1943 | 190 Squadron |

NAVAL RATINGS WAR DEATHS 1939—1948

| SKUES | CHARLES GILBERT | A/P.O. (Ty) | 1942 | President III, S.S. Cathay |

NAVAL WAR DEATHS 1914—1918

| SKEWIS | EDWIN H. | Boy Tel. | 1917 | Mignonette |

SUMMARY OF THE GENERAL REGISTERS AT ST CATHERINE'S HOUSE

The Indexes only were allowed to be searched at St. Catherine's House (formerly Somerset House), and these were copied exact. In many cases the spelling is incorrect. However, in all fairness to the General Register Office THEY copied names from the certificates sent in by the local Registrar. In the 19th century many surnames were spelt as they were pronounced.

From 1837 to 1866 all entries in the Index are handwritten on parchment and bound into volumes alphabetically, each volume being about 4 inches thick. More recently, and since the move to St Catherine's House, typed transcripts have appeared on the shelves which are not only a space saver, but a much quicker reference. As has been seen on the previous pages the entries list the surname, Christian name or names (or initials) & the district where the registration took place. If one purchases a certificate for £4.00 (eight shillings in 1970) the exact address is given.

Some of the SKEWES/SKEWIS/SKEWS/SKUES' did not appear to have a Christian name. They were listed as simply "male" or "female". This was normally due to the fact that at the time of registration of the child's birth, the Christian name had not been decided upon.

As from the year 1912 the maiden name of the mother was given in the Index. Altogether there are some 220 million records of births, marriages and deaths retained here.

For the section BIRTHS there are 1612 entries listed between 1837 and 1978 inclusive; 828 males and 784 females. There are 1126 MARRIAGES and 1124 DEATHS.

The total number of entries extracted from the General Registers at St Catherine's House is 3897.

The breakdown per year is as follows: —

1837 — 1847 inclusive

	BIRTHS	MARRIAGES	DEATHS
Total number	163	76	91
Number in Cornwall	127 (77.91%)	67 (88.15%)	63 (69.23%)
Number of Males	74 (45.40%)	40 (52.63%)	33 (36.26%)
Number of Females	89 (54.60%)	36 (47.37%)	58 (63.74%)

1968 — 1978 inclusive

	BIRTHS	MARRIAGES	DEATHS
Total number	67	94	82
Number in Cornwall	31 (46.26%)	35 (27.23%)	26 (31.71%)
Number of Males	29 (43.28%)	51 (54.26%)	43 (52.44%)
Number of Females	38 (56.72%)	43 (45.74%)	39 (47.56%)

1837 — 1978 inclusive

BREAKDOWN BY SURNAME			
	BIRTHS	MARRIAGES	DEATHS
Total	1612	1126	1124
SKEWES	695 (43.14%)	547 (48.58%)	569 (50.62%)
SKEWIS	142 (8.80%)	81 (7.19%)	74 (6.58%)
SKEWS	523 (32.44%)	330 (29.31%)	302 (26.87%)
SKUES	243 (15.07%)	161 (14.30%)	176 (15.66%)
OTHER SPELLINGS	9 (0.55%)	7 (0.62%)	3 (0.27%)

1837 — 1978 inclusive

	BIRTHS	MARRIAGES	DEATHS
MALE	828 (51.37%)	551 (48.93%)	541 (48.13%)
FEMALE	784 (48.63%)	575 (51.07%)	583 (51.87%)
TOTAL	1612	1126	1124

Total number of entries extracted from General Register Office (formerly Somerset House) including Overseas Registers and Adopted Children Registers for the years 1837 to 1978 inclusive: *3897*.
OLDEST PERSON: was MARIA SKEWES who died in 1976 at the advanced age of 97 years.
80 YEARS AND OVER (1866 — 1978) 132 out of 869 persons lived to be 80 years and over (15.18%): 56 (42.42%) were male and 76 (57.58%) were female.
DEATHS UNDER 21 YEARS
1883: Out of the 9 deaths, 6 (66.7%) died under the age of 21 years.
1886: Out of the 16 deaths, 11 (68.75%) died under the age of 21 years.
1906: All 5 deaths (100%) died under the age of 21 years.
1966 — 1978: Only 1 out of 90 (1.1%) died under the age of 21 years. This person died in a tractor accident.

1837 — 1978 inclusive

	BIRTHS	MARRIAGES	DEATHS
Average (arithmetic mean) number	11.5	8	8
Modal (most) number	25 (in 1886)	19 (in 1907)	17 (in 1842)
Range	from 2 (in 1837) to 25 (in 1886)	from 3 (in 1878) to 19 (in 1907)	from 1 (in 1927, 1967) to 17 (in 1842)

SEARCHES MADE IN THE GENERAL REGISTER OFFICE EDINBURGH, SCOTLAND
BIRTHS, MARRIAGES and DEATHS 1855 — 1979

The following entries were made between 1970 and 1981 covering all births, marriages and deaths registered in Scotland from 1855 to 1979 inclusive. The full areas for abbreviated towns and villages are as follows: —

Blackfriars	Glasgow
Blythswood	Glasgow
Bridgeton	Glasgow
Calton	Glasgow
Camalchie	Glasgow
College	Glasgow
Dennistoun	Glasgow
Gorbals	Glasgow
Govan	Glasgow
Highchurch	Glasgow
Hillhead	Glasgow
Hutchesontown	Glasgow
Logie	Stirling
Maryhill	Glasgow
Partick	Glasgow
Pollock	Glasgow
Shettleston	Glasgow
Shotts East	East District Shotts
St Rollox	Glasgow
Springburn	Glasgow
Tradeston	Glasgow

BIRTHS REGISTERED AT GENERAL REGISTER OFFICE, EDINBURGH, SCOTLAND 1855 — 1979

Year	Surname	Name	Place
1861	SKUES	MARGARET CAROLINE MACKENZIE	Aberdeen
1870	SKEWIS	JAMES	Glasgow
1870	SKEWIS	AMELIA	Glasgow
1872	SKEWIS	HELEN	Glasgow
1873	SKEWIS	ELIZABETH RUSSELL	Park
1875	SKEWIS	JOHN	Gorbals
1878	SKEWIS	JOSEPH	Glasgow
1880	SKEWIS	JOHN JACK	Old Monkland
1884	SKEWIS	JOHN	New Monkland
1885	SKEWIES	JAMES	Hamilton
1887	SKEWIES	JAMES	Camalchie
1888	SKEWIS	WILLIAM JAMIESON	Camalchie
1888	SKEWIES	ELIZABETH GEMMELL	Hamilton
1888	SKEWIS	MARY	Airdrie
1890	SKEWIS	WILLIAM	Coatbridge
1891	SKEWIS	GEORGE	Dennistoun
1891	SKEWIS	ANNIE	Airdrie
1892	SKEWIS	ELIZABETH	Dennistoun
1893	SKEWIS	THOMAS	Airdrie
1894	SKEWIS	ELLEN	Hutchesontown
1895	SKEWIS	DORINDA	New Monkland
1896	SKEWIS	JOHN	Calton
1896	SKEWIS	SARAH	Coatbridge
1898	SKEWIS	JAMES	Coatbridge
1898	SKEWIS	WILLIAM BENSON	Camalchie
1900	SKEWIS	JOSEPH RICHARD	Coatbridge
1901	**SKEWIS**	MARTHA McILROY	New Monkland
1902	SKEWIS	WALTER BLYTH	Blackfriars
1903	SKEWIS	JOHN CLIMPSON	New Monkland
1904	SKEWIS	ROBERT BLYTHE	Blackfriars
1906	SKEWIS	JOHN JAMIESON	Blackfriars
1907	SKEWIS	DAVID JAMIESON	Dennistoun
1908	SKEWIS	AGNES HASTINGS	New Monkland
1910	SKEWIS	WILLIAMINA AGNES	Dennistoun
1911	SKEWIES	JAMES	Hamilton
1913	SKEWIS	WILLIAM STARK	New Monkland
1917	SKEWIS	MARY ANN SMITH	New Monkland
1918	SKEWIS	JOSEPH RICHARD	Shotts E.
1918	SKEWIES	ISABEL ANDERSON	Hillhead
1919	SKEWIS	JOSEPH RICHARD	New Monkland
1919	SKEWIS	MARTHA S. BARCLAY	Shotts E.
1920	SKEWIES	ANNIE FYFE	Hamilton
1920	SKEWIS	SARAH NURSE	Shotts E.
1921	SKEWIES	JAMES FYFE	Hamilton
1921	SKEWIS	MARTHA McILROY	New Monkland
1922	SKEWIS	HANNAH B. SNEDDON	Blackridge
1923	SKEWIS	JOSEPH RICHARD	East Greenock
1923	SKEWIS	JOSEPH RICHARD	New Monkland
1924	SKEWIS	SARAH BELL	West Greenock
1924	SKEWIS	MARGARET	New Monkland
1925	SKEWIS	JOHN CLEMPSON	**St. Andrew, Dundee**
1925	SKEWIS	MARTHA McILROY	New Monkland
1925	SKEWIS	DAVID MARTIN BARCLAY	New Monkland
1925	SKEWIS	JAMES AIRNS	New Monkland
1925	SKEWIS	WALTER BLYTHE	Shettleston
1927	SKEWIS	JOHN CLEMPSON	New Monkland
1928	SKEWIS	JOSEPH RICHARD	St Andrew, Dundee
1928	SKEWIS	ANNIE GRANT ABERCROMBY	New Monkland
1929	SKEWIS	ELIZABETH A.A. Airns	New Monkland
1931	SKEWIS	JOSEPH RICHARD Grant	New Monkland
1931	SKEWIS	JAMES BROWN Brown	St Andrew, Dundee
1931	SKEWIS	JANET GRACE Thompson	Shettleston
1933	SKEWIES	ANDREW FYFE Clark	Hamilton
1933	SKEWIS	GRAHAM M.B.T. Thompson	Camalchie
1935	SKEWIS	ANNIE Brown	St. Andrew, Dundee
1936	SKEWIS	WILLIAM Thompson	Camalchie

Year	Surname	Name	Mother/Spouse	Place
1936	SKEWIS	WILLIAM IAIN	Jack	Pollock
1937	SKEWIS	DAVID J.W.	Wilson	Tradeston
1938	SKEWIS	SARAH BLACK	Thompson	College Glasgow
1939	SKEWIS	HUGH MacDONALD	Macdonald	Shettleston
1940	SKEWIS	MARGARET MUNRO	Jack	Pollock
1943	SKEWIS	MARY BELL	Thompson	College Glasgow
1949	SKEWIS	IAN	Wilson	College Park
1951	SKEWIS	JOSEPH RICHARD	Collins	St. Andrew, Dundee
1951	SKEWIS	BRIAN	Wilson	Gorbals
1951	SKEWIS	JOHN GLEN	Strachan	St. Andrew, Dundee
1951	SKEWIS	LINDA ANNE	Collins	St. Andrew, Dundee
1952	SKEWIS	ROBERT	Wilson	Gorbals
1953	SKEWIS	JANE S. O'NEIL	O'Neil	Camalchie
1954	SKEWIS	NEIL CRAIG	Strachan	Dundee East
1954	SKEWIS	CAROL	Collins	Dundee East
1955	SKEWIS	ELIZABETH I.	Fox	New Monkland
1956	SKEWIS	JOHN CLEMPSON	O'Neil	Bridgeton
1956	SKEWIS	DIANE	Collins	Dundee East
1956	SKEWIS	IRENE ANNE	Reid	Dundee East
1957	SKEWIS	JOHN JAMES	Reid	Dundee East
1958	SKEWIS	LINDA	Wilson	Govan
1959	SKEWIS	JAMES O'NEIL	O'Neil	Bridgeton
1961	SKEWIS	GEORGE O'NEIL	O'Neil	Bridgeton
1961	SKEWIS	JAMES CLEMSON	Reid	Dundee East
1961	SKEWIES	KAREN WILSON	Wilson	Bellshill
1962	SKEWIS	MICHAEL C.	Collins	Dundee East
1962	SKEWIS	KAREN	Hutchison	Springburn
1962	SKEWIS	LINDA	Maher	Blythswood
1963	SKEWIS	STEPHEN	Maher	Blythswood
1963	SKEWIS	THOMAS	Kilpatrick	Dennistoun
1964	SKEWIS	JOSEPH RICHARD	Kilpatrick	Glasgow North
1964	SKEWIS	CAROL	Kilpatrick	Glasgow North
1965	SKEWIES	PHILIPPA M.	Wilson	Bothwell
1965	SKEWIS	LYNNE	Hutchison	Glasgow
1966	SKEWIS	SHARON NANCY	Collins	Dundee East
1967	SKEWIS	ANGELA ROSE	Collins	Dundee East
1967	SKEWIS	MICHELLE	Skewis	Glasgow
1968	SKEWIS	JAN	Weir	Inverness
1969	SKEWIS	DAVID	Maher	Glasgow
1969	SKEWIS	ANNE	Riddell	Glasgow
1970	SKEWIS	IAN	Gillies	Dumbarton
1971	SKEWIS	ALAN	Weir	Inverness
1972	SKEWIS	LORRAINE MAHER	Maher	Glasgow
1972	SKEWIS	NICOLA	Riddell	Glasgow
1975	SKEWIS	PAUL WILLIAM	Doig	Dundee East
1975	SKEWIS	BRENDA	McAuley	Glasgow
1975	SKEWIS	JACQUELINE	Doig	Dundee East
1977	SKEWIS	KAREN	Doig	Dundee East

MARRIAGES FROM 1855 to 1979 inclusive

Year	Surname	Name	Spouse	Place
1859	SKEWIES	EMILIA		Muirkirk
1861	SKUES	VIOLETTA		Dundee
1868	SKEWIS	JAMES		Highchurch
1870	SKEWIS	JOSEPH		Highchurch
1873	SKEWIS	MARY JANE		Old Monkland
1876	SKEWIS	SARAH		Old Monkland
1880	SKEWIS	JESSIE		Old Monkland
1884	SKEWIES	JAMES		Hamilton
1885	SKEWIES	JAMES		Hamilton
1886	SKEWIS	WILLIAM		Calton
1886	SKEWIS	JOSEPH R.		Coatbridge
1889	SKEWIS	AMELIA		Dennistoun
1889	SKEWIS	AGNES		Coatbridge
1898	SKEWIS	WILLIAM		Dennistoun
1900	SKEWIS	HELEN		Camalchie
1906	SKEWIS	AMELIA		Blythswood
1907	SKEWIES	JAMES		Hamilton
1908	SKEWIS	MARY		New Monkland
1912	SKEWIS	JAMES		St Rollox
1913	SKEWIS	WILLIAM		Dennistoun
1913	SKEWIES	ELIZABETH GEMMELL		Hamilton
1916	SKEWIS	WILLIAM		Shotts E.
1917	SKEWIS	THOMAS		New Monkland
1918	SKEWIS	AMELIA		Possilpark
1918	SKEWIS	JAMES		New Monkland
1922	SKEWIS	JOSEPH RICHARD		New Monkland
1923	SKEWIS	MARTHA McILROY		New Monkland
1924	SKEWIS	JOHN CLEMPSON		St. Andrew, Dundee
1926	SKEWIS	WALTER BLYTHE		Shettleston
1933	SKEWIS	JOHN JAMIESON	Jack	Cadder
1934	SKEWIS	DAVID JAMIESON	Wilson	Dennistoun
1937	SKEWIS	WILLIAM	Mitchell	Cadder
1937	SKEWIS	MARTHA S.B.	Bell	Camalchie
1942	SKEWIS	HANNAH B.S.	Critchley	Shettleston
1943	SKEWS	HARRY	Adam	Logie
1943	SKEWIES	MARGARET S.	McKay	Hamilton
1944	SKEWIES	JOSEPH RICHARD	Bennet	Maryhill
1944	SKEWIES	ANNIE FYFE	Gillespie	Hamilton
1945	SKEWIS	JAMES AIRNS	Fox	New Monkland
1947	SKEWIES	ISABEL A.	Stuart	Hamilton
1947	SKEWIS	ELIZABETH A.A.	Wilson	New Monkland
1947	SKEWS	EILEEN SUSAN	Williamson	Stonehaven
1948	SKEWIS	JOHN CLEMSON	Strachan	Arbroath
1949	SKEWIS	JOSEPH RICHARD	Collins	St. Andrew, Dundee
1949	SKEWIS	WALTER BLYTHE	Wilson	Gorbals

Year	Surname	Name	Place
1949	SKEWIS	MARTHA McILROY Tod	Camalchie
1949	SKEWIS	SARAH NURSE Redmond	Shettleston
1950	SKEWIES	JAMES FYFE Dykes	Bellshill
1952	SKEWIS	JOHN CLEMPSON O'Neil	Camalchie
1952	SKEWIS	JANET GRACE Law	Camalchie
1953	SKEWIS	JAMES BROWN Forrest	Dalmeny
1953	SKEWIS	GRAHAM B.T. McDermott	Bridgeton
1957	SKEWIS	DOROTHY Taylor	New Monkland
1958	SKEWIES	ANDREW FYFE Wilson	Bothwell
1959	SKEWIS	ANNIE Peddie	Dundee West
1959	SKEWIS	SARAH BLACK Gillan	Bridgeton
1959	SKEWIS	MARY BELL Noble	Dennistoun
1960	SKEWIS	WILLIAM Lyons	Cadder East
1961	SKEWIS	DAVID J.W. Maher	Partick
1961	SKEWIS	HUGH MacDONALD Hutchison	Provan
1962	SKEWIS	JOSEPH RICHARD Kilpatrick	Bridgeton
1963	SKEWIS	WILLIAM IAIN Weir	Dollar
1964	SKEWIS	MARGARET MUNRO Penney	Glasgow
1966	SKEWIES	JAMES FYFE Stokhoe	Canongate
1967	SKEWIS	JOSEPH RICHARD Skewis	Glasgow
1967	SKEWIS	MARTHA McILROY Skewis	Glasgow
1968	SKEWIS	WALTER BLYTH Riddell	Glasgow
1969	SKEWIS	IAN Gillies	Dumbarton
1969	SKEWIS	ANNIE Macclusky	Dundee
1970	SKEWIS	GRAHAM Mcd B.T. Mccolligan	Glasgow
1972	SKEWIS	HANNAH BARCLAY S. Downie	Glasgow
1973	SKEWIS	BRIAN McAuley	Glasgow
1973	SKEWIS	LINDA ANN Craig	Dundee East
1974	SKEWIS	JOSEPH RICHARD Doig	Dundee East
1977	SKEWIS	DIANE Anderson	Dundee East
1979	SKEWIS	MARTHA STARK BARCLAY Laurie	Kirkcaldy

Year	Surname	Name	Age	Place
1900	SKEWIS	HELEN	aged 61	Dennistoun
1900	SKEWIS	SARAH	aged 4	Coatbridge
1907	SKEWIS	MARY JANE	aged 52	Coatbridge
1908	SKEWIS	AGNES HASTINGS	aged 0	New Monkland
1911	SKEWIS	CLARA	aged 56	Leadhills
1914	SKEWIS	MARTHA BARCLAY	aged 26	New Monkland
1914	SKEWIES	MARGARET BELL	aged 27	Hamilton
1915	SKEWIES	ELIZABETH	aged 77	Gorbals
1916	SKEWIS	WILLIAM	aged 50	Shettleston
1918	SKEWIS	MARY ANN SMITH	aged 0	New Monkland
1920	SKEWIS	AMELIA	aged 50	Possilpark
1921	SKEWIES	JAMES	aged 60	Hamilton
1921	SKEWIES	ANNIE	aged 68	Hamilton
1924	SKEWIS	HELEN	aged 55	Shettleston
1924	SKEWIS	MARGARET	aged 0	New Monkland
1924	SKEWIS	SARAH BELL	aged 0	West Greenock
1925	SKEWIS	JOSEPH RICHARD	aged 5	New Monkland
1926	SKEWIS	ROBERT BLYTH	aged 24	Possilpark
1927	SKEWIS	JOHN	aged 78	St Andrew, Dundee
1931	SKEWIS	THOMAS	aged 38	New Monkland
1933	SKEWIS	WILLIAM STARK	aged 19	Dennistoun
1935	SKEWIS	MARY	aged 46	New Monkland
1941	SKEWIS	JESSIE	aged 81	Springburn
1942	SKEWIS	DAVID MARTIN B.	aged 16	Shettleston
1945	SKEWIES	MARGARET MAIR	aged 55	Hamilton
1948	SKEWIS	MARTHA	aged 77	New Monkland
1948	SKEWIES	JAMES	aged 72	Bothwell
1951	SKEWIS	JOSEPH RICHARD	aged 51	Townhead, Glasgow
1951	SKEWIS	JOSEPH RICHARD	aged 83	New Monkland
1951	SKEWIES	AGNES	aged 66	Hamilton
1951	SKEWIS	HELEN	aged 79	Shettleston
1952	SKEWIS	ROBERT	aged 0	Shettleston
1955	SKEWIS	JOHN CLEMPSON	aged 30	Dundee East
1962	SKEWIS	MARTHA STARK	aged 74	Bridgeton
1963	SKEWIES	MARY MURRAY B.	aged 42	Carluke
1964	SKEWIES	ANDREW FYFE	aged 74	Shotts West
1964	SKEWIS	JOSEPH RICHARD	aged 36	Broughty Ferry
1966	SKEWIS	JAMES	aged 66	Glasgow
1970	SKEWIS	HELEN ANDREW	aged 70	Airdrie
1971	SKEWIS	WILLIAM	aged 70	Glasgow
1971	SKEWIS	ANNABELLA MACKENZIE	aged 67	Glasgow
1973	SKEWIS	MARGARET	aged 67	Galashields
1974	SKEWIS	DAVID JAMIESON	aged 66	Glasgow
1975	SKEWIS	WALTER BLYTHE	aged 73	Glasgow
1977	SKEWIS	ANNIE	aged 77	Sidlaw
1977	SKEWIS	ISABELLA	aged 54	Glasgow

DEATHS FROM 1885 to 1979 inclusive

Year	Surname	Name	Age	Place
1864	SKEWIS	ROBERT		Glasgow
1868	SKEWIS	MARY ANN	aged 63	Glasgow
1869	SKEWIS	JAMES	aged 64	Glasgow
1874	SKEWIS	ELIZA	aged 78	Glasgow
1874	SKUES	HELEN	aged 67	St Andrew, Dundee
1876	SKEWIS	JAMES	aged 3	Camalchie
1879	SKEWIS	ELIZABETH RUSSELL	aged 6	Hutchesontown
1880	SKEWIS	JOHN JACK	aged 0	Old Monkland
1884	SKEWIS	HELEN YATES GEMMELL	aged 5	Hamilton
1885	SKEWIES	CATHERINE	aged 22	Hamilton
1892	SKEWIS	ANNIE	aged 0	Airdrie
1895	SKEWIS	THOMAS	aged 67	Coatbridge
1896	SKEWIS	ELIZABETH	aged 33	Calton
1896	SKEWIS	JOHN	aged 0	Camalchie

5　Parish Registers

PARISH REGISTERS are probably the most important source of genealogical information and the first to be examined after the direct knowledge and family documents have been disposed of. Sometimes, however, they are not conclusive evidence by themselves. Confusion may arise where two identical names appear in the same parish. They may or may not be brothers and sisters.

Parish registers are not necessarily proof that an infant grew up to be an adult, as burials are quite often missing from records. This may perhaps explain the many cases of longevity. A son Richard is baptised say in 1759 and dies in the same year, the burial record being omitted. Twenty years later another Richard is baptised and he survives. His burial appears in the parish register in 1869 and may in error be related to the first baptism. Indeed it may only be a will naming older sons of seniority that brings the error to light.

Where registers are missing and large gaps appear, enquiries should be made as to the existence of the *bishop's transcripts*. These should be in the hands of the Diocesan Registrar who has charge of the official documents of the Bishopric. Generally, the transcripts will be in bundles by the year rather than arranged in parishes. In order to search one particular parish over a period of three or four hundred years a great deal of time and patience is needed to search through all the evidence in the transcripts[1].

Even if the parish registers have seen, it is well worth looking at the *bishop's transcripts*, if available, for a job worth doing is worth doing well. For genealogical purposes this job does not only have to be done well, but should be perfect. Whilst searching through the transcripts one may find a few unexpected entries which, by rights, should have been entered and recorded in the parish register. The writer has come across entries in the transcripts which do not appear in the registers which would indicate that perhaps an incumbent sometimes kept a notebook or list, and did not enter the name into the register (if at all) until he had sent the transcript through to the Diocesan Registrar.

In the year 1536 Thomas Cromwell, son of a Putney blacksmith, and who had been a soldier in Italy, became Vicar-General to Henry VIII. Originally a protégé of Cardinal Wolsey, he rose to great heights under Henry and introduced a practice which prevailed in various countries on the continent. Cromwell ordered that a system of parish registers should be kept throughout England and Wales. "Births, marriages and burials in future were to be recorded by the parish clergy!" At first there was great opposition to the scheme, but eventually it was started and still continues to this very day, and hopefully will until the end of time.

From the *Calendar of State Papers* dated 5th September, 1538 Thomas Cromwell said:

"In the name of God Amen. By the authorite and commision of the most excellent Prince Henry by the Grace of God, Kynge of Englande and of France, defensor of the faithe Lorde of Ireland, and in erthe supreme hedd undre Christ of the Church of Englande, I, Thomas Cromwell, lorde privie seall, Vicegerent within this realme do for the advancement of the trewe honor of almighty God, encrease of vertu and discharge of the kynges majestie, give and exhibite unto you theise injunctions following, to be kept observed and fulfilled upon the paynes hereafter declared...

That you and every person vicare or curate within this diocese shall for every churche kepe one boke or registere wherein ye shall write the day and yere of every weddyng christenyg and bureng made within yor parishe for yor tyme and so every man succeedyng you likewise. And shall there insert every persons name that shall be weddid christened or buried, and for the sauff keepinge of the same boke the parishe shall be bonde to provide of these comencharges one sure coffer with twoo lockes and keys whereof the one to remayne with you, and the other one with the said wardens, wherein the said boke shall be laid upp. Whiche boke ye shall every Sonday take furthe and in the presence of the said wardens or one of them write and recorde in the same all the Weddinges Christenyges and Buryenges made the hole weke before. And that every tyme that the same shall be omytted the partie that shall be in the faulte thereof shall forfeltto the said churche 111 shillyngs 1111 pence to be emlojed on the reparation of the same churche....."

THOMAS CROMWELL

---

[1] *Genealogy for Beginners*, Arthur J. Willis, London, 1955, pp. 32, 33

Cromwell was executed in 1540 after the failure of Ann of Cleves' marriage to Henry VIII, but his parish registers have lived on!

The Parish Register Abstract of 1830 shows that of 10,984 ancient parishes in England and Wales 812 parishes commenced logging their births, marriages and burials in the year 1538 such as Camborne, Cornwall. 1822 more parishes started before 1558 and a further 2448 between the years 1558 and 1603 like Frodsham in Cheshire. Between 1603 and 1650, 969 parishes commenced their registers and 2757 between 1650 and 1700. [2]

For over 300 years parish registers play a leading role in forming the mechanism by which a person can trace a family from the Middle Ages to the present day, provided the family has lived in the same area.

Until the end of the nineteenth century, when the tin mining depression swept across the county of Cornwall, the SKUES'/SKEWES'/SKEWS' dwelt in and around the Helston, Camborne and Redruth districts.

The arrangement of a parish register will not always be found in chronological order. Baptisms and burials may have become intermixed, especially with early registers. However, more and more registers are being transcribed and indexed alphabetically when surnames are placed in their correct order. However, the process is slow and on average there is about one parish per year being transcribed in Cornwall.

All variations of a surname must be taken into consideration, although each one should be copied in the exact spelling found. A number of variations the writer has found whilst compiling the Skues family history include: —

SCEUES, SCEUS, SCEWES, SCEWESE, SCEWIS, SCEWS, SCEWSE, SCEWIES, SCEWRES, SCEWYS, SCKEWES, SCKEWS, SCKEWIS, SCKEWSE, SCLUES, SCUES, SCOOSE, SCUSE, SCUESS, SCUIESS, SCUIS, SCUISH, SCUYS, SCUYSE, SCUYSS, SCUYSSE, SCUYSSHE, SCYWYS, SKEEWES, SKEUES, SKEUS, SKEWAS, SKEWERS, SKEWES, SKEWESE, SKEWIES, SKEWIS, SKEWISE, SKEWISH, SKEWS, SKEWSE, SKEWYS, SKEYWS, SKUCE, SKUESE, SKUESS, SKUIES, SKUIESS, SKUIS, SKUISH, SKUISS, SKUSE, SKUWSE, SKUYS, SKUYSE, SKUYSS, SKUYSSE, SKUYSSHE, SKRUES, SKYWYS, SQUCE, SQUES and SQUSE.

Including SKUES that makes a total of sixty-four versions of one surname and many of the above are still in use today. Although the basic spelling has an average of five letters not many families can qualify for so many permutations.

One interesting instance of misconception of spelling which the writer found was in the Redruth parish register in Cornwall. Between the years 1681 and 1686 three children were born to William and Jane SKUES . . . . . William, Jane and Stephen. All three were entered in the register as SKEWS.

Three more children (all daughters) were born between 1687 and 1700. They were entered in the register as Mary SKUIES, Jane SKUESS and Ann SKUES respectively. This just goes to prove that *all* variations *must* be taken into account to produce a true and accurate "family tree."

Before reading early parish registers it is wise to study different styles of handwriting. In many early registers the entries are in Latin, although mediaeval Latin went out of use in official documents around the end of the fifteenth century. However, it was used elsewhere up to 1733. Style can date handwriting fairly accurately and palaeography is an ever increasing hobby amongst genealogists and historians.

Looking through thousands of entries in a parish register one can easily become confused with surnames looking alike at first glance. Some examples the writer has found include: —

SKEWES   SKEWIS   STEVENS   SKERRIS   SHEARS   THOMAS

The most important entry in a parish register is for a marriage followed by a burial. Records of baptism are the least important as everyone was not baptized.

[2] *Catalogue of Parish Registers (1937) now in the possession of the Society of Genealogists, London.*

As regards the entries of burials in a register the majority simply mention the name and date of interment from the beginning to the end of a particular volume. In a minority of cases, however, we find a brief entry made when a death was caused by an accident. For example an entry taken from Dorking parish register in Surrey for 28th February 1562 states:

> "Owen Tonny was christened who (at a later date adds) scoffing at thunder standing under a beech tree, was stroke to death, his clothes stinking with sulphurious stenches, being about the age of twenty years or thereabouts."

In another instance we find:

> "Richard Tomason fallinge out of a tree as he was gatheringe ivie upon the Lords Daye took his death wound and was buried the xxii daye of the month of December, 1601."

That extract was taken from Blackesley parish register, Northants. Now two entries from Cornwall. First St. Hilary followed by Mylor:

> "Marriage between George Kelly, aged 22 and Catherine Dayce, aged 22 — the 23rd August, 1784. This Catherine Dayce is a remarkable dwarf said to be only thirty-four inches high. She died 18th October, 1785."

> "A woman aged 72 of Flushing of a wicked mind deliberately hung herself in a back cellar of her own house, which was unoccupied, having locked herself in. 27th June, 1857."

The vicar declined to attend the funeral, or to read the church service.

The Great Plague of London in 1664/1665 caused many thousands of deaths. In Cornwall a plague referred to by some as a "sweating sickness" spread through the county in 1591. From the Redruth parish register we find an entry which says "The Plague began on 11 August, 1591." A further entry on 11 November, 1592 gives the words "The Plague ceased."

Twenty-seven deaths are entered for just one month in June whereas the annual death rate around this period was under ten. This plague affected people when they felt dizzy. Many collapsed. Soon, swellings appeared under the arms and on their necks. Their faces were covered with black spots and boils which spread over the whole body. It took just four days for many of them to die in a raging fever.

Scarlet fever was also a very serious illness 150 years ago and in the parish of Gwennap, Cornwall it struck the SKEWES family:

> "Simon Davey SKEWES of Penance, Gwennap died of Scarlet Fever on 30 October, 1842, aged 6 years.

> Alexander SKEWES of Caernmarthe, Gwennap died of Scarlet Fever on 14 November, 1842, aged 8 years."

> Also in 1842 were the deaths of Mary SKEWES, aged 16 years, Elizabeth Ann SKEWES aged 4 years and Thomas SKEWES aged 10 years — all of Gwennap.

Four members of the SKUES family gained a place in the unusual section of Camborne parish register:

> "Ann, wife of John SKUES of Camborne, Cornwall, died of Apoplexy, aged 42 years on 18 March, 1835, after having given birth to five children."

> "Absalom SKUES, son of Absalom SKUES of Camborne, Cornwall died of decline on 25 January, 1836, aged 48 years. He was the father of five daughters and three sons."

> "Henry SKUES, son of Stephen SKUES, husbandman of Camborne, was scalded to death on 23 February, 1835, being aged 4 years."

> "Jane SKUES of Illogan, Camborne, Cornwall was buried on 5 May, 1822, aged 100 years."

Although the majority of the SKUES/SKEWES/SKEWS family have, through the ages, lived to a considerable age, Jane appears to have been the only person to score a century, thus making her the eldest member of the family as a whole. The youngest was Catherine SKEWES of Condurrow, Tuckingmill who died unbaptised on 6 February, 1901, aged just "one hour."

The author has searched hundreds of parish registers in Cornwall, Somerset and Devon and noted all entries. In some parishes there was no mention of the family, but those which did appear may be found in the following pages.

Phillimore has published many Marriage Registers for England and Wales. For the county of Cornwall he compiled 26 volumes of Marriages only, although there were only 150 copies of volumes 1 — 24 printed and 100 copies of volumes 25 and 26.

Also in the following pages are entries taken from Non Parochial Registers most of which are housed either at the Public Record Office in London or the County Record Office, Truro, Cornwall.

CORNWALL PARISH REGISTERS (Phillimore)
26 Volumes : Marriages only

All entries commence at the year given and end at 1812 unless otherwise stated.

VOLUME 1	Advent 1676-1801; St Breward 1558; St Clether 1640-1811; Davidstow 1676-1811; Forrabury 1676; St Juliot 1656; Lanteglos by Camelford 1588; Lesnewth 1569; Michaelstow 1548; Minster 1676; Otterham 1687-1811; St Teath 1558; Trevalga 1539.
VOLUME 2	Lanivet 1608; Tintagel 1588; St Tudy 1560; St Mabyn 1562; Laneast 1680; Egloskerry 1574; Tremaine 1674; Phillack 1572.
VOLUME 3	St Just-in-Penwith 1599; St Buryan 1654; St Sennan 1699; St Levan 1694; Gwithian 1560; Towednack 1676.
VOLUME 4	Shevioke 1570; Blisland 1539; Cardynham 1675; Endellion 1684; Helland 1677; Lanhydrock 1599; St Merryn 1689; St Minver 1559; Warleggan 1682.
VOLUME 5	St Breage 1559; St Germoe 1674; Ludgvan 1563; Sancreed 1559.
VOLUME 6	Egloshayle 1600; St Kew 1564; Padstow 1599; Warleggan 1547-1718; Withiel 1568; St Sampson or Golent 1568.
VOLUME 7	Mawnan 1553; Mylor 1673; Perranarworthal 1684; St Sithney 1654; Stythians 1654; Manaccan 1633.
VOLUME 8	Fowey 1568; Tywardreath 1642; Lostwithiel 1609; Luxulyan 1594; St Cleer 1678.
VOLUME 9	Lelant 1679; Paul 1598; Zennor 1617; St Hilary 1676.
VOLUME 10	St Ewe 1560; St Stephen's in Brannel 1681; St Winnow 1622; Lanlivery 1600; Menheniot 1554.
VOLUME 11	Bodmin 1559; St Wenn 1678; Lezant 1539; St Goran 1668.
VOLUME 12	Madron with Penzance 1674; Morvah 1617-1772 (Morvah marriages are included in the Madron Registers); Gulval 1686-1772; Gwinear 1560.
VOLUME 13	Budock 1653; St Gluvias 1599; St Colan 1665.
VOLUME 14	St Columb Minor 1560; St Issey 1596; Lewannick 1675; St Ives 1653; St Mawgan-in-Meneage 1563.
VOLUME 15	Wendron 1560; Constantine 1571; St Martin-in-Meneage 1571; Perranuthnoe 1589.
VOLUME 16	St. Crantock 1559; St Cubert 1608; St Ervan 1602; St Eval 1631; St Mawgan in Pydar 1608; St Newlyn in Pydar 1559; Perran-zabuloe 1619; St Petrock Minor 1636; St Columb Major 1781; Lanherne Convent 1710-1834.
VOLUME 17	Boyton 1568; Linkinhorne 1576; St Mellion 1558; Morwinstow 1558; South Petherwyn 1656; Pillaton 1557; Roche 1578.
VOLUME 18	St Agnes 1596; St Allen 1611; St Breock 1561; Crowan 1674.
VOLUME 19	Redruth 1717; Camborne 1538; Boylon 1756.
VOLUME 20	St Erth 1563; St Erme 1614; St Enoder 1571; Kilkhampton 1539; Poughill 1537; Botus Fleming 1550; St Anthony-in-Meneage 1726.
VOLUME 21	St. Denys 1610; Landulph 1541; Landrake 1583; St Erney 1555; Helston 1599; Stratton 1674.
VOLUME 22	Kenwyn 1559; Kea 1653; Tregony with Cuby 1661.
VOLUME 23	Marchamchurch 1558; St Stephens by Launceston 1566; Ladock 1686; Probus 1641; Cornelly 1679; Launcells 1642; St Veryan 1676.
VOLUME 24	Launceston, St Mary Magdalene 1559; St Keverne 1608.
VOLUME 25	Landewednack 1654; Ruan Major 1683; Ruan Minor 1667; Grade 1708; Poundstock 1615; Week St Mary 1602; Jacobstowe 1656; Treneglos 1694; Warbsto 1695; Gwennap 1660.
VOLUME 26	St Clement 1538-1837; St Michael Penkivel 1577-1837; Philleigh 1613-1837; Gerrans 1538-1837; St Just in Roseland with St Mawes 1538-1837; Creed with Grampound 1611-1837.

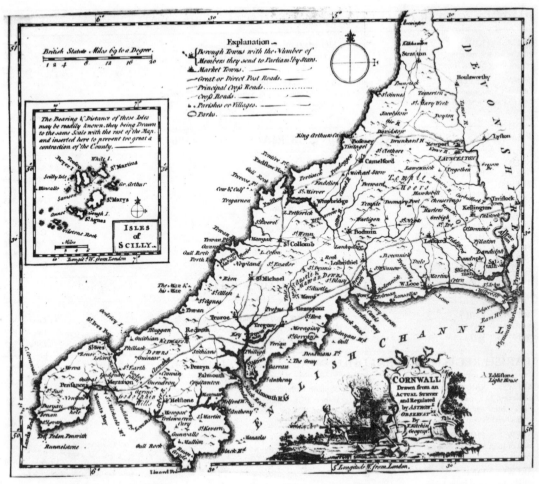

Kitchin's map of Cornwall, 1749

Now follows transcripts from parish registers relating to the county of Cornwall which the writer has compiled from Phillimore *Marriages* and from registers of parishes, copies of which are either still retained by the incumbent, or have been passed to the County Record Office, Truro, the Royal Institution of Cornwall, Truro or various reference libraries in Cornwall. Parishes are indexed alphabetically. Bishops' transcripts held in Exeter have also been checked.

PARISH REGISTER OF ALTARNUN   BAPTISMS   1853 – 1873

SKEWS	ELIZABETH JANE	dau of John William & Isabella	15 Sept	1853
SKEWS	JOHN GREGORY	son of John William & Isabella	15 Sept	1853
SKEWS	SAMUEL GREGORY	son of John William & Isabella	20 Oct	1856
SKEWS	FANNY GREGORY	dau of Peter and Elizabeth	20 Nov	1856
SKEWS	WILLIAM HENRY	son of Peter and Elizabeth	1 Nov	1858
SKEWS	JOHN WILLIAM	son of John and Isabella	16 Mar	1860
SKEWS	ALFRED	son of John and Isabella	7 Mar	1861
SKEWS	EMMA	dau of John and Isabella	1 Jan	1863
SKEWS	ALFRED	son of John and Isabella	20 Nov	1863
SKEWS	AMOS	son of John and Isabella	9 Mar	1865
SKEWS	CHARLES	son of John and Isabella	29 Dec	1866
SKEWS	MARY	dau of John and Isabella	5 Sept	1868
SKEWS	HENRY	son of John and Isabella	18 Apr	1870
SKEWS	DAVID	son of John and Isabella	29 Apr	1871
SKEWS	HARRY	son of John and Isabella	23 Oct	1873

Altarnun Parish Church

PARISH REGISTER OF ALTARNUN   MARRIAGES   1813—1907

SKEWS JOHN of Five Lanes, miner; son of Peter Skews, miner	and	Merrinia (Isabella) Gregory (minor), of Five Lanes; dau of Samuel Gregory, miner	
			26 Mar 1848
SKEWS PETER of Five Lanes, miner; son of Peter Skews, miner	and	Elizabeth Gregory (minor), of Five Lanes; dau of Samuel Gregory, miner.	
			26 Oct 1855

PARISH REGISTER OF ALTARNUN   BURIALS   1813—1961

SKEWS	JOHN GREGORY	of Five Lanes, aged 2 months	28 Sept	1853
SKEWS	JOHN GREGORY	of Trewint, aged 3 weeks	5 Mar	1855
SKEWS	ALFRED	of Trewint, aged 10 months	10 Mar	1861
SKEWS	EMMA	of Trewint, aged 1½ years	27 Nov	1863
SKEWS	ALFRED	of Trewint, aged 9 months	20 Mar	1864
SKEWS	THOMAS	of Trewint, aged 5 months	16 Mar	1866
SKEWS	MARY	of Trewint, aged 10 weeks	1 Oct	1868
SKEWS	HENRY	of Trewint, aged 13 months	7 Apl	1871
SKEWS	DAVID	of Trewint, aged 1 month	9 May	1871
SKEWS	JOHN	of Trewint, aged 58 years	16 Jan	1881

PARISH REGISTER OF BALDHU   BAPTISMS   1847—1975

SKEWES	EMILY	dau of Peter and Elizabeth of Hugus, Kea; miner	15 Oct	1850
SKEWES	LAVINIA	dau of John and Anne of Seveock, miner	4 Jun	1854
SKEWES	WILLIAM	son of John and Anne of Seveock, miner	4 Jun	1854

PARISH REGISTER OF BALDHU   MARRIAGES   1847—1978

SKEWS SARAH of Kerley, Kea, dau of Richard Skews, mine agent; in presence of Richard Skews	&	William Pollard miner of Chacewater, son of William Pollard, miner	
			11 Mar 1852
SKEWS PHILIPPA dau of John Skews of Baldhu, miner	&	John Symons son of Richard Symons, miner	
			19 Aug 1858
SKEWS JANE of Hugus; dau of Peter Skews, miner	&	William Francis Wasley, smith of Baldhu; son of Samuel Wasley, miner	
			10 Apl 1862
SKEWS WILLIAM miner of Baldhu; son of William Skews, miner	&	Jane Northey of Baldhu; dau of Josiah Northey, miner	
			29 Sept 1864
SKEWES MARY of Baldhu; dau of Peter Skewes, farmer; in presence of Grace Skewes.	&	Alfred Williams farmer of Baldhu, son of Solomon Williams, miner	
			8 Aug 1865
SKEWES GRACE of Baldhu; dau of Peter Skewes, farmer	&	Stephen Davey miner of Baldhu; son of William Davey, miner	
			29 June 1874
SKEWES MARIA of Baldhu; daughter of Peter Skewes, farmer	&	John Letcher miner of Baldhu; son of John Letcher, farmer	
			19 Sept 1876

PARISH REGISTER OF BALDHU   BURIALS   1847—1973

SKEWS	ANN	of Hugus, aged 82 years	16 Mar	1859
SKEWS	AGNES	of Kerley, Kea, aged 75 years	20 May	1860
SKEWES	PETER	of Kerley, Kea, aged 64 years	21 Jun	1867
SKEWES	RICHARD	of Kerley, Kea, aged 84 years	28 Jul	1867
SKEWES	MARY	of Kerley, Kea, aged 68 years	18 Sept	1867
SKEWES	JAMES	of Truro Union House, aged 54 years	3 Jul	1877
SKEWES	JANE	of Nangiles, aged 64 years	15 Jul	1894
SKEWES	GRACE	of Penstraze, Kea, aged 88 years	1 Mar	1896
SKEWES	HARRIET	of Kerley, Kea, aged 80 years	5 Oct	1899
SKEWES	RICHARD	of Penstraze, Kea, aged 74 years	15 Oct	1907

Grave of Richard Skewes. Left: *1907.* Right *1981. Interred in Baldhu cemetery, near Truro*

PARISH REGISTER OF BUDOCK   MARRIAGES ONLY   1653 — 1812

SKEWES	RICHARD	and	Frances Toy	11 Apl	1774

PARISH REGISTER OF CAMBORNE   BAPTISMS   1538 — 1960

				1619
SCUIS	PETERNESS	daughter of...	11 Sept	1638
SCEWIES	GEORG	son of Humfrey	26 Mar	1653
SCEWES	ROBART	son of Remfrey	21 Oct	1665
SCUES	THOMAS	son of William	29 Sept	1667
SCUES	ANNE	dau of William	17 July	1670
SCUES	ANNE	dau of William	21 July	1672
SCUES	HENRY	son of William	18 July	1675
SCUES	PRUDENCE	dau of William	8 Apl	1685
SCUES	RICHARD	son of Robert	2 Feb	1692
SKUES	ELIZABETH	dau of Robert	29 June	1693
SKUES	PETER	illegitimate son of Ann	20 Aug	1695
SKUES	JONE	illegitimate dau of Ann born 23 June 1695	4 July	1696
SCUES	REMFERY	son of Robert	1 Nov	1705
SCUIS	WILLIAM	son of Henery	2 June	1707
SKEWS	HENRY	son of Henery	6 May	1710
SKEWS	MARGARET	dau of Henery	26 Feb	1715
SKEWIS	MARY	dau of Henery	23 Nov	1717
SCUIS	JOHN	son of Henery	3 Sept	1721
SCUIS	JOHN	son of Henery		

SKEUES	ROBEN (ROBART)	son of Renfre (Renfry)		8 Apl	1726
SKUES	(SKEWIS) RENFERY	son of Renfery (Renfry)		26 Dec	1727
SKEWIS	WILLIAM	son of William		21 Feb	1735
SKEWIS	JOHN	son of William		20 Nov	1737
SKEWIS	JAMES	son of Henry		14 Jan	1739
SKEWIS	HENRY	son of Henry		24 June	1739
SKEWIS	RICHARD	son of William		24 Oct	1739
SKEWIS	JOHN	son of Henry		7 Mar	1741
SKEWIS	MARY	dau of William		25 Apl	1742
SKEWIS	MARGARET	dau of Henry		17 June	1744
SKEWIS	STEPHEN	son of William		20 Jan	1744
SKEWIS	SARAH	dau of William		8 Feb	1746
SKEWIS	WILLIAM	son of Henry		16 Aug	1747
SKEWIS	ABSALOM	son of Henry		29 June	1750
SKEWIS	HENRY	son of William		12 April	1752
SKEWIS	ROBERT	son of Robert	— privately	15 Aug	1752
				24 Sept	1752
SKEWIS	JANE	daughter of Robert		2 Feb	1754
SKEWIS	MARY	daughter of Robert		30 May	1756
SKEWIS	ANNE	daughter of Robin		21 Mar	1758
SKEWIS	MARGERY	daughter of Robin	— privately	21 Nov	1760
				30 Mar	1761
SKEWIS	JAMES	son of Robin		12 Sept	1762
SKEWIS	JAMES	son of James	— privately	7 June	1763
				12 June	1763
SKEWES	MARY	daughter of Richard		22 Feb	1767
SKEWIS	WILLIAM	son of John	— privately	19 Aug	1768
SKEWIS	WILLIAM	son of Richard		6 Nov	1768
SKEWIS	WILLIAM & MARY	twin children of John	— privately	20 Oct	1769
				13 Nov	1769
SKEWIS	MARY	daughter of Richard		9 Dec	1770
SKEWIS	CONSTANCE	daughter of James & Charity		10 March	1771
SKEWES	HENRY	son of Henry of Illogan		8 April	1772
SKEWIS	JOHN	son of John		29 Dec	1771
SKEWIS	RICHARD	son of Richard & Alice		9 May	1773
SKEWIS	SARAH	daughter of John		10 Oct	1773
SKEWIS	ELIZABETH	daughter of Henry & Elizabeth		16 Jan	1774
SKEWIS	JOHN	son of John & Philippa	— privately	15 Mar	1775
				9 April	1775
SKEWES	ALICE	daughter of Richard & Alice		19 May	1776
SKEWES	CATHERINE	daughter of John & Philippa		2 Feb	1777
SKEWES	HENRY	son of Richard & Alice		21 June	1778
SKEWES	STEPHEN	son of John & Philippa		26 Dec	1778
SKEWES	WILLIAM & JAMES	twin sons of James & Charity each aged 5 years		19 Dec	1779
SKEWES	ALICE	daughter of Richard & Alice		16 April	1780
SKEWES	HENRY	son of John & Philippa		21 Oct	1781
SKEWES	PHILIPPA	daughter of John & Philippa		30 Mar	1783
SKEWES	ELIZABETH	daughter of Richard and Alice		10 Apr	1785
SKEWES	RICHARD	son of John & Philippa		10 Apr	1785
SKEWES	WILLIAM	son of Absalom & Elizabeth		7 Nov	1786
SKEWES	JAMES	son of James & Elizabeth		22 Aug	1790
SKEWES	MARY ANN	daughter of James & Elizabeth		15 Jan	1792
SKEWES	JOHN & ANN	twin children of Absalom & Elizabeth		21 May	1793
SKEWES	WILLIAM	base son of Constance		31 May	1795
SKEWES	JAMES & EDWARD	twin sons of Absalom & Elizabeth		7 June	1795
SKEWES	MARGARET	daughter of Absalom & Elizabeth		8 Feb	1798
SKEWES	ELIZABETH TEMBY	base daughter of Constance		8 Feb	1798
SKEWES	MARGARET	base daughter of Constance		29 July	1799
SKEWES	STEPHEN	son of John & Jenefar		31 Aug	1800
SKEWES	MARIA	base daughter of Constance		24 Nov	1800
SKEWES	MARGARET	daughter of Henry & Margaret		24 Oct	1801
SKEWES	STEPHEN	son of William & Elizabeth		26 Dec	1803
SKEWES	WILLIAM	son of William & Elizabeth		9 Feb	1806
SKEWES	LAVINIA	daughter of Henry & Margaret		21 Dec	1806
SKEWES	MATILDA	daughter of Henry & Margaret		7 May	1809
SKEWES	BETSY	daughter of William & Elizabeth		19 May	1810
SKEWES	JANE PIPER	daughter of Absalom & Jane		7 April	1811
SKEWES	HENRY	son of William & Elizabeth		31 Oct	1812
SKEWES	MARY ANN	daughter of Absalom & Jane		12 Dec	1812
SKEWES	JAMES	son of James and Ann		26 Dec	1812
SKEWES	ELIZABETH	daughter of Absalom & Jane		2 Sept	1815
SKUES	JAMES	son of James & Joanna of Killivoase, miner		9 May	1818
SKEWES	HENRY	son of James and Joanna of Killivoase, miner		27 Nov	1819
SKUES	ELIZABETH	daughter of Absalom & Jane of Ramsgate, farmer		1 Jan	1820
SKEWES	JANE	daughter of John, widower of Illogan, farmer		31 Mar	1821
SKUES	WILLIAM	son of James and Joanna of Killivoase, miner		7 Oct	1821
SKUES	ABSALOM	son of Absalom and Jane of Ramsgate, miner		27 April	1822

SKUES	ANN	daughter of John and Ann of Town, miner		26 April	1823
SKUES	EDWARD	son of James and Joanna of Killivoase		11 Jan	1824
SKUES	MARY	daughter of John and Ann of Town, miner		7 Mar	1824
SKUES	WILLIAM	son of Absalom and Jane of Little Pendarves, miner		5 June	1824
SKUES	JOHN HOSKIN	son of Stephen & Margaret of Park Holly, farmer		25 Sept	1824
SKUES	CAROLINE	daughter of Absalom and Jane of Killivoase, miner		3 Sept	1825
SKUES	ABSALOM	son of Absalom and Jane of Killivoase, miner		26 Nov	1825
SKUES	JOHN	son of John and Ann of New Back Row, Town, miner		31 Jan	1826
SKUES	WILLIAM	son of Stephen & Margaret of Treswithian Lane, husbandman		8 July	1826
SKUES	JOHN RULE	son of James and Joanna of Killivoase, farmer		1 Dec	1827
SKUES	JOHN	son of John and Ann	privately	10 Jan	1828
SKUES	ELIZABETH	dau of Stephen & Margaret of Treswithian; husbandman		7 Mar	1829
SKEWES	STEPHEN	son of James and Joanna of Killivoase; farmer		21 Aug	1830
SKUES	HENRY JAMES and JULIANA	twin children of Absalom and Jane of Town; miner		16 July	1831
SKUES	WILLIAM HENRY	son of Henry and Grace of Ramsgate; miner		16 Feb	1833
SKUES	MARY	dau of John and Ann of Town; privately; miner		18 Apl	1833
SKUES	NANNY	dau of James & Joanna of Killivoase; farmer		20 Apl	1833
SKUES	RICHARD MARTIN	son of Henry and Grace of Penponds; miner		20 Sept	1834
SKUES	MARY	dau of James and Joanna of Killivoase; farmer		16 May	1835
SKUES	ELIZABETH	dau of Stephen & Margaret of Park Holly; husbandman		28 Nov	1835
SKEWISE	ELIZABETH	dau of Henry and Grace of Penponds; miner		30 Aug	1836
SKUES	STEPHEN	son of Henry & Grace of Penponds; miner		18 Aug	1838
SKUES	MARY ODGERS	dau of James & Alice of College Row, Town; cabinet maker		10 Apl	1839
SKUES	MARY	dau of John and Anne of College Row; miner		24 May	1839
SKEWES	PHILIP JAMES	son of Henry & Grace of Penponds; miner		13 Nov	1841
SKEWES	JAMES FEARGUS O'CONNOR	son of James and Alice of Town; cabinet maker		9 Mar	1842
SKEWES	JOANNA	dau of James and Sally of Pendarves Field; miner		4 Jan	1845
SKUES	HENRY JAMES	son of Henry and Grace of Penponds; miner		27 Nov	1845
SKUES	JOHN SAMUEL	son of Henry and Grace of Penponds; miner		27 Nov	1845
SKEWES	ANNIE MARY	dau of Elizabeth Ann, single woman of Gas Street; born 14 July, 1878		4 Sept	1878
SKEWES	FLORENCE ANNIE	dau of Richard & Louisa Jane of Braem; miner. Born 1 Jan 1885		25 Mar	1885
SKEWES	WILLIAM HENRY HERBERT	son of Richard & Louisa Jane of College Row; miner		11 May	1887
SKEWES	ELIZABETH MILDRED	dau of Richard and Louisa Jane of College Row; miner Born 22 January, 1889		3 Apl	1889
SKEWES	WILLIAM RICHARD	son of Richard and Louisa Jane of College Row; miner		17 Jan	1892
SKEWES	HAMES HENRY OSWALD	son of Harry Oswald and Emily Ann; plumber		17 Oct	1894
SKEWES	MATTHEW THOMAS	son of Matthew and Eliza Ann of Illogan Highway; miner		10 Sept	1899
SKEWES	MARY VERONICA	dau of Harry Oswald and Emily Ann of Moor Street; fitter		25 Nov	1899
SKEWES	DORIS MURIEL	dau of Harry Oswald and Emily Ann of Moor Street; fitter		28 June	1905
SKEWES	GEORGE HENNESSY	son of Harry Oswald and Emily Ann of 17 Moor Street; plumber		29 Jan	1909

PARISH REGISTER OF CAMBORNE   MARRIAGES   1538—1960

SKEWIS	JAMES	&	Agnes Ellis	21 Apl	1589
SKEWIS	HUMFREY	&	Christian Farmer	23 Oct	1637
SCUES	GEORG	&	Elizabeth Grills	3 Sept	1664
SCUES	WILLIAM	&	Margaret Thomas	24 Sept	1664
SCUIS	HENERY	&	Mary, his wife	9 Apl	1705
SKULES	ELIZABETH	&	Christopher Tellam	30 Dec	1714
SKEUES	REMFERY	&	Margry Bryant	26 Feb	1722
SKEWIS	WILLIAM	&	Mary Temby	15 July	1735
SKEWIS	JAMES	&	Charity Ellis	10 Apl	1763
SKEWES	MARY	&	Stephen Rowe	28 Oct	1764
SKEWES	RICHARD	&	Alice Knucky	17 Nov	1765
SKEWES	JOHN	&	Philippa King	1 Nov	1767
SKEWES	ANN	&	Matthew Brown, tinner	10 July	1785
SKEWES	JAMES, tinner	&	Elizabeth Handcock	1 Nov	1789
SKEWES	MARY	&	William Thomas, miner	18 Oct	1791
SKEWES	MARY (Witness: Henry Skewes)	&	William Smytheram of Breage	2 June	1793
SKEWES	SARAH	&	Gabriel Blewitt	2 July	1796
SKEWES	JOHN (Husbandman)	&	Jane Angove	8 Feb	1800
SKEWES	CATHERINE (Witness JOHN SKEWES)	&	George Prout	16 May	1801
SKEWES	PHILIPPA (Witness: JOHN SKEWES)	&	John Philips of Gwithian	14 Nov	1802
SKEWES	WILLIAM (miner)	&	Ann Ellis	28 Nov	1802
SKEWES	CONSTANCE	&	Richard Williams of Gwinear	1 Jan	1803
SKEWES	ABSALOM (miner)	&	Jane Piper	26 Dec	1810
SKEWES	JAMES (tinner)	&	Jane Richards, widow	16 Mar	1812
SKEWES	ELIZABETH	&	Richard Mill, miner	22 Nov	1813
SKUES	EDWARD (Witness JAMES SKEWIS)	&	Mary Pearce	3 Mar	1817

SKEWES JAMES (SKEWIS in signature)	&	Joanna Rule		8 April 1817
SKEWES MARY ANN (Witness JAMES SKEWES)	&	Richard Rogers, husbandman		24 Sept 1818
SKEWES MARIE (SKUES in signature)	&	William Shearman, miner		8 May 1819
SKUES JOHN, miner (SKEWISH in signature)	&	Ann Simmons		18 Feb 1822
SKUES STEPHEN, husbandman (SKEWES in signature)	&	Margaret Hoskin		29 July 1824
SKEWES WILLIAM, farmer	&	Eliza Vivian, w., lic.		7 Feb 1830
SKUES HENRY, miner (SKEWIS in signature) (Witness MARY SKEWES)	&	Grace Martin		2 June 1832
SKEWES MARIANNE (MARY ANN SKEWIS in signature)	&	James Rablin, miner		11 Oct 1834
SKEWES MARY (Witness HENRY SKEWES)	&	Thomas Martin, miner		5 Nov 1835
SKEWES ELIZABETH (SKEWIS in signature) (Witness WILLIAM SKEWES)	&	John Glasson		20 July 1836
SKEWES JANE (SKEWIS in signature)	&	William Simons, **sojourner**		19 Jan 1837
SKUES STEPHEN (SKEWIS in signature) widower, husbandman	&	Elizabeth Provis		2 April 1837
SKEWES HENRY miner of Killivoase, son of James Skewes, farmer	&	**Ann Bawden, dressmaker of Pengiggan,** dau of William Bawden, mine agent, deceased		27 Oct 1842
SKUES JAMES, the younger miner of Killivoase, son of James Skewes; farmer. In presence of James Skewis, senior	&	Sally Sems miner of Killivoase, dau of Samuel Sems, miner		25 Jan 1844
SKEWIS WILLIAM farmer of Killivoase, son of James Skewis, farmer. In presence of Henry Skewis.	&	Peggy Bawden of Vyvyan's Row, dau of William Bawden, dcsd.		29 Mar 1847
SKEWIS WILLIAM miner of Treswithian; son of Stephen Skewis, husbandman	&	Sarah Billing, minor of Treswithian; dau of John Billing, mine agent, deceased		26 Dec 1849
SKEWES ANNE of Trelowarren Street, dau of John Skewes, miner	&	Stephen Simmons miner of Newlyn Road, son of Stephen Simmons, miner, deceased		26 Dec 1849
SKEWES JAMES HENRY (24) carpenter of Chapel Street, son of John Skewes, labourer. In presence of Mary Skewes	&	Mary Jane Eudey (23) spinster of College Row, dau of Edward Eudey, labourer		5 Mar 1865
SKEWIS MARY JANE, widow dau of Edward Eudey, miner	&	James Gilbert, widower engineer of Camborne, son of Philip Gilbert, labourer		14 Dec 1871
SKEWES MATILDA of Camborne; dau of Henry Skewes, farmer, deceased	&	Robert Goodfellow, wdr., farmer of Mylor; son of Charles Goodfellow, farmer, deceased		3 Aug 1874
SKEWES RICHARD (21) miner of Treslothan; son of Philip Skewes, miner	&	Louisa Jane Tellam (19) of College Row; dau of Francis Tellam, miner		31 Aug 1884
SKEWES HARRY OSWALD (24) plumber of College Row; son of James Henry Skewes, carpenter	&	Emily Ann Taylor (21) factory girl of Rose Cottage; dau of George Taylor, Miner		12 Nov 1892
SKEWES MARY VERONICA (39) spinster of 4, Centenery Street, Camborne; dau of Henry Oswald Skewes, plumber In presence of Henry Oswald Skewes and James Henry Oswald Skewes	&	William Henry Cockram (56), widower; station master of Station House, Congresbury; son of Henry Cockram, carrier		19 July 1938
SKEWES GEORGE (27) motor body repairer of Palm Leigh, Four Lanes Redruth; son of Thomas Henry Skewes of Camborne, boilerman	&	Joyce Hawken (25) shop assistant, 31, Highville Street, Camborne; dau of William John Hawken, labourer		13 Dec 1948

PARISH REGISTER OF CAMBORNE   BURIALS   1538 — 1959

SCUIS		daughter of William (the whole of this entry is faded and indistinct)		24 Mar 1541
SCUES	THOMAS	son of William		21 Dec 1666
SKEWES	ELIZABETH	wife of George		13 Nov 1686
SCEWES	REMFRY			25 Jan 1686
SKEUES	PETTER			21 Sept 1693
SKEWES	GEORGE			22 Nov 1696

SKUES	JONE	daughter of Ann (illeg)	3 June	1697
SKEWES	MARGARET	(This entry appears to have been erased from the register)	Jan	1704
SCUIS	SEDWELL		11 July	1713
SCUIS	WILLIAM		13 Feb	1715
SCUIS	ROBARD	in the Church	20 Jan	1717
SCUIS	JOHN	son of Henery	19 Oct	1720
SCUIS	RICHARD	In the Church	20 Feb	1721
SCUIS	ROBARD		9 Mar	1721
SKEUES	JANE		29 Oct	1722
SKEUES	PRUEDENS (Prudence)		19 Dec	1723
SKEUES	MAREY (Mary)		12 Oct	1730
SKEWIS	JOHN		2 May	1743
SKEWIS	REMFREY	son of Remfrey	8 June	1743
SKEWIS	HENRY		21 Feb	1744
SKEWIS	MARY	daughter of Robin	30 Mar	1761
SKEWIS	WILLIAM	son of John	20 Aug	1768
SKEWIS	MARGERY	daughter of Robin	16 April	1761
SKEWIS	WILLIAM	son of Henry	8 Oct	1770
SKEWIS	MARY	daughter of Richard	28 Nov	1770
SKEWIS	JAMES	son of James	12 Jan	1772
SKEWIS	HENRY		2 May	1774
SKEWIS	JOHN		7 May	1774
SKEWES	HENRY		18 May	1776
SKEWES	ROBERT		27 June	1776
SKEWES	CONSTANCE		28 May	1776
SKEWES	ALICE	daughter of Richard	22 July	1777
SKEWES	MARGERY		16 Nov	1777
SKEWES	MARY	wife of William	22 Sept	1781
SKEWES	RICHARD	son of Richard and Alice	26 Oct	1785
SKEWES	CHARITY	wife of James (pauper)	3 July	1787
SKEWES	WILLIAM	Aged 85 years	21 June	1788
SKEWES	ELIZABETH	base daughter of Constance	21 Dec	1798
SKEWES	HONOUR	pauper	24 June	1791
SKEWES	STEPHEN	son of John	15 April	1799
SKEWES	MARGARET	base daughter of Constance	6 Feb	1801
SKEWES	JAMES		10 June	1804
SKEWES	WILLIAM	Aged 72 years	9 Dec	1807
SKEWES	HENRY	son of Absalom and Elizabeth	14 Oct	1808
SKEWES	MARGARET		27 Aug	1811
SKEWES	ABSALOM		12 Dec	1811
SKEWES	JOHN	Aged 77 years	26 April	1813
SKEWES	BETSY	Aged 3 years	7 Sept	1813
SKEWES	HENRY	Aged 75 years	7 Feb	1814
SKEWES	ELIZABETH	Aged 34 years	28 July	1814
SKEWES	ELIZABETH	Aged 5 weeks	3 Sept	1814
SKEWES	PHILIPPA	Aged 74 years	15 Aug	1815
SKEWES	JOHN	Aged 75 years	26 May	1816
SKEWES	RICHARD	Aged 31 years	9 Aug	1816
SKEWES	ELIZABETH Of Town	Aged 60 years	5 May	1818
SKUES	JANE Of Illogan	Aged 44 years	30 Mar	1821
SKUES	RICHARD Of Illogan	Aged 6 months	1 May	1821
SKUES	JANE Of Illogan	Aged 100 years	5 May	1822
SKUES	KATHERINE Of Illogan	Aged 9 years	25 Sept	1822
SKEWES	STEPHEN Of Treswithian	Aged 80 years	29 Sept	1823
SKUES	ROBERT Of Town	Aged 75 years	13 Nov	1823
SKUES	MARGARET Of Town	Aged 71 years	31 Dec	1823
SKUES	HENRY Of Carlean	Aged 44 years	19 May	1824
SKUES	FRANCES Of Illogan	Aged 14 years	6 Oct	1824
SKUES	WILLIAM Of Treswithian	Aged 56 years	17 Dec	1824
SKUES	MARY Of Town	Aged 20 months	23 Sept	1825
SKUES	STEPHEN Of Illogan	Aged 26 years	1 Jan	1826
SKUES	JOHN Of Park-en-bowen	Aged 6 weeks	5 Feb	1826
SKUES	MARY Of Illogan	Aged 23 years	23 Feb	1826
SKUES	JOHN Of Town	Aged 10 weeks	17 Jan	1828
SKUES	ELIZABETH Of Treswithian	Aged 3 years	25 Mar	1831
SKUES	ABSALOM The Younger of Town	Aged 10 years	31 Dec	1831
SKEWES	STEPHEN Of Killivoase	Aged 4 years	20 July	1834
SKEWES	MARY Of Town	Aged 4½ years	25 Nov	1834
SKUES	HENRY Of Treswithian	Aged 4, scalded to death	23 Feb	1835
SKEWISE	ANN Of Town	Aged 42, died of Apoplexy	18 Mar	1835
SKUES	ABSALOM Of Town	Aged 48, died of decline	25 Jan	1836
SKEWISE	ELIZABETH Of Town	Aged 4 years died of inflamation of the bowels	2 June	1836
SKEWISE	MARGARET Of Treswithian	Aged 33 — Scarlet Fever	30 Aug	1836
SKUES	HENRY of Penponds	Aged 75 years	20 Dec	1837
SKEWES	PHILIPPA	Town, aged 34	16 Oct	1838

SKEWIS	JOHN	Illogan, aged 64	29 Jan	1840
SKEWES	ELIZABETH	Town, aged 89	5 May	1842
SKEWES	ANNE	Killivoase, aged 23	18 July	1843
SKUES	WILLIAM	Town, aged 58 years	27 Apl	1844
SKEWIS	JOANNA	Killivoase, aged 54	7 Aug	1844
SKEWES	JOANNA	Town, aged 3 months	18 Jan	1844
SKEWIS	WILLIAM	Glebe Cottage, aged 71	22 Oct	1845
SKEWES	HENRY JAMES	Penponds, aged 4 weeks	1 Dec	1845
SKUES	CATHERINE	Town, aged 22	21 Feb	1846
SKEWES	GRACE	Town, aged 40	11 Apl	1847
SKEWES	JANE BAWDEN	Pengiggan Moor, aged 4	4 July	1852
SKEWES	ELIZABETH	Roskear, aged 58	27 Sept	1855
SKEWES	CAROLINE	Bassett Street, aged 43	10 Jan	1869
SKEWES	JAMES	North Parade, aged 85	15 Mar	1875
SKEWES	JAMES	William Street, aged 66	19 Oct	1879
SKEWES	JANE	Vyvyan's Row, aged 88	4 Nov	1878
SKEWES	ELIZABETH ANN	Redruth Union, aged 33	9 Oct	1885
SKEWES	SUSAN	Centenery Row, aged 64	4 Oct	1887
SKEWES	WILLIAM HENRY HERBERT	Of College Row, aged 14 Months	23 Apl	1888
SKEWES	LOUISA JANE	70, College Street, aged 69	16 Mar	1936
Philippa	SKEWES Heard	59 Enys Road, Camborne, aged 94 years	25 Mar	1947
SKEWES	MATILDA	99, Pendarves Road, Tuckingmill; Died in Barncoose Hospital, aged 88	26 Apr	1958

BAPTISMS (WESLEYAN/METHODIST) SOLEMNIZED IN THE CAMBORNE/REDRUTH CIRCUIT   1829 — 1837

SKEWES	HONOR	daughter of Edward (Miner) and Mary Skewes. Born 28 May, 1829	28 July	1829
SKEWES	HENRY	son of Edward and Mary Skewes. Born 17 September, 1831	24 Nov	1833
SKEWIS	ELIZABETH	daughter of John (Miner) and Ann Skewis, born 3 August, 1832	11 Oct	1832
SKEWIS	CAROLINE	daughter of Edward and Mary Skewis. Born 21 May, 1833	16 June	1833
SKEWES	WILLIAM	Son of Edward and Mary Skewes. Born 9 December, 1834	13 Mar	1835

PARISH REGISTER OF CHACEWATER   BAPTISMS   1828 — 1964

SKEWS	MARIA	daughter of Matthew and Mary Skews of Kenwyn, miner	15 Aug	1828
SKEWS	SAMUEL	son of William & Mary Skews of Kea, miner	12 Oct	1828
SKEWS	ELIZABETH	daughter of John & Ann Skews of Chacewood, miner	18 Dec	1828
SKEWS	ELIZABETH	daughter of John & Elizabeth Skews of Chacewater, miner	7 June	1829
SKEWS	SELINA	daughter of Thomas & Grace Skews of Chacewater, miner	11 Apl	1830
SKEWES	THOMAS	son of Richard & Agnes Skewes of Kerley, mine agent	7 Oct	1830
SKEWS	GRACE	daughter of Peter & Grace Skews of Kea, miner	31 July	1831
SKEWS	JULIA	daughter of Thomas & Grace Skews of Jolly's Bottom, miner	9 Oct	1831
SKUAZ	DANIEL	son of William and Mary Skuaz of Blackwater, miner	17 Oct	1831
SKEWS	ELIZABETH JANE	daughter of Thomas & Jane Skews of Kerley, miner	24 Nov	1833
SKEWES	EMMA JANE	daughter of Thomas and Grace Skewes of Kea, miner	18 May	1834
SKEWES	THOMAS	son of Thomas & Jane Skewes of Seveocke, miner	21 June	1835
SKEWES	ELIZABETH	daughter of Peter & Grace Skewes of Kerley, miner	16 June	1836
SKEWES	EMILY	daughter of Thomas & Grace Skewes of Jolly's Bottom, miner	10 Aug	1836
SKEWES	MARY	daughter of Peter and Grace Skewes of Kerley, miner	21 Feb	1837
SKEWES	MARTIN	son of Martin & Ann Skewes of Kerley, miner	26 Mar	1837
SKEWES	PHILIPPA	daughter of John & Harriet Skewes of Kerley, miner	9 July	1837
SKEWES	GRACE THERESA	daughter of Thomas & Grace Skewes of Jolly's Bottom, miner	16 Jan	1839
SKEWES	JOHN	son of Peter & Grace Skewes of Kerley, miner	17 Jan	1839
SKEWES	THOMAS	son of Martin and Ann Skewes of Blackwater, miner	9 June	1839
SKEWS	WILLIAM RICHARD FRANCIS DENNIS	son of William and Mary Skews of Chacewater, tailor	27 Sept	1840
SKEWS	MARY	daughter of Thomas and Jane Skews of Kerley, miner	17 Jan	1841
SKEWS	WALTER TREZIZE	son of Thomas and Grace Skews of Jolly's Bottom, miner	15 May	1842
SKEWS	WILLIAM TREZIZE	son of Thomas & Grace Skews of Kea, miner	6 Oct	1844
SKEWES	GRACE	daughter of James & Harriet Skewes of Kenwyn, miner	5 Oct	1845
SKEWES	JOHN	son of Martin and Ann Skewes of Kenwyn, innkeeper	10 Oct	1845
SKEWES	JOHN HENRY	son of John & Harriet Skewes of Kerley, miner	8 Aug	1847
SKEWES	AMELIA	daughter of John & Elizabeth Skewes of Chacewater	8 Mar	1848
SKEWS	SAMUEL	son of William & Susan Skews of Kerley, Kea, miner	2 Jan	1855
SKEWES	AMELIA	daughter of William & Susan Skews of Kerley, Kea, miner	2 Jan	1855
SKEWES	MATTHEW WARNE	son of John & Harriet Skews of Kerley, Kea, miner	11 Jan	1855
SKEWES	MARIA	daughter of Peter and Grace Skews of Kerley, Kea, miner	11 Jan	1855
SKEWES	WILLIAM HENRY	son of William Trezize and Maria Skewes of Camborne, miner	27 Dec	1863
SKEWES	RICHARD	son of Peter Skewes of River Cottage, Chacewater, mine agent	1 May	1874
SKEWES	BELLOTTA	daughter of Peter Skewes of River Cottage, Chacewater, mine agent	1 May	1874
SKEWES	JOHN	son of Peter & Elizabeth Skewes of Chacewater, mine agent	19 Sept	1878
SKEWES	GEORGE HARRIS	son of Peter & Elizabeth Skewes of Chacewater, mine agent	19 Sept	1878

SKEWES	JOHN HERBERT	son of John & Catherine Skewes of Chacewater, mine agent	29 Sept	1881
SKEWES	HILDA LAURA WILLIAMS	daughter of John & Catherine Skewes of Chacewater, mine agent	26 Nov	1882
SKEWES	KATIE BEATRICE	daughter of John & Catherine Skewes of Chacewater, mine agent	24 Jan	1886
SKEWES	LILIAN BEATRICE	daughter of Peter & Elizabeth Skewes of Redruth, mine agent	11 Mar	1887
SKEWES	HERBERT JOHN	son of Richard and Mary Skewes of Chacewater, mine agent	11 Mar	1887

PARISH REGISTER OF CHACEWATER   MARRIAGES   1837 — 1974

SKEWES WILLIAM miner of Jolly's Bottom; son of William Skewes, miner	and	Susan Oates of Jolly's Bottom, dau of John Oates, miner	24 Dec	1840
SKEWS MARY (Minor) daughter of William Skews, miner of Blackwater. In presence of William Skews	and	Thomas Trevethen miner; son of Henry Trevethen, miner	3 Mar	1842
SKEWS MARTIN, widower. Publican of Chacewater; son of Richard Skews, mine agent	and	Elizabeth Bennetts dau of Thomas Bennetts, farmer of Redruth	12 Mar	1851
SKEWES EMMA JANE dau of Thomas Skews, farmer, of Kea	and	Joel Wasley son of Joel Wasley, miner of Kea	25 June	1857
SKEWES MARY of Killiwerris; dau of John Skews, farmer. In presence of Emma Skews	and	George Warner of Killiwerris, smith; son of John Warner	24 Apl	1860
SKEWES EMMA of Chacewater; dau of John Skewes, farmer. In presence of Thomas Skewes Tonkin	and	Richard Furze of Chacewater; son of Richard Furze	24 July	1868
SKEWES JOHN mine agent of Chacewater; son of Peter Skewes, miner	and	Catherine Williams of Chacewater; dau of Michael Williams, grocer	4 Jan	1880
SKEWES HERBERT JOHN, 22 Gentleman of Chacewater; son of Richard Skewes, mining engineer	and	Henrietta Catalina Richards, 19, of Chacewater; dau of John Thompson Richards	25 Apl	1908

CHACEWATER PARISH REGISTER   BURIALS   1828 — 1936

SKEWS	JOHN HENRY	Chacewood	aged 2 years	18 Dec	1828
SKEWIS	MARIA	Chacewater	aged 2	31 Mar	1829
SKEWES	ELIZABETH	Kenwyn	aged 2	19 June	1829
SKEWS	GRACE	Salem	aged 46	6 Aug	1829
SKEWS	THOMAS	Kea	aged 5	29 Sept	1829
SKEWS	PETER	Blackwater	aged 67	11 July	1830
SKEWS	THOMAS	Kea	aged 1	21 Nov	1830
SKUAZ	MATTHEW	Chacewater	aged 2	20 Nov	1831
SKUAZ	SAMUEL	Kenwyn	aged 19	20 Nov	1831
SKEWS	PHILIPPA	Kerley	aged 12	24 Nov	1833
SKEWES	ANN	Chacewater	aged 62	3 July	1834
SKEWES	WILLIAM	Chacewater	aged 13	28 May	1836
SKEWES	SAMUEL	Kerley	aged 1	21 Feb	1837
SKEWES	RICHARD	Salem	aged 53	28 Mar	1837
SKEWES	MATTHEW	Kerley	aged 66	28 Mar	1838
SKEWES	JOHN	Hugus	aged 7	13 Feb	1839
SKEWES	GRACE	Kerley	aged 10	31 Mar	1840
SKEWES	GRACE THERESA	Kea	aged 5	9 May	1843
SKEWES	SELINA	Kea	aged 15	26 Dec	1843
SKEWES	LAVINIA	Kea	aged 11	15 Apl	1846
SKEWS	ELIZABETH	Kea	aged 85	23 Feb	1847
SKEWES	GRACE	Kerley in Kea	aged 12	9 Nov	1848
SKEWES	ANN	Chacewater	aged 36	27 Aug	1850
SKEWES	MARY	Wheal Busy, Kenwyn	aged 86	24 Mar	1853
SKEWS	ELIZABETH	Kerley in Kea	aged 21	11 Mar	1855
SKEWES	MATTHEW	Kenwyn	aged 60	28 Sept	1856
SKEWES	GRACE	Jolly's Bottom	aged 56	16 Nov	1857
SKEWES	MARY	Chacewater	aged 28	22 Mar	1861
SKEWES	JOHN	Killiwerris	aged 59	19 Jan	1862
SKEWES	WILLIAM	Camborne	aged 21	22 July	1864
SKEWES	ANN	Killiwerris	aged 61	16 May	1867
SKEWES	THOMAS	Jolly's Bottom	aged 83	19 Mar	1875
SKEWES	MARY	Kerley	aged 84	20 Nov	1882
SKEWES	KATIE BEATRICE	Chacewood	aged 18 months	19 Aug	1886

PARISH REGISTER OF CHARLESTOWN   BURIALS   1850—1890

| SKEWS | THOMAS | of Tregrehan, | aged 8 months | 16 Nov | 1872 |
| SKEWS | ELIZABETH JANE | of Boscoppa | aged 36 years | 14 Feb | 1878 |

No entries for Births or Marriages.

CONSTANTINE PARISH REGISTERS   BAPTISMS 1746—1943

SKEWES	MARY	daughter of HENRY & GRACE SKEWES	Bpt 6 July	1806
SKEWES	WILLIAM	son of HENRY & GRACE SKEWES	29 Nov	1807
SKEWES	GRACE	daughter of HENRY & GRACE SKEWES	23 July	1809
SKEWES	ALICE	daughter of HENRY & GRACE SKEWES	10 Mar	1811
SKEWES	ELIZABETH	daughter of HENRY & GRACE SKEWES	8 Aug	1813
SKEWES	HENRY	son of HENRY & GRACE SKEWES of Constantine, Farmer.	25 Dec	1818
SKEWES	JOSIAH	son of HENRY & GRACE SKEWES of Brill, Constantine, Farmer.	6 Aug	1820
SKEWES	FANNY	daughter of HENRY & GRACE SKEWES of Brill, Constantine, Farmer.	29 Sept	1822
SKEWES	CAROLINE	daughter of HENRY & GRACE SKEWES of Brill, Constantine, Farmer.	18 July	1824
SKEWES	ELIZA	daughter of HENRY & GRACE SKEWES of Brill, Constantine, Farmer.	26 May	1826
SKEWES	ANN	daughter of WILLIAM & REBECCA SKEWES of Churchtown, Constantine, Labourer.	29 Aug	1830
SKEWES	WILLIAM	son of WILLIAM & REBECCA SKEWES of Churchtown, Constantine, Labourer.	6 Apl	1834
SKEWES	ELIZA	daughter of JOSIAH & FANNY SKEWES of Bosawsack, Constantine, Farmer.	19 Nov	1862

Constantine Parish Church, circa 1910

CONSTANTINE PARISH REGISTERS   MARRIAGES   1571 — 1959

SKEWES	HENRY	of Cury and Judith Walters	28 Oct	1718
SKEWES	ALICE	and John Midlin. In the presence of Henry Skewes	24 Jan	1804
SKEWES	HENRY	and Grace Tremayne, special licence	9 Mar	1806
SKEWES	ELIZABETH	and John Rowe of Gluvias. In the presence of William Skewes and Henry Skewes	7 Feb	1810
SKUES	ANN	spinster of Constantine to Anthony Bafshar, bachelor, of Grade, miner	18 Feb	1823
SKEWES	WILLIAM	bachelor, and labourer, of Constantine to Rebecca Michell, spinster of Constantine	23 Mar	1828
SKEWES	MARY	spinster of Constantine to Stephen Eddy of Constantine	29 Mar	1828
SKEWES	JAMES	of Cury, farmer; to Grace Skewes of Constantine. In the presence of Henry Skewes	8 Apl	1834
SKEWES	ALICE	to Thomas Medlin, farmer. In the presence of Henry Skewes, Grace Skewes and Elizabeth Skewes	8 Oct	1835
SKEWES	ANN	Minor, of Trethowan Downs, Constantine, daughter of William Skewes, labourer, to Thomas Evans, of Trethowan Downs (son of Charles Evans), miner. In presence of William Skewes.	23 Dec	1847
SKEWES	FANNY	of Bosawsack (daughter of Henry Skewes, farmer) to Elias Geach, farmer of Budock. In presence of Josiah Skewes.	23 Feb	1848
SKEWES	CAROLINE	of Bosawsack, Constantine (daughter of Henry Skewes, deceased), to Alfred Knowles of Mabe, farmer (son of Caleb Knowles).	13 June	1849
SKEWES	JOHN	farmer, (son of John Skewes, farmer) to Elizabeth Jane Hill (daughter of William Hill, labourer).	3 Apl	1862
SKEWES	LAURA	aged 27 (daughter of Josiah Skewes, farmer) to Edwin Tregaskis, 30 (son of Edward Tregaskis). In the presence of James Skewes.	2 Mar	1882
SKEWES	HENRY	aged 28, farmer, (son of Josiah Skewes, deceased) to Ada Eliza Courage, 25 (daughter of William James Courage, farmer).	16 Sept	1896

CONSTANTINE PARISH REGISTER   BURIALS   1760 — 1911

SKURCE	WILLIAM	was buried	19 Nov.	1785
SKEWES	RICHARD	aged 68	1 Aug	1808
SKEWES	WILLIAM	of Penryn, aged 44	13 Oct	1813
SKEWES-HENDY, ALICE		of Churchtown, infant	29 Mar	1824
SKEWES	GRACE	of Brill, Constantine, aged 37	26 May	1826
SKEWES	HENRY	of Bosawsack, aged 66	5 June	1844
SKEWES	WILLIAM	of Trethowan Downs, aged 80	6 Mar	1846
SKEWES	ANN	of Trethowan Downs, aged 79	9 Apl	1847
SKEWES	WILLIAM	of Churchtown, Constantine, aged 65 years	11 Nov	1861
SKEWES	ELIZA	of Bosawsack, Constantine, aged 9 days	25 Nov	1862
SKEWES	JOSIAH	of Bosawsack, Constantine aged 58 years	5 June	1878
SKEWES	FANNY	of Bosawsack, Constantine, aged 68 years	24 June	1895

CROWAN PARISH REGISTER   BAPTISMS   1743 — 1869

SKEWIS	ABSALOM	son of Absalom & Elizabeth Skewes	Born 17 Oct	1787
			Bpt 26 Dec	1787
SKUES	ELIZABETH	dau of Absalom & Elizabeth Skues	Born 24 Mar	1789
			Bpt 2 Oct	1789
SKUES	HENRY	son of Absalom & Elizabeth Skues	Born 18 June	1791
			Bpt 7 Aug	1791

CROWAN PARISH REGISTER   MARRIAGES   1674 — 1889

SKEWIS	MARGARET	&	Henery Michell	28 Sept	1734
SKEWIS	MARY	&	Thomas Bastard	19 Apl	1737
SKEWES	HENRY	&	Constance Paul	9 July	1737
SKEWIS	ABSALOM	&	Elizabeth Clemence	6 Feb	1786
SKEWIS	ELONOR	&	Thomas Rowe	24 Sept	1786
SKEWES	ELIZABETH	&	Daniel Rowe	18 Nov	1787
SKEWES	WILLIAM	&	Elizabeth Thomas	* between July and Dec	1803 1803
SKEWES	JAMES	&	Jane Thomas	* between Nov and Dec	1807 1807

* date not printed in register

CROWAN PARISH REGISTER   BURIALS   1697 — 1947

SKEWES	WILLIAM JAMES	of Crowan, aged 4 years buried	27 Dec	1860
SKEWIS	JOHN	of Crowan, aged 48 years	6 Jan	1876
SKEWES	MARY ANN	of Crowan, aged 31 years	29 Dec	1881
SKEWES	PHILIPPA	of Crowan, aged 78 years	14 Aug	1883
SKEWES	RICHARD	or Crowan, aged 25 years	4 Jan	1885

| SKEWES | HETTY CATALINA | of the Vicarage, Crowan, aged 52 years. Burial service was conducted by H.S. Bancock, assistant priest of Camborne. Hetty was wife of Rev Herbert John Skewes, vicar of Crowan. | 4 Apl | 1942 |

CURY PARISH REGISTER   BAPTISMS FROM   1690 — 1956

SKEWES	WILLIAM	son of Edward and Elizabeth Skewes	13 July	1690
SKEWS	WELMOT	daughter of Henry and Elizabeth Skews	26 Dec	1694
SKEWES	EDWARD	son of Edward and Elizabeth Skewes (born 11 Feb 1695)	16 Feb	1695
SKEWES	JANE	daughter of James and Sarah Skewes	24 Mar	1705
SKEWES	ELIZABETH	daughter of James and Sarah Skewes	28 Mar	1708
SKEWES	WILLIAM	son of James and Sarah Skewes	22 Jan	1709
SKEWES	JAMES	son of James and Sarah Skewes	7 Nov	1711
SKEWES	SARAH	daughter of James and Sarah Skewes	27 Dec	1713
SKEWES	WILLIAM	son of James and Sarah Skewes	13 May	1716
SKEWES	MARY	daughter of James and Sarah Skewes	2 Mar	1717
SKEWES	ANNE	daughter of Henry and Judeth née Walters Skewes (married in Constantine 28 Oct 1718)	7 Dec	1718
SKEWES	BLANCH	daughter of James and Sarah Skewes	7 Feb	1719
SKEWES	ANN	daughter of Henry and Judeth Skewes	6 Aug	1721
SKEWES	JOHN	son of James and Sarah Skewes	25 Mar	1722
SKEWES	THOMAS	son of Henry and Judeth Skewes	14 Feb	1722
SKUES	EDWARD	son of James and Sarah Skues	1 Mar	1723
SKEWES	ANNE	daughter of Edward and Ann (née Beal of Gunwalloe) Skewes	1 Nov	1724
SKEWES	ANTHONY	son of Henry and Judeth Skewes	6 Dec	1725
SKEWES	GEORGE AND HENRY	sons of Henry and Judeth Skewes	6 Sep	1727
SKEWES	MARY	daughter of Edward and Ann Skewes	3 Nov	1728
SKEWES	JANE	daughter of Henry and Judeth Skewes	25 Jul	1731
SKEWES	JUDETH	daughter of Henry and Judeth Skewes	26 Mar	1733
SKEWES	BLANCH	daughter of Edward and Ann Skewes	8 May	1737
SKEWES	JOHN	son of Edward and Margaret née Rogers Skewes (married in Sithney 13 May 1743)	23 Sep	1744
SKEWES	ELEANOR	daughter of Edward and Margaret Skewes	16 Mar	1745
SKEWES	JAMES	son of John and Mary (née George) Skewes (married in Cury 12 Sep 1747)	12 Apr	1748
SKEWIS	JOHN	son of Edward and Margaret Skewis	7 Jun	1749
SKEWES	SARAH	daughter of John and Mary Skewes	4 Mar	1751
SKEWES	HENRY	son of Edward and Margaret Skewes	2 Dec	1753
SKEWES	JOHN	son of John and Margaret Skewes	24 Mar	1753
SKEWES	EDWARD	son of John and Mary Skewes	31 Oct	1756
SKEWIS	MARGERY	daughter of John and Mary Skewis	4 Mar	1759
SKEWES	ELIZABETH	daughter of John and Mary Skewes	13 Mar	1763
SKEWES	RICHARD	son of John and Mary Skewes	15 Jun	1768
SKEWES	WILLIAM	son of John and Mary Skewes	15 Jun	1766
SKEWES	FRANCES	daughter of John and Mary Skewes	11 Dec	1768
SKEWIS	JOHN	son of John and Mary Skewis	17 May	1775
SKEWES	EDWARD	son of John and Mary Skewes	6 Jan	1782
SKEWES	ELIZABETH	daughter of James and Ann Skewes	14 Jul	1782
SKEWES	MARY	daughter of John and Mary Skewes	15 Aug	1784
SKEWES	JAMES	son of James and Ann Skewes	13 May	1785
SKEWES	JAMES	base son of Mary Dorten	13 Aug	1786
SKEWES	MARY	daughter of John and Mary Skewes	21 May	1786
SKEWES	WILLIAM	son of John and Mary Skewes	1 Mar	1789
SKEWES	JANE	daughter of James and Ann Skewes	26 Jun	1791
SKEWES	BLANCH	daughter of John and Mary Skewes	7 Feb	1792
SKEWES	WILLIAM	son of John and Mary Skewes	6 Mar	1794
SKEWES	ALICE	daughter of William and Alice Skewes	19 Feb	1795
SKEWES	MARY	daughter of William and Alice Skewes	10 Jul	1796
SKEWES	JAMES	son of James and Ann Skewes	2 Apr	1797
SKEWES	JAMES	son of John and Mary Skewes	20 Aug	1797
SKEWES	JOHN	son of William and Alice Skewes	4 Jul	1798
SKEWES	ANN	daughter of William and Alice Skewes	15 Dec	1799
SKEWIS	ANN	daughter of John and Mary Skewis	17 May	1801
SKEWES	WILLIAM	son of William and Alice Skewes	28 Feb	1802
SKEWES	WILLIAM	son of William and Alice Skewes	22 May	1803
SKEWES	GRACE	daughter of John and Elizabeth Skewes (née Hendy married 23 Sept 1800)	24 Jul	1803
SKEWES	LOVEDAY	daughter of John and Elizabeth Skewes	7 Dec	1806
SKEWES	SARAH	daughter of William and Alice Skewes	9 Jun	1805
SKEWES	ELIZABETH	daughter of William and Alice Skewes	10 Mar	1807
SKEWIS	JAMES	son of James and Elizabeth née Tremayne Skewis (married 25 Jul 1808)	8 Oct	1809
SKEWES	JOHN	son of John and Loveday Skewes (pri)	2 Dec	1810
SKEWES	EDWARD	son of William and Alice Skewes	8 Dec	1810
SKEWES	MARY	daughter of James and Elizabeth Skewes	11 Apr	1811

			24	May	1812
SKEWES	HENRY	son of William and Alice Skewes	23	Feb	1812
SKEWES	JOHN	son of John and Loveday Skewes	29	Jul	1813
SKEWES	WILLIAM	son of James and Elizabeth Skewes of Gilly, labourer	27	Mar	1814
SKEWES	EDWARD	son of John and Loveday Skewes of Nantithet, labourer	15	Jan	1815
SKEWES	ELIZABETH	daughter of William and Alice Skewes of Treloskan, farmer	23	Apr	1815
SKEWES	JOHN	son of James and Elizabeth Skewes of Gilly, labourer	27	Aug	1815
SKEWES	SAMUEL	son of John and Loveday Skewes of Nantithet, labourer	8	Sep	1816
SKEWES	ELIZABETH	daughter of William and Alice Skewes of Treloskan, tinner	4	Apr	1817
SKEWES	HENRY	base son of Blanch Skewes of Treloskan	4	May	1817
SKEWES	ELIZABETH	daughter of James and Elizabeth Skewes of Gilly, labourer	18	May	1817
SKEWES	FRANCES	base daughter of Blanch Skewes of Nantithet privately / publicly	1	Jun	1817
			27	Jul	1817
SKEWES	ANN HENDY	daughter of John and Loveday Skewes of Nantithet, labourer	5	Jul	1818
SKEWES	HENRY	son of James and Elizabeth Skewes of Gilly, labourer	17	Feb	1820
SKEWES	MARY	daughter of John and Loveday Skewes of Nantithet	17	Feb	1820
SKEWES	ANN	daughter of James and Elizabeth Skewes of Gilly, labourer	5	Oct	1820
SKEWES	RICHARD	son of William and Alice Skewes of Treloskan, farmer	17	Mar	1822
SKEWES	WILLIAM	son of John and Loveday Skewes of Gilly, labourer	30	Jun	1822
SKEWES	JOSIAH	son of James and Elizabeth Skewes of Gilly, labourer	25	Apr	1824
SKEWES	LOVEDAY	daughter of James and Elizabeth Skewes of Gilly, labourer	4	Jul	1824
SKEWIS	HANNAH	daughter of John and Loveday Skewis of Nantithet, labourer	1	Aug	1824
SKUES	JANE JEFFREY	daughter of John and Avis Jeffrey Skues (married 4 Mar 1824)	30	Jan	1825
SKEWIS	JAMES	son of James and Simonette née Barnett Skewis of Treloskan (married 5 Oct 1824)	2	Apr	1826
SKEWIS	THOMAS	son of James and Elizabeth Skewis of Gilly, labourer	7	May	1826
SKEWIS	JAMES	natural son of Ann Skewis of Ruan Major	18	Jun	1826
SKEWIS	JOHN THOMAS	illegitimate son of Jane Skewis of Nantithet	10	Dec	1826
SKEWES	NANCY	daughter of James and Simonette Skewis of Little Treloskan	26	Oct	1828
SKEWIS	JOHN	son of John and Avis Skewes of Gilly, labourer	25	Dec	1828
SKEWIS	WILLIAM	son of James and Simonette Skewis of Little Treloskan, farmer	14	Aug	1831
SKEWIS	NANCY	daughter of James and Simonette Skewis of Little Treloskan, farmer	23	Feb	1834
SKEWES	ALICE	daughter of James and Simonette Skewis of Little Treloskan, farmer	1	Feb	1835
SKEWES	ELIZABETH MARY	daughter of William and Mary née Skewes Skewes of Nantithet, labourer (married 3 Nov 1834)	22	May	1836
SKEWES	JOHN	son of James and Simonette Skewes of Little Treloskan, farmer	14	Apr	1837
SKUES	JOSEPH	illegitimate son of Elizabeth Skues of Treloskan	4	Jun	1837
SKUES	ALICE ANN	daughter of William and Mary Skues of Polwin, labourer	16	Jul	1837
SKUES	JULIANNA HENDY	daughter of John (late of St. Hilary) and Julianna née Hendy Skues of Nantithet, labourer (married 3 Jan 1837)	10	Apr	1838
SKEWIS	JOHN	son of Edward and Martha Skewis of Church Town, shoemaker	6	May	1838
SKEWIS	EDWARD	son of James and Simonet Skewis of Treloskan, farmer	16	Dec	1838
SKEWES	WILLIAM HENRY	illegitimate son of Jane Skewes of Nantithet	5	Apr	1840
SKEWES	ELIZABETH JANE	daughter of James and Simonette Skewes of Meanley, farmer	20	Sep	1840
SKEWES	EMILY	daughter of William and Mary Skewes of Nantithet, labourer	1	Nov	1840
SKEWYS	JAMES HENRY	son of John and Julia Skewys of Gilly, labourer	29	June	1842
SKEWES	SAMUEL	illegitimate son of Ann Hendy Skewes of Nantithet — single woman	6	Jul	1844
SKEWES	ELIZA	daughter of William and Mary Skewes of Nantithet, labourer	2	Mar	1845
SKEWES	BLANCHE	daughter of James and Simonette Skewes of Little Treloskan, farmer	31	Jan	1846
SKEWES	ELIZA GRACE	daughter of James and Grace Skewes of Treloskan, farmer	19	Mar	1848
SKEWES	RICHARD LALY	son of Richard and Caroline Skewes of the Parish of St. Neot, miner	11	Mar	1849
SKEWES	ELLEN WILLCOCKS	daughter of James and Simonette Skewes of Meanley, farmer	4	Nov	1849
SKEWES	JOHN	son of John and Julianna Skewes of Trewellow, labourer	4	Nov	1849
SKEWES	MARIA	daughter of Henry and Ann Skewes of Meanley, miner	4	Apr	1852
SKEWES	SAMUEL LAITY	illegitimate son of Elizabeth Skewes, single woman of Nantithet	2	Nov	1852
SKEWES	JOHN FREDERICK	son of Francis and Julianna Skewes of Church Town, labourer	16	Apr	1854
SKEWES	THIRZA	daughter of Francis and Julia Skewes of Church Town, labourer	22	Feb	1856
SKEWES	ELIZABETH MARY	illegitimate daughter of Elizabeth Skewes, single woman of Nantithet	23	Mar	1856
SKEWES	SUSANNAH	daughter of Francis and Julia Skewes of Church Town, labourer	4	Dec	1857
SKEWES	FREDERICK THERIZE	illegitimate son of Julia Skewes of Chypons, single woman	5	Mar	1857
SKEWES	HENRY	son of Edward and Julia Skewes of Nantithet, shoemaker	29	Jul	1859
SKEWES	ELIZABETH MARIA HICKS	daughter of John and Susan Skewes of Nantithet, shoemaker	27	Jul	1860
SKEWES	JOHN WESLEY	illegitimate son of Alice Ann Skewes, single woman of Nantithet	4	May	1860
SKEWES	ANNE	daughter of Edward and Julia Skewes of Nantithet, cordwainer	15	May	1861
SKEWES	WILLIAM HICKS	son of John and Susan Skewes of Nantithet, cordwainer	6	Aug	1862
SKEWES	BESSIE	daughter of Edward and Julia Skewes of Gilly Lane, shoemaker	21	Jan	1863
SKEWES	EDITH	daughter of Edward and Julia Skewes of Nantithet, shoemaker	27	Aug	1865
SKEWES	LAURA	daughter of Edward and Julia Skewes of Nantithet, shoemaker	4	Jan	1867
SKEWES	EDWARD	son of Edward and Julia Skewes of Nantithet, shoemaker	3	May	1867
SKEWES	ARTHUR	illegitimate son of Alice Ann Skewes of Nantithet	24	Oct	1867
SKEWES	HARRY OSWALD	son of James Henry and Mary Jane Skewes of Central America, carpenter	8	Nov	1869
SKEWES	WILLIAM JOHN	son of William James and Susan Skewes of Nantithet, farm labourer	20	Jun	1869
SKEWES	JULIANNA	daughter of Edward and Julia Skewes of Nantithet, shoemaker	4	Nov	1872
SKEWES	LILLA EMMA	daughter of John and Thirza née Thomas Skewes of Chypons, labourer (married 17 Apr 1872)	4	Nov	1872
SKEWES	JAMES HENRY	son of John and Thirza Skewes of Chypons, labourer	26	Dec	1877
SKEWES	ELLEN JANE	daughter of John and Thirza Skewes of Chypons, labourer	26	Dec	1877
SKEWES	ELIZABETH MARY	daughter of John and Thirza Skewes of Chypons, labourer	18	Jan	1883
SKEWES	BESSIE	daughter of John and Thirza Skewes of Chypons, labourer			

| SKEWES | SUSAN | daughter of John and Thirza Skewes of Chypons, labourer | 18 Jan | 1883 |
| SKEWES | THIRZA | daughter of John and Thirza Skewes of Penhale, labourer | 13 Jan | 1887 |

CURY MARRIAGES (1608 — 1956)

SKEWES	MARY	&	Charles Betty	26 Dec	1693
SKEWES	URSELA	&	James Thomas of St Martin	27 Dec	1714
SKEWIS	WILMET	&	Peter Fayby of Mawgan	12 Nov	1726
SKEWIS	JANE	&	John James of Mullion	3 June	1727
SKEWIS	WELMET	&	Christopher Harris	12 April	1740
SKEWIS	ANNE	&	Joseph Dalle	6 Sept	1741
SKEWIS	ANNE	&	James Boaden	1 Nov	1744
SKEWES	JOHN	&	Mary George	12 Sept	1747
SKEWES	BLANCH	&	Robert Caddy	30 Dec	1758
SKEWES	ANTHONY	&	ELEANOR SKEWES	11 Dec	1760
SKEWES	SARAH	&	John Piercey of St Keverne	11 Feb	1777
SKEWES	MARY	&	William Jennings of Crowan	8 April	1777
SKEWIS	JOHN	&	Mary Williams	3 Jan	1778
SKEWES	MARGERY	&	John White	4 June	1783
SKEWES	FRANCES	&	Joseph Keverne	29 May	1792
SKEWES	MARY	&	Henry Williams	1 Oct	1793
SKEWES	ANN	&	John Tripconey of St Keverne	4 Feb	1795
SKEWES	JOHN	&	Elizabeth Hendy	23 Sept	1800
SKEWES	SARAH	&	Thomas Triggs, private in the Royal Cornwall Militia	12 Dec	1804
SKEWES	JAMES	&	Elizabeth Tremean (Tremayne)	25 July	1808
SKEWES	MARY	&	Richard Dudley	5 Nov	1810
SKEWES	JANE	&	Walter Bellman	4 April	1820
SKEWES	MARY	&	Thomas Piercey	24 April	1821
SKEWES	JOHN	&	Avis Jeffery	4 Mar	1824
SKEWES	JAMES	&	Simonette Barnett	5 Oct	1824
SKEWIS	SARAH	&	John Triggs	23 Oct	1827
SKEWIS	BLANCHE	&	Richard Oates	2 Dec	1828
SKEWIS	ELIZABETH	&	William James	29 Sept	1829
SKEWES	GRACE	&	Samuel Hendy	27 Dec	1831
SKEWES	WILLIAM	&	Sarah Hodge	6 July	1833
SKEWES	WILLIAM	&	MARY SKEWES	3 Nov	1834
SKEWES	EDWARD	&	Alice Triggs	11 Nov	1834
SKEWES	ANNE	&	James Freeman of Sithney	14 Dec	1836
SKEWES	JOHN of St Hilary	&	Julianna Hendy	3 Jan	1837
SKEWES	HENRY (26) carpenter of Skewes in Cury; son of James SKEWES and Elizabeth of Gilly, Labourer	&	Harriot Hodge (23) of White Cross, Cury. Daughter of Anthony Hodge, farmer	24 June	1845
SKEWIS	JAMES (25), husbandman of Cury; son of James Skewis, farmer.	&	Eleanor Harris (32) of Cury; daughter of James Harris, labourer	9 Jan	1848
SKEWIS	JANE (29) labourer of Nantithet. Daughter of John & Avis Skewis of Polsken, labourer	&	Francis Fox (25) of White Cross, Cury; son of Francis Fox, driver	22 Feb	1853
SKEWES	LOVEDAY HENDY (23) of Nantithet, Cury; daughter of Edward Skewes, shoemaker	&	John Penrose Crowl (22), Pattern-maker of St Erth; son of John Crowl, gardener	27 Nov	1864
SKEWES	MARTHA ELIZABETH (21) of Nantithet, Cury; daughter of Edward Skewes, shoemaker	&	Charles Courtis (21) farm labourer of Church Town; son of George Courtis, farm labourer	27 Nov	1864
SKEWES	ELIZA (19) of Cury, daughter of Edward Skewes, shoemaker	&	William Henry Blatchford (25) policeman of Illogan; son of William Blatchford, labourer	24 Oct	1867
SKEWES	JOHN (22) of Polglase, labourer; son of John Skewes, labourer	&	Thirza Thomas (19) of Cury White Cross; daughter of Francis Thomas	17 April	1872
SKEWES	JAMES (25) of Redruth, son of Edward Skewes, shoemaker	&	Susan Thomas (20) of Cury; daughter of Francis Thomas, labourer	11 Aug	1875
SKEWES	ANNIE (20) of Cury; daughter of Edward Skewes, shoemaker	&	Charles Evelyn Trerize (24) shoemaker; son of Edward Trerize, labourer	29 May	1879
SKEWES	ALFRED JOHN (27) Lorry driver of Mullion; son of Alfred John Skewes, moulder	&	Lily Matthews (29) of Cury; daughter of Frederick Pascoe Matthews, carpenter	30 June	1934

Cury Parish Church

CURY BURIALS   (1696 — 1941)

SKEWES	THOMAS	12 July	1696
SKEWES	ANN	30 May	1705
SKEWES	WILLIAM	20 June	1713
SKEWES	ELIZABETH	12 Feb	1715
SKEWES	THOMAS	11 Mar	1715
SKEWES	ANNE	17 July	1719
SKEWIS	GEORGE	24 Sept	1727
SKEWES	HENRY	5 April	1729
SKEWES	HENRY	26 Oct	1733
SKEWIS	ELIZABETH	25 Dec	1736
SKEWIS	WILLIAM	4 Feb	1737
SKEWIS	BLANCH	23 Feb	1737
SKEWIS	SARAH	8 April	1738
SKEWIS	JAMES	7 Feb	1741
SKEWIS	JOHN	26 Nov	1744
SKEWES	EDWARD	19 Mar	1747
SKEWIS	EDWARD	16 July	1758
SKEWIS	HENRY	25 Jan	1760
SKEWIS	EDWARD	19 Dec	1761
SKEWES	ELIZABETH	9 June	1762
SKEWIS	JUDETH	26 Nov	1764
SKEWES	MARY	23 Mar	1767
SKEWIS	SARAH	5 Feb	1771
SKEWIS	ELEANOR	8 Mar	1773
SKEWES	MARY	25 Dec	1784

SKEWES	JAMES		16 Dec	1785
SKEWES	WILLIAM		18 May	1788
SKEWES	JOHN		1 June	1789
SKEWES	WILLIAM		13 Mar	1790
SKEWES	MARIA		14 Nov	1794
SKEWES	ELIZABETH		23 Mar	1798
SKEWES	ELEANOR		15 Feb	1800
SKEWIS	MARY		21 April	1801
SKEWES	MARY		16 Oct	1802
SKEWES	WILLIAM		30 June	1804
SKEWIS	ELIZABETH	dau of William Skewis, aged 1 year	21 Apl	1808
SKEWES	JOHN	aged 62 years	5 Nov	1811
SKEWES	ELIZABETH	of Treloskan, aged 1 year	1 Dec	1815
SKEWES	JAMES	of Treloskan, aged 69 years	11 June	1817
SKEWIS	LOVEDAY	of Nantithet, aged 2 years	10 Jan	1826
SKEWIS	ANN	of Treloskan, aged 9 months	18 Aug	1827
SKEWES	JOHN	of Treloskan, aged 75 years	14 Dec	1828
SKEWES	ELIZA	of Gilly Lane, aged 11 years	20 Jan	1829
SKEWES	LOVEDAY	of Nantithet, aged 39 years	12 Aug	1830
SKEWIS	ALICE	of Treloskan, aged 54 years	17 Jan	1831
SKEWIS	ANN	of Treloskan, aged 82 years	8 Oct	1832
SKEWIS	ALICE	of Churchtown, aged 26 years	30 Jan	1834
SKEWES	ELIZABETH	of Nantithet, aged 43 years	19 Apl	1842
SKEWES	MARY	of Treloskan, aged 86 years	3 Oct	1842
SKEWES	MARTHA	of Nantithet, aged 26 years	17 Sept	1843
SKEWES	JAMES	of Skewes Gate, aged 56 years	12 Oct	1845
SKEWES	EDWARD	of White Cross, aged 90 years	27 June	1845
SKEWES	ANN HENDY	of Nantithet, aged 30 years	1 Aug	1848
		Surplus of blood in head. Inquest on body		
SKEWES	WILLIAM	of White Cross, aged 82 years. General decay	7 Feb	1849
SKEWES	AVIS	of Nantithet, aged 63 years. Hung herself in a fit of temporary insanity	27 July	1849
SKEWES	HENRY	of Nantithet, aged 38 years	29 Nov	1850
SKEWES	ELIZABETH	of Nantithet, aged 68 years	27 May	1851
SKEWES	JOHN	of Nantithet, aged 75 years	24 Oct	1852
SKEWES	ELIZABETH MARY	of Gilly Lane, aged 19 years	30 Jan	1854
SKEWES	MARY	of Nantithet, aged 43 years	26 July	1855
SKEWES	JAMES	of Treloskan, aged 58 years	22 Oct	1856
SKEWES	WILLIAM HENRY	of Gilly Lane, aged 18 years	14 Jan	1857
SKEWES	JOHN	of Nantithet, aged 64 years	22 July	1858
SKEWES	ELIZABETH JOANNA HICKS	of Nantithet, aged 5 months	4 Dec	1858
SKEWES	JOHN	of Chyponds, aged 46 years	20 June	1860
SKEWES	EDWARD	of Treloskan, aged 79 years	18 Jan	1861
SKEWES	FREDERICK AUGUSTUS	of White Cross, aged 2 years	9 Mar	1866
SKEWES	ALICE	of Nantithet, aged 77 years	21 July	1868
SKEWES	BLANCHE	of Maenley, aged 83 years	30 Apl	1871
SKEWES	ANN	of Gilly Lane, aged 73 years	26 Mar	1873
SKEWES	EDWARD	of Nantithet, aged 64 years	20 Apl	1875
SKEWES	JAMES	of Redruth, aged 27 years	11 Feb	1877
SKEWES	WILLIAM	of Nantithet, aged 68 years	22 July	1877
SKEWES	EDWARD	of Nantithet, aged 64 years	24 Feb	1878
SKEWES	SUSAN	of White Cross, aged 24 years	31 Oct	1880
SKEWES	WILLIAM	of Nancegollan, aged 6 months	5 Jan	1886
SKEWES	JANE	of Nantithet, aged 80 years	4 Feb	1886
SKEWES	THEODORA	of Ruan Minor, aged 6 weeks	12 Jan	1890
SKEWES	ELEANOR HENDY	of Grade, aged 66 years	6 Jan	1893
SKEWES	JOHN	of Ruan Major, aged 77 years	15 Dec	1895
SKEWES	ELIZABETH	of White Cross, aged 78 years	12 Mar	1895
SKEWES	JOHN	of Halwyn, St Keverne, aged 71 years	11 April	1922
SKEWES	THIRZA	of Chyrean, St Keverne, aged 87 years	13 Feb	1941

PARISH REGISTER OF FALMOUTH BAPTISMS (1663 — 1837)

SKEWES	THOMAS	son of Thomas & Eleanor Skewes; Born 13 October 1780	Bpt: 12 Nov	1780
SKEWES	ELIZABETH	daughter of Thomas & Eleanor Skewes; Born 10 August 1782	15 Sept	1782
SKEWES	ESTHER	daughter of Thomas & Eleanor Skewes Born 5 July 1786	27 Aug	1786
SKEWES	THOMAS	son of Thomas & Eleanor Skewes Born 15 April 1790	24 April	1790
SKEWES	CHARLES GILLES	son of Thomas & Eleanor Skewes Born 4 May 1793	14 July	1793
SKEWES	EDWARD JOHN	son of Edward and Grace Skewes Born 20 November 1794	2 Dec	1794
SKEWES	ELIZABETH MARY	daughter of Edward and Grace Skewes Born 13 September 1797	1 Oct	1797
SKEWES	BENJAMIN HELLINGS	son of Thomas & Eleanor Skewes Born 20 February 1822	25 Dec	1822
SKEWES	THOMAS HENRY	son of Thomas and Eleanor Skewes Born 25 February 1824	9 June	1824
		N.B. Mother is dead		

PARISH REGISTER OF FALMOUTH   MARRIAGES   (1663 — 1837)

SKEWES	CATHERINE	&	James Barnicoat	2 Feb	1752
SKEWES	ELIZABETH	&	Gideon Johns of Gluvias	3 Nov	1758
SKEWIS	HESTER	&	Phillip Eller	12 April	1777
SKEWES	AVICE	&	Richard Pike of Plymouth	15 Feb	1781
SKEWS	JANE	&	Andrew Mitchell of Paul	18 Nov	1787
SKEWES	ALICE	&	William Skewes of Cury	26 Sept	1794
SKEWES	ELEANOR	&	Peter Wood, widower of Massachusetts, America	6 Feb	1795
SKEWES	ELIZABETH	&	William Rontree	24 Feb	1800
SKEWES	THOMAS, widower	&	Grace Pollard	22 Aug	1829

PARISH REGISTER OF FALMOUTH   BURIALS   (1663 — 1846)

SKEWES	ELIZABETH		18 April	1730
SKEWES	THOMAS	aged 2 years	24 Nov	1782
SKEWES	ELEANOR	aged 46 years	1 Aug	1795
SKEWES	THOMAS	aged 58 years	12 Jan	1808
SKEWES	HESTER	aged 25 years	15 April	1811
SKEWES	ELEANOR	aged 45 years	9 June	1824

BAPTISMS SOLEMNISED IN THE FALMOUTH CIRCUIT
(Non Parochial Registers of the Methodist Chapel, Falmouth)

SKEWES	WILLIAM	son of William & Elizabeth Skewes of Constantine, farmer. Born 2 December, 1835	22 Jan	1836
SKEWES	JOSEPH HENRY	son of Wm & Elizabeth Skewes of Constantine. Born 29 April 1837	9 June	1837

Falmouth Harbour, from a print by J. M. W. Turner

PARISH REGISTER OF FEOCK   MARRIAGES   1600 — 1891

SKEWES	JOAN of Truro	and	William Walkham of St Clement	14 Sept	1724

PARISH REGISTER OF FOWEY   BAPTISMS   1830 — 1967

SKEWES	EDITH JANE	daughter of Lewis and Eliza Skewes of Church Yard, Fowey; mason.	6 May	1877
SKEWES	JAMES FREDERICK	son of Lewis and Eliza Skewes of Esplanade Street, Fowey; mason	23 Apr	1879
SKEWES	JAMES FREDERICK	son of Lewis and Eliza Skewes of St Catherine Street, Fowey; mason	29 Jun	1879
SKEWES	CHARLES	son of Lewis and Eliza Skewes of North Street, Fowey, mason	26 May	1881

PARISH REGISTER OF FOWEY   MARRIAGES   1850 — 1880

SKEWES LEWIS, 35 stone mason of St Mewan, son of John Skewes, stone mason	and	Eliza Pearn, 23 daughter of Joseph Pearn of Fowey, shoemaker	21 Jan	1877

PARISH REGISTER OF GERMOE   BURIALS   1700 — 1837

SKEWES	RICHARD	of Rejann, Germoe, aged 53 years	27 Mar	1825

PARISH REGISTER OF GERRANS   BAPTISMS   1538 — 1727

SKEWES	JAMES	son of John Skewes	26 Aug	1573
SKEWES	HUMFRY	son of Katherin Skewes, bastard	20 Nov	1574
SKEWES	WILLIAM	son of John Skewes	11 Mar	1577
SKEWES	STEPHEN	son of John Skewes	21 Jan	1580
SKEWES	JOHAN	daughter of Elnor Skewes, bastard	24 Sep	1581
SKEWES	JOHN	son of Humfry Skewes	8 Sep	1616
SKEWES	FLORENCE	daughter of Humfry Skewes	12 Sep	1618
SKEWS	JOHN	son of John Skewes	1 Sep	1650
SKEWS	PHILIPPA	dau of John Skews	10 July	1653
SKEWS	EDWARD	son of John Skews	6 Sep	1661

PARISH REGISTER OF GERRANS   MARRIAGES   1538 — 1727

SKEWES JANE daughter of Thomas Skewes	&	William Hayne	3 Oct	1563
SKEWES JOHN	&	Maud Penperth	23 Nov	1572
SKEWES MARY	&	John Babbe	5 Nov	1582
SKEWES ELNOR	&	Henry Fittack	17 Jan	1590
SKEWES AGNIS	&	Martin Luke	7 May	1611
SKEWES HUMFRY	&	Mary Evans	3 Nov	1612
SKEWES FLORENCE daughter of Humfry Skewes	&	Osborne Fittack	5 May	1646

PARISH REGISTER OF GERRANS   BURIALS   1571 — 1837

SKEWES	THOMAS	buried	7 Apl	1580
SKEWES	JOHN		6 Aug	1582
SKEWES	DORITER	daughter of Humfry Skewes	7 Aug	1639
SKEWES	HUMFRY		5 Nov	1641
SKEWS	MARY	widow	2 Jun	1651
SKEWS	EDWARD	son of John Skews	8 Aug	1661

PARISH REGISTER OF GRADE   BAPTISMS   1597 — 1837

SKEWES	HENRY	son of John and Jane Skewes of St Ruan, farmer	30 Jun	1834
SKEWES	THOMAS BOULDEN	son of John and Jane Skewes of St Ruan, farmer	18 May	1836

PARISH REGISTER OF GRADE   MARRIAGES   1716 — 1944

SKEWES	JOHN	&	Jane Boulden	18 June	1833

PARISH REGISTER OF GULVAL   BAPTISMS   1598 — 1837

| SCRUSE | GEORGE | son of George Scruse of Ludgvan | 21 May | 1716 |

PARISH REGISTER OF GUNWALLOE   BAPTISMS   1717 — 1812

SKEWES	EDWARD	son of Henry & Judith Skewes	3 Apl	1720
SKEWES	EDWARD	son of William & Avise Skewes	27 Aug	1721
SKEWES	LOVEDAY	daughter of William & Avise Skewes	22 May	1726
SKEWES	JOSEPH	son of Joseph & Jone Skewes	20 Mar	1733
SKEWES	JANE	daughter of Joseph & Jone Skewes	2 Nov	1736
SKEWIS	JUDETH	daughter of Anthony & Elanor Skewis of Cury	6 May	1764
SKEWES	JOHN	son of William & Ann Skewes	6 Nov	1791
SKEWES	WILLIAM	son of William & Ann Skewes	28 Dec	1794
SKEWES	WILLIAM	son of William & Ann Skewes	6 Nov	1796
SKEWES	JOHN	son of William & Ann Skewes	4 Mar	1798
SKEWES	JOSEPH	son of William & Ann Skewes	14 July	1799

Gunwalloe Church, circa 1899

PARISH REGISTER OF GUNWALLOE   MARRIAGES   1716 — 1837

SKEWES	WILLIAM	&	Avise Row	24 June	1718
SKEWES	EDWARD	&	Ann Boal	10 Nov	1723
SKEWES	JOSEPH	&	Jane Corien	5 Aug	1738
SKEWIS	LOVEDAY	&	George Jewil	25 May	1746
SKEWES	WILLIAM	&	Ann Williams	10 July	1791
(SKUIS in signature), husbandman					

PARISH REGISTER OF GUNWALLOE   BURIALS   1716 — 1812

SKEWES	JOSEPH	buried	20 July	1751
SKEWES	JONE		23 July	1757
SKEWIS	AVIS		10 Oct	1757
SKEWES	JOHN		1 Mar	1792
SKEWES	WILLIAM		19 Mar	1795
SKEWES	JOSEPH		31 Oct	1799

PARISH REGISTER OF GWENNAP   BAPTISMS   1670 — 1976

SKUES	THOMAS	son of Thomas Skues	19 May	1673
SKUES	JOAN	daughter of Thomas Skues	3 Sept	1676
SKEWES	WILLIAM	son of William Skewes	13 Nov	1692
SKEWS	JOAN (?)	daughter of William Skews	23 Apl	1698
SKEWS	ALEXANDER	son of William Skews	5 Dec	1700
SKEWS	JOHN	son of Thomas Skews, tinner	12 Aug	1704
SKEWS	MARY	daughter of William Skews	24 May	1708
SKEWES	BLANCH	daughter of Thomas Skewes	7 June	1707
SKEWES	MARGARET	daughter of Thomas Skewes	26 Mar	1709
SKEWS	BLANCH	daughter of William Skews	14 Oct	1710
SKEWS	THOMAS	son of Thomas Skews	6 Jan	1711
SKEWS	THOMAS	son of Thomas Skews	16 Dec	1712
SKEWS	JOAN	daughter of Thomas Skews	27 Sept	1715
SKEWS	RICHARD	son of Thomas Skews	3 May	1718
SKEWS	WILLIAM	son of Thomas Skews	6 Oct	1722
SKEWS	THOMAS	son of Thomas & Elizabeth Skews	10 Mar	1738
SKEWS	JOHN	son of Thomas & Elizabeth Skews	11 Oct	1740
SKEWS	WILLIAM	son of John and Mary Skews privately	10 Sept	1743
SKEWS	WILLIAM	son of Thomas & Elizabeth Skews	9 Feb	1744
SKEWS	RICHARD	son of John & Elizabeth Skews	9 June	1745
SKEWS	ALEXANDER	son of Thomas & Elizabeth Skews	26 Dec	1746
SKEWS	MARGARET	daughter of Thomas & Elizabeth Skews	13 May	1749
SKEWES	ELIZABETH	daughter of Thomas & Elizabeth Skewes	17 July	1751
SKEWES	ALEXANDER	son of Thomas & Elizabeth Skewes	15 Sept	1753
SKEWES	E...IZABETH	daughter of Thomas & Elizabeth Skewes	24 Apl	1756
SKEWES	JOAN	daughter of William & Ann Skewes	12 June	1756
SKEWES	ALEXANDER	son of Thomas & Elizabeth Skewes	22 Apl	1758
SKEWES	ANN	daughter of William & Ann Skewes	27 May	1758
SKEWES	THOMAS	son of John & Mary Skewes	26 Dec	1769
SKEWES	RICHARD	son of John & Mary Skewes	11 June	1771
SKEWES	RICHARD	son of John & Mary Skewes	11 Mar	1774
SKEWES	ELIZABETH	daughter of John & Mary Skewes	8 Apl	1776
SKEWES	JOHN	son of John & Mary Skewes	12 Oct	1777
SKEWES	RICHARD	son of John & Mary Skewes	16 July	1779
SKEWES	MARY	daughter of John & Mary Skewes	18 Mar	1781
SKEWES	SUSANNA	daughter of Richard & Jane Skewes	3 Oct	1782
SKEWES	ELIZABETH	daughter of John & Mary Skewes	5 Mar	1783
SKEWES	ELIZABETH	daughter of John & Mary Skewes	15 May	1785
SKEWES	MARY	daughter of John & Mary Skewes	15 Oct	1786
SKEWIS	GEORGE	son of Thomas & Ann Skewis	9 Sept	1787
SKEWIS	GRACE	daughter of John & Mary Skewis	21 Oct	1788
SKEWIS	PETER	son of Peter & Mary Skewis	3 Jan	1794
SKEWIS	GRACE	daughter of Alexander & Christian	12 Mar	1797
SKEWIS	MARGARET	daughter of Alexander & Christian	29 Nov	1798
SKEWIS	ELIZABETH	daughter of Richard & Mary Skewis	8 May	1800
SKEWIS	RICHARD	son of Alexander & Christian	23 Sept	1800
SKEWIS	ELIZABETH	daughter of Peter & Ann Skewis	21 June	1801
SKEWIS	COLLAN	son of Richard & Mary Skewis	8 Sept	1802
SKEWIS	JOANNA	daughter of Alexander & Christian	5 July	1803
SKEWIS	JOHN	son of Richard & Mary Skewis	28 Aug	1804
SKEWIS	CHRISTIAN MARTYN	daughter of Alexander & Christian	23 May	1805
SKEWIS	ELIZABETH	daughter of Alexander & Christian	3 Oct	1805
SKEWES	ALEXANDER	son of Alexander & Christian	7 Sept	1807
SKEWES	SUSANNAH	daughter of James & Susannah Skewes	6 June	1808
SKEWES	WILLIAM	son of Alexander & Christian Skewes	13 Aug	1808
SKEWES	ELIZABETH	daughter of Alexander & Christian	13 Mar	1810
SKEWES	MARY	daughter of Alexander & Christian	10 June	1812
SKEWES	JOHN	son of John & Jenifer Skewes	6 Dec	1812
SKEWES	CHARITY	daughter of James & Susannah Skewes of Lanner, Gwennap	23 Jan	1813
SKEWES	ANN	daughter of Alexander & Christian Skewes, mine clerk of Chenhale	12 Aug	1814
SKEWES	JOHN	son of Richard & Grace Skewes, miner, of Whitehall	17 Aug	1814
SKEWES	JOHN	son of John & Jenifer Skewes, miner of Shilstones	22 Mar	1816
SKEWES	JAMES HANLY	son of Richard & Grace Skewes of Whitehall, Kenwyn, miner	23 July	1817
SKEWES	MARY ANN	daughter of John & Jenifer Skewes, miner of Poldice	30 Mar	1819
SKEWES	JANE TREWEEK	daughter of John & Jenifer Skewes, miner of Poldice	5 June	1822
SKEWES	JAMES MARLY	son of Richard & Grace Skewes, miner of Kenwyn	6 June	1824
SKEWES	MARY	daughter of John & Anne Skewes, miner of Carharrack	14 Apl	1827
SKEWES	MARY	daughter of James & Charity Skewes, miner of Gordon	26 Jan	1829
SKEWES	WILLIAM	son of Henry & Anne, miner of Rough Street	24 Apl	1829
SKEWES	JOHN	son of John & Ann Skewes, miner of Carharrack	29 Oct	1829
SKEWES	CAROLINNE TREWEEK	daughter of John & Jenifer Skewes, farmer and miner of Poldice	17 Dec	1829
SKEWS	JOHN RULE	son of John & Mary Ann Skews, miner of Kenwyn	22 May	1831
SKEWS	JAMES	son of James & Charity Skewes, miner of Carvannel	25 Dec	1831
SKEWIS	THOMAS	son of John & Ann Skewis, miner of Crophendy	24 Oct	1832

SKEWES	ALEXANDER	son of John & Anne Skewes of Penance, miner	19 Nov	1834
SKEWES	SIMON DAVY	son of John & Anne Skewes, miner of Penance	25 Dec	1838
SKEWES	JOHN	son of John & Ann Skewes, miner and yeoman of Penance	16 Dec	1840
SKEWES	MARY JANE	daughter of Collan & Ann Skewes, miner of Lanner	17 Dec	1840
SKEWES	JAMES	son of Henry & Ann Skewes (6 years old) of Penstrathal, miner	22 April	1841
SKEWES	ELIZABETH EMMA	daughter of John & Ann Skewes of Carnwarth, Yeoman	12 Nov	1848
SKEWES	WILLIAM JOHN	son of William & Elizabeth Skewes, miner of Trevarth	20 July	1862

PARISH REGISTER OF GWENNAP   MARRIAGES   (1600 — 1976)

MARRIAGE LICENCES OF THE DIOCESE of EXETER (1631 — 1672) have been transcribed from the original records by the Devon & Cornwall Record Society in 1947. There are two entries for SKEWES.

| SKEWS | JOHN | of Gwennap & Elizabeth Symons of Penzance | 22 Aug | 1734 |
| SKEWES | ANN | of Clements, widow and John Williams of Gwennap, tinner | 2 Nov | 1742 |

The Marriage Registers

SKEWES	THOMAS	and Sidwell Millard	1 July	1665
SKEUIS	RICHARD	and Bridgett Williams	23 June	1675
SKEWS	BLANCH	daughter of Thomas Skews, and Martin Magor	16 Nov	1695
SKEWS	JOAN	daughter of Thomas Skews, and Anthony Michel	27 Nov	1701
SKEWS	THOMAS	son of Thomas Skews, and Margaret Richards daughter of Anthony Richards	7 Dec	1702
SKEWS	SIDEWELL	and Henry Rodgers of Illogan, tinner	28 April	1705
SKEWS	RICHARD	and Rebecca Boltenal of Sennan	6 Sept	1723
SKEWS	JOAN	daughter of Thomas Skews, and John Gregor	14 Aug	1735
SKEWES	THOMAS	& Elizabeth Webb	29 Apl	1738
SKEWES	JOHN	& Mary Webb of Kea	8 Nov	1740
SKEWES	WILLIAM	& Ann Bawdan	18 Aug	1753
SKEWES	PHILIPPA	& William Skinner	12 June	1763
SKEWES	WILLIAM	& Mary Hitchens	3 Jan	1765
of Helston
SKEWES	JOHN	& Mary Tregonning	18 Sept	1769
SKEWES	JOHN	& Mary Mitchell	17 June	1776
SKEWES	JOAN	& William Tregonning	23 May	1779
SKEWES	ANN	& Thomas Gregor	18 Apl	1780
SKEWIS	ELIZABETH	& Francis Tuckfield	21 Dec	1799
(In presence of JOHN SKEWIS)
SKEWIS	HENRY	& Ann Blamey	7 July	1801
SKEWIS	WILLIAM	& Margaret Edwards	6 July	1805
SKEWES	MARY	& Richard Tregaskis	14 Jan	1809
(In presence of
ALEXANDER SKEWES)
| SKEWES | JOHN | & Jennifer Treweek of Redruth | 24 Nov | 1810 |
| SKEWES | MARGARET | & John Tregaskis | 21 Mar | 1811 |
(widow)
| SKEWES | ELIZABETH | & Philip Lean | 5 Dec | 1812 |
(In presence of JOHN SKEWES)
| SKEWES | CONSTANCE | & Henry Hunt (widower) | 16 Dec | 1815 |
| SKEWES | GRACE | & Alexander Teague | 6 July | 1822 |
(In presence of ALEXANDER SKEWES)
| SKEWES | ELIZABETH | & Henry Morcom | 29 Sept | 1823 |
(In presence of JOHN SKEWES)
SKEWES	JOHN	& Ann Davy	30 July	1826
SKEWES	JAMES	& Charity Vial	17 Dec	1827
SKEWES	HENRY	& Ann Aunger	7 Sept	1828
SKEWES	CHRISTIAN MARTIN	& John Martyn	12 Feb	1829
(In presence of ALEXANDER SKEWES)
| SKEWES | JOANNA | & Ambrose Bray | 27 Oct | 1832 |
(In presence of ALEXANDER SKEWES
Snr and ALEXANDER SKEWES Jnr)
| SKEWES | CHARITY | & Thomas Grey | 2 Aug | 1834 |
| SKEWES | MARGARET | & Ambrose Bray, widower, mine agent | 8 Oct | 1837 |
of Trevarth Moor and daughter of
ALEXANDER SKEWES deceased
| SKEWES | JANE | & Edward Penna, of St. Day, | 2 Jan | 1843 |
of Polidice and daughter of
JOHN SKEWES, farmer deceased
| SKEWES | MARY aged 29, | & William Mitchell, 35, widower and carpenter of St. Day | 23 Nov | 1843 |
widow (father's name
RICHARD BAMPYLE, miner)
| SKEWES | ANN | & Walter Bray of Lanner, mine agent | 7 Mar | 1844 |
of Gwennap Moor, and daughter of
of Alexander Skewes, mine agent.
In presence of Alexander Skewes.
| SKEWES | SUSANNAH of | & Thomas Mills of Tryulla | 9 Apl | 1846 |
Lanner, daughter of James Skewes, miner
| SKEWES | WILLIAM (22) | & Eliza Jose (23) of White Stile | 26 July | 1856 |
miner and son of John Skewes,
miner of Carharrack. In
presence of William Skewes

SKEWES MARY AGNES (22) of Trevarth, dressmaker, and daughter of John Skewes, miner. In presence of Mary Ann Skewes   **&**   Edward Odgers (21) miner of Trevarth   28 July 1859

PARISH REGISTER OF GWENNAP   BURIALS   1658 — 1976

Surname	Name	Description	Date	Year
SKEWES	THOMAS	son of Thomas Skewes	7 Mar	1668
SKUES	ROBERT		3 Dec	1675
SKUES	SIDWELL	wife of Thomas Skues	18 Aug	1678
SKEWS	JOAN		8 June	1680
SKEWS	MARY	daughter of William Skews	1 Apl	1707
SKEWS	BLANCH	daughter of Thomas Skews	13 May	1708
SKEWS	THOMAS	son of Thomas Skews	7 Jan	1711
SKEWS	WILLIAM		22 April	1714
SKEWS	WILLIAM		27 July	1721
SKEWS	MARGARET		23 Dec	1738
SKEWS	PHILIPPA		28 Nov	1742
SKEWES	ALEXANDER	son of Thomas and Elizabeth Skewes	18 Mar	1748
SKEWES	MARGARET		28 Apl	1753
SKEWES	JOHN		3 May	1754
SKEWES	ALEXANDER	son of Thomas & Elizabeth Skewes	28 Nov	1754
SKEWES	ELIZABETH	daughter of Thomas and Elizabeth Skewes	3 Dec	1754
SKEWES	ELIZABETH		12 Aug	1757
SKEWES	THOMAS		29 Aug	1763
SKEWES	RICHARD		15 June	1766
SKEWES	RICHARD		6 June	1769
SKEWES	JOHN		8 July	1770
SKEWES	MARY		22 Dec	1770
SKEWES	JOHN		2 June	1772
SKEWES	MARY		19 July	1773
SKEWES	ANN		29 May	1779
SKEWES	RICHARD		5 Dec	1779
SKEWIS	ELIZABETH		14 July	1784
SKEWIS	WILLIAM		25 Dec	1784
SKEWIS	JOHN		22 Apl	1789
SKEWIS	GRACE		7 Nov	1796
SKEWIS	COLLAN		10 Feb	1797
SKEWIS	THOMASIN		21 Mar	1797
SKEWIS	THOMAS		16 Apl	1800
SKEWIS	MARY		24 June	1804
SKEWES	MARY		1 Feb	1808
SKEWES	WILLIAM		29 Nov	1808
SKEWES	RICHARD		19 Dec	1809
SKEWES	WILLIAM		13 Mar	1810
SKEWES	JOHN		18 May	1811
SKEWES	MARY		27 Nov	1811
SKEWES	WILLIAM	of Chenhale, aged 1	5 Feb	1813
SKEWES	MARGARET	of Chenhale, aged 65	25 Nov	1816
SKEWES	THOMAS	of Carharrack, aged 78	8 Dec	1816
SKUES	JAMES	of Whitehall, Kenwyn aged 1	27 Dec	1817
SKEWIS	WILLIAM	of Gwennap, aged 79	2 July	1824
SKEWES	RICHARD	of Chenhale, aged 27	13 July	1827
SKEWES	JAMES	of Bill, Gwennap, aged 56	11 June	1829
SKEWES	CHRISTIAN	of Chenhale, aged 63 (died of cunsumption)	7 Nov	1833
SKEWES	ALEXANDER	of Chenhale (no age given)	18 Mar	1835
SKEWES	SIMON DAVEY	of Penance, Gwennap, aged 6. Died of Scarlet Fever	30 Oct	1842
SKEWES	ALEXANDER	of Caernmarthe, aged 8. Died of Scarlet Fever	14 Nov	1842
SKEWES	MARY	of Caernmarthe, aged 16	14 Nov	1842
SKEWES	ELIZABETH ANN	of Caernmarthe, aged 4	20 Nov	1842
SKEWES	THOMAS	of Caernmarthe, aged 10	16 Nov	1842
SKEWES	SUSANNAH	of Caernmarthe, aged 80	6 Apl	1848
SKEWES	CHARITY	of Carvanell, aged 60	27 Feb	1858
SKEWES	ANN	of Lanner, aged 60	19 July	1859
SKEWES	ELIZABETH	of Lanner Hill, aged 1	11 Apl	1861
SKEWES	ALEXANDER	of Trevarth, aged 55	19 Dec	1862
SKEWES	HENRY	of Redruth, aged 66	2 Nov	1869
SKEWES	ANN	of Penryn, aged 72	14 Dec	1870
SKEWES	JECOLIAH	of Lanner, aged 35	3 Aug	1875
SKEWES	ELIZABETH	of Lanner Moors aged 66	17 May	1877
SKEWES	MARY	of Lanner House aged 66	14 Dec	1877
SKEWES	JOHN	of Little Carharrack, aged 80	13 Mar	1884
SKEWES	ANNIE	of Little Carharrack, aged 81	24 Oct	1888
SKEWES	MARY ANN	of Carharrack, aged 73	25 Oct	1904
SKEWES-TEAGUE, RICHARD		of Illogan, aged 76	1 June	1905
SKEWES-BRAY, CHRISTIANA ALEXANDRA		of Lanner House, aged 65	18 Dec	1923

BAPTISMS SOLEMNISED IN THE GWENNAP CIRCUIT (NON PAROCHIAL REGISTERS) OF WESLEYAN METHODIST CHAPEL, STITHIANS, IN THE PARISH OF GWENNAP 1848 — 1894

SKEWES	ELIZA	daughter of William & Elizabeth Skewes. Living in Crowan. Bpt at age of 2 mths.	19 Aug 1844

PARISH REGISTER OF GWINEAR   BAPTISMS   1737 — 1812

SKUES	ELIZABETH	daughter of Henry & Margaret Skues	23 Dec	1792
SKUES	MARY	daughter of Henry & Margaret Skues	14 Oct	1794
SKEWES	STEPHEN	son of Henry & Margaret Skewes	4 Feb	1798

PARISH REGISTER OF GWINEAR   MARRIAGES   1560 — 1812

SKEWIS	ELIZABETH (by licence)	&	William Cock, widower of Gwithian	30 Nov	1790
SKEWES	ELIZABETH	&	John Murley	1 Jan	1795

PARISH REGISTER OF GWITHIAN   MARRIAGES   1560 — 1837

SKEWES	HENRY	&	Margaret Phillips	11 Aug	1792

PARISH REGISTER OF GWITHIAN   BURIALS   1560 — 1917

SKEWIS-FARR,.	MARGARET	of Gwithian, aged 78	3 July	1902

PARISH REGISTER OF HELSTON   BAPTISMS   1600 — 1900

SKEWIS	JENEFAR	daughter of Richard	18 Oct	1730
SKEWIS	MARY	daughter of Richard & Jane	15 May	1733
SKEWES	WILLIAM	son of Richard and Jane	28 Oct	1735
SKEWIS	MARY	daughter of Richard & Jane	23 May	1738
SKEWIS	STEPHEN	son of Richard and Jane	11 Apl	1743
SKEWIS	JOHN	son of Richard and Jane	8 June	1744
SKEWIS	STEPHEN	son of Richard and Jane	16 Aug	1747
SKUES	WILLIAM	son of John and Mary P.	22 Dec	1776
SKEWES	WILLIAM	son of William & Mary	24 Mar	1776
SKEWES	STEPHEN	son of William & Mary	10 Aug	1778
SKUES	ELIZABETH	daughter of John & Mary P.	13 Dec	1778
SKUES	JOHN	son of John and Mary P.	20 Apl	1780
SKEWES	ISOBELL	daughter of John & Mary P.	27 May	1781
SKUES	RICHARD	son of John and Mary P.	24 Oct	1734
SKEWES	CHARLES	son of John and Mary P.	26 Mar	1786
SKEWES	JOSEPH	son of John and Mary P.	15 July	1787
SKUES	RICHARD	son of Richard & Ann; surgeon	4 Dec	1794
SKEWES	EDWARD	son of Richard and Ann	8 Oct	1795
SKUES	GEORGE	son of Richard and Ann	5 Oct	1797
SKEWIS	GRACE RICHARDS	daughter of Richard & Ann	24 Mar	1801
SKEWIS	MARY	daughter of Richard & Ann	24 Mar	1801
SKEWIS	WILLIAM	son of Richard and Ann	10 Feb	1802
SKUES	WILLIAM	son of Richard and Ann	26 Dec	1804
SKUES	ANN	daughter of Richard and Ann	26 Feb	1807
SKUES	GRACE	daughter of Richard & Grace	28 Dec	1819
SKEWES	JANE LUGG	daughter of Henry & Grace; innkeeper	5 Dec	1832
SKEWES	MARGARET ANN	daughter of Henry and Grace; schoolmaster	22 Feb	1837
SKEWES	HANNIBAL	son of Henry and Grace; schoolmaster	8 Nov	1838

PARISH REGISTER OF HELSTON   MARRIAGES   1600 — 1958

SKEWIS	ROBERT of Camborne	&	Jane Sandys of Helston	9 Nov	1751
SKEWIS	JENEFAR	&	James Gritton	19 Jul	1753
SKUES	MARY	&	Ralph Harvey	26 Dec	1757
SKUES	EDWARD	&	Honore Pearce	13 Apl	1762
SKEWES	EDWARD, mariner	&	Grace Pearce	23 Sept	1788
SKUES	ELIZABETH, by licence	&	James Byron, widower of Plymouth	20 Nov	1793
SKUES	RICHARD	&	Ann Richards of Truthall	4 Dec	1793
SKUES	MARY	&	William Mitchell	3 May	1802

(In presence of William and Ann SKUES)

SKUES	CHARLES	&	Mary Bennett		
SKUES	WILLIAM	&	Mary Staplis	5 Jan	1815
SKUES	GRACE	&	William Radford, Wesleyan Minister from Devon	27 Oct	1822
SKUES	JANE	&	Henry Pascoe	24 Aug	1824
(In presence of William and Ann SKUES)				17 Jul	1831
SKUES ANN		&	William Pearce, carpenter of Wendron Street	11 Dec	1838
of Wendron Street, Helston			Helston and son of William Pearce		
and daughter of William and					
Elizabeth SKUES					
SKEWES CATHERINE (19)		&	James Martin (22)		
from Redruth. Daughter of			baker and son of Martin Martin		
Henry SKEWES				23 Apl	1863
SKUES JOSIAH (55)		&	Ellen Hugo (38)		
widower, labourer. Son of James			Daughter of James Hugo, tinner		
SKUES, labourer				2 Jul	1881
SKEWES LORA (19)		&	William Tippett Tripp (29)		
Daughter of Edward SKEWES,				26 Sept	1882
shoemaker					

PARISH REGISTER OF HELSTON   BURIALS   1600 — 1964

SKEWIS	RICHARD	son of Richard		
SKEWIS	STEPHEN	son of Richard and Jane	3 Feb	1741
SKEWIS	STEPHEN	son of Richard and Jane	22 May	1743
SKEWIS	RICHARD		21 Aug	1747
SKEWES	HONNAR	daughter of Edward and Mary	23 Dec	1755
SKUES	WILLIAM	son of William	11 Feb	1764
SKEWES	MARY	wife of Edward	23 Aug	1771
SKEWES	STEPHEN	son of William	13 Dec	1774
SKEWES	JANE	widow	10 May	1781
SKEWES	EDWARD	aged 55 years	23 June	1782
SKEWES	JANE	daughter of John, aged 11 years	20 July	1782
SKUES	RICHARD	son of John, aged 11 years	20 Jan	1783
SKEWES	EDWARD	son of Mr Richard Skewes, infant	21 Dec	1794
SKEWIS	MARY	wife of John, aged 53 years	13 Oct	1795
SKEWIS	WILLIAM	son of William, aged 23 years. Ensign in Volunteers of the Borough	20 Aug	1799
SKEWIS	JOHN	aged 57 years	21 Aug	1800
SKEWIS	WILLIAM	son of Mr Richard Skewis; infant	20 Sept	1801
SKEWIS	WILLIAM	son of Richard and Ann; infant	17 Feb	1802
SKUES	MARY Mrs	aged 72 years	16 May	1805
SKUES	RICHARD Mr	Surgeon, aged 45 years	22 Oct	1809
SKUES	WILLIAM	of Helston, aged 81 years	20 Nov	1811
SKUES	ANN	aged 10 years	26 Feb	1817
SKUES	ANN	aged 62 years	4 May	1817
SKUES	MARY	aged 55 years	9 Feb	1838
SKUES-PASCOE, ELIZABETH		age 1 year	9 Feb	1838
SKUES-PASCOE, HENRY		infant	12 Jan	1839
SKUES	WILLIAM	aged 66 years	12 Apl	1840
SKEWS	ELIZABETH	aged 65 years	24 Nov	1842
SKEWES-MARTIN, RICHARD		aged 67 years	15 Dec	1879
			24 Nov	1897

Helston, from Loe pool, 1968

HELSTON CIRCUIT WESLEYAN CHAPEL (NON PAROCHIAL REGISTERS) BAPTISMS   1804 — 1837

SKUES	CHARLOTTE	daughter of Charles and Ann Skues of Helston in the parish of Wendron. Profession of father: tailor. Born 4 April, 1816	28 Apl	1816
SKUES	MARY BENNETT	daughter of Charles and Ann Skues of Helston in the parish of Wendron. Born 15 December 1817.	4 Jan	1818

REGISTERS OF HELSTON METHODIST CHURCH, FORE STREET MARRIAGES 1899 — 1968

Clara Jane SKEWES Benney (21) of Mill Lane, Helston, daughter of Thomas Benney, farmer	&	Ernest Opie (32) farmer of East Road, Stithians; son of Thomas Opie, deceased, grocer.	16 Dec	1910
William Thomas SKEWES Rowe (22) of Trelowarren, Mawgan; son of William Thomas Rowe, gardener, deceased	&	Sarah Jane Cooke (22) of Rosevear, Mawgan, daughter of William Thomas Cooke, builder	17 Jan	1917
ELLA SKEWES (28) Rose Villa. Mawgan, daughter of John Wesley Skewes, school attendance officer. In presence of John Wesley Skewes and Lilian Skews	&	Samuel Thomas Johns (27) carpenter of Mawgan; son of Samuel Thomas Johns, estate steward	20 Aug	1914
HARRY STANLEY SKEWES (28) market gardener (master) of Roseville, Mawgan, son of John Wesley Skewes, school attendance officer.	&	Beatrice Annie Rosevear (29) of Mawgan Cross, Mawgan; daughter of W. Rosevear, labourer	12 Jan	1921
ARTHUR SKEWES (23) farmer of Halwyn Farm, St Keverne; son of James Henry Skewes, farmer. In presence of Bertie Skewes	&	Violet Rashleigh (22) spinster of Porthallow, St Keverne; daughter of Cyril Blaur, stonemason	24 Feb	1926
HARRY STANLEY SKEWES (53) widower; Market Gardener (Master); of Roseville, Mawgan; son of John Wesley Skewes, school attendance officer. In presence of William Arthur Skewes	&	Rosa May Hockin (53), spinster; Ministry of Mines clerk; of 6, Holgrove Road, Bromley, Kent; daughter of Thomas Hockin, deceased, draper	9 Feb	1946

PARISH REGISTER OF ILLOGAN   BAPTISMS   1613 — 1882

SKEWIS	MARY	daughter of John and Jane	23 Oct	1803
SKEWIS	PHYLLIS	daughter of John and Jane	5 Jan	1806
SKEWIS	ELIZABETH	daughter of John and Jane	6 Dec	1807
SKEWIS	FRANCES	daughter of John and Jane. Born 17 September 1811	2 Nov	1811
SKEWIS	CATHERINE	daughter of John and Jane of Illogan, yeoman	18 Dec	1813
SKEWIS	JOHN	son of John and Jane of Illogan, yeoman	22 June	1816
SKEWES	JAMES HARRIS	son of James and Eleanor of Treskillard, labourman	20 July	1853
SKEWES	ELLEN (23) of Piece,	daughter of William and Priscilla of Carnkie, miner	29 Oct	1853
SKEWES	ANN AMELIA	daughter of William and Priscilla of Higher Treskillard, labourer	30 June	1856
SKEWES	MARIA	daughter of James and Nanny of Piece, Illogan, miner	23 July	1862
SKEWES	JOHN HENRY	son of John and Susan of Pool, policeman	11 Dec	1864
SKEWES	HENRY	son of William and Priscilla of Carnarthen, Illogan, farmer	25 Sept	1872
SKEWES	FLORENCE KATE	daughter of Thomas and Charlotte of Pennsylvania, USA, blacksmith	20 Apl	1873
SKEWES	RICHARD ERNEST	son of Francis and Grace of Illogan Highway, blacksmith	24 Feb	1874
SKEWES	JANE ROGERS	daughter of Francis and Grace of Illogan Highway, blacksmith	24 Feb	1874
SKEWES	JOHN	son of Francis and Grace of Illogan Highway, blacksmith	24 Feb	1874

PARISH REGISTER OF ILLOGAN   MARRIAGES   1721 — 1902

SKEWIS	ELIZABETH (In presence of John Skews)	&	William Rowe	23 Feb	1833
SKEWIS	JANE daughter of John Skewis, farmer of Park, Illogan	&	Henry Jenkin, miner; son of James Jenkin, farmer of Illogan Downs	13 Oct	1842
SKEWES	WILLIAM (23) miner of Carnkie, son of James Skewes, farmer. In presence of William Skewes	&	Priscilla Mill (24) of Carnkie, daughter of William Mill, miner	10 July	1853
SKEWES	THOMAS (23) miner, son of William Skewes, blacksmith	&	Charlotte Chigwyn (24) of Pool, daughter of William Chigwyn, horse dealer	19 Oct	1865
SKEWES	ELLEN (23) of Piece, Illogan, daughter of James Skewes, husbandman	&	Edwin Mills, miner, son of William Mills, miner of Camborne	20 Oct	1872
SKEWES	MARY (28) of Piece, Illogan, daughter of James Skewes, husbandman	&	William Carter (23) miner, son of James Carter, miner	27 Apl	1874

SKEWES EMMA (24) of Illogan Highway, daughter of William Skewes, blacksmith	&	John James Rule (23) of Redruth, miner; son of Elisha Rule, miner		4 Jan	1891
SKEWS JOHN (24) of Redruth, shoemaker; son of Matthew Henry Skews, miner. In presence of William Skews	&	Sarah Greenslade (22) of Portreath; daughter of Charles Greenslade, master mariner		16 June	1898
SKEWS MATTHEW (22) of Illogan Highway, miner; son of Matthew Skews, miner. In presence of Elizabeth Skews	&	Elizabeth Roberts of Illogan Highway; daughter of William Edward Roberts, carter		10 Dec	1898

PARISH REGISTER OF ILLOGAN   BURIALS   1619 — 1886

SKEWS	SARAH	of Illogan Highway, aged 1 year	2 Nov	1852
SKEWES	ELIZABETH ELLEN	of Piece, aged 4 months	28 July	1862
SKEWES	BLANCH	of West Wheal, aged 18 years	28 Oct	1862
SKEWES	WILLIAM	of Lannarth, Gwennap; 6 months	1 Dec	1862
SKEWES	JAMES	of Piece, aged 64 years	7 Feb	1964
SKEWS	MARY	of Illogan Highway, aged 49	7 Nov	1865
SKEWES	REBECCA	of Rayle Stamps, aged 67 years	15 Feb	1868
SKEWES	JAMES	of Piece, aged 78 years	19 Oct	1871
SKEWES	PRISCILLA	of Carnarthen, aged 43 years	2 Feb	1874
SKEWES	JAMES	of Carnarthen, aged 13 years	20 Aug	1874
SKEWES	JOHN	of Illogan Highway, aged 8	26 June	1880
SKEWS	EDWIN	of Cross Lanes, aged 17 months	6 Jan	1883
SKEWS	— male —	illegitimate male child of ELIZABETH ANN SKEWES of Cross Lanes; Coroner's Order. No funeral service	20 Mar	1886

BAPTISMS   PRIMITIVE   METHODIST   REGISTER,   ILLOGAN   1869   —   1934

SKEWES	ROSINA	daughter of Edwin and Elizabeth Skewes of Broad Lane, Illogan. Boilersmith. Born 27 Sept. 1878	18 Nov	1878
SKEWES	PRISCILLA	daughter of William and Jane Skewes of Treskillard, farmer.	20 Feb	1884
SKEWES	AMELIA JANE	daughter of William and Jane Skewes of Treskillard, farmer. Born 29 October, 1886	7 Oct	1887
SKEWES	JOHN HENRY	son of John and Edith Skewes of Carnkie, miner. Born 18 July, 1910	22 Sept	1910
SKEWES	MATTHEW JOHN	son of John and Sarah Skewes of Plain and Gwarry, Redruth. Bootmaker. Born 7 Aug. 1910	26 Oct	1910

PARISH REGISTER OF KEA   BAPTISMS   1612 — 1840

SKUSE	DIGGORY	son of Richard Skuse	11 Mar	1676
SCUSE	RICHARD	son of Richard Scuse	4 Apl	1680
SKEWS	RICHARD	son of Richard Skews	18 Oct	1724
SKEWES	JANE			
SKEWES	URSULA	daughter of Richard Skewes	12 July	1730
SKEWS	ELIZABETH	daughter of Henry Skews	12 Apl	1741
SKEWS	MARGERY	daughter of Henry Skews	24 Feb	1746
SKEWS	HENRY	son of Henry Skews	8 July	1749
SKEWES	ELIZABETH	daughter of Peter Skewes	29 Sept	1751
SKEWS	ANN	daughter of Peter Skewes	1 Jan	1754
SKEWS	JOHN	son of Peter Skews	25 Jan	1757
SKEWS	BIDDY	daughter of Henry Skewes	14 May	1758
SKEWES	PATIENCE	daughter of Henry Skewes	30 May	1762
SKEWES	RICHARD	son of Peter Skewes	25 Sept	1762
SKEWES	JOHN	son of John Skews	9 Aug	1763
SKEWES	RICHARD	son of John Skews	9 Dec	1765
SKEWES	ANN LUCY	daughter of John Skewes	8 July	1771
SKEWES	ELIZABETH	daughter of John and Alice Skewes	1 Apl	1774
SKEWES	MARGERY	daughter of Henry Skewes	24 Feb	1776
SKEWES	PETER	son of Martin and Mary Skewes	3 Aug	1777
SKEWS	HENRY	son of Henry Skews	8 July	1779
SKEWS	JOHN	son of Martin Skews	23 Aug	1779
SKEWS	RICHARD	son of Digory Skews, jnr	22 June	1783
SKEWES	DIGORY	son of Digory Skewes	6 Jan	1787
SKEWES	DIGORY	son of Digory Skewes	23 Dec	1787
SKEWES	DIGORY	son of Digory Skewes	7 June	1789
SKEWES	ELIZABETH	daughter of Digory Skewes	26 Feb	1792
SKEWES	WILLIAM	son of William Skewes	7 June	1794
SKEWES	MARY JOLLY	daughter of Henry and Catherine Skewes. Born 27 February, 1794	17 Aug	1794
SKEWES	MATTHEW	son of Digory Skewes	22 Mar	1796
SKEWES	EBENEZER JOHN	son of Henry and Catherine Skewes	17 Apl	1797
SKEWES	MARY	daughter of Digory and Elizabeth Skewes	26 Aug	1798
SKEWES	THOMAS	son of Henry and Catherine Skewes	31 Mar	1799

SKEWES	MARIA	daughter of Digory and Elizabeth Skewes	5 Apl	1801
SKEWES	WILLIAM	son of John and Temperence Skewes	29 Nov	1801
SKEWES	HENRY	son of Henry and Catherine Skewes	14 Nov	1802
SKEWES	ELEANOR	daughter of William and Ann Skewes	2 June	1805
SKEWES	RICHARD	son of Thomas and Mary Skewes	24 May	1807
SKEWES	PATIENCE	daughter of Richard and Mary Skewes	18 Oct	1807
SKEWES	MARY	daughter of Richard and Mary	23 Apl	1810
SKEWES	JENEFER	daughter of John and Ann	12 May	1811
SKEWES	SAMUEL TRUEN	son of William and Ann	6 Oct	1811
SKEWES	PEGGY	daughter of Richard and Mary	5 Apl	1812
SKEWES	JANE	daughter of Richard and Mary	14 May	1815
SKEWES	ANN ENYER	daughter of Richard and Mary	20 Nov	1817
SKEWES	ELIZABETH	daughter of Richard and Mary	18 June	1820
SKEWES	JENIFER	daughter of Peter and Grace, miller	24 Dec	1820
SKEWES	HARRIET	daughter of Richard and Mary of Nancevellan Common, labourer	12 Jan	1823
SKEWES	MARY ANN	daughter of Thomas & Jane of St. Clement, mason	5 Dec	1824
SKEWES	THOMASINE	daughter of Richard and Mary of Churchtown, miner	22 May	1825
SKEWES	ELIZABETH JANE	daughter of John and Ann of Kenwyn, miner	26 Mar	1826
SKEWES	HENRIETTA	daughter of Thomas & Jane of St. Clement, mason	5 Nov	1826
SKEWES	JOHN BEER	son of Thomas and Jane of Daniell Street, Kenwyn. Born 20 May, 1830	25 Aug	1830
SKEWES	PHILIPPA JANE	daughter of Thomas and Jane of Daniell Street, Kenwyn	22 Apl	1832
SKEWS	RICHARD	son of Peter and Ann of Gwennap		
SKEWS	MARY	daughter of Peter and Ann of Gwennap		
SKEWS	JULIA	daughter of Peter and Ann of Gwennap	9 July	1833
SKEWES	JANE	daughter of Peter and Ann of Gwennap (Father now dead)		
SKEWES	THOMAS	son of Thomas and Jane of Truro, mason	6 Apl	1834
SKEWES	MARY ANN	daughter of Jane Skewes of Hugus, Kea — single woman	6 Oct	1834
SKEWES	ELIZABETH	daughter of Peter & Elizabeth of Hugus, miner	3 Aug	1835
SKEWES	JANE	daughter of Peter & Elizabeth of Hugus, miner	8 Oct	1837
SKEWES	PETER	son of Peter & Elizabeth of Hugus, miner	19 Mar	1840

PARISH REGISTER OF KEA   MARRIAGES   1653 — 1858

SKEWES	RICHARD	&	Mary James	12 Nov	1710
SKEWS	PETER	&	Margaret Newton of St Columb Minor	11 June	1750
SKEWES	MARY	&	Ferdinando Behenna	18 Oct	1759
SKEWES	MARY	&	Thomas Shepherd	3 Feb	1781
SKEWES	ANN	&	William Lawry	19 Nov	1785
SKEWES	THOMAS	&	Mary Turner	7 Mar	1791
SKEWES	JOHN	&	Eleanor Philips	7 Mar	1791
SKEWES	WILLIAM	&	Ann Trewan	6 Oct	1793
SKEWES	ANN LUCEY	&	Anthony Sandoe	29 Oct	1795
SKEWES	ELIZABETH	&	Charles Dinnis	27 Dec	1796
SKEWES	JOHN	&	Ann Dinnis	21 Dec	1799
SKEWES	MARGARET	&	Matthew Wasley	17 Oct	1805
SKEWES	RICHARD	&	Agnes Jeffrey	4 Apl	1806
SKEWES	RICHARD	&	Mary Ninin	25 Apl	1807
SKEWES	DIGORY	&	Sophia Jordan	11 Sept	1811
SKEWES	ELIZABETH	&	Benjamin Baragwana (with special consent of their parents)	23 Mar	1814
In presence of Mary Skewes					
SKEWES	ANN	&	Charles Coad	10 June	1816
SKEWES	MATTHEW	&	Mary Jeffrey	22 June	1819
SKEWES	JOHN	&	Elizabeth Jeffrey of Kenwyn	10 Nov	1819
(Henry Skewes, Parish Clerk, was witness to the above wedding and many from 1814 onwards. Any extra Skewes' present will be mentioned)					
SKEWES	JOHN	&	Grace Bray	18 Nov	1820
(In presence of Richard Skewes)					
SKEWES	WILLIAM	&	Cordelia Pollard	9 Dec	1822
SKEWES	MARIA	&	William Jones	23 Nov	1823
SKEWES	ELIZABETH	&	William Holman	6 Aug	1825
SKEWES	ANN	&	William Dinnis	31 Mar	1827
SKEWES	PATIENCE	&	Michael Kent	20 June	1829
SKEWES	PETER	&	Grace Harris	16 Oct	1830
(In presence of Mary Skewes)					
SKEWES	MARY	&	Thomas Triganowan	31 Dec	1831
SKEWES	THOMAS	&	JANE SKEWES	11 June	1832
SKEWES	PEGGY	&	Thomas Chygwidden	24 Dec	1832
SKEWES	ANN	&	Joseph Rogers	21 Mar	1833
(In presence of John Skewes)					
SKEWES	MARIA	&	William Wasley	15 Feb	1834
SKEWES	PETER	&	Elizabeth Scoble	4 Oct	1834
SKEWES	CHARLOTTE	&	Caleb Jennins	7 July	1836
SKEWES	MARTIN	&	Ann Hocking	22 Sept	1836

Helston Parish Church
Kenwyn Parish Church

Kea Parish Church
Ruins of Ruan Major Parish Church

SKEWES JOHN	&	Harriet Francis		29 Sept	1836
(In presence of Matthew Skewes)					
SKEWES ELIZA	&	Peter Bonython		19 Nov	1836
SKEWES ELIZABETH	&	Thomas Pascoe		14 Jan	1837
SKEWES WILLIAM	&	Mary Dennis of Chacewater		4 June	1839
Tailor of Kerley (Father's name Richard Skewes, mine agent). Witnesses to wedding Richard Skewes and Tamson Skewes					
SKEWES JANE	&	James Goldsworthy of Bizzon			
of Kea Church Town. Son of Richard Skewes, Parish Clerk. Witnesses to wedding Tamson Skewes & Ann Skewes				26 Dec	1839
SKEWES RICHARD	&	Johanna Wasley of Kerley			
miner of Kerley. Son of Digory Skewes, miner				3 Sept	1840
SKEWES ELIZABETH	&	James Wasley of Kerley		20 Sept	1841
of Kerley. Dau of Peter Skewes, miner					
SKEWES THOMASINE (minor)	&	Thomas Williams excise man of Truro			
of Kea. Son of Richard Skewes, Parish Clerk. Witness: Harriette Skewes				14 Aug	1843
SKEWES ELIZA JANE	&	Thomas Gray			
of Seveock. Dau of John Skewes, miner. Witness: John Skewes				14 May	1846
SKEWES ANN EYNES	&	Thomas Eddy		13 June	1848
of Kea. Dau of Richard Skewes. Yeoman.					
SKEWES RICHARD	&	Mary Ann James of Kerley			
Cordwainer of Kerley. Son of Richard Skewes, mine agent. Witness Richard Skewes				15 May	1851

PARISH REGISTER OF KEA   BURIALS   1575 — 1915

SKEWS	RICHARD	son of Richard Skews was buried		19 Oct	1712
SKEWS	MARY	wife of Richard Skews		4 May	1721
SKEWS	JANE	wife of Richard Skews		12 July	1730
SKEWS	ELIZABETH	daughter of Richard Skews		7 Sept	1734
SKEWS	CHRISTIAN			14 July	1740
SKEWS	RICHARD			2 Mar	1741
SKEWS	KATHERINE	daughter of Martin Skews		16 May	1742
SKEWS	JOHN	son of Martin Skews		23 Aug	1749
SKEWS	MARY	wife of Martin Skews		22 Feb	1751
SKEWS	PETER	son of Martin Skews		26 Apl	1752
SKEWES	DIGORY			18 Jan	1757
SKEWES	ELIZABETH	daughter of Martin Skewes		15 June	1762
SKEWES	PETER	son of Digory Skewes		5 July	1763
SKEWES	PATIENCE	daughter of Henry Skewes		26 Sept	1763
SKEWES	MARTIN			17 Mar	1764
SKEWS	RICHARD	son of Peter Skews		8 Mar	1765
SKEWS	RICHARD Senior			10 Dec	1767
SKEWES	PETER			15 Oct	1768
SKEWES	MARGERY	daughter of Digory Skewes		5 July	1772
SKEWES	ELIZABETH			2 Aug	1772
SKEWES	THOMAS Junior			24 July	1779
SKEWES	MARGERY	daughter of Digory Skewes		8 Sept	1779
SKEWES	THOMAS Senior			15 Aug	1780
SKEWES	JOHN Senior			25 Apl	1781
SKEWES	MARGRETT	widow		8 Apl	1784
SKEWES	DIGORY Senior			6 Jan	1787
SKEWES	DIGORY	son of Richard Skewes of Kenwyn		20 May	1787
SKEWES	DIGORY	son of Digory Skewes Junior		19 May	1788
SKEWES	ANN	widow of Thomas Skewes		5 Nov	1788
SKEWS	ELIZABETH	daughter of John and Alice Skews		28 July	1790
SKEWS	JOHN			5 Jan	1792
SKEWES	ELIZABETH			28 Apl	1797
SKEWES	MARGERY			5 May	1797
SKEWES	PETER			1 Oct	1798
SKEWES	JAMES			4 Mar	1799
SKEWES	JOHN			30 Oct	1801
SKEWES	ANN			23 July	1802
SKEWES	PETER			11 Sept	1802
SKEWES	RICHARD			17 Mar	1803
SKEWES	MARY			12 Feb	1805
SKEWES	MARGERY	aged 74 years		1 Dec	1807
SKEWES	THOMAS			12 May	1808
SKEWES	MARY			12 June	1810
SKEWES	JOHN			22 May	1811
SKEWES	WILLIAM	aged 50 years		21 Dec	1815

SKEWES	ANN	aged 18 years	10 Mar	1818
SKEWES	ELEANOR	aged 54 years	30 July	1818
SKEWES	MARGERY	aged 77 years	14 July	1820
SKEWIS	DIGGERY	of Seveoke, aged 69 years	14 May	1824
SKEWES	ANN	of Jolly's Bottom, aged 51 years	17 Aug	1824
SKEWES	HENRY	Parish Clerk of Kea Church upwards of 40 years; aged 84 years	18 Feb	1833
SKEWES	JOHN	of Kerley, aged 67 years	9 July	1833
SKEWES	MARY ANN	of Baldhu, aged 18 years	23 Aug	1850
SKEWES	ELIZABETH	of Hugus, aged 42 years	12 Mar	1854
SKEWES	RICHARD	of Kea Church Town. Parish Clerk upwards of 20 years; aged 68 years	3 Oct	1854
SKEWES	MARY	of Kea Church town, aged 69 years	3 Oct	1854
SKEWES	PETER	of Hugus, aged 61 years	26 May	1865
SKEWES	WILLIAM	of Hugus, aged 1 year	12 Oct	1867

PARISH REGISTER OF KENWYN   BAPTISMS   1608 — 1955

SKUES	MARTIN	son of Degory Skues	25 May	1701
SKUES	( )	daughter of Degory Skues	6 Jan	1704
SKUES	MARGARET (?)	daughter of Degory Skues	3 Jan	1705
SKUES	ELIZABETH	daughter of Degory Skues	27 Dec	1707
SKUES	THOMAS	son of Richard Skues	18 Sept	1711
SKUES	RICHARD	son of Degory Skues	26 Dec	1714
SKUES	HENRY	son of Richard Skues	14 Jan	1714
SKUES	JOHN	son of Henry Skues	14 May	1716
SKUES	PETER	son of Richard Skues	17 July	1718
SKUES	ELIZABETH	daughter of Richard Skues	28 Feb	1719
SKEWES	CATHERINE	daughter of Martin Skewes	24 Feb	1738
SKEWS	MARY	daughter of Martin Skews	24 Feb	1740
SKEWS	MARY	daughter of Henry Skews	19 Dec	1743
SKEWS	RICHARD	son of Martin Skews	8 Apl	1744
SKEWS	JOHN	son of Martin Skews of Kea	6 June	1747
SKEWS	JOHN	son of Martin Skews of Kea	28 Apl	1750
SKEWS	PETER	son of Martin Skews of Kea	31 Jan	1752
SKEWS	JANE	daughter of Henry Skews of Kea	29 Mar	1752
SKEWEIS	ANN	daughter of Henry Skeweis	5 May	1755
SKEWEIS	DEGORY	son of Martin Skeweis	3 Sept	1757
SKUES	KATHERINE	daughter of Degory Skues of Kea	3 Feb	1760
SKEWES	MARY	daughter of Martin Skewes	2 April	1760
SKEWS	ELIZABETH	daughter of Thomas Skews of Kea	11 May	1760
SKEWIS	MARIA	daughter of John Skewis of Kea	1 June	1761
SKEWES	THOMAS	son of Thomas Skewes	31 Mar	1762
SKEWES	ELIZABETH	daughter of Martin Skewes of Kea	2 June	1762
SKEWES	PETER	son of Digory Skewes of Kea	14 May	1763
SKEWES	MARTIN	son of Martin Skewes of Kea	14 July	1764
SKEWES	PETER	son of Thomas Skewes of Kea	29 Jan	1765
SKEWES	MARY	daughter of Digory Skewes of Kea	24 Aug	1765
SKEWES	JOHN	son of Thomas Skewes	5 Oct	1766
SKEWES	JOHN	son of Martin Skewes of Kea	17 Apl	1767
SKEWES	JAMES	son of John Skewes of Kea	12 May	1767
SKEWES	ELIZABETH	daughter of Thomas Skewes (pri)	15 July	1768
SKEWES	PETER	sone of Digory Skewes of Kea	21 Aug	1768
SKEWES	WILLIAM	son of Thomas Skewes	11 Feb	1769
SKEWES	THOMAS	son of Martin Skewes of Kea	11 Aug	1770
SKEWES	ANN	daughter of Thomas Skewes of Kea	21 Oct	1770
SKEWES	MARGERY	daughter of Digory Skewes of Kea	13 April	1771
SKEWES	MARY	daughter of Richard Skewes	25 Mar	1771
SKEWES	ANNE	daughter of Richard Skewes of Kea	19 Mar	1772
SKEWES	MARY	daughter of Thomas Skewes	28 Oct	1770
SKEWES	CATHERINE	daughter of Thomas Skewes of Kea	31 May	1773
SKEWES	MATTHEW	son of Digory and Margery Skewes of Kea	9 Jan	1774
SKEWES	PHILIPPA	daughter of Thomas and Thomasine	6 Feb	1774
SKEWES	ELIZABETH	daughter of Martin and Mary Skewes of Kea	16 Apl	1776
SKEWES	ANN	daughter of Thomas and Thomasine Skewes of Kea	10 Feb	1776
SKEWIS	JENNY	daughter of Thomas and Ann Skewis	7 Oct	1776
SKEWIS	MARGERY	daughter of Digory and Margery Skewis of Kea	31 May	1777
SKEWES	THOMAS	son of Thomas and Thomasine Skewes	8 Aug	1778
SKEWES	HENRY	son of Henry & Mary Skewes	15 Aug	1784
SKEWES	RICHARD	son of Richard & Jane Skewes	10 Oct	1784
SKEWES	THOMAS	son of Degory and Elizabeth Skewes	11 Sept	1785
SKEWIS	RICHARD	son of Henry & Mary Skewis	20 Aug	1786
SKEWES	GRACE	daughter of John and Ann Skewes	5 Mar	1787
SKEWIS	JANE	daughter of Richard & Jane Skewis	27 July	1788
SKEWIS	MARIA	daughter of John and Ann Skewes	2 Sept	1791
SKEWIS	MARY	daughter of Richard & Jane Skewis (pri)	1 Aug	1792
SKEWIS	THOMAS	son of Thomas & Mary Skewis	25 Dec	1792

SKEWIS	ALICE	daughter of Richard and Roseanna Skewis	22 Dec	1793
SKEWIS	JOHN	son of Degory & Elizabeth Skewis	6 Oct	1794
SKEWIS	RICHARD	son of Thomas & Mary Skewis	1 May	1795
SKEWIS	JENNIFER	daughter of Peter & Peggy Skewis	12 July	1795
SKEWIS	ANN	daughter of William & Ann Skewis	27 Mar	1796
SKEWIS	PETER	son of Peter & Ann Skewis	9 May	1796
SKEWIS	JOHN	son of Richard & Roseanna Skewis	15 May	1796
SKEWES	MARIA	daughter of Peter & Margaret Skewes	11 June	1797
SKEWES	MARY	daughter of William & Ann Skewes	22 Apl	1798
SKEWES	JAMES	son of Richard and Roseanna Skewes	9 Sept	1798
SKEWES	JULIENA	daughter of Peter and Margaret Skewes	28 Apl	1799
SKEWES	MARY	daughter of Thomas and Mary Skewes	26 May	1799
SKEWES	MARY	daughter of Richard and Roseanna Skewes	9 Mar	1800
SKEWES	JOHN	son of Thomas & Mary Skewes	10 May	1801
SKEWES	SUSANNAH MOYLE	daughter of Peter and Peggy Skewes	28 June	1801
SKEWES	MARIA	daughter of Richard and Roseanna Skewes	6 Feb	1803
SKEWES	WILLIAM	son of Thomas & Mary Skewes	9 Apl	1803
SKEWES	PETER	son of Digory & Elizabeth Skewes	19 June	1803
SKEWES	PETER	son of John & Ann Skewes	24 June	1804
SKEWES	BETSY	daughter of Richard and Roseanna Skewes	26 Jan	1806
SKEWES	BETSY	daughter of John & Ann Skewes	11 May	1806
SKEWES	ANN	daughter of Thomas & Mary Skewes	8 Mar	1807
SKEWES	DANIEL	son of William & Ann Skewes	17 May	1807
SKEWES	RICHARD	son of Richard & Grace Skewes	6 Mar	1809
SKEWES	JOHN	son of John & Ann Skewes	4 June	1809
SKEWES	JENEFAR	daughter of William & Ann Skewes	18 June	1809
SKEWES	THOMAS	son of Richard & Jane Skewes	30 Sept	1810
SKEWES	PETER	son of Peter & Ann Skewes of St Agnes, miner	24 Apl	1814
SKEWES	ELIZABETH	daughter of William & Ann Skewes, miner	29 May	1814
SKEWES	JOHN	sonu of Richard and Agnes Skewes of Chacewater; miner	7 May	1815
SKEWES	ANN	daughter of William and Mary Skewes of Blackwater; miner	30 Dec	1817
SKEWES	WILLIAM	son of Richard and Agnes Skewes of Chacewater, miner	2 Aug	1818
SKEWES	ELIZABETH	daughter of Digory & Sophie Skewes of Kea; miner	27 Sept	1818
SKEWES	RICHARD	illegitimate son of Ann Skewes	22 Aug	1819
SKEWES	ELIZABETH	daughter of Matthew and Mary Skewes of Chacewater; miner	21 Jan	1820
SKEWES	WILLIAM	son of William & Mary Skewes of Blackwater; miner	8 Oct	1820
SKEWES	JAMES	son of John & Grace Skewes of Hugus; miner	1 July	1821
SKUES	MARY	daughter of Thomas and Grace Skues of Kea; miner	1 July	1821
SKUES	JANE	illegitimate daughter of Maria Skues of Hugus	17 Feb	1822
SKUES	RICHARD	son of Richard & Agnes Skues of Kea; miner	5 May	1822
SKUES	EMMA	daughter of John & Elizabeth Skues of Kea; miner	5 May	1822
SKUES	MARY	daughter of Matthew & Mary Skues of Kea; miner	5 May	1822
SKUES	ELEANOR	daughter of Thomas & Grace Skues of Kea; miner	18 May	1823
SKUES	THOMAS JENKIN	son of John & Margery of Chacewater; miner	18 May	1823
SKUES	AMELIA	daughter of Diggory & Sophia Skues of Kea; miner	25 Aug	1823
SKUES	DIGORY	son of Diggory & Sophia Skues of Kea; miner	25 Aug	1823
SKEWES	PHILIPPA	daughter of Richard & Agnes Skewes of Kerley	31 Aug	1823
SKEWES	MARY	daughter of William & Mary Skewes of Kea; miner	6 June	1824
SKEWES	SARAH	daughter of Richard & Agnes Skewes of Kea; miner	29 Mar	1825
SKEWES	ELIZA	daughter of Ann Skewes of Kea;	29 Mar	1825
SKEWES	THOMAS	son of Thomas & Grace Skewes of Kea; miner	10 July	1825
SKEWES	MATTHEW HENRY	son of Richard & Agnes Skewes of Kea; miner	21 May	1826
SKEWES	JEMIMA	daughter of Peter & Mary Skewes of the Poorhouse; miner	22 Oct	1826
SKEWES	PETER	son of Peter & Mary Skewes of the Poorhouse, Kenwyn; miner	22 Nov	1826
SKEWES	THOMAS	son of Peter & Elizabeth Skewes of the Poorhouse, Kenwyn	22 Nov	1826
SKEWES	JOHN WILLIAM	son of Peter and Mary Skewes of the Poorhouse. Kenwyn; miner	24 Dec	1826
SKEWES	ELIZABETH	daughter of Peter and Elizabeth Skewes of the Poorhouse, Kenwyn	22 Nov	1826
SKEWES	MARY WILLIAMS	daughter of Peter and Mary Skewes of Kea; miner	19 Feb	1827
SKEWES	ELIZABETH TRESIZE	daughter of Thomas and Grace Skewes of Chacewater; miner	10 June	1827
SKEWES	JOHN HENRY	son of John and Ann Skewes of Chacewater; miner	29 June	1828
SKEWES	JOHN	son of John and Anne Skewes of Kea; miner	15 Aug	1832
SKUES	ELLEN	daughter of John and Ann Skues of Kea; miner	20 Aug	1843
SKUES	JOHN	son of John and Ann Skues of Kea; miner	20 Aug	1843
SKUES	EMMA	daughter of John and Ann Skues of Kea; miner	20 Aug	1843
SKUES	GRACE	daughter of John and Ann Skues of Kea; miner	20 Aug	1843
Polkinghorne Mary Elizabeth		daughter of Arthur Dawe Polkinghorne (outfitters) and Eva (née Skewes) of Chy-an-Gwel, Boscolla, Truro. Adult baptism	4 Mar	1947

PARISH REGISTER OF KENWYN   MARRIAGES   1559 — 1963

SKEWES	AMY (MARY)	of Truro	&	John Freeman	30 Apl	1685
SKUES	DEGORY	of Kea	&	....	18 May	1700
SKUES	RICHARD		&	Jane Coombe	16 Dec	1722
SKUES	MARTIN		&	Mary Coad	15 June	1729
SKEWES	HENRY	of Kea	&	Margery Behenna of Kea	20 Dec	1740

SKEWES	DIGORY	of Kea	&	Margaret Spargo	27 Dec	1756
SKEWES	THOMAS	of Kea	&	Jane Crossman		
In presence of Mary					29 Dec	1759
SKEWES	MARTIN		&	Mary Polkinghorne	16 Feb	1760
In presence of Martin Skewes						
SKEWES	RICHARD		&	Mary Teague	20 Oct	1770
SKEWES	JOHN		&	Mary Dennis	23 Feb	1771
SKEWES	HENRY		&	Mary Jolly	4 Nov	1776
SKEWES	MARY		&	James Auery of St Agnes	19 July	1778
SKEWES	RICHARD		&	Jane Robins	26 Oct	1781
SKEWES	DEGORY OF Kea		&	Elizabeth Wasley of Kea	13 July	1782
SKEWES	CATHERINE of Kea		&	John Wasley of Kea	14 June	1783
SKEWES	ALICE		&	John Morcam of Gwennap	13 Nov	1784
SKEWES	MARIE		&	William Tamlyn	12 Nov	1785
SKEWES	JOHN		&	Ann Stephens	8 Nov	1787
SKEWES	BIDDY		&	Nicholas Trestraile both of Kea	6 Oct	1788
SKEWES	ELIZABETH		&	Thomas Trahear	18 Oct	1788
SKEWES	MARY		&	John Blackler, both of Kea	28 Mar	1789
SKEWES	PETER		&	Ann Crase	10 Sept	1791
SKEWES	PETER		&	Peggy Moyle, lic	7 Jan	1792
SKEWES	ANN		&	John Benny of Feock	29 Sept	1792
SKEWES	RICHARD		&	Rose Anthony	18 Feb	1793
SKEWES	HENRY		&	Catherine Wasley both of Kea	22 May	1793
SKEWES	CATHERINE		&	John James, both of Kea	8 Jan	1795
SKEWES	ANN		&	Daniel Hodge	1 May	1797
SKEWES	THOMAS		&	Mary Tippet, both of Kea	6 Jan	1798
SKEWES	JENNEFAR		&	John Bastian, both of Kea	27 Jan	1798
SKEWES	PEGGY		&	Thomas Roberts of Kea	30 Dec	1802
SKEWES	RICHARD		&	Grace Ford	10 Oct	1803
SKEWES	JANE		&	John Carthew of Illogan	8 May	1815
(In presence of Peter Skewes)						
SKEWES	ALICE		&	Joseph Mitchell	23 Dec	1815
(In presence of Richard Skewes and John Skewes)						
SKEWES	PETER		&	Mary Williams	21 Sept	1817
SKEWES	JOHN of Kea		&	ANN SKEWES of Kenwyn; by Licence	2 Sept	1818
SKUES	JULIANA		&	Thomas Davey	2 June	1819
SKEWES	MARY of Kea		&	Richard Tonkin	5 Mar	1820
(In presence of Henry Skewes)						
SKEWES	THOMAS of Kea		&	Grace Trezize	13 July	1820
(In presence of Henry Skewes)						
SKUES	JOHN		&	Margery Jenkin	14 Mar	1822
SKUES	MARY		&	Jacob Michell	17 Oct	1822
(In presence of Eleanor Skues)						
SKEWES	MARTHA		&	John Fenrell of Cullumpton, Devon	8 May	1823
By licence						
SKUES	SUSANNAH		&	William Harris	2 Aug	1823
SKEWES	THOMAS		&	Jane Beer of St. Mary's, Truro	12 Feb	1824
(In presence of Mary Jolly Skewes)						
SKUES	ELIZABETH		&	James Jones	21 May	1825
SKEWES	MARY JOLLY		&	Thomas Gilbert	3 July	1825
(In presence of Thomas Skewes)						
SKEWES	SUSANNAH		&	William Jeffery	18 Feb	1826
SKEWES	ELIZABETH		&	John Bawdyn	18 Feb	1826
SKEWES	ELEANOR		&	James Tonkin	13 Nov	1829
SKUES	JOHN		&	Mary Ann Stoddan	12 July	1830
SKUES	MARY		&	Robert Rabey	14 Aug	1830
SKUES	RICHARD, widower		&	MARY SKUES		
In Register "the mark of"			In signature "Marey Skewes"	17 Nov	1831
SKEWES	THOMAS		&	Grace Richards	24 Jan	1838
SKUES	ELIZA, 19		&	Thomas Hooper, 19,		
of Penstraze, Kenwyn. Father — Joseph Skues, carpenter			of Penstraze. Father — James Hooper, miner	2 June	1841
SKEWS	ELIZABETH, 21,		&	John Stripp, 31, of Chacewater Father — William Slade Stripp, carpenter		
of Chacewater. Father—Matthew Skews, miner; in presence of Matthew Skews				22 May	1842
SKUES	GRACE, 25, widow of		&	James Harry, 24, of		
Chacewater. Father — James Richards, miner.			Chacewater, miner. Father—Thomas Harry, miner	4 July	1842
SKEWS	JENIFER, 32, of Hugus;		&	James Rowe, 28, of Hugus,		
miner. Father—John Skews, miner			miner. Father — James Rowe, miner	11 Jan	1844
SKEWS	JAMES, 22,		&	Harriet Curno, 22, of Chacewater. Father — John Curno, miner.		
of Chacewater, miner. Father — Richard Skews, miner.				19 June	1844
SKEWES	JOHN, 20, of Daniell Street,		&	Mary Brown Windon, 19, of		
Truro; Cabinet Maker. Father — Thomas Skewes, mason. In presence of Thomas Skewes and Mary Ann Skewes			Kenwyn Street, Truro. Father—James Windon, shipwright	3 Dec	1849
SKEWS	JANE, 25,		&	Joseph Davey, 25, mason.		
of Chacewater. Father — Matthew			Father — Thomas Davey, mason.		

Skews; miner. In presence of Matthew Skews				21 Dec	1850
SKEWES JOHN, 20, of Chacewater, miner. Father— John Skewes, miner.	&	Mary Ann Sandoe, 21, of Chacewater. Father— William Sandoe, miner		27 Feb	1851
SKEWES HENRIETTA, 21, of Daniell Street, Truro. Father— Thomas Skewes, mason. In presence of Philippa Jane Skewes & Thomas Skewes.	&	William Henry Crewes, 25, of Kenwyn Street, Truro. Father—James Crewes; shoemaker.		17 Dec	1851
SKEWES RICHARD, 33, of Penstraze; carpenter. Father—William Skewes, miner	&	Elizabeth Rouse, 20, of Charles Street, Kenwyn. Father— Robert Rouse, labourer.		4 Mar	1852
SKEWES MATTHEW, 21, of Chacewater, miner. Father—Peter Skewes, miner.	&	Mary Hattam, 19, of Chacewater. Father—John Hattam, miner		4 Dec	1852
SKEWES ELIZABETH, 26, of Wheal Daniel. Father— Thomas Skewes, miner.	&	Thomas Oates, 28, of of Wheal Daniel, miner. Father—Joseph Oates, miner		31 Mar	1853
SKEWES MARY ANN, 28, of Daniell Street, Truro; Father—Thomas Skewes, mason. In presence of Thomas Skewes	&	John Mills, 26, of Daniell Street; tailor. Father— Philip Mills, lawyer		30 Apl	1853
SKEWES EMMA, 28, of Chacewater. Father—John Skewes, miner.	&	William Harris, 37, widower, mason of Chacewater. Father—John Harris, porter		19 Mar	1854
SKEWES AMELIA, 20, of Chacewater. Father—John Skewes, miner	&	William James, 23, of Chacewater; miner. Father—James James; blacksmith		16 Sept	1854
SKEWES ELIZABETH JANE, 27, of Kenwyn. Father—John Beer Skewes; cabinet maker. In presence of John Beer Skewes and Hetty Skewes	&	James Henry Flynn, 23, of St George's, Kenwyn; commercial traveller. Father— Henry John Flynn, storeman.		17 Aug	1879
SKEWES FLORENCE CECILIA, 21, of Trehaverne, Kenwyn. Father— Thomas Skewes; ironmonger. In presence of Annie Skewes & Thomas Skewes	&	William Thomas Tonkin, 30, of Victoria Place, St John's, Truro; butcher. Father—William Tonkin; butcher		18 Aug	1890
SKEWES-WASLEY, WILLIAM, 27, of Boscolla, Kenwyn; farmer; Father— William Wasley, deceased.	&	Lavinia Jane Hore, 28, Father—William Hore, market gardener		20 Apl	1905

KENWYN PARISH REGISTER   BURIALS   1608 — 1959

SKEWES	MARY	daughter of Richard Skewes	9 Jan	1773
SKEWES	MARY	wife of Richard Skewes	26 Jan	1774
SKEWES	MARY		27 Apl	1787
SKEWES	SUSANNAH	dau of Richard Skewes, pauper	25 Feb	1793
SKEWES	PETER	son of Henry Skewes of Kea	5 Aug	1793
SKEWES	RICHARD		26 Jan	1794
SKEWIS	MARY		1 May	1795
SKEWES	RICHARD	son of Thomas Skewes of Kea	11 Mar	1795
SKEWES	JAMES	son of John Skewes	9 Dec	1800
SKEWES	THOMAS		5 Sept	1806
SCKEWS	JANE	aged 55 years	7 July	1809
SCKEWS	THOMAS	aged 42 years	23 May	1811
SKEWES	PETER	of St Agnes. Aged 18 years	24 Apl	1814
SKEWES	RICHARD	of Hugus. Aged 57 years	14 Aug	1823
SKEWES	PETER	of Blackwater. Aged 12 years	22 April	1825
SKEWES	MARY	of Kea. Aged 5 years	5 June	1825
SKEWES	HENRY	of Fairmantle St. Aged 24 years	22 Oct	1826
SKEWES	THOMAS	of The Poorhouse. Aged 3 years	19 Feb	1827
SKEWES	HENRIETTA	of Newham Street. Aged 9 months	20 July	1827
SKUES	WILLIAM	of John Street. Aged 10 wks	23 Sept	1838
SKUES	ELIZABETH	of Truro. Aged 4 months	20 Nov	1840
SKEWES	HENRY	of St Mary's, Truro. Aged 6 yrs	7 Mar	1841
SKUES	ROSE	of Hugus. Aged 78 years	12 Mar	1843
SKEWES	HENRY CHARLES	of Truro. Aged 3 months	3 Feb	1844
SKEWES	MARGARET	of Kenwyn Street. Aged 78 yrs	20 Aug	1847
SKEWES	JAMES	of Truro. Aged 44 years	8 Feb	1849
SKEWES	PETER	of Charles Street. Aged 75 yrs	28 Dec	1864
SKEWES	MARY	of Truro Union. Aged 64 yrs	8 Dec	1864
SKEWES	MARY	of Richmond Hill. Aged 73 yrs	29 Mar	1868
SKEWES	LAVINIA	of Richmond Hill. Aged 60 yrs	12 July	1868
SKEWES	MARY ANN	of Truro Union House. Aged 70	5 May	1887
SKEWES	EMMA STEPHENS	of 8 St Clements Terrace, Truro. Aged 85 years	25 Mar	1926

PARISH REGISTER OF ST. KEVERNE   BAPTISMS   1580 — 1906

SKEWES	HUMFFREY	son of John Skewes	24 Sept	1625
SKEWES	LOWDYE	daughter of John Skewes	22 Nov	1628
SKEWES	WILMET	daughter of Richard Skewes	16 Mar	1633
SKEWES	ANN	daughter of John Skewes	17 Aug	1634
SKEWES	RICHARD	son of Richard & Jane Skewes	12 Dec	1636
SKEWES	DOROTHY	daughter of Richard & Joane Skewes	26 Aug	1638
SKEWES	JOHN	son of John & Margaret Skewes	12 May	1640
SKEWES	JOHN	son of Richard & Jane Skewes	5 June	1643
SKEWES	SAMUEL	son of Keverne Skewes	13 June	1665
SKEWES	EDWARD	son of John and Mary Skewes	22 Dec	1667
SKEWES	RICHARD	son of Keverne Skewes	11 Apl	1669
SKEWES	GRACE	daughter of John Skewes	24 Oct	1669
SKEWIS	ESTHER	daughter of Thomas & Esther	10 May	1747
SKEWIS	THOMAS	son of Thomas & Esther	15 Oct	1749
SKEWIS	MARY	daughter of Thomas & Esther	26 Jan	1752
SKEWIS	JUDITH	daughter of Thomas & Esther	24 Nov	1754
SKEWIS	HENRY	son of Thomas & Esther	19 Dec	1758
SKEWIS	JANE	daughter of Thomas & Esther	16 Nov	1760
SKEWIS	HENRY	son of Thomas & Esther	1 Jan	1764
SKEWIS	ANN	daughter of Thomas & Esther	27 Dec	1766
SKEWIS	ELEANOR	daughter of Thomas & Eleanor	20 Dec	1774
SKEWIS	HENRY	son of Thomas & Eleanor	15 June	1777
SKEWIS	MARGARET	daughter of Henry & Jane	26 Dec	1793
SKEWIS	EDWARD	son of Henry & Jane	19 July	1795
SKEWIS	JANE	daughter of Henry & Jane	2 July	1797
SKEWES	JOSEPH	base son of Blanch Skewes	24 Mar	1811
SKEWES	JAMES	son of William & Christiana of Tregarne; farmer	1 July	1827
SKEWES	WILLIAM	son of William & Christiana of Tregarne; farmer	28 Aug	1829
SKEWES	CHRISTIAN	daughter of William & Christiana of Tregarne; farmer	18 Mar	1832
SKEWES	GRACE	daughter of William & Christiana of Tregarne; farmer	29 June	1834
SKEWES	JOHN	son of William & Christiana of Tregarne; farmer	3 Apl	1836
SKEWES	RICHARD	son of Edward and Mary of Rosenithon; farmer	19 Apl	1838
SKEWES	SAMUEL HENRY	son of Henry & Grace, of Churchtown; school master	25 May	1845

PARISH REGISTER OF ST. KEVERNE   MARRIAGES   1608 — 1950

SKEWES	CHERITY	&	James Hockin	29 July	1623
SKEWES	JOHN	&	Ann Harwood	15 Nov	1624
SKEWES	JOHN	&	Margaret Cheran	20 Apr	1632
SKEWES	KEVERNE	&	Joanna Nicholas	11 Sept	1654
SKEWES	MARY	&	Gedeon Harrie	12 Jan	1659
SKEWES	MARY	&	Ambrose John	2 Feb	1659
SKEWES	WILLMOTE	&	Thomas Oliver	30 Dec	1661
SKEWES	JOHN	&	Mary Cornelius	15 Apl	1667
SKEWES	FLORENCE	&	Richard Row	6 July	1674
SKEWES	THOMAS	&	Esther James	23 Oct	1746
In presence of Thomas Skewes					
SKEWIS	THOMAS	&	Eleanor Giles	29 Oct	1774
SKEWES	JUDITH	&	John Mildren	11 Aug	1783
In presence of Thomas Skewes					
SKEWES	HENRY	&	Jane Pascoe	1 Jan	1787
SKEWES	HENRY	&	Jane Retallack; by licence	15 Aug	1793
In presence of John Skewes					
SKEWIS	ANN	&	John James	22 June	1794
SKEWIS	MARGARET	&	John Harris	10 Dec	1833
By Licence. In presence of Edward Skewis					
SKEWIS	EDWARD	&	Mary Lory. By licence	18 Feb	1835
SKEWES	EDWARD of Mawnan.	&	Mary Penticost Nicholls		
Son of William Skewes. In presence of			of Porthallow. Daughter of William Nicholls		
James Skewes. Edward was a blacksmith.					
				20 Aug	1844

PARISH REGISTER OF ST. KEVERNE   BURIALS   1597 — 1942

SKEWES	ELIZABETH	daughter of John	Buried	17 Dec	1626
SKEWES	AMYE	ux of John		25 Jan	1629
SKEWES	RICHARD	son of Richard		20 Dec	1636
SKEWES	JOHN	son of John		28 July	1640
SKEWES	DOROTHY	daughter of Richard		14 Feb	1643
SKEWES	ARTHUR			14 July	1654
SKEWES	TOMZIN	daughter of Walter		13 Jan	1661
SKEWES	WILLIAM	son of Richard		17 July	1664
SKEWES	JOANE	wife of Keverne		24 Apr	1673

SKEWES	JOHN		6 Apl	1674
SKEWES	RICHARD		17 Jan	1678
SKEWES	MARY	ux of Walter	19 Dec	1679
SKUIS	DOROTHY		28 Sept	1689
SKUIS	WALTER		20 Aug	1690
SKUIS	KEVERNE		7 Jan	1692
SKUIS	JANE		28 Aug	1695
SKUES	MARY	widow	22 May	1709
SKEWIS	ANN		6 Mar	1720
SKEWIS	PHILIPPA		10 Sept	1739
SKEWIS	HENRY	son of Thomas Skewis	28 Dec	1758
SKEWIS	—	a child of Thomas Skewis	20 July	1767
SKEWIS	THOMAS		28 Dec	1777
SKEWIS	JANE	wife of Henry Skewis	26 Nov	1792
SKEWIS	HESTER	widow of Thomas Skewis	5 Jan	1797
SKEWIS	MARGARET	daughter of Henry and Jane	14 May	1798
SKEWIS	JOHN	son of William & Christiana of Tregarne, aged 13 years	5 Feb	1830
SKEWES	MARY	from the parish of Grade, aged 40 years	21 July	1846

REGISTER OF LANNER WESLEYAN/METHODIST CHURCH   BAPTISMS   1840 — 1879

SKEWES	MARY JANE	daughter of John and Ann Skewes of Penance, aged 4 months	15 Feb	1843
SKEWES	SIMON DAVEY	son of John and Ann Skewes of Penance, aged 3 months, from the parish of Gwennap	3 Sept	1845
SKEWES	ALEXANDER	son of John and Ann Skewes of Penance, aged 4 months	25 June	1850

REGISTER OF LISKEARD WESLEYAN/METHODIST CHAPEL BAPTISMS   1838 — 1948

SKEWS	MORLEY DAVID	son of John and Louisa Skews of 1, Friends Place, Pound Street, Liskeard. Born 18 May 1919.	9 July	1919
SKEWES	CONSTANCE MARGARET	daughter of John and Mary Skews of Bay Tree Hill, Liskeard. Born 27 June 1920	2 Sept	1920
SKEWS	MARION RHODA	daughter of John and Mary Skews of Liskeard. Born 27 March 1924.	4 May	1924

PARISH REGISTER OF LUDGVAN — MARRIAGES — 1563 — 1966

SKEWES	GRACE	&	Nyclis Vybyst	20 Nov	1575
SKEWES	VIOLET MAY (23)	&	Thomas Francis Tresize (30)	12 Apl	1941

of Nancladra. daughter of William Trevena Skewes, farmer In presence of William Trevena Skewes.

farmer of Kerris Farm, Paul. Son of Richard Thomas Tresize, deceased.

PARISH REGISTER OF LUDGVAN — BURIALS — 1563 — 1812

SKEWES	RICHARD	son of Sandry Skewes	buried 20 Mar	1570
SKEWES	FRANCES	daughter of Sandry Skewes	3 Apl	1598
SKEWES	ENOUR	wife of Sandry Skewes	4 Oct	1598
SKEWES	SANDRY		20 Dec	1598
SCRUSE	DOROTHY	wife of Richard Scruse	23 Jan	1657
SCRUSE	GRACE	daughter of Richard Scruse	22 Apl	1657

(only checked to 1670)

PARISH REGISTER OF MADRON WITH PENZANCE — MARRIAGES — 1674 — 1812

SKEWIS	JOHN	&	Mary.....	31 Oct	1690
SKEWES	ANN of Penzance	&	John Richards of Madron. Marriage at Paul	5 July	1715
SKEWS	SAMUEL	&	Ann Quick	26 Dec	1719
SKEWS	JOHN of Gwennap	&	Elizabeth Symonds	25 Aug	1734
SKEWS	PHYLLIS of Penzance	&	Martin Hoskin	5 Jan	1771

REGISTER OF MARAZION WESLEYAN/METHODIST CHAPEL BAPTISMS 1841 — 1927

SKEWS	ANNIE	daughter of Samuel and Clara Skews of Marazion. Born 24 July 1866	21 Sept	1886
SKEWES	WILLIAM TREVENA	son of Samuel and Clara Skewes of Marazion. Born 11 June 1890	2 Sept	1890
SKEWES	AGNES CORONA	daughter of Richard and Hetty Skewes of Marazion. Born 14 June 1902	14 Oct	1902
SKEWES	VIOLET MAY	daughter of Wm Trevena & Edith Skewes of Gonew, Lelant. Bpt at White Cross.	Bn 8 Jan 1918. Bpt 14 Apl 1918	

PARISH REGISTER OF MARAZION   BAPTISMS   1848 — 1979

SKEWES	WILLIAM HANNIBAL	son of Digory and Frances of Marazion, miner. Born 2 March 1854	29 Sept	1854
SKEWES	THOMAS GEORGE	son of Digory and Frances of Marazion, miner. Born 15 March 1857	1 July	1857
SKEWES	JOHN WILLIAM	son of Thomas George and Jane of Marazion, labourer.	20 Feb	1881
SKEWES	GERTRUDE	daughter of Richard and Maria of Marazion, labourer. Born 1 Dec 1886	19 Jan	1887
SKEWES	RICHARD HENRY	son of Richard and Frenetta of Marazion, labourer. Born 5 Mar 1888	27 Apl	1888
SKEWES	JOSEPH JOHN	son of Richard and Frenetta of Marazion, labourer. Born 5 Dec 1889	23 Feb	1890
SKEWES	LAURA	daughter of Richard and Frenetta of Marazion, labourer. Born 26 Nov 1891	22 Jan	1892
SKEWES	ERNEST	son of Richard and Frenetta of Marazion, labourer. Born 29 Sept 1893	15 Dec	1893
SKEWES	HETTY LOUISE	daughter of Richard and Frenetta of Marazion, labourer. Born 29 Oct 1895	20 Dec	1895
SKEWES	JONATHAN BRADDON	son of Richard and Frenetta of Marazion, labourer. Born 2 Feb 1898	11 Mar	1898

Marriage registers not available

PARISH REGISTER OF MARAZION   BURIALS   1864 — 1944

SKEWES	DIGORY	aged 43 years	11 Mar	1868
SKEWES	FRENETTA	of Marazion, aged 31 years	19 Sept	1899
SKEWES	FANNY	of Marazion, aged 75 years	2 July	1902
SKEWES	ANNIE	of Fore Street, Marazion, aged 76 years	29 Apl	1920
SKEWIS	MARY JANE	of Fore Street, Marazion, aged 58 years	17 Nov	1922

PARISH REGISTER OF MAWGAN-IN-MENEAGE   BAPTISMS   1559 — 1914

SKEWES	JAMES	son of Elizabeth Skewes	19 July	1741
SKEWES	JOHN	son of Joseph and Philippa Skewes	21 Mar	1757
SKEWES	JOSEPH	son of Joseph and Philippa Skewes	8 Aug	1758
SKEWES	JOAN	daughter of Joseph and Philippa Skewes	8 Apl	1760
SKEWES	WILLIAM	son of Joseph and Philippa Skewes	28 Dec	1762
SKEWES	WILLIAM	son of Joseph and Philippa Skewes	5 May	1765
SKEWYS	ELINOR	daughter of Anthony and Elinor Skewys	23 Aug	1767
SKEWES	ANN	daughter of James and Anne Skewes	28 Dec	1773
SKEWES	MARY	daughter of James and Anne Skewes	10 Sept	1774
SKEWES	JAMES	son of Joseph and Elizabeth Skewes	22 June	1777
SKEWES	JAMES	son of James and Anne Skewes	29 June	1777
SKEWES	SARAH	daughter of James and Anne Skewes	21 Nov	1779
SKUES	MARIA	daughter of James and Anne Skues of Cury	2 Nov	1794

PARISH REGISTER OF MAWGAN-IN-MENEAGE   MARRIAGES   1563 — 1964

SKEWAS	GRACE of St. Keverne	&	Thomas Rownson	28 Aug	1703
SKEWIS	JOAN	&	Richard Traplyn	6 Nov	1755
SKEWIS	JANE	&	John Banfield, labourer	12 Feb	1760
SKEWES	JOSEPH	&	Elizabeth Pearce	14 Jan	1772
SKEWES	JAMES of Cury	&	Anne Richard	19 Oct	1773
SKEWES	MARY	&	Thomas Dale	31 Oct	1782
SKUES	MARY	&	Joseph Repper	1 Jan	1817
SKEWES	WILLIAM (28)	&	Amelia Odgers (23) of Mawgan. Father dead	7 Oct	1841
	labourer of Mawgan. Son of James Skewes, labourer. In presence of Henry Skewes and Josiah Skewes				
SKEWES	SAMUEL (26)	&	Mary Thomas (30) of Mawgan. Dau of Joseph Thomas (dead)	12 Apl	1842
	carpenter of Cury. Son of John Skewes, labourer. In presence of John Skewes				
SKEWES	ELIZABETH MARY (27)	&	Joseph Hollcomb Lugg (28) postman. Son of Henry Lugg, labourer	25 July	1871
	laundry-maid of Mawgan. Daughter of John Skewes, tailor. In presence of Mary Ann Mander Skewes and John Skewes				

(RKS note: The entry in the Register is incorrect. It lists ELIZABETH MARY SKEWES as the postman and Joseph Hollcomb Lugg as a laundry-maid. Even parish clerks make a mistake from time to time. I have taken the liberty of correcting the entry in this transcript.)

SKEWES	MARY JANE (22)	&	William Thomas Rowe (24)		
	of Mawgan. Daughter of William James Skewes, labourer. In presence of William Skewes		grocer of Mawgan. Son of William Hocking Rowe, labourer.	2 Nov	1893
SKEWES	ETHEL MAY (25)	&	Herbert Cooke (28)		
	of Mawgan. Daughter of William James Skewes, labourer.		carpenter of Mawgan. Son of William Thomas Cooke, carpenter	15 Oct	1908
SKEWES	OSWALD (42) farmer of	&	Celia Holbrook (31)		
	Higher Relouas, Mawgan. Son of John Skewes, farmer		of Higher Relouas, Mawgan. Daugher of Richard Henry Holbrook, gas meter collector.	27 Sept	1958

PARISH REGISTER OF MAWGAN-IN-MENEAGE   BURIALS   1559 — 1914

SKEWES	JAMES	was buried	10 May	1762
SKEWES	PHILIPPA	wife of Joseph SKEWES	18 Mar	1768
SKEWYS	JUDITH	daughter of Anthony SKEWYS	21 Oct	1769
SKEWES	JOHN		6 July	1777
SKEWES	ANN		30 Apl	1778
SKEWES	MARGARET		15 May	1786
SKUES	JOSEPH		18 May	1798

PARISH REGISTER OF MAWNAN   BAPTISMS   1812 — 1959

SKEWES	SAMUEL	son of William and Christian Skewes of Rosemullion, Farmer	10 Mar	1834
SKEWES	HESTER ANN	daughter of James and Frances Skewes (Parish Clerk) of Mawnansmith	5 July	1846
SKEWES	FRANCES MARIA	daughter of James and Frances Skewes (Parish Clerk) of Mawnansmith	23 Apl	1848
SKEWES	EDWARD	son of James and Frances Skewes (Parish Clerk) of Mawnansmith	16 Sept	1849
SKEWES	WILLIAM HENRY	son of James and Frances Skewes (Parish Clerk) of Mawnansmith	27 Apl	1851
SKEWES	EMILY KEMPTHORNE	daughter of James and Frances Skewes (Parish Clerk) of Mawnansmith	23 Oct	1853
SKEWES	JAMES LUGG	son of James and Frances Skewes (Parish Clerk) of Mawnansmith	7 Oct	1855
SKEWES	ALMA JANE	daughter of James and Frances Skewes (Parish Clerk) of Mawnansmith	17 May	1857
SKEWES	JAMES LUGG	son of James and Frances Skewes (Parish Clerk) of Mawnansmith	16 Jan	1859
SKEWES	KATE	daughter of James and Frances Skewes (Parish Clerk) of Mawnansmith	13 Sept	1863
SKEWES	ELLEN	daughter of James and Frances Skewes (Parish Clerk) of Mawnansmith	29 Apl	1866

PARISH REGISTER OF MAWNAN   MARRIAGES   1754 — 1960

SKEWES	JAMES	Farmer of Rosemullion, Mawnan (Father, William Skewes, farmer) to Frances Kempthorne (daughter of James Kempthorne, farmer) of Mawnan. In presence of Edward Skewes	2 Oct	1845
SKEWES	ELIZABETH	of Meadow, Mawnan (daughter of William Skewes, farmer) to Thomas Veal of Helford Passage (son of James Veal, farmer) In presence of Edward Skewes and William Skewes	2 Apl	1846
SKEWES	WILLIAM	Labourer of Little-in-Sight, Mawnan (son of William Skewes, farmer) to Jane Kempthorne of Mawnansmith (daughter of James Kempthorne, farmer). In presence of Henry Skewes.	5 Dec	1850
SKEWES	HENRY	Labourer of Little-in-Sight, Mawnan (son of William Skewes, farmer) to Ann Gribble of Falmouth (daughter of William Gribble). In presence of Grace Skewes.	24 Dec	1850
SKEWES	ANN	of Mawnan (daughter of William Skewes, farmer) to John Philips, farmer (son of John Phillips). In presence of Grace Skewes.	31 May	1855
SKEWES	GRACE	of Mawnan (daughter of William Skewes, farmer) to Samuel Phillips Veal, innkeeper of Helford Passage (son of James Veal). In presence of James Skewes.	15 Nov	1855
SKEWES	EDWARD	Aged 48, widower of Mawnansmith (son of William Skewes, farmer) to Mary Ellen Kempthorne, (25) spinster of Mawnansmith (daughter of John Kempthorne, carpenter of Mawnansmith). In presence of James Skewes	30 June	1867
SKEWES	EMILY KEMPTHORNE	aged 28; spinster of Mawnan (daughter of James Skewes, farmer) to Reuben Cobeldick (52), bachelor of Mawgan-in-Pydar, Gentleman (son of Richard Cobeldick, farmer). In presence of Hester Ann Skewes and Edward Skewes.	14 Dec	1883
SKEWES	KATE	Aged 24: spinster of Mawnan (daughter of James Skewes, farmer) to William John Chaffe Harman (24) innkeeper of Falmouth. In presence of Mary Skewes and Edward Skewes.	13 Dec	1888
SKEWES	ELLEN	Aged 24; spinster of Mawnan (daughter of James Skewes, farmer) to John Peter Sadler of Trebak, Derby (son of Robert Sadler, butler). In presence of Mary Skewes.	22 Apl	1890

PARISH REGISTER OF MAWNAN   BURIALS   1570 — 1959

SKEWES	GRACE	aged 20 from Helston	buried	12 Apl	1821
SKEWES	GRACE NOY	Aged 2 from Constantine		31 Dec	1821
SKEWES	JAMES LUGG	Aged 8 months of Mawnansmith		20 May	1856
SKEWES	WILLIAM	Aged 66 from Little-in-Sight		14 Aug	1861
SKEWES	CHRISTIAN	aged 70 from Little-in-Sight		14 Nov	1864
SKEWES	MARY	aged 40 from Mawnansmith		20 Feb	1867
SKEWES	WILLIAM HENRY	aged 18 from Mawnansmith		27 Oct	1869
SKEWES	EDWARD	aged 51 from Mawnansmith		26 June	1870
SKEWES	ALMA	aged 13 from Mawnansmith		12 Oct	1870
SKEWES	HESTER ANN	aged 46 from Mawnansmith		12 Oct	1893
SKEWES	JAMES	aged 84 Parish Clerk of Mawnan for fifty years		30 July	1899
SKEWES	FRANCES	aged 82 from Mawnansmith		13 May	1907
SKEWES	EDWARD	aged 92 from Mawnan		27 Jan	1942
SKEWES	MARY	aged 85 of Bareppa		23 Feb	1946

Mawnan Parish Church with table tomb of the Skues family in foreground

---

PARISH REGISTER OF MENHENIOT   BAPTISMS   1544 — 1837

SCOOSE	(Blank)	son of John	3 Apl	1563
SCOOSE	JESPER	son of John	2 Feb	1565
SCOOSE	MARY	daughter of John	18 Feb	1571
SCOOSE	FERNANDO		29 Nov	1573
SCORSEE	PETERNELL	daughter of John	28 June	1577
SCOOSE	GEORGE	son of John at St. Ive	24 Jan	1579

(Note: There are many entries for SCORSE throughout the 1550's)
The Registers for the year 1567 — 1569 inclusive are missing.

PARISH REGISTER OF MENHENIOT   MARRIAGES   1554 — 1812

SCOOSE	JOHN	and	Jane Piper	18 June	1562
SCOOSE	JANE	and	Thomas Hore	18 Sept	1587
SCOOSSE	PETERNELL	and	Christopher Hicks		
(died 16 April, 1655 at Menheniot)				26 Nov	1604
SCOOSSE	GEORGE	and	Ann Pethericke	9 Jan	1605

PARISH REGISTER OF MENHENIOT   BURIALS   1554 — 1837

SCOOSE	(Blank)	daughter of Jane	10 Mar	1580
SCOOSE	JOHN		20 Apl	1580
SCOOSE	JANE		16 May	1604

PARISH REGISTER OF MULLION   BAPTISMS   1747 — 1845

SKUES	JOSEPH	son of William and Ann SKUES	29 Nov	1801
SKEWIS	PHILIPPA	daughter of William and Ann SKEWIS from Gunwalloe	4 Mar	1804

PARISH REGISTER OF MULLION   BURIALS   1747 — 1869

SKEWIS	PHILIPPA	an infant	15 Mar	1804
SKEWES	JOSEPH		1 Nov	1804
SKEWES	MARY	from the parish of Ruan Major, aged 11 years	17 July	1843

PARISH REGISTER OF MYLOR   BAPTISMS   1729 — 1904

SKUES	JOHN BENNETT	son of William and Jane Skues	3 July	1803
SKUES	ELIZABETH	daughter of William and Jane Skues	24 Mar	1805
SKUES	MARY	daughter of William and Jane Skues	26 Oct	1806
SKUES	JANE	daughter of William and Jane Skues	24 Apl	1808
SKUES	ANN	daughter of William and Jane Skues	14 Jan	1810
SKUES	WILLIAM JOHN	son of William and Jane Skues of Lower Flushing	19 Nov	1815

PARISH REGISTER OF MYLOR   MARRIAGES   1673 — 1869

SKEWES	SARAH	and	William Anthony of St Keverne, widower	25 Jan	1797
In presence of William Skewes					
SKUES	WILLIAM	and	Jane John	10 June	1802
sojourner. In presence of Elizabeth Skues					

PARISH REGISTER OF MYLOR   BURIALS   1730 — 1925

SKEWES	JOHN BENNETT	son of William and Jane Skewes	24 Mar	1805
SKEWS	JOHN		4 Sept	1805
SKUES	WILLIAM JOHN	son of William and Jane SKUES, aged 1 year	27 May	1817
SKEWES	MARGARET	daughter of Henry and Margaret SKEWES, of Mylor, aged 22 years	15 Apl	1823

(Note: In the family of WILLIAM and JANE SKUES there is both a christening and burial on the same day — 24 March 1805)

PARISH REGISTER OF PAUL   BAPTISMS   1595 — 1812

SKEWYS	RICHARD	son of Richard	14 Jan	1704
SKEWS	MARGARET	daughter of Richard	14 Dec	1707
SKEWES	STEPHEN	son of Richard	19 Apl	1735
SKEWS	PHILIS	daughter of Richard	11 Nov	1736
SKEWISH	JOSEPH	base child of Margery	8 Nov	1747

PARISH REGISTER OF PAUL   MARRIAGES   1595 — 1812

SKEWS	RICHARD	and	Margaret Tregewe	2 Jan	1700
SKEUES	ANN of PENZANCE	and	John Richards	5 July	1715
SKEUES	MARGARET	and	Isaac Crusielieur	27 Apr	1726
SKEWS	RICHARD	and	Margery Warren	25 Feb	1734

PARISH REGISTER OF PERRANARWORTHAL   BAPTISMS   1684 — 1837

SKEWES	MARY	daughter of John and Alice of Kea	18 Sept	1759

PARISH REGISTER OF PERRANARWORTHAL   MARRIAGES   1597 — 1812

SKEWES	COLON	and	Elizabeth Warrine	9 June	1665
SKEWES	JOHN of Kea	and	Alice John (by licence)	23 June	1759
SKEWES	RICHARD	and	Mary Lean	24 June	1798

PARISH REGISTER OF PERRANARWORTHAL   BURIALS   1684 — 1837

SKUES	STEPHEN		4 Mar	1684

PARISH REGISTER OF PERRANUTHNOE   BAPTISMS   1813 — 1883

SKEWES	THOMAS HENRY	son of Thomas & Margaret, horse breaker of Goldsithney	25 Dec	1857
SKEWES	JOHN THOMAS	son of Richard & Caroline of Perran Downs; miner	22 Feb	1863
SKEWES	MARY JANE	daughter of James & Margaret of Goldsithney; groom.	Born: 17 Dec	1863
			Bpt: 28 May	1865
SKEWES	SUSAN ANNIE	daughter of Richard & Susan of Perran Downs; miner. Baptised Whit Sunday	28 May	1871
SKEWES	RICHARD HENRY	son of Richard & Susan of Perran Downs; fish salesman.	Born 25 Aug	1873
			Bpt 28 Sept	1873
SKEWES	WALTER	illegitimate son of Clarinda Ralph. Reputed father Thomas Henry Skewes of Henfon.	Born 1 Feb	1881
			Bpt 29 May	1881
SKEWES	ANNIE	daughter of Thomas Henry & Clarinda of Goldisthney; horse breaker.	Born 10 Feb	1882
			Bpt 26 Mar	1882

PARISH REGISTER OF PERRANUTHNOE   MARRIAGES   1589 — 1973

SKEWES WILLIAM (31) of Goldsithney. Labourer. Father dead.	&	Ann Prideaux Trezize (37), of Goldsithney. Father dead.	11 Feb	1854
SKEWES RICHARD (23) of Perran Downs; miner. Son of Richard Skewes; miner.	&	Susannah Donald (22) of Perran Downs; domestic servant. Daughter of Stephen Donald; farmer.	27 Aug	1870
SKEWES THOMAS HENRY (24) of Goldsithney. Son of Thomas Skewes of Goldsithney; horse breaker.	&	Clarinda Ralph (23) domestic servant. Dau of William Ralph, miner.	19 Feb	1881
SKEWES WILLIAM (full age) widower; small holder of Perranuthnoe. Son of Richard Skewes, farmer. In presence of R.H. SKEWES	&	Laura Allen of Prussia Cove, St. Hilary Daughter of Henry Allen; fisherman.	1 Oct	1921
SKEWES RICHARD JOHN (21) market gardener of Trebarvah, Perranuthnoe. Son of William Richard Skewes; market gardener. In presence of W.R. SKEWES.	&	Leonie Patricia Hall (22) bank clerk of Penlaynee, Perranuthnoe. Dau of Terence Osborne Hall, wholesale grocer.	6 Jan	1965

PARISH REGISTER OF PERRANUTHNOE   BURIALS   1813 — 1905

SKEWES	JOHN THOMAS	of Perran Downs, aged 10 month	21 Sept	1863
SKEWES	MARGARET	of Goldsithney, aged 67 years	1 July	1884
SKEWES	EMMA	of Perran Downs, aged 12 months	18 Feb	1885
SKEWES	JAMES	of Goldsithney, aged 72 years	26 Mar	1886
SKEWES	WILLIAM	of Primrose Hill, aged 14 months	19 Apr	1886
SKEWES	JOHN	of Goldsithney, aged 7 months	11 Jan	1890

REGISTER OF PERRANWELL CIRCUIT WESLEYAN/METHODIST BAPTISMS 1840 — 1874

SKEWS	ELIZABETH JANE	daughter of Richard & Joanna Skewes of Kea. Bpt aged 6 months & 15 days	6 Mar	1842
SKEWS	MARY	daughter of Peter & Elizabeth Skews of Kea. Born 1842.	7 Mar	1844
SKEWS	JOANNA	daughter of Peter & Elizabeth Skews of Kea. Born 18 October 1843	7 Mar	1844
SKEWS	GRACE	daughter of Peter and Elizabeth Skews of Kea. Born 16 September 1844	5 Jan	1845
SKEWES	MINNIE	daughter of Richard and Elizabeth Ann Skewes of Carharrack. Born 13 Mar 1867	11 Aug	1867

PARISH REGISTER OF PHILLEIGH   MARRIAGES   1613 — 1837

SKEWS	PHILIP	and Ann Webb	7 May	1743

PARISH REGISTER OF REDRUTH   BAPTISMS   1560 — 1878

SKUIS	NICHOLAS	son of Skuis	4 July	1595
SKEWS	WILLIAM	son of William and Jane	2 Oct	1681
SKEWS	JANE	daughter of William and Jane	5 Apl	1684
SKEWS	STEPHEN	son of William and Jane	5 Dec	1686
SKUIES	MARY	daughter of William and Jane	2 June	1689
SKUESS	JOAN	daughter of William and Jane	25 Apl	1698
SKUES	ANN	daughter of William and Jane	8 Feb	1700
SKEWES	ELIZABETH	daughter of Richard and Grace	19 Jan	1806
SKUES	JOHN PENROSE	son of Joseph and Elizabeth of Redruth town; soldier	5 Dec	1813
SKUES	MARY	daughter of Joseph and Elizabeth of Redruth town; soldier	18 June	1815
SKEWIS	LEWIS TUBB	son of John and Sally of Redruth town — mason	2 Feb	1840
SKEWES	JOHN	son of John and Sally of Redruth town — mason. Born 2 May 1838	2 Feb	1840
SKEWIS	THOMAS ALBERT JEFFERY	son of William and Mary of Redruth; tailor	9 July	1844
SKEWES	CHARLES PENROSE	son of John and Sally of Hodders Row, Redruth — mason	3 Mar	1850
SKEWES	ELIZABETH	daughter of John and Margery of Ford's Row, Redruth — engineer. Born 22 April 1837	7 Mar	1850

PARISH REGISTER OF REDRUTH   MARRIAGES   ·   1560 — 1885

SKUES	WILLIAM	and	Jane John	23 Sept	1680
SKUES	JANE	and	John William	5 Feb	1708
SKUIES	MARY	and	John Angove	20 May	1710
SKEWIS	STEPHEN	and	Francis Lydgey	4 Mar	1716
SKUESS	JOAN	and	John Cauldwell	2 Jan	1718
SKEWIS	STEPHEN	and	Jane Lydgey	9 Dec	1723
SKUES	ANN	and	Joseph Gribben	29 Oct	1725
(Note: Between 1725 and 1812 writing in register is very bad, so only briefly checked)					
SKEWES	JOSEPH, sojourner	and	Elizabeth Penrose	9 Feb	1813
SKEWES	JOHN, mason	and	Sally Tubb		
Son of John Skewes, engineer of					
Signs himself SKUES				16 July	1837
SKEWIS	JOHN, miner	and	Mary Barnfield		
Son of Richard Skewis, miner. Living at					
Shallow Adit, Redruth.					
In presence of James Skews				31 Dec	1837
SKUES	MARY	and	William Penrose,		
daught of Joseph Skues; mason			son of Thomas Penrose, mason	19 May	1839
SKEWES	JOHN	and	Caroline Ripper		
Son of John Skewes, engineer of			of Blight's Row. Dau of William Ripper, miner		
Foundary Row, Redruth. In presence of					
Thomas Jenkin Skewes				19 Apl	1845
SKEWES	MATTHEW (21)	and	Mary Jane Nettle (22)		
miner. Son of William Skewes, blacksmith,			daughter of Edward Nettle, miner of Blight's Row.		
of Blight's Row.				17 Aug	1873

PARISH REGISTER OF REDRUTH   BURIALS   1560 — 1887

Note: The whole register is in very bad writing. So only a brief check

SKUES	STEPHEN		28 Apl	1693
SKEWIS	FRANCIS	wife of Stephen Skewis who was a churchwarden in 1727	16 Oct	1717
SKEWIS	WILLIAM		6 Feb	1718
SKUES	JAMES		14 Dec	1737
SKUES	STEPHEN		17 Jan	1752
SKEWES	JANE	widow	20 Feb	1761
SKEWES	SALLY	of East End, Redruth, aged 42.	27 Mar	1853

SKEWES	JOHN	of East End, Redruth, aged 64.	28 July	1855
SKEWES	ANN	of Union House, Redruth, aged 84 or 54 (bad writing)	18 Mar	1856
SKEWES	JAMES	of Blight's Row, Redruth, aged 2.	8 May	1864
SKEWES	CLARA CAROLINE	of West End, Redruth, aged 1 year	31 Jan	1877

REGISTERS OF UNITED METHODIST CHURCH, FORE STREET, REDRUTH
MARRIAGES   1910 — 1964

SKEWES STEPHEN JAMES (30) gold miner of 2, Bullers Terrace, Redruth; son of Samuel Skewes, deceased, carter	&	Ethel Pollard (29) of Trefusis Terrace; daughter of Nathaniel Pollard, deceased, miner
		8 June 1911
SKEWES MARY MARGARET (29) of 1, Channel View Terrace Redruth; son of Samuel Skewes, deceased, carter	&	Alfred Thomas Bird (24) butcher of 2, Lansdowne Terrace, Newquay; son of Sydney Bird, engine driver
		11 Apl 1914
SKEWES DORIS (23) of Four Lanes, Illogan; daughter of John Henry Skewes, tin miner. In presence of John Henry Skewes	&	William Peters (24) general labourer of Higher North Country, Redurth; son of Daniel Laity Peters, mason
		31 Aug 1929
SKUES PHYLLIS (26) of 16, Trefusis Terrace, Redruth; daughter of James Frederick Skues; shoemaker. In presence of James Frederick Skues	&	Joel James Waters (22) tin miner of Lower Pumpfield Row, Illogan; son of William John Waters, deceased, tin miner
		1 Sept 1934
SKUES ADA MAY (30) of 16, Trefusis Terrace, Redruth; daughter of James Frederick Skues, shoemaker	&	Richard Leslie Pearce (29) dock labourer of Carnside, Lanner Hill; son of John Pearce, deceased, tin smelter
		12 Sept 1936

Fore Street Methodist Church, Redruth, circa 1910

BAPTISMS SOLEMNISED IN THE WESLEYAN/METHODIST CHAPEL IN THE REDRUTH
CIRCUIT (non parochial registers).   1822 — 1825 and 1839 — 1901

SKEWES	ANNE	daughter of Edward (miner) and Mary of Camborne	Born	1 Sept	1822
			Bpt	14 Nov	1822
SKEWES	CATHERINE	daughter of Edward (miner) and Mary of Camborne	Born	19 May	1824
			Bpt	6 June	1824
SKEWES	JAMES	son of Edward (miner) and Mary of Camborne	Born	10 Feb	1825
			Bpt	19 Mar	1825

PARISH REGISTER OF RUAN MAJOR   BAPTISMS   1700 — 1942

SKEWES	MARGARET	daughter of Henry & Jane Skewes	7 July	1799
SKEWES	HENRY	son of Henry & Jane Skewes	27 Dec	1801
SKEWES	JOHN	son of Henry & Jane Skewes	27 May	1804
SKEWES	THOMAS	son of Henry & Jane Skewes	1 July	1806
SKEWES	ANTHONY	son of Henry & Jane Skewes	20 June	1809
SKEWES	SAMUEL	son of Henry & Jane Skewes	8 Sept	1811
SKEWES	MARY	daughter of Henry & Jane Skewes of Ruan Major, farmer	9 Oct	1814
SKEWES	JAMES LUGG	son of William & Christian Skewes of Trelase; labourer	25 June	1815
SKEWES	JOHN	son of William & Christian Skewes of Trelugga; labourer	29 Dec	1816
SKEWES	EDWARD	son of William & Christian Skewes of Trelugga; farmer	7 Feb	1819
SKEWES	ELIZABETH	daughter of William & Christian Skewes of Trelugga; farmer	21 Jan	1821
SKEWES	ELIZABETH	daughter of William & Christian Skewes of Trelugga; farmer	10 July	1822
SKEWES	MARY	daughter of William & Christian Skewes of Trelugga; farmer	28 June	1824
SKEWES	ANN	daughter of William & Christian Skewes of Trelugga; farmer	23 Oct	1825
SKEWES	JAMES LUGG	son of Henry & Grace Skewes, of Hendra; schoolmaster	20 July	1834
SKEWES	MARY	daughter of Anthony & Christian Skewes of Chybarles; farmer	5 Apl	1835
SKEWES	ANN	daughter of Anthony & Christian Skewes of Chybarles; farmer	16 Apl	1837
SKEWES	EMMA	daughter of Anthony & Christian Skewes of Chybarles; farmer	23 Sept	1838
SKEWES	GEORGE EMMANUEL	son of Anthony & Christian Skewes of Chybarles; farmer	24 May	1840
SKEWES	BETSY	daughter of John & Jane Skewes of Chybarles; farmer	5 Jan	1841
SKEWES	CHRISTIAN	daughter of Anthony & Christian Skewes of Chybarles; farmer	26 Sept	1841
SKEWES	SAMUEL	son of Samuel & Catherine Skewes of Tresodden; farmer	27 Mar	1841
SKEWES	CATHERINE	daughter of Anthony & Christian Skewes of Tresodden; farmer	16 Apl	1843
SKEWES	JAMES	son of Anthony & Christian Skewes of Tresodden; farmer	20 Oct	1844
SKEWES	HENRY	son of Anthony & Christian Skewes of Tresodden; farmer	31 May	1845
SKEWES	SAMUEL	son of Anthony & Christian Skewes of Tresodden; farmer	26 Dec	1847
SKEWES	WILLIAM	son of Anthony & Christian Skewes of Tresodden; farmer	2 June	1849
SKEWES	EDWARD	son of Anthony & Christian Skewes of Tresodden; farmer	27 Mar	1853
SKEWES	HANNIBAL	son of Anthony & Christian Skewes of Tresodden; farmer	1 Apl	1855
SKEWES	GEORGE	son of Anthony & Christian Skewes of Tresodden; farmer	27 Aug	1856

PARISH REGISTER OF RUAN MAJOR   MARRIAGES   1700 — 1903

SKEWES	WILLIAM	and Christian Lugg	28 Mar	1815
In presence of Henry Skewes				
SKEWES	JANE	and James Lugg	16 July	1822
SKEWES	ELEANOR	and William Lugg	3 Nov	1824
In presence of Edward Skewes				
SKEWES	HENRY of Ruan	and Grace Lugg		
Minor; In presence of			28 July	1829
Edward Skewes				
SKEWES	ANTHONY	and Christian Lugg	30 Sept	1834
In presence of Henry Skewes				
SKEWES	MARY	and Josiah Boulden		
In presence of Anthony	of St Keverne; farmer		12 Jan	1837
Skewes & Samuel Skewes				
SKEWES	THOMAS	was a witness to the wedding of William Pengilly & Peggy Bray; 22 February 1837		
SKEWES	SAMUEL	and Catherine Lugg of Vendra;		
of Tresodden; farmer	daught of James Lugg; farmer		2 Mar	1841
Son of Henry Skewes, farmer; deceased				
SKEWES	MARY	and James Nicholls, junior of Treleage,		
of Tresodden; daughter of Anthony Skewes,	Ruan Minor; son of James Nicholls.		15 Apl	1868
farmer. In presence of James Skewes				
SKEWES	ANN	and Samuel Carter, carpenter of Ruan Minor;		
of Tresodden; daughter of Anthony Skewes,	son of Richard Carter, carpenter		18 Nov	1875
yeoman. In presence of Henry Skewes				
SKEWES	ELIZABETH MARY (27)	and Thomas Gilbert Carter (24)		
of Ruan Major; daughter of John Skewes,	labourer of Ruan Minor.			
farmer. In presence of John Skewes	Son of John Carter; tailor		16 June	1903
and Bessie Skewes				

PARISH REGISTER OF RUAN MAJOR   BURIALS   1700 — 1812

SKEWIS	EDWARD	was buried	23 Dec	1791
SKEWIS	ANTHONY		7 June	1796

PARISH REGISTER OF RUAN MINOR   BAPTISMS   1654 — 1882

SKEWES	EDWARD	son of Henry and Grace Skewes, innkeeper of Cadgwith	27 Mar	1830

PARISH REGISTER OF RUAN MINOR   MARRIAGES   1653 — 1836

SKEWES   THOMAS   and Loveday Mundy
of Ruan Major. In presence of
Edward Skewes

                                                        14 Dec   1831

Entry from Parish Register states:
In consequence of an Act of Parliament made on 10th March, 1801 to ascertain the population of the United Kingdom, this Parish was found to contain 71 Houses — 145 males and 172 females. Total number of Inhabitants 317. Signed Thomas Robinson, Rector.

10 years later the population was 60 families being 274 persons in total. There were 58 Inhabited houses and 15 Uninhabited houses.

Ruan Minor Church, circa 1910

PARISH REGISTER OF ST. ANTHONY IN MENEAGE   BAPTISMS   1608 — 1837

SKEWES	TAMSYN	daughter of John and Susannah	Born	2 Apl	1637
			Bpt	7 Apl	1637
SKEWES	GRACE	daughter of Richard & Jane SKEWES		21 Oct	1649

PARISH REGISTER OF ST. ANTHONY IN MENEAGE   MARRIAGES   1597 — 1725

Bishops Transcripts
SKEWES	ELIZABETH	and	James Secombe	29 Sept	1659
SKEWES	THOMASINE	and	Edward Sanders	3 Nov	1662

PARISH REGISTER OF ST. ANTHONY IN MENEAGE   BURIALS   1608 — 1837

SKEWES	(MARGA) RET	widow		26 May	1656

PARISH REGISTER OF ST. AUSTELL   BAPTISMS   1834 — 1961

SKEWS	WILLIAM	son of John and Jane of Porthpean; tinner		4 Oct	1835
SKEWS	THOMAS	son of John and Jane of Churchtown; beer shop keeper.	Born	6 Dec	1836
			Bpt	1 Apl	1838
SKEWS	JACQUELINE ANN	daughter of Thomas Henry and Constance Patricia Skews, Royal Navy of 25 Thornpark Estate, St Austell	Born	25 Feb	1949
			Bpt	1 May	1949

PARISH REGISTER OF ST. AUSTELL   MARRIAGES   1813 — 1941 and 1946 — 1961

SKEWES	JAMES	and Elizabeth Davey	3 July	1830
SKEWES	JOHN of St Ewe	and Jane Jago	8 Nov	1834
SKUES	MARY ANN	and James Rawling		
In presence of William Skues			28 Nov	1835
SKEWS	MARY	and Thomas Hancock,		
of Churchtown. Dau of John Skews, innkeeper		accountant. Son of William Hancock, accountant	16 July	1861

BANNS were published between THOMAS HENRY SKEWS of the Royal Naval Barracks at Devonport and Constance Patricia Harris, spinster of St. Austell on 29 August 1943; 5 September 1943 and 12 September 1943. According to Somerset House Registers the marriage took place in 1943.

PARISH REGISTER OF ST. AUSTELL   BURIALS   1813 — 1942

SKEWES	THOMAS	of Churchtown. Died of inflammation of the lung. Aged 2 years	10 July	1838
SKEWES	MARY	of Churchtown, aged 11 months	6 Nov	1840
SKEWES	JOHN	of Churchtown, aged 55 years	8 Sept	1855
SKEWES	ELIZABETH	of Union House, aged 75 years	16 Feb	1874
SKEWES	JAMES	of Union House, aged 73 years	18 Nov	1875

PARISH REGISTER OF ST. BREAGE   MARRIAGES   1559 — 1830

SKEWIS	JOAN of Mawgan	and James Meager, tinner	9 Sept	1793

Banns were published for LOVEDAY SKEWES & Thomas Cock 2 August; 9 August and 16 August 1835. (Married 19 Sept 1835)

PARISH REGISTER OF ST BURYAN   BAPTISMS   1654 — 1812

SKEWES	JOHN	son of John and Catherine	7 July	1717
SKEWS	RICHARD	son of John and Catherine	15 Mar	1718
SKEWS	WILLIAM	son of John and Catherine	12 Mar	1720
SKEWES	MICHAEL	son of John and Catherine	23 Mar	1722
SKEWES	CATHERINE	daughter of John and Catherine	18 June	1724
SKEWES	ROBERT	son of John and Catherine	15 July	1727

PARISH REGISTER OF ST BURYAN   MARRIAGES   1654 — 1812

SKEWS	JOHN	and Catherine Nicholas	13 Nov	1716

PARISH REGISTER OF ST BURYAN   BURIALS   1654 — 1812

SKEWES	MICHAEL	28 June	1722
SKEWES	ROBERT	20 July	1793

PARISH REGISTER OF ST CLEMENT   MARRIAGES   1538 — 1962

SKEWES	IDE	and	Garrat Sampson	19 July	1616
SKEWES	RICHARD of Kea	and	Ann Polgreen	15 Dec	1737
SKEWS	ANN	and	John Williams of Gwennap	7 Nov	1743
SKEWES	MARTIN	and	Elizabeth May	4 June	1786
SKEWES	JOHN	and	Ann Lanyon		
of Gwennap, farmer. Son of John Skewes, farmer			daughter of Simon Lanyon; farmer	28 Jan	1843
SKEWS	SUSAN JANE,	and	John Onear		
minor of St. Mary's, Truro. Daughter of Peter Skews, miner			Son of Frederick Onear, watchmaker	25 Mar	1862

PARISH REGISTER OF ST CLEMENT   BURIALS   1730 — 1856

SKEWS	ELIZA	of St Clement, aged 24 years	18 Apl	1843

PARISH REGISTER OF ST ENODER   MARRIAGES   1571 — 1812

SKEWES	ALICE widow	&	William Wiat		3 Feb	1576
SKEWES	ALEXANDER	&	Ann Carvett		19 May	1723

PARISH REGISTER OF ST EWE   BAPTISMS   1560 — 1959

SKEWS	ELIZABETH	daughter of Edward Skews by Anne		27	1713
SKEWS	ANNE	daughter of Edward Skews by Anne		6 Nov	1721
SKEWS	MARY	daughter of Edward & Anne Skews		21 Jan	1728
SKEWS	SARAH	daughter of Edward & Anne Skews		26 Jun	1731
SKEWS	JOHN	son of Philip & Anne Skews		19 May	1746
SKEWES	EDWARD	son of Philip & Anne Skews		8 Jan	1749
SKEWES	ELIZABETH	daughter of Philip & Anne Skews		13 Jan	1751
SKEWS	PHILIP	son of Philip & Anne Skews		10 Jun	1753
SKEWS	WILLIAM	son of Philip & Mary Skews		24 Aug	1755
SKEWS	ANN	daughter of Philip & Mary Skews		30 May	1757
SKEWS	JAMES	son of Philip & Mary Skews		6 Jul	1760
SKEWS	GEORGE	son of Philip & Mary Skews		8 Nov	1762
SKEWIS	SARAH	daughter of Philip & Mary Skewis		12 Aug	1764
SKEWS	FRANCES	daughter of John & Sarah Skews		5 Nov	1769
SKEWS	GRACE	daughter of James & Joanna Skews		5 Nov	1793
SKEWS	ANN	daughter of James & Joanna Skews		7 Feb	1795
SKEWS	JOANNA	daughter of James & Joanna Skews		15 Jan	1797
SKEWS	ANN	daughter of William & Nancy Skews	(bad writing)		...1802
SKEWS	JAMES	son of James & Joanna Skews		21 May	1802
SKEWS	JANE	daughter of James & Joanna Skews		28 Apl	1805
SKEWS	PHILIP	son of James & Joanna Skews		24 May	1806
SKEWS	ELIZABETH	daughter of William & Nancy Skews		5 July	1807
SKEWS	ELIZABETH	daughter of James & Joanna Skews		10 Sept	1809
SKEWS	MARY ANN	daughter of James & Joanna Skews of Livalsa.	pri...	7 Mar	1813
			pub...	23 Mar	1813
SKEWS	MARY	daughter of William & Nancy Skews of Nansladron, yeoman		17 Jan	1813
SKEWS	THOMAS TRUSCOTT	son of James & Joanna Skews, labourer		23 Aug	1815
SKEWS	THOMAS	son of James & Joanna Skews		17 Feb	1817
SKEUS	CHARLOTTE LOUISA	daughter of Jonathan & Jane Skeus, carpenter		20 Jun	1835
SKUS	WILLIAM THOMAS	son of Thomas & Ann Skus, farmer		27 Mar	1836
SKUS	JOSIAH	son of John & Elizabeth Skus, labourer		25 Sept	1853

St Ewe Parish Church

PARISH REGISTER OF ST. EWE   MARRIAGES   1560 — 1963

SKEWS	SARAH	and	John Warwick	11 Apl	1757
SKEWS	ANN	and	Hugh Tregensa	14 Aug	1784
SKUSE	SARAH	and	John Sweet	19 Dec	1790
SKEWES	JAMES	and	Joanna Truscott	4 Nov	1792
SKEWES	JOHANNA	and	John Toms	1 July	1820
SKEWES	ANN	and	John George	16 Feb	1822
SKEWES	MARY	and	Joseph Truscott		

of Nansladron.   labourer. Son of John
In presence of Philip   Truscott, farmer
Skewes. Mary was daughter of
William Skewes, farmer   10 Apl   1839

PARISH REGISTER OF ST. EWE   BURIALS   1560 — 1959

SKEWS	ELIZABETH		24 Aug	1732
SKEWS	JOHN		26 Feb	1734
SKEWES	ELIZABETH	daughter of Philip and Ann	9 Aug	1744
SKEWS	GEORGE		17 June	1763
SKEWS	ANN		20 Dec	1768
SKEWS	JOHN		3 June	1769
SKEWS	ELIZABETH		21 July	1771
SKEWS	THOMAS TRUSCOTT	infant	29 Aug	1815
SKEWS	PHILIPPA	aged 80 years	16 Apl	1828
SKEWS	JOHN	aged 31 years	14 Oct	1830
SKEWES	JAMES	of Lower Sticker, aged 78 years	8 July	1838
SKEWES	WILLIAM	of Nansladron, aged 84 years	23 Apl	1840
SKEWS	NANCY	of Nansladron, aged 72 years	14 Aug	1842
SKUES	HENRY	of Levatson Downs, aged 35 years	3 Jan	1847
SKEWES	THOMAS	of Parasnoon, aged 30 years	7 Nov	1847

PARISH REGISTER OF ST. FEOCK   MARRIAGES   1660 — 1670

SKEWES	ABIGAIL	and	Markes Maker	7 Oct	1665

PARISH REGISTER OF ST. GLUVIAS   BAPTISMS   1719 — 1837

SKEWS	HANNAH	daughter of William and Hannah SKEWS	1 Apl	1746
SKEWS	WILLIAM	son of William and Hannah SKEWS	24 Apl	1748
SKEWS	HENRY	son of William and Hannah SKEWS	28 Oct	1750
SKEWES	RICHARD	son of William and Hannah SKEWES	9 May	1753
SKEWES	CATHERINE	daughter of William and Hannah SKEWES	23 May	1756
SKEWES	MARY	daughter of William and Hannah SKEWES	17 Apl	1759
SKEWES	THOMAS	son of William and Hannah SKEWES	31 Aug	1760

PARISH REGISTER OF ST. GLUVIAS   MARRIAGES   1599 — 1812

SKEWS	WILLIAM of St Buryan	and Hannah Dayworth	30 Jan	1744
SKUSE	MOSES, sojourner	and Mary Thomas	26 Dec	1751
SKEWES	HANNAH of Penzance	and Charles Coleman of Penzance	2 Nov	1762
SKEWS	HONOR or Penryn	and James Pursell of Penryn	21 Jan	1788

PARISH REGISTER OF ST. GLUVIAS   BURIALS   1760 — 1837

SKEWES	MARY	daughter of William SKEWES, aged 2 years	5 Apl	1761
SKEWES	WILLIAM	son of William SKEWES, aged 24	12 Jan	1772
SKEWES	CATHERINE	daughter of William SKEWES, aged 17	11 Apl	1773
SKEWES	HENRY	son of William SKEWES, aged 24	20 Mar	1774
SKEWES	HANNAH	widow of William SKEWES, aged 57	16 Feb	1777

PARISH REGISTER OF ST HILARY including MARAZION & ST MICHAEL's MOUNT
BURIALS   1777 — 1812

SKREWS	MARGARET	spinster of Ludgvan	27 Jan	1735
SKREWS	GRACE	pauper of Crowan, aged 81 years	24 July	1791

PARISH REGISTER OF ST IVE   BAPTISMS   1864 — 1937

SKEWES	EDMUND	son of Peter and Elizabeth of Pensilva, miner	23 June	1867
SKEWES	SAMUEL GREGORY	son of Peter and Elizabeth of Pensilva, miner	29 Sept	1869
SKEWES	HARRY	son of Peter and Elizabeth of Pensilva, pauper	19 Jan	1871
SKEWES	ELLEN ANNIE	daughter of Peter and Elizabeth of Pensilva, pauper, late miner	30 Aug	1877
SKEWES	JAMES HENRY	son of Edmund and Maria Skewes of Pensilva, miner	22 Aug	1894
SKEWES	FLORENCE BEATRICE	daughter of Edmund and Maria of Pensilva, miner	22 Aug	1894
SKEWS	HARRY	son of Samuel Gregory and Harriet Ann of Pensilva, labourer	21 Apl	1903
SKEWS	ELIZABETH ANNIE	daughter of Samuel Gregory and Harriet Ann of Pensilva, labourer	21 Apl	1903
SKEWS	BEATRICE MELBA IRENE	daughter of Harry and Hilda Skews of Pensilva, labourer. Born 12 July 1920	2 Mar	1921
SKEWS	COURTENAY JOHN GREGORY	son of Harry and Hilda Skews of Pensilva, labourer. Born 17 Jan 1922, Albert Cottages	1 Mar	1922
SKEWS	JOSEPH HERBERT MARTYN	son of Harry and Hilda of 5, Albert Cottages, Pensilva, labourer. Born 11 August 1923	5 Sept	1923
SKEWS	WILFRED GERALD	son of Harry and Hilda of 5, Albert Cottages, Pensilva, labourer. Born 15 June 1925	5 Aug	1925
SKEWS	FREDERICK THOMAS	son of Harry and Hilda of 5, Albert Cottages, Pensilva, labourer. Born 5 October 1926.	12 Nov	1926
SKEWS	STANLEY GEORGE	son of Harry and Hilda of 5, Albert Cottages, Pensilva, labourer. Born 21 May 1929	21 Aug	1929

No entries for Marriages or Burials

PARISH REGISTER OF ST JUST IN PENWITH   MARRIAGES   1599 — 1812

SKEWES	TOBIAS	&	Elizabeth Davy	16 Apl	1754
SKUSE	SARAH	&	Richard Lobb	28 Aug	1757

PARISH REGISTER OF ST JUST IN ROSELAND   BAPTISMS   1600 — 1852

SKEWES	CHRISTOPHER	son of Stephen Skewes	24 Feb	1609
SCUES	STEPHEN	son of Stephan Scues	3 Jan	1612
SKEWES	ANN	daughter of Stephan Skewes	10 Mar	1615
SKEWES	JOHN	son of James Skewes	23 Nov	1617
SKEWES	CHRISTIAN	daughter of Stephen Skewes	7 May	1620
SKEWES	ABIGAIL	daughter of Stephen & Blanch Skewes	19 Jan	1639

PARISH REGISTER OF ST JUST IN ROSELAND   MARRIAGES   1538 — 1900

SKUES	STEVEN	&	Christian Jenkin	11 June	1605
SKEWES	JAMES	&	Tamson Tonkin	28 Jan	1607
SKEWS	ANN daughter of Stephen	&	Thomas Manley	26 Jan	1633
SKEWS	STEPHEN	&	Blanch Penrose	15 Jan	1638
SKEWS	MARY	&	Thomas Jack alias Peerse	14 July	1640
SKEWS	CHRISTIAN	&	Michael Buckseene	2 Nov	1646

PARISH REGISTER OF ST JUST IN ROSELAND   BURIALS   1545 — 1954

SKUES	CHRISTOPHER	son of Stephen Skues	28 Aug	1611
SKEWES	STEPHEN		2 May	1622
SKEWIS	JOHN		1 Mar	1639
SKEWS	JAMES		28 Feb	1644
SKEWS	THAMSEN		8 Aug	1644
SKEWS	CHRISTIAN	the elder	14 Sept	1662

PARISH REGISTER OF ST LEVAN   MARRIAGES   1694 — 1812

SKEWES	MARY of Madron	&	Tobias Richards	19 Feb	1708

PARISH REGISTER OF ST MARTIN IN MENEAGE   BAPTISMS   1700 — 1907

SKEWES	SARAH ANN	daughter of Henry and Grace, schoolteacher	13 June	1841

PARISH REGISTER OF ST MARTIN IN MENEAGE   MARRIAGES   1571 — 1963

SKEWES	THOMAS	and	Mary Retallack	22 Aug	1713

SKEWES JOSEPH		and	Philippa Martin	8 June	1756

husbandman of Mawgan.
Married by licence, but neither signed the
register

SKEWES-LUGG HENRY (26)		and	Eleanor Carlyon		

of St Martin. Son of James Lugg,   of St Martin. Daughter of John Carlyon,
labourer   schoolmaster of St Martin   2 Jan   1859

PARISH REGISTER OF ST MARTIN IN MENEAGE   BURIALS   1695 — 1956

SKEWES EDWARD	of Trecoose, aged 26 years		1 Sept	1857

PARISH REGISTER OF ST PINNOCK   BAPTISMS   1840 — 1870

SKEWES JOSEPH	son of Henry and Ann Skewes of The Highway, St Pinnock, miner		7 Apl	1852

PARISH REGISTER OF ST STEPHEN's IN BRANNEL   MARRIAGES   1681 — 1812

SKEWS MARY		and	William Coad	6 Feb	1774

PARISH REGISTER OF SANCREED   BAPTISMS   1566 — 1812

SKEWS	CHRISTOPHER	son of Richard and Rebecca	8 June	1729
SKEWS	REBECCA	daughter of Richard and Rebecca	1 Feb	1731
SKEWES	THOMAS	son of John and Elizabeth	4 Jan	1736

PARISH REGISTER OF SANCREED   MARRIAGES   1559 — 1812

SKUES	KATHLEEN of St Buryan	and	Simon Blagdon	21 Aug	1734
SKEWES	CHRISTOPHER	and	Honor Angwyn	31 July	1750

PARISH REGISTER OF SANCREED   BURIALS   1579 — 1812

SKEWES	RICHARD	son of Richard Skewes	20 Oct	1733
SKEWIS	WILLIAM		7 Jan	1742
SKEWIS	REBECCA		28 Jan	1761
SKEWES	CHRISTOPHER		29 Aug	1797
SKEWES	HONOUR		12 Sept	1797

PARISH REGISTER OF SITHNEY   MARRIAGES   1654 — 1862

SKEWIS EDWARD		and	Margaret Rogers	13 May	1743
SKEWIS JOHN (32)		and	Martha Harris (28)		

wheelwright of Sithney,   of Sithney, daughter of Christopher Harris, farmer
son of John Skewes, husbandman   8 Jan   1845

SKEWES JOSIAH (23)		and	Elizabeth Polglase (28)		

labourer of Sithney, son   of Sithney, daughter of George Polglase, miner
of James Skewes, labourer   28 July 1846

PARISH REGISTER OF SITHNEY   BURIALS   1813 — 1894

SKEWES	JOHN of Sithney,	aged 74 years	9 June	1886
SKEWES	MARTHA	of Tregoose, Sithney, aged 74 years	31 Dec	1891

PARISH REGISTER OF STITHIANS   MARRIAGES   1654 — 1812

SKEWES ALEXANDER	of Gwennap and Christian Martin		11 Sept	1794

PARISH REGISTER OF TOWEDNACK   MARRIAGES   1676 — 1812

SKEWIS GRACE, widow of Falmouth	and		Henry Dunstone	2 May	1793

PARISH REGISTER OF TRURO ST GEORGE'S   BAPTISMS   1847 — 1964

SKEWES	ELIZABETH JANE	daughter of John & Mary Browne Skewes of Kenwyn Street, Truro. Cabinet-maker	14 Dec	1850
SKEWES	FREDERICK AUGUSTUS	son of Alice Ann Skewes of Helston (reputed father)	7 Jan	1864

SKEWES	FLORENCE CECILIA	daughter of Thomas and Mary Jane Skewes of Parkvedras Terrace, Truro. Ironmonger	22 Dec	1888
SKEWES	FREDERICK JOHN CHARLES	son of Charles & Bessie Skewes of 76 Chapel Hill, Truro. Sailor, Royal Navy. Born 7 April, 1916	25 Apl	1916
SKEWES	ERNEST LLOYD	son of Charles & Bessie Skewes of 76 Chapel Hill, Truro. Chief Stocker, Royal Navy. Born 26 Nov, 1920	9 Jan	1921
SKEWES	PATRICIA ANNE	daughter of Ernest Lloyd and Doris Irene Patricia Skewes of 68 Chapel Hill, Truro. Mason. God parents—William Skewes & Gladys Skewes. Born 28 April, 1947	7 June	1947
SKEWES	LINDA ROSEMARY	daughter of Ernest Lloyd & Doris Irene Patricia Skewes of Boskyver Road, Truro. British Rail M & E Dept. Born 8 May, 1954	20 June	1954

Truro from Kenwyn. Print published by W. Lake

PARISH REGISTER OF TRURO ST GEORGE'S   MARRIAGES   1856 — 1969

SKEWES THOMAS Innkeeper of St George's, Truro; son of Thomas Skewes, builder. In presence of Thomas Skewes & Philippa Jane Skewes	&	Mary Jane Peters, daughter of John Peters, master mariner of St George's.	28 Apl	1860
SKEWES PHILIPPA JANE of St George's. Daughter of Thomas Skewes, mason. In presence of John Skewes	&	Richard Henry Philips of St George's. Carpenter. Son of Richard Philips, cordwainer.	29 Aug	1864
SKEWES GRACE (17) of St George's, Truro. Daughter of William Skewes, miner	&	Thomas Colenso (22) of St George's, Truro. Son of Michael Colenso, harness maker	3 Oct	1864
SKEWES ADA (23) of 1, John Street, Truro. Daughter of William Brown Skewes, painter. In presence of William Brown Skewes and Cereta Skewes.	&	William James Ellis (29) Labourer of 52 Fairmantle Street, Truro. Son of Robert James Ellis, postman	13 July	1907
SKEWES CERETA (25) of 9 St Dominic Street, Truro; Daughter of William Brown Skewes, housepainter. In presence of Henrietta Skewes and William Skewes	&	William Thomas Rowe (29) Labourer of Grampound Road; Son of John Rowe, labourer, deceased.	30 Dec	1911
SKEWES GRACE EMILY (24) of St Dominic Street, Truro. Daughter of William Skewes, painter. In presence of William Skewes	&	Edward Charles Moses (26) Soldier—Sergeant 2nd DCLI of Mark Road, Truro. Son of James Moses, labourer.	29 June	1918

SKEWES HENRIETTA (31) of St Dominic Street, Truro. Daughter of William Skewes, painter. In presence of Marion Skewes and William Skewes	&	Frederick James West (33) carpenter of Devon. Son of David West, carpenter	31 Dec	1921
SKEWES LIZZIE MARION (28) of St George's, Truro. Daughter of William Brown Skewes, painter. In presence of William Skewes	&	William John Vercoe (23) Plumber of St Paul's, Truro. Son of Charles Vercoe, plumber.	20 Dec	1926
SKEWES ERNEST LLOYD (25) Royal Air Force, of 53, Kenwyn Street, Truro. Son of Charles Frederick Skewes, retired. In presence of William Douglas Skewes and Bessie Skewes	&	Doris Irene Patricia Penhaligon (20) Shop Assistant of 6, Francis St., Truro. Daughter of Frederick Penhaligon, business proprietor	7 Sept	1946
SKEWES CERETA BETTY (23) laundry hand of 39a, Calenick Street, Truro. Daughter of William John Skewes, painter. In presence of William John Skewes	&	Auster Jack Charles Crawford Gosling (29), clerk of the Old Mansion House, Truro. Son of Samuel Auster Gosling, lorry-driver	14 Feb	1948

PARISH REGISTER OF TRURO ST JOHN'S   BAPTISMS   1852 — 1957

SKEWES	MARION JOYCE	daughter of William John & Rose Skewes of Charles Street, Truro. Painter. Born 2 April, 1921	19 July	1921
SKEWES	CERETA BETTY	Daughter of William John & Rose Skewes of Daniell Square. Born 29 September 1924	4 Nov	1924
SKEWES	WILLIAM JOHN	son of William Douglas & Gladys Maud Skewes, stoker, Royal Navy, of Carclew Cottages, Truro. Born 26 July, 1943	3 Sept	1943
SKEWES	MARGARET ROSEMARY	Daughter of William Douglas & Gladys Maud Skewes, Chief Petty Officer, Royal Navy, of Carclew Cottages, Truro. Born 6 December 1944	9 Feb	1945

PARISH REGISTER OF TRURO ST JOHN'S   MARRIAGES   1865 — 1966

| SKEWES WILLIAM JOHN (28) of Calenick Street, Truro. Painter. Son of William Skewes, painter | & | Rose Drew (29) of 24 Charles Street, Truro. Father not known. | 17 Feb | 1921 |

PARISH REGISTER OF TRURO ST MARY'S   BAPTISMS   1597 — 1867

SKEWES	WILLIAM	Illegitimate son of Ann Skewes. Born 9 August 1793. By charity	11 Aug	1793
SKEWIS	HENRY	Son of James & Ann Skewis of Kenwyn. Shoemaker	8 Mar	1835
SKEWES	HENRY	Son of James and Ann Skewes of Kenwyn. Shoemaker	10 Jan	1836
SKEWES	WILLIAM	Son of James and Ann Skewes of Kenwyn. Shoemaker	25 July	1838
SKEWES	ELIZABETH STEVENS	Daughter of James and Ann Skewes of Kenwyn. Shoemaker	29 July	1840
SKEWES	EMMA STEVENS	Daughter of James and Ann Skewes of Kenwyn. Shoemaker	16 Jan	1842
SKEWES	HENRY CHARLES	Son of James and Ann Skewes of St Mary's. Shoemaker	24 Nov	1843
SKEWES	ELLEN	Daughter of James and Ann Skewes of St Mary's. Shoemaker	18 Apl	1845
SKEWES	FLORENCE	Daughter of Amelia Skewes, single woman of St Mary's	10 Dec	1877
SKEWES	LILY	Daughter of Susan Skewes, laundress of St Mary's	20 Sept	1880
SKEWES	CHARLES	Son of Amelia Skewes of St Mary's, single woman	28 Aug	1882
SKEWES	FREDERICK	Son of Amelia Skewes of Tippets Backlet; single woman	6 June	1887
SKEWES	CERETA	Daughter of William & Blanche Skewes of Union Street. Painter	28 Nov	1887

PARISH REGISTER OF TRURO ST MARY'S   MARRIAGES   1597 — 1837

| SKUSE | ABRAHAM soldier of the Surrey Fencibles | & | Mary Bolitho | 29 Aug | 1799 |
| SKUES | ANN | & | William Scott, widower | 7 Feb | 1804 |

PARISH REGISTER OF TRURO ST MARY'S   BURIALS   1597 — 1943

SKUES	PHILIPPA		23 June	1806
SKEWS	MARTEN	of St Clement, aged 66 yrs.	13 Nov	1829
SKEWIS	ELIZABETH	of St Clement, aged 69 years	8 Apl	1834
SKEWIS	THOMAS	of St Clement, aged 5 years	5 Feb	1857
SKEWIS	HENRIETTA MARIA	of St Clement, aged 2 years	17 Feb	1857
SKEWES	THOMAS JOHN	of St Mary's, aged 1 year	5 Jan	1862
SKEWES	ELIZABETH ANN	of St Clement, aged 18 years	4 Apl	1869
SKEWES	FREDERICK	of St Mary's, aged 6 years	12 Dec	1875
SKEWES	LAURA	of St Mary's, aged 2 years	27 Apl	1882
SKEWES	LILY	of St Mary's, aged 3 years	29 July	1882
SKEWES	THOMAS	of Parkvedras Terrace, aged 59 years	30 Jan	1894
SKEWES	ANN BUCKLAND	of Choon, Kenwyn, aged 85 years	2 Mar	1896
SKEWES	SUSAN	of Tippets Backlet, aged 55 years	5 Apl	1900
SKEWES	MARY JANE	of Richmond Hill, aged 73 years	28 Apl	1908

East view of Truro, 1816. Drawn by T. Ashwin and published by W. Penaluna of Helston, 1816

PARISH REGISTER OF TRURO ST PAUL'S   BAPTISMS   1865 — 1913

SKEWES	ADA	Born 19 Feb 1885. Daughter of William & Blanche............................)	
SKEWES	FLORENCE BLANCHE	Born 27 Oct 1888 ....)	5 Aug 1891
SKEWES	HENRIETTA	Born 11 September 1890 ....)	

PARISH REGISTER OF TRURO ST PAUL'S   MARRIAGES   1865 — 1902

SKEWES   ELIZABETH ANN LANYON   &   Thomas Lambshead (33)
(28) of Prospect Place, St. Paul's,   Draper of Lambeth, Surrey, son of Samuel Lambshead, farmer.
Truro; daughter of John Skewes, farmer.

                                                                    10 Sept 1874

PARISH REGISTER OF TRURO WESLEYAN CHAPEL   BAPTISMS   1769 — 1837

SKEWES	CHARLOTTE	Married Robert Bryant & later gave birth to Emma Bryant who was baptised	21 Nov	1836
SKEWES	GRACE RICHARDS	Daughter of Thomas & Jane Skewes (daughter of William & Ann Skewes). miner of Kea. Born 10 September 1836	5 Mar	1837
SKEWES	JANE	Daughter of Matthew & Mary Skewes (daughter of Thomas & Elizabeth Jeffrey), miner of Chacewater. Born 4 December 1824	14 Mar	1837
SKEWES	ELIZA JANE &	Daughters of John & Elizabeth Skewes (daughter of Thomas & Elizabeth Jeffery),		
SKEWES	NANNY	miner of Kenwyn. Eliza Jane born 13 Aug 1823. Nanny, 7 Oct 1825	19 Mar	1837
SKEWES	THOMAS	Son of Peter & Mary Skewes (daughter of John & Elizabeth William), miner of Kenwyn. Born 8 December 1827	28 Mar	1837
SKEWS	JOHN	Born 24 June 1823		
SKEWS	JOSEPH	Born 3 Apl 1825		
SKEWS	MATTHEW	Born 24 June 1827		
SKEWS	SOPHIA	Born 24 June 1831		
SKEWS	MARY	24 Aug 1833		
		All children of Digory and Sophia (daughter of Joseph and Sarah Jordan),	28 Mar	1837

PARISH REGISTER OF TUCKINGMILL   BAPTISMS   1845 — 1930

SKEWES	LOUISA JANE	of Kea. Daughter of William Henry Skewes, moulder, and Alarina Skewes. Born 20 February 1885	6 Aug	1885

SKEWES	LILLIAN MAUD	of Edward Street. **Daughter of William Henry Skewes, moulder, and Alarina Skewes.** Born 8 February 1888	16 May	1888
SKEWES	EMILY ROSAMUND	Daughter of Alfred John & Matilda Skewes of Mayne's Row, moulder.		
SKEWES	FLORENCE MAY	Daughter of Alfred John & Matilda Skewes of Mayne's Row, moulder.		
SKEWES	BEATRICE MARY	Daughter of Alfred John & Matilda Skewes of Mayne's Row, moulder.		
SKEWES	ALFRED JOHN	Daughter of Alfred John & Matilda Skewes of Mayne's Row, moulder.		
SKEWES	SYLVIA DOREEN	Daughter of Alfred John & Matilda Skewes of Mayne's Row, moulder.	12 Sept	1917

PARISH REGISTER OF TUCKINGMILL   MARRIAGES   1845 — 1958

SKEWES WILLIAM TRESIZE (20) miner. Son of Thomas Skewes, farmer.	&	Maria Mitchell (18) Daughter of James Mitchell, miner	28 June	1862
SKEWES EDITH (22) of Condurrow. Daughter of John Skewes, railway guard. In presence of Kate Skewes.	&	John House (24) miner of Condurrow. Son of Nicholas House, deceased, engine driver.	18 July	1896
SKEWES MARY (23) of Higher Condurrow. Daughter of John Skewes, railway guard. In presence of John Skewes and Kate Skewes.	&	Samuel House (23) Blacksmith of Lower Condurrow. Son of Nicholas House, deceased, engine driver	27 Nov	1897
SKEWES-PHILIPS BERTRAM (25) Farm labourer of Gwithian. Son of John Skews-Philips	&	Christiana Laity (25) of 67 North Roskear Road, Tuckingmill. Daughter of William Thomas Laity, deceased	26 Dec	1940

PARISH REGISTER OF TUCKINGMILL   BURIALS   1845 — 1947

SKEWES	ANNIE	of Tuckingmill, aged 6½ yrs.	13 June	1867
SKEWIS	EDWARD FREDERICK	of Wheal Seton, aged 11	29 Nov	1893
SKEWES	EMILY	of Mayne's Row, aged 54	28 May	1898
SKEWES	ADA	of Condurrow, aged 1 month	11 Feb	1899
SKEWES	EDITH	of Condurrow, aged 22 months	10 Apl	1900
SKEWES	CATHERINE	of Condurrow, aged 1 hour (unbpt)	6 Feb	1901
SKEWES	ELIZABETH JOANNA	of Condurrow Croft, aged 2 months. Unbaptised	24 Feb	1902
SKEWES	SAMUEL JOHN	of Condurrow Croft, aged 14 months	23 Apl	1904
SKEWES	FREDERICK	of Condurrow, aged 10 months	17 Mar	1905
SKEWES	RICHARD CHARLES	of Maynes Row, aged 9 months	11 Dec	1906
SKEWES	EDWARD	of Pendarves Street, aged 70	2 May	1909
SKEWES	GLADYS MARY	of Brea, aged 38 years	31 Oct	1933

PARISH REGISTER OF WENDRON   BAPTISMS   1560 — 1947

| SCUIS | ELIZABETH | Daughter of Thomas & Phillip Scuis | 26 Jan | 1695 |
| SCUIS | MARY | Daughter of Thomas & Phillip Scuis | 22 Feb | 1701 |

PARISH REGISTER OF WENDRON   MARRIAGES   1560 — 1951

SKUES	AMY	&	Robert Hunt	26 Dec	1668
SKUES (STUES) ROBERT		&	Jane Mitchell	17 Feb	1682
SCUIS	THOMAS	&	Philippa Angove	23 May	1692
SKEWES	PHILIPPA	&	Henry Pascoe	30 Jan	1720
SKUES	MARY	&	James Williams	5 Jan	1722
SKUES	JAMES	&	Susannah Thomas	21 Sept	1799
SKUES	WILLIAM of Constantine	&	Elizabeth Glasson	11 Nov	1834

PARISH REGISTER OF WENDRON   BURIALS   1560 — 1927

SKEWES	WILLIAM		buried	8 Feb	1585
SKEWES	JANET			23 Apl	1590
SCUIS	ELIZABETH	Daughter of Thomas Scuis		24 Nov	1713
SKEWIS	PHILIPPA			25 Dec	1742
SKEWES	EMILY ANN	of Medlyn, aged 64 years		2 Jan	1915

PARISH REGISTER OF WITHIEL   MARRIAGES   1568 — 1812

| SKEWES | WILLIAM of St Ewe | & | Nancy Blewett | 13 Aug | 1790 |

PARISH REGISTERS OUTSIDE THE COUNTY OF CORNWALL

PARISH REGISTER OF OTTERY ST. MARY, DEVON   BAPTISMS   1600 — 1837

SCUSE	ELIZABETH	daughter of James Scuse	3 Mar	1604
SCUSE	JAMES	son of John Scuse	11 Jan	1628
SKUSE	GEORGE	son of Charles Skuse	16 Oct	1631
SKUSE	MARIE	daughter of Charles & Johan Skuse	14 Jan	1635
SKEWES	JONE	daughter of Charles and Jone Skewes	2 June	1639
SKUSE	ROBERT	son of Charles and Johan Skuse	23 May	1650

PARISH REGISTER OF OTTERY ST. MARY, DEVON   MARRIAGES   1600 — 1837

SKUSE	ELIZABETH	and	John Seaward	28 May	1630
SCUSE	CHARLES	and	Elizabeth Carwithen, daughter of James Carwithen	28 Oct	1630
SKUSE	CHARLES	and	Johan Clarke	3 Nov	1633
SKUSE	IZOTE	and	Christopher Harden	27 Dec	1648

PARISH REGISTER OF OTTERY ST. MARY, DEVON   BURIALS   1600 — 1837

SCUSE	JOHN	son of John	24 Mar	1621
SCUSE	JAMES		30 June	1622
SCUSE	RICHARD		23 Dec	1627
SKUSE	—	wife of Charles	19 Sept	1632
SKUES	—	a woman child of Charles SKUES	19 Oct	1634
SKUSE	MARY	daughter of Charles	19 July	1642
SCEWES	JOAN	widow	2 Dec	1644
SCEWES	CHARLES	son of Charles	26 Dec	1644
SKUSE	MARY	daughter of Charles	9 Apl	1660
SKUSE	ROBERT S.	son of Charles	26 Mar	1654
SKUES	CHARLES		27 Mar	1678
SKEWS	JOANE	(Witness at a burial)	5 Dec	1680
SKUSE	GRACE	an auncient mayde	19 Apl	1650

PARISH REGISTER OF BARNSTAPLE, DEVON   BURIALS   1538 — 1812

SKUSE	DOROTHY	daughter of Joseph SKUSE	buried	17 Nov	1716

PARISH REGISTER OF PLYMOUTH (ST. ANDREWS)   MARRIAGES   1825 — 1833

SKEWES	DANIEL	and Anna Dawe	1 Nov	1831

PARISH REGISTER OF ST. AUGUSTINE THE LESS, BRISTOL   BAPTISMS   1577 — 1700

SCUISE	ANN	daughter of Thomas and Elizabeth	13 July	1691

PARISH REGISTER OF ST. AUGUSTINE THE LESS, BRISTOL
MARRIAGES   1577 — 1700

SCRUES	JANE	and	William James	28 May	1690
SCUSE	ELIZABETH	and	Robert Addison	18 Apl	1700

PARISH REGISTER OF ST. AUGUSTINE THE LESS, BRISTOL
BURIALS   1577 — 1700

SCUISE	THOMAS		28 Aug	1694

Churchwardens and Collectors 1694 — 1695

SCUSE	THOMAS	John Price with assistance of Robert Naylor is to replace THOMAS SCUSE, deceased, in both offices.	3 Sept	1694

PARISH REGISTER OF ST ANTHONY & ST JOHN the BAPTIST, WALLBROOK, LONDON
MARRIAGES   1538 — 1754

| SKUCE HANNAH of Chelsea, Middlesex | and | John Cooper of St Edmund the King, London | 20 Sept 1715 |

PARISH REGISTER OF ST PETER and ST BENEDICT, PAUL'S WHARF, LONDON
MARRIAGES   1607 — 1834

| SKUELL KATHERINE | and | Samuel Bradwell | |

PARISH REGISTER OF BLACKCHURCH, LONDON   BURIALS   1538 — 1754

| SKERYS THOMAS | 25 Apl 1546 |

PARISH REGISTER OF ST GEORGE'S CHAPEL, HYDE PARK CORNER, LONDON
MARRIAGES   1680 — 1760

| SKUCE ANN | and | John Stevens | 14 Mar 1753 |

PARISH REGISTER OF ST KATHERINE BY THE TOWER, LONDON
MARRIAGES   1666 — 1686

| SKUSE MARY | and | Charles Blackmore | 19 Sept 1678 |

PARISH REGISTER OF ST MARGARET'S CHURCH, WESTMINSTER
BAPTISMS   1539 — 1660

| SKOOS RICHARD | 23 Mar 1550 |

PARISH REGISTER OF ST PAUL, COVENT GARDEN, LONDON
MARRIAGES   1658 — 1854

| SKUSE FRANCIS | and | Alice Bowan were married in the Parish Church of St Martin's in the Fields by Plaxton Dickenson, curate. Witness: THOMAZON SKUSE | 18 Apl 1796 |

PARISH REGISTER OF ST PAUL, COVENT GARDEN, LONDON   BURIALS   1658 — 1853

| THOMAZON SKUSE | aged 5 years — buried | 5 Feb 1805 |

INFORMATION RELATING TO PARISH REGISTERS (BAPTISMS & MARRIAGES) TAKEN FROM THE COMPUTER INDEX, LATTER DAY SAINTS, SALT LAKE CITY, UTAH, USA — NOT INCLUDED IN THE PREVIOUS PAGES FOR PARISH REGISTERS

SKEWS		child of Tobias & Elizabeth Bpt at St Just in Penwith	11 Apl 1757
SKEWS	ABIGAIL	daughter of Stephen & Blanch Bpt St Just in Penwith	19 Jan 1639
SKEWES	AGNES	daughter of John Skewes Bpt Gerrans	21 Dec 1575
SKEWS	ANN	daughter of John Skewes Bpt Mevagissey	1 Dec 1689
SKEWES	ANN	Mrd John Herring at St Mewan	15 Mar 1831
SKEWES	ANN	Mrd James Brown at St Agnes	5 Mar 1837
SKEWISS	ANNE	daughter of William Skewiss Bpt Madron	12 May 1793
SKEWIS	ANNIE	daughter of James and Margaret Skewis Bpt St Erth	7 Nov 1847
SKUES	BETSEY	daughter of William and Elizabeth Skues Bpt Lostwithiel	27 Oct 1773
SKEWES	BLANCH	daughter of Henry and Nancy Skewes Bpt St Hilary	13 Jan 1839
SKEWES	DIGORY	son of Martin and Mary Skewes Bpt St Enoder	19 Jan 1773
SKEWS	EDWARD	son of John Skews Bpt Mevagissey	31 Jan 1686
SKEWS	EDWIN	son of John and Jane Skewes Bpt Grade	2 Sept 1838
SKEWS	ELIZABETH	daughter of John Skews. Bpt Mevagissey	14 Oct 1688
SKEWS	ELIZABETH	daughter of John Skews Bpt Mevagissey	27 Nov 1692
SKUES	ELIZABETH	Mrd William Toms at Mevagissey	30 Jan 1831
SKEWES	ELIZA	daughter of William and Elizabeth Skewes Bpt Stithians Wesleyan/Methodist	19 Aug 1844
SKEWS	ELIZABETH	daughter of Philip and Ann Skews Bpt Cuby with Tregony	19 Sept 1743

SKEWS	ELIZABETH	daughter of James and Margaret Skews Bpt St Erth	24 Dec	1843
SKEWES	EMMA LAITY	daughter of Richard and Caroline Skewes Bpt St Hilary	20 July	1856
SKEWES	ESTHER JANE	daughter of Richard and Caroline Skewes Bpt St Hilary	2 Apl	1854
SKEWES	HENERY	son of Rabish Skewes Bpt St Mewan	26 Nov	1627
SKEWES	HENRY	son of Henry and Nancy Skewes Bpt St Hilary	16 Jan	1842
SKEWIS	JAMES	son of James and Charity Skewis Bpt Gwithian	10 Dec	1778
SCEWES	JANE	daughter of Edward and Jane Scewes Bpt Mevagissey	24 Jun	1724
SKEWS	JANE	Mrd Richard Edwards at St Blazey	19 Jan	1826
SKEWES	JENNIFER	Mrs John Viant at Mevagissey	3 Jun	1798
SKEWS	JOHN	Mrd Elizabeth Whitford at Mevagissey	23 Nov	1674
SKEWS	JOHN	son of John Skews. Bpt Mevagissey	23 Jun	1675
SKEWS	JOHN	son of John Skews. Bpt Mevagissey	19 Oct	1684
SKUES	JOHN	son of Peter and Ann Skues Bpt St Agnes	7 Dec	1797
SKEWIS	JOHN	Mrd Loveday Hendy at Maker	9 Jul	1810
SKEWES	JOHN	son of John and Margery Skewes Bpt Phillack	26 Jun	1825
SKEWS	JOHN	son of William and Lovelia Skews Bpt Mewan	28 May	1848
SKEWES	JOHN	son of John and Mary Skewes Bpt Egloshayle	25 Dec	1855
SKEWES	JOHN HOOPER	son of Thomas and Mary Skewes Bpt Egloshayle	5 Jun	1853
SKEWES	MARIA	Mrd Richard Hooper, St Agnes	17 Oct	1818
SKEWES	MARTIN	son of Martin and Mary Skewes Bpt St Enoder	5 Sept	1731
SKEWES	MARY	Mrd William Tripcony at Budock	29 Apl	1843
SKEWS	PHILIP	son of John Skews. Bpt Mevagissey	1 Jul	1683
SKUES	SARAH ANNE	daughter of Henry and Nancy Skues Bpt St Hilary	14 Jan	1844
SKEWES	STEPHEN	Mrd Susanna Woodman at Budock	12 Mar	1831
SKEWS	SUSANNAH	daughter of Richard and Grace Skews Bpt St Agnes	20 May	1804
SKEWES	SUSANNAH	Mrd Samuel Henwood at St Blazey	5 Feb	1829
SKEWES	THOMAS	son of Thomas Skewes. Bpt St Enoder	9 Aug	1574
SKEWS	WILLIAM	son of William and Lovelia Skews Bpt St Mewan	28 May	1848
SKEWS	WILLIAM HENRY	son of Stephen and Susannah Skews Bpt Budock	26 Nov	1831
SKEWES	WILLIAM HENRY	son of Richard and Caroline Skewes Bpt St Hilary	1 Aug	1858
SKEWS	WILLIAM	son of John and Elizabeth Skews Bpt Mevagissey	21 Oct	1677
SKEWS	WILLIAM	son of John Skews. Bpt Mevagissey	5 Jun	1682

6 John Skewys

JOHN SKEWYS was probably the most outstanding individual of the SKUES family. Born in 1467 he was the son of John SKEWYS of SKEWYS, Cury, Cornwall who married Joan, daughter of Richard Tomyowe. Skewys was bred a lawyer, becoming a confidential servant of the all powerful Cardinal Wolsey, and a Counsellor-at-Law.

It will be of interest to know what was happening both nationally and internationally when comparing dates and times.

The Lancastrians revolted and defeated the Royalists at Edgecote near Banbury in 1469. Shortly after, Richard Neville, Earl of Warwick captured Edward IV but released him in return for Pardons. Edward raised a large army which sailed to France in June, 1475. Louis XI made peace for seven years at the Treaty of Pecquigny, paying Edward a substantial amount of money.

When Skewys was ten William Caxton set up the first printing press in England and published "Dictes and Sayenges of the Phylosophers."

A change in Royalty occurred in 1483. Edward IV who came to the throne on 28 June, 1461 died suddenly from pneumonia on 9 April, 1483 at Westminster, aged 40 years.

He was succeeded to the throne by Edward, the twelve year-old son of Edward IV on 9 April, 1483 but who only stayed on the throne for a month. Historians believe Richard III, the ruthless younger brother of Edward IV, seized the throne himself and imprisoned young Edward, and his ten year-old brother Richard. By the autumn the boys had perished in the Tower of London.

Richard, the last of the Plantagenets, became King on 26 June, 1483, but his crown was far from secure and he survived his nephews by only two years, for on 22 August, 1485 he was killed by Henry Tudor at the Battle of Bosworth, near Leicester. His naked body was flung into an unmarked grave.

Henry claimed the throne and Parliament conferred the crown upon him and his rightful heirs. The Tudor dynasty had come to power! Also in the year 1485 the "Yeomen of the Guard" were formed for the protection of the King.

In January 1486 Henry married Elizabeth, daughter of Edward IV.

John Skewys was admitted to Lincoln's Inn Fields on 12 February, 1487. The numerous records of the Honourable Society were checked by the writer who found many references to Skewys in the "Black Books." (A.D. 1422 — 1586).

For example in 1493 (Folio 24) in the accounts of John Newport, the treasurer, receipts included ten shillings from Roger Fyrz in full payment of twenty shillings for pulling down the Hall, and six shillings and eight pence from John Skewys in part payment of the like. Also in 1493 John Skewys was elected as "Master of the Revels". (Folio 24) A Master of the Revels was elected for Christmastide when there was much merrymaking. He was normally from below the Bar, but usually elected by the Bench. On New Year's Day the Master of the Revels, during dinner time, took the post of Marshal who for that purpose sat as King. Music played a considerable part in these Revels and on Christmas Day a performance was given by a band of musicians hired for the purpose. Attendance at the Revels was apparently compulsory. Those who sang irreverently or mockingly were punished by fine.

In 1495 Skewys, together with Morys, was named as Auditor for the accounts of Thomas Byrley, the Steward (1495 — 1496) (Folio 37).

During the Michaelmas term, 13 Henry VII (1497) "Strikland gave 6/8d for admission to John Skewys's Chamber." (Folio 42) In the accounts of John Woode, the Treasurer (1497 — 1498) receipts included "6/8d from Thornburgh 'le tiers' for assignment to the Chamber of the late Skewys's; 6/8d from Strickland for assignment to the Chamber of the late Skewys in place of Skewys." (Folio 44).

Officers elected in Michaelmas terms, 14 Henry VII (1498) included John Skewys as Christmas

Steward. (Folio 46) The Officers elected comprised four Governors, a Lent Reader, and Autumn Reader, Treasurer, Marshal, Butler, Pensioner, Master of the Revels, Escheator and Christmas Steward. The Steward for Christmas was usually an Utter Barrister.

Skewys and Merland were named as Auditors (Folio 49) for the accounts of Roger Fitz, the Pensioner for 1498 — 1499.

On 4th May, 1501 "John Skewys was assigned to William Seintmaure's Chamber, with William; he gave 26/8d." (Folio 55)

Officers elected in Michaelmas Term, 17 Henry VII (1501) included "John Skuse as Butler" (Folio 59). The job of Butler comprised a variety of duties. This officer normally did all the writing for the Society; wrote the Pension Roll and Treasurers Roll; catalogued the Library and kept the Register Book. He checked the students who spoke loud in the hall; collected fees on admission, and occasionally superintended the erection of new buildings.

Folios 63, 68 and 72 cover Auditors. John Skewys was named Auditor with Merland for the accounts of William Wadham 1501 — 1502; and with Coloppe for Wadham's accounts (then Treasurer) for 1502 — 1503 and with Walter Stubbis for the accounts of William Ayloff, the Treasurer for 1503 — 1504.

On 14th April 1505 Richard Eryngton was elected Autumn Reader (Folio 75) "if he shall make default he shall be fined £10 without pardon and John Skewys shall be reader." The Reader was always a man of mark in Lincoln's Inn. The post was considered to confer distinction on the occupant. The Autumn Reader was paid £14, while the Lent Reader was paid just £8. Each Reader read for four weeks and gave a Dinner and Supper during the reading. It would appear that the aforementioned Richard Eryngton did not perform his duties, for in Folio 75 we find "20th July, 1505 — William Malom, one of the Masters of the Court of the King's Chancery, was admitted and pardoned all vacations, and admitted to repasts; he gave a hogshead of wine at the instance of John Skewys (Autumn Reader)". Richard Eryngton never appeared to have paid his fine and in 1507 his widow was asked to 'pay up'. The Folio did not say when he died or of what cause.

John Skewys had been a hard worker since he first went to Lincoln's Inn in 1487. It was presumably his wish that one day he would be elected as one of the Governors. This wish turned into reality 18 years later. Officers elected in Michaelmas Term, 21 Henry VII (1505) were Governors: James Hobbert, knight, the King's Attorney; William Frost, William Ayloff and John Skewys (Folio 80).

Governors were elected on the Feast of All Saints, from which festival the year of the Society ran. Most Governors served for one year and after that in no other office except, in a few instances, that of Reader. After a short break they could be re-elected as one of the Governors. John Skewys was re-elected as one of these Governors (with Calibut, Newport and Ayloff) in 1508 and was also named as Lent Reader (Folio 18). On 1st March, 1509 William Perpoynt, knight, was admitted to the Society. "He may be at Repasts. He shall give a hogshead of wine next Lent, to be delivered when Skewys holds his Reading." (Folio 20)

In Michaelmas Term, 1509 "Nudigate, Skuys, Roper and Moore were each amerced 40d for not attending the last Council." (Folio 22)

"Skewys, Aleyn, Straunge and Rokeby" were named as Governors at Michaelmas Term, 1510. (Folio 35)

In 1511 (Folio 46) "it was agreed at the request of Robert Thornburgh that he alone shall have the Chamber that Master Cutlard had when he was elected Serjeant, and that Sir Richard Fowler, who lay by sufferance in the same Chamber, shall have the Chamber with the chimney that William lies in, 'late translate by John Skewis', and that William Marshall have the Chamber by the kitchen that Master Alleyn late had. Thornburgh has paid 20 shillings."

Officers elected All Saints Day, 7 Henry VIII (1515) named John Skewys as one of the Governors with William Frost, William Marshall and Richard Clerk. (Folio 62) Five years later he was re-elected with Roper, Marshall and Treheyron (Folio 102).

In the accounts of William Marshall 1520 — 1521 (Folio 106), "a receipt of £3: 13: 4d was received from John Skewys being a loan (prestacia) for the building of the new gate."

John Skewys served further terms of office as one of the Governors of Lincoln's Inn Fields: In 1522 with Roper, Marshall and Jenney (Folio 116); 1524 with Wootton, Marshall and Densell (Folio 135); 1528 with Jenney, Honychurch and Curson (Folio 163) and finally in 1530 with Marshall, Chomeley and Dancaster (Folio 6).

There's a reference to a Richard Skoos, the Rector of Lincoln's Inn in the accounts of John Harvey (Folio 18) 1530 — 1531 in which it lists "an allowance of 7d to Richard Skoos for lead and for mending the dial (dielletta) of the Clock."

John Skewys was educated at Oxford University, matriculating at Exeter College, but does not appear to have taken a degree. Wood, translating the Latin words of Pits praises his "hapie genie accompanied with industry, prudence and dexterity." Skewys was entertained to wine by Exeter College in 1525 (Biographical Register of the University of Oxford 1501 — 1540 by A.B. Emden 1974) and gave him and his wife pairs of gloves in the summer of 1526 and gave him pairs of gloves in the Lent Term 1528 and winter of 1531. During this period he was one of Cardinal Wolsey's chief legal officers and concerned with the acquisition of a site for Cardinal College.

Whilst he was at university in Oxford and later as Governor of Lincoln's Inn many events were happening in the outside world. Caxton had died in 1490. Henry VII invaded France in 1492 with an army of more than 25,000 men, the first regularly paid and fully disciplined English army. Columbus discovered the West Indies that same year.

In 1497 Henry levied new taxes and 16,000 Cornish miners under Lord Audley (led by Michael Joseph[1] of St Keverne and Thomas Flammank[2], lawyer of Bodmin) marched in revolt to Kent. They were met at Blackheath by Giles Lord Daubeny, King Henry's General and three hundred soldiers on the King's part who dispersed the Cornishmen with the loss of 2,000 men dead. Joseph and Flammank were hanged, drawn and quartered and had their heads and quarters pitched upon stakes set up in London and other places on 26 June, 1497. Lord Audley's punishment was more drawn out. Taken to Newgate prison the night before his execution, he was then tied to a hurdle and drawn by horses through the city of London to Tower Hill, wearing a paper tabard, painted with his coat of arms, to show that he was no longer worthy of knighthood. But on Tower Hill he was given a quick death under the axe, followed by burial of everything except his head, which was set with the heads of Flammank and Joseph on London Bridge... obscene reminders to anyone entering or leaving the city of the penalties of rebellion.[3]

Perkin Warbeck sailed to Cornwall in 1497 and raised 6,000 men and attempted to take Exeter. On the eve of the Battle of Taunton with Henry, Warbeck abandoned his cause and he surrendered. He was executed at the Tower of London on 16 November, 1499.

John Cabot, under Henry's protection, sailed from Bristol in one ship with twenty men and reached North America and became the first seafarer to cross the North Atlantic since the Vikings in the 11th century.

In 1501 Henry VII's son Prince Arthur married Catherine of Aragon and England was united with Spain. The following year Arthur died and Catherine was contracted to his younger brother Henry who later became Henry VIII.

On 21 April, 1509 Henry VII died at Richmond from rheumatoid arthritis and gout and was buried at Westminster. He was 52. On 22 April, 1509, Henry VIII, the younger son of Henry VII ascended the throne at the age of eighteen. Henry married Catherine of Aragon in June, 1509.

Henry landed at Calais on 22 August, 1513 with 25,000 men and defeated the French at Guinnegatte (Battle of the Spurs).

The same year James IV in alliance with France invaded England from the north with 100,000 men, but was met by the Earl of Surrey and defeated at the Battle of Flodden with the loss of 10,000 killed. James IV was killed as indeed were the majority of Scottish peerage.

Surrey was made Duke of Norfolk in 1513.

In 1513, the Minister for the Duchy of Cornwall accounted for 66/8d of relief for the Manor

---

[1] Michael Joseph was a blacksmith from St. Keverne, Cornwall.
[2] Thomas Flammank is also referred to in many books as Thomas Flammock.
[3] *The Making of Henry VIII* (M.L. Bruce), 1977, pp 78, 79

of Polroda, described as parcel of the Duchy, and said to be held of the Castle of Launceston by the service of one Knight's fee of Mortaine — and at the same time he accounted for 6/8d received from John SKEWYS for relief of the same Manor; and also for £10: 5: 0¼d for the issue of the same Manor for the time it was in the hands of the King — it being stated that the Manor was worth per annum £19:19:8½d (Ministers Account, Duchy of Cornwall, 1513). It would seem that Sir Edmund Carew had alienated the Manor to John Skewys. At all events, the Manor was vested in the said John SKEWYS, who after being seized by his charter dated 6 February, 1539, granted the Manor of Polroda to William Reskymer (Skewys' younger step-son) on condition that he would pay John the annual rent of £90.

Three years afterwards proceedings were taken by William Hokkyn on behalf of Lawrence Courtenay, cousin of John Skewys for setting aside the settlement upon the ground that the rent had not been paid, which William Reskymer said was a great deal more than all the lands were worth. Accordingly, in the following year a fine was levied in which William Hokkyn and William Sydenham were querists and John Skewys was the defendant. The Manor of Polroda was settled upon John for his lifetime.

In 1514 John Skewys (then aged 47 years) had the pleasure of wearing his hat in the King's presence.

John Skewys entered the household of Cardinal Wolsey and was admitted to his private counsels being presumably one of the "four Counsellors learned in the lawe of the Realme who dwelt in his House". [4]

In May, 1523 he was entered in the subsidy roll of the Cardinal's officials for an assessment of 100 shillings. Christopher, Lord Conyers, granted to him and others in 1527 certain property for Wolsey's benefit; in June, 1529 he was appointed a member of the commission to adjudicate on cases in Chancery committed to them by the Cardinal, and in the same month the Bishop of Bangor complained of his action as "one of Wolsey's servants of law."

In 1529 Wolsey fell from favour following the failure of King Henry VIII's marriage to Catherine of Aragon. Henry secretly married Anne Boleyn in 1533. Cardinal Wolsey was arrested near York for treason in November, 1530. He died at Leicester Abbey on his way back to London for trial at Westminster.

John Skewys was the owner by inheritance and acquisition of a great amount of property in Cornwall including the Manor of Polroda in St. Tudy, and the lease of the Tolls in Tin in Tewington, Tywarnhaile and Helston. He was placed on commission for the county of Cornwall in 1510, 1511, 1514 and 1515 and was on commission for Middlesex in 1528, 1531, 1537 and 1539. In July, 1518 and July, 1521 he was appointed one of the commissioners for the Duchy of Cornwall; in 1521 he served as High Sheriff of Cornwall. Some deeds relating to his property are in Lansdowne M.S. British Museum 207f.

On 20 September, 1514 Skewys was included with William Lowre in a commission for assessing the possessions of the Duchy of Cornwall. His ancestor John de Skewys sued Adam, Prior of Launceston in 1344 for a corody in that Priory. The proceedings are very interesting as illustrating the manners and customs of the age and, moreover, enabling us to correct an error in the pedigree of Botreaux. [5]

In July, 1516 a grant of the next presentation to a Connonry at Windsor was made to Skewys and two others, and 1525 saw him elected as one of the commissioners for the suppression of St Fridewood's Convent at Oxford and other foundations. [6]

A fee of £61: 13: 4d for his services is entered in 1519 in the expenses of Henry Courtenay, Earl of Devon. The same peer, then the Marquis of Exeter, writing to Wolsey in October, 1525 recognised his relationship calling him "my cosyn Skewys". [7] As late as 1534 he was employed as Counsel.

---

[4] Cavendish, *Wolsey.* Edition 1827; page 100
[5] Maclean's *History of Trigg Minor*; ante volume 1, pp 640-641
[6] Dugdale *Monasticon*, ii, page 151
[7] Nichols, *Lawford Hall*, pp. 412-414

John Skewys spent a great deal of time writing, and was author of *Brevyat of a Cronacle*, made by Mathewe Paris of the *Conquests of Duke William of Normandy Uppon This Realme*. He wrote a treatise *De Bellor Trojano* and a history *Chronicorum Epitome*. He was credited by Bishop Bale with *Abbreviations Chronicorum*. His fame, however, chiefly rests upon another literary production called *The Black Book of Merthen*.

In 1979 the writer was shown the original copy of *Merthen* which is now in the possession of the Royal Institution of Cornwall, River Street, Truro. It measures 11 inches by 8 inches and has 62 leaves of parchment. It is a complete survey of the Reskymer Estate in Latin.

> *An Extent of all the Manors, Lands and Tenements of John Reskymer, Esquire, made at Merthen on the Feast of St. Michael the Archangel in the 22nd year of the reign of King Henry the Seventh (1506), from inspection of several Extents made in the time of Edward II[8], Edward III, Richard II, Henry IV and from other Inspections of Writings verifying the same; well and faithfully examined by JOHN SKEWYS and others."*

Except for a number of small notes the *Black Book of Merthen* does not appear to be in John Skewys' own hand-writing, but on the fly leaf he has written:

> *This boke made by JOHN SKEWYS uppon the syght and examynacion of Evydence of John Reskymer the fader and John Reskymer the sonne by good and long deliberacion: Anno Vicesimo Octavo regis Henrici Octavi (1536) fynyshid: per me Johannem Skewys manu propria.*

On the title page there is an achievement of the arms of Reskymer quartering Trevarthians. The land surveyed in the *Black Book of Merthen* includes the manors of Reskymer, Cutter, Reskymer-Manek, Rosowyk alias Lucyas, Merthyn, Hellogan, Tretheves, Trelowth-Hayle, Treforward, Trevarthyan and lands in Carveynek, Wynnyanton, Stikker, Trewynnyan and Rescurywll.

A copy of the survey made by John Skewys, and translated from Latin, now follows:

ABSTRACT OF AN "EXTENT OF THE MANOR OF MERTHEN".
Compiled by JOHN SKEWYS
from old Surveys in 1506

The Manor of Merthen near Gweek on the banks of the Helford River. Said John Skewys in the "Black Book of Merthen" — "From the time beyond the memory of man, the Lord of the Manor shall have the best fish called Porpos, Thorpole, Dolphyn and all other such great fishes in whatsoever place caught between the Passage and Gweek"

---

[8] By a fortunate chance this, the earliest of surveys used by JOHN SKEWYS and dated 1318, has been preserved in the Public Record Office: Rentals and Surveys, 6, 38.

FREE TENANTS

The heirs of Cereaux, now the Earl of Oxford, hold in Gweke Wolas, Men-Poule and Lestraynes and render yearly 5/-d and do Common Suit of Court.

The heir of Tremayn of Culcom holds the manor of Carthenek with lands in Carthenek, Trevasek-Meor, Trevasek-Vean, Lanharth, Gweke-Wartha and Kelter. (St Keverne).

The heir of Banathlek, now Gervas, holds there one acre Cornish in Polpry and Trethowyn and a ferling of land Cornish in Knight's service, rendering 4/-d yearly and doing Common Suit of Court for Trethowyn.

The heir of Trethowyn holds in Polpry one acre Cornish by Knight's service and renders 4/-d yearly and Common Suit.

The heir of Penkevall, viz Trefusis, holds in Vethnewas (Ethnevas) Polsodornek, Treworwell, Parke-Jak-Toma, Treglusowe Wolas, Treglusowe-Wartha, Nansarth Owe, Treaher-Veor one Knight's fee and renders 7/6d and Common Suit.

The heir of Polpenruth holds in Polpenruth Wolas in Knight's service and renders 6d yearly and Common Suit.

Sum of the free tenants rents 21/-d and one pound of Cummin. Merthen Demesne lands worth 43/4d yearly.

LEASEHOLD LANDS

Polpenruth-Wartha:	John Trelan. Rent 6/8d and Common Suite.
Langelong:	William Gervas. Rent 7/-d. He holds by demise to him and Emiline his wife and John their son for their lives, made by John Arundell of Talfern, a feofee of the manor.
Retalek:	Nicholas Pentacost. Rent 34/8d and Common Suit.
The Blowing Mill:	(Molendinum Sufflaticum) there (i.e. Retalleck) 4/-d.
The Old Wier	(Vetus Kydellum) 26/8d.
The New Wier:	26/8d.
The Wier House:	2/-d

Sum of the Leasehold Rents £8 : 1 0d
Total Rents of the Manor £9 : 0 0d

The manor is holden of the Duke of Cornwall as of his castle of Launceston by service of a third part of a twentieth part of one Knight's fee Mortain, as appears by the charters of Lord Richard and Edmund, Earls of Cornwall and of King Henry III made to Gervase de Hornicut granting him the Manors of Merthyn, Wynnyanton and Tamerton to hold by service of a twentieth part of a Knight's fee.

Wynnyanton is now held by Arundell, and Tamerton by Carewe, each of which do a third part of this service.

There now follows an account of the custom of the Lord of Merthen having "head fish" of the River Helford.

"There has been a certain custom within the Manor of Merthyn", said John Skewys when he began his survey of Merthen in 1506 "from the time beyond the memory of man, that the Lord of the Manor shall have the best fish called Porpos, Thorpole, Dolphyn and all other such great fishes in whatsoever place caught between the Passage and Gweke, Sent Maugan, Brygge, Polwheverer or Polpenryth or anywhere else between the Manor of Merthyn and the Passage and that all the fish of this sort shall be brought to Merthyn Greyn (i.e. Groyne Point) and there be divided, but not elsewhere."

Merthen Woods have long been the most extensive in the parish of Constantine, and are probably the remains of a forest of oak which covered all the lower part of the parish. The woods, at present, are on Merthen Barton and cover about 200 acres in area.

They remain unbroken all round the creeks. They are, in the main, of small coppice oak which have been cut at regular intervals since the sixteenth century, when the growth of mining required charcoal to burn in the smelting works or blowing houses. Prior to that the woods were the concern of the lord of the manor who, together with his tenants found fuel, burning material and feeding ground for his animals.

By the end of the sixteenth century, manors were slowly breaking up, and the highest price paid for charcoal by the smelters led to all the woods of Cornwall being treated as coppice, cut, and "coaled" most probably on the spot by the tinners.

In 1530 Reynold Tretherff, the agent (or deputy) of John Skewys, Lord of Merthen, and Walter Borlase, the Receiver of Sir John Arundell, agreed that if the "third part" of Merthen Wood lying next to Benatlek, except six acres adjoining the place of Merthen, was proved by legal verdict to belong to Sir John, then Reynold would hand over to Walter "all such cloes or the value thereof as is colyd or cutte there."

The wood was separated from Merthen in the year 1395.

Brill (anciently Brehylgh) takes its name from the isolated rounded hill (Bre) under which it lies. In 1337, as (Brehlgh), it was held under the manor freely by John SKEWYS, Lord of Skewys in Cury, who surrendered certain rights of pasture which it possessed in Bonallack Woods. It seems that he (John Skewys) exchanged these with James Gerveys for land in Syuwragh (Sewrah in Stithians) in 1386. The charter dated at Hellyston — Burgh describes the right as "land in Benadlek with common Estover and a Voleta and Pannage for one pig in the woods of Benadlek."

The Black Book of Merthen, written by John Skewys in Latin in 1536. "This boke made by John Skewys uppon syght and examynacion of Evydence of John Reskymer the fader and John Reskymer the sonne by good and longe deliberation. Anno Vicesimo Octavo regis Henrici Octavi (1536) fynished, per me Johannem Skewys manu propria"

John SKEWYS was Lord of Brehylgh at the time, and it was possible that the owner of Brill had the rights over Bonallack. Estover implies the right to take the wood for fire and building purposes. Voleta is the right of hawking and fowling and Pannage is the right to let pigs forage in the woods during autumn and winter. In this case the right appears to have extended to one pig only.

After the death of John Skewys, Lord of Skewys, the lands etc passed to his grandson John Skewys, Lord of Merthen who settled his estates, including the Manor of Skewys, (to which Brill was annexed) upon his step-son William Reskymer in marriage with his niece and heir-at-law, Alice Denzall. These lands eventually passed to the youngest of the four daughters and coheiress, Jane, who married Thomas Bower of St. Winnow.

Prior to this transaction, however, we see the Barton of Bonallack in the news in connection with a dispute which was between two overlords, John Skewys (as Lord of Merthen) in right of his wife's dower and Thomas Trefusis. Trefusis seized Richard Gerveys (grandson of the above mentioned James Gerveys) and entered into possession of his lands on the ground that certain lands of the Gerveys family in Ethnevas were held of his Manor of Treviades. John Skewys, who was a well known lawyer, sued him in the Court of Requests (see Proc. Henry VIII 1-91) for "Ravishment of Ward" and declared that the lands in Banathlek, Trethowyn, and Polpry (which adjoins Bonallack) were holden of Merthen. The matter was comprised before 1528 by John Skewys and his wife Katherine, selling their right in the wardship of Trefusis for 20 marks.[9]

In the *Black Book of Merthen*. John Skewys describes himself as the guardian of his step-son John Reskymer. The latter and his younger brother could only have been very young children when their father died, for their parents did not marry until the year 1498, and John was their step-father in residence at Merthen in 1506.

Among the deeds formerly at Trelawne was an Outlawry granted in 1514 against John Skewys at the suit of Sir William Trevanyon, Knight, and William Lytton for ravishing John, son and heir of John Reskymer, whom they claimed as their ward. (Henderson — History of Constantine). In all probability John Skewys had obtained the wardship from the Duchy of Cornwall, and as he had a great many connections, both personal and business, with Cardinal Thomas Wolsey, then at the height of his power, he was able to defend his worthy position.

---

[9] *History of Parish of Constantine*, Charles Henderson, 1937 pp 126, 127.

On the 13th September, 1509, Skewys was granted a lease of the Toll-tin on the Duchy manors and in 1514 he was exempted from serving on juries. This shows he was constantly at Court on the Cardinal's business, and there is every likelihood that he was a confidential friend of King Henry VIII himself until the fall of Wolsey in 1529. When Thomas Wolsey was Lord Chancellor, John Skewys quite often sat in the court of Chancery as his Vice-Chancellor. However, the latter years of his life were troubled by law-suits with his step-son, William Reskymer.

John Skewys, who married Katherine Tretherff daughter of John Tretherff had no children of his own; his sister was married to John Denzell of Denzall, near St. Columb, Serjeant-At-Law, another Cornish landowner who, like himself, had become a well-known laywer.

The Denzells had no son, but several daughters and it was arranged that one of these, Alice, should marry William Reskymer, John Skewys' younger step-son, and that John should settle his seven manors (in Cornwall) upon them and their children. This took place in 1538, and provided that if Alice die without issue male the lands should revert to John Reskymer, Skewys' eldest step-son. Such a settlement is proof enough that at this time the two Reskymers were so high in the estimation of their step-father that he even excluded his own relations in their favour. However, it is an ill wind that blows no good, and four years later all was changed. In 1542 we find William Reskymer described as "one of the King's Valett-Chambre", bringing a bill before the Court of Requests (P.R.O. Court of Requests, Proc Henry VIII., 1.5) against his step-father, John Skewys. He complained that John had induced him to marry his niece, Alice Denzell, on condition that he would settle the lands and manors upon them. Accordingly he married the lady and then his step-father took back the lands. In his defence Skewys said that "William Reskymer may spend yearly beyond £50", and that Mary (his mother-in-law) as executrix of John Denzell, her husband, had 1000 marks worth of goods and plate, and that William Reskymer had Denzell lands worth yearly the value of 40 marks, with Alice when he married her and that he had £10 yearly worth of his lands — in other words the marriage had made him a man of considerable wealth. John Skewys further asserted that he had only granted him his manors and lands after the marriage had taken place and also on condition that a yearly rent of £24 was paid. The rent was not paid, so he resumed possession.

Depositions of witnesses were taken in Cornwall by order of the Court. The first of John's witnesses was extremely interested in the proceedings. His name was Lawrence Courtenay of Ethy, and he was married to one of Alice Denzell's sisters. If the case went against the Reskymers, Alice stood a very good chance of obtaining her uncle John's inheritance.

Courtenay said that Skewys made the gift of his lands to William and Alice on condition that a yearly rent was paid, and as it was not, he re-entered them. Lawrence Courtenay was at John Skewys' house in St John's Lane, Smithfield, London when William Reskymer was a suitor to his step-father and desired him to be his *Good Father* and said to him *Sir, I do perceive ye have re-entered into your lands again that ye gave me and that ye are minded to put me from same contrary to the deed that you have made to me and my wife.* John answered *If the assurance that I have made you be not good already, ye shall have no other assurance of me than ye have, for ye have broken your covenants and have put me in the law full unkindly and ungently to my great costs and therefore ye have deserved no kindness of me.*

William Reskymer desired him *I pray you to be so good father as to give me the one half and to Mr Courtenay the other half.*

Noe Sir, replied John Skewys, *not soe, I will give my lands to him that doeth most for me and will be ruler of the same as long as I live.*

After this conversation William Reskymer left. William Perys, William Trubody, Thomas Horseman and also Skewys' Chaplain and Rose Woolman his servant were present on the day that Reskymer visited John Skewys in London, and all five witnessed the abovementioned dispute.

The final result of the suit was a decree in favour of the Reskymers, largely due to his being a Courtier of one of the Kings own bodyguards. The Court of Requests had always been amenable to court influence. Nevertheless John Skewys refused to be beaten. Now at the good age of 76 he felt his end drawing close and on 2 June, 1543 he made his will and desired that he should be buried at St John's, Clerkenwell, London next to his late wife Katherine, where already a marble tomb was prepared. There was to be an elaborate funeral with torches and many masses for his soul.

"Immediately after my death", he wrote "there to be three trentall of masses and dyryges said for my soul after the order and forme of Saint Gregories Trentall. Twelve poor men to be given black gowns with hoods, and thirteen to have a white gown with hood, and at the funeral service the man in white to stande at my heade with a Staffe Torche, and all the other twelve on both sides of my Corps, with twelve other Staffe Torches during all my funeral service. There to be fifty torches in all to wayte upon my Corps to the Churche. Thirteen.............(difficult to translate)..............in silver to be distributed to the poor.

"All my Bookes and Evydence to be keapte at my place at Skewys to the use of suche of my kynne and freends as shall fortune to be the Lord and Owner thereof."

John Skewys left £40 for the Church of St Carantyne, Cury towards the building of an ambulatory on the south side. The remainder of his Goods and Chattels were apportioned as follows:

"My servant Rose Woolman to enjoy the goods I have already given her and to have £20 in Gold Coin.
"Dame Elizabeth Byknell to whom I am executor bequeathed money for mending the highway besides Bekyngton yn Somersetsheer called Deadmanes Shade: she left 100 shillings of which I have delivered 40 to one Compton dwelling in Bekyngton — my executor to see about the payment of the rest.
"Sir Richard Conny my Chapleyn to have three pounds six and eight pence yearly for the rest of his life, and meate and drinck and a blacke gowne to pray for my soule and the soules of them that be comprysed in the Table Vppon the Aulter whereas the same Sir Richard saith his daily masse.
"John Woolman to have £10 and a blacke gowne.
"Philip Hill to have a blacke gowne and forty shillings.
"William Peerse to have a black gowne and forty shillings.
"My Horsekeap to have forty shillings and a blacke coate.
"To the Skollien of my kytchen a black coat and foure shillings.
"Rose Woolman a have a blacke gowne.
"Lawrence Courtenay to have ten pounds.
"Any who shall have my plate, not to put owte my Armes, but to leave them on pieces of plate to serve as a remembrance of me.
"The reste of my goodes, plate money and all my Evydences, Charters, Wrytings not already bequeathed to go to my cousen Lawrence Courtenay esquire and his heirs male.
"Sir Richard Page, knight, my sole executor to have twenty pounds for his pains, plus the twenty pounds I recently lente hym; also a standing Cupp all gyllte.
"Rose Woolman to have foure pounds yearly for her faithful, diligent and true servyce, from my Manor of Tredrym (St Just-in-Roseland) in Cornwall. My executor to pay Rose at the Font Stone in the Cathedral Church of St Paule in London. Rose also to have one haulfe of all manner of tynne hereafter wrought and gotten owte of any parte of my lands and tenements in the saide county of Cornwall. Lawrence Courtenay to have the other half."

The will was signed and sealed by John Skewys. An addition says:

"I feare the saide Sir Richard Page shall be so sore Laboured that he may not deny to healpe William Reskymer whome yn my conscience I cannot savor. Therefore I dyscharte Vtterly the said Sir Richard that he be not yn wise mine Executor, but Supervysor of this my Testament, so that he shall owte of blame to denye then that suyth Vnto hyn for his good will, so now I make and ordeyne my cousen Lawrence Courtenary and Richard Tomyawe myne Executors. This dated the last day of October, 1543."
Witnesses: Richard Coony, Preest; Willian Perde, Phillipp Hill, John Woolman and Thomas Farmer.

A second codicil dated 31st March, 1544 (and signed 6 May, 1544) said that Skewys was afraid that he may not have sufficient provision for the performance of his will; he said that the "issues" of his properties in Cornwall were to be used for this purpose, and he lists his "Manor, Lands and Tenements in Skewis, Fenton Venna, Botalecke, Polrode and Tredrynne" and all his tin works and tin in the county of Cornwall.

The Manor of Skawen and Bulland to go to Rose Woolman "for her good and diligent suite and attendance Vppon me in my sickness."

Her brother John Woolman to have money "for dyvers things that he hathe made for me, wythout moonay."

Philip Hill to have money to pray for John Skewys "and for himselfe."

William Peers to have money; likewise Thomas Farmer, John Skewys' servants.

Lawrence Courtenay to have the Manors of Skewis, Fenton Venna, Sellena, Tredrym, Polrode, Bullonde, Skawen and Sainte Crede in Cornwall.

John Skewys died 23 May, 1544 and his will was proved on 30 May, 1544 and led, as we may suppose, to litigation. Lawrence Courtenay was slain by the Scots at Haddington in Hertford's campaign in 1547. He left a son Francis Courtenay of Ethy.

William Reskymer died and his wife Alice survived him and in 1558 brought a suit in the Court of Requests (Proc XX 139) to compel Francis Courtenay to surrender the title deeds of the Skewys Estates — a case which the Reskymers won.

A few ancient deeds relating to John Skewys and other members of the Skewys family now follow.

A DESCRIPTIVE CATALOGUE
OF ANCIENT DEEDS

These Deeds date from the 12th century to the 16th century, and were all previously written in Latin. They are now in the possession of the Public Record Office, London.

The Deeds relating to members of the Skues/Skewys/Skewis family are referred to by numbers, and the paragraphs relating to them can be found on the next two pages. A. 8611, A. 9947, A. 10031, A. 10034, A. 10276, A. 10321, A. 10338, A. 10339, A. 10488, A. 10515, A. 12217, A. 12730, A. 12887, A. 12892, A. 13020, A. 13229, A. 13231.

CATALOGUE OF ANCIENT DEEDS

A. 8611 CORNWALL	Bond by Henry Talgarrek to JOHN SKEWYS in 20l., conditioned for the performance of covenants in indentures between them of even date. 30 June, 23 Henry VII. (Seal broken)
A. 9947 CORNWALL	Feoffment by John Reskymer, esquire, son and heir of John Reskymer, esquire, to Katherine his mother, in accordance with his father's last Will, (and to) JOHN SKEWYS, esquire, her husband, of his Manors of Merthyn, Cutter and Reskymer, to hold to the said JOHN SKEWYS (and Katherine) for the term of the life of the said Katherine; attorney to deliver seison, Nicholas Pentacost, 10 .... Henry VIII, (Seal, a gem).
A. 10031 CORNWALL	Counterpart indenture being a feoffment by Amicia late the wife of John Trevisa, widow to John Mohun, JOHN SKEWYS, Reginald Tretherff, James Veell and Peter Sentalbyn, of all her lands, etc., in Lannargh Meour, Marghasowe, Marghasvygham, Helston Burgh, Tresoward, Erlyn, Rescoll, Retalek, Tregoys and Gwenna and elsewhere in the county of Cornwall, to hold to the use of her, the said Amicia, for the term of her life, and after her decease to the use of Thomas Tretherff and Mary his wife and the heirs of their bodies, and in default of such issue to the use of her, the said Amicia's right heirs; attorneys to deliver seison John Densell and John Udy. 12 February, 23 Henry VII.
A. 10034 CORNWALL	Feoffment by Henry Talgarrek to JOHN SKEWYS, James Erysy, Richard Penros and Odo Geoff, of all his lands etc in Talgarrek and Redruyth, and elsewhere in the county of Cornwall; attorneys to deliver seison, William Tretherff, and John Robyn. Witnesses — John Arundell, knight, Richard Code, esquire, Peter Seyntawbyn. London, 8 February, 24 Henry VII. Seal. Memorandum endorsed of enrolment on dorse of close roll.
A. 10276 CORNWALL	Indenture being the defeasance of a recognisance, made in Exchequer, whereby William de Botreaux, Silvester de Trefruthken, John de Aldestowe, Robert de Forve, JOHN DE SKEWYS were bound to Master John de Hildeslegh £157 19s 5¼; £105 4s 6¼d therof to be paid to the said Master John at York in the quinzaine of St Hilary next, and £52 14 11ld in the quinzaine of Easter next, viz. on payment by the said William de Botreaux of £105 4s 6¼d into the King's exchequer at the quinzaine of Easter. York. 23 November, 9 Edward III. Seal of Arms: 1) Chequy on a bend three horshoes 2) A chevron between three oak leaves slipped 3) A bird, one wing expanded, within scroll works 4) A saltire five cinqufoils
A. 10321 CORNWALL	Release by JOHN SKEWYS to Oto Trevarthian, knight, of his right in lands, etc., in the Manors of Merthyn, Rosewyk, Trevarthian and Tretheves and in the towns of Layty, Chymeder, Willys and Sensowonao and in the advowsons of the parish churches of Ruan Major and Ruan Minor (Rumoni Magni et Parvi) and Landewednack (Wynwolay). Witnesses: William Bodrugan, Master Henry Wyngod, clerk, John Trethew, John Mertherderwa. Merthyn, Saturday before Epiphany, 1 .... Henry V. Seal
A. 10338 CORNWALL	Letter of attorney to John Trevarthian, to John Gerveys, Master Stephen Gerveys, Thomas Seynt Austell, clerk and Gregory Garlunyek to deliver seison to John Tremayn, James Gerveys, John Urban, JOHN SKEWYS, and John Trethewy the younger, of the Manors of Merthyn, Rosewyk, Trevarthian and Tretheves, with the advowsons of the churches of Landewednack, Ruan Major and Ruan Minor with rents and services of free tenants to the said Manors belonging, and of lands etc in Chymeder, Sensewana, Guylles, and Leyty, as in his charter therof to the said Tremayn and others made. Sunday after Ascension, 22 Richard II.
A. 10339 CORNWALL	Grant by Thomas Trevergy to Geoffrey Trelan of the rent and service, vis., fealty and Ws., of JOHN SKEWYS for a half acre of land Cornish in Nanfan in the parish of St. Corent in the county of Cornwall. Nanfan, 16 April-22 Henry VII.
A. 10488 CORNWALL	Indenture being a grant by Joan late the wife of John Trevarthian, knight, and Odo Trevarthian, John Trethiwy and JOHN SKYWYS to John Boskawen, of the custody of the land, etc., which they had by reason of the minority of the Henry brothers and heir of Roger Trewennert, with the marriage of the said Henry and the like of James, Henry's brother, and if he survive the said Henry. Monday before Whitsun, 6 Henry II.
A. 10515 CORNWALL	Indenture being of demise to John Trevarthian, esquire, to John Tremayn, James Gerveys, John Urban, John Trethewyn, JOHN SKEWYS and John Trethewy the younger, of his Manors of Merthyn and Rosewyk, Trevarthian and Tretheves, the advowson of the churches of Landewednack, Ruan Major and Ruan Minor, and his land etc., in Chymeder, Sensewana, Guylles and Leyty; to hold the said manors of Merthyn and Rosewyk, etc., and the said land in Chymeder, Sensewana, Guylles and Leyty, for the term of the life of Joan, his wife, and the said advowsons, for the term of their

lives, at the rent of a grain of corn at Michaelmas. Witnesses: John Penrose, James Treverbyn, John Trereys, Eurinus Boneython, Matthew SKEWYS.

Merthyn, Sunday before Ascension, 22 Richard II. Memorandum, endorsed, of enrolment in the Bench roll lof deeds enrolled Easter term, 22 Richard II.

A. 12217
HERTS

Indenture being a feoffment, by John Clyfford, of London, mercer, and Elizabeth, his wife, daughter and heir of John Sawyer, deceased, to Thomas More, knight, JOHN SKEWYS, esquire, Thomas Leynthorpe, Thomas Clyfford, the younger, William Barle, Richard Gylle and Humphrey Fitzharberd, and to Richard Clyfford of London, mercer, to the use of the said John & Elizabeth, of all their land etc., in Royston, Sondon, West Myll and Bontyngford, attorneys to deliver seison Thomas Brocas and Thomas Dourne. 18 July. 17 Henry VIII.

A. 12730
CORNWALL

Counterpart of demise by John Reskymer, alias Greber, of Merthen, esquire, and William Reskymer, alias Greber, in the same county, gentleman, to Baldwin (Baldewino) Perowe of the parish of Gunwallow Wyniaton, husbandman, (agricole), John Thomas, son of James Thomas, of the same, and Allan Bawden, son of the said Baldwin Perrowe, of all their tenements in Saint Sewannowe, within the said parish, which tenement the said Baldwin now holds; to hold for the term of their lives in survivorship, rendering therefore yearly to the said John Reskymer, and the heirs male of his body, or in default to the said William Reskymer, and the heirs male of his body, or in default to the heirs male of Richard Reskymer alias Greber, deceased 13s 4d at the four terms usual in the hundred of Kyrer, and the best beast for "heriot" of farley (farlevium) according to the customs used and approved in the said Hundred; attorneys to deliver seison, John Prigean and HENRY SKEWIS. 7 October, 25 Elizabeth, 1583. Names of witnesses: John Trethowan and others, endorsed.

A. 12887
CORNWALL

Counterpart indenture, 1 March, 21 Henry VIII between John Arundell of Talferne, the elder, John Arundell the younger, and JOHN SKEWYS, esquires, of the one part, and "Raynold" Tretherff, esquire, of the other, witnessing that it is agreed between them as follows: wheras John Tretherff, father of "Raynold" being seized in the fee the manors of Tretherff, Arallus alias Argallas, SKEWYS, Brongullowe, Trevelwyth, Petygrewe, Trewynyan and Tresamballe, in the county of Cornwall "and also of and yn" Chalonslegh alias Leigh Chalons and Strettewode Hedde alias Strette Raylegh, county Devon, enfeoffed the said John, the elder, John the younger, and JOHN SKEWYS therof, for the performance of his last will "as by the same John Tretherff is last wyll synke, partytd in dentyd" appears, now "Raynold" covenants with them; "they shall stond and be styll seasyd" of the said manors to the intent that the "seyd feffes" shall therewith fulfill the said last Will without "lette" or contradiction from him, and he shall make a true account to them of the profits therof "in case" he shall receive the same, the "feffes" covenanting that if his title be impleaded be shall be allowed his expenses. "Yevyn att Talfern." English. Signed Reynold Trertherff.

A. 12892
CORNWALL

Bond by Richard Penrose of Penrosemethele, gentleman, and John Penrose, of the same to "Reynold" (Reginaldo) Tretherff, in £200 as follows: Whereas the said "Reynold" Tretherff and "oon Margerye his wfee" by their deed indented of even date have enfeoffed John Arundell, of Talfern, the elder; JOHN SKEWYS, Thomas Tretherff, John Arundell, of Talfern, the younger, son and heir apparent to the said John, the elder, and James Ersey, esquires, William Trevenour, James Ersey, the younger, John Killygrewe, the younger, James Tripconyn and William Trewynnard, of all theirlands etc in Tremayn, Leen, Treveder, Chyenhall, Mogyan Vighan, Tregamynyon, Cornehegh, Knyehawes, Trefalserowe, Lesard and Helstonburgh, county Cornwall to the use of the said "Reynold" for life, with remainder to the use of the said Margery and to the heirs of her body by the said "Reynold" begotten, "and after to other uses as by same endentur" appears:" iff hytt fortune the foresaid Margery lyvyingthe said Reynold yo dye without heirs of the body", thenif the said "Reynold" take the rents, etc of the premises for his life "withoute interrupcion, lette, vaxacion or trebyll of the bounden Richard Penrose and John", the present obligation to be viod. 30 May, 14 Henry VIII Signed per me Ric'm Penros (Seals).

A. 13020
CORNWALL

Counterpart indenture being a feoffment by John Nanskylly to Benet (Benedicto) Tregooz and John Wolwedon, clerks, JOHN SKEWYS, William Gerves and Thomas Gerves, all of his land etc., in Penhale and Tregena with a garden in Helstonburgh called "Lovurth an Men", rendering therefore yearly for the next five years fifteen shillings, and thereafter forty shillings at the feast of St. Philip and St. James, Midsummer, Michaelmas and All Hallows. Witnesses: John Gotholghan, mayor, borough aforesaid, Peter Seyntaubyn, Thomas Seyntaubyn. Helston 10 April, Henry VIII.

A. 13229
CORNWALL

Indenture being a feoffment by JOHN SKEWYS, esquire to William Reskymer, second born son of John Reskymer, esquire, deceased, and to Alice Denssell, one of the daughters and heirs of John Denssell, late serjeant-at-law, nephew of him the said JOHN SKEWYS which Alice by God's Grace (William shall marry), and upon condition he marry her, of all his manors, lands etc., in SKEWYS, Polrode, Bulland, Scawen, Fontenvenna, Tredrym, Sulgena, Sent Crede and elsewhere in the county of Cornwall, all tin works (operibus stannariis) and toll of tine worked within the said manors, etc., excepted and reserved to him and the heirs of his body issuing; to hold said William and Alice and their heirs of their bodies, rendering therefore yearly to him and the heirs of his body ninety shillings by quarterly payments with remainder if the said Alice die without heir of her body, to the heir male of the body of the said William, rendering to him, and the heirs of his body the rent as aforesaid, with remainder, if William die without heir male of his body to John Reskymer, esquire, elder brother of the said William, and to the heirs male of his body rendering the rent as aforesaid, with remainder, if John die without heir male of his body, to the right heirs of him the said JOHN SKEWYS, etc attorneys to deliver seison, Warin Benet and William Bathe. 6 February, 30 Henry VIII.

A. 13231
CORNWALL

Indenture being feoffment by Isota late of the wife of Hugh Strange, cousin, and one of the heirs of John Carwynnek, widow, to Edward Tretherff, sonof John Tretherff, esquire, of all her land etc., in the parish of Sainte Crede, Leskerdburgh and Brendonnigh Leskard, county Cornwall, and in Plymouth, county Devon; to hold to him and the heirs of his body, of her and her heirs, by the rent of a grain of corn at Michaelmas in September, and to the chief lords the services due and accustomed; with remainder in default of his issue, to Reginald Tretherff, his brother, in tail, with remainder in default to Katherine, daughter of the said John Tretherff, in tail, with remainder in default to the said John Tretherff, esquire, his heirs and assigns: Witnesses: JOHN SKEWYS, William Tretherff, Edward Menwynnek, William Lour, John Joce, Carwynnek, 20 September 1 Henry VIII.

REFERENCES
Mathewe Paris: *Conquests of Duke William of Normandy*
Fullers Worthies (1811) i, 217
Pits: *De Angliae Scriptoribus,* page 709
Nicholas' *Testamenta Vetusta,* ii 495
Tanner *Bibl. Britannico Hibernica* (1748), page 677
Wilkins' *Concilia,* iii 705
Prynnes' *Writs,* iv 280, 780-783
Boase and Courtenay's *Bibl. Cornub,* ii 654-727; iii 1337
Maclean's *History of Trigg Minor* iii 333, 385-387
Harl M.S. 4031; f 77
Letters and Papers of Henry VIII; i, ii, iii & iv, passim, vii 607
Woods' *Athenae Oxon,* ed Bliss i, 58-59
Heritage of Britain — Readers Digest'
John Skewys *Black Book of Merthen*
Black Books of the Honourable Society of Lincoln's Inn (1422 — 1586)
History of Parish of Constantine, Charles Henderson, 1937, Royal Institution of Cornwall, pages 98 —
105, 126 — 127.
Cavendish, *Wolsey* (1827 Edition) page 100
Dictionary of National Biography, Vol. 52,
edited Sidney Lee, 1897, Smith, Elder & Co, London, pp 359-360.

7 Siege of Skewis

"If you have not found a murder in your genealogical travels, you have not thoroughly traced your family history", so goes a saying.

In the Skues family history there have been at least two members murdered — ANDREW de SKEWYS in 1335 and JAMES HENRY SKEWES in 1867.

The family also had a murderer — JOHN SKEWES of Chacewater who shot Alfred John Rule of Camborne in December, 1874. THOMAS SKEWES was transported for 14 years to Van Diemans Land following a court appearance where he was convicted of the manslaughter of a seaman in 1840. The charge of murder was dropped.

Murders have taken place at two of the three SKEWES manor houses — GREAT SKEWYS, St Wenn, 1335 and SKEWIS, Crowan in 1734.

This chapter deals with the murder at SKEWIS, Crowan, or to be precise the five murders.

SKEWIS is situated on the B3303 road from Helston to Camborne, close to what was originally the Nancegollan railway station.

In the seventeenth century the property was purchased by the Rogers family. Many generations had lived in the freehold property.

In January, 1723 a William Rogers married Anne Millett at St. Hilary and took over Skewis. However, eleven years later he suddenly died and his will caused somewhat of a disturbance.

William had a younger brother Henry Rogers who was a pewterer. In William's marriage allegation he is referred to as "Henricum Rogers de Falmouth, pewterer." In those days a pewterer was of considerable importance to Cornwall, although the trade is now virtually lost. A large portion of tin was exported in the shape of pewter made into plates, dishes etc., all of which have now been superseded by earthenware.

William Rogers had no children whereas Henry had several. Upon William's death his widow (maiden name Anne Millett, second daughter of John Millett of Gurlyn in St. Erth and Joan, daughter of John Davies, gent., of St Hilary) produced a will whereby her late husband had bequeathed all his freehold property to her.

In *Cornish Characters and Strange Events*, by S. Baring Gould, pages 364 and 365, he continues the Skewis saga and the outcome of the will in favour of Anne as follows:

This greatly exasperated Henry, who considered that as Skewis had been in the family for many generations, he was entitled to it, and he averred that the will had been wrung from his dying brother by the importunity of the wife, when he was feeble in mind as well as in body.

Forthwith, in place of disputing the will when proved, he took forcible possession of the house, and turned out of it some female servants left in charge whilst his sister-in-law was away from home.

The whole neighbourhood was satisfied that great wrong had been done to Henry Rogers, and was loud in its condemnation of the widow.

When Mrs Rogers returned to Skewis and found herself forcibly dispossessed, she appealed to the law, and judgement was given against Henry.

Stephen Tillie, who was then under-sheriff of the county of Cornwall, received orders to eject Rogers, and place Anne, the widow in possession, and on 18 June, 1734 he accordingly went to Skewis to serve the summons. But Henry stood at an upper window armed with a gun and dared the under-sheriff to approach. Tillie shouted to him that he had the King's writ and must have possession of the house, but assured him that he would not meddle with his person.

By this time a crowd of some 200 or 300 persons had assembled, all sympathisers with Henry Rogers and murmuring their disapproval of the ejection.

Henry, from his upper window, called out that the Lord Chancellor had made an unjust decree.

Tillie replied that Henry might appeal against his decision, but surrender the house he must. Rogers, in reply, fired and, as the under-sheriff stated "burned his wig and singed his face."

Skewis Farm, Crowan

Skewis Farm, Crowan

Cannonballs found in 1979 at Skewis, Crowan

This so frightened Tillie that he withdrew and sent to Helston for some soldiers; and Captain Sadler, who was then in charge of the military there, dispatched some to his aid.

So, reinforced on the morrow, Tillie went again to Skewis, and found the front door shut, with a hold in it. A gun barrel was protruding!

Again the under-sheriff demanded admittance, and in reply the gun was fired, and a bailiff by the name of William Carpenter was mortally wounded.

Another gun was discharged and Hatch, the under-sheriff's servant was struck. Anne Rogers, the plaintiff was in the rear of the house animating the soldiers against the occupants of the house.

Mrs Henry Rogers was within, loading and serving out the guns to her husband and to his servant John Street.

A soldier was shot in the groin, and two other men were wounded.

Thereupon the soldiers fired upon the house, and although the bullets flew in at the window none of those within were actually hurt.

Woolston, the soldier shot in the groin, was taken to the rear of the house where he died.

A bullet whizzed through Stephen Tillie's hat! (Discretion is the better part of valour.) Accordingly, the under-sheriff gave orders to "beat a retreat" and, like the Grand Old Duke of York's men, marched up a hill (towards Helston) and then marched down again.

Tillie and his posse of bailiffs and military retired from the battlefield, carrying their dead and wounded, without even having effected an entry.

In a kindly spirit Rogers had offered Tillie a dram, but the under-sheriff's courage was too much quailed to allow him to draw near enough to accept the hospitable offer.

Indeed it took Mr Tillie nine months to gather up sufficient courage to resume the attack, and then not until he had ordered up cannon from Pendennis Castle.

On the former occasion there had been at least ten soldiers under the command of an officer.

Within the house were only Henry Rogers and his wife, his small children and his servant man.

Clowance House, home of Sir John St Aubyn

On March 16th, in the year following, another party was sent to apprehend Rogers and take possession of the house. On this occasion, apparently, Mr. Stephen Tillie did not put in an appearance, but left the duty to be discharged by the constables.

Henry Rogers was prepared for them and fired, whereupon one named Andrew Willis, alias Tubby, was shot dead. Rogers then, with the utmost coolness, came out of the door and walked round the man he had shot and again on this occasion offered the besiegers a drink. The besiegers then retired, but not till a second man had been shot. That night, probably realising the game was up, Henry Rogers effected his escape. He went out of the back door into the yard, and through the hedge across the field and came out onto the Helston-Camborne Road.

He travelled on foot to Salisbury with the intention of making his case known to the King. St John Aubyn, of Clowance (which is situated about a mile to the north of Skewis) now took an active part in endeavouring to secure the fugitive, and hand bills descriptive of Rogers were circulated along the road to London, whither it was known Rogers was making his way. On 21 March 1734 a reward of £350 was offered for his capture, dead or alive. He was wearing a white fustian frock, with bastard pearl buttons and blue riding coat. Near Salisbury a post boy, driving homewards a post-chaise, was accosted by a stout man walking with a gun in his hand, who requested to be given a lift. The boy drove him to the inn, where he procured a bed, but the circumstances and description had excited strong suspicion and he was secured in his sleep. The prisoner was removed to Cornwall. There he was convicted of murder, together with John Street, who seems to have been his principal partisan. Both were tried at Launceston in August 1735, were both found guilty of murder and were sentenced to death.

"August 6th, at the Assizes at Launceston, Henry Rogers and John Street received sentence of death for two murders they committed in opposing the Sheriff of Cornwall in Execution of his Office and were this day executed; they seemed very penitent, particularly Rogers, who did not care for any sustenance but bread and water. He said he was guilty of one of the murders, but knew nothing of the other, but had it been in his power he would have killed as many more again, and thought he had committed no crime."

Gates of Skewis Farm, Crowan. The spelling was changed to Skewes by 1979

Street, who was his servant had little to say, but that what he did was to defend his Master, and he was willing to Die, for by the course of his years he could not live much longer, and he hoped God would receive his poor Soul."

In his book *Parochial History of Cornwall*, Davies Gilbert tells us of an interesting encounter he had with Henry Rogers' son in 1812 when he relates:

On 30th October 1812, I called on Mr. Henry Rogers, formerly a saddler at Penzance, but then residing there in great poverty, being supported by a small allowance from a club, and by half-a-crown a week given him by the corporation, nominally for yielding up the possession of a house, but in truth to prevent his becoming a common pauper.

Mr. Henry Rogers was then eighty-four years of age, and remembered the unfortunate transactions at Skewis perfectly well; he was between seven and eight years old at the time. He recollected going out with his father into the court after there had been some firing. His father had a gun in his hand and enquired what they wanted. On this his father was fired at, and had a snuff box and powder-horn broken in his pocket by a ball, whilst he stood on the other side.

He recollected that whilst he himself was in bed several balls came in through the window of the room, and after striking against the wall rolled about on the floor. One brother and a sister, who were in the house, went out to inquire what was wanted of their father, and they were not permitted to return.

On the last night, no one remained in the house but his father, himself, and the servant maid. In the middle of the night they all went out, and got some distance from the house. In crossing a field, however, they were met by two soldiers, who inquired their business, &c. The maid answered that they were looking for a cow, when they were permitted to proceed. The soldiers had their arms, and his father had his gun. The maid and himself were left at a farm-house in the neighbourhood, and Mr. Rogers proceeded on his way towards London. Mr. Henry Rogers said that he was born in Crowan, and he apprehended so were most of his children; that his father, although bred a pewterer, had for many years occupied land in that parish.

All these circumstances, after so long an interval, were related to me by the old man with tears in his eyes.
It is curious to compare this account of the escape of one man, a woman, and a child, with the proclamation of the next day.

On the 8th January, 1816, I called at Skewis, and saw several holes in the partitions, made by shot of different sizes, when Mr Henry Rogers resisted the law in 1735.

I have an extract from a letter written by a Cornish gentleman in May 1735, who states that he had seen Rogers in the prison at Salisbury, when he seemed to rejoice in what he had done. And I have found in an account book of my great uncle, Mr Henry Davies, the following receipt:

"1st July 1735. Received of Mr Henry Davies, towards the taking of Henry Rogers, two pounds two shillings, per Francis Arthur."

A print of Rogers was soon after published with the following legend:

"Henry Rogers lived at a village called Skewis. He was so ignorant of the reason as well as the power of the law, that when a decree in Chancery went against him, he resisted all remonstrances, and fortified his house, making loopholes for his muskets, through which he shot two men of the posse comitatus who attended the Under-sheriff. A little after he shot one Hitchens, as he was passing the high road on his private business. He also fired through the window and killed one Tony, and would not suffer his body to be taken away to be buried for some days. At length the neighbouring justices of the peace assisted the constables, and procured an aid of some soldiers, one of whom he killed and afterwards made his escape; but at Salisbury, on his way towards London, he was apprehended and brought down to Cornwall when at the assizes in August 1735 five bills of indictment were found against him by the grand jury for the five murders aforesaid; to save the court time he was tried only on three of them, and found guilty of every one, before Lord Chief Justice Hardwick. As he lay in gaol after his conviction, the Under-sheriff coming in, he attempted to seize his sword, with a resolution to kill him, swearing he should die easy if he could succeed in that design. He was attended by several clergymen; but they could make no impression on his brutal stupidity, and he died at the gallows without any remorse."

Although no one attempted to justify the murders committed by Henry Rogers, there was, for a very long time after his death, a strong feeling of compassion entertained for his case, and it was popularly held in the neighbourhood that none of the subsequent proprietors of old Skewis would ever prosper in its possession. Some stated that it was later haunted. No one seems able to prove that theory, although a very interesting story was told to the writer when he visited Skewis in 1958. It came from Mrs Gordon Simmons of Skewis Cottage, a small residence on the opposite side of the road to Skewis farm. In 1897 she was living with her parents in Nancegollan. Suddenly her mother was taken ill, and so her father, Daniel Harrington went for the doctor, the nearest being at Camborne about five miles distant. In those days, of course, there were no motor vehicles in these country districts and the only transport was by horse or foot. On this occasion he travelled by the former. As Mr. Harrington was passing Skewis House the horse came to a standstill. Seemingly it had a premonition of an occurrence here in earlier days.

Mr. Harrington gave the horse a lump of sugar and it continued on its way safely. He reported this incident to the local police constable at Praze. Harrington collected the doctor at Camborne, together with the priest. On the return the policeman accompanied the trio back to Nancegollan. When the party reached Skewis all the horses shied, and stopped. The priest seemed the most surprised of all, and said a prayer against evil spirits. The horses were patted, given some more sugar, and then they carried on their way, as if nothing had happened. All arrived safely at Nancegollan.

Perhaps the finale of the story came in the evening when the priest was returning to Camborne. The horse did *not* stop at Skewis.

Various items of correspondence in connection with "The Siege of Skewis" have been preserved in Cornwall. At Penzance Library in the Borlase Collection we find a brief letter from Henry Rogers to Sir John St Aubyn.

SKEWIS; 9th March, 1743.
I was this day shot at three times by Bennetts, Pengwedna and Arthur Tuby and they say it was by your order, and if it is not your order I desire you may write to the bearer or any of your servants, but if it is, forebeare writing to your Honours Humble Servant.
(Signed)   H. ROGERS

Also in the Borlase Collection we find a draft letter from William Borlase dated at Ludgvan, 11 April, 1736. There is no clue to whom it is intended. The spelling is copied exactly:

As you desire me to give you the whole of the Skewish affair I cannot better than relate it in the words of Sir John St Aubyn who being nearest neighbour to the scene of the villainy consequently for his own sake, and his conscience as well as the reason of his office as Justice of the Peace exerting himself more than persons more remote thought themselves obliged to do, drew upon himself the particular odium of Rogers, and was not without just apprehensions of his house being burned down and himself assassinated.
When Rogers was brought to trial at Launceston, Lord Chief Justice Hardwicke returned thanks in the most publick and handsome manner to St Aubyn for his steady endeavours to put the laws of his country in execution and the regulation St John Aubyn got among all good men, and the consciousness of having done his duty during so open and unparralled defyance of all laws of humanity and England was all the recompense he had or desired for all his expense (which I have heard was not less than £500) and for what was much worse his being forced to have his own house and removed his family to Launceston where his lady even there not free from fears contracted so ill an habit of body as brought on a sensyble decay.

When the affair was over and Rogers hanged St. John drew up a short narration of the whole, and gave the papers to me. They are written in his own hand and the contents these:

"Henry Rogers was the second son of *(illegible)* Rogers and served his apprenticeship to a pewterer, he was a good workman, but being naturally idle, he ran himself in debt and deserted his business. His elder brother William Rogers at his death bequeathed his estate to his widow and not to his next brother, by which Henry Rogers thinking himselfe injured commenced a Chancery suit against the widow, and by violence turned her out of possession of the mansion house called Skewis. Chancery determining this suit in her favour. Henry Rogers in contempt of the decree kept possession, and upon the under-sheriff's coming in June 1734 to put her into possession, he and his wife appeared at the window with a gun between them, and though the undersheriff shewed him the authority by which he came, advised him to submit the decree, to seek redress in a legal way by appealing to the House of Lords, they both declared that they would rather dye than give up the estate, and that if he did not depart immediately they would shoot him, insisting upon a natural right to the estate (though by that rule Rogers' father's elder brother who was disinherited by the grandfather and is still alive would have had the best title). The undersheriff then read the proclamation hoped he would do him no personal injury for performing his duty and told him the danger of obstructing an officer in the execution of it, but this produced no other effect, but his damning the King, House of Lords and my Lord Chancellor and immediately the gun was discharged; then the undersheriff retired advising him to consider cooly of the matter till the next day, when he hoped he should find him in a better temper, but they no other wise considered of it than to engage a sett of foolhardy fellows by large promises to come into the house who were armed with guns which his wife had brought there, and she advised them to drink that they might be better qualified to assist them in this outrageous resistance. Having thus provided matters within doors, upon the second day of the undersheriff's coming, the wife was met with in the lanes solliciting others to stand by them in their villainys, and the undersheriff bringing her before three Justices of the Peace who mett at this time and making a proper deposition, they committed her to jail; this was all proved upon her by the evidence for the Crown the Grandjury found two bills against her, but she was not brought to tryal in hopes of her *(illegible)* and that the examples which were made would prove sufficient to prevent the like practises for the future.

At this second coming of the undersheriff (who had then required soldiers to the assistance of his possee) he found Rogers in a worse temper than before, for Rogers fired a gun at him from a narrow window which luckily missed him, but shot one of his bailiffs who dyed soon after this, and immediately after another gun went off from the house which killed a soldier upon the spot; the soldiers then discharged their muskets upon the house, and happily retired without further mischief.

The authority of the law being thus for a while suspended there arose many strange disorders at this time; Skewis became an asylum for all villains, the gentlemen of the two western Hundreds in a full body met, and their resolutions were printed and read by the authority of the Bishop by the ministers in the church of every parish, who likewise enforced the duty and advantage of submission to the laws; all sober people joyned in this work and His Majesty issued a proclamation enjoyning all magistrates to do their duty and offering great rewards for bringing Rogers and his accomplices to justice.

Rogers now grew jealous of many people, and one Hichens going accidentally through Skewis, which is a high road, on private business, unhappily mett him, and upon a bare suspicion only that he was not his friend, he insulted him and shot him, and dyed shortly after of the wound, and so far was he lost to all sensations of humanity, that when the corps was carrying through Skewis to his grave, he declared that if he thought he was not dead he would shoot him again.

After this he sent several messages to the constables that he would burn their houses and kill them, and he wrote a menacing letter to Sir John St. Aubyn a neighbouring Justice, and in order to get some of them within his reach, lay concealed in the house without fire or candlelight, meditating murder all that time; accordingly as one Tuby who was engaged with the constables was going through the place imagining him to be gone off for the reasons mentioned Rogers shot him from the window twice; and afterwards went out of his house, insulted the dead body with his gun, he threatened to shoot those who out of decency offered to carry off the dead man to his grave, and afterwards shot at one Richards who was active in it, declaring that he would cutt the other off in the same manner. The body lay there so long that it became very offensive, and the dogs licked about it, and he said he would cutt off the head and stick it upon his chimney and stiled it by the ignominious character of the black bull. The Civil Magistrates being unable to restrain these violences any longer were forced to call in the military power, and accordingly required soldiers to attend the constables in the discharge of their duty, they surrounded the house to prevent his escape and his receiving any provisions, but he soon grew impatient of this restraint, sally'd out of his house and fired at the commanding officer, but immediately retreated and then shot one of the soldiers from a window who died in a short time; afterwards they besieged the house in form but he found means to make his escape, and soon after by the vigilance of the magistrates in searching after him, and the large reward which the gentlemen of the country offered for taking him he abandoned the country.

It is remarkable that during the time of his rebellion against the lawes and murder, he committed theft and lived in a state of adultery with his servant maid, who escaped with him big with child and they lay by some time near Tavistock but being pursued there very narrowly he proceeded towards London. All the Mayors and Postmasters of the several towns and seaports were now advertised of him, and accordingly he was apprehended at Salisbury where he pretended to be one Cornish, and kept himselfe perpetually drunk; from thence he was brought by Habeas Corpus to Launceston where he was at the last Assizes try'd by my Lord Chief Justice Hardwick.

The Grand Jury found five bills of murder against him but to save time he was try'd upon three only and was convicted upon all three; he had nothing to say for himself, but even in court reviled the judge and his jury; after he was condemned he was most narrowly guarded to prevent his making away with himselfe, which he had often declared he would do; his wife was allowed to see him only in the presence of others for fear of her assisting him in that purpose, and indeed it would have been happy if she had not seen him at all for in their last interview instead of making his peace with God, she advised him to dye brave and with courage.

He was attended by several clergymen but to no purpose, for he attempted by catching the under sheriff's sword to kill him (but was prevented by the guard) and declared that he should dye easy if he could murder him and Sir John St. Aubyn; and though he was attended at the gallows by another clergyman, he did indeed dye with that false bravery with which too many such abandoned wretches go out of the world, reviling all law and authority and denouncing woe to them who were instruments of bringing him to justice. As he had in all five murders shown the greatest cowardice so when he came to dye he gave a further instance of his want of generosity and the baseness of his spirit by expressing no manner of concern for his fellow sufferer John Street though he kept constantly appealing to him as the author of his misfortunes. Thus the world got rid of this most audacious villain who bad difiance to the laws of God and man and was for breaking down those fences of that Society in which he lived.

There is a further draft letter from William Borlase dated at Ludgvan 14th April, 1735.

The resistance Rogers made to the under sheriff in which two men were killed was in the middle of June last. St. John Aubyn wrote circular letters to all Justices and Gentlemen of the two Hundreds of Penwith and Kerrier to meet at Redruth in order to concert measures how to remove so great a scandal to our country and apprehend and bring to justice the authors of it. They met accordingly in August and the declaration then drawn up and agreed upon to be made publick. There was also a private letter sent to the Sheriff to acquaint him that the opinion of the Gentlemen there present was that the most effectual method to the violint profession Rogers kept at Skewis and of apprehending him and bring him to justice was to make use of the assistance of the military power and to bring some cannon and batter down the house in order to save the lives that might be lost in storming it. What use the Sheriff made of this letter and of the unanimous resolution of these Gentlemen to assist him is yet a secret.

Things were now at a standstill for six months. Rogers in the meantime keeping his musket pointed out of the window and going armed where he pleased in open defyance of all law much to the regret of all sober men till about the middle of February last Rogers having killed another man and in March last a fourth walking the highway to his own home found themselves under necessity to call in the military power.

You will see by the above that our country could not express more detestation of the offence nor a more earnest desire to have such a flagrant contempt of all government brought to its deserved punishment and since his Majesty's kind orders for the Military to assist the civil power everything has been done by both to wipe off the reproach from this country by apprehending Rogers but hitherto indeed without effect.

I hope therefore that you and all other friends to our country as you justly may take all occasions of setting this matter in so candid a light as to let the reproach fall only when its entirely due I mean on the low illeterate vulgar in the neighbourhood of Skewis.

I have taken up a great deal of your time to inform you that our country gentlemen have neither been insensible of Rogers' offence nor looked idly on and saw open rebellion and murder committed. But since his Majesty has been graciously pleased to express all manner of satisfaction at the several steps his magistrates here have taken a vindication is happily become . . . . however just and proper a right information may be. We are very sensible how much we are obliged to his Majesty in the first place and all that we have to be concertied at now is that we did not apply sooner to those that have shown themselves in this affair such hearty friends to all law and government in general and (illegible) in particular.

I remain with respect to Mr. Harn.
W.B.

In Davies Gilbert's *Parochial History of Cornwall* (Pages 284-287) we find an address given to the Parish of Crowan by Sir John Aubyn.

As I am obliged to attend at the assizes, I must earnestly recommend the care of the parish in my absence to you, and hope that you will do your endeavours to prevent the very great expense and mischief which must otherwise fall upon us; although you do not at present seem to perceive the danger that threatens us; for the outrage and murder which happened in our parish have justly alarmed the government, and induced his majesty to issue out a proclamation, wherein he offers a reward of two hundred pounds for apprehending Henry Rogers, and one hundred pounds for each of the other offenders, together with a pardon to any who shall discover and apprehend them. He likewise commands all civil magistrates, upon pain of his majesty's displeasure, to be diligent in suppressing this riot, and bringing the authors of it to the punishment which their crimes deserve.

In obedience to this, I think myself obliged, in the faithful discharge of my duty for the preservation of the public peace, and the good of our own parish in particular, to admonish you and the principal inhabitants of it, to give me your aid and assistance in this dangerous and troublesome affair. His Majesty, as he declares in the proclamations, being firmly resolved to put an effectual stop to such enormous practices, hath by his warrant from the Secretary of War, sent orders to the commanders of regiments of soldiers at Exeter, to send to the Sheriff so many soldiers as he shall require and think sufficient to suppress this notorious violation of the laws of the land, and which certainly will be done by force of arms, if it cannot be stopped by a gentle and careful process. This is a true and exact state of cause; and whoever consider it with due temper, must be filled with the most melancholy apprehensions of the mischief that must happen, if every good subject and christian does not endeavour to keep off this evil, by endeavouring, as far as his influence can prevail, to make the usual method of bringing crimes to justice effectual.

It is for this reason I now write this letter to you, which I hope you will read with serious attention more than once, that it may have a good effect upon you. I myself can foresee, and I wish you likewise could, the dreadful inconvenience and expense of a regiment of soldiers sent down and quartered upon us; particularly this parish, being the unfortunate place of this disorder, must, in a much heavier manner, feel the burden of it. Consider the charges and the trouble of having every house in the parish filled with soldiers; consider what must be the consequence of abetting and supporting Rogers, whose house will be fired about his ears, and those lives which may be lost if he continues in his extravagance. Take notice, that I have done my duty as justice of the peace and a parishioner; and if you all likewise do yours, by encouraging a proper subjection to authority, and aiding the civil magistrates in discovering and bringing the offenders to justice, these dismal calamities may be prevented.

I think more reasonable to advise you of this, because there is too general a mistake and prejudice, or rather vicious encouragement shown, and that too by many who should and do know better, to the unhappy author of this disturbance. To pity the unfortunate is a virtuous character, even to those whose vices have made them so; but at the same time we ought to detect their crimes, and it is for the public good they should be punished; and this consideration ought to prevail over the concern we may feel for a private person. Murder is a crime of the basest nature, and what the law in common cases never forgives; but when it is committed on any officer in the execution of his duty, and in supporting the usurpation of another's right, and what the law shall determine such, it is certainly a more complicated guilt. Whosoever abets a murderer, or does what he can to conceal and defend him from justice, is in the eyes of God a murderer himself in cold blood. To justify a murderer is the strongest indication of a most base temper; and whosoever does not cry out against the misguided spirit of the people in behalf of Henry Rogers, deserves that character.

Whilst the law-suit was depending all people were at liberty to weigh on either side. It does at first sight seem a little hard that one brother should give away an estate from another; and there must be some strong provocation to make it appear reasonable; but the circumstances of the whole case are not known, and therefore no man is able to form a true judgement of it; not even to pass harsh censures on particular persons; but when the law has determined right, all people must submit to that determination; otherwise no man is secure in his property, but a number of idle resolute fellows may wrest it from him, and declare that in their opinion he has an unjust title to it. So that if you give your estate by will unequally among your children, as they may have behaved more or less dutiful to you, that which has the least may take the other's part from him; or another relation may possibly hire such another mob, to take away the whole from them. We shall not at such times see property determined by judge and jury, but by force of arms, and the richest and most powerful man will be able to swallow up all the estates of his lesser neighbours.

The law is the only protection of our lives and estates, and if that is once set aside, we must hold them only by the base sanction of a giddy rabble. The law therefore should be strictly maintained by all such who have any possessions. The inferior people indeed, who have nothing to lose, will be at all times for breaking down the fences, that they may have some share of the common plunder. I should mention one instance. Suppose any of you had bought this estate of the late Rogers, being advised by your lawyer that he had the power to sell it, (which he certainly had, as the law has declared he had a right of giving it away,) you would then think it very hard that the present Rogers, with his wicked crew, should come and take it away by force, and afterwards keep it as he now does. Suppose the money you paid him for it he gave to his widow; should you in such a case agree that 'tis his brother's right to have the estate? Let every one make this his own case.

I believe you all honest men, and won't suspect any one of you to justifying this affair; but I have put these arguments into your mouths to warn other people from this vicious way of thinking, and that you may exert yourselves in keeping this hardship from the parish, from which I could never learn this Rogers deserved so much kindness as to suffer on his account; for he never paid church, priest, or poor, when he was in possession of the estate, and withheld from many their just due. The character of the honest and just man is to relieve the poor, to pity the unfortunate; but to use their utmost endeavours to punish the guilty, and to recommend and enforce an obedience to the laws of the land, which are the only protection of our lives and properties.

> I am, gentlemen,
> Your friend and servant,
> JOHN ST. AUBYN.

At the County Museum, Truro in the Hawkins Manuscript Collection there is further correspondence in connection with "The Siege of Skewis".

1. Letter:
    James Tillie to (Sir John St. Aubyn)
    Asks if Rogers has given up possession of Skewis I presume you will not think it prudent to suffer such an insult upon the laws to pass without making use of other means in order to shew your detestation and abhorrence of it, and to bring the offenders to justice, the contrary whereof would be giving encouragement to the whole body of tinners to triumph upon the noble stand their Bro. Rogers has made and from his example to defy the execution of the law... my under sheriff shall attend you in order to communicate your orders to the forces now at Penzance — as soon as I know your sentiments whether an attack upon the house may be made with any tolerable security without cannon, or whether any safer approach may be made underground".
    August 11th 1734

2. Letter:
Sir John St. Aubyn to Mr. Pawley at Ginevin Lelant. Enclosing copy of letter from the Sheriff (Tillie).
*The forcible possession of Henry Rogers at Skewis and the murders which have happened upon the
sheriff's attempting to remove it by his authority, the disposition of the low people too prone to resist all
law, and the little effect which the endeavours of the Justices of the Peace (who have hitherto acted in this
affair, and who now find themselves unequal to so great a task) in order to suppress this unruly spirit, and
to bring the offenders to punishment have met with us likewise the contempt which has been shewn to
the more immediate authority of the Crown, which has been so justly alarmed as to think it proper to
issue out a Proclamation upon this occasion, are so many melancholy considerations, that it now becomes
a matter of such universal concernment, that I doubt not but that all gentlemen who have properly to
preserve, and are willing to live under the sanction and protection of the laws, will think it their interest
as well as duty, in obedience to his Majesty's Proclamation immediately to consider of measures pro-
perest to be taken by the sheriff to facilitate the execution of the laws, and to prevent the effusion of any
more blood......... The flame is kindled here, but it has so much combustible matter to prey upon that
God only knows where it may end.*

Proposes meeting of JPs and local gentry (from Clowance) August 1734.

3. Letter:
Sir John St. Aubyn to Christopher Hawkins. Asks his opinion on action to be taken and to meet him and
Davy Haweis *"tomorrow"*. (from Clowance) August 25th, 1734

4 . (Corrected draft) Letter from JPs and gentry of the two western Hundreds — to the Sheriff.
*"We are of the opinion that any other methods in order to remove this force at Skewis than battering
down the house with some cannon proper for that purpose and laying it flat with the ground, will greatly
hazzard the lives of severall of his Majesty's subjects, and at the last prove allso uneffectual. In order
therefore to do this we are of opinion that it would be proper for you to require part of the detachment of
soldiers now at Penzance to attend you who have orders from his Majesty to act in obedience to your commands, if this madman at Skewis shall make it necessary for you to use force to strengthen your
authority".*
(from Redruth) August 29th, 1734

5 . Letter: The Duke of Newcastle to Sir John St. Aubyn. *To the effect that His Majesty approves of the JPs
having called in the aid of the Military from Penzance has ordered Brigadier General Barrell's Regiment
at Exeter to be ready if further assistance required. (from Whitehall) March 25th, 1735*

6 . Letter: Lord Pembroke to Sir John St. Aubyn. Announcing Rogers' capture.

*"Rogers gott up behind the Blanford coach to Salisbury, and the coachman knowing him by the descrip-
tion to (illegible) care to drink with him so as to have a good opportunity of taking him, which he did and
found in his pockets two brace of pistols with 15 bullets.........*

*I believe the man that took him is one Twogood who lets coach horses and not the man that drove the
Blanford coach which he got behind for his passage".* April 19th, 1735

PAPERS FROM THE TRIAL OF HENRY ROGERS

TO SAVE TIME AT LAUNCESTON ASSIZE COURT, ROGERS WAS TRIED ON ONLY THREE
OF THE MURDERS AND FOUND GUILTY, TOGETHER WITH JOHN STREET, HIS PRIN-
CIPAL PARTISAN, OF THEM ALL.

Launceston, August 1st, 1735.

The King against Henry Rogers and John Street.

Indictment for murder of William Carpenter, by shooting him in the back with a gun charged with
leaden bullets, 19th June, 1734, at Crowan, in com. Cornub.

Plea, Not Guilty.

Sergeant Chapple pro Rege.

STEPHEN TILLIE was under-sheriff in 1734. 8th June, 1734 received a writ of assistance under the
great seal. 31 Maij, 7 Geo. II. writ of assistance, reciting the writ of execution of the decree and writ of injunction, whereby possession was to be delivered to Anne Rogers, commanding to put Anne Rogers into
possession and to remove and expel the said Henry Rogers, his tenants, and accomplices, from possession
of the premises.

18 June he went to the house; the prisoner was in the window, and held a gun at him; he called to him,
and told that he had the King's writ, and must have possession; would not meddle with his person.

Prisoner said Lord Chancellor made an unjust decree. He said that then he might deliver possession and
appeal. Swore, damm him, he would not deliver possession. Saw two or three hundred people. Read the
proclamation. The prisoner fired a gun, burned his wig and singed his face. One of the officers said he

was shot through the head. Expostulation again. Then he swore if the King and Lord Chancellor came he would not deliver it. Several guns were fired. He told him he would give him till tomorrow morning eight o'clock.

Sent to Captain Sadler for a few soldiers; and captain sent them; he went with them; he demanded entrance. Prisoner said, "Damm you, are you come again?"

A gun mounted out of the hole cut in the door within an inch of his body discharged; and it shot Carpenter, who fell with it, and said he was a dead man.

Another gun fired, and shot Hatch, his servant. Rogers had a gun in his hand when he first saw him, and afterwards came out with a gun in his hand. Carpenter was a bailiff to the sheriff, and he had commanded him to go to his assistance. Mrs. Rogers, the plaintiff, was there both times.

GEORGE ELLIS. 18 June was desired by Mrs. Rogers to go with them. Rogers and his wife in the window, and had a gun between them. Mr. Tillie demanded possession. Prisoner said he would not, swore and cursed, and said he had strength enough to defend his possession against any person; insisted the estate was his. The under-sheriff expostulated with him, and told him if he had a right, his best way was to submit to the law. Sheriff read the proclamation. Rogers asked him to drink a dram; he went for it, and in the meantime his wife held a gun; guns were fired.

19 June went again. Under-sheriff told him he hoped he was in a better mind now, and would deliver him possession. Refused. A gun fired from the house. Soon after, heard it called out that Carpenter was shot in the back, and a soldier shot in the groin. He is a surgeon, and dressed Carpenter; found him shot from about the fourth rib to the buttock; many slugs and jagged pieces of lead on it.

Between two and three hundred men were there the first day, and a great many the second day, but not so many. Sir J. St. Aubyn having sent out his steward, heard the under-sheriff ask him who were in the house. He said only his own servants.

No gun was fired or any force used by any of the under-sheriff's company till Carpenter was shot.

Mr. LUKEY, surgeon. Found a gun-shot wound in the small of his back. He saw him on Wednesday the 19th, died on Friday. It was a great quantity of small shot; thinks the wound went through into his belly.

SAMUAL HATCH, servant to Mr. Tillie, the under-sheriff. 18th was there. The under-sheriff read the King's writ to him. He did not see who fired the gun, but saw no man in the house that day but Rogers, whom he knows.

Cannot say he saw Rogers fire the first time. Carpenter was shot, and another soldier shot, and two men wounded before any of the soldiers or sheriff's company fired. He was shot with slugs.

RICHARD VINSAM. Was there the first day and the sheriff read and showed him the writ; told Rogers that if he would try the cause again he should be as ready to put him in as to take him out. He was there again the second day. The sheriff told him he was come again to do his office, and desired him to be easy. Gives same account, and that the soldiers did not fire till after Carpenter was shot.

AS TO STREET

EDWARD WILLIAMS. Was at Skewis House on the 19th day of June, 1734. Saw John Street there in the house, with a sword in his hand. Kept people in the house, and said he would run anybody through that offered to go away, said now was the time to do a friend service; assisted Rogers by keeping persons in by force; the sheriff was then come to demand possession.

Street was in the house when the firing was.

Rogers' wife was apprehended by the time the under-sheriff came to the house.

MR. BLACK, ensign, was there with the soldiers; with the others; had orders from the commanding officer to attend the sheriff. No firing by the soldiers or the sheriff's company till Carpenter and soldier killed.

JOHN ELLETT was one of the soldiers; with the others who went with the under-sheriff to assist him. Agrees with the rest that Carpenter was shot from that part of the house where he saw Rogers. There was no firing by the soldiers or the sheriff's assistants till Carpenter was wounded.

HENRY JEFFRIES was corporal to the party, heard the under-sheriff read the proclamation, demand entrance; when Rogers refused.

Carpenter went up and struck at the door; and as he turned about was shot in the back; he was shot in the leg; had orders from the under-sheriff to fire.

THE PRISONER. Had good counsel, and thought he had a good right to the estate; was unwilling to deliver it up the first day; told him he intended to appeal; said if he did not deliver possession he might bring a writ of rebellion against him.

Sheriff swore he would have possession. Sheriff went off and did not expect to see him again. Next morning heard the soldiers were coming; sent his wife out; they seized her. With beat of drum Sheriff and soldiers came and fired at him; the soldiers fired about five rounds a piece.

HENRY BERRIMAN. 18 day of June saw the Sheriff go, and heard him demand entrance; and the prisoner said he should have none. The next day the Sheriff came with the soldiers: but he was two coits cast off; the soldiers were on the eastern side of the house: the soldiers fired three rounds; but he did not see the gun from out of the house.

Carpenter was shot on the eastern side of the house; and he was on the western side of the house; the under-sheriff desired him to carry him off. Did not see Carpenter receive the shot.

Was not on the same side of the house when Carpenter was shot; as far off as the tower of this town from this place. (Carpenter was on the eastern side of the house when he was shot)

THOMAS PENDARVES. Rode through the town just as the soldiers came with the sheriff; saw Henry Rogers' wife; was on the south side of the house where the firing was first; but that was on the east side of the house; however, thinks he could distinguish whether it came from the house or the soldiers, because the firing from the house was by single pops now and then, and the soldiers shot many together. To his sight and perception the first firing was by the soldiers. Can't say anymore. He was not on the east side at all. A great number of people assembled. HENRY JOHNS was in company with Carpenter; said he forgave Mr Rogers.

JOHN ROGERS saw Carpenter in his bed, and drank with him. He asked how he came to throw a great stone. He said he did not know; but he freely forgave the man that shot him; for if they had not been merciful they might have destroyed them all.

JOHN STREET was at the house at his labour. Writ of execution of the decree then read.

MR JOHN HAWKINS was solicitor for Mrs Rogers; went with the Sheriff; demanded possession; saw a gun fired from the house: did not hurt; saw Carpenter actually shot and fall; no firing by the soldiers till after that of two other guns.

VERDICT: BOTH GUILTY OF MURDER
SENTENCE: DEATH BY HANGING.

The King against Henry Rogers and John Street. Indictment for the murder of George Woolston alias Wilson, with a gun charged with leaden bullets 19th June 1734, at Crowan, in com. Cornub.

Plea, Not Guilty.

Sergeant Chapple, pro Rege.
Writ of Execution, Injunction, and Writ of Assistance, put in.

MR TILLIE. Gives the same account that he did before. Second day after Carpenter was shot, Henry Rogers came to the window with his gun on the east side, fired, and a shot went through his hat, and a soldier wounded. He ordered the soldiers to fire. Woolston was on the west side, and was shot there. No gun was fired by the soldiers, or any person in the assistance of the sheriff, now a sword drawn, nor any force, till after Carpenter was shot and Hatch wounded, and Jeffries shot through the leg. Woolston declared that Rogers had shot him, on his asking him. Died in about half an hour after. Soldiers went to the assistance of him; ordered them to use no force till resistance.

JOHN ELLET. He was on the east side of the house; he carried off Woolston; was shot from the waistband of his breeches to the buckle of his shoes. Gives the same account as to the occasion. There was no firing on the eastern side of the house till after Carpenter was killed and Jeffries shot in the leg.

NICHOLAS DANIEL was serjeant, and went to Skewis House. After the first firing William Carpenter was killed. The officer ordered him to go with ten men to the west side of the house. As soon as he came into the court, saw the prisoner Rogers come to the window and fire his gun and shot Woolston, of which he died in an hour.

Cross-examined. After Carpenter was killed, some of the soldiers had fired on the east side of the house before he went to the west side.

Samuel Hatch gives the same account as before of the facts on 18th and 19th June. The first guns which were fired were by persons that were withinside of the house, and not by persons that were withoutside of the house. No firing by the soldiers, or any in assistance of the sheriff, till after one was killed and two wounded.

GEORGE ELLIS. The same as before. Saw Woolston go with the soldiers to the west side of the house. Soon afterwards heard a cry that Woolston was shot. Went and saw him. He was shot from the groin to the ankle. He was then in a manner dying; died of that wound. The first firing from within the house, before the Sheriff had finished the concluding words of the proclamation; three guns fired before the soldiers fired.

RICHARD VINSAM. Saw Rogers looking out at the window. Several guns fired before the sheriff had quite finished the proclamation. No guns fired by the soldiers till they had fired from the house.

MR. BLACK. After the firing from the east side, ordered eight or ten soldiers to go round to the west

HENRY ROGERS Pewterer of the County of *CORNWALL*.

Henry Rogers liv'd at a Village call'd Skewis. He was so ignorant of the Reason as well as of the Power of the Law, that when a Decree in Chancery went against him, he resisted all remonstrances, and fortify'd the House, making loup Holes for his Muskets, through which he shot two men of the Posse Comitatus, who attended the under Sheriff. A little after, he shot one Hitchens as he was passing the high Road on his private Business. He also fir'd through the Window and kill'd one Toby and would not suffer his Body to be taken away to be buried for some Days. At length the neighbouring Justices of the Peace, assisted the Constables and procur'd an Aid of some Soldiers, one of whom he kill'd and afterward made his Escape; but at Salisbury on his way towards London, he was apprehended and brought down to Cornwall, where at the Assizes in August 1735, five Bills of Indictment were found against him by the Grand Jury, for the five Murders aforesaid, to save the Court Time, he was try'd only on three of them, and found, guilty of every one, before Ld. cheif Justice Hardwick. As he lay in Gaol after his Condemnation, the under Sheriff coming in, he Attempted to seize his Sword with a Resolution to kill him; swearing he should die easy if he could succeed in ye Design. He was attended by several Clergymen, but they could make no impression on his brutal Stupidity, and he died at the Gallows without any remorse.

side, and soon heard Woolston was shot. No firing by the soldiers till after from the house.

MR. JOHN HAWKINS. 19th, no gun fired from the soldiers till after Carpenter dropped.

PIERCY PRICE. 18th March last at Skewis. Was with the soldiers when they took possession. Rogers looked out of the little door. Asked him how he came to let a man lay unburied who was there? Owned "I killed him. As to the old soldier that was killed, I had no animosity against him. It is true I killed him, but it was time, he was too proud; intended to kill the sheriff and his men."
AS TO STREET.

EDWARD WILLIAMS. Was there when Woolston was killed. Street was on the inside of the house at the western door when Woolston was killed. Had a sword drawn. He asked to go out. Street said if he offered to do it he would run through; hindered him and another from going out; said if they would do a friend any good or service now was the time; the service was to keep the possession against the sheriff. The prisoner Rogers thought his appeal had been lodged.

HENRY BERRYMAN. The soldiers fired upon the house about three times before they parted to different sides of the house; did not see Carpenter shot, nor does not know when he was shot; was as far off as the length of the whole hall; did not see Street there.

THOMAS PENDARVES. By his perceivance the soldiers fired first. Stood on the south side of the house, two hundred yards off; did not see either Carpenter or Woolston shot.

John Street had no evidence.
VERDICT: BOTH GUILTY. OF MURDER
SENTENCE: DEATH BY HANGING.

The King against Henry Rogers.

Indictment for the murder of Andrew Willis, alias Tubby, by shooting him in the breast on the 16th of March at Crowan.
Plea, Not Guilty.
Serjeant Chapple, pro Rege.

EDWARD BENNETT. Was a constable, and on 16th March called Andrew Willis, alias Tubby, to give his assistance to take the prisoner Rogers at Skewis House on account of murders that he had committed. Tubby was about sixty yards from the house, and he saw a gun fired from a window of the house; immediately on that Tubby fell down; he ran off; immediately saw Rogers in the window from which the fire came; afterwards saw Rogers come out to the man and walk round him and take Tubby's gun, but before Rogers came out another gun was fired; saw one or two more at the window afterwards; intended to apprehend him and bring him to Launceston.

JOHN WILLIAMS. Was with Bennett and Tubby at the constable's desire to take Mr. Rogers, but ordered them not to shoot without necessity; about sixty yards off the house saw Tubby on his knee, almost before he heard the report of the gun; immediately saw Rogers in the window with a gun in his hand; thought Rogers was gone out of his house. Tubby cried, "Lord! Lord!" and fell down. Another gun fired, and he crept away through the hedge.

HENRY THOMAS. Saw Rogers on 16th March, with a gun walk by the dead body forwards and backwards. Said, "Here lies the black Bill."

HENRY JAMES. Was called to assist William John the constable the Sunday that Tubby lay dead at Skewis; saw the prisoner with a gun within twelve feet of the body. Prisoner said, "Sir Andrew, thou didst make thy brag last Sunday that thou wouldst lend me a brace of bullets, but I think I have paid thee." Asked them to come in and drink a dram; refused. He said, "If he would, he would make them come into the castle." They went away, and we retired. Rogers stood in the lane with a gun in his hand, bid them turn in; said, Sir John St. Aubyn would be angry if they had any thing to do with any body in the house. He said, "Damn them, if they did not he would shoot them." Asked, if they knew who killed the man? "No." Said, "There was a black man lay dead in the moor, if any body would own him they should have him. I have the bill," produced the gun; "Damn him, if they don't come and own him, I'll cut off his head and stick it on the chimney."

JAMES FALL. Heard the gun go off. Heard somebody say, "Take up the man." He ran out, and Rogers looked out of his window, asked, what he was going for? said, "To see what you have done: you will be hanged at last." Said,
"If you do not go back, I will shoot you too." Said to him, "Did not I tell you to tell Sir John, that I would take them off as he would fetch them." He said "fetch them?"

Prisoner. That these people followed him and endeavoured to shoot him.

VERDICT: GUILTY OF MURDER
SENTENCE: DEATH BY HANGING.

An addition which appears to have been made to a charge delivered by Lord Hardwicke, Chief Justice on Western Circuit in 1735.

Of the truth of this observation and of the pernicious consequences of lawless force, you of this country have lately had a flagrant but an instructive instance. In that you have seen from what small springs a torrent of violence may arise. How people once engaged in such practices, go on from invading the property, to taking away the lives of their subjects; and from an obstinate contemptuous opposition to the regular decisions of the ordinary Courts of Justice, they advance almost to open rebellion.

The honourable and indefatigable endeavours of the gentlemen of this country to reform and suppress such daring outrages cannot be sufficiently commended, and must always be remembered highly to their honour. And happy it is that these endeavours, enforced by the seasonable and gracious assistance of his majesty, had the desired effect. To consider this affair in its full extent, it ought on the one hand to be looked upon as a strong proof that the King will make use of the extraordinary as well as the ordinary powers of his government, only for protection and security of his people; and on the other hand, that the gentlemen of England will unite in the support of the laws, and of legal, well established government, against all attempts of any kind whatsoever to introduce disorder and confusion.

So great were the apprehensions entertained of a man who had in this extraordinary manner, and for months set at defiance the whole authority of the country, that, immediately after his absconding, the magistrates of the hundred issued the following proclamation:

Cornwall. — To all Magistrates, Headboroughs and Officers of Towns and Parishes, to whom these presents shall come.

Whereas several murders have lately been committed by Henry Rogers, of Skewis, in the parish of Crowan, in the county of Cornwall, and whereas the said Henry Rogers and his gang did last night abscond and withdraw themselves from justice, notwithstanding a strict guard of soldiers and others which were placed about the house at Skewis to prevent their escape, and any further mischiefs that might ensue from their wicked intentions and intrigues of the said Henry Rogers and his abettors; And whereas they withhdrew from Skewis with their guns and ammunition, whereby it is suspected that they will plunder and ravage the whole country: — We therefore desire you to transmit this to the next town, that it may go through the whole country, not only that all his Majesty's good and peaceable subjects may be guarded against the said Rogers and his gang, but that they may do their utmost endeavours to apprehend them, and bring them to their trial, that all such horrid practices, which threaten destruction to society and government, may for the future be prevented, the public peace preserved, and the authors of such infamous disorders be brought to condign punishment.

We are, with much respect, gentlemen,

Your most humble servants,

> John St Aubyn
> John Borlase
> William Arundell

Launceston, August 1 1735[1]

This day came on before the Lord Chief Justice Hardwick, the trials of Henry Rogers and John Street, one of his assistants, for murders committed in opposing the Sheriff of Cornwall in the execution of his office.

Rogers was arraigned upon five indictments, and Street upon two. The trials began about seven in the morning and ended about two in the afternoon. Rogers was tried upon the three first indictments, and being found guilty on all three, the Court thought it unnecessary to proceed upon the other two. Street was found guilty of the two indictments against him. And they both received sentence of death before the Court rose.

The Counsel for the king were Mr. Serjeant Chapple and Fortescue, jun. The Counsel for the criminals Mr. Pratt and Mr Draper. The Solicitor for the Treasury Richard Pacton, Esq. was also there on the part of the Crown, he being sent down purposely to prosecute the affair.

THE ROGERS FAMILY of KILLIVOSE in the Parish of CAMBORNE and later of CROWAN[2]

The purpose of this research into the Rogers family of Camborne is an attempt to establish the ancestry of the unfortunate Henry Rogers of Crowan who was to be hung, at Launceston in 1735 for defending his right to the ownership of a farm of the name of Skewis in Crowan, claimed by his sister-in-law, widow of his elder brother William. Henry Rogers was said to have been a pewterer and it will be easier in this narrative if he is distinguished from his grandfather by calling him 'the pewterer'.

The story of the siege of Skewis is told in Baring-Goulds 'Cornish Characters and Strange Events' and even more fully in Davies Gilbert's Parish History of Crowan. This is not an attempt to vindicate Rogers, who was hung for the murder of men attempting to evict him from Skewis, but to suggest that the property had, in fact, been left to him under the will of his father Matthew Rogers of Camborne and that he was correct in his claim of ownership.

---

1 Weekly miscellany; Saturday, 9th August 1735. No CXXIX kept at British Museum.

[2]Mrs Betty Farrell of Mawnansmith compiled some valuable notes on the Rogers Family and with her kind permission they are reproduced above.

To recount the story — Briefly; after the death of William Rogers, who was childless, a will had been produced, giving, it was said all the property at Skewis where he was apparently living at the time of his death, to his widow Ann, but Henry who believed the will to be spurious, waited until his sister-in-law was away from home, turned the servants out of the house and took possession. It appeared that Henry had public sympathy and had he waited and restrained from violence, he might even have received the support of Sir John St. Aubyn of Clowance, in Crowan, a leading figure in both Parish and County. However, William's widow had appealed to the law, the Sheriff received instructions to evict Henry by force, and in June 1734, two men were killed by shots from the house and the Sheriff himself only narrowly escaped.

The following day the Sheriff returned, with some soldiers, one of whom was shot and killed. After this, for some reason, Henry was allowed to remain quietly in possession until March 1735 when soldiers were again brought in and the siege was said to have continued for several days, with the loss of two more men. Cannon were then brought from Pendennis Castle and the following night Henry escaped and travelled on foot as far as Salisbury, his intention being to bring his case before the King (George II) but he was apprehended and removed to Cornwall where he, with John Street an accessory were tried, sentenced to death and duly executed. Murder had been committed and the penalty had been paid, but was Henry within his rights in claiming that Skewis was his property and was the will produced by his sister-in-law, a forgery?

Wills now available at the Cornwall County Record Office, would seem to indicate that this was the case, namely a will made in 1702 by Matthew Rogers, father of Henry and William, by which William received property in Camborne and Henry received tenements in Skewis in Crowan, and William's own will made in 1725 and proved in 1728 in which no specific properties are mentioned. The inventory to the will, however, names the properties in Camborne, but again there is no mention whatsoever of Skewis.

To clarify the ancestry of this family, it is now necessary to return to Camborne, and to an area known as Killivose, lying to the south of the parish and not a great distance from the Crowan parish boundary. Killivose lies close to the road leading from Camborne to Helston, about 3½ miles north of Skewis, the subject of the later troubles. The Camborne Parish Church Rate Book shows an entry in 1666 when Henry Rogers, grandfather of Henry of Crowan, paid a rate of 5/- for 'his part in Killivose'. The previous year, this rate was paid by Peter Pendarves, Gent. Henry Rogers had married, in Camborne, in 1660, one Rebecca Coath. No record has been found in the Parish Registers of the baptisms of either Henry or Rebecca, and it may well be that they both came from Illogan families, where the names of Coath and Rogers appear earlier. Although the name of Coath does appear twice in the early entries in the Rate Book, namely William Coath, of 'Laytie' and Henry Coath of Buswin, in 1649.

Henry of Camborne was a yeoman, as was his second son Matthew, father of William and Henry, the Pewterer. His eldest son, Edward, was described as 'of Gwinear'. Edward does not come into the story, although he received property under his father's will and was married in Camborne. Henry and Rebecca had a number of children, but only three appear to have survived, Edward, Matthew and a daughter named Rebecca, who married John Davy of Crowan. Henry increased his property considerably before his death in 1702. In 1667 he was also paying a rate on 'part of Tolkarne' and in 1671 on property in 'Chengweth'(Chynoweth). In 1678 he added Humphrys Tenement in Killivose, previously owned by Richard Pendarves, and after Henry's death occupied by his widow, Rebecca. By 1668 'Condurra' and 'part of Meanes Tenement' had been added to his holding and according to his will made in 1697, he held a number of 'tyn bounds'. His name appears many times in the Rate Book as one of the "Twelve Men" and by 1697 the Accounts show him as 'Mr Henry Rogers', an indication that his status had risen in the Parish. He and many of his family were buried within the Parish Church, and he left £2.10 in his will to the Poor of Camborne and a similar amount to the Poor of Illogan. A detailed account appears in the Camborne Accounts of the disposal of this money which had been received from his Executor, Matthew Rogers, on October 20th 1702. A list of names was added together with the amounts received. At the time of Henry's death he was paying a total rate of 27/6 for his various properties, and his will indicated that an earlier deed or marriage article had been executed before he made his will in 1697, had made provision for his son Matthew, and his wife Rebecca, because thy are not given any specific property by the will.

Matthew, in fact only survived his father by about eighteen months, and his name does not appear in the Rate Book at all, the next entry following Henry's being the name of 'The Widdow Rogers'. This is not Henry's widow, who now paid the rate on Humphry's Tenement in Killivose, but Matthew's widow, Mary, who continued to pay the rates for Killivose and Chynoweth, Condurrow and part of Mean's tenement until her own death in 1709.

Matthew Rogers had married in Breage in 1695. He would have been about 23 years of age and he married Mary Rowe. An interesting entry in the Camborne Rate Book for 1697 'Mr Henry Rogers kept of his 3 rates towards the buryall of a poor man of Breage that dyed in his house, 4/-' is another indication of the family connection with Breage. Matthew and Mary were the parents of William and Henry of the Skewis tragedy. There was also a daughter, Jane, who married Richard Morris of Crowan, and John, a younger son, who was to marry Margaret Hocken at Camborne and was probably the 'John Rogers' who was paying rates for part of Killivose at least until 1760.

Matthew was about 30 when he died. His will is clear and comprehensive. Although his children were so young, ranging from 5 years down to ten months, he appointed them executors of his will, with his wife, his father in law, John Rowe, and his brother, Alexander Rowe of Helston, to be guardians and overseers of his will... His first bequest is to Henry, his second son, two tenements in Skewis, Next he bequeaths to John, his youngest son, Trevean in Perranuthnoe, and to Jane the tenement and appurtenances in Buscaverran in Crowan. To his mother, Rebecca, he leaves two of his best cows.

The remainder of his goods and chattels he leaves to his four children. Mary his wife, does not specifically receive anything, but her own will a few years later shows that she had a tenement in Killivose known as Treweek's Tenement, so Matthew had evidently made provision for her prior to his death. William Trevarthen, according to Matthew's will, was an uncle 'late in possession of Buscaverran'. Perhaps Skewis and Buscaverran both came into Matthew's hands through his relationship with this family, no mention having been made of either property until 1702. Edward Rogers was probably his uncle, his father's elder brother. His signature to the inventory was well written but William Trevarthen only made his mark.

Also attached to the will is a document made in 1708 concerning the guardianship of the children, signed by John and Alex. Rowe, Edward Rogers and Mary Rogers made her mark. She herself died the following year. Rates were paid in her name until 1709 and from 1710 until 1717, by 'the heirs of Matthew Rogers'. In 1717 William came of age and the rates are paid in his name. Rebecca, his grandmother, again becomes 'The Widdow Roggers' paying 4/- for her 'tenement in Killivose': William pays a total of 19/- for the 'heirs' property.

In 1720 Rebecca's name appears in the church account; when 6/8 was paid for her grave, but there is no entry of her death in the registers until 1721, so she may have anticipated her death by ensuring her place in the church with her husband. Rebecca is an interesting figure. Taking her age at the time of her marriage in 1660 to have been 20 or thereabouts, she lived to quite a good age for those days, and outlived at least one of her two remaining sons. She had borne eight children but only three had survived to marry and have children themselves. Her name 'Coath' is of interest because of the famous Dolcoath Mine in Camborne, one of the early mines, said to have been working by 1720 'if not before'. Unfortunately, no will or inventory are available for Rebecca.

The next will of interest is that of Mary Rogers (née Rowe), but there is no inventory. She only survived her husband, Matthew, by seven years and the children were still young, the eldest being 13 and the youngest 7. Mary had property of her own to leave, in Marazion, and this she left to William, the eldest. To Henry and John, she left a tenement in Killivose known as Treweeks Tenement. This may have been the part of Killivose occupied, in 1688 by Richard Treweeke and by 1696 by the 'Widdow Treweek' and in 1705 by 'Zenoby Treweeks'.

Mary owned part of a messuage or tenement here which was evidently producing a rent, because she directs Henry and John to pay to their sister, Jane an amount of £40 when she should attain the age of 21. To James Hawking of the parish of Camborne she bequeathed a field or close of barley then growing, known by the name of Parkwreglas in Killivose and to the poor of Camborne the sum of 55/- to be paid at the festival of all saints next following her death.

She appoints her eldest son, 13 year old William, to be her executor, he to pay his sister Jane a further £20 on attaining the age of 21 and her brothers John and William Row and her cousin Alexander Row of Resugian in the parish of St. Hilary and her brother in law, John Davy of Crowan (husband of Matthew's sister, Rebecca) to be guardians and overseers of her will.

The four children, William and Henry, the subject of the Skewis drama, and Jane and John, were now orphaned, but as Rebecca their grandmother was still living at Humphrys Tenement in Killivose, it is reasonable to suppose that at least some of them remained there, because William took over the responsibility for paying rates there in 1717 and, later, after William's death, it seems that the youngest brother, John was still there and the rates continued to be paid in his name until 1760, after which the name of Rogers ceases. One interesting thing about John and his family is that his daughter, Mary, was to marry Andrew Mill in 1750 and in 1741 one Thomas Mill paid 7/6 rates for 'Killivose and Chynoweth', the same amount that was paid by Matthew's Heirs in 1712.

Now we come to William, whose widow was to cause all the trouble at Skewis. In 1722 he was paying 24/6 rates which by then included his grandmother's part, Humphry's Tenement. In 1723 he married, at St. Hilary, Ann Millet of St. Erth. The Millets were quite a prominent family in those parts. The marriage was witnessed by Humphry and Leonard Millet, Churchwardens. These may well have been the pewterer family of Marazion (J.R.I.C. 1969 etc.) and there was 'Wheal Millet' in Crowan (Essays in Cornish Mining History etc.). William and Ann were childless and, again the husband was to die before he reached the age of 30.

William made his will in 1725 when he was described as 'of Camborne'. He was buried in 1729 again in the Church at Camborne. At the time the will was made, there was obviously no ill-feeling to his younger brother, Henry, because his first bequest is £5 to be paid to Henry within a month of his brother's death. He gives exactly the same amounts to his brother John and sister Jane, now the wife of Richard Morrish of Crowan. To William son of John Davies of Crowan he gives 'the sume of one broad piece of Gold to the value of 25/-' and to the poor of the parishes of Camborne and Crowan £2.10 each. He makes his wife, Anne, his sole heiress and executrix of all his lands and tenements etc., to do with as she thought proper and there is no mention at all of any specific property. The will is witnessed by William Davies (twice) and George Davies.

Now comes the query as to what happened between the making of the will and William's death in 1729. An interesting point is that in the very full inventory to the will made in 1729 by John Davey of Camborne, Yeoman, William Davies of St. Hilary and Martin Harry of Lugan, Gent, William, is described as 'late of the parish of Crowan......... Gent.........' This may indicate that he had left Killivose and moved into Skewis where his widow was said to have been living after his death. However, it does not seem to have been regarded as his property because there is no mention of it in the inventory which does give in detail all his other holdings at Killivose. There is one clue to the situation contained in the inventory and that is that Henry apparently owed his brother £15 'on Judgment' at the time of William's death and this could have been the widow's reason for claiming Skewis. To claim it was her husband's 'patrimony' was quite wrong in view of the father's will. Anne only survived her husband *by nine years and she too was buried in Camborne Church. No will is available of hers and how the Killivose property was disposed of is not known. When John's name appears in the Camborne Parish Church Rate Book in 1738 his holding is described as 'Mr Bassett's Killivose' and the rate was 4/4, a very small portion. There were at that time ten other names all but one paying much less, and that one paying the same amount as John. By 1741 he had added 'for Tolgarrick 3/4' to his property and in 1760 the entry is 'Mr John Rogers pt. of Killivose 3/3 Mr John Rogers pt. called Mr. Bassett's 3/3.'*

Henry was a figure of mystery until his notoriety in the Skewis affair. He was said to have been a pewterer in Helston, but no record of his marriage or the baptisms of his children appear in those registers. In fact the only marriage that has so far been traced and could have been his took place in Redruth in 1723 with Catherine Webster and the only baptisms of children that may have been connected with the Camborne family were at Falmouth as follows:

19 Sept 1724	*Luce daughter of Henry Rogers*
3 July 1726	*Matthew Rogers son of Mr. Henry Rogers*
19 July 1728	*William son of Mr Henry Rogers*
1 Jan 1733	*Mary daughter of Mr Henry Rogers*

Matthew and William were the names of his father and brother and Mary, his mother's name.

Davies Gilbert in his account of the family says that in 1812 he called on Mr Henry Rogers, 'formerly a saddler at Penzance', but then residing there in great poverty, being supported by a small allowance from a club, and by half-a-crown a week given him by the corporation, nominally for yielding up the possession of a house, but in truth to prevent his becoming a common pauper.........' He continues that Mr Henry Rogers was then 84 years of age. If this was correct, then he would have been born in 1728. William was the name of the child baptised in Falmouth in 1728, but there was time for another child to have been born the same year and baptised elsewhere.

The old man at Penzance remembered much of the siege and also said that he was born in Crowan and that his father *though bred a pewterer* had for many years occupied land in Crowan.

References for SKEWIS incident include:

Weekly Miscellany; British Museum 9 August 1735 No. CXXXIX
Life of Lord Chancellor Hardwicke I, George Harris; pp 295-303
Portraits of Remarkable People; Caulfield, 1813.

Parochial History of Cornwall I; David Gilbert; pp 267-287
Cornish Characters and Strange Events; S. Baring Gould pp 364-369.
Gentleman's Magazine, 1735; page 497
Documents and correspondence at the Penzance Library — Borlase Collection
Documents and correspondence at the County Museum, Truro — Hawkins Collection
Notes on the Rogers Family — Betty Farrell

8 In a Skewes Manor

THREE SKEWES MANOR HOUSES and their adjoining lands have seen the turn of history. GREAT SKEWES and LITTLE SKEWES (St Wenn) have been with us since Domesday as indeed has SKEWES (Cury). SKEWIS in Crowan parish hit the headlines in 1734 with 'The Siege of Skewis' — preceding chapter. There were manors at TRESKEWES in the parishes of St Keverne and Stithians. All the manors are now farmsteads.

GREAT SKEWES & LITTLE SKEWES (ST WENN)

Situated in the deanery and hundred of Pydar the parish is bounded by St Issey and St Breock on the north side; on the west by St Columb Major; on the east by Withiel and on the south by Roche. The estimated tithable lands of St Wenn amount to 3858 acres. There is one bus a month to St Austell. Electricity was introduced into the parish in 1959, but as late as 1975 there was no main supply of water. As one might gather St Wenn is a little off the beaten track.

The parish church is fifteenth century and on its sundial are written the words "Ye Know no When". "Punny" as it many seem very few people know St Wenn. But it is the hamlet that is first connected with the Skues (Skewys) family.

It is believed that an ancestor of the family was granted the manor of Great SKEWYS having saved the life of a bishop during one of the Crusades to the Holy Land. On return to this country the bishop is reputed to have granted the man — John — Great Skewys.

Great Skewes, St Wenn, Cornwall. Photo taken 1968

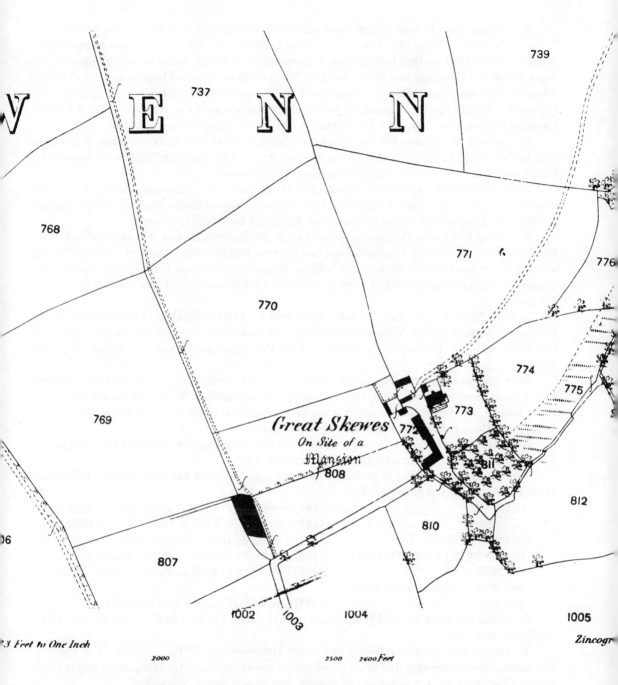

V E N N

739

737

768

771

776

770

774

775

769

773

772

Great Skewes
On Site of a
Mansion
808

811

812

810

807

06

1002   1003   1004   1005

3 Feet to One Inch   *Zincogr*

2000   2500   2600 *Feet*

Skewes, St Wenn, Cornwall based on the 1880 Ordnance Survey map

At a time so early in history, surnames were taken from a variety of sources and John became "John of the Manor House called Skewys" — John de Skewys. In time the "de" (meaning 'of') was dropped and in 1343 we find John Skewys, Commissioner of Peace, living there with his wife who was a daughter of Fortasse Benalleck. In 1386, Matthew Skewys (son of John) was Lord of Skewys and lived there with his wife Mary, a daughter of Andrew Ferners of Trelowarin. In turn the property passed to his son Matthew, grandson John and great grandson John, who was Legal Adviser to Cardinal Wolsey. (See Chapter 6 for Biography of John Skewys who died in 1544).

John Skewys had no sons but two daughters who married Mohun and Courtenay. The former inherited the estate of Skewys and from the Mohuns it passed through the families of Vivian, Silly, Parkin and Wise. In 1867 the Rawlings family were the owners.

In the will of Thomas Vivian of Trenowith in St Columb, Gent., (will was proved at Exeter, 9th August, 1617) he bequeathed to his son Michael Vivian the sum of £300 and all his lands in Skewes, St Wenn which he bought off John Courtenay, Esq., and his brother, Edward.

According to Charles Henderson (History of St Wenn, unpublished, but original at County Museum, Truro, Cornwall), by 1666 Skewes had reverted half the elder branch of Vivian of Trewan whereas seven years earlier Skewes was held by Courtenay, formerly Oley Vivian, Speaker-in-Socage as half acre Cornish by suit only. John Perkin held the other half acre Cornish by Suit-in-Socage.

In 1659 Edward Wise, Esq., of Sydenham, sold for £180 halfendeal of Skewes Vean (Little Skewes), St Wenn to Francis Vivian of St Columb. The tenants were named as John Silly, Esq., and his brother Richard. (Henderson Collection, Volume VII, page 181 — retained at County Museum, Truro).

Since 1867 when the Rawlings family owned Skewes the property was sold to the Hawkey family who in turn passed the estate to their son Captain Whitford Hawkey. Tenants at Great Skewes were Harry Lander, and before him his father (total tenancy approx. 100 years); Dick Burnett (two years) Tom Glover (four years), and Harry Hawkey (four years).

James Hawkey purchased Great Skewes in 1954 following Captain Whitford Hawkey's death. They had previously been tenants from 13th October, 1949.

Skewes (meaning shaded or sheltered spot) through the years has been referred to in many deeds and documents. These include: —

SKEWYT	(1284) Assize (Plea) Rolls at Public Record Office
SKYUES	(1327) Lay Subsidy Rolls at Public Record Office
SKEWIS BIGHAM	(1327) Placita de Banco Rolls at Public Record Office
SKYWYS JUXTA CRUKMAGON	(1370) Assize (Plea) Rolls at Public Record Office
SKEWYS	(1408) Assize (Plea) Rolls at Public Record Office
SKYWYS MOER and SKYWYS	
VIAN	(1443) Calender of Inquisitions Post Mortem

In the Subsidy Rolls for 1327 John Skyues paid 12 pence Tax Roll on Great Skewes and Adam de Skewys, sixpence.

In *Ancient Indictments* (collected by Charles Henderson 32 Ed III — 1358): "The jury present Andrew Crukmagon for that he on Monday next before the feast of St Margaret (1335) in Cruxmagon killed Andrew, son of Juliana de Skewes. But he was found "not guilty".

According to Bassett Papers, in 1642 the Royalist leaders confiscated the estates of Richard and John Silly for their nonherence to the Parliament. The brothers were tenants of Skewes and Trelever, both in St Wenn parish.

By the Tithe Communication Act of 1836 tithes were charged to fixed charges on land and this necessitated a detailed survey, apportionment and valuation. This resulted in the best and most comprehensive land record since Domesday was made. Each parish had its copy of the Tithe map, which, in conjunction with the Tithe Apportionment lists, showed each field and house with its boundaries and the name of the owner and occupier.

Today Great Skewes comprises just over 130 acres and in the 1841 Tithe Apportionment plan when the landowner was Rawlings and occupier Henry Hawkey the make-up of fields (which remain the same today) were as follows: —

	Field name	Acres	Roods	Perches
783	Goose Close Moor	2	2	30
784	Waste			38
785	Waste			34
786	Outer Goose Close	10	1	6
787	Little Goose Close	5	0	6
883	Humphrys Close	5	1	1
884	Pool			9
885	Church Park	5	1	1
886	Church Town Close	8	3	19
887	Road			35
888	Outer Beef Park Moor	1	2	27
889	Inner Beef Park Moor	1	1	30
890	Pool			27
891	Mowhay Meadow	3	2	9
892	Road			9
893	Outer Beef Park	7	3	13
894	Beef Park	7	1	3
895	Road			18
896	Goose Close	8	0	25
897	Road		1	29
898	Waste			6
899	Waste			6
900	Outer Goose Close Moor	1	3	11
901	Road			14
902	North Close	9	0	0
903	Marsh		3	0
904	River			32
905	Lower Way Close	7	3	4
906	Marsh		1	0
907	Grove		1	6
908	Road		1	6
909	Tanners Moor	4	0	28
910	Watering			10
911	Lower Meadow	1	1	39
912	High Way Close	7	0	30
913	Road		2	35
914	Garden			11
915	Homestead, Farmyard etc	1	3	22
916	Kitchen Meadow		2	28
917	Garden			5
918	Higher Meadow	2	1	26
919	Orchard		1	34
920	Garden			14
921	Potato Meadow	1	2	16
922	Town Moor	1	2	13
923	Shoot Meadow	1	0	17
924	Waste			32
925	Great close	10	1	25
926	East Humphys close	7	0	8
	Total	130	2	7

Amount of Rent apportioned upon several lands — Payable to Vicar £6, 17; 6d; payable to Impropriator £8: 6 : 8d.

LITTLE SKEWES
In 1841 the Owner was Hon. Anna Maria Agar and Occupier Joseph Blake.

	Field names	Acres	Roods	Perches
999	Inner Higher Ground	9	0	20
1000	Outer Higher Ground	9	0	25
1001	Church Park	7	2	14
1002	Marsh		1	33
1003	Front Hill	4	0	0
1004	Road		1	12
1005	Hill	1	1	10
1006	Great Meadow	5	3	0
1007	Middle Meadow	1	1	24
1008	Orchard		1	14
1009	Farm Yard		2	32
1010	Garden			4
1011	Mowhay Meadow			29
1012	Dry Park	5	2	1
1013	Road			25
1014	Grim Park	11	0	22
1015	Little Meadow	1	0	36
1016	Little Park Mear	6	1	0
1017	Great Park Mear	7	3	4
1018	Marsh	1	0	34
1019	Park Mear Moor	5	1	22
1020	Grim Park Moor	8	1	36
		87	1	37

Amount of Rent payable to Vicar   £ 4 : 0 : 6d
and Rent payable to Impropriator   £ 4 : 17 : 6d
The figures for 1975 were: payable annually to Inland Revenue.
LITTLE SKEWES
                                                               £ 8 : 90 pence

payable annually to Inland Revenue.
GREAT SKEWES
                                                               £13 : 49 pence

In the year 1919 we find "Sale by Auction", Hancock and Sons of Sydney Place, St Austell who announced they were selling LITTLE SKEWES (Lot 18) on Saturday, 13th December, 1919 at 3 o'clock in the afternoon together with other freehold farms, tenements, cottages and granite quarries. The land agent was named as Mr John Gilbert, Landhydrock, St Austell and the Solicitors, Messrs Walker Martinear and Co., of 36, Theobalds Road, Grays Inn, London WC.

In November, 1975 the owner of Little Skewes was Mrs Lilian Blake and the occupier Mrs Lavinia Rowse.

Little Skewes, St Wenn, Cornwall. Photo taken 1970

The Crest for SKEWES, St Wenn is: —

"VERT, A CHEVRON BETWEEN THREE THISTLES, OR"

When the 1851 Census was taken the following people were living at GREAT SKEWES: Thomas Slick (25), his wife Elizabeth (23), brother James Slick (21) and servants Mary Ann Callicot (16), Thomas Lobb (18) and Thomas Magor (14).

At LITTLE SKEWES were Peggy Blake (46) and her children Elizabeth (23), Mary Jane (18), Richard (16), William Henry (14), Amelia (10), Jemima (8) and Marshall (6). Also living in the house was servant John Harris (57).

There had been a change of residents at GREAT SKEWES by 1871. Living there was Christopher Lander (52), together with his wife Maria (49) and their children Nicholas (23), Francis (16), Maria (11), Annie (10) and Harry (5). Henry Verran (16) was a servant and ploughboy and Ruana Trevail (30) was a domestic servant.

The Blakes were still at LITTLE SKEWES in 1871. Marshall Blake who was the youngest member of the family in the 1851 Census had taken over as householder. Now aged 26 he had married and was living with his wife Jane (27) and children Mary (3), Emma (2) and Richard Henry (1). Mary G. Nicholls (16) was a domestic servant, John Rowe (20) a carter and Richard Osborne (11) a ploughboy.

SKEWES in the parish of CURY

CURY is in the western division of the Hundred of Kirrier, and lies about five miles south west from Helston. Anciently called Corantyn, Cury is bounded on the north and west by Mawgan; on the east by Ruan Major and on the south by Mullion and Gunwalloe. The estimated tithable lands of the parish amount to 2723 acres, although the gross acreage by actual measurement amounts to 2770 acres.

Cury and Gunwalloe form one perpetual curacy. They were, with Germoe, formerly daughter churches to Breage. Cury church was dedicated by Walter Bronescombe, Bishop of Exeter, 1st September, 1261 to Saint Corentine. There are no monuments of any kind in the church, but in the south part of the churchyard is a monolith granite cross nine feet high. Saint Corentine is said to be the first Cornish apostle of note to be found. Born in Brittany, he preached first in his own country until

Skewes Farm, Cury, Cornwall. Photo taken 1968

being driven away by violence, so he decided on the life of a hermit. He settled at the foot of a mountain called Menhont, in the diocese of Cornwall, which is thought to mean Menheniot. Here the fame of his preaching spread and he was consecrated Bishop of Cornwall by St. Martin, Bishop of Tours in France and, it is said, having converted all Cornwall, died in the year 401.[1]

The poet Henry Wadsworth Longfellow (1807 — 1882) was interested in the village of Cury because he could trace his family back to the third daughter of Richard Bonythan. Richard settled in America in 1631 and there is a 20th century window dedicated to his family in the church. By all accounts Bonythan was one of the first emigrants to America.

In the parish of Cury is SKEWES, originally a manor owned by the Skewes family but which was dismembered around 1770. The manor and lands were here in Domesday and for the King's demesne lands in Cornwall, Cheneret held the Manor called ESCHEWITT, Exch. SCHEWIT (Skewes in Cury), and "it geld for one virgate. One team can plough this. Now it is unoccupied (vacua) and when the Count received it, it was worth 15 shillings". (Domesday Book — Survey for Cornwall, page 63, folio 99).

Further reference (774b; folio 225b) says "The Count of Mortain has one manor which is called ESCHEWITT (SKEWES in Cury) wherein is a virgate of land. And it rendered geld for one ferling. One team can plough this. Cheveret holds this on the Count. This was of the Kings which is called Vinneton (Winnington). And it has been entirely wasted and when the Count received it, it was worth 15 shillings." It may be of interest here to mention the layout of those holding land in Cornwall:

1)   King William
2)   Bishop of Exeter
3)   Church of Tavistock
4)   Churches of Certain Saints
5)   Earl of Mortain
6)   Judhail of Totnes
7)   Goscelm

Matthew SKEWYS of SKEWYS, Cury witnessed a charter dated at Merthyn held sometime by the powerful family of Carminow — on the 12th May, 1398. He was present with John Penrose of Penrose near Helston.[2]

On 19 May 1398 (Calendar of Close Rolls) a memorandum of a main prize (an undertaking to be responsible for the appearance of a released prisoner in court on a day appointed), under a pain of 100 marks, was made in Chancery by John Syreston, Henry Gerves, Eurinos Boneithon and JOHN SKEWYS of Cornwall, for John Rosemeryn that he shall do or procure no hurt or harm to William Cullynge, and on 18 July a writ of superseadeas by main prize John Tregoys, JOHN SKEWYS, Eurinos Boneithon and Robert Syreston of Cornwall to the Sheriff of Devon in favour of John Syreston at suit of Master Hugh Hickerlinge.

In the Subsidy Rolls for Cury (1327) "JOHN SKEWYS payed six pence Tax Roll", which compares with a maximum in the parish of two shillings at Bonythan. In 1523 THOMAS SKEWYS was assessed on ten pounds and paid five shillings for property he owned. The value of the SKEWYS estate had risen considerably and was amongst the highest in the parish.

In the "Kalender of Deeds relating to Merthen and Grylls estate for Bonnallack in the year 1387", we find "JOHN SKEWYS, Dominus de Banadlek grants to James Gerveys, Dominus de Banadlek and his heirs a yearly rental of ten pounds out of his (SKEWYS) lands in SKEWYS, Brehylgh, Trvythyan, Syvwragh and Tredenek payable at the usual terms. Witnesses: William Tregoos, Mathew Bretz, John Tremaen, Peter Erysy and Michael Gerveys at Hellyston Burgh, Saturday before St Luke II R II." (October, 1387).

---

[1] From *A Complete Parochial History of Cornwall*, Gilbert, 1867.
[2] *De Banco Roll*, 860m 449 Mich lb Edward IV.

On 7 June 1437 the Bishop, when at Helston, granted a licence to JOHN SKEWYS and his wife Marina for Divine Service within their mansion at SKEWYS in the parish of St Corontin (Cury). [3]

In 1543 John Skewys left the then large sum of £40 towards the building of an aisle in the south side of Cury Church. John died in May 1544 and his will was proved on 30 May 1544, but since the aisle was never built it would appear that religious trouble caused the project to be abandoned. [4]

After the death of JOHN SKEWYS the MANOR of SKEWYS passed to his niece and heir-at-law Alice Denzell. Dismembered about 1770 the property then passed to the family of Lemon.

In 1639 the Manor of SKEWES comprised Brilleigh or Bream in Constantine, Trelanvere the Higher, Bahow in St Keverne, Nanfan in Cury, Trevithian and Trewithan in St Keverne, Caguricke in Grade, Tregrassick in Mawgan in Meneage, Kalignon in Mawgan, Wavall in Mawgan and Seawroth in Stithians. Also Gooneetho and fields called Boscayth, Two Parks, Carracks, Park-an-Yeate on the Barton of Skewes.

In "A Perfect Rentall or Survey of the Estate of the late John Rooper, Esq., deceased, within the county of Cornwall (1710)", Henderson Records, volume 9 — the Manor of SKEWES was listed as follows: —

"Trevithian in St Keverne, a quarter of an acre; Trewythian in St Keverne, 76 acres; Cuguricke in Grade, 26 acres; Nanfan in Cury, 21 acres; Tregassick in Cury, 43 acres; and Seawroth in Stithians, 57 acres.

"SKEWES Capital, Messuage, Barton and Domesues fallen in and on the death of Renatus Bellott, Esq., who died on 22nd May, 1710, aged 36 years. Viz. The hall, spence, large parlour wainscoted and ceiled, three chambers and entry open to the top of the house (there was a floor, but nothing but beams) and other rooms (now four cottages).

"Fields were Polscath, Park Garrocks, The Stray, Parken Bath, Crouchy Guidden, Parkenhall and Gooreath.

Manor of SKEWES also included Bahow in St Keverne; Trelanvere in St Keverne, one eighth of an acre; Kellenen in Mawgan in Meneage, 45 acres; and Bream in Constantine, 28 acres.

Total purchase value — £3242."

On 2nd November, 1721 a Lease was drawn up by "Charles Henshaw to Robert Cross of St Martin in Meneage, Gent., on the lives of Robert Cross, Thomas Lukey, junior of Helston and Samuel Polkinghorne of St Martin in Meneage."

An Indenture was made 14th January, 1754 between Sir Edward Doring of Surrondon Doring in the county of Kent, Baronet, Sir Roland Winn and William Strickland.

On 4th March, 1755 a 99 year Lease was drawn up for the Manor of SKEWES. Nanfan, Cury, Rent £5. Sir John St Aubyn of Clowance to Simon Hendy of Cury, yeoman. Consideration £109. Property called Nanfan.

For Lady Day, 1759 to Lady Day 1760 the Rental for the Manor of SKEWES was as follows: —

Free Tenants: Philip Enouf, gent, for the tenement of Trewithen in Stithians, yearly rent seven shillings; Sir Richard Vyvyan, Bart for a water course to Skiburio Mile at a yearly rent of one shilling; Heirs of Robinson for the tenement of Polglase in Cury at a yearly rent of two shillings; Heirs of Robinson for the tenement of Trenoweth in Cury at a yearly rent of four shillings; Heirs of Smaley for lands in Penryn at a yearly rent of twelve shillings and one penny; and Heirs of John Penrose, Esq., for tenement of Tregiddle in Cury at a yearly rent of fourteen shillings and one penny.

Convencionaries: John James for tenements in Trewithian in St Keverne at a yearly rent of £17:1:10d.

William Sandys, gent for tenement in Trewithian in St Keverne at a yearly rent of £18 : 18 : 0d.

John James for tenement in Trewithian in St Keverne at a yearly rent of £8 : 3 : 6d.

Thomas Lugg for tenement in Trewithian in St Keverne at a yearly rent of £10 : 7 : 0d.

Thomas Lugg for tenement in Trewithian in St Keverne at a yearly rent of £11 : 14 : 8d.

Thomas Boulden for tenement in Cagericke in Grade at a yearly rental of £20 : 19 : 0d.

3, 4 *Ecclesiastical History of Cornwall*, Charles Henderson, 1923, unpublished.

William Hendy for tenement Nanfan in Cury at a yearly rental of £18 : 0 : 0d.

Joseph Hendy for tenement Tregassick in Mawgan at a yearly rental of £33 : 0 : 0d.

William Bath and Henry Bath for tenement in Seawroth in Stithians at a yearly rental of £40 : 19 : 0d.

William Pearce for tenement in Treland Veor the higher and Bahow in St Keverne at a yearly rental of £10 : 10 : 0d.

Richard Grills for tenement in Breleigh also Bream in Constantine at a yearly rental of £20 : 1 : 0d.

Jo Davies for tenement Keleenan also Calignan and Waval in Mawgan at a yearly rental of £29 : 3 : 7d.

Robert Grosse for tenement Moreby of the Barton of SKEWES and the other Moreby at a yearly rental of £70 : 9 : 6d.

The rental for SKEWES was much the same in 1769 as it was in 1759/60.

In the year 1805 Free Tenants were: — The Heirs of Philip Enouf for the tenement of Trewithen in Stithians at a yearly rent of seven shillings; Sir H. Trelawney for Tenement Polglase in Cury at a yearly rent of two shillings; Mrs Moore for tenement Trenoweth in Cury at a yearly rent of four shillings; heirs of John Penrose, Esq., for tenement Tregiddle in Cury (no rent) and the heirs of Smalley for lands in Penryn (no rent).

Conventionary Rents were for various tenements in Trewithian, St Keverne; Nanfan, Cury; Seawrough in Stithians; Treland Vean and Bahow in St Keverne and SKEWES Barton in Cury.

In "Index of Lemon Papers" (County Record Office, Truro — DD. WH 905) Title Deeds for the Manor of SKEWES — 26 March, 1771. Release: 1) Sir Edward Dering 2) Sam Phipps, trustee of Sir Roland Winn 3) John Freeman 4) William Strickland 5) Simon, Lord, Irnham 6) Grace Lombard to 7) Sir Richard Vyvyan and 8) John Richards and Thomas Daniel.

Consideration: £4184 : 11 : 1d and £2005 : 8 : 11d.

Property: Manor of SKEWES in Stithians, Penryn, Cury, St Keverne, Grade, St Mawgan in Meneage and Constantine.

On 29th September, 1780 a 99 year lease was drawn up for SKEWES BARTON: Rent £3:10:0d. Sir William Lemon of Carclew to Sam Grosse of Cury, gent. Consideration of £112:10:0d. Property comprising houses, orchards, gardens, and fields — part of SKEWES Barton on right hand side or south side of lane leading from Cury Parish Church to the Four Cross Lanes, Bonithan and Goonhilly Downs, late occupied by lessee's father Rob. Grosse.

On the same date (29th September, 1780) a 99 year lease for other lands on the Barton of SKEWES was signed. Rent £3 : 10 : 0d Sir William Lemon of Carclew to Sam Grosse of Cury, gent. Consideration £112. For property comprising dwelling house, lands and premises called Goonreaths with fields all part of Skewes Barton, being on the left hand side or north side of land from Cury Parish Church to the Four Cross Lanes, Bonithan and Goonhilly Downs, late occupied by Rob. Grosse, John Jenkin and William Tregidgeon.

On 16th December, 1807 an "Assignment of Leasehold of 400 years" was drawn up:

1)   Sir John St Aubyn of Clowance 2) Thomas Grylls of Helston, gent., 3) Sir William Lemon of Carclew 4) John Borlase of Helston, gent., to 5) Francis Paynter of St Columb, gent.

An Indenture was made 21st March, 1894 between Charlotte Anne Head of the Church Town, Mullion, widow of Samuel Robert Grosse Head, late of the parish of Cury in the county of Cornwall of the first part; Charlotte Sobey, wife of Thomas Sobey of the first part; Charlotte Sobey, wife of Thomas Sobey of the Church Town, in the said parish of Mullion, farmer, of the second part; of the third part Sarah Hawken of Padstow in the said county of Cornwall, wife of John Hawken, Master Mariner. The Indenture mentions a mortgage for Priske in the parish of Mullion, Trenance in the parish of St Keverne and Nanplough and SKEWES in the parish of Cury "to secure £400 and interest and further advances."

On 22nd April, 1899 an Indenture was made between Sarah Hawken, Charlotte Ann Head, Charlotte Sobey, Thomas Sobey, Gerard Noel Cornwallis Mann and Emily Mary Tyacke.

On 10th August, 1901 an Agreement was made between Arthur Tremayne and James Boaden for the Lease of the Barton of SKEWES for a term of 14 years from 29th September, 1900 at a yearly rent of £94 : 2 : 9d, plus additional rent of £13 : 10 : 0d.

An Agreement was made on 31st January, 1905 between Arthur Tremayne (then a retired Lieut Colonel) and Howard Orchard Boaden of Skyburriowe, Mawgan-in-Meneage and James Boaden of SKEWES, Cury in which Tremayne agreed to sell to the Boadens for the price of £3000 the Barton of SKEWES. This comprised all that messuage or dwelling house, farm tenement or closes of land together with buildings known as the Barton of SKEWES containing 69 acres 2 roods and 3 perches. The purchase was completed on 25th March, 1905 at the offices of Messrs Whitford and Sons at St Columb.

On 25th March 1905 a conveyance was made between Arthur Tremayne of Carclew and Francis Alexander of 30 Belgrave Square and Douglas James Proby of 2 Draycott Place, Cadogan Gardens, London (a Lieut-Colonel of the Irish Guards) of the first part; and Howard Orchard Boaden of Skyburriowe of the second part; and James Boaden of SKEWES of the third part.

A Mortgage Indenture dated 27th March 1905 requested Alexander and Proby to lend the Boadens £2000. This they did with an interest rate of £3 : 10 : 0d per centum per annum.

A Conveyance was made 21 December, 1909 between Howard Orchard Boaden of Skyburriowe, Mawgan-in-Meneage, farmer of the one part and James Boaden of SKEWES, farmer of the second part.

An Indenture was made 24th October 1925 between Douglas James Proby of Elton Hall, Peterborough, Northants, a retired Colonel in His Majesty's Army of the one part and James Boaden of SKEWES, Cury, farmer, of the other part.

An Agreement was made on the 15th March, 1937 between James Boaden and George Bosustow of Silverbirch in Cury, retired postman, in which Bosustow became a tenant from 29th September, 1936 at Silverbirch for the annual tenancy of £25.

A Conveyance was made 9th November, 1938 between James Boaden of SKEWES and the County Council of Cornwall in which Boaden sold land to the council which contained one rood fourteen perches and twenty-one square yards with the dwelling house known as Polscarth and garage and shop thereon situate Cury Cross Lanes. The price was £501 : 12 : 0d. and the property numbered 453 and 454 parts on the twenty-five inch ordnance survey map (second edition, 1907).

Consideration £890 for property at Nanfan, Cury. In occupation Simon Hendy as tenant to St. Aubyn.

Sir Charles Lemon of Carclew, near Truro inherited SKEWES from his father. According to Sir Charles' will dated 16th May, 1866 he appointed his nephews Arthur Tremayne and William Charles Buller executors and bequeathed all his real and personal estate, property and effects to Arthur Tremayne. Sir Charles Lemon died 12th February, 1868 and his will was proved in the District Registry at Bodmin Court of Probate.

On 4th April, 1884 an Agreement for Sale for the tenement Trevithian, in the Manor of SKEWES was drawn up between Arthur Tremayne of Carclew to Geo. Williams of Scorrier, Esq.; Consideration £6000. For property at Trevithian, also Schedule of Deeds, requisitions on title, draft accounts, survey, valuation and allied papers.

On 13th August, 1890 an Indenture was made between Arthur Tremayne and William Francis Tremayne of Carclew (eldest son and heir apparent of the said Arthur Tremayne) and also Zoe Anna Judith de Robeck (daughter of John Henry Edward Baron de Robeck) of Gowran Grange Nass in the county of Kildare; Francis Alexander of 41, Eccleston Square, London; George Henry Boscawen of Liverpool and Douglas Hamilton of Shortlands in the county of Kent.

This Indenture mentioned that a marriage had been agreed upon between William Francis Tremayne and Zoe Anna Judith de Robeck and that Arthur Tremayne had agreed to execute such a settlement. The marriage took place on the 19th August, 1890.

On 3rd April, 1891 George Henry Boscawen died in Liverpool and was buried at Lamonan on 7th April, 1891. As there was no appointment of new Trustees, Francis Alexander and Douglas James Proby were named as Trustees.

An Assent was made 29th November 1948 between John Carter Boaden of SKEWES, Cury, farmer and Thomas Boaden of 19 Treliske Close, Truro, bank official and William John Trewhella of Lanner Farm, Helston, farmer (hereinafter together called the executors) of the one part and the said John Carter Boaden (hereinafter called the beneficiary) of the other part.

James Boaden died on 26th March, 1947 and his will was proved 6th October, 1947 in the Bodmin District Probate Registry. He demised the property of SKEWES to his wife Annie Boaden during her life, with the remainder to his son the beneficiary in fee simple.

Annie Boaden predeceased the testator having died on 16th February, 1944. The Executors assented to the vesting in John Carter Boaden all that Messuage or farm dwelling house, farm tenement of closes of land together with the building belonging to the same, commonly called the Barton of SKEWES situate in the parish of Cury and containing by estimation 69 acres 2 roods and 3 perches statute measure and also a bungalow known as Boscathe erected thereon and then in the possession of J.J. James.

Antony Boaden (son of John Carter Boaden) and his wife Sandra now farm SKEWES and live on the premises.

TITHE APPORTIONMENT FOR SKEWES, CURY, 1841

			Acres	Roods	Perches
567	Higher Crowgie Widdon	Arable	5	1	16
568	Gew	Arable	9	3	29
569	Park Jet	Arable	6	3	36
570	Garrack	Arable	11	3	5
571	Lower Crowgie Widden	Arable	6	—	21
572	Park in Hale	Arable	6	1	33
573	Homestead and waste	—	2	—	13
574	Moor	Arable	2	2	26
575	Lane	—			13
576	Orchard	Willow Orchard		2	12
577	Orchard	Pasture and Orchard		2	22
578	Meadow	Arable	1	3	22
579	Garden	Garden		1	25
580	Orchard	Orchard	3	1	34
581	Polscarth	Arable	11	—	19
			69	2	6

Payable to Vicar   £8 : 1 : 3d
Payable to Impropriate Rector   £11 : 11 : 0d

Owner : Sir Charles Lemon
Occupier: Samuel Grosse

582	SKEWIS — CARPENTERS SHOP AND GARDEN — COTTAGE				35
583	Long Garden	Arable		1	27
584	Well Close	Arable	2	3	26
585	Gweal Reeth	Arable	8	2	23
586	Sounding Pan Croft	Pasture	5	1	3
587	Smiths Croft	Arable	2	—	28
588	Sounding Pan	Arable	8	—	26
589	Half Green Lane	—			5
			27	3	13

Payable to Vicar   £2 : 4 : 3d
Payable to Gerveys Grills   £3 : 3 : 0d

Owner : Sir Charles Lemon
Occupier: Samuel Grosse

The SKEWES estate is now much reduced in size to 400 years ago, although not much different to the Apportionment of 1841. Today SKEWES Farm comprises stone cattlehouse with barn over, bulls house, cattle houses and stables of stone and slate; calves and furnace house of stone and slate; piggeries of concrete and asbestos; cow house and fodder house of concrete and asbestos (interesting to note that although the walls are very old indeed, the roof was retiled in the 19th century). Inside we find "John Penn, 1863". One would gather that Mr Penn was the man who retiled the fodder house. SKEWES Farm also comprised garage and dwelling house which has five bedrooms and a bathroom (upstairs), three reception rooms, a kitchen and a dairy downstairs; a Dutch barn 18 feet x 75 feet of galvanised steel; and a Dutch barn 20 feet x 30 feet of asbestos and wood.

The field names for SKEWES in Cury with numbers and acreage according to the 1907 Ordnance Survey map are as follows: —

449	Parc Jette	6.872 acres
450	Outer Garrax	8.887
451	Outer Boscaythe	6.935
452	Little Garrax	2.946
453	Little Boscaythe	3.709
467	Higher Kerchighidden	4.127
469	Gew	9.779
470	Lower Kerchighidden	5.949
471	Parc Hale	6.336
472	Moor	3.211
473	Road and shoot	.696
474	Bank	1.120
479	Mowhay, Dutch Barn, Stackyard, Inner Yard, Gardens, Dwelling House	.761
480	Orchard	1.285
481	Lawn	.567
482	Meadow	3.811
		66.991 acres

Sign outside Skewes Farm, Cury, 1980

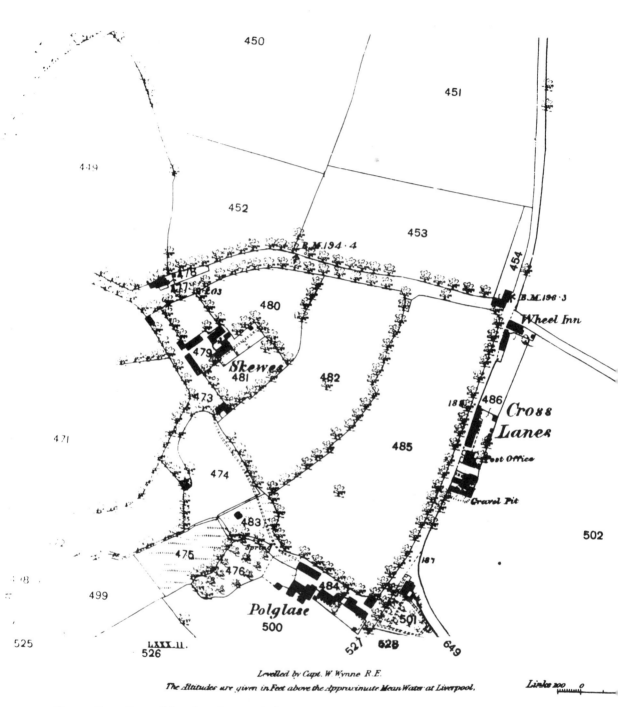

Skewes, Cury, Cornwall based on the 1880 Ordnance Survey map

The annual tithage (payable each September) amounts to *£17.64 pence*.

In June, 1966 Antony Boaden purchased more fields to add to the SKEWES holding. This was 11 acres in Cury known as Parc Drea, and in June 1968 a complete holding of 25 acres known as Venton Arriance.

The Crest for SKEWES, Cury is:

GULES, A CHEVRON BETWEEN THREE STUMPS OF TREES, OR.

It is known that a number of the SKEWES family resided in the village of Cury (see Census Returns for full details) but to end this section of "In a Skewes Manor" on a lighter note here is an extract from an unpublished book "Memoirs of John Boaden, J.P., of Mawgan-in-Meneage" which is kept at Truro Reference Library. It is dated 1902.

> I have seen horses ridden through White Cross, Cury at full gallop in the dark of an evening to prevent being known, going for anchors. At this time there were three cottages at Nantithet where smuggled brandy could be obtained by the initiate privately. Their keeps called Richard Dudley, JAMES SKEWIS (Little JIMMY who fell over the Clies Quarry at Helston one night with an anchor of brandy was unhurt) and another SKEWIS called Old Cooley."[5]

On 11 January 1980 Antony and Sandra Boaden were decorating the first floor of their home. A blow lamp had been used to remove paintwork.

They were taking a break for lunch downstairs when fire destroyed the roof of the main building and spread like a roaring furnace.

Firemen and neighbours helped to remove a considerable amount of furniture from the burning farmhouse, but furniture in the two upper bedrooms was severely damaged.

Antony and Sandra, together with their four children, all of school age, moved to a bungalow lent by a friend until the roof had been repaired.

SKEWIS in the parish of CROWAN

Crowan is situated in the rural district and deanery of Kerrier, and the Hundred of Penwith. The parish and township is bounded by Illogan on the east, by Wendron on the south, Germoe and St. Hilary on the west and Camborne and Gwinear on the north. Crowan contains 7478 statute acres and the inhabitants were 2587 in the year 1807 but had decreased to 1838 by the year 1931.

The Church Town is situated nearly in the centre of the parish, about 6 miles north of Helston.

The Church of St. Crewenna is chiefly 15th century but very much renewed with a Tudor Arcade running into the chancel. There is a Norman font. The church was restored and re-pewed in 1872.

For 300 years the family of St Aubyn lived at Clowance in the parish.

The first mention of SKEWIS in Crowan which the author has found appears in a Bill which was made 18th January, 1573 when John St Aubyn, Lord of Binnerton received from Roger Rise (alias Retinne) gentleman, cousin and heir to Thomas Retinne, gent, deceased, the sum of 6/3d for a "reliffe on the death of Thomas Retinne for half an acre of land in SKEWIS and Polcrebowe" (Henderson — Cornish Manuscripts, Volume 16, page 59, referring to the Manor of Binnerton in Crowan.)

In 1641 according to the will of William Pendarves of Roskrowe (11 January, 1641) he bequeathed to his son William "all those lands which I purchased in the name of John Enys, gent, and Winifred his wife, and after his death all the premises I bequeath to my grandchild and godsonne Samuel, son of my son William and issue male of his body. To the said Samuel when he be 21 years he shall convey my lands in SKEWIS, Crowan; Co SKEWIS, Crowan and Chypons and Pokerebowe — viz a quarter part of all the lands I bought of Arthur Lavellis and William Thomas unto his brother John Pendarves.

---

[5] Boaden refers to a servant man WILLIAM SKEWIS who, with his family, moved to Bejarrow in 1839.

Skewis, Crowan, Cornwall, based on the 1880 Ordnance Survey map

William Pendarves' will was proved at Exeter, 5 October, 1643.

In the previous chapter we read about "The Siege of Skewis" in the parish of Crowan.

The Rev. S. Baring-Gould in his book *A Book of Cornwall* (first published 1899) says that "SKEWIS had been for many generations the freehold patrimony of the Rogers family, and that it was the suspicion that William Rogers' widow Anne would make over the property to her own relatives which so upset Henry Rogers.

"Anne may not have long survived the tragic events of 1734 when her brother-in-law Henry Rogers was hanged. She was born in 1702 and baptised at St. Hilary, 28th December, 1702. It is possible she died before 1743.

"Alternatively her name may have been omitted deliberately, on account of the scandal attached to the SKEWIS incident."

According to an article written in *Devon and Cornwall Notes and Queries*, January 1959 (page 28) by Vincent Vivian Millett "The outcome of the affair, when the violence had come to an end, was that the estate of SKEWIS must have passed to the Milletts after all. There is mention in the Will of John Millett of Gurlyn (dated 1777), the nephew of Anne Rogers (son of her brother Rev John Millett) of, among other unspecified lands in Crowan, "All that part of Curskewis in the said parish of Crowan now rented by George Reynolds as tenant to me........." John Millett married Sarah Rawle. His death in 1778 was at an early age of 26. The property then passed to his son William Millett, who was a surgeon at Liskeard. William Millett married Josepha, daughter of the Rev Malachi Hichens, vicar of St. Just. He died in 1829. SKEWIS was then inherited by his son John Fortescue Millett, a solicitor, who was unmarried and he died in 1852. It is mentioned in his will (dated 1844) "all my freehold estates in or called SKEWIS, KUS-SKEWIS, LITTLE KUS-SKEWIS.............. situate in the parish of Crowan in the said County of Cornwall." All this property was bequeathed to his nephew, the late Mr Fortescue William Millett (already mentioned), who was the only son of Fortescue Millett and Johanna Teague. Fortescue William Millett never married, and with his death in 1915 at Brixham the estate which, despite the ghost of Henry Rogers, had remained with them for nearly two hundred years, finally left the Millett family.

In 1861 Census Returns living at Skewis were William Trevenen, 39, farmer and his wife Jane, 30, and two daughters and one brother Henry Trevenen (farmer) and one servant. Also at Skewis were Elizabeth Dunn, pauper, widow, 77, and daughter Ann, miner. Also Ann Williams, pauper, widow, 41, and three sons and three daughters and one lodger.

At KUS SKEWIS were Elizabeth Thomas, 52, miner's wife, living with two sons and four daughters. At KIS SKEWIS were Grace Vivian, widow, 62, and daughter Grace, dressmaker, 23. Also Henry Ward, 41, miner and wife Elizabeth and six sons and one daughter. Also Thomas Cliff, widower, miner, 52, and two sons and one daughter. Also Grace Williams, widow, 59 and one son Benjamin, 24.

SKEWIS Farm, Crowan was purchased by Leslie Jenkin, and his wife Carol in 1967 and they are the current owners (1981).

Redvers Rodgers was tenant until 1967.

Follows now a copy of the Tithe Apportionment for SKEWIS, Crowan (1841); Landowners — John Fortescue Millett: Occupier John Trevenen.

			Acres	Roods	Perches
1872	Further Grove	Arable	5	1	7
1873	Nearer Grove	Arable	5	2	1
1874	Yonder Churchway	Arable	6	—	35
1875)	Nearer Churchway	Arable	5	2	6
)	Quarry in Churchway	Waste			28
1876	The Hults	Arable	7	—	13
1877	The Green	Arable	7	3	32
1878	Green Meadow	Arable	1	2	10
1879	Mowhay	Arable			37
1880	Mowhay Meadow	Arable		2	33
1881	Dwelling House Homestead	—	1	1	13
1882	Addit Meadow	Arable		2	32
1883	Cot, house and plot	—			21
1884	Park Stevens	Arable	7	—	16
1885	Guel Nance	Arable	6	—	4
1886	Chypons Field	Arable	7	—	19
1887	Higher Guel Mala	Arable	4	—	17
1888)	Guel Mala	Arable	5	—	3
)	Burrow in Guel Mala	Waste	1	1	8
1889	Yonder Guel Row	Arable	6	—	5
1890	Near Guel Row	Arable	5	—	33
1891	Cot, House and Plot	—			31
1892	Inner Moor	Arable	1	2	11
1895	Quillet	Arable		1	19
1894	Skewis Green	Waste	1	1	38
1893	Kellas Moor	Arable	2	—	25
1896	Minnis Croft	Pasture	5	—	19
1900	Meadow	Arable		1	10
1901	House and Plot	—		1	10
1902	Long Field	Arable	2	1	8
1903	Town Field	Arable	1	3	23
1904	The Croft	Arable	1	3	6
1905	The Round	Arable		1	20
1906	Higher Dence Field	Arable	1	1	17
1907	Higher Middle Field	Arable	1	1	0
1908	Two Acres	Arable	2	2	19
1909	Lane Field	Arable	1	1	10
1910	Downs Field	Arable	2	—	30
1911	Middle Field	Arable	2	—	4
1912	Shop Field	Arable	3	—	18
			116	1	31

Payable to Vicar   £10 : 15 : 0d
Payable to the Impropriate Rector   £10 : 15 : 6d

KUS-SKEWIS

			Acres	Roods	Perches
1947	Kus Skewis	Pasture	7	2	25
1948	Great Kus Skewis	Pasture	13	1	9
1949	Kus Skewis Croft	Pasture	8	1	30
1950	Kus Skewis Croft	Pasture	5	—	14
1951	Kus Skewis Croft	Pasture	7	—	19
1952	Great Downs	Pasture	18	0	0
			59	2	27

Landowner: John Fortescue Millett
Occupier : John Trevenen

Payable to the Vicar   £1 : 9 : 4d
Payable to Impropriate Rector   Nil

ENCLOSURE FROM SKEWIS COMMON

			Acres	Roods	Perches
1897	Cot. house and plot	Arable	—	—	33
1898	Plot	Arable	—	3	4
1899	Plot	Arable	—	—	26
			1	0	23

Owner : John Fortescue Millett. Lessee: William
Williams
Occupier: William Williams

Payable to the Vicar £- : 1 : 0d

ENCLOSURE FROM SKEWIS COMMON

			Acres	Roods	Perches
1913	High Plot	Arable		2	32
1914	Higher Plot	Arable		—	32
1915	House and plot	—		1	32
1916	Little Meadow	Arable		1	22
1917	Well Field	Arable	1	—	36
1918	Lower Field	Arable	1	—	17
1919	Higher Field	Arable	1	—	12
1920	Slip outside	Waste			22
			5	1	5

Payable to Vicar 7/2d
Payable to Impropriate Rector 7/9d

Owner: John Fortescue Millett: Lessee Rachel
Reynolds
Occupier: Richard Symonds

1921 SKEWIS COMMON MOOR

		Acres	Roods	Perches
	Waste	16	3	27

No Moneys payable
Owner: John Fortescue Millett: Lessee Richard
Symonds
Occupiers: John Trevenen, Joseph Williams
William Williams, Charles Vivian, John Reynolds
and William Moyle.

KUS SKEWIS

			Acres	Roods	Perches
1922	Little Kus Skewis	Pasture	13	1	13
1923	Little Moor	Pasture		3	28
1924	Little Croft	Arable	1	2	8
1932	Moor	Pasture	1	—	25
1933	Croft	Pasture	1	1	13
1934	Moor Field	Arable	1	1	14
1935	Long Field	Arable	1	2	27
1936	Stamps Field	Arable		2	15
1937	Common	Pasture	2	1	12
1938	Meadow	Arable		2	30
1939	Plot	Arable			37
1940	Orchard Field	Arable		1	7
1941	House and Plot	—			18
1942	Lower Field	Arable	2	1	12
1943	Three Cornered Field	Arable	1	3	11
1944	Middle Field	Arable	2	—	32
1945	Higher Field	Arable	1	3	8
1946	The Croft	Pasture	2	—	25
			35	3	15

Payable to the Vicar £1 : 8 : 9d
Payable to Impropriate Rector £1 : 11 : 2d
Owner : John Fortescue Millett
Lessee : Joseph Williams
Occupier : Joseph Williams

Higher Skewes sign, Crowan

KUS SKEWIS

1925	The Moor	Pasture		3	22
1926	Eastern Field	Arable	1	2	24
1927	Well Field	Arable	1	2	30
1928	House and Plot	—			30
1929	Higher Field	Arable		3	17
1930	Higher Field	Arable		3	19
1931	Higher Field	Arable		3	32
			6	3	14

Payable to Vicar 9/9d
Payable to Impropriate Rector 10/7d
Owner   : John Fortescue Millett
Lessee : Joseph Williams
Occupier : Joseph Williams

KISS SKEWIS

1953	Plot	Pasture	2	1	18
1954	Plot	Arable		2	24
1955	Plot	Arable	1	—	—
1956	Plot	Arable		1	8
1957	Plot	Arable		2	14
1958	Plot	Arable		3	0
1959	Plot and House	Arable			20
			5	3	4

Payable to Vicar 3/11d
Payable to Impropriate Rector 4/3d
Owner   : John Fortescue Millett
Lessee : Sarah Vivian
Occupier: Christopher Vivian

KISS SKEWIS

1960	Plot	Arable		1	20
1961	Plot	Arable		1	0
1962	Plot	Arable			20
1963	Plot	Arable		1	34
1964	Plot	Arable		1	12
1965	Plot	Arable			26
1966	Plot	Arable		2	4
1967	House and Waste	—			20
1968	Plot	Pasture			20
1969	Plot	Pasture	2	3	31
			5	1	27

Payable to Vicar 2/8d
Payable to Impropriate Rector 2/11d
Owner : John Fortescue Millett
Lessee : Ann Reynolds
Occupier: Ann Reynolds

KISS SKEWIS

1970	Waste	Waste		1	33
1971	House and Plot	Arable		1	0
1972	Plot	Arable		1	32
1973	Plot	Arable		2	21
1974	Plot	Arable		2	5
1975	Plot	Arable		1	25
1976	Plot	Pasture	2	3	18
			5	2	14

Payable to Vicar 3/7d
Payable to Impropriate Rector 3/10d
Owner   : John Fortescue Millett
Lessee : John Reynolds
Occupier: James Goldsworthy

KISS SKEWIS		Acres	Roods	Perches
1977 Croft	Pasture	6	0	3
1978 Plot	Arable		2	24
1979 Plot	Arable	1	—	16
1980 House and Plot	—		1	8
1981 Plot	Arable		1	20
		8	1	31

Payable to Vicar   5/4d
Payable to Impropriate Rector   5/9d
Owner : John Fortescue Millett
Lessee : William Moyle
Occupier: William Moyle

TRESKEWES in the parish of ST. KEVERNE

St Keverne is in the Hundred of Kerrier. To the north is St Martins, to the east St Anthony, to the west Ruan Minor and to the south the Bristol Channel. It measures 8792 statute acres.

To the north the scenery is wooded; to the west there are vast expanses of heathland on which is built the international UHF communication station at Goonhilly which made history in July 1962 by exchanging the first intercontinental picture transmissions with the United States of America via a space satellite.

The old parish church was rededicated to St. Keverne in 1266. It has a spire 40 feet high set above its 60 foot tower as a landmark to sailors. There is a fine view from the churchyard over Falmouth Bay.

The earliest reference to TRESKEWES in the parish was in 1315 (Seldon Soc 41) and in 1334 TRESKEWYS (Feet of Fines) — Public Record Office — meaning "Farm in a sheltered spot."

TITHE APPORTIONMENT FOR TRESKEWES, ST. KEVERNE, 1845

Lessor: Henry Sincock   Occupier: Himself

No. on plan	Field name	State of cultivation	Quantities in statute measure		
			Acres	Roods	Perches
1765	The Gew	Arable	3	0	18
1766	Gew Moor	Pasture	1	1	9
1767	Pit Orchard	—		3	7
1768	House, yard, buildings, mowhay etc	—		3	1
1769	Higher Orchard	Arable		1	23
1772	Home Little Field	Arable	1	3	13
1773	Home Bongey	Arable	4	1	3
1774	Watering place	Waste	1	0	0
1775	Stubb's Moor	Arable	2	1	8
1776	Outer Bongey	Arable	3	0	16
1777	Middle Little Field	Arable	2	0	30
1778	Higher Little Field	Arable	2	1	3
1779	Chywoon Crossfield	Arable	4	1	30
1780	Well Crop-him	Arable	2	0	5
1781	Red Gate Field	Arable	3	1	0
1782	Blue Gate Field	Arable	2	0	31
1783	Higher Field	Arable	3	2	12
1784	Hay Croft	Arable	3	3	15
1784a	Manacle Croft	Pasture	1	0	36
1785	Fowling Pool Croft	Pasture	7	0	24
1859	Dolly's Croft	Pasture	13	0	26
			64	0	30

Amount of Rent Charge apportioned upon the several lands and to whom payable.
Payable to Henry Sincock   £12 10 0d
Payable to Vicar   £ 4 0 0d

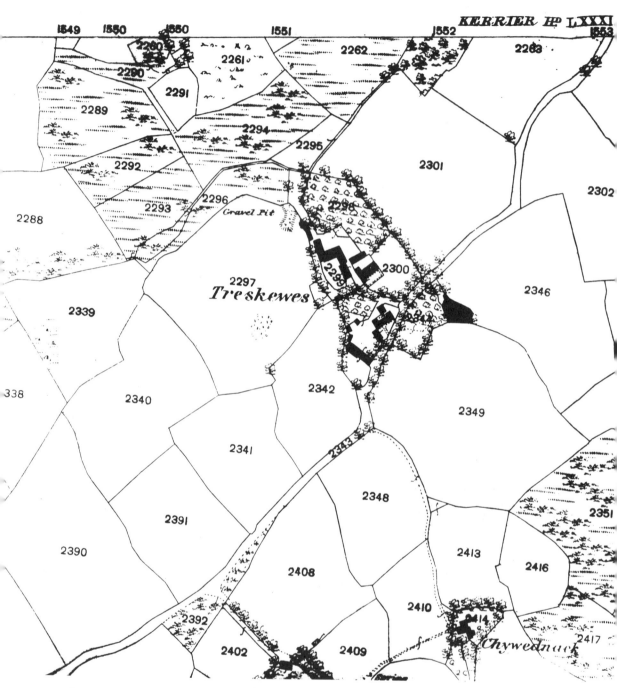

Treskewes, St Keverne, Cornwall based on the 1880 Ordnance Survey map. All Ordnance Survey maps retained at the Local Studies Library, Redruth

Treskewes Farm, St Keverne, Cornwall. Photos taken 1980

Lessor: Thomas James   Occupier: James Lory

1701	Moor	Pasture	2	0	24
1702	Moor	Pasture	5	1	6
1703	Great Croft Mainer	Arable	4	0	20
1704	Little Croft Mainer	Arable	1	3	22
1705	Park-an-starve-us	Arable	2	2	18
1706	Long Field	Arable	1	3	39
1707	Little Park-an-starve-us	Arable	1	1	10
1707a	Garden	—			11
1748	Gew Moor	Pasture	4	1	32
1756	Park-an-Jora Field	Arable	2	2	29
1757	Park-an-Jora Moor	Arable		3	32
1758	Little Gew Moor	Arable	1	1	20
1759	Little Moor	Arable		1	30
1760	Higher Gew	Arable	5	0	22
1761	Orchard	—		1	19
1762	Lower Gew	Arable	4	0	16
1763	Park Crays	Arable	2	0	3
1764	Park Bean	Arable	1	0	14
1770	Orchard	—			38
1771	House, yard, building, Mowhay, etc	—		1	32
1715	Rocky Garden	Arable		1	9
1716	Rocky Field	Arable	2	1	38
1717	Park-an-Grouse	Arable	2	0	3
			42	2	7

Amount of Rent Charge apportioned upon the several lands and to whom payable.

Payable to James Lory   £ 9 0 0d

Payable to the Vicar   £ 3 5 0d

EDWARD SKEWES (of Rosenithon, St Keverne) was occupier of Bannel Tenement, St Keverne. (Lessor Rev John Kempthorne, Trustees under the will of). Lessee: Lieut William Lugg R.N. EDWARD SKEWES was also occupier of Cliff Tenement. Lessees and Lessors same as before.

1066	Cliff Gate Stitch	Arable	1	1	34
1067	Clover Field	Arable	2	1	7
1068	Middle Field	Arable	1	1	7
1069	Well Cliff	Arable	2	1	7
1070	Waste	—		3	38
1071	Lower Cliff	Arable	1	1	10
1072	Waste	—		3	19
1073	Long Hill	Arable	1	1	12
1074	Lower Boscarnon	Arable		2	25
1075	Higher Boscarnon	Arable	1	1	36
1083a	Garden	—			16
1084	Lower Holt's Field	Arable	1	0	34
1085	Higher Holt's Field	Arable	1	0	8
1092	Inner Holt's	Arable	1	0	31
1156	Cottage, buildings and yard	—			12
			17	2	16

Amount of Rent Charge apportioned upon the several lands and to whom payable.

Payable to EDWARD SKEWES   £3 14 6d

Payable to Vicar   £1 8 0d

BANNEL TENEMENT

1172	Turn Hal	Arable	1	3	24
1173	Mowhay, House & Garden	Garden			32
1176	Nursery	—			24
1177	Park Grouse	Arable	2	1	34
1178	The Bannel	Arable	2	1	17
			7	0	11

Payable to Edward Kempthorne   £2 7 0d

Payable to Vicar   £- 17 6d

ROSENITHON
Lessors: Sir Richard Rawlinson Vyvyan, Bart
Lessees: Lieut William Lugg, R.N.
Occupier: EDWARD SKEWES

			Acres	Roods	Perches
1115	Barn and yard	—			8
1116	Long field	Arable	1	1	22
1134	Park-an-drea	Arable	1	2	31
1165	Part of Orchard	—			22
			3	1	3

Payable to Edward Kempthorne   £1 0 0d
Payable to Vicar   £- 9 0d

			Acres	Roods	Perches
1169	Vineyard	Arable	2	0	8
1170	Vineyard	Arable	1	3	32
			4	0	0

Payable to Edward Kempthorne   £1 8 0d
Payable to Vicar   £- 9 0d

LITTLE TRESKEWES, St Keverne

			Acres	Roods	Perches
147	House and Mowhay	—			25
148	Mowhay Field	Arable	1	1	22
150	Little Field	Arable		3	30
152	Withy Garden	Willows			35
153	Withy Garden	Willows			9
			2	3	1

Rent charge in lieu of Tithes
Payable to Grace Daniel   £2 10 0d
Payable to Vicar   £- 7 6d

Grace Daniel was Lessee and Occupier Rev John Kempthorne
Trustees under the will of: Lessors

LITTLE TRESKEWES, St Keverne

			Acres	Roods	Perches
149	Long Field	Arable	1	2	3
151	Further Field	Arable	1	0	6
154	The Moor	Arable		1	24
			2	3	33

Payable to Grace Daniel   Nil
Payable to Vicar   7/6d

Occupier was Ralph Randal, late, Daniel
Rev John Kempthorne Trustees under the will of: Lessors

LITTLE TRESKEWES, St Keverne

			Acres	Roods	Perches
138	Waste	Waste			13
139	Building and Mowhay	—			9
141	Buildings	—			8
142	Lower Field	Pasture	2	1	2
145	Middle Field	Arable	1	2	14
146	Lower Field	Arable	2	1	21
140	Waste	Pasture		1	2
			6	2	29

Payable to Joyce John and Mary Cock   £2 9 0d
Payable to Vicar   £- 16 0d

Lessee was Mary Cock. Occupier Francis Roskruge
Rev John Kempthorne Trustees under the will of: Lessors

LITTLE TRESKEWES, St Keverne			Roods	Perches
135	House and Garden	—	1	9
136	Garden	—		17
137	Orchard			39
			2	25

Payable to Joyce John and Mary Cock   2/6d
Payable to Vicar   2/-d

Lessee was Mary Cock. Occupier: Mary Cock
Rev John Kempthorne Trustees under the will of: Lessors

Estate sign at Treskewes, St Keverne

According to the 1841 Census Returns the people living at TRESKEWES, St Keverne were: Elizabeth Lory and family: Henry Sincock (40) his wife Elizabeth (35) and children Mary (20), Jane (17), William (15), Hannah (13), Martha (11), Henry (10), and Henry Williams, farm servant (15).

In the 1851 Census Returns we find: James Lory (35), his wife Elizabeth (34) and children Jacob (5), Elizabeth (4), and James (2); along with servants Thomas Mitchell (15), Thomas Hocking (36) and Ann Hocking (16).

Also at Treskewes were Elizabeth Sincock (50) and her son William (26): with servants Joanah Collins (14) and William Philips (13) and Henry Martin (14), who was a lodger.

At LITTLE TRESKEWES were Thomas Downing (36), his wife Mary (31), and children Robert (7), John (4), Thomas (3), Henry (2) and Susanna (4 months).

By 1871 those living at Treskewes were William James (38), his wife Alice (33) and their son Thomas (5). Also Alfred Allan (26) and his wife Elizabeth (34).

At Little Treskewes were Henry Retallack (34), his wife Mary (34), and children George (9), Henry (6), Mark (5) and Ruth (11 weeks).

In 1883 the Directory for Cornwall listed James James, farmer as resident; 1926 gave the name of Andrew James, farmer and 1970 William and Mary James and Harry Pascoe.

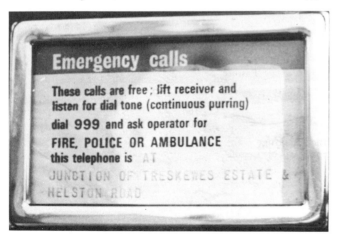

Inside the phone box on the Treskewes Estate

Gate Sign at Treskewis Farm, Stithians

TRESKEWIS in the parish of STITHIANS

Stithians, according to Hals (1838) is situated in the Hundred of Kirrier and has upon the north Gwennap; west Gwendron; east Gluvias and Perranwell and south Mabe.

During Tudor times was the Barton and Manor of Penalmicke, is est, the head of chief coat of mail order, so called that such armour was lodged there in former ages by the professors or proprietors thereof; which place gave name and origin to an old family of Gentlemen from thence came Penalmicke (Penalurick) from whose heirs it passed to SKEWIS, tempore 3d of James I (1605)[6] who sold the same to Sir Nicholas Hals, who sold the same to William Pendarves.[7] The Manor on which there were two farm houses passed to Stephen Ustick, Thomas Hocker and Josiah Tremayne.

In 1872 the tithable lands in the parish of Stithians amounted to 3446 acres.

The earliest reference to TRESKEWIS was in Early Chancery Proceedings, 1523 (TRESKYWIS) and the following year in Lay Subsidy Rolls, Public Record Office. The meaning of TRESKEWIS is 'farmstead in a shady or sheltered place'.

TITHE APPORTIONMENT FOR TRESKEWIS, STITHIANS, 1840

			Acres	Roods	Perches
766	Homestead, garden and lane	Garden		3	0
767	Barn Close	Arable	2	3	38
837	Churchway	Arable	1	1	38
836	Trembroth Field	Arable	3	0	35
770	Long Field	Arable	2	3	39
769	Roadway Field	Arable	2	0	3
757	Greenland Field	Arable	3	1	38
699	Higher Moor	Moor	3	0	14
479	Middle Moor	Arable	3	0	10
758	Sheeps Close	Arable	3	2	32
768	Francis Field	Arable	1	3	27
759	Well Close	Arable	5	3	8
765	Orchard Meadow	Arable	3	0	22
840	Three Cornered Field	Arable	2	0	19
845	Pond Field	Arable	2	3	39
846	Little Hill	Arable	1	2	36
839	Middle Hill	Arable	2	3	11
838	Way Field	Arable	3	2	18
			50	3	27

Payable to Impropriator   £4 3 6d
Payable to the Vicar   £4 18 6d

Landowner: Michael Williams
Occupier: Hugh Phillips

Treskewis Farm, Stithians in 1958

[6] *Magna Brittania*, Lysons 1814
[7] *Parochial History of Cornwall*, Gilbert 1838, page 303

In 1803 the Impropriator was John Williams, Gent. The Occupier was Jone Martyn. (Contract drawn up 14 December, 1790). The Contractor was John Williams.

Living at Treskewis when the 1851 Census was taken were: John Spargo (49), his wife Ann (42), with their son Edward John (7) and a visitor to the house Mary Ann Spargo (15). Also at Treskewis were John Oppy (34), his wife Elizabeth (33) and their children John (8), William (5), Elizabeth (4) and Thomas (3). Elizabeth Oppy (14) was a servant.

Yet another family were resident at Treskewis. William Dunstan (53), his wife Tonie (50), and children Hugh (24), Joseph (20), Elizabeth (21), Henry (18) and Richard (14).

In the 1883 Directory of Cornwall Henry Bawden was farming Treskewis followed by Nicholas Pearce for four years. In the 1926 Kelly's Directory for Cornwall Richard Rowe was the farmer. His nephew Edwin Trewartha Rowe became tenant in 1950 and currently farms 47 acres (1980). The owner of Treskewis is Mr Charles Williams of Caerhays Castle, Gorran, St Austell.

Three acres of moor was sold off just before 1900 to Hercules Collins, a mason.

Treskewis Cottage was sold in 1965, but retains its original name. It has changed hands three times since that date.

9 Westward Ho

QUEEN VICTORIA came to the throne as an eighteen-year-old girl in 1837, and reigned for 64 years, the longest in British history. It was an exciting era in which to live — the country was linked by railways, there were electric trams and even motor cars. Sail gave way to steam. Britain held the Great Exhibition of 1851 in Hyde Park. There was the Crimean War, and Charles Dickens' novels exposed the evils of Victorian society.

In the early Victorian days, Britain was larger than ever before in its history. In 1801 there were 15.8 million people living in Great Britain. In 1831 the census returns gave us a population of 24.1 millions and by 1841 the total was 26.7 millions.

In 1851 despite a large exodus of people from Cornwall and a massive emigration from Ireland, the figure had reached 27.3 millions.[1]

From the census returns of 1831 we see that 28% of the total population of England, Scotland, Wales and Ireland was employed in agriculture. In these surroundings there must also have been the local village shop, together with local craftsmen, which would bring the total to over 40% of people in Britain living and working in rural areas.

Emigration from Ireland was most noticeable. In the 1840's Ireland suffered a famine and about 750,000 people died and a quarter of the population was without work.

Since 1800 1.5 million people had emigrated to settle in the New World and 0.5 million to work in new factories in England and Scotland[2].

Britain was plunged into the darkest period of the 1800's. The trade boom of good harvests collapsed. Industry came to a standstill, unemployment reached hitherto unknown proportions with high food prices and the population at large faced hunger and destitution.[3]

The majority of ordinary people in Britain were simply known as "the poor", normally defined as a person who had to work with his hands to support himself and his family. The social structure in these early Victorian days appeared to be a pattern of poverty.

In later life when even more hardship arose with the possibility of not earning money, as before, the poor faced the fears of the workhouse and, most shameful of all, a pauper's funeral.

Very few could either read or write as is witnessed in the certificates of births and marriages, when the vast majority signed simply "X".

As well as all these problems the working people of Cornwall had to face another major setback — the tin mining depression. Many families emigrated to North America and Australia to look for a brighter future.

One such family who were typical of this era were the SKEWIS' of Camborne, Cornwall who left England in the 1840's. Edward Skewis set sail for North America in 1848 and the following year was joined by his wife Mary and their children, Mary, Elizabeth, Edward, Ann, Eliza, Honor, Henry, Caroline, William and the person who was to document so much valuable information, James Skewis. Also on the journey were cousin Absalom Skewis, his sister Nanny and cousin Harry Skewis.

The Skewis family resided at Vyvyan's Row, Camborne. James remembers his earliest days:[4]

---

[1] *Abstract of British Historical Statistics* (B.R. Mitchell & Phyllis Dean), Cambridge, 1962.
[2] *Atlas of World Population History*, Colin McEvedy & Richard Jones; Penguin Books, 1978, London; p.46.
[3] *Early Victorian Britain*, JFC Harrison, Fontana /Collins, London, 1979, pp 27, 34, 43, 46.
[4] For the many references to James Skewis and his family from Camborne the writer is indebted to Miss Dorothy Skewis of Storm Lake, Iowa, and to her relations Maude Skewis, Anita Skewis Rosendahl and Bettie Skewis Balou who collated information from note books and letters of James Skewis (1826-1911).

My first school was a private house two minutes walk northwest from where I lived. I was very young but do not remember making any progress in my learning there. My next school was with a Mrs Roberts. This was also a private house and two minutes walk southeast from our house. My next school was with a man teacher by the name of Joseph Toy. By this time I was big enough to be able to understand the good that might be got by going to school, and learned fairly well. I continued at this school until Mr Toy left for New York in the employment of a safety fuse company. He was a good master and well beloved by the whole school.

James continued his schooling under Samuel Whear, a very capable but hard master who was very partial and showed favour to children who came from good class families. But it was a good school and he learned a lot.

We did much work in school and every class had a monitor and there was a card hung on the wall. If it were spelling the words were printed on a card. We had to spell the words by singing the letters of each ten or twelve times when the monitor, who had a pointer staff in hand, would raise it, then all hands would begin on the next word and always the same tune. We had regular writing and arithmetic lessons, besides considerable mental arithmetic questions and it was very remarkable how quick the children were in answering.

During the breaks in between lessons the boys played an assortment of games. The bigger boys would throw apples or marbles or anything of that kind to get the younger boys to scramble and retrieve the object. The boys would pile on top of each other often causing problems for the ones underneath. On one occasion James Skewis found himself injured.

Well do I remember being under when I got my knee hurt and it was hard work to reach my home about half a mile away. My knee was much swollen and I was for months unable to go to school. My knee was poulticed by many compounds, but the most effective was vinegar brand, mixed with the waste from the brewery. I was finally able to go to school by the use of crutches.

I remember a gentleman visitor came to the school; our master was asking questions to let the visitor see and hear how well the scholars could answer. When I was called up to the stand and requested to hold out my hand and received a severe blow on it I heard the master say to the gentleman that he was sorry to chastise the little cripple. From that day to this I have not known of doing anything to merit chastisement. I think children can always forgive their masters for a flogging when they know they deserve it and soon forget the whole affair, but when they are whipped for nothing, they ever remember it.

James was ten years old when this incident happened at school. At home he and his friends would amuse themselves with games of marbles, tennis and rounders. They would tell stories they had either read in books or heard from other people. During the school holidays in summer they would visit the seaside three miles away.

I think it impossible for those who live distant from the sea to understand the pleasure in seaside pastimes. In digging into the sands for shrimps, and knocking limpets and periwinkles and searching for crabs. When cooked they are very nice eating. Thousands of these are brought to market already cooked, and many who have left their native land would gladly have such old time treats.

Sunday School played an important part in the life of James Skewis. He attended Camborne Wesleyan Methodist Sunday School from an early age. It was a large school with hundreds of boys and girls attending. The superintendents were James Richards and Henry Vivian and there were between twelve and fourteen scholars in each class. School began at 9.00am. At 10.30am the children walked into the Great Chapel two by two, teachers leading. There was more preaching in the Chapel from 2.00pm until 4.00pm and again at 6.00pm.

Although we are not told what age James Skewis began work, he was very young. His first month's pay packet brought him five shillings, from work undertaken at a local mine. By the age of 15 James was working in a mine three miles from his home and left for work at 6 o'clock in the morning to arrive there by seven.

In winter it was very cold and quite often he would go into the Engine House in the early evening to keep warm.

In 1841 two other boys and myself waited until after the others had left to have all the room to ourselves so as we could roast some potatoes. As we came to the door with a basket of potatoes we met a woman by the name of Shelby Martin who said "My dear boys, don't go in as I think there is something wrong with the boiler." So we left. A few minutes later the boiler burst and killed the only girl that was there by the name of Mitchell. Some people who were near got hurt. I have ever been thankful to God that we escaped that fearful accident. The names of the other boys were Anthony Cock and Toby Stephens. I have heard that Anthony became a very good man, and many have been brought to know the Lord through him.

When James was sixteen years of age his father Edward Skewis became very ill and doctors said he would die. There was an elderly gentleman in Camborne, John Vivian, who understood herbs and was an expert in making them up into medicine. Edward Skewis held his head over burning tar and inhaled hop steam. He also took regular exercise and made a remarkable recovery.

James Skewis

Illness set in again with the Skewis family in 1846; this time Catherine Skewis (aged 22) died, although the best medical aid had been employed. She was a devout Christian and a member of the Church.

In the spring of 1846 Edward Skewis (aged 26 years) left Camborne for the United States of America. He wrote many letters home describing the wealth of the country, and sent money through to help the family. Land could be purchased for as little as one dollar and twenty-five cents per acre. Finally Edward (senior) decided on making a move to the "new world." He went to America in 1848 and was well pleased with what he saw. The following year the whole family left Camborne.

We left our home on 6 January and took the boat at Hayle for Bristol, then travelled by rail road to Liverpool. Some of us were seasick on the water, but in the train it was delightful riding through that part of England.

Liverpool was the largest city we had ever seen, and to see the hundreds if not thousands of vessels it was like a great forest. We could hardly think there were so many ships in the world.

We secured a passage in the ship "Mary Ward" for New Orleans. When we were out about two weeks, there came on a heavy storm which made the ship creak and tremble, and the big waves dashed against the sides of the vessel, and broke in some of her bulwarks. We were all pretty well tossed with the waves of the ocean, but when the storm was gone we had a calm, and the ship would roll from side to side as though it would roll over. That was the only storm we had on the trip and we soon got into the southern climate and had nice warm weather and saw thousands of porpoise fish. They would appear as if they wanted to keep up with the ship. Some of the sailors would throw a harpoon at them and would bring them on board and cut them up and cook them.

We saw schools of flying fish. I think they flew two hundred feet, and some would fly on board the ship and cause great excitement.

One morning there was a cry of land in sight which turned out to be Cuba and Haiti. We sailed between them and for some days were in sight of land which made it appear comfortable. After we lost sight of land we had a fair wind up the mouth of the river to New Orleans. Then a tug boat pulled us to New Orleans.

We saw lots of negroes working on the plantations and the beautiful mansions of the owners with a host of little houses in which the negroes and their families lived. We landed in New Orleans in early March and the climate was very warm.

James Skewis found New Orleans a very pretty place — a large city which had some fine streets and buildings. There was plenty of fruit and everything looked abundant. He was impressed by the numerous sailing vessels and river boats. But James was saddened by slave auctions.

The slaves were being sold to the highest bidder. Thus families would be separated perhaps for ever. Some would be bought to be transported to the different States. It looked awful to us who had never seen anything like it before, and it was astonishing to us how any person could by custom become so hard hearted. It looks as if the more one is under the influence of such habits the worse they become. We soon found out that the white folks were not pleased for us to be free with these poor, helpless negroes.

In this country in 1849
I crossed the briny sea.
In New Orleans we landed
There were many sights to see.
And all so strange to foreigners
As anything could be.
It was the month of February
If I remember right
There were a host of river boats
To us a novel sight.
The river was a full mile wide
It must be that or more
Such a large river like that
We never saw before.
The negroes were under slavery
And sold by auction then.
It was a most awful sight
For us to comprehend.
The child was sold from mother
The husband from the wife.
We never saw such barbarity
Before in all our life.

The Skewis family of Inwood, Iowa, USA. Left to right: *Edward Skewis, William Skewis, Harry Skewis, Charles Absalom Skewis and George Skewis.* Front row, from left: *Anita Skewis, James Skewis, Jane Skewis, Elmer Arthur Skewis and Jennie Skewis*

From New Orleans James Skewis travelled by steamboat for St Louis. On the banks of the river there were tens of thousands of trees straight as arrows which added to the beauty of the scenery.

Within five days the ship had arrived in Cairo where the Ohio unites with the Mississippi. Another day's journey by boat and the Skewis family arrived in St. Louis. Although there was a rail road under construction it had not arrived at St Louis by 1849. So the journey continued by river in a smaller boat. Galena was the destination and that took four days to reach. They stayed at the Rabling Hotel and sent word to Shullsburg to friends that they had arrived safely.

The following day a gentleman arrived on horseback. James knew it to be either his father or Uncle James (they were twins) and it was difficult to distinguish between the two. It turned out to be his father and there was a great reunion as the family had not seen each other for twelve months. The Skewis' travelled on to Shullsburg, which in those days was not a large town. It had a church or two, numerous saloons, stores which sold liquor and customers could have all they wanted.

A brief interlude followed when the Skewis family moved to Dodgeville, but did not like it as much, so returned to Shullsburg which was basically a mining town. Here James Skewis (senior) bought a house and the family soon settled in.

In 1850 there was a big rush to the gold fields of California and a number of people from Shullsburg made a lot of money. Edward Skewis was one such person and within a year his two brothers Henry and James arrived at Deer Creek. It was here that James wrote letters home, normally in rhyme. Here is one example.

Thousands of men with tools in hand,
Travelling all o'er the land,
This they did with greatest pleasure
Searching for the hidden treasure.
And fixed their Toms[5] close by their side
And washed a piece about eight feet wide.
And at the close of every day
Took their little scales to weigh
The gold they had taken from the pit,
By this they knew how much they got.
And thus they would work from day to day,
As long as they could make it pay.
All bachelors in a cabin three,
While there they lived in harmony.
Potatoes, beef, onions and bread,
Well buttered daily, they were fed.
As morning came, so noon and night
Found them with a good appetite.
They drank neither rum nor gin,
But water from a sparkling spring.
As night and day rolled along
They continued robust and strong.
From six to noon, from one 'til night,
Work for them was a great delight.
Six ounces daily, they to their pile would add,
Enough to make the hearts of miners glad.
No time was lost, active in getting more,
Every day adding gold to their store.
Though in number only three men,
They wanted to do the work of ten.
No idleness, no waste of time,

From breakfast until supper time.
They cooked as bachelors always eat,
Fried and boiled and roasted meat.
But Sunday was their day of rest,
They changed and wore their very best.
And quite respectable would go
To Town if possible some news to know,
And learn of tidings from their home,
If any letters through the mail had come.
And to their cabins would return,
Some hours before the setting sun,
Read our letters with much delight,
And fixed things tidy 'ere it was night.
Then to our beds we all turned in,
Early in the morning to be up again,
After breakfast to the diggins' went
More gold to find was our intent.
We picked and shovelled the dirt away,
To get to bedrock without delay.
'Twas there the gold was mostly found,
Twelve ounces only made a pound.
The rocks glistened with the shining stuff,
And hard we worked hoping to have enough
That at some future time we might retire,
With all the gold we might require.
To buy a home like to some paradise,
And find an Eve that is beyond all price,
That perchance some shrubs might come
To remember the old tree when dead and gone
The sweetness of the thought we all may see,
And the longing desire of all remember me.

The onward journey to California was long and drawn-out. In addition to James Skewis there were five other colleagues who made the trip. The first day they reached Galena. From there the roads were very bad via Elizabeth and Dixon, Illinois. The journey continued down the Illinois River to Peoria and St. Louis, New Orleans and Havana in Cuba. But the party were not allowed to land at Havana without passports, and they had none.

---

[5] A long trough used in washing gold

The passengers were not well pleased, and many expressed their willingness to fight against a government so unliberal. About thirty hours after stopping at the Cuban port we left for Chagres. There was a river there by which we had to go up some miles in a row boat. We had to pay a high price. The natives of that town were queer people. They all spoke the Spanish language, and were many colours. Some had their feet swollen out of shape by some insect that lived in the sand. They called them "jiggers". Their feet were terrible objects to look at.

In some places they would use long poles, and put it to the bottom and push the boat along. Where the rapids were, we would have to jump in the water to help to get the boat over short places. There was one place where we came to what they told us by walking a quarter of a mile we would save miles of river travel, so five or six of us agreed to do it, and got lost.

The sun being overhead, we could not tell north from south, and the forest was so dense we could hardly see any distance through it. There were wild beasts in the jungle and we were afraid. We were burning with thirst and in an awful fix, and afraid we would not be able to find the way back again. After a while we came to a trail we agreed to follow, and we came back to the point we started from. The first thing was to throw ourselves down beside the river to quench our thirst. We had to pay to be taken around the bend, about seven miles, and there we found our boat, and the rest of our comrades waiting for us. We passed a point in the river where they told us a whole boat load of passengers were killed, among them women and children, for robbery.

The party eventually arrived at the head waters of navigation and then travelled into Panama where they slept on the ground that night.

The following day more steamship travel and not without dramas. At about one o'clock one early morning one of the ship's engineers sent a lad for a pot of whiskey. The lad put the pot under the tap, and fell asleep. The liquor came up equal with his light, and caught fire. A cry of "fire" and all hands were on deck. Flames were belching forth from the many bottles of whiskey and the whole store room appeared to be on fire. Near panic overtook many including one Jew who offered to sell his jewellery stock worth three thousand dollars for twenty. Some men were waiting to cut the ropes, and to get the first chance to jump in the water if the fire could not be overcome. All who were on board that fearful time would be apt to remember it as long as life lasted. What rejoicing when the pumps were in full play! Soon all was safe. Glad was the poor Jew that no one took him up on his offer to sell his stock for twenty dollars.

Among the passengers on board that night were James Skewis, his brother Henry and their cousin Will Skewis.

Acapulco was the first port the ship put into.

The houses in this old Mexican town were mostly one storey high, covered with tiles. The port had a very narrow entrance, I should say no more than a quarter of a mile, but after we got in perhaps a mile wide. It was very deep, and the little boys were the best swimmers. They could dive like fish. We would throw a small silver coin in the water, and they would dive after it and bring it up everytime. We went ashore and had a comfortable time.

The Mexicans did not need much clothing, and did not appear to have more than necessary.

The port and town was shut in by high hills, and the cannons they fired reverberated against the hills as though there were many. I should imagine there was not a more secure harbour in the world than that of Acapulco.

And all too soon it was time to leave Mexico. After the ship had taken on her cargo and coal, not forgetting the passengers, she left for San Francisco. It was just four weeks from the time the Skewis family left Shullsburg that they saw the Golden Gate as they entered the great bay of San Francisco. In the 1850's San Francisco was only a small town built very hastily for the business that was literally thrust upon them because of the discovery of gold. It was a gambling town. Dens of men with stacks of money, and bags of gold dust, and every device and contrivance to induce people to gamble.

There were no railroads in California at this time, so once again James, Henry and Will Skewis took to the boat, this time bound for Sacramento. The fare was eight dollars. Stage coach was the next form of transport, although the journey was mainly uphill, and the surrounding country was rough and mountainous. They eventually arrived at Deer Creek where they teamed up with brother Edward Skewis.

> *An incident happened one day there, just after dinner. Moyle and his partner, who worked a mile or so above us, came to us and enquired if we had seen a man pass by. We said that one just went along. They said the fellow had robbed them of a bag of gold, and asked if we would go with them to recover it. We went with all the men we could gather up, and went to a little town at that time called Newtown, and we found the man in a saloon. He had just taken a glass of beer. We arrested him as our prisoner, accused him of the theft, but he denied the whole of it, expressing his willingness to be searched which we did and found the identical bag of gold dust. The bag was given to the landlord to hold until Mr Moyle and his partner could prove it was theirs.*
>
> *There was a Miner's Court established, a Judge appointed, and two of the best talented men to defend each side. The one who defended the prisoner was a Mr Hartsough, a very able Defender. The name of the other I do not remember now, but he understood the work very well.*
>
> *The bag was produced. Mr Moyle said that if that bag was theirs it weighed so many ounces, and there were pieces containing so much weight, and described their shape. Everything was found as stated. The prisoner was found "guilty." There was a difference of opinion in regards to that one party was for hanging, the other for branding with a red hot iron in the shape of the letter "R", to signify thief. This was to be burned on the side of his face, besides receiving on the bare back two dozen lashes by Mr Moyle who was a very powerful man.*
>
> *Before the division of the crowd Mr Hartsough argued in relation to the seriousness of sending the poor man into eternity not having time to prepare to meet his God, and so eloquently did he argue that when division was made, it was found there were two or three more for branding and flogging, than hanging.*
>
> *So the iron was shaped into the letter "R", and the thief tied to a tree and stripped to the bare back. A rough whip was made for the flogging and he got it severely. His back was a mass of torn flesh, then the iron was applied to his face, but it was too hot to leave any readable letter. He was loose with these words "If caught again to be hanged by the neck until dead." I have heard since that he continued robbing and was finally arrested by the civil authorities, and hanged in the same county Nevada, California.*

That winter, as the rainy season set in, James Skewis and his colleagues moved up into the ravines. By day the countryside was beautiful. There were massive oak trees and pine trees, some of which stood two or three hundred feet high. But at night there were the haunting unearthly yells by the many wolves that abounded there. The grizzly bear also prowled about by night.

Close by was Grass Valley which had become a popular town. A Methodist church had been built. Mr Blain was reputedly a good man and a good preacher. But one Sunday there was an unusual occurrence which disrupted the normally peaceful town.

> *There was a man caught for stealing horses, and there was a fuss between the sheriff and his party, and the miners. The former wanted to arrest him, and the latter wanted to lynch him. There were thousands of people there. The miners grabbed him and dragged him along and the poor fellow trembled like the wind. Finally the sheriff got him and had him in prison. What became of him I never heard.*

James Skewis moved on in the search of gold to Sullivan's Creek, Sonora, Springfield and Carson Creek but with little luck. He set his mind on San Francisco with a view to going into the dray business. But no sooner had he arrived when he met a group of people who were about to embark on a trip to Australia looking for gold. Comments they had received from friends who were out there pointed to a very bright future. In 1853 James and his newly acquired friend set sail on a barque bound for Australia.

There was a good crowd of passengers and everyone got on well with each other. There were on board twelve or thirteen Mormon apostles, as they called themselves, who did not appear too well informed. This was apparently unnecessary for they had the "light" and whenever the gentiles seemed to have them cornered they would simply say "You are in the dark, and cannot understand the light."

One day we were about 130 degrees north latitude when we espied a boat pulling towards us. We could not tell what to make of it, but when they came alongside they told us their ship was wrecked off the island yonder. They had been whaling, and had a considerable quantity on board, and as the weather was favourable they thought they could save most of it. They wanted some little provisions, and wanted our Captain to take five or six men with us to the next island we might put into. They came on board; one of them was the doctor of the wrecked vessel. He professed to be an infidel, and he argued his views with the Mormons and Christians, so there was a new theme every day. We soon put into the Samoa Islands. Here we found both Catholic and Protestant missionaries. The natives were fine looking people, and well behaved. They did all they could to please the passengers and ship's crew.

We set sail having left behind the wrecked crew and very soon one of the Mormons was taken ill with smallpox. There was a suggestion to throw him overboard, but the other Mormons assured the gentiles that the disease would spread no further for they had laid hands on him. But the next morning one of the gentiles was taken down with it. Then there was a great to do — a big stir — and all acted as though they were sure to be marked if the two who were ill were not thrown overboard. However, no one else caught the disease. Eventually land was sighted and we drew into Sydney harbour. A doctor came on board and said we would have to remain in quarantine for the usual time. Smallpox was not known in Australia and they wanted to be very careful to prevent it taking hold in that country.

Once out of quarantine James Skewis and friends landed in Sydney and spent a week looking around the town which had beautiful churches, good preachers, exciting walks and a wonderful climate. Then it was en route for Melbourne by steamboat which took five days. The town was only small, but full of life and business, and one day it would become a great commercial city.

Four days were spent sightseeing before the next part of the journey — to the gold fields of Bendigo. They walked all the way . . . ninety miles! The weather was hot and dry and the party had to pass through the Black Forest where murders and robberies took place almost every day. People travelling from the gold mines were often attacked and many lives would be lost and much gold stolen.

The Bendigo Mines comprised seven hills, and extended five to seven miles in measurement. Each of the hills was rich in gold, but by the time James Skewis arrived there the best part of them had been worked out. He and his friends built a log cabin, covered it with canvas; cooked their own victuals and generally speaking had a good time, although good water was not always easy to find. A fee of one pound and ten shillings for a licence per month was payable to the government for the privilege of working the mines. James Skewis was fairly successful at finding gold, his most successful "clean up" being thirty ounces in ten days.

James (then 29) and his cousin Will Skewis (47) later moved to Castle Main and Creswick Creek. They were accompanied by a Mr Henry Davis. It seems that one has never to spend too much time in one place and soon the party were on the road again to Ballarat and a new town called Avoca where gold had just been discovered. There was lots of gold — stained black, caused by the iron in the gravel with water. But after a few months here the Skewis boys became homesick and made up their minds to return to see the home folks once more.

After taking in the sights of Melbourne they secured a third class passage on the ship *Anglesey* bound for London. The ship sailed on 5 January 1855. When the ship drew near to Cornwall off Penzance, a pilot boat drew alongside and offered to land anyone in Penzance for the price of one pound. About twelve passengers transferred, but no sooner had they climbed aboard the pilot boat when a big storm blew up. Most were seasick and it took thirty-six hours to land. The crew remarked that in all their seafaring lives they had never seen it more rough.

James Skewis and his cousin Will had been away from Cornwall for just over six years. They made their way to Camborne by train where they were met by relatives and friends.

This was the spring of 1855 and I spent my time visiting places and surrounding towns that I had never seen before which greatly pleased me. I met with people who were glad to see me from the knowledge I possessed of dear friends and relatives of theirs in Australia. By having seen their likenesses in picture albums, I was able to address them by name much to their astonishment, never having seen me before.

On this visit to England, cousin Will and myself went up to London to see the capital, and likely the most populous city of the world. While there we visited many noted places historically and otherwise. One beautiful evening, the city being lit up, the Queen of the English nation and her husband, with hosts of aristocracy in their elegant carriages and finely dressed attendants, passed in the street in which we happened to be, so we had a tolerable good view of the whole procession. As we wanted to see as much of London as possible, we were glad to have had a sight of one who certainly, on account of her blessed qualities, all England is proud of and never hesitates to pray God's blessings on her.

We also went to the great St. Paul's Cathedral while divine service was rendered, and was pleased with the delightful singing and to look up to the dome and to note all its grandeuer was pleasing in the extreme.

We took pleasure in crossing London Bridge on the River Thames, beheld the ships and crafts from all countries of the world and all peoples, languages and colours. But what could one see of London in three or four days? Very little indeed when you take the whole city in question. To a stranger it seems as though it has no end of attractions, and as time was precious we had to leave the British capital.

Will and James Skewis returned to Cornwall by train and spent the remainder of their time visiting friends and relations. Just before they left for America James surprised a lot of people by suddenly announcing his engagement to Jane Thomas Rabling. They married in Camborne in 1855 and shortly afterwards departed for New York on board the good ship *Esmeralda*, which was loaded with tin plate for the States. The journey took almost eight weeks. From New York it was by land to Chicago and Shullsburg.

James and his newly acquired wife Jane bought a farm with seventy acres, a mile east of Shullsburg. There was a good farmhouse and several outhouses for horses and cattle. Their spirits were high, but sadly the crops and profits were poor. However James and Jane had plenty of chickens and turkeys as well as cows and hogs, so they could live reasonably cheaply.

Three children were born to James and Jane Skewis between 1856 and 1860 — Anita, (born 12 November, 1856), William James (27 February, 1858) and Francis Harry (18 January, 1860).

James sold the farm in March, 1861 at a similar time to the inauguration of President Abraham Lincoln, the sixteenth President of the United States of America. The Skewis family sailed down the Mississippi to New Orleans and arrived there at a time when the South was drilling men to fight for independence from the North. All the problem was brought about through the question of slavery.

The Skewis' were heading for Mexico, but having come from the North there was considerable hard feeling against northern folk. They waited several days at a hotel awaiting a steamboat and managed to sail just before the port was blocked from all commerce. On the journey to Mexico were two colleagues Harry Oates and Joseph Rule who were going to work in the silver mines.

We arrived in Mexico without accident. The Port of landing was Vera Cruz. At certain seasons of the year yellow fever prevailed.

At that time there were no finished roads by rail. There was a commencement, and some ten or twelve miles of track laid. Our coach was drawn on a car, and pulled by mules to the end of the track, then we were drawn by mules on the old road to Mexico.

The first long days ride brought us to Orizaba where we got good meals and a bed for a few hours. Then off again, and that night arrived at Publa which was to us a beautiful town. Here we were refreshed by a good meal and a few hours sleep, and after a cup of good coffee we were off again.

Every day we had to pass a long plain, then would have to go up another flight of high mountains, and the descent to the great plain of the city of Mexico. After a brief stop in the city we made for Pachuca arriving the same day. We were received at the house of the wife's father William Rabling, also brother William Rabling and sister Elizabeth Rabling.

The first job James Skewis had at Pachuca was working underground in a mine where the pay was very good. The majority of the workers were Mexicans who were generally speaking a cheerful bunch of fellows — great singers and superb whistlers.

In due course James was promoted to look after the company's stamp and to receive the ore when brought from the mines to be stamped. He later took over in charge of the ore yards when he saw that the boys separated the waste from the ore, and made sure it was fit to be taken to the stamps to be crushed.

James Skewis and the family spent seven years in Mexico and in 1868 they decided on a return to the United States.

> By this time there had been many changes in the Mexican government. While the United States had on one hand the great war between the north and the south, the French had landed a large body of troops in Mexico and subdued it so to put Maximillian at the head of the Mexican government, as Emperor of Mexico. He once came to visit our mine, and the English people cheered him lustily. He said that was the heartiest cheer he had heard since landing, and he gave us 500 dollars to have a good breakfast, which we did. However, in 1867 he was shot, and many were sad at the event.
>
> While there were many encounters with the soldiers, about two or three miles from us sixty Austrians were going to Real del Monte to relieve a force there. They were laid by three or four thousand Mexican troops, and all were killed with the exception of two who made a break over the mountains, bullets flying all around them. We were near enough at other times to hear the bullets rattling on the top of the houses near us, and many a poor fellow lost his life. Sad indeed it is to live in the midst of revolutions.

Two more children had been born to Jane and James Skewis whilst they were in Mexico: Edward John (born 12 January, 1865) and George Absalom (25 January 1867). Once back in Shullsburg the family expanded by a further three — Charles Samuel (born 21 February, 1869), Jennie Rabling (1 December, 1872) and Elmer Arthur (25 December, 1877) who incidentally celebrated his 100th birthday on 25th December, 1977.

The Skewis family moved to Iowa, in the north central state of America. A prairie tableland, it is drained by tributaries of the bordering Mississippi and Missouri and has great climatic extremes.

In 1876 the family went to LeMars on the Illinois Central Railway, and then had to travel by wagon. It was necessary to ford the Rock River on the trip. A farm was rented from Tom Warren and cattle, horses and equipment were bought. The family lived there for a year or two, meanwhile building a house on their own farm. Beloit, on the Sioux river, was the closest town.

The town of Inwood was started in the late 1880's and was built on the Milwaukee Railroad a mile north of the Skewis farm.

One of the first buildings was a small store run by Mrs Billie Skewis who was the widow of James Skewis' first cousin Will Skewis, who accompanied him on his trip to California and Australia.

The Skewis brothers built a warehouse to store grain and a lumber yard.

Anita Skewis started a school in a store building, which was the first school in Inwood, and she was the first teacher.

Mr Mack and Ed Lyon started a newspaper *The Inwood Herald* about 1898 which was later bought by the Skewis brothers, and for a time Miss Jennie Skewis was its editor.

The Skewis family lived on the farm for ten years before moving to the town of Inwood. During this time James Skewis made many trips to Mexico and would be gone several months at a time; the farm work would be done by his sons.

As Inwood grew, a bank was started. James Skewis was the President and Ed and Jennie Skewis worked in the bank. It appeared that James Skewis had a finger in most new enterprises in Inwood. He wrote a rhyme about the town:

Inwood the little town in which I live	*We have some by the name of Bahnson*
Some go by the name of Brown	*And quite a few by the name of Lyon*
For which we should not grieve.	*We are proud of our Jacksons*
And some by the name of Anderson	*And also of our Albertsons*
Others by the name of Johnson	*We have many Jensens*
And through the darkest night	*But perhaps more Hansons*
Some by the name of White.	*Quite a few Ericksons*
Then there is Doctor Lewis	*A small number of Larsons*
And also James Skewis	*Then there is Mr Iverson*
Then comes Mr Liddel	*And our old friend Halverson*
And our distinguished Doctor Strubbel	*The lumber man Richardson*

And the ticket agent Flanagan.
We are glad to have Shoemakers,
And some few Bakers
Then come the Stefens
And auctioneer Lambkins
Our butcher Henry Khurts
Must be followed by the Devonports.
The Herald's editor Stern
And Mr and Mrs Washburn.
A plenty by the name of Harris
And there is a family of Lowerys
Sam Mack, the postmaster
And Clarence Ladd, restaurateur
Minister Hainch, the Presbyterian
Leslie Foote the creameryman
Again we have Moons
And a nice family of Shermans
William Oates and family

And veterinarian Badgely
Then there is Bill Iyves
And the one-armed man Ives
We are blessed with Helgersons
And just as good Storajham
Boys like Professor Flitvier
And girls — ice cream Hatcher
Fred Bucknam the grain buyer
Martin the grain and coal seller.
John Bullock and his mother
They have married Will his brother
Miss Colvin the lady hat-maker
Mr Manwaring the banker
Miss Royce high school teacher
Berge, Lutheran preacher.
Herb Rensham and Mr Craft
Likely will vote for Mr Taft
We must not forget Mr Frank Ream
Nor bachelor Lamkin Romain.

Without any doubt whatsoever Mexico was very close to the heart of James Skewis who wrote at length on his visits to the country.

Mexico as a mining country is second to none. It has every known mineral—gold and silver is quite plentiful. These loades are mostly found in the mountains, because they crop out at the surface and are visible for miles, so that by driving tunnels and sinking shafts mines may be opened up, and by good judgement, made very profitable.

And the countryside was grand. Here he describes a journey from Tampico:

Soon after leaving the town we had to pass a deep wide river a full quarter of a mile wide. We got a native with a canoe to take us across. We unsaddled our horses and held the halter in our hands. The horses had to be kept by the canoes, and we had enough to do to keep their heads above the water. When we landed, the horses were exhausted and we were glad we got across so well. Then we rode through a flat country but very fertile. That night we slept on a bench in the open air.

Early next day we were off over more elevated ground—here and there a few natives huts with patches of maize, vegetables and fruits. When hungry we would ask for a meal off them and always got it. They would kill a chicken, fry or boil eggs, and give us a splendid meal for fifteen cents apiece.

Finally we came to a river not very wide, but deep and swift, which we had to cross on horse back. I was fearful to do this, but my comrade took the lead and I had to plunge in also, and risk it. I had no experience in such work and was very tired, but thankful we got through in safety.

After that we passed a big stream with a rocky bottom and by keeping the ford were able to cross without the horse having to swim. I think through the journey we crossed the same stream twenty-seven times.

Finally we came to a mountain which we had to go up until we arrived on top. They call it El Monte del Cachillo, which is the knife mountain. We had to travel a considerable distance where it was very narrow. Both on our right and on our left we could look down thousands of feet. In all my journeys I never met its equal. One place we passed was a great forest of all kinds of trees and there were oranges growing wild. We saw no habitation near, and we had to stand on our horses to reach the lower branches to get at the oranges.

By present indications Mexico will become a powerful nation. Everything is being fostered to that end, and many of the old customs one by one are done away with. As the light comes, darkness through ignorance disappears.

James Skewis celebrated his 80th birthday on 10th February, 1906 and received a letter from his son William James Skewis:

Dear Father,
As it is your birthday, and your 80th at that, I thought I would write you a letter.
For one to look ahead to that number of years it looks a long way off, but after the time has passed, it does not seem so long after all; and yet when one stops and thinks of what strides the world has made in

that time you cannot but be astonished. It was in the year of your birth that Stephenson and Erickson were trying their first locomotives. I believe that about twelve miles of track were the entire length of railroads in the world. And to think of the miles of roads there are today, and the great number of engines, and also the improvements made in other lines, and all in your day and lifetime.

If someone could have told you when you were a boy what you would see accomplished during your life, it would have sounded like a remarkable fairy tale. Many of the things that children of today consider just everyday affairs you would not believe could ever be accomplished.

I often sit and look back and wonder what man is that it should be given to him to work out the great forces for his use that God has stored away for him when he made the world, and kept hidden until it was time to use them. There are other wonders stored away ready for the time for which they are needed and then they will be found.

But how can man take and use the wonders of God without giving him scarcely a thought for His share, I do not understand.

Well, coming back to the present, I think that we as a family have a great cause to be thankful for, more so than the average family. We have all grown up with very little sickness, and it is a rare thing indeed for a family of children to all live to the Golden Wedding Day as yours have, and to be as little separated from each other as we have been.

It would be very pleasant if we could all gather together tomorrow to wish you well, but I guess we have had so many blessings that we ought not to grumble because we don't have everything we wish for.

It is my wish that you may have a good many more birthdays with good health, and a contented mind as long as God permits you to live, and to remain on the earth, and that we may gather together again many times.

With best love to Ma and Jennie and yourself.

I remain your loving son,

W.J. SKEWiS

There were to be two more happy years together as a family, but on 18th May, 1908 Jane Skewis died at the age of 74 years and was interred in Inwood Cemetery in a brick vault.

In September, 1908 James and his daughter Jennie, together with Hazel Prichard spent the winter months in Mexico, via Sheldon, Sioux, Kansas City, Dallas, Texas, San Antonio and Monterrey. They visited many friends and also the rich silver mines of Pachuca and Real del Monte.

For those who can afford to leave their northern homes and spend a winter in California or Mexico, I cannot see how there will be cause for regret. For our kind need a change such as these countries can give for health, as well as educationally. Many places give such pure water that it does one much good. Pure sparkling water is a delight of no small matter.

James Skewis had attended Camborne Wesleyan Methodist School, Cornwall as a boy and it made a lasting impression upon him. Throughout his life he would reminisce about the people he had met or listened to preaching. He often made reference to passages from the Bible.

I well remember a man I heard when a boy by name Billy Bray preach in the Bible Christian Church. He was very unlearned, and full of simplicity but never the less a holy Christian. Every time he came the church would be full, and very often many would not be able to get in. He used many simple expressions and very effective. He would say he was not a very good singer, but his heavenly Father liked to hear him do his best. That God made the crow as well as the nightingale, or the lark. All that was required was to do your best. It is thought that a great number were converted by his preaching. His trust was in God, and God honoured him, by having power with God and man. In those days local preachers were in great repute. I have seen great revivals for weeks, conducted without seeing any regular preacher all through, and I never saw more effective revival work anywhere in my life. Preachers and prayer leaders filled with the love of Christ, and sinners knew they got their power at the fountain head, and there could be no more cause for any to say it is all for pay, as they very often do when conducted by paid ministers.

I often think how differently God's word may read. If properly, the greatest boon, sweeter than the honey or the honeycomb. It imparts life spiritual, and there is no doubt of the source from which it comes. There is nothing second-handed about it. One can get no closer to the fountain than here, and I may not condemn other good books, but sometimes think it would be better if there were less, and none of the worthless ones which lead to one's ruin without government, just as surely as drunkenness, if continued.

One would suppose by reading a few cases of some youths to have devoted all their life to the service of the church, more particularly those whose office consecrated them as ministers or priests, and of one especially who knew the scriptures from youth, and none can be known too soon. But children like to play, and have all the enjoyment which their activity enables them, and likely this is the spirit of youth in past ages as well as in our day. Yet there may have been some in all ages opposed to children playing. I would judge such as never knew what it was to be boys, much less men.

The broadmindedness of St Paul "When I was a boy, I thought as a boy and acted as a boy, but when I became a man I put away childish things and acted like a man" felt the greater responsibilties connected therewith, and most boys with all their love of play look forward to the time when they will become themselves as the very height of their ambition, and no doubt girls think just the same. The apostle did not compass his views to one town or parish, he was a man of the world, and appeared to enter into all phases of life. First a boy, then a man, and God's chosen to preach the news of God's eternal salvation to every creature — bond or free, white or black — and in every sense worthy to be called the great apostle, to suffer and die for his master. His challenge to the church "Follow me, as I follow Christ" is an example of all ages, and the church could perhaps do nothing better to hasten the Kingdom of God on earth than by praying God to give the world many like him.

By the witness of his spirit the church knows Jesus to be the way, the truth and the life. The disciples did not like the idea of losing him, but he comforted them by saying "I go to my Lord and my God, to your Lord and your god, and will come again and will receive you to myself. My presence shall be always with you. I will never leave you, nor forsake you. Heaven and earth may pass away, but my word never. Be not faithless, but believing."

I read when I was a boy how that the house of Mr Wesley's father burned up when he and the other children were small and lost everything, but the clothes about their persons, and when his father knew that all his children were spared, he and the children knelt down and thanked God that all were spared, safe and sound. If that family shall be found saved, and none found wanting in the day of judgement there will be a thousand times greater cause for gratitude.

I do admire the family arrangement. There seems to be a love gathered around one's own family that gives the deepest concern for the happiness, and welfare for everyone, and though the Christian is charitable to all the world in gifts and prayers, but much more for his own family, there is nothing inconsistent in that. For a man is responsible for the welfare of his family. We know that man is a two-fold being and he has to be careful and faithful to the interest of both, or he cannot glorify God in the fullest sense.

Negligence, slothfulness and ignorance are the causes of all poverty in temporal, as well as spiritual affairs. The wise man said he passed by the field of the slothful, and by the vineyard of the man void of understanding, and thorns and nettles covered the face thereof, and the walls thereof were broken down. He saw and considered it well, looked upon it, and received instruction. Thus the wise will learn from the foolishness and follies of others. The means and appliances in those days were so crude and slow, that there must have been very little stimulus as we find it in our day.

Within the last few years men have shown such wonderful activity mentally as to turn things in the world upside down, and one is continually looking and expecting to hear of or see something invested that will displace or make useless the things that preceded them.

When I was a boy I heard a lecture by a man who hinted at the inventions that were being brought forth by the brainthought of man, so that one old woman saw men making a road for a train to run on, and wanted to know what they doing. They told her she could ride in the cars from town just as comfortable as sitting in her house, and in almost no time at all. In later years she often saw the train flying along, but was afraid to ride in it. The next time she saw men digging pits and putting in poles to stand up with wire stretched on top of them, she asked what they were doing. They said it would convey news around the world in about eight minutes. She replied "Get me to ride on that if you can". She believed in caution.

We are glad to know there are millions of people who have set their hearts on things that are not material, but spiritual, to satisfy the longings and desires of their hearts, and their honour is the glory of God, and people of all nations and colours, rich or poor, learned or unlearned.

James Skewis died 13 May 1911 and was buried at Inwood. He was 83 years of age. He had always led a good Christian life and was always thankful to others:

WHAT LIFE MEANS
First of all, life means to me an unceasing gratitude to God who gave it. There is no day of my existence on which I forgot to give thanks to that Eternal Power, who, out of unconscious

past, beneficiently called me into the present of this world; a world so lovely in its natural beauty that we can imagine nothing lovelier save Heaven. To be allowed to dwell at all in such a paradise, made fair with everything that can delight the eyes or charm the senses, is to me sufficient cause for beauty that we can imagine no greater ingratitude than unthankfulness. And if I were to try and count up the blessings which just the one joy of sight bestows, I should be beggered of all words.

     *   *   *   *   *   *

God hath blessed us, and so we must
Annually and daily trust
Him the author of all good
Who sends us daily, our daily food
Our hearts to Him we strive to love
And praise Him ever, who dwells above.

And so we need not faint nor fear
To trust Him for the coming year.
His hands are open, and will bestow
On all his creatures, here below
Milk and butter, bread and honey
And feed his children that are hungry
Receive the thanks of this our country.

     *   *   *   *   *   *

MEANWHILE BACK IN CORNWALL

SAMUEL SKEWES was the son of Henry and Jane Skewes of Ruan Major, Cornwall. He was born 10 July 1811 and later farmed at Tresodden and Chybarles, Ruan Major.

The agricultural labourer had the lowest standard of living of any large occupational group. His food was more coarse and less plentiful, his living accommodation more overcrowded and insanitary and his wages lower than any regularly employed town worker. During the 1840's agricultural labourers received in the region of eight to ten shillings a week.

Tresodden Farm, Ruan Major, Cornwall, 1930

The lifeboat "Edith" being launched at Mullion. She was built in 1887 and served Mullion from 1887 to 1894. Photo circa 1890 — Royal Institution of Cornwall

Chybarles Farm, Ruan Major, Cornwall, 1930

The farmer worked hard, with little compensation in those early Victorian days. He would work in all weathers for very long hours and with very little aid from machinery until late in the century. They happily went about their daily chores like ploughing, sowing, reaping and mowing.[6]

Very few agricultural labourers left biographies of themselves, but Samuel Skewes kept a diary. Perhaps not as detailed as the diary written by James Skewis of Camborne and Wisconsin, but it gives an insight as to his activities in Cornwall.

A brief look at 1839.

In January the majority of the month was taken up by "bringing in the turnips". On 9 February he bought five pigs. Good Friday fell on 29 March and there was much rain. On 2 April he visited Redruth fair when he remarked that there were few cattle, and those which were on sale seemed very expensive.

On 4 April Samuel logged that the weather was "very wet and stormy. Four vessels were driven on shore at Mullion." Although he does not name the vessels they were the *Albion, Penrice Castle, Tamar* and the *William and Catherine.*[7]

Much of May was spent "ploughing in potatoes". The family had a feast on 3 June. On 18 July more trouble on the Cornish coast when "six men were drowned after a vessel ran aground at Gunwalloe." The storm happened about midday when a schooner, laden with coals, the *Perseverance* of Leith bound for Truro, was driven on the Loe-pool bar of sand in Mount's Bay. Five men and a boy were drowned and the vessel broke into fragments.[8]

In 1839 Samuel Skewes attended church four times, chapel, twenty-four; he visited Helston twenty-seven times and St Keverne, seven. On the farm forty-eight days spent on ploughing, eleven days on threshing, in addition to working in the orchard, carrying dung, winnowing and sawing timber.

Corn was cut with a short "badging" hook and hay was cut with a scythe. On average a man could cut half an acre of corn a day and bind it into sheaves. He would take hold of the corn stalks and hold them with his left hand and sever them near the base, holding them until he had collected enough to make a sheaf. This was then tied with a straw "bant."[9]

Of note from his 1840 diary Samuel reported that January was a very wet and windy month. In March he went to Helston and returned a warrant to "Earby and Harris for assault". On 14 August he killed the "great sow for the market", and received 5/4d.

A major event took place in his life on 2 March 1841 when he married Catherine Lugg at Ruan Major Church. She was the daughter of James Lugg, farmer of Hendra on the Lizard. Samuel and Catherine did not have a honeymoon. They spent the day at Hendra on 3rd March and the following day Samuel was back on the farm "thrashing barley."

On 21 May he reports in his diary "Began to till potatoes. Flood of rain. Went to Mullion to have tooth drawn out."

Samuel celebrated his 30th birthday on 10 July by spending the day "tilling the turnips."

On 9 February 1842 "Catherine had child." This, according to Ruan Major parish register, was a son Samuel who was christened on 27 March 1842.

There was no indication from the notes made in Samuel's diary that there were plans for the family to emigrate to America. Our first knowledge that plans were being made came in two entries for 25 and 26 May, 1852. "To Helston with wife buying clothes. Preparing things for our voyage."

A month later he went to Camborne with Edward Dale and F.H. Foxwell and "agreed with Mr Vivian for *The Cornwall* to go to Quebec at £3.00 per head."

On 4 August Samuel Skewes went to Falmouth with three chests and two casks of luggage. He was still working on the farm winnowing and going to Helston with corn. On return from Helston on 8 August, where he had purchased another cask and articles for the trip, he learned that *The Cornwall* would probably be sailing from Falmouth on the 9 August.

---

[6]*Useful Toil*, John Burnett; Penguin Books, London, 1977; p. 29.
[7]*Royal Cornwall Gazette* 12 April 1839.
[8]*Royal Cornwall Gazette* 26 July 1839.
[9]*Useful Toil*, John Burnett; Penguin Books, London, 1977, p. 65.

The remainder of the day was spent packing, and the family left for Falmouth placing their luggage on board. They spent the night "sleeping on the shore." The weather was fair. There was a long delay in the barque leaving. Three days were spent on board in the harbour. On Saturday 13 August 1842 Samuel went ashore and posted a letter to his mother.

The Cornwall eventually set sail at 11 o'clock in the morning of the 13th heading south-east. "There was a light breeze. We sailed south-east until 6.00pm. Becalmed. Steered south-west. Saw the Falmouth and Lizard lights, the last marks of old England which we had a chance to see."

The diary notes he made of the journey continued.[10]

18 August	*Came on stormy in evening. Got sick.*
1 September	*Storms, wind and gale. Got sick. Sea continued very rough.*
19 September	*Becalmed the whole of the day in sight of Newfoundland and Cape Britton. Caught 16 codfish.*
1 October	*Wayed anchor. Came up the river slowly with the tide. Anchored in the evening within sight of Quebec. The old town is very dirty. The new town has many fine buildings which together with its impregnable fortyfications makes it an interesting place.*
4 October	*Put our baggage on the Montreal steam boat and proceeded to Montreal in the evening.*
5 October	*Arrived Montreal at 5 o'clock in the morning. Took our luggage out of the wharf. Engaged a passage to Kingston by the canals and the Ottawa river for 3 dollars per head and two shillings luggage. Started in the evening. Whent on a few miles and lay too for the night, it being dark.*
6 October	*Proceeded on our journey. Came upto a steamer stuck in the mud. Made a rope fast to her and pulled her out.*
7 October	*Ran into a creek in fog and got fast in the mud. Paddled out again after a long struggle and proceeded on the river, passed Carrillion locks. Came up the five docks to Bytown in the evening. Whent on shore and bought some beef and bread. This is a flourishing village.*
8 October	*When we got up in the morning found ourselves crammed in between some trees, it being dark towards the morning they could not see the proper channel. However, after a long struggle we got out and whent on at a fine rate.*
9 October	*Came into Kingston longside of the 'Princes Royal'. Booked for Toronto at 2 dollars per head on a steamer. Put our luggage on board and remained in harbour until Monday evening. Kingston is a pretty place. Rainey. Taken ill with bowel complaint.*
10 October	*Left for Toronto. Stormy nights. Our accommodation aboard this boat is horrible.*
11 October	*Arrived Toronto this evening. The females slept on the shore at Mrs Roberts, a Cornish woman. This is the prettiest place we have seen.*
12 October	*Whent on board the transit steamer and came up to Lewes town. Got our baggage up to the rail carrs by waggons kept for the purpose. Proceeded onto Niagara where we stopped for the night after visiting the falls. Took lodgings.*
13 October	*Started for Buffalo at 6 o'clock. Arrived 8 o'clock. Put our baggage on board 'The Wisconsin' bound for Racine. Price eight dollars. Started in the evening.*
14 October	*Proceeded on the lake. Rather rough. Came into Cleveland and stopped for the night.*
15 October	*Left Cleveland and arrived at Detroit about midnight, and remained till morning.*
16 October	*Whent on shore. Bought some milk and cheese. Proceeded on our journey up Lake St Clare. Took in a great quantity of wood in the afternoon. Finds myself getting better.*
17 October	*Crossed Lake Huron.*
18 October	*On Lake Michigan. Sheltered a storm in the leward of an island. Remained for the night.*

---

[10] For these references I am grateful to Ruth Viall Skewes of St. Cloud, Minnesota, USA and Alice Eve Kennington of College Park, Maryland, USA for the loan of Samuel Skewes' diaries.

| 19 October | *Proceeded straight for Milwaukee.* |
| 20 October | *Arrived at Milwaukee in the morning and landed at Racine in the evening. Moderate rain.* |

The diaries of Samuel Skewes of Ruan Major and later Ives Grove, Racine, Wisconsin, USA, written between 1839 and 1880

It took nine weeks from leaving Cornwall for Samuel Skewes and his family to reach their final destination, Yorkville. The remainder of October was spent visiting friends Messrs T. Moyle, Thomas, Shepherd and Coles.

By November Samuel had purchased three forty-acre tracts of land, and then entered land from the Government adjoining that farm. Indians still passed through the neighbourhood and wild animals were quite plenty. At one time Samuel saw thirteen deer in a grove. These and wild fowl furnished many a meal for the early settlers. Samuel spoke of the danger from prairie fires which many times threatened homes so that they were compelled to plough all around their premises to protect their buildings. Out of the land that he purchased only six acres had been broken, and it was no easy task to develop raw land, but he laboured untiringly until he had developed a good farm. [11]

---

[11]*Biographical Album of Racine County*, Chicago, 1892, pp. 616, 617

The Mud House, Grovean, Ives Grove, Racine County, Wisconsin, USA to which Samuel Skewes and Jacob Lory and their families moved from Ruan Major, Cornwall after they emigrated in 1842

The winter of 1842 was spent in a shanty on Shanty Knoll at the north-west corner of Grovean Farm. But Samuel had made preparations to build his own house with out-houses for cattle. From his diary of November 1842:

"Building an oxen house and working on a new frame for apartment. Purchased 13 acres of woodland on a river, formerly of Isaac Place. Weather snowy, frosty and cold."

The "Mud House" was completed in 1843 and sheltered the family until 1874 when the property was rebuilt. "Grovean Farm" still remains in the Skewes family possession four generations later.

Grovean Farm, Racine County, Wisconsin, USA

From Samuel's diary of 1874 much of the year was spent writing letters, building a new cellar, mowing hay, cutting corn, sinking a well, fetching logs, mending shoes and making a bookcase. Visits included Yorkville, Milwaukee and Racine. He had begun to pick up the local dialect for on 31 March 1843 he reports "making shoes. Yankee doodle!" In 1844 he was granted a Certificate of Naturalisation.

> Be it remembered That at a Circuit Court of the State of Wisconsin, held at the Court House, in the town of Racine, for the County of Racine, in the State of Wisconsin, in the United States of America on the 25th day of October in the year of our Lord one thousand eight hundred and forty eight, SAMUEL SKEWES a native of England exhibited a petition, praying to be admitted to become a citizen of the United States, and it appearing to the said Court that he had declared on oath before the Clerk of the District Court for the County of Milwaukee on the 21st September A.S. 1848, that it was bona fide his intention to become a citizen of the United States and to renounce forever all allegiance and fidelity to any foreign Prince, Potentate, State or Sovereignty whatsoever, and particularly to Victoria, Queen of Great Britain and Ireland of whom he was at that time a subject; and the said Samuel Skewes having on his solemn oath declared, and also made proof thereof by competent testimony of William Cole and Charles Morris, citizens of the United States, that he had resided one year and upwards within the State of Wisconsin, and within the United States of America upwards of five years, immediately preceding his applications; and it appearing to the satisfaction of the Court, that during that time he had behaved as a man of good moral character; attached to the principles of the Constitution of the United States, and well disposed to the good order and happiness of the same; and having on his solemn oath declared before the said Court, that he would support the Constitution of the United States, and the State of Wisconsin, and that he did absolutely and entirely renounce and abjure all allegiance and fidelity to every foreign Prince, Potentate, State and Sovereignty whatever, and particularly to Victoria Queen of Great Britain and Ireland of whom before he was a subject — Thereupon the Court admitted the said SAMUEL SKEWES to become a citizen of the United States, and ordered all the proceedings aforesaid to be recorded by the clerk of the said Court, and which was done accordingly.

> In Witness whereof, I have hereunto affixed my hand and the seal of the said Circuit Court, at Racine, this 25th day of October in the year one thousand eight hundred and forty eight and of the sovereignty and independence of the United States of America the seventy second.
>
> ALBERT KNIGHT, Clerk.

Three more children were born to Samuel and Catherine in Wisconsin: George (1844), Sarah (1846) and Margaret (1848). His wife Catherine was taken ill in 1854 and died 21 August that year. His diary reports:

> *Friday 21 August 1854.*
>
> *Died in peace hanging on her Redeemer, my beloved wife and sharer of my joys and sorrows for these last 13 years and 6 months, leaving me a lonely widower and four motherless children — Samuel aged 12 years 7 months; George 10 years 2 months; Sarah Jane aged 8 years 3 months and Margaret Anne aged 6 years 1 month.*
>
> *May the Lord of Life and Glory enable me to hold fast whereunto I have attained, to walk in the paths of wisdom and virtue and bring up these dear children in the ways of piety, that parents and children may all meet again in Heaven and sing the praises of our Redeemer and Saviour throughout Eternity. Amen.*

The funeral took place on 27 August leaving the house at 11 o'clock after singing the hymn "Give Me The Wings of Faith". The procession arrived at Yorkville about 12 o'clock. There was a long train of 35 trams.

It was a bad period for Samuel. He had heard from James Lugg in England that his mother had died in 1853, aged 85 years. The same year his sister Jane died suddenly. She had married James Lugg and they had 5 sons and 4 daughters.

On 5 March 1853 Samuel Skewes had written to a young lady seeking help in the house:

> *To Miss Ruth Bottomley of Burlington*
>
> *Ives Grove,*
> *5 March 1853*
> *Madame,*
> *I learn by Mr John Hay that you have thoughts of hiring out this season. My wife would like me to have you come and live with us.*
> *You will therefore please to write us a few lines to say whether you can come — or not. We can*

wait a few weeks for you.
If you conclude to come I will bring a conveyance for you anytime you may appoint.
Yours very respectfully,

SAM SKEWES

Ruth accepted the job and commenced work just prior to the death of Catherine Skewes. She was the daughter of Edwin and Martha Bottomley and born in Huddersfield, Yorkshire 16 February 1832 and came to Wisconsin with her parents in 1842.

Within four years Samuel Skewes married Ruth Bottomley — on 20 March 1857. Four children were born to them: Edwin Bottomley (1858), Emma (1860), Eleanor Jessop (1864) and Thomas Henry (1869).

On 18 October 1857 Samuel Skewes wrote a letter to William Lugg at Geelong, Victoria, Australia:

15 years ago I was tossed on the broad Atlantic. I believed I was going in the path that providence had pointed out. So I went, nothing doubting. We were 21 passengers besides a young man from the east of Cornwall and out of that number six have already gone the way of all the earth. John Lory died from the kick of a horse. Mary Carter wife of T.H. Foxwell died of consumption. Alice Dale died of consumption. Charles Hosking, T.H. Foxwell's boy went to California and died there.

Old Mrs Dale died of consumption or something similar. Poor Catherine (Skewes) died in peace after a lingering disease of a consumptive kind of three years standing. And now Edward Dale has died.

In 1859 Grovean Estate was valued at 5140 dollars. It comprised 264 acres in one block, 17 acres of woodland in Ives Grove and 30 acres in what is called the Milwaukee Woods situated along the coast of Lake Michigan.

On 21 June 1859 Samuel began planning his new home to replace the "Mud House". This was successfully completed in 1867. On the occasion, after the old building had been razed, and had been replaced by the present structure nearby, a grove of thirteen sugar maple trees was planted on the site. From Samuel Skewes' diary we read:

Saturday 21 October 1876

Preparing site of old house for planting trees, digging pits and trimming trees. Family gathering on the occasion of planting centennial trees consisting of 13 Sugar Maples and planted by persons named hereunder, ten of whom were born on the premises and the other three children came with us on our settlement here in 1842, viz James L., Jane Lory and Samuel. Weather gloomy and chilly.

EDWIN B. SKEWES	EMMA SKEWES	JANE L. LUGG
SAMUEL SKEWES Jnr	MARGARET A. SKEWES	GEORGE SKEWES
THOMAS H. SKEWES	ELEANOR J. SKEWES	WILLIAM G. SKEWES
JAMES LUGG	WILLIAM LORY	MARY E.L. PHILLIPS
JAMES L. SKEWES		

As well as his property in Ives Grove, Samuel Skewes also had property back in Cornwall. A letter received in Wisconsin in 1872 from his brother Anthony Skewes of Tresodden Farm, Ruan Major read as follows:

Written at the Bell Inn, Helston, Cornwall, 30 March 1872.

My Dear Brother,

I have enclosed in this letter the money order which I received for you and party concerned on the Troons sale. I will also send herewith the bill of expenses which John Lobb and I had of Mr Trengrouse. You will please pay over to Henry two pounds less his money as I had to pay two pounds to Peter Williams' wife. The cost and postage of sending the cash is five shillings, so the cash now is £88 6s 6d. I hope it will find you all right. Please excuse anymore writing at the moment as I am in a Publick House and talking all around me.

Remember me kindly to Aunt Ruth and all your family. And my son James. I believe Henry will to my home on winter move. He is getting much better. I will send you a letter soon.

Yours truly

ANTHONY SKEWES

Resale of Troon

	£	s	d
Purchase money	152	0	0
plus interest	3	1	0
Already paid: notices and posting	1	8	6
For tracing from parish map		2	6
Hotel bill	1	2	6
Registration of Deed to America; London and back. Postage	—	7	6
Auction and special conditions	1	1	0
	4	2	0
	152	0	0
Plus	3	1	0
	155	1	0
Less	4	2	0
	150	19	0

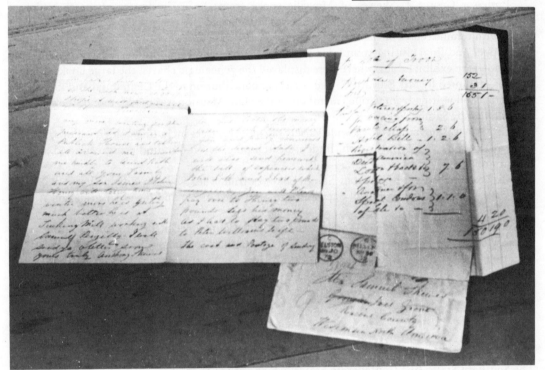

Letter and bill sent from Anthony Skewes of Ruan Major, Cornwall to Samuel Skewes of Ives Grove, Wisconsin, USA dated 30 March 1872

Samuel Skewes was also in receipt of money from Anthony Skewes when he received £147 10s 0d on 13 November 1866.

There had been quite an exodus of the Skewes family from Ruan Major in Cornwall to Wisconsin. The following had emigrated since 1842 up to 1860. Samuel Skewes and family; Mary Skewes who married Josiah Boulden; John and Mary Jane Skewes and their children Henry, Thomas Boulden, Edwin, Betsy and George, James Lugg Skewes; Samuel L. Skewes; William John Skewes and Hannibal Skewes.

Hannibal Skewes was born in Ruan Major 19 October 1838, son of Henry and Grace (née

Lugg) Skewes. He set sail for America on 17 April 1858. He boarded the *Charles Chalmer* at Falmouth and reached Grovean Farm, home of his uncle Samuel Skewes on 25 May 1858. On 15 June 1865 he married Miss Eliza Phillips. The ceremony was conducted by Rev William Jolliffe and afterwards a large party was held.

The couple later had five children: Edith Grace, Edward Henry, Manley Thomas, Clinton Hannibal and Lillie Ann.

On 11 July 1942 one hundred years after Samuel Skewes and his family arrived in Wisconsin a Centennial party was held when their descendants celebrated the occasion.

In the 1890's there were 17 first cousins who were descended from the Skewes family. In 1942 only a handful survived, but it was a perfect day for the picnic which was held at the Old Settlers Park, Union Grove. The oldest son of the oldest son of Samuel Skewes, Doctor William G. Skewes presided with the next oldest member of the clan Edward H. Skewes acting a secretary. Greetings were read from absent members and friends. The most distant came from Howard and Jessie Skewes in Los Angeles; James Skewes the editor, and Grace his wife, had sent besides their telegram their 13 year-old son as their representitive from Meridian, Mississippi; greetings were received from George and Boulden Skewes of Luverne, Minnesota.

Later in the afternoon nearly 80 persons gathered for the Centennial programme, which consisted of historical sketches and of music.

Professor George J. Skewes of Mayville spoke from the early diaries about the original settlement in Racine County. Edward H. Skewes represented the Hannibal Skewes branch of the family with reminiscenses of the seventeen cousins.

Supper and final visiting completed a perfect day, during which interested groups of people surrounded the exhibit tables, where were displayed the genealogic charts; the large book of family pictures, mounted by Mrs Edward G. Skewes as her contribution to the Centennial and samples of handicraft and writing from various members of the clan. Mention was made, too, of the groves of trees planted by Samuel Skewes.[12]

Grovean was surrounded by a wide variety of colourful trees including golden willows, maple, Lombardy poplar, apple, pear, ash, linden, Scotch pine, seven hundred evergreens and a black walnut grove.

Grovean has been the home of Samuel Skewes from 1867, his son Edwin (born 1858 died 1913), his grandson Arthur Edwin Skewes (born 1891 died 1921) and his great grandson Arthur Russell Skewes (born 1922).

In August 1965 a wayside park was given to Racine County by Doctor Arthur Russell Skewes in memory of his great grandfather Samuel Skewes, and others to whom over the years Grovean has been their home. Today a grove of black walnut trees, hand planted in 1895 by Samuel Skewes, provides shade for picnickers at Skewes Park located at County Trunk "C" and 51st Drive in Yorkville, a mile and a half from Ives Grove.

*   *   *

AMERICAN CIVIL WAR

The American Civil War was fought throughout America between the years 1861 — 1865. The Southern States (the Confederate States) which wished to maintain their "states' right" went to war against the Northern States (The Union) who fought to keep the Union, and to abolish slavery.

Various members of the Skewes family from Wisconsin enlisted. The Wisconsin Army was referred to as the Badger Boys in Blue[13] They bore quite unequally the burden of war service and sacrifice. Some, including many of the early volunteers, served as long as three and even four years, saw a great deal of battle action, and were frequently exposed to the risk of disablement or death.

Of the estimated 80,595 individual enlistments from Wisconsin, more than 11,000 men died from wounds or disease, or were reported missing in action. There were approximately 15,000 men

---

[12] *Union Grove Sun*, 22 July 1942.
[13] *History of Wisconsin* Vol 2, Richard N. Current. State Historical Society of Wisconsin, 1976, p 352.

discharged for disabilities incurred in the service.

Roughly one soldier in three became a casualty of some kind, and one in every seven failed to survive the war.[14]

The 2nd Wisconsin Cavalry was organised under special authority from the General Government, granted to the Honourable Cadwalader C. Washburn, Governor Randall endorsing the action, and commissioning him as Colonel, 10 October 1861. Each Company had 2 majors, 12 captains, 12 first lieutenants and 12 second lieutenants.

Engagements for the 2nd Wisconsin Cavalry during the Civil War were Yellville, Helena, Prairie Grove, and La Grange (Arkansas), 1862.

Lick Creek, Arkansas, Vicksburg, Siege of Mississippi, Red Bone, Ingraham's Plantation, Mississippi, 1863.

Red Bone, Clinton, Jackson, Port Gibson, Fayette and Cole Creek (Mississippi), Fort Adams, Los Angeles and Yazoo City, Mississippi, 1864 and 1865.

The following members of the Skewes family served in the American Civil War.

SKEWES	EDWARD H.	Private with G Company, 2nd Cavalry. Enlisted 3 February 1862. Single. Aged 25 years. Deserted 20 January 1863.
SKEWES	EDWIN	Major with F and S Companies, 2nd Cavalry. Lived at Yorkville. Promoted to Major 29 July 1865. After the war he settled at Neosho, Missouri.
SKEWES	HENRY	Sergeant with G Company, 2nd Wisconsin Cavalry. Enlisted 18 November 1861. Single. Aged 26 years. Lived at Yorkville.
SKEWES	JOSEPH T.	Private with H Company, 22nd Infantry. Enlisted 15 August 1862. Single. Aged 19 years. Lived at Yorkville. Was wounded at Resaca. Was absent sick at muster out of the Regiment 15 November 1865.
SKEWES	THOMAS B.	Private with K Company 8th Infantry. Enlisted 5 September 1861. Single. Lived at Racine. Aged 40 years. Fought in Mississippi between 1861 and 1864 and Los Angeles, 1864.

The Civil War lasted four years. The Confederate States chose Jefferson Davis as President whereas the North was represented by President Abraham Lincoln. During the war years 90,000 people emigrated from Britain to the United States of America of whom almost half became Union soldiers. The Skewes family with their blue uniforms fought for the North (Union).

The Confederacy urgently needed British recognition, but all it got was popular sympathy as Britain did not take sides.

At first the Confederates were successful under General Robert E. Lee at the Battles of Bull Run in July, 1861 and August, 1862, but Lee suffered a repulse at Gettysburg in July, 1863. General Ulysses S. Grant succeeded in bringing the whole of the Mississippi under Northern control.

On Palm Sunday, 9 April 1865, Lee surrendered 13,000 survivors in Confederate grey to General Grant at Appomattox Court House, and a month later the world's largest, most costly civil war was over.[15]

The number of dead on both sides was estimated at 600,000. Slavery was ended as four million slaves achieved freedom, and it was hoped that the United States would be a better place for the ordinary citizen. As General Sherman had commented during the fighting: "War, at best, is barbarism."

But although the war was over trouble lay just around the corner for the President. Abraham Lincoln was assassinated on 14 April 1865 at Ford's Theatre in Washington by an actor and a Confederate fanatic, John Wilkes Booth, who escaped from the theatre, but was tracked down in Virginia and shot dead.

Ulysses S. Grant became President of the United States in 1869.

[14] *War of the Rebellion*, published by The State 1914.

[15] *Illustrated American Civil War*, edited by H.S. Commager; Orbis Publishing, London, 1976, p 262.

10 The Mining Brigade

FROM TIME immemorial Cornwall has produced miners. The county is rich in ores, and few can compare with it for the variety of minerals found.

The export of tin has been the very life of the community from the earliest times. In the year 1201 King John established four stannary towns in Liskeard, Helston, Truro and Lostwithiel. Penzance was added at a later date — 1663. All tin was brought to these towns for testing, taxing and sale. When smelted and moulded it was carried to the stannary town to be assayed by the stamping office. The block tin was "coined" (a corner was cut off) and the block, if found pure, was stamped with the Duchy seal. By an old stannary law, if any man adulterated the metal, three spoonsful of melted tin were poured down his throat.

On 13 September 1509 JOHN SKEWYS was granted a lease of the Tolls of tin in the Duchy Manors of Tewington, Tywarnhaile and Helston-in-Kerrier. In his will dated 2 June 1543 Skewys says:

"My servant Rose Woolman to have one haulfe of all manner of tynne hereafter wrought and gotten owte of any parte of my lands and tenements in the said county of Cornwall. Lawrence Courtenay to have the other half."

Tin remained Cornwall's most important mineral until the early years of the 18th century when the presence of copper became more appreciated. By the middle of the 19th century there were about 340 tin and copper mines employing 50,000 people; Cornwall was producing three-quarters of the world's copper.

From 1823 to 1840 Great Britain produced 231,163 tons of copper, of which 198,200 tons (or 82.6%) were produced in Cornwall.

The discovery of larger and cheaper supplies of tin and copper in other parts of the world including Chile and Lake Superior, Canada in the latter part of the 19th century led to falls in price which closed many mines throughout the country and in turn made thousands of people redundant.

In recent years a number of old Cornish mines have re-opened, but the success rate generally has been rather poor. Mines were seldom worked by one person alone, the persons comprising a company on the cost-book system, a form of partnership in transferable shares, being termed "adventurers." The practical direction of the mines was in the hands of the mine agent, termed "Mine Captain."

The life of the miner was hard, harsh and dangerous. Men, women and children worked in or on the mines. There were no lifts. Miners had to climb down ladders maybe 1,000 feet deep and work for long periods of time in temperatures of 100 degrees Fahrenheit plus.

In Helston WILLIAM SKUES was secretary of the Tinners' Association for Cornwall and Devon for 50 years from 1755, and it was agreed to pay him to "take the book of resolutions around all the tinners and associates who had not attended a meeting on 26 February, 1788 and to print 500 copies of the articles for circulation amongst the proper rank of this country."[1]

One major mining area in Cornwall was Gwennap and its various mines from 1823 to 1832 produced 30.1% of the total production of Great Britain and 37.7% of the Cornwall total. Tin was priced at £100 a ton in 1850. In 1982 it reached a staggering £9,000 a ton.

Gwennap is named after a saint and is situated seven miles north west of Falmouth and the same distance from Truro, and to the east is Kenwyn and Kea which were rich in Skewes'. To the north is St. Agnes and Redruth and to the west Redruth, whereas Stithians and Perranarworthal lie to the south. In the year 1837 the acreage for the parish of Gwennap was 5291 acres.

There were many members of the Skewes family living and working in Gwennap. Of this total

---

[1] *Cornwall in the Age of the Industrial Revolution*, John Rowe, Liverpool, 1953.

a large proportion were miners and they included:

ALEXANDER SKEWES, mine clerk from Chenhale (1814), mine agent by 1844.
RICHARD SKEWES, miner of Whitehall, Gwennap (1814). [2]
THOMAS SKEWES, miner who died 1817.
JOHN SKEWES, miner of Shilstones (1816) and later Poldice (1819 — 1829).
JOHN SKEWES, miner of Carharrack (1827 — 1829) and later of Penance (1834 — 1840). [3]
HENRY SKEWES, miner of Rough Street, Gwennap (1829).
JAMES SKEWES, miner of Carvannel, Gwennap (1831).
COLLAN SKEWES, miner of Lanner (1840).
WILLIAM SKEWES, miner of Trevarth (1862).
RICHARD SKEWES, miner of Penance (1841).
THOMAS SKEWES, miner of Penance (1841).
JOHN SKEWES, copper miner of Wheal Virgin (1851).
WILLIAM SKEWES, copper miner of Wheal Virgin (1851).
JOHN SKEWES, miner of Penance (1851).
JOHN SKEWES, copper miner of Carharrack (1851).
JOHN SKEWES, miner who died in Cuba 1859, but formerly of Gwennap.
RICHARD SKEWES, copper miner of Little Carharrack (1861).
WILLIAM SKEWES, miner of Trevarth (1861).
JOHN SKEWES, miner of Carharrack (1871).

The many mines in the Gwennap area included:

Andrew, Bell and Lanarth, Carvannal Cathedral, Clifford Amalgamated, South Clifford, West Clifford United, East Damsel, St Day United, Wheal Friendship, South Gorland, West Wheal Gorland, Grambler, Great Consuls, Wheal Jewell, Wheal Peevor, Tresavean and Treskerby.

A glance across the whole county from the Census Returns of Cornwall 1841-1871 lists the following as miners — exluding Gwennap.

1841
MATTHEW SKEWES, copper miner of Navy Row, Chacewater.
EDWARD SKEWES, copper miner of Veryan Row, Camborne.
JAMES SKEWES, copper miner of Veryan Row, Camborne.
WILLIAM SKEWIS, copper miner of Veryan Row, Camborne.
JOHN SKEWIS, copper miner of Union Street, Camborne.
JAMES, HENRY and WILLIAM SKEWES of Killivose, copper miners.
JOHN SKEWES, copper miner of Treswithian.
HENRY SKEWIS, copper miner of Higher Penponds.
JOHN, PETER, JOHN and RICHARD SKEWS, copper miners of Hugus, Kea.
RICHARD SKEWS of Kerley, Kea, mine agent.
JOHN and PEGGY SKEWS, copper miners of Kerley, Kea.
DIGORY and THOMAS SKEWS, copper miners of Kerley, Kea.
THOMAS SKEWS of Jolly's Bottom, Chacewater, copper miner.
WILLIAM SKEWS of Jolly's Bottom, Chacewater, copper miner.
JOHN SKEWS of Hugus, Kea, copper miner.

1851
JOHN SKEWS, tin miner of Trewint, Altarnun, Launceston.
DIGORY, MATTHEW and MARY SKEWES, copper miners of Dobwalls, Liskeard.
JOSEPH SKEWS, copper miner of Dobwalls, Liskeard.
HENRY SKEWES, lead miner of East Taphouse, St Pinnock.
THOMAS SKEWES, lead miner of St Allen, Truro.
PETER SKEWES, copper miner of Hugus, Kea.
RICHARD SKEWS, mine agent of Kerley, Kea.
JOHN SKEWS, mine agent of Kerley, Kea.
JOHN and SAMUEL SKEWS, copper miners of Seveock, Kea.
WILLIAM SKEWES, copper miner of Chacewater.
JOHN SKEWES, copper miner of Miners Row, Redruth.
WILLIAM SKEWES, copper miner of Pengegan, Camborne.
JAMES SKEWIS, copper ore labourer of Higher Treskillard.
HENRY, WILLIAM HENRY and RICHARD MARTIN SKEWIS, copper miners of Berriper,
Penponds, Camborne.
WILLIAM SKEWES, copper ore miner of Piece, Illogan

---

[2]Whitehall although then in Gwennap parish, is generally regarded as being in Scorrier.
[3] Modern spelling is Pennance.

1861
JOHN SKEWS, tin miner of Trewint, Altarnun, Launceston.
SAMUEL SKEWS, copper miner of St Cleer, Liskeard.
PETER SKEWS, miner of Hugus Common, Kea.
RICHARD, JOHN, THOMAS and PETER SKEWES, copper and tin miners of Kerley, Kea.
PETER SKEWES, copper miner of Charles Street, Truro.
WILLIAM SKEWES, copper and tin miner of Seveock Hill, Kea.
JOHN SKEWES, copper miner of Horse Downs, Crowan.
JOHN and EDWARD SKEWIS, copper miners of Treskillard, Illogan.
WILLIAM SKEWES of Roskear Fields, Camborne, mine agent.
WILLIAM SKEWS, miner of Illogan Downs.
SKEWES HENRY, mine agent of Beacon Hill, Camborne.
WILLIAM SKEWES, copper miner of Bolenowe Carn, Camborne.
HENRY SKEWES, mine agent of Lamin, Gwinear.
PHILIP SKEWES, copper miner of Lamin, Gwinear.
DIGORY SKEWES, copper and tin miner of Trevenner, Marazion.

1871
JOHN SKEWS, tin miner of Trewint, Altarnun, Launceston.
SAMUEL, JOHN and MATTHEW SKEWS, copper and tin miners of Commonmoor, St Cleer,
                                                                Liskeard.
MATTHEW HENRY and JOHN, copper and tin miners of Illogan.
HENRY and EDWARD SKEWES, miners of Rewlya Lane, Gwinear.
RICHARD SKEWIS, tin miner of Millpool, Perranuthnoe.

Mines around the CAMBORNE area included:

Camborne Consols, West Camborne, Camborne Vean, Camborne Vean and Wheal Frances, Carn Brea, Condurrow, Condurrow South, Condurrow West, Crane, Carnarthen Consols, West Dolcoath, North Frances, East Wheal Grenville, Wheal Nelson, North Wheal Crofty, New Dolcoath, North Dolcoath, South Dolcoath, Pendarves United, Wheal Rome, Roskear, Roskear North, Roskear South, Roskear West, North Wheal Seton, South Wheal Seton and Trevorrian.

Mines in the KENWYN area were:

Great Wheal Busy, North Wheal Busy, North Busy United, Creegbrawse and Penkevil United, Hallenbeagle, Wheal Henry, Killifreth, St Michael Penkevil, Penhaldarva, Great Wheal Prosper and Silver Valley.

KEA was represented by the mines of Great Wheal Baddern, East Wheal Clifford, Wheal Jane, Sperries and Falmouth and West Cornwall Consols.

REDRUTH mines included: Great Wheal Basset, North Wheal Basset, Wheal Buckets, Bullen and Basset United, Carn Brea South, Clyjah and Wentworth, Wheal Cupid, Grambler North, Wheal Harmony, Harmony and Montague, Mount Carbis, North Downs, Wheal Sparnon, Pednandrea Consols, Wheal Prussia, Great North Tolgus, Great South Tolgus, Old Tolgus, West Tolgus, Wheal Trefusis, East Trefusis, Treleigh United, New Treleigh and Treleigh Wood.

ILLOGAN mines were: Wheal Agar, Basset Consols, South Wheal Basset, West Basset, Buller Consols, Cooks Kitchen, Wheal Emily Henrietta, West Wheal Frances, Pool East, Pool North, East Seton, Old Tincroft, New Wheal Towan, West Wheal Towan, Wheal Union and West United Hills.

Mines in the Crowan area were: Wheal Abraham Consols, East Wheal Abraham, Carzise, Crenver and Abraham, Crowan, Wheal Curtis, Great Wheal Fortescue, New Wheal Frances, Wheal Hender, Wheal Osborne, Polcrebo and West Briton.

Members of the Skewes family also worked in mines further to the east. ST CLEER was represented by East Wheal Agar, Caradon Consols, South Caradon, South Caradon Wheal Hooper, West Caradon and Wheal Norris. ALTARNUN mines were: Halvana and Great Tregune.

The following are names of directors or members of committees, managers, under-managers and staff associated with Devon and Cornwall mines in the 19th and 20th centuries.[4]

---

[4] I am indebted to Justin Brooke of Marazion for so kindly preparing the list of SKEWES/SKEWIS' from his card index of mines and miners.

Part of the Wheal Busy complex, Chacewater, Cornwall.

SKEWES	Captain A.	clerk, Wheal Damsel, Gwennap, 1835.
SKEWES	Captain ALEXANDER	son of Captain A. Skewes. Chief clerk, Burncoose Copper Office, Illogan, 1835.
SKEWES	Captain DANIEL	manager, West Shepherd's, Perranzabuloe, 1845—47.
SKEWES	Captain DANIEL HODGE	manager, Sithney Wheal Buller, Sithney, 1852—53.
SKEWES	Captain H.	agent, East Alfred Consols, Gwinear, 1857-62. manager, Roskear, Camborne, 1863—64.
SKEWES	Captain H.	manager, Wheal Fanny Adela, Lelant, 1868—70.
SKEWES	Captain HENRY	agent, West Wheal Kitty, St Agnes, 1864. agent, South Alfred Consols, Phillack, 1866.
SKEWES	Captain PHILIP	agent, Wheal Hartley, Gwinear, 1863—66.
SKEWES	Captain RICHARD	purser, Hallenbeagle, Scorrier, 1841—42.
SKEWES	Captain WILLIAM	agent, Tincroft, Illogan, 1855.
SKEWES	Captain WILLIAM	agent, Stray Park, Camborne, 1860—66.
SKEWIS	Captain .	manager, Devon Copper and Blende, Lamerton, 1880.
SKEWIS	Captain A.	manager, Shepherd's United (East Wheal Rose section), Newlyn East, 1885—86.
SKEWIS & BAWDEN of Tavistock		pursers and managers, Drake Walls, Gunnislake, 1873. managers, Dunsley Wheal Phoenix, Linkinhorne, 1873.
SKEWIS	D.H.	director, Wheal Julian, Plympton St Mary and Shaugh Prior, 1855.
SKEWIS	EDWIN	Mining Journal, 1875 (5.6). Mining and mechanical engineer, surveyor, valuer; Washford near Taunton. Mining Journal, 1907 (2.3). Surveyor, Brendon Hills Mining Company to 1879.
SKEWIS	Captain H.	manager or agent, West Wheal Russell, Tavistock 1853—54.
SKEWIS	Captain HENRY	resident agent, Drake Walls, Gunnislake, 1851—3.
SKEWIS	Captain HENRY	agent, Wheal Seton, Camborne, 1856—61. agent, Calvadnack, Wendron, 1860. manager, Crane, Camborne, 1860—62.
SKEWIS	Captain H.	manager, Wheal Curtis, Crowan, 1864—65.
SKEWIS	Captain HENRY	manager, Wheal Crofty, Illogan, 1864—65.
SKEWIS	Captain HENRY	manager, Brendon Hills, Somerset, 1867—84. manager, Eisen Hill (part of Brendon Hills), 1867—74.
SKEWIS	Captain JOHN	manager, Castle Dinas, St Columb Major, 1851—52.
SKEWIS	Captain P.	agent, Florence Consols, Perranuthnoe, 1874—75.
SKEWIS	Captain PETER	manager, Florence Consols, Perranuthnoe, 1874—75.
SKEWIS	R.	agent, Garras, 1848, Kenwyn.
SKEWIS	Captain WILLIAM	secretary (or purser), Roskear, Camborne, 1867. manager, South Roskear, Camborne, 1872—76.
SKEWIS	Captain WILLIAM	manager, Exmouth, Christow, 1858—60.
SKEWIS	Captain W.	manager, North Exmouth, Christow, 1860—61.
SKEWIS	Captain WILLIAM	manager, Crelake, Tavistock, 1861-70.
SKEWIS	Captain W.	manager, Lydford Consols, Lydford, 1861—62. manager, Kit Hill, Callington, 1862—68.
SKEWIS	Captain WILLIAM	manager, Gunnislake Clitters, 1863—83. manager, New Birch Tor and Vitifer, 1864—71. purser, New Birch Tor and Vitifer, 1864—71. manager, West Maria and Fortescue, Lamerton, 1864—77. manager, New East Birch Tor, North Bovey and Manaton, 1865—66.
SKEWIS	Captain W.	manager, Great Devon and Bedford, Tavistock, 1866.
SKEWIS	Captain WILLIAM	manager, New East Birch Tor and Vitifer, North Bovey and Manaton, 1868. manager, Colcharton, Tavistock, 1868. manager, Victoria, Ashburton, 1868. manager, King's Oven and Water Hill, North Bovey, 1869—70.
SKEWIS	Captain W.	agent, Calstock Consols, Calstock, 1870. manager, East Kit Hill, Stoke Climsland, 1870. manager, South Kit Hill, Stoke Climsland, 1870 and 1872. manager, Hawkmoor, Gunnislake, 1870. manager, Wheal Arthur, Calstock, 1872—73. manager, New Victoria, Ashburton, 1870—71. manager, White Works, Princetown, 1869—70. manager, Dunsley Wheal Phoenix, Linkinhorne, 1872—75.
SKEWIS	Captain WILLIAM	manager, Slimeford Tin Waste Dressing Company, 1873.

Miners waiting to go down Dolcoath Mine,
Camborne. Circa 1900

SKEWIS	Captain W.	manager, Wheal Arthur, Calstock, 1873.
SKEWIS	Captain WILLIAM	manager, Drake Walls, Gunnislake, 1873 — 75.
		consultant, Wheal Luskey, North Hill, 1881.
		manager, Wheal Luskey, North Hill, 1882 — 84.
SKEWIS	Captain W.	manager, Trebartha Lemarne, North Hill, 1881-84.
SKEWIS	Captain WILLIAM	manager, Sortridge, Whitchurch, 1881 — 83
		manager, Collacombe, Lamerton, 1883 — 84.
SKEWIS	Captain W.	manager, Old Gunnislake, Gunnislake, 1880 — 83.
SKEWIS	Captain WILLIAM	manager, East Wheal Rose, Newlyn East, 1881 — 85.
SKEWIS	WILLIAM BAWDEN	secretary, Devon Copper Blende, Lamerton, 1880 — 82.
SKEWS	Captain JOHN	manager, Wheal Spry, St Columb Minor, 1851.
SKUES	G.E.M.	director, Cornwall Tailings Company Ltd., Illogan, 1910 — 13.

One of the most colourful members of the mining family was WILLIAM SKEWIS of Crelake, near Tavistock who was secretary of the Roskear Mining Company in Camborne. He owned 4000 shares out of the 6000 shares which were issued. However a petition was filed in May 1866 to wind up the company.[5] He appeared before the court of the Vice-Warden of the Stannaries and the mine was subsequently sold on 22 June 1866 and the company was wound up on 27 April 1871.

---

[5] Full details of court cases appear in Appendix.

Skewis made further appearances before the courts. In 1876 he was accused as Principal Agent of Adventurers of damaging land in Calstock, as well as polluting streams of pure drinking water. He was fined £42 11 6d which he was ordered to pay within four days as well as a further £51 15 3d for costs incurred in the case.

The following year he was found guilty of not paying monies he owed to various parties in connection with South Roskear Mine of which he was Principal Agent.

William Skewis was actively involved with a number of Devon and Cornwall tin mines as the list prepared by Justin Brooke confirms.

In Cornwall the miner did not necessarily have to find his own tools — the company for whom he worked could charge them to his account each month. [6] Generally speaking he was better off than the collier.

The copper and tin mines where he worked were let out to pairs or gangs of men, a group which might vary from two men to a dozen or more, on tribute. Contracts were taken out for periods of two weeks and upwards, on the basis of the miners receiving a fixed proportion, expressed as so many shillings and pence in the pound, of each pound's worth of mineral raised. Out of their share the miners had to pay for their tools, candles, gunpowder, "sick club" and monthly haircut. Such superintendence as was necessary underground was done by the captain or manager in small mines and by underground captains in large ones. In small mines the manager kept the books, but in most mines an official called the purser did the book-keeping and saw to the ordering of materials, selling of ore, calling of meetings of adventurers and generally dealing with the business of mining.

There were very few captains in relation to the number of workers employed — 28 at the Consolidated Mines, Gwennap in 1836 when 2,387 workers were employed.

Over at Fowey Consols there were 14 mine captains, or agents, working with 1,706 miners. [7]

According to Friedrich Engels' book *Conditions of the Working Class in England,* [8] there were 19,000 men and 11,000 women and children employed in Cornish tin, lead, copper and zinc mines in 1841.

The Children's Employment Commission's Report [9] describes working conditions down the mines:

> Those employed in the Cornish Mines suffer from serious diseases of the lungs, heart and digestive organs, caused by inhaling air deficient in oxygen and impregnated with particles of dust and smoke from gunpowder used in blasting operations. Miners have to climb up and down long ladders in the mine shafts and sometimes it takes even strong young men over an hour a day both before and after their work to ascend and descend the ladders.

> Consequently those male underground workers who enter the mines at an early age are much inferior in physique to the female labourers who work at the surface. Many of the men die young of galloping consumption, and those who live to middle age succumb to slow consumption.

> Many miners become unfit to continue work between the ages of 35 and 45. Under these conditions a severe bronchial cold will prove fateful to a miner whose respiratory organs have already been weakened by the nature of his work.

> The tasks at the top of the mine shafts — the breaking up and sorting of the ore — are performed by women and children and are said to be very healthy because the work is carried on in the open air.

The miner lived in pretty appalling conditions. Generally speaking he would live in a back to back house, sometimes with two rooms, certainly not more than four and with a cellar for coal and food. [10]

6,7 *Cornwall, Its Mines and Miners*, London, 1885, pp 146, 173, 179 and Lord Kinnaird's Commission Part 1:Q8731 (1864).
8   Written in 1884. Translated by W.O. Henderson and W.H. Chaloner. Published by Basil Blackwell, Oxford, 1971, page 274.
9   *Children's Employment Commission* by Doctor Charles Barham, 1842: Mines: Part 11, pp 780 and 796.
10   The conditions applied mainly to coal miners.

In these cramped conditions the miner and his wife together with his often sizeable family of seven or eight children would have to eat, wash, run a home and sleep.

In the early Victorian times it was not unusual for the whole family, married and single persons, to huddle together in one small room.

There was a danger of illness, through lack of sanitation. In these back to back terraced houses water had to be drawn from a common tap in the yard, or on the "privy" wall. The earth-closet was normally outside the house. Disease took the toll in typhus fever, smallpox and cholera.

The terraced house would have little furniture — a table, a few wooden chairs, a fireplace or open hearth, a number of pots and pans and upstairs two or three simple beds. [11] The walls would be bare, and the floor made of either stone or mud.

In the 1850's and 1860's world over-production of copper, tin and lead resulted in a slump in Cornwall. The price of a commodity was fixed in the market-place, over which producers had no control whatsoever. Copper was the first to be affected. The market had been ruined some years earlier when in the 1790's copper had been over-produced in Anglesea. In 1854 there were 24 active mines in the Liskeard area. In the same year copper production for Devon and Cornwall was 185,000 tons of over 7.5% copper ore containing 14,000 tons of metal. [12]

But the decline was just around the corner. Some of the Camborne and Redruth mines had already become tin mines which had also suffered a severe setback in production. So the great exodus began. Some 7300 miners emigrated after the 1866 slump. Two years earlier there had been 173 productive copper mines in Devon and Cornwall. By 1878 there were only 80. The great collapse reduced output from 160,000 to 80,000 tons by 1870 and the metal price fell sharply from

Countryside around Drake Walls mine, Gunnislake, Cornwall, 1981

---

[11] *Early Victorian Britain*, J.F.C. Harrison, London, 1979. pp 84, 114.
[12] *Report of Mineral Development Committee*, HMSO, July 1949, page 26.

Right: The sign which greets the visitor to the Cornish Section of Mineral Point, Wisconsin, USA
Below: Many Cornishmen and women moved to this American Mid-west mining town in the 1850's and built their houses and cottages in a similar style to the ones they left behind in Cornwall

1860, when it was £115, to £38 a ton in 1890. By 1875 only four major copper mines survived — Devon Great Consols, South Caradon, Marke Valley and Mellanear. [13] By 1880 West of England production was only 1/350th part of the world's output. [14]

A few smaller mines continued but found the going more difficult. From *The Cornish Mines Year Book, 1918* we read:

> "Cornwall Tailing Company Ltd. Directors: A Richards (Managing) and G.E.M. SKUES. Address: 522 — 525, Salisbury House, London EC. The nominal capital of £50,000 all of £1 shares all of which are issued and fully paid."

The company was treating the sands of Carn Brea Mine at Illogan, Redruth, but operations ceased at the end of 1918 and the company was liquidated the following year.

All that is left of the great copper mining era are the roofless engine houses surrounded by ivy, with heather creeping over the floor and foundations.

For those Cornishmen and women who decided to stay on in their own county a new mineral industry emerged in the 19th century. William Cookworthy, a Plymouth merchant, took out the first patent in 1773 to manufacture porcelain and Josiah Wedgwood set up his first works in 1791. Nearly 200 years later the St. Austell China Clay Works is still the major supplier to the Staffordshire potteries.

Emigration had taken its toll on Cornwall. Copper and tin miners sold their houses, cottages, farms and stock and made for Falmouth where mail packets sailed weekly to New York and Quebec.

For many of the miners their eventual destination was Wisconsin in America's Mid-west, whereas farmers emigrated to the Lake Michigan area. The fare aboard ship in 1843 was £6 on packets and £4 on trading vessels. As the route became more popular the fare dropped to £4 and £2 respectively.

There were a number of routes to Wisconsin. The cheapest was via Quebec, but also it carried more risks with the probability of high winds, ice and fog. There was a route via New Orleans, thence by river boat up the cholera infected Mississippi river. Others travelled to Detroit and even more to New York and then made their way across country.

By 1850 some 5000 emigrants had gone to Wisconsin. [15] In America they were referred to as "Cousin Jacks", probably because all had "cousins" back in Cornwall eager and willing to come over to the new land. A similar expression developed with the Cornish miner who emigrated to Australia. But so ubiquitous were the Cornish on the mining frontier that a popular saying had it that wherever there was a hole in the ground a "Cousin Jack" would be at the bottom of it.

As more and more Cornish emigrated so the number of new mines opened in America. By 1880 the Cornishman had moved from Wisconsin to Michigan, Colorado, Nevada, Idaho, Utah and Arizona.

In Cornwall they had carried on their jobs of mining, farming and fishing. In *The Cornish Miner in America*, Arthur Cecil Todd says "Political awareness has never been a marked characteristic of the Cornish because of the peculiarities of their occupations. Mining, farming and fishing by their very nature demand a withdrawal from the crowd or group, where political ideas are generated, to the field, the open sea and the underground passage where men gather only in twos and threes, making them reflective rather than revolutionary, and content to play a minor role in local government and in the development of freemasonry. Many indeed were elected sheriffs."[16]

---

[13] Mellanear went on working until June, 1899 and was the last Cornish copper mine to pay a dividend.
[14] *Metal Mining*, J.B. Richardson, London, 1974, pp 101, 102.
[15] "Wisconsin the Miners' Refuge". Article by Keith Skues in *West Briton*, 30th August 1979. See Appendix for full story.
[16] *The Cornish Miner in America*, AC Todd, Truro, 1967, page 24.

Another important quality which marked a Cornishman was his deeply religious beliefs as was seen in the previous chapter concerning James Skewis. Methodism was a most important part of their lives. When one looks through the history of American towns time after time we read that the first permanent building which was erected was the Methodist church.

Today there may be eight times as many people of Cornish descent in the USA as there are in Cornwall.[17]

EDWARD SKEWIS left Camborne in 1846 for a short visit, but returned home the same year singing the praises of Wisconsin saying there was a great future for anyone who wished to emigrate. He took up permanent residence in America's Mid-west in 1848, his family joining him the following year. The route Edward took was from Falmouth to New Orleans and by steamer to Peoria on the Illinois River via St Louis. From there he travelled by stage coach from Galena to Shullsburg.

Edward's brother JAMES SKEWIS emigrated in 1849. (Chapter Nine.) He had begun his mining career at the age of twelve as a "mucker" toiling at the heavy work of loading and pushing wheelbarrows of rock, blasted out from the drifts, a distance of 300 yards to the bottom of the shaft.

In 1851's. Edward, Henry and James Skewis moved to the outskirts of Nevada City where they opened up a rich claim for the summers work and apparently did quite well. This journey had taken a month travelling west from Shullsburg via the wastes of Utah, through Nevada, scaling the heights of the Sierra Nevada, crossing the Sacramento River and eventually arriving at Deer Creek. Almost every day the Skewis boys collected 6 ounces of gold. That was until the rainy season set in. Then they washed in smaller creeks between hills, which also paid quite satisfactorily.[18] The gold was much larger in size and was called rough or nugget gold.

Mining dominated the economy of Nevada from the 1850's. The rush to Nevada to the Comstock Lode began in a small way. Several hundred men came over the mountains in a frenzy, staked claims wildly and gouged a few small holes in the mountainside. Only in 1860 did the first big influx of wealth seekers reach Mount Davidson and they came in their thousands. Between 1864 and 1881 the Comstock Lode produced hundreds of millions of dollars worth of silver and gold and created fabulous fortunes.[19]

States James Skewis:

> *Just about this time there was a strike at Grass Valley on a slide from a hill and we got a claim and sold it for a hundred dollars. One day a man gave me 10 dollars for one day's work on that hill to do some timbering work as he was not used to that kind of work; and that was the wages paid at that time. Then we went south to Sonora and Springfield. However, we did not find it any better from the place we left, nor as good, for some days we made 15 dollars in gold dust.*

It was whilst at Sonora, a mountainous state which was mainly arid, but nevertheless rich in minerals, especially copper, gold, lead and zinc, that the Skewis boys heard of a gold strike in Australia. So they made for Bendigo in Victoria about 85 miles north-west of Melbourne. It was in 1851 that gold was discovered and the town developed.

We are not told what happened to Edward Skewis. He disappears from the pages of James Skewis' letters, which mention only his brother Henry Skewis and cousin Will Skewis. They stayed in Bendigo for a year making up to thirty dollars a day by washing pay-dirt from the wastes of miners who had already departed for pastures new.

The boys who had gone three years before presented a striking spectacle on the road to the goldfields. Some looked tense and impatient, and others looked almost ashamed of being there; some looked downcast and preoccupied: but all their faces showed the same determination. They went on foot, on horseback, in carts or in drays pulled by ten bullocks all hurrying to reach Bendigo, Ballarat or Mount Alexander. There were no roads or paths, only the barest tracks which became gradually impassable under the wheels of the many heavy vehicles. The diggers wore what almost amounted to a uniform; the inevitable cabbage-tree hat, a blue shirt, trousers of indeterminate shade usually turned yellow by mud and clay, and a leather belt bearing a knife or pistol.

---

[17] *Cornish in America*, A.L. Rowse, London, 1969, page 4.
[18] Diary of James Skewis (1826—1911) unpublished.
[19] *The Nevada Adventure*, James W. Hulse, 1966. University of Nevada Press, Reno, Nevada, USA.

A model reconstructing the Eureka Stockade, Ballarat, Victoria, Australia
Below: *A print produced by F.W. Niven & Co of Ballarat Flat, from the Black Hill. Local residents of the town are now going back to the original spelling — Ballaarat*

BALLAARAT FLAT, FROM THE BLACK HILL — 1855.

Sign outside memorial to the miners who were killed in the Eureka Stockade, Gold Hill, Ballarat on 3 December 1854
Below left: *Monument in Ballarat old cemetery*
Below right: *Memorial in Ballarat*

Their tools were a short handled shovel, a pick of the smallest design, a strongish rope, a washing pan, a sieve, a bucket and a wooden basin, in addition to a frying pan, a saucepan and a billy can. [20]

Relates James Skewis:

> We could see gold often very thick, almost close onto a chalk bed. The drifts were in the chalk below the gravel. The pay dirt we would cart about a mile to water, and wash to get the gold. Besides we washed about three months the wastes that the first workers threw away, and we could earn 15 to 16 dollars very regular each day. It was very easy work.

James, Henry and Will Skewis paid £1 10s English money to the Australian Government for a licence to work in the mines and this gave them protection in the form of policemen who kept an eye open for thieves.

> There were many people prospecting, and it took months to develop the work they undertook to do before getting gold, and the men had to live. For them to pay for a licence when they had nothing, and to lose their title to the claim was too hard, and this made a riot between the miners and Government forces.

In addition the Government of Victoria gazetted the right to all gold in Crown Lands and *doubled* the licence fee. This led to the famous Eureka stockade which took place on the morning of Sunday, 3rd December 1854 and has since been described as a "bloody massacre." 200 miners helped to shape Australia's destiny by their rebellious stand when they took up arms in defiance of oppressive government and military rule.

Troops and police stormed the stockade in the early hours and 21 miners and 6 soldiers died. The "diggers" were overcome and arrested. Between 6th and 7th December 1854 the majority of the prisoners were liberated, but 13 were committed for trial on a charge of high treason and taken to Melbourne. All were found "not guilty."

Relating what he could recall of the incident in his diary James Skewis said that some stray shots here and there killed people not actually in the fight.

> One man hearing the shooting went out of his tent to see what was the matter and got killed. One woman was shot in her tent. Some of the miners were arrested. All the miners were in a deep gloom. But this riot caused a change in the law and everyone could work where they chose. However, a duty of 2/6d per ounce was put on all gold raised and shipped out of the country. There were other incidents here at Ballarat where fights broke out, but they were normally between British or American people against the Irish.

Following the outcome of the trial the government reversed its policies on miners' licences and abandoned them in favour of a yearly £1 miners' right, a document which also gave the miners a right to vote. The miners' stand had hastened the arrival of political democracy in the State of Victoria.

From reports in *West Briton* one learns that other members of the Skewes family had gone out from Cornwall to Ballarat:

> Mr. R. SKEWES of Ballarat Diggings, whose wife gave birth to a daughter in St Day, Cornwall in November, 1858.

> On 16 May 1863 the death occurred at Ballarat Diggings of ANN, wife of HENRY SKEWES, formerly of Mawnan, Cornwall, aged 36 years.

Notices placed in Ballarat Post Office listed unclaimed letters:

THOMAS SKEWES	1 July 1857
RICHARD SKEWES	2 February, 2 March, 3 August and 2 October 1857
THOMAS SKEWES	1 February, 2 March 1858
HENRY SKEWES	1 June 1858
SAMUEL SKEWES	1 February 1858 [21]

---

[20] *A Concise History of Australia*, Robert Lacour-Gayet, 1976 (Aus) page 201.
[21] Information taken from *Ballarat Star*, 1857 and 1858.

"GOLDEN POINT" AND THE BALLARAT GOLD WASHERS, 1851

Gold Point and the Ballarat Gold Washers, 1851, produced by F.W. Niven and Co

Today Ballarat is a tourist attraction with 250,000 visitors a year going to the site of the Eureka Stockade which is now a park with a memorial to those who fell in the battle. The soldiers and diggers are all buried in the Old Cemetery at Ballarat.

Just outside the town is Sovereign Hill, a fine re-creation of the first hectic 10 years of Ballarat's development. One can see the Diggings, tents and humpies, mud-brick and slab huts with an opportunity to explore a gold mine. Sovereign Hill shows how men lived and laboured — a township where every building has been researched and reconstructed with infinite care: and a Mining Museum relating the later developments of company mining.

There is still a sizeable branch of the Skewes family living in Ballarat to this day, together with descendants from many other Cornish families.

Another area where a mini gold rush took place was Charters Towers and the Palmer River, Queensland. Gold was discovered here in 1871 and mined from 1875. JOHN SKEWES was born in Cornwall and in 1862 arrived in Charters Towers. He was a gold miner and later married Miss Margaret Wood in September, 1889. His children and grandchildren were also born in Charters Towers. One grandson JACK SKEWES was a foreman employed by Mount Isa Mines Limited, Queensland. SKEWES Street, Mount Isa was named after him.

Australia actually displaced America as the favourite goal for British emigrants — most of whom came looking for gold — in 1852 when the total reached 85,000. Almost as many emigrated in 1853 and again in 1854. This exodus from Britain carried on well into the 1870's. In the first six months of 1875 no less than 10,576 Cornishmen and women left for Australia. [22]

WILLIAM SKEWES emigrated from Cornwall in 1853. He married Elizabeth Northey in Sydney three years later and they moved north to Rocky River Gold Diggings, Uralla, New South Wales. They had 12 children and today there are over 100 descendants still living in this part of Australia.

---

[22] *West Briton*, 27 September 1875.

Bucket dredger from Watsons Creek, New South Wales, Australia. Dirt was washed off the river bed into the treatment area. The tin was extracted and sent to the smelter. The tailings were then deposited on the nearby dump. Photo circa 1910

In its boom days Rocky River Gold Field, which is situated to the south of Armidale, covered an area of 23 square miles to the west of Uralla. Gold was discovered here in September, 1851. Panning and cradling were the most common methods of extracting the gold from the washdirt.

The population of Uralla shot up from 1000 in July 1856 to 5000 by December 1856. Buildings sprang up overnight. There were three public houses, six stores, five butchers, two bakers, six public and a number of private boarding houses, four blacksmiths, together with shoemakers and bankers.[23]

The alluvial gold deposits accumulated on river bars, behind boulders, in roots of trees and in gutters and hollows.

Generally speaking Europeans mined only the most accessible gold on their claims before leaving for a more promising area. When the Europeans moved out, the Chinese moved in. Working in gangs of 100 the Chinese quickly stripped an area of payable gold. By 1860 the Chinese outnumbered European diggers in New South Wales by 12,000 to 8000. Disputes and fights often arose with many fatal results.

1856 was the great bonanza year at Rocky River Diggings with an estimated 40,000 ounces of gold being won. But the good fortune did not last, and by 1857 the population of the gold field had been drastically cut to 2500 persons. In 1877 there was only one hotel, one public school and a general store. Today it is hard to believe Uralla was such a bustling town 130 years ago. There is little to remind the visitor of the pioneering spirit which prevailed in the mid 1800's. The corrugated and wood buildings have gone. There are no footprints on dirt roads — just scars on a fairly barren landscape dotted with elm trees, which in 1981 were dying out at an alarming rate.

The total production of gold in New South Wales to the end of 1927 was 14,968,346 ounces fine, valued at £63,581,454[24]

Watsons Creek is some 35 miles west of Uralla and an area to where many of the Skewes family moved in search of tin. The alluvial tin is shed out of the reef and concentrated in the rivers, creeks and gulleys. In its boom days Watsons Creek was mined by 40 workers, but today there is little activity. NOEL SKEWES followed his father and grandfather into tin mining.

> "We would use explosives on the Den Mountain which in turn would break the boulders into smaller sediments and dirt. The smaller rocks would go through a gravel pump, and larger ones would be picked out and stacked.

> "The rocks and sand would then go into the sluice boxes where the tin would be concentrated and tailings or waste would be separated. Much processing would be done by the boxman who would also supervise the work. He would end up with a concentrate of 50% tin which would then be put through a flotation process which separated the remaining impurities resulting in a tin concentrate of a 75% assay. Payment by the tin buyer would be on 75%. This would be smelted in Sydney."

In 1971 the Gillie Prospecting and Drilling Service of New South Wales conducted a survey in Watsons Creek which confirmed areas of tin occurring. Several washings of tin and monazite were found in a 14 inch dish located in the South Molong Creek area. There was also a presence of scheelite, copper, antimony and several quartz reefs which indicated a presence of gold in Watsons Creek.

In South Australia the Yorke Peninsula divides Spencer and St Vincent Gulfs and is one of the country's most attractive and productive regions. Today most of its money comes from agriculture, but its "claim to fame" is not the present but the past; not its physical beauty, but its history. In the 1860's vast deposits of copper were discovered at Moonta and Kadina and for many years the district boomed. The people who brought success to both the Yorke Peninsula and themselves were the Cornishmen and women who had despaired at the tin mining depression in the mid 1800's. They boarded a vessel at Plymouth for a journey which would take them on average 106 days to Adelaide, Australia.

---

[23] *Armidale Express*, 7 June 1856.
[24] *Mineral Industry of New South Wales*, E.J. Kenny, 1928; page 69.

Some ships like *Osprey*, *Merchantman*, *Phoebe Dunbar*, *Fairlie*, *Geelong*, *Colonial Empire* and *Mount Stuart Elphinstone* sailed from Plymouth to Port Phillip, Melbourne. Others including *Trevelyan* which left Plymouth on 15 December 1865 with 423 passengers on board headed for Port Adelaide, South Australia. The ship arrived on 21 March 1866. Sixty per cent of the passengers had come from Cornwall — the others from Devon and South Wales.

From Port Adelaide the Cornishmen and women made their way by stage-coach for the 90 mile journey to the Yorke Peninsula, via Port Wakefield. There were normally two or three changes of horses en route and the journey would take the best part of a day.

A triangle of towns covering some 104 square miles in area became known as "Australia's Little Cornwall." Furthest north on the coast is Wallaroo; 10 miles south is Moonta and 6 miles east inland is Kadina.

Copper was mined at Moonta and Kadina and sent to Wallaroo for smelting. The ore was transported in bullock-waggons, two or three tons at a time. The railway came later.

The discovery of copper at Kadina was by pure accident. In 1859 the Yorke Peninsula was virtually uninhabited except for a few Aboriginal tribes. The only Europeans were Walter Watson Hughes, a retired ship's captain from Scotland; his brother-in-law John Duncan, their respective families and a few shepherds.

On 17 December 1859 James Boor, a shepherd working on the Wallaroo sheep station, caught his foot in a wombat's furrow. When he looked down he found the furrow full of small stones of copper ore. His boss Mr Hughes immediately took out a mineral lease on 80 acres covering the area.

Strangely enough copper was found in Moonta in a similar manner. Shepherd Paddy Ryan, also employed by Hughes, was walking on the Wallaroo sheep run and noticed green stones at the opening of a marsupial rat's burrow. This was in May, 1861 and he reported his findings to Hughes. Ryan was a wise Irishman and he insisted on being in with the action. Two mines were formed, "The Moonta Mining Company" and the "Wallaroo Mining and Smelting Company", which amalgamated in 1889 to form the "Wallaroo and Moonta Mining and Smelting Company" with its first Superintendent, Captain H.R. Hancock.

The site for the township of Moonta was selected in 1863 and the town incorporated in 1872.

Paddy Ryan signed an agreement with Captain Hughes for a one tenth share of the mine and £6 a week until the payment of a dividend. In those far away days it sounded like a good bargain, but alas he did not enjoy the rewards of his discovery for he died within a year.

The pioneer miners lived in tents or shelters built of a framework of pine post covered with canvas. As they became more established the miner moved into a cottage of wattle and daub with paling roofs. Walls were normally whitewashed. The floor was of hard earth. They were simple constructions, but gave a sense of security to those who dwelt within.

Before the days of the steam engine the copper was hauled to the surface in a bucket by means of a horse-whim, the first being built in Moonta Mines by RICHARD SKEWES, a carpenter who had come out to Australia from Redruth in 1848.

Cornwall Hotel, Moonta, South Australia

Hughes Pumphouse, Moonta, South Australia built by Cornishmen of fossilised limestone

WELCOME TO MOONTA
AUSTRALIA'S LITTLE CORNWALL

All the ore dressing was done by hand. The broken ore was wheeled onto a table and young lads selected the rich pieces which were then dropped into wooden trays. This ore was later sent to the smelters in Wallaroo.

The Moonta Mine is probably unique in the annals of mining history (including all Cornish tin mines) in that it paid well over £1 million in dividends without calling on shareholders to subscribe one penny in working capital. At a depth of about 120 feet below the surface copper pyrites was struck and that class of ore continued to an indeterminate depth either as yellow ore which was assayed at 30% copper or purple ore (50% copper).

An unnamed journalist visiting Moonta Mines in 1887 at the request of Captain Hancock wrote:

> Bump, bump, bump; down, down, down. The cage jolted and jumped along at a pace that I thought would have shaken every rivet out of it. The sensation was a most peculiar one, and anyone in search of excitement should make a descent in a copper mine in this manner.

> We emerged from the cage 1440 feet below surface and away below us miners could be seen quarrying on the rock for the purpose of carrying the shaft still lower.

> We made our way through a lengthy drive at the end of which was a boring machine. The noise was deafening. The holes being bored by it would be utilised for blasting.

> Leaving these sturdy toilers we retraced our steps and entered another level and came upon a body of men taking out a stope. Hard work it was and busty fellows they were. There is no mistake, the miners deserve all they get. Little do the bulk of our population think of the hardships that have to be endured by the miners before those metals on which we all set such a price can be obtained."

Cornish cottage restored at Moonta, South Australia

At Moonta the miners met harsh conditions and at one stage, because of lack of water on the ground, 110 deaths were recorded in one week.

The Wallaroo Mining and Smelting Company had a working life of 63 years and produced copper worth £21 million and extracted an estimated 6¼ millions tons of ore from the ground.

Mining ceased production in 1923 when the copper industry world wide went into a slump. In South Australia the mining installations fell idle, hundreds of people left the area and everything that could be sold was dismantled and sent back to Adelaide. However, a breath of history still hangs in the air. Old slag heaps, smelting works, installations and old cottages are a reminder of the heritage built by Cousin Jacks and Jennies in "Australia's Little Cornwall."

The majority of Cornish cottages were demolished in 1923, but at Moonta Mines there is a fine restored cottage, furnished in period style, which is now one of the town's main attractions. Another is Moonta Mines National Trust Museum, which was originally the town's Primary School, until it closed in 1968, and houses many of the relics of the mining days.

Today in Moonta (Aboriginal word meaning "impenetrable scrub") one can visit Ryan's Shaft, where copper was originally discovered; Taylor's Shaft which, at a depth of 2520 feet was the deepest mine of its kind in South Australia, and the Hughes Pumphouse which was built in 1865 of fossilised limestone. The engine drained the underground workings continuously for 60 years without any major overhaul. It was a 60 inch cylinder by 10 ft stroke and had been made at the foundry of Harvey and Company of Hayle, Cornwall in 1863.

Cartoons drawn by Oswald Pryor depicting the Cornish-Australian sense of humour on the Yorke Peninsula, South Australia

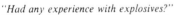
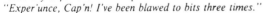

"Had any experience with explosives?"
"Exper'unce, Cap'n! I've been blawed to bits three times."

"Psst! Ask my missus if it's time to put the pasties in th' oven?"

Many of the miners lie at rest in Kadina and Moonta cemeteries. The ground is brown and parched as the sun beats down with no mercy. The headstones on graves paint a graphic picture of the hardship and personal anguish faced by the early settlers. Walking along the rows of graves we see familiar names like Polglase, Uren, Bolitho, Pascoe, Retallack and Spargo. And there are the epitaphs:

> *The miner dieth and wasteth away.*
> *Yea, he giveth up the ghost and where is he?*
>
> *Rock of Ages Cleft for Me*
>
> *Rest for the toiling hand. Rest for the anxious brow.*
> *Rest from the weary way. Rest from all labour now.*

The population of Moonta at its height in 1875 was 12,000 and, apart from Adelaide 108 miles south-east, was the largest town in South Australia. Today there are only 1200 people living here and half the population is over the age of 55.

Every two years the triangle of towns (Kadina, Moonta and Wallaroo) hold a Cornish Festival "Kernewek Lowender" — a festival of Cornish customs, food and song. It provides a chance to enjoy the Furry Dance which is based on the Helston ritual, Cornish pasties, a gathering of the Celts, a specially brewed concoction which the locals call "Swanky" and an opportunity to take part in a Cornish wheelbarrow race. All these, and street dances, a cavalcade of vintage motor cycles and cars, brass band shows and community singing, together with the crowning of the festival's "Cousin Jack and Jenny".

Thanks to the Cornishmen and women's skills and industry the mining brigade helped bring great prosperity to Australia.

The Skewis family of Wisconsin who had been prospecting for gold in Australia returned home via England in 1855. JAMES SKEWIS found himself a wife in Jane Thomas Rabling and they were married in Camborne in the autumn of 1855. Both her father and grandfather were very rich, most of their finances being collected from the silver mines of Pachuca and Real del Monte, Mexico.

Harvey Pumphouse, Kadina, South Australia built and operated by Cornishmen

It was to Pachuca that the new Skewis family — James, Jane and their three children — moved in 1860, and so were united two Cornish families by a long loop which encircled England, the United States of America and Mexico. And in Pachuca it seemed as if there were almost as many Cornish as they had left behind in Wisconsin, some of whom they had known in Cornwall. From his diary James Skewis says:

> *Here were Englishmen and ladies that we had known in former days whom we were glad to see. We formed many agreeable acquaintances.*

Mining had been in operation in Pachuca for nearly three hundred years.[25]

Destruction of official records, first during the War of Independence and then during the many internal strifes which at different subsequent periods marked the history of Mexico, has handicapped historians so much they have had to resort to church records in an endeavour to gain a picture of the early history of this most attractive territory.

Pachuca is situated at the base of the west side of a divide, whose summit has an average elevation of 10,000 feet. The country on the west side of the divide is semi-arid, but the east side has abundant vegetation with forests of oak and fir. Pachuca and Real del Monte lie within a mountain range known as the Sierra de Pachuca which forms part of the north east rim of the topographic basin of the valley of Mexico.

The first reference to Pachuca is in 1324 under the name of Patlachiuhcán and nomadic aborigines in quest of agricultural sites are credited as discovering silver in the region.

Spanish Conquistadores first reached Pachuca in 1528, thirty-six years after the discovery of the New World. Francisco Telléz, an officer at Cortés, arrived in Pachuca and established Spanish rule and became the first recognised authority in the territory.

The founding of Real del Monte is not as clearly defined. History first detects the presence of the white man in 1531 from information taken from a church report.

The first mines worked by the Spaniards in this area were known as "El Jacal" (Pachuca) and Almoloya (Real del Monte). Parochial records of 1531 describe these mines as "old workings", thereby supporting the theory commonly held by historians, that mining in the area was undertaken by aborigines long before the advent of the white man.

Nothing is known of the metallurgical process employed in those early times, but it is generally assumed that silver was produced entirely by fusion.

Smelting was introduced by the Spaniards and this process was exclusively used up to 1557 when Bartolomé de Medina discovered and introduced the patio amalgamation process. This new process revolutionised the mining industry throughout the world and it continued to hold sway in the metallurgical field for the next 350 years.

The Spaniards were reported to have been hard task masters. It is said that many of them railroaded Indians to the mines for life, the proprietor of the mine having the power to do with them what he pleased. The Indians were sent down the mines and obliged to stay there, eating and sleeping underground. The working day was from 4.00 am until 11.00 pm with half an hour for lunch.

The men were cruelly treated, many of them lasting no longer than three days, dying in the mines. Those that died were taken to the surface and thrown to the vultures.[26]

In the latter half of the 18th century the bonanza deposits produced great wealth and contributed largely to the riches that Spain drew from Mexico. The outstanding figure in this romantic epoch of Pachuca's mining was Pedro de Terreros; who it is said entered the district a comparatively poor man. His mining activities soon made him Pachuca's premier mining operator and brought him very great wealth. His large donations to the Spanish throne gained him the title of Count of Regla.

---

[25] John Herbert Skewes wrote *History of Mexico's Richest Silver Mines* for the *Compressed Air Magazine*, published London and New York, February and March, 1930. The article appears in the Appendix.

[26] *Pachuca Real Del Monte Mining Camp*, W.H. Johnson of the Efficiency Department of Cia Santa Gertrudis, Mexico, June 1925.

Pachuca, Mexico from Real del Monte

Salaries offered to miners in Mexico were very substantial. In 1830 working miners earned £15 a month and Captains £1000 a year. Compare those figures to a miner in Cornwall who would earn 50 shillings a month and a mine Captain £80 a year.

At the beginning of the 19th century, the crude facilities became inadequate for handling the large quantities of water encountered with increasing depth of the workings. At one time a total of about 2000 horses were being used in the district to operate whims for raising water from the mines. Due to this difficulty, and also because of the disturbance occasioned during the period of Mexico's War of Independence, mining at Pachuca became dormant for a period of years.[27]

As Pachuca fell into a period of poverty and decay, people outside Mexico were not slow to comment on speculating on the stock market. In 1831 Cochrane and M'Crone of London published a paper dissuading members of the public from investing their money in mines:

THE REAL DEL MONTE MINING CONCERNS UNMASKED

An eager and inordinate solicitude to obtain the gifts of fortunes, through the medium of speculative enterprise has, in an eminent degree, characterised the public in the commercial transactions of the present age.

Amongst the numerous bubble schemes which with a few years past have been projected, the Real del Monte Mining Concern stands pre-eminent. It was the prolific source of various projects, adapted to entangle the public in the snares of stock jobbers and adventurers, and it therefore claims our particular attention and consideration.

We have conversed with many purchasers of the Real del Monte shares on the subject of profit they expected to derive from their respective speculations and we found their opinions to be, that, as the shares once sold at £1500 each, although they might not rise that high again, yet at all events they would advance a few hundred each, and, when they were assured that the present price (low as it seemed) was actually higher than the shares had fetched at any period they could not apprehend our assertion.

In 1831 shares were £10 — in 1824 £1500.

Another important fact is not generally known, namely that before the shareholders can receive one shilling dividend, a debt of a quarter of a million pounds sterling must be paid out of the profits of the mine.

If the circumstances should appear exaggerated we would beg to remind them that within the last ten years more than a dozen large mining concerns under the management of the same gentleman, after having been raised to various premiums, from one to eight hundred pounds per share, have been successfully abandoned as hopeless, without producing the speculators one single shilling in return, save the few pounds arising from the sale of the machinery; these concerns were under the conduct of the same scientific manager and derived all the advantages that would result from his personal superintendence, skill and experience, before he recommended them to the notice of his friends.

If our remarks should induce a single individual to pause and reflect on the pernicious consequences of rushing ignorantly into expensive speculations, and thereby save him from irretrievable ruin, our object will be accomplished, and labour sufficiently recompensed.

---

[27] *Ax-I-Dent-Ax*, Salt Lake City, August 1929.

Cautious words indeed! So one must look at facts.

In 1824 some English capitalists, headed by John Taylor, one of the most respected mine managers in Britain, entered into negotiation with the 3rd Count of Regla, the principal owner of Pachuca mines in those days and formed "A Company of Gentleman Adventurers", which afterwards became "Cia de Real del Monte y Pachuca". This company spent a large amount of money to re-open and equip the mines with the best machinery at the time. The mines were in a state of ruin, workings caved, and machinery destroyed or stolen.

Back in Cornwall James Vetch, who had seen active service as a young subaltern in the Royal Engineers with the Duke of Wellington in the Peninsular War, was given the job of recruiting men.

John Taylor had given Vetch the job because of his ability to give orders and expecting them to be obeyed instantly, and for his initiative and determination, and for his zeal in planning this venture as a military expedition.

John Rule, of Camborne, superintendent at United Mines, was given the task of shipping the technical material over to Mexico. [28]

The expedition left Liverpool aboard the transatlantic packet *The Corinthian* on 24 March 1824 and arrived in Real del Monte on 11 June. However, a year was taken in moving the heavy machinery by mule power from the coast up the eastern slope of the Mexican plateau to the mines which lay at an altitude of 10,000 feet above sea level.

From the outset they encountered problems both large and small. Production date was set for May, 1827 but Vetch ran into serious disputes about the payment of wages to Mexican employees.

It was not until the end of September, 1827 that the first shipment of silver was despatched to the mint in Mexico City which was $19,272 and was the first return on investment which had cost $1,526,250, half as much again as had been originally planned.

Vetch had suffered arguments with miners, both Mexican and English, and his morale was at an all time low, as it had taken three years to get production under way. He sailed for England in the summer of 1827 to face his critics in London and was replaced by Commissioner Charles Tindal. [29]

On arrival in Mexico Tindal also found problems and by June 1830, after six years of exploration and development, the company had lost $3,188,505. [30] Nothing could be worse for shareholders' morale.

In July, 1832 Tindal resigned and handed over the mine to John Rule and for the next fifteen years Real del Monte remained under Cornish control with Commissioner William Rule taking over from his brother in 1843.

After 14 years of operation the company was $4,229,059 in debt and after 23 years the loss made by the end of 1847 was $4,930,158.

In 1849 the mine was sold to two Mexicans, Don Manuel Escandon and Don Nicanor Veistequi for £1½ million, so although shareholders lost money they did at least receive a token dividend. Ironically Real del Monte then turned into a profit situation making $12,125,656 between the years 1849 and 1865. [31] It is interesting to note that the mine was managed during this time by a British man, John Hitchcock Buchan, who was responsible for transporting the first load of steam engines and machinery, equipment and stores from England in April, 1825. [32]

The author visited both Real del Monte and Pachuca in 1979 and witnessed the many huge masonry buildings with Cornish pumps, and the steeply sloping shingled roofs, which still exist. But today it is difficult to realise how many Cornishmen died of fever. Half the men and a third of the supervisors died, and because they were Protestant, they could not be buried in hallowed ground, so were interred in shallow graves dug in sand-dunes outside the walls of Vera Cruz.

---

[28] *Search for Silver*, A.C. Todd; Padstow, 1977; pp 32-34
[29] *Geology and Ore Deposits of the Pachuca*, A.R. Geyne (Mexico, 1863), page 92.
[30] *Search For Silver*, A.C. Todd (Padstow, Cornwall), page 74.
[31] *History of Mexico*, H.H. Bancroft (San Francisco 1886-1888), page 515.
[32] *Search For Silver*, A.C. Todd (Padstow, 1977), page 151.

With the population of 5000 in 1850 increasing to 40,000 by the year 1895 the financial climate in Mexico improved. The *Mining Journal*, 14 March 1868 reports under "Letters to the Editor":

> Ever since I have been a shareholder in this company in Real del Monte, I have been constantly annoyed and persecuted with letters "Private and Confidential" and in reference to its not only gloomy prospects, but absolute and certain ruin.
>
> It is really sickening the amount of gratuitous information which has been conveyed to me respecting the company, advising me if I would only save a little from the "wreck", and to sell at once.
>
> Of late the efforts would have been redoubled and every morning's post brings its quota of abuse. I should think that the means adopted, these friendly and "disinterested" parties must take every shareholder to be an absolute dolt and fool. We know full well in what enterprise we have embarked, and are perfectly willing to abide the result. Signed "A Shareholder."

From the *Mining Journal*, 9 July, 1870, H. Sewell wrote a "Letter to the Editor".

MEXICAN MINES ARE PRODUCING GOOD PROFITS

> The profits of Guatizmotzin Mine next year will be double this year's profit of £120,000. This is proof that Mexican mining companies flourish, when properly managed by competent and intelligent persons. Like Guatizmotzin you have many mines in Mexico not known to the English public in general, as they are mostly worked by native companies, and these keep up the regular supply of bullion to the English market.
>
> I am confident that a few English mining companies in Mexico would do wonders, providing competent persons are placed in management, and especially conversant with metallurgical knowledge which is most essential in conducting the affairs of Mexican mining companies.

From the *Mining Journal*, 21 November, 1874; R. Tredinnick on the subject of "MEXICO and its MINERS."

> The history of Mexico from the moment when Cortez, Spanish adventurer bound its sovereign in chains, degrading him in the eyes of its subjects, reflects no honour upon civilisation. How Spain treated this dependency, with its vast riches and resources, is only too well known.
>
> The annals of the emancipated colony, from the day it threw off the Dominion of its European rulers, present one uniform tale of turbulence, anarchy and bloodshed. The Independence of Mexico was recognised by the principal powers of Europe in the year 1821, but the existence of the Government as a Federal Republic was of short duration, and from the period of the reconstruction of the Empire under the Sovereignty of Maximillian, the country passed through no less than 36 revolutions and 72 personages have successfully held the Chief Executive Office of the State. The unhappy fate of the last Emperor has again sunk Mexico into deeper trouble, anarchy and confusion.[33]
>
> Mexico is wondrously productive as the life sustaining elements of both man and beast, though its agricultural capacity is comparatively underdeveloped, only about one eighth portion of its land being under cultivation. Its population is scanty, people are inert and indifferent as to the future, to a degree incomprehensible to the hardy, ready and industrious citizens of Europe. This wonderful feel for agricultural industry will never attain its natural standard of wealth unless the natives become renovated, enriched, and enlightened through the encouragement of emigration from the more hardy and sustaining surplus labourers of the colder climates.
>
> The mineral produce of Mexico is remarkable even when compared to the richest countries of the world. The annual silver coinage is about 20 million dollars — £4 million sterling. These miners, however, may be considered at the moment not only neglected, but really and substantially in a state of embryo though labour and the implication of capital are alone required to develop their established and unquestionable wealth.
>
> There are no geological surveys, and the richest district of Mexico—Sonora—is still a "terra in cognita".
>
> There are upwards of 500 mines in Mexico, and between 3000 and 4000 silver veins have been discovered.

---

33 Mr Tredinnick was not to know that the last and indeed bloodiest revolution of all would happen between 1910 and 1924 when 2,000,000 Mexicans were to die.
Real del Monte did not escape the tortures and many people realising their lives would be lost, buried their silver coins. Only in 1941 when a new road was being constructed did workmen find barrels full of silver coins. No one can put a figure on the amount of money found, as much was stolen.

Writing in the *Mining Journal*, 8 September, 1883, F.W. Bawden in Pachuca said:

> No country in the world offers such inducements for the profitable employment of capital as Mexico does at the present time. The climate of this part of the world is in general healthy after climatisation has been effected; the mean temperature for the year averages about 70 degrees Fahrenheit, but the seasons are much the same throughout, but owing to the extreme elevation from 8000 to 10,000 feet above sea level the air is very rarefied.

The War of Reform, the civil conflict that engulfed Mexico from 1858 to 1861 began, as most Mexican wars, with a new plan, this time the "Plan de Tacubaya", proclaimed by conservative general Felix Zuloaga, who promptly dissolved the Congress and arrested the chief liberal spokesman for the government, Benito Juarez, who was next in line for the presidency had a vacancy occurred.

President Comonfort resigned. When the army declared Zuloaga as the new president, Juarez escaped north to Queretaro, where his liberal cohorts proclaimed him president.

With two presidents, two governments and two uncompromising ideologies, Mexico plunged headlong into the most passionate and horrifying civil war up to that time.

During the first two years of the war the liberals had a hard time holding their own. The conservative army, better trained, equipped and led, won most of their major engagements and held the most populous states of central Mexico.

The conservatives shot captured prisoners in the name of holy religion, and the liberals did the same in defence of freedom and democratic government. [34]

Priests who refused the sacraments to the liberal rank and file were placed summarily before firing squads.

The liberals ordered all births and marriages to be made into civil ceremonies; all cemeteries were secularized; monastic orders were outlawed; all church properties nationalised and the church and state were separated.

By 1860 the tide of the battle had turned in favour of the liberals. On New Year's Day, 1861 the liberals, some 25,000 strong, entered Mexico City to a tumultuous welcome. But the war had left its scars. The landscape was dotted with burned haciendas, unrepaired bridges, neglected fields and sacked villages. Tens of thousands of Mexicans were exhausted, crippled and aggrieved. Soldiers slowly drifted back to their villages to find no work. Bandits continued to infest the highways.

In 1863 when the issue had not quite been resolved the war almost reached the Skewis household in Pachuca. James's cousin Richard Rabling had been captured by the Mexicans whilst on his way to Mexico City. It took three weeks to arrange the ransom money for his release which was 2,500 Mexican dollars. This was in return for his safe conduct to the hacienda in San Miguel where he lived.

James Skewis did not leave too much information as to his investments in Mexico, although he filled many pocket notebooks with his observations about mines, minerals and earnings. In addition he made notes of the clothing he would take with him on a trip from Iowa to Pachuca. For example on 12 March 1888: 3 coats; 2 vests; 3 pants: 5 woollen shirts; 3 linen shirts; 4 drawers; 5 flannel shirts; 9 handkerchiefs; 3 pairs of socks; 3 pairs of shoes; 1 hat; 1 heavy rug; 1 blanket; 1 razor; 1 razor strop; 1 shaving brush and 1 clothes brush.

In 1890, at the age of 65 he was employed as a mine captain at a salary of $100 a month. In 1892 he called at the office of No. 9, Calle de Empedrabille, Mexico where he had a financial interest. He owned titles to the Ludlow Silver Mine, and possessed a quarter share in La Florencia Mine. In 1897 he received $200 dividends from Fresimillo, Guadalupe.

In his notebook for this time he mentions a mine in Mineral del Monte, but gives no date, nor name to whom it is intended:

---

[34] *The Course of Mexican History*, Meyer/Sherman, Oxford University Press, 1979, pp. 381—385.

A MINE IN REAL DEL MONTE

Richard Stephens denounced, paid taxes, till taken sick. It is called Soledad—located south of the English burying ground half a mile or more east. Mr Lugo is the engineer that made the survey. The Deputado de Mininia can tell if it is free to denounce. Shaft 40 or 50 Varas deep. Lode as wide as the shaft. Will average 2½ marks per Monton of 30 Crats which is $20 and I think a good prospect in the run of good paying mines..

50 pertenencias is about 120 acres — the tax for the year would be $250 Mexican.

I think it would be well to denounce the mine. Costs $3. You have 90 days to do anything to satisfy yourself that the prospect is good. If it is then get the legal title and secure as many pertenencias as you think best.

JAMES SKEWIS

We learned earlier that machinery for Mexican mines was being made in Cornwall and exported in the 1820's and 1830's. But this practice continued well into the middle of the nineteenth century:

El Constitucianal, 21 January, 1873

The Real del Monte and Pachuca Mines bought a new pumping engine for use at their Acosta shaft, reputedly one of the best in the country. It was constructed by Messrs Harvey and Company, Hayle, Cornwall, England.

West Briton, 14 August 1879.

More equipment was shipped out to Mexico this summer including a new 50 inch engine, with pumping and other machinery. It left Hayle aboard *Henry Harvey* and arrived at Vera Cruz 69 days later destined for the Santa Gertrudis Mine.

Commenting on the richness of the mines around Real del Monte and Pachuca, James Skewis dictating biographical notes on 20 October, 1909 relates:

There are many millions of dollars of silver and gold taken from its mines and the mountains are hardly scratched for mining. Its possibilities are great and no doubt for ages to come rich mines will be found.

There are very many rich mines employing thousands of men and paying thousands of dollars in dividends to the owners.

It is a great and interesting sight to see the various processes necessary to extract the silver and gold contained in the rock. The veins or lodes in which the ore is found in the Real del Monte and Pachuca districts are called Fissures. That means the lodes are without break. Whatever their course they continue their regular course down, and east and west, or north or south or whatever course the lode runs. But it is noticeable that I believe all the best mines are on lodes east or a little north east. These lodes are mostly a considerable width—say from four feet to thirty feet or more. And for miles they are being worked. Although the lodes are continuous there are poor places in these lodes that are worthless. We think there are reasons for this such as the various turns of the lode—from an easterly to a south easterly or north easterly, and by other lodes entering into contact and being carried along with the same lode. These are called feeders and often make very rich deposits or "bonanza's" as often termed. So there is, or ought to be, great care in selecting a mine.
Very little silver is found in the upper parts of the lodes in Pachuca. If you find a little to begin it is a good sign of being better in depth and there are many mines of great depth.

Large pumps are required to draw the water from the mine so it is expensive and requires a fairly good mine to pay expenses. And the rich one is a great stimulus for men to venture and try to find a similar good one and no doubt, but what there will be for all time, rich ones discovered. For such is the science of mining in all ages.

At this time there are many Americans in the mining business. They are seldom afraid to speculate and are finding good mines. The present mode of mining seems to be much better than formerly, that mines worthless thirty or forty years ago now pay good profits. Considering all things—climate and regularity of wages and reasonable laws of the Mexican Government — I doubt if there is any better place to invest money than in that industry.

Real del Monte, Mexico

Various members of the Skewes family were employed in the mines of Mexico and the following extracts from "births, marriages and deaths" in the *West Briton* give some indication as to dates, times and locations.

REAL DEL MONTE

25 May 1870.	Marriage of PETER SKEWES (son of PETER SKEWES of Kerley, Cornwall) to Elizabeth Bray of Lanner at Real del Monte.
25 January, 1872.	Marriage at St Austell of RICHARD SKEWES of Kerley, Cornwall, late of Mexico, to Miss E. Stripp of St Austell.
6 January, 1874.	Death at Real del Monte of THOMAS SKEWES, late of Kerley, Cornwall, after four days of illness, aged 33 years.
21 May, 1891.	Death at Real del Monte of Captain PETER SKEWES, formerly of Redruth and Chacewater, aged 48 years.
4 February, 1897.	Birth at Real del Monte to the wife of Captain DICK SKEWES of a son.
18 January, 1906.	Marriage at Johannesburg, South Africa, 14 December, 1905, LILIAN B. SKEWES, daughter of the late Captain PETER SKEWES, Real del Monte, to Arthur Everington of Kimberley.

MINERAL DEL MONTE

Various:	The wife of RICHARD SKEWES (late of Chacewater) gave birth to a daughter in 1881 and a son in 1882 at Mineral del Monte, but returned to Chacewater by 1885 for the birth of another son.
24 October, 1884.	Death at Mineral del Monte of MAUD MARY SKEWES, only child of Captain RICHARD SKEWES, aged 6 months.
2 September, 1884.	Birth at Mineral del Monte 18th July, the wife of Captain PETER SKEWES of a daughter.
23 January, 1885.	Death at Mineral del Monte, 10th December, 1884 of GEORGE HARRIS, second son of Captain PETER SKEWES, aged 10 yrs.

PACHUCA

18 April, 1889.	Death at Ivy Cottage, Chacewater, 12th April the dearly beloved wife of JOHN SKEWES of Pachuca, aged 34 years.
30 March, 1899.	Death at Pachuca from injuries sustained by being thrown from a horse, Mr RICHARD SKEWES, of Redruth, aged 28 years.
30 April, 1908.	Marriage at St Paul's, Chacewater of HERBERT JOHN SKEWES, only son of the late Captain RICHARD SKEWES and the late Mrs SKEWES of Pachuca to Henrietta C. Richards.

Pachuca Cemetery, Mexico — one of the highest locations in the world

ROSARIO
A new mine opened in 1850, and between 1855 and 1862 produced 16,125,656 ounces of silver. In five years the population of the town went up from 8000 to 40,000. Between 1863 and 1868 Rosario Mine paid dividends of £1,400,000 to shareholders. [35]

Captain RICHARD SKEWES spent much of his life working away from Cornwall and was latterly identified with the mining industry in Mexico where he held some lucrative appointments including that of Manager of Gertrudis Mine for many years. He had a large amount of capital invested in Real del Monte Mining Company. He died at his son-in-law's at Penstraze, Cornwall. He left one nephew in Mexico, Captain J.H. SKEWES, manager of Barron Mine, Pachuca and two nieces, Mrs John Rabling of Guanajuato and Mrs F.J. Pratt of Real del Monte.

ZACATECAS
This was a bustling area in the 1840's and boasted a population of 35,000. "The mines here are amongst the most important in the country, their outworks appear like immense castles reared against the face of the barren rock, and long strings of mules, proceeding to the smelting-house, enliven the dreary landscape."[36]

Captain J.W. SKEWES of Algoma, Ontario, Canada worked here and he was the son of Captain HENRY SKEWES of Gwinear. J.W. SKEWES died at Zacatecas 3 May, 1894, aged 46 years.

COMPANIA MINERA de PENOLES
The death was reported at Compania Minera de Penoles, Mapami Estado du Durango, 22 August, 1905 of Edith Gertrude Saunders, wife of THOMAS SKEWES-SAUNDERS, (formerly of Gwinear) who was manager of the world famed gold mine of Dos Estrellas.

A hundred years ago Mexico boasted thousands of Cornish emigrants. Today there are but a handful left.

---

[35] *Mining Journal,* 29 December, 1883. F. Bawden on Mining Prospects in Mexico.
[36] *Mexico Landscape & Popular Sketches* by Carl Sartorius, Darmstadt, 1858.

There is a Cornish cemetery on the pine enclosed hill outside Real del Monte which tells the long tale of those who elected to stay amongst the cactus, maguey and orchards of apples. [37]

Three hundred men, women and children of Cornish background are buried there, most of them belonging to families who came from the mining districts west of Truro like Gwennap, Illogan, Redruth, Kenwyn, Chacewater and Kea.

In the cemetery which holds the remains of twelve members of the Skewes family we find the gravestone of JOHN SKEWES, born Cornwall 21 August 1838 — copper and tin miner — who died in an accident at Rosario Mine, Pachuca on 29 November, 1903, aged 65 years.

To him goes the credit of the Mexican branch as it is today. He was a colourful character, with sad eyes and a long white flowing beard.

He came to Mexico as a young man in his early twenties all set to discover the wealth of Mexican silver and to carve out a new life. He met a young Mexican girl, Luisa Garcia, whom he married in Real del Monte in 1866. Seven children were born to them between 1867 and 1874.

John then returned to England, leaving his wife and children in Mexico. There he met a Miss Catherine Williams, daughter of Michael Williams, grocer whom he married at Chacewater Parish Church, Cornwall on 4 January 1880. He was at this time still legally married to Luisa (Garcia) Skewes. Five children were born to John and Catherine between 1881 and 1886. Two died very young. Catherine died 12 April 1889, aged 34 years.

In 1891 John returned to Mexico with his three children to join his first wife and family. But reports indicate the two families led separate lives.

The Mexican branch blossomed and between 1866 and 1979 a total of 80 children have been born to the Skewes'. All speak Spanish and live in Mexico City, Pachuca and Real del Monte.

Today Pachuca is an important town and has a population of 100,000, whereas Real del Monte only has 3000 residents.

Centre of Pachuca, Mexico

La Rica Mine, Mexico

[37] *Search For Silver*, A.C. Todd, p.158

With the exception of La Rica Mine all other silver mines have been closed in Real del Monte, the highest town in Mexico where people live — 10,000 feet above sea level.

Intermarriage still continues today. The following is an extract from a Mexican Traders Directory:

> Residence: Calle Puerto Real 28, Colonia, Condesa, Mexico, 11, Distrido Federal were GUILLERMO SKEWES ROSATI (Mexican), his wife Ma Teresa Bonnett (American) and their children Guillermo, Eduardo and Ricardo (Mexican).

In the 1979 Telephone Directory for Mexico City (not including Real del Monte and Pachuca) we find the following:

SKEWES	HERMININA ROSATI de	Priv Corrigidora 6ZP20	(905) 593 5813
SKEWES	GUILLERMO	Priv Corrigidora 6ZP20	(905) 593 5813
SKEWES	HERMINIA, ROSATI de	Circ Navegantes A. Malaspina 56ZPEM	(905) 562 4268
SKEWES	MARTINEZ MAGDALENA	Apicultura 227ZP2	(905) 789 9808
SKEWES	VARELA CLARA	T-Avenida 11 No 178ZP13	(905) 532 5293
SKEWES	GUILLERMO	Calle Puerto Real No. 28, Colonia Condesa, M. 11	(905) 553 4961

*   *   *   *   *   *   *   *   *   *

A descendant of Cornish immigrants, who lives in Wisconsin where others share a similar background to her own, was asked how she felt about her ancestors and whether being Cornish was important to her. She replied:

> Yes, it is important because it's our roots. It's where we came from and why we are here... of course we're Americans, there's no question of that... it's just that our heredity is Cornish. I think it's still the Cousin Jack feeling because there's a strong sense of family and cousinship among the Cornish in this area, and the fact that we are all related and share the same roots makes for a happy neighbourhood.[38]

On the west coast of America lies Virginia City, another area where the Cornish settled in their search for gold. From time to time physical weakness, nervous exhaustion and economic anxiety all produced their strains and stresses and often made men unpredictable. [39]

On Saturday 19 December 1874 four miners sat around a table in the bar room of the Washington House on the Divide in Virginia City playing their usual game of pedro... Thomas Trembath, Joseph Hodges, Michael Roach and JOHN SKEWES.

About midnight they were joined by Alfred Rule, originally from Camborne, who suggested they should play for drinks instead of "for pastime". This was a grave mistake as it happened, for it made them quarrelsome.

When only Trembath, Hodges and Skewes were left in the game, Rule suddenly accused Skewes of cheating by looking at Trembath's cards. In a flash tempers were flared. Skewes denied the charge and Rule called him a "goddammed liar". Skewes told him he must take back that statement. The 25-year-old Rule said he would take nothing back, and being heavily built struck Skewes across the shoulder with his left hand, grasped him by the collar of his coat and forced him backwards onto the table top.

Impulsively Skewes dragged a six shooter from his pocket and said "If you don't take it back, I'll kill you." Rule declared he would take nothing back, so Skewes fired on him. The bullet struck Rule at the back of his left ear, passing into his head and killing him instantly. The shocked onlookers were more horrified since Skewes was normally a mild man who had never been known to quarrel. It was in keeping with his character that he at once surrendered to Police Officers Jackson and Merrow, whilst sympathetic Cousin Jacks somehow raised no less than 10,000 dollars bail.

---

[38] *Destination America*, M.A. Jones (Glasgow, 1976) pp 205, 206.
[39] *Cornish Miner in America*, A.C. Todd (Truro, 1967) pp 196, 197

It is said that both men were sober at the time of the shooting and nobody present had the least idea that the little war of words was going to end in anything serious. [40]

The *Virginia City Territorial Enterprise* devoted its Editorial to the event on Wednesday 23 December 1874.

> On Saturday night last, in this city, two men, both bearing the reputation of being steady, peaceable and hard-working men, engaged in a trifling game of cards; one called the other a liar; a few words followed, a scuffle, and then one shot the other dead. So little is life prized here that the tragedy is now well forgotten except among the acquaintances of the two actors in the tragedy. And yet it is none the less terrible; and it is time that here in Virginia, with our city government and police, our country government with its courts and sheriffs, with our churches and clergymen, with our schools filled with innocent children; it is time, we repeat, that these causeless murders should cease. To stop an effect we must find and stop the cause. There are two causes for this homicide. The first was the practice, so prevalent here, of carrying weapons.

> The participants in the affair were Cornishmen. Cornishmen often have disputes and often engage in fisticuffs. They cannot very well help it. The disposition has been transmitted down through their English forefathers for two score generations. A little row, a punch in the head or a black eye, are simply matters of course with them. But not murder. They shrink from that as shocked and loathingly as any people.

> But one of these men had a pistol in his pocket, as has almost everybody else in Virginia. This was the first cause of what resulted in an untimely death. The second cause is that unexplainable but almost universal disposition of people here to say, if a man does not resent an insult, he is a coward, and if he does, and slays a fellow man, he is a murderer. In this we are all in part to blame for the killing of Rule. When Rule called Skewes a liar, Skewes was not much shocked nor much angry. Had there been none present but the two, there is every reason to think nothing more would have come of it, and by the next day the men would have been drinking together again. But Skewes had a friend who advised him that he ought not to let the insult pass without redress, and while the friend advised, Skewes felt the pistol warm in his pocket, and in five minutes the result was a dead man lying on the floor, and another with his peace of mind gone forever, and with a felon's cell opening before him.

> The law ought to forbid the carrying of concealed weapons, and the officers ought to mercilessly execute this law. Then our wealthy men ought from their abundance to provide a hall with books, periodicals, daily papers and other innocent attractions, to lure miners from the groggeries, which are now too often their places of resort. It would be but a trifle for our rich men to do, but it would be the commencement of the saving of human life in our midst.

John Skewes was tried for the murder of Alfred Rule in April 1875. Evidence was given by Thomas Trembath and Joseph Marks. Trembath said "I have known Skewes for seven years. We are friendly. I never knew him to have a quarrel with anybody."

Skewes, who weighed 140 pounds, was said to be an engineer by trade, but had recently been working in the Belcher blacksmith shop.

The jury failed to agree on a verdict, so a fresh trial was ordered and on 20 May 1875 the bail reduced to 6000 dollars. Unfortunately for Skewes a recession had set in; the population of Washoe had dropped from 1500 to 500 and the money could not be raised, so into the county jail went the unfortunate Mr Skewes to await trial the following September.

J. Ross Brown, an author, visited Virginia City about the time of the great gold rush to the Comstock Lode. His description as to the countryside leaves little to the imagination:

> Every foot of the canyon was claimed, and gangs of miners were at work all along the road, digging and delving into the earth like so many infatuated gophers. Many of these unfortunate creatures lived in holes dug into the side of a hill, and here and there a blanket thrown over a few stakes served as a domicile to shield them from the weather.

> The district is said to be exceedingly rich in gold and I fancy it may well be so, for it is certainly rich in nothing else. A more barren-looking and forbidding spot could scarcely be found elsewhere on the face of the earth. The whole aspect of the country indicates that it must have been burned up in hot fires many years ago and reduced to a mass of cinders, or scraped up from all over the desolate spots known to the world, and thrown over the Sierra Nevada Mountains in a confused mass to be out of the way.

---

[40] *Virginia City Territorial Enterprise*, 20 December 1874.

Sickness is bad enough at the best of time, but here the conditions of the sick was truly pitiful. There was scarcely a tenement in the place that could be regarded as affording shelter against the piercing wind.

Many had come with barely means sufficient to defray their expenses to the Diggings, in the confident belief that they would immediately strike upon "something rich" or, if they failed in that, they could work a while on wages. But the highest wages here for common labour were three dollars a day, while meals were a dollar each and lodgings the same. No records of deaths were kept. The mass of emigration were strangers to each other, and it concerned nobody in particular when a man 'pegged out', except to put him in a hole somewhere out of the way."

For one reason and another the Skewes murder trial was further delayed, but eventually set for 1st November 1875. Now by a strange quirk of fate a fire began in Crazy Kate's lodging house on October 26th and spread through the whole city, roaring through the main streets with such terrible force that it destroyed churches, business buildings, mills and hundreds of homes.

Skewes now disappears completely from the pages of the local newspaper except for a note which said, at the height of the conflagration, he was lodged for safety in a tunnel of the Sierra Nevada mine and then in Gold Hill Jail.

As for Rule he was almost forgotten, for his friends were so terrified that none dared tell his relatives back in Cornwall of his fate for a year. [41]

Whether Skewes was found "guilty" or "not guilty" or if the trial eventually took place we are not told.

From a Skewes who allegedly killed in America, to a Skewes who *was* killed in America. This incident happened about 1867. From a very faded press cutting (no date — no newspaper) retained by his grandson GEORGE HENNESSY SKEWES of Camborne we read:

DEATH OF A CORNISHMAN IN NICARAGUA
Intelligence has just been received of a shocking occurrence which took place in Nicaragua, Central America, by which a Cornishman, named JAMES HENRY SKEWES, a native of the Lizard, and for many years a resident of Camborne, lost his life under most painful circumstances.

It appears that on Sunday 24 May last, Skewes, who was employed as foreman carpenter of the Chontales Mines, was invited by the doctor of the company to go with him on a visit to a patient who resided some fifteen or twenty miles distant, and not having been out of the mines for many months Skewes consented.

On their way back they called at the Company's farm, where they found one of the underground agents, Captain James White (formerly of St Ives), and a miner, both of whom had been drinking rather freely during the day. Refusing the invitation to drink also the doctor and Skewes rode homewards, accompanied by Captain White and his companion. The latter, being exceedingly intoxicated, very soon lagged behind the rest of considerable distance, and on Skewes pointing out the danger of the man's being left to take care of himself in such a locality, White became annoyed, and after a few angry words rode up to Skewes and struck him a severe blow with his fist. In self-defence the latter dismounted, and upon White repeating his attack, Skewes being a fine stalwart man about thirty years of age, soon got the best of the encounter, knocking his antagonist down two or three times. White who was also a big, powerful man, and of a violent overbearing disposition, became so enraged that he drew out his revolver, and with an oath placed it close to Skewes and fired. The ball penetrated the right breast & perforated the lung, causing internal hemorrhage which resulted in death within half an hour after the wound was received.

The doctor gave the alarm as soon as possible, and the body was removed to the mines for interment, White being placed in prison. The unfortunate deceased was universally liked and respected at the mines, by natives as well as the English, and it was with great difficulty that his murderer escaped being 'lynched.'

Skewes was a remarkably steady, inoffensive man, besides being a most useful servant to the company. In a letter of condolence to the widow of the deceased, the secretary to the company says, "I feel deeply for your position, and having known Skewes at the mines, can bear testimony to the loss we suffer in the death of so good a workman."

White according to the last advices, had been sentenced to be hanged, but having caught the yellow fever, the execution was deferred for a time. [42]

---

41 *Cornish Miner in America*, A.C. Todd (Truro, 1967) p197

42 There is no indication as to which newspaper this article appeared in. Various editions of *Royal Cornwall Gazette* and *West Briton* were searched, but with no success.

The Chontales Mines were situated in Nicaragua nestled in the hills between the town of La Libertad and the village of Santa Domingo, Central America. There were fourteen mines in operation in 1883.

As well as the United States of America, Mexico and Australia to where the Skewes' emigrated, some went to South Africa including HENRY SKEWES, formerly of Condurrow Croft, Camborne and a miner who had been working for a time at Reitfontein Lazaretto, Transvaal Colony and who died on 13 June 1905.

Another member of the family went to the mining area of Portugal, and to the second largest city, Oporto. However, minerals were little exploited owing to poor communications and the lack of fuel. MATTHEW SKEWES worked for Polhol Mines, and on 15th September 1855 married Anna Maria Nettle (of Redruth) in Oporto. Matthew was the son of MATTHEW SKEWES of Chacewater, Cornwall.

Photograph taken in 1867 shortly before the murder of James Henry Skewes
Below: *The reverse of the picture on which he wrote "For Father from his son James from Central America."*

As well as members of the family emigrating during the tin mining depression, others migrated. Five areas within the British Isles to where they moved were Somerset, South Wales, Durham, South Yorkshire and Nottinghamshire.

HENRY SKEWIS was born in Camborne in 1819 and had been captain of Crane Mine, Cornwall, but moved to Somerset in March, 1867 when he took over as mine captain at Brendon Hills, a post formerly held by Morgan Morgans. He proved to be a sound, practical miner, if something of a disciplinarian. For part of his time at the mines he was assisted by his son EDWIN SKEWIS, who prepared most of the plans which survive. A sturdy, bearded man, he was best remembered for organising the Wesleyan Sunday School outings on the mineral railway for he was a staunch Methodist.[43]

Iron working in the Brendon Hills area of West Somerset could have started as long ago as Roman times. German iron workers were there in the 16th century. But the Brendon Hills complex really came into its own during Victorian times.

Situated 1200 feet above the Bristol Channel, it is today a quiet spot noted for farming and forestry. Only the old engine house at Burrow Farm is still visible. 120 years ago the county of Somerset linked with South Wales. Iron ore fed the smelting furnaces of Ebbw Vale Steel, Iron and Coal Company Ltd which was incorporated in 1855 for £65,000 to connect the workings on the Hills to Watchet Harbour. From the Brendons iron ore was shipped to Newport across the Bristol Channel. The mines employed 300 workers who lived in the nearby villages of Gupworthy, Luxborough and Withiel Florey.

Burrow Farm and Kennesome Hill mines both had rotary beam engines serving the dual functions of pumping and winding. The buildings were constructed under Captain Skewis' direction and their design closely resembled such engine houses in Cornwall. They contained 25-inch and 28-inch cylinder engines respectively, each with a 9 foot stroke. As the engine houses were each set back about 50 feet from the drift collar, the pump rods ran horizontally close to the ground until reaching the drift, when the change of direction was effected by means of bell cranks. Burrow Farm, built in 1880, had two winding drums whereas Kennesome Hill completed some seven years earlier, only had one.

On average in the 1860's Brendon Hills mines were producing 30,000 tons a year. In 1877 a record 52,000 tons of ore were sent to South Wales.

Two prosecutions were brought against the Ebbw Vale Company in 1877, for contravening the Metalliferous Mines Regulation Act 1872. In November the company was fined for failing to provide adequate ventilation and proper accommodation for the men to dry and change their clothes, and for not fencing shafts at Langham Hill, while in December it was fined again for not providing platforms at Kennesome Hill.

Wages at the Brendon Hills mines in 1870 were approx. 10/- a week for a labourer and 18/- for a skilled worker.

Due to cheaper imports of Spanish ore, Welsh smelters turned their affections away from Somerset. By 1883 the mines at Elsen Hill, Burrow Farm, Florey Hill, Carew, Roman, Colton and Elworthy were silent. The Cornish miners who had moved there had slipped away. One hundred years after Henry Skewis built his engine house at Burrow Farm (1980), there was a move to make a museum on the original site.

Captain Skewis quit as mines captain in 1883 and took over as manager of the West Somerset Mineral Railway. He died in Watchet on 29 October 1889. The railway closed on 7 November 1898, although it was briefly re-opened again in 1907 for a short while. However the tracks were lifted for scrap metal during the First World War.

[43] *West Somerset Mineral Railway*, Roger Sellick, Newton Abbot, 1962; pp 36, 53, 62, 64.

A number of the Skewis family moved to mid and west Glamorgan and Gwent in South Wales to join the several large steel, iron and tin-plate works and collieries. They moved from west Cornwall to Merthyr Tydfil, Bedwellty, Aberdare, Neath, Ebbw Vale, Pontypridd and Tredegar.

Four great iron works at Merthyr became a thriving industry and iron working spread into the Monmouthshire valleys. Originally the foundries had been fuelled by wood. But due to the discovery of coal the iron works expanded during the 19th century. The coal field, 56 miles in length, stretched from Carmarthen to Pontypridd and on average was 16 miles wide. Coal was also mined at Aberdare and Rhymney Valley. By 1870 there were some 5000 miners producing nearly 2 million tons of coal a year.

But at a similar time there was a decline in the iron industry which led to large scale emigration in the 1870's. 15,000 people left Glamorgan and many of them went to Pennsylvania, USA.

Members of the family who moved away from Cornwall to Yorkshire, Durham and Nothinghamshire became coal miners.

MATTHEW SKEWS moved north from Liskeard, Cornwall to live at 17, Best View Terrace, Shiney Row, County Durham. Another member of that family,

Burrow Farm, built by Captain Henry Skewis, located in the Brendon Hills, Somerset

WILLIAM JOHN SKEWS, left St Columb, Cornwall to set up house at 44, Elemore Lane, Hetton-le-Hole, County Durham, and his descendants still live in that part of the world today and are connected with the colliery business.

THOMAS SKEWS was born in Truro in 1867. He left Cornwall as a youth and travelled north to Sheffield where he became a coal ripper. He married in Ecclesall, Sheffield in 1886. His son THOMAS SKEWS was a trammer and later a coal ripper in Wombwell Main and Cortonwood collieries from 1925 to 1951 and, in turn, his son ROY SKEWS worked as an underground official in Elsecar colliery until 1978 when he retired.

76-year-old EDGAR SKEWS, talking in May, 1980, about his days in the South Yorkshire pits said:

> I come from a mining family. My father and my five brothers all worked down the pit. I believed that the coal face was really quite safe. Nothing would go wrong that would hurt me.
>
> I left school at 13 and went to work at Mitchell's Main colliery, Wombwell at the pit top on screens. I first went down the pit at 15½ and was not in any way scared. Really I was not aware of the real dangers that confronted me.
>
> I started work on the coal face in 1926, just before the General Strike. We worked eight hours a day, five days a week in appalling conditions, and I remember my pay packet at the end of the week — 42/5d.
>
> You would crawl down the seam which was four-foot-six deep, and only inches would separate the roof from your soaking wet body. Your head would be turned to the side, and perhaps there was a two

inch gap above your head before you hit the roof. You would slide forward, arms out in front and your legs spreadeagled behind, pushing yourself forward. And all the time the roof would be creaking above your head. All the time water would be dripping from the roof.

I wore a dirty old raincoat with a pair of swimming trunks underneath. There were no baths, so I washed at home. I used to laugh at the state I got in. But my wife said "You may laugh now, but you'll be sorry later." How right she was.

There were twenty of us working at the coal face and we had 125 pit ponies who were stabled underground. They hauled the tubs of coal, which we filled, to the pit bottom. We got one shilling for every ton of coal we mined, and if we pulled out 10 tons of coal in a day, we thought we had done right well.

In 1966 I had to give up working at the coal face, because I had developed an arthritic spine, so was given lighter work controlling the conveyer belts extracting the coal from the pit. When I left the coal face I was earning £8 a week. Now the lads today can earn £100 a week, and sometimes, with productivity deals, even more.

TOM SKUSE was born in Keynsham, Bristol on 25 November 1902. At the age of 17 he moved to Kirkby in Ashfield, Nottinghamshire. He became one of the operators on the control panel of the Remotely Operated Longwall Face machines. Tom had four sons who became miners — Dale, Dean, Gordon and Trevor. Now, together with their sons, the Skuse family have worked a total of 120 years at Newstead Colliery, Nottinghamshire.

Says 43-year-old GORDON SKUSE: "The modern day coal cutting machines are very powerful, and where machinery is operated in very confined spaces, accidents sometimes occur, although the standard of safety in British mines is very good indeed and being improved all the time. Hydraulic roof supporters have been invaluable in the modern coving in system of long wall faces. The National Coal Board are also working very hard on dust problems, installing extractor fans, fitters and dust sprays wherever possible, together with safety clothing. Safety in mines has greatly improved over the last 30 years considering the size and power of today's mining equipment."

The "mining brigade" have been hard workers, sometimes willing to travel many thousands of miles, long before the birth of the motor car, the luxury liner or the aeroplane.

Their work was highly skilled, but the conditions in which they worked were so bad, with little oxygen in the air, and in so much heat, it was impossible to work for more than twenty minutes without a break. All stood the risk of suffering from congestion of the lungs caused by coal dust.

Overseas the money was good for the miner, but his wage depended on sheer physical strength and manual dexterity.

11 Boyd's Marriage Index

BOYD'S MARRIAGE INDEX is an alphabetical list of names extracted from parish registers which are classified by counties and come in groups of either 25 or 50 years per volume. The Marriage Index covers the period 1538-1837 in 531 volumes kept at the Society of Genealogists in London. In Cornwall there are 202 parishes from which names have been taken, but in all, Boyd's Marriage Index covers 4200 registers containing over seven million names.

Although the names are in alphabetical order the Index is now incomplete as many other parish registers have been copied since Boyd compiled it between 1925 and 1955. All entries are typewritten.

It is a very useful source of information. As the majority of marriages in the SKEWES/SKEWIS/SKEWS/SKUES families took place in the 17th, 18th, and 19th centuries it is obvious that the bulk of names will be in Boyd's Marriage Index for the county of Cornwall.

In addition to the various county records on the shelves at the Society of Genealogists there are two additional series of miscellaneous volumes containing marriages from many other counties, as well as a large number of marriage announcements in the "Gentleman's Magazine."

Follows now a list of all the entries found appertaining to SKUES and the variations in spelling. All abbreviations as per the typewriter of Mr Percival Boyd.

1575	SKEWES	GRACE	and	Nic Vybyst	Ludgvan
1576	SKEWES	ALICE	and	Wm Wiat	St Enoder
1589	SKEWIS	JAS	and	Agn Ellis	Camborne
1623	SKEWES	CHARITY	and	Jas Hockin	St Keverne
1624	SKEWES	JN	and	Ann Harwood	St Keverne
1632	SKEWES	JN	and	Mgt Cheren	St Keverne
1637	SCEWES	HUM	and	Xtian Farmer	Camborne
1654	SKEWES	KEVERNE	and	Joan Nicholas	St Keverne
1654	SKEWES	ISAATT	and	Herc Niclas	Truro, St Mary
1659	SKEWES	MARY	and	Ambrose John	St Keverne
1661	SKEWES	WILMOT	and	Thos Olivy	St Keverne
1664	SCUES	WILLIAM	and	Mgt Thomas	Camborne BT
1664	SCUES	GEORGE	and	Eliz Grills	Camborne
1665	SKEWES	ABGALL	and	... rkes Maker	St Feock BT
1665	SKEWES	THOMAS	and	Sidwell Millard	Gwennap
1665	SKEWES	COLON	and	Eliz Warrine	Perranarworthal BT
1667	SKEWES	JN	and	Mary Cornelius	St Keverne
1668	SKUES	AMY	and	Bob Hunt	Wendron
1674	SKEWES	FLORENCE	and	Ric Row	St Keverne
1675	SKEUIS	RIC	and	Brid Williams	Gwennap
1680	SKEWS	WM	and	Jane John	Redruth
1685	SKEWES	AMY (MARY)	and	John Feeeman	Kenwyn
1690	SKEWIS	JN	and	Mary	Madron
1692	SCUIS	THOM	and	Philip Anguin	Wendron
1695	SKEWS	BLANCH	and	Martin Magor	Gwennap
1700	SKUES	DEGORY	and	......	Kenwyn
1700	SKEWS	RIC	and	Mgt Tregew	Paul
1701	SKEWS	JOAN	and	Anth Michel	Gwennap
1702	SKEWS	THOMAS	and	Mgt Richards	Gwennap
1703	SKEWAS	GRACE	and	Thos Rownson	St Mawgan-in-Meneage
1705	SKEWS	SIDWELL	and	Henry Rogers	Gwennap
1705	SCUIS	HENRY	and	Mary	Camborne
1708	SCUES	JANE	and	John Williams	Redruth
1708	SKEWES	MARY	and	Tobias Richards	St Levan
1710	SCUES	MARY	and	Jn Angove	Redruth
1710	SKEWES	RIC	and	Mary James	Kea
1713	SKEWES	THOS	and	Mary Retallack	St Martin-in-Mge
1714	SKEWES	ELIZ	and	Chris Tellam	Camborne
1715	SKEUES	ANN	and	Jn Richards	Paul
1716	SKEUS	JN	and	Cath Nicholas	St Buryan
1716	SKEWIS	STE	and	Fran Lydgy	Redruth
1718	SKEWIS	JONE	and	Jn Caudwell	Redruth
1718	SKEWIS	HENRY	and	Judith Walters	Constantine
1719	SKEWS	SAM	and	Ann Quick	Madron
1722	SKEWES	PHILIPPA	and	Henry Pascoe	Wendron
1722	SKUES	RIC	and	Jane Coombe	Kenwyn
1722	SKEWES	REMFREY	and	Mgy Bryant	Camborne
1722	SKUES	MARY	and	Jas Williams	Wendron

Year	Surname	Name		Spouse	Parish
1723	SKEWES	ALEX	and	Anne Carveth	St Enoder
1723	SKEWIS	STEP	and	Jane Lydgy	Redruth
1724	SKEWS	RIC	and	Reb Botteral	Gwennap
1724	SKUES	MARY	and	Walter Staple	Kenwyn
1725	SKUES	ANN	and	Jos Gribben	Redruth
1726	SKEUES	MGT	and	Isaac Crusilier	Paul
1729	SKUES	MARTIN	and	Mary Coad	Kenwyn
1734	SKUES	MARGARET	and	Henry Michel	Crowan
1734	SKUES	KATH	and	Simon Blagdon	Sancreed
1734	SKEWS	RIC	and	Mgy Warren	Paul
1734	SKEWS	JOHN	and	Eliz Symonds	Madron
1734	SKEWS	WM	and	Mary Temby	Camborne
1735	SKEWS	JOAN	and	Jn Gregor	Gwennap
1737	SKEWS	MARY	and	Thomas Bastard	Crowan
1737	SKEWS	HENRY	and	Constance Paul	Crowan
1738	SKEWES	THOMAS	and	Eliz. Webb	Gwennap
1740	SKEWES	JOHN	and	Mary Webb	Gwennap
1740	SKEWES	HENRY	and	Mary Behenna	Kenwyn
1743	SKEWES	EDWARD	and	Margaret Rogers	St. Sithney
1744	SKEWS	WM	and	Hannah Dayworth	St Gluvias
1746	SKEWS	THOS	and	Esther James	St Keverne
1750	SKEWS	PETER	and	Margaret Newton	Kea
1750	SKEWS	CHRIS	and	Honor Angwyn	Sancreed
1751	SKEWIS	ROB	and	Jane Sandys	Helston
1751	SKUSE	MOSES	and	Mary Thomas	St Gluvias
1752	SKEWS	CATH	and	Jas Barnicoat	Falmouth
1753	SKEWIS	JENNEFAR	and	Jas Gritten	Helston
1753	SKEWIS	WM	and	Ann Bawden	Gwennap
1754	SKEWIS	TOBIAS	and	Eliz Davy	St Just in Pnwth
1755	SKEWIS	JOAN	and	Ric Traplyn	St Mawgan in Mge
1756	SKEWIS	DIGORY	and	Mgt Spargo	Kenwyn
1756	SKEWIS	JOS	and	Philippa Martin	St Martin in Mge
1757	SKUES	MARY	and	Ralph Harvey	Helston
1757	SKUSE	SARAH	and	Ric Lobb	St Just in Pnwth
1757	SKEWS	SARAH	and	Jn Warrick	St Ewe
1758	SKEWS	ELIZ	and	Gidgeon Johns	Falmouth
1759	SKEWS	MARY	and	Ferninando Behenna	Kea
1759	SKEWS	THOS	and	Jane Crossman	Kenwyn
1760	SKEWS	MARTIN	and	Mary Polkinhorne	Kenwyn
1759	SKEWS	JN	and	Alice John	Perranarworthal
1760	SKEWIS	JANE	and	Jn Banfield	St Mawgan in Mge
1762	SKEWIS	HANNAH	and	Chas Coleman	St Gluvias
1762	SKEWIS	JUDITH	and	Thos Harry	Helston
1762	SKUES	EDWARD	and	Honor Pearce	Helston
1763	SKEWES	PHILIPPA	and	William Skinner	Gwennap
1763	SKEWIS	JAS	and	Charity Ellis	Camborne
1764	SKEWIS	MARY	and	Stephen Rowe	Camborne
1765	SKEWIS	RIC	and	Alice Knucky	Camborne
1765	SKEWIS	WM	and	Mary Hitchens	Gwennap
1767	SKEWES	JN	and	Philippa King	Camborne
1769	SKUES	JOHN	and	Mary Hockins	Helston
1769	SKEWES	JN	and	Mary Tregonning	Gwennap
1770	SKEWES	RIC	and	Mary Teague	Kenwyn
1771	SKEWES	JN	and	Mary Dennis	Kenwyn
1771	SKUEIS	JANE	and	Ric Harris	St. Mary, Truro
1771	SKEWS	PHYLLIS	and	Martin Hoskin	Madron
1772	SKEWES	JOS	and	Eliz Pearce	St Mawgan in Mge
1773	SKEWES	JAS	and	Anne Richard	St Mawgan in Mge
1774	SKEWIS	THOS	and	Elnr Giles	St Keverne
1774	SKEWES	RIC	and	Fran Toy	Budock
1774	SKEWS	MARY	and	William Coad	St Stephen in B.
1776	SKEUES	JN	and	Mary Mitchell	Gwennap
1776	SKEWES	HENRY	and	Mary Jolly	Kenwyn
1777	SKEWIS	HESTER	and	Phil Eller	Falmouth
1778	SKEWES	MARY	and	Jas Avery	Kenwyn
1779	SKEWES	JOAN	and	Wm Tregonning	Gwennap
1780	SKEWES	ANN	and	Thos Gregor	Gwennap
1781	SKEWES	RIC	and	Jane Robins	Kenwyn
1781	SKEWES	MARY	and	Thos Shepherd	Kea
1781	SKEWES	AVICE	and	Ric Pike	Falmouth
1782	SKEWES	MARY	and	Thomas Dale	St Mawgan in Mge
1782	SKEWES	DEGORY	and	Elizabeth Wasley	Kenwyn
1783	SKEWES	CATH	and	Jn Wasley	Kenwyn
1783	SKEWES	JUDITH	and	Jn Mildren	St Keverne
1784	SKEWS	ANN	and	Hugh Tregensa	St Ewe
1784	SKEWES	ALICE	and	Jn Morcam	Kenwyn
1785	SKEWES	MARIE	and	Wm Tamlyn	Kenwyn
1785	SKEWES	ANN	and	Wm Lawry	Kea
1785	SKEWES	ANNE	and	Math Brown	Camborne
1786	SKEWIS	ABSALOM	and	Eliz Clemance	Crowan
1786	SKEWIS	ELNR	and	Thos Rowe	Crowan
1787	SKEWES	ELIZ	and	Dan Rowe	Crowan
1787	SKEWES	HEN	and	Jane Pascoe	St Keverne
1787	SKEWES	JN	and	Ann Stephens	Kenwyn
1787	SKEWS	JANE	and	Andr Mitchell	Falmouth
1788	SKEWES	EDWARD	and	Grace Pearce	Helston
1788	SKEWS	HONOR	and	Jas Russell	St Gluvias
1788	SKEWES	BIDDY	and	Nic Trestraile	Kenwyn

1788	SKEWES	ELIZABETH	and	Thomas Trahaer	Kenwyn
1789	SKEWES	MARY	and	Jn Blackler	Kenwyn
1790	SKUSE	SARAH	and	Jn Sweet	St Ewe
1790	SKEWES	ELIZ	and	Wm Cock	Gwinear
1791	SKEWES	PET	and	Anne Crase	Kenwyn
1791	SKEWES	THOS	and	Mary Turner	Kea
1791	SKEWES	JN	and	Elnr Phillips	Kea
1791	SKEWES	MARY	and	Wm Thomas	Camborne
1792	SKEWES	HENRY	and	Mgt Phillips	Gwithian
1792	SKEWS	JAS	and	Joanna Triscott	St Ewe
1792	SKEWES	PET	and	Peggy Moyle	Kenwyn
1792	SKEWES	ANN	and	Jn Benney	Kenwyn
1793	SKEWES	RIC	and	Rose Anthony	Kenwyn
1793	SKEWES	HENRY	and	Cath Wasley	Kenwyn
1793	SKEWES	GRACE	and	Hen Dunstone	Towednack
1793	SKEWES	MARY	and	Wm Smetheran	Camborne
1793	SKEWES	WM	and	Ann Trewan	Kea
1793	SKUES	RICHARD	and	Ann Richards	Helston
1793	SKUES	ELIZABETH	and	Jas Byron	Helston
1793	SKEWIS	JOAN	and	Jas Meager	St Breage
1793	SKEWES	HEN	and	Jane Retallack	St Keverne
1794	SKEWIS	ANN	and	Jn James	St Keverne
1794	SKEWES	ALICE	and	WILLIAM SKEWES	Falmouth
1794	SKEWES	ALEX	and	Christian Marten	Stithians
1795	SKEWES	CATH	and	Jn Thomas	Kenwyn
1795	SKEWES	ELIZ	and	Jn Murley	Gwinear
1795	SKEWES	ANN LUCEY	and	Anth Sandoe	Kea
1796	SKEWES	ELIZ	and	Chas Dennis	Kea
1796	SKEWS	WM	and	Nancy Blewett	Withiel
1796	SKEWS	SARAH	and	Gabriel Blewett	Camborne
1796	SKEWES	ELNOR	and	Pet Wood	Falmouth
1797	SKEWES	SARAH	and	Wm Anthony	Mylor
1797	SKEWES	ANN	and	Dan Hodge	Kenwyn
1798	SKEWES	THOS	and	Mary Tippet	Kenwyn
1798	SKEWES	JENNIFER	and	Jos Bastian	Kenwyn
1798	SKEWES	RIC	and	Mary Lean	Perranarworthal
1799	SKEWIS	ELIZ	and	Fran Tuckfield	Wendron
1799	SKUES	JAS	and	Sus Thomas	Wendron
1799	SKEWES	JN	and	Ann Dinnis	Kea
1799	SKUSE	ABRAH	and	Mary Bolitho	St Mary, Truro
1800	SKEWES	ELIZ	and	Wm Rontree	Falmouth
1800	SKEWES	JN	and	Jane Angove	Camborne
1801	SKEWES	CATH	and	Geo Prout	Camborne
1801	SKEWIS	HY	and	Ann Blamey	Gwennap
1802	SKEWES	PHILIPPA	and	Jn Phillips	Camborne
1802	SKEWES	WM	and	Anne Ellis	Camborne
1802	SKUES	WM	and	Jane John	Mylor
1802	SKUES	MARY	and	Wm Mitchell	Helston
1802	SKEWES	PEGGY	and	Thos Roberts	Kenwyn
1803	SKEWES	CONSTANCE	and	Ric Williams	Camborne
1803	SKEWES	WM	and	Eliz Thomas	Crowan
1803	SKEWES	RIC	and	Grace Ford	Kenwyn
1804	SKEWES	ALICE	and	Jn Midlin	Constantine
1804	SKUES	AN	and	Wm Scott	St Mary, Truro
1805	SKEWIS	WM	and	Mary Edwards	Gwennap
1805	SKEWES	MGT	and	Math Wasley	Kea
1806	SKEWES	HEN	and	Grace Tremayne	Constantine
1806	SKEWES	RIC	and	Agn Jeffry	Kea
1807	SKEWES	JAS	and	Jane Thomas	Crowan
1807	SKEWES	RIC	and	Mary Ninis	Kea
1809	SKEWES	MARY	and	Ric Tregaskis	Gwennap
1810	SKEWES	ELIZ	and	Jn Rowe	Constantine
1810	SKEWS	JN	and	Jennifer Treweek	Gwennap
1810	SKEWES	ABSALOM	and	Jane Piper	Camborne
1811	SKEWES	DIGORY	and	Sophia Jordan	Kea
1811	SKEWES	MARY	and	Jn Tregaskis	Gwennap
1812	SKEWES	JAS	and	Jane Richards	Camborne
1812	SKEWES	ELIZ	and	Phil Lean	Gwennap
1813	SKUES	JOS	and	Eliz Penrose	Redruth
1824	SKUES	ELIZ	and	Jas Lanksbury	Redruth
1837	SKEWES	JN	and	Sally Tub	Redruth
1837	SKEWIS	JN	and	Mary Banfield	Redruth

BT following the name of a parish means that Boyd took information from Bishop's Transcripts.

BOYD'S MARRIAGE INDEX — MISCELLANEOUS

All parishes are in Cornwall, except where stated.

1563	SKEWES	JANE	and	William Hain	St Gerrans
1572	SKEWES	JN	and	Maud Penperth	St Gerrans
1582	SKEWES	MARY	and	Jn Babbe	St Gerrans
1590	SKEWES	ELNOR	and	Hen Fittack	St Gerrans
1605	SKUES	STE	and	Xtian Jenkin	St Just in Roseland
1607	SKEWS	JAS	and	Tamsen Tonkin	St Just in Roseland
1611	SKEWS	AGN	and	Martin Luke	St Gerrans

1612	SKEWS	HUM	and	Mary Evans	St Gerrans
1616	SKEWS	ISA or IDA	and	Garret Samson	Clement
1617	SKEWS	XTIAN	and	Nic Vinicom	Exeter, Devon
1633	SKEWS	STE	and	Tho Manly	St Just in Roseland
1638	SKEWS	STE	and	Blanch Penrose	St Just in Roseland
1638	SKEWS	JOANE	and	Jn Mills	St Martin, Exeter
1640	SKEWS	MARY	and	Thos Pearce	St Just in Roseland
1646	SKEWS	FLORENCE	and	Osborne Fittack	Gerrans
1646	SKEWS	MARY	and	Thos Jack	St Just in Roseland
1646	SKEWS	XTIAN	and	Mick Buskeen	St Just in Roseland
1647	SKEWS	ELIZ	and	Jas Southen	Hemel Hempstead, Herts
1650	SKEWS	STE	and	Sar Wilkeson	Southwark, St Thomas
1648 *	SKUES	MARY	and	Wm Bastone	Ottery St Mary
1655	SKEWES	FLO	and	Jn Heale	Plymouth, St Andrew
1665	SKUES	JN	and	Pasco Tomkins	Portsmouth, Hants
1687	SKEWS	SAR	and	Chas Betty	Cury
1693	SKEWS	MARY	and	Tho Beech	Wheathampstead, Herts
1701	SKEWS	RIC	and	Eliz Oakley	Friends
1718	SKEWS	WM	and	Avis Rowe	Gunwalloe
1723	SKEWS	EDW	and	An Beal	Gunwalloe
1733	SKEWES	JOS	and	Jane Corien	Gunwalloe
1737	SKEWS	RIC	and	An Polgreen	St Clement
1743	SKEWS	PHILIP	and	An Webb	Philleigh
1743	SKEWS	AN	and	Jn Williams	St Clement
1747	SKEWES	JN	and	Mary George	Cury
1758	SKEWES	BLANCH	and	Rob Caddy	Cury
1760	SKEWES	ANT	and	ELNR SKEWES	Cury
1777	SKEWES	MARY	and	Wm Jennings	Cury
1777	SKEWES	SARA	and	Jn Piercy	Cury
1778	SKEWIS	JN	and	Mary Williams	Cury
1782	SKEWES	ELIZ	and	Thos White	Cury
1783	SKEWES	MGY	and	Jn White	Cury
1786	SKEWES	MARTIN	and	Eliz May	St Clement
1792	SKEWES	FRAN	and	Jose Keverne	Cury
1793	SKEWES	MARY	and	Hen Williams	Cury
1791	SKEWES	WM	and	An Williams	Gunwalloe
1795	SKEWES	AN	and	Jn Tripconey	Cury
1796	SKEWES	ELEANOR	and	Peter Wood, widower of Falmouth, also of Massachusetts, America	Falmouth
1800	SKEWES	JN	and	Eliz Hendy	Cury
1802	SKEWES	ELIZ	and	Rob Triggs	Cury
1804	SKEWES	SARAH	and	Tho Triggs	Cury
1808	SKEWES	JAS	and	Eliz Tremayne	Cury
1810	SKEWES	MARY	and	Rich Dudley	Cury
1820	SKEWES	JANE	and	Walter Bellman	Cury
1821	SKEWES	MARY	and	Tho Piercy	Cury
1824	SKEWES	JAS	and	Simonet Barnet	Cury
1824	SKEWES	JN	and	Avis Jeffrey	Cury
1827	SKEWIS	SARA	and	Jn Triggs	Cury
1829	SKEWIS	ELIZ	and	Wm James	Cury
1828	SKEWES	BLANCH	and	Ric Oates	Cury
1831	SKEWES	GRACE	and	Sam Hendy	Cury
1831	SKEWES	THOMAS	and	Loveday Mundy	Ruan Minor
1833	SKEWES	WM	and	Sara Hodge	Cury
1834	SKEWES	EDW	and	Alice Triggs	Cury
1834	SKEWES	WM	and	MARY SKEWES	Cury
1834	SKUES	WM	and	Eliz Glasson	Wendron
1836	SKEWES	AN	and	Jas Freeman	Cury
1837	SKEWES	JN	and	Julian Hendy	Cury

(Note: Probably *SKUSE as four other weddings took place at the same church within a period of ten years.)

12 Various Branches of the Family

THE SKEWES family took its roots in Cornwall and remained there for many generations. The big exodus did not occur until the tin mining depression in the mid nineteenth century. Many branches emigrated. Others migrated. Of those who went to Australia, America, Canada and Mexico the families and their descendants survive to this day.

The first indication we have of members of the family moving away from Cornwall came from studying Probate Registers. For example between the years 1622 and 1650 there was a branch of the family at Ottery St Mary in Devon and another at Colliton Rayleigh, Devon around 1637 — 1646.

A large number of SKUSEs sprang up around Bristol and that spelling is still popular to this day. There seems to be no connection between that side of the family and the county of Cornwall.

By 1800 a number of SKUCEs and SKUSEs appeared in Northern Ireland. From 1840 the spelling SCUSE was popular in Gloucester and Wiltshire. A family of SKEWIS appeared in South Wales about 1830 at a similar time to a branch of SKEWIS in Scotland.

By the end of 1875 the various spellings had spread more or less throughout England, Scotland and Wales. Although a number of SKEWES' intermarried in Cornwall the writer has not come across a SKUSE marrying a SKUES, or a SKEWS marrying a SKEWIS.

The most popular profession of the Cornish Skewes' were farmers and miners, but also in Cornwall we meet a wheelwright, school master, a few carpenters and blacksmiths, a licensee, doctors, apothecaries, auctioneers and surveyors and many others.

There are now 50 pedigrees listing members of the family. Many branches have died out. Others list just a handful of names. Individual pedigrees have been drawn by the author, but are too large for inclusion in this book. They may be obtained from the publishers. Let us look briefly at information extracted from these different charts.

CHART 1   SKEWYS of CURY and ST WENN, CORNWALL 1340 — 1600

The first branch which is known to the author. JOHN SKEWYS married a daughter of Fortesse Benalleck. He was Commissioner for Peace in 1343. His grandson John Skewys was Lord of Skewys in 1386 and the title and the property remained in the family until the death of John Skewys in 1544 (see Chapter Six). This property went to the stepsons of Skewys — William and John Reskymer, and this branch of the family is now extinct. A coat of arms was granted to John Skewys in the 16th century (see Chapter 14).

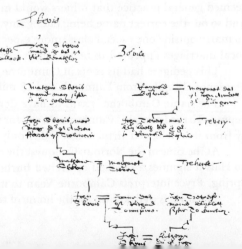

Early pedigree of Skewys family kept at British Library

Skewes' of South Australia. Left to right: *Henry Josiah Skewes, Annie May Skewes, Leila Mavis Skewes, Ronald George Skewes, Annie Ellen Muir Skewes, Henry Skewes and Archibald William Skewes. Photo circa 1930*

CHART 2   SKEWES/SKEWIS/SKUES of CAMBORNE, CORNWALL 1637—1980

A large branch with over 300 names appearing on the pedigree. The earliest known person was Humfrey Scewies who married Christian Farmer at Camborne Parish Church on 23 October 1637. Their descendants lived in Camborne for seven generations before "uprooting." No less than 23 members of the family left for North America in the mid 1800's: William Henry Skewes and Henry Skewes emigrated to Carlton, Missouri; William and Sarah Skewes went to Massachusetts; Absalom, Edward, William and Henry Skewis to Shullsburg, Wisconsin, likewise Edward and Mary Skewis.

From the same pedigree others emigrated to Australia including John Skewes and William Henry Skewes. The Skewes line in Britain was depleted by almost 50%.

Within the county of Cornwall the family moved away from Camborne to Mabe, Sithney to Gwinear. Others migrated to Plymouth, Devon and as far north as Huddersfield, West Yorkshire. One branch moved to London.

As we have already discussed, the majority of Skewes' were either miners or farmers and it seemed general practice that miners would marry miners' daughters; farmers, farmers' daughters and so on, the correct name being endogamy. However, in recent years there has been a tendency to marry outside one's social class, more especially in larger cities. But with village life in Cornwall local marriages appeared to be the order of the day.

This pedigree had its roots in Camborne, a market town and parish 14 miles north east from Penzance, 14 miles from Falmouth and 12 miles south west from Truro.

The name Camborne is said to have derived from a famous well, and was formerly in high repute. To the fountain "Camburne Well" for many years the aged and infirm visited to seek sanctity from its celebrated virtues. But today only the tales of tradition survive.

At the time of the Norman Conquest the current name of Camborne was unknown. According to Hals it signifies a crooked or arched burne or well pit of water, so called from its consecrated spring. Pryce interprets Camborne Vean to mean "little crooked well."

The town is well-known for the home of the great engineer Richard Trevithick, the inventor of

Skewes' of Victoria, Australia. Back row, from left: *Linda Laura Skewes, William James Skewes, Cerceda Emily Skewes, Beryl Colville Skewes and Clarence George Skewes.* Front row: *Eric William Skewes, Catherine Skewes and Coryl Isabel Skewes.* Photo circa 1935

the high pressure steam engine in 1796. The chief industry over the past 200 years has been mining and Camborne was one of the earliest locations to produce tin.

There is a modern School of Mines close to the town and also a fine Holman's Mining Museum.

The population of Camborne in 1871 was 14,920 and in 1971 was 16,410.

The residences in Camborne of the Skewes family were Vyvyan Row, Killivoase, Treswithian, Higher Penponds and Berrispiper.

On this pedigree there are six illegitimate Skewes'.

Twins run in this side of the family and there are no less than nine sets of twins born between 1770 and 1940.

Infant mortality was high in the 18th and 19th centuries and the chances were that one in every three children born would perish in the first year of life, and that only one out of every two would reach the age of 21 years.[1]

Although today there are members of the Skewes family living in Camborne none are descendants from this particular pedigree.

The last person on Chart 2 to die in Camborne was James Skewes of Roskear Crofts in 1875, aged 85 years.

There are more members from this branch now living in the United States than anywhere in the United Kingdom, including Cornwall. Australia would come a close second.

CHART 3   *SKEWIS/SKEWES/SKUES of HELSTON 1750—1980*

Helston existed as early as the reign of Edward the Confessor. Mentioned in Domesday Book, its first charter was granted by King John on 5 April 1201 when Helston ("old Court town") was made a free borough, the second oldest in Cornwall, Launceston being the oldest.

Of the historical and architectural features of interest surviving in Helston, the Parish Church of St Michael is probably the most prominent. It replaces a very fine church destroyed by fire in 1763.

---

[1] *Making of a Modern Family*, Edward Shorter, Glasgow, 1976, p34.

South-west view of Helston, Cornwall, 1815. From a sketch by M.P. Moyle. Published by the Helston firm of W. Penaluna, September 1815. Local History Library, Redruth

The old Grammar School which stands in Wendron Street is often referred to as "The Eton of Cornwall" — Charles Kingsley was a scholar here. Helston (also called "fortress on the marsh") was formed into an ecclesiastical parish on 5 December 1845 from the parish of Wendron. It is a municipal borough and market town 10 miles south from Camborne and 10 miles south west from Redruth.

The town is naturally very closely associated with the ancient industries of Cornwall, tin and copper mining. Tradition has it that Cornish tin was used for the building of King Solomon's Temple. Tin has certainly been mined here for at least 2000 years and probably for more than 4000.

In Elizabeth I's time Cornwall was divided into four districts for purposes of tin testing, the result of which ended in four stannary towns being created — Helston, Truro, Lostwithiel and Liskeard. They were known as coinage towns and each had its coinage hall where the tin was tested. Helston still maintains proof of this evidence in the name of its main street, Coinagehall Street. The actual hall was pulled down during the last century, due to the modernisation in transport facilities. Coinage Hall originally stood in the middle of the street. William Skues (1735-1817) was Secretary to the Tinners Association in 1788 for upwards of fifty years and worked for the Office of Tin Coinage for Cornwall and Devon under the Duke of Cornwall. He was succeeded in his office by his grandson Richard Skues.

The tin mining industry in Cornwall had from its earliest times its own peculiar code of custom which was enforced by the Stannary Courts, and the tinners were exempt from all other jurisdiction than that of their own courts. One of the most important functions of the courts, it seems, was to maintain the purity of the standard of the tin. The smelted blocks were tested by cutting off a "coin", or corner, after which if passed, the newly exposed surface was given the official stamp of purity. No tin could be disposed of until this had been done. The tin mining industry has seriously declined due mainly to the importation of Banca tin from abroad, but ivy grown chimneys, ruined engine houses and heaps of refuse, which scatter the Cornish countryside, all serve as reminders of its past importance.

Eightieth birthday party of Clara Skues (née Roberts) at Stockport, Cheshire with her sons and daughter. Back row, from left: *Jack Skues, Vincent Skues and Richard Skues.* Front row: *Florence Muriel Skues and Clara Skues. Photo taken in 1955*

Below: *The Skues family of Barnsley.* From left: *Clara Skues, Cecil Skues, Jack Skues (baby), Vincent Skues, Florence Skues, Ernest Skues and Richard Skues*

Helston is reputed to have been at one time a port and an important one in the ancient pre-Christian tin trade. It stands on the river Cober which runs into a deep valley and forms a lake, the water ultimately seeping through the sand and shingle ridge which now closes the mouth. There could have been a harbour which would shelter the ships of those days before the shingle bank closed the mouth. But its name belies its size and beauty, for the Loe is the largest of Cornwall'a lakes and probably the most beautiful. Legend has it that the Bar (the sand and shingle ridge) was formed when the wicked Tregeagle was chased by the Devil whilst carrying a sack of sand and he let it drop in the entry to the pool. However, it is generally understood that Loe Pool rose until it overflowed into the lower parts of the town. Nowadays the council has made a culvert which has been driven through the rocks. Should a future occasion arise when flooding seems imminent the culvert will let off the water as soon as it has attained a certain height.

As regards Helston in Parliament, there is a report which bears the date 20 October 1802 and is headed "Report Respecting The Borough of Helleston". It begins by giving a short sketch of its history and refers briefly to events and happenings both before and after the grant of the new charter. In due course it sets out "The Present State of the Borough" and gives the name of the Mayor, Aldermen, and the twelve Freemen. Included in the names of twelve Freemen we find William Skues, aged 63 years who was elected on 23 September 1786. On 15 September 1804 and 20 January 1820, Richard Skues was elected to the Freedom of the Borough. (Taken from *History of Helston*, Spencer Toy).

On checking through the various records, one is bound to come across confusions. For example the writer was endeavouring to trace the birthdate of one Richard Skues Martin. It was known that he died in Helston in 1897, in fact on 24 November, but his birthplace was not known. All Cornish parish registers were checked and in Camborne we find Richard Skues Martin, son of Henry and Grace of Penponds, miner, born on 20 September 1834. All appears to be in order as we learn that Richard died in his 60's, and then, quite by accident, one comes across more information stating that he died aged 67 years. Helston Parish Register was rechecked and there as bold as brass — "Richard Skues Martin died in Helston on 24 November 1897, aged 67 years." This means he was born approximately 1830. Putting two and clue together one comes to the conclusion they are not in fact one and the same. After much searching the eventual answer came to light in the records of the General Register office in London. There were two different Richard Skues Martins.

Today Helston is a municipal borough and market town situated 10 miles south from Camborne and 10 miles south from Redruth. The population in 1931 was 3026 — in 1971, 6830 persons. The town has long been remarkable as the scene of the Furry or Flora Dance, celebrated with rejoicing on 8 May by all classes of inhabitants. Numerous members of the Skues and Skewes family have taken part in the annual celebrations. A song was written about the dance by Katie Moss and popularised by Peter Dawson, and more recently (1977) an instrumental version by the Brighouse and Rastrick Band under the title *Floral Dance*. Disc jockey Terry Wogan also had a hit record with the song in 1978.

The exodus of the Skues branch of the family happened when Richard Skues, surgeon moved to Plymouth in 1830. His son Richard moved north to Halifax. Another brother went into the Royal Marines and his descendants went into the army as surgeons. Today the Helston branch is spread as far as Cheshire, Lancashire, West Yorkshire, Leicestershire, South Yorkshire, Surrey, Dorset, London and Canada.

Although this pedigree was sizeable in the 19th century the number of males to carry on the line is now down to four.

There are still Skewes' living in Helston, but none are from this branch. They appear on Chart 12.

CHART 4   SKUES of REDRUTH, CORNWALL 1680—1770

A small chart comprising one family, information being taken from Redruth Parish Register. William Skues married Jane John in 1680. They had six children — two sons and four daughters.

The writing in the parish register is very bad so it is difficult to ascertain whether the family continued (which is probable) and the descendants formed Chart 5.

CHART 5   SKUES of REDRUTH, CORNWALL 1800—1980

A pedigree of fifty names. The earliest known information is that Joseph Skues, sojourner and soldier married Elizabeth Penrose in Redruth, 1813. They remained in Redruth until about 1850, then some grandchildren moved away from Cornwall to Buckinghamshire, another to Australia, others to America. One branch remained in Redruth and the only remaining male in this line is Lewis Skues who lives in Tresadderns Road, Redruth. The oldest member was William John Skues who died in Probus, Truro in 1976, aged 95 years.

Redruth is a market town and parish formerly called Dredruith or Druids Town. It is 10 miles north west from Falmouth, 10 miles north from Helston and 18 miles north east from Penzance. The parish church of St Euny, erected in 1768 is chiefly a Georgian building situated about a mile from the town centre. The registers date from 1560 (Baptisms, Marriages and Burials). William Murdock, the inventor of the application of gas to lighting purposes lived in Cross Street — the first house in England that was lit by gas and it bears a memorial stone "William Murdock lived in this house 1782 — 1798. Made the first locomotive here and tested it in 1784. Invented gas lighting and used it in this house, 1792."

The population of Redruth in 1871 was 10,685. In 1971 it was 41,250 (Camborne/Redruth Urban District).

Frederick Skues was a boot and shoe repairer in 1939 and lived at 16, Trefusis Street, Redruth.

The American and Australian branches survive to this day and should continue into the next century.

Derek Peter Skues (foreground Jessie Skues), Diana Katherine (née Skues), Katherine Pepita Skues and Kenneth Frederick Skues in Melbourne, January 1981

CHART 6   SKEWES/SKEWS of KENWYN AND WISCONSIN, U.S.A. 1789—1980

A small branch which begins with Peter Skewes in Kenwyn 1789 who married Mary Williams in September 1817 at Kenwyn. One son at least emigrated to Mineral Point, Wisconsin, USA in the mid 1800's. Although there was quite a sizeable family by 1910 the recent additions to the branch have been girls and there is every likelihood that it will die out by early next century.

CHART 7   SKUES of LONDON AND KENT 1854—1980

The earliest known person, Thomas Skues, came from London and married Elizabeth Harris at St George's, Hannover Square in 1874. They had three sons and three daughters. The family moved to Kent and their descendants are very much alive and well and living in Sussex and Kent.

CHART 8   SKUES OF LONDON 1800—1980

William Henry Skues was a coal whipper and married Sarah Young and they lived in London. One grandson Walter Edward Skues did much to continue the Skues line. He fathered no less than 18 children, via two wives between 1893 and 1924. The family now live in London and the county of Essex. There is a strong male line to carry on the branch well into the twenty-first century.

Lucy Skues (born 1862) with her brother Claude Skues (born 1881)

The Skues family of London. The Ruby Wedding on April 16, 1938 of Walter Edward Skues. Back row, from left: Alfred Skues, Herbert Skues, Sidney Skues, Walter Skues, Arthur Skues and Ernest John Skues. Middle row: Ruby Skues, Atalanta Skues, Walter Edward Skues, Lucy Skues and Dora Skues. Front row: Maud Skues and Olive Skues

George Henry, Mary Sophia and Claude Skues

CHART 9   SKEWS/SKUES of ST EWE and LONDON 1755—1980

The earliest known generation goes back to Philip and Mary Skews (1755) who provided three sons and two daughters. The family lived and worked in St Ewe near Mevagissey which is a parish and village. It is likely that Philip Skews came from a family of Skews who resided in Mevagissey a century before. St Ewe had a population of 300 in the year 1871. In 1971 it was 650.

The parish church is dedicated to St Eval. William Truscott Skues was born at St Ewe in 1812 and moved to London where, as a carpenter, he was employed to make window frames for the Houses of Parliament, as well as putting the facing on Big Ben. He married and his family remained in the south of England.

This branch continues with the majority of persons living in London, Kent and Surrey. Every chance this branch will continue well into the next century.

Roy Skues, Gillian Skues, Barry Skues, Joan Skues and John Skues of Ashford, Kent

Skewes' of Mexico. Guillermo Skewes and Aaron Skewes, taken in Pachuca, Mexico in July 1979

The Skewes family in Mexico. Taken at La Casa San Vicente, in Mineral del Monte, Hidalgo circa 1897. Foreground, from left: Louie Pratt Skewes, Catherine M. Honey and Richard H. Skewes holding George Owen Skewes in his arms. In the background is the "moso" (servant)

John Herbert and Beatrice Mary (née Pratt) Skewes on their 50th wedding anniversary, 25 September 1955

CHART 10 SKEWES/SKEWS of ILLOGAN, KEA, KENWYN, LISKEARD, ST AUSTELL (CORNWALL), PLYMOUTH (DEVON), HAMILTON, ONTARIO (CANADA), PHILADELPHIA, VIRGINIA, CALIFORNIA (UNITED STATES OF AMERICA) and REAL DEL MONTE and PACHUCA (MEXICO) 1700—1980

A very large branch with over 500 names. It began with a Digory Skues who married at Kenwyn 18 May 1700. This branch produced a good number of males called Digory and Martin. With their respective families they lived in the Kenwyn and Kea districts, just outside Truro.

Kenwyn is a parish, and the church is three quarters of a mile north west from Truro. The population in 1871 was 9740; 1931 was 1212 and in 1971 was 1790. By 1800 the descendants had moved away to Chacewater, Illogan and St Austell.

Kea is a parish 2½ miles south from Truro, 8½ miles north from Falmouth. The former church of St Kea was built in 1802, but pulled down in 1894. The present church of All Hallows was raised upon the site at a cost of £4500 and consecrated on 4 June 1896. The Old Kea Church is three miles east. The population of Kea in 1871 was 3000 and 1610 in 1971.

Chacewater is a parish five miles west from Truro and four miles east from Redruth. The population in 1871 was 900 and in 1971 was 1310. Thomas Skewes and his wife Grace (née Trezize) moved from Kenwyn around 1830 to settle in Chacewater with their 11 children.

Illogan is a large and populous mining parish 2½ miles north west from Redruth, three miles north east from Camborne. The population in 1931 was 6842, a drop of some 3500 persons from 1871. By 1971 the figure was 9945. Many marriages and baptisms took place at Illogan Parish Church. A number of Skewes' lived in the hamlet of Treskillard, three miles north.

Iron miner Peter Skewes married Elizabeth Jane Youren and they moved to St Austell with their two daughters and one son. Peter (junior) was responsible for the continuation of the Skewes/Skews line. He married Maud Mary Rickard in 1901 and had six sons and three daughters. Their descendants continue to this day living in St Austell which is a market town, parish and head of a county court district.

It is 40 miles from Plymouth and 11 miles south south west from Bodmin. The town, seated on the southern slope of a hill, is of comparatively modern date, and owes its prosperous condition to the numerous china clay works in the surrounding district. Thousands of tons of clay are annually transported to the Potteries and into Lancashire where it is largely used in the calico weaving districts of Blackburn and other cotton towns, the china clay being the pricipal ingredient in the sizing from which the cloth is heavily loaded. It is also used in chemical works. Carclaze Tin Mine and Works are two miles north of the town at an altitude of 665 feet. From the summit of this rising ground the mine is sunk to a depth of 150 feet, open, and somewhat in the shape of an enormous basin, the surface of which measures upwards of 15 acres, with a circumference of two miles. It is supposed to have been worked for over 450 years. Until 1851 it produced tin, but now only produces china clay (Kaolin). The population of St Austell in 1871 was 11,790 and in 1971 — 24,280. One branch of this widespread family emigrated to Hamilton, Ontario, Canada, another to Michigan, USA and another to Martinez, California. The Hamilton branch continues to this day.

Of those in Cornwall families live in Falmouth and St Austell. Another lives at Plymouth, Devon.

During the mass exodus from Cornwall during the tin mining depression a number of Skewes' went over to Mexico including Peter Skewes and his brothers John, Richard and Thomas who worked in silver mines in Real del Monte and Pachuca. Of the children born to Peter the descendants live in California. John Skewes appeared to be a popular man for he became a bigamist, having a wife in Cornwall and another in Mexico. By his wife from Cornwall, Catherine Williams, he had two sons and three daughters. The family continues to this day with descendants living in Virginia, USA. On the Mexican side John married Luisa Garcia and they had five sons and two daughters. Between 1870 and 1930 the family grew at an astonishing rate. Today's generation (1980 plus) has 15 sons to take the family into the next century. Most live in Pachuca, Real del Monte and Mexico City.

Left: *Wedding picture of Richard Henry Skewes and Louie Pratt on 25 December 1893 in Mexico*

Below left: *Jonathan Braddon Skewes aged 18 in 1916 in the uniform of the 134th Kiltie Battalion (Canadian). Served in France with the 19th Infantry Battalion, 4th Brigade, 2nd Division. Now lives in Hamilton, Ontario, Canada*

Below right: *Joseph John Skewes (1865-1931) with his wife Catherine Mary (née Richards). Emigrated to Hamilton, Ontario in 1906*

The author with Guillermo Skewes in Mexico, July 1979

Below: *Skewes' of Canada. From left: Mabel (née Skewes) Bryant, Hettie Louise (née Skewes) Davis and Lillian (née Skewes) Woodworth. (Toronto July 1979)*

Below right: *Skewes' of Canada. From left: Tamara Skewes, Ann Marie Skewes (both of Toronto), Robert Skewes (of Waterdown), Beverley (née Skewes) Titley, Lillian Skewes (wife of Robert), Lillian (née Skewes) Woodworth and Karen Skewes, daughter of Robert Skewes. (Waterdown, Ontario July 1979)*

Mr and Mrs John Skewes and their children Dennis (14), Dick (16½) and Rex Owen (9½). (Johannesburg, South Africa, Christmas 1932)

CHART 11 SKEWES of CAMBORNE and SAN DIEGO and SEATTLE (USA) 1800 — 1980

James and Ann Skewes had a son, James Skewes, a carpenter and cabinet maker of Camborne. Of the family he had one son, Thomas John Skewes who emigrated to the United States of America in the mid 1800's. He married Laura B. Gest in Cincinatti 19 May 1880 and had four sons and three daughters. This chart covers six generations and contains 22 names. The Cornish side has died out, but the American connection looks likely to continue into the 21st century.

CHART 12 SKEWES of CURY, HELSTON, ST AGNES, MULLION, ST KEVERNE, ST MAR-
*   TIN and CAMBORNE 1786—1980*

A sizeable chart with 150 names which began when a single girl from Cury called Mary Dorten named her illegitimate son James Skewes about 1786. The family and surviving eight generations remained in Cornwall with the exception of one James Henry Skewes who went to work in Central America and was murdered in 1858.

The main villages where the Skewes' lived were Cury and Landewednack. Cury is a village and parish five miles south south east from Helston and twelve miles south west from Falmouth. The parish registers of births, marriages and deaths date from 1690. Cury has been the seat of the Skewes family for many generations. In the village is SKEWES, a residence at one time of the family; also Nantithet. In the late 1400's John Skewys, Lord of Skewys had his main residence at Skewes.

Today members of this branch can be found in Helston, Illogan, Redruth, Camborne, Porthallow, St Agnes, Ruan Major, St Keverne, Mawgan, Cadgwith and St Austell. Still an impressive looking chart with a number of males who can continue the line for generations yet to come.

Golden Wedding anniversary of William John and Bessie (née Curnow) Skewes in December 1975. From left:
Mary Skewes, Bill Skewes, William John Skewes, Ronald Skewes, Bessie Skewes, Maurice Skewes, Wendy Skewes
and Nan Skewes

Three generations of Skewes of Helston, Cornwall. From back: *William John Skewes (born 1927), Christopher John Skewes (born 1948) and Mark Christopher Skewes (born 1978)*

Natalia Eve, Ronald and Diana Rose Skewes of St Austell. Chart 12

Christopher John Skewes leads the children's dance in the Helston Furry Dance 8 May 1960. The Mayor, James Henry Thomas, heads the Helston Church of England School

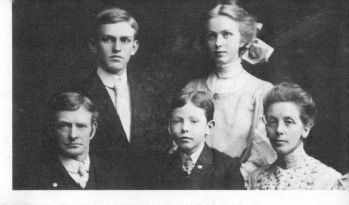

Right: *The Edwin Bottomley Skewes family of America.* Front row, from left: *Edwin Bottomley Skewes, George Jessop Skewes and Alice Ada Collier Skewes.* Back row: *Arthur Skewes and Ruth Skewes*

Left: *Skewes' of America. Irene Olson Skewes with Alice Ruth Skewes Ford, taken in Lexington, Kentucky in August 1979*

Below: *Some American Skewes'.* Front row, from left: *Duayne Skewes, Le Mar Skewes, Helen Skewes (wife of George Boulden Skewes), Mortier Skewes (baby) and George Edwin Skewes.* Back row: *May Skewes (wife of Duayne Skewes), Boulden Skewes and Emma Skewes (wife of George Edwin Skewes)*

CHART 13 SKEWS of MEVAGISSEY AND ST. EWE (CORNWALL) 1674—1700

A small chart of two generations listing baptisms at Mevagissey and St Ewe.

CHART 14 SKEWES of RUAN MAJOR, CURY, ST KEVERNE (CORNWALL) IVES GROVE,
*   RACINE and YORKVILLE, WISCONSIN (UNITED STATES OF AMERICA),*
*   1700—1980.*

A large branch containing 150 names spanning eight generations. Earliest known person was Henry Skewes who married Judith Walters in Constantine 18 October 1718. Their children and grandchildren lived in Cury. By 1750 the next generation had moved to St Keverne and were farmers.

St Keverne is a parish close to the shore of the English Channel 19 miles south from Falmouth, and 11 miles south east from Helston. The church is dedicated to St Keverne and was founded around 1155. Numerous wrecks have occurred on the coast and the churchyard contains the graves of many persons including the victims of *The Mohegan* which sank on 14 October 1898 when 106 persons lost their lives. Betty Skewes lives in Mullion, near Helston and in 1977 wrote a song, with the help of 100 school children, aged between eight and nine years old, and was recorded by boys and girls from St Keverne School which went as follows:

The Mohegan was filled with the good and the bad
This dreadful tale is told.
And the story we tell is both true and sad
Of the waters wild and cold.
She was sailing by neath the autumn sky
With never a thought of fear
When the coastguard said "Don't go ahead
For the Manacle Rocks are near."
This mighty fine ship on her Atlantic trip
Was sailing through the storm.
As people ate their meal in the ship of steel
They seemed both safe and warm.
That they felt the shock as they struck the rock
And the sea came running through.
The boats were filled, though many were killed
For they didn't know what to do.
Women launched the lifeboat, and they made it float
Already for the crew.
As the men ran down from St Keverne Churchtown
The wind still roared and blew
Oh the waves they crashed, but the men were lashed
To their seats by the Coxswain brave.
They hauled for the wreck with the listing deck
There were so many souls to save.
As the boat came near the Captain said "Keep clear
For God's sake if you can."
People swam around, many folks were drowned.
And then appeared one man. From the old Sharks Fin
He called the lifeboat in
Drop sails and man your oars.
200 men will help you when you reach old P'roustocks shores.
So they brought in the men, and the little children
And the women who were dead.
In the church we prayed where the bodies were laid
And many tears were shed.
It was long ago, but our hearts still glow with pride
When we recall old P'roustocks crew, so staunch and true.
They were the bravest men of all.

In 1842 Samuel and Catherine (née Lugg) Skewes, together with their son Samuel emigrated to

Wisconsin, USA and were soon joined by Skewes brothers Henry and John and sister Mary. Another sister Eleanor emigrated to Geelong, Victoria, Australia. Samuel Skewes' nephews William John and Samuel set up their homes in Racine, Wisconsin, USA.

Today the family is spread throughout the States with descendants living in Washington, D.C., Kentucky, Minnesota, Mississippi, Illinois, Arizona and Wisconsin.

There are a dozen males to carry on the line into the next century.

CHART 15 SKEWS of ALTARNUN, PENSILVA, ST GERMANS, LISKEARD and CALLINGTON (CORNWALL) and PLYMOUTH (DEVON) 1800 — 1980

Peter Skewes had two sons, Peter and John who lived in Altarnun, a parish on the tributary of the River Inny, six miles south west from Egloskerry, nine miles east from Camelford. Population in 1871 was 1000. In 1971 it had dropped to 700. John lived at Trewint and Peter at St Ive.

The branch flourished in the early 1900's and it is one of the few charts where the family has stayed together in Cornwall and Devon. There are 75 names in all with many male Skews' to carry on the line.

CHART 16 SKEWES/SKEWIS of NEWTON ABBOT 1861 — 1920

A list of 34 names of those Skewes/Skewis' born, married and died in the Newton Abbot district.

CHART 17 SKEWS of GRAVESEND, AYLESFORD, BETHNAL GREEN, DEVONPORT, EDMONTON, ENFIELD, KETTERING, SHOREDITCH, NORTHAMPTON, PETERBOROUGH, WEST HAM, HULL, SHREWSBURY, MACCLESFIELD and SWANSEA 1840 — 1980

George Skews, son of William Skews, confectioner, married Charlotte Dane in Gravesend, Kent in 1843. Their two sons moved to Bethnal Green. The following generation spread further afield to Poplar, Hammersmith, Shrewsbury, Edmonton and Swansea. Today this branch is located in ten areas of England and Wales. It spans six generations listing 80 names. The family still has a strong male line which should carry on into the next century.

John William Skews and wife Isabella

Above: *During First World War. From left: Harold Skewes, Arthur George and John Edward Skewes, sons of Edward and Eliza Skewes of Chorlton, Manchester*

Left: *Eliza Skewes (née Maddocks). Married Edward Skewes, hosiery warehouseman, 1885, Chorlton, Manchester. Children: Harold Skewes, John Edward Skewes, Charles Skewes, William Frederick Skewes and Arthur George Skewes*

Below: *The Skewes family of Wilmslow, Cheshire. From left: Anne, Anthony Robert, Jane and Frank Robert*

CHART 18 SKEWES of KEA, KENWYN (CORNWALL), BERE ALSTON, BEER FERRIS and
PLYMOUTH (DEVON) and BRISTOL 1750 — 1980

This branch originated in Kerley, Kea. Three brothers and four sisters carried on the line in the Kenwyn area for two generations and then the family split and moved to Bere Alston and Beer Ferris in Devon. That particular branch then moved to Plymouth with three brothers becoming tailors and outfitters. Another generation only produced three sons, one of whom died as an infant, another killed in the First World War and the third producing two sons and one daughter. The only surviving male has been married twice and there are no children. On his death this branch, which spans seven generations with fifty names, will die out.

CHART 19 SKEWES of GWENNAP (CORNWALL) and WAREHAM (DORSET) 1665—1951

It started in Gwennap when Thomas Skewes married Sidwell Millard in 1665. The family remained in Gwennap for six generations. The name Skewes was one of the most popular in the village in the 19th century. Situated 3 miles south east of Redruth the population of Gwennap in 1931 was 1081. In 1971 — 1215 persons. One mile north is Carharrack which in 1770 had only 12 cottages. The close proximity of the mines was the main reason for its growth. Several rows of houses were built in the 1830's. Several Skewes' resided here and at Lanner, which before 1800 had only six cottages and like Carharrack many houses were built in the 1830's and miners who worked at Tresavean moved in.

The Gwennap branch, which had amongst its ranks many mine agents and miners, died out by 1888. One section had moved to Wareham in Dorset mainly in the educational field running boarding schools. The last surviving member was Albert Edward Skewes who died in 1951, aged 89 years.

CHART 20 SKEWES of GWENNAP (CORNWALL) Various

A selection of very small sections which do not link into any other Gwennap branches. All are now extinct.

CHART 21 SKEWES/SKEWIS of TAVISTOCK (DEVON) 1838 — 1916

A list of 24 names of those Skewes/Skewis' born, married and died in the Tavistock area between 1838 and 1916.

CHART 22 SKEWES of KEA (CORNWALL) Various

Four small "twigs" of Skewes' of Kea and Kenwyn (not related). All now extinct.

CHART 23 SKEWS of ST. AUSTELL, FALMOUTH and CAMBORNE (CORNWALL) and
SWINDON (WILTSHIRE) 1862 — 1980

Three generations beginning with the marriage of William Skews to Jane Bullock in 1862. The family moved to Wiltshire in 1880. This branch will die out by the end of this century.

CHART 24 SKEWES of NEW SOUTH WALES, (AUSTRALIA) 1858 — 1980

Dating from the birth of John Skewes of Sofala, New South Wales, in 1858 this is a chart of three dozen names. There are six males to carry on the line into the next century.

The wedding of Arthur George Skewes to Ruth Hacking in Manchester in May 1927. Arthur, back row left, was born 15 April 1897 and died 4 November 1978, aged 81 years. Also in the back row is Charles Skewes, born 1889, married 1914 and died 1943, aged 54 years

CHART 25 SKEWES of FALMOUTH and ST KEVERNE (CORNWALL), SALFORD, CHORLTON (MANCHESTER) and WILMSLOW, and MACCLESFIELD (CHESHIRE) 1745 — 1980

Eight generations which began in 1746 when Thomas Skewes married Esther James at St Keverne. This branch has fifty names and resided in the Falmouth district for four generations. Their main residences were Brook Street and Smithwick Hill. Falmouth is a sea port, market town and county court town, municipal and parliamentary borough 11 miles from Truro and 24 miles from Penzance. Its harbour is one of the finest in England. The entrance is between two bold headlands and is defended by St Mawes Fort on the east and Pendennis Castle on the west. The population in 1871 was 10,471. In 1971 it was 16,630 (Metropolitan Borough).

Charles Skewes moved north to Salford, Manchester around 1875 with his wife Elizabeth and four sons and two daughters. This branch grew considerably in size and today still thrives in Lancashire and Cheshire. There are three sons to carry on the line which is likely to continue into the next century.

CHART 26 SKEWES of CONNECTICUT (UNITED STATES OF AMERICA) 1850 — 1980

Five generations of Skewes' from Connecticut, USA. The current generation has 11 children with five sons to carry on the line which should continue well into the next century.

CHART 27 SKUES of BATH 1840 — 1871

A very small chart circa 1840 which sprang up in the Bath area with the registration of six births. It is likely their spelling changed to SKUSE, or failing that the family emigrated after 1871 as there are no references to marriages or deaths.

CHART 28 SKEWES of KEA 1750 — 1900

A small chart commencing in 1750 with Henry Skewes marrying Mary Jolly at Kenwyn. This branch has twelve names, but the last generation produced eight daughters and the Skewes line died out by 1900.

CHART 29 SKEWES of KENWYN 1780 — 1820

A small chart with 14 names which began with John Skewes marrying Alice John at Perranarworthal in 1759. There were three generations but the line is now extinct.

CHART 30 SKEWES of KEA, KENWYN, TRURO (CORNWALL) and EXETER (DEVON) 1790 — 1980

Henry Skewes married Catherine Worsley in 1793 at Kenwyn. This chart has 31 names. The family remained in Cornwall for three generations, mainly in the Truro area.

Truro (dwelling on the slope) is a city and municipal borough, head of a county court district and a port. It is situated 23 miles south west from Bodmin, 11 miles north from Falmouth and 17 north east from Helston. Truro was formerly one of the towns having the privilege of coining or more properly "stamping" tin and possessed this right as early as the reign of King John.

The Cathedral Church of St Mary is designed in the early English style of the early part of the 13th century. Also here in Truro are the churches of St George's (an ecclesiastical parish), St John's (an ecclesiastical parish) and St Paul's (an ecclesiastical parish).

The Royal Institution of Cornwall was founded in 1818 for the encouragement of literature and promotion of knowledge in natural history, archaeology, ethnology and the fine and industrial arts, especially in relation to the county of Cornwall. It stands above the County Museum and Art Gallery in River Street, which was opened on 11 June 1919 by HRH Duke of Windsor, then Prince of Wales.

The Royal Institution of Cornwall is one of the most useful sources of information for the genealogist as is the County Record Office which stands in the grounds of Old County Hall and has a mass of Cornish wills, parish registers, mine maps and all things Cornish.

The population of Truro in 1931 was 11,801. In 1971 — 13,920.

Movement in the Skewes family had begun by 1880 in Truro. One member left for Exeter and two for London. The male side of this branch died out with the death of Frederick Henry Skewes in 1969, aged 78 years.

CHART 31 SKEWS of ST. AUSTELL (CORNWALL) 1800 — 1973

Two small charts of families residing in St. Austell — one at the General Wolfe Hotel and the other at Carthew. Both branches are now extinct.

CHART 32 SKEWES of KEA, KENWYN and GWENNAP (CORNWALL) circa 1800

A very small chart with only five names covering two generations. Now extinct.

Skewis' of Devon: Ronald Skewis with his daughter Eileen and wife Lilian

CHART 33 SKEWES/SKEWIS of KENWYN and CHACEWATER (CORNWALL) and ASHBURTON and TOTNES (DEVON) 1817 — 1980

This branch originated in Kenwyn with William and Mary Skewes. Some of their children remained in Truro, but this side of the family is now extinct. Others moved to Devon and changed their spelling to SKEWIS. In 1920 there were 24 members of the family but today only a handful remain. Every chance this branch will be extinct by the end of this century.

CHART 34 SKEWES/SKEWIS of CAMBORNE (CORNWALL), WILLITON (SOMERSET) and CANTERBURY, STURRY and TUNBRIDGE WELLS (KENT) 1820—1980

A small branch of five generations which began in Camborne, moved to Somerset and finally settled in Kent. One male to carry on the line.

CHART 35 SKEWES of CURY (CORNWALL) circa 1690

A handful of names from a very early parish register in Cury.

CHART 36 SKEWES of CURY, MAWNAN SMITH, ST HILARY, ILLOGAN, CAMBORNE, TUCKINGMILL, TRURO and REDRUTH (CORNWALL), WISCONSIN (USA) and SOUTH AUSTRALIA, WEST AUSTRALIA, VICTORIA and NEW SOUTH WALES (AUSTRALIA) 1700—1980

An enormous chart which commenced in 1700 with the marriage of James and Sarah Skewes who had ten children and lived in Cury. The majority of these early Skewes' were farmers who lived at Treloskan, Cury.

There is one intermarriage of Skewes' in Cornwall and another in Australia. James Skewes of Cury married Grace Skewes of Constantine in 1834. William Skewes married Ida Olive Skewes in New South Wales, in 1922.

The village of Constantine is very scattered and lies on the Helford River 7 miles south-west from Penryn. The parish church is a foundation of antiquity and there is evidence that a church existed here as early as the Domesday Survey. The population in the year 1871 was 2093 persons — in 1971 there were 1860 persons living in the village.

Skewes' of Uralla, New South Wales, Australia in January 1981. From left: Lois Ada (née Skewes) Barnden, Gloria June (née Skewes) Bullen, Mary Elizabeth (née Skewes) Nelson and Una Irene Skewes

Skewes' of Perth and Safety Bay, Western Australia, January 1981

One branch of the family headed by William Skewes moved to the parish of Mabe where they became farmers at Little Insight Farm. The family spread to Mawnan, a parish at the mouth of the Helford River about 4½ miles south-west from Falmouth. The parish registers date from 1582; marriages and burials from 1553. There is a beautiful outlook from the church and is one of the most picturesque and peaceful settings in Cornwall. Many Skewes' have been laid to rest here and their headstones (a number over 100 years old) are still clearly visible today. The population of Mawnan in 1871 was 573. In 1971 there were 1085 persons living in the village. There are people in Mawnan and Mawnansmith (a village 1½ miles north-east of Mawnan) who are related to the Skewes', but the male line died out in 1942 with the death of farmer Edward Skewes, aged 92 years.

Of this branch of the family 145 Skewes' were born, married and died in Cornwall. But there were more Skewes' who chose to emigrate. Some to Wisconsin, USA — the majority to Australia.

Samuel Skewes married Mary Thomas at Mawgan-in-Meneage on 12 April 1842. They boarded a ship for Wisconsin. This branch of the family has now become extinct.

William Skewes from Cury emigrated to New South Wales, Australia in 1853. Once in Sydney he married Elizabeth Northey and they had a sizeable family: 6 sons and 6 daughters. Their descendants moved to Tamworth, Uralla and Watsons Creek, all in New South Wales.

William and Elizabeth Skewes produced descendants totalling 150 Skewes'. Today there are 30 males to carry on the line.

Henry Skewes married Ann Gribble in Mawnan on 24 December 1850 and emigrated to the goldfields of Ballarat, Victoria. From this offshoot came another big family with 60 descendants. There are 13 males to carry on the line. Travelling out from Plymouth with the family was a cousin Samuel Skewes from Nantithet in Cury. He later married Mary Ann Waters at Gawler, South Australia in 1870. From this branch stems 40 Skewes' with a strong male line of 10 to carry the family into the next century.

John Henry Skewes became a policeman in Cury. He married Susan Hicks and they emigrated with their two children to South Australia in December, 1865. There were 60 Skewes descendants through this marriage with 20 males to carry on the line.

William Skewes of New South Wales married his first cousin Ida Olive Skewes in 1922 and they had 9 children and 19 Skewes grandchildren.

This section of the "tree" is stronger today than 60 years ago.

It is hard to believe that there have been 700 Skewes' born in this branch of the family. Certainly the Australian branch will go on for many generations.

Family of William Vere at Robert Skewes's wedding in 1965

A selection of Skewes' living in Watsons Creek and Tamworth, Australia in January, 1981. Below: Mary Jane Skewes of Australia celebrating her 89th birthday in 1936, surrounded by her family

Charles Harold Vivian Skewes outside his father William Hicks Skewes's shop in Rundle Street, Adelaide in 1899

Glenleigh Skewes and his family in Sebastopol, Australia, January, 1981. Below: Descendants of William & Elizabeth Skewes of Uralla, Australia. Taken at Rocky River gold field in January, 1981

Skewes' in Adelaide, South Australia in 1979. From left: Bonnie, Trevor, Cherylyn, Gwyn, Dorothy and Jack Roe Skewes

Bruce, Max, Bob and Bill Skewes of Tamworth, Australia in 1965. Below: Children of Percy and Muriel Skewes of Tamworth, Australia in 1970

CHART 37 SKEWES of SYDNEY (AUSTRALIA) 1880 — 1980

Four generations with 13 names which dates back to Ballarat, Victoria. No connection with the previous chart. Richard John Skewes was a coach builder who was living in Ballarat in 1880. His descendants are now living in Sydney and there is every chance that this branch will grow and continue into the next century.

CHART 38 SKEWES of SOUTH AUSTRALIA 1850—1980

Richard Skewes, copper miner, was born in Cornwall. He married Elizabeth Stephens. They emigrated to South Australia and Burra where he became a mine superintendent. One of his children William Henry set up a business as a chemist in Port Pirie which was taken over by his children and grandchildren. Another son Richard Skewes became a carpenter in Moonta. He married Mary Jane Reynolds in 1882 and they had 11 sons and 1 daughter. By 1920 there were over 60 members of the Skewes family in South Australia. Now the present generation live in Adelaide, Kadina, Port Pirie, Modbury North and Blair Athol (South Australia) and Broken Hill (New South Wales).

CHART 39 SKEWES/SKEWS of WALES 1837—1980

A list of births, marriages and deaths recorded in Wales in Merthyr Tydfil, Abergavenny, Bedwellty, Holyhead, Swansea, Chepstow and Hereford not already accounted for on other charts and pedigrees.

Skewes' of Watsons Creek, New South Wales, Australia in 1905. From left: Amy Skewes, James "Scissors" Skewes, William Skewes (sitting), Lily Skewes, Percy Skewes, William Junior and Hannah Jane (née Gale) Skewes

Left: *Daughters of William and Edith Skewes of New South Wales in 1914. From left: Eva Skewes, Dulcie Skewes and May Skewes*

Right: *William Hicks and Elizabeth Skewes with their family in Orroroo, South Australia in 1896. From left: Winifred Charles, Harold Vivian, William Hicks, Hubert E. Mervyn (with racquet), Gytha Eveleen Morna, William and Elizabeth*

Below left: *Samuel Skewes laying the foundation stone for Millicent Methodist Church, South Australia on 20 February 1908*

Below right: *Dedication to Samuel Skewes, Millicent Methodist Church, South Australia*

Millicent Methodist Church and Manse

Skewes' of South Australia outside Pirie Street Methodist Church, Adelaide in 1945. From left:
Richard James Skewes, Gertrude Olive Skewes and Stanley Victor Skewes

*Richard James Skewes, Harold Edward
Skewes and Sydney Howard Skewes in
Adelaide, 1940*

*Geoffrey Garfield Skewes, Donna
Louise Skewes and Grayson Paul Skewes
in Melbourne*

A group of Skewes' of South Australia at a reunion outside Adelaide, January 1981

Skewes' of Adelaide, South Australia in 1967. From left:
Neil David, Irene Kaye and Brian Wayne Skewes

Three ex-Skewes' of South Australia. From left: *Joyce
Brown (née Skewes), Doreen Hancock (née Skewes) and
Kathleen Deed (née Skewes)*

CHART 40 SKEWES of MARAZION, ST. MARTIN, PENZANCE (CORNWALL) 1820 — 1980

This chart commenced with Richard Skewes, a miner born 1823 who lived at Perranuthnoe.
Today, six generations later the family still farms the locality which is a parish on the coast of
Mount's Bay, 5 miles east of Penzance. The land is chiefly owned by farmers and is good for broc-
coli, potatoes and cabbage, as well as for flowers.

William Richard Skewes (born 1913) is a market gardener.

The population in 1871 was 1190 persons and it is much the same today.

This branch of the family continues to this day with two sons to carry on the line.

CHART 41 SKEWS of ST. ALLEN (CORNWALL), ECCLESALL, SHEFFIELD, BARNSLEY, and WOMBWELL (SOUTH YORKSHIRE), HETTON-LE-HOLE, HOUGHTON-LE-SPRING and EASINGTON (DURHAM) 1830 — 1980

Matthew Skews of St. Allen, Cornwall had
six children and moved north to Durham about
1868. He was a miner. One son remained in the
Durham area and descendants of his sizeable
family still live and work in the area.

Another son, also a miner, went to Ecclesall,
Sheffield where he married and helped raise 10
children. His descendants, of whom there are
many, also went into the mining profession. Today there are Skews' living in Wombwell, Darfield and Barnsley (South Yorkshire). There are
over 100 names on this branch of the family with
16 males to carry on the line into the next century.

*Jennie, Roy and David Skews of Wombwell, Barnsley,
South Yorkshire*

The wedding of Roy and Jennie Skews of Barnsley, South Yorkshire at Harrogate, Yorkshire. From left: *Thomas Skews, Jane Skews (seated), Miriam Shackleton, Ernest Skews, Roy and Jennie Skews. Jack Boynton, Joan Boynton (child), Elsie Dennison, Ernest Shackleton and Ellen Shackleton*

Below: *Skews family of County Durham in December 1954.* Back row, from left: *George David Skews, Roland Gerald Skews, Janet Audrey Skews, William Clifford Skews and John Hilary Skews.* Front row: *William John Skews (died February 1955), Mary Hannah Rump Skews (died July 1979) and Kirtley Skews (died November 1979)*

CHART 42 SKEWES of NEW SOUTH WALES (AUSTRALIA) 1898 — 1980

A small chart covering five generations which began when Thomas Skewes married Annie McDowell. Descendants all live in New South Wales and there are 8 males to carry on the line.

CHART 43 SKUES/SKEWIS of SHEFFIELD (SOUTH YORKSHIRE) 1840 — 1890

A small chart of three generations which commenced with Samuel Skues. He had a son Charles Skues who married Sarah Haynes on 31 December 1873 at Sheffield Parish Church (now Cathedral). They had six children — three sons and three daughters. There do not appear to be any records in the General Register Office, London as to the children's marriages or deaths; this could indicate a possible emigration. The spelling changed from Skues to Skewis in 1873.

CHART 44 SKEWES/SKEWIS of ABERGAVENNY (WALES) 1810 — 1875

Two small charts containing a total of 16 names. Both branches are now extinct.

CHART 45 SKEWES of CURY (CORNWALL) 1794 — 1875

A small branch with two generations and a family of thirteen children, but no evidence of a continuation. Most were farmers at Treloskan and Nantithet, Cury.

CHART 46 SKEWES of FALMOUTH and TRURO (CORNWALL) 1870—1980

A small branch of 5 generations, but with only 10 names which began in Falmouth with the birth of an illegitimate son to Rebecca Annie Skewes (son of William Skewes, labourer). The son, Charles, later moved to Truro where his descendants live to this day. There is one son to carry on the line.

CHART 47 SKEWES/SKEWS of CALLINGTON and LAUNCESTON (CORNWALL) 1895—1960

A very small chart with only three generations, the male line of which died out in 1954. Peter Skews from Kelly Bray, Callington began the line. He was married in Liskeard in 1890.

CHART 48 SKEWES of TRURO (CORNWALL), WIGAN (LANCASHIRE), CROYDON (SURREY) and DONCASTER and LEEDS, YORKSHIRE 1875—1980

A small branch of five generations which stemmed from the illegitimate son of Amelia Skewes of Truro. A generation later William (Verdayne) Skewes moved to Wigan, Lancashire. His descendants remain in the north. William Skewes married again in London in 1910 and settled in Croydon where his daughter lives to this day. As there are no sons to carry on the line this branch will die out by early next century.

CHART 49 SKEWES/SKEWIS/SKEWS of TOTNES (DEVON) 1876—1964

A list of 43 names of SKEWES/SKEWIS/SKEWS' born, married and died between 1876 and 1964.

CHART 50 SKEWIS of SOUTH WALES, SCOTLAND, NORTH YORKSHIRE and PENNSYLVANIA, (USA) 1800 — 1980

James Skewis was born in 1805. He married Mary Ann Griffiths in Llanover, Monmouthshire on 25 July 1825. They had 12 children. The family moved north to Scotland about 1850. According to records at General Register Office, Edinburgh, James Skewis was convicted of bigamy at the Sheriffdom of Lanark on 31 December 1869.

Some of his "legal" children emigrated to Pennsylvania, USA . At least 30 Skewis descendants are still living in the States. Another of James Skewis' sons emigrated to Ontario, Canada. His descendants live in Burlington and Toronto.

Of those Skewis' who chose to remain in Scotland it would be true to say there is confusion in the ranks as to who actually belongs to which section of the pedigree.

Some older members of the clan are reluctant to talk about the past. There have been a number of intermarriages. At its height in the 1920's the family lived in Old and New Monkland, Dennistoun, Hamilton and Camalchie. Today the family are to be found in Glasgow, Dundee, Inverness, Dumbarton and Dennistoun.

A record number of 104 births were recorded in the General Register Office, Edinburgh between 1855 and 1977 for the Skewis family. This excludes 9 births for Skewies of which James Skewis is also reported to have been the founder.

13 Census Returns

ONE OF THE most important lists of documents giving information of families and their whereabouts are Census Returns. Since 1801 these returns have been made every ten years.

However, only in 1841 was it decided to list the parish, borough, house name, individual names of the occupants, age, sex, profession and where born. The exact age was given for those persons under the age of 15, but to the lowest five years for those over that age. For instance a person of 39 would be listed as 35.

The Census Returns for 1851, 1861 and 1871 are far more explicit listing parish, borough, name of street, forename and surname, relationship to head of household, sex, age, married or unmarried, widow or widower, occupation, the parish in which he or she was born, whether deaf, dumb or blind, an imbecile, a lunatic or an idiot. In 1861 and 1871 the returns gave the added information of ships in port and those persons on board.

The returns for 1841 were made on 7 June; 1851 on 30 March; 1861 on 7 April; and for 1871 on 2 April.

Returns from recent times (within the last hundred years) are kept with the Registrar General at St Catherine's House, London. He works on the assumption that recent returns may refer to a living person, and therefore may not be viewed by the general public.

The following pages have been compiled from the Census Returns for the years 1841-1871 inclusive which are held at the Public Record Office in London. The searches were made by the author between 1964 and 1978. During the 1960's this entailed looking through 88 volumes (each volume containing over 200 pages of names and addresses all in handwriting, sometimes very difficult to read and unindexed!) and transcribing the relevant information. By 1970 microfilms had been introduced by the Public Record Office at Portugal Street, London for the use of the general public, and the returns for 1851, 1861 and 1871 were transcribed from many hundreds of feet of film.

Public Record Office references are as follows:

1841	HO 107 (133 — 154)
1851	HO 107 (1897 — 1917)
1861	RG 9 (1512 — 1600)
1871	RG 10 (2214 — 2347)

The searches were made in all towns, villages and hamlets for the county of Cornwall as well as one or two towns in Devon. Entries for people called SKEWIS, SKEWES, SKEWS and SKUES are listed as well as place names GREAT SKEWES, LITTLE SKEWES, SKEWES, SKEWIS and TRESKEWES.

Since the first census in 1801 through to the latest available returns for 1871, the population had increased by 88% in the county of Cornwall. The number of persons had increased by 170,062 (males 78,013 and females 92, 049).

In 1871 Cornwall comprised nine "Hundreds" — The Scilly Islands and the Municipal Boroughs of Bodmin, Falmouth, Helston, Launceston, Liskeard, Penryn, Penzance, St Ives and Truro. In April, 1974 new districts for Cornwall were introduced as follows: — Caradon, Carrick, Kerrier, North Cornwall, Penwith and Restormal. The Scilly Islands are now administered by an all purpose administrative body and are no longer part of Cornwall.

Cornwall was 869,878 statute acres in area in 1871.[1] It had 73,950 inhabited houses, 4648 uninhabited houses and 264 under construction. There were 362,343 persons giving 0.42 persons to an acre and 2.40 acres to a person.

---

[1] British Parliamentary Papers 1871 Census England and Wales. Population 16. University Press Series 1970.

COMPARISON OF POPULATION FIGURES 1841-1871 inclusive

YEAR	TOTAL POPULATION	MALES	FEMALES	INCREASE IN POPULATION BETWEEN CENSUSES NUMBER OF PERSONS	RATE%
1841	342,159	165,112	177,047	40,853	14
1851	355,558	171,636	183,922	13,399	4
1861	369,390	176,384	193,006	13,832	4
1871	362,343	169,706	192,637	-7,047	-2

The failure and abandonment of copper and tin mines in Western Cornwall and the consequent migration and emigration of miners are the causes for the decrease of population in the area.

CENSUS RETURNS FOR THE COUNTY OF CORNWALL — 1841

PUBLIC RECORD OFFICE REFERENCES AND DISTRICTS   ALL NUMBERS ARE PREFACED BY HO 107/

133 CALLINGTON, CALSTOCK, ST DOMINICK, ST IVE, ST MELLION, MENHENIOT, PILLATON, QUETHIOCK, SOUTH HILL.

134 EGLOSKERRY, LANEAST, LAUNCESTON, LAWHITTON, LEWANNICK, LEZANT, TREWARLET, LINKINGHORNE, NORTH HILL, SOUTH PETHERWIN, ST STEPHENS WITH NEWPORT, STOKE CLIMSLAND, ST THOMAS THE APOSTLE, TREMAYNE, TRESMEER, TREWEN.

135 ST JACOB ANTHONY, BOTUS FLEMING, ST BUDEAUX, ST GERMANS, ST JOHN, LANDRAKE WITH ST ERNEY, LANDULPH, MAKER, RAME, SHEVIOCK, ST STEPHENS BY SALTASH, SALTASH.

136 ST ANTHONY, BREAGE, BUDOCK, CONSTANTINE, CURY.

137 GERMOE, ST GLUVIAS, PENRYN, GRADE, GUNWALLOE, GWENNAP.

138 ST KEVERNE, LANDEWEDNACK, MABE, MANACCAN, ST MARTIN IN MENEAGE, MAWGAN IN MENEAGE, MAWNAN, MULLION, MYLOR, PERRAN-AR-WORTHAL, RUAN MAJOR, RUAN MINOR.

139 SITHNEY, STITHIANS, WENDRON.

140 ADVENT, ALTARNUN, ST CLETHER, DAVIDSTOW, FORRABURY, ST GENNYS, ST JULIOT, LANEAST, LANTEGLOS BY CAMELFORD, LESNEWTH, MICHAELSTOW, MINSTER, OTTERHAM, POUNDSTOCK, TINTAGEL, TRENEGLOSS, TREVALGA, WARBSTOW.

141 ST BURYAN, CAMBORNE, CROWAN.

142 ST ERTH, GULVAL, GWINEAR, GWITHIAN, ST HILARY, MARAZION, ST MICHAEL's MOUNT, ILLOGAN, ST IVES, ST JUST, LELANT, ST LEVAN, LUDGVAN.

143 MADRON, PENZANCE, MORVAH, PAUL, PERRANUTHNOE, PHILLACK, REDRUTH.

144 SANCREED, SENNAN, TOWEDNACK, ZENNOR.

145 FOWEY, GORRAN, LADOCK, LANLIVERY, LOSTWITHIEL, LUXULLION, MEVAGISSEY.

146 ST MEWAN, ST CARHAVES MICHAEL, ST SAMPSON, ST STEPHEN IN BRANNEL, TYWARDREATH.

147 ST ALLEN, ST ANTHONY IN ROSELAND, ST CLEMENTS, CORNELLY, CREED, GRAMPOUND, CUBY, ST JAMES WITH TREGONY, ST ERME, ST FEOCK, GERRANS, ST JUST IN ROSELAND, ST MAWES, KEA, KENWYN.

148 LAMORRAN, MERTHER, ST MICHAEL PENKEVIL, PHILLEIGH, PROBUS, GRAMPOUND, RUAN LANIHORNE, TRURO ST MARY, VERYAN.

149 ST AGNES, ST BREOCK, COLAN, ST COLUMB MAJOR, ST COLUMB MINOR, CRANTOCK, CUBERT.

150 ST ENODER, ST ERVAN, ST EVAL, ST ISSEY, LANHYDROCK, LANIVET, ST MAWGAN IN PYDAR, ST MERRYN, NEWLYN, PADSTOW, PERRANZABULOE, LITTLE PETHENICK, ST WENN, WITHIEL.

151 BOYTON, BRIDGERULE, JACOBSTOWE, KILKHAMPTON, LAUNCELLS, MARHAMCHURCH, MORWINSTOW, POUGHILL, STRATTON, NORTH TAMERTON, WEEK ST MARY, WHITSTONE.

152 BODMIN, BLISLAND, ST BREWARD, EGLOSHAYLE, ST ENDELLION, HELLAND, ST KEW, ST MABYN, ST MINVER, TEMPLE, ST TUDY, ST TEATH.

153 BOCONNOCK, BRADOCK, CARDINHAM, ST CLEER, DULOE, ST KEYNE, LANREATH, LANSALLOES, LANTEGLOS BY FOWEY, POLRUAN, LISKEARD, ST MARTINS, LOOE (EAST & WEST), MORVAL, ST NEOT, PELYNT, ST PINNOCK, TALLAND, ST VEEP, WARLEGGON, ST WINNOW.

154 LAUNCESTON (ST MARY MAGDELINE), FALMOUTH, SCILLY ISLANDS.

ADDRESS	NAME		AGE	PROFESSION	WHERE BORN
CURY (HO107/136)					
SKEWES	SKEWES	JOSIAH	15	Male servant	Cornwall
	Boaden	Edward	50	Farmer	ditto
	Boaden	Joan	40		ditto
	Boaden	Elizabeth	15		ditto
	Boaden	Mary	12		ditto
White Cross	SKEWES	EDWARD	25	Shoemaker	ditto
	SKEWES	MARTHA	20		ditto
	SKEWES	JOHN	3		ditto
White Cross	SKEWES	WILLIAM	15	Apprentice	ditto
Broadhow	SKEWES	JANE	15	Female servant	ditto
	SKEWES	JOHN	16	Male servant	ditto
Treloskan	SKEWES	EDWARD	59	Farmer	ditto
	SKEWES	JAMES	42	Farmer	ditto
	SKEWES	GRACE	31	Farmer	ditto
	SKEWES	MARY	85	Widow	ditto
Treloskan	SKEWES	JAMES	45	Farmer	ditto
	SKEWES	SIMONETTE	36		ditto
	SKEWES	JAMES	16		ditto
	SKEWES	WILLIAM	12		ditto
	SKEWES	JOHN	5		ditto
	SKEWES	EDWARD	3		ditto
	SKEWES	ANN	10		ditto
	SKEWES	ALICE	7		ditto
	SKEWES	ELIZABETH	1		ditto
	SKEWES	BLANCH	55	Female servant	ditto
Nantithet	SKEWES	JOHN	63	Agricultural labourer	ditto
	SKEWES	ELIZABETH	40		ditto
	SKEWES	SAMUEL	25	Carpenter	ditto
Gilly Lane	SKEWES	ALICE	45	Servant	ditto
	SKEWES	JANE	30	Servant	ditto
	SKEWES	JAMES or JOHN H.	2		ditto
Gilly Lane	SKEWES	JOHN	46	Agricultural labourer	ditto
	SKEWES	AVIS	45		ditto
Gilly Lane	SKEWES	JAMES	50	Agricultural labourer	ditto
	SKEWES	ELIZABETH	55		ditto
	SKEWES	HENRY	20	Carpenter	ditto
	SKEWES	ANNEY	20	Dressmaker	ditto
	SKEWES	THOMAS	15	Agricultural servant	ditto
Gilly Lane	SKEWES	WILLIAM	25	Agricultural labourer	ditto
	SKEWES	MARY	25		ditto
	SKEWES	ELIZABETH MARY	6		ditto
	SKEWES	ALICE ANN	4		ditto
	SKEWES	EMILY	4 months		ditto
Gilly Lane	SKEWES	JOHN	25	Agricultural labourer	ditto
	SKEWES	JULIA	25		ditto
	SKEWES	JULIANA	4		ditto
	SKEWES	JAMES	14 months		ditto
CONSTANTINE (HO 107/136)					
Bosawsack	SKEWES	HENRY	60	Farmer	ditto
	SKEWES	ELIZABETH	25	Farmer	ditto
	SKEWES	JOSIAH	20	Farmer	ditto
	SKEWES	FANNY	18	Farmer	ditto
	SKEWES	CAROLINE	16	Farmer	ditto
	SKEWES	ELIZA	15	Farmer	ditto
Tresohn	SKEWES	HANNAH	15		ditto
Trewardreva Vean	SKEWIS	WILLIAM	44	Labourer	ditto
	SKEWIS	REBECCA	44		ditto
	SKEWIS	ANN	11		ditto
	SKEWIS	WILLIAM	8		ditto

Treloskan	SKEWES	WILLIAM	77		Farmer	Cornwall
	SKEWES	SARAH	45			ditto
	SKEWES	EDWARD	30			ditto
	SKEWES	HENRY	27			ditto
	SKEWES	EDWARD	84		Agricultural labourer	ditto
	SKEWES	JOSEPH	4			ditto

PENRYN (HO 107/137)

Higher Market Street	SKEWES	MARY	20		Independent means	ditto
Lower Market Street	SKEWIS	STEPHEN	40		Labourer	ditto
	SKEWIS	SUSANNA	35			ditto
	SKEWIS	WILLIAM	9			ditto
	SKEWIS	EDWARD	5			ditto
	SKEWIS	LOUISA	3			ditto
	SKEWIS	PHILIPPA	2	months		ditto

GRADE

Kugger	SKEWES	MARY	8		Staying with Sarah and William Mundy	ditto
Givavas	SKEWES	LOVEDAY	30		Housekeeper	ditto

GUNWALLOE

Trenoweth	SKEWES	ELIZABETH	20		Farm servant	ditto

ST DAY	SKEWES	ANN	60		Widow	ditto
	SKEWES	JULIA	26			ditto

GWENNAP (HO 107/137)

Poldice	SKEWES	JANE	50		Widow	ditto
	SKEWES	JOHN	20		Agricultural labourer	ditto
	SKEWES	JANE	13			ditto
	SKEWES	COLLAN	10			ditto
Belle	SKEWES	SUSAN	65		Widow	ditto
Lanner	SKEWES	JAMES	40		Farmer	ditto
	SKEWES	CHARITY	40			ditto
	SKEWES	MARY	12			ditto
	SKEWES	JAMES	10			ditto
	SKEWES	CHARITY	7			ditto
	SKEWES	JOHN	5			ditto
Lanner	SKEWES	HENRY	35		Miner	ditto
	SKEWES	ANN	40			ditto
	SKEWES	WILLIAM	12			ditto
	SKEWES	MARY	9			ditto
	SKEWES	HENRY	6			ditto
	SKEWES	JAMES	3			ditto
Gwennap Moor	SKEWES	ALEXANDER	30		Clerk	ditto
	SKEWES	MARGARET	35			ditto
	SKEWES	ELIZABETH	25			ditto
	SKEWES	MARY	23			ditto
	SKEWES	ANN	20			ditto
Penance	SKEWES	JOHN	37		Farmer	ditto
	SKEWES	ANN	34			ditto
	SKEWES	MARY	14			ditto
	SKEWES	JOHN	12			ditto
	SKEWES	THOMAS	9			ditto
	SKEWES	ALEXANDER	7			ditto
	SKEWES	SIMON	5			ditto
	SKEWES	ELIZABETH	3			ditto
	SKEWES	RICHARD	8	months		ditto
Penance	SKEWES	ANN	38		Widow	ditto
	SKEWES	RICHARD	16		Miner	Not born in Cornwall
	SKEWES	THOMAS	13		Miner	Not born in Cornwall
	SKEWES	MARY	7			Cornwall

MULLION (HO 107/137)

Angrouse	SKUES	ANN	30		Farm servant to Thomas and Ann Shephard	ditto

ST MARTIN (HO 107/137)

Trezise	SKEWES	JANE	70			ditto

MAWNAN (HO 107/137)

Rosemullion	SKEWES	WILLIAM	46	Farmer	ditto
	SKEWES	CHRISTIAN	45		ditto
	SKEWES	JAMES	25		Cornwall
	SKEWES	ELIZABETH	18		ditto
	SKEWES	MARY	16		ditto
	SKEWES	ANN	15		ditto
	SKEWES	HENRY	13		ditto
	SKEWES	WILLIAM	11		ditto
	SKEWES	CHRISTIAN	9		ditto
	SKEWES	GRACE	7		ditto
	SKEWES	JOHN	5		ditto
	SKEWES	SAMUEL	2		ditto

ST KEVERNE (HO 107/138)

Rosinithon	SKEWES	EDWARD	40	Farmer	ditto
	SKEWES	MARY	30		ditto
	SKEWES	EDWARD	5		ditto
	SKEWES	RICHARD	3		ditto
	SKEWES	SUSANNA	3 months		ditto
Roskowrule	SKEWES	EDWARD	20		ditto
TRESKEWES	Lory Elizabeth		24	and family	ditto
	Sincock Henry		40	and his wife Elizabeth (35) and children Mary (20), Jane (17), William (15), Hannah (13), Martha (11) and Henry (10). Also Henry Williams (15) farm servant	ditto

MABE (HO 107/138)

Highersparga	SKEWES	HENRY	20	Male servant	ditto
	SKEWES	ANN	20	Farm servant	ditto
	SKEWES	MARY	20	Farm servant	ditto
	SKEWES	JAMES	13	Male servant (All working on the farm of Alice — née SKEWES — and Thomas Midlin. Alice (30), Thomas (25), and children Mary (5) and Thomas (4).	ditto

RUAN MAJOR (HO 107/138)

Chybarlis	SKEWES	JOHN	35	Farmer	ditto
	SKEWES	JANE	25		ditto
	SKEWES	HENRY	7		ditto
	SKEWES	THOMAS	5		ditto
	SKEWES	EDWIN	3		ditto
	SKEWES	BETSY	3 months		ditto
Tresoddern	SKEWES	SAMUEL	25	Farmer	ditto
	SKEWES	CATHERINE	20		ditto
	SKEWES	THOMAS	30		ditto
	SKEWES	MARGARET	4		ditto

SITHNEY (HO 107/139)

Tregadjack	SKEWES	ELIZABETH	30	Housekeeper	ditto
	SKEWES	WILLIAM	5		ditto
	SKEWES	JOSEPH	3		ditto
	SKEWES	CHRISTIAN	2		ditto
	SKEWES	GRACE	4 months		ditto
Tregoose	SKEWES	JOHN	25	Carpenter	ditto

HELSTON (HO 107/139)

Wendron Street	SKUES	WILLIAM	60	Carpenter	ditto
	SKUES	ELIZABETH	30		ditto

CAMBORNE (HO 107/141)

College Street	SKEWES	JAMES	25	Cabinet maker	ditto
	SKEWES	ALICE	20		ditto
	SKEWES	MARY	3		ditto
Glebe	SKEWES	WILLIAM	65	Agricultural labourer	ditto
	SKEWES	ANN	60		ditto
Town	SKEWIS	CAROLINE	20	Female servant	ditto
Veryan Row	SKEWES	EDWARD	45	Copper miner	ditto
	SKEWES	MARY	45		ditto
	SKEWES	MARY	20	Fuze factory	ditto

	SKEWES	EDWARD	20	Copper miner	ditto
	SKEWES	ANN	15	Dressing ore	ditto
	SKEWES	CATHERINE	15	Dressing ore	ditto
	SKEWES	JAMES	15	Copper miner	ditto
	SKEWES	ELIZA	13	Dressing ore	ditto
	SKEWES	HONOR	12	Dressing ore	ditto
	SKEWES	HENRY	9		Cornwall
	SKEWES	CAROLINA	8		ditto
	SKEWES	WILLIAM	6		ditto
Veryan Row	SKEWIS	WILLIAM	50	Copper miner	ditto
	SKEWIS	ELIZABETH	85	Independent means	ditto
Veryan Row	SKEWES	JANE	45	Independent means	ditto
	SKEWES	WILLIAM	15	Copper miner	ditto
	SKEWES	ELIZABETH	20	Dressing ore	ditto
	SKEWES	CAROLINE	14	Dressing ore	ditto
	SKEWES	HENRY	9		ditto
	SKEWES	LAVINIA	5		ditto
Veryan Row	SKEWES	JULIA	12		ditto
Race Gate	SKEWIES	WILLIAM	14	Male servant	ditto
Union Street	SKEWIS	JOHN	45	Miner	ditto
	SKEWIS	ANN	45		ditto
	SKEWIS	ANN	15	Mine girl	ditto
	SKEWIS	MARY	3		ditto
Killivoase	SKEWES	JAMES	45	Farmer	ditto
	SKEWES	JOHANNA	50		ditto
	SKEWES	JAMES	20	Copper miner	ditto
	SKEWES	HENRY	20	Copper miner	ditto
	SKEWES	WILLIAM	15	Copper miner	ditto
	SKEWES	EDWARD	15		ditto
	SKEWES	ABSALOM	15		ditto
	SKEWES	JOHN	13		ditto
	SKEWES	NANNY	9		ditto
	SKEWES	MARY	7		ditto
Treswithian	SKEWES	STEPHEN	35	Agricultural labourer	ditto
	SKEWES	ELIZABETH	40		ditto
	SKEWES	JOHN	15	Copper miner	ditto
	SKEWES	ELIZABETH	6		ditto
Higher Penponds	SKEWIS	HENRY	25	Copper miner	ditto
	SKEWIS	GRACE	30		ditto
	SKEWIS	WILLIAM	8		ditto
	SKEWIS	RICHARD	6		ditto
	SKEWIS	ELIZABETH	4		ditto
	SKEWIS	STEPHEN	2		ditto

CROWAN (HO 107/141)

SKEWIS	Williams	Joseph	— farmer — his wife Grace, and nine children
	Moyle	William	— miner — his wife Jane, and four children
	Austin	Richard	and Philippa
	Dower	William	
	Goldsworthy	James	— his wife Ann and four children
	Reynolds	Ann	and her five children
	Vivian	Christopher	— his wife Grace, and six children
	Reynolds	Richard	— and his four children
	Williams	William	— his wife Mary and four children
	Ward	Elizabeth	and her family of seven
	Pascoe	John	— his wife Ann and six children
	Pool	John	— his wife Philippa and three children

ILLOGAN (HO 107/142)

Illogan Park	SKEWIS	JOHN	25	Farmer	ditto
	SKEWIS	PHILLEY	35		ditto
	SKEWIS	JANE	26		ditto

REDRUTH (HO 107/143)

Blights Row	SKUES	JOHN	25	Mason	ditto
	SKUES	SALLY	25		ditto
	SKUES	JOSEPH	3		ditto
	SKUES	LEWIS	1		ditto

Foundry Row	SKEWES	JOHN	40	Blacksmith	Cornwall
	SKEWES	JOHN Jnr	15		ditto
	SKEWES	TH (ALE)	15		ditto
	SKEWES	MATTHEW	14		Not born in Cornwall
	SKEWES	RICHARD	11		Not born in Cornwall
	SKEWES	JOHN	7		Born in Cornwall
Foundry Row	SKEWES	MARGERY	35		ditto
	SKEWES	MARGERY	4		ditto
	SKEWES	MARY	1		ditto
Foundry Row	SKEWES	ELIZABETH	14	Servant	ditto
Green Lane	SKEWES	SUSAN	32	Female servant	ditto

ST AUSTELL (HO 107/146)

Workhouse Lane	SKEWES	WILLIAM	6	Staying with John and Mary Jago, each aged 70 years	ditto

ST MEWAN

Coombe	SKEWS	LOVILIA	24		ditto
	SKEWS	JOHN	9 months		ditto

ST EWE

Lanhadron	SKUWYS	ANN	70	Independent means	ditto
	SKUWYS	HENRY	30	Tin miner	ditto
	SKUWS	PHILIP	40	Agricultural labourer	ditto
	SKUWS	LUCHRECIA	40	Agricultural labourer	ditto
Polgooth	SKEWS	JOANNA	65		ditto
	SKEWS	THOMAS	20	Agricultural labourer	ditto

ST CLEMENTS (HO 107/147)

East Brown Row	SKEWES	ELIZA	20		ditto

KEA (HO 107/147)

New Church Town	SKEWS	RICHARD	50	Agricultural labourer	ditto
	SKEWS	MARY	50		ditto
	SKEWS	ANN	21		ditto
	SKEWS	THOMASINE	15		ditto
Hugus	SKEWS	JOHN	30	Copper miner	ditto
	SKEWS	MARY	30		ditto
	SKEWS	JOHN	10		ditto
	SKEWS	WILLIAM	6		ditto
	SKEWS	MARY	4		ditto
Hugus	SKEWS	PETER	35	Copper miner	ditto
	SKEWS	ELIZABETH	25		ditto
	SKEWS	ELIZABETH	6		ditto
	SKEWS	JANE	4		ditto
	SKEWS	PETER	1		ditto
Hugus	SKEWS	ANN	60		ditto
	SKEWS	JANE	30		ditto
	SKEWS	MARY	8		ditto
Hugus	SKEWS	JOHN	35	Copper miner	ditto
	SKEWS	ANN	35		ditto
	SKEWS	ELIZA	15		ditto
	SKEWS	ELIZABETH	12		ditto
	SKEWS	SAMUEL	6		ditto
	SKEWS	MARY	4		ditto
	SKEWS	GRACE	2		ditto
	SKEWS	JOHN	1		ditto
Hugus	SKEWS	RICHARD	25	Copper miner	ditto
	SKEWS	JOHANNA	20		ditto
Kerley	SKEWS	RICHARD	55	Mine Agent	ditto
	SKEWS	AGNES	55		ditto
	SKEWS	RICHARD	20		ditto
	SKEWS	SARAH	15		ditto
	SKEWS	MATTHEW	15		ditto
Kerley	SKEWS	JOHN	25	Miner	ditto
	SKEWS	HARRIET	20		ditto
	SKEWS	PHILIPPA	1		ditto

Kerley	SKEWS	ELIZABETH	80	Independent means	Cornwall
Kerley	SKEWS	MARY	45	School mistress	ditto
Kerley	SKEWS	PEGGY	35	Copper miner	ditto
	SKEWS	GRACE	30		ditto
	SKEWS	RICHARD	8		ditto
	SKEWS	ELIZABETH	6		ditto
	SKEWS	MARY	4		ditto
	SKEWS	JOHN	2		ditto
	SKEWS	THOMAS	10 months		ditto
Kerley	SKEWS	DIGORY	50	Miner	ditto
	SKEWS	SOPHIA	45		ditto
	SKEWS	ANN	20		ditto
	SKEWS	ELIZABETH	20		ditto
	SKEWS	AMELIA	15		ditto
	SKEWS	DIGORY	15		ditto
	SKEWS	JOSEPH	14		ditto
	SKEWS	JOHN	12		ditto
	SKEWS	SOPHIA	10		ditto
	SKEWS	MATTHEW	8		ditto
	SKEWS	MARY	6		ditto
	SKEWS	SAMUEL	3		ditto
Kerley	SKEWS	THOMAS	30	Miner	ditto
	SKEWS	JANE	30		ditto
	SKEWS	ELIZABETH	8		ditto
	SKEWS	THOMAS	6		ditto
	SKEWS	GRACE	4		ditto
	SKEWS	SAMUEL	3		dotto
	SKEWS	MARY	1		ditto
Jolly's Bottom	SKEWS	THOMAS	45	Copper miner	ditto
	SKEWS	GRACE	40		ditto
	SKEWS	ELEANOR	15		ditto
	SKEWS	SELINA	12		ditto
	SKEWS	JULIA	10		ditto
	SKEWS	EMMA	8		ditto
	SKEWS	EMILY	6		ditto
	SKEWS	GRACE	3		ditto
	SKEWS	WALTER	2 months		ditto
Jolly's Bottom	SKEWES	WILLIAM	20	Copper miner	ditto
	SKEWES	SUSANNAH	20		ditto
	SKEWES	MARY	4 months		ditto
Chacewater	SKEWS	WILLIAM	20	Tailor	ditto
	SKEWS	MARY	20		ditto
	SKEWS	WILIAM	1		ditto
Chacewater	SKEWS	MARY	20		ditto

KENWYN (HO 107/147)

Daniell	SKEWES	THOMAS	42	Mason	ditto
Street	SKEWES	JANE	42		ditto
	SKEWES	MARY	16		ditto
	SKEWES	HENRIETTA	12		ditto
	SKEWES	JOHN	11		ditto
	SKEWES	PHILIPPA	9		ditto
	SKEWES	THOMAS	7		ditto
Kenwyn Street	SKEWES	HENRY	65	Innkeeper	ditto
	SKEWES	MARGARET	72		ditto
	SKEWES	MARY	30		ditto
	SKEWES	LARMEA?	25		ditto
	SKEWES	MATILDA	20		ditto
	SKEWES	MARGARET	15		ditto
Comprigney	SKUES	ISABELLA	60	Female servant	ditto
	SKUES	MARY	35	Female servant	ditto
Hugus	SKEWS	ROSE	77	Independent means	ditto
Hugus	SKEWS	JOHN	40	Copper miner	ditto
	SKEWS	GRACE	40		ditto
	SKEWS	JAMES	15	Agricultural labourer	ditto

CHACEWATER

Navy Row	SKEWS	MATTHEW	40	Copper miner	Cornwall
	SKEWS	MARY	35		ditto
	SKEWS	ELIZABETH	15		ditto
	SKEWS	MARY	15		ditto
	SKEWS	MATTHEW	12	Carpenter's apprentice	ditto
	SKEWS	JANE	13		ditto
Navy Row	SKEWS	ELIZABETH	45		ditto
	SKEWS	EMMA	20		ditto
	SKEWS	ELIZA	15		ditto
	SKEWS	NANNY	13		ditto
	SKEWS	AMELIA	5		ditto
Wheal Busy	SKEWS	MARY	25	Independent means	ditto
	SKEWS	SUSAN	3		ditto
	SKEWS	MARY	1		ditto
BLACKWATER	SKEWS	MARTIN	30	Innkeeper	ditto
	SKEWS	ANN	25		ditto
	SKEWS	MARY	4		ditto
	SKEWS	THOMAS	2		ditto
Blackwater	SKEWS	WILLIAM	45	Engineer	ditto
	SKEWS	MARY	45		ditto
	SKEWS	MARY	18		ditto
	SKEWS	THOMAS	15		ditto
	SKEWS	SAMUEL	13		ditto
	SKEWS	DANIEL	10		ditto
	SKEWS	ELIZABETH	6		ditto

TRURO ST MARY's (HO 107/148)

HIGHCROSS	SKEWES	JAMES	30	Boot and shoe maker	ditto
	SKEWES	ANN	30		ditto

FALMOUTH (HO 107/154)

Dispersan	SKEWES	THOMAS	45	Shoemaker	ditto
Green	SKEWES	GRACE	35		ditto
	SKEWES	CHARLES	11		ditto

ABERDARE, WALES

Village:	SKEWES	THOMAS	age 25	Turner	Born outside Wales
	SKEWES	CHARLOTTE	25	Turner	Born outside Wales
	SKEWES	THOMAS	8	Turner	Born outside Wales
	SKEWES	GEORGE	4	Turner	Born outside Wales
	SKEWES	SAMUEL	1	Turner	Born outside Wales

Would appear to have moved away from Aberdare by 1851 Census.

CENSUS RETURNS FOR THE COUNTY OF CORNWALL-1851

PUBLIC RECORD OFFICE REFERENCE AND DISTRICTS ALL NUMBERS ARE PREFACED BY HO 107/(1897-1919 inc)

1897	STRATTON	1909	TRURO
1898	CAMELFORD	1910	TRURO
1899	LAUNCESTON	1911	FALMOUTH
1900	ST GERMANS	1912	HELSTON
1901	LISKEARD	1913	HELSTON
1902	LISKEARD	1914	REDRUTH
1903	LISKEARD	1915	REDRUTH
1904	BODMIN	1916	REDRUTH
1905	ST COLUMB	1917	PENZANCE
1906	ST AUSTELL	1918	PENZANCE
1907	ST AUSTELL	1919	PENZANCE
1908	ST AUSTELL		and SCILLY ISLANDS

ADDRESS	NAME	RELATION TO HEAD OF HOUSEHOLD	STATUS	AGE	PROFESSION	WHERE BORN
ALTARNUN, LAUNCESTON (HO 107/1898)						
Trewint	SKEWS JOHN	Head	Married	28	Tin miner	Kenwyn
	SKEWS ISABELLA	Wife	Married	19		Altarnun
	SKEWS ELIZABETH JANE	Dau	Unmarried	1 month		Altarnun
	Gregory Elizabeth	Sister-in-law	Unmarried	16		Altarnun
LISKEARD (HO 107/1902)						
Dobwalls	SKEWES DIGORY	Head	Married	62	Copper miner	Kea
	SKEWES SOPHIA	Wife	Married	57		Truro
	SKEWES MATTHEW	Son	Unmarried	17	Copper miner	Kea
	SKEWES MARY	Daughter	Unmarried	15	Copper miner	Kea
	SKEWES SAMUEL	Son	Unmarried	11	Sunday scholar	Kea

Place	Surname	First name	Relationship	Status	Age	Occupation	Birthplace
Dobwalls	SKEWS	JOSEPH	Head	Married	24	Copper miner	Kea
	SKEWS	ELIZABETH	Wife	Married	20		Kenwyn
	SKEWS	ELIZA	Daughter	Unmarried	10 months		Liskeard
EAST TAPHOUSE	SKEWES	HENRY	Head	Married	33	Lead miner	Cury
St Pinnock	SKEWES	ANN	Wife	Married	33		St Hilary
	SKEWES	BLANCHE	Daughter	Unmarried	12		St Hilary
	SKEWES	HENRY	Son	Unmarried	10		St Hilary
	SKEWES	MARIA	Daughter	Unmarried	2		St Pinnock
	SKEWES	SARAH ANN	Daughter	Unmarried	8		St Hilary
	SKEWES	JOSEPH	Son	Unmarried	7 months		St Pinnock

ST WENN (HO 107/1905)

Place	Surname	First name	Relationship	Status	Age	Occupation	Birthplace
GREAT SKEWES	Slick	Thomas	Head	Married	25	Farmer of 70 acres emloying 4 men	Roche
	Slick	Elizabeth	Wife	Married	23		Roche
	Slick	James	Brother	Unmarried	21	Farmer of 70 acres	Roche
	Callicot	Mary Ann	Servant	Unmarried	16	Servant	St Wenn
	Lobb	Thomas	Servant	Unmarried	18	Employed on farm	St Wenn
	Magor	Thomas	Servant	Unmarried	14	Employed on farm	St Wenn
LITTLE SKEWES	Blake	Peggy	Head	Widow	46	Farmer of 60 acres employing 1 man	St Merryn
	Blake	Elizabeth	Daughter	Unmarried	23		St Wenn
	Blake	Mary Jane	Daughter	Unmarried	18		St Wenn
	Blake	Richard	Son	Unmarried	16		St Wenn
	Blake	William Henry	Son	Unmarried	14		St Wenn
	Blake	Amelia	Daughter	Unmarried	10		St Wenn
	Blake	Jemima	Daughter	Unmarried	8		St Wenn
	Blake	Marshall	Son	Unmarried	6		St Wenn
	Harris	John	Servant	Widower	57	Waggoner	St Columb

ST AUSTELL (HO 107/1908)

Place	Surname	First name	Relationship	Status	Age	Occupation	Birthplace
Charlestown	SKEWS	JAMES	Head	Married	49	Labourer	St Ewe
	SKEWS	ELIZABETH	Wife	Married	50		St Perrant
Polgooth	SKEWS	JOANNA	Wife's mother	Widow	77		St Ewe
	Herring	John	Head	Married	55	Carpenter	Probus
	Herring	Ann	Wife	Married	56		St Ewe
	Herring	Elizabeth	Daughter	Unmarried	19	Dressmaker	St Mewan
Little Lavalsa	SKEWS	PHILIP	Head	Married	53	Farmer of 8 acres employing 1 boy	St Ewe
	SKEWS	LUCCRETIA	Wife	Married	50		St Mewan

ST AGNES, TRURO (HO 107/1909)

Place	Surname	First name	Relationship	Status	Age	Occupation	Birthplace
Churchtown	SKEWES	JULIA	Servant	Unmarried	20	House servant	Kea

ST ALLEN, TRURO (HO 107/1910)

Place	Surname	First name	Relationship	Status	Age	Occupation	Birthplace
St Allen	SKEWES	THOMAS	Head	Married	42	Lead miner	Kea
	SKEWES	JANE	Wife	Married	41		Kea
	SKEWES	ELIZABETH JANE	Daughter	Unmarried	18	Dresser of lead ore	Kea
	SKEWES	THOMAS	Son	Unmarried	16	Lead miner	Kea
	SKEWES	SAMUEL	Son	Unmarried	12	Dresser of lead ore	Kea
	SKEWES	MARY	Daughter	Unmarried	11	Dresser of lead ore	Kea
	SKEWES	EMILY	Daughter	Unmarried	7	Scholar	Kea
	SKEWES	RICHARD	Son	Unmarried	3		Kea
High Cross	SKEWES	ANN	Head	Widow	42	Assembly rooms attdnt.	St Clements
	SKEWES	EMMA	Daughter	Unmarried	9	Scholar	Truro

KENWYN

Place	Surname	First name	Relationship	Status	Age	Occupation	Birthplace
Daniel Street	SKEWES	THOMAS	Head	Married	52	Mason	Kea
	SKEWES	JANE	Wife	Married	52		St Teath
	SKEWES	MARY ANN	Daughter	Unmarried	26		Kenwyn
	SKEWES	HENRIETTA	Daughter	Unmarried	22	Dressmaker	Kenwyn
	SKEWES	PHILIPPA	Daughter	Unmarried	19	School mistress	Kenwyn
	SKEWES	THOMAS	Son	Unmarried	17	Ironmongers asst.	Kenwyn

KEA

Place	Surname	First name	Relationship	Status	Age	Occupation	Birthplace
Goodern	SKEWES	ANN	Mother-in-law to James Rowe	Widow	73	Pauper	Kea
Kilserd	SKEWES	JANE	Visitor	Unmarried	13		Kea
Hugus	SKEWES	PETER	Head	Married	46	Copper miner	Kea
	SKEWES	ELIZABETH	Wife	Married	38		Kea
	SKEWES	ELIZABETH	Daughter	Unmarried	15	Mine labourer	Kea
	SKEWES	PETER	Son	Unmarried	11	Mine labourer	Kea

	SKEWES	MARY	Daughter	Unmarried 8	Scholar	Kea
	SKEWES	GRACE	Daughter	Unmarried 6	Scholar	Kea
	SKEWES	ELLEN	Daughter	Unmarried 4		Kea
	SKEWES	EMILY	Daughter	Unmarried 2		Kea
Kerley	SKEWS	MARY	Head	Widow 52	School mistress	Kea
Kerley	SKEWS	RICHARD	Head	Married 67	Mine agent	Kea
	SKEWS	AGNES	Wife	Married 65		St Columb
	SKEWS	RICHARD	Son	Unmarried 30	Copper miner	Kea
	SKEWS	SARAH	Daughter	Unmarried 26	At home	Kea
Kerley	SKEWS	JOHN	Head	Married 36	Mine agent	Kea
	SKEWS	HARRIET	Wife	Married 32		Kenwyn
	SKEWS	PHILIPPA	Daughter	Unmarried 14		Kea
	SKEWS	JOHN HENRY	Son	Unmarried 3		Kea
Seveock	SKEWS	JOHN	Head	Married 48	Copper miner	Kenwyn
	SKEWS	ANN	Wife	Married 45		Kea
	SKEWS	SAMUEL	Son	Unmarried 16	Copper miner	Kea
	SKEWS	MARY	Daughter	Unmarried 14		Kea
	SKEWS	GRACE	Daughter	Unmarried 12		Kea
	SKEWS	JOHN	Son	Unmarried 11	Agricultural lab.	Kea
	SKEWS	EMMA	Daughter	Unmarried 9	Scholar	Kea
	SKEWS	ELLEN	Daughter	Unmarried 7	Scholar	Kea
	SKEWS	LAVINIA	Daughter	Unmarried 6	Scholar	Kea
	SKEWS	WILLIAM	Son	Unmarried 5	Scholar	Kea
Hugus	SKEWS	JOHN	Head	Married 35	Farmer of 20 acres	Gwennap
	SKEWS	ANN	Wife	Married 34		St Allen
	SKEWS	ELIZABETH ANN	Daughter	Unmarried 6		Gwennap
	SKEWS	CHARLOTTE MARY	Daughter	Unmarried 4		Gwennap
	SKEWS	MARY ANN	Daughter	Unmarried 2		Kenwyn
Hugus	SKEWS	JAMES	Son of Head — Grace Coad	Unmarried 30	Ag. labourer	Kenwyn
Chacewater	SKEWS	ELIZABETH	Head	Widow 57	Housekeeper	Kenwyn
	SKEWS	EMMA	Daughter	Unmarried 26		Kenwyn
	SKEWS	AMELIA	Daughter	Unmarried 14	Scholar	Kenwyn
Chacewater	SKEWES	MARTIN	Head	Married 40	Innkeeper	Kea
	SKEWES	ELIZABETH	Wife	Married 32		St Erth
	SKEWES	MARTIN	Son	Unmarried 14	Blacksmith	Kea
	SKEWES	THOMAS	Son	Unmarried 13	Scholar	St Agnes
	SKEWES	ELIZABETH JANE	Daughter	Unmarried 11	Scholar	Kenwyn
	SKEWES	JOHN	Son	Unmarried 6	Scholar	Kenwyn
Chacewater	SKEWES	THOMAS	Head	Married 58	Ag. labourer	Kea
	SKEWES	EMMA	Daughter	Unmarried 17	Dressmaker	Kea
	SKEWES	EMILY	Daughter	Unmarried 15		Kea
	SKEWES	WALTER	Son	Unmarried 10		Kea
	SKEWES	WILLIAM	Son	Unmarried 7	Scholar	Kea
Chacewater	SKEWES	ELIZABETH	Servant	Unmarried 24	General servant	Kea
	SKEWES	WILLIAM	Head	Married 30	Copper miner	Kea
	SKEWES	SUSANNE	Wife	Married 31		Kenwyn
	SKEWES	MARY	Daughter	Unmarried 10		Kenwyn
	SKEWES	WILLIAM	Son	Unmarried 8		Kea
	SKEWES	SUSAN	Daughter	Unmarried 6		Kea
	SKEWES	GRACE	Daughter	Unmarried 4		Kea
	SKEWES	ELIZABETH	Daughter	Unmarried 1		Kea

PENRYN (HO 107/1911)

Truro Lane	SKEWES	STEPHEN	Head	Married 53	Dock labourer	Gwinear
	SKEWES	SUSANNAH	Wife	Married 44	Dressmaker	Budock
	SKEWES	LOUISA	Daughter	Unmarried 13	Scholar	Penryn
	SKEWES	JOHN	Son	Unmarried 7	Scholar	Penryn

MABE

Little Insight	SKEWES	WILLIAM	Head	Married 56	Farmer of 9 acres	Cury
	SKEWES	CHRISTIAN	Wife	Married 55		Ruan Major
	SKEWES	GRACE	Daughter	Unmarried 16		St Keverne
	SKEWES	JOHN	Son	Unmarried 14	Ag. labourer	St Keverne
	SKEWES	SAMUEL	Son	Unmarried 12	Scholar	Mawnan
	SKEWES	EDWARD	Lodger	Unmarried 20	School master	Ruan Major

Mawnan Smith	SKEWES	JAMES	Head	Married	34	Ag. labourer	Ruan Major
	SKEWES	FRANCES	Wife	Married	26		Mawnan
	SKEWES	HESTORA	Daughter	Unmarried	4	Scholar	Mawnan
	SKEWES	FANNY	Daughter	Unmarried	3		Mawnan
	SKEWES	EDWARD	Son	Unmarried	1		Mawnan
Mawnan Smith	SKEWES	EDWARD	Head	Married	32	{ Blacksmith	Ruan
	SKEWES	MARY	Wife	Married	30	{ employing 2 men	Southwark, London
Bosawsack	SKEWES	JOSEPH	Head	Unmarried	30	{ Farmer of 30 acres	Constantine
	SKEWES	ELIZA	Sister	Unmarried	24	{ employing 2 labrs.	Constantine
	SKEWES	JOSIAH	Nephew	Unmarried	3		Stithians

CURY (HO 107/1912)

Trewolla	SKEWES	JOHN	Head	Married	35	Farm labourer	Cury
	SKEWES	JULIA	Wife	Married	38		Cury
	SKEWS	JULIANNA	Daughter	Unmarried	13	Scholar	Cury
	SKEWES	JAMES	Son	Unmarried	10	Scholar	Cury
	SKEWES	ELIZABETH	Daughter	Unmarried	7	Scholar	Cury
	SKEWES	JOHN	Son	Unmarried	2		Cury
Nanturit	SKEWES	ELIZABETH	Head	Married	31	Farm labourer	Cury
	SKEWES	JOSEPH	Son	Unmarried	12	Farm labourer	Cury
	SKEWES	SAMUEL	Son	Unmarried	9	At home	Cury
	SKEWES	EDWARD	Brother	Unmarried	40	Pauper	Cury
Nanturit	SKEWES	JOHN	Head	Widower	72	Ag. labourer	Cury
	SKEWES	HANNAH	Daughter	Unmarried	25	At home	Cury
	SKEWES	SAMUEL	Grandson	Unmarried	8	Scholar	Cury
Nanturit	SKEWES	EDWARD	Head	Married	37	{ Shoemaker employing	Cury
	SKEWES	JULIA	Wife	Married	27	{ three men	Cury
	SKEWES	JOHN	Son	Unmarried	13	At home	Cury
	SKEWES	LOVELIA	Daughter	Unmarried	9	Scholar	Cury
	SKEWES	MARTHA	Daughter	Unmarried	7	Scholar	Cury
	SKEWES	MARY	Daughter	Unmarried	3	Scholar	Cury
	SKEWES	ELIZA	Daughter	Unmarried	3	At home	Cury
	SKEWES	JAMES	Son	Unmarried	11 months	At home	Cury
Nanturit	SKEWES	WILLIAM	Head	Married	44	Ag labourer	Cury
	SKEWES	MARY	Wife	Married	34		Cury
	SKEWES	ALICE	Daughter	Unmarried	12	Scholar	Cury
	SKEWES	EMILY	Daughter	Unmarried	9	Scholar	Cury
	SKEWES	ELIZA	Daughter	Unmarried	7	Scholar	Cury
	SKEWES	WILLIAM JAMES	Son	Unmarried	1		Cury
Nanturit	SKEWES	JOHN	Head	Widower	54	Ag. labourer	Cury
	SKEWES	JANE	Daughter	Unmarried	26	At home	Cury
Gilly Cove	SKEWES	RICHARD	Head	Married	27	Ag. labourer	Cury
	SKEWES	CAROLINE	Wife	Married	28	Labourer's wife	St Hilary
Gilly Cove	SKEWES	ALICE	Head	Unmarried	56	Labourer	Cury
	SKEWES	ANN	Sister	Unmarried	52	Labourer	Cury
	SKEWES	JANE	Sister	Unmarried	47	Labourer	Cury
	SKEWES	WILLIAM H.	Nephew	Unmarried	11	Scholar	Cury
Gilly Cove	SKEWES	ELIZABETH M.	Servant	Unmarried	16	House servant	Cury
Treloskan	SKEWES	BLANCHE	Head	Widow	64	Washerwoman	Cury
Treloskan	SKEWES	JAMES	Head	Married	52	{ Farmer of 90 acres	Cury
	SKEWES	GRACE	Wife	Married	41	{ employing 2 men	Constantine
	SKEWES	ELIZA GRACE	Daughter	Unmarried	5	At home	Cury
	SKEWES	EDWARD	Brother	Unmarried	69	Assistant	Cury
	SKEWES	MARY	Niece	Unmarried	26	House servant	Cury

MAWGAN in MENEAGE (HO 107/1912)

Belofsack	SKEWES	WILLIAM	Head	Married	36	Ag. labourer	Cury
	SKEWES	AMELIA	Wife	Married	33	Ag. labourer	Mawgan
	SKEWES	EDWARD WILLIAM	Nephew	Unmarried	3		Mawgan
Lower Tregadra	SKEWES	JAMES	Servant	Unmarried	25	Farm labourer	Ruan Major

SITHNEY (HO 107/1912)

St Elvin	SKEWIS	JOSIAH	Head	Married	28	Farm labourer	Cury

St Elvin	SKEWIS	ELIZABETH	Wife		Married	35		Sithney
	SKEWIS	ELIZA	Daughter		Unmarried	4		Sithney
Tregoose	SKEWES	JOHN	Lodger		Married	39	Carpenter	Cury
Old Town, Sithney	SKEWES	WILLIAM	Head		Unmarried	28	Cordwainer	Cury

ST KEVERNE (HO 107/1913)

Laddewean	SKEWES	HENRY	Head		Married	49	School master	Ruan Major
	SKEWES	GRACE	Wife		Married	42		Ruan Major
	SKEWES	JANE	Daughter		Unmarried	18	Dressmaker	Helston
	SKEWES	HANNIBAL	Son		Unmarried	12	Scholar	St Martin
	SKEWES	SARAH ANN	Daughter		Unmarried	10	Scholar	St Martin
	SKEWES	SAMUEL HENRY	Son		Unmarried	6	Scholar	St Keverne
TRESKEWES	Sincock	Elizabeth	Wife		Married	50	Farmer's wife	St Keverne
	Sincock	William	Son		Unmarried	26	Farmer's son	St Keverne
	Peters	Thomas	Servant		Unmarried	20	Farm labourer	St Keverne
	Collins	Joanah	Servant		Unmarried	14	House servant	St Keverne
	Phillips	William	Servant		Unmarried	13	Farm labourer	St Keverne
	Martin	Henry	Lodger		Unmarried	14	Millers boy	St Keverne
TRESKEWES	Lory	James	Head		Married	35	⎧ Farmer of 25 acres	St Keverne
	Lory	Elizabeth	Wife		Married	34	⎩ emp. 1 lab & 1 boy	St Anthony
	Lory	Jacob	Son		Unmarried	5	Scholar	St Keverne
	Lory	Elizabeth	Daughter		Unmarried	4	Scholar	St Keverne
	Lory	James	Son		Unmarried	2		St Keverne
	Mitchell	Thomas	Servant		Unmarried	15	Servant	St Keverne
	Hocking	Thomas	Servant		Unmarried	36	Servant	St Keverne
	Hocking	Ann	Servant		Unmarried	16	Servant	St Keverne
LITTLE	Downing	Thomas	Head		Married	36	Ag labourer	St Keverne
TRESKEWES	Downing	Mary	Wife		Married	31		St Keverne
	Downing	Robert	Son		Unmarried	7		St Keverne
	Downing	John	Son		Unmarried	4		St Keverne
	Downing	Thomas	Son		Unmarried	3		St Keverne
	Downing	Henry	Son		Unmarried	2		St Keverne
	Downing	Susanna	Daughter		Unmarried	4 months		St Keverne

RUAN MAJOR (HO 107/1913)

Chybarlis	SKEWES	SUSAN J.	Niece to William & Eleanor Lugg		Unmarried	5	Visitor	Grade
Hendra	SKEWES	MARGARET A.	Granddaughter of Sarah Lugg		Unmarried	14	With her grandmtr.	Helston
Tresodden	SKEWES	ANTHONY	Head		Married	42	⎧ Farmer of 45 acres	Ruan Major
	SKEWES	CHRISTIAN	Wife		Married	38	⎩ employing 1 lab.	Ruan Major
	SKEWES	MARY	Daughter		Unmarried	16		Ruan Major
	SKEWES	ANN	Daughter		Unmarried	14		Ruan Major
	SKEWES	CATHERINE	Daughter		Unmarried	8		Ruan Major
	SKEWES	JAMES	Son		Unmarried	6		Ruan Major
	SKEWES	HENRY	Son		Unmarried	4		Ruan Major
	SKEWES	SAMUEL	Son		Unmarried	3		Ruan Major
	SKEWES	WILLIAM J.	Son		Unmarried	1		Ruan Major
	SKEWES	JANE	Mother		Widow	83	Annuitant	St Anthony
	SKEWES	THOMAS	Brother		Married	45	Employed on farm	Ruan Major

GRADE (HO 107/1913)

Kugger	SKEWES	LOVEDAY	Head		Married	42	Annuitant	Ruan Minor
Carne	SKEWES	EDWARD	Head		Widower	55	Farmer of 20 acres	St Keverne
	SKEWES	EDWARD H.	Son		Unmarried	15	Employed at home	St Keverne
	SKEWES	RICHARD L.	Son		Unmarried	13	Employed at home	St Keverne

RUAN MINOR (HO 107/1913)

Treal	SKEWES	JANE	Niece to John Evans, widower		Unmarried	16		Ruan Minor

CROWAN (HO 107/1913)

SKEWIS	Richards	Henry	Head		Married	55	Farm labourer	Crowan
	Richards	Jane	Wife		Married	56	Farmer's wife	Crowan
	Richards	William	Son		Unmarried	18	Copper miner	Crowan
	Richards	James	Son		Unmarried	14	Horse boy	Crowan
	Keveran	William	Lodger		Unmarried	23	Labourer	Crowan
SKEWIS	Reynolds	Ann	Head		Widow	66	Housekeeper	Crowan
	Reynolds	Ann	Daughter		Unmarried	39	Mine girl	Crowan
	Reynolds	George	Son		Unmarried	32	Tailor	Crowan
	Vivian	Jane	Servant		Unmarried	19	Tailor	Crowan

SKEWIS	Ward	Henry	Head	Married	31	Miner	Crowan
	Ward	Elizabeth	Wife	Married	30	Housewife	Crowan
	Ward	Elizabeth A.	Daughter	Unmarried	5		Crowan
	Ward	Thomas	Son	Unmarried	4		Crowan
	Ward	Mary J.	Daughter	Unmarried	2		Crowan
	Ward	William	Son	Unmarried	2 months		Crowan
SKEWIS	Cliff	Mary	Wife	Married	44		Breage
	Cliff	Ursella	Daughter	Unmarried	17		Breage
	Cliff	Thomas	Son	Unmarried	11	Horseboy	Breage
	Cliff	James	Son	Unmarried	10	Horseboy	Breage
	Cliff	Margaret	Daughter	Unmarried	7		Breage
	Cliff	John F.	Son	Unmarried	6		Breage
	Cliff	Elizabeth	Daughter	Unmarried	5		Breage
	Edwards	Ursella	Mother	Widow	69		Crowan
	Midlyn	Elizabeth	Relation	Unmarried	6		Crowan

BREAGE (HO 107/1913)

Pengelly	SKEWES	JOHN	Servant to John & Jane Wear, farmer of 105 acres	Unmarried	21	Ag. labourer	Cury

LANDEWEDNACK (HO 107/1913)

Lizard Village	SKEWIS	HENRY	Head	Married	31	Carpenter	Cury
	SKEWIS	HARRIET	Wife	Married	28		Cury
	SKEWIS	JAMES HENRY	Son	Unmarried	2		Land/nck
	SKEWIS	JOHN	Son	Unmarried	2 months		Land/nck

CROWAN (HO 107/1913)

Bolitho	SKEWES	WILLIAM	Head	Married	43	Farmer of 40 acres employing 1 lab.	Constantine
	SKEWES	ELIZABETH	Wife	Married	43		Sithney
	SKEWES	JOSEPH	Son	Unmarried	13	Farm labourer	Constantine
	SKEWES	CHRISTIAN	Daughter	Unmarried	12		Budock
	SKEWES	GRACE	Daughter	Unmarried	10		Sithney
	SKEWES	JAMES	Son	Unmarried	8		Sithney
	SKEWES	JOHN	Son	Unmarried	5		Crowan
	SKEWES	ELIZABETH	Daughter	Unmarried	2		Crowan

STITHIANS (HO 107/1914)

TRESKEWIS	Spargo	John	Head	Married	49	Copper miner	Stithians
	Spargo	Ann	Wife	Married	42	Housekeeper	Gwennap
	Spargo	Edward John	Son	Unmarried	7	Scholar	Stithians
	Spargo	Mary Ann	Visitor	Unmarried	15	Scholar	Stithians
TRESKEWIS	Oppy	John	Head	Married	34	Miner	Stithians
	Oppy	Elizabeth	Wife	Married	33		Stithians
	Oppy	John	Son	Unmarried	8	Scholar	Stithians
	Oppy	William	Son	Unmarried	5	Scholar	Stithians
	Oppy	Elizabeth	Daughter	Unmarried	4		Stithians
	Oppy	Thomas	Son	Unmarried	3		Stithians
	Oppy	Elizabeth	Servant	Unmarried	14	Servant	Gwennap
TRESKEWIS	Dunstan	William	Head	Married	53	Roper	Stithians
	Dunstan	Tonie	Wife	Married	50		Stithians
	Dunstan	Hugh	Son	Unmarried	24	Miner	Stithians
	Dunstan	Joseph	Son	Unmarried	20		Stithians
	Dunstan	Elizabeth	Daughter	Unmarried	21		Stithians
	Dunstan	Henry	Son	Unmarried	18	Farm labourer	Stithians
	Dunstan	Richard	Son	Unmarried	14	Farm labourer	Stithians

STITHIANS (HO 107/1914)

Rosemanowis	SKEWES	HENRY	Head	Married	30	Farmer of 40 acres	Constantine
	SKEWES	AVIS	Wife	Married	27		Stithians
	SKEWES	WILLIAM HENRY	Son	Unmarried	5		Stithians
	SKEWES	JAMES	Son	Unmarried	2		Stithians
	SKEWES	ALFRED	Son	Unmarried	2 months		Stithians
	Jenkin	John	Servant	Unmarried	16	Servant	Stithians
	Martin	Mary	Servant	Unmarried	16	Servant	Stithians

GWENNAP (HO 107/1914)

Chapel Street	SKEWES	ELIZABETH	Servant to John & Mary Rogers	Unmarried	20	House servant	Kenwyn
Wheal Virgin	SKEWES	JOHN	Head	Married	41	Copper miner	Kea
	SKEWES	MARY	Wife	Married	45		Camborne
	SKEWES	WILLIAM	Son	Unmarried	16	Copper miner	Kea
	SKEWES	MARGRY or MARY (difficult to read)	Daughter	Unmarried	13	Dressmaker asst.	Kea

Penance	SKEWES	JOHN	Head	Married	45	Farmer	Gwennap
	SKEWES	ANN	Wife	Married	43		Gwennap
	SKEWES	JOHN	Son	Unmarried	22	Miner	Gwennap
	SKEWES	RICHARD	Son	Unmarried	11		Gwennap
	SKEWES	MARY	Daughter	Unmarried	8	Works to miner	Gwennap
	SKEWES	SIMON	Son	Unmarried	6		Gwennap
	SKEWES	ELIZABETH A.	Daughter	Unmarried	3		Gwennap
	SKEWES	ALEXANDER	Son	Unmarried	1		Gwennap
Carharrack	SKEWES	JOHN	Head	Married	20	Copper miner	Gwennap
	SKEWES	MARY ANN	Wife	Married	21		Gwennap
Lanner	SKEWS	ANN	Head	Widow	61	House keeper	Gwennap
	SKEWS	RICHARD	Son	Unmarried	26	Grocer	Mould, Flints.
Carvannar	SKEWES	JAMES	Head	Married	41	Mine labourer	Gwennap
	SKEWES	CHARITY	Wife	Married	52	—	Constantine
	SKEWES	MARY	Daughter	Unmarried	22	—	Gwennap
	SKEWES	JAMES	Son	Unmarried	19	Agricultural labourer	Gwennap
	SKEWES	ROBERT	Son	Unmarried	15	Agricultural labourer	Gwennap
Carharrack	SKEWES	JOHN	Head	Married	41	Copper miner	Kea
	SKEWES	MARGARET A.	Wife	Married	45	—	Camborne
	SKEWES	WILLIAM	Son	Unmarried	16	Copper miner	Kea
	SKEWES	MARGERY A.	Daughter	Unmarried	13	Dressmaker's assistant	Kea

CAMBORNE (HO 107/1914)

College Street	SKEWES	MARY	Visitor to house of Thos & Mary Moyle	Unmarried	4		Camborne
New Road	SKEWIS	MARY	Visitor	Unmarried	54		Gwinear
	SKEWIS	LAVINIA	Visitor	Unmarried	44		Gwinear
	SKEWIS	MATILDA	Visitor	Unmarried	38		Gwinear
Gass Street	SKEWES	JAMES	Head	Married	60	Agricultural labourer	Camborne
Chapel Street	SKEWIS	EDWARD	Lodger	Unmarried	27	Butcher	Camborne
Cottage, Back Lane	SKEWIS	NANCY	Head	Widow	72	Annuitant	Scilly Islands
Pendarves Row	SKEWIS	JAMES	Head	Married	33	Miner	Camborne
	SKEWIS	SALLY	Wife	Married	30	—	Camborne
	SKEWIS	EMILY	Daughter	Unmarried	5	Scholar	Camborne
	SKEWIS	STEPHEN	Son	Unmarried	3	—	Camborne
	SKEWIS	MARY J.	Daughter	Unmarried	1	—	Camborne
Trelowarren St.	SKEWES	ANN	Head	Married	73	Small house property	Camborne
Vyvyan's Row	SKEWIS	JANE	Head	Widow	59	Miner's widow lodging	Camborne
	SKEWIS	ELIZABETH	Daughter	Unmarried	30	House keeper	Camborne
	SKEWIS	CAROLINE	Daughter	Unmarried	24	—	Camborne
	SKEWIS	JULIA	Daughter	Unmarried	21	—	Camborne
	SKEWIS	LAVINIA	Daughter	Unmarried	16	—	Camborne
Treswithian Village	SKEWIS	STEPHEN	Head	Married	47	Farm labourer	Camborne
	SKEWIS	ELIZABETH	Wife	Married	52		Camborne
	SKEWIS	ELIZABETH	Daughter	Unmarried	15	At home	Camborne
Bell Lake	SKEWES	JOHN	Head	Unmarried	34	Farmer of 15 acres	Illogan
	SKEWES	PHILLEY	Sister	Unmarried	46	—	Illogan
	SKEWES	MARY ANN	Daughter	Unmarried	4	—	Illogan
Pengegan	SKEWS	WILLIAM	Head	Married	29	Copper miner	Camborne
	SKEWS	PEGGY	Wife	Married	27	—	Camborne
Berriper, Penponds	SKEWIS	HENRY	Head	Married	38	Copper miner	Camborne
	SKEWIS	HANNAH	Wife	Married	37		Camborne
	SKEWIS	WILLIAM HENRY	Son	Unmarried	18	Copper miner	Camborne
	SKEWIS	RICHARD MARTIN	Son	Unmarried	16	Copper miner	Camborne
	SKEWIS	ELIZABETH	Daughter	Unmarried	14		Camborne
	SKEWIS	STEPHEN	Son	Unmarried	12	Miner	Camborne
	SKEWIS	PHILIP	Son	Unmarried	9	Scholar	Camborne
	SKEWIS	MARY	Daughter	Unmarried	7		Camborne

	SKEWIS	SAMUEL	Son	Unmarried	6		Camborne
	SKEWIS	HENRY	Son	Unmarried	1		Camborne

ILLOGAN (HO 107/1915)

Highway	SKEWS	WILLIAM	Head	Married	33	Blacksmith	Kea
	SKEWS	MARY	Wife	Married	32	—	Gwennap
	SKEWS	WILLIAM	Son	Unmarried	11	—	Kea
	SKEWS	THOMAS	Son	Unmarried	9	—	Kea
	SKEWS	MARY	Daughter	Unmarried	5	—	Kenwyn
	SKEWS	TERESA	Daughter	Unmarried	3	—	Camborne
	SKEWS	MATTHEW	Son	Unmarried	1	—	Illogan
Piece	SKEWES	WILLIAM	Head	Married	26	Copper ore miner	Camborne
	SKEWES	SARAH	Wife	Married	20	—	St Agnes
	SKEWES	JOHN	Son	Unmarried	1	—	Camborne
Higher Treskillard	SKEWIS	JAMES	Head	Married	26	Copper mine labourer	Cury
	SKEWIS	ELEANOR	Wife	Married	35	—	Mawgan
	SKEWIS	ELIZABETH M.	Daughter	Unmarried	2	—	Mawgan
Treskillard	SKEWES	JAMES	Head	Married	54	{ Occupier of 8 acres of	Cury
	SKEWES	SIMONETTE	Wife	Married	48	{ land and ag. labourer	Cury
	SKEWES	WILLIAM	Son	Unmarried	22	—	Cury
	SKEWES	ANN	Daughter	Unmarried	20	—	Cury
	SKEWES	ALICE	Daughter	Unmarried	17	—	Cury
	SKEWES	JOHN	Son	Unmarried	16	—	Cury
	SKEWES	EDWARD	Son	Unmarried	13	—	Cury
	SKEWES	ELIZABETH	Daughter	Unmarried	10	—	Cury
	SKEWES	MARY	Daughter	Unmarried	9	—	Cury
	SKEWES	BLANCH	Daughter	Unmarried	6	—	Cury
	SKEWES	ELLEN	Daughter	Unmarried	2	—	Cury

REDRUTH (HO 107/1915)

Trefusis	SKEWIS	HENRY	Head	Married	47	Copper miner	Gwennap
	SKEWIS	ANN	Wife	Married	51	—	Gwennap
	SKEWIS	WILLIAM	Son	Unmarried	22	Copper miner	Gwennap
	SKEWIS	HENRY	Son	Unmarried	16	Copper miner	Gwennap
	SKEWIS	JAMES	Son	Unmarried	12	Copper miner	Gwennap
	SKEWIS	SUSAN	Daughter	Unmarried	9	Scholar	Gwennap
	SKEWIS	CATHERINE	Daughter	Unmarried	7	Scholar	Gwennap
Sparnon	SKEWES	MARY	Servant	Unmarried	19	{ General servant to John Trevena and family	Redruth
9, Hodders Row	SKEWES	JOHN	Head	Married	37	Mason	Redruth
	SKEWES	SARAH	Wife	Married	39	—	Redruth
	SKEWES	JOSEPH	Son	Unmarried	12	Apprentice cabinet maker	Redruth
	SKEWES	LEWIS	Son	Unmarried	10	Mason's labourer	Redruth
	SKEWES	JOHN	Son	Unmarried	9	—	Redruth
	SKEWES	JANE	Daughter	Unmarried	6		Redruth
	SKEWES	CHARLES	Son	Unmarried	4	—	Redruth
Blight's Row	SKEWES	THOMAS	Head	Married	29	Engine fitter	Kenwyn
	SKEWES	MARY ANN	Wife	Married	29	—	Redruth
	SKEWES	MARY JANE	Daughter	Unmarried	3	—	Redruth
	SKEWES	ISABELLA R.	Daughter	Unmarried	1	—	Redruth
26, Fords Row	SKEWES	MARGERY	Head	Married	48	Annuitant engineer's wife	Kenwyn
	SKEWES	ELIZABETH	Daughter	Unmarried	14	Scholar	Illogan
	SKEWES	MARY	Daughter	Unmarried	10	Scholar	Illogan
	SKEWES	MATTHEW	Son	Unmarried	9	Scholar	Redruth
	SKEWES	WILLIAM S.	Son	Unmarried	4	Scholar	Redruth
	SKEWES	JOHN WILLIAM	G/son	Unmarried	4	—	Redruth
Miners Row	SKEWES	JOHN H.	Head	Married	38	Copper miner	Camborne
	SKEWES	ANN	Wife	Married	38	—	Redruth
	SKEWES	MARY	Daughter	Unmarried	12	—	Camborne

PERRANUTHNOE (HO 107/1918)

Goldsithney	SKEWES	JAMES	Head	Married	41	Farm labourer	Cury
	SKEWES	MARGARET	Wife	Married	35	—	St Just
	SKEWES	ELIZABETH	Daughter	Unmarried	6	At home	St Erth
	SKEWES	ANNIE	Daughter	Unmarried	5	At home	St Erth

ST HILARY (HO 107/1918)

Colenso	SKEWES	RICHARD	Visitor	Unmarried	14	{ Visitor to home of Ralph and Mary Laity	Germoe

CENSUS RETURNS FOR 1851 — PLYMOUTH DEVON HO 107/1878

15, Camden Street:

Boulter	Fanny	Head	Widow	47	Annuitant	Stratton
SKUES	RICHARD	Son	Unmarried	18	Printers compositor	Plymouth
SKUES	ELLEN	Daughter	Unmarried	16	Dressmaker	Plymouth
SKUES	JAMES	Son	Unmarried	13	Scholar at home	Plymouth
Colton	Mary	Sister	Unmarried	49	Annuitant	Bude

5, Week Street:

SKEWS	MARY	Head	Widow	47	Coopers widow	Plymouth
SKEWS	ELLEN	Daughter	Unmarried	20	—	Plymouth
Smith	Joseph	Brother in law	Unmarried	60	Cooper	Plymouth

72, Coburg Street:

SKEWES	WILLIAM	Head	Married	30	Potato dealer	Stonehouse
SKEWES	HANNAH	Wife	Married	40	—	Devonport

18, Stillman Street, Sutton on Plym, Plymouth

SKEWS	JOHN	Head	Widower	52	Coal porter	St Agnes

CENSUS RETURNS FOR 1851 — ABERGAVENNY, MONMOUTH HO 107/2448

East Place, Tredegar, Bedwellty, Monmouth

SKEWES	JAMES	Head	Married	41	Engineer	Tredegar
SKEWES	ELIZABETH	Wife	Married	33	—	Tredegar
SKEWES	MARY	Daughter	Unmarried	12	—	Tredegar
SKEWES	JANE	Daughter	Unmarried	7	—	Tredegar
SKEWES	ROBERT	Son	Unmarried	5	Scholar	Tredegar
SKEWES	ELIZABETH	Daughter	Unmarried	2	—	Rhymney

In this area there are many iron and coal works: Iron foundries at Victoria and Rhymney.

CENSUS RETURNS FOR 1851 NEATH, GLAMORGAN, SOUTH WALES

Mile End Row,	SKEWES	HARRIET	Head	Widow	28	Cook	Cornwall
Lower Lantwit	SKEWES	MARY	Daughter		5	Scholar	Glamorgan
	SKEWES	RICHARD	Son		3		Glamorgan

CENSUS RETURNS FOR CORNWALL — 1861

1861 PUBLIC RECORD OFFICE REFERENCES AND DISTRICTS   ALL NUMBERS ARE PREFACED BY "RG 9"

1512	KILKHAMPTON	No Entry	1542	ST COLUMB	No Entry	1572	HELSTON	See Over
1513	STRATTON	No Entry	1543	ST COLUMB	See Over	1573	ST KEVERNE	See Over
1514	WEEK ST MARY	No Entry	1544	NEWLYN	No Entry	1574	BREAGE	No Entry
1515	BOSCASTLE	No Entry	1545	FOWEY	No Entry	1575	CROWAN	See Over
1516	CAMELFORD	No Entry	1546	FOWEY	No Entry	1576	GWENNAP	See Over
1517	ALTARNUN	No Entry	1547	ST AUSTELL	See Over	1577	GWENNAP	See Over
1518	NORTH PETHERWIN	No Entry	1548	ST AUSTELL	No Entry	1578	GWENNAP	See Over
1519	ST STEPHEN	No Entry	1549	ST AUSTELL	No Entry	1579	REDRUTH	See Over
1520	LAUNCESTON	No Entry	1550	MEVAGISSEY	See Over	1580	REDRUTH	See Over
1521	NORTHILL	No Entry	1551	GRAMPOUND	No Entry	1581	ILLOGAN	See Over
1522	ANTONY	No Entry	1552	PROBUS	No Entry	1582	ILLOGAN	See Over
1523	ANTONY	No Entry	1553	ST JUST	No Entry	1583	CAMBORNE	See Over
1524	ST GERMANS	No Entry	1554	ST AGNES	No Entry	1584	CAMBORNE	See Over
1525	SALTASH	No Entry	1555	ST AGNES	No Entry	1585	PHILLACK	No Entry
1526	CALLINGTON	See Over	1556	ST AGNES	See Over	1586	PHILLACK	See Over
1527	CALLINGTON	No Entry	1557	ST CLEMENT	See Over	1587	UNY LELANT	No Entry
1528	LISKEARD	See Over	1558	ST CLEMENT	See Over	1588	UNY LELANT	No Entry
1529	LISKEARD	See Over	1559	KENWYN	See Over	1589	ST IVES	No Entry
1530	LISKEARD	No Entry	1560	KENWYN	See Over	1590	ST IVES	See Over
1531	LOOE	No Entry	1561	KENWYN	See Over	1591	MARAZION	No Entry
1532	LERRIN	No Entry	1562	KEA	See Over	1592	PENZANCE	No Entry
1533	LANLIVERY	No Entry	1563	KEA	See Over	1593	PENZANCE	No Entry
1534	LANLIVERY	No Entry	1564	MYLOR	No Entry	1594	PENZANCE	No Entry
1535	ST MABYN	No Entry	1565	FALMOUTH	See Over	1595	PENZANCE	No Entry
1536	BODMIN	No Entry	1566	FALMOUTH	See Over	1596	ST JUST	No Entry
1537	BODMIN	No Entry	1567	PENRYN	See Over	1597	ST JUST	No Entry
1538	EGLOSHAYLE	No Entry	1568	CONSTANTINE	See Over	1598	ST JUST	No Entry
1539	EGLOSHAYLE	No Entry	1569	WENDRON	See Over	1599	ST BURYAN	No Entry
1540	PADSTOW	No Entry	1570	WENDRON	No Entry	1600	SCILLY ISLANDS	No Entry
1541	PADSTOW	No Entry	1571	WENDRON	See Over			

ADDRESS	NAME		RELATION TO HEAD OF HOUSEHOLD	STATUS	AGE	PROFESSION	WHERE BORN
ALTARNUN, LAUNCESTON (Public Record Office Reference RG 9 — 1517)							
Trewint	SKEWS	JOHN	Head	Married	38	Copper miner	Chacewater
	SKEWS	ISABELLA	Wife	Married	30		Altarnun
	SKEWS	ELIZABETH	Daughter	Unmarried	10		Altarnun
	SKEWS	SAMUEL	Son	Unmarried	5		Altarnun
	SKEWS	JOHN	Son	Unmarried	2		Altarnun
	SKEWS	ALFRED	Son	Unmarried	8 months		Altarnun
ST IVE, CALLINGTON (RG 9 — 1526)							
Woolston	SKEWS	ELIZABETH	Wife	Married	25	Miner's wife	Altarnun
	SKEWS	FANNY GREGORY	Daughter	Unmarried	4	Scholar	Altarnun
	SKEWS	WILLIAM HENRY	Son	Unmarried	2		Altarnun
	SKEWS	JOHN GREGORY	Son	Unmarried	6 months		Altarnun
ST CLEER, LISKEARD (RG 9 — 1528)							
St Cleer	SKEWS	SOPHIA	Head	Ibid	67	Housekeeper	Truro
Village	SKEWS	SAMUEL	Son	Unmarried	21	Copper miner	Kea
LISKEARD (RG 9 — 1529)							
Green Lane	Cock	Ann	Head	Widow	51	Charwoman	Liskeard
	SKEWS	MARY GRACE	Granddaughter	Unmarried	3		St Cleer
ST WENN, St Columb (RG 9 — 1543)							
GREAT	Slick	Thomas	Head	Married	35	Farmer of 140	Roche
SKEWES	Slick	Elizabeth	Wife	Married	32	acres, employing	Roche
	Slick	Tom	Son	Unmarried	5	2 boys and	St Wenn
	Slick	Nicholas	Son	Unmarried	2 months	2 labourers	St Wenn
	Slick	Hannah	Daughter	Unmarried	9	Scholar	St Wenn
	Slick	Elizabeth	Daughter	Unmarried	6	Scholar	St Wenn
	Slick	Emily	Daughter	Unmarried	3		St Wenn
	Harris	Mary	House servant	Unmarried	17	Servant	St Columb
	Bray	Harriet	Servant	Unmarried	14	House servant	Llanivet
	Cleave	Thomas	Servant	Unmarried	21	Carter	St Wenn
	Stephens	Richard	Servant	Unmarried	14	Ploughboy	St Wenn
LITTE SKEWES	Blake	Peggy	Head	Widow	53	Farmer of 50	St Merryn
	Blake	Amelia	Daughter	Unmarried	19	acres; empl.	St Wenn
	Blake	Jemima	Daughter	Unmarried	17	1 lab & 1 boy	St Wenn
	Blake	Marshall	Son	Unmarried	16		St Wenn
ST AUSTELL (RG 9 — 1547)							
125, Back	SKEWS	JAMES	Head	Married	59	Lime burner	St Ewe
Row, Charlestown	SKEWS	ELIZABETH	Wife	Married	60		St Austell
ST EWE, MEVAGISSEY (RG 9 — 1550)							
Polgooth	SKEWS	JOANNA	Head	Widow	87	Pauper	St Ewe
	Thoms	Grace	Daughter	Widow	67	Pauper	St Ewe
ST AGNES, TRURO							
Hamlet of Goonvrea	SKEWES	WALTER	Brother to head of household James Mayne (34) and wife Julia (30) and Baby Clara (6 months)	Unmarried	20	Engine driver	St Agnes
ST CLEMENT, TRURO							
No 3,	SKEWES	ANN BUCKLAND	Head	Widow	50		St Allen
Prospect	SKEWES	ELIZABETH ANN	Daughter	Unmarried	15	Scholar	Gwennap
Place	SKEWES	CHARLOTTE M.	Daughter	Unmarried	12	Scholar	Gwennap
	SKEWES	MARY ANN	Daughter	Unmarried	10	Scholar	Kenwyn
St Paul's Row	SKEWES	JOHN	Head	Married	30	Cabinet maker	Kenwyn
	SKEWES	MARY	Wife	Married	29		Padstow
	SKEWES	ELIZABETH J.	Daughter	Unmarried	11	Scholar	St Clement
	SKEWES	JOHN	Son	Unmarried	4		St Clement
	SKEWES	WILLIAM B.	Son	Unmarried	2		St Clement
	SKEWES	HENRIETTA	Daughter	Unmarried	6 months		St Clement
Solar Row	SKEWES	ANN	Head	Widow	45	Charwoman	St Clement
	SKEWES	EMMA STEPHENS	Daughter	Unmarried	19	Dressmaker	Truro
TRURO (RG 9 — 1558)							
Castle Street	SKEWES	SUSAN J.	Housekeeper to Parkin family	Unmarried	18	Housekeeper	Cornwall
Charles Street	SKEWES	PETER	Head	Married	69	Copper miner	Kea
	SKEWES	MARY	Wife	Married	64		Kenwyn

PARISH of KENWYN, TRURO (RG 9 — 1560)

Richmond Hill	SKEWES	MARY	Head	Unmarried	66	Retired publican (blind)	Gwinear
	SKEWES	LAVINIA	Sister	Unmarried	54		Gwinear
	SKEWES	MATILDA	Sister	Unmarried	52		Gwinear
Daniel Street	SKEWS	GRACE	Servant	Unmarried	16	House servant	Kea
Daniel Street	SKEWS	THOMAS	Head	Married	62	Builder & grocer	Kea
	SKEWS	JANE	Wife	Married	62		St Erth
	SKEWS	PHILIPPA	Daughter	Unmarried	29		Truro
Penstraze	SKEWS	RICHARD	Head	Married	42	Small farmer	Kea
	SKEWS	ELIZABETH ANN	Wife	Married	32	Small farmer	Kea
	SKEWS	RICHARD	Son	Unmarried	2		Kenwyn
Tomperrow	Coode	Grace	Head	Married	66	Miner's wife	Perranzabuloe
	SKEWS	JAMES	Son	Unmarried	40	Agricultural lab.	Kenwyn

PARISH of CHACEWATER, TRURO (RG 9 — 1561)

Back Lane Chacewater	SKEWS	MARY	Head	Widow	62		Blackwater
Chacewater	Hatton	Dinah	Head	Widow	61	Former tailoress	St Agnes
	Hatton	John	Son	Unmarried	37		St Agnes
	Hatton	Dinah	Daughter	Unmarried	19	Dressmaker	St Agnes
	Hatton	Elizabeth	Daughter	Unmarried	15	Housekeeper	St Agnes
	SKEWS	EMMA	Granddaughter	Unmarried	4		Liskeard

PARISH of KEA, TRURO (RG — 1562)

Hugus Common	SKEWS	PETER	Head	Widower	56	Miner	Kea
	Holman	Elizabeth Ann	Daughter	Widow	25	Miner's widow	Kea
	SKEWS	PETER	Son	Unmarried	21	Miner	Kea
	SKEWS	MARY	Daughter	Unmarried	18	Miner's daughter	Kea
	SKEWS	EMILY	Daughter	Unmarried	11	Scholar	Kea
Kerley	SKEWES	RICHARD	Head	Widower	77	Farmer of 4 acres	Kea
	SKEWES	HARRIET	Daughter-in-law	Widow	41	Housekeeper	Kea
	SKEWES	JOHN	Grandson	Unmarried	14	Mine engine man	Kea
	SKEWES	MATTHEW	Grandson	Unmarried	9	Scholar	Kea
Kerley	SKEWES	PETER	Head	Married	37	Farmer of 12 acres	Kea
	SKEWES	GRACE	Wife	Married	53	Farmer's wife	Penryn
	SKEWES	RICHARD	Son	Unmarried	28	Copper & tin miner	Kea
	SKEWES	MARY	Daughter	Unmarried	24	Dressmaker	Kea
	SKEWES	JOHN	Son	Unmarried	22	Copper & tin miner	Kea
	SKEWES	THOMAS	Son	Unmarried	20	Copper & tin miner	Kea
	SKEWES	PETER	Son	Unmarried	18	Copper & tin miner	Kea
	SKEWES	GRACE	Daughter	Unmarried	16	House maid	Kea
	SKEWES	MARIA	Daughter	Unmarried	14	Scholar	Kea
Kerley	SKEWES	MARY	Head	Widow	60	School mistress	Kea
Seveock Hill	SKEWES	SUSANNAH	Head	Married	39	General servant	Kenwyn
	SKEWES	WILLIAM	Son	Unmarried	18	Copper & tin miner	Kenwyn
	SKEWES	ELIZABETH	Daughter	Unmarried	9	Copper mine girl	Kenwyn
	SKEWES	SAMUEL	Son	Unmarried	8		Kenwyn
	SKEWES	AURELIA	Daughter	Unmarried	6	Scholar	Kenwyn

PARISH of CHACEWATER (RG 9 — 1563)

Killiwerris	SKEWES	JOHN	Head	Married	58	{ Farmer of 60 acres	Kea
	SKEWES	ANN	Wife	Married	54	{ emp. 2 men & 2 boys	Kea
	SKEWES	GRACE	Daughter	Unmarried	26	Tailoress	Kea
	SKEWES	JOHN	Son	Unmarried	22	Farm labourer	Kea
	SKEWES	EMMA	Daughter	Unmarried	19	House assistant	Kea
	SKEWES	ELLEN	Daughter	Unmarried	18	Dressmaker	Kea
	SKEWES	LAVINIA	Daughter	Unmarried	16	House assistant	Kea
	SKEWES	WILLIAM	Son	Unmarried	15	Farm labourer	Kea
Bivvlet Vale, Feock	SKEWS	EDWIN	Boarder	Unmarried	15	Carpenter	St Austell

PARISH of FALMOUTH (RG 9 — 1565)

Porhan Street	SKEWES	THOMAS	Head	Married	68	Cordwainer	Falmouth
	SKEWES	GRACE	Wife	Married	66		Constantine
Smithick Hill	SKEWES	BENJAMIN HELLINGS	Head	Married	35	Cordwainer	Falmouth
	SKEWES	CAROLINE	Wife	Married	34		St Hilary

Smithick	SKEWES	CHARLES	Head	Married	30	Shoemaker	Falmouth
Hill	SKEWES	ELIZABETH	Wife	Married	32		Marazion
	SKEWES	CHARLES	Son	Unmarried	4	Scholar	Falmouth
	SKEWES	WILLIAM JOHN	Son	Unmarried	1		Falmouth
Treverna	Bath	May	Head	Widow	75	Charwoman	Mabe
	SKEWIS	AVIS	Daughter	Widow	37	Charwoman	Stithians

PARISH of PENRYN (RG 9 — 1567)

Quay Road	Millar	Hannah	Wife	Married	62	Seaman's wife	Devonshire
	SKEWES	SUSANNAH	Sister	Widow	54	Labourer's wife	Budock

PARISH of MAWNAN (RG 9 — 1568)

Little	SKEWES	WILLIAM	Head	Married	66	⎰Farmer of 8 acres	Cury
Insight	SKEWES	CHRISTIAN	Wife	Married	66	⎱employing 1 boy	Ruan Major
Farm	SKEWES	JOHN	Son	Unmarried	22	Agricultural lab.	St Keverne
	Phillips	William	Grandson	Unmarried	4	Scholar	St Keverne
Mawnan	SKEWES	EDWARD	Head	Married	42	Blacksmith	Ruan Major
Smith	SKEWES	MARY	Wife	Married	40		Southwark, London
	SKEWES	SAMUEL	Brother	Unmarried	21	Blacksmith	Mawnan
	Oates	John	Cousin	Unmarried	20	Apprentice	St Keverne
Mawnan	SKEWES	JAMES	Head	Married	45	⎰Farmer of 30 acres	Ruan Major
Smith	SKEWES	FRANCES	Wife	Married	35	⎱emp. 1 man & 1 boy	Mawnan
	SKEWES	HESTER ANN	Daughter	Unmarried	14	Farmer's daughter	Mawnan
	SKEWES	FRANCES MARIA	Daughter	Unmarried	13	Scholar	Mawnan
	SKEWES	EDWARD	Son	Unmarried	11	Scholar	Mawnan
	SKEWES	WILLIAM HENRY	Son	Unmarried	9	Scholar	Mawnan
	SKEWES	EMILY KEMPTHORNE	Daughter	Unmarried	7	Scholar	Mawnan
	SKEWES	ALMA JANE	Daughter	Unmarried	4	Scholar	Mawnan
	SKEWES	JAMES LUGG	Son	Unmarried	2		Mawnan
	SKEWES	MARY	Daughter	Unmarried	6 months		Mawnan

PARISH of CONSTANTINE (RG 9 — 1568)

Church	SKEWES	WILLIAM	Head	Married	56	Ag. labourer	Gunwalloe
Town	SKEWES	REBECCA	Wife	Married	56		Breage
Bosawsack	SKEWIS	JOSIAH	Head	Married	39	⎰Farmer of 100 acres	Constantine
	SKEWIS	FANNY	Wife	Married	34	⎱emp. 3 men & 2 boys	Budock
	SKEWIS	LAURA	Daughter	Unmarried	6	Scholar	Constantine
	SKEWIS	JAMES	Son	Unmarried	3		Constantine
	SKEWIS	WILLIAM HENRY	Nephew	Unmarried	14	Shepherd	Stithians
	SKEWIS	JOSIAH	Nephew	Unmarried	13	Carter	Stithians

PARISH of WENDRON (RG 9 — 1569)

Degibua	SKEWES	WILLIAM	Head	Married	46	Agricultural labourer	Cury
	SKEWES	ARMELIA	Wife	Married	41		Mawgan
St Elvan,	SKEWES	JOSIAH	Head	Married	37	Agricultural labourer	Cury
Sithney	SKEWES	ELIZABETH	Wife	Married	47		Sithney
	SKEWES	ELIZA ANN	Daughter	Unmarried	14		Sithney
Trannack	SKEWES	JOHN	Head	Married	47	Wheelwright	Cury
	SKEWES	MARTHA	Wife	Married	43		Sithney

PARISH of GUNWALLOE (RG 9 — 1572)

Gwills	SKEWES	WILLIAM	Servant	Unmarried	16	Farm servant	Cury

PARISH of CURY, HELSTON (RG 9 — 1572)

Crosslanes	SKEWES	JULIA	Lodger	Unmarried	23	Washerwoman	Cury
Chypons	SKEWES	JOHN	Head	Married	46	Farm labourer	Cury
	SKEWES	ELIZABETH	Daughter	Unmarried	17	Charwoman	Cury
	SKEWES	FREDERICK	Grandson	Unmarried	3		Cury
	(It is likely that John married someone with surname of HENDRY)						
Lanfom	SKEWES	JOHN	Servant	Unmarried	11		Cury
Nanplough	SKEWES	ELIZA	Servant	Unmarried	17	Servant	Cury
Polun	SKEWES	BLANCH	Head	Unmarried	73	Poultry dealer	Cury
Penvesse	SKEWES	JANE	Servant	Unmarried	34	Washerwoman	Cury
Nantithet	SKEWES	EDWARD	Head	Married	47	⎧Farmer of 8 acres	Cury
	SKEWES	JULIA	Wife	Married	36	⎨employing 1 man &	Landewednack
	SKEWES	LOVEDAY HENDY	Daughter	Unmarried	19	⎩3 boys	Cury

	SKEWES	MARTHA ELIZABETH	Daughter	Unmarried 17	Shoebinder	Cury
	SKEWES	ELIZA	Daughter	Unmarried 13	Scholar	Cury
	SKEWES	JAMES	Son	Unmarried 10	Scholar	Cury
	SKEWES	THOMAS WILLIAM	Son	Unmarried 8	Scholar	Cury
	SKEWES	HENRY	Son	Unmarried 4	Scholar	Cury
	SKEWES	ANNIE	Daughter	Unmarried 2		Cury
	SKEWES	BESSIE	Daughter	Unmarried 3 months		Cury
	SKEWES	SAMUEL	Nephew	Unmarried 18	Apprentice	Cury
Nantithet	SKEWES	EDWARD	Head	Unmarried 46	Cripple	Cury
	SKEWES	ELIZABETH	Sister	Unmarried 42	Washerwoman	Cury
	SKEWES	ELIZABETH MARY	Daughter	Unmarried 7	Scholar	Cury
Nantithet	SKEWES	JOHN	Head	Married 25	Cordwainer	Cury
	SKEWES	SUSAN	Wife	Married 27	Wife	Feock
	SKEWES	WILLIAM H.	Son	Unmarried 3 months		Cury
Gilly Lane	SKEWES	WILLIAM	Head	Widower 52	Agricultural labourer	Cury
	SKEWES	ALICE	Daughter	Unmarried 23	Dressmaker	Cury
	SKEWES	EMILY	Daughter	Unmarried 21	Housekeeper	Cury
	SKEWES	WILLIAM	Son	Unmarried 12	Agricultural workboy	Cury
	SKEWES	JOHN WESLEY	Grandson	Unmarried 11 months		Cury
Gilly Lane	SKEWES	ALICE	Head	Unmarried 65	Infirm	Cury
	SKEWES	ANN	Sister	Unmarried 63	Farm labourer	Cury
Treloskan	SKEWES	GRACE	Head	Widow 50	⎰ Farmer of 80 acres	Constantine
	SKEWES	ELIZA GRACE	Daughter	Unmarried 15	⎱ emp. 3 men & 1 boy	Cury

PARISH of St MARTIN, HELSTON (RG 9 — 1573)

Trecoose	SKEWES	HENRY	Head	Married 59	⎰ Clerk to Sir R.R.	Ruan Major
	SKEWES	GRACE	Wife	Married 51	⎱ Vyvyan, Trelowarren	Ruan Major
	SKEWES	JANE LUGG	Daughter	Unmarried 28	Milliner	Helston
	SKEWES	MARGARET H.	Daughter	Unmarried 24	Milliner	Helston
	SKEWES	SARAH ANN	Daughter	Unmarried 20	Milliner	St Martin
	SKEWES	SAMUEL HENRY	Son	Unmarried 16	Scholar	St Martin

PARISH of St KEVERNE, HELSTON (RG 9 — 1573)

Trabo Village	SKEWES	JOSEPH	Servant	Unmarried 25	Carter	Cury
Carne Farm	SKEWES	EDWARD	Head	Widower 61	Farmer of 20 acres	St Keverne
House, Grade	SKEWES	RICHARD LORY	Son	Unmarried 23	Farmer's son	St Keverne
	SKEWES	SUSAN I.	Daughter	Unmarried 14	Farmer's daughter	Grade

PARISH of RUAN MINOR, HELSTON (RG 9 — 1573)

Churchtown	SKEWES	LOVEDAY	Head	Married 52	Grocer	Ruan Minor

PARISH of RUAN MAJOR, HELSTON (RG 9 — 1573)

Tresodden	SKEWES	ANTHONY	Head	Married 52	⎰ Farmer of 20 acres	Ruan Major
	SKEWES	CHRISTIANA	Wife	Married 40	⎱ employing 2 labs.	Ruan Major
	SKEWES	MARY	Daughter	Unmarried 26	Farmer's daughter	Ruan Major
	SKEWES	ANN	Daughter	Unmarried 24	Farmer's daughter	Ruan Major
	SKEWES	CATHERINE	Daughter	Unmarried 18	Farmer's daughter	Ruan Major
	SKEWES	JAMES	Son	Unmarried 16	Farmer's son	Ruan Major
	SKEWES	HENRY	Son	Unmarried 15	Scholar	Ruan Major
	SKEWES	SAMUEL	Son	Unmarried 13	Scholar	Ruan Major
	SKEWES	WILLIAM	Son	Unmarried 11	Scholar	Ruan Major
	SKEWES	HANNIBAL	Son	Unmarried 6	Scholar	Ruan Major
	SKEWES	GEORGE	Son	Unmarried 3	Scholar	Ruan Major

PARISH of LANDEWEDNACK (RG 9 — 1573)

Three Tuns Hotel	SKEWES	HENRY	Head	Married 41	Carpenter master emp. 1 boy	Cury
	SKEWES	HARRIET	Wife	Married 38	Hotel keeper	Cury
	SKEWES	JAMES HENRY	Son	Unmarried 12	Scholar	Landewednack
	SKEWES	JOHN	Son	Unmarried 10	Scholar	Landewednack
	SKEWES	WILLIAM	Son	Unmarried 8	Scholar	Landewednack
	SKEWES	MARY ANN M.	Daughter	Unmarried 6	Scholar	Landewednack
	SKEWES	THOMAS	Son	Unmarried 4	Scholar	Landewednack
	SKEWES	SARAH	?	Widow 63	House servant	Redruth

Private house near Three Tuns Hotel

	SKEWES	MARY	Visitor	Unmarried 15	Domestic	Cury

PARISH of CROWAN (RG 9 — 1575)

Horse Downs	SKEWES	JOHN	Head	Married	35	Copper miner	Crowan
	SKEWES	GRACE	Wife	Married	37	Copper miner	Crowan
	SKEWES	JOHN	Son	Unmarried	7		Crowan
	SKEWES	RICHARD	Son	Unmarried	1		Crowan
	Carusen	Richard	Brother in law	Unmarried	22	Copper miner	Crowan
Cargenwen	SKEWES	JOHN	Head	Unmarried	43	Farmer of 22 acres	Illogan
	SKEWES	PHILIPPA	Sister	Unmarried	51	Farmer's sister	Illogan
	SKEWES-CRASE	MARY ANN	Illegitimate daughter	Unmarried	14	Farmer's daughter	Camborne
Bolitho	SKEWES	WILLIAM	Head	Married	55	Farmer	Constantine
	SKEWES	ELIZABETH	Wife	Married	53	Farmer's wife	Sithney
	SKEWES	JOSEPH	Son	Unmarried	23	Farm labourer	Constantine
	SKEWES	CHRISTIAN	Daughter	Unmarried	22	House maid	Budock
	SKEWES	GRACE	Daughter	Unmarried	20	House maid	Sithney
	SKEWES	JAMES	Son	Unmarried	18	Farm labourer	Sithney
	SKEWES	JOHN	Son	Unmarried	15	Farm labourer	Crowan
	SKEWES	ELIZABETH	Daughter	Unmarried	13	Scholar	Crowan

PARISH of GWENNAP (RG 9 — 1576)

Churchtown	SKEWS	JOHN	Head	Married	30	Miner	Gwennap
	SKEWS	MARY	Wife	Married	30	Miner's wife	Gwennap
	SKEWS	JOHN	Son	Unmarried	9	Scholar	Gwennap
Simmons Street	SKEWES	MARY ANN	Head	Married	30	Dressmaker & milliner	Kenwyn
	SKEWES	MARY	Daughter	Unmarried	9	Scholar	Gwennap
	SKEWES	FANNY JANE	Daughter	Unmarried	2		Gwennap
Pink Moor	SKEWES	JULIA	Head	Unmarried	50	Former schoolmistress	Kenwyn
Little Carharrack	SKEWES	JOHN	Head	Married	57	⎰ Agent on commercial	Gwennap
	SKEWES	ANNE	Wife	Married	53	⎱ stores	Gwennap
	SKEWES	RICHARD	Son	Unmarried	20	Copper miner	Gwennap
	SKEWES	MARY J.	Daughter	Unmarried	18	House maid	Gwennap
	SKEWES	SIMON D.	Son	Unmarried	15	Copper miner	Gwennap
	SKEWES	ELIZABETH	Daughter	Unmarried	13	Dressmaker	Gwennap
	SKEWES	ALEXANDER	Son	Unmarried	11	Scholar	Gwennap
Trevarth	SKEWES	WILLIAM	Head	Married	26	Miner	Kenwyn
	SKEWES	ELIZA	Wife	Married	27		Gwennap
Carharrack	SKEWES	MARY ANN	Head	Widow	53	House proprietor	Camborne
Lanner Moor	SKEWES	ALEXANDER	Head	Unmarried	54	Clerk to copper business	Gwennap
	SKEWES	MARY	Sister	Unmarried	46	Land owner	Gwennap
Lanner Hill	SKEWES	RICHARD	Head	Unmarried	35	Druggist	St Keverne
Lanner Hill	SKEWS	JAMES	Head	Married	60	Farmer of 5 acres	Gwennap
	SKEWS	ANN	Wife	Married	31	Farmer's wife	Cury
	SKEWS	SUSAN	Daughter	Unmarried	1		Gwennap
	SKEWS	ELIZABETH	Daughter	Unmarried	4 months		Gwennap
	SKEWS	MARY	Boarder	Unmarried	17	Copper mine labourer	Cury
	SKEWS	ELLEN	Servant	Unmarried	13	House servant	Cury

PARISH of REDRUTH (RG 9 — 1579)

West End	SKEWES	SEMINITTA	Servant	Married	53	Charwoman	Cury
Fore St.	SKEWES	GRACE	Boarder	Unmarried	14	Domestic servant	Kenwyn
Clinton Square	SKEWES	MARY	Visitor	Unmarried	23	House servant	Camborne
Highway	SKEWES	ELIZABETH	Aunt	Unmarried	45	Landed income	Gwennap
	(Teague being head of the household)						
Cal Downs	SKEWES	HENRY	Head	Married	65	Carrier and farmer	Gwennap
	SKEWES	ANN	Wife	Married	65		St Cleer
	SKEWES	CATHERINE	Daughter	Unmarried	17		Gwennap
	SKEWES	JOHN	Head	Married	47	Mason-journeyman	Redruth
	SKEWES	ELIZABETH	Wife	Married	34		Ludgvan
	SKEWES	LEWIS	Son	Unmarried	21	Mason-journeyman	Redruth
	SKEWES	JOHN	Son	Unmarried	19	Mason-journeyman	Redruth
	SKEWES	JANE	Daughter	Unmarried	16	Dressmaker	Redruth
	SKEWES	CHARLES	Son	Unmarried	14	Cabinet maker's app.	Redruth
	SKEWES	ELIZABETH	Daughter	Unmarried	6 months		Redruth

PARISH of ILLOGAN (RG 9 — 1581)

Treskillard	SKEWIS	JAMES	Head	Married	66	Agricultural labourer	Cury
	SKEWIS	SIMONETTE	Wife	Married	55		Cury
	SKEWIS	ALICE	Daughter	Unmarried	25		Cury
	SKEWIS	JOHN	Son	Unmarried	23	Copper miner	Cury
	SKEWIS	EDWARD	Son	Unmarried	21	Copper miner	Cury
	SKEWIS	ELIZABETH JANE	Daughter	Unmarried	20	Copper ore dresser	Cury
	SKEWIS	BLANCH	Daughter	Unmarried	16	Copper ore dresser	Cury
Carnkie	SKEWIS	ELIZABETH	Head	Widow	46	Charwoman	Cury
	SKEWIS	ELIZABETH M.	Daughter	Unmarried	12	Copper mine girl	Cury
	SKEWIS	JAMES	Son	Unmarried	8	Scholar	Illogan
Illogan Downs	SKEWS	WILLIAM	Head	Married	43	Blacksmith	Kea
	SKEWS	MARY	Wife	Married	44		Gwennap
	SKEWS	WILLIAM	Son	Unmarried	20	Blacksmith	Kenwyn
	SKEWS	THOMAS	Son	Unmarried	18	Miner	Kenwyn
	SKEWS	MARY ELIZABETH	Daughter	Unmarried	15	Mine girl	Kenwyn
	SKEWS	TERESA HERMINA	Daughter	Unmarried	13	At home	Camborne
	SKEWS	MATTHEW HENRY	Son	Unmarried	11	Scholar	Illogan
	SKEWS	JOHN	Son	Unmarried	7	Scholar	Illogan
	SKEWS	EDWIN	Son	Unmarried	5	At home	Illogan
	SKEWS	SARAH	Daughter	Unmarried	1	At home	Illogan

PARISH of CAMBORNE (RG 9 — 1583)

Trelowarren Street	SKEWIS	JAMES H.	Lodger	Unmarried	21	Carpenter	Cury
Roskear Fields	SKEWES	WILLIAM	Head	Married	34	Mine agent	Camborne
	SKEWES	SARAH	Wife	Married	30		St Agnes
	SKEWES	JOHN BILLING	Son	Unmarried	12	Smith	Camborne
	SKEWES	EMILY LOUISA	Daughter	Unmarried	9	Scholar	Illogan
	SKEWES	WILLIAM	Son	Unmarried	5	Scholar	Illogan
	SKEWES	ROBERT BILLING	Son	Unmarried	1 month		Camborne
North Parade	SKEWIS	CAROLINE	Boarder	Unmarried	33	Miner	Camborne
Vyvyan Row	SKEWIS	ANN	Lodger	Widow	79	Fund holder	Scilly Isles
Vyvyan Row	SKEWES	JANE	Head	Widow	69	Housekeeper	Camborne
	SKEWES	ELIZABETH	Daughter	Unmarried	40	Mine girl	Camborne
	SKEWES	WILLIAM	Son	Unmarried	36	Independent	Camborne
	SKEWES	CAROLINE	Daughter	Unmarried	34	Mine girl	Camborne
	Bullock	Richard W.	Grandson	Unmarried	5	Scholar	Camborne
Red River	SKEWIS	JAMES	Head	Widow	70	Farmer	Camborne
	SKEWIS	MARY	Daughter	Unmarried	14		Camborne
	SKEWIS	ELIZABETH	Daughter	Unmarried	12		Camborne
Beacon Hill	SKEWES	HENRY	Head	Married	41	Mine agent	Camborne
	SKEWES	ELIZABETH	Wife	Married	40		Camborne
	SKEWES	EDWIN	Son	Unmarried	7	Scholar	Camborne
Bolenowe Carn	SKEWIS	WILLIAM	Head	Married	31	Copper miner	Cury
	SKEWIS	PRISCILLA	Wife	Married	31		Illogan
	SKEWIS	ELIZA ELLEN	Daughter	Unmarried	8	Scholar	Illogan
	SKEWIS	ANN AMELIA	Daughter	Unmarried	5		St Erth
	SKEWIS	MARY JANE	Daughter	Unmarried	3		Illogan
	SKEWIS	WILLIAM JAMES	Son	Unmarried	1 month		Illogan

PARISH of GWINEAR (RG 9 — 1586)

Lamin	SKEWES	HENRY	Head	Married	48	Mine agent	Camborne
	SKEWES	ANNA	Wife	Married	47		Camborne
	SKEWES	ELIZABETH	Daughter	Unmarried	24		Camborne
	SKEWES	PHILIP	Son	Unmarried	19	Copper miner	Camborne
	SKEWES	MARY	Daughter	Unmarried	17	Milliner	Camborne
	SKEWES	SAMUEL	Son	Unmarried	15	Scholar	Camborne
	SKEWES	HENRY	Son	Unmarried	11	Scholar	Camborne
	SKEWES	EDWARD	Son	Unmarried	9		Camborne
	SKEWES	SARAH ANN	Daughter	Unmarried	6		Camborne
	SKEWES	ANNIE	Daughter	Unmarried	4		Camborne

PARISH of GWITHIAN (RG 9 — 1586)

Churchtown	Far	Augustus	Head	Married	42	Seafaring man	Dorset
	Far	Margaret Skewis	Wife	Married	34		Gwithian
	Far	John Philips	Son	Unmarried	10	Scholar	Gwithian
	Far	Margaret Skewis	Daughter	Unmarried	5	Scholar	Gwithian
Churchtown	Phillips	William	Head	Married	44	Ag labourer	Gwithian

Phillips	Honour	Wife	Married	34		Gwithian
Phillips	Philippa Skewis	Daughter	Unmarried	8	Scholar	Gwithian

PARISH of MARAZION (RG 9 — 1590)

Trevenner	SKEWES	DIGORY	Head	Married	35	Copper & tin miner	Kea
	SKEWES	FANNY	Wife	Married	34		Marazion
	SKEWES	WILLIAM	Son	Unmarried	7	Scholar	Marazion
	SKEWES	THOMAS GEORGE	Son	Unmarried	4	Scholar	Marazion
	SKEWES	ELIZABETH MARY	Daughter	Unmarried	2		St Ewe
	SKEWES	SAMUEL	Son	Unmarried	1		St Cleer

PARISH of PERRANUTHNOE (RG 9 — 1590)

Goldsithney	SKEWES	JAMES	Head	Married	45	Groom to W.J. Trevelyan	Cury
	SKEWES	MARGARET	Wife	Married	51	Groom's wife	St Just
	SKEWES	JAMES	Son	Unmarried	18	Groom to J. Laity	St Erth
	SKEWES	ELIZABETH	Daughter	Unmarried	16	Charwoman	St Erth
	SKEWES	ANNE	Daughter	Unmarried	14	Scholar	Perranuthnoe
	SKEWES	SARAH	Daughter	Unmarried	7	Scholar	Perranuthnoe
	SKEWES	THOMAS	Son	Unmarried	4	Scholar	Perranuthnoe
Downs	SKEWES	WILLIAM H.	Head	Married	38	Tin miner	Cury
	SKEWES	CAROLINE	Wife	Married	36	Miner's wife	St Hilary
	SKEWES	RICHARD	Son	Unmarried	13	Tin miner	Germoe
	SKEWES	HESTER ANN	Daughter	Unmarried	7	Scholar	Perranuthnoe
	SKEWES	EMMA	Daughter	Unmarried	5	Scholar	Perranuthnoe
	SKEWES	WILLIAM HARRY	Son	Unmarried	3		Perranuthnoe

CENSUS RETURNS FOR 1861 — DEVONSHIRE — Parish of Bere Alston (RG 9 — 1458)

Crocers Shop, Pepper Street	SKEWS	DANIEL HODGE	Head	Married	52	Grocer	Kea, Cornwall
	SKEWS	MARY ANN	Wife	Married	44		Beerferris
	Brown	Elizabeth A.	Servant	Unmarried	13	Servant	Beerferris
Fore Street	SKEWES	SAMUEL DAWE	Head	Married	29	Druggist & chemist	St Austell
	SKEWES	JANE	Wife	Married	33		Bere Alston
	SKEWES	MARY A.C.	Daughter	Unmarried	2		Bere Alston
	SKEWES	JANE	Daughter	Unmarried	1		Bere Alston

CENSUS RETURNS FOR THE COUNTY OF CORNWALL — 1871

1871 PUBLIC RECORD OFFICE REFERENCES AND DISTRICTS   ALL NUMBERS ARE PREFACED BY "RG 10"

2214	KILKHAMPTON	No Entry
2215	STRATTON	No Entry
2216	STRATTON	No Entry
2217	WEEK ST MARY	No Entry
2218	BOSCASTLE	No Entry
2219	CAMELFORD	No Entry
2220	CAMELFORD	No Entry
2221	CAMELFORD	No Entry
2222	ALTARNUN	See Over
2223	NORTH PETHERWIN	No Entry
2224	ST STEPHEN	No Entry
2225	LAUNCESTON	No Entry
2226	NORTHILL	No Entry
2227	NORTHILL	No Entry
2228	ANTONY	No Entry
2229	ANTONY	No Entry
2230	ST GERMANS	No Entry
2231	SALTASH	No Entry
2232	SALTASH	No Entry
2233	CALLINGTON	No Entry
2234	CALLINGTON	No Entry
2235	CALLINGTON	No Entry
2236	LISKEARD	No Entry
2237	LISKEARD	See Over
2238	LISKEARD	No Entry
2239	LISKEARD	See Over
2240	LISKEARD	No Entry
2241	LOOE	No Entry
2242	LOOE	No Entry
2243	LOOE	No Entry
2244	LERRIN	No Entry
2245	LERRIN	No Entry
2246	LERRIN	No Entry
2247	LANLIVERY	No Entry
2248	ST MABYN	No Entry
2249	BODMIN	No Entry
2250	BODMIN	No Entry
2251	EGLOSHAYLE	No Entry
2252	EGLOSHAYLE	No Entry
2253	PADSTOW	No Entry
2254	PADSTOW	No Entry
2255	ST COLUMB	No Entry
2256	ST COLUMB	See Over
2257	NEWLYN	No Entry
2258	FOWEY	No Entry
2259	FOWEY	No Entry
2260	FOWEY	No Entry
2261	FOWEY	No Entry
2262	ST AUSTELL	No Entry
2263	ST AUSTELL	See Over
2264	ST AUSTELL	No Entry
2265	ST AUSTELL	No Entry
2266	ST AUSTELL	No Entry
2267	ST AUSTELL	No Entry
2268	MEVAGISSEY	No Entry
2269	MEVAGISSEY	No Entry
2270	GRAMPOUND	No Entry
2271	GRAMPOUND	See Over
2272	PROBUS	No Entry
2273	PROBUS	No Entry
2274	PROBUS	No Entry
2275	ST JUST	No Entry
2276	ST AGNES	No Entry
2277	ST AGNES	No Entry
2278	ST AGNES	No Entry
2279	ST AGNES	No Entry
2280	ST CLEMENT	No Entry
2281	ST CLEMENT	See Over
2282	ST CLEMENT	See Over
2283	KENWYN	See Over
2284	KENWYN	See Over
2285	KENWYN	No Entry
2286	KENWYN	See Over
2287	KEA	See Over
2288	KEA	No Entry
2289	KEA	No Entry
2290	MYLOR	See Over
2291	MYLOR	No Entry
2292	FALMOUTH	No Entry
2293	FALMOUTH	See Over
2294	FALMOUTH	No Entry
2295	FALMOUTH	No Entry
2296	PENRYN	No Entry
2297	PENRYN	No Entry
2298	CONSTANTINE	See Over
2299	WENDRON	See Over
2300	WENDRON	See Over
2301	WENDRON	No Entry
2302	WENDRON	No Entry
2303	HELSTON	See Over
2304	HELSTON	See Over
2305	ST KEVERNE	See Over
2306	ST KEVERNE	See Over
2307	BREAGE	See Over
2308	BREAGE	No Entry
2309	CROWAN	See Over
2310	CROWAN	See Over
2311	GWENNAP	No Entry
2312	GWENNAP	No Entry
2313	GWENNAP	See Over
2314	GWENNAP	See Over
2315	REDRUTH	See Over
2316	REDRUTH	See Over
2317	REDRUTH	No Entry
2318	REDRUTH	See Over
2319	ILLOGAN	No Entry
2320	ILLOGAN	See Over
2321	ILLOGAN	See Over
2322	ILLOGAN	See Over
2323	CAMBORNE	See Over
2324	CAMBORNE	See Over
2325	CAMBORNE	No Entry
2326	CAMBORNE	See Over
2327	PHILLACK	No Entry
2328	PHILLACK	See Over
2329	PHILLACK	See Over
2330	UNY LELANT	No Entry
2331	UNY LELANT	No Entry
2332	UNY LELANT	No Entry
2333	ST IVES	No Entry
2334	ST IVES	No Entry
2335	ST IVES	No Entry
2336	MARAZION	See Over
2337	MARAZION	See Over
2338	PENZANCE	No Entry
2339	PENZANCE	No Entry
2340	PENZANCE	No Entry
2341	PENZANCE	See Over
2342	PENZANCE	See Over
2343	ST JUST IN PENWITH	No Entry
2344	ST JUST IN PENWITH	No Entry
2345	ST JUST IN PENWITH	No Entry
2346	ST BURYAN	No Entry
2347	SCILLY ISLANDS	No Entry

ADDRESS	NAME		RELATION TO HEAD OF HOUSEHOLD	STATUS	AGE	PROFESSION	WHERE BORN
ALTARNUN, LAUNCESTON (Public Record Office Reference RG 10 — 2222)							
Trewint	SKEWS	JOHN	Head	Married	49	Miner	Altarnun
	SKEWS	ISABELLA	Wife	Married	42		Altarnun
	SKEWS	JOHN	Son	Unmarried	12	Scholar	Altarnun
	SKEWS	AMOS	Son	Unmarried	6	Scholar	Altarnun
	SKEWS	CHARLES	Son	Unmarried	5		Altarnun
	SKEWS	HARRY	Son	Unmarried	1		Altarnun
Lewannick	SKEWES	SAMUEL	Servant	Unmarried	15	Stable boy	Altarnun
ST CLEER, LISKEARD (RG 10 — 2237)							
Commonmoor	SKEWS	SAMUEL	Son in law to Juliana Mildern	Unmarried	18	Copper & tin miner	St Cleer
	SKEWS	JOHN	Son in law to Juliana Mildern	Unmarried	14	Copper & tin miner	St Cleer
	SKEWES	MATTHEW	Son in law to Julia Mildern	Unmarried	12	Copper & tin miner	St Cleer
St Ive, Pensilva	SKEWS	PETER	Head	Married	39	Blind	Chacewater
	SKEWS	ELIZABETH	Wife	Married	35		Altarnun
	SKEWS	FANNY GREGORY	Daughter	Unmarried	14	Mine worker	Altarnun
	SKEWS	WILLIAM HENRY	Son	Unmarried	12	Scholar	Altarnun
	SKEWS	JOHN GREGORY	Son	Unmarried	10	Scholar	St Ive
	SKEWS	EDMUND	Son	Unmarried	4		St Ive
	SKEWS	SAMUEL	Son	Unmarried	1		St Ive
LISKEARD (RG 10 — 2239)							
Dobwalls	SKEWS	ELIZA	Servant to William and Jane Pascoe	Unmarried	20	Domestic servant	Liskeard
ST WENN, ST COLUMB (RG 10 — 2256)							
GREAT SKEWES	Lander	Christopher	Head	Married	52	Farmer employing 1 man and 2 boys and farming 144 acres	Blisland
	Lander	Maria	Wife	Married	49	Farmer's wife	St Tudy
	Lander	Nicholas	Son	Unmarried	23	Farmer's son	Lanteglos
	Lander	Francis	Son	Unmarried	16		Lanteglos
	Lander	Maria	Daughter	Unmarried	11		Lanteglos
	Lander	Annie	Daughter	Unmarried	10		Lanteglos
	Lander	Harry	Son	Unmarried	5		St Wenn
	Verran	Henry	Servant	Unmarried	16	Servant & ploughboy	Luxillian
	Trevail	Ruana	Servant	Unmarried	30	Domestic servant	Luxillian
LITTLE SKEWES	Blake	Marshall	Head	Married	26	Farmer of 70 acres employing 1 man and 1 boy	St Wenn
	Blake	Jane	Wife	Married	27		Withiel
	Blake	Mary	Daughter	Unmarried	3		St Wenn
	Blake	Emma	Daughter	Unmarried	2		St Wenn
	Blake	Richard H.	Son	Unmarried	1		St Wenn
	Nicholls	Mary G.	Servant	Unmarried	16	Domestic servant	Luxillian
	Rowe	John	Servant	Unmarried	20	Carter	Helland
	Osborne	Richard	Servant	Unmarried	11	Ploughboy	St Columb
ST. AUSTELL (RG 10 — 2263)							
CHARLESTOWN	SKEWS	JAMES	Head	Married	69	Retired lime burner	St Ewe
	SKEWS	ELIZABETH	Wife	Married	70		St Austell
ST MEWAN, GRAMPOUND (RG 10 — 2271)							
Sticker	SKEWS	PHILIP	Head	Widower	73	Retired farmer	St Ewe
ST CLEMENT, TRURO (RG 10 — 2281)							
Paul's Row	SKEWES	ELIZABETH JANE	Niece of Constance Hobbs, widow (80)	Unmarried	21	Annuitant	Truro
Prospect Place	SKEWES	ANN BUCKLAND	Head	Widow	60	Retired farmer's wife	St Allen
	SKEWES	ANNIE L.	Daughter	Unmarried	25		Gwennap
Back Prospect Place	SKEWES	ANN	Head	Widow	62	Billiard maker's widow	St Clement
	SKEWES	EMMA	Daughter	Unmarried	28	Dressmaker	Truro
ST MARY, TRURO (RG 10 — 2282)							
Tippets Backlet	SKEWES	SUSAN	Head	Widow	51	Annuitant	Kenwyn
	SKEWES	AMELIA	Daughter	Unmarried	13	Scholar	Kea
	SKEWES	JAMES	Nephew	Unmarried	5	Scholar	Kea
Edward Street	SKEWES	THOMAS	Head	Married	37	Ironmonger	Truro
	SKEWES	MARY JANE	Wife	Married	37	Ironmonger's wife	Truro
	SKEWES	MARY ANN PETERS	Daughter	Unmarried	8	Scholar	Truro

	SKEWES	HERBERT	Son	Unmarried	5	Scholar	Truro
	SKEWES	ELIZABETH J.	Daughter	Unmarried	2		Truro
	SKEWES	FLORENCE	Daughter	Unmarried	15 months		Truro
Union Workhouse,	SKEWES	SUSAN	Inmate	Unmarried	24	Domestic Servant	Chacewater
Truro	SKEWES	FREDERICK	Inmate	Unmarried	1		Truro Union

KENWYN, TRURO (RG 10 — 2283)

Calenick Street	SKEWES	JAMES	Boarder	Unmarried	50	Labourer	Kenwyn
Daniell Street	SKEWES	JANE	Head	Widow	72	Retired grocer	St Teath
	(Granddaughter Minnie Mills, aged 14; scholar in Truro)						

KENWYN, TRURO (RG 10 — 2284)

Kenwyn Street	SKEWES	JOHN BEER	Head	Married	40	Cabinet maker	Truro
	SKEWES	MARY BROWN	Wife	Married	39		Padstow
	SKEWES	JOHN BROWN	Son	Unmarried	14	Compositor	Truro
	SKEWES	WILLIAM BROWN	Son	Unmarried	13	Scholar	Truro
	SKEWES	HARRIET MARIA	Daughter	Unmarried	10	Scholar	Truro
	(Incorrect entry in Census Returns — should be HENRIETTA MARIA SKEWES)						
	SKEWES	THOMAS JAMES	Son	Unmarried	7	Scholar	Truro
	SKEWES	PHILIPPA MARY	Daughter	Unmarried	4		Camborne
	SKEWES	RICHARD HENRY	Son	Unmarried	1 month		Truro

KENWYN, TRURO (RG 10 — 2286)

Chacewater	SKEWES	JOHN	Lodger	Unmarried	32	Retired farmer	Kea
Chacewater	SKEWES	MARY	Head	Widow	72		Kenwyn

KENWYN, TRURO (RG 10 — 2287)

Chacewater	SKEWES	THOMAS	Head	Widower	79	Farmer of 7 acres	Kea
Killiwerries	SKEWS	JAMES	Lodger	Unmarried	48	Labourer	Kenwyn
Hugus, Kea	Holman	Elizabeth Ann	Head	Widow	35		Kea
	SKEWES	GRACE	Sister	Unmarried	26	Domestic servant	Kea
Baldhu, Kea	SKEWS	HARRIET	Head	Widow	52	Miner's wife	Kenwyn
	Symons	Philippa	Daughter	Married	33	Dressmaker	Kea
	Symons	Catherine G.	Granddaughter	Unmarried	11		Kea
Baldhu, Kea	SKEWS	GRACE	Head	Widow	63	Miner's widow	Penryn
	SKEWS	GRACE	Daughter	Unmarried	22		Kea
	SKEWS	MARIA	Daughter	Unmarried	20		Kea

MYLOR (RG 10 — 2290)

High Street	SKEWES	EMILY KEMPTHORNE	Boarder	Unmarried	17	Assistant school teacher. Boarder at house of Thomasine Lawrence (23), school mistress.	Mawnan

FALMOUTH (RG 10 — 2293)

Retreat	SKEWES	THOMAS	Head	Married	77	Shoemaker	Falmouth
Higher Brook, Penryn	SKEWES	FANNY	Boarder	Unmarried	20	Draper's assistant	Mawnan
Brook Street,	SKEWES	CHARLES	Head	Married	39	Shoemaker	Falmouth
Falmouth	SKEWES	ELIZABETH	Wife	Married	41		St Michael's Mnt
	SKEWES	CHARLES	Son	Unmarried	13	Baker's errand boy	Falmouth
	SKEWES	WILLIAM JOHN	Son	Unmarried	11	Grocer's errand boy	Falmouth
	SKEWES	GEORGE	Son	Unmarried	9	Scholar	Falmouth
	SKEWES	EDWARD	Son	Unmarried	7	Scholar	Falmouth
	SKEWES	LOUISA J.	Daughter	Unmarried	1		Falmouth

MAWNAN (RG 10 — 2298)

Goldmartin House	SKEWES	MARY ELLEN	Daughter to head of household Ann Kempthorne, widow (61)	Widow	30	Annuitant	Mawnan
	SKEWES	JOHN	Grandson to head of household	Unmarried	1		Mawnan
Mawnan Smith	SKEWES	JAMES	Head	Married	54	Farmer	Ruan Major
	SKEWES	FRANCES	Wife	Married	46		Mawnan
	SKEWES	HESTER ANN	Daughter	Unmarried	24		Mawnan

	Surname	Forename	Relation	Status	Age	Occupation	Birthplace
	SKEWES	FANNY	Daughter	Unmarried	22	Draper's assistant	Mawnan
	SKEWES	JAMES LUGG	Son	Unmarried	12	Scholar	Mawnan
	SKEWES	MINNIE	Daughter	Unmarried	10	Scholar	Mawnan
	SKEWES	KATE	Daughter	Unmarried	7	Scholar	Mawnan
	SKEWES	ELLEN	Daughter	Unmarried	5	Scholar	Mawnan
CONSTANTINE							
Bosawsack	SKEWES	JOSIAH	Head	Married	50	Farmer of 127 acres employing 2 labourers	Constantine
	SKEWES	FANNY	Wife	Married	44		Budock
	SKEWES	LAURA	Daughter	Unmarried	16		Constantine
	SKEWES	JAMES	Son	Unmarried	13	Scholar	Constantine
	SKEWES	JOSIAH	Son	Unmarried	6	Scholar	Constantine
	SKEWES	HENRY	Son	Unmarried	3		Constantine

WENDRON (RG 10 — 2299)

	Surname	Forename	Relation	Status	Age	Occupation	Birthplace
Gwealgears	SKEWES	ELEANOR	Head	Widow	56	Charwoman	Cury
Mankey	SKEWIS	WILLIAM	Head	Married	55	Agricultural labourer and grocer	Cury
	SKEWIS	AMELIA	Wife	Married	49	Grocer	Mawgan

WENDRON (RG 10 — 2300)

	Surname	Forename	Relation	Status	Age	Occupation	Birthplace
Carthvean	SKEWES	JOSIAH	Head	Married	46	Agricultural labourer	Cury
	SKEWES	ELIZABETH	Wife	Married	56		Sithney
Carthvean	SKEWES	JAMES	Head	Unmarried	21	Agricultural labourer	Cury

SITHNEY (RG 10 — 2302)

	Surname	Forename	Relation	Status	Age	Occupation	Birthplace
Trannack	SKEWIS	JOHN	Head	Married	59	Carpenter	Cury
	SKEWIS	MARTHA	Wife	Married	54	Carpenter's wife	Sithney

HELSTON (RG 10 — 2303)

	Surname	Forename	Relation	Status	Age	Occupation	Birthplace
Meneage Street	SKEWES	JAMES	Servant	Unmarried	20	Coachman	Cury

HELSTON AND CURY (RG 10 — 2304)

	Surname	Forename	Relation	Status	Age	Occupation	Birthplace
Wendron Street	SKEWIS	ELIZABETH A.	Niece of Obadiah & Anna Harris	Married	26	Copper miner's wife	Gwinear
Polglase, Cury	SKEWES	JOHN	Servant	Unmarried	21	Farm servant	Cury
Maenley, Cury	SKEWES	BLANCH	Head	Unmarried	82	Poultry dealer	Cury
Gilly Lane, Cury	SKEWES	JANE	Head	Unmarried	50	Washerwoman	Cury
	SKEWES	ANN	Sister	Unmarried	60	Farm labourer	Cury
Nantithet	SKEWES	WILLIAM JAMES	Head	Married	20	Labourer	Cury
	SKEWES	SUSAN	Wife	Married	20	Labourer's wife	Wendron
Nantithet	SKEWES	EDWARD	Brother to Mary Percy, head of household	Unmarried	57		Cury
	SKEWES	ELIZABETH	Sister to Mary Percy, head of household	Unmarried	45	Field labourer	Cury
	SKEWES	ELIZABETH MARY	Niece to Mary Percy, head of household	Unmarried	17	Field labourer	Cury
Nantithet	SKEWES	EDWARD	Head	Married	59	Shoemaker	Cury
	SKEWES	JULIA	Wife	Married	46	Shoemaker's wife	Lizard
	SKEWES	THOMAS	Son	Unmarried	18		Cury
	SKEWES	HENRY	Son	Unmarried	14		Cury
	SKEWES	ANNIE	Daughter	Unmarried	12		Cury
	SKEWES	BESSIE	Daughter	Unmarried	10		Cury
	SKEWES	EDITH	Daughter	Unmarried	8		Cury
	SKEWES	LAURA	Daughter	Unmarried	6		Cury
	SKEWES	EDWARD	Son	Unmarried	4		Cury
	SKEWES	JULIA ANNA	Daughter	Unmarried	2		Cury
Nantithet	SKEWES	WILLIAM	Head	Widower	63	Agricultural labourer	Cury
	SKEWES	ALICE ANN	Daughter	Unmarried	31	Dressmaker	Cury
	SKEWES	JOHN WESLEY	Grandson	Unmarried	10	Scholar	Cury
	SKEWES	ARTHUR WESLEY	Grandson	Unmarried	4		Cury

ST KEVERNE (RG 10 — 2305)

	Surname	Forename	Relation	Status	Age	Occupation	Birthplace
TRESKEWES	James	William	Head	Married	38	Farmer of 30 acres	Cury
	James	Alice	Wife	Married	33	Farmer's wife	St Keverne
	James	Thomas	Son	Unmarried	5		St Keverne
TRESKEWES	Allan	Alfred	Head	Married	26	Agricultural labourer	St Keverne
	Allan	Elizabeth	Wife	Married	34		Lizard

LITTLE TRESKEWES	Retallack	Henry	Head	Married	34	Agricultural labourer	St Keverne
	Retallack	Mary	Wife	Married	34		St Keverne
	Retallack	George	Son	Unmarried	9	Scholar	St Keverne
	Retallack	Henry	Son	Unmarried	6	Scholar	St Keverne
	Retallack	Mark	Son	Unmarried	5		St Keverne
	Retallack	Ruth	Daughter	Unmarried	11 weeks		St Keverne

ST KEVERNE (RG 10 — 2306) HENRY SKEWES was the Enumerator

Churchtown	SKEWES	LOVEDAY	Head	Widow	62		Ruan Minor

Churchtown   SKEWES-NICHOLLS, HENRYSon of James Nicholls (43) and Mary Nicholls (36) — 9 months old

Tresodden	SKEWES	ANTHONY	Head	Married	69	Farmer of 145 acres employing one man	Ruan Major
	SKEWES	CHRISTIAN	Wife	Married	58		Ruan Major
	SKEWES	ANN	Daughter	Unmarried	34		Ruan Major
	SKEWES	CATHERINE	Daughter	Unmarried	28		Ruan Major
	SKEWES	HENRY	Son	Unmarried	25	Farmer's assistant	Ruan Major
	SKEWES	SAMUEL	Son	Unmarried	23	Farmer's assistant	Ruan Major
	SKEWES	WILLIAM JOHN	Son	Unmarried	21	Farmer's assistant	Ruan Major
	SKEWES	HANNIBAL	Son	Unmarried	16	Farmer's assistant	Ruan Major
	SKEWES	GEORGE	Son	Unmarried	13	Farmer's assistant	Ruan Major
Lizard Town	SKEWES	JOHN	Head	Married	21		Landewednack
	SKEWES	LOUISA	Wife	Married	22		Landewednack
	SKEWES	ADA L.	Daughter	Unmarried	1		Landewednack
	SKEWES	MARY	Daughter	Unmarried	7 months		Landewednack
	SKEWES	THOMAS	Brother	Unmarried	15	Scholar	Landewednack
Lizard Town	SKEWES	HARRIET	Head	Widow	48	Out of business	Cury
Lizard Town	SKEWES	JAMES H.	Head	Married	22	Carpenter	Landewednack
	SKEWES	ELIZABETH	Wife	Married	23		Landewednack
	SKEWES	SARAH ANN	Daughter	Unmarried	11 months		Landewednack
Lizard Town	SKEWES	WILLIAM	Boarder at home of Sampson Hill	Unmarried	18	Carpenter	Landewednack

BREAGE (RG 10 — 2307)

Sethnoe	SKEWES	GRACE	Mother-in-law to Jacob Rowe	Widow	61		Constantine
Frew	SKEWES	MARIA	Visitor	Widow	27		Perranzabuloe

CROWAN (RG 10 — 2309)

SKEWES	Trevenen	William	Head	Married	48	Farmer of 35 acres	Crowan
	Trevenen	Jane	Wife	Married	42		Crowan
	Trevenen	Joanna	Daughter	Unmarried	16		Crowan
	Trevenen	Mary	Daughter	Unmarried	12		Crowan
	Trevenen	John	Son	Unmarried	11		Crowan
	Trevenen	Laura	Daughter	Unmarried	9		Crowan
	Trevenen	William	Son	Unmarried	7		Crowan
	Bond	Elizabeth	Servant	Unmarried	28		Crowan
SKEWES	Dunn	Anne	Head	Unmarried	39	Worker in a bone mill	Crowan
	Dunn	Elizabeth	Daughter	Unmarried	9		Crowan
SKEWES	Bond	William	Head	Married	55	Agricultural labourer	North Devon
	Bond	Grace	Wife	Married	60		North Devon
	Bond	Grace	Daughter	Unmarried	15	Scholar	Gwinear
Horse Downs	SKEWES	JOHN	Head	Married	41	Miner	Cury
	SKEWES	GRACE	Wife	Married	47	Miner's wife	Crowan
	SKEWES	JOHN H.	Son	Unmarried	17	Miner	Crowan
	SKEWES	RICHARD	Son	Unmarried	10	Scholar	Crowan
	SKEWES	ANNIE J.	Daughter	Unmarried	8	Scholar	Crowan

CROWAN (RG 10 — 2310)

Praze	SKEWIS	LEWIS	Boarder at home of Elizabeth Hocking, widow (67)	Unmarried	28	Mason	Redruth
Cargenwen	SKEWES	JOHN	Head	Unmarried	53	Farmer of 25 acres	Illogan
	SKEWES	PHILIPPA	Sister	Unmarried	65		Illogan
	SKEWES	MARY ANNE	Daughter	Unmarried	23		Camborne
Bolitho	SKEWES	WILLIAM	Head	Married	63	Farmer of 200 acres employing 2 men & 2 boys	Constantine

	SKEWES	ELIZABETH	Wife	Married	63	Farmer's wife	Sithney
	SKEWES	GRACE	Daughter	Unmarried	30		Sithney
	SKEWES	JAMES	Son	Unmarried	28	Farmer	Sithney
	SKEWES	JOHN	Son	Unmarried	24	Undergraduate at University of Oxford	Crowan

GWENNAP (RG 10 — 2313)

Carharrack	SKEWES	MARY ANN	Head	Widow	41	Domestic	Kenwyn
	SKEWES	JOHN	Son	Unmarried	19	Miner	Gwennap
Croft Row	SKEWIS	ELIZABETH A.	Head	Married	26	Wife of miner who is in Mexico	Gwennap
	SKEWIS	MINNIE	Daughter	Unmarried	4	Scholar	Gwennap
Lanner House	SKEWES	MARY	Sister to Ann Bray	Unmarried	50		Gwennap
Lanner House	SKEWES	ELIZABETH	Head	Unmarried	60	Rents annuitant	Gwennap

GWENNAP (RG 10 — 2314)

Lanner	SKEWES	EDWARD	Head	Married	30	Railway labourer	Cury
	SKEWES	JECOLIAH	Wife	Married	31		Gwennap
	SKEWES	EDWARD J.	Son	Unmarried	10	Scholar	Gwennap
	SKEWES	WILLIAM	Son	Unmarried	7	Scholar	Gwennap
	SKEWES	ELIZA J.	Daughter	Unmarried	2 months		Gwennap

REDRUTH (RG 10 — 2315)

Bond Street	SKEWES	MINNIE	Servant	Unmarried	20	Domestic servant to Peter Renfree and family	Tuckingmill

REDRUTH (RG 10 — 2316)

Dopps Row	SKEWES	MINNIE	Visitor	Unmarried	8	Visitor to house of Eliza Davey (48)	Redruth

REDRUTH (RG 10 — 2318)

Hodders Row	SKUES	JOHN	Head	Married	57	Mason	Redruth
	SKUES	ELIZABETH	Wife	Married	42		Ludgvan
	SKUES	BESSIE	Daughter	Unmarried	10	Scholar	Redruth

ILLOGAN (RG 10 — 2320)

Carnarton	SKEWES	WILLIAM	Head	Married	42	Agricultural labourer	Cury
	SKEWES	PRISCILLA	Wife	Married	42		Illogan
	SKEWES	WILLIAM	Son	Unmarried	10	Scholar	Camborne
	SKEWES	JAMES	Son	Unmarried	7	Scholar	Camborne
	SKEWES	ELIZA	Daughter	Unmarried	18	Worker in a tin mine	Illogan
	SKEWES	HANNAH	Daughter	Unmarried	16	Worker in a tin mine	St Erth
	SKEWES	MARY	Daughter	Unmarried	13		Illogan
	SKEWES	EDWARD	Son	Unmarried	4	Scholar	Camborne
Treskillard	SKEWIS	JAMES	Head	Widower	77	Retired farmer	Cury
	SKEWIS	MARY	Daughter	Unmarried	25	Tin dresser	Cury
	SKEWIS	ELLEN	Daughter	Unmarried	22	Tin dresser	Cury
Treskillard	SKEWIS	NANNY	Head	Widow	37	Copper ore dresser	Cury
	SKEWIS	SUSAN	Daughter	Unmarried	12	Tin dresser	Gwennap
	SKEWIS	MARIE	Daughter	Unmarried	6	Scholar	Gwennap

ILLOGAN (RG 10 — 2321)

Highway	SKEWES	FRANCIS	Head	Married	30	Blacksmith	Chacewater
	SKEWES	GRACE	Wife	Married	31		Illogan
	SKEWES	WILLIAM	Son	Unmarried	5	Scholar	Illogan
	SKEWES	SAMUEL	Son	Unmarried	3	Scholar	Illogan
	SKEWES	JANE R.	Daughter	Unmarried	7 months		Illogan

ILLOGAN (RG 10 — 2322)

Illogan Highway	SKEWS	WILLIAM	Head	Married	54	Blacksmith	Kea
	SKEWS	JANE	Wife	Married	46		Redruth
	SKEWS	MATTHEW HENRY	Son	Unmarried	21	Tin and copper miner	Illogan
	SKEWS	JOHN	Son	Unmarried	17	Tin and copper miner	Illogan
	SKEWS	EDWIN	Son	Unmarried	16	Blacksmith	Illogan
	SKEWS	SARAH	Daughter	Unmarried	12	Scholar	Illogan
	SKEWS	MARTIN	Son	Unmarried	8	Scholar	Illogan
	SKEWS	EMMA	Daughter	Unmarried	4	Scholar	Illogan

CAMBORNE (RG 10 — 2323)

Chapel Street	SKEWES	EDWARD	Head	Widower	75	Retired miner	Camborne
	SKEWES	MARY	Daughter	Unmarried	53	Housekeeper	Crowan
Gas Street	SKEWES	ELIZABETH A.	Boarder	Unmarried	22	Seamstress	Camborne

CAMBORNE (RG 10 — 2324)

Address	Surname	Name	Relation	Status	Age	Occupation	Birthplace
Trelowarren Street	SKEWIES	MARY J.	Lodger	Widow	29	Boot & shoe assistant	Pennsylvania, U.S.A.
Lower Vyvyan Row	SKEWES	JANE	Head	Widow	79	Tailoress — unemployed	Camborne
Roskear Crofts	SKEWIS	JAMES	Head	Married	81		Camborne
	SKEWIS	SUSAN	Wife	Married	45		Camborne
	SKEWIS	ELIZA ANN	Daughter	Unmarried	22		Camborne
Edward Street	SKEWES	WILLIAM H.	Grandson of James (62) & Mary Mitchell (63)	Unmarried	8	Scholar	Camborne
	SKEWES	ALFRED	Grandson of James (62) & Mary Mitchell (63)	Unmarried	6	Scholar	Tuckingmill

CAMBORNE (RG 10 — 2326)

Address	Surname	Name	Relation	Status	Age	Occupation	Birthplace
Lower Penponds	SKEWS	WILLIAM	Head	Married	33	Carpenter & joiner	St Austell
	SKEWS	JANE	Wife	Married	30		St Columb
	SKEWS	EDDY	Son	Unmarried	8	Scholar	Falmouth
	SKEWS	JANE	Daughter	Unmarried	4	Scholar	Camborne
	SKEWS	ANNIE	Daughter	Unmarried	3		Camborne
	SKEWS	LELIA M.	Daughter	Unmarried	9 months		Camborne

GWINEAR (RG 10 — 2328)

Address	Surname	Name	Relation	Status	Age	Occupation	Birthplace
Carnell Green	SKEWES	ELIZABETH	Head	Married	34	Miner's wife. Husband in California	Gwinear
	SKEWES	GRACE	Daughter	Unmarried	9	Scholar	Gwinear
	SKEWES	RICHARD	Son	Unmarried	8	Scholar	Gwinear
	SKEWES	JOHN	Son	Unmarried	6	Scholar	Gwinear
	SKEWES	HARRY	Son	Unmarried	5	Scholar	Gwinear
	SKEWES	JOSEPH V.	Son	Unmarried	4	Scholar	Gwinear

GWINEAR (RG 10 — 2329)

Address	Surname	Name	Relation	Status	Age	Occupation	Birthplace
Rewlya Lane	SKEWES	HENRY	Head	Married	58	Miner	Camborne
	SKEWES	HANNAH	Wife	Married	57		Camborne
	SKEWES	EDWARD	Son	Unmarried	19	Miner	Camborne
	SKEWES	SARAH A.	Daughter	Unmarried	16		Gwinear
	SKEWES	ANNE	Daughter	Unmarried	14	Domestic	Gwinear

MARAZION (RG 10 — 2336)

Address	Surname	Name	Relation	Status	Age	Occupation	Birthplace
Chymorvah	SKEWIS	ELIZABETH	Servant	Unmarried	25	Cook & domestic Servant to Ambrose B. Michelle, land owner and house owner	St Erth

PERRANUTHNOE (RG 10 — 2337)

Address	Surname	Name	Relation	Status	Age	Occupation	Birthplace
Goldsithney	SKEWES	JAMES	Head	Married	62	Colt breaker	Cury
	SKEWES	MARGARET	Wife	Married	52		St Just
	SKEWES	ANNIE	Daughter	Unmarried	23		St Erth
	SKEWES	MARY JANE	Daughter	Unmarried	7	Scholar	Perranuthnoe
Goldsithney	SKEWES	SARAH A.	Servant	Unmarried	16	Servant to Mary Gundry, merchant's widow	Perranuthnoe
Colenzoe	SKEWIS	HENRY	Servant	Unmarried	13	Farm servant to Hugh Lory	Perranuthnoe
Millpool	SKEWIS	RICHARD	Head	Married	48	Tin miner	Cury
	SKEWIS	CAROLINE	Wife	Married	47	Tin miner's wife	St Hilary
	SKEWIS	EMMA	Daughter	Unmarried	15	Farm servant	Penryn
Carbaws, St Hilary	SKEWYS	THOMAS H.	Servant	Unmarried	15	Servant to John Verrant	Perranuthnoe

PENZANCE (RG 10 — 2341)

Address	Surname	Name	Relation	Status	Age	Occupation	Birthplace
Cornwall Terrace	SKEWES	HESTER A.	Servant	Unmarried	17	Servant to James Beckerley	Perranuthnoe

MADRON (RG 10 — 2342)

Address	Surname	Name	Relation	Status	Age	Occupation	Birthplace
Union Workhouse, Madron	SKEWES	RICHARD	Inmate	Unmarried	7	Scholar	Marazion
	SKEWES	JOSEPH	Inmate	Unmarried	6	Scholar	Marazion
	SKEWES	HENRY	Inmate	Unmarried	5	Scholar	Marazion

BEER FERRIS, TAVISTOCK, DEVON (RG 10 — 2142)

Address	Surname	Name	Relation	Status	Age	Occupation	Birthplace
Fore Street	SKEWES	SAMUEL DAWE	Head	Married	39	Druggist and grocer	St Austell
	SKEWES	JANE	Wife	Married	42		Bere Alston
	SKEWES	MARY A.C.	Daughter	Unmarried	12	Scholar	Bere Alston
	SKEWES	JANE	Daughter	Unmarried	11	Scholar	Bere Alston
	SKEWES	ALICE K.	Daughter	Unmarried	9	Scholar	Bere Alston
	SKEWES	JOHN C.	Son	Unmarried	7	Scholar	Bere Alston

	SKEWES	ELLEN M.	Daughter	Unmarried	5	Scholar	Bere Alston
	SKEWES	FLORENCE R.	Daughter	Unmarried	3		Bere Alston
	SKEWES	HOWARD	Son	Unmarried	6 months		Bere Alston

ASHBURTON, DEVON (RG 10 — 2127)

Bell Mount	SKEWIS	DANIEL	Head	Married	38	Tin miner	Kea, Cornwall
	SKEWIS	ELIZABETH	Wife	Married	38	Wool sorter	Ashburton
	SKEWIS	ELIZABETH	Daughter	Unmarried	17		Ashburton
	SKEWIS	JOHN	Son	Unmarried	13	Scholar	Ashburton
	SKEWIS	SARAH	Daughter	Unmarried	11	Scholar	Ashburton
	SKEWIS	MARY	Daughter	Unmarried	9	Scholar	Ashburton
	SKEWIS	HENRIETTA	Daughter	Unmarried	6	Scholar	Ashburton
	SKEWIS	CLARA	Daughter	Unmarried	4	Scholar	Ashburton
	SKEWIS	DANIEL	Son	Unmarried	1		Ashburton
Crockalow	SKEWIS	SAMUEL	Head	Married	43	Tin miner	Kea, Cornwall
	SKEWIS	SUSAN	Wife	Married	44		Ashburton
	SKEWIS	MARY	Daughter	Unmarried	19	Weaver	Ashburton
	SKEWIS	SAMUEL	Son	Unmarried	12	Scholar	Ashburton
	SKEWIS	WILLIAM	Son	Unmarried	9	Scholar	Ashburton
	SKEWIS	DANIEL	Son	Unmarried	6	Scholar	Ashburton

14   Armorial Splendour

HERALDRY BEGAN in mediaeval times when it was custom for the more distinguished families to identify themselves in battle with "coat armour" on a shield, banner or on their person.

However, by Tudor times heraldry changed from prominence on the battle field to a sign of gentility. A grant of arms is one of outward expressions of inward grace of gentle blood.[1]

Heraldry became big business between 1530 and 1688 when Heralds visited counties throughout England giving nobility and the gentry the opportunity to register arms and genealogical pedigrees. These Heralds had the power to deface and mutilate monuments which bore arms used without authority, to proclaim publicly that persons to whom the Heralds confirmed no authority to bear arms were not entitled to them and to require disclaimers of the use of arms for such persons.[2]

Two coats of arms were borne by the family of SKEWES during this time, but only one is officially recorded at the College of Arms.

Many people are confused as to "a coat of arms." There is no such thing as "family arms". Each coat of arms or shield is granted to an individual and all his descendants in the male line. No two families may bear the same arms.

All records of arms granted in England, Wales and Northern Ireland and the Commonwealth are kept in the offices of the College of Arms in London. The College was incorporated by Royal Charter of Richard III in 1484 at a building called Cold Harbour, formerly Poultney's Inn, City of London. When Richard was killed at Bosworth, the Heralds lost their chief, the Duke of Norfolk, who was also killed. The grant of Cold Harbour was declared void, and it was not until the Heralds obtained a new charter from Queen Mary in 1555 reaffirming their privileges, that they were granted a property called Derby House, in the parish of St Benedict and St Peter, City of London.[3]

This building was destroyed by the Great Fire of London in 1666, but fortunately the majority of the records were saved. The new college was rebuilt and completed in 1683 and remains on the original site three centuries later.

The post of Garter King of Arms came into being in 1415 when King Henry V appointed William Bruges as his chief Herald. Today Garter is supported by two other Kings of Arms, Clarenceux who has a responsibility for granting armorial bearings in the area south of the River Trent in Nottinghamshire and Norroy and Ulster, who has a similar task from north of the River Trent to the Scottish border. Ulster King of Arms was a separate title, but in 1943 his office was ended and his title annexed to that of Norroy King of Arms.

The title Herald dates back to the end of the 12th century. The College of Arms has six Heralds: Lancaster, Chester, York, Richmond, Windsor and Somerset.

Heralds Extra-Ordinary include Norfolk, Fitzalan, Wales, Maltravers and Surrey and they are nominated for particular occasions.

There are four Pursuivants. Recognised as junior or probationary Heralds their title goes back to the 15th century. They are known as Rouge Croix, Bluemantle, Portcullis and Rouge Dragon.

All Heralds are appointed by the Crown and are members of the Royal Household by letters patent under the great seal on the nomination of the Duke of Norfolk, as Earl Marshal of England.

1,2,3. *Heraldry and Genealogy*, L.G. Pine, London, 1957, pp. 130.

The Duchy of Cornwall were granted supporters for their arms in August, 1968. Cornish choughs with ostrich feathers as a badge of Royalty. The motto is one used by the Black Prince (the first Duke of Cornwall) and may be found on his tomb in Canterbury Cathedral

Description: Sable fifteen bezants in pile within a Bordure barry wavy of eight argent and azure and over the crest on a wreath argent and azure a chough proper resting the dexter claw upon a ducal coronet Or; on the dexter side a fisherman holding over the exterior shoulder a net, and on the sinister side a miner resting the exterior hand on a sledge hammer all proper

Heralds assist the Earl Marshal of England in all the great ceremonies of State, including the State opening of Parliament. They make Royal Proclamations and attend those Royal occasions to which they are summoned.[4]

The College of Arms contains the finest collection of heraldic and genealogical material in the world. However, neither the College nor its officers receive any subsidy from public funds, and its building and records have to be maintained from their fees. On average there are some 200 armorial bearings granted to new peers, civic bodies and private citizens each year.

Grants made to Scottish families and clans are kept at the Lyon Office in Edinburgh.

No man can demand, as a matter of right, that he has qualifications to bear arms and he must first of all obtain a formal patent of arms from the Crown. A grant will not be made to a person who is notorious for any improper reason.[5]

Normally a heraldic device consists of the arms or shield and designs upon it — helmet; mantling or lambrequin; wreath or torse; crest and the motto.

There are five primary colours used in heraldry: azure (blue), gules (red), sable (black), vert (green) and purpure (purple). There are two metallic colours: or (gold) and argent (silver).

Towards the end of the nineteenth century WILLIAM MACKENZIE SKUES is reputed to have convinced the College of Arms in London that he qualified to bear arms (a coat of arms, not weapons!). It was generally recognised amongst his family these arms were genuine. Furthermore he used to display them on his private notepaper and documents.

The reputed arms of Skues included the quartering of Mackenzie. Lieutenant George Skues ran away with, and later married, Mary Gibbs Mackenzie of Breda (Scotland) who was a niece of the Chieftain of the Clan Mackenzie. The objection to George Skues was not on account of birth or character, however, but because he was only a Lieutenant of Marines on half pay and with no prospects.

He was forgiven and his family adopted into the Clan. All his children, grandchildren and great grandchildren were called "Mackenzie Skues."

There are three mottoes displayed on the Skues arms. Mottoes, by the way, occasionally refer to the name of the bearer, often the bearings, and more frequently are short, quaint sentiments based on the mind or humour of the person who first adopted them. As with Skues the mottoes refer to some particular action or circumstance which they are meant to perpetuate.

"Sans Tache" is the first motto meaning "Without Stain" (the motto of the Mackenzie Clan). On the opposite corner are the words "Scutum Crusis" which refer to an ancestor (no doubt a mail clad warrior in those early days) who went on one of the Crusades to the Holy Land. The third motto, under the shield, is "Data Fata Secutus", Latin for "freely following my allotted fate" or "following the destiny allotted to me."

Enlargement of coat of arms as used on headed notepaper by William Mackenzie Skues

---

[4] *The Pageantry of Britain*, Julian Paget, 1979, London, pp 168-170.
[5] *Heraldry Explained*, Fox-Davies, 1906, Newton Abbot, page 17.

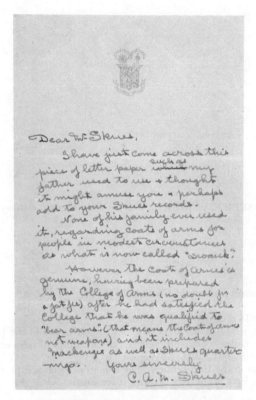

A copy of a letter sent to the author by Charles Ayre
Mackenzie Skues of Beckenham, Kent in 1958

To confirm the above grant the writer contacted the College of Arms and a search was made into the records in March, 1958. Two months later Walter J.G. Verco, MVO, Rouge Croix Pursuivant of Arms wrote to say that "William Mackenzie Skues appears never to have registered here his right to armorial bearings."[6]

As the supposed arms incorporated the Mackenzie Quarterings a search was made at the Lyon Office in Edinburgh, but with no success.

Various works published since 1740 list SKEWES in their link with heraldry.

In the book *Memorandums of Heraldry*, published in 1740 and retained at Penzance Library, Cornwall, MATTHEW SKEWYS circa 1400 is shown as having a coat of arms as follows:

Gules, a chevron Or between three quivvers Or.

From Gilbert's *Cornwall*, published in 1820.

SKEWIS of SKEWIS, Cury.
Arms: Gules, a chevron between three stumps of trees, Or, which seems to be quartered by Tredinnick. The name Skewis still remains with a respectable family at Helston which is probably descended from the same house.
SKEWIS of SKEWIS, St Wenn.
The Coheiresses are said by Messrs Lysons to have married Mohun and Courtenay in the 16th century. It is, however, very evident that an heiress or coheiress of this family married Denzell, as the arms are quartered by that family on many different shields in St Tudy Church.
Arms: Vert, a chevron, between three thistles, Or.

---

[6] Walter J.G. Verco is now KCVO. He subsequently became Chester Herald of Arms and later Norroy and Ulster King of Arms. He retired in 1980 when he was knighted and appointed Surrey Herald Extraordinary.

SKEWES of SKEWES, Cury, Cornwall. 16th century

From Lyson's *History of Cornwall* (1814).

SKEWIS of SKEWIS, Cury
The heiress married Denzall about the latter end of the 15th century.
Arms: Gules, a chevron, between three stumps of trees erased, Or.
SKEWIS of SKEWIS, St Wenn
Extinct in the 15th century. The coheiresses married Mohun and Courtenay.
Arms. Vert, a chevron between three thistles, Or.

The General Armory (Burke), 1884 confirmed the above mentioned entries. The book gave an additional example of arms and crest in the name of SKEWSE for the county of Cornwall.

Gules, a chevron between three escallops Or, on a chief of second a griffin passant, azure enclosed by two torteaux, each charged with a fleur-de-lys, Or.
Crest: A wolf passant proper collared and charged on the body with six stars, Or.

The College of Arms also confirmed this entry for the 16th century, although had no county listed or any entry of pedigree.

Gules, a chevron between three stocks of trees eradicated Or on a chief of the last a griffin passant between two torteaux each charged with a fleur-de-lys gold.
Crest: A wolf passant proper semee of estoiles Or and collared gold.
(Patent of Sir Christopher Barker, Garter Principal King of Arms).

SKEWES of SKEWES, St Wenn, Cornwall. 16th century

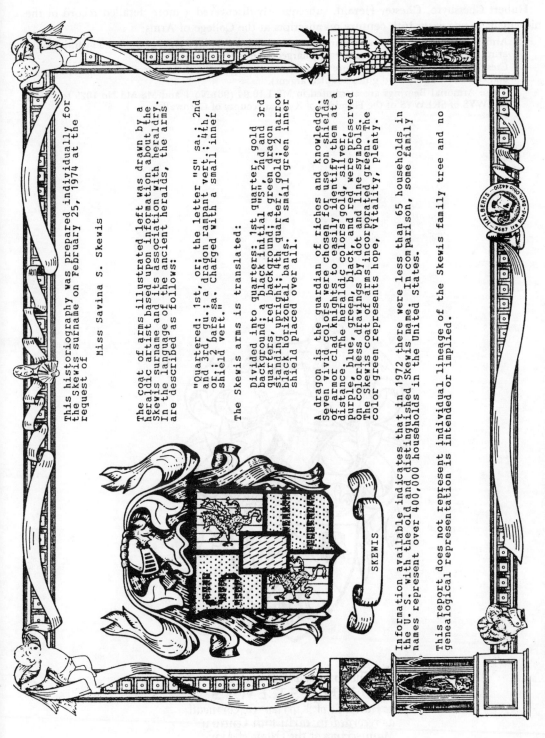

This historiography was prepared individually for the Skewis surname on February 25, 1974 at the request of

Miss Savina S. Skewis

The coat of arms illustrated left was drawn by a heraldic artist based upon information about the Skewis surname and its association with heraldry. In the language of the ancient heralds, the arms are described as follows:

"Quartered: 1st, or; the letter "S" sa.; 2nd and 3rd, gu..; a dragon rampant vert.; 4th, or;2 bars.sa. Charged with a small inner shield vert.."

The Skewis arms is translated:

Divided into quarters: 1st quarter, gold background; a black initial "S", 2nd and 3rd quarters, red background; a green dragon standing upright; 4th quarter,gold;2 narrow black horizontal bands. A small green inner shield placed over all.

A dragon is the guardian of riches and knowledge. Seven vivid colors were chosen for use on shields of armor clad knights to easily identify them at a distance. The heraldic colors gold, silver, purple, blue, green, black, and red were preserved on colorless drawings by dot and line symbols. The Skewis coat of arms incorporated green. The color green represents hope, vitality, plenty.

Information available indicates that in 1972 there were less than 65 households in the U.S. with the old and distinguished Skewis name. In comparison, some family names represent over 400,000 households in the United States.

This report does not represent individual lineage of the Skewis family tree and no genealogical representation is intended or implied.

SKEWIS

A copy of arms of SKEWIS in the United States of America sent by Miss Savina S. Skewis

Hubert Chesshyre, Chester Herald, subsequently discovered a more detailed record of the achievement in two early 16th century manuscripts at the College of Arms:

> Arms: Gules, a chevron between three stumps eradicated Or on a chief of the last a griffin passant azure between two roundels gules each charged with a fleur-de-lys Or.
>
> Crest: On a wreath argent and azure a pantheon statant purpure semy of estoiles and eared, unguled and collared Or (Mantled gules doubled argent).
>
> These Armorial Bearings are attributed in MS L10.94 (96) No 1 and MS M3 No 1025 to JOHN SKEWYS of SKEWYS of the Hundred of Kyrryar, county of Cornwall.

The Armorial Bearings of
JOHN SKEWYS
of the Hundred of Kyrryar, Co. Cornwall
as recorded in early 16th Century
Manuscripts at the College of Arms.

College of Arms,
London, MCMLXXX

Chester Herald.

A coat of arms hanging in the home of Dot and
Garfield Skewes of Adelaide, South Australia

The College of Arms confirmed a grant of arms and crest for Scott (pursuant to a Royal Warrant of the 6th February 1827 authorising the grantee to assume the name of Scott in lieu of that of SKUES) to RICHARD SKUES of Devonport, county Devon, Deputy Steward of His Majesty's Coinages of Cornwall and Devon and to Susannah Maria Martha his wife, only surviving child of John Scott of Saltash, county Cornwall, Esquire, sometime Principal Officer in His Majesty's Dockyard at Devonport aforesaid, deceased.

The grant is dated 19th March 1827 and it would appear therefore that the said Richard Skues had not established his right to paternal arms and crest since none are mentioned in the grant.

By Letters Patent dated 4 May 1978, honorary armorial bearings were granted to JAMES BUCKINGHAM SKEWES of Meridian, Mississippi, United States of America:

> Arms: Or on a chevron engrailed between three fleurs de lis gules as many tree stocks of the field, on a chief azure between two mullets a griffin passant or beaked and legged gules.
> Crest: On a wreath of the colours a tree stock thereon a pantheon statent or semy of estoiles and unguled gules.
> Motto: We endure.

American citizens do not qualify for grants of arms in the normal way, but if they can prove and register with the College of Arms a descent from an English ancestor, or else an ancestor residing in America before the Declaration of Independence, they can be granted honorary armorial bearings.[7]

The Armorial Bearings of
James Buckingham Skewes

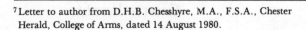

College of Arms,
London.

Windsor Herald of Arms.

Arms of James Buckingham Skewes of the United
States of America

---

[7] Letter to author from D.H.B. Chesshyre, M.A., F.S.A., Chester
Herald, College of Arms, dated 14 August 1980.

By Letters Patent dated 4 March 1981, armorial bearing were granted to **RICHARD KEITH SKUES** of England.

> Arms: Or on a chevron sable between in chief two treestocks eradicated each sprouting an oak branch leaved and fructed and in base a thistle slipped and leaved gules, a plate between two bezants.
>
> Crest: On a wreath Or and gules a pantheon sejant gules semy of estoiles or supporting with the dexter forefoot a roundel sable pierced and charged with five concentric annulets argent.
>
> Motto: Perseverantia et Prudentia.

The Armorial Bearings of
RICHARD KEITH SKUES

College of Arms,
London, MCMLXXXI

Hubert Chesshyre
Chester Herald.

15 Wills & Administrations

A WILL deals with Real Estate — one's house and grounds. A TESTAMENT on the other hand usually lists the personal belongings from furniture to a fur coat and from money to a motor vehicle. It has been practice to link the two together as "The last Will and Testament of..."

Wills, which can be in any language or hand on paper or parchment, are one of the main sources of information for a genealogist.

Latin was used in wills until around the middle of the sixteenth century. One will find many gaps in the 16th/17th centuries following the death of a particular member of the family. There was no necessity in those days to make a will as many people were tenants of a manor, and there was no real estate to dispose of.

Prior to 1882 women tended not to leave wills unless a spinster or widow. It was only in 1882 that the Married Women's Property Act became law which meant she could bequeath items to family and friends. Before this date everything in law belonged to her husband.

Before 1858 wills and administrations were looked after by the Church. England is divided into two church provinces, Canterbury and York. Wills and administrations for the Prerogative Court of Canterbury are kept at the Public Record Office in London and run from 1383 to 1858. Wills and administrations for similar years for the Prerogative Court of York are retained at the Bothwick Institute of Historical Research in York.

Many County Record Offices now retain copies of wills and administrations for that particular county.

After 1858 wills and administrations are housed at the Principal Probate Registry at Somerset House, London. All are indexed by the year.

Wills and administrations for Scotland are kept at the Probate Registry, Edinburgh.

Information which can be taken from wills include the name of the testator, occupation, parish, date of execution of will, names of beneficiaries, particulars of the estate mentioned and the names of witnesses and executors.

In this chapter it is not the intention of the writer to trace the history of wills and administrations. Anthony J. Camp has produced an excellent book *Wills and Their Whereabouts*, London, 1974.

Throughout the following pages there is a list of wills and administrations "tracked down" in Great Britain and where possible relevant information extracted.

The majority of the early SKEWES wills and administrations are to be found in Cornwall and Devon. The County Record Office, Truro has a very good collection of Cornish wills, but there are gaps. Some wills were lost in a move from St. Neot to Lostwithiel in 1753. Others went astray in a further move to Bodmin in 1773.

In Devon the building housing many old wills was completely destroyed during the Second World War and the only ones remaining are those indexed in the Prerogative Court of Canterbury. The printed catalogue of Devon wills, however, does remain with us to show what records have been lost for ever.

All variations of the name are included up to the year 1837, after which date only SKEWES, SKEWIS, SKEWS and SKUES are included.

The author is grateful to the County Record Office, Truro for permission to reproduce extracts from older wills and administrations to 1858 and to the Lord Chancellor's Office, Somerset House, London for wills and administrations since 1858.

Names of beneficiaries since 1900 have been purposely omitted so as not to embarrass either themselves or their descendants.

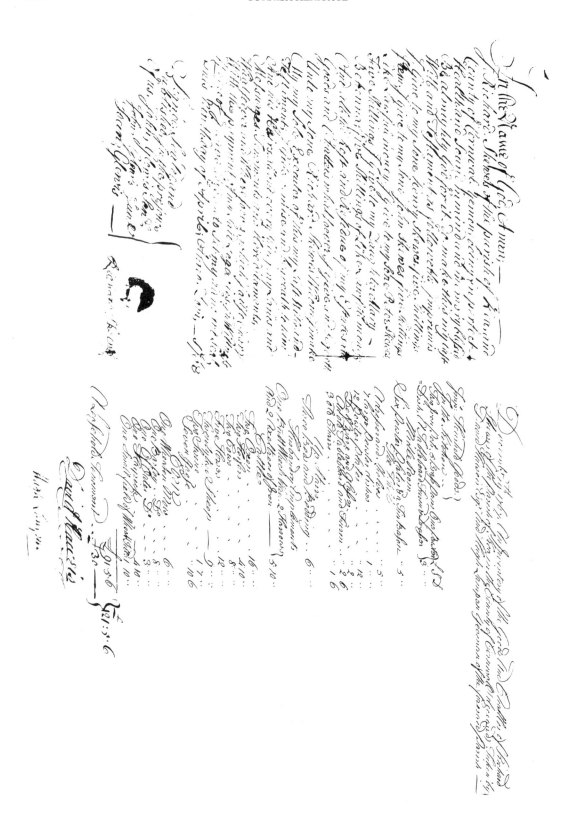

Copy of the will of Richard Skewes, dated 9 April 1763

INDEX OF WILLS 1383 — 1980

ABBREVIATIONS
W   Will
A   Administration
D   Destroyed by fire in Exeter in 1944
SH   Retained at Somerset House (General Registry)
CRO   Retained at County Record Office, Truro, Cornwall
DRO   Retained at Devon Record Office, Exeter, Devon

Year	Name		District	Where held	W or A
1544	SKEWYS	JOHN	Cury & London	SH	W
1586	SKEWES	JOHN	Gwennap	CRO	W
1604	SKEWES	ALEXANDER	Ludgvan	CRO	A
1622	SKUES	JOHN	Mullion	CRO	A
1622	SKEWES	JAMES	Ottery St Mary	D	A
1622	SKEWES	STEPHEN	St Just in R/land	CRO	A
1637	SKEWES	PETER	Colliton Rayleigh	D	W
1640	SKEWES	MARY, widow	Colliton Reyleigh	D	W
1643	SKEWES	JOHN	St Gorran	CRO	W
1643	SKEWES	THOMAZINE	Colliton Rayleigh	D	A
1644	SKEWES	BEATON	St Gorran	CRO	W
1644	SKEWES	PEARCE	Werrington	CRO	W
1646	SKEWES	JOHN, Jnr	Colliton Rayleigh	D	W
1650	SKEWES	GRACE	Ottery St Mary	D	A
1672	SKUES	RICHARD	Stebonheath	SH	W
1679	SKEWS	ROBERT	Honiton	D	A
1681	SKEWS	MARY	Sidmouth	D	A with W
1694	SKUES	THOMAS	Bristol	SH	W
1704	SKUSE	EDWARDIUS	Died overseas	SH	W
1707	SKUSE	DANIEL	Wiltshire	SH	W
1708	SKUSE	EDWARDUS	Died overseas	SH	A
1718	SKEWS	JOHN	Mevagissey	CRO	A
1718	SKUES	RICHARD	Bristol	Bristol	W
1718	SKUES	ELIZABETH	Bristol	Bristol	W
1735	SKEWS	THOMAS	Gwennap	CRO	W
1736	SKEWES	ALEXANDER	Gwennap	CRO	A
1738	SKEWS	RICHARD	Sancreed	CRO	W
1741	SKUES	RICHARD	Kea	CRO	W
1748	SKEWYS	WILLIAM	Kent	SH	W
1748	SKUSE	JOHN	Wiltshire	SH	W
1749	SKUCE	ANN	Gloucester	Bristol	W
1751	SKEWIS	JOSEPH	Gunwalloe	CRO	A
1752	SKUES	STEPHEN	Redruth	CRO	W
1756	SKUES	RICHARD	Helston	CRO	W
1758	SKUES	JOAN	Mawgan in Meneage	CRO	W
1760	SKEWES	RICHARD	Sancreed	CRO	W
1764	SKEWS	THOMAS	Gwennap	CRO	W
1768	SKEWES	RICHARD	Kea	CRO	W
1772	SKEWES	JOHN	Gwennap	CRO	A
1781	SKEWES	EDWARD	Mevagissey	CRO	W
1781	SKEWES	JOHN	Kenwyn	CRO	W
1786	SKEWES	DIGORY	Kea	CRO	W
1786	SKEWES	EDWARD	St Keverne	CRO	W
1787	SKEWES	WILLIAM	Camborne	CRO	W
1787	SKEWES	DIGORY	Kea	CRO	W
1789	SKEWES	WILLIAM	Camborne	CRO	W
1790	SKEWES	JOHN	Cury	CRO	A
1791	SKEWES	JOHN	Gwennap	CRO	A
1792	SKEWES	EDWARD	St Keverne	CRO	W
1795	SKUSE	WILLIAM	London	SH	W
1799	SKUSE	THOMAS	Ireland	SH	W
1802	SKEWES	JOHN	Kea	CRO	W
1802	SKEWES	PETER	Kenwyn — innkeeper	CRO	W
1807	SKEWES	RICHARD	Devon (late Gwennap)	SH	W
1808	SKEWES	RICHARD	Constantine	CRO	A
1808	SKEWES	WILLIAM	Gwinear — yeoman	CRO	A
1811	SKEWES	WILLIAM	At sea	SH	A
1811	SKEWES	JOHN	Gwennap	CRO	W
1812	SKUES	RICHARD	Helston	SH	A
1813	SKUSE	MARY	Wiltshire	SH	W
1813	SKEWES	WILLIAM	Constantine	CRO	W
1813	SKEWES	JOHN	Camborne - yeoman	CRO	W
1814	SKEWES	JOHN	Kenwyn	CRO	W

Year	Name		District	Where held	W or A
1814	SKEWES	HENRY	Camborne - yeoman	CRO	W
1816	SKEWES	PHILIPPA	Camborne - widow	CRO	W
1816	SKEWES	WILLIAM	Kea - yeoman	CRO	W
1816	SKUCE	JOHN	In Army	SH	W
1817	SKEWES	MARGARET	Gwennap - spinster	CRO	W
1817	SKUES	WILLIAM	Helston	SH	A
1817	SKEWES	THOMAS	Gwennap - miner	CRO	W
1819	SKUSE	NATHANIEL	Middlesex	SH	W
1823	SKEWS	RICHARD	Kenwyn - miner	CRO	W
1824	SKUES	STEPHEN	Camborne - yeoman	CRO	W
1824	SKEWES	JOHN	Cury	CRO	W
1824	SKEWES	DIGORY	Kea - miner	CRO	W
1824	SKEWES	HENRY	Camborne - yeoman	CRO	W
1829	SKEWES	JOHN	Cury - yeoman	CRO	W
1829	SKUCE	JOHN	Wiltshire	SH	W
1830	SKEWES	THOMAS	Gwennap	CRO	W
1830	SKUSE	GEORGE	Wiltshire	SH	W
1830	SKEWES	MARTIN	St Clement	CRO	W
1831	SKEWES	HENRY	Ruan Major	CRO	W
1834	SKEWS	JOHN	Kerley, Kea	CRO	W
1835	SCUSE	WILLIAM	Gloucester	SH	W
1837	SKEWES	RICHARD	Kenwyn - miner	CRO	W
1837	SKEWES	HENRY	Camborne - yeoman	CRO	W
1838	SKEWES	THOMAS	Gwennap - miner	CRO	W
1839	SKEWES	JOHN	Gwennap - yeoman	CRO	W
1840	SKEWES	WILLIAM	St Ewe - yeoman	CRO	W
1843	SKEWES	JOHN	Kenwyn	CRO	W
1844	SKEWES	HENRY	Constantine	CRO	W
1844	SKEWES	JOHN	Kenwyn - miner	CRO	A
1847	SKUES	ANN	East Stonehouse	DRO	W
1852	SKEWES	JOHN	Cury - yeoman	CRO	W
1854	SKEWES	RICHARD	Kea - parish clerk	CRO	W
1856	SKEWES	JAMES	Cury - farmer	CRO	W
1857	SKEWES	MATTHEW	Kenwyn - innkeeper	CRO	A
1859	SKEWES	JOHN	St Erme	CRO	W
1859	SKEWES	JOHN	Gwennap	SH	W
1859	SKEWS	JOHN	St Austell	CRO	W
1860	SKEWES	WILLIAM	Devon	SH	W
1863	SKEWES	JOHN	Killiwerris, Kea	SH	W
1863	SKEWES	ALEXANDER	Gwennap	SH	W
1864	SKEWES	DANIEL HODGE	Beerferris, Devon	SH	W
1867	SKEWES	PETER	Kea	SH	W
1868	SKEWES	THOMAS	Truro	SH	W
1869	SKEWES	THOMAS	Ruan Major	SH	W
1869	SKUES	MARY BENNETT	Wiltshire	SH	W
1870	SKEWES	EDWARD	Mawnan	SH	W
1871	SKEWES	HENRY	Redruth	SH	W
1871	SKEWES	ANN	Penryn	SH	W
1872	SKEWES	JAMES	Neath	SH	W
1872	SKUES	GEORGE	Middlesex	SH	W
1872	SKEWS	PHILIP	St Mewan	SH	W
1873	SKEWES	ANTHONY	Ruan Major	SH	W
1873	SKEWES	RICHARD	Kenwyn	SH	W
1875	SKEWES	THOMAS	Kea	SH	W
1875	SKEWIS	JAMES	Camborne	SH	W
1875	SKEWIS	THOMAS	Chacewater	SH	W
1876	SKUES	WILLIAM	London	SH	W
1877	SKEWES	ELIZABETH	Gwennap	SH	W
1877	SKEWES	FRANCIS	Illogan	SH	W
1877	SKEWES	LAVINIA	Truro	SH	W
1878	SKEWES	EDWARD	Cury	SH	W
1878	SKEWES	JOSIAH	Constantine	SH	W
1878	SKEWES	MARY	Gwennap	SH	W
1879	SKUES	WILLIAM	Gloucester	SH	W
1881	SKEWES	HRY BLEWETT	St Ewe	SH	A
1884	SKEWES	JOHN	Gwennap	SH	W
1884	SKEWES	RICHARD	Kenwyn	SH	W
1885	SKUES	GEORGE	Middlesex	SH	W
1887	SKEWES	WILLIAM	Crowan	SH	W
1889	SKEWES	JANE	Truro	SH	W
1890	SKEWES	MARIA	Liverpool	SH	A
1890	SKEWIS	HENRY	Somerset	SH	W
1890	SKUES	MARGARET	Surrey	SH	A
1891	SKEWES	LOVEDAY	Ruan Minor	SH	A
1892	SKUES	WM. MACKENZIE	Surrey	SH	A
1894	SKEWES	THOMAS	Truro	SH	A

Year	Name		District	Where held	W or A
1896	SKEWES	ANN	Kenwyn	SH	A
1896	SKEWES	JANE	Kea	SH	A
1896	SKEWES	FANNY	Constantine	SH	W
1897	SKUES	GEORGE HENRY	Paddington	SH	W
1897	SKUES	JOHN	Redruth	SH	W
1898	SKEWES	JOSEPH HENRY, Rev.	Liverpool	SH	A
1899	SKEWS	JOHN	Callington	SH	A
1900	SKEWES	JAMES	Mawgan	SH	W
1901	SKEWES	LOUISA JANE	Middlesex	SH	A
1902	SKEWS	ELIZABETH	Middlesex	SH	A
1902	SKUES	MOSES	Minety	SH	W
1903	SKEWES	SAMUEL DAWE	Bristol	SH	W
1903	SKEWES	JOHN JAMES	Middlesex	SH	A
1903	SKEWES	THOMAS LEAN	Devonshire	SH	W
1903	SKUES	GEORGINA MARY	Middlesex	SH	A with W
1904	SKUES	MARY ELIZABETH	Kent	SH	A
1906	SKEWES	HENRY	Camborne	SH	A
1906	SKEWIS	GEORGE	America	SH	A
1908	SKEWES	MARY JANE	Truro	SH	W
1909	SKEWES	FRANCES	Mawnan	SH	A
1910	SKUES	FREDERICK MACKENZIE	Surrey	SH	W
1911	SKUES	LUCY	Halifax	SH	W
1912	SKEWES	THOMAS	Truro	SH	A
1912	SKEWIS	MARY LANGMEAD	Devonshire	SH	W
1913	SKEWS	JOHN WILLIAM HENRY	Plymouth	SH	W
1913	SKEWES-COX	SIR THOMAS	Surrey	SH	W
1914	SKEWS	WILLIAM	St Columb Minor	SH	W
1915	SKEWES	EDWARD	Huddersfield	SH	W
1915	SKEWES	EMILY ANN	Wendron	SH	W
1916	SKEWES	ARTHUR COURTIS	Devonshire	SH	A
1917	SKEWES	ANNIE	St Austell	SH	W
1917	SKEWES	JAMES	Plymouth	SH	W
1917	SKUES	JOHN	Surrey	SH	W
1918	SKEWES	SAMUEL	Australia	SH	A
1919	SKEWES	ADA ELIZA	Mabe	SH	W
1922	SKEWES	EMMA	Bere Alston	SH	W
1922	SKEWES	HENRY	Camborne	SH	W
1922	SKUES	FREDERICK MACKENZIE	South Africa	SH	A with W
1924	SKUES	WINIFRED	Cricklewood	SH	A
1925	SKUES	ELIZABETH	Devonshire	SH	A
1926	SKEWES	HENRY	Cury	SH	W
1928	SKEWES	GWENDOLINE	Exeter	SH	A
1928	SKEWES	HANNIBAL	Ruan Major	SH	A
1928	SKEWS	EDMUND	Plymouth	SH	A
1929	SKEWS	JANE	Falmouth	SH	W
1929	SKEWS	JOHN	Redruth	SH	A
1930	SKUES	PHILIP HENRY	Surrey	SH	A
1930	SKEWES-COX	JESSICA	Petersham	SH	W
1931	SKEWES	FRANCES ANN	Cury	SH	A
1932	SKEWES	AGNES	Huddersfield	SH	W
1932	SKEWES	WILLIAM	Landewednack	SH	A (Ltd)
1932	SKEWES	WILLIAM	Falmouth	SH	A
1933	SKUES	EDWARD GEORGE	South Africa	SH	A with W
1934	SKEWS	ELIZABETH SARAH	Plymouth	SH	W
1935	SKEWES	LIZZIE MARION	Newquay	SH	W
1935	SKEWIS	WILLIAM BAWDEN	Brighton Ladock	SH	A with W
1935	SKEWS	MATTHEW	County Durham	SH	W
1935	SKEWS	WILLIAM JOHN	County Durham	SH	W
1935	SKUES	JOHN GILBERT	London	SH	W
1936	SKEWES	JOHN COURTIS	Crediton	SH	W
1936	SKEWS	AMELIA	County Durham	SH	W
1936	SKEWS	JOHN	St Austell	SH	W
1937	SKEWS	MINNIE	Finchley	SH	W
1937	SKEWS	MAY LOUISA	Plymouth	SH	W
1937	SKEWS	SAMUEL FRANCIS	South Africa	SH	W
1938	SKEWES	EDITH	Cury	SH	W
1938	SKEWES	LILY	Gidleigh	SH	A
1938	SKEWES	WILLIAM	Chiverton	SH	A
1939	SKEWES	MARY ELLEN	Essex	SH	W
1939	SKEWES	NELLIE	Redruth	SH	A
1939	SKEWIS	HELEN THOMASINE	Penzance	SH	W
1940	SKEWES	ALFRED JOHN	Somerset	SH	A
1940	SKEWES	EMILY ANN	Camborne	SH	A
1940	SKEWES	HARRY OSWALD	Camborne	SH	A
1940	SKEWES	JOHN KEMPTHORNE	London	SH	W
1940	SKUES	FRED W. MACKENZIE	Croydon	SH	W

Year	Name		District	Where held	W or A
1940	SKUES	MARGARET GEORGINA SARAH	Devon	SH	W
1941	SKEWES	ANN	Crediton	SH	W
1941	SKEWES	CHARLES	Manchester	SH	W
1941	SKEWIS	ALFRED	At sea	SH	A
1942	SKEWES	EDWARD	Mawnan	SH	W
1942	SKEWES	HENRIETTA CATALINA	Crowan	SH	A with W
1942	SKEWES	EDITH	Preston	SH	A
1942	SKEWS	ELIZA	Swindon	SH	A
1943	SKEWES	MAUD ANNA	Falmouth	SH	W
1944	SKEWES	FREDERICK WILLIAM	Manchester	SH	A
1944	SKEWS	HENRY JAMES	Walthamstow	SH	W
1944	SKEWS	WILLIAM THOMAS	Bethnal Green	SH	A
1945	SKUES	MARY THERESA	Devonshire	SH	W
1945	SKEWES	HOWARD	Gidleigh	SH	W
1946	SKEWES	ANNIE	Manchester	SH	A
1946	SKEWES	MARY	Mawnan	SH	W
1946	SKEWS	JOHN HENRY	Plymouth	SH	W
1946	SKUES	ERNEST	Stockport	SH	W
1946	SKUES	DORIS GAMBLE	Surrey	SH	W
1946	SKUES	FLORENCE MARY	Halifax	SH	W
1947	SKEWES	DOROTHY MARION	Doncaster	SH	W
1947	SKEWS	JOHN EDWIN	Swindon	SH	W
1947	SKUES	MARY ISOBELLA MACKENZIE	Croydon	SH	W
1948	SKEWES	JOSIAH	Finchley	SH	W
1948	SKEWS	ALICE	Edmonton	SH	A
1948	SKEWS	GEORGE FRANCIS	Winchmore Hill	SH	A
1948	SKUES	ALBERT EDWARD	Wandsworth	SH	A
1948	SKUES	ELIZABETH	Wood Green	SH	W
1948	SKUES	ELIZABETH	Redruth	SH	W
1949	SKEWES	MAGGIE ISABELLA SIMPSON	Durham	SH	W
1949	SKEWIS	FRANK	Kent	SH	A
1949	SKEWS	MATTHEW	Durham	SH	A with W
1949	SKUES	EDWARD ALFRED	Tonbridge	SH	A
1949	SKUES	GEORGE EDWARD MACKENZIE	Beckenham	SH	W
1950	SKUES	CLORINDA EMMA	London	SH	A
1950	SKEWES	HARRY STANLEY	Mawgan	SH	W
1950	SKEWES	WILLIAM JOHN	Redruth	SH	W
1950	SKEWS	ALFRED DAVID RICHARD	Edmonton	SH	W
1950	SKUES	HAROLD FREDERICK CLAUDE	Wood Green	SH	W
1951	SKEWES	ALBERT EDWARD	Wareham	SH	A with W
1951	SKEWES	JOHN WESLEY	Mawgan	SH	W
1951	SKEWS	VICTOR GEORGE	Gravesend	SH	A
1951	SKUES	JANE EMILY	Chalft. St Giles	SH	A
1951	SKUES	ELIZABETH MACKENZIE	Beckenham	SH	W
1952	SKEWES	EDWARD	Helston	SH	W
1952	SKEWES	ELIZABETH	Manchester	SH	W
1952	SKEWES	LILIAN LINDA MAY	Penzance	SH	A
1953	SKEWES	ALARINA	Monmouth	SH	W
1953	SKUES	BESSIE ANNIE	Chalft St Giles	SH	W
1954	SKEWES	GEORGE ERNEST	Sale	SH	W
1954	SKEWES	JAMES HENRY OSWALD	Camborne	SH	A
1954	SKEWES	SAMUEL JOHN	Callington	SH	W
1954	SKEWES	WM. FDCK. CHARLES	Doncaster	SH	A
1954	SKEWES	WILLIAM TREVENA	Penzance	SH	A
1954	SKEWS	JOHN HENRY	Plymouth	SH	A
1955	SKEWS	BERTHA	St Austell	SH	A
1955	SKEWS	FREDERICK	Durham	SH	W
1955	SKEWS	WILLIAM	St Austell	SH	A
1955	SKEWS	WILLIAM JOHN	Durham	SH	A with W
1956	SKEWES	WILLIAM HENRY	Carnkie	SH	A
1956	SKEWS	FRANCES	Durham	SH	W
1956	SKUES	ERNEST	Redruth	SH	A
1957	SKEWES	ANN MARIE	Bridgwater	SH	A with W
1957	SKEWES	FLORENCE LUCY	Exeter	SH	A
1957	SKEWES	WILLIAM VERDAYNE	Croydon	SH	W
1957	SKEWIS	LAURA	Pembrokeshire	SH	A
1957	SKUES	JOAN MACKENZIE	Bromley	SH	A
1958	SKEWES	HERBERT JOHN	Redruth	SH	W
1958	SKEWIS	SAMUEL	Pembrokeshire	SH	A
1958	SKUES	LILY	Worcester	SH	W
1958	SKUES	CHARLES AYRE MACKENZIE	Market Drayton	SH	W

Year	Name		District	Where held	W or A
1959	SKEWES	ALFRED JOHN	Truro	SH	W
1959	SKEWES	JOHN HENRY	California	SH	A (Ltd)
1959	SKEWES	MATILDA	Tuckingmill	SH	W
1959	SKEWS	ETHEL	Durham	SH	W
1959	SKUES	CHARLES HENRY	Bucks	SH	W
1960	SKEWES	ARTHUR DAW	Plymouth	SH	W
1960	SKEWES	JANIE	Falmouth	SH	W
1960	SKUES	MARGARET ROSEMARY	Gloucester	SH	A
1961	SKEWS	GEORGE WEALE	London, E.1.	SH	W
1961	SKUES	MARGARET ELIZABETH	London, N 13	SH	A
1962	SKEWES	CHARLOTTE	Callington	SH	W
1962	SKEWS	MATTHEW	Durham	SH	A with W
1962	SKUES	MINNIE MACKENZIE	Shropshire	SH	W
1963	SKEWES	ETHEL	Redruth	SH	W
1963	SKEWS	ALICE ELIZABETH	Kent	SH	A
1963	SKEWS	ALICE MARTHA ROSE	Sussex	SH	A
1963	SKEWS	GERTRUDE ALBERTA	St Austell	SH	A
1963	SKEWS	MINNIE	Redruth	SH	A
1964	SKEWS	BEATRICE	Newquay	SH	W
1964	SKEWS	MABLE COOPER	Kettering	SH	W
1964	SKUES	THOMAS GEORGE	Cricklewood	SH	W
1965	SKEWS	BELLA CLARKE	Devon	SH	A
1965	SKEWES	ELIZABETH	Croydon	SH	W
1965	SKEWES	GEORGE	Plymouth	SH	W
1965	SKEWES	LIONAL JAMES	Mabe	SH	W
1965	SKEWES	WILLIAM HEDLEY	Redruth	SH	W
1965	SKEWS	ANNIE EDITH	Preston	SH	W
1965	SKEWS	ELIZ. ETHEL GRACE	Plymouth	SH	W
1965	SKEWS	EVA MARY	Kent	SH	W
1965	SKUES	ELSIE KATE	Wood Green	SH	A
1966	SKEWES	RACHEL CARDWELL	Bournemouth	SH	W
1966	SKEWS	MINNIE	Redruth	SH	W
1966	SKEWS	SARAH	Hayle	SH	W
1966	SKUES	EVA	Probus	SH	A withW
1966	SKUES	REGINALD PENROSE	West Looe	SH	W
1967	SKEWES	EDWARD MORLEY	Tuckingmill	SH	A
1967	SKUES	PHILIP ERNEST	Ewell	SH	W
1968	SKEWES	ERNEST JOHN	Exeter	SH	W
1968	SKEWES	HAROLD	Manchester	SH	A
1968	SKUES	WALTER EDWARD	Walton on Naze	SH	W
1969	SKEWES	FREDERICK HENRY	Exeter	SH	A
1970	SKEWES	ANNIE	Penzance	SH	A
1970	SKEWS	ALBERT EDWARD VICTOR	Plymouth	SH	A
1970	SKEWS	WILLIAM DAVID	Sussex	SH	A
1971	SKEWES	BESSIE SARAH	Truro	SH	A
1971	SKEWES	EMMA	Redruth	SH	W
1971	SKEWES	GEORGE	Camborne	SH	A
1971	SKEWES	IDA MAY	Ealing	SH	W
1971	SKEWES	JOHN EDWARD	Poole	SH	W
1971	SKEWES-COX	THOS. EDMUND	Southwald	SH	W
1971	SKEWIS	SAMUEL LESLIE	Gillingham	SH	A
1971	SKEWS	EDWIN ARTHUR	Shrewsbury	SH	A
1971	SKUES	ARTHUR LEONARD PETER	Barrow in F.	SH	A
1971	SKUES	THOMAS HENRY JAMES	Ashford	SH	A
1971	SKUES	VINCENT	Chorley	SH	A
1973	SKEWES	VIOLET	St Keverne	SH	A
1973	SKEWS	ESME ETHEL	Lincs	SH	A
1973	SKEWS	WILLIAM HEDLEY	St Austell	SH	A
1973	SKUES	CARMELLA	Ewell	SH	A
1974	SKEWES	FANNY	Manchester	SH	A
1974	SKEWES	SIDNEY ARTHUR	St Keverne	SH	A
1975	SKEWES	AVIS MAY	Camborne	SH	A
1975	SKEWS	DAVID GEORGE	Dagenham	SH	A
1976	SKEWES	HARRY	Penzance	SH	A
1976	SKUES	ANNIE MARIE	Clacton	SH	W
1976	SKUES	VICTOR CLAUDE	Clacton	SH	W
1976	SKUES	WILLIAM JOHN	Probus	SH	W
1978	SKEWS	CLARENCE	Callington	SH	W
1978	SKUES	ERNEST	Banstead	SH	W
1979	SKEWES	ARTHUR GEORGE	Paignton	SH	W
1979	SKEWIS	MARJORIE CONSTANCE	Tunbridge Wells	SH	W
1980	SKEWS	ALFRED GEORGE WILLIAM	Clacton	SH	W
1980	SKEWS	KIRTLEY	Tyne & Wear	SH	A
1980	SKUES	LUCY	Halifax	SH	W
1980	SKUES	MARJORIE HELEN	Barrow in Furness	SH	A
1980	SKEWES-COX	MILES L.D.	Ashburton	SH	W

In early wills and administrations there are variations in the spelling of both Christian and surnames, as well as items mentioned in an inventory. Exact spelling as per will or administration has been maintained.

EXTRACTS FROM WILLS

1544 SKEWYS JOHN of Cury & London. For details of will please refer to Chapter 6 "John Skewys".

1622 SKUES JOHN of Mullion. Inventory only. Very bad writing which cannot be read. Will dated March, 1622.

1622 SKEWES STEPHEN of St Just in Roseland. An unreadable inventory. Will dated July, 1622.

1643 SKEWES JOHN of St Gorran. Very fragile document. Names Margarett daughter of Floursse (?) and 100 other bequests for people in Gorran. He left a large inventory totalling £268 : 08 : 0d ... a considerable amount in those days.

1644 SKEWES BEATON of St Gorran. In Latin. Totally unreadable.

1644 SKEWES PEARCE of Werrington. Written 19 May, 1642. Lists JOHN JAMES (?) TAMOR SKEWES, son; CAMPON (CAMSON) SKEWES, daughter, MARGOROTT, daughter; and EIDOTH, wife. Gives a long inventory, but totally unreadable.

1718 SKEWES JOHN of Mevagissey. Inventory of his goods dated 27 October, 1718. Includes the following on Inventory and names his wife Elizabeth SKEWS.

	£	s	d
Purse and wearing apparoll	—	10	0
One small feather bed with an old bedhood			
One old covershed, one slutt, one old blankett with two old pillows	1	0	0
Two little brass pans	—	6	0
One brass crork	—	7	0
Five pewter dishes	—	6	0
One old table and frame and forms	—	2	0
Two little old horses	2	0	0
One little old cow	1	5	0
Three yearlings	3	0	0
One little old bouso	2	0	0
	£10	16	0

1735 SKEWES THOMAS of Gwennap. Will proved 11 February, 1735. Names MARGARET, wife; JOHN, RICHARD, WILLIAM & THOMAS, sons; & MARGARET & JOAN, daughters. Executor: THOMAS SKEWS, son.

A true inventory of all and singular goods and chattels of THOMAS SKEWS, late of the parish of Gwennap, in the county of Cornwall; tinner. Taken and appraised this 6th day of February, 1735 by us Mark Moyle & Philip Tom jnr.

	£	s	d
Purse and wearing apparoll	2	0	0
8 pewter platters; 12 pewter plates and other goods in the hall	4	0	0
3 brass pans and brass pot and 3 iron pots & other goods in the kitchen	3	10	0
4 feather beds with appurtonies and other goods in the chambers	15	0	0
Imp winsuss belonging to this bandry and tin affairs	3	0	0
A sack of Hay	1	1	0
2 Hoggs	4	0	0
3 Cows and a yearling	7	10	0
Tin and tin stuff	10	0	0
Chattel estate called Cownhale with Stamping Mill	90	0	0
Chote estate called Bowl's Jonson	35	0	0
3 Ewe sheep	—	12	0
Debts sporate and desporate	15	0	0
For things misson	1	0	0
	£191	13	0

1736 SKEWES ALEXANDER of Gwennap. Inventory taken 14 October, 1736. Alexander was a tinner and bond and inventory granted to his brother RICHARD SKEWES.

	£	s	d
Wearing apparroll	4	0	0
Cash in his possession	3	0	0
Bed tick with feathers in it	2	0	0
Small chattel estate on three lives	60	0	0
Debts good and bad	2	0	0
	£71	0	0

1738 SKEWS RICHARD of Sancreed. Will written 4 January, 1737. Proved 10 May, 1738. Names WILLIAM, CHRISTOPHER, RICHARD (sons), REBECAH (wife), brother-in-law John Cattrall, daughters GRACE and REBECAH; his sister JANE and BROTHER JOHN SKEWS.

1741 SKUES RICHARD of Kea. Will dated 26 Feb. 1741. Proved 22 March, 1741. Names DIGORY SKUES (father) to whom he gave his estate in Kea, also 40 shillings. Gave his brothers, brothers-in-law and sister one shilling. To his wife ANN SKUES all the remainder of his Goods and Chattels. There is very bad writing on the will, but it looks as if his brother is named MARINO(?) and family and brother-in-law Francis Holman and family.

1751 SKEWIS JOSEPH of Gunwalloe. Bond of Administration dated 8 October, 1751. Mentions JOAN SKUES (wife).

	£	s	d
Two cows	4	0	0
Two horses	2	10	0
Two maids	3	0	0
Corn in the ground	1	1	0
Two bedds, stools and furniture	2	0	0
Nine pewter dishes and two dozen of pewter plates	1	10	0
Six brass panns	1	16	0
Two iron potts and one brass pot	—	5	0
One case of shelves	—	1	6
One hanging pot	—	2	6
Two round tables, one long table	—	7	6
Five chairs	—	5	0
Two brass skillotts	—	2	0
For wearing apparollo	1	0	0
For things forgotten	2	5	0
	£20	5	6

1752 SKUES STEPHEN of Redruth; tinner. Names his brother Executor, RICHARD SKUES; mentions his wife JANE SKUES to whom he gives £3 per year as long as she may live. Gives his sister Jone Cadgwith five shillings; sister Ann Gobey five shillings; his nephew Mary Goodman five shillings; his nephew STEPHEN SKUES of Newland twenty shillings. To his brother RICHARD SKUES he bequeathed his Goods and Chattels.
Note: Stephen Skues was son of William & Jane Skues of Redruth. He died 16 January, 1752 at Redruth.

1756 SKUES RICHARD of Helston. Will proved 2 April, 1756. Deeds of the will were granted to his widow, and also WILLIAM SKUES (son) and JOHN SKUES (son). He left five shillings to his daughter JENNIFER (Gritton) and £5 to his daughter MARY SKUES. RICHARD SKUES was a tinner.

1758 SKUES JOAN of Mawgan in Meneage. Will written 30 May, 1757. Proved 2 May, 1758. Mentions son JOSEPH SKUES junior, Executor; her daughter Joan Traplin as well as Frances, Thomas, William and Jane Cornish.
Note: Jane was a widow. Her husband Joseph died in 1751.

1760 SKEWES RICHARD of Sancreed. Served aboard His Majesty's Ship *Royal George.* His mother, REBECCA SKEWS of St. Criets. was Executrix.

1764 SKEWS THOMAS of Gwennap. Will written 25 August, 1763. Proved 15 May, 1764. Mentions his wife ELIZABETH (Executrix); sons THOMAS, JOHN, RICHARD, WILLIAM and ALEXANDER and daughter MARGARET.

1768 SKEWES RICHARD of Kea; yeoman. Will written 9 April, 1763. Proved 11 June, 1768. Names son HENRY to whom he gave five shillings; son JOHN-five shillings; son PETER-five shillings; daughter MARY Bekenna-five shillings; and to his son RICHARD (Executor) "All my lands, messuages, tenements and heridaments, whatsoever and wheresoever."
19 December, 1767. An Inventory of the Goods and Chattels of RICHARD SKEWES of the Parish of Kea, in the county of Cornwall (Deceased). Taken by David Hawkers, Esq., and Hugh Lampson, yeoman of the aforesaid parish.

	£	s	d
Imp' Household Goods in Kitchen			
Two iron pots, five brass pans, one pewter dish, a tableboard, form, dressor	3	0	0
Middle Room			
Six pewter plates and tin basin		5	0
The Halls			
A dresser and shelves		5	0
Seven large pewter dishes	1	0	0
Twelve pewter plates		12	0
Dressware and glasses		2	0
An old tableboard and form		2	6
Three old chairs		1	6

	£	s	d
Up Stairs			
Three beds and bedding	6	0	0
Husbandry Implements			
One butt wheels wain, two harrows and two axeltrees of iron	5	10	0
Cattle			
Two oxen	16	0	0
Two heifers	4	10	0
Two cows	8	0	0
Five horses	12	0	0
Twenty two sheep	9	0	0
Two swine	1	7	0
Seven geese		10	6
Corn			
One Wheaton Mow	6	0	0
One Barley Mow	8	0	0
One of Oats Mow	3	0	0
One hairpick	4	10	0
One small field of wheat	1	10	0
A Leasehold Tenement	30	0	0
	£121	5	6

1772 SKEWES   JOHN of Gwennap. Bond dated 5 September, 1772. Names son WILLIAM SKEWES as Executor.

1781 SKEWES   EDWARD of Mevagissey; mariner. Will dated 18 November, 1779. Proved 15 June, 1781. Gave all his Goods to Ann, wife of William Covings.

1781 SKEWES JOHN of Kenwyn; tinner. Mentions his, daughter MARY to whom he gave half a guinea; daughter MERRIA-half a guinea and to his wife ALICE and sons JOHN, RICHARD and JAMES and daughter ELIZABETH all his Goods, Chattels and Effects to share and share alike. Wife ALICE was appointed Executrix. Legacies to be paid one year and one day after his decease. Will dated 16 April, 1781. Proved 15 June, 1781.

1786 SKEWES DIGORY of Kea; tinner. Will dated 26 December, 1786. He left a long will with the following bequests.
DIGORY SKEWES (son) Two pounds and two shillings.
CATHERINE (daughter), wife of John Wasley-five shillings. Both amounts to be paid as soon as his son MATTHEW SKEWES attained the age of 21 years.
MARY SKEWES (daughter)-Two pounds and two shillings to be paid within one month after the decease of his wife MARGERY. MARY also to receive 24 shillings yearly, to be paid quarterly out of the premises in which they lived from the date of the death of his wife during the remainder of Mary's life, or until she became married. Mary also to receive the dwelling house on the Skewes premises, then let at a yearly rate to John Polkinghorne.
MARGERY (daughter) to receive three pounds and three shillings, as soon as she attained the age of 21.
To MARGERY (wife) Digory bequeathed the dwelling house and premises leased from Viscount Falmouth, situated in the parish of Kea. She also received all the household goods and furniture and chattels and effects, provided she remained a widow. If she married again, then she would only receive one shilling.
Digory also stated that his sons PETER and MATTHEW and daughter MARGERY be maintained by his wife out of the effects given until they reach the age of 21 or become married. Funeral expenses, just debts and cost of proving his will to be paid by his wife Margery.

1786 SKEWES EDWARD of St Keverne (Carnhervis). Will written 4 June, 1786. He died 1792 and it was proved 15 May, 1792. He mentioned sons JOHN and HENRY SKEWES (executor).

1787 SKEWES WILLIAM of Camborne; yeoman. Will proved 22 May, 1787. "I Give and bequeath to my son JOHN SKEWES one Annuity, or yearly rent charge, of Five Pounds to be paid to him out of the rent and profits of my Estate or Tenement in Treslothan, Camborne." He gave to his son RICHARD SKEWES all the estate in Treslothan in which he then lived. Also responsible for paying rent, rates and taxes. He gave to his son WILLIAM ten pounds and to his daughters MARY (wife of Stephen Rowe), SARAH and son STEPHEN one shilling. All living grandchildren to be given one shilling. To his son WILLIAM SKEWES (Executor) he gave the remainder of his goods, chattels and effects. Also mentioned in the will is grandson WILLIAM SKEWES, son of John Skewes.

1790 SKEWES JOHN of Cury. Bond dated 11 May, 1790. Mentions his wife MARY SKEWES and also WILLIAM SKEWES.

1791 SKEWES JOHN of Gwennap. Bond dated 20 January, 1791. Mentions his wife MARY SKEWES.

1792 SKEWES EDWARD of St Keverne. Will dated 4 June, 1786. Proved 15 May, 1792. Names JOHN
SKEWES (son) to whom he gives his estate known as Carhewis, St Keverne. The remainder of his goods
and chattels to HENRY SKEWES who is named sole executor who also is given Chybarles in Ruan Major.

1802 SKEWES PETER of Kenwyn; innkeeper. Will dated 24 September, 1802. Mentions his wife PEGGY
SKEWES and five children, but does not give their names.

1802 SKEWES JOHN of Kea. Bond dated 27 July, 1802 which was granted to his cousin Henry Behenna and
his only next of kin.

1807 SKEWES RICHARD of Shillingford, Devon, late of Gwennap. Will dated July, 1807. Mentions
THOMAS SKEWES, WILLIAM SKEWES, ALEXANDER SKEWES and MARGARET SKEWES all
of Gwennap. ALEXANDER SKEWES (Executor) was bequeathed £20 amongst various items of personal effect.

1808 SKEWES RICHARD of Constantine. Bond dated 27 July, 1808. Names two sons WILLIAM SKEWES
and HENRY SKEWES and daughter MARY (wife of William Hendy), daughter ELIZABETH
SKEWES. Wife was ALICE SKEWES.

1808 SKEWES WILLIAM of Gwinear. Names his brother HENRY SKEWES (lately deceased) and Henry's
wife ELIZABETH. Also Henry and Elizabeth's daughter ELIZABETH SKEWES, and son HENRY
SKEWES. Names his other brothers RICHARD SKEWES, JOHN SKEWES, STEPHEN SKEWES and
sisters MARY SKEWES and SARAH SKEWES. Will proved 28 April, 1809.

1811 SKEWES WILLIAM. Died at sea. "Administrations of Warrant Officers and Petty Officers, seamen
and soldiers belonging to ships or dying abroad." Ser. "Dictator"—July, 1811.

1811 SKEWES JOHN of Gwennap. Will proved 6 November, 1811. Names his daughters ELIZABETH
SKEWES and MARY SKEWES. Also THOMAS SKEWES son of his brother WILLIAM SKEWES
(lately deceased). Names ELIZABETH SKEWES, daughter of his son RICHARD SKEWES (lately
deceased) and COLLAN SKEWES, son of the said RICHARD SKEWES. ALEXANDER SKEWES
was named as Trustee and JOHN SKEWES, son of his late son Richard, as Executor.

1812 SKUES RICHARD of Helston. Bond dated 28 March, 1812. Administration of the Goods, Chattels
and Credits of RICHARD SKUES, late of the Borough of Helston in the county of Cornwall; surgeon,
deceased was granted to ANNE SKUES, widow, the relinct. £2000.

1813 SKEWES JOHN of Camborne. Will proved 23 October, 1813. Mentions sons WILLIAM SKEWES,
HENRY SKEWES, JOHN SKEWES, RICHARD SKEWES and daughter MARY (married to William
Smytheram), SARAH (married to Isaac Jenkin), CATHERINE (married to John Prout), PHILIPPA
(married to John Phillips). Widow was PHILIPPA SKEWES.

1813 SKEWES WILLIAM of Constantine; yeoman. Will proved 16 December, 1813. Names Mary Thomas,
Alice Hendy and Elizabeth Rowe, sisters of the deceased.

1814 SKEWES HENRY of Camborne, yeoman of Killivoase. Will proved 17 May, 1814. Names the wife of
Richard Williams being his niece to whom he gives Killivoase. Also names his brother JOHN SKEWES,
brother ABSALOM SKEWES, deceased, and *his* son JAMES SKEWES. Also gives another JAMES
SKEWES and his children but no names.

1815 SKEWES PHILIPPA of Camborne. Widow of JOHN SKEWES. Names two sons RICHARD SKEWES
and HENRY SKEWES to whom she gave her whole estate—they to pay funeral expenses. Both also
named Executors. Will dated 9 August, 1815.

1816 SKUCE JOHN, Quartermaster 3rd Regiment of Guards. Administration dated May, 1816.

1816 SKEWES WILLIAM of Kea; yeoman. Will dated 20 May, 1816. Names son WILLIAM SKEWES,
daughters ANN SKEWES, MARY SKEWES, JANE SKEWES and ELIZABETH SKEWES; sons
SAMUEL SKEWES, DANIEL SKEWES and JOHN SKEWES and daughter ELEANOR SKEWES.
Also names his brother JOHN SKEWES and brothers-in-law Daniel Hodge and John Thomas.

1817 SKEWES MARGARET of Gwennap; spinster. Will dated 12 May, 1817. Names brothers ALEX-
ANDER SKEWES and WILLIAM SKEWES, both of Gwennap, miners. Two nieces Mary Tregaskis
and Elizabeth Tuckfield. Also ELIZABETH SKEWES the daughter of her nephew RICHARD
SKEWES, deceased. Also names THOMAS SKEWES, son of nephew RICHARD SKEWES, and the
daughters of brother ALEXANDER SKEWES. THOMAS SKEWES is also named as a brother of
MARGARET SKEWES, lately deceased.

1817 SKEWES THOMAS of Gwennap; miner. Dated 12 May, 1817. Proved 5 September, 1817. Names brother ALEXANDER SKEWES, brother WILLIAM SKEWES and sister MARGARET SKEWES. Also ELIZA SKEWES, daughter of his nephew RICHARD SKEWES and JOHN SKEWES son of his nephew RICHARD SKEWES and THOMAS SKEWES, son of his nephew RICHARD SKEWES. Also THOMAS SKEWES, son of his nephew WILLIAM SKEWES. He lists the children of his brother ALEXANDER SKEWES as GRACE SKEWES, MARGARET SKEWES, JOANNA SKEWES, CHRISTIAN SKEWES and ELIZABETH SKEWES. Also mentions his nephew ALEXANDER SKEWES, son of ALEXANDER SKEWES (brother) and two nieces Elizabeth Tuckfield and Mary Tregaskis. Finally names the Methodist Society of Carharrack, Gwennap.

1817 SKUES WILLIAM of Helston. Administration of the Goods, Chattels and Credits of WILLIAM SKUES, late of Helston in the county of Cornwall — gentleman — a widower, deceased, was granted to RICHARD SKUES, grandson and next of kin, being first sworn by common duly to Administration.
£600

1823 SKEWS RICHARD of Kenwyn. Administration dated 24 October, 1823. Miner. Granted to ROSEANNAH SKEWS, widow of deceased.

1824 SKUES STEPHEN of Park Colly, Camborne; yeoman. Will dated 13 September, 1823. Proved 6 August, 1824. Leaves his estate to STEPHEN SKEWES and HENRY SKEWES sons of his nephew WILLIAM SKEWES. His nephew was appointed Executor.

1824 SKEWES JOHN of Cury. Will dated 12 June, 1824. He gave to his wife the sum of £10 per year to be paid quarterly out of his freehold estate "so long as she do live and also the use of that house that JAMES SKEWES do now live in. And my best bed and bedding and such other of my household goods as she have need of so long as she do live. Also I give to my two sons JOHN SKEWES and WILLIAM SKEWES and to my daughters MARY SKEWES, BLANCH SKEWES and ANN SKEWES the sum of one shilling each. Also I give unto my sons EDWARD SKEWES and JAMES SKEWES my freehold estate in Nantithet, Cury with their paying their mother her annuity as aforesaid, during her life. After her death then they pay my son WILLIAM SKEWES the sum of one pound per year or his heirs for ever."
EDWARD SKEWES and JAMES SKEWES were named as Executors.

1824 SKEWES DIGORY of Kea; miner. Will dated 14 June, 1824. Names widow ELIZABETH SKEWS, sons PETER SKEWS, DIGORY SKEWS, RICHARD SKEWS, JOHN SKEWS and MATTHEW SKEWS. Names daughters MARY SKEWS and MARIA SKEWS and daughter MARGERY Wasley.

1824 SKEWES HENRY of Camborne; yeoman. Will dated 6 August, 1824. Names his daughter CAROLINE SKEWES as Executrix. Names JOHN SKEWES of Illogan as guardian of CAROLINE SKEWES.

1829 SKEWES JOHN of Cury; yeoman. See 1824. Will proved 8 January, 1829.

1830 SKEWES THOMAS of Gwennap. Died 3 March, 1838. Will dated 16 November, 1830. He was son of the late RICHARD SKEWES. Names his brother COLLAN SKEWES, brother JOHN SKEWES and sister ELIZABETH (Morcam). JOHN to be Executor and ELIZABETH to be Executrix. Effects under £800

1830 SKEWES MARTIN of St Clement, Truro; cordwainer. Will dated 14 June, 1830. Names his widow ELIZABETH SKEWES as Executrix. Effects under £100

1831 SKEWES HENRY of Ruan Major; yeoman. Will dated 19 December, 1831. Executors named as ANTHONY SKEWES and SAMUEL SKEWES, sons of the deceased. Occupied the freehold estate of Tresodden, Ruan Major. Names sons EDWARD SKEWES, HENRY SKEWES, THOMAS SKEWES and JOHN SKEWES and daughters JANE SKEWES, MARGARET SKEWES and MARY SKEWES.

1834 SKEWES JOHN of Kerley, Kea; miner. He died 7 July, 1833. Will was proved 4 January, 1834. Names wife ANN SKEWES, nephew THOMAS SKEWES (son of his brother THOMAS SKEWES, deceased). Effects under £100

1837 SKEWS RICHARD of Kenwyn; miner. Will dated 6 March, 1837. He died 26 March, 1837. Names wife MARY SKEWS (Executrix), sons JAMES SKEWS and THOMAS SKEWS; daughters SUSANNAH (Jeffrey) and ELIZABETH (Bawden). Wife is to have the property, but if she married again, then only one shilling. Joseph Walters on Cregbraws Common, constable, to act as guardian over wife and family. Effects under £200

1837 SKEWES HENRY of Camborne; yeoman. Will dated 27 January, 1837. Proved 3 January, 1838. Gives to his wife the house in which she now lives. He names Redruth Savings Bank in which she has £95 (interest £10 per year). When she has spent this he gives her £10 yearly during her life. He gives his brother WILLIAM SKEWES (Executor) all the interest arising from the money in Redruth Savings Bank in the hands of Copper House Company with all the interest and profits of all his property of every description. Names his brother JAMES SKEWES and his daughters CHARITY SKEWES and SUZANNE SKEWES (each to receive £50 if WILLIAM SKEWES should die before his wife). Also names brother JAMES SKEWES' sons, JAMES SKEWES and HENRY SKEWES.

Effects under £800

1838 SKEWES THOMAS of Gwennap; miner. Will dated 16 November, 1830. He died 3 March, 1838. See 1830.

1839 SKEWES JOHN of Gwennap; yeoman. Will dated 25 June, 1839. He died 1 July, 1839. Names JENEFAR SKEWES (wife) and Executor JOHN SKEWES (son). Daughters JANE TREWEEK SKEWES and CATHERINE TREWEEK SKEWES.

Effects under £600

1840 SKEWES WILLIAM of St. Ewe; yeoman. Dated February, 1839. He died 6 October, 1840. Lived at leasehold property called Nansladdron. Names NANCY SKEWES (widow) and PHILIP SKEWES (son), Executor. To his sons JOHN SKEWES he left £20; HENRY SKEWES (£10). To his daughters MARY SKEWES (£6 13 4d); ELIZABETH Tom (£6 13 4d) and ANN SKEWES (widow), £6 13 4d. To his wife he left his household furniture, goods and effects, farming and other live and dead stock as well as farming implements.

1843 SKEWES JOHN of Kenwyn; miner. He died 31 March, 1843. Administration granted to Mary Michell, wife of William Michell, widow of the aforesaid. Mary Michell, formerly Skewes.   Effects under £200

1844 SKEWES HENRY of Constantine; yeoman. Lived at Bosawsack, Constantine. Died 3 June, 1844. Names MARY (wife of Stephen Eddy) and daughter ALICE (wife of Thomas Midlin), also daughters ELIZABETH SKEWES, GRACE SKEWES, FANNY SKEWES, CAROLINE SKEWES and ELIZA SKEWES and sons JOSIAH SKEWES, WILLIAM SKEWES and HENRY SKEWES.
He left MARY (Eddy) one shilling; ALICE (Midlin) two guineas; ELIZABETH SKEWES £27; JOSIAH SKEWES — all the interest that Henry Skewes may have at the time of his death in the farm and premises of Bosawsack, subject to yearly rents and covenants. He left WILLIAM SKEWES £50; HENRY SKEWES £150; GRACE SKEWES £50; FANNY SKEWES £100; CAROLINE SKEWES £100 and ELIZA SKEWES £100. Will dated 15 January, 1842.   Effects under £2000

1847 SKUES ANN of East Stonehouse, Devon; widow. She died 8 February, 1847. Will was proved 12 October, 1847. ". . . . . I give unto my daughter GRACE Richards Radford, widow, the sum of £10. I give John Gedye of Devonport, scrivener, £5, I also give unto my daughter Grace all my clothes and wearing apparel of every description, and as to all the rest, residue and remainder of my Estate and Effects of what nature and kind so ever I give unto John Beer of Devonport, Attorney-at-Law and John Gedye . . . . . and as soon as shall conveniently may be after my deceased lay out and invest a competent sum thereof in the purchase of one hundred pounds Three per cent consolidated bank Annuities in their joint names and to pay the dividends, interest and produce unto my said daughter Grace Richards Radford during the term of her natural life . . . immediately after the decease of my said daughter upon trust that they my said trustees and the survivor of them and the Executors and administrators of such survivors do and shall assign and transfer the said principal sum of one hundred pounds Three per cent consolidated bank Annuities unto my grand daughter GEORGINA MARY SKUES, daughter of my son GEORGE SKUES upon her attaining the age of 21 years, or upon her marriage whichever shall first happen . . . . and to pay over the same to my daughter MARY (Rodd), the wife of Richard Rodd of the parish of East Stonehouse, attorney at law to pay the interest and dividends thereof for the term of her natural life."
Executors named as John Beer of Stoke Damerell, Devon, gentleman and John Gedye, of the same place, scrivener.   Effects under £450

1852 SKEWES JOHN of Cury; yeoman. Will proved 24 November, 1852. John died 21 October, 1852. He asks that his freehold property at Nantithet be sold either by public auction or private contract. Out of the proceeds he gave to his grandson SAMUEL SKEWES (son of NANCY SKEWES) £20 to be lodged with Mr John Thomas of Tregigeon to be used for his education and support according to his discretion. SAMUEL also to receive the bed, watch and chest. The other portion of his furniture he gave to his daughter HANNAH. He names his son EDWARD SKEWES as Executor.
Will dated 17 April, 1852.   Effects under £20

1854 SKEWES RICHARD of Kea; parish clerk. Died 30 September, 1854. Will proved 8 December, 1854. Names his wife MARY SKEWES, and daughter MARY Tregeynowan, wife of Thomas Tregeynowan and other daughter ANN Eddy.   Effects under £200

1856 SKEWES JAMES of Cury; farmer. Will dated 17 October, 1856. He died 19 October, 1856. Left to his wife freehold property (Messuage, tenement and cottage) in Nantithet, Cury. Names his daughter

ELIZA GRACE SKEWES; his brother EDWARD SKEWES; his sister ANN (Freeman); his nephew JOHN SKEWES (son of brother WILLIAM SKEWES). Good friends ANTHONY SKEWES of Ruan Major and James Freeman of Sithney who are appointed guardians of ELIZA GRACE SKEWES until she attains the age of twenty-one years.

1857 SKEWES MATTHEW of Kenwyn; innkeeper. Will dated 11 March, 1857. Names his wife MARY SKEWES and son MATTHEW SKEWES and daughters ELIZABETH (Stripp) and JANE (Davey). Witness to signature on will was RICHARD SKEWES, a housekeeper of Kea.   Effects under £100

1859 SKEWES JOHN formerly of Gwennap, but late of Cuba. Admin. proved 22 September, 1859. John Skewes, miner, died 10 August, 1859 in Cuba, South America. Granted to MARY ANN SKEWES of Gwennap, widow.

1859 SKEWS JOHN of St Austell; innkeeper of General Wolfe Inn. Bequeathed his freehold house known by the name or sign of the "London Inn", situated on the left hand side of the street leading from Market House in St Austell to Tregonissey now in the occupation of George Bennallack to his good friends William Simmonds of Falmouth, innkeeper and John Lovering of St Austell, clay merchant. He also bequeathed his other freehold house in Fore Street, St Austell now in the occupation of Mr Furniss to them, for the use of his sons WILLIAM SKEWS and EDWIN SKEWS their heirs and assigns for ever equally as tenants in common and to his daughter MARY SKEWS her heirs and assigns for ever to be held and disposed of as her own separate estate and independently of any husband she may at any time have. Will dated 20 December, 1856. On 11 February, 1859 will was proved.   Effects under £100

1859 SKEWES JOHN of St Erme; farmer. Bequeathed all and singular his Estate to John Clyma of Truro, hatter and John Lanyon of Truro, saddler. And that they pay the annual income that may be derived from the Estate to his wife ANN SKEWES during her life, for the support and maintenance of his un-married children. He gave £40 to his sister JANE TREWEEK Perma. Clyma and Lanyon were named Executors. Will dated 15 May, 1858. Will was proved 17 May, 1859.   Effects under £800

1860 SKEWES WILLIAM of Bideford; mine agent. Died 29 October, 1860. Will proved 26 December, 1860.   Effects under £200

1863 SKEWES JOHN of Killiwerris, Kea; yeoman. Will dated 30 December, 1861. Proved 2 February, 1863. Names his wife ANN SKEWES to whom he bequeaths Killiwerris and Deerpark Farms with all the stock thereon until his youngest son WILLIAM SKEWES is of age. If she shall marry the property will revert to his two oldest sons SAMUEL SKEWES (to have Killiwerris) and JOHN SKEWES (Deer-park). He gave to his daughter ELIZABETH ANN SKEWES £2; daughter ELLEN SKEWES £2 and daughter LAVINIA SKEWES £2. To his youngest son WILLIAM SKEWES to receive £1 upon the death of his mother ANN SKEWES. The whole of the farm stock with all household furniture to be equally divided between his sons SAMUEL SKEWES and JOHN SKEWES.
John Skewes died 16 January, 1862.   Effects under £300

1863 SKEWES ALEXANDER of Gwennap Moors, Gwennap; accountant. Will dated 22 November, 1862. He died 12 December, 1862 and the will was proved 5 February, 1863. A very long will covering many pages. He gave tea kettle and stand to his nephew Alexander Teague; a tea service of plate to his nephew RICHARD SKEWES Martin; a family tea pot to his nephew Walter Rufus Bray; and a clear legacy or sum of £100 to his nephew GEORGE SKEWES Bray for his kind attention. His sister was ANN (Bray), mother of Walter Rufus Bray and George Skewes Bray. He names his three sisters ELIZABETH SKEWES, MARY SKEWES and ANN (Bray), widow. Nephews were RICHARD SKEWES Martin and RICHARD SKEWES Teague. Brother in law John Martin. He had three married sisters: Mrs Loam, wife of Michael Loam; Mrs Martin, wife of John Martin and Mrs Teague, wife of Alexander Teague.
          Effects under £14,000

1864 SKEWES DANIEL HODGE late of Bere Alston, Devon; grocer. Died 20 December, 1863 at Bere Alston. Will was proved at Exeter by the oath of SAMUEL DAW SKEWES of Bere Alston, grocer, the son and one of the Executors.   Effects under £200

1867 SKEWES PETER of Kea; miner. Died 18 June, 1867 at Kea. Will was proved at Bodmin by the oath of GRACE SKEWES, widow, sole executrix.

1868 SKEWES THOMAS of Truro; builder and grocer. Died at Truro 15 July, 1868. Will proved at Bodmin by the oath of JANE SKEWES, widow, sole executrix, 19 August, 1868.   Effects under £600

1869 SKEWES THOMAS of Ruan Major; labourer. Died at Ruan Major 22 January 1869. Will proved at Bodmin by the oath of ANTHONY SKEWES, farmer and brother, sole Executor.   Effects under £100

1869 SKUES MARY BENNETT of Champmanslade, Wiltshire. Died 14 September, 1869 at Champ-manslade. Will was proved at Salisbury by the oath of Rev. James Hay Waugh, of the Rectory, Corsley,

Wiltshire, clerk, the sole Executor. In her will she asks that all books of hers that may be of value be given to the Western College, Plymouth. She mentions her late uncle Ambrose Garrett. She bequeaths her Plate, 12 teaspoons, 2 table spoons, 3 salt spoons and one pair of old fashioned Tongues to her sister CHARLOTTE Bryant... but later revoked this bequest and then gave the aforementioned to her niece Charlotte Cornell, wife of Richard Cornell. The will was proved 22 November, 1869.

Effects under £100

1870   SKEWES EDWARD of Mawnan; blacksmith. Died 22 June, 1870 at Mawnan. Will was proved at Bodmin by the oaths of MARY ELLEN SKEWES, widow and Edwin Boaden, farmer; Executors, 20 July, 1870.   Effects under £300

1871   SKEWS HENRY of Redruth; farmer. Died 29 October, 1869 at Redruth. Will was proved at Bodmin by the oath of Thomas John Hancock of Redruth, grocer, sole Executor.   Effects under £300

1871   SKEWES ANN of Penryn; widow. Died 11 December, 1870 at Penryn. Will was proved 13 March, 1871 at Bodmin by Catherine Martin (wife of James Martin, baker) of Penryn, the daughter and sole Executrix.   Effects under £200

1872   SKEWES JAMES of Neath, Glamorgan. Died 22 June, 1849 at Melicrythan, Neath. He was a collier. Will was proved at Llandaff by the oath of Harriet West (wife of John West, grocer — formerly SKEWS, widow) of Melincrythan, the relict, 20 December, 1872.   Effects under £100

1872   SKUES GEORGE of 8, St John's Road, Upper Holloway, Middlesex, Lieutenant of Marines. Died 9 January, 1872 at 8, St John's Road, Upper Holloway. Will was proved by John Duncan of Aberdeen, one of the Executors, 9 Mar 1872. Double Probate issued February, 1885.   Effects under £1000

1872   SKEWS PHILIP of Lower Sticker, St Mewan; farmer. Died 28 March, 1872 at Sticker. Will was proved at Bodmin by Joseph Truscott of Pentewan, St Austell, farmer, sole Executor, 10 April, 1872.
Effects under £200

1873   SKEWES ANTHONY of Ruan Major; yeoman. Died 14 February, 1873 at Ruan Major. Will was proved at Bodmin by Hannibal Lyne of St Martin in Meneage, yeoman and James Lugg, of Mawgan, yeoman and CHRISTIAN SKEWES of Ruan Major, the Relict, the Executors, 11 June, 1873.
Effects under £600

1873   SKEWES RICHARD of Kenwyn; farmer. Died 8 February, 1873 at Kenwyn. Admin with will was granted at Bodmin under the usual limitations to James Andrew, farmer and Edward Hooper, miner, both of Kenwyn, the guardians of RICHARD SKEWES and DANIEL SKEWES, minors, the sons and the Executors. Another grant 1884.   Effects under £200

1875   SKEWES THOMAS of Jolly's Bottom, Kea. Died 15 March, 1875 at Kea. Will was proved at Bodmin by Elizabeth Oates (wife of Thomas Oates, miner) of Kenwyn, the daughter and sole Executrix, 27 March, 1875.   Effects under £100

1875   SKEWIS JAMES of Camborne; farmer. Died 10 March 1875 at Camborne. Will was proved at Bodmin by William Temby of Camborne, gentleman, the sole Executor, 20 May, 1875.   Effects under £200

1875   SKEWIS THOMAS formerly of Chacewater. Died 1 December, 1873 at Real del Monte, Mexico. He was a miner. Administration was granted at Bodmin to PETER SKEWIS of Kenwyn; sharebroker, the brother, 2 June, 1875.   Effects under £50

1876   SKUES WILLIAM of 6, William Street, Gibson Street, Lambeth, Surrey; builder. Died 21 February, 1876 at 6, William Street. Will was proved at Principal Registry by John Little, otherwise SKUES of 6, William Street, carpenter, one of the Executors, 7 April, 1876.   Effects under £600

1877   SKEWES ELIZABETH of Lanner House, Gwennap. Died 12 May, 1877 at Lanner House. Spinster. Will proved at Bodmin by Ann Bray of Lanner House, widow, the sister, the sole Executrix, 12 November, 1877. Resworn March, 1878. 1877: Effects under £1500. 1878: Effects under £2000

1877   SKEWES FRANCIS of Illogan; blacksmith. Died 23 April, 1876 at Coquimbo, Chile, South America. Administration was granted at Bodmin to GRACE SKEWES of Illogan, widow, Relict, 6 February, 1877.   Effects under £200

1877   SKEWES LAVINIA of Truro; spinster. Died 12 July, 1868 at Truro. Administration granted at Bodmin to LOUISA JANE SKEWES of Walsall, Staffordshire, spinster, niece and one of the persons entitled to distribution, 18 January, 1877.   Effects under £200

1878   SKEWES EDWARD of Cury, farmer and shoemaker. Died at Lower Poleskan, Cury 20 February, 1878. Will was proved at Principal Registry by Julia Roberts, widow, and Henry Roberts, cordwainer, both of Cury, the Executors, 23 September, 1878.   Effects under £200

1878 SKEWES JOSIAH of Constantine; yeoman. Died 2 June, 1878 at Constantine. Will was proved at Bodmin by Alfred Knowles of Lower Spargo, Mabe, Thomas Medlin of Higher Spargo, Mabe and Robert
Knowles of Bonalack, Mabe, yeomen, the Executors, 25 July, 1878.   Effects under £4000

1878 SKEWES MARY of Lanner House, Gwennap; spinster. Died 10 December, 1877 at Lanner House.
Will was proved at Bodmin by Ann Bray of Lanner House, widow and sister, the sole Executrix, 4
January, 1878.   Effects under £3000

1879 SKUES WILLIAM of Thicket Lane, Stapleton, Gloucester. Died 7 February, 1878 at the Bristol Royal
Infirmary. Was a labourer. Will proved at Bristol by MARY SKUES, of Thicket Lane, widow, the
relict, the sole Executrix, 3 February, 1879.   Effects under £20

1881 SKEWES HENRY BLEWETT of St Ewe; labourer. Bachelor. Died 1 January, 1847 at St Ewe. Admin
Bodmin 22 December, 1881 granted to Joseph Truscott of Pentewan, St Austell, agent, the husband
and administrator of the personal estate of Mary Truscott, the sister of one of the next of kin.
                                                                       £44   10   5d

1884 SKEWES JOHN of Carharrack, Gwennap; farmer. Died 10 March, 1884 at Carharrack. Will proved
at Bodmin 8 April, 1884 by ANNE SKEWES of Carharrack, widow, the relict and sole Executrix.
                                                                      £275   8   6d

1884 SKEWES RICHARD of Kenwyn; farmer. Died 8 February, 1873 at Kenwyn. Will was proved at Bodmin 4 April, 1884 by RICHARD SKEWES of Scorrier, engine driver and son, and one of the Executors. The Admin with will was granted at Bodmin February 1874 having ceased and expired.
                                                                      £150   0   0d

1885 SKUES GEORGE of 8, St John's Road, Upper Holloway, Middlesex; Lieutenant of Marines. Died 9
January, 1872 at 8, St John's Road, Upper Holloway. Will was proved at the Principal Registry on 12
February 1885 by FREDERICK MACKENZIE SKUES of 4, Springfield Crescent, Trinity Road, in the
Isle of Jersey, M.B., the son of George Skues and one of the surviving Executors. Will with two codicils.
Former grant — Principal Registry March, 1872.   £980   9   4d

1887 SKEWES WILLIAM of Crowan. Died 23 December 1886 at Crowan. Will was proved at Bodmin 9
December, 1887 by John Roberts of Wendron and William Rowe of Sithney, farmers, two of the Executors.   £628   14   6d

1889 SKEWES JANE of Daniell Street, Truro; widow. Died 19 September 1889 at Daniell Street. Will was
proved at Bodmin 31 October, 1889 by THOMAS SKEWES of Parkvedras Terrace, Truro, ironmonger, the son and sole Executor.   £456   7   0d

1890 SKEWES MARIA (wife of Rev. JOSEPH HENRY SKEWES, clerk, late of Islington, Liverpool). Died
29 January, 1890 at Islington. Administration granted at Liverpool to the said Rev JOSEPH HENRY
SKEWES.   £87   12   6d

1890 SKEWIS HENRY of Watchet, St Decuman's, Somerset; mining agent. Died 29 October, 1889 at Watchet. Will was proved at Taunton 13 January 1890 by John White of Stogumber, Somerset, gentleman
and John Risdon, the younger of Wiveliscombe, Somerset, auctioneer and surveyor, the Executors.
                                                                     £4220   18   1d

1890 SKUES MARGARET (wife of WILLIAM MACKENZIE SKUES) of Shrublands, 17, Linden Grove,
Nunhead, Surrey. Died 5 June, 1890 at Avoca Carysfort Road, Boscombe, Southampton. Administration was granted at the Principal Registry 2nd July 1890 to GEORGE EDWARD MACKENZIE SKUES
of 34, Essex Street, Strand, London, Middlesex, solicitor and son and one of the next of kin.
                                                                       £98   18   8d

1891 SKEWES LOVEDAY of Ruan Minor; widow. Died 21 February, 1890 at Ruan Minor. Administration
was granted at Bodmin to John Chapman Mundy of Ruan Minor, blacksmith, the nephew and one of
the next of kin, 24 February, 1891.   £60   0   0d

1892 SKUES WILLIAM MACKENZIE of Shrublands, 17, Linden Grove, Nunhead, Surrey, M.D., retired
Brigade Surgeon, Army Medical Department. Died 10 June, 1892. Administration, London 10
August, 1892 to GEORGE EDWARD MACKENZIE SKUES, solicitor.   £2482   2   5d

1894 SKEWES THOMAS of Truro; ironmonger. Died 26 January, 1894 at Guy's Hospital, London. Administration, Bodmin, 18 September, 1894 to MARY JANE SKEWES, widow.
Further grant March, 1912.   £446   5   2d

1896 SKEWES ANN of Choon, Kenwyn; widow. Died 27 February, 1896. Admin, Bodmin 21 April, 1896 to
Charlotte Mary Mitchell (wife of Henry Mitchell).   £298   3   5d

1896 SKEWES FANNY of Bosawsack, Constantine; widow. Died 18 June, 1895. Probate Bodmin 20 March, 1896 to Laura Tregaskis, widow.   £104   17   0d

1896 SKEWES JANE of Kea; spinster. Died 9 July, 1894. Administration (Limited) Bodmin 11 June, 1896 to Francis Hearle Cock, solicitor, the attorney of Harriet Hicks, widow.   £216   0   0d

1897 SKUES GEORGE HENRY of 14, Sale Street, Paddington, Middlesex. Died 23 April, 1897. Probate London 14 May, 1897 to WINIFRED SKUES, widow.   £671   7   6d

1897 SKUES JOHN of Redruth; mason. Died 11 May, 1896. Probate Bodmin 11 March, 1897 to ELIZABETH SKUES, widow.   £58   0   0d

1898 SKEWES Rev JOSEPH HENRY of Fitzclarence Street, Liverpool; clerk. Died 18 March, 1898. Administration Liverpool 5 April, 1898 to BESSIE MAUD SKEWES, spinster.   £264   2   6d

1899 SKEWS JOHN of Callington; miner. Died 16 September, 1898, at Coulterville, Mariposa County, California, America. Administration Bodmin 7 January, 1899 to EMMA SKEWS, widow.
                                                                                                                                                £425   0   0d

1900 SKUES MARY of Purton, Wiltshire (wife of MOSES SKUES). Died 7 March, 1899. Administration London 18 January 1900 to the said MOSES SKUES, labourer.   £46   8   0d

1900 SKEWES JAMES of Mawgan, Cornwall; farmer. Died 30 July, 1899. Probate Bodmin 30 January 1900 to FRANCES SKEWES, widow, EDWARD SKEWES, farmer and Reginald Nankivell Rogers, solicitor.   £751   9   6d

1901 SKEWES LOUISA JANE of 10 Zion Road, Twickenham, Middlesex; spinster. Died 29 May 1901 at St Thomas' Hospital, Surrey. Admin London 14 June.   £203   0   0d

1902 SKEWS ELIZABETH of 153 Wandsworth Bridge Road, Fulham, Middlesex (wife of EDWIN SKEWS). Died 6 April 1900. Admin London 12 June.   £44   2   4d

1902 SKUES MOSES of Minety, Wiltshire. Died 24 June 1902. Probate London 25 August.
                                                                                                                                                £41   1   9d

1903 SKEWES SAMUEL DAWE of Bere Alston, Devonshire and of 10 Chesterfield Road, St Andrews Park, Bristol. Died 15 August 1903 at 10, Chesterfield Road, Bristol. Probate London 21 October.
                                                                                                                                                £776   15   7d

1903 SKEWES JOHN JAMES of 10 Zion Road, Twickenham, Middlesex; naval pensioner. Died 12 October 1903. Admin 29 October.   £196   8   6d

1903 SKEWES THOMAS LEAN of 31 Elm Grove, Bideford, Devonshire; retired school master. Died 17 February 1903. Probate Exeter 24 March.   £5390   1   6d

1903 SKUES GEORGINA MARY of Mackenzie Cottage, Hastings Road, Ealing Down, Middlesex; spinster. Died 7 October 1903. Admin (with will) London 5 December.   £286   6   5d

1904 SKUES MARY ELIZABETH of 51 Ringstead, Catford, Kent (wife of FREDERICK MACKENZIE SKUES). Died 21 December 1903 at 282 High Street, Lewisham, Kent. Admin London 15 February.
                                                                                                                                                £811   18   0d

1906 SKEWES HENRY of Condurrow Croft, Camborne; miner. Died 13 June 1905 at Reitfontein Lazaretto, Transvaal Colony, South Africa. Admin Bodmin 26 April.   £65   0   0d

1906 SKEWIS GEORGE of New Brunswick, Middlesex, New Jersey, United States of America. Died 18 February 1905. Admin (with will) London 1 March.   £1436   13   2d

1908 SKEWES MARY JANE of 6 Richmond Hill, Truro, Cornwall; widow. Died 24 April 1908. Probate London 10 August.   £554   11   8d

1909 SKEWES FRANCES of Mawnan, Cornwall; widow. Died 10 May 1907. Admin Bodmin 21 January.
                                                                                                                                                £32   1   9d

1910 SKUES FREDERICK MACKENZIE of 58 Riggindale Road, Streatham, Surrey. Died 13 August 1910. Probate London 7 September.   £3711   5   0d

1911 SKUES LUCY (wife of RICHARD SKUES). Died 2 January 1911. Probate Wakefield 18 January.
                                                                                                                                                £260   6   0d

1912 SKEWES THOMAS of Truro; ironmonger. Died 26 January 1894 at Guys Hospital, London. Admin Bodmin 12 March. Former grant 1894.   £27   1   0d

1912 SKEWES MARY LANGMEAD of Totnes, Devon; widow. Died 4 February 1912. Probate Exeter 21 June.   £505   9   0d

1913 SKEWS JOHN WILLIAM HENRY of 10, Hazelwood Terrace, Peverell, Plymouth; retired Lieutenant, Royal Navy. Died 26 January 1913. Probate Exeter 16 April.   £827   9   5d

1913 SKEWES-COX, Sir THOMAS of the Manor House, Petersham, Surrey, and of 8 Lancaster Place, Strand, Middlesex; knight. Died 15 November 1912 at the Manor House, Petersham. Probate London 17 January.   £5050   2   6d

1914 SKEWS WILLIAM of Penrlos House, St Columb Minor, Cornwall. Died 5 January 1914. Probate Bodmin 7 February.   £385   1   9d

1915 SKEWES EDWARD of Yew Tree Road, Birchencliffe, Huddersfield, West Yorkshire. Died 23 May 1915. Probate Wakefield 23 June.   £3903   2   11d

1915 SKEWES EMILY ANN of Medlyn, Wendron, Cornwall; widow. Died 29 December 1914. Probate Bodmin 11 February.   £20   0   0d

1916 SKEWES ARTHUR COURTIS of 7 Cotham Road, Bristol; temporary Second Lieutenant 11th (Reserve) Battalion, Devonshire Regiment. Died 19 July 1916 in France. Admin Bristol 18 November.   £590   6   2d

1917 SKEWES ANNIE of the Anchorage, Holmbush, St Austell, Cornwall; widow. Died 7 December 1916. Probate London 10 July.   £305   4   7d

1917 SKEWES JAMES of Mutley Park Villas, Plymouth. Died 24 September 1917 at the Cattle Market, Yealmpton, Devon. Probate London 20 November.   £2653   1   0d

1917 SKUES JOHN of 8 Coral Street, Lambeth, Surrey. Died 6 March 1917. Probate London 20 March.   £1574   13   10d

1918 SKEWES SAMUEL of Geelong, Victoria, Australia. Died 21 February 1864. Admin (Limited) London 8 April.   £8   0   0d

1919 SKEWES ADA ELIZA of Packsaddle, Mabe, Cornwall (wife of HENRY SKEWES). Died 28 February 1919 at Falmouth. Probate London 12 June.   £692   18   0d

1922 SKEWES EMMA of Fore Street, Bere Alston, Devon; widow. Died 6 February at Upperton Farm, Bickleigh, Devon. Probate London 23 August.   £97   6   0d

1922 SKEWES HENRY of Camborne, Cornwall. Died 21 February 1922. Probate Bodmin 4 May.   £278   11   6d

1922 SKUES FREDERICK MACKENZIE of Green's Hotel, Bethlehem, Orange Free State, South Africa. Died 18 August 1921 at Bloemfontein, South Africa. Admin (with will) London 28 April.   £1735   0   11d

1924 SKUES WINIFRED of 47 Ashford Road, Cricklewood, Middlesex; widow. Died 23 February 1924 at Park Royal Hospital, Acton Lane, Middlesex. Admin London 13 June.   £554   9   9d

1925 SKUES ELIZABETH of the village of Chardstock, Devon; widow. Died 24 March 1925. Admin Exeter 6 May.   £168   14   0d

1926 SKEWES HENRY of Bonython House, Cury, Cornwall. Died 12 September 1926. Probate Bodmin 10 November.   £1621   12   0d

1928 SKEWES GWENDOLINE of 80 Wellington Road, St Thomas, Exeter; spinster. Died 22 March 1928 at Royal Devon and Exeter Hospital, Exeter. Admin Exeter 8 May.   £154   7   1d

1928 SKEWES HANNIBAL of Chybarles, Ruan Major, Cornwall. Died 12 April 1928. Admin Bodmin 28 April.   £246   0   0d

1929 SKEWS EDMUND of 123 King Street, Plymouth. Died 22 March 1928 at Homeopathic Hospital, Plymouth. Admin London 13 April.   £132   3   4d

1929 SKEWES JANE of 2 Arwenack Avenue, Falmouth, Cornwall; widow. Died 27 March 1929 at 19 Poplar Road, Merton, Surrey. Probate London 1 June 1929. £307 0 4d

1929 SKEWS JOHN of 5 Cauldfield Place, Redruth. Died 3 May 1929. Admin London 14 June. £87 14 8d

1930 SKUES PHILIP HENRY of 170 Lion Street, New Kent Road, Walworth, Surrey. Died 20 September 1930 at St Thomas' Hospital, Lambeth, Surrey. Admin London 27 November. £396 16 9d

1930 SKEWES-COX JESSIE of Laburnham Cottage, Petersham, Surrey; widow. Died 18 May 1930. Probate London 6 August. £1901 16 4d

1931 SKEWES FRANCES ANN of Merris, Cornwall; widow. Died 16 July 1931. Admin Bodmin. £106 10 0d

1932 SKEWES AGNES of 41 George Street, Linley, Huddersfield; widow. Died 2 June 1932. Probate Wakefield 21 July. £8021 1 5d

1932 SKEWES WILLIAM of Landewednack, the Lizard, Cornwall. Died 2 October 1930. Admin (Limited) Bodmin 23 March. £812 19 5d

1932 SKEWES WILLIAM of 10 Golf Villas, Falmouth, Cornwall. Died 12 August 1932. Admin Bodmin 19 September. £670 8 9d

1933 SKUES EDWARD GEORGE of Quiet Street, Claremont, Wynberg, Cape Colony, South Africa. Died 30 June 1933. Admin (with will Ltd) London 8 December. £344 10 3d

1934 SKEWS ELIZABETH SARAH of 11 Ford Park Road, Plymouth; widow. Died 4 July 1934. Probate Exeter 1 October. £1094 1 10d

1935 SKEWS MATTHEW of 17 Best View Terrace, Shiney Row, County Durham. Died 17 December 1934. Probate Bodmin 16 March. £2863 2 6d

1935 SKEWIS WILLIAM BAWDEN of Myrtle Cottage, Brighton Ladock, Cornwall. Died 14 June 1935. Admin (with will) Bodmin 28 October. £76 17 9d

1935 SKEWS MATTHEW of 17 Best View Terrace, Shiney Row, County Durham. Died 17 December 1944. Probate Newcastle Upon Tyne 5 March. Further grant 18 December 1962. £1235 8 7d

1935 SKEWS WILLIAM JOHN of 44 Elemore Lane, Easington Lane, Hetton-le-Hole, County Durham. Died 21 November 1935. Probate Durham 2 December. £163 0 0d

1935 SKUES JOHN GILBERT of 24 Tintern Road, Lordship Lane, Wood Green, Middlesex. Died 3 May 1935. Probate London 5 July. £2183 9 8d

1936 SKEWES JOHN COURTIS of Newcombes, Crediton, Devon. Died 13 May 1936. Probate Bristol 26 June. £66,773 13 10d
Resworn: £71,683 14 6d

1936 SKEWS AMELIA of 17 Best View Terrace, Shiney Road, County Durham; widow. Died 4 April 1935. Probate Durham 28 May. £346 17 6d

1936 SKEWS JOHN of Cocksbarrow, St Austell, Cornwall. Died 18 February 1936. Probate Bodmin 8 April. £506 0 0d

1937 SKEWES MINNIE of 212 Ballards Lane, Finchley, Middlesex (wife of JOSIAH SKEWES). Died 14 January 1937. Probate London 26 May. £5980 17 7d

1937 SKEWS MAY LOUISA of 68 Glen Park Avenue, Plymouth (wife of JOHN SKEWS). Died 26 June 1937. Probate Exeter, 30 October. £3526 11 8d

1937 SKEWS SAMUEL FRANCIS of 39a South Street, Boksburg, Transvaal, South Africa. Died 17 October 1922. Probate Bodmin 17 July. £5 0 0d

1938 SKEWES EDITH of Nantithet, Cury, Cornwall; spinster. Died 21 April 1938. Probate Bodmin 13 May. £515 9 7d

1938 SKEWES LILY of the Old Rectory, Gidleigh, Chagford, Devon (wife of HOWARD SKEWES). Died 24 May 1938 at Southmead Hospital, Bristol. Admin Bristol 6 July. £2581 1 6d

1938   SKEWES WILLIAM of Chiverton Farm, Perranuthnoe, Cornwall. Died 5 October 1937 at Penzance. Admin Bodmin 30 June.   £3257   19   7d

1939   SKEWES MARY ELLEN of 51a Cranley Road, Westcliffe on Sea, Essex; widow. Died 14 May 1939. Probate Exeter 26 June.   £480   12   11d

1939   SKEWES NELLIE of 61 East End, Redruth, Cornwall (wife of WILLIAM HEDLEY SKEWES). Died 7 December 1938. Admin Bodmin 4 February.   £655   19   1d

1939   SKEWIS HELEN THOMASINE of 4 Regence Terrace, Penzance; widow. Died 13 April 1939. Probate Bodmin 30 October.   £117   11   3d

1940   SKEWES ALFRED JOHN of Barford Farm, Spaxton, Somerset. Died 18 December 1939. Admin Bristol 1 February.   £1050   18   4d

1940   SKEWES EMILY ANN of 4 Centenary Street, Camborne; widow. Died 20 October 1940. Admin Bodmin 27 November.   £883   15   10d

1940   SKEWES HARRY OSWALD of 4 Centenery Street, Camborne. Died 15 September 1940 at Hayle, Cornwall. Admin Bodmin 31 October.   £880   8   4d

1940   SKEWES JOHN KEMPTHORNE of the Averade Hotel, Lancaster Gate, London. Died 23 November 1939 at Prince of Wales Hospital, Plymouth. Probate London 29 January.   £31,154   14   2d
                                                                    Resworn: £33,285   13   7d

1940   SKUES FREDERICK WILLIAM MACKENZIE of 5 Campden Road, South Croydon, Surrey. Died 27 May 1940. Probate London 24 June.   £1452   4   11d
                                                            Resworn: £1391   16   11d

1940   SKUES MARGARET GEORGINA SARAH of the Retreat, Cullompton, Devonshire; spinster. Died 21 September 1940 at 35 Southern Hay, West Exeter. Probate Llandudno 15 November.
                                                                    £3883   13   3d
                                                            Resworn: £3864   1   0d

1941   SKEWES ANN of South View, Crediton, Devon; widow. Died 16 March 1941. Probate Exeter 3 June.
                                                                    £3739   8   1d

1941   SKEWES CHARLES of 15 Horton Street, Rusholme, Manchester. Died 26 July 1941. Probate Manchester 13 October.   £1011   11   8d

1941   SKEWIS ALFRED of 13 Dartmouth Gardens, Milford Haven, Pembrokeshire. Died on or since 24 December 1940 at sea. Admin Camarthen 6 May.   £271   8   11d

1942   SKEWES EDWARD of West Close, Mawnan, Cornwall. Died 24 January 1942. Probate Bodmin 8 May.   £4397   16   2d

1942   SKEWES HENRIETTA CATALINA GOLDSWORTHY otherwise HENRIETTA of The Vicarage, Praze, Crowan, Cornwall (wife of HERBERT JOHN SKEWES). Died 2 April 1942. Admin (with will) Bodmin 24 July.   £396   18   0d

1942   SKEWES EDITH of 24 Margaret Road, Penwortham, Preston, Lancashire; widow. Died 5 May 1942. Admin Lancaster 28 May.   £302   10   0d

1942   SKEWS ELIZA of 6 Horsall Street, Swindon, Wiltshire (wife of JOHN EDWIN SKEWS). Died 13 August 1942. Admin Winchester 11 November.   £205   0   0d

1943   SKEWES MAUD ANNA of 1 Penmere Terrace, Falmouth, Cornwall; widow. Died 7 April 1943. Probate Llandudno 25 June.   £3123   6   0d

1944   SKEWES FREDERICK WILLIAM of 75 Palmerston Street, Manchester 16. Died 15 March 1944 at 20 Nell Lane, Manchester 20. Admin Manchester 31 May.   £449   5   8d

1944   SKEWS HENRY JAMES of 39 Shakespeare Road, Walthamstow, London E17. Died 14 November 1944. Probate Llandudno 7 December.   £162   8   6d

1944   SKEWS WILLIAM THOMAS of 51 Sale Street, London E2. Died 10 December 1943 at Bethnal Green Hospital, London E2. Admin Llandudno 17 June.   £150   0   0d

1944 SKUES MARY THERESA of 4 Gravel Walk, Cullompton, Devon; spinster. Died 4 May 1944. Probate Llandudno 3 July. £5862 10 3d

1945 SKEWES HOWARD of Berry Down Farm, Gidleigh, Chagford, Devon. Died 11 May 1945 at Melvin Nursing Home, Newton Abbot. Probate Bristol 22 August. £6084 8 8d

1946 SKEWES ANNIE of 15 Horton Street, Rusholme, Manchester; widow. Died 31 January 1946. Admin Manchester 1 August. £118 17 8d

1946 SKEWES MARY of West Close, Mawnan, Cornwall; spinster. Died 20 February 1946. Probate Bodmin 6 December. £1935 5 8d

1946 SKEWS JOHN HENRY of Wallaford Venn Close, Plymouth. Died 13 September 1946. Probate London 22 November. £245 10 2d

1946 SKUES DORIS GAMBLE of Baddow, 4 The Highway, Sutton, Surrey (wife of ERNEST SKUES). Died 21 November 1945. Probate London 20 June. £1200 1 7d

1946 SKUES ERNEST of 1 Ashburn Grove, Heaton Norris, Stockport, Cheshire. Died 29 March 1945 at the Infirmary, Stockport. Probate Llandudno 17 January. £221 5 9d

1946 SKUES FLORENCE MARY of 1 Willow Bank, Hyde Park, Halifax, West Yorkshire; spinster. Died 23 October 1945. Probate Durham 18 February. £1137 8 5d

1947 SKEWES DOROTHY MARION of 9 St Augustine's Road, Bessecar, Doncaster, South Yorkshire (wife of WILLIAM FREDERICK CHARLES SKEWES). Died 19 July 1947. Probate Wakefield 19 September. £2113 11 4d

1947 SKEWS JOHN EDWIN of 6 Horsell Street, Swindon, Wiltshire. Died 11 March 1947. Probate Oxford 29 April. £2050 4 6d

1947 SKUES MARY ISABELLA MACKENZIE of 14 Moreton Road, South Croydon, Surrey; spinster. Died 14 April 1947 at Warlingham Park Hospital, Surrey. Probate London 9 July. £6083 11 0d

1948 SKEWES JOSIAH of 212 Ballards Lane, Finchley, Middlesex. Died 16 September 1948. Probate London 25 November. £13,394 13 3d

1948 SKEWS ALICE of 6 St George's Road, Lower Edmonton, London N9 (wife of ALFRED DAVID RICHARD SKEWS). Died 2 August 1948. Admin London 1 September. £216 16 3d

1948 SKEWS GEORGE FRANCIS of 18 Cambridge Gardens, Winchmore Hill, Middlesex. Died 3 October 1948 at Sunken Garden Village Road. Edmonton, Middlesex. Admin London 25 October. £409 4 5d

1948 SKUES ALBERT EDWARD of 149 Tilson House, Tilson Gardens, Wandsworth, London SW2. Died 27 August 1947 near St. Bartholomew's Hospital, London. Admin London 18 June. £300 19 0d

1948 SKUES ELIZABETH of 22 Tintern Road, Lordship Lane, Wood Green, Middlesex; widow. Died 4 December 1946. Probate London 12 January. £2414 8 9d

1948 SKUES ELIZABETH of Barncoose Lane, Illogan Highway, Redruth, Cornwall; spinster. Died 7 February 1948. Probate Bodmin 13 September. £263 9 8d

1949 SKUES GEORGE EDWARD MACKENZIE of 23 Kelsey Park Road, Beckenham, Kent. Died 9 August 1949. Probate London 12 October. £13,848 8 1d

1949 SKUES EDWARD ALFRED of 209 Shipbourne Road, Tonbridge. Died 30 August 1948. Admin London 1 January. £346 10 1d

1949 SKEWES MAGGIE ISABELLA SIMPSON of 11 Station Road, Shiney Row, County Durham; widow. Died 16 November 1948. Probate Durham 7 January. £809 16 2d

1949 SKEWIS FRANK of 17 Deansway Avenue, Sturry, Kent. Died 8 January 1949 at the Kent and Canterbury Hospital. Admin Lewes 29 April. £444 0 0d

1949 SKEWS MATTHEW of 17 Best View Terrace, Shiney Row, County Durham. Died 17 December 1934. Admin (with will) London 6 July. Former grant D.R. Newcastle Upon Tyne 5 March 1935. £835 0 0d

1950 SKUES CLORINDA EMMA of 149 Tilson House, Tilson Gardens, Brixton Hill, London; widow. Died 20 October 1949. Admin London 11 January.   £204   15   4d

1950 SKEWES HARRY STANLEY of Garras, Mawgan in Meneage, Cornwall. Died 21 August 1950 at Helston, Cornwall. Probate Bodmin 12 September.   £58   14   5d

1950 SKUES HAROLD FREDERICK CLAUDE of 20 Tintern Road, Wood Green, Middlesex. Died 13 September 1950 at Royal Free Hospital, St Pancras, London. Probate London 31 October. £2195 9 4d

1950 SKEWES WILLIAM JOHN of 28 Albany Road, Redruth, Cornwall. Died 8 October 1949. Probate Bodmin 26 January.   £4435   19   4d

1950 SKEWS ALFRED DAVID RICHARD of 447 Hertford Road, Lower Edmonton, Middlesex. Died 31 March 1950. Probate London 27 April.   £376   12   6d

1951 SKEWES ALBERT EDWARD of Elm House, Wareham, Dorset. Died 15 May 1951. Admin (with will) Winchester 30 May.   £313   6   1d

1951 SKEWES JOHN WESLEY of Garras, Mawgan in Meneage, Cornwall. Died 3 February 1951 at Mount View Hospital, Madron. Probate Bodmin 19 March.   £783   11   0d

1951 SKEWS VICTOR GEORGE of 39 Peppercroft Street, Gravesend, Kent. Died 3 November 1951. Admin London 21 December.   £291   0   4d

1951 SKUES JANE EMILY of Mawgan, Priory Road, Chalfont St. Peter, Bucks. Died 17 March 1951. Admin London 13 June.   £1000   16   11d

1951 SKUES ELIZABETH MACKENZIE of 20 Copers Cope Road, Beckenham, Kent (wife of CHARLES AYRE MACKENZIE SKUES). Died 30 March 1951. Probate London 9 July. £10,879   18   6d

1952 SKEWES EDWARD of Winsford, Ashton, Helston, Cornwall. Died 14 August 1952 at Helston and District Cottage Hospital. Probate Bodmin 13 September.   £3298   6   3d

1952 SKEWES ELIZABETH of 15 Horton Road, Rusholme, Manchester; spinster. Died 23 June 1952 at 20 Nell Lane, Manchester 20. Probate Manchester 8 October.   £1540   14   10d

1952 SKEWES LILLIAN LINDA MAY of Ivy Court, Perran Downs, Rosudgeon, Penzance; spinster. Died 22 May 1952 at St Michael's Hospital, Hayle, Cornwall. Admin Bodmin 14 September.
                                                                                            £1114   12   11d

1953 SKEWES ALARINA of West End Shop, Caldicot, near Chepstow, Monmouth; widow. Died 30 June 1951. Probate Llandaff 1 September.   £754   4   8d

1953 SKUES BESSIE ANNIE of Mawgan, Priory Road, Chalfont St. Peter, Bucks; spinster. Died 20 November 1951. Probate London 12 February.   £420   11   0d

1954 SKEWES GEORGE ERNEST of 8 Hunstan Road, Sale, Cheshire. Died 26 December 1953 at Royal Hospital, Cheadle, Cheshire. Probate Manchester 20 May.   £4265   11   5d

1954 SKEWES JAMES HENRY OSWALD of Trecarne, 12 Atlantic Terrace, Camborne, Cornwall. Died 27 March 1954. Admin Bodmin 10 May.   £2152   5   5d

1954 SKEWES SAMUEL JOHN of The Railway Hotel, Kelly Bray, Callington, Cornwall. Died 16 October 1954. Probate Exeter 17 November.   £3018   1   6d

1954 SKEWES WILLIAM FREDERICK CHARLES of 12 South Parade, Doncaster, South Yorkshire. Died 29 November 1953 at Western Hospital, Springwell Lane, Doncaster. Admin Wakefield 7 April.
                                                                                            £2015   6   0d

1954 SKEWES WILLIAM TREVENA of Mount Carne Farm, Nancledra, Penzance. Died 14 September 1953 at St. Michael's Hospital, Hayle, Cornwall. Admin Bodmin 5 January. £2007   1   6d

1954 SKEWS JOHN HENRY of 4 Shenstone Gardens, Honicknowle, Plymouth, Devon. Died 7 August 1954. Admin Exeter 14 September.   £474   15   4d

1955 SKEWS BERTHA of Coxbarrow, Carthew, St Austell, Cornwall; widow. Died 26 December 1954. Admin Bodmin 14 April.   £498   5   6d

1955 SKEWS FREDERICK of Bowthorpe South, Hetton-le-Hole, County Durham. Died 8 June 1955. Probate Durham 11 July.   £1308   17   10d

1955 SKEWS WILLIAM of Coxbarrow, Carthew, St Austell, Cornwall. Died 10 January 1904. Admin Bodmin 28 June.   £250   0   0d

1955 SKEWS WILLIAM JOHN of St Nicholas House, Hetton-le-Hole, County Durham. Died 29 January 1955. Admin (with will) Durham 17 March.   £437   5   7d

1956 SKEWES WILLIAM HENRY of Fernside Farm, Carne Lane, Carnkie, Cornwall. Died 19 April 1956 at St Michael's Hospital, Hayle. Admin Bodmin 28 May.   £1500   0   0d

1956 SKEWS FRANCES of Bowthorpe South, Hetton-le-Hole, County Durham; widow. Died 5 February 1956. Probate Durham 1 March.   £588   6   8d

1956 SKUES ERNEST of 20 Tresoddern Road, Redruth, Cornwall. Died 11 October 1955 at Royal Cornwall Infirmary, Truro. Admin Bodmin 7 March.   £103   18   10d

1957 SKUES JOAN MACKENZIE of 20 Copers Cope Road, Beckenham, Kent; spinster. Died 13 January 1957 at Bickley Railway Station, Kent; Admin London 5 April.   £4939   11   3d

1957 SKEWES ANN MARIA of Banford Farm, Spaxton, Bridgwater, Somerset; widow. Died 3 June 1957. Admin (with will) Bristol 1 November.   £8048   18   5d

1957 SKEWES FLORENCE LUCY of 7 Courtenay Road, St Thomas, Exeter (wife of ERNEST JOHN SKEWES). Died 16 June 1957. Admin Exeter 23 August.   £112   10   0d

1957 SKEWES WILLIAM VERDAYNE of 49 Addiscombe Road, Croydon, Surrey. Died 9 January 1957 at General Hospital, Croydon. Probate London 19 March.   £8348   7   4d

1957 SKEWIS LAURA of Redbraes, 2 Hayston Avenue, Milford Haven, Pembrokeshire (wife of SAMUEL SKEWIS). Died 31 May 1957 at Withybush Hospital, Haverfordwest. Admin Camarthen 13 August.
                                                                                                                                                                                 £440   0   8d

1958 SKEWES Rev. HERBERT JOHN of Gilmore, Crowan, Cornwall. Died 11 October 1958 at 10, Trewirgie Road, Redruth. Probate Bodmin 14 November.   £981   6   0d

1958 SKEWIS SAMUEL of Redbraes, 2 Hayston Avenue, Milford Haven, Pembrokeshire. Died 8 March 1958. Admin Camarthen 27 March.   £645   6   11d

1958 SKUES LILY of Rosedale Park Road, West Malvern, Worcester (wife of ERIC SKUES). Died 8 August 1958. Probate London 13 October.   £997   0   7d

1958 SKUES CHARLES AYRE MACKENZIE of Yew Tree House, Stafford Street, Market Drayton, Shropshire. Died 12 April 1958. Probate London, 6 August.   £18,843   7   5d

1959 SKEWES ALFRED JOHN of the Vicarage, Kenwyn, Truro. Died 25 April 1959. Probate Bodmin 17 June.   £1324   7   0d

1959 SKEWES JOHN HENRY of 451a Hill Street, Laguna Beach, California, United States of America. Died 18 February 1959 at Hoag Memorial Hospital, Newport Beach, California. Admin (with will) London 28 July.   £1324   7   1d

1959 SKEWES MATILDA of 99 Pendarves Street, Tuckingmill, Camborne, Cornwall (wife of ALFRED JOHN SKEWES). Died 24 April 1958 at Barncoose Hospital, Illogan, Redruth. Probate Bodmin 21 January.   £700   0   0d

1959 SKEWS ETHEL OF 11 Garden Lane, Cleadon, County Durham; widow. Died 15 February 1959 at the General Hospital, Ryhope, County Durham. Probate Newcastle Upon Tyne 4 March.
                                                                                                                                                                                 £1048   17   0d

1959 SKUES CHARLES HENRY of Mawgan, 11 Priory Road, Chalfont St. Peter, Bucks; retired office accountant. Died 28 December 1958 at White Lodge Court Road, Maidenhead, Berkshire. Probate London 24 March.   £2501   16   5d

1960 SKEWES ARTHUR DAWE of 24 Western College Road, Mannamead, Plymouth, Devon. Died 2 August 1960 at Greenbanks, Agar Road, Redruth. Probate Exeter 16 September.
                                                                                                                                                                                 £107,849 16   11d

1960 SKUES ROSEMARY MARGARET of Watermoor Parsonage, Cirencester, Gloucester (wife of Rev. JOHN ANTHONY SKUES). Died 23 August 1960 at General Hospital, Cheltenham. Admin Gloucester 8 November.   £229   2   9d

1960 SKEWES JANIE of 52 Trevethan Road, Falmouth, Cornwall; widow. Died 30 August 1960. Probate London 14 September.   £1821   0   3d

1961 SKUES MARGARET ELIZABETH of 75 Derwent Road, Palmers Green, London, N13; widow. Died 4 June 1961. Admin London 21 August.   £174   7   0d

1961 SKEWS GEORGE WEALE of the Church Army Hostel, 22 Johnson Street, Stepney, London E1. Died 28 April 1961 at Mile End Hospital, Stepney. Probate London 20 June.   £966   13   0d

1962 SKUES MINNIE MACKENZIE of Yew Tree Cottage, Stafford Street, Market Drayton, Shropshire; spinster. Died 21 June 1962. Probate London 21 August 1962.   £20,814   15   8d

1962 SKEWES CHARLOTTE of Dunmere, Kelly Bray, Callington, Cornwall; widow. Died 26 November 1961. Admin London 7 March.   £476   11   10d

1962 SKEWS MATTHEW of 17 Best View Terrace, Chester Road, Shiney Row, Houghton-le-Spring, County Durham. Died 17 December 1934. Admin (with will) Newcastle Upon Tyne 18 December (Former grant: Newcastle 5 March 1935).   £100   0   0d

1963 SKEWES ETHEL of 27 Cardrew Close, Redruth, Cornwall; widow. Died 4 July 1963 at Barncoose Hospital, Redruth. Probate London 18 November.   £859   14   0d

1963 SKEWS ALICE ELIZABETH of 84 High Street, Swanscombe, Kent; widow. Died 12 March 1963. Admin London 30 April.   £157   1   6d

1963 SKEWS ALICE MARTHA ROSE of 13 Lashmar Road, East Preston, Sussex. Died 18 April 1963 at Swandean Hospital, Worthing, Sussex. Probate Lewes 4 June.   £3194   10   2d

1963 SKEWS GERTRUDE ALBERTA of Coxbarrow, Carthew, St Austell, Cornwall; spinster. Died 9 March 1963. Admin Bodmin 10 April.   £737   19   0d

1963 SKEWS MINNIE of 1 Fords Row, Redruth, Cornwall; widow. Died 19 August 1963 at Barncoose Hospital, Redruth. Admin Bodmin 6 November.   £147   14   0d

1964 SKUES THOMAS GEORGE of 47 Ashford Road, Cricklewood, Middlesex. Died 12 January 1964 at Neasden Hospital, London NW10. Probate London 11 March.   £5018   0   0d

1964 SKEWS BEATRICE of 19 Alexander Road, Newquay, Cornwall; spinster. Died 31 May 1964 at Bodmin. Probate Bodmin 6 August.   £342   0   0d

1964 SKEWS MABEL COOPER of 109 Centre Parade, Kettering, Northants (wife of JOHN GEORGE SKEWS). Died 27 December 1963 at Victoria Hospital, Lewes, Sussex. Probate Leicester 13 January.
                                                                                    £2515   0   0d
      As from 1965 Somerset House 'rounded off' wills and administrations to the nearest £.

1965 SKEWES BELLA CLARKE of St Peter's Convent, Plympton House, Plympton, Devon. Died 9 January 1965. Admin Exeter 28 March.   £192

1965 SKEWES ELIZABETH of 49 Addiscombe Road, Croydon, Surrey. Died 17 February 1965. Probate London 25 May.   £13,894

1965 SKEWES GEORGE of 75 South Milton Street, Plymouth. Died 9 March 1965. Probate Bodmin 16 June.   £376

1965 SKEWES LIONAL JAMES of 3 Corpascus Cottages, Mabe, Penryn, Cornwall. Died 23 February 1965 at Miners Hospital, Redruth. Probate London 6 April.   £2050

1965 SKEWES WILLIAM HEDLEY of Trevarth Vean Lanner Moor, Redruth, Cornwall. Died 9 November 1964 at Barncoose Hospital, Redruth. Probate Bodmin 14 January.   £2340

1965 SKEWES ANNIE EDITH of 24 Margaret Road, Penworthan, Preston, Lancashire. Died 22 December 1965. Probate Manchester 2 February.   £995

1965 SKEWS ELIZABETH ETHEL GRACE of 167 Pasley Street, Stoke Devonport, Plymouth, Devon. Died 30 September 1964. Probate Bodmin 5 November.   £548

1965 SKEWS EVA MARY of 34 Station Road, Sidcup, Kent. Died 2 November 1965. Probate London 17 December.   £414

1965 SKUES ELSIE KATE of 28 Tintern Road, Wood Green, Middlesex. Died 1 March 1965 at North Middlesex Hospital, Edmonton. Admin London 2 April.   £207

1966 SKEWES RACHEL CARDWELL otherwise RACHEL of 25 Surrey Road, Bournemouth, Hampshire. Died 1 November 1966 at St. Leonard's Hospital, Ringwood, Hants. Probate Winchester 15 December.   £1950

1966 SKEWS MINNIE of 36 Adelaide Road, Redruth, Cornwall. Died 8 November 1965 at Barncoose Hospital, Redruth. Probate Bodmin 18 May.   £2119

1966 SKEWS SARAH of 65 St John Street, Copperhouse, Hayle, Cornwall. Died 24 October 1966. Probate Bodmin 9 November.   £911

1966 SKUES EVA of Fern Cottage, Probus, Truro, Cornwall. Died 3 July 1966. Admin (with will) Bodmin 23 November.   £1600

1966 SKUES REGINALD PENROSE of Trebron, The Downs, West Looe, Cornwall. Died 23 April 1966. Probate Bodmin 5 July.   £4703

1967 SKEWES EDWARD MORLEY of 13 Bartles Row, Tuckingmill, Camborne, Cornwall. Died 19 September 1967 at 77 Higher Fore Street, Redruth. Admin Bodmin 14 November.   £4762

1967 SKUES PHILIP ERNEST of 16 Ruxley Close, Ewell, Surrey. Died 27 December 1966 at Cuddington Hospital, Cheam, Surrey. Admin Lewes 21 February.   £6794

1968 SKEWES ERNEST JOHN of 7 Courtenay Road, St Thomas, Exeter. Died 6 March 1968. Probate Exeter 25 March.   £2420

1968 SKEWES HAROLD of 117 Yew Tree Road, Manchester. Died 20 May 1968. Admin Manchester 17 June.   £1037

1968 SKUES WALTER EDWARD of 6 Newgate Street, Walton on Naze, Essex. Died 6 September 1968. Probate Ipswich 1 October.   £2100

1969 SKEWES FREDERICK HENRY of 80 Wellington Road, St Thomas, Exeter. Died 6 July 1969. Probate Bristol 7 August.   £3200

1970 SKEWES ANNIE of West End, Goldsithney, Penzance. Died 3 September 1969. Admin Bristol 13 March.   £1308

1970 SKEWS ALBERT EDWARD VICTOR of 25 Acklington Place, Ernesettle, Plymouth. Died 17 May 1970. Admin Bristol 10 August.   £818

1970 SKEWS WILLIAM DAVID of 1 Holm Oak Cottages, East Kingston, East Preston, Sussex. Died 7 July 1970. Admin Winchester 9 October.   £2033

1971 SKEWES BESSIE SARAH of 53 Kenwyn Street, Truro. Died 18 February 1971. Admin Bristol 6 April.   £735

1971 SKEWES EMMA of Trevarth Vean, Lanner, Redruth, Cornwall. Died 11 January 1971. Probate Bristol 23 March.   £5155

1971 SKEWES GEORGE of 39 Coronation Avenue, Camborne, Cornwall. Died 29 August 1971. Admin Bristol 18 October.   £816

1971 SKEWES IDA MARY of 24 Cecil Court, 73 Eaton Rise, London, W5. Died 2 April 1971. Probate London 24 May.   £9055

1971 SKEWES JOHN EDWARD of 17 Mornish Road, Branksome Park, Poole, Dorset. Died 8 January 1971. Probate Bristol 2 April.   £11,115

1971 SKEWES-COX, THOMAS EDMUND of Providence Cottage, South Green, Southwold, Suffolk. Died 26 March 1971. Probate London 21 October.   £5387

1971 SKEWIS SAMUEL LESLIE of 9 Bearstead Close, Gillingham, Kent. Died 13 March 1971. Admin Brighton 8 April.   £1080

1971 SKEWS EDWIN ARTHUR of 3 Featherbed Lane, Harlescott, Shrewsbury, Salop. Died 29 October 1970. Admin Sheffield 15 March.   £5389

1971 SKUES ARTHUR LEONARD PETER of 42 Priory Path, Barrow in Furness. Died 6 October 1971. Admin Liverpool 12 November.   £552

1971 SKUES THOMAS HENRY JAMES of 172 Bybrook Road, Kennington, Ashford, Kent. Died 23 August 1971. Admin Brighton 8 October.   £559

1971 SKUES VINCENT of Vinclyn, Dawson Lane, Whittle le Woods, Chorley, Lancashire. Died 18 July 1970. Probate Manchester 24 June.   £3100

1973 SKEWES VIOLET of Rose Glen, Porthallow, St Keverne, Cornwall. Died 31 January 1972. Admin Bristol 11 July.   £7133

1973 SKEWS ESME ETHEL of 28 South Street, Crowland, Lincs. Died 12 October 1973. Probate Ipswich 30 November.   £929

1973 SKEWS WILLIAM HEDLEY of Oak View, Coxbarrow, Carthew, Cornwall. Died 26 March 1973. Admin Bristol 21 May.   £5887

1973 SKUES CARMELLA of 16 Ruxley Close, Ewell, Surrey. Died 17 January 1973. Admin Brighton 23 May.   £14,949

1974 SKEWES FANNY of 24 Bradshaw Avenue, Withington, Manchester. Died 2 June 1974. Admin Manchester 9 July.   £749

1974 SKEWES SIDNEY ARTHUR of Rose Glen, Porthallow, St Keverne, Cornwall. Died 13 December 1973. Admin Bristol 16 May.   £13,817

1975 SKEWES AVIS MAY of 39 Coronation Avenue, Camborne, Cornwall. Died 15 April 1975. Admin Bristol 9 July.   £2164

1975 SKEWS DAVID GEORGE of 35 Rothwell Road, Dagenham, Essex. Died 16 March 1975. Admin London 6 August.   £1034

1976 SKEWES HARRY of 2 South Terrace, Penzance. Died 31 May 1975. Admin Bristol 27 May.   £2686

1976 SKUES ANNIE MARIE of 228 Point Clear Road, St Osyth, Clacton, Essex. Died 23 September 1975. Probate London 26 May.   £15,533

1976 SKUES VICTOR CLAUDE of 228 Point Clear Road, St Osyth, Clacton, Essex. Died 16 May 1975. Admin London 11 May.   £17,764

1976 SKUES WILLIAM JOHN of Fern Cottage, Fore Street, Probus, Cornwall. Died 21 March 1976. Probate Bristol 4 May.   £6857

1978 SKEWS CLARENCE of 25 Valentine Row, Callington, Cornwall. Died 12 November 1977. Probate Bristol 3 January.   £8462

1978 SKUES ERNEST of 36 Well House, Woodmanstone Lane, Banstead, Surrey. Died 24 November 1977. Probate Brighton 3 February.   £67,770

1979 SKEWES ARTHUR GEORGE of 6 Blackbrook Avenue, Paignton, Devon. Died 4 November 1978.
                                                                                              £24,027

1979 SKEWIS MARJORIE CONSTANCE of 31 Farncombe Road, Tunbridge Wells, Kent. Died 17 June 1979.   £4634

1980 SKEWS ALFRED GEORGE WILLIAM of 86 North Road, Great Clacton-on-Sea, Essex. Died 8 December 1979. Probate London 28 February 1980.   £16,960

1980 SKEWS KIRTLEY of 29 Wordsworth Avenue East, Houghton-le-Spring, Tyne and Wear. Died 6 November 1979. Admin Newcastle Upon Tyne 15 May 1980.   £6234

1980   SKUES LUCY of 11 Bell Hall Terrace, Savile Park, Halifax, West Yorkshire. Died 4 September 1980.
       Probate Leeds, 31 October 1980.   £5735

1980   SKUES MARJORIE HELEN of 42 Priory Path, Barrow in Furness, Cumbria. Died 29 July 1980. Admin Liverpool 18 November 1980.   £13,250

1980   SKEWES-COX, MILES LEICESTER DUNNING of Uphill, Ponsworthy, Devon. Died 26 December
       1979. Probate London 1 August 1980.   £173,950

16 International Who's Skewes, Skewis, Skews, Skues and Skuse

The following pages are a complete list of names in alphabetical order of SKEWES/SKEWIS/ SKEWS/SKUES and SKUSE known to the author whether it be personal contact or simply names extracted from census returns, parish registers or street directories. Spellings, unusual at times, have been copied exactly.

Although the family had its roots in Cornwall, by the mid 1800's people were migrating as well as emigrating. There are entries for people living in Mexico, Chile, South Africa, Canada, Australia, New Zealand, Portugal and the United States of America, where various branches of the family still exist to this day.

A mini "Who's Who" is out of date from the very day it appears as a published work. New members arrive and senior citizens move on; time and tide wait for no man! However, with thousands of names arranged in alphabetical and chronological order, the task of updating will be made easier in the future.

This chapter, which has been constantly updated over the last 25 years, covers the period circa 1300 to 1980. All forenames appear in chronological order; so for example a Richard Skues born in 1769 would appear before a Richard Skues born 1919.

ABBREVIATIONS

A(SH)	Administration held at Somerset House, London
Bpt	Baptised
Chart "X"	Contained on a particular pedigree. See Chapter 12 "Various Branches of the Family."
CRO	Document held at the County Record Office, Truro, Cornwall.
Mrd	Married
W(SH)	Will held at Somerset House, London

ABBREVIATIONS FOR TOWNS AND VILLAGES IN MORE DETAIL

Aberdare	Glamorgan, South Wales
Abergavenny	Gwent, South Wales
Adelaide	South Australia
Altrincham	Cheshire
Ashburton	Devon
Baldhu	Cornwall
Ballarat	Victoria, Australia
Barnsley	South Yorkshire
Bedwellty	South Wales
Beer Ferris	Devon (now spelt "Beer Ferrers")
Bendemeer	New South Wales, Australia
Bere Alston	Devon
Blackwater	Truro, Cornwall
Broken Hill	New South Wales, Australia

Calstock	East Cornwall
Camborne	Cornwall
Chacewater	Truro, Cornwall
Crowan	Cornwall
Devonport	Devon
Dobwalls	Liskeard, Cornwall
Ebbw Vale	Gwent, South Wales
Falmouth	Cornwall
Geelong	Victoria, Australia
Gwennap	Cornwall
Halifax	West Yorkshire
Hamilton	Scotland
Hamilton	Ontario, Canada
Helston	Cornwall
Huddersfield	West Yorkshire
Illogan	Cornwall
Ives Grove	Racine, Wisconsin, USA
Lambeth	London
Liskeard	Cornwall
Lizard	Cornwall
Marazion	Cornwall
Mawgan	Helston, Cornwall
Mawnan	Falmouth, Cornwall
Mawnan Smith	Falmouth, Cornwall
Merthyr Tydfil	Mid Glamorgan, South Wales
Moonta	South Australia
Mount Kurrangai	New South Wales, Australia
Mullion	Helston, Cornwall
Neath	West Glamorgan
Penryn	Falmouth, Cornwall
Penzance	West Cornwall
Pachuca	Mexico
Pontypridd	South Wales
Real del Monte	Mexico
Redruth	Cornwall
Rosudgeon	Penzance, Cornwall
St Agnes	Cornwall
St Ewe	Cornwall
St Ive	Liskeard, Cornwall
St Ives	North Cornwall
St Just in Roseland	Cornwall
St Keverne	Cornwall
St Wenn	Bodmin, Cornwall
Stithians	Helston, Cornwall
Tamworth	New South Wales, Australia
Tavistock	Devon
Totnes	Devon
Tredegar	South Wales
Trewint	Launceston, Cornwall
Tuckingmill	Cornwall
Uralla	New South Wales, Australia
Virginia City	Nevada, United States of America
Watchet	West Somerset
Watsons Creek	New South Wales, Australia
Wendron	Helston, Cornwall
Williton	West Somerset

A

SKEWES A.
Lived at 26 Mount Street, Devonport 1920-1921.

SKEWES A.
Farmer living in Ruan Major, Helston, 1856.

SKUES A.
Sent a letter to *The Times* newspaper about cigarettes being issued to the Forces in France. Letter dated 14 February 1939. He lived at 157 Regent Road, London, W.1.

SKUES A.
of Highbury, London. Was a winner of a competition in *News of the World*, August, 1956. Prize was a cruise lasting six days to the Canary Islands, Christmas, 1956.

SKUES A.E.
B.A. Downing College, Cambridge, 1954. Territorial Army Reserve for Officers. Lieutenant (414396) from active service (unattached) made Lieutenant 1st March 1957 retaining present seniority.

SKEWIES A.F.
Author of *Analysis of Uranium-Zirconium Alloys*, 1953. H.M.S.O. 2/6d.

SKEWES A.J.
Lived at 31 Wyndham Street, Plymouth 1920-1921.

SKEWS A.J.
Lived at 74 Cecil Street, Plymouth 1920-1921.

SKEWES AARON
Chart 2, Son of Luis Enrique Skewes. Mexican. Born 1 July 1937. Married Maria Teresa Navarrete. Children: Martha (1962), Lilia (1966), Nancy (1968) and Miriam and Isela — twins (1970).

SKEWES AARON ERNESTO
Chart 10. Son of Ernesto Skewes. Born 1 July 1969, Mexico.

SKEWES AARON MICHAEL
Chart 10. Son of Michael Thomas and Mary Skewes. Born Hamilton, Ontario, Canada 13 June 1979.

SKEWES ABIGAIL
Son of Stephen and Blanch Skewes. Bpt St Just in Roseland 19 January 1639. Married Markes Maker at St Feock 7 October 1665.

SKUSE ABRAHAM
Soldier of the Surrey Fencibles. Married Mary Bolitho at St Mary's, Truro 29 August 1799.

Tombstone of Absalom Skewis (1825-1880) in Shullsburg, USA

SKEWES ABRIL
Chart 10. Mexican. Daughter of Juan and Leonor Skewes. Born Mexico 23 April 1965.

SKEWIS ABSALOM
Chart 2. Son of Henry Skewis. Baptised Camborne 29 July 1750. Married Elizabeth Clemmence at Crowan 6 February 1786. Children: William, Margaret, John and Ann (twins), Absalom and James and Edward (twins).

SKEWES ABSALOM
Chart 2. Son of Absalom and Elizabeth Skewes of Camborne. Born 17 October 1787. Bpt Crowan 26 December 1787. Married Jane Piper 26 December 1810 at Camborne Parish Church. Miner. Children: Jane Piper, Mary Ann, Elizabeth, William, Caroline, and Henry Janes and Juliana (twins).

SKEWES ABSALOM
Chart 2. Son of Absalom and Jane Skewes of Ramsgate, Camborne. Bpt Camborne 27 April 1822. Buried Camborne 31 December 1831, aged 10 years.

SKUES ABSALOM
Chart 2. Son of James and Joanna Skues of Camborne. Born 4 November 1825. Bpt Camborne 26 November 1825. Married Jane T. Osborne (she born 9 March 1828 died 14 November 1866). Emigrated to United States of America 1849. Children: Mary Ellen (1851), Emily Jane (1854), Elizabeth Adeline (1857), John Rule (1858) and Bennett Osborne (1862). Spelling changed to SKEWIS. Freemason. Lived at Shullsburg, Wisconsin. Died 14 April 1880, aged 55 years. Buried in Shullsburg cemetery, Wisconsin. Masonic emblem on tombstone.

SKEWES ABSALOM
Born Neath, 1884.

SKEWES ADA
Born Redruth 1856. Married. Died Redruth 1930 aged 74 years.

SKUES ADA
Chart 3. Née Dawson of Halifax. Born 1861. Married Frederick Gordon Skues in Halifax 1884. In 1905 Trade Directory of Halifax she was listed as a milliner of 23 Boothtown Road, Halifax. Children: Ernest (1885) and Arthur (1891). Died Wandsworth 1945 aged 84 years.

SKEWES ADA
Chart 2. Daughter of William Henry and Catherine Skewes. Born 3 September 1872. Died 6 December 1949, aged 77 years. Married Henry Watson. No issue.

SKEWIS ADA
Born Sheffield 1880.

SKEWES ADA
Chart 30. Daughter of William Brown and Blanche Skewes, painter of Middle Rosewin Row, St Paul's, Truro. Born 19 February 1885. Bpt St Paul's, Truro 5 August 1891. Married 13 July 1907 to William James Ellis (29), labourer of 52 Fairmantle Street, Truro and son of Robert James Ellis, postman. Married at St George's, Truro, in presence of William Brown Skewes and Cereta Skewes.

SKEWES ADA
Chart 12. Daughter of Frederick Tresize Skewes. Born 1885. Married Jenkin.

SKUES ADA
Chart 6. Née Tregonning. Born 1886. Married James Frederick Skues 1905. Lived at 16 Trefusis Road, Redruth, 1922. Children: Ada May (1905) Phyllis (1908), James Frederick Junior (1909), Lewis (1912) and Ernest (1923). Died 1946, aged 60 years.

SKEWES ADA
of Condurrow. Born 1899. Buried Tuckingmill Parish Church 11 February 1899, aged 1 month.

SKEWS ADA
Chart 41. Née Sheldon. Married Thomas Skews 1886, Ecclesall, Sheffield, South Yorkshire. Children: Thomas (1886), Minnie (1889), Louisa (1891), Elizabeth (1892), Mabel (1893), Ernest (1895), George (1897), Olive (1900), Joseph (1901), Samuel (1903) and Edgar (1905). After the death of Thomas Skews in 1911, Ada married John Michael Dolan 1913 in Barnsley, South Yorkshire.

SKEWES ADA
Lived at South Carn, Carn Brea, Illogan in 1922 with Frederick Skewes.

SKEWES ADA
Lived at 10 Condurrow Road, Beacon, Camborne in 1922 with Mary Marjorie Skewes. In 1949 she lived at the same address, but on her own.

SKEWES ADA
Lived at 37 Dolcoath Avenue, Camborne in 1922.

SKEWES ADA
Married Whitford 1940 in Redruth.

SKUES ADA ALICE
Chart 7. Born 1889 Tonbridge. Married Wood 1909 Tonbridge. Five or six children.

SKEWES ADA ELIZA
Born 1872. Chart 16. First wife of Henry Skewes. One son: Lional

James. Died 28 February 1919 aged 47 years.

SKEWS   ADA IVY
Chart 41. Daughter of Thomas and Jane (née Renshaw) Skews. Born 21 October 1911. Married Rev. William Richie Harrison Hesketh 24 December 1932 in Barnsley, South Yorkshire. Now lives in Lichfield. Issue: two sons.

SKUES   ADA J.
Born 1877. Died 1968 Lambeth, aged 91 years.

SKEWES   ADA J.
Lived at 14 Pendarves Road, Camborne in 1968.

SKEWES   ADA JANE
Chart 36. Born 4 February 1882. Married Richard Charles Skewes 1907, Redruth. Lived at White Cross Hill, Illogan and later 10 Condurrow Road, Beacon. Child: Mary Margery (1907). Died 1976, aged 94 years.

SKEWES   ADA JOHANNA
of Lambeth. Born 1875.

SKEWES   ADA LOUISA
Chart 12. Daughter of John and Louisa Skewes. Born Helston 1870. Married 1891.

SKEWES   ADA MARY
Lived at Kornane Road, Murranbeena, Henty, Victoria, Australia in 1913 with Raymond Kenwyn Skewes, gasfitter.

SKUES   ADA MAY
Chart 5. Eldest daughter of James Frederick Skues of 16 Trefusis Terrace, Redruth. Born 1905. Married Richard Leslie Pearce, dock labourer of Lanner Hill, and son of Mr and Mrs John Pearce, tin smelter, 12 September 1936 at Fore Street Methodist Church, Redruth. Brother Fred Skues "gave her away."

SKEWES   ADAM DAVID
Chart 36. Son of Gary Earl and Jennifer Joy (née Matthews) Skewes. Born 26 November 1973 Tamworth, New South Wales, Australia.

SKEWES   ADAM LEIGH
Chart 36. Son of Leigh and Kerry Gail (née Dobbyn) Skewes. Born 1 September 1976. Lives at 5 Woolway, Delacombe, Victoria, 3356, Australia.

SKEWES   ADELAIDE
of Truro. Born 1865. Died 1865, aged 0.

SKEWES   ADELINE HARRIET R.
of Helston. Born 1880. Married 1903 at Landewednack Parish Church, Lizard.

SKEWES   ADRIAN GEORGE
Lived at 4 Palm Street, Coffs Harbour, New South Wales, 1959. Labourer.

SKEWES   AERIAL
Chart 10. Son of Juan and Leonor (née Munoz) Skewes. Born Mexico 9 December 1959.

SKEWES   AGATHA BLANCHE
Née Johns. Daughter of William and Emma Johns. Born 22 December 1888, Kadina, South Australia. Married Horace Henry Skewes, 31 August 1907, Kadina, South Australia. In 1959 was living at 164 Chapple Street, Broken Hill West, New South Wales. Children: Richard Horace Henry, Frank Horace, Violet Blanche, Gladys May, Clarice Olive, Dorothy Alice, Eva Lorraine, Harry, Laurel Jean, Muriel Melbanear, Horatio Gerald and Harold Melville. Died 9 September 1977, aged 89 years.

SKEWES   AGNES
Daughter of John Skewes. Bpt St Gerrans 21 December 1575.

SKEWES   AGNES
Wife of Edward Skewes (who died Huddersfield 23 May 1915). Born 1864. Lived at 41 George Street, Lindley, Huddersfield. Died 2 June 1932, aged 68 years.

SKEWIS   AGNES
Chart 17. Daughter of James Arthur Skewis of Stepney. Mother's maiden name Jarvis. Born 1919. Died 1919, aged 0.

SKEWS   AGNES
Chart 26. Wife of Richard Skews of Kerley, Kea. Born 1786. Children: John, Richard, William, Philippa and Sarah. Buried 20 May 1860 at Baldhu, aged 75 years.

SKEWIES   AGNES
Born 1883. Died 1951, Hamilton, Scotland, aged 66 years.

SKEWIS   AGNES
Married 1889, Coatbridge, Scotland. Prior to marriage had an illegitimate son John Hastings. Father was James Hastings. Baby born 5 December 1884.

SKEWES   AGNES CORONA
Chart 10. Born 14 June 1902, Penzance. Daughter of Richard and Hetty Skewes of Marazion. Bpt Marazion Circuit 14 October 1902. Married William Snowden.

SKEWIS   AGNES HASTINGS
Born 1908, New Monkland, Scotland. Died New Monkland, 1908, aged 0.

SKEWES   AGNES RICE
Lives at 33 Graduate Crescent, Mulgrave, 3170, Victoria, Australia

with Ronald Oswald Skewes, panel beater.

SKEWES   AGNES VERONICA
Lived at 4 Netherby Street, Wahroonga, Normanhurst, New South Wales, Australia in 1959 with Edward Skewes, postal officer. Children: Michael James Skewes and Anthony Joseph Skewes. Now lives at 27 Eastern Valley Way, Northbridge, 2063, New South Wales, Australia.

SKEUES   AGNIS
Married Martin Luke at Gerrans Parish Church, 7 May 1611.

SKEWIS   AGNES FORBES
of Kettering. Born 27 July 1894. Died 1971, aged 77 years.

SKEWES   AIDA
Chart 10. Mexican. Daughter of Alfredo and Juila (née Varela) Skewes. Born 20 April 1950, Mexico. Spinster. Lives in Mexico City.

SKEWES   AILEEN MAY
Chart 10. Daughter of Jonathan Braddon and May Evelyn (née Gallagher) Skewes. Born 21 April 1927, Hamilton, Ontario, Canada. Married Norman Arthur Epps 14 April 1951. Issue: 3 daughters.

SKEWES   AINSLIE HERBERT
Chart 36. Son of Thomas Herbert and Catherine Ann (née Harvey) Skewes. Born 7 November 1912. Married Muriel Edith Garnham 19 July 1941. Son: Brian Ainslie Skewes (1948). Lives at 12 Scammell Court, Mount Waverley, 3149, Victoria, Australia.

SKEWES   ALAN
Chart 38. Son of Stanley Victor and Gertrude Olive (née Trimper) Skewes. Born 1914. Married Gwen Pudney. Lives at Port Hughes, Kadina, South Australia.

SKEWES   ALAN
Son of William Henry and Clara Bertha Skewes. Born 1933, Missouri, USA. Died 1937, aged 4 years.

SKEWES   ALAN
Chart 24. Son of Jack and Betony Skewes. Born 6 August 1947. Lived at 6 Cardigan Street. Stockton, 2295, Victoria, Australia. Married Shirley Rutherford December 1968. Children: Terri (1972), adopted; Grant (1973), adopted; and Shirley Jane (1975). Now lives in Christchurch, New Zealand.

SKEWS   ALAN
Lived at 207 Brighton Road, St Kilda, Victoria, Australia in 1959. Carter.

SKEWIS   ALAN
Born 1971, Inverness, Scotland.

SKEWS   ALAN DAVID
Chart 15. Son of Peter and Mary (née Sylvester) Skews of Liskeard. Born 1958.

SKUES   ALAN J.
Chart 9. Son of Philip Ernest Skues. Mother's maiden name Lucchesi. Born 1952. Married Kathleen Buck in Barking, Essex 1973. Divorced. Married Linda S. Vesma 1978, Canterbury, Kent.

SKEWIS   ALAN LOWELL
Born 27 June 1936, USA. Line Ensign, United States Navy, 1959. In 1967 Seattle, Washington Street Directory was technical analyst, Boeing at 2603 NE 130th, Seattle, Washington. Married to Lee R. Skewis.

SKIWERS   ALAN de
"Appointment of H. de Montfort to take assize by Alan de Skiwers and Annora his wife, against Matthew de Skiwers and Dodus de Skiwers, touching a tenement in Skewes." (Patent Rolls 3 Edward I). The year 1275.

SKEWES   ALARINA I.
of West End Shop, Caldicot, near Chepstow, Monmouth. Widow. Born 1862. Died 30 June 1951, aged 89 years. Still listed in 1980 Telephone Directory — Caldicot 420214.

SKEWS   ALBAN EDGAR
of Dartford, Kent. Born 1883. Married Eliza Crowhurst in Gravesend 1915. No children. Died at sea aboard vessel *Unity* 1920, aged 37 years. His wife Eliza remarried 1921 to Midson in Gravesend.

SKEWIS   ALBERT
Chart 43. Born 1878, Sheffield, South Yorkshire.

SKEWS   ALBERT
of Devonport. Listed in 1950/1953 Plymouth Street Directory living at 137 Pasley Street, Plymouth.

SKUES   ALBERT E.
Chart 9. Son of Albert Edward Skues. Mother's maiden name Cullingham. Born 1930, Southwark.

SKEWES   ALBERT E.
of Salford. Born 1936. Mother's maiden name SKEWES.

SKEWS   ALBERT E.
Married Wills in Plymouth, 1958.

SKEWES   ALBERT EDWARD
Chart 19. Son of Thomas Lean and Emma M.M. Skewes. Born 1862. Lived at Elm House, Wareham, Dorset. Married 1890. Died 15 May 1951.

SKUES   ALBERT EDWARD

Albert Edward Skues (1893-1947)

Chart 9. Born 19 January 1893. Married Louisa A. Cullingham in Southwark 1926. Children: Eileen (1928) and Albert E. (1930). Died 1947, aged 54 years.

SKEWS ALBERT EDWARD
Chart 15. Born 10 July 1894, Stoke Devonport. Married Weston 1921, East Stonehouse. Children: Albert Edward Victor (1923). Died 1969, aged 75 years.

SKEWS ALBERT EDWARD
Chart 17. Son of Alfred David Richard and Alice Skews of 6 St George's Road, Lower Edmonton, London N9. Born 1902. Married Jane Harding 1932, Edmonton. Children: Dorothy J. (1934) and Brian A.E. (1938).

SKEWS ALBERT EDWARD
Son of Albert John Skews, cement labourer. Born 1903 Dartford, Kent. Was a wheelman at Cement Office Works and lived at 11 The Grove, Swanscombe, Kent. Married Daisy Atkinson, house maid at training colony, and daughter of Joseph Atkinson of 6 Graylands Lane, Swanscombe, Kent at Register Office, Dartford, Kent on 1 August 1925. Children: Eunice D. (1927) and Brian A.A. (1934). Died 1946, aged 43 years, in Dartford.

SKEWS ALBERT EDWARD
Chart 50. Son of John Edwin and Eliza (née Wells) Skews of 6 Horsall Street, Swindon, Wiltshire. Born 7 December 1904. Married Henly (she born 12 March 1915) 21 May 1952. No children. Lives at 6 Horsall Street, Swindon. Coach finisher.

SKEWS ALBERT EDWARD VICTOR
Chart 50. Born 22 July 1923. Mother's maiden name Weston. Lived at 25 Acklington Place, Ernesettle, Plymouth. Married Lowe 1958, Plymouth. Children: Martyn R. (1959) and Mark H.V. (1962). Died 7 May 1970, aged 47 years, Plymouth.

SKEWES ALBERT HENRY
Chart 19. Son of Thomas Lean Skewes. Born 1863.

SKEWES ALBERT J.
Born 1913, Redruth. Mother's maiden name Ford. Died 1913, aged 0.

SKEWES ALBERT JAMES
Lived at Highbury East, South Australia, 1959 with Mary Elizabeth Skewes. He was a miner.

SKEWS ALBERT JOHN
Born 1880 Dartford, Kent. Married 1903. Died 1936, aged 55 years. Son: Albert Edward Skews (1903).

SKEWS ALBERT JOHN
Chart 38. Son of Ernest Richard and Lena Mary (née Hass) Skewes. Born 17 April 1941. Married Kathleen Mavis Clark 7 March 1964, South Australia. Children: Joanna Kay (1964), Kym John (1965) and Ricky Wayne (1971). Lives at Government Road, Bute, 5560, South Australia. Supervisor with South Australian Highways Department.

SKEWES ALBERT MILTON
Chart 38. Son of Richard and Mary Jane (née Reynolds) Skewes, Born 24 February 1889, Moonta, South Australia. Married Myrtle Emma Marks 11 February 1911. Died 21 November 1952, aged 63 years. Buried in Kadina Cemetery, South Australia.

SKEWES ALBERT MURRAY
Chart 38, Son of Edgar William and Mary Bridget (née Kavanagh) Skewes. Born 20 September 1913. Married Olive May Brand 19 April 1947. Children: Edward Kent Skewes and Leanne May Skewes. Lived at 2 William Street, Croydon, South Australia. Fireman. Died 11 October 1962, aged 49 years.

SKEWS ALBERT PETER
Chart 15. Born Liskeard 1932. Mother's maiden name Jane.

SKUES ALBERT VICTOR
Twin to Winifred Violet Skues. Born 1884 Westminster. Died 1884, aged 0.

SKEWES ALBERT VICTOR
Chart 38. Son of Richard and Mary Jane (née Reynolds) Skewes.

Born 11 March 1885, Moonta, South Australia. Died 5 April 1886, aged 1 year.

SKEWS ALBERT WILLIAM
Born 1869 North Aylesford, Kent. Died 1894, aged 24 years.

SKEWES ALBERTA
Daughter of William and Elizabeth Alberta Mary Jessop Skewes. Born 1 June 1902, Kearsage, Houghton, Michigan, USA. Married Louis J. Haga.

SKEWES ALEXANDER
Son of William Skews of Gwennap. Bpt Gwennap 5 December 1700.

SKEWES ALEXANDER
Married Ann Carvett 19 May 1723 at St Enoder.

SKEWES ALEXANDER
Chart 19. Owned estate on three lives worth £60. Had a brother Richard Skewes. Will (CRO) proved 15 October 1736.

SKEWES ALEXANDER
Chart 19. Son of Thomas and Elizabeth Skewes. Bpt Gwennap 26 December 1746. Died 18 March 1748, aged 2 years.

SKEWES ALEXANDER
Chart 19. Son of Thomas and Elizabeth Skewes. Bpt Gwennap 15 September 1753. Died 28 November 1754, aged 1 year.

SKEWES ALEXANDER
Chart 19. Son of Thomas and Elizabeth Skewes. Bpt Gwennap 22 April 1758. Mine agent. Lived at Chenhale, Gwennap. Married Christian Martin of Stithians 14 September 1794 at Stithians. Children: Grace, Richard, Margaret, Christian Martyn, Alexander, William, Elizabeth Mary and Ann. Buried Gwennap 18 March 1835.

SKEWES ALEXANDER
Chart 19. Son of Alexander and Christian Skewes. Bpt Gwennap 7

Albert Milton Skewes (1889-1952) taken in South Australia, 1920

September 1807. Account clerk in Copper. Died 12 December 1862, aged 55 years. Will proved 1863. Effects under £14,000.

SKEWES ALEXANDER
of East Kerrier. Lent his name to "The Roman Catholic Question" (1829). See Chapter 3 for full details.

SKEWES ALEXANDER
Chart 19. Son of John & Ann Skewes of Penance, Gwennap, miner. Bpt Gwennap 19 November 1834. Died of scarlet fever. Buried 14 November 1842 at Gwennap.

SKEWES ALEXANDER
Son of John and Ann Skewes of Little Carharrack, Gwennap. Born February 1850. Bpt Gwennap Wesleyan Church 25 June 1850.

SKUES ALEXANDER JAMES
Chart 8. Son of George Henry Skues. Born 1876 at 6 Little Chapel Street, Soho, London. Died 1877, aged 0.

SKEWES ALEXANDER McLEOD
Chart 36. Son of Bruce and Judith Rosemary (née Taylor) Skewes. Born 18 July 1978, Tamworth, New South Wales, Australia.

SKEWES ALEXANDER RICHARD
Chart 19. Born 1858, Wareham, Dorset. Died 1858, aged 0.

SKEWES ALEXANDRA
Chart 36. Daughter of Anthony Joseph and Bronwyn (née Gapp) Skewes. Born 14 September 1972, New South Wales, Australia.

SKUES ALFRED
Chart 27. Born 1843, Bath.

SKEWES ALFRED
Chart 2. Son of Henry and Avis (née Bath) Skewes. Born 14 January 1851. Died 13 February 1852 at Roseworthy, aged 1 year. Buried in Camborne Churchyard.

SKEWES ALFRED
Chart 2. Son of Henry and Avis (née Bath) Skewes. Born 16 April 1852. Died 20 April 1852, aged 4 days. Buried in Gwinear Churchyard alongside his father.

SKEWES ALFRED
Chart 15. Son of William Skews. Born 1859. Married Margaret Simmonds (20), factory girl and daughter of William Simmonds, at Christ Church, St Olave, London, 15 February 1885. Alfred was resident at 19 Cherry Tree Garden Street, St Olave in 1885. Children: Elizabeth Martha (1888), Alfred William (1890), William George (1893), Emily Anne (1895), Henry Frederick (1897), George Thomas (1899) and Martha Margaret (1901). Died 1902, aged 39 years.

SKEWS ALFRED
Chart 15. Born 1860, Launceston. Son of John and Isabella Skews. Bpt Altarnun 7 March 1861. Died 1861, aged 10 months.

SKEWS ALFRED
Born 1862, Launceston.

SKEWS ALFRED
Born Liskeard 1862. Died Liskeard 1862, aged 0.

SKEWS ALFRED
Chart 15. Born 1863, Launceston. Son of John and Isabella Skews. Bpt Altarnun 20 November 1863.

SKEWS ALFRED
Chart 15. Born 1864, Launceston. Died 1864, aged 9 months.

SKEWES ALFRED
Chart 10. Born 1865, Redruth. Son of William Trezize and Maria (née Mitchell) Skewes.

SKEWIS ALFRED
Chart 50. Son of Daniel and Sarah (née Matthias) Skewis, copper miner. Born 13 September 1887 at Trimley St Mary, Woodbridge, Suffolk. Moved to South Wales and lived at 13 Dartmouth Gardens, Milford Haven, Pembrokeshire. Married Edith Alice Hughes in Haverfordwest, 1913. Died at sea approx 24 December 1940, aged 53 years. Children: Delilah C (1913), Alfred W. St. E. (1916), Brenda G.S. (1924) and Gretta J. (1934). Edith Alice died 1975, aged 82 years.

SKEWES ALFRED
Chart 10. Son of Richard Skewes late of Marazion. Born 28 March 1914 at Hamilton, Ontario, Canada. Married Pearl Armstrong 1945.

SKEWES ALFRED
Was killed in action in 1915. He was Lance Corporal with Royal Fusiliers, London.

SKEWS ALFRED DAVID RICHARD
Chart 17. Son of George Alfred and Lucy Caroline (née Moore — late Bernard) Skews 39 Gee Street, St Luke, Holborn. Born 7 April 1871, Holborn. Married Alice.... 1898 (she died 2 August 1948). Was a grocer's assistant of 6 St George's Road, Lower Edmonton, London N9, and later lived at 447 Hertford Road, Lower Edmonton. Children: Albert Edward, George Francis and Alice D. Died 31 March 1950, aged 78 years.

SKUES ALFRED EDGAR
Chart 8. Son of Walter Edward Skues. Mother's maiden name Bond. Born 1914. Married Catherine E.N. Brassett in Finsbury, 1940. Son Terence F. (1947) and daughter Shirley C.J. (1941). In 1964 Alfred living at 13 Almorah Road, Islington, London.

SKEWS ALFRED GEORGE WILLIAM

Born 1899. Married Annie L. Snowshill, 1927, Edmonton, London. Daughter Betty F. (1938). Lived at 86 North Road, Great Clacton, Clacton on Sea, Essex. Died 8 December 1979, aged 80 years.

SKEWES ALFRED HERBERT
Born 1871. Admitted to paternity to an illegitimate child of Jessie Agnes Steward, aged 23, Presbyterian, pianist at a public house in Port Adelaide. Single. Skewes, who was born in Victoria, was employed on the railways as a fireman, but in 1895 was out of work living with J. Fahey of Hindley Street, Adelaide. He signed a written statement saying that he would pay all expenses in connection with the girl's confinement, as soon as he obtained employment. She was penniless at the time. She left hospital in Adelaide with the child on 25 April 1895. Skewes later lived at 16 Bewes Street, Adelaide. Buried in the public cemetery, Adelaide, 13 May 1947, aged 76 years.

SKEWS ALFRED J.
Born 1915, Whitechapel. Died 1915, aged 0.

SKEWES ALFRED JOHN
Born 1869, Redruth. Died 1869, aged 0.

SKEWES ALFRED JOHN
Born 1875. Married Ann Maria... Lived at Barford Farm, Spaxton, Bridgwater, Somerset. Died 18 December 1939, aged 64 years.

SKEWES ALFRED JOHN
Chart 36. Son of Edward Skewes. Born 6 May 1877. Mining engineer... Married Matilda Hill (she died 25 April 1959 at Barncoose Hospital, Redruth). Lived at Pengellys Row 1923; Maynes Row, 1926; Bartles Row 1940-1949 and 99 Pendarves Street, Tuckingmill, 1959. He spent 30 years in Detroit, Michigan. Retired in 1957 and returned to Cornwall. Children: Rosamund Emily, Florence May, Beatrice Mary, Alfred John, Sylvia Doreen, Matilda Joan and Edward Morley. Died 25 April 1959, aged 81 years.

SKEWES ALFRED JOHN
Married 1901 in Holyhead.

SKEWES ALFRED JOHN
Married 1900, Redruth.

SKEWES ALFRED JOHN
Married 1904, Bideford, Devon.

SKEWES ALFRED JOHN
Chart 36. Son of Alfred John and Matilda Skewes of Maynes Row, Tuckingmill. Born 6 May 1907. Bpt with his sisters at Tuckingmill Parish Church 12 Sept 1917. Married Lily Matthews (daughter of Frederick Pascoe Matthews, carpenter) at Cury Parish Church 30 June 1934. Was a lorry driver. No children. Died 21 February 1982, aged 74 years.

SKEWIS ALFRED W. St E.
Chart 50. Son of Alfred and Edith Alice (née Hughes) Skewis. Born 1916, Haverfordwest. Died 1916, aged 0.

SKEWS ALFRED WILLIAM
Born 1890, St Olave, London.

SKEWES ALFREDO
Chart 10. Mexican. Son of Nazario and Dolores (née Riofrio) Skewes. Born 25 January 1911. Married Juila Varela, Mexico. Children: Alfredo (1941), Clara Thawsnelda (1944), Dolores (1948) and Aida (1950).

SKEWES ALFREDO
Chart 10. Mexican. Son of Alfredo and Juila (née Varela) Skewes. Born 25 August 1941. Married Leticia Bello. Children: Julio (1974) and Leticia (1976). Lives in Mexico City.

SKEWES ALICE
Widow. Married William Wiat at St Enoder 3 Feb 1576.

SKEWES ALICE
Chart 29. Maiden name John. Married John Skewes at Perranarworthal 23 June 1759. Children: Mary, Maria, John, Richard, James, Ann Lucey & Elizabeth.

SKEWES ALICE
Chart 2. Daughter of Richard and Alice Skewes. Bpt Camborne 19 May 1776. Died 22 July 1777, aged 1.

SKEWES ALICE
Chart 36. Of Treloskan, Cury. Maiden name Skewes. Married William Skewes of Cury at Falmouth 26 Sept 1794. Children: Alice, Mary, John, Ann, William, Sarah, Elizabeth, Edward, Henry & Richard.

SKEWES ALICE
Chart 2. Daughter of Richard & Alice Skewes. Bpt Camborne 16 Apl 1780. Married William Hendy. An Alice Skewes Hendy died in Constantine 29 March 1824.

SKEWES ALICE
Married John Morcam of Gwennap at Kenwyn 13 November 1784.

SKEWES ALICE
Born 1791. Died Helston 21 July 1868, aged 77 years.

SKEWES ALICE
Chart 29. Daughter of Richard and Roseanna Skewes. Bpt Kenwyn 22 December 1793.

SKEWES ALICE
Daughter of William Skewes. Bpt Falmouth 26 Sept 1794.

SKEWES   ALICE
Chart 45. Daughter of William and Alice Skewes of Treloskan, Cury. Bpt Cury 19 February 1795.

SKEWES   ALICE
Married John Midlin at Constantine 24 January 1804, in presence of Henry Skewes.

SKEWES   ALICE
of Churchtown, Cury. Born 1808. Buried Cury 30 Jan 1834, aged 26 years.

SKEWES   ALICE
Chart 2. Daughter of Henry & Grace Skewes. Bpt 10 March 1811, Constantine. Married Thomas Midlin 8 Oct 1835 at Constantine in presence of Henry, Grace and Elizabeth Skewes.

SKEWES   ALICE
Married Joseph Michell at Kenwyn 23 Dec 1815 in presence of Richard and John Skewes.

SKEWES   ALICE
Chart 36. Daughter of James & Simonette Skewes. Bpt Cury 23 February 1834.

SKEWES   ALICE
Married Joseph Henry Gribble 23 December 1861 at Redruth. Great great grandson Peter Brian Jelbert (born 29 October 1944 at Camborne) lists Skewes/Gribble in his birth brief at Society of Genealogists, London (September 1976). Alice Skewes was 13 generations past.

SKEWS   ALICE
Chart 54. Born 1871. Wife of Alfred David Richard Skews. Lived at 6 St George's Road, Lower Edmonton and later 447 Hertford Street, Lower Edmonton, London, N 9. Children: Albert Edward (1902), George Francis (1905) and Alice D. (1912). Married 1898. Died 2 August 1948, aged 77 years.

SKUES   ALICE
Chart 27. Daughter of William and Mary Skues of Bath. Born 1871. Died 1871, aged 0.

SKEWES   ALICE
Born 1873. Died Salford 1907, aged 34 years.

SKUSE   ALICE
Daughter of Daniel and Louisa (née Clouder) Skuse. Born 1878. Married Len Rayner. Issue two sons and two daughters.

SKEWS   ALICE
Married 1888, Dartford, Kent.

SKEWS   ALICE
Chart 41. Née Lumb. Second wife of Joseph Skews. Married 1928, Barnsley, South Yorkshire. Children: Rita (1929), Desmond (1930), Raymond (1931), Brenda (1932) and Brian J. (1946).
Joseph died 1963, Barkeston Ash, aged 61 years. Alice married Slade, a Salvation Army man, 1969, Staincross.

SKEWES   ALICE
Chart 12. Daughter of William and Mary Skewes of Gilly Lane, Cury. Born 1837. Bpt Cury 4 June 1837. Dressmaker. Had two illegitimate sons — Arthur Skewes (1867) and John Wesley Skewes (1860). In 1871 Census Returns was living at Nantithet, Cury. Unmarried. Died Cury 1926, aged 89 years.

SKEWIS   ALICE
Wife of Robert L. Skewis. Lives at 1263 Farrington Drive, San Jose, California, United States of America.

SKUES   ALICE
Daughter of William and Mary Skues. Bpt Cury 4 June 1837.

SKEWS   ALICE ANNIE
Born 1878, Bethnal Green. Married 1904.

SKEWES   ALICE BEATRICE
Chart 36. Daughter of William and Elizabeth (née Northey) Skewes. Born 20 December 1879, Uralla, New South Wales, Australia. Married Richard Young, 1899. Issue: 4 sons and 9 daughters. Died 25 April 1977, Uralla, aged 97 years.

SKEWS   ALICE D.
Chart 17. Daughter of Alfred David Richard and Alice (née Fawcett) Skews. Born 1912, Edmonton, London. Died 1925, aged 13 years.

SKEWS   ALICE E.
Born 1868, Limerick. Information taken from Regimental Registers at General Registry Office, London.

SKEWES   ALICE EDITH
Lived at Stanhope Street, Malvern East, Australia in 1913, with Matthew Skews.

SKEWES   ALICE ELIZABETH
Born 1883. Lived at 84 High Street, Swanscombe, Kent. Widow. Died 12 March 1963, aged 80 years.

SKEWS   ALICE ELIZABETH
Born 1906 Strood, Kent. Married Law, 1925, in Gravesend, Kent.

SKEWES   ALICE EMILY
Chart 36. Daughter of Edward Skewes. Born 1885, Redruth. Married 1909 to Alfred Trebilcock.

SKEWES   ALICE EVE
M.A. Chart 14. Daughter of George Jessop and Ruth (née Viall)

Skewes. Born 20 August 1935, America. Educated at Hamline University, St Paul, Minnesota. B.A. (High Honours), 1957. Studied at Tübingen, Heidelberg and Göttingen, West Germany from 1955 to 1956 and from 1959 to 1963. Also studied at the University of Chicago, Pennsylvania State University and University of Maryland. Married Karl-Wolfgang Michel, 20 August 1959 at Göttingen, West Germany. One daughter Alice Ellinor Michel (1961). Divorced November 1964.
Married Professor Richard Kennington 11 December 1964 at Bellefonte, Pennsylvania, USA.
M.A. (University of Maryland), 1980. Teacher and Instructor at various universities in the United States and Germany. Lives at 4710 College Avenue, College Park, Maryland, 20740, United States of America. Telephone number (301) 927 6242.

SKEWS   ALICE GERTRUDE
Born 1887, Preston, Lancashire. Died 1888, aged 1 year.

SKEWES   ALICE HENDY
of Churchtown, Constantine. Born 1824. Buried Constantine 29 March 1824.

SKEWS   ALICE J.
Born 31 July 1861. Married William Skews. Lived in Mineral Point, Wisconsin, United States of America. Children: Thomas (1882) and Harvey (1883). Died 4 July 1896, aged 34 years. Buried in Jackson Cemetery, Mineral Point.

SKEWES   ALICE JEAN
Lived at 103 Greenhill Road, Toorak Gardens, Rose Park, South Australia in 1959. Lived with Henry Skews. Now lives at 5 Mariner Street, London Park, 5065, South Australia.

SKEWES   ALICE KATE
Chart 18. Daughter of Samuel Dawe Skewes of Beer Ferris, Bere Alston, Devon. Born 1862. Married 1892 to Tonkin. She was married again twice, one husband being called Anderson. In 1871 Census Returns she was living at Fore Street, Bere Alston, Devon.

SKEWES   ALICE LENORE
In 1959 lived at West End, Uralla, New South Wales, Australia. Now lives at 29 Queen Street, Uralla, 2358, New South Wales, Australia.

SKEWES   ALICE LYNN
Chart 10. Daughter of Richard Herbert and Alice Skewes. Born 1 November 1955, Ontario, Canada.

SKEWS   ALICE MARTHA R.
Born 1898, Bethnal Green.

SKEWS   ALICE MATILDA
Born 1865, North Aylesford, Kent.

SKEWS   ALICE MAY
Lives at 58 St James Road, Heidelberg, 3084, Victoria, Australia.

SKEWES   ALICE RUTH
M.A. Chart 14. Daughter of Edwin Bottomley and Alice (née Collier) Skewes. Born 19 March 1894. Teacher at High School, Greenwood, Wisconsin, USA (1917-1918); at Racine High School (1918-1920) and Wichita, Kansas (1920-1923).
Married Reverend Eddy L. Ford, 7 August 1933. He died January, 1951.
She took Masters Degree in English Literature at the University of California at Berkeley in 1924. Taught at Madison, Wisconsin 1924-1933.
Managing Editor and researcher for the Journal of the National Educational Association from 1951 to 1973. Lives at 1884 Dalton Court, Lexington, Kentucky, 40505, United States of America.

SKUES   ALICIA ANN
Chart 9. Daughter of David J. Skues.
Mother's name Weighill. Born 1971, Dartford, Kent.

SKEWES ALISON BOYD
In 1959 lived at 54 Moray Avenue, Wembley Park, Victoria, Australia with David Thomas Skewes. Now lives at 29 Darke St, Torrens, 2607, Canberra, Australia.

SKEWES ALISON MARY
Lives at 49 La Perouse Avenue, Flinders Park, 5025, South Australia with Dulcie Elma Skewes. Teacher.

SKEWS   ALISTAIR DEREK
Chart 15. Son of Derek Thomas and Linda (née McManaman) Skews. Born 19 October 1976. Lives at 4 Moonfield, Callington, Cornwall.

SKEWES   ALLAN
In 1959 lived at 21 Gainsborough, St Ferryden, South Australia. Coach painter. Now lives at 13 Cuncliffe Street, Port Hughes, 5558, South Australia with Gwendoline Euphemia Skewes.

SKEWS   ALLAN CLAUDE
Lives at 5/203 Brighton Road, Elwood, 3182, Victoria, Australia with Margaret Isobel Skewes.

SKEWS   ALLAN ROBERTSON
Lived at 37 Newry Street, Prahan, Victoria, Australia in 1959 with Florence Rose Skews. Plasterer.

SKEWES   ALLEN BRENT
Chart 26. Son of Frank Anson and June Beverley (née Spaulding) Skewes. Born 25 September 1950. Married and divorced. No

Alice Eve Skewes

Alice Ruth Skewes, aged 17 years

children.

SKEWS   ALLEN E.
Born 1885, Romford, Essex. Died 1920, aged 35 years.

SKEWES   ALLISON ELIZABETH
Chart 25. Daughter of Joseph Frederick and Doreen (née Isaac) Skewes. Born 13 January 1960. Lives at 12 Walnut Walk, Stretford, Manchester M32 9AQ.

SKEWES   ALLISON MARY
Chart 36. Daughter of Douglas Arthur and Coleen Marie (née McKenzie) Skewes. Born 31 August 1954. Single. Teacher in Queensland, Australia.

SKEWES   ALMA BERNICE
Née Walker. Born 6 April 1909, Victoria, Australia. Married Harold William Skewes at Warragul, Australia. Issue: Patricia (1931), Harold Grenville (1932) and Judith (1946). Lives at 31 Clifford Street, Warragul, 3820, Victoria, Australia.

SKEWES   ALMA JANE
Chart 36. Daughter of James and Frances Skewes of Mawnan Smith, Falmouth. Born 1857. Bpt Mawnan Parish Church 17 May 1857. Died 12 October 1870, aged 13 years.

SKEWES   ALMA MAE
Chart 14. Daughter of Edward Henry and Helen (née Gilmore) Skewes. Born 1899, America. Married William Siewert. Issue: 1 son and 1 daughter.

SKEWES   ALMA PHOEBE
Chart 36. Daughter of Henry John and Phoebe Marie (née Holdsworth) Skewes. Born January 1905. Married approx. 1943. Issue: 1 son and 1 daughter. Lives in Dytes Parade, Ballarat, 3356, Victoria, Australia.

SKEWES   AMANDA
Chart 36. Daughter of William and Margery (née Moran) Skewes. Born Watsons Creek, Bendemeer, New South Wales, Australia.

SKEWES   AMANDA ELIZABETH
Chart 12. Daughter of John Osburn and Pat (née Williams) Skewes. Born 30 October 1977.

SKEWES   AMELIA
Chart 10. Daughter of Digory and Sophia Skewes of Kea, miner. Bpt Kenwyn 25 August 1823.

SKEWES   AMELIA
Born 1827, Helston. Died 1907, aged 80 years.

SKEWES   AMELIA
Born 1834, Truro. Daughter of John and Elizabeth Skewes. In 1851 Census Returns was living with her widowed mother (housekeeper born in Kenwyn) and her sister Emma (spinster aged 26 years) in Chacewater. Her father was a miner. Married William James (23) at Kenwyn Parish Church 16 September 1854. William James was son of John James, blacksmith.

SKEWES   AMELIA
Died 1847, Liskeard.

SKEWES   AMELIA
Daughter of John and Elizabeth Skewes of Chacewater. Bpt Chacewater 8 March 1848.

SKEWS   AMELIA
Daughter of Joseph Skews (miner) and Elizabeth (née Stanaway). Born 22 September 1853 at St Cleer. Married 1872 at Liskeard.

SKUES   AMELIA
Chart 8. Daughter of George Gilbert and Isabella Skues. Bpt St Luke, Westminster 19 May 1853. Died 1853, aged 0.

SKEWES   AMELIA
Chart 33. Daughter of William and Susan Skewes of Kerley, Kea, miner. Baptised Chacewater 2 January 1855.

SKEWS   AMELIA
Chart 42. Born 1856. Wife of Matthew Skews of 17 Best View Terrace, Shiney Row, Durham. Died 4 April 1935, aged 79 years.

SKEWES AMELIA
Chart 10. Daughter of Digory & Fanny Skewes of Trevenner, Marazion. Born 8 Jan 1862. In 1883 she was residing at Princes Buildings, Lambeth and on 2 December 1883 she married Joseph Draper, bachelor, and bricklayer of Cox's Buildings, son of Benjamin Draper, carpenter; at Lambeth Parish Church.

SKEWES AMELIA
Chart 34. Second wife of Edward James Skewes, porter on railway. Born 1868. Married 28 January 1888 at Redruth Register Office. Died 1901, aged 33 years.

SKEWIS   AMELIA
Born 1870, Glasgow. Died Possilpark, Scotland, 1920, aged 50 years.

SKEWIS   AMELIA
Chart 50. Illegitimate daughter of James Skewis (iron roller) and Helen Jamieson. Born 1 January 1870 at 130 Gargnd Road, Glasgow. Reference in register: "Helen Jamieson, housekeeper, who was married to James Skewis at Glasgow, 23 December 1864, who in respect of such marriage has since been convicted of bigamy." James Skewis was also known as "Davidson."

SKEWIS   AMELIA
Married 1906, Blythswood, Scotland.

SKEWES   AMELIA
Chart 10. Daughter of Thomas George and Jane (née Mitchell) Skewes. Born 12 June 1883, Marazion. Married William Gluyas in March, 1905. Emigrated with her family to Michigan, USA, 1896.

SKEWES   AMELIA
Married 1908, Redruth to Mr. T. Harry (1st January).

SKEWS   AMELIA
Lived at Isabella Street, Malvern East, Australia in 1913.

SKEWIS   AMELIA
Married 1918, Possilpark, Scotland.

SKEWS   AMELIA E.
Married Burgess, Essex SW, 1946.

SKEWES   AMELIA JANE
Daughter of William and Jane Skewes of Treskillard, farmer. Born 29 October 1886. Bpt 7 October 1887 at Camborne Wesleyan/Methodist Church.

SKEWIS   AMELIA JANE
Chart 50. Daughter of Joseph Richard and Marion (née Hamilton) Skewis. Born 14 April 1894, Farmington, Pennsylvania, USA. Married J. Howard Carothers in McKeesport, Pennsylvania, USA, 1921. Children: Robert Joseph Carothers, Charles John Carothers and Marion Carothers Blaine who lives at 1930 Lincoln Avenue, Northbrook, Illinois, 60062, USA. Died 1953, aged 58 years.

SKEUES   AMELIA KATE
Married 1907, Bath, Somerset.
SKEWES   AMELIA MADELINE
Lived at 8 Claire Street, Bentleigh, Victoria SE 14, Australia in 1959 with Matthew Herbert Skewes and Neville Herbert Skewes.
SKUES   AMELIA MARY ANN
Born 1846, Medway, Kent.
SKEWS   AMOS
Chart 15. Son of John and Isabella (née Gregory) Skews. Born 1864, Bpt Altarnun 9 March 1865. In 1871 Census Returns was living at Trewint, Altarnun, Launceston. Married 1890, Stoke Devonport. Children: John Henry, Elizabeth Ethel Grace, Albert Edward, Frederick Charles and Maud. Died 1925, aged 60 years.
SKEWS   AMY
Born 1881, Helston Married 1909.
SKUES   AMY
Married Robert Hunt at Wendron Parish Church, 26 December 1668.
SKEWES   AMY
Chart 50. Née Post. Wife of Richard James Skewes whom she married 20 August 1924, North Sydney, Australia. In 1959 she lived at 57 Burlington Street, Crows Nest, New South Wales, Australia with Joseph Mark Skewes (plumber) and Kenneth Skewes (truck driver). Children: Kenneth Richard (1925), Jack (1927), Valerie (1930) and Joan (1933).
SKEWES   AMY
In 1959 was living at 110 Ellen Street, Port Pirie, South Australia with Robert John Skewes and Thomas Nesbitt Skewes.
SKEWES   AMY EDITH
Chart 36. Daughter of William and Hannah (née Gale) Skewes. Born 23 April 1885, Australia. Married Alfred Howarth, 20 December 1911. Issue: 5 daughters and 1 son. Lived at Watsons Creek, via Bendemeer, New South Wales, Australia. Died 12 January 1968, aged 82 years.
SKEWES   AMY EDITH
Chart 36. Daughter of William and Elizabeth (née Northey) Skewes. Born 18 October 1873, Australia. Married James Wood. Issue: 3 daughters. Died 8 July 1963, aged 90 years.
SKEWIS   AMY EILEEN
Chart 2. Daughter of Richard Edward and Deanne Skewis of America. Born 4 July 1968.
SKEWS   AMY EMMA
Chart 15. Born 1893. Married John Henry Skews in 1918, Devonport. Lived at 4 Shenstone Gardens, Honicknowle, Plymouth. Died 1961, aged 68 years.
SKEWES   AMY RUTH
In 1959 lived at 18 Ridge Street, Coffs Harbour, New South Wales, Australia with George Roy Skewes, Shire employer.
SKEWES   ANDREA ALICE
Chart 10. Daughter of Michael Thomas and Mary Skewes of Hamilton, Ontario, Canada. Born 15 June 1977.
SKEWIS   ANDREA DAWN
Chart 50. Daughter of Michael Ian and Audrey (née Humphries) Skewis. Born 18 October 1966, Hull.
SKEWES   ANDREA LOUISE
Chart 36 Daughter of Robert Skewes. Born 4 October 1974, Victoria, Australia.
SKEWES   ANDREW CUTHBERT
Lives at 8 Leeworthy Street, Victor Harbour, 5211, South Australia with Susan Patricia Skewes. Principal.
SKEWIES   ANDREW FYFE
Born 1890. Died Shotts West, Scotland, aged 74 years in 1964.
SKEWIES ANDREW FYFE
Born 1933, Hamilton, Scotland. Married Wilson in Bothwell, 1958.
SKEWIES ANDREW F.
Married Anita G. Holt-Knockwell, Oxford, 1947.
SKEWS ANDREW J.
Chart 15. Son of Courtenay John Gregory and Sylvia (née Arnold) Skews. Born 1950. Married Pamela E.L. Searle, 1974, St Germans. Children: Victoria Ann (1975) and Zowie (1976). Lives at 19 Fairfield Estate, St Germans, Bodmin. Tel: 05033 557.
SKUES ANDREW J.
Chart 8. Son of Sydney Thomas Skues. Mother's maiden name Parnell. Born 1956, Hackney, London.
SKUES ANDREW JOHN
Chart 9. Son of David J. Skues. Mother's maiden name Weighill. Born 1973, Dartford, Kent.
SKEWES ANDREW JOHN
Lives at O'Connor Street, Uranquinty, 2650, New South Wales, Australia with Mary Millar Skewes. Technician.
SKUES ANDREW P.
Chart 8. Mother's maiden name Cox. Born 1955, Brentwood, Essex.
SKEWS ANDREW P.
Chart 10. Son of Stanley and Mavis (née Soady) Skews. Born 1956, St

Amy Edith Skewes (left) with her sister Lily Skewes of Watsons Creek, New South Wales, Australia

Austell. Married Sandra E. Stephens, St Austell, 1979.
SKEWES ANDREW PHILIP
Son of Henry Snowden and Marjorie Joyce (née Munro) Skewes. Born 19 April 1949. Lives at Yarrawonga, Victoria, Australia.
SKEWES ANDREW WILLIAM
Chart 2. Son of William John and Barbara Mackay (née Carroll) Skewes. Born 12 January 1964, Australia.
SKEWS ANGELA
Chart 41. Daughter of Eric Skews. Mother's maiden name Rasburn. Born 1947, Bradford. Married Binney, 1967, Staincross.
SKEWES ANGELA DAWN
Chart 36. Daughter of Aubrey Rupert and Annie (née Townsend) Skewes. Born 4 January 1925, Uralla, New South Wales, Australia. Married Reginald McMillan. Issue: 2 daughters. Lives at Vincent St, Uralla, 2356, New South Wales, Australia.
SKEWIS ANGELA ROSE
Born 1967, Dundee East, Scotland.
SKEWES ANGELICA
Chart 10. Mexican. Daughter of Nazario and Dolores (née Riofrio) Skewes. Born 28 September 1907. Married Esteban Ruiz. Issue: 3 sons and 2 daughters. Lives in Mexico City.
SKEWES ANGELINA MARY
Chart 24. Daughter of John and Mary Jane (née Cole) Skewes. Born 1893, New South Wales, Australia. Married with 4 children.
SKEWES ANGUS LOCKWOOD
In 1959 lived at 680 High Street, Kew North, Victoria E 5, Australia. Chemist.
SKEWIS ANITA
Chart 2. Daughter of Francis Harry and Annie Skewis. Born 26 April 1889, America. Married Ole Moen. Both killed in a car crash 15 July 1950. Issue: 4 daughters and 2 sons.
SKEWIS ANITA MARY
Chart 2. Daughters of Elmer Arthur and Maude Skewis. Born 14 November 1910. Married Edward Rosendahl. Issue: 1 daughter and 2 sons. Lives at 602 North 7th Street, Estherville, Iowa, 51334, United States of America.
SKEWS ANNE
Daughter of Steven and Christian Skews. Born St Just in Roseland 10 March 1615. Married Thomas Manley 26 January 1633.
SKEWES ANN
Daughter of John Skewes of St Keverne. Bpt St Keverne 17 August 1634.
SKUES ANN
Chart 2. Daughter of William & Margaret Skues of Camborne. Bpt Camborne 29 September 1667. Died before 1670.
SKUES ANN
Chart 2. Daughter of William and Margaret Skues of Camborne. Bpt Camborne 17 July 1670. Had two illegitimate children: Peter (1693) and Jone (1695). Both died young.

SKEWES ANN
Chart 37. Daughter of James and Simonette Skewes of Cury.

SKEWS ANN
Chart 13. Daughter of John and Elizabeth (née Whitford) Skews. Bpt Mevagissey 1 December 1689.

SKUES ANN
Chart 4. Daughter of William and Jane Skues. Bpt Redruth 8 February 1701. Married Joseph Gribben of St Agnes, 29 October 1725.

SKEWES ANNE
Chart 14. Daughter of Henry and Judith (née Walters) Skewes of Nantithet, Cury. Bpt 7 December 1718, Cury. Buried 17 July 1719, Cury, aged 8 months.

SKEWES ANN
of Penzance. Married John Richards of Madron at Paul 5 July 1715.

SKEWIS ANN
Buried St Keverne 6 March 1720.

SKEWES ANNE
Chart 14. Daughter of Henry & Judith Skewes of Cury. Bpt Cury 6 August 1721.

SKEWS ANNE
Daughter of Edward & Ann Skews. Bpt St Ewe 6 November 1721.

SKEWES ANNE
Daughter of Edward & Anne (née Beale) Skewes of Gunwalloe. Bpt Cury 1 November 1724.

SKEWIS ANNE
Married Joseph Dalle at Cury 6 September 1741.

SKEWES ANN
of Clements, widow married John Williams, tinner of Gwennap. Marriage licence granted at Exeter 2 November 1742. Marriage took place at St Clement 7 November 1743.

SKEWIS ANNE
Married James Boaden at Cury 1 November. 1744.

SKEWES ANN
of Treloskan, Cury. Born 1750. Buried Cury 8 October 1832.

SKEWES ANN
Daughter of Peter Skewes. Bpt Kea 1 January 1754.

SKEWS ANN
Chart 9. Daughter of Philip & Mary Skews. Bpt St. Ewe 30 May 1757. Married Hugh Tregensa at St Ewe 14 August 1784.

SKEUS ANN
Chart 2. Daughter of Roben (Robart) Skeus. Bpt Camborne 21 March 1758. Married Matthew Brown, tinner, sojourner 10 July 1785 at Camborne Parish Church.

SKEWES ANN
Daughter of William and Ann Skewes. Bpt Gwennap 27 May 1758.

SKEWES ANN
Daughter of Henry Skewes of Kea. Bpt Kenwyn 5 May 1755.

SKUES ANN
Chart 3. Born 1764. Wife of Richard Skues, Surgeon. Lived at Durnford Street, East Stonehouse, Plymouth, formerly of Helston. Children: Grace Richards Skues, George Skues; granddaughter Georgina Mary Skues. Died at Durnford Street, East Stonehouse at residence of her son in law Richard Rodd, solicitor. Reference to her death in *Gentleman's Magazine* 1847, page 329. Will at Devon Record Office £450. Died 8 Feb 1847, aged 83 years.

SKEWIS ANN
Daughter of Thomas & Esther Skewis. Bpt St Keverne 27 December 1766.

SKEWIS ANN
of Trethowan Downs. Born 1768. Died 1847. Buried Constantine 9 April, 1847, aged 79 years.

SKEWES ANN
of Hugus, Kea. Born 1769. Buried Baldhu, 16 March 1859, aged 82 years.

SKEWES ANN
Daughter of Thomas Skewes of Kea. Bpt Kenwyn 21 October 1770.

SKEWIS ANN
Chart 25. Daughter of Thomas and Esther Skewis. Bpt St Keverne 27 December 1766. Married John James of St Keverne 22 June 1794.

SKEWIS ANN
Daughter of Edward and Honor Skewis. Bpt Helston 25 September 1771.

SKEWES ANN
Born 1772. Buried Chacewater 3 July 1834, aged 62 years.

SKEWES ANN
Daughter of Richard Skewes of Kea. Bpt Kenwyn 19 March 1772.

SKEWES ANNE
of Jolly's Bottom, Kea. Born 1773. Buried Kea 17 August 1824, aged 51 years.

SKEWES ANNE
Chart 36. Daughter of James and Anne Skewes. Bpt Mawgan in Meneage 28 December 1773.

SKUES ANN

SKEWES ANN
Chart 3. Daughter of John and Mary Skues of Helston. Born 6 September 1775. Died 9 February 1838, aged 62 years (the same day as her sister-in-law Mary Skues — wife of William Skues, carpenter — died).

SKEWES ANN
Chart 18. Daughter of Thomas and Thomasine Skewes of Kea. Bpt Kenwyn 10 February 1776. Married Daniel Hodge at Kenwyn Parish Church 1 May 1797.

SKEWES ANN
of Camborne. Born 1778. Died 1 February 1861, aged 83 years. Widow.

SKEWES ANN
Buried Mawgan in Meneage 30 April 1778.

SKEWES ANN
Buried Gwennap 29 May 1779.

SKEWES ANN
Married Thomas Gregor at Gwennap 18 April 1780.

SKEWES ANN
Married Matthew Brown at Camborne 10 July 1785.

SKEWES ANN
Married William Lawry at Kea 19 November 1785.

SKEWES ANN
Widow of Thomas Skewes of Kea. Buried Kea 5 November 1788.

SKEWES ANN
Married John Benney of Feock at Kenwyn 29 September 1792.

SKEWISS ANN
Daughter of William Skewiss of Madron. Bpt Madron 12 May 1793.

SKEWES ANN
Chart 2. Born 1793. Was twin to John Skewes and daughter of Absalom and Elizabeth Skewes. Bpt Camborne 21 May 1793. Died of apoplexy. Buried Camborne 18 March 1835, aged 42 years.

SKEWES ANN
Married John Tripconey of St Keverne at St Keverne 1 February 1795.

SKEWS ANN
Born 1795. Died Plymouth 1869, aged 74 years.

SKEWS ANN
Chart 9. Daughter of James & Joanna Skews of Lower Sticker, St Ewe. Bpt St Ewe 7 February 1795. Married John George at St Ewe 16 February 1822.

SKEWIS ANN
Chart 18. Daughter of William & Ann Skewis. Bpt Kenwyn 27 March 1796.

SKEWES ANN
Born 1798. Died 1870, Falmouth, aged 72 years.

SKEWES ANN
of Penryn. Born 1798. Buried Gwennap 14 Dec 1870, aged 72 years.

SKEWES ANN
of Lanner, Gwennap. Born 1799. Buried Gwennap 19 July 1859, aged 60 years.

SKEWES ANN
Chart 36. Daughter of William & Alice Skewes of Treloskan, Cury. Bpt Cury 15 December, 1799.

SKEWES ANN
of Gilly Lane, Cury. Born 1800. Buried Cury 26 March 1873, aged 73 years.

SKEWES ANN
Born 1800. Buried Kea 10 March 1818, aged 18 years.

SKEWIS ANN
Daughter of Robert and Sarah Skewis. Bpt St Swithen, Worcester 20 July 1800.

SKEWES ANN
of Kenwyn. Wife of James Skewes.

SKEWS ANN
Chart 9. Daughter of William and Nancy Skews. Bpt St Ewe 8 February 1801.

SKEWES ANN
Chart 36. Daughter of John & Mary Skewes. Bpt Cury 17 May 1801. Married James Freeman of Sithney at Cury 14 December 1836.

SKEWES ANN
Buried Kea 23 July 1802.

SKUES ANN
Married William Scott 7 February 1804, Truro.

SKEWES ANN
of Killiwerris. Born 1806. Buried Chacewater 16 May 1867, aged 61 years.

SKUES ANN
Chart 3. Daughter of Richard and Ann Skues of Helston. Born 29 January 1807. Bpt Helston 26 February 1807. Died 4 May 1817, aged 10 years.

SKEWES ANN
Chart 18. Daughter of Thomas and Mary Skewes of Kenwyn. Bpt 8 March 1807, Kenwyn.

SKUES ANN
Daughter of William and Jane Skues of Mylor. Bpt Mylor 14 January 1810.

SKEWES ANN
Born 1810, St Clement. Wife of James Skewes. In 1871 Census lived at Back Prospect Place, St Clement. Had daughter Emma born Truro, 1843. In 1851 Census was an attendant at Assembly Rooms and lived at High Cross, St Mary, Truro. Died 1887, aged 77 years.

SKEWES ANN
Chart 19. Daughter of Alexander (Mine Clerk of Chenhale) and Christian Skewes. Bpt Gwennap 12 August 1814. Married Walter Bray at Gwennap 7 March 1844.

SKEWS ANN
of Chacewater. Born 1814. Died 1850, aged 36 years. Buried Chacewater 27 August, 1850.

SKEWES ANN
Married Charles Coad at Kea 10 June 1816.

SKEWES ANN
Chart 33. Daughter of William & Mary Skewes. Bpt Kenwyn 30 December 1817. William was a miner and lived in Blackwater.

SKEWES ANN
Married John Skewes of Kenwyn at Kenwyn 2 Sept 1818. By licence.

SKEWES ANN
Chart 12. Daughter of James & Elizabeth Skewes of Cury. Bpt. Cury 17 February 1820. In 1841 Census was a dressmaker living at Gilly Lane, Cury.

SKEWIS ANN
Born 1820. Wife of Henry Skewes of Pengigan, Camborne. Died 1843 (July), aged 23 years. Buried Camborne 18 July, 1843.

SKEWES ANN
Chart 2. Maiden name Simmons (Born 1793); married John Skewes at Camborne 18 February 1822.

SKEWES ANN
Chart 2. Daughter of Edward and Mary Skewes. Born 14 Sept 1822. Bpt Redruth Circuit 14 Nov 1822. Married William Gilham and emigrated to America in 1849 to Red Cloud, Nebraska. Issue: three sons.

SKEWES ANN
Married Anthony Bafsher of Grade, miner at Constantine Parish Church 18 February 1823.

SKUES ANN
Chart 2. Daughter of John and Ann Skues of Camborne. Bpt Camborne 26 April 1823. Was a mine girl in 1841 Census Returns.

SKEWES ANN
Chart 36. Daughter of William and Christian Skewes. Bpt Ruan Major 23 October 1825. Married John Phillips, son of John Phillips, at Mawnan Parish Church 31 May 1855 in presence of Grace Skewes.

SKEWES ANN
Chart 36. Daughter of William Gribble of Illogan. Born 1825. Married Henry Skewes 24 December 1850 at Mawnan Parish Church. Emigrated to Victoria, Australia about 1852. Children: Mary, Jack and William. Died Ballarat, Victoria, 16 May 1863, aged 38 years. Buried in Ballarat Old Cemetery within 20 yards of the Eureka Stockade victims.

SKEWES ANN
Married William Dinnis at Kea 31 March 1827.

SKEWES ANN
of Treloskan. Buried Cury 18 August 1827, aged 9 months.

SKEWES ANN
Chart 17. Daughter of William & Rebecca Skewes of Churchtown, Constantine, labourer. Bpt Constantine 29 August 1830. Married Thomas Evans, miner (son of Charles Evans) 23 December 1847 in presence of William Skewes. Before marriage she lived at Trethowan Downs.

SKEWES ANN
Aged 34 was charged with stealing printed cotton in July 1830. She was acquitted at Cornwall Quarter Sessions at Bodmin.

SKEWES ANN
Married John Herring at St Mewan 15 March 1831.

SKEWES ANN
Married Joseph Rogers at Kea 21 March 1833 in presence of John Skewes.

SKEWES ANN
Two entries in *Royal Cornwall Gazette* 21 March 1835 list her with different ages.
Entry 1: "Died at Camborne, March 1835, aged 32. She went to bed in good health, was taken ill, but had died by morning."
Entry 2: "Died at Camborne, March 1835, aged 40 years. She went to bed in good health, but died during the night. She was a consistent member of the Wesleyan Society for 13 years and walked worthy of her profession."

SKEWES ANN
Married James Brown 5 March 1837, St Agnes.

SKEWES ANN
Chart 14. Daughter of Anthony & Christian Skewes of Tresodden,

Ruan Major. Born 16 April 1837 at Ruan Major. Married Samuel Carter, carpenter of Ruan Minor, son of Richard Carter, carpenter of Ruan Major 18 November, 1875, in presence of Henry Skewes. At Ruan Major Parish Church.

SKUES ANN
Daughter of William & Elizabeth Skues of Wendron Street, Helston. Married William Pearce 11 December 1838 at Helston Parish Church.

SKEWIS ANN
Born 1845, Penzance.

SKEWES ANN
Daughter of Allan and Ann MacDonald. Born 1847. Married Skewes. Lived in South Australia. Died 30 November 1892, aged 46 years. Buried in Clare Gaelic Cemetery, South Australia.

SKEWES ANN
Married 1845, Plymouth.

SKEWES ANN
Married 1845, Liskeard.

SKEWES ANN
Died 1846, Redruth.

SKEWES ANN
Born 1849. Wife of Matthew Skewes. Died Redruth 3 January 1898, aged 49 years.

SKEWES ANN
of Trelowarren Street, Camborne. Daughter of John Skewes, miner. Married 26 December 1849 to Stephen Simmons, miner of Newlyn Road at Camborne Parish Church.

SKEWS ANN
Born 1851, Liskeard.

SKEWES ANN
Married 1851, Helston.

SKEWES ANNE
Chart 25. Wife of Charles Skewes whom she married in Chorlton, 1883. Lived at 15 Horton Road, Rusholme, Manchester. Daughter: Elizabeth (1886). Died 31 January 1946, aged 95 years.

SKEWIS ANNE
Born 1856, Redruth. Died Redruth aged 0.

SKEWES ANNE
Died 1856, Redruth.

SKEWES ANN
of Union House, Redruth. Buried Redruth Parish Church 18 March, 1856 aged either 54 or 84. (Writing in parish register very bad.)

SKEWES ANN
Married 1858, Redruth.

SKEWES ANNE
Chart 13. Daughter of Edward & Julia Skewes of Nantithet, cordwainer. Bpt 4 May 1860, Cury. Married Charles Evelyn Trerize (24) shoemaker (son of Edward Trerize, labourer) 29 May 1879 at Cury Parish Church.

SKEWES ANN
Died 1861, Redruth.

SKEWES ANN
of South View, Crediton, Devon. Widow. Born 1862. Died 16 March 1941, aged 79 years.

SKEWS ANN
Died 1862, Greenwich.

SKEWS ANN
Died 1864, North Aylesford.

SKEWSE ANN
Died 1865, Bethnal Green.

SKEWES ANN
Married 1876, Redruth.

SKEWES ANN
Chart 40. Née Morgan. Married Matthew Henry Skewes in Eltham, London, 11 October 1945. Children: Carol (1946), Susan Barbara (1949), Jill Alexandra (1953) and William Clive (1954). Lives at Trewince Farm, St Martin, Helston. Telephone number: 0326 23304.

SKUSE ANN
Daughter of Henry and Margery (née Bishop) Skuse. Born 1935.

SKEWES ANN
Chart 36. Daughter of Percy and Muriel (née Norris) Skewes. Born November 1943, Australia.

SKEWES ANN
Chart 36. Daughter of William George and Eunice (née Howard) Skewes. Born August 1964, Coffs Harbour, New South Wales, Australia. Lives at Burleigh Heads News Agency, Gold Coast, Queensland, 4220, Australia.

SKEWIS ANN
Born 1969, Glasgow, Scotland.

SKEWES ANN AMELIA
Chart 36. Daughter of William and Priscilla (née Mill) Skewes of Higher Treskillard, agricultural labourer. Bpt St Erth, 29 December 1855.

SKEWIS ANN BAWDEN
Daughter of Captain Henry Skewis. Born 1849, Liskeard. Died at Drake Walls mine, 14 December 1851, aged 3 years.

SKEWES ANN BUCKLAND
of Choon, Kenwyn. Farmer's wife. Born 1811, St Allen. Daughter Annie L. (1846). In 1871 Census Returns was living at Prospect Place, St Clement, Truro. Died 27 February 1896, aged 85 years. Buried St Mary's, Truro, 2 March 1896.

SKEWS ANN ELIZABETH
Born 1866, North Aylesford. Married 1888 at Dartford.

SKEWES ANN EYNES
Chart 28. Daughter of Richard and Mary Skewes of Nancevellan Common, Kea, yeoman. Bpt Kea, 20 November 1817. Married at Kea to Thomas Eddy, 13 June 1848.

SKEWES ANN HENDY
Chart 36. Daughter of John and Loveday Skewes. Bpt Cury 27 July 1817. Had illeg. son Samuel (1842). Died 1 August 1848, aged 30 years — surplus of blood in her head. Inquest on the body.

SKEWS ANN JANE
Born 1827, Plymouth. Died 1892, aged 65 years.

SKEWES ANNE JANE
Daughter of John & Grace Skewes of Crowan. Born 1862. In 1871 Census living at Horse Downs, Crowan with her parents and brothers John H. and Richard H. Married 1885.

SKEWES ANN LUCEY
Chart 29. Daughter of John & Alice Skewes; bpt Kea 8 July, 1771. Married Anthony Sandoe at Kea 1795.

SKEWES ANN MARGARET
Daughter of Henry Snowden and Marjorie Joyce (née Munro) Skewes. Born 14 March 1959. Lives at Yarrawonga, Victoria, Australia.

SKEWES ANN MARIA
Born 1880. Lived at Barford Farm, Spaxton, Bridgwater, Somerset. Died 3 June 1957, aged 77 years.

SKEWES ANN MAREE
Lives at Farm 1265, Cor Hill, 2705, New South Wales, Australia.

SKEWES ANN MARIE
Chart 10. Daughter of Claude Jocelyn and Honourah Bridget Millar. Born 28 November 1938, Somerset. Emigrated to Canada. Registered Industrial Accountant. Married Richard Albert Skewes at St. Michael's Cathedral, Toronto, Ontario 28 April 1962. Children: Mark Alexander (1963), Kevin Richard (1964), Tamara (1965) and Michael James Patrick (1967). Lives at 1207 Royal York, Islington, Toronto, Canada. Tel No: 0101 (416) 233 9864.

SKEWES ANNE MARIE
Chart 48. Daughter of Cyril William Marsh and Marie Florence (née Ambrose) Skewes. Born 7 August 1944. Married Rudolf Hans Pittl at St Jacob's Cathedral, Innsbruck, Austria 27 September 1969. Issue: 2 daughters and 1 son. Lives in Austria.

SKEWES ANN MARIE
In 1959 lived at 4 West Avenue, Cammery, New South Wales. Secretary. Lived with Kathleen Lillian and Leonard Francis Skewes.

SKEWES ANNA
Born 1814. Died Redruth 1896, aged 82 years.

SKEWES ANNA
Daughter of Edward Hosking of Helston. Born March, 1876. Married Sidney Hope Skewes in Montreal, Canada, 1894. Children: Gladys E. (1895), Harold A. (1897) & Arthur H. (1899). Moved to New York, 1899.

SKEWIS ANNA
Wife of Francis H. Skewis living at 625 South Trafton, Tacoma, Washington, USA in 1911.

SKEWIS ANNA MARIE
Chart 50. Daughter of James Skewis. Mother's maiden name Smart. Born 1975, Hull.

SKEWES ANNA MARIE MARY
Chart 19. Daughter of Charles Young, gentleman. First wife of Thomas Lean Skewes. Married Parish Church, Plumstead, London 13 July 1852. Born 1829, she died 1879, aged 50 years.

SKEWIS ANNABELLA MACKENZIE
Born 1904. Died Glasgow, 1971, aged 67 years.

SKEWES ANNETTE
Born 1947, Redruth. Mother's maiden name SKEWES.

SKEWIS ANNETTE
Lived at 248 Corbelt Avenue, San Francisco, 1961.

SKEWES ANNIE
of Little Carharrack. Born 1807. Buried Gwennap 24 October 1888, aged 81 years.

SKEWES ANNIE
Born 1844. Died 29 April 1920 at Fore Street, Marazion, aged 76 years.

SKEWIS ANNIE
Daughter of James and Margaret Skewis. Bpt St Ewe 7 November 1847.

SKEWES ANNIE
Chart 19. Daughter of Thomas Lean and Elizabeth Ann Skewes. Born 1855. Ran private ladies school at 6 Bestwell Villas, East Street, Wareham, Dorset, in 1895. Her brother ran the boys school at Elm House, North Street, Wareham and her father was a former schoolmaster in Wareham.

SKUES ANNIE
Chart 2. Daughter of Henry and Grace Skues. Born 1857 at Gwinear.

SKEWES ANNIE
of The Anchorage, Holmbush, St Austell. Widow. Born 1853. Died 7 December 1916, aged 63 years.

SKEWIES ANNIE
Born 1853. Died Hamilton, Scotland, 1921, aged 68 years.

SKEWES ANNIE
Born 1857. Died Salford, 1913, aged 56 years.

SKEWS ANNIE
Born 1860, Stoke Devonport.

SKEWES ANNIE
of Tuckingmill. Born 1861. Died 1867, aged 6½ years. Buried Tuckingmill Parish Church 13 June 1867.

SKEWES ANNIE
Born 1866, Redruth.

SKEWS ANNIE
Chart 50. Daughter of William and Jane (née Bullock) Skews. Born 1868, Camborne. Married in Swindon, 1910.

SKEWS ANNIE
Chart 15. Née Gartrell. Born 1869. Married John Gregory Skews, 1890. Children: John (1894), Clarence (1896), Winifred Mary (1898), Edith Jane (1901) and Fernley Walter (1907). Died 1944, St Germans, aged 75 years.

SKEWES ANNIE
Eldest daughter of the late John Skewes of Trevella Farm. Married T. Lambshead of London at St Paul's Church, Truro 10 September 1874.

SKEWES ANNIE
Married 1880 at Pancras, London.

SKEWES ANNIE
Born 10 February 1882. Daughter of Thomas Henry and Clarinda Skewes. Bpt at Perranuthnoe Parish Church 26 March 1882. Spinster. Lived at West End, Goldsithney, Penzance. Died 3 September 1969, aged 87 years.

SKEWES ANNIE
Married 1884, East Stonehouse.

SKEWES ANNIE
Chart 10. Daughter of Samuel and Clara Skewes of Marazion. Born 24 July 1886. Bpt 31 Sept 1886 at Wesleyan/Methodist Chapel, Marazion. Married Johns in Penzance, 1909.

SKEWIS ANNIE
Born 1892, Airdrie, Scotland. Died 1892, aged 2 years.

SKEWES ANNIE
Born 1895. Died 1950, Salford, aged 55 years.

SKEWS ANNIE
Born 1892, Died Liskeard 1892.

SKEWIS ANNIE
Mother's maiden name Brown. Born 1900. Died Sidlaw, Scotland, 1977, aged 77 years.

SKEWIS ANNIE
Married 1903, Haverfordwest.

SKEWS ANNIE
Lived at Scotsburn, Ballarat, Victoria, Australia in 1912 with William Skews, engine driver.

SKEWIS ANNIE
Born 1935, St Andrew, Dundee, Scotland. Married Edward Thomas Peddie in Dundee West, 1959.

SKEWES ANNIE
Lived at Lower Pengegon, Camborne, 1949.

SKEWES ANNIE
Lived at Palmleigh, Four Lanes, Redruth, 1949.

SKEWES ANNIE
Lived at Meneage Hospital, Helston, 1969.

SKEWIS ANNIE
Married MacClusky, 1969, Dundee, Scotland.

SKEWES ANNIE AMELIA
Married 1882, Redruth.

SKEWES ANNIE DORIS
Chart 12. Daughter of John Henry and Annie Williams of St Keverne. Worked at Treskewes, St Keverne 1914-1918. Married William Frank Skewes, 27 September 1927 at Helston Wesleyan/Methodist Church. Children: Lilian Gladys (1929), William Arthur Raymond (1931), John Trevor (1935) and Peter Marsden (1941). Lived at Lovely Vale, Mithian, St Agnes 1927-1934; Lower Tregidden 1934-1944 and Chybarles, Ruan Major 1944-1970. Present address: 30 Glebe Place, Ruan Minor, Helston.

SKEWES ANNIE DOROTHEA
In 1959 lived at 28 Anderson Road, Auburn, Victoria, Australia with
Dorothea Alison and Philip Randolph Skewes.

SKEWES ANNIE EDITH
Born 1886. Spinster who lived at 24 Margaret Road, Penworthan,
Preston, Lancashire. Died 22 December 1964, aged 79 years.

SKEWIS ANNIE ELIZABETH
Née Jones. Daughter of John Jones, Baptist Minister. Married Edwin
Skewis 1 September 1875 at Parish Church Bedwellty, Monmouth.
Born 1851 and died 1910, aged 59 years in Rhayader.

SKEWES ANNIE ELLEN
Chart 2. Daughter of Henry and Annie May (née Cross) Skewes.
Born 7 March 1912. Married 1)..... Issue: 3 children. Married 2)
Clifford Freeman, 1951. No children in second marriage. Lives at 38
Town Hall Avenue, Preston, 3072, Victoria, Australia.

SKEWES ANNIE EMILY
In 1959 lived at 61 Hawkestone Street, Cottesloe, Victoria, Australia
with Henry Ernest Skewes.

SKUES ANNIE FRANCES
Born 1876, Devizes, Wiltshire. Spinster. Died 1958 Exeter, aged 82
years.

SKEWIES ANNIE FYFE
Born 1920, Hamilton, Scotland. Married Gillespie, 1944, Hamilton.

SKEWIS ANNIE GRANT ABERCROMBIE
Born 1928, New Monkland, Scotland.

SKEWS ANNIE LOUISA
Born 2 March 1900. Née Snowshill. Married Alfred George W.
Skews, 1927 in Edmonton, London. Daughter: Betty F. (1938). Died
1969, aged 69 years in Colchester, Essex.

SKEWES ANNIE M.
Lived at Fernside, Carn Lane, Carnkie, Redruth with Priscilla
Skewes in 1968.

SKEWES ANNIE M.
Chart 50. Daughter of George and Elizabeth Skewes. Mother's
maiden name Caddy. Born 1927, Pontypridd.

SKEWES ANNIE M.
Married Skinner, Redruth, 1966.

SKUES ANNIE MARIA
Chart 8. Wife of Victor Claude Skues of 228 Point Clear Road, St
Osyth, Clacton, Essex. Born 28 February 1895. Died 23 September
1975, aged 80 years.

SKEWES ANNIE MARY
Daughter of Elizabeth Ann Skewes, single woman. Born 14 July
1878. Bpt Camborne Parish Church 4 September 1878.

SKEWES ANNIE MAUD
Lived at Bowling Green, Illogan with Frederick Tresize Skewes,
1922.

SKEWES ANNIE MAUD
Chart 15. Born 1894. Married Thomas Henry Skewes, 1915. Lived at
Redruth Coombe, 1922 and Higher Carnkie 1932. Children: Iris M.,
Enid, George, Veronica T., Rosemary and Maureen. Lived at Four
Lanes, Redruth 1960. Died 1962, aged 68 years. Maiden name Jory.

SKEWES ANNIE PHILLIPS
In 1959 lived at 174 Mont Albert Road, Canterbury, Victoria,
Australia with Robert Skewes.

SKEWES ANNIE REBECCA
Chart 36. Née Strain. Born 21 April 1904, Gympie, Queensland,
Australia. Married William Vere Skewes at Childers, Queensland,
24 August 1926. Children: Mary Irene (1927), William George
(1929), Joan Bentley (1931), Jill (1933), Robert (1939), Max (1942)
and Bruce (1944). Died 9 September 1980 in Tamworth, New South
Wales, aged 76 years.

SKEWES ANTHONY
Chart 14. Son of Henry and Judith (née Walters) Skewes. Bpt Cury 6
December 1725. Married ELEANOR SKEWES of Cury, 11
December 1760 at Cury. Children: Elinor and Judith. Buried Ruan
Major 7 June 1796, aged 71 years.

SKEWES ANTHONY
Chart 14. Son of Henry & Jane Skewes. Born 1809. Bpt Ruan Major 20
June 1809. Farmer of 145 acres employing one man. Married at Ruan
Major 30 Sept 1834 to Christian Lugg in presence of Henry Skewes.
Children: Mary; Ann; Catherine; James; Henry; Samuel; William; Ed-
ward Hannibal and George. Died 14 Feb 1873, aged 63 years. Lived at
Tresodden.

SKEWES ANTHONY
Born 1954, Truro. Mother's maiden name Skewes.

SKUES ANTHONY
Chart 9. Twin of Paul Skues. Mother's maiden name Whincop. Born
1956, Woolwich. Married Sandra R. Burley in Greenwich, 1979.

SKEWES ANTHONY JOHN
Chart 12. Son of Maurice and Mary Skewes. Born 1970, Kerrier.
Mother's maiden name Payne.

SKEWES ANTHONY JOSEPH
Chart 36. Lives at 4 Netherby Street, Wahrnga, 2076. Son of James
Edward and Agnes Veronica Skewes of Australia. Married Bronwyn

Gapp 4 March 1969. Children: Alexandra (1972), Edwin (1973) and
Patrick (1975).

SKEWES ANTHONY ROBERT
Chart 25. Son of Frank Robert Skewes. Mother's maiden name Anne
Taylor. Born 28 December 1958, Cheadle Hulme, Cheshire. Lives at
21 Caperthorne Road, Wilmslow, Cheshire, SK9 6LU.

SKEWES ANTHONY RONALD
Chart 12. Son of William John and Nora (née Thomas) Skewes. Born
25 September 1933, Manaccan. Builder. Married Margaret Betty
Coward (née Healey) 23 August 1969 at Helston Register Office.
Lives at Kittiwake, Churchtown, Mullion, Helston, Cornwall.
Telephone number 0326 240727.

Anthony Ronald and Betty Skewes of Mullion

SKEWES ANTHONY WAYNE
Chart 36. Son of Ronald Edgar and Janice Kathleen (née Egan)
Skewes. Born 5 June 1960. Lives at Head Goolwa Z, Goolwa, 5214,
South Australia. Accountant.

SKEWES APRIL LYNN
Chart 2. Daughter of Charles Armington and Cindy Skewes. Born 20
May 1974. Lives in Bountiful, Utah, United States of America.

SKEWES ARCHER WILLIAM
Son of Samuel and Mary Ann (née Waters) Skewes of Millicent,
South Australia. Born 27 August 1886. Married Elsie May Handley
at Malborough, Queensland, Australia, 22 October 1918. Children:
Colin Archer (1918), John Locke (1921), Geoffrey (1923) Douglas
Arthur (1926) and May Dorothy (1937). Grazier of Maroomba,
Queensland. Died 31 August 1964, aged 78 years.

SKEWIS ARCHIBALD
Chart 2. Twin of Arthur Lawrence Skewis. Born Sebastopol, California, USA. Became a Canadian citizen, but later returned to America
to become a citizen of Oregon.

SKEWIS ARCHIBALD WILLIAM
Chart 2. Son of Henry and Annie May (née Cross) Skewes. Born 27
June 1916, Footscray, Victoria, Australia. Married Gwendoline Jones
at Sunshine, Victoria. Children: Graham Henry (1942), Barbara
Ann (1947), Helen Elizabeth (1949) and Robert William (1951).
Lives at 34a Kerford Street, Essendon, 3041, Victoria, Australia.
Electrical fitter.

SKEWIS ARCHIE R.
Lives at 1380 Furlong Road, Sebastopol, California, United States of
America. Tel No: (707) 823 2840.

SKEWES ARDYTH EVONNE
Chart 2. Daughter of Arthur Wayne and Lorene (née Parker) Skewes.
Born 6 September 1931, Shattuck, Oklahoma, USA. Married James
R. Atkins 20 August 1950 at Guymon, Oklahoma, USA.

SKEWES ARTHUR
Born 1864, Helston.

SKEWES ARTHUR
Born Cury 28 February 1868. Left Penzance when he was 30 (1898)
to emigrate to USA. In Cornwall he was a coachman. He left Cornwall on 16 April 1898 to go to Camden Main, USA. Occupation
abroad: Motor driver. Died in USA 8 March, 1953 aged 85 years.

SKEWES ARTHUR
Mentioned in Cornwall Protestation Returns, 1642.

SKUES ARTHUR
Chart 3. Son of Frederick Gordon and Ada Skues. Born 6 September
1891. Married Gladys Thompson in Downham, 1922. Son: George
Ernest Skues. Lived at 32 Blaby Road, South Wigston. Tel No South
Wigston 6985. Died 1 September 1976, aged 85 years.

SKEWES ARTHUR
Married 1900, Helston.

SKEWIS ARTHUR
Chart 36. Born 5 May 1905. Married Ethel Winifred Peters of Pool at
Illogan Parish Church 22 February 1930. One daughter Elizabeth
Joan Skewes (1932). Lived at Lower Pumpfield Row, Pool, Illogan,
1932. Present address Cantor, 31 Agar Road, Illogan Highway,
Redruth. Tel No: Redruth 216576.

SKEWES ARTHUR COURTIS
Chart 18. Son of John Courtis Skewes. Born 1896. Was a Temporary
2nd Lieutenant, Devonshire & Gloucesters. Died in France on active
service, 1916.

SKEWS ARTHUR DAVID RICHARD
Chart 17. Born Holborn 1871. Married Alice Fawcett, 1898 at

Shoreditch. Lived at 6 St George's Road, Lower Edmonton and later 447 Hertford Street, Lower Edmonton, London N.9. Children Albert Edward, George Francis and Alice D. Wife Alice died Aug., 1948. He died 31 March, 1950, aged 78 years.

SKEWES ARTHUR DAWE
Chart 18. Son of Samuel and Jane Skewes of Bere Alston, Devonshire. Born 17 April 1873. Married Eva Valentine 1902 (she died 1943, aged 65 years). He was a tailor and outfitter of 32 and 33 Old Town Street, Plymouth (1939 Street Directory) and later 31 Old Town Street. He was in business with his brother Howard Skewes. In 1906-1907 Directory listed as 23 Drake Street, Plymouth, and home address 10 Resavoir Road, Plymouth. By 1920 had moved to Lanecost, Tavistock Road, Plymouth. Old Town Street was destroyed by fire in Second World War. Children: Bella Clark (1905), Mary Elizabeth (1911) and Winifred Jean (1920). In 1953 Directory, Skewes Brothers were at 9 George Street, and 23-26 Centre Stalls, Plymouth Fruit and Fish and Poultry Market, Plymouth. He lived at 24 Western College Road, Mannamead, Plymouth from 1950's until his death. He had retired only two days when he died at Greenbanks, Agar Road, Redruth 2 August 1960.

SKEWES ARTHUR EDWIN
Chart 14. Son of Edwin Bottomley and Alice Ada (née Collier) Skewes. Born 11 August 1891. Relates his sister Alice Ruth Skewes Ford: "My arrival in the family when Arthur was 2½ years old probably kept him from being spoiled, for he was an entrancing little boy with shining blue eyes, a roseleaf complexion and a lively responsiveness. He was brought up at Grovean and like other children before and after him he used to slide down the smooth cherry bannister, and swinging in the high swing under the big oak."
Arthur began school at the age of 7, walking the mile to Ives Grove. In 1900 the family moved for a short while to Madison.
Like most boys he had his ups and downs: At the age of 7 he was walking the upper hall bannister, slipped and gashed his forehead on the heating stove. Three years later he fell from a crossbeam in his Uncle Thomas's hay mow and hurt his back.
Arthur spent three years at Rochester Academy and a year and a half at Lawrence College. He loved music and learned the violin. He was a natural leader in group activities of all sorts.
After his father's death in 1913, Arthur took up the responsibilities of running the farm at Grovean. With the optimism and self-confidence of youth, he persuaded his mother to let him rebuild and enlarge the barn, though to do so meant increasing the mortgage. He worked hard and learned by experience. On 25 October 1919 he married Miss Irene Olson. Together they took over Grovean from their mother who sadly died within four months from pneumonia. In the autumn of 1921 Arthur developed back pains and he visited an osteopath. He thought he had strained his back when cleaning the cistern in the kitchen the previous day. Within a week two doctors had diagnosed polio. By that night paralysis had developed and by the following day he had lost his sight. Within 24 hours he was dead — a mere thirty years old. He died 8 September 1921. He left one son Arthur Russell Skewes (1922).

SKEWES ARTHUR ERNEST
Chart 12. Son of John Wesley Skewes. Born 1890. Died 1905, aged 15 years. Buried in Mawgan Churchyard, Helston.

SKUES ARTHUR E.W.
Chart 8. Born 1919, Shoreditch. Mother's maiden name Harris. Married Winifred E. Jackson, 1940, Islington. Son: Kenneth (1948). Emigrated to New Zealand 1976. Died January 1980, aged 61 years.

SKEWES ARTHUR G.
Born 1911, Strood, Mother's maiden name Davis. Died 1920, aged 8 years.

SKEWES ARTHUR GEORGE
Chart 25, Born 15 April 1897, Chorlton. Married Ruth Hacking in Manchester May, 1927. Lived at Dalton Avenue, Moss Side Manchester 1927-1934; 6 The Oval, Heald Green, Cheshire 1934-1961; Templars Way, Kingsteignton, Newton Abbot, Devon 1961-1963 and 6 Blackbrook Avenue, Paignton, Devon 1968-1978. Child: Frank Robert (1928). Ruth died 1972, aged 69 years. He died 4 November 1978, aged 81 years.

SKEWES ARTHUR GEORGE
Chart 10. Son of John William Skewes of Marazion. Born 23 October 1907. Married Borghild Hansen, 4 July 1930 in America. Died 23 April 1935. No children.

SKEWES ARTHUR H.
Son of Sidney Hope and Anna (née Hosking) Skewes. Born September 1899, New York.

SKEWIS ARTHUR J.
Married Fideline Mahiew in Cardiff, 1919. No children.

SKEWES ARTHUR J.
Born 1925, Bristol. Mother's maiden name Morrison. Died 1926, aged 0.

SKEWS ARTHUR JAMES
Born 1875, Dartford, Kent.

SKEWIS ARTHUR LAWRENCE
Chart 2. Twin to Archibald Skewis. Son of Benjamin Peters Skewis

and Amelia. Born in America. Plumber. Married Elizabeth Ballard and became an American citizen, then a Canadian citizen and finally back to an American citizen of Oregon. In 1932 was living at 1797 Center, Salem, Oregon, United States of America.

SKUES ARTHUR LEONARD PETER
Chart 9. Born 28 June 1896, London. Married Marjorie Helen Lamont, 1925, Barrow-in-Furness. Children: Beryl E. and Doreen M. (twins), 1927. Sanitary Inspector in Barrow-in-Furness. Lived at 42 Priory Road, Barrow. Died 6 October 1971, aged 75 years.

SKEWES ARTHUR RUSSELL D.V.M.
Chart 14. Son of Arthur Edwin and Irene (née Olson) Skewes. Born 21 May 1922, Wisconsin. He received his degree of Doctor of Veterinary Medicine from Iowa State University in 1949.
He married Helen Roberta Horr (she born 10 January 1931) 30 June 1951.
Arthur was commissioned as Captain with the United States Air Force looking after the USA Vet Corps. During the Korean conflict he was in charge of 100 sentry dogs.
He is now an equine practitioner and an associate veterinarian with Hagyard, Davidson, McGee and Associates PSC.
Children: Russell Frank; Martha Rene; Melinda Irene; Rodrick Arthur and Roberta Glee.
After graduating from college Arthur Skewes practised at Union Grove, Wisconsin and was also resident veterinarian at Castleton Farm in Lexington from 1964 to 1966.
The Skewes family have played an active role in church activities. Prior to moving to Lexington they were active in the Ives Grove Methodist Church where Helen served as Sunday School Superintendent and in youth development. Since moving to Kentucky their activities have won them special honour.
The Skewes' were chosen "Family of the Year" at the Aldersgate Methodist Church in 1965. Doctor Skewes was also one of the initial members of the Board of Directors for Christ Centre. Arthur and Helen Skewes are both active at First United Methodist Church in Lexington. He serves on the church board and she is a youth coordinator.
Doctor Skewes was a member of No.288 F and A.M., past master and past patron of O.E.S. No 71 at Union Grove. He also started a memorial scholarship for Union Grove High School.
Arthur has served as President of the Bryan Station Senior School PTA in Lexington. Helen is also secretary of the County Council for the Fayette County PTA.
Arthur Skewes is a member of the American Simmental Association and secretary/treasurer of Kentucky Simmental Association, American Association of Equine Practitioners, American Veterinary Medical Association, the Thoroughbred Club, Farm Managers Club and the Kentucky Livestock Improvement Association.
He has appeared on several veterinary medical programmes as a guest lecturer. In addition he is author of the chapter on "Equine Dentistry" in the book *Equine Medicine and Surgery*.
Arthur Skewes is also president of the Lexington Rodeos which own and operate the "dunking machine" each year at the Lions Club Bluegrass Fair. While in Wisconsin he was director and general manager of the Racine County Fair where he introduced several innovations that have been used ever since.
The Skewes family lives at 157 Swigert Avenue, Lexington, Kentucky, 40505, United States of America.

Skewes Brothers shop in Old Town Street, Plymouth, Devon

Arthur Edwin Skewes of Wisconsin, USA taken in 1919   *Arthur George Skewes (1897-1978)*

Arthur Russell Skewes

SKEWS ARTHUR S.
Chart 41. Son of Joseph and Nellie Skews. Mother's maiden name Randerson. Born 1926, Barnsley, South Yorkshire.

SKEWS ARTHUR S.
In 1969 Street Directory for Exeter he is listed for the first time living at 18 Queens Crescent, Exeter.

SKEWS ARTHUR S.A.
Chart 17. Son of James Arthur Skews. Born 1914, London. Mother's maiden name Jarvis. Married Stroud in Romford, Essex. Children: Patricia (1944) and Elizabeth (1949).

SKEWES ARTHUR VIVIAN
Lives at 79 Payten Street, Kogarah, 2217, New South Wales, Australia with Gwendoline Joyce Skewes. Boilerman.

SKEWES ARTHUR WAYNE
Chart 2. Son of John Billing and Lydia Skewes of America. Born 26 September 1910 at Moab, Utah, USA. Married Lorene Parker 26 November 1930. Children: Ardyth Evonne (1931), Harry Blaine (1935) and Linda Ann (1940). Freemason with Top of Texas Lodge No 1381. Industrial electrician. Lives at 2345 Aspen, Pampa, Texas, 79065, USA. Telephone number (806) 669 6416.

Arthur Wayne Skewes

SKEWES ARTHUR WEATHERBY
Born 1892, Helston, Cornwall.

SKEWES ARTHUR WESLEY
Chart 12. Born 1867, Cury, Helston. Illegitimate son of Alice Ann Skewes of Cury. Bpt Cury 3 May 1867. Lived at Nantithet in 1871 Census Returns. Had two illegitimate brothers, John Wesley and Frederick Augustus. Went abroad.

SKEWS ASHLEY JANE
Daughter of Lawrence Skews. Mother's maiden name Brown. Born 1967, Sunderland,

SKEWES ATHOL HENRY
In 1959 was living at Farm 1425, Leeton, New South Wales, Australia as a farm labourer. Also on the farm were John Reginald & Nora Louise Skewes.
Now lives at 24 Cudgerie Avenue, Leeton, 2705, New South Wales, Australia.

SKUES ATLANTA EMILY
Chart 8. Née Bond. Born 1872, Shoreditch. Married Walter Edward Skues 23 April 1893. Children: Walter Edward (1894), Percival

Walter (1893), Elizabeth (1895), Atlanta Violet (1896), Florence Ruby (1904), Maud Evelyn (1909), Olive Emily (1910), Ernest John (1912) and Alfred Edgar (1914). Died 1915, aged 43 years.

SKUES ATLANTA VIOLET
Chart 8. Daughter of Walter Edward Skues. Born 1896, Edmonton. Married 1921 to William Bignall in Islington. Issue: one son and one daughter.

SKEWES AUBREY RUPERT
Chart 36. Son of George and Mary (née Dowling) Skewes. Born 27 April 1895. Married Annie Lovinia Townsend. Children: Gloria June (1923), Angela Dawn (1925), Cyrus Lyle (1926), Vemba Merrill (1928), and Lois Ada (1932). In 1959 lived at Jubilee, Uralla, New South Wales, Australia.
Died 30 August 1976, aged 87 years. Annie died 24 October 1948.

SKUES AUDREY
Chart 3. Née Hiscock. Born 20 July 1915, Southampton. Daughter of a solicitor. Her great grandparents (mother's side) came from Denmark. Married Ernest Skues at Highfield Church, Southampton 2 October 1948. It was his second marriage. No children with this marriage. Ernest died 24 November 1977, aged 92 years.
Lives at 36 Well House, Woodmanstone Lane, Banstead, Surrey. Tel. No: Burgh Heath 52403.

SKUES AUDREY F.
Chart 9. Born 1928, Camberwell. Mother's maiden name Bremer. Married David D. Johnson, 1949, Woolwich, London.

SKUES AUGUSTA
Born 1888. Née Kretschmann. Married Thomas Mackenzie Skues, 17 June 1915. Died 1961, aged 74 years in Marylebone.

SKEWES AURELIA
Born 1855. Died Truro, 1926, aged 71 years.

SKEWES AVIS
Née Rowe. Wife of William Skewes. Married at Gunwalloe, 24 June 1718. Buried Gunwalloe 10 October 1757. Children: Edward (1721) and Loveday (1726).

SKEWIS AVIS
Daughter of Edward and Honour Skewis. Bpt Helston, 28 August 1762.

SKEWES AVIS
Married Richard Pike of Plymouth at Falmouth, 15 February 1781.

SKEWES AVIS
Born 1786. Lived at Nantithet, Cury. Hanged herself in a temporary fit of insanity. Buried Cury, 27 July 1849, aged 63 years.

SKEWES AVIS
Chart 2. Daughter of Malachi Bath, farmer of Roseminowes, Stithians. Born 8 February 1824. Married Henry Skewes at Stithians Parish Church 26 July 1845. Children: William Henry (1846), Josiah (1847), James (1849) and Alfred (1852). Lived at Angarrack, Phillack. Died 1865, Bodmin, aged 41 years.

SKEWES AVIS MAY
Born 15 August 1912. Lived at 39 Coronation Avenue, Camborne in 1968 with George Skewes. Died 15 April 1975, aged 63 years.

B

SKEWS B.W.
Author of "Profiles in Diffracting Shockwaves", an analysis based on Whitham's Theory. University of Witwatersrand, Johannesburg, South Africa. Department of Mechanical Engineering, 1966.

SKUES BAE LUCY
Chart 5. Wife of Laurence Penrose Skues, dentist. Lives at Boongala, Rosehill Road, Lower Plenty, Victoria, Australia, 3093.

SKUSE BARBARA
Daughter of Horace Sydney and Ada (née Tomsett) Skuse. Born 1928. Married Eric Cox, 1950. Issue: two daughters and one son.

SKEWES BARBARA
Chart 25. Daughter of Henry and Agnes (née Lally) Skewes of 117 Yew Tree Road, Manchester. Born 1930. Married Bernard Logue 2 July 1955 at St Kentigern's, Fallowfield. Issue one son and one daughter.

SKEWES BARBARA ALLEN
Lived at Newtown, Kadina, Wallaroo, South Australia in 1959 with Cecil John Skewes. Now lives at 10/32 Eaton Street, Cumberland Park, 5041, South Australia.

SKEWES BARBARA ANN
Chart 48. Daughter of William Frederick Charles and Dorothy (née Hornby) Skewes. Born 30 March 1931, Doncaster, South Yorkshire. Married Thomas Jeffrey Pickering, February 1958, Holderness. Issue: two daughters.

SKEWES BARBARA ANN
Chart 2. Daughter of Archibald William and Gwendoline (née Jones) Skewes. Born 4 November 1947 at North Essendon, Australia. Married Trevor William McBain. Now lives at 23 Wattleblossom Road, Warrandyte, 3113, Victoria, Australia. Issue: 2 daughters.

SKEWES BARBARA HANNAH
Chart 36. Daughter of James and Stella Margaret (née Farrell) Skewes. Born 2 April 1928, Watsons Creek, Bendemeer, Australia. Married Ronald James. Issue: 1 son and 1 daughter.

SKEWES BARBARA HELEN
Lives at 12 Grevillia Street, Chester Hill, 2162, New South Wales, Australia with Leonard James Skewes, linotype operator.

SKEWES BARBARA JESSIE
Chart 36. Née McKinley. Married Brian Lock Skewes 12 November 1955. Children: Janet Barbara (1957), David Brian (1958), Neville John (1962) and Kathryn Mary (1963). Lives at Currency Creek, Y, 5251, South Australia.

SKEWES BARBARA JO
Daughter of Leonard and Virginia (née Sterler) Skewes. Born 14 March 1953. Lives at 304 Elm Street, Marshall, Minnesota, 56528, United States of America.

SKEWES BARBARA JOAN
Chart 12. Daughter of William John and Nora (née Thomas) Skewes. Born 5 October 1934. Married Norman Johnson at Helston Register Office, 1957. Issue: one son and one daughter. Is now divorced.

SKEWES BARBARA JOYCE
Lives at 40 Kitchener Road, Broadmeadows, Victoria, Australia, 3047 with William John Skewes, driver. Dressmaker.

SKEWS BARBARA KATHLEEN
Chart 17. Daughter of Stanley and Marjorie (née Hardcastle) Skews. Born 17 February 1953. Married Graham Smith 21 July 1973, Hull. Issue: 2 sons.

SKEWES BARBARA KAY
Chart 36. Daughter of Andrew and Olga Stephen. Born 28 November 1949. Married Warren Benjamin Skewes in Tamworth, New South Wales, Australia, 11 November 1972. Lives at George Street, Moonbi, Tamworth, 2352, New South Wales, Australia. No children.

SKEWIS BARBARA M.
Chart 34. Daughter of Frank and Winifred Kate (née Baker) Skewis. Born 5 October 1931, Sheppey.

SKEWES BARBARA MACKAY
Lives at 15 Acheron Street, Doncaster, 3108, Victoria, Australia.

SKEWES BARBARA MAY
Lived at 27 Barkl Avenue, Padstow, Revensby, New South Wales, Australia in 1959 with Harold George Skewes, labourer.

SKEWS BARON S.
Chart 41. Son of Joseph and Nellie (née Randerson) Skews. Born 1924 Barnsley, South Yorkshire. Married Lilian Barson, 1943, Staincross. Married Cielemecka, 1952, Calder. Married Ramsden, 1967, Calder. Married Sherburn, 1973, Calder. Children: Barry S. (1943) and Nicholas (1947).

SKEWES BARRINGTON
Eldest son of T. Skewes. Born 1887, Helston. Died 23 September 1889, aged 12 years at Common Cross, Lizard.

SKEWES BARRY
Born 1962, Redruth. Mother's maiden name Williams.

SKEWS BARRY J.
Chart 10. Son of Thomas H. Skews. Mother's maiden name Harris. Born 1955, St Austell.

SKEWES BARRY JOHN
Chart 38. Son of Ray Samuel and Betty (née Sloan) Skewes. Born 6 April 1959, Adelaide, South Australia. Freezer hand. Married Linda Patricia Sneyd (she born 20 May 1962, Colchester, Essex), 18 October 1980. Lives at Flat 4, 18 Prospect Terrace, Prospect, South Australia, 5082.

Barry John Skewes

SKUES BARRY RUSSELL
Chart 9. Son of Roy Arthur and Joan D. (née Causton) Skues. Born 1 January 1954, Wandsworth, London. Married Gillian Ann Epps 20 November 1976. Children: Emma Catherine (1978) and Russell Thomas (1980). Lives at "The Hollies", Bromley Green Road, Ruckinge, near Ashford, Kent. Tel no: 023 373 2948.

SKEWS BARRY S.
Chart 41. Son of Baron S. Skews. Mother's maiden name Barson. Born 1943, Staincross. Married Campbell, 1975, Staincross.

SKEWS BEATRICE
Chart 10. Daughter of William Francis Dennis and Jane Skews. Born 1880. Spinster of 19 Alexander Road, Porth, Newquay. Died 31 May 1964, aged 84 years.

SKEWES BEATRICE ANNIE
Born 1889, Redruth. Died 1889, aged 0.

SKEWES BEATRICE ANNIE
Chart 12. Née Rosevear. Daughter of W. Rosevear, labourer of Mawgan Cross. Born 1891. First wife of Harry Stanley Skewes whom she married in 1921 at Helston United Methodist Church — 12 January 1921. Died 1945, aged 54 years.

SKEWES BEATRICE DONNA
Daughter of Byron James and Margaret Cecilia (née Morrison) Skewes. Born 14 December (year not known), New York. Married Michael Keane 16 May 1980, New York.

SKEWES BEATRICE MARY
Chart 36. Née Reynolds. Born 1903. Married William Henry Skewes, 1936. Lived at Carnbone Farm, Wendron. Died following a car crash on 21 July 1951, aged 48 years, in Helston Cottage Hospital. She was a passenger — her husband was driving. Child: Priscilla (1938).

SKEWES BEATRICE MARY
Chart 36. Daughter of Alfred John & Matilda Skewes of Maynes Row, Tuckingmill. Born 10 February 1904. Was baptised with her sisters and brother at Tuckingmill Parish Church 12 September 1917. Married John Henry Harvey, 1924, Redruth. Lived at 77 Higher Fore Street, Redruth, 1967.

SKEWES BEATRICE MELBA IRENE
Chart 15. Born 12 July 1920. Daughter of Harry and Hilda (née Jane) Skews. Bpt St Ive 2 March 1921. Married Cyril Congdon, 1940, Liskeard.

SKEWES BEATRICE PAULINE
Lives at Lower Watsons Creek, Bendemeer, 2352, New South Wales, Australia with James William Skewes, tin dredger.

SKEWES BEDE KEVIN
Chart 36. Son of Leslie Kevin and Jill Cecelia (Pullman) Skewes. Born 16 December 1952, Bendemeer, New South Wales. Lives at Caroline Street, Bendemeer, 2352, New South Wales, Australia.

SKEWES BELINDA ANN
Chart 36. Daughter of Geoffrey John and Margaret (née Shanley) Skewes. Born 31 August 1974. Lives at 17 Willie Street, Werris Creek, 2341, New South Wales, Australia.

SKEWES BELINDA O.M.
Born 1918, Devonport. Mother's maiden name Webber. Married Rossiter, 1940, Portsmouth.

SKEWES BELITA
Chart 10. Daughter of Peter Skewes of River Cottage, Chacewater, Cornwall. Mine agent. Born 12 April 1873. Bpt Chacewater 1 May 1874. Married Nicholas James in Redruth, 1897. Emigrated to South Africa. No children. Died 2 June 1963, aged 90 years.

SKEWES BELLA CLARK
Chart 18. Daughter of Arthur Dawe Skewes. Spinster of St Peter's Convent, Plympton, Plymouth, Devon. Born 1905. Died 9 January 1965, aged 59 years in Plympton.

SKEWIS BENJAMIN
Chart 2. Son of Charles Elmer & Leotice Skewis. Born 16 March 1949, America. Married Nancy Brodie. Now divorced. Children: Deborah Lynn (1969) and Benjamin James (1974).

SKEWES BENJAMIN HELLINGS
Chart 25. Born 20 Feb 1822, Falmouth. Son of Thomas and Eleanor Skewes. Bpt 25 December 1822, Falmouth. In 1841 (30 June) he appeared before Magistrates at Bodmin accused of stealing copper in the parish of Budock, but was acquitted. Married Caroline.......... 1859 (She died 16 January 1909, aged 79 in Truro). Died at Bissoe 24 February 1913, aged 91 years.

SKEWIS BENJAMIN JAMES
Chart 2. Son of Benjamin & Nancy Skewis. Born 9 January 1974, America.

SKEWIS BENJAMIN PETERS
Chart 2. Son of Edward and Catherine Skewis. Born 1 February 1845, Wisconsin, USA. Married Amelia Bennett. Children: Arthur Lawrence and Archibald (twins), Florence Clyde, Percy Vernon, Myrl Leone and John Bennett. In 1932 lived at 960 North 20th Street, Salem, Oregon. Died 6 March 1936 in Salem, Oregon.

SKEWES BENJAMIN ROBERT
Chart 36. Son of Robert Skewes. Born 20 December 1968, New South Wales, Australia.

Bernard Erick Skuse

SKEWES BENJAMIN SAMUEL
Chart 36. Son of James Robert and Pearl Isabel (née Chapman) Skewes. Born 26 May 1926. Married Gweneth Adams, 22 September 1945, New South Wales. Children: Warren Benjamin, Daryl, Dianne Gweneth and Marilyn Pearl. Lives at Glenelg, Watsons Creek, Bendemeer, 2352, New South Wales, Australia.

SKEWES BENNETT
Son of John and Judeth Skewes. Bpt St Keverne March 1630.

SKEWIS BENNETT OSBORNE
Chart 2. Son of Absalom and Jane Skewis. Born 8 March 1862, America. Married Martha Morten. Children: Catherine, Martha and Shirley. In 1911 he was President/Manager of the Eastern Mill Company, 509 NE, Tacoma, Washington. Died 19 July 1924, aged 62 years.

SKEWS BERNARD
Born 1885, Dartford, Kent. Married Kate Murphy, 1916, Dartford. Died 1925, aged 40 years.

SKEWES BERNARD
Chart 36. Son of Francis James and Valerie (née Foster) Skewes. Born Watsons Creek, Australia.

SKUES BERNARD E.
Chart 7. Son of Francis Albert Skues. Mother's maiden name Jeffrey. Born 1919, Dartford, Kent. Died 1921, aged 1 year in Dartford.

SKUSE BERNARD ERICK
Son of Harold James and Edith Marion (née Lamerton) Skuse. Born 3 March 1915, Keynsham, Bristol. At the age of 13 stowed away on a sailing schooner bound for America from Bideford, North Devon, returning home a year later. He was made to work his passage and took part in most activities to work the ship.
On return to England he became an apprentice blacksmith, but within twelve months transferred to coal mining. Two years later he joined a circus for a short while, and after returning home worked on building sites as a general labourer.
An opening came to join a firm doing "spider" work on constructional metal erection where he learned his trade thoroughly working all over the country as a top rigger for many leading companies.
He took every opportunity to lead an open air life spending much time in the woods living in makeshift shelters and hunting with a bow and arrow. In winter he wore a jerkin and shorts and in summer just a leotard.
The local press heard about the young man of the woods who had taken up residence at a local beauty spot. This led to a short feature film "Tarzan of the Trees" in which he played the part of Tarzan.
Motor cycle riding was an interest and led to "Wall of Death" riding and stunt riding for films. He admits he broke many bones.
In between the repair of more broken bones and the offer of more films he returned to steel erecting. Working out of London he met Johnny Weissmuller by chance at a swimming pool who invited him to do some diving.
After joining the merchant navy during the Second World War he returned home to Bristol and started his own business as a general builder, decorator and signwriter.
In the early 1950's he was approached by a man for whom he had done under-water salvage work who wanted him to go to Cornwall and drop three radar masts at Downderry — a job which nobody would tackle because of their height topping 300 feet — and made of wood. He accepted the challenge, after which time a local landowner offered further employment in building and maintenance. His family joined him and he made an entirely new life in Cornwall.
He is a popular character around the Tideford and St Germans area. Looking like a pirate, he wears a gold tassled hat, gold earring and sports a Van Dyke beard. His first marriage was to Dorothy Joan Janaway and they had two children: Dorothea and Christine. His second marriage is to Jean Marie Patricia (née Clark). They live at Tideford Lodge, Tideford, Saltash, Cornwall. Bernie still enjoys the "big outside", stalking through the woods or paddling upstream in his canoe.

SKEWS   BERTHA
Chart 23. Born 1871, St Austell. Married John Skews of Coxbarrow. St Austell. Children: William Hedley, Gertrude Alberta and Mabel Millicent. Died 1954, aged 83 years.

SKEWS   BERTHA C.
Wife of Walter Skews. Lived at 316 Douglas, San Francisco, United States of America in 1917.

SKUES   BERTHA ELIZABETH
Chart 8. Daughter of John Gilbert Skues. Born 1895. Married 1928 to Walter J. Humphrey in Edmonton, London.

SKUES   BERTHA ELIZABETH
Married Jenkins, 1919, Edmonton, London.

SKEWES BERTIE
Chart 36. Son of William and Annie (née Taylor) Skewes. Born December, 1898, Victoria, Australia. Married Ada Carroll in 1924. Children: Amelia, Thomas, William, John, May, Annie, Margaret, Beatrice, Donald, Mary, Shirley, Jack, Edward, Ernest and James. Died 1950, aged 52 years.

SKEWES BERTIE COLE
Chart 24. Son of John and Mary Jane (née Cole) Skewes. Born 1894, New South Wales, Australia. Wife's name Doris. Children: John Richard, Lesley, Roy, Molly, Ella, Dorothy and Laurel.

SKEWES BERTRAM
Chart 12. Son of James Henry Skewes. Born 1902. Married Elizabeth "Lily" Prowse, 1930, Truro. Lived at Kai Ping, Goonvrea, St Agnes and later Chegwyn Gardens, St Agnes, Cornwall. Children: Elizabeth Marlene and Pamela J. Died 14 December 1976, aged 74 years. Buried at St Agnes Methodist Church.

SKEWES BERYL
Chart 36. Daughter of Percy and Mary (née Farrell) Skewes. Born 7 June 1917, Watsons Creek, Australia. Married Lloyd Griffin. Issue: one daughter.

SKEWES BERYL COLVILLE
In 1959 was living at 284 Mitcham Road, Mitcham, Victoria, Australia with Clarence George Skewes, engineer.

SKUES BERYL I.
Chart 9. Daughter of Arthur Leonard P. Skues. Twin to Doreen M. Skues. Mother's maiden name Lamont. Born 1927. Married George L.H. Houlden, 1955, Barrow in Furness.

Twins Beryl and Doreen Skues taken about 1932

SKEWES BERYL MAY
Chart 36. Née Johnson. Married John David Skewes 25 February 1961. Children: Robyn May (1962), Mark Andrew (1964) and Philip John (1966). Lives at Ackland Hill Road, Cherry Gardens, 5157, South Australia.

SKEWES BESSIE
Chart 13. Daughter of Edward and Julia Skewes, shoemaker, of Nantithet, Cury. Bpt Cury 6 August 1862. Lived at Nantithet in 1871 census returns.

SKEWES BESSIE
Chart 12. Born 1882. Daughter of John & Thirza Skewes of Chypons, labourer. Bpt Cury 18 January 1883. Married Richard Hill, 1909. Lived at St Day after marriage. Issue one daughter.

SKUES BESSIE
Chart 5. Daughter of Joseph Penrose Skues. Emigrated to Australia from Redruth, Cornwall around 1860.

SKEWES BESSIE
Married 1890, Helston.

SKEWES BESSIE
Married 1909, Helston

SKEWES BESSIE
Chart 12. Born 2 September 1899. Married William John Skewes 10

December 1925 at Landewednack Church, Lizard. Children: William John (1927), Ronald (1929) and Maurice (1933). Died 30 April 1979, aged 80 years.

SKUES BESSIE ANNIE
Chart 5. Daughter of Charles Penrose Skues. Born 1875. Spinster. Died 1951, aged 76 in Amersham.

SKEWES BESSIE ANNIE
Living at Helstonwater, Perranwell Station, Kea in 1932 with Charles Skewes.

SKEWES BESSIE E.A.
Married Allen in Redruth, 1922.

SKEWES BESSIE EDITH A.
Born 1886, St Columb.

SKEWES BESSIE ELLEN
Born 18 February 1883, Redruth. Daughter of C. Skewes of Roaches Row, Redruth. Admitted Redruth East End School 1 March 1887.

SKEWS BESSIE HARRIET
Born 1892, Preston, Lancashire. Married Theodore F. Thomas, 1936, Amounderness.

SKEWES BESSIE SARAH
Born 10 October 1881. Married Charles Skewes. Lived at Helstonwater, Perranwell 1920-1930. Later moved to 53 Kenwyn Street, Truro. Died 18 February 1971, aged 90 years.

SKEWES BETONY IRENE
Chart 50. Lives at 6 Cardigan Street, Stockton, 2295, New South Wales, Australia. Maiden name Roach. Married Jack Skewes 1 February 1947. Children: Alan (1947), Harry (1949), Julie (1954), Donna May (1959).

SKUES BETSEY
Daughter of William and Elizabeth Skues. Bpt 27 October 1773, Lostwithiel.

SKEWES BETSY
Chart 29. Daughter of Richard and Roseanna Skewes of Kenwyn. Bpt Kenwyn 26 January 1806.

SKEWES BETSY
Chart 10. Daughter of John and Ann Skewes of Kenwyn. Bpt Kenwyn 11 May 1806.

SKEWES BETSY
Chart 2. Daughter of William and Mary Skewes of Camborne. Bpt Camborne 19 May 1810. Died 7 September 1813, aged 3 years.

SKEWES BETSY
Chart 14. Daughter of John and Jane Skewes of Chybarles, Ruan Major, farmer. Bpt Ruan Major 5 January 1841. Emigrated with her parents to Yorkville, Wisconsin arriving 29 May 1850. Married Mr Smith. Issue: one daughter.

SKEWS BETSY
Chart 41. Née Tresider. Daughter of John Tresider, labourer of Wadebridge. Born 1842, Redruth. Married Matthew Skews, widower, at St Breock Parish Church, 13 July 1861. Children: William John (1862), Matthew (1864) and Thomas (1867). Died 1895, aged 53 years, in Redruth.

SKEWS BETSY
Chart 41. Daughter of Thomas and Ada (née Sheldon) Skews. Born 1892, Barnsley, South Yorkshire. Married 1911, Easington.

SKEWIS BETTIE ANNIE
Chart 2. Daughter of Robert and Ruth Skewis. Born 16 March 1959, United States of America.

SKEWES BETTY
In 1959 lived at 7 Nerong Road, Lambton, Jesmond, New South Wales, Australia with Leo William Skewes.

SKEWES BETTY
Chart 26. Daughter of Grant Phillip Skewes of Connecticut, United States of America.

SKEWES BETTY ELAINE
Chart 50. Daughter of Cyril Thomas and Annie Mary (née Leathan) Skewes. Married. No children.

SKEWS BETTY F.
Daughter of Alfred George and Annie L. (née Snowshill) Skews. Born 1938, Paddington. Married Archer, 1957, Edmonton, London.

SKEWES BETTY GRACE
Lived at Watsons Creek, Bendemeer, New South Wales, Australia, 1959 with Francis John Skewes. Now lives at 37 Croydon Avenue, Tamworth, New South Wales.

SKEWIS BETTY HAZEL
Chart 2. Daughter of Elmer Arthur and Maude Skewis. Born 10 December 1914. Married Leland Ballou 15 May 1939, Greenville, Iowa. Issue: two daughters. Lives in Storm Lake, Iowa, USA. Together with her cousin Dorothy Delphine Skewis she helped to develop the Art Gallery in Storm Lake which opened in 1974.

SKUES BETTY IRENE
Chart 7. Born 1924, Tonbridge, Kent. Mother's maiden name Madge Irene Meades. Married Bertie H. Bishop, 1946, Tonbridge. Issue: Three sons.

SKEWES BETTY J.
Married Proctor, 1973, Chichester, Sussex.

SKEWES BETTY JOY
Chart 38. Daughter of Sydney and Dora (Milde) Sloan. Born 22 May 1928. Married Ray Samuel Skewes, St. Aiden's Parish Church, Payneham, Adelaide, 28 April 1948. Issue: Sandra (1950) and Barry John (1959). Lives at 31 Browning Street, Clearview, South Australia, 5085.

SKEWES BEULAH
Is a member of the Charter of Professional and Business Women of Union Grove, Wisconsin, USA. The ladies held a charter night on 29 February 1964, at The Golden Lantern, Racine.

SKEWES BEVERLEY DIANE
Chart 10. Daughter of Robert Arthur and Lillian (née Foster) Skewes. Born 8 September 1944, Hastings, Sussex. Married Gary Allan Titley 2 June 1967 in Hamilton, Ontario, Canada. Now lives at Box 538, Waterdown, Ontario, Canada.

SKEWS BEVERLEY J.
Chart 41. Daughter of Kenneth D. Skews. Born 1959, Worth Valley. Mother's maiden name Lord. Killed in a car crash with her mother and brother Nigel in South Africa about 1970.

SKUES BEVERLEY JEAN
Chart 5. Daughter of Leigh Harold and Ethel Maude (née Poynton) Skues. Born 18 February 1953, Victoria, Australia. Killed in a car crash in Melbourne, 1971, aged 18 years.

SKEWES BEVERLEY KAREN
Chart 10. Daughter of Richard John and Edna May (née Manson) Skewes. Born 17 September 1947, South Africa. Married Preston in South Africa, 23 March 1968. Issue: 2 sons.

SKEWES BEVERLEY MAY
Chart 26. Daughter of Frank Anson and June Beverley (née Spaulding). Born 6 May 1944, America. Twice married: 1) Paul Watress – issue one daughter and 2) Martin Deford – issue one son and one daughter. Lives in East Lyme, Connecticut.

SKEWES BIDDY
Daughter of Henry Skewes of Kea. Bpt Kea 14 May 1758. Married Nicholas Trestraile of Kea at Kenwyn Parish Church 6 October 1788.

SKEWES BLADIMIR
Chart 2. Mexican. Son of Franz and Atala (née Castaneda) Skewes. Born 17 December 1976.

SKEWES BLANCH
Chart 19. Daughter of Thomas Skewes of Gwennap. Married Martin Magor 16 November 1695 at Gwennap.

SKEWES BLANCH
Chart 19. Daughter of Thomas and Margaret Skewes of Gwennap. Bpt Gwennap 7 June 1707. Buried Gwennap 13 May 1708, aged 1 year.

SKEWS BLANCH
Daughter of William Skews of Gwennap. Bpt Gwennap 14 October 1710.

SKEWES BLANCH
Chart 36. Daughter of James and Sarah Skewes of Cury. Bpt Cury 7 Feb 1719.

SKEWES BLANCH
Brd Cury 23 February 1737.

SKEWES BLANCH
Daughter of Edward and Ann Skewes of Cury. Bpt Cury 8 May 1737.

SKEWES BLANCH
Married Robert Caddy, Cury 30 December 1758.

SKEWIS BLANCH
Daughter of Edward & Honour Skewis. Bpt Helston 1 January 1767.

SKEWES BLANCH
Daughter of James and Ann Skewes. Bpt Cury 26 July 1788. Spinster. Buried Cury 30 April 1871, aged 83 years. Poultry dealer.

SKEWES BLANCH
Married Richard Oates 2 December 1828, Cury.

SKEWES BLANCH
Daughter of Henry and Ann Skewes of East Taphouse, St Pinnock, Liskeard. Born 1838 at St Hilary. Brothers: Henry and Joseph. Sisters: Maria and Sarah Ann.

SKEWES BLANCH
of Illogan (West Wheal). Born 1844. Buried Illogan 28 October 1862, aged 18 years.

SKEWES BLANCH
Chart 36. Daughter of James and Simonette Skewes of Treskillard, Cury. Bpt Cury 2 March 1845. In 1861 census returns is listed as a copper ore dresser.

SKEWES BLANCH
Born 1862. Wife of William Skewes. Died Truro 29 January 1917 at St Dominic Street, Truro, aged 55.

SKEWES BLANCH
Born 1888, Truro.

SKEWES BLANCH
Chart 38. Daughter of Sydney Howard and Cordelia (née Blight)

Skewes. Born 7 January 1916. Twice married:
1) Leslie Louis Cassay.
2) Clement Edward Gifford 5 May 1952. No children. Lives at 111 Botting Street, Albert Park, South Australia, 5014.

SKUES BLANCHE LOUISA
Chart 7. Daughter of Thomas Skues. Born 1880, Chelsea area. Married 1905 to James Botten at Tonbridge. Issue: five or six children. Died 1971, aged 91 years.

SKEWES BLANCHE MARY
Lives at 132 Ellesmere Rd, Gymea, 2227, NSW, Australia.

SKEWES BLANCHE S.
Chart 36. Daughter of John and Mary Skewes of Cury. Bpt Cury 7 February 1792.

SKEWES BLASA
Chart 10. Daughter of Juan and Luisa (née Garcia) Skewes. Born Mexico. Married Ricardo Richards and had 18 children. Prior to marriage had an illegitimate son Isaac Skewes (1905). Lived in Real del Monte, Mexico. Died 27 June 1922, aged 66 years.

SKEWES BLASA
Chart 10. Mexican. Daughter of Juan and Fransisca (née Meneses) Skewes. Born 25 June 1906. Married.

SKEWS BOBBIE
Chart 41. Daughter of Eric Skews. Mother's maiden name Rasburn. Born 1961, Barnsley, South Yorkshire.

SKEWES BONNIE MAULE
Chart 6. Daughter of Donald and Effie Kite. Born 18 October 1944. Married Trevor John Skewes at St Cuthbert's, Prospect, South Australia. Children: Cherylyn Kay (1964) and Gwyn Martin (1968). Lives c/o P.O. Box 96, Stirling, South Australia, 5152.

SKEWES BRADLEY JOHN
Chart 42. Son of Dennis Paul and Kayleen Daphne (née Bourke) Skewes. Born 2 December 1975, Nowra Hill. Now lives at 25 McKay Street, Nowra Hill, 2540, New South Wales, Australia.

SKEWES BOULDEN JOHN
Chart 14. Son of George Boulden and Helen Skewes. Born 30 December 1874, America. Bachelor. Died 1 April 1959, aged 85 years.

SKEWS BRENDA
Chart 41. Daughter of Joseph and Alice (née Lumb) Skews. Born 1933, Barnsley, South Yorkshire. Died 1933, aged 0.

SKEWIS BRENDA
Born 1975, Glasgow, Scotland.

SKEWIS BRENDA G.S.
Chart 50. Daughter of Alfred and Edith Alice (née Hughes) Skewis. Born 1924, Haverfordwest. Married Parsons, 1945, Haverfordwest.

SKEWS BRENDAN ASHLEY JAY
Lives at 32 Frome Avenue, Frankston, 3199, Victoria, Australia with Edmond John Skews and Hilda Margaret Skews. Labourer.

SKEWES BRETT LANIER
Chart 10. Son of Oswald and Alice (née Obenchain) Skewes of USA. Born 5 November 1974, Manassas, Virginia, 22110, USA.

SKEWIS BRIAN
Born 1951, Gorbals, Scotland. Married Patricia McAuley, 1973, Glasgow.

SKEWES BRIAN AINSLIE
Son of Ainslie Herbert Harvey and Muriel Edith (née Garnham) Skewes. Born 3 February 1948, Kew, Victoria, Australia. Lives at 12 Scammell Court, Mount Waverley, 3149, Victoria, Australia.

SKEWS BRIAN A.A.
Born 1934, Dartford, Kent. Mother's maiden name Atkinson. Married Alldis, 1958, Shoreditch. Children: Tina P. (1959) and Diana (1961).

SKEWS BRIAN A.E.
Chart 17. Son of Albert E and Jane (née Harding) Skews. Born 1938, Edmonton, London. Married Newby 1965, Edmonton. Children: Helen Dorothy (1969) and Theresa Jane (1973).

SKEWES BRIAN C.
Chart 36. Son of Cecil Skewes. Mother's maiden name Millett. Born 1937.

SKEWS BRIAN J.
Chart 41. Son of Joseph Skews. Mother's maiden name Lumb. Born 1946. Married Wharam, 1972, Barnsley.

SKEWES BRIAN LAWRENCE
Lives at 8 Maysbury Avenue, Elsternwick, 3185, Victoria, Australia with Yvonne Marie Skewes. Television mechanic.

SKEWES BRIAN LOCK
Chart 36. Son of Samuel Edgar and Erlestoun Minneta (née Mudge) Skewes. Born 14 September 1932. Married Barbara Jessie McKinlay 12 November 1955. Children: Janet Barbara (1957), David Brian (1958), Neville John (1962) and Kathryn Mary (1963). Lives at Currency Creek, Victor Harbour, 5251, South Australia.

SKEWES BRIAN SAMUEL
Chart 36. Son of William and Ida Olive (née Skewes) Skewes. Lives at 88 Rawson Avenue, Tamworth, 2340, New South Wales, Australia. Transport driver.

SKEWIS BRIAN W.
Married Coe in Lincolnshire, 1979.

SKEWES BRIAN WAYNE
Chart 38. Son of Norman and Ruth Melva (née Ellis) Skewes. Born 1 October 1946, Hindmarsh, Adelaide, South Australia. Married Irene Kaye Shammall 6 January 1968 at Enfield Methodist Church. Child: Rebecca Jade (1980). Lives at 18 Launceston Avenue, Banksia Park, 5091, South Australia.

SKUES BRIDGET MARY
Chart 3. Daughter of Reverend John Anthony and Rosemary (née Bamber) Skues. Born 12 March 1959. Lives at 8 Shirley Road, Walsgrave, Coventry. Telephone number 0203 614193.

SKEWES BRONWYN MAY
Chart 36. Daughter of Geoffrey and Dorothy May (née Chapman) Skewes. Born 21 August 1964. Lives at 35 Jean Street, Grange, 4051, Queensland, Australia.

SKEWES BRONWYN RUA MARY
Lives at 4 Netherby Street, Wahroonga, 2076, New South Wales, Australia. Retail buyer.

SKEWES BRUCE
Chart 36. Son of Glenleigh Bertie William and Mary Evelyn Harriet (née Watkins) Skewes. Born 21 May 1949. Married December, 1968. Children: David (1969) and Jodi Lynne (1972).

SKEWES BRUCE
Chart 36. Son of William Vere and Annie Rebecca (née Strain) Skewes. Born 24 November 1943, Australia. Married Judith Rosemary Taylor 10 February 1973. Printer. Children: Josie McLeod, Libby McLeod and Alexander McLeod. Lives at 21 Ridge Street, Tamworth, 2340, New South Wales, Australia.

SKEWES BRUCE ALEXANDER
Son of Henry Snowden and Marjorie Joyce (née Munro) Skewes. Born 24 November 1956. Lives at 1/45 Liberty Parade, Ivanhoe, 3079, Victoria, Australia.

SKEWES BRUCE PHILIP
Chart 36. Son of Edward Keith and Maisie (née Lawson) Skewes. Born 29 October 1953, Western Australia. Lives at 28 Perkins Road, Melville, Western Australia. Bachelor.

SKEWES BRYON ANTHONY
Chart 38. Son of William Seymour and Glenda Lorraine (née Walter) Skewes. Born 1 October 1974. Lives at 15 Alawa Avenue, Modbury North, Adelaide, 5000, Australia.

SKEWES BRYON PATRICK
Chart 42. Son of Jack and Shirley Beryl (née Callaghan) Skewes. Born 17 August 1955. Lives at 120 Smart Street, Fairfield, 2165, New South Wales, Australia. Motor mechanic.

SKEWES BYRON JAMES
Son of James Edward and Wilma (née Bacon) Skewes. Born 30 April 1918, New York. Married Margaret Cecilia Morrison, 13 September 1947, New York. Electronics technician. Served in US Army from 1940-1944 and 1950-1952. Later worked for Sperry Company and Grumman Company. Spent six years working on Grumman Moon Module which landed on the moon in 1969. Now works for the New York Telephone Company.
Children: Beatrice Donna, James William, Margaret Gail, Edward Nelson and William Byron.
Lives at 126 Toronto Avenue, Massapequa, New York, United States of America. Tel no: (516) 541 7627.

C

SKEWES CALVIN CHARLES
Lives at 21 Wangaroa Crescent, Mount Druitt, 2770, New South Wales, Australia.

SKEWES CARL
Chart 12. Son of Horace and Iris Verbina (née Jose) Skewes. Born 20 June 1940. Married Elizabeth Clackworthy September 1965 at Penzance. Children: Ian (1966) and Susan (1968). Divorced. Married Doreen Berryman of Brea, 1971. Child: Katherine (1971). Lives at 33 Roskear Road, Camborne. Works at Redruth Post Office.

SKEWES CARLTON B.
Chart 12. Son of John Henry and Florence (née Blenes) Skewes. Born 1950, Redruth.

SKUES CARMELA
Chart 9. Née Pinto. Born 16 June 1901. Married Philip Ernest Skues, 1922. Lived at 16 Ruxley Close, Ewell, Surrey. Children: Raymond Anthony (1929), Miriam M. (1937) and Sandra J. (1944). Died 17 January 1973, aged 71 years.

SKEWES CARMEN
Chart 10. Mexican. Daughter of Juan and Maria de Jesus (née Ortega) Skewes. Lives in Pachuca, Mexico.

SKEWES CARMEN VICTORIA
Chart 38. Daughter of Edward Kent and Susan Glenys (née Schramm) Skewes. Born 16 May 1974. Lives c/o Ungarra Post Office, 5610, Australia.

SKEWES   CAROL
Chart 40. Daughter of Henry and Ann Skewes. Mother's maiden name Morgan. Born 6 December 1946. Married John Lawrence 26 February 1972.

SKEWIS   CAROL
Born 1954, Dundee, Scotland.

SKEWIS   CAROL
Born 1964, Glasgow North, Scotland.

SKEWES   CAROL ANN
Chart 2. Daughter of Harry Blaine and Elizabeth Ann (née Laycock) Skewes. Born 1 March 1964, Houston, Texas, USA.

SKEWIS   CAROL ANN
Lives at 90 Mapleton Road, Nambour, 4560, Queensland, Australia with Noel Ernest Skewis.

SKEWES   CAROL ANN
Chart 38. Née Wright. Married Peter William Skewes 26 January 1968. Son: Craig Richard Skewes (1972). Her husband was killed in a car accident on 3 May 1972, aged 26 years in Sydney, Australia. Lives at 26 Geraint, Bracken Ridge, 4017, Queensland, Australia.

SKUES   CAROL C.A.
Chart 8. Mother's maiden name Kethro. Born 1942. Married Alan R. Cox in Weston, 1960.

SKEWES   CAROLE MARY
Chart 12. Daughter of Gilbert and Kathleen Skewes. Mother's maiden name Dennis. Born 20 May 1965, Kerrier.

SKEWES   CAROL WENDY
Chart 12. Daughter of William John and Wendy Violet (née Williams) Skewes. Born 19 January 1947, Helston. Lived at 27 Beacon Parc, Helston. Married John Treloar at St Michael's Church, Helston, 28 February 1969. Led the Helston Furry Dance (7.00 am and 5.00 pm) 7 May 1977 with her brother Peter. Issue: 1 son and 1 daughter. Lives at 32 Manor Way, Helston.

SKEWES   CAROLINE
Chart 2. Daughter of Henry and Grace Skewes, farmer. Bpt Constantine Church 18 July 1824. Married Alfred Knowles of Mabe, farmer, at Constantine 13 June 1849.

SKUES   CAROLINE
Chart 2. Daughter of Absalom and Jane Skues. Bpt Camborne 3 September 1825. Died 1869, aged 43 years.

SKEWES   CAROLINE
Née Laity. Born 1825. Married Richard Skewes of Mill Pool, Perranuthnoe, Penzance. Daughter: Emma (1856). Died 1903, aged 78 years.

SKEWES   CAROLINE
Born 1826, Camborne. Lived at Bassett Street, Camborne. Buried Camborne 10 January 1869, aged 43 years.

SKEWES   CAROLINE
Chart 25. Born 1830. Married Benjamin Hellings Skewes at Falmouth, 1859. Died 16 January 1909, aged 79 years at Carnon Crease, Perranwell.

SKEWES   CAROLINE
Chart 2. Daughter of Edward and Mary Skewes. Born 21 April 1833. Bpt Camborne Wesleyan/Methodist Chapel 16 June 1833. Married John Madrill. Emigrated.

SKEWES   CAROLINE
Married 1842, Redruth.

SKEWES   CAROLINE
Died 1848, Stoke Devonport.

SKEWES   CAROLINE
Married 1851, Plymouth.

SKEWES   CAROLINE
Married 1870, Lambeth.

SKEWES   CAROLINE
Chart 23. Née Nottage. Born 1872. Married George William Skews, 1892, Bethnal Green. Children: John George Skews (1897) and Francis (1900). Died Kettering, 1961, aged 89 years.

SKEWIS   CAROLINE
Born 1888, Redruth.

SKEWES   CAROLINE
Chart 36. Daughter of Samuel Sidney and Sarah (née Pennall) Skewes. Born 7 July 1902, New South Wales, Australia. Married David Dally Watkins in Sydney. Mother of June Dally Watkins, famous Australian model. Divorced and later married Bill James, musical director of Australian Broadcasting Commission. Died 6 October 1979, aged 77 years. Ashes interred in Bendemeer Cemetery, New South Wales, Australia.

SKEWS   CAROLINE ANNE
Born 1862, North Aylesford.

SKEWS   CAROLINE CHARLOTTE
Born 1902, Bethnal Green. Married Askew in Kettering, 1922.

SKEWIS   CAROLINE GRACE
Chart 2. Daughter of Edward George and Margaret Skewis of America. Born 2 October 1944. Married Michael Sigler in America 19 December 1963. Issue two sons. Died 9 October 1973, aged 29

Caroline Skewes (1902-1979)

years.

SKEWES   CAROLINE LOUISE
Born 1910, Truro. Died 1914, aged 4 years.

SKEWES   CAROLINE MARY
Chart 36. Daughter of William and Elizabeth (née Northey) Skewes. Born 13 January 1876, Uralla, New South Wales, Australia. Married Frank Fearby, 1896, Uralla. Issue: 1 son and 1 daughter. Died 22 June 1956, aged 80 years in Warwick, Queensland, Australia.

SKEWES   CAROLINE TREWEEK
Chart 19. Bpt Gwennap 17 December 1829. Daughter of John and Jennifer Skewes, farmer and miner of Poldice.

SKEWES   CAROLO
Chart 10. Mexican. Son of Henry and Lourdes (née Escudero) Skewes. Born 3 February 1973. Lives in Real del Monte, Mexico.

SKEWES   CAROLO FEDERICO
Chart 10. Mexican. Son of Salvador and Carmen (née Ramirez) Skewes. Born 15 March 1950. Died following being hit in the stomach. Lived in Real del Monte, Mexico. Died 6 July 1967, aged 17 years.

SKEWIS   CAROLYN
Chart 2. Daughter of William and Martha Skewis of United States of America. Born 19 September 1876. Married Henry F. Storjohakn. Died 4 February 1918, aged 41 years.

SKUES   CAROLYN LOUISE
Chart 7. Daughter of Roydon Thomas and Valerie (née Cooke) Skues. Born 15 February 1971. Lives at 16 Lower Drive, Seaford, Sussex.

SKEWES   CARRIE
Married 1908, Redruth.

SKEWES   CARYL I.
Married Muntz in Kensington, 1956.

SKEWIS CATHERINE
Chart 2. Daughter of Bennett Osborne and Martha Skewis of America.

SKEWES   CATHERINE
Daughter of John and Catherine Skewes. Bpt St Buryan Parish Church, Cornwall 18 June 1724.

SKEWES   CATHERINE
Daughter of Martin Skewes. Bpt Kenwyn 24 February 1738.

SKEWS   CATHERINE
Married James Barnicoat at Falmouth 2 February 1752.

SKEWES   CATHERINE
Daughter of William and Hannah Skewes. Bpt St Gluvias, Cornwall 23 May 1756. Buried St Gluvias 11 April 1773, aged 17 years.

SKEWES   CATHERINE
Chart 10. Daughter of Digory and Margery Skewes. Bpt Kea 3 February 1760. Married John Wasley at Kea Parish Church 14 June 1783.

SKEWES   CATHERINE
Chart 18. Daughter of Thomas Skewes of Kea. Bpt at Kea 31 May 1773. Mrd John Thomas at Kenwyn 8 Jan 1795.

SKEWIS   CATHERINE
Chart 2. Daughter of John and Philippa Skewis. Bpt Camborne 2 February 1777. Married George Prout, husbandman, 16 May 1801. Witness: John Skewes.

SKEWES CATHERINE
Chart 30. Née Wasley. Married Henry Skewes at Kenwyn Parish Church 22 May 1793. Children: Mary Jolly, Ebenezer John Thomas and Henry.

SKEWIS   CATHERINE
Chart 36. Daughter of John and Jane Skewis of Illogan, yeoman. Bpt Illogan 18 December 1813.

SKUES   CATHERINE
Chart 2. Daughter of Edward and Mary Skues. Born 19 May 1824. Bpt 6 June 1824 at Camborne/Redruth Wesleyan Chapel. In 1841 Census Returns was "Dressing Ore". Buried Camborne 21 February 1846, aged 22 years.

SKEWES   CATHERINE
Chart 14. Daughter of Anthony and Christian Skewes of Tresodden. Bpt Ruan Major 16 April 1843. Living at Tresodden in 1871 Census Returns.

SKEWIS   CATHERINE
Living in Jo Daviess County, Melville, Illinois, United States of America, 1850.

SKEWES   CATHERINE
Chart 10. Née Williams. Daughter of Michael Williams, grocer. Second wife of John Skewes of Pachuca, Mexico. Married at Chacewater Parish Church 4 January 1880. (She was born 16 June 1854.) Children: John Herbert (1881), Hilda Laura Williams (1882), Grace Elizabeth (1883), Katie Beatrice (1885) and Thomas Edgar (1886). Died 12 April 1889, aged 34 years at Ivy Cottage, Chacewater.

SKEWS   CATHERINE
Died 1862, Greenwich.

SKEWIES   CATHERINE
Born 1863. Died Hamilton, Scotland, 1885, aged 22 years.

SKEWES   CATHERINE
Daughter of Henry Skewes of Redruth. Married James Martin, baker, aged 22 (son of Martin Martin) at Helston 23 April 1863.

SKEWES   CATHERINE
Born 1870, Redruth.

SKEWES   CATHERINE
Born 1897, Redruth.

SKEWES   CATHERINE
of Condurrow, Redruth. Born 6 February 1901. Died 6 February 1901, aged 1 hour. Unbaptised. Buried Tuckingmill 6 February 1901.

SKEWES   CATHERINE
Married Phillips, 1930, Redruth.

SKEWES   CATHERINE
Chart 36. Born 23 January 1889. Married Walter Nicholas Skewes 16 April 1913, St John's Church, Treslothan. Lived at 42a Fore Street, Beacon and later 36 Coronation Avenue, Camborne. Children: Cecil (1916) and Leslie (1920). Died Redruth 1971, aged 82 years.

SKEWS   CATHERINE
Chart 41. Daughter of Thomas Ernest and Lily R. (née Brayford) Skews. Born 1954, Wombwell, Barnsley, South Yorkshire. Married Stephen Lowe 11 November 1978. Lives at St Annes, Blackpool, Lancashire.

SKEWES   CATHERINE ANN
Chart 50. Daughter of Leo William and Betty (née Thompson) Skewes. Born 18 March 1955, New South Wales, Australia. Bank clerk. Lives at 2/11 William Street, Lambton, 2229, New South Wales, Australia with her sister Vicki Louise Skewes.

SKEWES   CATHERINE ANN S.
Born 1881, Redruth.

SKEWS   CATHERINE ELIZABETH
In 1959 lived at Lot 45, Arlunya Avenue, Cloverdale, Belmont, Western Australia. Machinist. Now lives at 23 Valentine Street, Morawa, 6623, Western Australia with Kenneth Harold Skews.

SKEWS   CATHERINE ELIZABETH MARY

Born 1839, Derby. Died 1840, aged 1 year.

SKUES   CATHERINE ELIZABETH N.
Chart 8. Née Brasset. Married Alfred Edgar Skues 1940. Children: Terence F. (1947) and Shirley C.J. (1941). Died 1975, aged 59 years.

SKEWES   CATHERINE M.
Born 1841. Died 1916, Falmouth, aged 75 years.

SKEWES   CATHERINE M.
Chart 38. Daughter of Ernest William Seymour and Eleanor May (née Stapleton) Skewes. Born 16 November 1924. Married Michael Shuttleworth. Issue: one son and three daughters.

SKEWES   CATHERINE MARY
Chart 10. Née Richards. Lived at Germoe, Ashton, Helston. Married Joseph John Skewes of Marazion. Emigrated to America in the 1890's. Children: William Joseph Skewes (1895) and Herbert Tregonning Skewes (1898). Her sister Elizabeth Richards married Joseph John's brother Henry Skewes who also emigrated to America.

SKEWES   CATHERINE MARY
Chart 14. Daughter of William John Skewes of America.

SKEWES   CATHERINE MARY
Born 1882, Helston.

SKEWES   CATHERINE PATRICIA
Lives at 28 Leawarra Crescent, Doncaster East, Victoria, 3109, Australia, with Jennifer Ann Skewes.

SKEWES   CECILIA
Chart 38. Née Andrew. Married Richard James Skewes, 20 September 1902, Moonta, South Australia

SKEWES   CECILIA
Chart 50. Daughter of Thomas and Sarah Ann (née Lord) Skewes. Born Australia. Married Retallick. Died 14 March 1930.

SKEWES   CECELIA
Chart 36. Daughter of Neville Percy and Helen (née O'Lockland) Skewes. Born 17 September 1962, Australia.

SKUES   CECIL
Chart 3. Son of Ernest and Clara (née Roberts) Skues. Born 14 June 1897, Nottingham. Attended Barnsley Grammar School. During his school days he owned, printed and produced the Form Magazine of which he was chief editor and principal contributor. He was called up for military duty in the First World War, having left school in 1913 and become a clerk to an accountant. Private Cecil Skues became a signaller with King's Own Rifle Corps and was killed in action whilst signalling in France, 20 May 1917, aged 19 years. A year previous he had attended his grandfather Richard Skues' funeral in Halifax. He is mentioned on his grandparents grave at Salterhebble, Halifax, West Yorkshire (All Saints Cemetery).

SKEWES   CECIL
Chart 36. Son of Walter Nicholas and Kate (née Ford) Skewes. Born 1916. Married Dolores E. Millett in Redruth, 1937. Lives at 51 Pendarves Street, Beacon, Redruth. Children: Brian C. (1937) and Shirley A. (1939).

SKEWES   CECIL
Married Williams, 1952, Redruth.

SKEWES   CECIL JOHN
In 1959 was living at Newton Kadina, South Australia, with Barbara Allen Skewes. Farmer.

SKEWES   CELIA
Chart 10. Daughter of Juan and Sereto (née Castro) Skewes. Spinster. Lives in Mexico City.

SKEWES   CELIA
Chart 12. Née Holbrook who lived at Higher Relouas, Mawgan. Married Oswald C. Skewes 27 September 1958, at Mawgan Parish Church. Children: Susan (1959) and John (1963). Lived at Goonhilly Downs (Telstar) Filling Station until 1970. Now lives at Trezemper Farm, Goonhilly Downs, Mawgan, Helston. Tel. No: Mawgan 607.

SKEWES   CELIA ELIZABETH
Chart 50. Daughter of Thomas Grenville and Ilma Elizabeth (née Dodd) Skewes. Born 1 January 1943, Victoria, Australia. Married Roger D'Orr 19 December 1963. Issue: three children.

SKEWES   CERCEDA EMILY
Chart 2. Daughter of William Henry and Catherine (née Collins, née Tregonning) Skewes. Born 18 August 1881, Australia. Spinster. Died 6 July 1942, aged 61 years.

SKEWES   CERETA
Chart 30. Daughter of William Brown and Blanche Skewes, housepainter of Union Street, Truro. Born 1887. Bpt St Mary's, Truro 28 November 1887. Lived at 9 St Dominic Street, Truro. Married William Thomas Rowe (29), labourer of Grampound Road and son of John Rowe, labourer, deceased; at St George's, Truro 30 December 1911.

SKEWES   CERETA BETTY
Daughter of William John and Rose (née Drew) Skewes of Charles Street, Truro, painter and later Daniell Square. Born 29 September 1924. Bpt St John's, Truro 4 November 1924. Married Auster Jack Charles Crawford Gosling (29), clerk, of Old Mansion House, Truro, son of Samuel Auster Gosling, lorry driver; at St George's, Truro 14 February 1948.

SKEWES CHARITY
Chart 2. Née Ellis. Wife of James Skewes, pauper. Married 10 April 1763, Camborne. Died 3 July 1787.

SKEWES CHARITY
of Carvanell. Born 1798. Buried Gwennap 27 February 1858, aged 60 years.

SKEWES CHARITY
Daughter of James and Susannah Skewes of Lanner, Gwennap. Bpt Gwennap 23 January 1813. Married Thomas Grey at Gwennap 2 August 1834.

SKUSE CHARLES
Married Johanna Clarke, 1633, Ottery St Mary.

SCUES CHARLES
Son of Charles Scues. Bpt Ottery St Mary 19 January 1645.

SKUES CHARLES
Chart 3. Son of John and Mary Skues of Helston. Bpt Helston Parish Church 26 March 1786. Married Mary Bennett 5 January 1815 at Helston. Later moved to London where he became a druggist and tailor living at 18 Lower Queen Street, Westminster (1827 London Street Directory). Children: Charlotte and Mary Bennett Skues. He died 11 January 1841, aged 55 years at 42 Dean Street, London W.1.

SKEWES CHARLES
Chart 14. Son of Samuel Skewes of America and twin to Earl Skewes. Children: Charles J. Jnr and Helen Ann.

SKUES CHARLES
Chart 5. Eldest son of Joseph Penrose Skues. He emigrated to Australia from Redruth, Cornwall around 1860. Children: Oliver Harold Skues and Reginald Skues.

SKEWES CHARLES
Chart 25. Born 1838, Falmouth, Cornwall. Son of Thomas Skewes. Married Elizabeth.....of St Michael's Mount in 1857. In 1861 Census Returns was living at Smithwick Hill, Falmouth. In 1871 Census Returns was living at Brook Street, Falmouth. Children: Charles (1857), William John (1860), George (1861), Edward (1864) and Louisa Jane (1870). Left Falmouth in 1870's (trade: shoemaker) to carry on his trade in Rossendale Valley, Lancashire. Later moved to Manchester and was employed as bootmaker, St Anne's Square. Died 1911, aged 73 years. Buried Weaste Cemetery. His wife Elizabeth died 1892, aged 62 years.

SKUES CHARLES
Born 1843. Died Grimsby 1910, aged 66 years.

SKEWS CHARLES
Born 1845. Died 1922, Poplar, London, aged 77 years.

SKUES CHARLES
Born 1845. Son of Samuel Skues. Married Sarah Haynes (30) at the Parish Church, Sheffield 31 December 1873. Both of them resided at Barkers Pool, Sheffield, South Yorkshire. Mason.

SKEWES CHARLES
Chart 5. Son of John and Sarah (née Tubb), mason of East Turnpike, Redruth. Born 20 June 1846 at 2.00am. Married 1865, Pancras, London.

SKEWES CHARLES
Chart 25. Son of Charles and Elizabeth Skewes of Smithwick Hill, Falmouth. Born 1857. Was a baker's errand boy in 1871 Census Returns. Moved north with his parents in 1870's. Married Ann.....1883, Chorlton, Manchester. Lived at 15 Horton Street, Rusholme, Manchester. One daughter Elizabeth (1886). Died 26 July 1941, aged 83 years. Wife Ann died Manchester, 1946, aged 95 years.

SKEWES CHARLES
Died 1864, Redruth.

SKEWES CHARLES
Born 1865, Helston. Died 1865, aged 0.

SKEWS CHARLES
Chart 15. Son of John and Isabella Skews of Launceston. Bpt Altarnun 29 December 1866. In 1871 Census Returns living at Trewint, Altarnun with his brothers Amos, John and Harry. Emigrated to Napier, New Zealand about 1880.

SKEWES CHARLES
Born 6 September 1881. Son of William Skewes of Roaches Row, Redruth. Attended Redruth East End Primary School from 23 March 1885 to 19 July 1886. Died 1904, aged 24 years.

SKEWES CHARLES
Born 19 March 1881, son of Amelia Skewes, single woman of Truro. Bpt St Mary's, Truro 28 August 1882. Attended St George's School, Truro from 31 January 1888. Married 1905.

SKEWES CHARLES
of Truro. Baker. Married Ellen Hawkins 20 June 1884 at Truro Cathedral.

SKEWES CHARLES
Born 1889, Chorlton, Manchester. Died 1895, aged 5 years.

SKEWES CHARLES
Chart 25. Son of Edward and Eliza (née Maddocks) Skewes. Born 1889, Manchester. Married Mary Gichero, 1914, Chorlton, Manchester. One son Edward (1915). Was a civil servant in Inland Revenue. Served in ar-

my in France in World War I. Was badly gassed and suffered from tuberculosis for rest of his life. Died 1943, aged 54 years in Salford.

SKEWES CHARLES
Born 1892. Died Redruth, 1892, aged 0.

SKEWS CHARLES
Married 1896, St Austell.

SKEWS CHARLES
Married 1898, Salford.

SKEWS CHARLES
Born 1908, Bethnal Green. Died 1909, aged 0.

SKEWES CHARLES
Chart 36. Lived at Whitecross Hill, Illogan, 1922. Wife's name Ada Jane (née Collins).

SKEWES CHARLES
Lived at Penpol, Chariot Road, Illogan Highway, 1949.

SKEWES CHARLES
Lived at Helstonwater, Perranwell Station, Kea in 1932 with Bessie Annie Skewes.

SKEWES CHARLES ANDREW
Chart 11. Son of Thomas John III and Virginia Ann (née Day) Skewes. Born 4 October 1964, Seattle, Washington, USA.

SKEWES CHARLES ARMINGTON
Chart 2. Son of John Billing III and Mary Jo (née Armington) Skewes of Utah, USA. Born 4 February 1949, San Juan County, Utah, USA. Graduated from Utah State University, 1975 with BSc (Bachelor of Science) in Civil Engineering; Married Lucinda Lee 25 September 1971. Children: April Lynn (1974), Matthew Charles (1976) and Katy Lee (1980).

SKEWIS CHARLES ARTHUR
Chart 2. Son of Robert and Ruth Skewis of Iowa. Born 21 January 1955. Bachelor.

SKUES CHARLES AYRE MACKENZIE
Chart 3. Youngest son of William Mackenzie Skues, M.D. and Margaret (née Ayre). Born 2 October 1875. Attended Dulwich College. Was in Rugby Football XV in 1894. Captain in Royal Garrison Artillery (Special Reserve) in First World War. Married Elizabeth Gaute 12 August 1903. Children: Sheila Mackenzie and Joan Mackenzie (twins, 1904). He was the first SKUES on the telephone (1914). He became a surveyor with Smallpiece and Allen. Later qualified F.R.I.C.S. working from 45 Lincoln's Inn Fields, London WC2 (1920-1950) and later 16 Tooks Court, London EC4. In 1939 he was Secretary of the "Pure Rivers Society."
Often mentioned in The Field alongside his brother GEM Skues, the angler.
Lived at 20 Copers Cope Road, Beckenham, Kent until 1957 when his daughter Joan Mackenzie Skues took her life at Bickley railway station, Kent. He moved north to Yew Tree Cottage, Stafford Road, Market Drayton, Shropshire where he died 12 April 1958, aged 82 years.

SKEWES CHARLES COLLAN
Chart 19. Son of Thomas Lean and Elizabeth Ann Skewes. Born 1856. Died 1856, Wareham, aged 0.

SKEWIS CHARLES EDWARD
Chart 2. Son of Charles Elmer and Leotice Skewis. Born 17 February 1940, America. Married Sharon Rajchel, September 1952. Son Lawrence Charles and daughter Tamara.

SKEWIS CHARLES ELMER
Chart 2. Son of Francis Harry and Annie Skewis and twin brother to Edward George Skewis. Married Leotice Hartman, 4 February 1934.

SKEWES CHARLES FREDERICK
Chart 46. Born 4 October 1883. Sailor. Married Bessie Teague 12 May 1907 at Falmouth. Lived at 76, Chapel Hill, Truro. Was in the navy for 22 years. Became chief stoker. Children: William Douglas, Frederick John Charles and Ernest Lloyd.

SKEWES CHARLES GEORGE
Chart 14. Adopted son of Richard Edwin and Victoria (néeLohman Holey) Skewes. Born 6 February 1962. Died 23 November 1976, aged 14 years. Took his own life.

SKUES CHARLES GILBERT
Chart 8. Son of John Gilbert Skues. Born 1898. Married Elsie K. Wyatt in Edmonton, 1928. One daughter Sylvia G. Skues. Awarded DSM in March 1943 for bravery as a temporary acting leading seaman serving in South Africa. Later was made Acting Petty Officer (temp). Drowned at sea during Second World War aboard S.S. Cathay. Elsie died 1965, aged 69 years.

SKEWES CHARLES GILLES
Chart 25. Son of Thomas and Eleanor Skewes. Born 4 May 1793, Falmouth. Bpt 14 July 1793, Falmouth.

SKEWES CHARLES HAROLD VIVIAN
Chart 36. Son of William Hicks Skewes formerly of Cury. Born 30 May 1885, Australia. Married Emiline Lamphee 18 March 1912, West Midland, Western Australia. Lived at 16 Grant Street, Scarborough, Balcutta, Australia. Children: Douglas William (1912), Edward Keith (1913), Olive (1916), Mervyn (1919), Edith (1922) and Kenneth (1924). Died 28 September 1970, aged 85 years.

Charles Harold Vivian Skewes (1883-1970)

Helen; one brother Earl, of Dayton, Ohio and one sister Mrs G. Francher.

SKEWES   CHARLES J. Jnr
Chart 14. Son of Charles J. and Mamie Skewes of Racine, Wisconsin. Married Loretta Jean Swanson. Lives at Route 1, Box 282 Weyanwega, Wis. 54983, United States of America. Children: Michael Jess, Clint Charles, Jane, William Raymond and Sarah Marie.

SKUES   CHARLES JOHN
Chart 9. Born 1843. Worked with the Post Office. Died 1878, aged 35 years.

SKUES   CHARLES JOSEPH
Lived at Barclay Place, Bendigo, Victoria, Australia in 1912. Agent.

SKEWES   CHARLES LESLIE
Chart 38. Son of Richard and Mary Jane (née Reynolds) Skewes. Born 26 January 1896, Moonta, South Australia. Married Ellen Jane Ritter, 22 September 1917. Died 23 March 1948, aged 52 years.

SKUES   CHARLES PENROSE
Chart 5. Son of John Penrose and Sally (née Tubb) Skues. Born 20 June 1846 (2.00am), Redruth. Lived at East Turnpike, Redruth, and later Hodder's Row, Redruth. Bpt Redruth Parish Church 3 March 1850. Later moved to London. Married Emily.....1869, Marylebone. Children: Emily Jane, Eleanor Lucy, Bessie Annie, William John, Charles Henry and Reginald Penrose. In 1894 Trades Directory for London he was listed as a cabinet maker of 59 Stone Road, Shepherd's Bush, London. His wife Emily was listed as a dressmaker at the same address. Died 1939, aged 92 years in Amersham.

SKEWES   CHARLES PERCIVAL
Chart 38. Son of Edgar William and Mary Bridget (née Kavanagh) Skewes. Born 28 November 1916. Miner. Married Nancy Merle Ham 23 July 1948, Broken Hill, Australia. Children: James Charles (1950), Thomas Edgar (1954) and Francine Jean (1956). Died 28 December 1970, aged 54 years. Worked as a shift boss at the Zinc Corporation in Broken Hill. Served in the Royal Air Force during the Second World War.

SKUES   CHARLES PICKARD
Chart 3. Born 1864, Halifax, Yorkshire. Died 1865, aged 0.

SKEWS   CHARLES R.
Chart 10. Son of Peter Skews. Mother's maiden name Rickard. Born 1916.

SKEWIS   CHARLES SAMUEL
Chart 2. Son of James and Jane (née Rabling) Skewis. Born 21 February 1869, Wisconsin, USA. Married Myrtle Howe 23 October 1895 (she was born 1869, Illinois, USA and died 21 December 1954). Children: Dorothy Delphine (1900), Margaret Josephine (1905) and Elizabeth Marion (1908). Died 21 December 1954, aged 80 years.

SKEWES   CHARLES STEPHEN
Born 1863 Redruth, Cornwall.

SKEWES   CHARLES TREVALYAN
In 1959 was living at Kitchen Avenue, Belgrave, Ferntree Gully, Victoria, Australia with Ethel May Skewes.

SKUES   CHARLES WILLIAM
Born 1869, Westminster. Died 1871, aged 2 years.

SKEWS   CHARLES WILLIAM
Born 1896, Liskeard, Cornwall.

SKEWES   CHARLOTTE
Chart 2. Daughter of Raymond and Lottie Skewis. Born in America.

SKUES   CHARLOTTE
Daughter of Charles and Ann Skues of Helston, tailor. Born 4 April 1816. Bpt Helston Circuit 28 April 1816.

SKEWS   CHARLOTTE
Chart 17. Born 1820. Née Dane. Daughter of Nathaniel Dane, shoe manufacturer. Married George Skews at St Paul's Church, Chalk, North Aylesford, Kent. Children: Richard Nathaniel Edwin (1844) and George Alfred (1846). Died Chelsea 1902, aged 82 years.

SKEWES   CHARLOTTE
Married Caleb Jennine at Kea 7 July 1836.

SKEWES   CHARLOTTE
Daughter of Charles and Mary Skewes. Married Robert Bryant. Daughter Emma Bryant bpt 21 November 1836 at Truro Wesleyan Chapel.

SKEUSE   CHARLOTTE
Born 1839, Portsea.

SKEWES   CHARLOTTE
Chart 47, Born 1891. Married Samuel John Skewes 1915, Bodmin. Lived at Dunmere, Kelly Bray, Callington, Cornwall. Children: Winifred A. (1915) and Rose Pearl Skewes (1926). Died 26 November 1961, aged 70 years.

SKEUS   CHARLOTTE LOUISA
Daughter of Jonathan and Jane Skeus. Bpt St Ewe, Cornwall 20 June 1835.

SKEWES   CHARLOTTE LOUISE
Chart 40. Daughter of Colin Skewes. Mother's maiden name Jordan. Born 1972, St Austell.

SKEWES   CHARLES HENRY
Chart 2. Son of William and Sarah Skewes of Roskear Fields, Camborne. Born 1 April 1865, Camborne. Emigrated to USA with his family (Salt Lake City), 1871. Undertaker. Married Clara Heath. Died America 29 March 1948 at Portland, Oregon, aged 82 years. Child: One daughter Doris, spinster who died in Salt Lake City.

SKUES   CHARLES HENRY
Chart 5. Son of Charles Penrose Skues. Born 1877, Marylebone. Lived at "Mawgan", 11 Priory Road, Chalfont St Peter, Bucks. Was an office accountant. Died 28 December 1958, aged 81 years.

SKEWES   CHARLES J.
Chart 14. Son of Samuel and Mary Skewes of Racine, Wisconsin. Born 30 October 1893. They lived on 11th Street, Racine. He was educated in local schools and during the years 1923 and 1924 he served as deputy under Sheriff George Wherry. In 1927 he was elected Sheriff and served two years, his administration of that office being declared exceptionally efficient. When the county board of supervisors came to the decision that workers on the county highways needed the protection of an officer, Charles was selected for that duty. He served in that capacity for two years, but was taken ill and had to undergo an operation in January 1932. He took early retirement at his residence at 1021 Hayes Avenue, but a second operation was found necessary. He died at St Mary's Hospital at 10.10pm on Friday 18 March 1932, aged 38 years.
Charles Skewes was a member of the American Legion having served at Camp Taylor during World War One and was a member of Belle City Lodge of Free and Accepted Masons.
He was survived by his widow, one son Charles J. Junior; one daughter

SKEWES CHARLOTTE MARY
Daughter of John and Ann Skewes of Three Mile Stone, Kea. Born 1847, Gwennap. In 1851 Census living at Three Mile Stone, Kea with her parents and sisters Elizabeth Ann and Mary Ann.

SKEWES CHARLOTTE MARY JANE
Born 1847, Redruth.

SKEWS CHARLOTTE REBECCA
Born 1883, Bethnal Green. Married 1910.

SKUES CHARLOTTE SOPHIA
Born 1854, St James, London. Married 1876, Westminster.

SKEWES CHARMAINE
Née Burles. Married Ian Thomas Skewes, grocer. Children: Penny (1974) and Jason (1978) Lives at Clyde Road, Clyde, 3978, Victoria, Australia.

SKEWES CHERITY
Married James Hockin at St Keverne Parish Church 29 July 1623.

SKEWES CHERYL ANNE
Chart 36. Née Sproule. Married Maxwell Charles Skewes, 13 January 1968, Tamworth, Australia. Children: Tania Maree (1968) and Jason Maxwell (1971). Lives at 12 Julia Place, Moree, 2400, New South Wales, Australia.

SKEWES CHERYLYN KAY
Chart 36. Daughter of Trevor John and Bonnie (née Kite) Skewes. Born 2 January 1964. Lives c/o P.O. Box 96, Stirling, 5152, Australia.

SKEWES CHRISTIAN
Wife of Stephen Skewes (married St Just in Roseland, 7 May 1605). Buried 14 September 1622, St Just in Roseland.

SKEWES CHRISTIAN
Daughter of Stephen and Christian Skewes. Bpt St Just in Roseland 7 May 1620. Married Michael Buckseene at St Just in Roseland 2 November 1646.

SKEWS CHRISTIAN
Married Nicholas Vinicom at Exeter, 1617.

SKEWES CHRISTIAN
Chart 19. Born 1770. Married Alexander Skewes of Gwennap. Children: Grace, Margaret, Richard, Joanna, Christian Martyn, Alexander, William, Elizabeth, Mary and Ann. Died 7 November 1833 of consumption, aged 63 years.

SKEWS CHRISTIAN
Buried Kea, 14 March 1740.

SKEWES CHRISTIAN
Chart 14. Born 1814. Wife of Anthony Skewes of Ruan Major. Children: Mary, Ann, Catherine, James, Henry, Samuel, William, Edward, Hannibal and George. In 1871 Census Returns living at Tresodden, Ruan Major. Died 1887, aged 73 years.

SKEWES CHRISTIAN
Chart 36. Daughter of William and Christian Skewes. Bpt St Keverne 18 March 1832. Emigrated to Australia aboard "Merchantman", which sailed from Plymouth, 11 January 1854 and arrived in Melbourne 20 April 1854. Engaged by Edward Cotton of Richmond at a rate of £27 per annum, including rations, for a period of one month.

SKEWES CHRISTIAN
Chart 2. Daughter of William and Elizabeth Skewes of Bolitho, Crowan. Born 1838, Budock. In 1851 Census Returns living at Bolitho with her parents and sisters Grace and Elizabeth and brothers Joseph, James and John.

SKEWES CHRISTIAN
Chart 14. Daughter of Anthony and Christian Skewes of Tresodden, Ruan Major. Bpt Ruan Major 26 September 1841.

SKEWES CHRISTIAN
Died 1842, Helston.

SKEWES CHRISTIAN
Chart 36. Née Lugg. Married William Skewes at Ruan Major 28 March 1815. Children: James (1815), John (1816), Edward (1819), Elizabeth (1821), Ann (1825), Henry (1827), William (1829), Christian (1832), Grace (1834), John (1836) and Samuel (1838). Buried in Mawnan churchyard 11 November 1865.

SKEWES CHRISTIAN KATE
Married 1870, Helston.

SKEWES CHRISTIAN MARTYN
Chart 19. Daughter of Alexander and Christian Skewes. Bpt Gwennap 23 May 1805. Married John Martin at Gwennap 12 February 1829. Children called Skewes Martin.

SKEWES CHRISTINA A.
Mother's maiden name Lundell. Born Edmonton, 1940.

SKEWES CHRISTINE
Married Simcock in Calder, 1965.

SKEWIS CHRISTINE
Married Dalee in Hull, 1974.

SKEWES CHRISTINE ANNE
Daughter of Marjorie Keeler and John A. Gallagher. Born 4 June 1950. Married James William Skewes, 23 June 1973, New York, USA.

SKEWES CHRISTINE ANN
Chart 50. Daughter of David Buick and Irene Margaret (née Murphy) Skewes. Born 20 April 1952, Ballarat, Victoria, Australia. Married Francis John Bongiorno, 23 April 1973. Issue: 3 sons. Lives at Booruga Place, P.O. Box 95, Popondetta, Papua New Guinea.

SKEWES CHRISTINE CAROL
Lives at Noosa Woods Caravan Park, Noosa Heads, 4567, Queensland, Australia with Francis Raymond Skewes.

SKUES CHRISTINE EVELYN
Chart 7. Daughter of Edwin Thomas Skues. Mother's maiden name Hawkins. Born 1945, Dartford, Kent. Married Bourne, 1972 in Chanctonbury.

SKEWIS CHRISTINE J.
Mother's maiden name Gilbert. Born 1938, Tonbridge, Kent. Married Harrison, 1963.

SKEWES CHRISTINE JOY
Chart 50. Daughter of Leo William and Betty (née Thompson) Skewes. Born 2 July 1953, New South Wales, Australia.

SKEWES CHRISTINE MARGARET
Lives at 64 Arnott Street, Trigg, 6022, Western Australia. Bookbinder.

SKEWES CHRISTINE THIRZA
Lives at 66 King Street, Solomontown, 5540, South Australia with Ronald Leonard Skewes.

SKEWES CHRISTOPHER
Son of Steven and Christian Skewes. Bpt St Just in Roseland 24 February 1609. Buried St Just in Roseland 28 August 1611, aged 2½ years.

SCUES CHRISTOPHER
Son of Christopher Scues. Bpt Camborne 16 May 1680.

SKEWS CHRISTOPHER
Son of Richard and Rebecca Skews. Bpt Sancreed 8 June 1729. Married Honor Angwyn at Sancreed 31 July 1750.

SKEWS CHRISTOPHER
Bpt Sancreed 29 August 1797.

SKEWS CHRISTOPHER
Chart 23. Son of John G.P. and Dorothy (née Boyland) Skews. Born 1954, Bourne. Lives at 5 Lime Tree Avenue, Peterborough. Tel no: 0733 62073.

SKEWES CHRISTOPHER ALLEN
Chart 36. Son of Jack Roe and Dorothy May (née Burn) Skewes. Born 1 August 1954, Adelaide, South Australia. Lives at 16 Alawa Road, Ingle Farm, South Australia, 5098.

SKUES CHRISTOPHER A.J.
Mother's maiden name Falk. Born Hammersmith, 1965.

SKUES CHRISTOPHER HERBERT VICTOR
Chart 8. Son of Walter Edward and Florence Skues. Born 1917. Married Winifred C. Kethro in Bristol, 1941. One daughter Carol C.A. (1942). Winifred remarried Morgan, 1952.

SKEWS CHRISTOPHER J.
Mother's maiden name Berryman. Born 1940, Brentford.

SKEWES CHRISTOPHER JAMES
Chart 38. Son of James Charles Skewes. Born 7 February 1979. Lives in Broken Hill, 2880, New South Wales, Australia.

SKEWES CHRISTOPHER JOHN
Chart 12. Son of William John and Wendy (née Williams) Skewes. Born 1 December 1948, Helston. Lived at 27 Beacon Parc, Helston. Lorry driver. Married Hazel Williams 28 February 1976. Children: Mark Christopher (1978) and David John and Michelle (1980), twins. Lives at 23 St John's Terrace, Helston. Tel no: 03265 2064.

SKEWES CHRISTOPHER LINDSAY
Lives at 6 Tuart Street, Blakehurst, 2221, New South Wales, Australia. Accountant.

SKEWS CHRISTOPHER R.
Chart 17. Son of Ernest W. and . . . (née Falconer) Skews. Born 1946, Essex SW. Married Kempson, 1968, Waltham Forest. Children: David Falconer (1972) and Nicola Jane (1975).

SKUES CHRISTOPHER RAYMOND
Chart 3. Son of Richard and Doris Eileen (née Hughes) Skues. Born 2 July 1949, Manchester. Died 19 February 1950 at "Richleen", 21 Buckingham Grove, Timperley, Cheshire, aged 7 months. Service at St George's Church, Stockport, Cheshire followed by cremation at Stockport Crematorium.

SKUES CLAIR
Chart 8. Daughter of Terence F. and Jean Skues. Mother's maiden name Moore. Born 1971, Barking.

SKEWIS CLARA
Born 1855. Died Leadhills, Scotland, 1911, aged 56 years.

SKEWES CLARA
Chart 10. Née Trevena. Born 1861. Married Samuel Skewes of Marazion, 1885. Children: Annie (1886) and William Trevena (1890). Died 1945, aged 83 years.

Children: Ryan James (1974) and Kerry Ann (1975). Lives at 169 Westwood Drive, Brentwood, New York, 11717, United States of America.

SKUES CLARA
Chart 3. Née Roberts of Nottingham. Born 11 June 1875. Married Ernest Skues, 1897, Nottingham. Children: Cecil (1897), Vincent (1898), Richard (1904), Florence Muriel (1905) and Jack (1911). Lived at 1 Ashburn Grove, Heaton Norris, Stockport, Cheshire. Died February, 1961 at Hazel Grove, Cheshire, aged 86 years.

SKEWES CLARA
Born 1877, Redruth. Married 1902.

SKEWS CLARA
Born 1883, Houghton. Died 1884, aged 1 year.

SKEWES CLARA ANN
Chart 33. Daughter of Daniel and Elizabeth Skewes. Born 1866, Newton Abbot, Devon. Married 1889 to Eggbeer from Ashburton, Devon. Issue: 2 daughters. Emigrated to United States of America in 1914.

SKEWES CLARA CAROLINE
Born 1876, West End, Redruth. Died 1877, aged 1 year. Buried Redruth 31 January 1877.

SKEWES CLARA CAROLINE S.
Born 1880, Penzance. Died 1881, aged 1 year.

SKEWES CLARA F. HEATH.
Born April 1870. Stepdaughter to Emry and Sarah H. Ward of Salt Lake City. Married and a widow by 1900. School teacher. Died 1905, aged 35 years. Buried in Mount Olivet Cemetery, Salt Lake City, Utah, USA.

SKEWS CLARA JEANETTE
Born 1860. Maiden name Babcock. Married John Skews, stonemason of Mineral Point, Wisconsin. Died 1950, aged 90 years. Buried in Jackson Cemetery, Mineral Point, Wisconsin.

SKEWES CLARA THAWSNELDA
Chart 10. Mexican. Daughter of Alfredo and Juila (née Varela). Born 12 August 1944. Married Miguel Alva 1971. Issue one son. Lives in Mexico.

SKEWS CLARENCE
Chart 15. Son of John Gregory and Annie Skews. Born 1896, Liskeard. Married Ethel Duke in St Germans, 1937. Lived at 25 Valentine's Row, Callington, Cornwall. Child: Marion (1938). Died 12 November 1977, aged 81 years.

SKEWS CLARENCE
Born 1891 Liskeard. Died 1892, aged 0.

SKEWIS CLARENCE G.
Chart 2. Son of Ed and Kittie Skewis of Shullsburg, Wisconsin, USA. Born 25 March 1873, Shullsburg. Was a partner in Skewis Brothers, Meats of Shullsburg. Died 5 February 1953, aged 78 years. Buried in Shullsburg Cemetery.

SKEWES CLARENCE GEORGE
Chart 2. Son of William James and Laura Annie Skewes. Born 12 March 1897 at Fitzroy, Melbourne, Victoria, Australia. Married Beryl Colville Keage (she born 13 January 1900 — died 15 November 1978, aged 78 years), 1 December 1925 at South Yarra, Melbourne, Australia. Children: Coryl Isabel (1927) and Eric William (1929). Was appointed Engineer for Watersheds and Channels in 1934 by the Melbourne Water Supply Authority, the Melbourne and Metropolitan Board of Works. Retired 1962.
Active member of Toc H., Australia, incorporated since 1950. Appointed President of Toc H., **Australia** (Victoria) and awarded the Order of Australian Medal in 1978 for outstanding service to the community in introducing and promulgating the Emergency Alarm Service for people living alone. Hobbies include philately. Past President of Royal Victorian Philatical Society, Melbourne. Has a collection of some 1500 gramophone records, including many rare 78's. Lives at 4 Windouran Drive, Mitcham, Victoria, Australia, 3132.

SKEWIS CLARENCE JAMES
Chart 33. Son of William Richard and Elizabeth Jane (née Willcott) Skewis. Born 1911, Buckfastleigh, Devon. Married Elsie Maddick, Totnes, 1947. She died 22 October 1975, aged 81 years.

SKEWES CLARENDA
Born 1895, Redruth. Married Garnet Mayne, 1920 in Redruth.

SKEWES CLARICE ARCADIA
Chart 38. Daughter of Richard and Mary (née Reynolds) Skewes. Born 7 February 1894, Moonta, South Australia. Married Alfred James Galliford, 25 February 1913. Issue: 3 sons and 3 daughters. Died 24 October 1975, aged 81 years.

SKEWES CLARICE MARGARET
Chart 36. Daughter of James and Stella Margaret (née Farrell) Skewes. Born 20 January 1925, Australia. Married Max Gardener. Issue: 2 sons.

SKEWES CLARICE OLIVE
Chart 38. Daughter of Horace Henry and Agatha Blanche Skewes. Born 7 February 1913. Married 14 Sept 1931 to Alfred Charles Boynton. Lives in South Australia.

SKEWES CLARINDA
Née Ralph. Daughter of William Ralph, miner. Born 1858. Married Thomas Henry Skewes at Perranuthnoe Parish Church 19 Feb 1881. Children: Walter (illeg. son via Thomas Henry Skewes) 1881 and Annie, 1882. Died 1922, aged 64 years in Penzance.

Clarence George Skewes

Clarence James Skewis

SKEWES CLARINDA
Born 1899, Redruth.
SKEWES CLARINDA JANE
Born 1882, Helston. Married Arthur Thomas in Falmouth, 1915.
SKUES CLAUDE
Gold and silver mounter of 21 St John's Square, London, E.C.1. (1930 Street Directory of London).
SKEWS CLAUDE
In 1959 lived at 21 Maud Street, Bentleigh North, Victoria, Australia with Rhoda Eleanor Skews.
SKUES CLAUDE WILLIAM
Chart 8. Son of Walter Edward Skues. Born 1899. Died 1900, Shoreditch, aged 1 year.
SKEWES CLAUDINE ELIZABETH
Chart 50. Daughter of Geoffrey Grenville and Ruth Lois (née Philp) Skewes. Born 24 February 1973, Victoria, Australia. Lives at 33 Howard Street, Warrnambool, 3280, Victoria, Australia.
SKEWES CLIFFORD
Chart 14. Son of Samuel and Betsy (née Phillips) Skewes of Ives Grove, Wisconsin. Born 25 December 1873. Bachelor. Died 1904, aged 31 years.
SKEWES CLINT CHARLES
Chart 14. Son of Charles J. and Loretta Skewes of Racine.
SKEWES CLINT EDWARD
Chart 36. Son of Gary William & Lynette Mary (née Smith) Skewes. Born 8 February 1974. Lives at 9 Surrey Road, Wilson, 6107, Western Australia.
SKEWES CLINTON HANNIBAL
Chart 14. Son of Hannibal and Eliza (née Phillips). Born 14 August 1880, Yorkville, Wisconsin, USA. Married Grace Vivyan 14 March 1898. No issue. She died 1940. Clinton Hannibal married Eleanor Hanson 26 September 1945. Again no issue. Lived on a farm in Yorkville during first marriage. During second marriage lived at 5401 East Covina Road, Mesa, Arizona, 85205. Died Mesa, Arizona 3 January 1979, aged 98 years.

Clorinda Doris Skues

SKUES CLIVE P.
Chart 9. Mother's maiden name Lucchesi. Son of Philip Ernest Skues. Born 1960, Sidcup, Kent.
SKEWES CLIVE RAYMOND
Lives at 393 Murray Road, Preston, 3072, Victoria, Australia with Margaret Rose Skewes and Elsie Miriam Skewes. Minister.

SKUES CLORINDA A.
Chart 9. Mother's maiden name Pinto. Born 1923, Lambeth. Killed during bombing raid, 1940, aged 16 years.
SKUES CLORINDA DORIS
Chart 9. Born 1906, Southwark. Spinster. Daughter of Philip Henry Skues.

Clinton and Grace Skewes. Photo taken in 1945

SKUES CLORINDA EMMA
Chart 9. Born 1871. Married Philip Henry Skues, 1890, Wandsworth, London. Children: John Philip W., Albert Edward, Thomas Henry I., Arthur Leonard Peter, Philip Ernest, Clorinda Doris and Ivy Margaretta. Died 1949, aged 78 years.
SKEWES COLAN
Mentioned in Cornwall Protestation Returns in 1642 living in Gwennap.
SKEWES COLEEN MARIE
Née McKenzie. Married Douglas Arthur Skewes. Lives at 62 Shamrock Street, Blackall, Queensland. 4723, Australia.
SKEWS COLIN
Chart 41. Son of Samuel Skews. Mother's maiden name Parden. Born 1926, Barnsley, South Yorkshire. Died 1930, aged 3 years — in Sheffield.
SKEWES COLIN
Chart 40. Mother's maiden name Moon. Born 1947, Penzance. Married Edwina A. Jordan in Penzance, 1970. Children: Charlotte Louise (1972), Emily Clare (1974) and Rebecca Phyllis (1976). Lives at Roche, Cornwall.
SKEWIS COLIN
Mother's maiden name Lyons. Born 1965, Kettering, Northants.
SKEWES COLIN ARCHER
Son of Archer William and Elsie May (née Handley) Skewes. Born 16 November 1919. Married Flora McKenzie at Mineeda, Blackall, Queensland, 7 November 1949. One daughter Lynette Margaret (1950). Killed in a car accident in Sydney, Australia, 3 May 1972, aged 25 years.
SKEWES COLIN ARTHUR
Chart 36. Son of William Roe and Evelyn Dorothy Skewes. Born 13 December 1927. Married Joyce Eva Boundy 24 June 1950. Children: John Arthur and Julie Lorraine. Lives at 4 Parkhouse Avenue, Seaton, 5023, South Australia. Butcher.
SKUES COLIN CAMPBELL
Son of William and Margaret Skues, Born 21 January 1895. Lived in New South Wales, Australia.
SKEWES COLIN DOUGLAS
Chart 36. Son of Douglas Arthur and Coleen Marie (née McKenzie) Skewes. Born 20 April 1963. Lives at 62 Shamrock Street, Blackall, 4723, Queensland, Australia.

SKUES COLIN JOSEPH
Lives at 21 Lord's Avenue, Asquith, Hornsby, 2078, New South Wales, Australia with Esther Mary Skues.

SKEWES COLLAN
Son of John and Mary Skewes. Bpt Gwennap 26 December 1771. Buried Gwennap 10 February 1797.

SKEWES COLLAN
Chart 19. Son of Richard and Mary Skewes. Bpt Gwennap 8 September 1802. Married Ann...(who died 15 July 1859, aged 60 years). Children: Mary Jane, Richard and Thomas Lean.

SKEWES COLLEEN RUTH
Chart 38. Daughter of Cyril George and Dorothy Melva (née James) Skewes. Born 11 June 1947, South Australia. Married John Willis, 6 January 1968 at Kadina Church of Christ, South Australia. Issue: 1 son and 1 daughter.

SKEWES COLON
Married Elizabeth Warrine at Perranarworthal, Cornwall, 9 June 1665.

SKEWES CONSTANCE
Chart 2. Daughter of James and Charity Skewes of Camborne. Bpt Camborne 10 March 1771. Married Richard Williams of Gwinear at Camborne Parish Church, 1 January 1803. Prior to her marriage she had four illegitimate children: William (1795), Elizabeth Temby (1798), Margaret (1799) and Maria (1800).

SKEWES CONSTANCE
Buried Camborne, 28 May 1776.

SKEWES CONSTANCE
Married Henry Hunt (widower) at Gwennap 16 December 1815.

SKUSE CONSTANCE
Daughter of Sydney and Nellie (née Cox) Skuse. Born 1901. Married George Soper. Issue: one son. Died 1940, aged 39 years.

SKEWES CONSTANCE
Chart 12. Daughter of Samuel Percy and Hilda Skewes. Mother's maiden name Tremayne. Born 1943, Kerrier.

SKEWES CONSTANCE
Chart 12. Daughter of John and Cissie Skewes. Born 1907. Married Reggie Cannicot, 1930, Helston. One daughter.

SKEWS CONSTANCE MARGARET
Chart 15. Daughter of John and May Louisa (née Mallet) Skews of Baytree Hill, Liskeard. Born 27 June 1920. Bpt 2 September 1920 at Liskeard Wesleyan/Methodist Church. Married Thomas Hurst, 1942, Mutley Baptist Church. Issue: 1 son and 1 daughter. Lives at 8 Salcombe Road, Plymouth.

SKEWS CONSTANCE MARY
Chart 41. Born 18 July 1901. Née Royston. Married Edgar Skews in Barnsley, 1931. No children. Died 1977, aged 76 years.

SKEWS CONSTANCE PATRICIA
Chart 23. Née Harris. Born 15 June 1923. Married Thomas Henry Skews, 1943, St Austell. Children: Peter B (1945), Jaqueline A. (1949) and Barry J. (1955). Died 1975, aged 52 years.

SKEWES CONSTANCE SHIRLEY
Lives at 58 Clifford Street, Warragul, 3820, Victoria, Australia with Harold Grenville Skewes, clerk and Peter Andrew Skewes.

SKEWES CORAL ISABEL
Chart 36. Daughter of Reginald John and Mary Mildred (née Rooney) Skewes. Born 3 March 1927, Uralla, New South Wales. Married John Carpenter. Issue: 2 daughters. Deputy Matron, Tamworth Hospital. Lives at 16 Sapphire Crescent, Tamworth, 2340, New South Wales, Australia.

SKEWES CORDELGER
Died 1861, Bideford, North Devon.

SKEWES CORDELIA ANNE
Chart 38. Daughter of Garfield Sydney and Doris Margaret Skewes. Born 24 January 1956. Lives at 55 Maesbury Street, Kensington Park, Adelaide Beach, South Australia. Single.

SKEWES CORYL ISABEL
Chart 2. Daughter of Clarence George and Beryl Colville (née Keage) Skewes. Born 9 May 1927, Lilydale, Victoria, Australia. University of Melbourne B.Sc. (1948). Married Edward Keith Muntz 27 August 1956. Issue: 1 son — David William Skewes Muntz (1957). Compiles indexes for books. Lives in Melbourne, Victoria, Australia.

SKEWS COURTENAY JOHN GREGORY
Chart 15. Son of Harry and Hilda (née Jane) Skews. Born 17 January 1922, Pensilva, Liskeard. Bpt St Ive 1 March 1922. Married Arnold, St Germans, 1950. Son: Andrew (1950). Listed in Exmouth Street Directory 1968-1973 inclusive living at 2 Caroline Close, Exmouth, Devon.

SKEWS CRAIG LESLIE
Son of David Leslie and Irma Margaret (née Green) Skewes. Born 23 February 1959. Lives at 7/12 Vine Street, Blackburn, 3130, Victoria, Australia. Clerk.

SKEWES CRAIG RICHARD
Chart 38. Son of Peter William and Carol Ann (née Wright) Skewes. Born 7 December 1972. Lives at 26 Geraint Street, Bracken Ridge, Queensland, 4017, Australia.

Skewes. Born 9 March 1964. Lives at Goolwa, 5214, South Australia.

SKEWES CRAIG WILLIAM
Chart 38. Son of William Seymour and Glenda Lorraine (née Walter) Skewes. Born 13 July 1969, North Adelaide, South Australia. Lives at 43 Fletcher Road, Elizabeth East, 5112, South Australia.

SKEWES CRAWFORD STANLEY
In 1959 lived at 21 Rockbourne Street, Elizabeth North, Gawler, South Australia with Evelyn Mary Skewes. Process worker.

SKEWES CRISTINA
Chart 10. Mexican. Daughter of Nazario and Dolores (née Riofrio) Skewes. Born 19 July 1913. Married Antonio Rodriguez. Issue: 3 sons and 3 daughters.

SKEWES CUTHBERT GEORGE
Chart 36. Son of George and Mary (née Dowling) Skewes. Born 7 October 1897. Married Violet Ferris, October, 1926. Lived at 93, O'Dell Street, West Armidale, 2350, Australia. Children: Gwendra, Harvey and Verna Joy. Died 29 April 1941, aged 43 years.

SKEWES CYNTHIA ELAINE
Chart 10. Daughter of Rex Owen and Jean Lilian (née van Rensburg) Skewes. Born 2 April 1954, Transvaal, South Africa. Married Henry Doran.

SKUES CYRIL ALBERT J.
Chart 9. Son of John Philip W. Skues. Mother's maiden name Bremer. Born 1917. Married Jessie H. Norris, 1940, Woolwich, London. Child: David J. (1944).

SKEWES CYRIL GEORGE
Chart 38. Son of Albert Milton and Myrtle Emma (née Marks) Skewes. Born 20 June 1918, Kadina. Married Dorothy Melva James, 7 April 1943. Served in Australia Imperial Forces during Second World War for five years. Children: Colleen Ruth (1947) and Helen Joyce (1949). Postal officer for 30 years in Kadina, South Australia. Retired in 1976. Lives at 23 Doswell Terrace, Kadina, 5554, South Australia.

Cyril George & Myrtle Emma Skewes of Kadina, South Australia

SKEWES CRAIG STEPHEN
Chart 36. Son of Ronald Edgar and Janice Kathleen (née Egan)

SKEWES CYRIL JAMES
Lives at 19 Thompson Street, Woonona, 2517, New South Wales, Australia with Judith Ann Skewes. Driver.

SKEWES CYRIL THOMAS
Chart 50. Son of John and Mary Jane (née Cole) Skewes. Born 1889, New South Wales, Australia. Married Annie Mary Leathan. Children: John William, Sirrel Arthur, Ruby and Betty Elaine.

SKEWES CYRIL WILLIAM
Chart 48. Born 4 January 1912, Croydon. Son of William Verdayne Skewes and Elizabeth (née Marsh). District manager. Lived at 19 Green Court Avenue, Addiscombe, Surrey (Tel. No. Addiscombe

C. W. (Bill) Skewes

2746) in 1947. By 1978 had moved to 9 Croft Rise, Menston, Yorkshire. Tel. No: 0943 73051. Married Marie Florence Ambrose in Croydon, Surrey, 1939. Children: Anne Marie (1944) and Linda Rosemary (1947).

SKEWES CYRUS LYLE
Chart 36. Son of Aubrey Rupert and Annie (née Townsend) Skewes. Born 17 March 1926, Uralla, New South Wales, Australia. Married Alice Welbourne. Children: Lenore and Virginia. Lives at 2/21 Merlin Street, North Sydney, Australia.

D

SKEWS D.B.
In 1979 living at 19 Valleywood Road, North York, Toronto, Canada. Tel. No: (416) 444 1720.

SKEWS DAISY
Née Atkinson. Daughter of Joseph Atkinson, labourer of 6 Craylands Lane, Swanscombe, Kent. Married Albert Edward Skews, of 11 The Grove, Swanscombe, Kent 1 August 1925, at the Register Office, Dartford. He died 1946, aged 43 years. She married Dean in Dartford, 1951.

SKEWES DAISY
Lived at 46 Brighton Road, Glenelg, South Australia in 1959 with William Percival Skewes.

SKEWS DAISY EMILY
Born 1889, Bethnal Green. Married Deway in Bethnal Green, 1912.

SKEWIS DALE
Chart 2. Twin to Donald Earl Skewis. Son of Raymond and Lottie Skewis. Born 16 April 1921. Married Shirley Helen... Two sons: Ronald James (1949) and Robert Don (1951).

SKUSE DALE
Son of Gordon and Janet (née Mellor) Skuse. Born 5 March 1961. Lives at 30 Abbey Road, Newstead Village, Mansfield, Nottingham.

SKEWS DANIEL
Chart 33. Son of William and Mary Skews of Blackwater, miner. Bpt Chacewater, 17 October 1831. In 1852 was a miner residing at Ashburton, Devon. Married Elizabeth Jane Willcott, daughter of Richard Willcott, post boy; at Parish Church, Ashburton, Devon 28 November 1852. Children: Elizabeth (1854), John (1858), Sarah (1860), Mary (1862), Henrietta (1863), Clara (1866), Daniel (1869) and William Richard (1872).
Elizabeth Jane died 1874. Daniel, then aged 44, married Mary Langmead Trebilcock at the Register Office, St Thomas, Devon, 19 June 1877. She was aged 40, widow, and daughter of Robert Northcott, farmer.

SKUSE DANIEL

Youngest son of James Skuse. Born 30 August 1847, Horton, Bucks. Farm labourer and later coachman. Lived in Uxbridge, Middlesex but eventually moved to Brixton. Married Louisa Clouder, 1869. Children: Sydney (1870), Herbert Henry (1874) and Alice (1878).

SKEWES DANIEL
Born 1863, Truro. Son of Richard and Elizabeth Skewes.

SKEWES DANIEL
Chart 33. Son of Samuel and Susan Skewes of Crockalow, Ashburton, Devon. Born 1864, Newton Abbot, Devon.

SKEWES DANIEL
Chart 33. Son of Daniel and Elizabeth Skewes of Bell Mount, Ashburton, Devon. Born 1869, Newton Abbot, Devon.

SKEWIS DANIEL
Married Sarah Matthias, 1877, St Thomas, Exeter. Child: Alfred (1887).

SKEWES DANIEL
Chart 36. Son of Timothy Lester and Lynette Skewes. Born 16 November 1974, Australia.

SKEWES DANIEL HODGE
Chart 18. Son of William and Ann (née Trewan) Skewes. Bpt Kenwyn 17 May 1807. Married Anna Dawe St Andrews Parish Church, Plymouth, Devon, 1 November 1831. She died 23 March 1832, aged 32. Remarried Mary... Lived at Grocer's Shop, Pepper Street, Bere Alston, Tavistock, Devon, in 1861 Census. Was listed as a mine agent. One son Samuel Dawe Skewes. One daughter Mary Ann Lipsom Skewes. Died 1863, aged 56 years.

SKEWS DANIEL RICHARD
Chart 10. Son of Michael J. Skews. Mother's maiden name Clifft. Born 1977, Truro.

SKEWES DANIELLE ELIZABETH
Chart 36. Daughter of John Michael and Janice Elizabeth (née Miles) Skewes. Born 14 May 1973, Ballarat, Victoria, Australia. Lives at 702 Neil Street, Ballarat, Victoria, 3350, Australia.

SKEWES DANNY
Chart 36. Son of Neville Percy and Helen (née O'Lockland) Skewes. Born 8 February 1959, Australia. Married Jacqueline Fairall 8 September 1979. Child: Kelly (1980).

SKEWS DAPHNE GRACE
Living at 306 Dorcas Street, South Melbourne, Victoria, Australia in 1959 with Stanley Richard Skews. She was a tailor — he an accountant. Now lives at 268 Wade Avenue, Mildura, 3500, Victoria, Australia.

SKEWIS DARLENE F.
Chart 2. Wife of Dale R. Skewis. Lives at 1525 21st NE, Salem, Oregon, USA. Child: Bonnie J.

SKEWIS DARREN ANDREW
Chart 50. Son of David and Patricia (née Gibson) Skewis. Born 1976, Hull.

SKEWES DARREN VERNON
Mother's maiden name Hall. Born 1973, Truro.

SKEWES DARYL
Chart 36. Son of Benjamin Samuel and Gweneth (née Adams) Skewes. Born 24 February 1955. Married Jeanette Noon, 14 February 1981 at Tamworth, New South Wales. Lives at Kootingal, 2352, New South Wales, Australia.

SKEWS DARYL ANDREW
Lives at 39 Amiel Street, Springvale, 3171, Victoria, Australia with Lynette Skews. Salesman.

SKEWES DARYL JAMES
Lives at Glenelg, Bendemeer, 2352, New South Wales, Australia. Welder.

SKUES DARYL JAMES
Lives at 56 Frances Street, Merrylands, 2160, New South Wales, Australia. Labourer.

SKEWES DARRYL JOHN
Lived at 72 Rundle Street, Kent Town, Adelaide, South Australia. Died 1949. Buried Adelaide Public Cemetery, 17 November 1949, aged 25 days.

SKEWS DAVID
Chart 15. Son of John and Isabella (née Gregory) Skews, of Trewint, Launceston. Bpt Altarnun 29 April 1871. Died 1871, aged 0.

SKEWS DAVID
Chart 41. Son of Roy and Jennie (née Boynton) Skews. Born 19 February 1943, Wortley, South Yorkshire. Attended Hemingfield Church of England School and later Barnsley Holgate Grammar School.
Craft apprentice at Corton Wood Colliery 1960-1965; Associated Electrical Industries 1965-1968; British Ropes, Doncaster, 1969; electrical engineer with British Steel, Tinsley Park, Sheffield 1970 to present date.
Married Helen Ackroyd at Jump Parish Church, 21 March 1975. Daughter Emma Jane (1975). Hobbies: golf, squash, badminton and singing. Lives at 11 Woodlands View, Wombwell, Barnsley, South Yorkshire.
Tel. number Barnsley 753530.

David Skews

SKEWIS   DAVID
Chart 50. Son of James Airns and Irene (née Fox) Skewis. Born 14 March 1950, Hull. Married Christine Brattan, 1967, Hull. Children: Karen Jayne (1968) and Zquin James B. (1974). Lives at 10 Devon Street, Gypsyville, Hull. Tel. No: 0482 501627.

SKEWS   DAVID
Mother's maiden name Pascoe. Born 1958, Plymouth. Died 1958, aged 0.

SKEWS   DAVID
Chart 41. Son of George David and Olwynne (née Thirwell) Skews. Born 1962, Sunderland.

SKEWIS   DAVID
Chart 50. Son of David and Bridie (née Maher) Skewis. Born 24 February 1970. Lives at 9 Drumry Place, Glasgow 15, Scotland. Telephone number: 041 944 1426.

SKEWIS   DAVID
Chart 50. Married Patricia Gibson, 1973, Holderness. Child: Darren Andrew (1976).

SKEWES   DAVID
Chart 12. Son of Gilbert James and Kathleen (née Dennis) Skewes. Born 7 January 1962, Kerrier, Cornwall.

SKEWES   DAVID
Chart 36. Son of Bruce Skewes. Born 7 July 1969, Victoria, Australia.

SKUES   DAVID A.
Chart 8. Son of Sydney V. Skues. Mother's maiden name Cox. Born 1958, Brentwood, Essex.

SKEWS   DAVID A.H.
Chart 17. Son of John G.P. and Dorothy (née Boyland) Skews. Born 1952, Peterborough. Lives at 5 Lime Tree Avenue, Peterborough.

SKEWES   DAVID B.
Married Brunsdon, 1939, Pancras, London.

SKEWES   DAVID BRIAN
Chart 36. Son of Brian Lock and Barbara Jessie (née McKinley) Skewes. Born 25 October 1958. Lives at Currency Creek, Y, 5251, South Australia.

SKEWES   DAVID BUICK
M.B. FRCS (Edinburgh), FRACS. Chart 50. Son of Thomas Garland and Marion Edith Alfreda (née Wilson) Skewes. Born 26 February 1910, Ballarat, Victoria, Australia. University of Melbourne. Graduated Bachelor of Medicine 1935. Perth Hospital 1936-1937; London House, London 1938-1939; Edinburgh 1939. At outbreak of war returned to Australia arriving in January 1940. Joined Royal Australian Air Force, July 1940. Squadron Leader. Commanded No 7 RAAF Hospital, Adelaide and later No 4 Medical Receiving Station. Responsible for service and civilian personnel throughout north west of Australia. In August, 1945 transferred to RAAF Reserve. Married Irene Margaret Murphy, 28 February 1942. Returned to Edinburgh 1950. Became Fellow of Royal College of Surgeons (Edinburgh), January 1951. In September, 1951 appointed Honorary Surgeon to Ballarat and District Base Hospital and held various offices including Consultant to the Queen Elizabeth Geriatric Centre and Consultant Surgeon to the Repatriation Department.

Retired from staff of Ballarat and District Base Hospital in 1971 and appointed Honorary Consultant Surgeon of Ballarat Base Hospital. In January, 1975 retired from private practice. Regional Geriatrician, Central Highlands Region, Queen Elizabeth Geriatric Centre, Ballarat. Acting Medical Superintendent 1975-1978. Part time Medical Officer to RAAF Unit, Ballarat from 1961. Children: Helen Margaret (1942), Gillian Mary (1944), David Garland (1946), Margaret Alison (1949) and Christine Ann (1952). Lives at "Windarra", 213 Sim Street, Ballarat, Victoria, Australia. Tel. No: Ballarat 326909.

Skewes' of Ballarat, Victoria, Australia. Left to right: Gillian Mary, Dr David Buick Skewes, Hilary Skewes, Lorelle Skewes and Dr David Garland Skewes

SKEWS   DAVID CHARLES
Chart 17. Son of George Alfred Skews. Born 1880, Bethnal Green.

SKEWES   DAVID DARROW
Chart 26. Son of Robert Ernest and Elaine Helen (née Albanese) Skewes. Born 26 July 1956. Athlete. Works at Coast Guard Academy, USA.

SKEWES   DAVID ERIC
Chart 36. Adopted son of Owen Eric Edward and Stella Tabitha (née Harris) Skewes. Born April, 1943. Married Janis Williams in Sebastopol, Ballarat, 1968. Children: Shane, Narelle and Brett. Lives at 205 Victoria Street, Ballarat, 3350, Victoria, Australia.

SKEWS   DAVID FALCONER
Chart 17. Son of Christopher R. Skews. Mother's maiden name Kempson. Born 1972, Redbridge.

SKEWS   DAVID G.
Chart 15. Son of Stanley Skews. Mother's maiden name Fishleigh. Born 1960, Liskeard.

SKEWES   DAVID GARLAND
M.B., B.S., F.F.A.R.C.S (London). Chart 50. Son of David Buick and Irene Margaret (née Murphy) Skewes. Born 9 November 1946, Ballarat, Victoria, Australia. University of Melbourne. Graduated 1971. Junior Resident Doctor at Austin Hospital, Melbourne. Went to Europe May, 1973 touring for five months. Became Senior House Officer at Kenton, Canterbury Hospital; Royal Sussex County Hospital, Brighton, 1974: New Addenbrookes Hospital, Cambridge 1974-1977; London Hospital, Whitechapel 1977-1978; Hammersmith Hospital, London 1978-1981 (Senior Registrar); Royal Marsden Hospital, Fulham, London 1981. Professional opera singer and has sung at Aldeburgh and Glyndebourne. Married Lorelle Davey, 11 May 1970. Child: Hilary (1970). Lives at 27 Riverside Grove, Chiswick, London W4 3Q1.

SKEWS   DAVID GEORGE
Chart 17. Son of William Thomas and Emily (née Homan) Skews, wood turner of 29 Gales Gardens, Bethnal Green, London. Married Emily Lampey, 23 December 1923, Bethnal Green. Lived at 35 Rothwell Road, Dagenham, Essex. Children: David George, William A., Joan L.D. and Iris D. Died 16 March 1975, aged 76 years.

SKEWS DAVID GEORGE
Chart 17. Son of David George Skews. Mother's maiden name Lampey. Born 7 September 1924. Married Doris Adelaide Parrott, 1947, Ilford, Essex at St. Alban's Church, Dagenham (1st February). Children: One daughter Gwendoline D. (1948). Lives at 60 Valentine's Way, Dagenham, Essex. Previous address: 645 Gale Street, Dagenham, Essex.

SKUES DAVID J.
Chart 9. Son of Cyril A.J. Skues. Mother's maiden name Norris. Born 1944, Wellingborough. Married Elizabeth A. Weighill, 1967, Dartford, Kent. Lives at 43 Priory Close, Dartford, Kent.

SKEWS DAVID J.
Mother's maiden name Duff. Born 1965, Birmingham.

SKEWES DAVID J.
Married Janis S. Blazy, Surrey Mid East, 1979.

SKEWIS DAVID JAMIESON
Chart 50. Son of William and Ellen (née Blythe) Skewis. Born 8 December 1907, Dennistoun, Scotland. Married Grace Wilson at Manse Westercraig's Parish Church, Dennistoun, 1934. Child: David Jamieson Wilson Skewis (1937). Lived at 42 Kaystone Road, Glasgow, 15. Telephone number 041 944 2034. During Second World War served with RAF. On demobilisation returned to his job as a bus conductor. Retired as Patrol Inspector on buses, Glasgow Corporation. For many years sang with Clydebank Male Voice Choir. Freemason with Ruckhill Lodge, Glasgow. Died Glasgow, 1 July 1974, aged 66 years.

SKEWIS DAVID JAMIESON WILSON
Chart 50. Son of David Jamieson and Grace (née Wilson) Skewis. Born 10 June 1937, Tradeston. Sang with Kirkintilloch Junior Choir in his youth. National Service with RAOC in Hong Kong (1957-1959). Married Bridie Maher at Old Drumchapel Parish Church, 29 March 1961. Children: Linda (1962), Stephen (1963), David (1970) and Lorraine (1972). Lives at 9 Drumry Place, Glasgow, 15, Scotland. Tel. number 041 944 1426. Taxi driver.

SKEWES DAVID JOHN
Lives at 8 Epping Street, Malvern East, 3145, Victoria, Australia with Lynette Skewes.

SKEWES DAVID JOHN
Lives at 45 Glenhuntley Street, Woodville South, 5011, South Australia with Gwendra Pearl Skewes, Ralph Edward Skewes and Steven Melville Skewes.

SKEWES DAVID JOHN
Chart 12. Son of Christopher John and Hazel (née Williams) Skewes. Born 26 June 1980, Helston. Twin to Michelle Clair. Lives at 23 St John's Terrace, Helston. Tel no: 03265 2064.

SKEWES DAVID LANCE
Chart 37. Son of Vernon John and Margaret Janet (née Williams) Skewes. Born 13 June 1979, Berowra Heights, Australia 2080.

SKEWES DAVID LESLIE
Son of Leslie Henry Irving and Edith Ann (née White) Skewes. Born 10 October 1929. Married Irma Margaret Green 12 April 1952. Children: Gregory David (1956), Craig Leslie (1959) and Susan Margaret (1964). Lives at 35 McNally Street, Yarrawonga, Victoria, Australia, 3730.

SKEWIS DAVID MARTIN BARCLAY
Born 1925, New Monkland. Died Shettleston, 1942, aged 16 years.

SKEWES DAVID MICHAEL
Chart 36. Son of Earl William and Fay (née Chad) Skewes. Born 10 December 1954, New South Wales, Australia. Married Janelle Heyward, 10 June 1978. Child: Simon David (1980).

SKEWES DAVID MICHAEL
Chart 36. Son of Michael James and Millie (née van Naerssen) Skewes. Born Victoria, Australia 17 May 1968.

SKEWES DAVID NEAL
Chart 2. Son of William Henry and Clara Bertha (née Ahlvers) Skewes. Born 22 September 1935, Missouri, USA. Married 1955. Wife's name Patricia. Children: Pamela (1958), Michael (1961) & Kathy (1966).

SKEWS DAVID P.
Chart 10. Son of Stanley Skews. Mother's maiden name Soady. Born 1953, St Austell. Married Reseigh in Truro, 1974.

SKEWES DAVID REGAN
Chart 10. Son of Norman David and Linda Skewes of Hamilton, Ontario, Canada. Born 18 November 1975.

SKEWES DAVID ROBERT
Chart 36. Son of Robert Keith and Shirley Cicely (née Jacobs) Skewes. Born 1 August 1963, Australia. Lives at Laurel Street, Kootingal, 2352, New South Wales, Australia.

SKEWES DAVID THOMAS
Son of Norman Leslie Skewes. Married Alison Boyd Gregg. Issue: 1 son and 1 daughter. Lives at 29 Darke Street, Torrens, 2607, Canberra, Australia. Tel No: (062) 862464.

SKEWES DAWN
Chart 12. Daughter of James Harry Skewes. Mother's maiden name Woolcock. Born 1946, Truro. Married Mike Trevethan, 1966,

Truro. Issue: one son.

SKEWES DAWN FLORENCE
Lived at 74 Daly Street, Kurralta Park, Plympton, South Australia in 1959 with Terence Allan Skewes, tool maker. Now lives at 53 Elgin Avenue, Christie's Beach, 5165, South Australia with Leanne Margaret Skewes and Terence Allan Skewes.

SKUSE DEAN
Son of Tom and Muriel (née Goodhead) Skuse. Born 12 January 1945. Married Margaret Barnes 1 October 1966. Children: Lisa (1967) and Jason (1971). Lives at 26 Fraser Street, Newstead Village, Nottinghamshire.

SKEWES DEAN ANTHONY
Chart 36. Son of Noel James and Veronica Elaine (née Cooper) Skewes. Born 28 January 1963. Lives at Bantry, Watsons Creek, Bendemeer, 2352, New South Wales, Australia.

SKEWES DEAN MAURICE
Lived at 72 Rundle Street, Kent Town, Adelaide, South Australia. Buried 17 November 1949, aged 23 days in Adelaide Public Cemetery.

SKEWIS DEAN JOHN
Mother's maiden name Kennedy. Born 1980, Kettering, Northants.

SKEWS DEBBIE
Chart 41. Daughter of Eric Skews. Mother's maiden name Rasburn. Born 1963, Sheffield, South Yorkshire.

SKEWIS DEBBIE
Mother's maiden name Kilpatrick. Born 1966, Kettering, Northants.

SKEWES DEBBIE GAY
Chart 36. Daughter of Noel James and Veronica (née Cooper) Skewes. Born 8 December 1964. Lives at Watsons Creek, via Bendemeer, 2352, New South Wales, Australia.

SKEWES DEBORAH
Chart 10. Daughter of Ronald Lanier and Patricia (née Fountain) Skewes of USA. Born 4 February 1968, Manassas, Virginia, 22110, USA.

SKUES DEBORAH JESSIE
Chart 5. Née McMillan. Married Derek Peter Skues 26 May 1969. Children: Jeremy Derek (1972) and Jessie Pepita (1974). Lives at 467 Thurgoona Street, Albury, 2640, New South Wales, Australia.

SKEWES DEBORAH LEANNE
Chart 36. Daughter of Robert Skewes. Born 28 August 1967, Australia.

SKEWIS DEBORAH LYNN
Chart 2. Daughter of Benjamin and Nancy Skewis. Born 18 February 1969, United States of America.

SKEWES DEBRA CHRISTINE
Chart 2. Daughter of William John and Barbara McKay (née Carroll) Skewes. Born 27 June 1965, Australia.

SKEWES DEBRA KAY
Née Ginger. Married Ian Geoffrey Skewes, January 1975. Child: Ian Guy Skewes (1980). Lives at 20 Deakin Street, Hampton, 3188, Victoria, Australia.

SKEWES DEGORY
of Kea, miner. Died 1824.

SKEWIS DELIGHT D.
Wife of William A. Skewis. Lived at 550 North Winter, Salem, Oregon, USA in 1950.

SKEWIS DELILAH C.
Chart 50. Daughter of Alfred and Edith Alice Skewis. Mother's maiden name Hughes. Born 1913, Haverfordwest. Married Gough, 1934, Haverfordwest.

SKEWES DELMA
Chart 38. Daughter of Sydney Howard and Ruby Maud (née Smith) Skewes. Born 27 May 1932. Married Eric Jonathan Patching, 8 March 1952 at Church of Christ, Adelaide, South Australia. Issue: 1 son and 2 daughters. Lives at 18 Golden Glow Avenue, Underdale, South Australia, 5032.

SKEWES DELSIA
Lives at 60 Queenscroft Street, Chelmer, 4068, Queensland, Australia with George Alton Skewes.

SKEWES DELYSE MERLE
Chart 10. Daughter of Richard John and Edna Thelma (née Manson) Skewes. Born 11 December 1943, South Africa. Married Beltramo, 5 June 1965. Issue: two daughters.

SKEWS DENA
Chart 6. Daughter of Harvey Thomas and Bernice (née Shackley) Skews. Born 14 November 1942, Mineral Point, Wisconsin, USA. Married Roger Holmes 13 April 1963. Issue: 2 sons and 3 daughters. Lives in Middleton, Wisconsin, USA.

SCUSE DENNIS GEORGE MBE
Son of Charles H. and Katherine Scuse. Educated at Park School, Ilford, Essex and Mercers School, London. His first job was working at Martins Bank, 1937.
Was mobilised at the outbreak or war, September, 1939 into the Royal Artillery. Served in this country until 1942 when posted to Ceylon as Command Entertainments Officer. Joined Army Broad-

casting Service and commanded stations at Bari, Rome and Athens, 1945/1946. Demobilised in September, 1946 at rank of Captain, he joined overseas division of BBC and was seconded to War Office with Forces Broadcasting Service in Benghazi, Canal Zone as Chief Programmes Officer, 1947/1948. Posted to British Forces Network, Hamburg 1949/1950 (Assistant Director) and Director 1950/1957. He was responsible for the move from Hamburg to new premises in Cologne. Awarded MBE. He was a familiar voice as regular presenter in Germany of "Two Way Family Favourites", 1952/1957. Joined BBC Television as Senior Planning Assistant 1958/1959; Chief Assistant Light Entertainment BBC TV, 1960. Took up office in New York, September, 1960 as Chief Assistant, and two years later became BBC Representative in United States. In 1963 returned to London to set up BBC TV Enterprises as General Manager, a position he held for nine years. He was also General Manager for BBC Radio Enterprises. Moved to Independent Television in 1972 and became Managing Director of Trident Television International TV Enterprises 1972/1976. Is now Managing Director of Dennis Scuse Limited, a public relations firm. Joint Chairman and Managing Director of Charter Marketing Ltd. Married Joyce Evelyn, younger daughter of Frank and Frances Burt. They have one son and live at 246 Sheen Lane, London SW 14. Telephone number 01 876 2372. Recreations — wine making and watching television.

SKEWES   DENNIS IVOR JOHN
Chart 12. Son of Arthur and Violet Skewes. Mother's maiden name Rashleigh. Born 30 April 1934. Married June Letcher 26 December 1964, Redruth. Children: John Anthony (1967) and Richard Andrew (1970). Lives at Rose Glen, Porthallow, St Keverne, Helston, Cornwall.

SKEWES   DENNIS MILNER
Chart 10. Son of John and Lilian May (née Maynard) Skewes. Born 27 December 1918, Johannesburg, South Africa. Married Madge Pallas. No children. Lived at 21 Lynford Place, Durban North, Durban, Natal, South Africa. Died 1 May 1980, aged 61 years. His wife died two weeks previous.

SKEWES   DENNIS PAUL
Chart 42. Son of Jack and Shirley Beryl (née Callaghan) Skewes. Born 12 August 1951, North Ryde, Australia. Married Kaylene Daphne Bourke 6 December 1970, Wagga Wagga, Australia. Children: Tracey Lee (1971), Terry Paul (1972) and Bradley John (1975). Lives at 25 McKay Street, Nowra Hill, 2540, New South Wales, Australia.

SKEWS   DEREK
Married Margaret A. Gould, 1972, Worth Valley.

SKEWES   DEREK
Chart 42. Son of Michael Bruce and Dianne (née Dickson) Skewes. Born 14 November 1979, Nowra, Australia. Now lives: c/o 725 Squadron, R.A.N.A.S., Nowra Hill, 2540, New South Wales, Australia.

SKUES   DEREK A.
Chart 9. Mother's maiden name Bremer. Born 1933. Camberwell. Died 1933, aged 0.

SKUES   DEREK PETER
Chart 5. Son of Kenneth Frederick and Katherine Pepita (née Shaw) Skues.Born 14 May 1945, Melbourne, Australia. Married Deborah Jessie McMillan, 26 May 1969, Presbyterian Church, Toorak, Victoria. Children: Jeremy Derek (1972) and Jessie Pepita (1974). Lives at 467 Thurgoona Street, Albury, 2640, New South Wales, Australia. Telephone number: (060) 215010. Architect.

SKEWS   DEREK THOMAS
Chart 15. Son of Harry and Jean Jamieson (née Adam) Skews of Pensilva. Born 21 January 1951. Married Linda McManamon, St James Parish Church, Pollock, Glasgow, 17 August 1974. Children: Michele Rosemary (1970-adopted) and Alistair Derek (1976). Lives at 4 Moonsfield Callington, Cornwall.

SKEWS   DESMOND
Chart 41. Son of Joseph and Alice (née Lumb) Skews. Born 1930, Thorne. Married Lunn, 1954 in Thorne. Children: Sharon (1958) and John Michael (1966).

SKEWS   DIANA
Daughter of Brian A.A. Skews. Mother's maiden name Alldis. Born 1961, Dartford.

SKUES   DIANA KATHERINE
B.V.Sc., M.R.C.V.S. Chart 5. Daughter of Kenneth Frederick and Katherine Pepita (née Shaw) Skues. Born 1 September 1947, Melbourne, Victoria. Attended St Leonard's Presbyterian Girls College, Melbourne; University of Melbourne. Graduated 1970. Married Richard Szafranski on 28 September 1974 at Melbourne Trinity College Chapel. Issue: 1 son and 1 daughter. Lives at 78 Brice Avenue, Mooroolbark, Victoria, 3138, Australia.

SKEWES   DIANA ROSE
Chart 12. Daughter of Ronald and Natalia Eve (née Curtis) Skewes. Born 10 May 1958. Married Robert Anthony Foster, 2 October 1976, Parish Church, Charlestown, St Austell. Now lives at Beningbrough Hall, North Yorkshire.

SKEWIS   DIANE

Derek Peter Skues

Born 1956, Dundee East, Scotland. Married Bruce Anderson, 1977, Dundee East.

SKEWES   DIANNE GWENETH
Chart 36. Daughter of Benjamin Samuel and Gweneth (née Adams) Skewes. Born 10 June 1949. Married Donald Alexander 9 March 1968, Tamworth, New South Wales, Australia. Issue: 2 sons.

SKEWES   DIANE JANE
Lives at 9 Beryl Street, Woodville West, 5011, South Australia with Enid Merle Skewes and Robin Skewes. Clerk.

SKEWES   DIANNE LEE
Lives at 22 Queensborough Street, Nowra Hill, 2540, New South Wales, Australia. Nurse.

SKEWES   DIANE MARGARET
Chart 25. Daughter of John H. Skewes. Mother's maiden name Wynne. Born 1944, Manchester. Married Richard Guest in Manchester, November. 1963.

SKEWES   DIANE REBECCA
Chart 36. Daughter of Douglas Arthur and Coleen Marie (née McKenzie) Skewes. Born 1 October 1956. Married Ronald James Vagg, 5 July 1980. Lives in Queensland, Australia. Nursing sister.

SKEWES   DIANE THERESE
Lives at 10 Boronia Avenue, Administration Heights, 2289, New South Wales, Australia.

SKUES   DIGORY
Chart 10. Married 18 May 1700 at Kenwyn Parish Church. Lived at Kea. Children: Martin (1701), Margaret (1705), Elizabeth (1707) and Richard (1714).

SKEWES   DIGORY
Chart 10. Son of Martin and Mary Skewes. Bpt St Enoder 19 January 1733. Married Margery Spargo at Kenwyn Parish Church 27 December 1756. Children: Digory (1756). Catherine (1760), Peter (1763), Mary (1765), Peter (1768), Margery (1771), Matthew (1774) and Margery (1777). Will dated 26 December 1786. Margery (wife) died 1 December 1807, aged 74 years.

SKEWES   DIGORY
Chart 10. Miner of Seveoke. Son of Digory and Margery Skewes (née Spargo). Born 1755. Married Elizabeth Wasley of Kea at Kenwyn 13 July 1782. Buried Kea 14 May 1824, aged 69 years. Children: Thomas, Peter, Digory, Richard, Elizabeth, John, Matthew, Mary, Margery and Maria. Will proved 14 June 1824.

SKEWES   DIGORY
Bpt Kenwyn 3 September 1757. Son of Martin Skewes.

SKEWS   DIGORY
Buried Kea 18 January 1757.

SKEWES   DIGORY
Chart 10. Son of Digory and Elizabeth Skewes. Bpt 6 January 1787. Buried 19 May 1787, aged 4 months.

SKEWES   DIGORY
Son of Richard Skewes of Kenwyn. Buried Kea 20 May 1787.

SKEWES   DIGORY
Chart 10. Son of Digory Skewes. Bpt Kea 23 December 1787. Died 19 May 1788, aged 16 months.

SKEWES   DIGORY
Chart 10. Son of Digory and Elizabeth (née Wasley) Skewes. Bpt Kea 7 June 1789. Married Sophia Jordan 11 September 1811 at Kea. Children: Digory, Elizabeth, Amelia, Joseph, Matthew, Sophia, Mary and Samuel.

SKEWES   DIGORY
Chart 10. Son of Digory and Sophia Skewes. Born 1823. Bpt Kenwyn 25 August 1823. Married Fanny Tregonning, 1856. Children: William, Thomas, George, Elizabeth, Mary, Samuel, Amelia, Richard, Joseph and Henry. Buried Marazion 11 March 1868, aged 43 years. Fanny died 30 June 1902, aged 75 years.

SKEWS   DIGORY
Died 1859, Liskeard.

SKEWES   DOLORES
Chart 10. Mexican. Née Riofrio. Second wife of Nazario Skewes of Real del Monte, Mexico. Married 1902. Children: Rodolfo, Piedad, Angelica, Alfredo, Cristina, Eloisa, Elvira, Elmina and Guillermo.

SKEWES   DOLORES
Chart 10. Daughter of Alfredo and Juila (née Varela) Skewes. Born 20 September 1948. Spinster. Lives in Mexico City.

SKEWES   DOLORES ELIZABETH
Chart 36. Born 28 July 1922. Married Cecil Skewes, 1937, Redruth. Lived at 51 Pendarves Street, Beacon, Camborne. Children: Brian C. (1937) and Shirley A. (1939). Died 1974, aged 52 years.

SKUES   DONALD
Chart 3. Son of Vincent and Eva (née Rowland) Skues. Born June 1929, Leeds South. Died 1936, aged 7 years in Blackburn, Lancashire.

SKEWIS   DONALD EARL
Chart 2. Twin to Dale Skewis. Son of Raymond and Lottie Skewis. Born 16 April 1921, USA.

SKEWIS   DONALD G.
Engraver living at 1755 Dolores, San Francisco, USA in 1951. Wife's name Ruth.

SKEWES   DONALD HERBERT
Lives at Boundary Road, Warrenheip, 3350, Australia with Frances Anita Skewes.

SKEWS   DONALD IAN
Railway employee living at 141 Hare Street, Kalgoortie, Victoria, Australia in 1959 with Lois Violet Skews.

SKEWES   DONALD IAN
Lives at Lot/36 Hardy Road, Glen Forrest, 6071, Western Australia with Valerie Skewes.

SKEWES   DONALD JAMES
Chart 40. Son of William and Laura (née Allen) Skewes. Born 1932. Married Anita E. Thomas in Penzance, 1976.

SKEWIS   DONALD JAMES
Son of James Skewis of Toronto, Canada. Born 1974.

SKEWES   DONALD LLOYD
Chart 36. Son of William and Ida Olive (née SKEWES) Skewes. Married Elizabeth Blair Fisher. Children: Timothy Donald, Donna Elizabeth, Tania Jane, Matthew Charles and Simon William. In 1959 lived at 4 Brewery Lane, Tamworth, New South Wales, Australia.

SKEWES   DONALD RICHARD
Chart 37. Son of John Richard Skewes.Born 26 June 1919, Australia. Commissioned into 4 Australian Field Regiment (Jungle Division), Lieutenant, 3 October 1940. Lives at 26 Inmarna Avenue, Caringbah, 2229, New South Wales. Australia with Phyllis Marian Skewes. Public servant.

SKEWIS   DONNA
Chart 2. Daughter of Mason and Clara Skewis. Born 24 September 1946, America. Married Lynn William Dunn. Issue: 1 son.

SKEWES   DONNA ANN
Chart 36. Daughter of Gary William and Lynette Mary (née Smith) Skewes. Born 15 March 1968. Lives at 9 Surrey Road, Wilson, 6107, Western Australia.

SKEWES   DONNA ELIZABETH
Chart 36. Daughter of Donald Lloyd and Elizabeth Blair (née Fisher) Skewes. Born 9 November 1963, Tamworth, New South Wales, Australia.

SKEWES   DONNA LOUISE
Chart 38. Daughter of Kenneth Thomas and Joan Helen (née Bach) Bridge. Born 27 September 1949. Married Geoffrey Garfield Skewes 12 April 1971, St Kilda's Methodist Church, Australia. Son: Grayson Paul (1972). Lives at 28 York Street, South Caulfield, Melbourne, 3162, Victoria, Australia. Computer operator.

SKEWES   DONNA MARIE
Chart 36. Daughter of Geoffrey John and Margaret (née Shanley)

Skewes. Born 16 December 1976. Lives at 17 Wilkie Street, Werris Creek, 2341, New South Wales, Australia.

SKEWS   DONNA MARIE
Mother's maiden name Whitfield. Born 1977, St Austell.

SKEWS   DONNA MAY
Chart 24. Daughter of Jack and Betony (née Roach) Skewes. Born 24 November 1959. Lives at 6 Cardigan Street, Stockton, New South Wales, Australia, 2295. Married John Skey, 26 April 1980.

SKEWES   DORA.
Chart 10. Mexican. Daughter of Juan and Fransisca (Meneses) Skewes. Born 24 July 1952. aged 4 years.

SKUES   DORA BEATRICE
Chart 8. Born 1907, Shoreditch. Spinster. Lives in Loughton, Essex.

SKEWES   DORA MARIA
Chart 10. Mexican. Daughter of Humberto and Laura (née Borja) Skewes. Born 1 August 1957. Lives in Pachuca, Mexico.

SKEWES   DORA MARIA
Chart 10. Mexican. Daughter of Juan and Leonor (Munoz) Skewes. Born 18 June 1968.

SKEWS   DORA N.J.
Chart 15. Daughter of Frederick C. Skews. Mother's maiden name Charles. Born 1929, Totnes, Devon. Married Hickman in Wednesbury, 1950.

SKEWES   DORCAS
Born 1886, Penzance. Died 1886, aged 0.

SKEWES   DOREEN
Daughter of Frederick Thomas and Rose (née Trudgeon) Skewes. Born 28 September 1914. Married Winston Cuthbert. Lives in Canal Fulton, Ohio, United States of America.

SKUES   DOREEN
Chart 3. Née Arnold. Married Frèderick Mackenzie Skues, 1948. Divorce case 1968, London Divorce Court. She later married Patrick Ernest Bushnell in Manchester, 1968.

SKEWES   DOREEN
Chart 25. Married Joseph F. Skewes at Edge Lane Methodist Church, Stretford, Manchester 5 July 1958. Children: Allison Elizabeth, Melanie Anne and Jill Katheryn. Lives at 12 Walnut Walk, Stretford, Manchester.

SKEWES   DOREEN M.
Mother's maiden name Ford. Born 1915, Redruth. Married Foster in Redruth, 1935.

SKUES   DOREEN M.
Chart 9. Twin to Beryl I. Skues. Daughter of Arthur Leonard Peter Skues. Mother's maiden name Lamont. Born 1927, Barrow in Furness. Married Colin Peterson, 1955, Barrow in Furness.

SKEWES   DOREEN NELLIE
Chart 38. Daughter of Charles Leslie and Ellen Jane (née Ritter) Skewes. Born 12 August 1918. Married Eric Arthur Hancock, 19 December 1942. Issue: 2 daughters. Lives at 7 Blacker Avenue, Plympton Park, Adelaide, 5038, South Australia.

SKEWIS   DORINDA
Born 1895, New Monkland, Scotland.

SKEWES   DORIEL
Chart 12. Born 16 September 1926. Daughter of William John and Edith Mary Skewes. Lived at 1 Penhallick, Carn Brea, 1949. Married Fernley Harfoot, 1961. No issue.

SKEWES   DORIS
Born 1881. Died 1967 in America. Buried in Mount Olivet Cemetery, Salt Lak⌐ City, Utah.

SKEWES   DORIS
Born 1909, Truro. Died 1942, aged 32 years.

SKEWS   DORIS
Daughter of William and Susan Skews. Mother's maiden name Childs. Born 1920, Hackney, London. Died 1920, aged 0.

SKEWES   DORIS
Chart 36. Daughter of John Henry and Eliza Jane (née Bartle) Skewes. Married William Peters 31 August 1929 at Redruth Methodist Church. He was a general labourer and son of Daniel Laity Peters, mason of Higher North Country.

SKEWES   DORIS
Lived at 35 North Parade, Camborne 1949.

SKEWS   DORIS
Married Cocks, 1952, Kerrier.

SKEWES   DORIS
Lived at 60 Adrian Street, Palmyra, Melville, Victoria, Australia in 1959 with Roy Edward Skewes. Now lives at 332 Marmion St Melville, 6156, Western Australia.

SKUES   DORIS A.
Mother's maiden name Brissendon. Born 1914, Lewisham, London. Died 1914, aged 0.

SKUES   DORIS EILEEN
Chart 3. Daughter of John Frederick and Elizabeth (née Franklin) Hughes. Born 8 March 1913, Cheshire. Married Richard Skues at Frodsham Parish Church, Cheshire 5 March 1938. Children:

Doris Eileen Skues (1913-1974)

Dot and Garfield Skewes of South Australia

Richard Keith (1939), Margaret Elaine (1947) and Christopher Raymond (1949). Was a very active church worker, especially for "Mothers Union." Lived at "Bearwood", 19 De Redvers Road, Parkstone, Poole, Dorset. Previous address: "Richleen", 21 Buckingham Grove, Timperley, Cheshire. Died 23 March 1974, aged 61 years, at Poole General Hospital, Dorset.

SKEWES   DORIS EMMA
Wife of John Skewes. Born 1895. Lived at 505 Port Road, West Croydon, Brompton, South Australia in 1959. Died 18 November 1960, aged 65 years. Buried Hindmarsh Cemetery, South Australia.

SKUES   DORIS GAMBLE
Chart 3. Née Marsh. Born 1889. Married Ernest Skues, March 1919. Child: Margaret Pamela (1924). Died 1945 in Surrey Mid E., aged 56 years.

SKUES   DORIS HOPE
Chart 5. Daughter of Victor Ernest and Christina (née Bedwell) Hope. Born 7 February 1918. Married Jack Sydney Skues, 10 August 1940. Children: Margaret Lorraine (1941) and John Barry (1945). Lives at 202 Were Street, East Brighton, 3187, Victoria, Australia.

SKEWES   DORIS MARGARET
Chart 38. Daughter of Thomas Paul and Elvina Daisy May (née Skeer) Sandford. Born 13 August 1923, Prospect, South Australia. Served in Australian Women's Army Service 1943-1945 in Fremantle, Perth, Western Australia. Married (in uniform) Garfield Sydney Skewes, 25 May 1943 at Pirie Street Methodist Church, Adelaide. Children: Geoffrey Garfield Skewes (1946), Philip Graham (1949) and Cordelia Anne (1956). Lives at Chapmans Road, Inglewood, 5133, South Australia. Tel. no: Adelaide 380 5269.

SKEWES   DORIS MARY
Chart 25. Daughter of Harold and Agnes Skewes of 117 Yew Tree Road, Manchester. Mother's maiden name Agnes Lally. Born 12 December 1941. Married Albert McKenna 8 October 1932. Widowed 29 November 1954. One daughter June. Remarried Thomas Lane 4 February 1961.

SKEWS   DORIS MARY CARMELLA
Graduate of Exeter University 1926-1929. B.A. Hons (English) II (I), 1928. C.S.T.D. (II) 1929. Information from "Exeter University Register 1893-1962."

SKEWS   DORIS MAY
Born 1898, Redruth. Died 1898, aged 0.

SKEWS   DORIS MAY
Author of *Letter Writing for General and Commercial Courses* (1935) and *Principles of Precis* (1959).

SKEWES   DORIS MURIEL
Chart 12. Daughter of Harry Oswald and Emily Ann (née Taylor) Skewes. Born 1901. Bpt Camborne Parish Church 28 June 1905. Lived at 4 Centenery Street, Camborne. Married Richard Rogers in Camborne, 1934. Issue: 2 sons.

SKEWES   DORIS ROSE
Lives at 107 Caringbah Road, Caringbah, 2229, New South Wales, Australia.

SKEWES   DORITER
Daughter of Humfry Skewes. Buried Gerrans 7 August 1639.

SKEWES   DOROTHEA ALISON
Lived at 28 Anderson Road, Auburn, Victoria, Australia in 1959, with Annie Dorothea Skewes and Philip Randolph Skewes. Typist.

SKEWES   DOROTHEA HOPE
Daughter of Wilfred J. and Ann Louisa (née Borgas) Skewes. Born South Australia. Married Robert Edward Armstead. Issue: 2 sons and 1 daughter.

SKEWES   DOROTHY
Daughter of Richard and Joane Skewes. Bpt St Keverne 26 August 1638.

SCRUSE   DOROTHY
Wife of Richard Scruse. Buried Ludgvan 23 January 1657.

SKEWES   DOROTHY
Daughter of John Skewes. Bpt St Keverne 22 December 1667.

SKEWES   DOROTHY
Chart 14. Daughter of Manley and Eva (née Reed) Skewes. Born Yorkville, Wisconsin, USA, 1903. Married Ernest Melton. Issue: 4 sons and 1 daughter.

SKEWIS   DOROTHY
Married John M. Taylor in New Monkland, Scotland, 1957.

SKEWES   DOROTHY ALICE
Chart 38. Daughter of Horace Henry and Agatha Blanche Skewes. Born 5 August 1914, Broken Hill, New South Wales. Married 26 September 1931 to Horace Plane in Australia.

SKEWES   DOROTHY BARBARA
Chart 40. Daughter of William and Laura Skewes. Mother's maiden name Allen. Born 1926. Spinster. Farms at Chiverton, Rosudgeon, Cornwall.

SKEWES   DOROTHY CATHERINE
Lived at Fox Street, Narrogan, Williams, Victoria in 1959 with William Wilfred John Skewes, piano tuner. Now lives at 3b Goldsmith Street, Narrogin, 6312 Western Australia.

SKEWES   DOROTHY CHERYL
Chart 2. Née Fitzclarence. Married Graham Henry Skewes 27 August 1942 at Maffra, Victoria, Australia. Children: Katrina Louise (1972) and Jacqueline Ann (1974). Lives at 15 Crossen Street, Eshuca, 3625, Victoria, Australia.

SKEWES   DOROTHY DAINTRY
Daughter of William and Elizabeth Alberta Mary Jessop Skewes. Born 18 October 1906 at Superior, Houghton, Michigan. Married Ralph Matthews.

SKEWES   DOROTHY DAWN
Chart 36. Daughter of William and Ida Olive (née Skewes) Skewes. In 1959 lived at 4 Brewery Lane, Tamworth, New South Wales, Australia, with her brother Donald Lloyd Skewes. Married Dale Ross. Issue: one son and one daughter.

SKEWIS   DOROTHY DELPHINE
Chart 2. Daughter of Charles Samuel and Myrtle Skewis. Born 10 May 1900, America. Graduated from Morningside College, Sioux City, Iowa, 1922. B.A. Wayne University, Detroit, Michigan. M.A. (1942). Studied graphic arts for two years at Chicago Art Institute. Taught Latin and English at high school in Greenville for one year. She taught for 29 years at Cass Technical High School, and for six years was head of the department. She left in 1954 and returned from Detroit to Iowa.
Dorothy taught for 14 years at Buena Vista College, Storm Lake, Iowa. In all she spent 42 years in the teaching profession. Today she is an unofficial reference point in Storm Lake for any queries on graphic art.

To her credit are *Handwriting in the United States*, a study of the American copy books in the Rickett's collection (Wayne University, 1943) and *Neoferkephtar and the Book of Troth*, Chicago, 1925, compiled from a collection of old Egyptian legends. Designed, set and printed with an illustration cut in wood by Dorothy. She helped develop the Art Gallery in Storm Lake (a very going concern today) with Betty Skewis Ballou and which was opened in 1974. In 1977 University College, Storm Lake honoured Dorothy with the degree "Doctor of Fine Arts." She has done much to collate her branch of the Skewis family with the help of diaries written by her grandfather James Skewis.
Lives at 303 Lake Avenue, Storm Lake, Iowa, 50588, United States of America.

SKEWES   DOROTHY EDNA
Lives at 4 Oakington Street, Torrensville, 5031, South Australia.

SKEWES   DOROTHY GWENDOLINE
Born 1895, Newton Abbot, Devon.

SKEWES DOROTHY HELEN
Lives at 61 Acacia Street, Seacliffe, 5049, South Australia. Nurse.

SKEWS   DOROTHY J.
Chart 17. Daughter of Albert Edward Skews. Mother's maiden name Harding. Born 1934. Married Harvey in Edmonton, 1958.

SKEWES   DOROTHY JESSIE
Lived at 13 Longeuville Road, Lane Cove, New South Wales, Australia in 1959 with James Robert Skewes.

SKUES   DOROTHY KATHLEEN
Chart 8. Daughter of John Gilbert Skues. Born 1899, Edmonton. Married 1924 to Charles L. Abbott in Edmonton.

SKEWIS   DOROTHY M.
Chart 33. Daughter of William Richard Skewis. Mother's maiden name Shute. Born 1912, Totnes. Died 1913, aged 1 year.

SKUES   DOROTHY MARGARET
Born 1906, Shoreditch. Died 1906, aged 0.

SKEWES   DOROTHY MARINA
Chart 12. Daughter of John Henry and Evelyn May (née Cork). Born 1939, Redruth. Married 1957 to Philips in Falmouth. Prior to marriage she was a former Carnival Queen of Mylor.

SKEWES   DOROTHY MARION
Chart 48. Née Hornby. Born 1898. Married William Frederick Charles Skewes, 1929, Doncaster. Died 19 July 1947, aged 49 years. Children: Barbara Ann (1931) and John Hornby (1933).

SKEWES   DOROTHY MAY
Née Chapman. Born 12 December 1929. Married Geoffrey Skewes 27 January 1951. Children: Gregory Archer (1952), Ian Charles (1953), Rosalie Anne (1956), Helen Elizabeth (1960) and Bronwyn May (1964). Lives at 35 Jean Street, Grange, 4051, Queensland, Australia.

SKEWES   DOROTHY MAY
Chart 36. Née Burn. Born 6 June 1923. Married Jack Roe Skewes 2 May 1942. Children: Trevor John (1944), Timothy Lester (1948), Christopher Allen (1954) and Peter Nathaniel (1955). Lives at 16 Alawara Road, Ingle Farm, South Australia, 5098.

SKEWES   DOROTHY MELVA
Chart 38. Daughter of Nicholas John and Emiline (née Harrop) James. Born 28 May 1916, South Australia. Married Cyril George Skewes, 7 April 1943. Children: Colleen Ruth (1947) and Helen Joyce (1949). Lives at 23 Doswell Terrace, Kadina, 5554, South Australia.

SKEWES   DOROTHY T.E.
Mother's maiden name Webber. Born 1934, Totnes, Devon.

SKEWES   DOUGLAS
Chart 38. Son of Stanley Victor and Gertrude Olive (née Trimper) Skewes. Married Lorna May Webb. Adopted one son Ian Douglas. Lives at 2 Miller Street, Kidman Park, 5025, South Australia. Mechanic.

Skewis' of America. Left to right: Dorothy Delphine standing behind her cousins Robert & Betty Hazel.

Woodcut picture "Forces and Energies" produced by Dorothy Delphine Skewis

SKEWES DOUGLAS ARTHUR
Chart 36. Son of Archer William and Elsie May (née Handley) Skewes. Born 7 September 1926. Married Coleen Marie McKenzie of Mineeda, Queensland 6 April 1953. Children: Allison Mary (1954), Diane Rebecca (1956), Kay Elizabeth (1957) and Colin Douglas (1963). Lives at 62 Shamrock Street, Blackall, 4723, Queensland, Australia.

SKEWES DOUGLAS GEORGE
Born 6 December 1941 at Bluefield, MacDowell, West Virgina, USA. Son of Harold Hershell Skewes and Gladys J. (née Batty) Skewes. Married 24 January 1961, North Hollywood to Sue Simrell. Child: Michael Douglas Skewes (1964).

SKEWES DOUGLAS JAMES
Chart 36. Son of James Henry and Elsie (née Snow) Skewes. Born 4 August 1948. Married Madeline Kingston, 12 June 1971, Australia. No children. Lives at 78 Taylor Street, Woy Woy, 2256, New South Wales, Australia. Engraver.

SKEWES DOUGLAS WESTMORE
Son of Thomas Westmore and Isobel (née Sommerville) Skewes. Born 11 May 1922, Warragul, Victoria, Australia. Married Lorna Jean Farquhar, 28 February 1948 at Wangaratta, Victoria. Children: Craig Douglas (1949), Ian Thomas and Lynette Mary-twins (1951). Lives at 13 Barton Drive, Mount Elizabeth, 3930, Victoria, Australia.

SKEWES DOUGLAS WILLIAM
Chart 36. Son of Charles Harold Vivian and Maude (née Lamphee) Skewes. Born 28 September 1912. Married Elsie May Smith, 18 June 1938. She died 1955. Married Jean Gladys Lovell, 30 March 1968. Lives at 6 Hillcrest Road, Kewdale, 6105, West Australia. Sub foreman.

SKEWIS DUDLEY WALTER KENT
Lived at Gormleys Road, Chinchilla, Marona, Queensland, Australia in 1959. Benchman. Now lives at 15 Henney Street, Chilla, 4413, Queensland, Australia with Janice Florence Skewis. Sawmill hand.

SKEWES DUANE WILLIAM
Chart 14. Son of George Boulden and Helen Skewes. Born 4 April 1873, America. Married May Farrington. Child: La Mar (1903). Died 1912, aged 39 years.

SKEWES DULCIE
Lived at Asquith Street, Austinmer, New South Wales, Australia in 1959 with Ronald Leslie Skewes. Now lives at 15/20 Springvale Avenue, Potts Point, 2011, New South Wales, Australia. Storewoman.

SKEWES DULCIE EMMA
Lives at 49 La Perouse Avenue, Flinders Park, 5025, South Australia with Alison Mary Skewes.

SKEWES DULCIE JEAN
Lives at 7 Nerong Road, Lambton, 2229, New South Wales, Australia with Leo William Skewes.

E

SKUSE E.
Author of "*Skuse's Complete Confectioner*". Lived at 1, Ashmore Road, London W.

SKEWS E.S.
Lived at 11, Ford Park Road, Plymouth, 1920/1921.

SKEWES EARL
Chart 14. Son of Samuel Skewes of Yorkville, Wisconsin, USA. Twin to Charles J. Skewes. Married with one daughter Mary. Lives at 5801 16th Street, Racine, Wisconsin, USA.

SKEWES EARL
Chart 14. Adopted son of James Lugg and Jane Skewes. Born 1898. Died 1904. Buried in Yorkville Cemetery.

SKEWES EARLE WILLIAM
Chart 36. Son of William and Ida Olive (née SKEWES) Skewes. Born 14 April 1924, Watsons Creek, New South Wales. Lived at 520 Peel Street, Tamworth, New South Wales, Australia. Married Edna Fay Chad, 29 December 1950. Children: Gary Earle (1951), David Michael (1954), Lynda Suzanne (1956), Sharon Gae (1958) and Jillian Fay (1959). Labourer.

SKEWES EBENEZER JOHN
Chart 30. Son of Henry and Catherine Skewes. Bpt Kea 17 April 1797.

SKEWES EDGAR
Son of Harry and Mary Skewes. Born January 1890, New York. In 1900 was living at New Hempstead, Nassau, New York, USA.

SKEWES EDGAR
Chart 14. Son of Lyman and Lilian (née Bertke) Skewes. Born 1928. Married Beulah Haverwas. Children: Linton and Jeffrie. Lived at 927, 67th Drive, Union Grove, Wisconsin, 53182, USA.

SKEWIS EDGAR
Chart 2. Son of John Rule and Jane Skewis of America. Married Myrtle ..... Child: Russell Skewis.

SKEWS EDGAR
Chart 41. Son of Thomas and Ada (née Sheldon) Skews. Born 23

December 1904, Jump, Barnsley, South Yorkshire. Educated at King's Road School, Wombwell and Hemingfield Church of England School. Left school at 13 and joined Mitchell's Main Colliery at Wombwell working at the pit top on screens.
He went down the pit at 15½ as a pony driver, a job he held for a year. He then went to Cortonwood Colliery on haulage and tramming for four years. This was followed by three years at Elsecar Colliery "tramming" and from 1926 to 1970 at Houghton Main working at the coal face, although his last four years were spent controlling conveyor belts, extracting coal from the face.
He married Constance Mary Royston on 26 December 1931 at Darfield Parish Church, South Yorkshire. She died 21 March 1977, aged 76 years.
He is a champion crown green bowler.
Lives at 10, Woodall Flats, Darfield, Barnsley, South Yorkshire.

Wedding of Edgar Skews to Constance Mary Royston at Darfield Parish Church, Barnsley, 26 December 1931

SKUES EDGAR CLAUDIUS
Chart 8. Born 1888, Edmonton, London. Died 1889, aged 6 months from fits.

SKEWES EDGAR ERNEST
Lived at 3, Dew Street, The Barton, South Australia in 1959 with Florence Louisa Skewes. He was a "striker."

SKEWES EDGAR WILLIAM
Chart 38. Son of Richard and Mary Jane (née Reynolds) Skewes. Born 8 February 1884, Moonta, South Australia. Married 24 October 1904 to Mary Bridget Kavanagh. Children: Richard Skewes, Murray Skewes and Charles Percival Skewes. Died 29 June 1947, aged 63 years.

SKEWS EDITH
Born 1861. Widow who lived at 24 Margaret Road, Penwortham, Preston, Lancashire. Died 5 May 1942, aged 81 years.

SKEWES EDITH
Chart 36. Born 1862. Daughter of Edward and Julie Skewes of Poleskan, Cury. Bpt Cury 21 January 1863. Spinster living at Nantithet, Cury in 1871 Census Returns. Died 21 April 1938, aged 75 years. Buried in Cury Churchyard.

SKEWES EDITH
Chart 36. Daughter of John Skewes, railway guard. Born 1873. Married John House (24), miner of Condurrow, and son of Nicholas House, deceased, engine driver at Tuckingmill Parish Church 18 July 1896. Married in presence of Kate Skewes.

SKUES EDITH
Born 1879, Thetford. Died 1879, aged 0.

SKEWES EDITH
Chart 18. Daughter of Samuel Dawe and Emma Skewes. Born 1889. Died 17 March 1916, Tavistock, Devon, aged 26 years. Buried at Bere Alston, Devon.

SKEWES   EDITH
Chart 36. Née Howarth. Born 19 October 1889. Married William
Skewes, 1907. Lived at Watsons Creek, New South Wales, Australia.
Children: May (1908), Eva (1910), Dulcie (1912), William (1915), Roy
(1918), Daphne (1921) and Frank (1925).
Died 29 March 1975, aged 85 years. Buried in Methodist Section of
Bendemeer Cemetery, New South Wales, Australia.
SKEWES   EDITH
Chart 10. Née Jenkin. Married William Trevena Skewes, 1915,
Penzance. Child: Violet May (1918). Lives at at Carn Villa, Crowlas,
Ludgvan, Penzance, Cornwall.
SKEWES   EDITH
Born 1898. Lived at Condurrow, Redruth. Died 1900 aged 22 months.
Buried Tuckingmill 10 April 1900.
SKEWES   EDITH
Born 1899, Penzance.
SKEWES   EDITH
Born 1900, Redruth. Died 1901, aged 1 year.
SKEWIS   EDITH
Chart 2. Daughter of Frank and Daisy Skewis of America.
SKEWES   EDITH
Mother's maiden name Skewes. Born 1920, Penzance. Married Milton
in Penzance, 1944.
SKEWES   EDITH
Lived at Bosleake Row with James Skewes in 1922, Redruth.
SKEWES   EDITH
Lived at 1, Penhalik, Carn Brea, Illogan, Redruth in 1949 with Doriel
and Muriel Skewes.
SKEWIS   EDITH ALICE
Chart 50. Née Hughes. Born 5 November 1893. Married Alfred Skewis
in Haverfordwest, 1913. Lived at 13, Dartmouth Gardens, Milford
Haven, Pembrokeshire.Children: Delilah C. (1913), Alfred W. St E.
(1916).Brenda G.S. (1924) and Gretta (1934). Died 1975, aged 82 years.
SKEWES   EDITH ANN
Née White. Married Leslie Henry Irving Skewes 1925. Children: Henry
Snowden (1926), Dulcie Margaret (1927) and David Leslie (1929).
Lived at 43 Tom Street, Yarrawonga, Victoria, Australia. Died 21
October 1976.
SKEWES   EDITH BERYL
Lives at 7 Cormack Road, Beacon Hill, 2100 New South Wales,
Australia with William Ashdown Skewes, mechanic.
SKEWES   EDITH FLORENCE
Born 1882, Stoke Devonport. Married 1907, Plymouth.
SKEWIS   EDITH G.
Wife of Joseph R. Skewis, junior. Private residence 1423 Magnolia
Avenue, Los Angeles, USA.
SKEWES   EDITH GRACE
Chart 14. Daughter of Hannibal and Eliza Skewes. Born 7 June 1866,
Yorkville, Wisconsin, USA. School teacher. Married Thomas Hay 25
December 1890. Issue: 4 sons. Died 1911.
SKEWES   EDITH JANE
Chart 5. Daughter of Lewis and Eliza Skewes of Fowey, Cornwall,
miner. Born 1877. Bpt Fowey 6 May 1877. Married 1905, Redruth.
SKEWS   EDITH JANE
Born 1890, Easington. Died 1890, aged 0.
SKEWS   EDITH JANE
Chart 15. Daughter of John Gregory and Annie Skews of Callington,
Cornwall. Had illegitimate son Kenneth W.W. (1923). Married
Andrew Kenny, 1927, Devonport. Died 1975, aged 74 years.
SKEWES   EDITH L.
Born 1878, Redruth. Died 1925, aged 47 years.
SKUES   EDITH MARY
Born 1882, Eton. Died 1883, aged 1 year
SKEWES   EDITH MARY
Born 1891. Died 1956, aged 65 years, Redruth.
SKEWES   EDITH MARY
Chart 36. Daughter of Charles Harold Vivian and Maude Emiline (née
Lamphee) Skewes. Born 5 June 1922, Brookton, Western Australia.
Married Victor Albert Blair 29 May 1946 at St Matthew's Church,
Guildford, Australia. Issue: one daughter. Lives at 20 Wallsend Street,
Safety Bay, Western Australia.
SKEWS   EDITH S.
Married Frost in Preston, 1925.
SKEWS   EDITH SARAH
Born 1900, Bethnal Green.
SKEWS   EDMOND JOHN
Lives at 32 Frome Avenue, Frankston, 3199, Victoria, Australia with
Brendan Ashley Jay Skews and Hilda Margaret Skews.
SKEWS   EDMUND
Chart 15. Born 1867. Bpt St Ive Parish Church 23 June 1867. Son of
Peter and Elizabeth Skews of Pensilva, Callington. Married Maria . . . . .
1892, Liskeard. Died 22 March 1928, aged 61 years at the Homoepathic
Hospital, Plymouth. Children: James Henry (1893) and Florence
Beatrice (1894). Maria died 1955, aged 87 years.

SKEWS   EDMUND JOHN
Lived at 82 Stuart Avenue, Manley, New South Wales, Australia, 1959,
with Esther Deller Skews.
SKEWES   EDMUNDO
Living at 3109 Cadbury Drive, Las Vegas, 8912, USA in 1979. Tel No:
(702) 458   7758.
SKEWES   EDNA
Chart 25. Mother's maiden name Barrett. Daughter of Barry and
Sarah E. Skewes. Born 1922. Halifax, Yorkshire. Married Waller in
Halifax, 1946.
SKEWES   EDNA
Lived at 22 Ellesmere Street, North Perth in 1959 with Herbert Skewes,
civil servant. Now lives at 59 Gale Street, Busselton, 6280, Western
Australia.
SKEWES   EDNA FAY
Chart 36. Née Chad. Married Earl William Skewes 29 December 1950.
Lived at 520 Peel Street, Tamworth, New South Wales, Australia in
1959. Children: Gary Earl (1951), David Michael (1954), Lynda
Suzanne (1956), Sharon Gae (1958) and Jillian Fay (1959).
SKUES   EDNA JOYCE
Chart 3. Née Littlewood. Married George Ernest Skues in Melton
Mowbray, 1949. Two sons: Richard Anthony (1953) and Mark Alastair
(1957). Lives at 31 Eastern Road, Sutton Coldfield, Warwickshire.
SKEWES   EDNA MAVIS
Chart 36. Daughter of Robert Northey and Sarah Agnes (née Connell)
Skewes. Born 24 June 1909, Tingha, NSW, Australia. Known as Sister
Agnes. B.A. University of Sydney. Religious Sister of Charity. Author of
Life Comes to Newness (Brisbane, 1982). Lives at Mount Olivet
Hospital, 411 Main Street, Kangaroo Point, Brisbane, Queensland,
4169, Australia.
SKEWES   EDNA MAY
Chart 25. Daughter of Harry and Agnes (née Lally) Skewes of 117 Yew
Tree Road, Manchester. Born 3 December 1923, Chorlton. Married
Booth in Manchester, 1843.
SKEWES   EDNA PHYLLIS
Chart 24. Lives at Boat Harbour Road, Boat Harbour, 2301, New
South Wales, Australia with Sirrel Arthur Skewes, bricklayer.
SKEWES   EDUARDO GUSTAVO
Chart 10. Son of Guillermo and Teresa (née Bonnett) Skewes. Mexican.
Born 28 August 1972, Mexico City.
SKEWES   EDWARD
Mentioned in Cornwall Protestation Returns, 1642, Cury.
SKEWES   EDWARD
Chart 35. Married Elizabeth . . . . . Children: William and Edward.
Lived at Cury.
SKEWES   EDWARD
Chart 35. Son of Edward and Elizabeth Skewes. Born 11 February 1695.
Bpt Cury 16 February 1695.
SKEWS   EDWARD
Buried Gerrans 8 August 1661.
SKEWS   EDWARD
Son of John Skews. Bpt Gerrans 6 September 1661.
SKEWS   EDWARD
Chart 13. Son of John and Elizabeth (née Whitford) Skews. Bpt
Mevagissey 31 January 1686.
SKEWIS   EDWARD
Chart 2. Son of James Edward and Alice Skewis. Legally changed his
name to Brown in America.
SKEWES   EDWARD
Son of Edward and Elizabeth Skewes. Bpt Cury 16 February 1695.
SKEWES   EDWARD
Chart 14. Son of Henry and Judith Skewes. Bpt Gunwalloe 3 April 1720.
Married Margaret Rogers at Sithney 13 May 1743. Children: John,
Henry and Eleanor. Buried Ruan Major 23 December 1791.
SKEWES   EDWARD
Son of William and Avise Skewes. Bpt Gunwalloe 27 August 1721.
SKEWES   EDWARD
Married Ann Boal at Gunwalloe 10 November 1723.
SKEWES   EDWARD
Chart 36. Son of James and Sarah Skewes. Bpt Cury 1 March 1723.
SKEWES   EDWARD
Buried Cury 19 March 1747.
SKEWES   EDWARD
Son of Philip and Anne Skewes. Bpt St Ewe 8 January 1747.
SKEWES   EDWARD
Chart 36. Son of John and Mary Skewes. Bpt Cury 31 October 1756.
Lived at White Cross, Cury. Labourer. Died 27 June, 1845 ,aged 90
years.
SKEWES   EDWARD
Buried Cury 16 July 1758.
SKEWES   EDWARD
Bpt Cury 1 March 1761. Son of John and Mary Skewes.
SKEWES   EDWARD
Buried Cury 19 December 1761.

SKEWES EDWARD
Born 1727. Buried Helston 20 July 1782, aged 55 years.

SKEWES EDWARD
Bpt St Ewe 13 January 1751. Son of Philip and Ann Skewes.

SKEWES EDWARD
Married Honore Pearce 13 April 1762, Helston. Banns read 31 January, 7 February and 15 February.

SKEWES EDWARD
Chart 36. Son of John and Mary Skewes. Born 1781. Bpt Cury 6 January 1782. Lived at Treloskan, Cury with his brother James Skewes in 1841 and 1851 Census Returns.
Was a farmer. Died Cury 18 January 1861, aged 79 years.

SKEWES EDWARD
Mariner. Married Grace Pearce 23 September 1788 at Helston.

SKEWES EDWARD
Chart 2. Twin to James Skewes and son of Absalom and Elizabeth Skewes. Bpt Camborne 7 June 1795. Married Mary Pearce 3 March 1817, Camborne in presence of James Skewis. Children: Mary, Edward, Ann, Catherine, James, Eliza, Honor, Henry, Caroline and William. Emigrated to Wisconsin. Died 28 January 1872, aged 77 years. Buried in Shullsburg Cemetery, Wisconsin, USA. Mary (born 17 December 1793) died June 1858, aged 64 years.

SKEWIS EDWARD
Chart 14. Son of Henry and Jane Skewis. Bpt St Keverne 19 July 1795.

SKUES EDWARD
Chart 3. Son of Richard and Ann Skues. Born 14 September 1795. Died 13 October 1795, aged one month.

SKEWES EDWARD
Chart 36. Son of William and Alice Skewes of Treloskan, Cury. Bpt Cury 8 December 1810. Died Nantithet 20 April 1875, aged 64 years.

SKEWES EDWARD
Chart 36. Son of John and Loveday Skewes of Nantithet. Shoemaker. Born 1814. Bpt Cury 27 March 1814. In 1871 Census Returns was living at Nantithet, Cury. Had a sister Mary Percy, another sister Elizabeth Skewes and a niece Elizabeth Mary Skewes. Married three times. 1) Martha who was buried 17 September 1843, aged 26 years. 2) Mary died 1844 and 3) Julia Roberts at Register Office, Helston 13 February 1845. She died 13 August 1910, aged 85 years. Children: John, Loveday Hendy, Martha Elizabeth, Eliza, James, Thomas William, Henry, Annie, Bessie, Edith, Laura, Edward and Juliana. Died 20 February 1878 at Poleskan, Cury, aged 64 years. Buried in Cury Churchyard 24 February 1878. Julia is also buried in Cury Churchyard.

SKEWES EDWARD
Chart 36. Son of William and Christian Skewes of Ruan Major. Born 1819. Bpt Ruan Major 7 February 1819. Blacksmith at Mawnan. Twice married. 1) Mary Penticost Nicholls at St Keverne Church 20 August 1844. 2) Mary Ellen Kempthorne, daughter of John Kempthorne, carpenter; at Mawnan Parish Church 30 June 1867, in presence of James Skewes.
Died 22 June 1870, aged 51 years.

SKUES EDWARD
Chart 2. Son of Edward and Mary Skues of Camborne. Born 3 August 1820. In 1841 Census Returns was a copper miner. Married Catherine Jeane Peters, a divorcee. Emigrated to California, USA in 1846. Died America 6 October 1899, aged 79 years.

SKUES EDWARD
Chart 2. Son of James and Joanna Skues. Bpt Camborne 11 January 1824. Mining engineer. Emigrated to Shullsburg, Wisconsin, USA 1849. Married Kittie .... from England. Edward later became a butcher. Children: Emma, Harriet, Mary, Edward J., William H., and Clarence G. Died 28 January 1899, aged 74 years. Buried in Shullsburg Cemetery.

SKEWES EDWARD
Chart 14. Son of Henry and Grace Skewes, innkeeper at Cadgwith. Bpt Ruan Minor 27 March 1831.

SKUSE EDWARD
Married Sarah Coles, 1831 at Mangotsville, Gloucester.

SKEWES EDWARD
Married Alice Triggs 11 November 1834 at Cury.

SKEWES EDWARD
Chart 14. Son of Henry and Jane Skewes. Born 1795. Farmer of 50 acres. In 1851 Census Returns living at Carne, St Keverne. Married Mary Lory (by licence) at St Keverne 18 February 1835. Mary had died by 1851. Children: Edward H., Susan J. and Richard Lory. Died 1866, aged 70 years.

SKEWES EDWARD
Chart 36. Son of James and Simonette Skewes, farmer of Cury. Bpt Cury 6 May 1838. Copper miner. Twice married. 1) Jecoliah Uren, daughter of William Uren, miner, at Parish Church, Lannarth 27 April 1861. She was buried at Gwennap 3 August 1875. 2) Elizabeth Emily Bennett Semmens (32), daughter of John Semmens, in presence of John Skewes at Parish Church, Treslothan, Camborne, 3 August 1876. Lived in Cury during his youth and later Troon. He was a railway guard. Children: Edward James, William, Elizabeth Jane, Mary, Catherine, Alfred John and Alice Emily. Buried Tuckingmill 2 May 1909, aged 70

years.

SKEWES EDWARD
Chart 36. Son of James and Frances Skewes, parish clerk. Bpt Mawnan Parish Church 16 September 1849. Bachelor. Lived at West Close, Mawnan, Falmouth. Died 24 January 1942, aged 92 years.

SKEWS EDWARD
Born 1849, North Aylesford, Kent. Died 1912, aged 63 years in Dartford, Kent.

SKEWES EDWARD
Chart 2. Son of Henry and Hannah Skewes of Gwinear. Lived at Rewlya Lane, Gwinear, 1871 Census Returns. Wife Agnes (born 1864-died 1932 and 68 years at 41, George Street, Linley Huddersfield, Yorkshire). In diary of James Skewis of Inwood, Iowa, Edward is listed with the addresses: Joy House, Linley, Huddersfield; 35 Lemon Street, Truro and Ivey House, Huddersfield. Diary dated 1910. Died at Yew Tree Road, Birchencliffe, Huddersfield 23 May 1915, aged 63 years.

SKEWES EDWARD
Chart 14. Born 1853. Bpt Ruan Major 27 March 1853. Son of Anthony and Christian Skewes, farmer of Tresodden. Died Ruan Major 25 August 1857, aged 4 years.

SKEWES EDWARD
Married 1861, Redruth.

SKEWES EDWARD
Chart 25. Son of Charles and Elizabeth Skewes, shoemaker of Falmouth. Born 1864. In 1871 Census Returns living at Brook Street, Falmouth with his parents and sister Louisa J. and brothers Charles, William John and George. Married Eliza Maddocks, 1885, Chorlton. Hosiery warehouseman. Children: John Edward (1886), Charles (1889), Harold (1892), William Frederick (1894) and Arthur George (1897). Died 1899, aged 35 years.

SKEWES EDWARD
Chart 36. Son of Edward (shoemaker) and Julia Skewes of Cury. Bpt 4 January 1867, Cury. In 1871 Census Returns at Nantithet, Cury. Lived at Wood View, Gweek — farmer. Later lived at Bonython House, Cury. Was a regular attender at Cury Methodist Church and also Ashton Methodist Church. Died at Winsford, Ashton, Helston 14 August 1952, aged 86 years. Buried in Cury Churchyard.

SKEWES EDWARD
Born 1868, died 1893, aged 25 years in Helston.

SKEWES EDWARD
Chart 36. Son of William and Priscilla Skewes of Camborne. Born 1867.

SKEWES EDWARD
Married 1872, Chelsea.

SKEWES EDWARD
Wrote essay on Gwinear Mining District — 1875.

SKEWIS EDWARD
Lived at Newton, Camborne 1885/1886.

SKEWS EDWARD
Born 1886, Easington. Died 1888, aged 1 year.

SKEWIS EDWARD
Married 1892, Redruth.

SKEWIS EDWARD
Born 1893, Redruth. Died 1893, aged 0.

SKEWES EDWARD
Chart 36. Born 1896, Redruth. Son of Henry and Elizabeth Johanna Skewes. Emigrated to America in 1920's. One son — Reginald.

SKEWES EDWARD
Married 1901, Chorlton.

SKEWES EDWARD
Born 1904, Salford. Died 1906, aged 1 year.

SKEWES EDWARD
Chart 10. Son of Juan and Fransisca (Meneses) Skewes. Born Real del Monte, Mexico, 1912. Died 18 May 1914, aged 2 years.

SKEWES EDWARD
Lived at Condurrow, Camborne, 1922.

SKEWES EDWARD
Chart 26. Son of Grant Phillip Skewes of Connecticut, USA.

SKEWES EDWARD
Chart 25. Son of Charles and Mary Skewes. Mother's maiden name Gichero. Born 1915, Chorlton. No children.

SKEWES EDWARD
Lived at Bartles Row, Tuckingmill, Camborne, 1949, with Alfred John and Matilda Skewes.

SKEWES EDWARD
Married Minnie Ingleby, Stockport, 1964.

SKEWES EDWARD ALBERT
Born 1867, Redruth. Died 1869, aged 1 year.

SKEWES EDWARD ALBERT
Born 1868, Falmouth. Died 1869, aged 1 year.

SKUES EDWARD ALBERT
"Alfred". Chart 7. Born 13 August 1893. Son of Thomas and Elizabeth (née Harris) Skues of Commercial Road, Paddock Wood, Tonbridge, Kent. Married Madge Irene Meads, 1920, Tonbridge. Children: Eric Edward Alfred (1922), Betty Irene (1924) and Roydon Thomas (1929).

Died 1948, aged 55 years in Tonbridge, Kent. Madge died 1971, aged 78 years, Tonbridge.

SKEWES   EDWARD ANTHONY
Chart 26. Son of Robert Ernest and Elaine Helen (née Albanese) Skewes, of Connecticut, USA. Born 18 May 1955.

SKEWES   EDWARD C.
Living at 104 Walden Drive, Manassas Park, Virginia, 22110, USA (1980). Comes from New Jersey.

SKEWES   EDWARD ERNEST
Lived at 178 York Street, Warrenheip, Victoria, Australia, 1959, with Joyce Margaret Skewes. Now lives at 24 Pico Avenue, Point Lonsdale, 3225, Victoria, Australia. Plumber.

SKEWES   EDWARD FOSTER
Graduated from University of Adelaide LL B. (1917). In 1959 lived at Elderstie Road, Naracoorte, South Australia. Now lives at 17 Arthur Street, Naracoorte, 5721 with Effie Una Skewes. Solicitor.

SKUES   EDWARD FRANCIS
Born 1858, Strand. Died 1899, aged 41 years.

SKEWES   EDWARD FREDERICK
Chart 12. Son of Frederick Tresize Skewes, of Wheal Seaton. Born 1882, Helston. Died 1893, aged 11 years. Buried Tuckingmill 29 November 1893.

SKEWES   EDWARD G.
Lived at 1430 Glenwood Avenue, San Jose, USA (1960). Wife: Ann L. Skewes.

SKEWES   EDWARD GARY
Chart 26. Son of Frank Anson and June Beverley (née Spaulding) Skewes of Connecticut, USA. Born 24 December 1958. Bachelor. Lives in East Lyme, Connecticut, USA.

SKUES   EDWARD GEORGE
Chart 3. Son of Frederick Mackenzie and Mary Skues. Born 1869, Islington, London. Emigrated to Bethlehem, Orange Free State, South Africa. Lived at Quiet Street, Claremont, Wynberg, Cape Colony, South Africa. Veterinary surgeon. Died 30 June 1933, aged 64 years.

SKEWS   EDWARD GEORGE
Born 1873, Dartford, Kent. Died 1937, aged 64 years, Dartford.

SKEWIS   EDWARD GEORGE
Chart 2. Twin to Charles Elmer Skewis, and son of Francis Harry and Annie Skewis. Born 13 June 1909, America. Married Margaret Johnson 20 August 1932. Children: Marienne, Richard Edward and Caroline Grace.

SKEWES   EDWARD HENRY
Chart 14. Son of Edward and Mary Skewes. Born 1836, St Keverne. Died 1868, aged 32 years. He had run away to sea with his brother Richard Skewes. He eventually ended up in Yorkville, Wisconsin, USA and lived at Grovean. During the American Civil War he served with 2nd Wisconsin Cavalry as a private enlisting on 3 February 1862. Bachelor. He deserted 20 January 1863.

SKEWES   EDWARD HENRY
Chart 14. Son of Hannibal and Eliza Skewes, farmer. Born 12 May 1869. Married Helen Gilmore, 18 March 1897. Children: Alma May (1899) and Lyman Hannibal (1904). Was secretary of the Union Grove Telephone Company when it celebrated its 100th anniversary in 1938. Lived in Yorkville, Wisconsin, USA.

SKEWES   EDWARD HENRY
Married 1864, Penzance.

SKEWES   EDWARD HENRY
Born 1864. Died 1911, aged 47 years in Redruth.

SKEWIS   EDWARD J.
Chart 2. Son of Edward and Kittie Skewis. Born June, 1863, Shullsburg, Wisconsin, USA. Butcher in Shullsburg.

SKEWES   EDWARD JAMES
Chart 36. Son of Edward (railway guard) and Jecoliah Skewes. Born 1861. In 1871 Census Returns was living with his parents and brother William, and sister Eliza J., at Lanner, Gwennap. Porter on the railway. Married Amelia Symons (20) of Treskillard, daughter of Walter Symons, retired miner, at the Register Office, Redruth, 28 January 1888. He was first married in 1883, Redruth.

SKEWES   EDWARD JAMES
Chart 26. Son of Thomas John and Louisa (née Brookes) Skewes. Born 14 November 1867, Cobalt, Connecticut, USA. Married Harriet A. Rockwell. Children: Flora L. (1892), Frank Edward (1898), Grant Phillip (1903) and Wallace R. (1894).

SKEWES   EDWARD JAMES
Born 1890, Redruth. Died at St Clement, Truro 1897, aged 7 years.

SKEWES   EDWARD JAMES
Marrried 1906, Redruth.

SKEWES   EDWARD JOHN
Born 20 November 1794. Son of Edward and Grace Skewes. Bpt Falmouth 2 December 1794.

SKEWIS   EDWARD JOHN
Chart 2. Son of James and Jane Skewis. Born 12 January 1865, Mexico. Married Franc Scandrett (born 1876, died 1976, aged 100 years), 9 December 1904. Children: Jane Rabling and James Edward. Lived at Shullsburg, Wisconsin, USA.

SKEWES   EDWARD JOHN R.
Born 1901, Redruth. Died 1902, aged 1.

SKEWES   EDWARD JOHN R.
Born 1902, Redruth. Died 1902, aged 0.

SKEWES   EDWARD KEITH
Chart 36. Son of Charles Harold Vivian and Maude Emiline (née Lamphee) Skewes of Western Australia. Born 30 December 1913. Married Maisie Lawson, February 1942. In 1959 lived at 22 Wilcock Avenue, Tuart Hill, Balcutta, Western Australia. Bitumen contractor. Children: Jeanette C. (1942), Norman J.H. (1943), Ronald E. (1944), **Gary W.** (1949), Robert A. (1950) and Bruce P. (1953). Died 3 August 1974, aged 61 years.

SKEWES   EDWARD KENT
Chart 38. Son of Albert Murray and Olive May (née Brand) Skewes. Born 13 April 1948, Hindmarsh, South Australia. Married Susan Glenys Schramm 20 February 1971. Two daughters: Verity Kate (1974) and Carmen Victoria (1977). After leaving school he spent five years surveying for Australian Highways Department at Adelaide Institute of Technology. Now a farmer working on 2000 acres of cereal as well as looking after 1000 sheep.
Lives: c/o Ungarra Post Office, 5610, South Australia.

SKEWES   EDWARD MORLEY
Chart 36. Son of Alfred John and Matilda Skewes. Born 30 January 1920, Redruth. Mother's maiden name Hill. Lived at 13 Bartles Row, Tuckingmill, Camborne. Died at the home of his sister at 77 Higher Fore Street, Redruth 19 September 1967, aged 47 years.
Bachelor. Electrician.

SKEWES   EDWARD NELSON
Son of Byron James and Margaret Cecilia (née Morrison) Skewes. Born 16 February 1954, New York. Married Kathleen O'Brien, 19 May 1974. Children: Edward Thomas (1974) and Michael James (1977).
Lives at 120 Magwar Place, Babylon, Suffolk, New York, USA. Tel no: (516) 422 6114.

SKEWES   EDWARD SIMON
Chart 40. Son of Richard John and Leonie Patricia Skewes. Mother's maiden name Hall. Born 1974, Truro.

SKEWES   EDWARD THOMAS
Son of Edward Nelson Skewes. Born 10 November 1974, New York, USA.

SKUES   EDWARD WALKER M.B.
Chart 3. Son of George and Mary Gibbs (née Mackenzie) Skues. Born 17 July 1830, Aberdeen, Scotland. Licentiate Royal College of Surgeons (Edinburgh) 1852. M.B. Maris College, Aberdeen 1852. Commissioned into Army 11 June 1852, Assistant Surgeon to Forces. Surgeon to Forces 11 September 1860. Bachelor. Died in Calcutta 15 March 1862, aged 32 years.

SKEWES   EDWARD WILLIAM
Married 1869, Redruth.

SKEWIS   EDWIN
Chart 2. Son of Percy Vernon Skewis of America.

SKEWES   EDWIN
Chart 14. Son of John and Jane Skewes. Born 1838. Emigrated from Grade, Cornwall to Wisconsin, USA, arriving Yorkville 29 May 1850. Printer by trade. Worked in Pierce City and later Carthage. During the American Civil War he served with "F" and "S" Companies, 2nd Wisconsin Cavalry. Was promoted to Major, 29 July 1865.
After the Civil War he settled in Neosho, Missouri and formed a hardware business with J.R. Wolfendon. Married Virginia Drake (she born 28 April 1846 – died 1929, aged 83 years) in 1869. She was daughter of Silas Drake of New York State. They had a daughter who died in infancy.
Very involved with church and civic affairs. Was a Charter Member of the Congregational Church.
Died 1922, aged 84 years.

SKEWS   EDWIN
Chart 31. Son of John and Jane Skews. Bpt St Austell 2 February 1845. Died 1912, aged 67 years in Fulham, London.

SKEWIS   EDWIN
Chart 43. Son of Thomas and Elizabeth Skewis. Born 1850, Bedwellty, South Wales. Iron turner. Married Louisa Day, 1875, Bedwellty. Moved to Sheffield, South Yorkshire. Child: Mary Emma (1876).

SKEWIS   EDWIN
Chart 34. Son of Henry and Elizabeth (née Bennetts) Skewis, mine agent. Born 21 November 1853, Liskeard. Drew plans for the Brendon Hills Mining Complex where his father was mine manager from 1867 to 1883. Lived in Watchet, Somerset. Married Annie Elizabeth Jones (24), daughter of John Jones, Baptist Minister of Ebbw Vale, at the Parish Church, Bedwellty, Monmouth, South Wales, 1 September 1875. Children: Edwin Henry (1899), Ernest Ronald (1900), Frank (1902) and George (?).
Elizabeth Skewis died at Rhayader, Wales, 1910, aged 59 years.
Edwin moved to London where he was an auctioneer and surveyor at 29 Park Place, London W. Married Emily Tozer 1907. Children: Wilfred Roy (1908) and Leslie (1909). Edwin died at Tonbridge, 1909, aged 56 years. Emily died 1936, Tunbridge Wells, aged 62 years.

SKEWS   EDWIN

Edwin Skewis (1853-1909)

Chart 10. Son of William Skews of Illogan. Born 1856, Redruth. Married 1878, Redruth. Wife's name Elizabeth: she born 1854; died 28 May 1917, aged 63 years.
Emigrated to South Africa. Died 27 September 1935, aged 79 years. Buried in Brixton Cemetery, Johannesburg, South Africa.

SKEWES   EDWIN
Born 1881, Redruth. Illegitimate son of Elizabeth Ann Skewes. Lived at Cross Lane, Illogan. Died 1883. Buried at Illogan Parish Church 6 January 1883, aged 17 months.

SKEWIS   EDWIN
Born 1883. Died 1883, aged 0.

SKEWS   EDWIN
Married 1884, Islington.

SKEWES   EDWIN
Chart 36. Son of Anthony Joseph and Bronwyn (née Gapp) Skewes. Born 15 August 1973, New South Wales, Australia. Lives at 4 Netherby Street, Wahrnga, 2076, Australia.

SKEWS   EDWIN ARTHUR
Chart 17. Son of Richard Nathaniel Edward and Sarah (née Harding) Skews. Born 11 January 1884 at 1A Granby Street, Bethnal Green, London. Married Smith in Bethnal Green, 1912. Children: Sarah E.E., Kathleen P.H. and Arthur. Died Bournemouth, 1962, aged 79 years.

SKEWS   EDWIN ARTHUR
Chart 17. Son of Edwin Arthur Skews. Born 20 Nov 1919, Brentford. Married Lewis, 1943, Camarthen. Lived at 3 Featherbed Lane, Harlescott, Shrewsbury. Children: Roger D. (1946) and Patricia E. (1950). Died 1970, Shrewsbury.

SKEWES   EDWIN BOTTOMLEY
Chart 14. Son of Samuel and Ruth Skewes of Wisconsin, USA. Born 30 January 1858 at Grovean Farm, Racine County, Wisconsin. He was educated at Racine High School and graduated from Lawrence University with Honours in 1887. He married Alice Collier 22 October 1890. Children: Arthur Edwin (1891), Alice Ruth (1894) and George Jessop (1900).
His daughter Alice Ruth wrote in 1967:
"His own mother must have been proud when Edwin graduated with high honours from Lawrence University, one of the first, and I believe one of the relatively young people in the community and in his generation of the family to earn such a college degree.
"He would have made an excellent teacher. Two things kept him from going into teaching — a hearing loss, and the fact that his father looked to him to take over the responsibility for the home farm, Grovean. My father was a man of deep Christian commitment and vital faith, expressed in a life of integrity, service to others, and high standards of personal conduct. Bible reading every morning at breakfast, grace before every meal, and regular attendance at church and Sunday school were part of the fabric of our life. Having seen the harm done to persons, families and society by the use of alcoholic beverages, Father was not only a total abstainer, but an active crusader against the liquor traffic. He sought to curb the traffic by working through local option to increase dry areas, and by voting the Prohibition ticket. Convinced that tobacco also was harmful to health and morals, he was uncompromising in his opposition to its use. He was an initiator and active leader in community betterment. He was the Sunday school superintendent for 25 years, taught the adult class, and was on the official board of the church.
"Father was serious by temperament and strict in his judgements of himself and others. He could be stern, but he enjoyed good fun and there was often a twinkle in his blue eyes.
"Never a robust man, he often pushed himself beyond his strength. Dairy farming those days didn't allow much in the way of vacations, but Father entered into the good times we had at home — games in winter evenings, birthday parties, Fourth of July picnics and our own special observances of holidays.
"Accidents came without warning. At the end of a day of silo filling at Chybarles, as Father stooped to clean up the debris where he had been feeding the cutter, a light puff of breeze blew his denim work jacket against the exposed cogs of the still-running machine. Instantly he was jerked backwards, and the cogs seemed to leap out to devour his clothing and his flesh.
"In the shock and pain, he still had the presence of mind to call to the other men 'Throw off the belts!'
"Dr Fred Peehn, summoned from five miles away, operated right there on the long table in Uncle Thomas's kitchen, cutting away the damaged flesh, cleaning and closing the jagged wound which extended from the right shoulder blade to below the left arm, and inserting a tube for drainage. If only there had been antibiotics in 1913!
"It was a long time before Father could be moved to Grovean. Mother nursed him, Arthur carried on the farm work. After our first two anxious weeks, Father began fretting over my not being in college, and the doctor said 'She'd better go.'
"So for five weeks I attended Northwestern as had been planned.
Father nearly won his intrepid fight for recovery. Then came mother's letter telling of a setback, a day or so later the diagnosis, confirmed by a specialist from Milwaukee — meningitis — and then the summons 'Come quickly.'
"All the way home from Evanston, I prayed 'Father, wait!' He did. That evening, despite fever, pain, and ebbing strength, he asked that he might talk with each member of the family alone. One of the things he asked me to remember was that in any relationship, love is not merely emotion, but is stabilized by purpose and loyalty."
Edwin Bottomley Skewes died 8 November 1913, aged 55 years. Alice died 8 February 1920.

SKEWES   EDWIN CHARLES
Lived at Prince Street, Grange, Enoggera, Queensland, Australia, 1959 with Monica Doris Skewes. He was a telephone engineer.

SKEWIS   EDWIN GEORGE
Chart 43. Born 21 March 1873 at 33 Newhall Road, Brightside, Sheffield, South Yorkshire. Son of Edwin and Louisa (née Day) Skewis, iron turner.

SKEWES   EDWIN H.
Living at Woodbrier Drive, Florida, USA (1980). Telephone number (813) 694 4617.

SKEWIS   EDWIN HENRY
Chart 34. Son of Edwin and Emily (née Tozer) Skewis. Born 23 March 1899 at 4 Cotswold Terrace, Tylers Avenue, Southend, Essex, Died at sea aboard HMS *Wellington*, bound for Mignonette, 1917, aged 18 years.

SKEWES   EDWIN M.
Chart 14. Son of William M. and Mary Skewes of Yorkville, Wisconsin, USA. Auto mechanic. Married Olive Jacobson 5 October 1946 at Yorkville Methodist Church.

SKUES   EDWIN MICHAEL
Chart 7. Son of Edwin Thomas and Joan Skues of 54 Lansbury Crescent, Dartford, Kent. Born 1942. Married Brothwell, 1972, Dover, Kent.

Edwin Henry Skewis (1899-1917)

Edwin Bottomley Skewes (1858-1913)

SKEWS   EDWIN NATHANIEL
Chart 17. Born 9 January 1846, Medway, Kent. Son of George and Charlotte (née Dane) Skews, confectioner, High Street, Chatham, Kent.
SKEWES   EDWIN SCOTT WARNE
Born 1860, Truro.
SKUES   EDWIN THOMAS
Chart 7. Son of Francis Albert Skues. Mother's maiden name Jeffery. Born 13 December 1911.
Lived at 54 Lansbury Crescent, Dartford, Kent (1952). Married Joan M. Hawkins, 1940, Dartford. Children: Edwin Michael (1942) and Christine Evelyn (1945). Died 1974, aged 63 years in Cuckfield, Sussex.
SKEWES   EFFIE UNA
Lived at 21 Philips Street, Somerston, Glenelg, South Australia, in 1959.
Now lives at 17 Arthur Street, Naracoorte, 5721, South Australia, with Edward Foster Skewes, solicitor.

SKEWS   EILEEN
Chart 17. Daughter of James Arthur Skews. Mother's maiden name Jarvis. Born 1920, Stepney. Married Dickerson, 1939, Romford, Essex.
SKUES   EILEEN
Chart 9. Daughter of Albert Edward Skues. Mother's maiden name Cullingham. Born 1928, Camberwell.
SKEWES   EILEEN
Lived at 23 Tamar Street, Sutherland, New South Wales, Australia in 1959 with Lional Skewes, labourer.
SKEWES   EILEEN ANTOINETTE
Lived at 51a Wycombe Road, Neutral Bay, New South Wales, Australia in 1959 with Leonard Joseph Skewes. She was a librarian. Now lives at 23 Bannerman Street, Cremore, 2090, New South Wales, Australia.
SKEWES   EILEEN MARGARET
Chart 25. Daughter of Arthur George and Ruth (née Hacking) Skewes. Born 1942, North East Cheshire. Married Cooper in Newton Abbot, 1966.
SKEWIS   EILEEN MAY
Chart 33. Daughter of Ronald and Lilian Margaret (née Wyatt) Skewis. Born 4 August 1941, Totnes, Devon. As a youngster was active with Girl Guides, local swimming club and various school activities. Attended Technical College, taking a two-year commercial course. Joined local

government in the Town Clerk's Office. Married David Reeves Drennan on 7 March 1964 at St Mary's Parish Church, Totnes, Devon. Issue: 2 sons. Lives at Springcroft, Woodbrook Road, Bridgetown, Totnes, Devon.

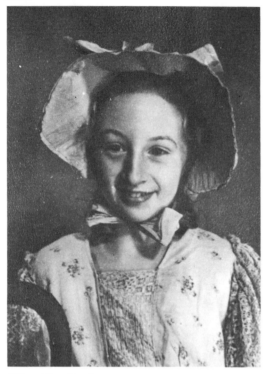

Eileen May Skewis

SKEWES   EILEEN MARGARET
Chart 2. Née Tritchler. Married Gordon William Skewes, bank manager, 4 August 1928. Children: Margaret Laura (1929) and William John (1934).
In 1959 lived at 18a Churchill Street, Surrey Hills, Victoria, Australia.

SKEWS   EILEEN SUSAN
Chart 17. Daughter of William George Alfred and Susan (née Childs) Skews. Born 1927 Hackney, London. Married James Masson Williamson, 1947, Stonehaven, Scotland.

SKEWES   ELAINE ELEANOR
Chart 26. Daughter of Frank Anson and June Beverley (née Spaulding) Skewes of Connecticut. Born 6 May 1952. Married Timothy Reeves in Connecticut 1972. Issue: one son and one daughter.

SKEWES   ELAINE MADOLINE
Chart 2. Born 28 July 1908, Moab, Utah, USA. Daughter of John Billing and Lydia Skewes. Married W. Golden Peterson 28 May 1931. Lives at 33N 3rd E, Moab, Utah, USA. Member of Church of Latter Day Saints.

SKEWES   ELAINE MARY
Chart 36. Daughter of James William and Pauline Beatrice (née Seymour) Skewes. Born 3 May 1940, Watsons Creek, Bendemeer, New South Wales, Australia.

SKEWES   ELEANOR
Daughter of Edward and Margaret Skewes. Bpt Cury 16 March 1745.

SKEWES   ELEANOR
Chart 25. Born 1748. Wife of Thomas Skewes. Died 1 August 1795, aged 46 years in Falmouth.

SKEWES   ELEANOR
of Cury. Married Anthony Skewes at Cury Parish Church 11 December 1760.

SKEWES   ELEANOR
Born 1764. Buried Kea 30 July 1818, aged 54 years.

SKEWYS   ELINOR
Daughter of Anthony and Elinor Skewys. Bpt Mawgan in Meneage 23 August 1767.

SKEWES   ELEANOR
Buried 8 March 1773, Cury.

SKEWIS   ELEANOR
Chart 25. Daughter of Thomas and Eleanor Skewis. Bpt St Keverne 20 December 1747. Married Peter Wood, widower of Massachusetts, USA

6 Feb 1795 at Falmouth.

SKEWES   ELEANOR
Chart 25. Born 1779. Wife of Thomas Skewes. Children: Benjamin Hellings and Thomas Henry. Died 9 June 1824, aged 45 years.

SKEWIS   ELEANOR
Married Thomas Rowe at Crowan 24 September 1786.

SKEWES   ELEANOR
Buried Cury 15 February 1800.

SKEWES   ELEANOR
Chart 14. Daughter of Henry and Jane Skewes. Twin of John Skewes. Bpt Ruan Major 27 May 1804 (born 30 Jan 1804). Married William Lugg 3 Nov 1824, Ruan Major. Emigrated to Australia and lived in Freshwater Creek, Geelong, Victoria. Issue 6 sons and 2 daughters. Died 24 October 1891, aged 87 years. Buried at Duneed, Victoria, Australia.

SKEWES   ELEANOR
Born 1815, Cury. In 1871 Census lived at Gwealgears, Wendron as a charwoman. Died 1880, aged 65 years.

SKEWES   ELEANOR
Married James Tonkin at Kenwyn 13 November 1829.

SKUES   ELEANOR
Chart 3. Born 1872. Née Chorley. Married Richard James Skues 13 September 1897. Children: Lucy, Evelyn, Frederick and Eric. Died 1960, aged 88 years.

SKEWES   ELEANOR
Chart 18. Daughter of William and Ann Skewes. Bpt Kea 2 June 1805.

SKUES   ELEANOR
Chart 10. Daughter of Thomas and Grace Skues. Bpt Kenwyn 18 May 1823.

SKEWES   ELEANOR HENDY
Born 1827, Grade. Died 6 January 1893 in Cury, aged 66 years.

SKEWES   ELEANOR JESSOP
Chart 14. Daughter of Samuel and Ruth Skewes of Grovean, Ives Grove, Yorkville, Wisconsin, USA. Born 18 January 1864. Spinster. Died 30 June 1893, aged 29 years.

SKUES   ELEANOR LUCY LUCAS
Chart 5. Born 1871, Marylebone. Daughter of Charles Penrose Skues. Married Bradshaw, 1895. Died 1957, aged 86 years.

SKEWES   ELEANOR MAY
Chart 38. Née Stapleton. Married Ernest Seymour Skewes. Children: Catherine and William Seymour Skewes. Lived at 7 Fisher Street, Welland, Flinders Park, Hindmarsh, South Australia in 1959. Died 26 October 1978.

SKEWES   ELISA
Chart 10. Mexican. Daughter of Juan and Fransisca (née Meneses) Skewes. Born 1900. Had an illegitimate son Humberto (1926). Lived in Real del Monte, Mexico. Died 11 September 1962, aged 62 years.

SKEWIS   ELIZA
Born 1796. Died Glasgow, 1874, aged 78 years.

SKEWES   ELIZA
Chart 2. Daughter of Absalom and Jane Skewes. Bpt Camborne 20 September 1815.

SKEWES   ELIZA
Chart 36. Daughter of James and Elizabeth. Bpt Cury 4 May 1817. Lived at Gilly Lane, Cury. Buried Cury 20 January 1829, aged 11 years.

SKEWS   ELIZA
Born 1819. Buried St Clement 18 April 1843, aged 24 years.

SKEWES   ELIZA
Daughter of Richard and Mary Skewes. Bpt Kea 18 June 1820.

SKUES   ELIZA
Born 1822. Daughter of Joseph Skues, carpenter. Mrd Thomas Hooper, son of James Hooper, of Penstraze at Kenwyn Parish Church 2 June 1841.

SKEWES   ELIZA
Daughter of Ann Skewes of Kea. Bpt 29 March 1825, Kenwyn.

SKEWES   ELIZA
Chart 2. Daughter of Henry and Grace Skewes of Bosawsack. Bpt Constantine 26 May 1826.

SKUES   ELIZA
Chart 2. Daughter of Edward & Mary Skues. Born 14 November 1827. In 1841 Census Returns was "dressing ore". Married James Craze. Issue: one daughter. Emigrated to USA, 1849. Buried in California.

SKEWES   ELIZA
Married John Glasson, 20 July 1836, Camborne.

SKEWES   ELIZA
Married Peter Bonython at Kea 19 November 1836.

SKUES   ELIZA
Chart 3. Daughter of George & Mary Gibbs Skues. Born 6 June 1837. Died 1858, aged 21 years.

SKEWS   ELIZA
Born 1839, North Aylesford, Kent.

SKUES   ELIZA
Died St George's East, 1842.

SKEWIS   ELIZA
Died Truro, 1843.

SKEWES   ELIZA
Chart 12. Born 1844. Bpt 6 July 1844, Cury. Daughter of William & Mary Skewes of Cury. Was a servant at Nanplough aged 17 in 1861 Census Returns.

SKEWES   ELIZA
Born 1844. Daughter of William & Elizabeth Skewes of Crowan. Bpt Wesleyan Methodist Chapel, Stithians, 19 August 1844.

SKEWES   ELIZA
Died 1845, Helston.

SKEWES   ELIZA
Born 1849, Truro.

SKEWES   ELIZA
Married 1852, Falmouth.

SKEWES   ELIZA
Born 1854, Died 1905, aged 51 years, Devonport.

SKEWES   ELIZA
Died 1864, Rochford, Essex.

SKUES   ELIZA
Born 1855. Died 1883, aged 28 years, Whitechapel.

SKEWES   ELIZA
Chart 2. Daughter of Josiah & Fanny Skewes of Bosawsack, farmer. Bpt Constantine 19 November 1862. Buried Constantine 25 November 1862, aged 9 days.

SKEWES   ELIZA
Chart 25. Daughter of Charles and Elizabeth Skewes of Falmouth. Born 1863, Falmouth. Died 1915, aged 52 years in Chorlton, Manchester.

SKEWS   ELIZA
Married 1863, Lambeth.

SKEWES   ELIZA
Born 1865. Wife of John Edwin Skews (married 1896). Died 13 August 1942, aged 77 years.

SKUES   ELIZA
Born 1883, Whitechapel. Died 1883, aged 0.

SKEWS   ELIZA
Widow of Alban Edgar Skews who died 1920. Married Midson, 1921, Gravesend.

SKEWES   ELIZA
Living at Mithian, St Agnes, 1932 with Bertram Skewes.

SKEWES   ELIZA ANN
Chart 12. Daughter of Josiah and Elizabeth Skewes of Sithney. Born 1847. Bpt Sithney 19 May 1847.

SKEWES   ELIZA ANN
Chart 36. Daughter of Edward and Julia Skewes of Nantithet. Born 1847, Cury. In 1851 Census Returns living at Nantithet. Married William Henry Blatchford, policeman, of Cury (son of William Blatchford, labourer) at Cury Parish Church 24 October 1867.

SKEWES   ELIZA ANN
Chart 2. Born 1849. Daughter of James and Susan Skewes. Unmarried. In 1871 Census Returns living in Camborne.

SKUES   ELIZA E.
Chart 5. Born 1847. Married Charles Penrose Skues. 1869, Redruth. Children: Emily Jane, Eleanor Lucy, Bessie Annie, William John and Charles Henry.
Died Amersham 1915, aged 68 years. Charles Penrose Skues died 1939, Amersham, aged 92 years.

SKEWES   ELIZA E.
Born 1850. Died 1928, aged 78 years in Redruth.

SKEWES   ELIZA ELLEN
Married 1874, Redruth.

SKEWIS   ELIZA ELLEN
Born 1891. Died 1893, aged 2 years in Redruth.

SKEWES   ELIZA EMMA
Living at Carnmarth Cove, Gwennap, 1922 with Thomas William Skewes.

SKEWES   ELIZA GRACE
Chart 2. Daughter of James and Grace (née Skewes) of Cury. Born 1846. Bpt 31 January 1846. In 1851 Census Returns living at Treloskan, Cury. Married 1866, Helston district.

SKUES   ELIZA HELEN
Born 1873, Marylebone.

SKEWES   ELIZA JANE
Born 13 August 1823. Bpt Truro Wesleyan Chapel 19 March 1837. Daughter of John and Elizabeth Skewes (née Jeffrey), miner of Kenwyn.

SKEWES   ELIZA JANE
Daughter of John and Anne Skewes. Bpt 26 March 1826, Kea.

SKEWES   ELIZA JANE
Chart 36. Née Semmens. Born 1844. Married John Skewes at St John's, Treslothan 19 March 1862. Died 1902, aged 58 years in Camborne.

SKEWES   ELIZA JANE
Daughter of John Skewes of Kea, miner of Seveock, Kea. Married Thomas Gray 14 May 1846 at Kea. Witness to wedding, John Skewes.

SKEWS   ELIZA JANE
Chart 10. Born 1850. Daughter of Joseph and Elizabeth Skews. In 1871 Census Returns was a domestic servant to William and Jane Pascoe

living at Dobwalls, Liskeard.

SKEWES   ELIZA JANE
Chart 33. Daughter of Edward and Jecoliah Skewes, railway labourer. Born 1871. In 1871 Census Returns living at Lanner, Gwennap with her parents and brothers Edward James and William.

SKEWES   ELIZA JANE
Born 1882. Wife of John Henry Skewes, miner. Child: Doris Skewes who married William Peters. Lived at Four Lanes, 1932. Was a member of Fore Street Methodist Church. Died at 10 Sparnon Hill, Redruth 25 February 1959, aged 77 years.

SKEWES   ELIZA JANE
Married 1889, Redruth.

SKEWES   ELIZA JANE
Married 1906, Helston.

SKEWS   ELIZA MAY
Born 1895, Bethnal Green. Married Hawkes in Mile End, 1916.

SKUES   ELIZA SUSANNAH
Born 1850, St George's East, London.

SKEWES   ELIZABETH
Daughter of Sandry Skewes. Bpt 13 June 1567, Ludgvan.

SKEWES   ELIZABETH
Daughter of Thomas Skewes. Bpt 8 February 1609, Exeter.

SKEWES   ELIZABETH
Daughter of Thomas Skewes. Bpt 8 June 1617, Exeter St Mary Major.

SKEWS   ELIZABETH
Daughter of John Skewes. Bpt 3 December 1626, Martin in Meneage.

SKEWES   ELIZABETH
Chart 35. Married Henry Skewes of Cury. Child: Welmot Skewes.

SKEWES   ELIZABETH
Chart 35. Married Edward Skewes of Cury. Children: William and Edward.

SKEWS   ELIZABETH
Married James Southern at Hemel Hempstead, Herts, 1647.

SKEWES   ELIZABETH
Married James Secombe 29 September 1659, St Anthony in Meneage.

SKEWES   ELIZABETH
Chart 2. Née Grills. Wife of George Skewes. Married 3 September 1664. Died 13 November 1686.

SKEWS   ELIZABETH
Chart 13. Daughter of John and Elizabeth (née Whitford) Skews. Bpt 14 October 1688, Mevagissey.

SKEWS   ELIZABETH
Chart 13. Daughter of John and Elizabeth (née Whitford) Skews. Bpt 27 November 1692, Mevagissey.

SKUES   ELIZABETH
Chart 2. Daughter of Robert Skues. Bpt 2 February 1693, Camborne. Married Christopher Tellam, 30 December 1714.

SCUIS   ELIZABETH
Daughter of Thomas and Philippa Scuis. Bpt 26 January 1695, Wendron. Buried Wendron 24 November 1713, aged 18 years.

SKUES   ELIZABETH
Chart 10. Daughter of Digory Skues of Kenwyn. Bpt Kenwyn 27 December 1707.

SKEWES   ELIZABETH
Chart 36. Daughter of James and Sarah Skewes. Bpt Cury 28 March 1708.

SKEWS   ELIZABETH
Daughter of Edward Skews. Bpt St Ewe 1713.

SKEWES   ELIZABTH
Buried Cury 12 February 1715.

SKUES   ELIZABETH
Daughter of Richard Skues. Bpt 18 February 1719, Kenwyn.

SKEWS   ELIZABETH
Daughter of James Skews. Bpt St Mary, Lewisham, Kent 22 May 1724.

SKEWES   ELIZABETH
Buried at Falmouth 18 April 1730.

SKEWIS   ELIZABETH
Daughter of Edward and Anne Skewis. Bpt Cury 2 January 1731.

SKEWS   ELIZABETH
Buried St Ewe 24 August 1732.

SKEWS   ELIZABETH
Daughter of John Skews. Bpt Penzance 5 March 1735.

SKEWES   ELIZABETH
Buried Cury 25 December 1736.

SKEWS   ELIZABETH
Daughter of Henry Skews. Bpt Kea 12 April 1741.

SKEWS   ELIZABETH
Daughter of Philip and Ann Skewes. Bpt Cuby with Tregony 19 September 1743. Buried St Ewe 9 August 1744.

SKEWS   ELIZABETH
Daughter of Philip and Anne Skews. Bpt St Ewe 19 May 1746.

SKEWES   ELIZABETH
Daughter of Philip and Anne Skews. Bpt St Ewe 13 January 1750.

SKEWES   ELIZABETH
Chart 19. Daughter of Thomas and Elizabeth Skewes. Bpt Gwennap 27
July 1751. Died 3 December 1754, aged 3 years.
SKEWES   ELIZABETH
Daughter of Peter Skewes. Bpt Kea 29 September 1751.
SKEWES   ELIZABETH
Born 1753. Lived at Town, Camborne. Buried Camborne 5 May 1842,
aged 89 years.
SKEWES   ELIZABETH
Daughter of Tobias & Elizabeth. Bpt St Just in Penwith 14 July 1754.
SKEWES   ELIZABETH
Chart 19. Daughter of Thomas and Elizabeth Skewes. Bpt Gwennap 24
April 1756.
SKEWES   ELIZABETH
Born 1758. Buried Camborne 5 May 1818, aged 60.

SKEWES   ELIZABETH
Married Gideon Johns of Gluvias at Falmouth 3 November 1758.
SKEWS   ELIZABETH
Daughter of Thomas Skews of Kea. Bpt Kenwyn 11 May 1760.
SKEWIS   ELIZABETH
Daughter of Anthony & Eleanor. Bpt Cury 18 January 1762.
SKEWES   ELIZABETH
Chart 10. Daughter of Martin and Mary Skewes of Kea. Bpt Kenwyn 2
June 1762. Buried Kea 15 June 1762.
SKEWES   ELIZABETH
Buried Cury 9 June 1762.
SKEWES   ELIZABETH
Daughter of Martin Skewes. Buried Kea 15 June 1762.
SKEWES   ELIZABETH
Chart 36. Daughter of John & Mary Skewes. Bpt 13 March 1763, Cury.
SKEWES   ELIZABETH
Daughter of William and Mary Skewes. Bpt Helston 6 January 1765.
SKEWES   ELIZABETH
Born 1765. Née May. Married Martin Skewes of St Clement, 4 June
1786 at St Clement. Buried St Mary's, Truro 8 April 1834, aged 69
years.
SKEWES   ELIZABETH
Chart 18. Daughter of Thomas Skewes. Bpt Kenwyn privately 15 July
1768.
SKEWS   ELIZABETH
Buried St Ewe 21 July 1771.
SKEWES   ELIZABETH
Buried Kea 2 August 1772.
SKEWIS   ELIZABETH
Daughter of Henry and Elizabeth Skewis. Bpt Camborne 16 January
1774.
SKEWES   ELIZABETH
Chart 29. Daughter of John and Alice Skewes. Bpt Kea 1 April 1774.
Probably married Charles Dennis at Kea, 1796.
SKEWES   ELIZABETH
Chart 10. Daughter of Martin and Mary Skewes of Kea. Bpt Kenwyn 16
April 1774.
SKEWES   ELIZABETH
Born 1762. Lived at Kea. Buried Chacewater 23 February 1847.
SKEWES   ELIZABETH
Chart 19. Daughter of John and Mary Skewes. Bpt 8 April 1776.
Married Francis Tuckfield 21 December 1799 at Gwennap.
SKUES   ELIZABETH
Chart 3. Daughter of John and Mary Skues. Bpt Helston 13 December
1778.
SKEWES   ELIZABETH
Born 1780. Buried Camborne 28 July 1814, aged 34.
SKEWES   ELIZABETH
Née Wasley. Married Digory Skewes of Kea at Kenwyn 13 July 1782.
Children: Thomas, Peter, Digory, Richard, Elizabeth, John, Matthew,
Margery and Maria.
SKEWES   ELIZABETH
Chart 36. Daughter of James and Ann Skewes. Bpt Cury 14 July 1782.
SKEWES   ELIZABETH
Chart 25. Daughter of Thomas and Eleanor Skewes. Born 10 August
1782. Bpt Falmouth 15 September 1782.
SKEWES   ELIZABETH
Married Thomas White, Cury, 1782.
SKEWES   ELIZABETH
Daughter of John and Mary Skewes. Bpt Gwennap 5 March 1783.
SKEWES   ELIZABETH
Chart 12. Born 1783. Lived at Nantithet, Cury. Married James Skewes
at Cury Parish Church 25 July 1808. Children: James (1809), Mary
(1811), William (1813), John (1815), Elizabeth (1817), Henry (1818),
Ann (1820), Josiah (1824), Loveday (1824) and Thomas (1826). Died 27
May 1851, aged 68 years.
SKEWIS   ELIZABETH
Buried Gwennap 14 July 1784.

SKEWES   ELIZABETH
Chart 2. Daughter of Richard and Alice Skewes. Bpt Camborne 10
April 1785. Married John Rowe of Gluvias 7 February 1810 at
Constantine.
SKEWES   ELIZABETH
Daughter of John and Mary Skewes. Bpt Gwennap 15 May 1785.
SKEWES   ELIZABETH
Married Daniel Rowe at Crowan 18 November 1787.
SKUES   ELIZABETH
Chart 2. Daughter of Absalom and Elizabeth Skues. Born 24 March
1789. Bpt Crowan 2 October 1789. Married Richard Mill (with issue) at
Camborne Parish Church 22 November 1813.
SKEWES   ELIZABETH
Married Thomas Trahear at Kenwyn 18 October 1788.
SKEWES   ELIZABETH
Daughter of John and Alice Skewes. Buried Kea 28 July 1790.
SKEWIS   ELIZABETH
Married William Cock, widower of Gwithian at Gwinear 30 November
1790. By licence.
SKEWES   ELIZABETH
Chart 10. Daughter of Digory and Elizabeth Skewes. Bpt Kea 26
February 1792.
SKEWES   ELIZABETH
Daughter of Henry and Margaret Skewes. Bpt Gwinear 23 December
1792.
SKUES   ELIZABETH
Chart 3. Daughter of William and Mary Skues of Helston. Married Rev.
James Byron, widower of the Wesleyans, Plymouth at Helston 20
November 1793.
SKEWES   ELIZABETH
Married John Murley 1 January 1795 at Gwinear.
SKEWES   ELIZABETH
Born 1797. Died 25 September 1855 aged 58 at Tuckingmill.
SKEWES   ELIZABETH
Buried 28 April 1797 at Kea.
SKEWES   ELIZABETH
Buried Cury 23 March 1798.
SKEWES   ELIZABETH
Illegitimate daughter of Constance Skewes. Buried Camborne 21
December 1798.
SKEWES   ELIZABETH
Born 1799. Buried Cury 19 April 1842, aged 43 years.
SKEWES   ELIZABETH
Born 1799, St Perran. Wife of James Skewes of Charlestown, St Austell;
lime burner who was born at St Ewe. Lived at Charlestown in 1851, 1861
and 1871 Census Returns. Died 1874, aged 75 years at St Austell.
SKEWES   ELIZABETH
Married William Rontree 24 February 1800, Falmouth.
SKEWIS   ELIZABETH
Chart 19. Daughter of Richard and Mary Skewis. Bpt 8 May 1800.
Married Henry Morcam 29 September 1823 at Gwennap.
SKEWES   ELIZABETH
Daughter of James & Elizabeth Skewes. Bpt Cury 11 January 1801.
SKEWIS   ELIZABETH
Daughter of Peter and Ann Skewis. Bpt Gwennap 20 June 1801.
SKEWES   ELIZABETH
Married Robert Triggs at Cury, 1802.
SKUES   ELIZABETH
Daughter of William and Jane Skues. Bpt Mylor 24 March 1805.
SKEWES   ELIZABETH
Daughter of Alexander and Christian Skewes. Bpt Gwennap 3 October
1805.
SKEWES   ELIZABETH
Daughter of Richard & Grace Skewes. Bpt Redruth 19 January 1806.
SKEWES   ELIZABETH
Chart 36. Daughter of William and Alice Skewes of Treloskan, Cury.
Bpt Cury 10 March 1807. Buried Cury 21 April 1808, aged 1 year.
SKEWS   ELIZABETH
Daughter of William and Nancy Skews. Bpt St Ewe 5 July 1807.
SKEWES   ELIZABETH
Daughter of James & Elizabeth. Bpt Constantine 14 August 1808.
SKEWIS   ELIZABETH
Daughter of John and Jane Skewis. Bpt Illogan 6 December 1807.
SKEWES   ELIZABETH
Chart 17. Née Glasson. Born 1808. Born Truthall, Sithney (20 March
1808); daughter of Joseph and Bathsheba Glasson. Married William
Skewes. Was a member of the Wesleyan Society for 54 years. Died 9
April 1882, aged 74 years.
SKEWS   ELIZABETH
Chart 9. Daughter of James and Joanna Skews of Lower Sticker. Bpt 10
September 1809, St Ewe.
SKEWES   ELIZABETH
Chart 19. Daughter of Alexander and Christian Skewes. Bpt Gwennap
13 March 1810. Lived at Lanner House, Gwennap. Spinster. Died 12
May 1877, aged 67 years. Buried at Gwennap 17 May 1877.

SKEWES ELIZABETH
Chart 26. Née Scoble. Born 1812. Married Peter Skewes of Hugus, miner at Kea 4 October 1834. Children: Elizabeth, Jane, Peter, Mary, Grace, Ellen and Emily. Lived at Hugus, Kea. Buried Kea 12 March 1854, aged 42 years.

SKEWES ELIZABETH
Married Philip Lean at Gwennap 5 December 1812. In presence of John Skewes.

SKEWES ELIZABETH
Born 1813. Died 1905, aged 92 years in Swansea.

SKUES ELIZABETH
Chart 5. Née Penrose. Married Joseph Skues at Redruth Parish Church 9 February 1813. Children: John Penrose and Mary.

SKEWES ELIZABETH
Chart 2. Daughter of Henry and Grace Skewes of Bosawsack. Bpt 8 August 1813 at Constantine.

SKEWES ELIZABETH
Married Benjamin Baragwana (with consent of their parents) at Kea 23 March 1814. In presence of Mary Skewes.

SKEWES ELIZABETH
Chart 18. Daughter of William and Ann Skewes, miner. Bpt Kenwyn 29 May 1814.

SKEWES ELIZABETH
Daughter of William & Elizabeth. Bpt Camborne 28 June 1814.

SKEWES ELIZABETH
Chart 2. Daughter of Absalom and Jane Skewes. Born July 1814. Died 3 September 1814, aged 5 weeks.

SKEWES ELIZABETH
Born 1814, Sithney. Married Josiah Skewes of Cury. Buried Helston Parish Church 15 December, 1879, aged 65 years. Josiah remarried: Ellen Hugo (38) at Helston Parish Church 2 July 1881.

SKEWES ELIZABETH
Chart 10. Daughter of Digory and Sophia Skewes. Bpt 27 September 1818 at Kenwyn.

SKEWES ELIZABETH
Chart 36. Daughter of William and Alice Skewes of Treloskan, Cury. Bpt Cury 15 January 1815. Buried Cury 1 December 1815, aged 1 year.

SKEWES ELIZABETH
Chart 36. Daughter of William and Alice Skewes of Treloskan, Cury; tinner. Bpt 8 September, 1816, Cury.

SKEWES ELIZABETH
Chart 12. Daughter of James and Elizabeth Skewes of Cury. Bpt Cury 4 May 1817.

SKEWES ELIZABETH
Born 1817. Lived at White Cross, Cury. Buried Cury 12 March 1895, aged 78 years.

SKEWES ELIZABETH
Chart 10. Daughter of Digory & Sophia Skewes. Bpt Kenwyn 27 September 1818.

SKEWES ELIZABETH
Daughter of Edward and Mary Skewes. Bpt Camborne 28 August 1819.

SKUES ELIZABETH
Chart 2. Daughter of Absalom and Jane Skues. Bpt Camborne 1 January 1820.

SKEWES ELIZABETH
Chart 28. Daughter of Richard and Mary Skewes of Nancegollan Common, Kea. Bpt Kea 18 June 1820.

SKEWES ELIZABETH
Chart 10, Daughter of Matthew and Mary Skewes of Kea. Bpt 21 January 1821 at Kenwyn.

SKEWES ELIZABETH
Chart 36. Daughter of William and Christian Skewes of Ruan Major. Bpt 10 July 1822, Ruan Major Church. Married Thomas Veal at Mawnan Parish Church 2 April 1846 in presence of Edward Skewes and William Skewes. Descendant Mary McLelland lives at 3716 St. Mark's Road, Durham, North Carolina, 27707, United States of America.

SKUES ELIZABETH
Married James Lanksbury at Redruth, 1824.

SKUES ELIZABETH
Born 1825. Died 1900, Bethnal Green, aged 75 years.

SKUES ELIZABETH
Married James Jones at Kenwyn 21 May 1825.

SKEWES ELIZABETH
Married William Holman at Kea 6 August 1825.

SKEWES ELIZABETH
Married John Bawdyn 18 February 1826 at Kenwyn.

SKEWES ELIZABETH
Daughter of Peter and Elizabeth Skewes of the Poorhouse, Kenwyn. Bpt Kenwyn 22 November 1826.

SKEWES ELIZABETH
Born 1827. Buried Chacewater 19 June 1829, aged 2.

SKEWS ELIZABETH
Daughter of John and Ann Skews of Chacewood; miner. Bpt Chacewater 18 December 1828.

SKEWS ELIZABETH
Daughter of John and Elizabeth Skews of Chacewater, miner. Bpt Chacewater 7 June 1829.

SKUES ELIZABETH
Chart 5. Born 1829, Ludgvan. Second wife of John Penrose Skues of Hodders Row, Redruth. Married 1859, Penzance. Children Elizabeth and James. Died 1903, aged 74 years, Redruth.

SKUES ELIZABETH
Chart 2. Daughter of Stephen and Margaret Skues of Treswithian. Bpt Camborne 7 March 1829. Died 25 March 1831.

SKEWIS ELIZABETH
Chart 2. Born 15 August 1819. Daughter of Edward and Mary Skewis. Emigrated to Wisconsin, USA. Married Henry Ford. Issue 2 daughters and 1 son. Died 10 January 1852. Buried in Shullsburg.

SKEWES ELIZABETH
Married William James, Cury 29 September 1829.

SKEWES ELIZABETH
Chart 36. Daughter of William and Christian Skewes, farmer. Bpt Ruan Major 21 January 1821. Died very young.

SKEWIS ELIZABETH
Born 1820. Died 1887, aged 67 years, Williton.

SKEWES ELIZABETH
Born 1821. Daughter of Matthew Skewes, miner. Married 22 May 1842 to John Stripp (31) of Chacewater, son of William Slade Stripp, carpenter in Truro district.

SKEWES ELIZABETH
Chart 10. Born 1830, Kenwyn. Married Joseph Skewes in Liskeard, 1849. Lived at Dobwalls, Liskeard. Child: Eliza (1850). Died 1919, aged 89 years.

SKEWES ELIZABETH
Chart 48. Born 1830, St Michael's Mount. Married Charles Skewes, shoemaker, Falmouth, 1857. Children: Charles, William John, George, Edward and Louisa J. Died 1892, aged 62 years, Salford, Lancashire.

SKEWES ELIZABETH
Born 1832, Buried Camborne 2 June 1836, aged 4 years. Died of inflammation of the bowels.

SKEWIS ELIZABETH
Daughter of John (miner) and Ann Skewis. Born 3 August 1832. Bpt Camborne/Redruth Wesleyan Methodist Church 11 October 1832.

SKUSE ELIZABETH
Married John Webster, 1832, Stoke Gifford, Gloucester.

SKEWS ELIZABETH
Born 1833. Died 1897, aged 64 years.

SKEWES ELIZABETH
Chart 36. Daughter of Robert Northey. Born 24 September 1833, Truro. She sailed for Australia aboard ship *Sultana*, which arrived in Sydney in May, 1855. She was accompanied by her widowed mother (44) and two brothers James (20) and William (18). The journey on board ship had taken three months. On 4 August 1856 she married William Skewes, labourer, at 24 Lower Fort Street, Sydney, the service according to the rites of the Presbyterian Church being conducted by Alexander Salmon. Children: James (1857), William (1858), Samuel (1859), Elizabeth (1860), John (1862), Frances Charlotte (1864), Robert Northey (1867), Emily Susan (1869), George (1871), Amy Elizabeth (1873), Caroline Mary (1876) and Alice Beatrice (1878). Moved to Rocky River, Uralla in the boom days of the gold field arriving by horse and dray on 17 March 1857. Seven of her grandsons fought in the First World War, all of whom returned. Died 13 August 1926, aged 93 years.

Elizabeth Northey Skewes (1833-1926)

SKEWIS ELIZABETH
Married William Rowe at Illogan, 23 February 1833.
SKUES ELIZABETH
Chart 2. Daughter of Stephen and Margaret Skues of Park Holly, Camborne, husbandman. Bpt Camborne 28 November 1835.
SKUES ELIZABETH
Chart 2. Daughter of Henry and Grace Skues. Bpt Camborne 30 August 1836.
SKEWES ELIZABETH
Married John Glasson at Camborne Parish Church 20 July 1836. Witness William Skewes.
SKEWIS ELIZABETH
Born 1837. Daughter of John and Margery Skewes of Ford's Row, Redruth, engineer. Born 22 April, 1837. Bpt Redruth 7 March 1852. Died 1874, aged 37 years, Redruth.
SKEWES ELIZABETH
Born 1838. Died 1916, aged 78 years in Bolton.
SKEWS ELIZABETH
Died 1839. Plymouth.
SKEWES ELIZABETH
Born 1834. Lived at Kerley, Kea. Died 1855, aged 21 years. Buried Chacewater 11 March 1855.
SKEWES ELIZABETH
Daughter of Peter and Grace Skewes of Kerley, Kea, miner. Bpt Chacewater 16 June 1836.
SKEWES ELIZABETH
Chart 26. Daughter of Peter and Elizabeth. Bpt Kea 3 August 1835. Lived at Hugus, Kea. In 1851 Census Returns listed as a mine labourer.
SKEWES ELIZABETH
Married Thomas Pascoe at Kea 14 January 1837.
SKEWIES ELIZABETH
Born 1838. Died Gorbals, Scotland, 1915, aged 77 years.
SKUSE ELIZABETH
Married Thornbury, 1841.
SKEWES ELIZABETH
Daughter of Peter Skewes, miner of Kerley, Kea. Married James Wasley at Kea 20 September 1841.
SKEWES ELIZABETH
Married Henry Ford at Madron, 1842.
SKEWES ELIZABETH
Married 1842, Truro.
SKEWS ELIZABETH
Born 1842. Died 1900, aged 58 years in Fulham.
SKEWS ELIZABETH
Daughter of James and Margaret Skews. Bpt St Erth 24 December 1843.
SKUES ELIZABETH
Born 1844. Died 1925, aged 81 years, Axminster.
SKEWS ELIZABETH
Married 1845, Liskeard.
SKEWS ELIZABETH
Died 1845, Bodmin.
SKEWS ELIZABETH
Died 1846, East London.
SKEWES ELIZABETH
Chart 2. Daughter of William and Elizabeth Skewes of Crowan. Born 1848. In 1851 Census Returns living with her parents and brothers Joseph, John and James and sisters Christian and Grace.
SKEWES ELIZABETH
Born 1848, Helston district.
SKUES ELIZABETH
Chart 27. Born 1848, Bath.
SKUES ELIZABETH
Married William Pearce 10 December 1848 at Breage.
SKEWIS ELIZABETH
Married 1848, Penzance.
SKEWES ELIZABETH
Chart 11. Born 1849. Wife of James Henry Skewes. In 1871 Census Returns living at Lizard Town with her husband and daughter Sarah Ann.
SKEWIS ELIZABETH
Chart 44. Born 1849, Abergavenny. Daughter of James and Elizabeth Skewis.
SKEWES ELIZABETH
Chart 33. Daughter of William and Susanne Skewes of Chacewater. Born 1849, Kea. In 1851 Census Returns was living with her parents and sisters Mary, Susan and Grace and brother William.
SKEWES ELIZABETH
Living in Morris County, Rockaway, New Jersey, 1850,
SKEWIS ELIZABETH
Daughter of Thomas and Elizabeth Skewis of Abergavenny. Born 1852.
SKUES ELIZABETH
Chart 7. Née Harris. Daughter of John Harris. Born 1853. Married Thomas Skues 6 September 1874 at St George's, Hannover Square.

Children: Noah James, Edward Alfred, Blanche Louisa, Ada Alice, Florence Emily and Francis Albert. Died 1925, aged 72 years in Cuckfield, Sussex.
SKEWES ELIZABETH
Married 1853, Bedford.
SKEWES ELIZABETH
Born 1854, Redruth. Moved to South Africa. Married a Skewes? Buried in Brixton Cemetery, Johannesburg, South Africa, 28 May 1917.
SKEWES ELIZABETH
Married 1855, West Stonehouse.
SKEWIS ELIZABETH
Born 1856, Redruth.
SKEWES ELIZABETH
Born 1856. Chart 30. Daughter of Thomas Whether of St Austell, Cornwall. Married John Beer Skewes, compositor, at St Geo's, Hannover Square 8 May 1880. Lived at 80 Wellington Road, St Thomas, Exeter. She ran Westgate Coffee Tavern at Edmund Street, Exeter 1912-1916. Children: Ernest John (1881), Gwendoline (1884) and Frederick Henry (1891). Died 1928, aged 72 years, in Exeter.
SKEWS ELIZABETH
Married 1857, Merthyr Tydfill.
SKEWES ELIZABETH
Married 1858, Truro.
SKEWES ELIZABETH
Died 1858, Redruth.
SKEWES ELIZABETH
Born 1859, Abergavenny.
SKEWES ELIZABETH
Born 1860. Lived at Lanner Hill, Gwennap. Died 1861. Buried Gwennap 11 April 1861, aged 1 year.
SKUES ELIZABETH
Chart 5. Daughter of John Penrose and Elizabeth Skues of Hodders Row, Redruth. Born 1860. Spinster. Died 7 February 1948, aged 87 years.
SKEWS ELIZABETH
Died 1860, Abergavenny.
SKEWS ELIZABETH
Died 1860, Bodmin.
SKUES ELIZABETH
Chart 8. Born 1861. Widow. Lived at 24 Tintern Road, Wood Green, London. Died 1948, aged 87 years in Redruth.
SKEWES ELIZABETH
Married 1861, Bodmin.
SKUES ELIZABETH
Chart 8. Born 1863. Married John Gilbert Skues, 1887, Edmonton. Lived at 24 Tintern Road (later moved to 22 Tintern Road), Wood Green, London. Died 4 December 1946, aged 83 years.
SKEWES ELIZABETH
Daughter of Thomas and Marianne Skewes. Bpt Gunwalloe, 18 January 1863.
SKEWIS ELIZABETH
Née Shaw. Daughter of Martin and Ann (née McLeod) Shaw. Born 1862. Married William Skewis 22 October 1886 at Broad Street, Glasgow. Children: James (1887), George (1891) and John (1896). Died Calton, Scotland, 1896, aged 33 years.
SKEWIS ELIZABETH
Born 1865, Chorlton.
SKEWIS ELIZABETH
Married 1866, Crickhowell.
SKEWES ELIZABETH
Married 1868, Helston.
SKUES ELIZABETH
Chart 3. Née Gaute. Born 1876. Married Charles Ayre Mackenzie Skues 12 August 1903. Lived at 20 Copers Cope Road, Beckenham, Kent. Children: Sheila Mackenzie and Joan Mackenzie (twins). Died 1951, aged 75, Bromley, Kent.
SKEWIS ELIZABETH
Married 1873, Sheffield.
SKEWIS ELIZABETH
Married 1874, Penzance.
SKEWIS ELIZABETH
Chart 33. Daughter of Daniel and Elizabeth Jane (née Willcott) Skewis. Born 1876, Williton, Somerset. Married a Mr Beavis from Ashburton, Devon. Emigrated to Canada. Issue: 2 sons.
SKEWS ELIZABETH
Married 1877, Plymouth, Devon.
SKEWIS ELIZABETH
Chart 50. Born 1877. Had a son James Airns Skewis (1925). Died 1940, aged 63 years in Hull.
SKEWS ELIZABETH
Married 1880, Bedwellty, South Wales.
SKEWES ELIZABETH
Chart 25. Born 1886. Daughter of Charles and Ann Skewes of 15 Horton

Street, Rusholme, Manchester. Spinster. Died 23 June 1952, aged 66 years at 15 Horton Road, Rusholme, Manchester.

SKEWS   ELIZABETH
Married 1887, Pancras.

SKEWS   ELIZABETH
Chart 17. Née Hilliard. Born 1890. Married Henry James Skews, 1909, West Ham. Children: Henry George (1911), Frederick (1914) and Stanley (1919). Died 1920, aged 30 years, in West Ham.

SKEWES   ELIZABETH
Née Richards. Born in Cornwall. Lived at Gurma, Ashton, Helston. Married Henry Skewes 28 April 1891. Emigrated to Martinez, California. Children: John Henry and Frederick Charles. Her sister Catherine Mary Richards of Gurma, Ashton, Helston married Joseph John Skewes, brother to Henry Skewes. Died 22 March 1947.

SKEWIS   ELIZABETH
Born 1892, Dennistoun, Scotland.

SKEWES   ELIZABETH
Lived at Bassett Street, Redruth, 1897.

SKEWS   ELIZABETH
Chart 41. Daughter of Thomas and Ada (née Sheldon) Skews. Born 1898, Barnsley, South Yorkshire. Married George Fletcher, 1917. Issue: 1 daughter and 3 sons. Divorced. Married Herbert Townend, 1943, Staincross. Lives at Clayton, South Yorkshire.

SKEWES   ELIZABETH
Married 1899, Truro.

SKEWES   ELIZABETH
Chart 10. Mexican. Daughter of Juan and Fransisca (née Meneses). Born 23 February 1900, Real del Monte, Mexico.

SKEWES   ELIZABETH
Married 1900, Truro.

SKEWS   ELIZABETH
Born 1904 Bethnal Green. Married Eaton, 1932, Bethnal Green.

SKEWES   ELIZABETH
Chart 50. Daughter of George and Elizabeth J. (née Caddy) Skewes. Born 1930 Pontypridd. Died 1930, aged 0.

SKEWES   ELIZABETH
Lived at Illogan Highway, 1932.

SKEWES   ELIZABETH
Chart 36. Adopted daughter of Percy John and Muriel (née Norris) Skewes. Born 30 August 1937. Married Lance Hazelwood, April 1957. Issue: 4 daughters and 1 son. Lives in Australia.

SKEWES   ELIZABETH
Mother's maiden name Moon. Born 1947, Penzance.

SKEWIS   ELIZABETH
Chart 50. Daughter of James Airns and Irene (née Fox) Skewis. Born 20 March 1955.

SKUES   ELIZABETH
Lived at 53 Cambridge Street, Lidicombe South, New South Wales, Australia in 1959.

SKEWES   ELIZABETH A.
Daughter of John Skewes. Born 1829. Married Richard Skewes, widower, at Register Office, Truro, 18 February 1858. Lived at Penstraze, Kenwyn, 1861. Died 1866, aged 37 years.

SKEWS   ELIZABETH A.
Born 1860. Died 1924, aged 64 years, Redruth.

SKEWES   ELIZABETH A.
Married 1910, Barnstaple, North Devon.

SKEWS   ELIZABETH A.
Chart 17. Daughter of Arthur S.A. Skews. Mother's maiden name Stroud. Born 1949, Stepney.

SKEWIS   ELIZABETH A.A.
Born 1929, New Monkland, Scotland. Married Robert Alexander Wilson, 1947, New Monkland.

SKEWIS   ELIZABETH ADELINE
Chart 2. Daughter of Absalom and Jane Skewis. Born 3 April 1857, America. Died 5 July 1857.

SKEWES   ELIZABETH ALBERTA MARY
(Née Jessop) Born 4 April 1878, Boston, Ontario, Canada. Married William Skewes 7 March 1899. Children: William Jessop (1900), Alberta (1902), Walter George (1904), Harold Herschell (1905), Dorothy Daintry (1906), Robert (1908), James Robert (1914) and June Patricia (1918). Died 18 June 1954 at Michigan, aged 76 years.

SKEWES   ELIZABETH ANN
Daughter of Peter and Elizabeth Skewes. Bpt Kea 3 Aug 1835.

SKEWES   ELIZABETH ANN
Born 1838. Lived at Carnmarthe, Gwennap. Buried Gwennap 20 November 1842, aged 4 years.

SKEWES   ELIZABETH ANN
Born 1874, Helston.

SKEWES   ELIZABETH ANN
Born 1851. Died 1869, St Clement. Buried St Mary's Truro 4 April 1869, aged 18 years.

SKEWES   ELIZABETH ANN
Born 1852. Buried Camborne 9 October 1885, aged 32 years in

Redruth.

SKUES   ELIZABETH ANN
Born 1860, St James, London. Died 1864, aged 4 years.

SKUES   ELIZABETH ANN
Chart 8. Daughter of George Gilbert and Isabella Skues. Bpt St Luke, Westminster 14 April 1864.

SKEWES   ELIZABETH ANN
Born 1860, Truro.

SKEWES   ELIZABETH ANN
Chart 36. Born 14 October 1860, Australia. Married Richard Cooper. Issue: 4 sons and 1 daughter. Died 9 June 1896, aged 36 years.

SKEWES   ELIZABETH ANN
Born 1863, Truro.

SKEWES   ELIZABETH ANN
Born 7 August 1865, Greenbottom, Truro. Daughter of William and Jane (née Northey) Skewes. Emigrated with her parents to Michigan, USA around 1867. Married William John Northey 6 February 1883.

SKEWS   ELIZABETH ANN
Died 1875, aged 0 in Houghton.

SKEWS   ELIZABETH ANN
Chart 49. Born 1876. Daughter of William and Harriet Skews. Died 1895, aged 19 years in Totnes, Devon.

SKEWS   ELIZABETH ANN
Married 1888, St Austell.

SKEWES   ELIZABETH ANN
Lived at 79 Higher Fore Street, Redruth 1906-1922.

SKEWES   ELIZABETH ANN
Chart 37. Daughter of K.M. Skewes of Australia. Born 1 February 1956.

SKEWES   ELIZABETH ANN
Chart 14. Daughter of Glen Wilson and Patricia (née Manthey) Skewes of Wisconsin, USA. Born 18 July 1976. Lives at 918 South Ninth Street, La Crosse, Wisconsin, 54061.

SKEWES   ELIZABETH ANN LANYON
Born 1845, Redruth. Daughter of John Skewes, farmer. Lived at Prospect Place, St Paul's, Truro. Married Thomas Lambshead (33) draper of Lambeth, Surrey, son of Samuel Lambshead, farmer, 10 September 1874 at St Paul's Church, Truro.

SKEWS   ELIZABETH ANNIE
Chart 15. Daughter of Samuel Gregory and Harriet Ann Skews of Pensilva, labourer. Born 1902. Bpt St Ive 21 April 1903. Married Drew 1927. Issue: one son and one daughter.

SKEWES   ELIZABETH CHARLOTTE
Born 1848, Isle of Thanet.

SKEWS   ELIZABETH CHARLOTTE
Died 1850, Bethnal Green.

SKEWS   ELIZABETH DENNIS
Born 1845, Truro.

SKEWES   ELIZABETH ELLEN
Chart 36. Daughter of William and Priscilla Skewes of Carnkie, miner. Born 1853. Bpt Illogan Parish Church 29 October 1853.

SKEWES   ELIZABETH ELLEN
Born 1860, Redruth.

SKEWES   ELIZABETH ELLEN
Born 1862. Buried Illogan Parish Church 28 July 1862, aged 4 months.

SKEWES   ELIZABETH ELLEN R.
Born 1883. Married 1908, Redruth.

SKEWS   ELIZABETH EMILY
Born 1882. Married 1905, Bethnal Green.

SKEWES   ELIZABETH EMMA
Daughter of John and Ann Skewes of Carnwarth; yeoman. Bpt Gwennap 12 November 1848.

SKEWS   ELIZABETH ETHEL GRACE
Chart 15. Daughter of Amos Skews of Trewint, Altarnun. Spinster. Lived at 167 Pasley Street, Plymouth. Born 1892. Died 30 Sept 1965, aged 73 years.

SKEWES   E.H.
Married Joseph Spencer in Wakefield, 1920.

SKEWES   ELIZABETH FRANCES
Chart 24. Daughter of John and Mary Jane (née Cole) Skewes. Born 1897, New South Wales, Australia. Married with three children.

SKEWIS   ELIZABETH GEMMELL
Born Hamilton, Scotland, 1885.

SKEWIS   ELIZABETH GERTRUDE
Born 1889, Sheffield, South Yorkshire.

SKEWS   ELIZABETH GRACE
Born 1900, Devonport. Died 1900, aged 0.

SKEWS   ELIZABETH H.
Mother's maiden name Skews. Born 1921, Devonport. Married Clements, 1942, Plymouth.

SKUES   ELIZABETH HARRIET
Born 1871, Lambeth. Married 1899 in Rochford.

SKEWIS   ELIZABETH I.
Born 1955, New Monkland, Scotland. Married Short, 1973, Grantham, Lincs.

SKEWES   ELIZABETH J.
Born 1840. Died 1922, Redruth, aged 82 years.
SKEWES   ELIZABETH J.
Born 1892. Died Bodmin 1954, aged 62 years.
SKEWIS   ELIZABETH J.
Married Brown in Falmouth, 1952.
SKEWES   ELIZABETH JANE
Daughter of John and Ann Skewes of Kenwyn, miner. Bpt Kea 26 March 1826.
SKEWES   ELIZABETH JANE
Chart 50. Daughter of Thomas and Jane Skewes of Kerley, Kea, miner. Bpt Chacewater 24 November 1833. Emigrated to Australia aboard vessel "Phoebe Dunbar", which sailed from Plymouth 5 September 1854 and arrived in Melbourne 25 December 1854. Engaged by Mr Bushby of Lonsdale Street, Melbourne at an annual rate of £20 for a period of 3 months and which included rations.
SKEWES   ELIZABETH JANE
Born 1842. Died 1866, aged 24 years in Redruth.
SKEWIS   ELIZABETH JANE
Chart 33. Née Willcott. Daughter of Richard Willcott, post boy of Ashburton, Devon. Married Daniel Skewis, 28 November 1852 at the Parish Church, Ashburton. Children: Elizabeth (1854), John (1858), Sarah (1860), Mary (1862), Henrietta (1863), Clara Ann (1866), Emma (1868), Daniel (1869) and William Richard (1872). Died Totnes district 1874, aged 42 years.
SKEWES   ELIZABETH JANE
Chart 2. Daughter of Henry and Grace Skewes. Bpt Camborne 30 August 1836.
SKEWES   ELIZABETH JANE
Chart 36. Born 1840. Bpt Cury 5 April 1840. Daughter of James and Simonette Skewes of Meanley, Cury. Unmarried in 1861 Census Returns.
SKEWS   ELIZABETH JANE
Chart 10. Née Youren. Born 1842. Married Peter Skews at Truro, 1862. Buried Charlestown 14 February 1878, aged 36 years. Lived at Boscappa.
SKEWES   ELIZABETH JANE
Born 1845. Died 1900, Brentford, aged 55 years.
SKEWES   ELIZABETH JANE
Died 1848, Helston.
SKEWES   ELIZABETH JANE
Chart 15. Daughter of John and Isabella Skews of Trewint, Altarnun, Launceston. Born 1851. Bpt Altarnun 15 September 1853. Married 1872, Launceston.
SKEWS   ELIZABETH JANE
Born 1880, Newton Abbot. Died 1880, aged 0.
SKEWES   ELIZABETH JANE
Married 1863, Redruth.
SKEWS   ELIZABETH JANE
Daughter of Richard and Joanna Skews of Kea. Born 21 September 1841. Bpt 6 March 1842.
SKEWS   ELIZABETH JANE
Daughter of Martin and Elizabeth Skews of Chacewater. Born 1842, Kenwyn. In 1851 Census living at Chacewater with her parents and brothers Martin, Thomas and John.
SKEWES   ELIZABETH JANE
Chart 30. Daughter of John Beer and Mary Browne Skewes. Born 1850. Bpt St George's, Truro 14 December 1850. Married James Henry Flynn of St George's, Kenwyn at Kenwyn Parish Church 17 August 1879. Flynn was son of Henry John Flynn, storeman. Wedding in presence of John Beer Skewes and Hetty Skewes. In 1871 Census Returns had been living at Paul's Row, St Clement, Truro as Annuitant. (Niece of Constance Hobbs, widow, aged 80 years.)
SKEWES   ELIZABETH JANE
Married 1851, Truro.
SKEWS   ELIZABETH JANE
Daughter of William and Jane Skews of Kenwyn; miner. Bpt at Bible Christian Chapel, Greenbottom, Truro, 12 October 1865.
SKEWES   ELIZABETH JANE
Chart 30. Daughter of Thomas and Mary Skewes, ironmonger, of Truro. Born 1868. In 1871 Census Returns living in Edward Street, Truro with sisters Mary Ann Peters and Florence and brother Herbert. Married Joseph Stephens Argall, ironmonger of Plymouth at New Methodist Connection Chapel, Truro 7 June 1892 by Rev P. Baker.
SKEWS   ELIZABETH JANE
Chart 10. Daughter of Peter and Maude Mary Skews. Born 1904, St Austell. Died 1905, aged 0.
SKEWIS   ELIZABETH JOAN
Chart 36. Daughter of Arthur and Effie Skewis. Mother's maiden name Peters. Born 19 July 1931. Married David Brown of Falmouth, 1952. Divorced. Married Paul Nesbett in Barry, Canada, May 1960. Lives in Canada.
SKEWES   ELIZABETH JOANNA
Born 1902, Condurrow, Redruth. Buried Tuckingmill Parish Church

(unbaptised) 24 February 1902, aged 2 months.
SKEWES   ELIZABETH JOANNA
Married 1907, Redruth.
SKEWES   ELIZABETH L.
Married 1874, Truro.
SKEWES   ELIZABETH LUCINDA
Chart 2. Daughter of William Henry and Catherine Skewes. Born 27 February 1877 in Australia. Died 23 July 1906, aged 29 years. Spinster.
SKEWES   ELIZABETH M.
Born 1880. Died 1962, Penzance, aged 82 years.
SKEWES   ELIZABETH M.
Born 1889. Died 1911, aged 22 years in Redruth.
SKEWES   ELIZABETH M.
Chart 40. Née Roberts. Born 1889. Married William Skewes, 1910, Penzance. Children: William Richard (1913) and Leonard (1919). Died 1921, aged 32 years in Penzance.
SKEUSE   ELIZABETH M.
Married 1911, Bath.
SKEWES   ELIZABETH MARGARET
Chart 36. Daughter of John Lock and Heather Leonne (née McKenzie) Skewes. Born 24 April 1961, Queensland, Australia. Nurse at Toowoomba Hospital, Queensland.
SKEWES   ELIZABETH MARGARET EDWARDS
Born 1851. Bpt St Mary, Swansea, Glamorgan 8 February 1852. Died 1852, aged 9 months.
SKEWES   ELIZABETH MARIA HICKS
Chart 36. Daughter of John and Susan Skewes of Nantithet, Cury; shoemaker. Bpt Cury 29 July 1858. Buried Cury 4 December 1858, aged 5 months.
SKEWIS   ELIZABETH   MARIE
Chart 2. Daughter of Richard Edward and Deanne Skewis. Born 3 August 1962, America.
SKEWIS   ELIZABETH MARION
Chart 2. Daughter of Charles Samuel and Myrtle Skewis. Born 10 June 1908. Married William Bradley 28 August 1931. Issue: one son and one daughter.
SKEWES   ELIZABETH MARLENE
Chart 12. Daughter of Bertram and Elizabeth Skewes. Mother's maiden name Prowse. Born 1938, Truro. Married John Ball in Truro, 1959.
SKEWS   ELIZABETH MARTHA
Born 1888, St Olave, London. Married George Hewitt in St Olave, 1912.
SKEWES   ELIZABETH MARY
Daughter of Edward and Grace Skewes of Falmouth. Born 13 September 1797. Bpt Falmouth 1 October 1797.
SKEWES   ELIZABETH MARY
Chart 12. Born 24 December 1843 at Gilly, Cury, Helston. Daughter of John and Julianna (née Hendy) Skewes of Cury. Bpt Gunwalloe 3 November 1844. Married John Hollcomb Lugg of Mawgan, postman and son of Henry Lugg, labourer. At the time of marriage Elizabeth Mary was a laundry maid. They married at Mawgan-in-Meneage Church 25 July 1871 in presence of Mary Ann Mander Skewes and John Skewes.
They later ran a hotel on the Lizard prior to emigrating to the United States of America about 1890. Issue: one son and one daughter. Died at Berkeley, California, USA 31 October 1918, aged 75 years.
Descendant: Mrs. Sarah Isabelle Anderson lives at 10 Scenic Road, Fairfax, California, 94930, USA.
SKEWES   ELIZABETH MARY
Daughter of James and Eleanor Skewes of Cury. Bpt Cury 16 July 1848. Died 1870, aged 21 years in Helston.
SKEWES   ELIZABETH MARY
Chart 12. Daughter of William and Mary (née Skewes) Skewes of Gilly Lane, Cury. Bpt Cury 1 February 1835. Died at Gilly Lane, Cury and buried 30 January 1854, aged 19 years.
SKEWES   ELIZABETH MARY
Born 1851, Redruth.
SKEWES   ELIZABETH MARY
Daughter of Edward and Elizabeth Skewes of Nantithet, Cury. Born 1854.
SKEWES   ELIZABETH MARY
Illegitimate daughter of Elizabeth Skewes of Nantithet. Bpt Cury 22 February 1856. Listed in 1871 Census Returns living at Nantithet with her mother and uncle Edward Skewes. She was a field labourer.
SKEWS   ELIZABETH MARY
Chart 10. Daughter of Digory and Fanny (née Tregonning) Skewes. Born 1858, St Ewe. In 1861 Census Returns was living with her parents at Trevenner, Marazion.
SKEWES   ELIZABETH MARY
Married 1877, Lambeth, London.
SKEWES   ELIZABETH MARY
Chart 12. Daughter of John and Thirza Skewes. Bpt Cury 26 December 1877. Had an illegitimate son William John Skewes in 1900. Later married Thomas Gilbert Carter (24), labourer at Ruan Minor, son of

Ellen Skewes (1866-1940) of Mawnan Smith

Elizabeth Mary Skewes (1843-1918)

Elizabeth Mary Skewes of Ontario, Canada

Betty Skewes with her mother Elizabeth Skewes. Photo taken in 1927

John Carter, tailor on 16 June 1903 at Ruan Major Church in the presence of John Skewes and Bessie Skewes. She died in the early 1900's. Thomas Carter then married Bessie Skewes (sister of Elizabeth Mary) at Helston Register Office in 1909.

SKEWES ELIZABETH MARY
Married 1879, Helston.

SKEWES ELIZABETH MARY
Chart 12. Daughter of James Henry and Maude Mary Skewes of Golla Farm, Callestick, Helston. Born 1908. Married William Henry Eustace of Me-Hall-Hill, St Keverne 1 November 1930 at St Keverne Wesleyan Church. Lives in Helston. Issue: 1 daughter.

SKEWES ELIZABETH MARY
Chart 48. Daughter of William (Verdayne) and Elizabeth (née Marsh) Skewes. Born 4 October 1926, Croydon, Surrey. Educated at a series of private schools. At the age of 14 took a year's course at Lamport Commercial College to learn Gregg shorthand, typing, book-keeping and general business studies. First professional job was as secretary to one of the Directors of Down Brothers Ltd, surgical instrument manufacturers.
This was followed by a job with Tuck and Co. Ltd., asbestos manufacturers. Within a year she had moved to be secretary to the Editor of *Poultry World* — and was the only chicken working on the staff! All the other employees were men.
Elizabeth Mary, known as Betty, stayed with the same journal for 20 years (1947-1967) and covered a variety of jobs from production assistant to technical journalist and Home Feature editor.
From 1968-1971 she worked for a small public relations agency and handled a number of industrial accounts.
She was Press Officer for the Dust Control and Air Cleaning Exhibition at Olympia, London in 1969 and 1971.
In 1972 Betty founded "Skewes Press Services", looking after publicity for a variety of firms ranging from picture framing to drawing office equipment and tank cleaning machines to pressure washing equipment.
Spinster. Hobbies include: dressmaking, embroidery, gardening, cine photography, cookery, DIY decorating, painting in oil and water colour, walking and generally keeping fit.
Lives at 49 Addiscombe Road, East Croydon, Surrey, CR0 6SB. Telephone number 01 688 3925.

SKEWES ELIZABETH MARY J.
Married 1873, Clifton, Bristol.

SKEWES ELIZABETH MARY TRERIZE
Born 1865, Helston. Died 1866, aged 0.

SKEWS ELIZABETH MAUD
Born 1886 Bethnal Green. Died 1886, aged 0.

SKEWES ELIZABETH MAY
Born 1875, Helston.

SKEWES ELIZABETH MILDRED
Born 22 January 1889. Daughter of Richard and Louisa Skewes of College Row, Camborne. Bpt Camborne Parish Church 3 April 1889.

SKEWES ELIZABETH PHILIPS
Daughter of Henry and Margaret Skewes. Bpt Gwinear 23 December 1792.

SKEWIS ELIZABETH RUSSELL
Chart 50. Daughter of Joseph Skewis, iron foreman and Marion (née Hamilton) Skewis. Born 13 January 1873, Park, Scotland. Died 1879, Hamilton, Scotland, aged 6 years.

SKEWES ELIZABETH RUTH
Lives at 2/105 Avenue, Tamworth, 2340, New South Wales, Australia with Graeme Trevor Skewes, welder.

SKEWES ELIZABETH S.
Chart 12. Née Clackworthy. Married Carl Skewes, September 1965, Penzance. Children: Ian (1966) and Susan (1968). Lived at 33 Roskear Road, Camborne. Now divorced.

SKEWS ELIZABETH SARAH
Born 1858. Married Lieut. J.W.H. Skews, R.N. 1877. Lived at Coryton House, 11 Ford Park Road, Plymouth. Died 4 July 1934, aged 76 years. Buried Mutley Methodist Churchyard.

SKEWES ELIZABETH STEVENS
Daughter of James and Ann Skewes of St. Mary's, Truro. Bpt St Mary's 29 July 1840. Buried Kenwyn 20 November 1840.

SKEWES ELIZABETH TEMBY
Chart 2. Illegitimate daughter of Constance Skewes. Bpt Camborne 8 February 1798. Died 21 December 1798, aged 10 months.

SKEWES ELIZABETH TRESIZE
Daughter of Thomas and Grace Skewes of Chacewater, miner. Bpt Kenwyn 10 June 1827. Married Thomas Oates, son of Joseph Oates at Kenwyn 31 March 1853.

SKEWES ELLA
Born 1850. Married Frank Bush Adams at Yorkville, Wisconsin, USA. Died 1911, aged 61 years. Buried at Union Grove, Racine County, Wisconsin.

SKEWES ELLA
Chart 12. Daughter of John Wesley Skewes, school attendance officer. Born 1886. Married Samuel Thomas Johns (22), carpenter of Mawgan,

son of Samuel Thomas Johns, estate steward at Helston United Methodist Street Church 20 August 1914. In presence of John Wesley Skewes and Lilian Skewes.

SKEWES ELLA
Chart 36. Née O'Toole. Married Sydney Samuel Skewes in New South Wales, Australia.

SKEWES ELLA BARBARA
Chart 36. Daughter of Simon Skewes. Born 17 July 1897. Spinster. Lives at 6 Warner Street, Malvern East, 3144, Victoria, Australia.

SKEWES ELLA GWENDOLINE
Born 1885. Died 1886, aged 0 in Helston.

SKEWES ELLEN
Daughter of John and Ann Skews of Kea, miner. Born 1843. Bpt Kenwyn 20 August 1843.

SKUES ELLEN
Born 1836. Died 1908, aged 72 years in Islington, London.

SKEWES ELLEN
Daughter of James and Ann Skewes, shoemaker, Bpt St Mary's Truro 18 April 1845. Died 1845, aged 0.

SKEWES ELLEN
Chart 10. Born Truro 1847. Daughter of Peter and Elizabeth Skewes.

SKEWES ELLEN
Daughter of James Skewes, husbandman of Piece, Illogan. Born 1849, Redruth. Married Edwin Mills, miner (son of William Mills, miner) of Camborne at Illogan Parish Church, 20 October 1872.

SKEWES ELLEN
Married 1849, Truro.

SKEWES ELLEN
Born 1853. Died Dartford 1933, aged 80 years.

SKEWES ELLEN
Died 1853, Truro

SKEWES ELLEN
Chart 36. Youngest daughter of James and Frances Skewes, farmer and parish clerk of Mawnan. Born 1866. Bpt 29 April 1866, Mawnan. Married John Peter Sadler of Derby, son of Robert Sadler, butler 22 April 1890 at Mawnan Parish Church, in presence of Mary Skewes. Lived in a cottage in Mawnan now called Windyridge Dairy. Children: Arthur, Russell and Edward. Died 31 May 1940.

SKEWES ELLEN
Chart 14. Daughter of Samuel and Betsy (née Phillips) Skewes. Born 1883, Yorkville, Wisconsin, USA. Married 1) Francis J. Florent (1875-1921) and 2) Thomas H. Donald. Died 1941, aged 68 years.

SKEWIS ELLEN
Born 1894, Hutchesontown, Scotland.

SKEWES ELLEN
Married 1897 in Helston.

SKEWS ELLEN
Married 1897 in Liskeard.

SKUES ELLEN
Married 1909 in Amersham

SKEWS ELLEN ANNIE
Chart 15. Daughter of Peter and Elizabeth Skews of Pensilva, Liskeard. Bpt St Ive 30 August, 1877.

SKUES ELLEN EMMA
Chart 3. Daughter of Richard Skues. Born 1835. Married J. Harrison in Halifax, 1865. Issue: one daughter and two sons.

SKEWS ELLEN JANE
Married 1906, in Redruth.

SKEWS ELLEN KAY
Chart 2. Daughter of Harry Blaine and Elizabeth Ann (née Laycock) Skewes. Born 22 August 1961, Lake Jackson, Texas, USA.

SKEWES ELLEN LOUISA
Died 1865, Redruth.

SKEWES ELLEN LOUISE
Born 1864, Redruth.

SKEWES ELLEN MAUD
Born 1866, Tavistock. Married 1894 in Plymouth.

SKEWS ELLEN M.
Chart 17. Daughter of Robert Albert Skews. Mother's maiden name Waite. Born 1919, Poplar, London. Married Gowers in Stepney, 1940.

SKEWES ELLEN WILLCOCKS
Chart 36. Born 1849. Daughter of James and Simonette Skewes of Cury. Bpt Cury 11 March 1849. In 1871 Census Returns was living at Treskillard, then aged 22, unmarried; tin dresser.

SKEWES ELLINER
Daughter of Richard Skewes. Bpt Mullion 22 February 1627.

SKEWIS ELMER ARTHUR
Chart 2. Son of James and Jane (née Rabling) Skewis. Born 25 December 1877. Lived in America. Married Maude Seymour 7 December 1909 (she born 16 March 1885; died 1976). Celebrated his 100th birthday on 25 December 1977. Died September 1978, aged 100 years. Children: Anita Mary (1910), Betty Hazel (1914) and Robert (1917).

SKEWES ELMINA
Chart 10. Mexican. Daughter of Nazario and Dolores (née Riofrio) Skewes. Born 4 July 1922. Married Daniel Pacas. Issue 3 sons and 3 daughter. Lives in Mexico.

SKEWES ELNOR
Married Henry Fittack at Gerrans, 17 January 1590.

SKEWES ELOISA
Chart 10. Mexican. Daughter of Nazario and Dolores (née Riofrio) Skewes. Born 15 April 1915. Married Mario Bobadilla. Issue 3 sons and 2 daughters. Lives in Mexico.

SKEWES ELSA
Chart 10. Mexican. Daughter of Juan and Leonor (née Munoz) Skewes. Born 28 April 1958. Lives in Mexico.

SKEWIS ELSIE
Born 1910, Helston.

SKEWS ELSIE
Chart 17. Daughter of William George Alfred and Susan (née Childs) Skews. Born 1917, Bethnal Green, London.

SKUES ELSIE
Chart 5. Née Eadon. Daughter of Arthur and Mary Eadon of Sheffield, South Yorkshire. Born 11 April 1892. Married Reginald Penrose Skues at St Mary's Church, Walkley, Sheffield 6 June 1919. He died 23 April 1966, aged 80 years. Lives at Trebron, The Downs, West Looe, Cornwall. Tel No: 05036 2739. No children.

SKEWS ELSIE
Born 1926. Died 1962, Wharfendale, aged 36 years.

SKEWES ELSIE
Chart 40. Only daughter of R.H. Skewes of Bolenna, Fore Street, Marazion. Married Archie Laity, son of Mrs A. and the late Mr Z. Laity of Rosudgeon, at Gulval Parish Church 1 February 1956, by Canon C.H. Buckley.

SKEWS ELSIE
Lived at 2 Hudson Grove, Brunswick South, Victoria, Australia in 1959.

SKEWIS ELSIE ALICE
Chart 33. Née Maddick. Born 30 October 1894. Married Clarence James Skewis, 1947, Totnes, Devon. Died 22 October 1975, aged 81 years.

SKEWES ELSIE BERYL
Chart 36. Daughter of Samuel Sidney and Sarah (née Pennall) Skewes. Born 22 August 1893, New South Wales, Australia. Married Jack Kennedy. Died 18 April 1953, aged 59 years. No children. Buried at Bendemeer, New South Wales.

SKUES ELSIE F.R.
Chart 8. Mother's maiden name Harris. Born 1924, Shoreditch. Married Dennis Martin, 1947, Islington. Issue: 2 sons and 1 daughter.

SKUES ELSIE K.
Born 1896. Died 1965, aged 69 years in Edmonton.

SKUES ELSIE MACKENZIE; LRAM.
Chart 3. Daughter of William Mackenzie and Margaret (née Ayre) Skues. Born 14 December 1872. Married Ernest Allan, August 1903 in Croydon. Issue: 3 sons.

SKEWES ELSIE MARY
Chart 36. Daughter of Samuel and Mary Ann (née Waters) Skewes. Born 20 August 1875. Lived in Queensland, Australia. Married Neil McCall, 6 August 1900. Issue: 4 sons and 1 daughter.

SKEWES ELSIE MAY
Chart 36. Née Smith. Married Douglas William Skewes, 18 June 1938. Lived at 138 Norwood Road, Riverdale, Belmont, Western Australia. Died 1955.

SKEWES ELSIE MAY
Chart 36. Née Handley. Born 12 October 1897, Alton Downs, Queensland, Australia. Married Archer William Skewes at Marlborough, Queensland, 22 October 1918. Children: Colin Archer (1919), John Locke (1921), Geoffrey (1923), Douglas Arthur (1926) and May Dorothy (1937). Lives at 53 Morcombe Street, Brighton, 4107, Queensland, Australia.

SKEWES ELSIE MIRIAM
Chart 2. Née Barry. Married Henry Josiah Skewes at Sunshine, Australia, 1935. Children: Beverley Lorraine (1938) and Glenice Marilyn (1943). Lives at 5 Dalgety Street, Preston, 3072, Victoria, Australia.

SKEWES ELVA
Chart 38. Daughter of Sydney Howard and Cordelia (née Blight) Skewes. Born 20 February 1917, South Australia. Married Donald Norman Bell. Died 28 September 1948, aged 31 years.

SKEWES ELVA BERYL
Lives at 14 Wexcombe Street, Elizabethville, 5112, South Australia with Kenneth Mervaine Skewes, Leon Donald Skewes and Stanley Crawford Skewes.

SKEWES ELVINA
Chart 50. Daughter of Thomas and Sarah Ann (née Lord) Skewes. Born Australia. Married Swan. Died 1922.

SKEWES ELVIRA
Chart 10. Mexican. Daughter of Nazario and Dolores (née Riofrio) Skewes. Born 1 October 1918. Married Juan Rodrigues. Issue: 4 sons

and 4 daughters. Lives in Mexico.

SKEWIS EMILIA
Born 1839, Merthyr Tydfil, Wales. Married 1859, Muirkirk, Scotland to Graham.

SKEWES EMILY
Chart 10. Daughter of Thomas and Grace Skewes of Jolly's Bottom, Chacewater, miner. Bpt Chacewater 10 August 1836. Married 1858, Truro.

SKEWES EMILY
Chart 12. Born 1840. Daughter of William and Mary Skewes of Cury. Bpt Cury 20 September 1840. Married Williams in 1864. Issue: four children. Died in Cury.

SKEWES EMILY
Chart 50. Daughter of Thomas and Jane Skewes of Seveocke, miner. Born 1844, Truro. Emigrated with her parents to Australia in 1850's.

SKEWES EMILY
Born 1844. Lived at Maynes Row, Tuckingmill. Buried Tuckingmill 28 May 1898, aged 54 years.

SKEWES EMILY
Chart 10. Daughter of Peter and Elizabeth Skewes of Hugus, Kea; miner. Bpt Baldhu 15 October 1850.

SKEWES EMILY
Chart 19. Born 1859. Daughter of Thomas Lean and Elizabeth Ann Skewes. Born in Wareham, Dorset.

SKEWES EMILY
Married 1870, Truro.

SKEWES EMILY
Daughter of William and Jane (née Northey) Skewes. Born 29 January 1871 at Wilksburg, Pennsylvania, USA. Married Thomas Strick. Died 4 March 1954, aged 83 years.

SKEWIS EMILY
Born 1874. Died Tonbridge 1936, aged 62 years.

SKUES EMILY
Married 1875, Croydon, Surrey.

SKEWS EMILY
Chart 10. Daughter of Peter and Elizabeth Skews. Born 1876, St Austell. Died 1876, aged 0.

SKEWES EMILY
Born 1879, Redruth.

SKEWES EMILY
Married 1896 in Bideford, North Devon.

SKEWS EMILY
Married 1907 in Redruth.

SKEWES EMILY
Chart 36. Née Mann. Married Oswald Percy Skewes in New South Wales, Australia.

SKEWIS EMILY A.
Chart 2. Born 1857, Wisconsin, USA. Daughter of Edward and Kittie Skewis of Shullsburg, Wisconsin.

SKEWES EMILY ANN
Born 1850. Lived at Medlyn, Wendron. Died 29 December 1914, aged 64 years. Buried Wendron 2 January 1915.

SKEWES EMILY ANN
Chart 12. Née Taylor. Born 1871. Married Henry "Harry" Oswald Skewes, 1892. Lived at Moor Street, Camborne in 1922; 4 Centenary Street, Camborne, 1932. Children: James Henry Oswald, Doris Muriel, Veronica Mary and George Hennessy.

SKEWS EMILY ANNIE
Born 1895, Died 1896, aged 1 in St Olave, London.

SKEWES EMILY CLAIRE
Chart 40. Daughter of Colin Skewes. Mother's maiden name Jordan. Born 1974, Truro.

SKUES EMILY CONSTANCE
Born 1871, Westminster. Died 1873, aged 2 years.

SKEWES EMILY EVELYN
Lives at 52 Albion Street, Annandale, 2038, New South Wales, Australia.

SKEWS EMILY GERTRUDE
Born 1888. Died 1900, Preston, aged 11 years.

SKEWS EMILY J.
Born 1866. Died 1921, aged 55 years.

SKEWIS EMILY JANE
Chart 2. Daughter of Absalom and Jane Skewis. Born 9 July 1854. Married Frank Spensley in America (he died 1919). Died 13 September 1929.

SKEWES EMILY JANE
Born 1862, Redruth. Married 1884, Redruth.

SKUES EMILY JANE
Chart 5. Daughter of Charles Penrose Skues. Born 1871, Pancras, London. Spinster. Lived at Chalfont St Peter. Died of coronary thrombosis, 30 March 1951, aged 78 years

SKEWS EMILY JANE
Born 1874, Liskeard.

SKEWES   EMILY KEMPTHORNE
Chart 36. Daughter of James (farmer and parish clerk of Mawnan) and Frances Skewes of Mawnan Smith. Bpt Mawnan 23 October 1853. In 1871 Census Returns was a boarder at High Street, Mylor and was listed as an assistant school teacher. Married Reuben Cobeldick, bachelor, aged 52 of Mawgan in Pydar, gentleman and son of Richard Cobeldick, farmer 14 December 1883 at Mawnan Parish Church, in presence of Hester Ann Skewes and Edward Skewes.

SKEWES   EMILY LOUISA
Chart 2. Daughter of William and Sarah Skewes. Born 1852, Illogan. Married Dwight. Died 21 September 1937.

SKEWS   EMILY LOUISA
Born 1879, North Aylesford, Kent. Died 1880, aged 0.

SKEWS   EMILY MAUD
Lived at 9 Naroon Road, Alphington, Victoria, Australia in 1959.

SKEWES   EMILY ROSAMUND
Chart 36. Daughter of Alfred John and Matilda Skewes of Maynes Row, Tuckingmill. Born 29 June 1900. Bpt at Tuckingmill Parish Church 12 September 1917 with her sisters and brother. Married Samuel J. George in Redruth 1926 and later John Lawry, 1952. Died 1966.

SKEWS   EMILY S.
Born 1882. Died 1945, aged 61 years in Hendon.

SKEWES   EMILY SUSAN
Chart 36. Daughter of William and Elizabeth (née Northey) Skewes. Born 5 October 1869, Australia. Married Donald Anderson. Issue: 4 sons and 4 daughters. Died 23 December 1968, aged 99 years.

SKEWES   EMMA
Chart 22. Bpt Kenwyn 5 May 1822.

SKEWS   EMMA
Chart 14. Daughter of Anthony and Christian Skewes of Chybarles; farmer. Bpt Ruan Major 23 Sept 1838.

SKEWIS   EMMA
Died 1839, Abergavenny.

SKEWS   EMMA
Born 1841, London. Daughter of John & Elizabeth Skews. Bpt St Botolph without Aldersgate 8 May 1842.

SKEWES   EMMA
Daughter of John and Ann Skewes of Kea; miner and farmer. Born 1841. Bpt Kenwyn 20 August 1843. Lived at Killiwerris. Married R. Trice of Bere Alston, Devon 24 July 1868 at St Paul's Church, Chacewater.

SKEWES   EMMA
Died 1842, Helston.

SKEWIS   EMMA
Born 1843, Crickhowell.

SKUES   EMMA
Daughter of John and Ann Skues of Kea; miner. Bpt Kenwyn 20 Aug 1843 along with her brother John and sister Grace.

SKEWS   EMMA
Died 1845, East London.

SKEWES   EMMA
Chart 19. Born 1847. Lived at Fore Street, Beer Ferris, Devon. Died at Upperton Farm, Bickleigh, Devonshire 6 Feb 1922, aged 75.

SKEWES   EMMA
Daughter of John Skewes, miner. Married William Harris at Kenwyn Parish Church 19 March 1854. Was aged 28 in the year 1854.

SKEWS   EMMA
Born 1855, Liskeard.

SKEWS   EMMA
Born 1857, Launceston.

SKEWS   EMMA
Born 1858. Died 1904, aged 46 years in Sedgefield.

SKEWIS   EMMA
Chart 2. Daughter of Edward and Kittie Skewis. Born Wisconsin, USA 29 October 1857. Spinster. In 1900 lived at Webster City, Hamilton County, Iowa. Died 25 February 1928, aged 71 years.

SKEWES   EMMA
Chart 14. Daughter of Samuel and Ruth Skewes. Born 15 August 1860, Wisconsin, USA. Lived at Ives Grove, Racine County. Educated at Beloit High School from where she graduated and for four years was a teacher in Milwaukee public schools. Married Eugene Hoyt. Issue: one son and one daughter. Died November 1927, aged 67 years.

SKUES   EMMA
Chart 27. Daughter of William and Mary Skues of Bath. Born 1861. Had died by 1865.

SKEWS   EMMA
Chart 15. Daughter of John and Isabella Skews of Trewint, Altarnun, Launceston. Born 1862. Bpt Altarnun 1 January 1863. Died 27 November 1863, aged 1½ years.

SKEWIS   EMMA
Married Samuel Pritchard 7 December 1862 at Manchester Cathedral.

SKUES   EMMA
Born 1865, Strand.

SKUES   EMMA
Chart 27. Daughter of William and Mary Skues of Bath. Born 1866.

SKEWES   EMMA
Chart 10. Daughter of William and Jane Skewes of Illogan Highway; blacksmith. Born 1867. Married John James Rule (23), son of Elisha Rule, miner at Illogan Parish Church 4 January 1891.

SKEWS   EMMA
Married 1869, Brentford.

SKEWS   EMMA
Born 1868, Newton Abbot. Died 1868, aged 0.

SKEWIS   EMMA
Born 1875, Newton Abbot. Died 1875, aged 0.

SKEWS   EMMA
Born 1875. Died 1926, aged 51 years, Stepney.

SKEWS   EMMA
Married 1882, Plymouth.

SKEWES   EMMA
Born 1884. Daughter of Richard Skewes of Ivy Court, Perranuthnoe, Penzance. Died 1885, aged 12 months.

SKEWES   EMMA
Born 10 February 1893. Lived at Trevarth Farm, Lanner and was married to William Skewes. Died 11 January 1971, aged 78 years.

SKUES   EMMA CATHERINE
Chart 9. Daughter of Barry Russell and Gillian Ann Skues. Born 20 February 1978. Lives at "The Hollies", Bromley Green Road, Ruckinge, near Ashford, Kent.

SKEWES   EMMA E.
Married Bowson in Devonport, 1912.

SKUES   EMMA ELIZABETH
Married 1865, St Martin.

SKEWS   EMMA FRANCES
Born 1873, North Aylesford. Married 1893, North Aylesford.

SKEWS   EMMA G.
Born 1857. Died Bournemouth 1928, aged 71 years.

SKEWES   EMMA JANE
Chart 10. Daughter of Thomas and Grace Skewes, farmer. Bpt Chacewater 18 May 1834. Married Joel Wasley, son of Joel Wasley of Kea 25 June 1857 at St Paul's Church, Chacewater.

SKEWS   EMMA JANE
Born 1867, Chorlton, Manchester.

SKEWS   EMMA JANE
Chart 41. Daughter of David and Helen (née Ackroyd) Skews. Born 1975, Barnsley, South Yorkshire. Lives at 11 Woodlands View, Wombwell, Barnsley.

SKEWES   EMMA LAITY
Chart 40. Daughter of Richard and Caroline (née Laity) Skewes. Bpt St Hilary 20 July 1856. Married Helston, 1883.

SKEWES   EMMA MAUD
Born 1861, Truro.

SKEWIS   EMMA NORTHCOTT
Born 1877, Newton Abbot. Married Pethybridge in Totnes, 1913.

SKEWES   EMMA STEPHENS
Daughter of James and Ann Skewes of Truro, shoemaker. Bpt St Mary's, Truro 16 January 1842. In 1861 Census Returns she was living with her widowed mother at Solar Row, St Clement, Truro. Was a dressmaker. Spinster. Died at 8 St Clement Terrace, Truro, aged 85 years. Buried Kenwyn 25 March 1926.

SKEWES   ENID
Chart 12. Mother's maiden name Jory. Daughter of Thomas Henry and Annie Maud Skewes. Born 1920 Redruth. Married Curnow in Redruth, 1952.

SKEWS   ENID
Chart 15. Daughter of William and Gladys Pascoe from Liskeard. Born 14 October 1924. Married Kenneth W.W. Skews at Congregational Church, Liskeard, 24 November 1951. Lives at 11 Bodgara Way, Liskeard. One adopted son Stephen Kenneth Skews (1957).

SKUES   ENID ELIZABETH
Chart 7. Daughter of Francis Albert Skues. Born 1908, Dartford. Married Stanley A. Bayes, 1931, Dartford.

SKEWES   ENID MERLE
Lives at 9 Beryl Street, Woodville West, 5011, South Australia with Robin Skewes and Diane Jane Skewes.

SKEWES   ENOUR
Wife of Sandry Skewes. Buried Ludgvan 4 October 1598.

SKUES   ERIC
B.A. Chart 3. Reverend. Son of Richard James and Eleanor (née Chorley) Skues. Born 14 October 1899. Educated at Clare Road Secondary School, Halifax, Yorkshire. Married Lily Brearley in Halifax, 1924. (She died 1958, aged 64 years.) Graduated University of Leeds with B.A. 1922. Previously at College of Resurrection, Mirfield, 1919. Deacon, 1924 Sheffield for Shantung. Priest 1926. Mission at Yenchow 1924/1928; Furlough 1928/1929 and 1934/1935; Pingyin 1929/1934; Shantung Chaplain Missionary at

Weihaiwei 1935/1940; Tsing-Tao 1940/1945; Furlough, 1946. Society for the Propagation of the Gospel (S.P.G.) Area Secretary, Diocese of Coventry 1947/1953; Diocese of Gloucester and Worcester 1947/1965; Diocese of Hereford 1953/1965; United Society for the Propagation of the Gospel, Diocese of Hereford and Worcester from 1965. Permission to officiate Diocese of Coventry 1947/1953; Diocese of Gloucester 1947/1965; Diocese of Hereford from 1953; Licence to officiate Diocese of Worcester from 1947. Worked in bookshop for United Society for the Propagation of the Gospel, London from 1970 to 1979. Retired 1979. Children: Joyce (1925) and (Rev) John Anthony (1930). Author of *Shensi—China's Mission to the Chinese* (1935).
Address: Juxon, Lollards Tower Chambers, Lambeth Palace Road, London, S.E.I.

Rev. Eric Skues with his daughter Joyce. Photo taken in China, 1925

SKEWS   ERIC
Chart 41. Son of Joseph and Nellie Skews. Mother's maiden name Randerson. Born 1923, Barnsley. Married Rasburn, 1945, Barnsley. Children: Angela, Lynn, Trevor, Paul, Bobbie and Debbie.
SKEWES   ERIC
Chart 10. Mexican. Son of Hector and Georgina (née Cardoso) Skewes. Born 28 January 1974. Lives in Mexico.
SKUSE   ERIC ALBERT
Son of Edwin Charles and Bessie Marian (née Adams) Skuse. Born 6 October 1914, Tooting, London. Married Winifred Kathleen Palmer in Morden, Surrey, 12 August 1939. Children: Frank Eric (1944) & Helen (1947). Draughtsman. Emigrated to Australia in 1959. Retired May, 1979. Lives at Menzies Creek, Victoria, 3159, Australia. Tel no: (059) 684 978.
SKEWIS   ERIC EDWARD
Chart 2. Son of Richard Edward and Deanne Skewis. Born 10 May 1966 in the United States of America.
SKUES   ERIC EDWARD ALFRED
Chart 7. Mother's maiden name Madge Irene Meades. Born 1922, Tonbridge, Kent. Bachelor. Lives at 128 Hop Garden Road, Tonbridge, Kent.
SKEWES   ERIC LAWRENCE
Chart 36. Lived at 36 Mount Carmel Road, Boonah, Queensland, Australia in 1959 with Evelynne Roseina Skewes. Now lives at 7 May Street, Boonah, 4310, Queensland, Australia. Children: Brett, Toni and Shaylene. Taxi driver.
SKEWES   ERIC WILLIAM
Chart 2. Son of Clarence George and Beryl Colville (née Keage) Skewes. Born 11 April 1929, Darlington, New South Wales, Australia. Married Pamela Drummond (she born 17 February 1933) on 13 August 1953. Children: Gillian Wendy (1955), Michael James (1957) and Peter William (1971).
Lives at Lot/422, Galoola Drive, Nelson Bay, 2315, New South Wales, Australia. Yacht proprietor.
SKEWES   ERLESTOUN MINNETA
Chart 36. Née Mudge. Married Samuel Edgar Skewes 25 February 1931. Children: Brian Lock (1932), Ronald Edgar (1934) and John David (1937). Lives at Charles Street, Port Elliot, 5212, South Australia.
SKEWES   ERMA DEONE
Chart 2. Daughter of John Billing and Lydia Skewes. Born 20

Eric Albert Skuse

September 1920, Moab, Utah, USA. Spinster.
SKUES   ERNEST
Chart 3. Son of Richard and Lucy (née Pickard) Skues. Born 19 September 1868, Halifax. Married Clara Roberts, 1897, in Nottingham. Was connected with the multiple firm of Messrs Goodsons and later Ryans of Stockport, Cheshire. He was a well-known figure on the Lancashire and Yorkshire cricket grounds, where for 12 years he never missed a match. Celebrated golden wedding anniversary, February 1945.
Children: Cecil (1897), Vincent (1898), Richard (1904), Florence (1905) and Jack (1911).
Lived at 3 Ashburn Grove, Heaton Norris, Stockport, Cheshire and later 1 Ashburn Grove, Heaton Norris, Stockport where he died 29 March 1945, age 76 years. Clara died 1961, aged 86 years. Both are buried at Cheadle cemetery, Cheshire.
SKUES   ERNEST
Chart 3. Son of Frederick Gordon and Ada Skues. Born Halifax, Yorkshire 8 July 1885. Lived at Portland Place, Halifax and attended Trinity Church School. Was apprenticed to H.C. Brierley (Chemists) of Halifax; gained experience in Leeds with Reynolds and Branson for eight years and qualified 1909.
He moved to London in 1909 and registered with the Pharmaceutical Society (17634) on 10 July 1909, his address being 3 Broadwater Road, London SW 17. He managed a shop in Bermondsey and later bought Barkers Cash Chemists (Croydon) Ltd.
In 1939 he, and a number of enterprising independent pharmacists, founded an organisation designed to further the common interest of the proprietor chemists and to safeguard the future of private retail pharmacy in Britain. The wholesale company was floated for £680. Now Unichem (United Chemists) has an annual turnover of £250 million (1981). A portrait of Ernest Skues still hangs in their boardroom at Crown House, Morden, Surrey. He retired from the Board of Unichem in August 1960. Writing in *Unichem News and Views* Chairman Trevor Cale wrote: "Unichem's progress and success is largely due to Ernest Skues' acumen and inspired direction over the past 21 years. He possesses that exceptional quality of mental orderliness which enabled him to apply a carefully considered reasoning in his approach to every problem. He has rarely been proved wrong in his judgement of people.

Drawing by Eric Skuse of his home at Menzies Creek, Victoria, Australia, December, 1981

Ernest Skues (1868-1945)

Ernest Skews (1893-1918)

Ernest Skues (right) at his resignation party in 1960 as a director of Unichem, handing over a portrait of himself for the Boardroom

This attribute in the calibre of our executive staff is exemplified by their high esprit de corps together with the obvious enthusiasm in the way they set about their work."

Ernest Skues was made a Freeman of the City of London 19 December 1952, and later joined the Guild of Freemen. He attended the Lord Mayor's Banquets annually.

He has served as President of the Proprietary Articles Trades Association, The Photographic Dealers' Association, The London Pharmaceutical Association.

He was a member of the Pharmaceutical Society and later made Honorary Fellow of the Pharmaceutical Society.

After his retirement Ernest Skues kept on one or two pharmacies but sold his interests in 1968. He was a senior officer in the craft of Freemasonry. He was made a Paul Harris Fellow for his services to the Rotary movement... "Ernest Skues is hereby named a Paul Harris Fellow in appreciation of tangible and significant assistance given for the furtherance and better understanding and friendly relations between peoples of the world. April, 1976." (Paul Harris founded the Rotary Movement in America in 1905). Ernest Skues founded the Rotary Club of Tooting and was founder President from 1929 to 1970.

Ernest Skues married Doris Gamble Marsh in March, 1919 (who died 21 November 1945, aged 56 years). They had one child, Margaret Pamela Skues (born 7 August 1924) who married Maxamillion J. Pawlack of Canada, 1945.

He married Audrey Hiscock of Southampton, 2 October 1948. They lived at 36 Well House, Woodmanston Lane, Banstead, Surrey. Tel no: Burgh Heath 52403.

Ernest Skues died 24 November 1977, aged 92 years.

SKEWES   ERNEST
Chart 10. Son of Richard and Frenetta Skewes of Marazion. Born 29 September 1893. Bpt Marazion 15 December 1893. Emigrated to America with his parents and family. Married Marjorie Jane Coomber 27 March 1916 at Hamilton, Ontario, Canada. Children: Ernest William, Richard, Robert, Vera and Shirley. Lived at 117 Young Street, Hamilton, Ontario. Died 23 December 1977, aged 80 years.

SKEWES   ERNEST
Chart 18. Born 1888, Tavistock, Devon. Son of Samuel Dawe and Emma Skewes. Killed in First World War serving in France with 364th Infantry US Army 28 September 1918, aged 30 years.

SKEWS   ERNEST
Chart 41. Son of Thomas and Ada (née Sheldon) Skews. Born 1895, Barnsley, South Yorkshire. Was a driver with Royal Horse Artillery in First World War. Killed in action 17 August 1918 in France, aged 23 years.

SKEWS   ERNEST
Born 1911, Bethnal Green. Died 1911, aged 0.

SKUES   ERNEST
Chart 5. Son of James Frederick Skues. Mother's maiden name Tregonning. Born 1923, Redruth. Was deaf and dumb. Lived at 16 Trefusis Terrace, Redruth. On 11 October 1955 he was travelling as a pillion passenger on a motor cycle which collided with a stationary van at Mount Pleasant, Roche. He was 32 years old. He was buried in St Day Road Cemetery, Redruth.

SKEWS   ERNEST EDGAR
Born 1904, Bromley, Kent.

SKEWES   ERNEST JOHN
Chart 30. Son of John Beer and Bessie (née Whether) Skewes. Born 1881, London. Married Florence Lucy Showbrooke. Lived at 103 Regent Street, Exeter and later 7 Courtenay Road, St Thomas, Exeter. Was a capstan setter and brass finisher. No children. Died 1968, aged 87 years. Funeral service was at Exwick Road Cemetery Church 11 March 1968.

SKUES   ERNEST JOHN
Chart 8. Son of Walter Edward and Atalanta Emily (née Bond) Skues. Born 25 May 1912, Shoreditch. Married Jennie E. Franklin, Shoreditch, 16 February 1935. Daughter: Jean Margaret (1935).
Served with Royal Artillery 1941-1945 in Germany, France, Belgium and Holland.
Compositor with Williams Lea 1945-1978. Retired 1978. Now does part time work for Metropolitan Police at Hendon.
Married Sarah Minnie Ellen Porter 20 May 1961. Lives at 13 Blundell Road, Edgware, Middlesex. Telephone number: 01 959 0582.

SKEWS   ERNEST JOSEPH
Chart 17. Son of George Alfred and Lucy Caroline (née Moore, formerly Bernard) Skews, wood turner. Born 1 April 1889 at 10 Granby Row, Bethnal Green, Died 1953, aged 63 years in Ilford, Essex.

SKEWES   ERNEST LLOYD
Chart 46. Son of Charles and Bessie (née Teague) Skewes of 76 Chapel Hill, Truro. Born 26 November 1920. Bpt St George's, Truro 9 January 1921. Married Doris Irene Patricia Penhaligon in St George's, Truro 7 September 1946. He was then serving in the Royal Air Force. Witnesses at wedding: William Douglas Skewes and Bessie Skewes. Later lived at 68 Chapel Hill, Truro. Children: Patricia Ann and Linda Rosemary. Now lives at 9 Albany Road, Truro.

SKEWES   ERNEST RICHARD
Chart 38. Son of Albert Milton and Myrtle Emma (née Marks) Skewes.

Ernest John Skues

Born 30 August 1914. Married Lena Mary Hass, 30 November 1940. Children: Albert John (1941) and Peter William (1946). Lived at 40 Perry Road, Wallaroo Mines, South Australia. Died 13 October 1974, aged 60 years. Buried in Kadina Cemetery, South Australia.

SKEWIS   ERNEST RONALD
Chart 34. Son of Edwin Skewis. Born 8 May 1900, Cochrane Street, Marylebone, London. Married Joyce Elizabeth Gilbert 22 June 1935 at St Peter's Church, Tunbridge Wells, Kent. Lives at 20 Claremont Gardens, Tunbridge Wells, Kent TN 2 5DD. Issue: one daughter Christine J. (1938).

Ernest Ronald Skewis

SKEWES   ERNEST SEYMOUR
Chart 38. Son of Richard and Mary Jane (née Reynolds) Skewes. Born 23 May 1900, Moonta, South Australia. Married Eleanor May Stapleton 10 March 1924. Children: William Seymour (1925) and Cathrine (1924). Lived at 7 Fisher Street, Welland, Flinders Park, South Australia. Labourer. Died 12 July 1963, aged 63 years.

SKEWS   ERNEST W.
Chart 17. Son of Nathaniel Edward Richard Skews. Mother's maiden name Hilliard. Born 1911, West Ham. Married 1937 to Falconer in Croydon. Children: Evelyn M. (1938), Irene M. (1939), Robert W. (1941) and Christopher R. (1946).

SKEWES   ERNEST WILLIAM
Chart 10. Son of Ernest Skewes of Marazion. Born 8 August 1917, Hamilton, Ontario, Canada. Married Gladys Hennings in Canada.

SKEWES   ERNESTINE MARY
Chart 10. Daughter of Rev. Herbert John and Henrietta Catalina (née Richards). Born 13 June 1911. Lived at Churchtown, Praze, Camborne. Spinster. She worked as a civilian clerk at Redruth Police Station for 30 years (1942 to 1972). Previously she was a teacher. Died following a fire at her garage. Died at the Royal Cornwall Hospital, Treliske, Truro, 8 October 1972, aged 61 years. At an inquest in Camborne a verdict of misadventure was recorded in October 1972. Ernestine Mary Skewes lived alone at Gilmore House, Crowan. She was an arthritis sufferer. On the day of the fire (25 September) she had told a neighbour she was going to clear out the garage. Her only words were "I was smoking ..... a can." Assistant Divisional Officer of Camborne Fire Station said there was a strong smell of petrol in the garage. There had been at least two explosions.

SKEWES   ERNESTO
Chart 2. Mexican. Son of Francisco Skewes of Pachuca, Mexico. Born 4 August 1928. Children: Aaron Ernesto (1969) and Gabriela (1970).

SKEWS   ESME ETHEL
Born 23 September 1904. Lived at 28 South Street, Crowland, Lincs. Died 1973 (12 October), aged 69 years.

SKEWES   ESTHER
Chart 25. Née James. Married Thomas Skewes of St Keverne 23 October 1746 at St Keverne. Died 5 January 1797 (he died 28 Dec 1777). Children: Esther, Thomas, Mary, Judith, Henry, Jane, Ann and Eleanor.

SKEWIS   ESTHER
Chart 25. Daughter of Thomas and Esther Skewis. Bpt St Keverne 10 May 1747.

SKEWES   ESTHER
Chart 25. Daughter of Thomas and Eleanor Skewes. Born 5 July 1786. Bpt Falmouth 27 August 1786. Died Falmouth 15 April 1811, aged 25 years.

SKEWES   ESTHER
Chart 50. Daughter of Samuel and Mary (née Sanders) Skewes. Born 1875. Died Redruth 1885, aged 10 years.

SKEWES   ESTHER
Married 1876, Ulverston.

SKEWS   ESTHER
Manager Sahara Apartments, 7500 Tenton Avenue, Apartment 11, Seattle, Washington, USA (1967). Married to Wesley Skews.

SKEWES   ESTHER ANN
Daughter of James and Frances Skewes. Bpt Mawnan 5 July 1846.

SKEWES   ESTHER ANN
Chart 40. Daughter of Richard and Caroline (née Laity) Skewes. Bpt St Hilary 2 April 1854.

SKEWS   ESTHER DELLER
Lived at 82 Stuart Avenue, Manley, New South Wales, Australia in 1959 with Edmund John Skews.

SKEWS   ESTHER ISABEL
Born 1888, Plymouth.

SKUES   ESTHER MARY
Lives at 21 Lord's Avenue, Asquith, 2078, Australia with Colin Arthur Skues.

SKEWES   ETHEL
Chart 50. Née Pollard. Born October 1881. Married Stephen James Skewes at Redruth Methodist Church 8 June 1911. Children: Harry (1915) and James (1919).
Lived at 23 Trefusis Road, Redruth and later at 27 Cardew Close, Redruth.
She had a long association with Fore Street Methodist Church and was a teacher and chorister in the Sunday School and Church before marriage. Died at Barncoose Hospital, Redruth 4 July 1963, aged 81 years.

SKEWS   ETHEL
Born 1885. Lived at 11 Garden Lane, Cleadon, County Durham. Died 15 February 1959, aged 74 years at General Hospital, Ryhope, County Durham.

SKEWS   ETHEL
Born 1889. Died 1902, aged 13 years in Plymouth.

SKUES   ETHEL
Married 1907, Chippenham, Wiltshire.

SKEWS   ETHEL
Married Harris in Plymouth, 1944.

SKEWS   ETHEL
Lives at 36 Manley Parade, The Entrance, 2261, New South Wales, Australia.

SKEWS   ETHEL ADELAIDE
Lived at B.S.L. Carrum Downs, Cranbourne, Victoria, Australia, 1959.

SKEWES   ETHEL CATHERINE
Chart 10. Daughter of Herbert Tregonning Skewes and Florence Martha of Ontario, Canada. Born 24 July 1925 at Victoria Harbour, Ontario. Married Bruce Cowie 9 November 1944. Issue: one son and one adopted son.

SKUES   ETHEL EMMA
Born 1877, Bath.

SKEWES   ETHEL EVA
Chart 36. Daughter of Samuel Sidney and Sarah (née Pennall) Skewes. Born 22 December 1889, Uralla, New South Wales, Australia. Married Robert Streeting. Issue: 3 sons and 3 daughters. Died 27 November 1974, aged 84 years.

SKEWES   ETHEL IVY
Lives at 73 Ashburton Road, Glen Iris, Victoria, 3147, Australia with Ivan Herbert Skewes.

SKEWES   ETHEL JANE
Born 1883, Eton. Married 1907, Eton.

SKEWS   ETHEL JANE
Chart 10. Born 1890, Redruth. Married Martin Skews at Redruth, 1915. Children: Rex Skews (1919). Lived at Bellvue, Redruth. Died 29 January 1963, aged 73 years at Mayday Hospital, Croydon, Surrey. Cremated at Croydon 4 February 1963. Ashes interred at Treleigh, 11 February 1963.

SKEWES   ETHEL MABEL
Lived at 21 Blackwall Point Road, Chiswick, Abbotsford, New South Wales, Australia in 1959.

SKEWS   ETHEL MARY
Born 1888, Dartford, Kent. Married 1907 in Strood.

SKEWES   ETHEL MAUDE
Lived at Poplar Grove, Murrembeena, Henty, Victoria, Australia in 1913 with Norman William Skewes.

SKUES   ETHEL MAUDE
Lives at 73 Wattle Drive, Doveton, 3177, Victoria, Australia with Leigh Harold Skues, painter.

SKEWES   ETHEL MAY
Chart 12. Daughter of William James Skewes of Mawgan. Born 1883. Married Herbert Cooke (28), carpenter of Mawgan, and son of William Thomas Cooke, carpenter of Mawgan at Meneage Church, 15 October 1908.

SKEWES   ETHEL MAY
Lived at Kitchen Avenue, Belgrave, Ferntree Gully, Victoria, Australia in 1959 with Charles Trevalyan Skewes.

SKEWS   ETHEL MAY
Lived at 125a Park Street, Abbotsford, Victoria, Australia in 1959 with Herbert Skews.

SKEWES   ETHEL TUNNICLIFFE
Chart 25. Née Ashton. Born 6 September 1896. Married George Ernest Skewes, 25 July 1925, Broughton Park, Salford. No children. Lived at 8 Hunstan Road, Sale, Cheshire until 1966 when she moved to 11 Eastway, Sale, Cheshire. Current address. Telephone number 061 973 2722.

SKEWIS   ETHEL WINIFRED
Chart 36. Née Peters. Married Arthur Skewis, Illogan Parish Church 22 February 1930. Lived at Lower Pumpfield Row, Pool, Illogan, 1932. One daughter Elizabeth Joan (1931). Lives at Cantor, 31 Agar Road, Illogan Highway, Redruth. Tel No: Redruth 216576.

SKEWES   ETHEL WOODMAN
Born 1880, East Stonehouse. Died 1880, aged 0.

SKEWIS   ETTIE
Chart 33. Daughter of William Richard Skewis. Born 1909, Totnes. Died 1910, aged 1 year.

SKEWS   EUNICE D.
Mother's maiden name Atkinson. Born 1927, Dartford. Married Phillips, Dartford, 1949.

SKEWES   EUNICE ELAINE
Lives at 1968 Gold Coast Highway, Miami, 4220, Queensland, Australia with William George Skewes, newsagent.

SKEWES   EUNICE J.
Wife of Thomas J.D. Skewes. Lived at B6 — 1729 Boylston Avenue, Seattle, Washington, USA (1912).

SKUES   EVA
Born 1875, St Olave. Died 1904, aged 29 years.

SKEWES   EVA
Chart 18. Née Valentine. Born 1878. Married Arthur Dawe Skewes, 1902, Plymouth. Children: Bella Clark, Mary Elizabeth and Winifred Jean. Lived at Lanecost, Tavistock Road, Plymouth 1906-1935. Died 1943, aged 65 years.

SKUES EVA
Chart 5. Born 1889. Née Garvey. Married William John Skues in Amersham, Bucks, 1911. Child: Vivian William Skues. Later moved to Fern Cottage, Fore Street, Probus. Died 3 July 1966, aged 77 years. William John Skues died 1976.

SKUES EVA
Chart 3. Née Rowland. Married Vincent Skues, 1922 in Blackburn. Children: Muriel M. (1926), Vera Joan (1924) and Donald (1929). Lives at "Vinclyn", Dawson Lane, Whittle-le-Woods, Chorley, Lancashire. Vincent died 18 July 1970.

SKEWES EVA
Married Arthur Dawe Polkinghorne (outfitters of Chy-an-Gwel, Boscolla, Truro). Adult baptism of daughter Mary Elizabeth at Kenwyn 4 March 1948.

SKEWS EVA
Married Mirza in Hull, 1967.

SKEWES EVA
Lived at 12 Donald Street, Panama, New South Wales, Australia in 1959 with Norman William Skewes.

SKEWES EVA
Chart 10. Mexican. Daughter of Henry and Lourdes (née Escudero) Skewes. Born 26 January 1975. Lives in Real del Monte, Mexico.

SKEWES EVA KATHERINE
Chart 14. Daughter of Samuel and Betsy (née Phillips) Skewes of Wisconsin, USA. Born 13 August 1869. Died 16 March 1892, aged 21 years. Spinster.

SKEWIS EVA L.
Lived at 475 Northern, San Jose, California, USA in 1960.

SKEWES EVA LORRAINE
Chart 38. Daughter of Horace Henry and Agatha Blanche Skewes. Born 4 September 1916, Broken Hill, Australia. Married 15 June 1935 to Francis John James Campbell in Australia.
Issue: 2 sons and 2 daughters. Lives at 86 Williams Lane, Broken Hill, New South Wales, Australia.

SKEWES EVA LOUISE
Chart 43. Born 1874, Sheffield.

SKEWS EVA MARY
Born 1881. Lived at 34 Station Road, Sidcup, Kent. Died 2 November 1965, aged 84 years.

SKUES EVELYN
Chart 3. Daughter of Richard James and Eleanor (née Chorley) Skues. Born 9 November 1902 at Willow Cottage, Rochdale Road, Halifax. Attended Hough Shaw Primary School, Parkinson Lane Junior School and Miss Glendenning's Private School, Hopwood Lane, Halifax. Joined Skues' Cafe in Princess Street, Halifax in her teens. Worked to her aunt (Florence Mary Skues) who was proprietor. Skues' Cafe was bought out by Burtons the Tailors in 1949. The Cafe then moved to Wade Street, Halifax. Evelyn started Confectioners Shop with her sister Lucy at 66 King Cross Street, Halifax around 1950. Retired to 11 Bell Hall Terrace, Halifax. Tel No: Halifax 58604. Spinster.

Evelyn Skues

SKEWES EVELYN JUNE
Chart 10. Daughter of Jonathan Braddon and May Eve (née Gallagher) Skewes of Marazion. Born 7 August 1922 at Hamilton, Ontario, Canada. Married Michael Werne, 17 April 1948. Issue: 1 son and 2 daughters. Lives at Limeridge Road West, Hamilton, Ontario, Canada, L9C2T9.

SKEWS EVELYN M.
Chart 17. Daughter of Ernest W. Skews. Mother's maiden name Falconer. Born 1938, Croydon, Surrey.
Advert in *Picture Show* magazine 20 September 1958: "Miss E.M. Skews of 48 Ardleigh Road, Walthamstow, London E17 wants a pen-friend in Iraq, Turkey or Greece. Interests: general. Own age 20. Photograph appreciated."
Married Genovese in SW Essex, 1962.

SKEWES EVELYN MARY
Chart 12. Née Cork. First wife of John Henry Skewes. She later married Pustelnyk in Truro, 1951. Had lived at Carnarthen Villas, Carn Brea, 1932.

SKEWES EVELYN MARY
Lived at 21 Rockbourne Street, Elizabeth North, Gawler, South Australia in 1959 with Stanley Crawford Skewes. Now lives at 43 Fletcher Road, Elizabethville, 5112, South Australia.

SKUES EVELYN ROSE
Chart 8. Born 1878 at 6 Little Chapel Street, Westminster. Married 1898 to Lloyd. Died 14 February 1960 in Golders Green, London.

SKEWES EVELYNNE ROSEINA
Lived at 36 Mount Carmel Road, Boonah, Queensland, Australia in 1959 with Eric Lawrence Skewes, truck driver.
Now lives at 7 Mary Street, Boonah, 4310, Queensland, Australia.

F

SKUSE F.A.A.
Author of *British Stalk Eyed Crustaceans & Spiders*. An extract from Australian Encyclopaedia Volume III relates: "The studies of Diptera in Australia were started by F.A.A. Skuse (1888-1896) working on the Nematocera."

SKUSE FAITH HOPE CHARITY
Daughter of James and Rachel Skuse. Born 30 January 1831, Horton, Bucks. Died 25 September 1845 of consumption.

SKEWES FANNY
Chart 2. Daughter of Henry and Grace Skewes of Bosawsack; farmer. Bpt Constantine 29 Sept 1822. Married Elias Geach of Budock, farmer at Constantine 23 Feb 1848.

SKEWES FANNY
Chart 17. Born 1827, Budock. Wife of Josiah Skewes. Lived at Bosawsack, Constantine. Died 18 June 1895, aged 68 years. Buried in Constantine Churchyard alongside her husband and five infant children. Children included Laura, James, Josiah and Henry (all living in 1871 Census at Bosawsack).

SKEWES FANNY
Chart 10. Née Tregonning. Born 1827. Married Digory Skewes of Liskeard, 1856. Children: William Hannibal, Thomas George, Elizabeth, Mary, Samuel, Amelia, Richard, Joseph and Henry. Buried 2 July 1902, aged 75 years in Marazion.

SKEWSE FANNY
Born 1838, Malmsbury.

SKEWIS FANNY
Chart 44. Daughter of Thomas and Elizabeth Skewis. Born 1855, Abergavenny.

SKEWS FANNY
Born 1859. Died 1896, aged 37 years, Bristol.

SKEWIS FANNY
Married 1876, Newport, Mon.

SKEWES FANNY
Chart 25. Born 16 June 1894. Née Denton. Married Frederick William Skewes in Chorlton, Manchester, 1920. Lived at 24 Bradshaw Avenue, Withington, Manchester. Died 2 June 1974, aged 80 years. No children. Frederick William Skewes died 1944, aged 49 years.

SKEWES FANNY ELIZABETH
Chart 36. Daughter of Samuel and Mary Ann (née Waters) Skewes. Born 30 March 1873. Lived in Queensland, Australia. Married Alfred Collins 3 June 1895. Issue: 5 sons. Died 16 December 1954, aged 81 years.

SKEWS FANNY GREGORY
Chart 15. Daughter of Peter and Elizabeth Skews of Woolstan, Callington. Bpt Altarnun, 20 November 1856.

SKEWES FANNY JANE MANLEY
Daughter of Mary Ann Skewes of St Day, Gwennap. Bpt Gwennap Primitive Methodist Church 31 January 1860.

SKUCE FAY
Daughter of Stewart Tennyson and Gertrude (née Roe) Skuce. Born 1926, Australia. Married Moon. Issue four children and five grand-children.

SKEWES   FAY ELSIE
Lived at 33 Guthrie Street, Brunswick South, Victoria N 12, Australia in 1959 with Hazel Netta Skewes and William Thomas Skewes.

SKEWIS   FEARNLEY JOHN
Chart 33. Son of William Richard Skewis. Born 1901, Totnes. Died 1902, aged 1 year.

SKEWES   FEDERICO
Chart 10. Son of Juan and Luisa (née Garcia) Skewes. Born 1884. Mexican. Bachelor. Died 30 April 1922, aged 38 years.

SKEWIS   FEODORA
Born 1890 at Ruan Major. Died 1890, aged 6 weeks. (12 January 1890).

SKEWES   FERNANDO
Bpt Menheniot 29 November 1573.

SKEWES   FERNANDO
Chart 10. Mexican. Son of Juan and Maria (née Mendosa) Skewes. Born 15 July 1907.

SKEWS   FERNLEY WALTER
Chart 15. Son of John Gregory and Annie Skews. Born 1907, Liskeard. Married Susan Wilcocks, St Germans, 1938. One son: John Walter (1939). Died 1940, aged 33 years.

SKEWES   FIONA
Chart 36. Daughter of Maxwell Skewes. Mother's maiden name Walls. Born 1969, Truro.

SKEWES   FLORA
Born 12 July 1883. Lived in South Australia. Sister of Gertrude Skewes, Allen Skewes and Jess Skewes. Married J. Vivian. Died 12 July 1947, aged 64 years. Buried in Church of England Cemetery, South Australia.

SKEWES   FLORA HEATHER
Née McKenzie. Married Colin Arthur Skewes. Child: Lynette Margaret Skewes. Lives at Mineeda, Blackall, Queensland, 4732, Australia.

SKEWES   FLORA L.
Chart 26. Daughter of Edward James and Harriet (née Rockwell) Skewes. Born Connecticut, USA 28 November 1892.

SKEWS   FLORA LEE
Born 1879, Redruth.

SKEWES   FLORENCE
Daughter of Humfrey Skewes. Bpt Gerrans 12 September 1618. Married Osborn Fittack 5 May 1646 at Gerrans.

SKEWES   FLORENCE
Married John Heale at St Andrew's, Plymouth, 1655.

SKEWES   FLORENCE
Married Richard Row at St Keverne 6 July 1674.

SKEWES   FLORENCE
Daughter of Amelia Skewes, single woman. Bpt St Mary. Truro, 10 December 1877. Married 1904, Truro.

SKEWES   FLORENCE
Mother's name Allcock. Born 1914, Salford.

SKEWES   FLORENCE
Married Phillips, 1949 in Salford.

SKEWES   FLORENCE
Chart 12. Née Blenes. Second wife of John Henry Skewes. Lived at Western Froggeries, Carnkie, Redruth. Divorced after five weeks. One son: Carlton B. Skewes.

SKEWES   FLORENCE
Lived at 27 Tresavean Estate, Lanner, Redruth, 1968.

SKUES   FLORENCE
Died 1970, Pancras, London.

SKEWS   FLORENCE A.
Married Powell in Maidenhead 1923.

SKEWES   FLORENCE ANNIE
Born 1885. Daughter of Richard and Louisa Jane Skewes of Bream, miner. Bpt Camborne 25 March 1885 (born 1 January 1885). Married 1908 in Redruth.

SKUES   FLORENCE AUGUSTA
Born 1886. Died Eton, 1900, aged 14 years.

SKEWS   FLORENCE BEATRICE
Chart 15. Daughter of Edmund and Maria Skews of Pensilva, Liskeard. Bpt St Ive 22 August 1894. Died 1894, aged 0.

SKEWES   FLORENCE BLANCHE
Born 27 October 1888. Daughter of William and Blanche Skewes, painter, of Middle Rosewin Row, St Paul's, Truro. Bpt St Paul's, Truro, 5 August 1891. Married 1910, Truro.

SKEWES   FLORENCE CECILIA
Chart 30. Youngest daughter of Thomas and Mary Jane Skewes of Parkvedras Terrace, Truro, ironmonger. Born 3 January 1870. In 1871 Census Returns living with her parents and sisters Mary A.P., Elizabeth J. and brother Herbert at Edward Street, Truro. Bpt St George's, Truro, 22 December 1888. Married 18 August 1890 at Kenwyn Parish Church to William Thomas Tonkin (30), butcher of Victoria Place, St John's, Truro and son of William Tonkin, butcher. In presence of Annie Skewes and Thomas Skewes.

SKEWIS   FLORENCE CLYDE
Chart 2. Daughter of Benjamin Peter and Amelia Skewis. Married C.H. Whitmore. Issue: one daughter. Lives in America.

SKEWS   FLORENCE ELIZABETH
Born 1876, Edmonton. Married 1895, Bethnal Green.

SKUES   FLORENCE EMILY
Chart 7. Daughter of Thomas Skues. Born 1887, Tonbridge. Married William J. Marjoram, 1913, Chelsea district. Issue: 4 sons.

SKEWS   FLORENCE EMMA
Born 1884, Liskeard. Married 1905, Liskeard.

SKEWS   FLORENCE JANE
Born 1902, Devonport. Died 1902, aged 0.

SKEWS   FLORENCE KATE
Born 1873. Daughter of Thomas and Charlotte of Pennsylvania, USA; blacksmith. Bpt Illogan Parish Church 20 April 1873.

SKUES   FLORENCE LILIAN
Chart 5. Daughter of John Charles Skues. Born 1906, Redruth. Died 1914, aged 8 years.

SKEWES   FLORENCE LOUISA
Lived at 30 Dew Street, The Barton, South Australia in 1959 with Edgar Ernest Skewes.

SKEWES   FLORENCE LUCY
Chart 30. Born 1880. Married Ernest John Skewes. Lived at 7 Courtenay Road, St Thomas, Exeter. Died 23 August 1957, aged 77 years.

SKUES   FLORENCE M.
Chart 9. Born 1890. Married John Philip Skues. Children: Cyril Albert J., Philip Ernest, Joseph John G., Audrey F. and Derek A. Died 1955, aged 65 years, in Woolwich.

SKUES   FLORENCE MARY
Chart 3. Daughter of Richard and Lucy Skues. Born 29 May 1875. Spinster. Lived at 38 Hough Shaw Road, Halifax in 1936 and later 1 Willow Bank, Hyde Park, Halifax. Was a proprietor of Skues Cafe at 4 Princess Street, Halifax. She wished to be a rescue worker but her mother would not spare her from the cafe. Died 23 October 1945, aged 70 years.

Florence Mary Skues (1873-1945)

SKEWES   FLORENCE MAY
Chart 36. Daughter of Alfred John and Matilda Skewes of Mayne's Row, Tuckingmill. Born 25 November 1902. Bpt at Tuckingmill Parish Church with her sisters and brother 12 September 1917. Married David Vincent, 1929. Issue: One son.

SKUES   FLORENCE MURIEL
Chart 3. Daughter of Ernest and Clara (née Roberts) Skues. Born 23 September 1905, Halifax. Attended schools in Barnsley and Blackburn. Married Harry L. Coulthurst at Christ Church, Heaton Norris, Stockport 11 June 1938. Lived at 1 Ashburn Grove, Heaton Norris, Stockport, Cheshire. Issue: one daughter Anne who lives in Ottawa, Canada.
Address: 17 Peveril Drive, Hazel Grove, Stockport, Cheshire. Tel no: 09967 873581.

Florence Muriel Skues

SKUES   FLORENCE RACHAEL
Chart 5. Née Rosenburg. Born 21 February 1887, Victoria, Australia.
Married Samuel Francis Skues. Child: Jack Sydney (1918). Lived at 70
Tennyson Street, Elwood, Victoria, Australia. Died 10 December 1961,
aged 74 years.
SKEWES   FLORENCE ROSALIE
Chart 18. Daughter of Samuel Dawe and Jane (née Courtis) Skewes of
Bere Alston, Devon. Born 1868. Died 1874, aged 6 years.
SKEWS   FLORENCE ROSE
Lived at 37 Newry Street, Prahran, Victoria, Australia in 1959 with
Allan Robertson Skews.
SKUES   FLORENCE RUBY
Chart 8. Born 1904. Daughter of Walter Edward and Atlanta Emily
(née Bond) Skues. Married John C. Barrett, 1938, Shoreditch. Issue:
one son.
SKEWIS   FLORENCE SANDRA
Daughter of William Skewis of Burlington, Ontario, Canada. Born
1948. She is a teacher in Canada and lives at Apartment 1606, 2200
Avenue Road, Toronto, Canada.
SKEWES   FLORENCE WILLIAMS
Born 3 August 1913. Married . . . . . . Skewes. Died 1977, aged 64 years.
SKEWES   FRANCES
Daughter of Sandry Skewes. Buried Ludgvan 3 April 1598.
SKEWES   FRANCES
Daughter of John and Mary Skewes. Bpt Cury 11 December 1768.
SKEWS   FRANCES
Daughter of John and Sarah Skews. Bpt St Ewe 5 November 1769.
SKEWES   FRANCES
Married Joseph Keverne at Cury 29 May 1792.
SKUES   FRANCES
Born 1810. Lived at Illogan. Died 6 October 1824, aged 14 years.
SKEWIS   FRANCES
Chart 36. Daughter of John and Jane Skewis; yeoman. Bpt Illogan 2
November 1811. (Born 17 September 1811).
SKEWES   FRANCES
Illegitimate daughter of Blanch Skewes of Nantithet, Cury. Bpt Cury
privately 18 May 1817; publicly 1 June 1817.
SKEWES   FRANCES
Chart 36. Née Kempthorne. Born 1824. Married James Skewes at
Mawnan Parish Church 2 October 1845. Children: Hester Ann,
Frances Maria, Edward, William Henry, Emily Kempthorne, James
Lugg, Alma Jane, Kate, Mary and Ellen.
Died 10 May 1907, aged 82 years.
SKEWS   FRANCES
Married 1878, Plymouth.
SKEWS   FRANCES
Chart 42. Née Smith. Daughter of William Smith, miner. Born 1882.
Married Frederick Skews at Lyons Parish Church 29 May 1909.
Children: Frederick Crago, Leslie, Irene, and Mabel and Lily (twins).
Lived at South Hetton Road, Hetton-le-Hole, County Durham. Died, a
widow, 5 February 1956, aged 74 years.
SKEWES   FRANCES ANITA
Lived at 10 Stawell Street, Warrenheip, Victoria, Australia in 1959 with
John Albert Skewes. In 1980 was living at Boundary Road, Broken Hill,
Warrenheip, Australia, 3350 with Donald Herbert Skewes.

SKEWES   FRANCES ANN
Chart 14. Born 1855. Married Hannibal Skewes, 1890. Lived at
Chybarles, Ruan Major. Died 16 July 1931, aged 76 years.
SKEWES   FRANCES CHARLOTTE
Chart 36. Daughter of William and Elizabeth (née Northey) Skewes.
Born 17 March 1864, Australia. Married Henry John Cooper. Issue: one
daughter.
Died 17 March 1885, aged 21 years exactly.
SKEWES   FRANCES MARIA
Chart 36. Daughter of James and Frances Skewes of Mawnansmith.
Born 1848. Bpt 23 April 1848 at Mawnan Parish Church. In 1871
Census Returns was listed as a draper's assistant. Married Arthur
Liddicoat of Falmouth at St Michael's Church, Mawnan 15 May 1879.

Frances Maria Skewes of Mawnan Smith

SKEWES   FRANCINE JANE
Chart 38. Daughter of Charles Percival and Nancy Merle (née Ham)
Skewes. Born 29 February 1956.
Works for Department of Trade and Resources, Adelaide, South
Australia. Married Ian Matthews, 10 October 1981 at Broken Hill, New
South Wales. Lives at 59 Myrtle Road, Seacliff, 5049, South Australia.
Tel no: Adelaide: 298 7965.

Francine Jane Skewes

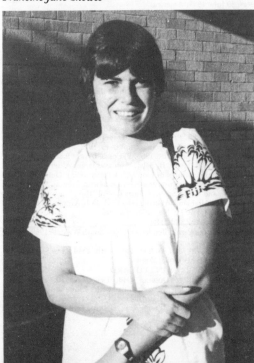

SKEWES   FRANCIS
Chart 36. Wife's name Grace. Lived at Illogan Highway; blacksmith. Children: Jane Rogers (1870), Samuel Francis (1868), John (1872) and Richard Ernest (1874).

SKEWIS   FRANCIS
Wife of Stephen Skewis, churchwarden at Redruth Parish Church. Buried Redruth 16 October 1717.

SKUSE   FRANCIS
Married Alice Bowen at St Paul, Covent Garden, 1796.

SKEWES   FRANCIS
of Mullion. Married at Register Office, Helston July, 1842 to Mrs Catherine Chirgwin of Cury.

SKEWIS   FRANCIS
Born July, 1875, Missouri, USA. Father born in England. Mother born in Missouri. Lived with his brother in Tywappily Township, Mississippi in 1900.

SKEWS   FRANCIS
Chart 23. Son of George William and Caroline (née Nottage) Skews. Born 1900, Shoreditch.

SKUES   FRANCIS ALBERT
Chart 7. Son of Thomas and Elizabeth (née Harris) Skues, footman. Born 4 October 1882 at 33 North Street, Chelsea. Married Nellie Jeffrey (19), of 64 Anne of Cleves Road, Dartford, Kent — servant — 23 November 1907 at Holy Trinity Church, Dartford. She was daughter of James Henry Jeffrey, rug weaver. Children: Edwin Thomas, Herbert, Leslie James, Raymond J., Bernard E., Enid Elizabeth and Francis Henry. Died 1954, aged 72 years.

SKEWES   FRANCIS BARRY
Lived at 9 Clyde Street, Glen Iris, Victoria, Australia in 1959 with Frank Bullivant Skewes. Now lives at 8 Epping Street, Malvern East, Victoria, Australia.

SKEWES   FRANCIS CLYDE
Chart 11. Son of Thomas John and Laura B. Skewes. Born 23 September 1888, USA. Served in United States Navy.

SKEWIS   FRANCIS HARRY
Chart 2. Son of James and Jane Skewis. Born 18 January 1860, Wisconsin, USA. Twice married. 1) Annie Albertson 19 October 1887 (she was born 17 May 1864; died 15 September 1954) 2) Mabel Ransom. Children: Anita, Francis James, Isabel, Victoria, Grace Rabling, Mary Alberta, Ruth Genevieve, Edward George and Charles Elmer (twins). Lived at 625 South Trafton, Tacoma, Washington. Lumberman. Died 19 September 1954, aged 94 years.

SKUES   FRANCIS HENRY
Chart 7. Son of Francis Albert Skues. Born 1909, Dartford, Kent. Married Norah E. Henson, 1946, Dartford. Died 1950, aged 40 years in Dartford. Children: Jeffrey (1947).

SKEWIS   FRANCIS HENRY II
Chart 2. Son of Francis James and Lucretia Skewis. Born 15 October 1917, America. Married Mary Jane Carpenter 23 February 1943.

SKEWIS   FRANCIS HENRY III
Chart 2. Son of Francis Henry II and Mary Jane (née Carpenter) Skewis. Born 30 June 1947, America.

SKEWES   FRANCIS JAMES
Chart 36. Son of James and Stella Margaret (née Farrell) Skewes. Born 9 October 1922, Australia. Married Valerie Foster. Children: Phillip, Stephen, Bernard and Graham.

SKEWIS   FRANCIS JAMES
Chart 2. Son of Francis Harry and Annie Skewis. Born 10 March 1891. Attended University of Washington, Seattle. Graduated in Law, 1914 (LLB). Lived in Greenville, Iowa from 1914 to 1929. Manager of grain elevator business; lumber and coal yards. Sold out in 1929. Travelled west to Tacoma, Washington State. Production manager of the Forest Greens Company. Lived in Coose Bay, Oregon from 1933 to 1945 developing the forestry business. Was head of Office of Prices Administration for 35,000 people from 1942 to 1945. President of the Rotary Club, 1938. President of Chamber of Commerce, 1939, all in Coose Bay. He retired from business in 1975. Twice married. 1) Lucretia Callison, who died 1963. 2) Cassie Bryant 9 September 1964. Children: Francis Henry II, Sylvia Ann and James Alderton.
Is now an active member of Lion's Club (since 1973). University Lion's Club, Seattle, Washington. Is a Freemason with Evening Shade Lodge No 312, F and A.M., Spencer, Iowa since 1918.
Lives at 314 Highland Apartments 11501 15th Avenue N.E. Seattle, Washington, USA. Tel No: (206) 362 8987.

SKEWES   FRANCIS JOHN
Lived at Watsons Creek, Bendemeer, New South Wales in 1959. He was a station hand.
Now lives at 37 Croydon Avenue, Tamworth, 2340, New South Wales, Australia with Betty Grace Skewes.

SKUCE   FRANCIS JOHN LEONARD
B.A. Trinity College Dublin, 1948. Deacon, 1950. Priest 1951. Dromore College of Warrenpoint with Clonallan 1950-1953. Incumbent of Innishmacsaint, Diocese of Clogher from 1953. Address: Rectory, Derrygonnelly, Enniskillen, County Fermanagh, Northern Ireland.

Francis James Skewis

SKEWES   FRANCIS RAYMOND
Lived at Noosa Woods Caravan Park, Noosa Heads, 4567, Queensland, Australia with Christine Carol Skewes.

SKEWIS   FRANCIS THOMAS
Married Julia Thomas of Mullion at Helston Register Office, 11 October 1851.

SKEWES   FRANCISCO
Chart 2. Son of James Enrique and Juana Brito Skewes. Born 7 February 1905. Married. Child: Ernesto (1928).

SKEWIS   FRANK
Chart 2. Son of John Rule and Elizabeth Skewis of America. Married Daisy Howry. Children: Edith, Lynette and James.

SKEWIS   FRANK
Chart 34. Born 1902. Married Winifred Kate Baker, 6 December 1930, Tunbridge. Lived at 17 Deansway Avenue, Sturry, Kent. Died 8 January 1949 at the Kent and Canterbury Hospital, Canterbury, Kent. Children: Barbara M. (1931) and Trevor (1942). She remarried Worgan, 1949 in Bridge.

SKEWES   FRANK
Chart 36. Son of William and Edith (née Howarth) Skewes. Born 18 November 1925. Lives at Watsons Creek, via Bendemeer, New South Wales, Australia.

Frank Skewis (1902-1949)

SKEWES   FRANK
Chart 38. Son of Albert Milton and Myrtle Emma (née Marks) Skewes. Bachelor. Lived at 41 Digby Street, Kadina, South Australia in 1959. Now lives at 10/2 Phillips Court, Northcote, 3070, Victoria, Australia.

SKEWES   FRANK ANSON
Chart 26. Son of Frank Edward and Eleanor May (née Darrow) Skewes. Born 3 April 1921, New London, Connecticut, USA. Served in United States Navy 30 years as a Lieut. Commander. Twice married. 1) June Beverley Spaulding. Children: Beverley May (1944), Frank Anson Jnr (1947), Allen Brent (1950), Jacquelynn Ann (1953), Elaine Eleanor (1952), Edward Gary (1958) and Jennine Mary (1962). 2) Married Mary Wier from Scotland. Child: Ian (1972). Lives at 979 Bucknell Place, Rockledge, Florida, USA. Tel. No: (305) 632 1134.

SKEWES   FRANK ANSON Jnr
Chart 26. Son of Frank Anson and June Beverley (née Spaulding) Skewes. Born 21 December 1947. Bachelor. Works for Electric Bolt, Groton, Connecticut, USA. Lives in New London, Connecticut.

SKEWES   FRANK BULLIVANT
Lived at 9 Clyde Street, Malvern, Victoria, Australia in 1959 with Francis Barry Skewes. He was a traveller.

SKEWES   FRANK EDWARD
Chart 26. Son of Edward James and Harriet A. (née Rockwell) Skewes. Born 28 September 1898, Buckingham, Connecticut, USA. Married Eleanor May Darrow. Children: Robert Ernest (1924) and Frank Anson (1921).

SKUSE   FRANK ERIC
Son of Eric Albert and Winifred Kathleen (née Palmer) Skuse. Born 5 August 1944, Carshalton, Surrey. Emigrated with his parents to Australia in 1959. Returned to England 1971. Bachelor. Lives at 58 Empress Avenue, Woodford Green, Essex.

SKEWES   FRANK HORACE
Chart 38. Son of Horace Henry and Agatha Blanche (née Johns) Skewes. Born 15 April 1909, Kadina, South Australia. Died 4 December 1909, infant.

SKUSE   FRANK RICHARD
B.A. Trinity College, Dublin, 1942. Deacon, 1942. Priest, 1943, Clogher; Curate of Monaghan 1942-1945; Drumcondra with North Stroud 1945/1950; Curate in Charge, Clonaslee with Rosenallis Union 1950/1954. Incumbent of Kinneigh with Balleymoney, Diocese of Cork, from 1954. Lived at Rectory, Balineen, Cork, Eire. In 1970 was Secretary of the Diocesan Council of Clogher and Rector of Derrygonnelly.

SKEWES   FRANK ROBERT
Chart 25. Son of Arthur George and Ruth (née Hacking) Skewes. Born 25 January 1928, Rusholme, Manchester. Educated at Broadway School, Cheadle, Cheshire until 1942. Joined an accountants firm as an articled clerk until he was called up for National Service in February, 1946. RAF Chivenor, Handforth and Keble. Worked on air frames with Spitfire and Hurricane aircraft. Demobbed June, 1948. Married Anne Taylor at Henbury Parish Church, Macclesfield, Cheshire 6 August, 1956.
Children: Anthony Robert (1958) and Jane (1961). After leaving Royal Air Force he worked for Gaskell's (brewery engineers) in Manchester for 22 years, then became office manager for northern headquarters in Sheffield, South Yorkshire.
In 1967 he joined Taylor's Stainless Metals for two years until taking a job with Weldall Engineering from 1969 to 1973.
He is a sales executive for Tubesales (UK) Ltd.
Address: 21 Capesthorne Road, Wilmslow, Cheshire, SK9 6LU.

SKEWES   FRANKLIN
Chart 10. Mexican. Son of Salvador and Carmen (née Ramirez) Skewes. Born 27 October 1945, Real del Monte, Mexico. Married Margarita Sanchez. Children: Roman (1966), Teodoro (1968) and Magdalena (1972).

SKEWES   FRANSISCO BRITO
Chart 2. Mexican. Son of James Enrique and Juana (née Brito) Skewes. Born 7 February 1905. Married ..... Mares. Child: Ernesto (1928). Died 28 December 1943, aged 38 years.

SKEWES   FRANZ
Chart 10. Mexican. Son of Salvador and Carmen (née Ramirez) Skewes. Born 4 October 1943. Married Atala Castaneda. Children: Franz (1974) and Bladimir (1976). Lives in Mexico City.

SKEWES   FRANZ
Chart 10. Mexican. Son of Franz and Atala (née Castaneda) Skewes. Born 17 December 1974.

SKEWES   FRED
Chart 10. Mexican. Son of Juan and Leonor (née Munoz) Skewes. Born October 1961. Died 23 January 1962, aged 3 months.

SKEWES   FRED C.
Lived at 5200 Marathon, Los Angeles, USA in 1939. Accountant. Wife's name Vera.

SKUES   FREDERICK
Born 1847. Married 29 February 1876 at the Parish Church Northwold, Norfolk to Elizabeth Eliza Nurse, daughter of William Nurse, farmer. He was son of John Skues, labourer and a gardener.

Frank Robert Skewes

SKEWES   FREDERICK
Born 1870. Illegitimate son of Susan Skewes. Was an inmate with his mother at Union Workhouse, Truro where he was born. His mother was born in Chacewater. Died 1875, aged 6 years.

SKEWES   FREDERICK
Chart 30. Son of John Beer and Mary Skewes. Born June 1874 in Pydar Street, Truro. Died 7 March 1875, aged 9 months.

SKEWES   FREDERICK
Chart 25. Son of Charles and Elizabeth Skewes. Born 1872. Married Alice Taylor (24), daughter of John Taylor, saw maker of 35 Duke Street, Broughton, Salford, at Lower Broughton Wesleyan Methodist Church, Sussex Street, 8 December 1894. Son Henry (Harry) 1898. Lived at 1 Kempston Street, Broughton. Calico printer. Died Salford, 1958, aged 86 years.

SKEWES   FREDERICK
Chart 25. Son of William and Jane (née Jameson) Skewes. Born 1885. Died 1885, Salford, aged 0.

SKEWS   FREDERICK
Chart 41. Born 1885. Son of William John Skews, miner. Married 29 May 1909 at the Parish Church of Lyons, Houghton to Frances Smith, daughter of William Smith. She died 5 February 1956.
Children: Frederick Crago Skews, Irene Skews, Leslie Skews, Mabel Skews and Lily Skews (twins). Lived at 44 Elemore Lane, Hetton-le-Hole, County Durham.
Died 8 June 1955, aged 70 years.

SKEWES   FREDERICK
Born 7 August 1886, St Clement, Truro. Son of Amelia Skewes, charwoman and single. Bpt Truro St Mary's, 6 June 1887.

SKUES FREDERICK
Lived at 15 Oval Road, Gloucester Gate, London, NW in 1890. (London Street Directory).

SKEWES   FREDERICK
Born 1899, Rochford, Essex.

SKUES   FREDERICK
Chart 3. Son of Richard James and Eleanor (née Chorley) Skues. Born 31 October 1900, Sowerby Bridge. Attended Haugh Shaw School, Halifax and Halifax Technical College. Joined Gordon Highlanders in August 1918. One year later was transferred to Duke of Wellington's Regiment and served in Palestine and Egypt. Demobilised 1922. Joined W & RK Lee (cotton doublers) at Sowerby Bridge as an electrician. This firm became Cross Lee Yarns, part of Carpets International. Retired 1965.
Married Theresa Kaye, at St Paul's Church, Halifax, 11 April 1929. No children.

Theresa died 12 July 1980, aged 75 years. Lives at 14 Second Avenue, Manor Drive, Halifax, West Yorkshire.

Frederick Skues

SKEWES   FREDERICK
Born 1904. Lived at Condurrow, Redruth. Died 1905, aged 10 months. Buried Tuckingmill 17 March 1905.

SKEWES   FREDERICK
Son of Frederick Thomas Skewes and Rose (née Trudgeon) Skewes. Born 3 January 1908.

SKEWES   FREDERICK
Married 1909, Ashton.

SKEWES   FREDERICK
Lived at South Carn, Brea, Illogan with Ada Skewes in 1922.

SKEWS   FREDERICK
Married Joyce in Islington, 1936.

SKEWS   FREDERICK
Living at 167 Pasley Street, Devonport, Plymouth. (1950-1953 Street Directory).

SKEWS   FREDERICK
Chart 17. Son of Henry James and Elizabeth Skews. Mother's maiden name Hilliard. Born 5 August 1914, West Ham. Married Eileen Joyce, 1936, Islington. Children: Patricia and Valerie B. Lives at 5 The Willows, Mercea Road, Colchester, Essex.

SKEWES   FREDERICK AUGUSTUS
Chart 12. Illegitimate son of Alice Ann Skewes. Born 1863. Bpt at St George's, Truro 7 January 1864. Died 1866 (9 March), aged 2. Lived at White Cross, Cury.

SKEWS   FREDERICK C.
Born 1910, Dartford, Kent.

SKEWS   FREDERICK C.
Born 1884. Died Redruth, 1958, aged 74 years.

SKEWES   FREDERICK CECIL
Born 1898, Helston. Died 1898, aged 0.

SKEWES   FREDERICK CHARLES
Chart 10. Son of Henry Skewes of Ashton, Helston. Born 27 May 1895 at Wilkes, Bourne, Luzerne, Pa, USA. Married Ruth E. Madden, 1 December 1917. Died 16 April 1966, aged 70.

SKEWS   FREDERICK CHARLES
Chart 15. Son of Amos Skews. Born 1896 Stoke Devonport. Married Charles in Totnes, 1917. Lived in Plymouth on his own in 1968 at 81 Castle Street, Plymouth. Died Plymouth 1976, aged 80 years. Children: Dora N.J. (1929) & Lilian L. (1925).

SKEWS   FREDERICK CRAGO
Chart 41. Son of Frederick and Frances (née Smith) Skews. Born 1911, Houghton. Colliery Clerk. Married Ruth Thompson, 1936, Easington. Children: Renee and Lawrence.

SKEWS   FREDERICK E.
Married Meadows, 1947, Leeds.

SKUES   FREDERICK GORDON
Chart 3. Son of Richard and Lucy (née Pickard) Skues. Born 14 April 1860 at 4 Colbeck Street, Halifax. Married Ada Dawson, 1884. Worked with his father in publishing. From 1890-1894 published *Halifax Free Press* at 18 Barum Top, Halifax. Children: Ernest (1885) and Arthur (1891). Ada Skues ran milliners shop at 23 Boothtown Road, Halifax. Died 29 September 1895, aged 35 years. Interred in All Saints Cemetery, Halifax.

SKUES   FREDERICK HAROLD
Chart 8. Son of Walter Edward Skues. Born 1898, Edmonton. Died 1898, aged 0.

SKUES   FREDERICK HENRY
Chart 5. Son of Joseph Penrose Skues who emigrated to Australia from Redruth about 1860. Born 27 May 1875. Married Ellen Hosking (she born 1 June 1871 — and died April, 1958, aged 87 years). Children: Kenneth Frederick (1905) and Laurence Penrose (1907). Accountant. Lived at 97 Wills Street, Bendigo, Victoria, Australia. Died October, 1955, aged 80 years.

SKEWES   FREDERICK HENRY
Chart 30. Son of John Beer and Bessie (née Whether) Skewes. Born 12 January 1891. Married Charlotte L. Lithiby in St Thomas, Exeter, 7 August 1920. Lived at 80 Wellington Road, St Thomas, Exeter. No children. Died 6 July 1969, aged 78 years.

SKEWS   FREDERICK JOHN
Born 1871, North Aylesford. Died 1938, aged 66 years.

SKUES   FREDERICK JOHN
Born 1875, St George's, Hannover Square, London.

SKEWES   FREDERICK JOHN CHARLES
Chart 46. Son of Charles and Bessie (née Teague) Skewes. Born 7 April 1916. Bpt St George's, Truro 25 April 1916. Lived at 76 Chapel Hill, Truro. Died 1918, aged 1 year.

SKUES   FRED MACKENZIE
M.B. Chart 3. Son of George and Mary Gibbs Skues. Born 21 October 1833, Aberdeen. Bachelor of Medicine (M.B.), Maris College, Aberdeen, 1855. Licentiate Royal College of Surgeons, (Edinburgh), 1855.
Assistant Surgeon to the Forces 1st West Indian Regiment 28 Feb 1855. Staff 11 September 1860. Surgeon to the Forces 14 October 1862; 26 Regiment of Foot 1 April 1870; Army Medical Department Surgeon Major 14 October 1868; Brigade Surgeon 28 July 1880. Retired with rank of Deputy Surgeon General 16 December 1882. Married Mary Theresa Malcolm (she died 21 December 1903 in Lewisham). Lived at 21 Linden Grove, Peckham, London S.E. in 1894 London Street Directory. Last address 58 Riggindale Road, Streatham, Surrey. Children: Fred Mackenzie, Edward, Mary and Margaret. Died Streatham 13 August 1910, aged 76 years.

SKUES   FREDERICK MACKENZIE
Chart 3. Born 1866. Son of Fred Mackenzie and Mary Theresa Skues. Went to Bethlehem, Orange Free State, South Africa. Was a veterinary surgeon. Died 18 August 1921, aged 55 years. Bachelor.

SKUES   FREDERICK MACKENZIE
Chart 3. Son of Thomas Mackenzie Skues, auctioneer. Married Doreen Arnold, waitress of 23 Wright Street, Chorlton on Medlock, Manchester, daughter of William Charles Arnold, commercial traveller. Frederick lived at 15 Bridge Street, Ardwick, Manchester. He was born 1920 and married 26 April 1948 at Register Office, Manchester. Divorce case London Divorce Court 1968. She remarried Patrick Ernest Bushnell in Manchester, 1968. Frederick Mackenzie Skues was a snake charmer and fire eater and known as Prince Neekeyzolo.

SKEWS   FREDERICK THOMAS
Chart 15. Son of Harry and Hilda (née Jane) Skews of Albert Cottages, Pensilva, Liskeard. Born 5 October 1926. Bpt St Ive 12 November 1926. Died 1943, aged 17 years in Liskeard.

SKEWES   FREDERICK THOMAS
Went to America aged 18 years in 1903. Married Rose Trudgeon from Helston about 1906 in Michigan. He was a copper miner and later ordained as a Methodist minister in 1918. Children: Frederick (1908), Doreen (1914), Kenneth William (1917) and Leonard (1919). Died about 1930.

SKEWES   FREDERICK TRESIZE
Chart 12. Born 1857. Illegitimate son of Julia Skewes of Chypons, Cury. Bpt Cury 4 December 1857. Married Annie Maud ..... 1880, Helston. Lived at Loscombe Lane, Four Lanes, Illogan 1932; Bowling Green, Illogan, 1922 and Carnkie 1906. Children: Ada (1885), Edward Frederick (1882), Thomas Henry (1893), Mary Eliza (1886), Sarah Annie (1889) and William John (1891). Died 1935 at Four Lanes, Redruth, aged 78 years.

SKEWS   FREDERICK WILLIAM
Born 1877, Dartford, Kent. Died 1877, aged 0.

SKEWES   FREDERICK WILLIAM
Born 1894. Married Fanny Denton in Chorlton, 1920. Lived at 75 Palmerston Street, Manchester 16. No children. Died 15 March 1944 at 20 Nell Lane, Manchester 20, aged 49 years.

SKUES   FREDERICK WILLIAM MACKENZIE
Chart 3. Son of Brigade Surgeon William Mackenzie and Margaret Skues. Born 15 June 1867. Was a civil engineer for Rhodesian Railways. Died 27 May 1940, aged 72 years in Croydon. Bachelor.

SKEWES   FRENETTA
Chart 10. Née Littleton. Born 1868. First wife of Richard Skewes. Children: Gertrude, Richard Henry, John Joseph, Laura, Ernest, Hettie Louise and Jonathan Braddon. Died 15 September 1899, aged 31 years at West End, Marazion. Buried Marazion 19 September 1899.

G

SKUSE   G.
Rifleman with 9th London Regiment (Queen Victoria's Rifles). Lived at 194 Kilburn Lane, London W 10. Died in First World War.

SKEWES   GABRIELLA
Chart 2. Mexican. Daughter of Ernesto Skewes. Born 5 September 1970, Pachuca, Mexico.

SKEWES   GAIL MAREE
Daughter of John A. and Shirley Skewes. Lives at 337 Richard Street, Ballarat, Victoria, 3350, Australia with Rodney Craig Skewes.

SKEWS   GALE
Chart 6. Daughter of William Alexander and Gale (née Julson) Skews. Born 23 October 1927, Wisconsin, USA. Married Dick F. Cary. Issue: 3 daughters. Lives in Jefferson, USA.

SKEWES   GARFIELD SYDNEY
Chart 38. Son of Sydney Howard and Cordelia (née Blight) Skewes. Born 3 March 1922, South Australia. Educated in North Adelaide and Walkerville, South Australia. During Second World War spent 5 years in army. Started his working life as a butcher, but transferred to the catering world. Was a wine waiter for 26 years at the South Australian Hotel, Adelaide; beverage executive manager for 1 year (1966) and Manager, Strathmore Hotel, Adelaide 1967-1973. Purchased North East Highway Restaurant, Tee Tree Gully and was manager from 1973-1979. Semi retirement since 1979.
Married Doris Margaret Sandford, 25 May 1943 at Pirie Street Methodist Church, Adelaide. Children: Geoffrey Garfield (1946), Philip Graham (1949) and Cordelia Anne (1956). Lives at Chapmans Road, Inglewood, 5133, South Australia. Telephone number: Adelaide 380 5269.

SKEWES   GARY B.
Lives at 126N 28th Place, Great West Palm Beach, Florida, USA.

SKEWES GARY DOUGLAS
Son of Douglas Westmore and Lorna Jean (née Farquhar) Skewes. Born 1 August 1949, Victoria, Australia. Married Sandra Wooton. Children: Andrew (1973), Scott (1974), Paul (1976) and Krishy (1978). Lives at 11 Jillian Street, Cranbourne, 3977, Victoria, Australia with Sandra Skewes. Printer.

SKEWES   GARY EARLE
Chart 36. Son of Earle William and Fay (née Chad) Skewes. Born 1 November 1951, New South Wales, Australia. Married Jennifer Joy Matthews, 27 February 1971. Children: Jason Gary (1971) and Adam David (1973). Lives at 1 King Street, Tamworth, 2340, New South Wales, Australia.

SKEWES   GARY LEONARD
Chart 2. Son of John Herbert and Thelma Jean (née Ettridge) Skewes. Born 26 April 1967, Australia. Lives at Lot/85, Eclipse Drive, Albany, 6330, Western Australia.

SKEWES   GARY REGINALD
Lives at Farm/404, Dalbata Road, Leeton, 2705, New South Wales, Australia with Laurence John Skewes, Pearl Louisa Skewes and Reginald Lionel Skewes.

SKEWES   GARY WILLIAM
Chart 36. Son of Edward Keith and Maisie (née Lawson) Skewes. Born 13 January 1949. Married Lynette Mary Smith (she born 20 October 1948), 25 November 1966. Children: Donna Ann (1968), Teasha Maree (1970), Marc William (1973) and Clint Edward (1974). Lives at 9 Surrey Road, Wilson, 6107, Western Australia. Contractor.

SKEWES   GAY YVONNE
Lived at 4 Bonleigh Avenue, Elsternwick, Victoria, Australia in 1959 with William Henry Skewes. Now lives at 8 Cassia Court, Wantirna, 3152, Victoria, Australia with Mandy Louise Skewes.

SKEWES   GAYE LORRAINE
Lives at 8 Douglas Street, Townsville, 4810, Queensland, Australia with John Leslie Skewes.

SKEWS   GAYLE M.
Chart 6. Lived in Mineral Point, Wisconsin, USA. Born 1909. Died 1927, aged 18 years.

SKUES   GENE M.
Chart 8. Mother's maiden name Woodyer. Born 21 May 1930, Edmonton, London. Married Jerzy Gola, 1953 in St Alban's.

SKEWES   GEOFFREY
Chart 36. Son of Percy and Muriel (née Norris) Skewes. Born October, 1949, New South Wales, Australia.

SKEWES   GEOFFREY
Chart 36. Son of Archer William and Elsie May (née Handley) Skewes. Born 3 March 1923. Married Dorothy May Chapman (she born 12 December 1929), 27 January 1951. Children: Gregory Archer (1952), Ian Charles (1953), Rosalie Anne (1956), Helen Elizabeth (1960) and Bronwyn May (1964). Taxi driver. Lives at 35 Jean Street, Grange, 4051, Queensland, Australia.

SKEWES   GEOFFREY GARFIELD
Chart 38. Son of Garfield Sydney and Doris Margaret (née Sandford) Skewes. Born 13 October 1946. Educated at Brighton High School, Adelaide, South Australia (1959-1964). Studied art at Western Teachers College 1964-1966. Resigned from Education Department of South Australia in 1966 to become a professional musician. He moved to Melbourne in July, 1966. Joined a band called The Vibrants, one of Australia's most popular groups in the 1960's. He played keyboards and had two national top five records "Something About You Baby" and "My Prayer."
Met Donna Louise Bridge in Perth, Western Australia in 1968 and they married on Easter Monday, 12 April 1971 at St Kilda's Methodist Church. Son: Grayson Paul (1972).
In 1972 Geoff left The Vibrants and formed a band called Skylight and recorded two singles and one album. In 1975 he gave up music professionally and became involved in the management side and worked for a number of years in self orientated study programmes as a booking agent, record company and management company. He promoted venues from hotel lounges to international concerts.
He moved back to Adelaide in July 1977 with a view to learning the restaurant business which his parents were running. He continued to keep up his contacts in the music business and wrote a weekly column for the pop magazine *Juke*.
It was through his writing that he heard about a young Australian singer Christie Allen who had come to Adelaide from Perth. He took over as personal manager from March 1978. Since then she has recorded two top selling albums and in April 1980 was voted Top Female Performer of Australia. She has also had two top ten hits in the singles market.
Geoff Skewes moved to Melbourne in May 1979. Current address: 28 York Street, Cauldfield South, Victoria, Australia, 3162. Telephone number Melbourne 5237184. Hobbies: Modelling and flying model aircraft, fishing, playing cricket and listening to music.

SKEWES   GEOFFREY GRENVILLE
Chart 50. Son of Thomas Grenville and Ilma Elizabeth (née Dodd) Skewes. Born 13 August 1939. Married Ruth Lois Philp, 13 June 1964. Children: Joanna Robin Skewes (1971) and Claudine Elizabeth Skewes (1973). Solicitor. Lives at 33 Howard Street, Warrnambool, 3280, Victoria, Australia. Telephone number: (055) 621109.

SKEWES   GEOFFREY IAN
Chart 36. Son of Owen Eric Edward and Stella Tabitha (née Harris) Skewes. Born March 1947. Married Aivonne Wendy Lowe 1977. Children: Elizabeth and Rachel.
Lives at 182 Victoria Street, Ballarat, 3350, Victoria, Australia.

SKEWES   GEOFFREY JOHN
Chart 36. Son of Percy and Muriel (née Norris) Skewes. Born 5 October 1949. Married Margaret Joyce Shanley, 2 September 1972. Children: Nicole Louise (1974), Belinda Ann (1976) and Donna Marie (1978). Lives at 17 Wilkie Street, Werris Creek, 2341, New South Wales, Australia.

Wedding of Geoffrey Skewes to Donna Bridge in Melbourne, Australia, April, 1971

Geoffrey John Skewes and his family of New South Wales, Australia

SKEWES   GEOFFREY ROBIN
Lives at 19 Wolgarra Street, Salisbury, 5108, South Australia. Motor mechanic.

SKEWIS   GEOFFREY WILFRED
Lived at Claydon Street, Chinchilla, Marona, Queensland, Australia in 1959. Now lives at 8 Gormleys Road, Chilla, 4413, Queensland with Valma Aileen Skewis and Malcolm Geoffrey Skewis. Labourer.

SCOOSSE GEORGE
Son of John Scoosse of St Ive. Bpt Menheniot 24 January 1579. Married Ann Pethericke at Menheniot 9 January 1605.

SCEWIES   GEORGE
Chart 2. Son of Humphrey Scewies. Bpt Camborne 11 September 1638. Married Elizabeth Grills, 3 September 1664 at Camborne Parish Church. Died 22 November 1698, aged 60 years.

SCRUSE   GEORGE
Bpt 21 May 1716 at Gulval. Son of George Scruse of Gulval, Cornwall.

SKEWES   GEORGE
Chart 14. Twin to Henry Skewes. Son of Henry and Judith Skewes. Bpt Cury 6 September 1727. Buried Cury 24 September 1727, infant.

SKEWS   GEORGE
Chart 9. Son of Philip and Mary Skews. Bpt St Ewe 8 November 1762. Buried St Ewe 17 June 1763.

SKEWES   GEORGE
Son of Thomas and Ann Skewes. Bpt Gwennap 9 September 1787.

SKUES   GEORGE
Lieut. R.N. Chart 3. Son of Richard and Ann Skues. Born 3 March 1797. Bpt Helston 5 October 1797. Married Gibbs Mackenzie, daughter of the late Alexander Mackenzie of Breda, Esq., at St Paul's Chapel, Aberdeen, Scotland 25 March 1827. Commissioned into Royal Marines, 2nd Lieut. In Army Lists 1820-1870. On half pay from 1 September 1815-1870. Children: William Mackenzie, Richard Alexander, John Richard, Fred Mackenzie, Edward Walker, Gertrude and Georgina Mary. Died 9 January 1872, aged 74 years. Buried in Lair No 30, Section G of Old Machar Churchyard, Aberdeen, 16 January 1872. Monumental tomb erected by Garden and Company, monumental masons of King Street, Aberdeen.

SKUSE   GEORGE
Son of William Skuse. Married Mary Ann Smart, 1833, Stroud, Gloucester.

SKUES   GEORGE
Chart 3. Son of Charles and Mary Skues. Tailor. Married Lucy Bird (Minor) at St Martins in the Fields, London 7 July 1840. Lucy was daughter of Henry Bird, wire worker. George lived at Castle Street, St Martins in the Fields. Married in the presence of Mary Skues.

SKEWES   GEORGE
Born 1841, Tiverton, Devon.

SKEWES   GEORGE
Married 1841, Truro.

SKEWS   GEORGE
Chart 17. Son of William Skews, confectioner. Married Charlotte Dane of Canal Cottages, Milton, Gravesend, Kent, daughter of Nathaniel Dane, shoe manufacturer, at St Paul's Church, Chalk, North Aylesford, Kent, 26 March 1843. Children: Richard Nathaniel Edward (1844), Edwin Nathaniel (1844) and George Alfred (1846). Confectioner.

SKEWES   GEORGE
Chart 14. Son of Samuel and Catherine Skewes of Wisconsin, USA. Born 26 June 1844, Yorkville, Wisconsin. Married Ruth Hoyt from Yorkville. Children: Jessie (1874) and Howard (1878). School teacher. Died 19 February 1897, aged 53 years.

Grave of Lieutenant George Skues (1797-1872)

Drawing by Minnie Mackenzie Skues of St Machar's Cathedral, Aberdeen, Scotland where her grandfather Lieut. George Skues is buried. Drawing completed in 1900

George Skewes (1844-1897)

George and Mary Skewes and family of Uralla, New South Wales, Australia. Photo taken in 1915

SKEWES GEORGE
Chart 14. Son of John and Jane Skewes. Bpt Ruan Minor 11 December 1844.

SKEWES GEORGE
Chart 14. Son of Anthony and Christian Skewes of Tresodden, Ruan Major; farmer. Bpt Ruan Major 27 August 1856. In 1871 Census Returns was living at Tresodden.

SKEWS GEORGE
Born Mevagissey, 1875.

SKEWES GEORGE
Died 1857, Abergavenny.

SKEWES GEORGE
Chart 25. Son of Charles and Elizabeth Skewes of Brook Street, Falmouth. Born Falmouth 1861. In 1871 Census Returns was listed as a "scholar, aged 9 years." Moved north with his parents to Salford, Manchester and lived at 1 Kempster Street, Lower Broughton, Salford. Married Annie Houghton (38), widow of 61 Kempster Street, Lower Broughton at Lower Broughton Wesleyan Methodist Chapel, Sussex Street, 6 January 1894. Child: George Ernest (1894).
Is reported to have been "fond of his drink." He was a calico printer's foreman.
Buried in a pauper's grave, in Agecroft Cemetery, Salford, 1939, aged 79 years.

SKEWIS GEORGE
Son of Thomas Skewis, fitter. Lived at Robert Street, Ardwick, Manchester. Married Ellen Booth (a preparer of gum), daughter of William Booth, spinner of Robert Street, Ardwick at St Thomas' Church, Ardwick, 30 September 1862, in presence of Samuel Skewis.

SKEWES GEORGE
Chart 36. Son of William and Elizabeth (née Northey) Skewes. Born 31 October 1871, Maitland Point, Uralla, New South Wales, Australia. Married Mary Ann Dowling, 20 June 1894. Children: Aubrey Rupert, William Vere, James, Irene, Cuthbert George, Reginald John and Mary Elizabeth.
Engaged in various spheres of bush work. Later he selected land and established an apple and stone fruit orchard at Rocky River, Uralla from which he retired in 1940. Died 9 March 1955, aged 84 years. Buried in Methodist portion of New Cemetery, Uralla.

SKEWES GEORGE
Chart 49. Born 1879, Totnes. Married 1905 to Maria ..... Moved to Plymouth and lived at 75 South Milton Street. Died 9 March 1965, aged 85 years.

SKUES GEORGE
Born 1887. Died 1888, aged 1 year in Halifax.

SKEWIS GEORGE
Chart 50. Son of William and Elizabeth (née Shaw) Skewis, fruit store keeper. Born at 128 Cardross Street, Glasgow, 1 January 1891.

SKEWES GEORGE
Born 23 August 1893. Lived at 39 Coronation Avenue, Camborne. Died 29 August 1971, aged 78 years.

SKEWS GEORGE
Chart 41. Son of Thomas and Ada (née Sheldon) Skews. Born 20 June 1897. Married Minnie Addy in Barnsley, South Yorkshire, 1929. Child: Gordon (1934). Died Rother Valley, 1973, aged 76 years. Lived at 12 Wilson Street, Wombwell, Barnsley.

SKEWS GEORGE
Chart 34. Born 26 July 1904, Park Place, Paddington, London. Married 26 January 1937 to Marjorie Constance Crook. No children. Lives at 31 Farncombe Road, Tunbridge Wells, Kent.
Marjorie Constance died 17 June 1979.

SKEWES GEORGE
Chart 50. Son of Thomas Henry Skewes, assistant timber man. Born 1893. Colliery timber man. Married Margaret Phelps, daughter of George Phelps, colliery engine driver at St David's Chapel, Pontypridd 23 November 1918. Children: Gwenllian F. (1919), Thomas G. (1920) and Iestyn (1922). Lived at 1 Aely Cryn, Panleygraigeven, Pontypridd.
Margaret, his wife, died 1922, aged 25 years. Married Elizabeth J. Caddy in Pontypridd, 1925. Child: Annie M. (1927).

SKEWES GEORGE
Chart 12. Son of Thomas Henry Skewes, boilerman. Mother's maiden name Jory. Born 1921, Redruth. Married Joyce Hawken (25), shop assistant and daughter of William John Hawken, labourer at Camborne Parish Church 13 December 1948. Children: Jeffrey Keith Skewes (1950) and Joanathan Ross Skewes (1957). Lives at "Rosskeith", 140 Agar Road, Illogan Highway, Redruth having moved from 12 Lower Pumpfield Row, Pool, Illogan where they were living in 1949.

SKEWS GEORGE
Chart 41. Son of Joseph and Nellie Skews. Mother's maiden name Randerson. Born 1921, Barnsley, South Yorkshire. Married Littledike in Barnsley, 1944. Child: Sandra (1946). Lives at 1 Wharf Street, Barnsley. Tel No: Barnsley 41664.

SKUES GEORGE
Also listed as SKUSE. Married Lily Ashcroft, 1948 in Ince.

SKEWES GEORGE
Lived at 32 Wellington Road, Camborne with Phyllis Skewes in 1949.

SKEWES GEORGE
Married Gilbert in Redruth, 1960.

SKEWS GEORGE
Married Proudly in Barnsley, 1965.

SKEWES GEORGE
Lived at 39 Coronation Avenue, Camborne in 1968 with Avis M. Skewes.

SKEWIS GEORGE ABSALOM
Chart 2. Son of James and Jane (née Rabling) Skewis. Born 25 January 1867, Mexico. Married Martha Townsend, 14 October 1903. No children. In 1900 lived at Lloyd Township, Dickinson County, Iowa, USA. Banker. Died March, 1963 aged 96 years. Martha died January, 1962, aged 89 years.

George Edward Mackenzie Skues (1856-1949)

SKEWS GEORGE ALFRED
Chart 17. Son of George Skews. Born 1846, Bethnal Green. Ring polisher. Married Caroline Moore, formerly Bernard, 1870, Strand, London. Lived at 39 Gee Street, Old Street, St Luke, Holborn. Children: Alfred David Richard (1871), and George Francis W. (1872). Died 1918, aged 72 years.

SKEWS GEORGE ALFRED
Born 1901, Bethnal Green. Died 1905, aged 4 years.

SKEWES GEORGE ALLWORTH
Born 1857, Helston. Died 1936, aged 80 years in Penzance.

SKEWES GEORGE ALTON
Chart 36. Son of James Henry and Elsie (née Snow) Skewes. Married Delsia Lucy Pearson, 19 August 1961, Australia,. Lives at 60 Queenscroft Street, Chelmer, 4068, Queensland, Australia.Issue: two sons. Engineer.

SKEWES GEORGE BENNETTS
Born 1841, Truro.

SKEWES GEORGE BOULDEN
Chart 14. Born in Ruan Major, Cornwall. Son of John and Jane Skewes. Emigrated to America with his parents and lived in Racine County, Wisconsin. Married Helen Herrick (she died 6 November 1913). Children: Duane William (1873), Boulden John (1874) and George Edwin (1881). Lived at Fond Du Lac, Fairwater, Wisconsin, USA. Died 4 September 1881.

SKUES GEORGE CHARLES
Born 1868, Marylebone, London. Died 1893, aged 25 years.

SKEWS GEORGE CHARLES
Born 1901, Bethnal Green.

SKEWS GEORGE DAVID
Chart 41. Son of William John and Mary (née Rump) Skews. Born 23 March 1931, Houghton. Married Olwynne Thirwell in Durham East, 23 March 1957. Children: Lynn (1959), David (1962) and Olwynne (1966). Now divorced.

SKEWIS GEORGE EDWARD
Chart 2. See SKEWIS EDWARD GEORGE.

SKUES GEORGE EDWARD MACKENZIE
Chart 3. Eldest son of Brigade Surgeon William Mackenzie and Margaret (née Ayre) Skues. Born 13 August 1858 at St John's, Newfoundland. His father was a surgeon with The Newfoundland Company. On his mother's side of the family his "roots" contained the last Lord Seaforth, the title being preserved in one of his pen names "Seaforth and Soforth." G.E.M. returned to Britain in 1859 with his parents to live in Scotland with his paternal grandparents who had a house in Aberdeen. In 1861 William Mackenzie Skues, together with his wife Margaret left for India leaving G.E.M. and his two sisters Mary Isabella and Margaret Caroline (known as Lina) in the care of his grandparents.
Shortly afterwards they all moved to Langford, Somerset, followed by another move to Wrington, Somerset.
G.E.M. Skues was to become one of the world's finest trout fishermen. It was here at Wrington where a small tributary of the River Yeo passed through the garden and here he saw his first trout. He was then five years old. At the age of seven he was sent to boarding school near Bristol, for one year. At the end of that period his parents returned from India and after brief family stays in Portsmouth and Southsea, G.E.M. settled with his mother near Hornsey Rise, London, his father departing for Germany. His first attempts at fishing came on the New River where he spent many hours fishing for perch and roach with a cheap cane winder, float and line. Before he could save enough money for a proper rod he was packed off to boarding school once more, this time to Stokes Bay near Gosport.
At the age of 14 he sat a scholarship for Winchester College and to his surprise gained 14th place out of 150. He passed and entered this fine establishment as a Foundation Scholar. Winchester College later described G.E.M. as a "Winchester Worthy."
He left Winchester in 1877 for the Channel Islands, his parents being resident there by now. In 1878 G.E.M. Skues became an articled clerk in the legal office of Mr James Powell, at the time the solicitor to the Skues family. G.E.M. earned the small annual wage of £80. He remained with this firm (latterly called "Powell, Skues and Graham Smith") for the remainder of his long working life, being made a partner in 1895 and serving this solicitors' practice at 34 Essex Street, off the Strand, London, until the age of 82.
His father William Mackenzie Skues died on 3 October 1887. G.E.M. at the age of 29, being the eldest of the family, became responsible for the welfare of his two brothers and five sisters. In November 1892 G.E.M. almost died from double pneumonia, but a very strong constitution pulled him through. In 1893 he went on a voyage to South Africa, and after this he was fully recuperated.
Although he applied himself to the profession of law his off-duty hours were spent fishing, mainly on the River Itchen in Hampshire.
In 1888 he commenced his angling literature to the press. It was a letter to the *Fishing Gazette*, signed "Val Conson" (lawyers' language for 'valuable consideration'). Over the years G.E.M. used a variety of pen-names. These included: "E.O.E.", 'Seaforth and Soforth", "S.A.S.", "Capt Stoke", "A. Fluker", "A. Limity Dincombe", "Integer Vitae", "A.

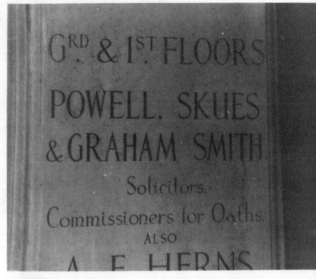

Sign outside offices of George Edward Mackenzie Skues. Photo taken 1958

Butt", "Simplex Mundishes", "M.C.", "Spent Naturalist", "I. Caunter Fordham", "Current Calomel", "The Unspoilt Child", and many others.
His books were: *Minor Tactics of the Chalk Stream* published 1910, reprinted 1974; *The Way of a Trout With a Fly*, 1921 reprinted 1961; *Side Lines, Side Lights and Reflections*, 1932, reprinted 1976 with *Chalk Stream Angler* and *Nymph Fishing for Chalk Stream Trout*, 1939 reprinted 1974. Two further books were published after his death, *Silk, Fur and Feathers* and *Itchen Memories*. C.F. Walker edited *Angling Letters of G.E.M. Skues* in 1957. In 1977 Donald Overfield wrote *G.E.M. Skues — The Way of a Man with a Trout*. G.E.M. Skues also wrote for a number of magazines including *Encyclopaedia of Sport*, *The Field*, *Fishing Gazette*, *The Salmon and Trout Magazine*, *The Bulletin of the Anglers' Club of New York* and *The Journal of the Fly Fishers' Club*.
As a chalk stream fisherman he had few, if any, equals. In his book *Angling Letters of G.E.M. Skues*, C.F. Walker describes him as "unselfish, generous and sympathetic. He also possessed a delightful sense of humour, and, on occasions, showed a ready wit which those who did not know him well sometimes found a trifle disconcerting."
Skues became one of the best loved and most prolific writers on angling in his day.
It is of interest to learn the derivation of surnames and place names. It is equally as interesting to know the story behind a particular book, for example *The Way of a Trout with a Fly*, which Skues dedicated to the Fly Fishers' Club in gratitude for many happy hours and some priceless friends.
In the Bible in Proverbs 30 verses 18 and 19 we read "There be three things which are too wonderful for me, yea, four, which I know not. The way of an eagle in the air, the way of a serpent upon a rock, the way of a ship in the midst of the sea, and the way of a man with a maid." Rudyard Kipling used this reference in *The Long Trail* (1886). George Edward Mackenzie Skues expounded the aforementioned:
"Some future Solomon will end with a fifth — the way of a trout with a fly — for it combines the poise of an eagle in the air, the swift certainty of a serpent upon a rock, and the mystery of the way of a ship in the midst of the sea, with the incalculableness of the way of a man with a maid. Our aviators seem to be on their way towards a solution of the way of an eagle in the air. The mystery of the way of a ship in the midst of the sea has yielded all its secrets to the persistence of modern man, but the way of a man with a maid and the way of a trout with a fly remain with us to be a delight and a torment to thousands of generations yet unborn."
G.E.M. Skues fished the River Itchen, a clear, unpolluted chalk stream

Plaque on the Skues seat on the banks of the River Itchen, Hampshire

Fishermen gather on the banks of the river Itchen, Hampshire for the dedication of a seat to the memory of George Edward Mackenzie Skues

from 1883 to 1938. He never caught a four-pounder in the Itchen, but he does speak nonchalantly in *Itchen Memories* of catching many three-pounders. On another occasion he caught 27 grayling in one day. G.E.M. Skues was a Director of Cornwall Trailings Company Limited of 522-525 Salisbury House, London, E.C. Having a nominal capital of £50,000 of £1 shares all of which were issued and fully paid, the company treated the Carn Brea Sands, Illogan, Redruth, Cornwall until operations ceased at the end of 1918. The company was liquidated the following year. G.E.M. remained on the board until the closure of the company.

Although Skues kept generally healthy throughout his long life, he was almost blind in one eye and had impaired vision in the other. He had damaged wrists and suffered from deafness later in life. He would not suffer angling fools gladly. He used to get annoyed if his surname was spelt incorrectly. In a letter to *The Times*, 16 June 1936 he wrote "I have abandoned the collection of misspellings of my name, having recorded upwards of 600 in the course of a few years. This does not include the same misspelling from several different sources."

In 1940 he retired from the legal world. He also moved from Hyrst View, 5 Campden Road, South Croydon, Surrey where he had lived with his sisters since 1894, and took up residence at the Nadder Vale Hotel, on the banks of the River Nadder in Wiltshire. Eight years later the hotel was sold and converted into flats.

G.E.M. then moved to Beckenham, Kent to reside near his younger brother Charles Ayre Mackenzie Skues. He died on 9th August 1949 at 23 Kelsey Park Road, Beckenham, Kent, of an internal haemorrhage, just four days short of his 91st birthday. He had remained a bachelor all his life.

From his obituary in *The Times* (12 August 1949) we read: "Skues' predecessor, Halford, was one of the great fly-fishermen, who some 70 years ago set a new fashion of approach by perfecting the use of the floating fly as a definite technique and fly-fishermen all over the world went dry-fly crazy. For these dry-fly purists the whole aqueous insect world then lives only on the surface of the water, and those who caught large trout on the wet, sunk fly concealed the fact and were in danger of blackballing if found out! Thus, as Lord Balfour remarked in another fishing connection, the 'odium theologicum' had a parallel in the 'odium ichtyologicum.' If the bitter feeling has to some extent died down and less jealousy subsists between the two schools, no little credit for the change is due to Mr Skues. At some time in the nineties he developed the nymph fashion. The nymph is the life-form of most water-borne insects between the larval stage in the mud or gravel bottom and their water-borne and ephemeral existence as duns and spinners. Having discovered that the nymph was just as attractive to trout as the imago, and being an expert fly-dresser, Skues set himself to produce tiny nymphs, which were marvels of close imitation, and fished them sunk below the surface — with results that seemed wonderful to the older rule-of-thumb anglers. It was all so simple when there came a man who fished 'with brains', and that discovery revolutionized trout fishing. Being the result of acute observation and logical reasoning, Skues' methods changed when conditions changed. While he 'nymphed' greatly and successfully, he was also unquestionably a great master of the use of the dry-fly at the proper time, so that thanks to his writing all can fish with a new pleasure in the knowledge of what they are doing and why."

In his will G.E.M. Skues asks that his ashes be scattered on the banks of the River Itchen as follows: "I desire that my body shall be cremated and the ashes scattered by the River Itchen on the Abbots Barton Fishery, preferably in the tussocky paddock on the east bank of the main river adjoining the clump of trees near the Winchester Gas Works."

In 1977, T. Donald Overfield was drawing near to the completion of his book about G.E.M. Skues. Michael Gale was the editor at Ernest Benn Publishers. He wrote a letter to the *Hampshire Chronicle* enquiring whether the request of Skues was ever carried out. Gale was lucky. He received a letter from Mrs. B.D. Ford who was the daughter of William Mullins who was head keeper for the syndicate for years on the River Itchen. It was William Mullins that scattered the ashes of G.E.M.Skues as requested. On the fly-leaf of *Itchen Memories*, Charles Ayre Mackenzie Skues, executor to the will had written: "There could be no more suitable person to do this than his old friend and keeper W.Mullins. As the author's brother and executor I therefore brought the ashes in the winter following his death and Mullins scattered them as desired on the east bank of the main river not far from the gas works."

Talking at his home in Abbots Barton, Winchester in August, 1980, former physician to Queen Elizabeth II, 93 year-old Sir John Mcknee said: "G.E.M. Skues was a stocky man. During his youth he had damaged both his wrists and his left shoulder. He had hands like a coal hewer. His casting was very unusual — half horizontal, rather than vertical. When I first witnessed this it fascinated me and I watched him for hours. He really was a very fine angler. Skues proposed me into the Fly Fishers' Club and Doctor Barton seconded me. I am now the oldest member of that very elite club."

On exactly the 31st anniversary of the death of G.E.M. Skues (9th August 1980), a large seat in Purbeck stone was unveiled and dedicated to his memory. It was placed on the bank of his beloved stream at Abbots Barton opposite where his ashes were scattered, the land which is now owned by Mrs Iris Whitfield.

A memorial fund had been set up be Roy Darlington who had helped bring back Abbots Barton Fishery to its former glory. It had been a long-held dream to erect a permanent memorial to Skues. Anglers from many parts of the world had sent contributions and offered suitable suggestions for an epitaph.

The one chosen was submitted by Doctor Christopher Jarmen: "In Memory of G.E.M. Skues who fished these waters from 1883-1938. A man who had a way with a trout."

Among the guests at Abbots Barton was Donald Overfield, the angling historian, who said "Abbots Barton was a unique place which the fishing holds in the history of trout fishing. Thanks were due to Roy Darlington who had put so much effort into honouring this grand old Itchen fisherman G.E.M. Skues."

SKEWES   GEORGE EDWIN
Chart 14. Son of George Boulden and Helen Skewes. Born 8 July 1881, America. Married 6 June 1906 to Emma Hagedorn. Children: Mortier Boulden (1909) and Kenneth F.(1911). Died 12 February 1966, aged 86 years. Emma died 20 October 1957. Freemason with Ben Franklin Lodge No 114, Luverne, Minn.

SKEWES   GEORGE EMMANUEL
Chart 14. Son of Anthony and Christian Skewes. Born 1840. Bpt Ruan Major 24 May 1840. Lived at Chybarles but died there in 1842, aged 2 years.

SKEWES   GEORGE ERNEST
Chart 25. Son of George Skewes. Mother's name Horton (divorcee). Born 1 July 1894, Salford. Married Ethel Tunnicliffe Ashton in Broughton Park, 25 July 1925. Foreman of Instrument Assembly Department at Metropolitan-Vickers, Manchester. Retired due to ill-health, 1945. Lived at 8 Hunstan Road, Sale, Cheshire. No children. Died 26 December 1953, aged 59 years at Royal Hospital, Cheadle, Cheshire.

SKUES   GEORGE ERNEST
Chart 3. Son of Arthur and Gladys Skues. Mother's maiden name Thompson. Born 4 February 1924. Married Joyce Littlewood in Melton Mowbray, 1949. Children: Richard Antony and Mark Alastair. Lives at 31 Eastern Road, Sutton Coldfield, Warwickshire.

SKEWS   GEORGE FRANCIS
Chart 17. Born 1905. Married Ivy Grace Cudgeon in Edmonton, 1935. Lived at 18 Cambridge Gardens, Winchmore Hill, Middlesex. Died 3 October 1948 at Sunken Garden Village Road, Edmonton, Middlesex, aged 43 years.

SKEWS GEORGE FRANCIS WM.
Chart 17. Born 1872. Married Caroline Nottage, 1892, Bethnal Green. Children: John George (1897) and Francis (1900). Died 1959, aged 86 years in Holborn, London.

SKUES   GEORGE GILBERT
Married 1848, Strand, London. Died 1861, Marylebone, London,

SKEWES   GEORGE HARRIS
Chart 10. Son of Captain Peter and Elizabeth Skewes of Chacewater. Born 29 March 1871. Lived in Mexico. Died of lockjaw and typhoid fever, 13 December 1884, aged 10 years. Buried in English cemetery, Real del Monte, Mexico: "We shall gather the lambs in his arms and carry him in his bosom."

SKEWES   GEORGE HENNESSY
Chart 12. Son of Harry Oswald and Emily Ann Skewes of 17 Moor Street, Camborne. Born 29 August 1908. Bpt Camborne Parish Church 29 January 1909. Married Phyllis Jane Capel at Treslothan Parish Church 27 April 1946. No children.
He spent six years in army during Second World War. Seconded to ENSA in 1939 for one year. Left Camborne in August 1939 for France and Belgium. Served one year with Royal Engineers and five years with Royal Artillery. With ENSA was a leading comic with Cyril Maude's Starlight. He returned to civilian life and became a supply manager for ICI in Cornwall. He was a keen actor and a member of Redruth Operatic Society for 30 years playing comedy roles.
Lives at 53 Tehidy Road, Camborne, Cornwall.
Tel No: 0209 713518.

SKUES   GEORGE HENRY
Chart 8. Son of William Henry (coal whipper) and Sarah (née Young) Skues. Born 15 August 1841 at 20 Dock Street, St George's East, London. Married Mary Sophia Birch at St Pancras Church 13 April 1862. (She died 1909, aged 66 years). Children: John Gilbert, Walter Edward, Evelyn Rose, George Henry, Harold Frederick Claude and Alexander James. Died 28 July 1924, aged 82 years in Edmonton.
Was a tailor at 6 Little Chapel Street, Soho, London W. in 1886, 1887, 1888, 1889 and 1890 London Street Directory.

SKUES   GEORGE HENRY
Died 1849, St Georges East, London.

SKUES   GEORGE HENRY
Chart 8. Son of George Henry (tailor) and Mary Sophia (née Birch) Skues. Dairyman. Born 13 December 1866 at 18 Air Street, St James, Westminster. Listed in London Street Directory for 1890-1895 as a dairyman. Married Winifred Sebright, 1888. Died of double pneumonia (4 days) and influenza (5 days) 23 April 1897 at 14 Sale Street, Paddington. Father-in-law Thomas Sebright present at death.

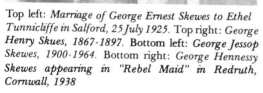

Top left: *Marriage of George Ernest Skewes to Ethel Tunnicliffe in Salford, 25 July 1925.* Top right: *George Henry Skues, 1867-1897.* Bottom left: *George Jessop Skewes, 1900-1964.* Bottom right: *George Hennessy Skewes appearing in "Rebel Maid" in Redruth, Cornwall, 1938*

George Owen Skewes

Photograph of an oil painting by George Owen Skewes in 1968 of the house in which he was born in Real del Monte, Mexico in 1897

SKEWES   GEORGE HOLDSWORTH
Lived at Coswinsawsen, Gwinear, 1932.

SKEWES   GEORGE JESSOP
Chart 14. Professor. PhD. Son of Edwin Bottomley and Alice (née Collier) Skewes. Born 16 September 1900. Lived at Grovean Farm, Ives Grove, Wisconsin, USA. Attended Ives Grove School from the age of eight. He became critically ill with pneumonia in 1910, but recovered. He attended Racine High School for three and a half years, and then worked to save money in order to attend college. Graduated from Lawrence University with Bachelor of Science, 1925. PhD University of Wisconsin, 1933. Whilst at college George had thoughts of becoming a doctor, hoping that he might help find ways to fight polio and meningitis. But teaching proved to be a better choice for him, a calling for which his interest in people and his gifts of mind and spirit fitted him.
A new teacher came to Lawrence University from Simpson, Iowa, and told George about a Margaret Skewis from Storm Lake, Iowa. George wrote to her to raise the question of kinship. Though her father's people had come from Cornwall and the same given names ran through both families, the kinship, if any, was too distant to trace.
George Skewes taught at Norway, Michigan and Jefferson, Wisconsin. On 22 August 1934 George married Ruth Viall, who had a Bachelor of Science degree from the University of Wisconsin, at the Wesleyan Memorial Chapel, Madison, Wisconsin. Children: Alice Eve (1935), Richard Edwin (1937) and Glen Wilson (1941). He later taught at Mayville State Teachers College, North Dakota and St Cloud College, Minnesota.
In 1955 it was confirmed George Skewes was suffering from Parkinson's disease but he carried on his teaching and adapted to his changed future.
He died 6 August 1964, aged 63 years.

SKEWS   GEORGE JOHN A.
Born 1892, Bethnal Green. Died 1894, aged 1 year.

SKEWIS   GEORGE O'NEIL
Born 1961, Bridgeton, Scotland.

SKEWES   GEORGE OWEN
Chart 10. Son of Richard Henry and Louie (née Pratt) Skewes. Born 4 February 1897, Mineral del Monte, Mexico. As a youngster lived in Pueblo, Mexico with his mother's parents.
He left Mexico 1 August 1907 and moved to California where he attended a private school in Los Angeles for 5½ years.
Later lived in Hermosa Beach, California, and worked for three years at California Cornice Works, Los Angeles.
During the First World War enlisted in US Army on 22 April 1918 and served with 2nd Field Artillery (Pathfinder Division) in France. Received Victory Medal (with clasp).
"In those days patriotism and love for our country was very high. I wanted to enlist as soon as war broke out, but my mother didn't want me to be in too big a hurry and urged me to wait for a while. When I did eventually enlist my mother took it a bit hard. But I explained that I felt it was my duty."
On return to civilian life in 1919 George found a job in the citrus industry in San Fernando where the fruit was prepared for the market. In 1923 he became foreman of the Placentia Mutual Orange Association where he worked for seven years. It was here that George met his future wife Etta Robins. They were married 14 December 1927 at Placentia, Orange County, California. No children.
In 1930 he was made foreman of the Escondido Lemon Association where he remained for 10 years during which time he spent 17 months nursing a compound fracture with seven breaks in his right ankle.
A Federal Marketing Order controlled the shipping of oranges and lemons throughout the states of Arizona and California. George took a job with the Lemon Administrative Committee as a field supervisor for San Diego County. He retired at the age of 65 years.
His spare time activities include stamp collecting, gardening, making hanging baskets and oil painting. He also has a sizeable shell collection and is a member of San Diego Shell Club.
He has 61 years of continuous membership in the American Legion as well as being a life member.
George is also a life member of Escondido Barracks No 449, Veterans of World War I.
Attends First United Church of Escondido.
Freemason with Consuelo Lodge No 325, Escondido, California. Worshipful Master 1951. Lives at 130 West 10th Avenue, Escondido, California, 92025, United States of America. Telephone number (714) 745 4637.

SKEWES   GEORGE PERCY
Chart 38. Son of Richard and Mary Jane (née Reynolds) Skewes. Born 31 March 1897, Moonta, South Australia. Bachelor. Lived at 7 Fisher Street, Flinders Park, Hindmarsh, South Aust. Died 29 January 1977, aged 79 years.

SKEWES   GEORGE ROY
Lived at 18 Ridge Street, Coffs Harbour, New South Wales, Australia, 1959, with Amy Ruth Skewes. He was a shire employer.

SKEWES   GEORGE STANLEY
Chart 14. Son of Henry and Winifred (née Oehls) Skewes. Born in Wisconsin, USA. Married May Oakleaf. No children.

George Percy Skewes (1897-1977)

SKEWS   GEORGE THOMAS
Born 1899 St Olave. Died 1899, aged 0.

SKEWS   GEORGE WEALE
Born 1901. Married Hill in Stourbridge, 1936. Lived at the Church Army Hostel, 22 Johnson Street, Stepney, London E.l. Died 28 April 1961, aged 59 years at Mile End Hospital, Stepney. Wife's name Hilda Marjorie Skews.

SKEWS   GEORGE WILLIAM
Chart 23. Married Caroline Nottage, 1892, Bethnal Green, London. Children: John George (1897) and Francis (1900).

SKEWS   GEORGE WILLIAMS
Chart 41. Son of Matthew and Betsy (née Tresider) Skews. Born 1869, Guisborough. Miner. Lived at 3 Seventh Street, Horden, County Durham. Married 1889, Easington. On 16 December 1907 he had a quarrel with another miner, John Richards (34). They met on a beach at Dean Holme and fought for nearly an hour and a half.
Richards stripped to his singlet and Skews stripped to his top shirt, but afterwards stripped bare to his waist. There was no time arranged for the number of rounds or the duration of the encounter.
Both men were in an exhausted condition and in the last round both fell to the ground. Skews gave up the fight. He walked away with a man on each side of him. There had been about 60 people present. About 30 rounds had been fought. On his return home Skews became seriously ill and died the following morning of compression of the brain, due to a fracture of the skull. At a Coroner's Court the jury returned a verdict of manslaughter. John Richards was sent for trial at the Durham Assizes. George Skews' widow married again in Easington, 1911. Full story in Appendix. Press Cuttings, 1907.

SKEWES   GEORGINA FRANCES
Born 1877. Died Holyhead 1901, aged 24 years.

SKUES   GEORGINA MARY
Chart 3. Spinster. Daughter of George and Mary Gibbs Skues. Born 31 October 1840. Died 7 October 1903, aged 63 years at Mackenzie Cottage, Hastings Road, Ealing Down, Middlesex.

SKEWS   GEORGINA MARY
Lives at 3/146 Queenscliffe Road, Harbord, 2096, New South Wales, Australia. Nurse.

SKEWES   GEORGINA MAY
Lives at Halls Creek, 2346, New South Wales, Australia with Samuel Thomas William Skewes, labourer.

SKEWES   GEORGINA MIRIAM
Daughter of Alfred John & Ann Maria Skewes. Born 1904, Bideford, N. Devon. Spinster. Lives at Barford Farm, Spaxton, Bridgwater, Somerset. Tel Spaxton 266.

SKEWS GERALD N.
Chart 17. Son of John G.P. and Dorothy Skews. Mother's maiden name Boyland. Born 1957. Lives at 5 Lime Tree Avenue, Peterborough. Tel No: 0733 62073.

SKEWS GERTRUDE
Chart 10. Daughter of Richard Skewes of Marazion. Born 1 December 1886 at Marazion. Emigrated to Canada with her parents and family. Married Samuel Bulley 1 June 1908 at Burkes Fall, Ontario, Canada. Issue 4 daughters and 2 sons. Died 13 May 1970 in Detroit, Michigan, USA, aged 84 years.

SKEWS GERTRUDE A.
Married 1910, Kensington.

SKEWS GERTRUDE ALBERTA
Born 1896. Spinster. Daughter of John and Bertha Skews of St Austell. Lived at Coxbarrow, Carthew, St Austell. Died 9 March 1963, aged 66 years.

SKEWIS GERTRUDE ALICE
Born 1878, Wellington, Somerset.

SKEWES GERTRUDE ANNIE
Born 1899, Redruth.

SKUES GERTRUDE ELIZA MACKENZIE
Chart 3. Daughter of George and Mary Gibbs (née Mackenzie) Skues. Bpt Aberdeen 16 February 1832. Died 16 February 1835, aged 3 years.

SKUES GERTRUDE ELIZA MACKENZIE
Chart 3. Daughter of Brigade Surgeon William Mackenzie and Margaret (née Ayre) Skues. Born 30 October 1862. Married Doctor Walter Watkins, July 1894. Died 5 June 1905. Issue: 2 sons and 1 daughter.

SKEWES GERTRUDE M.
Born 1880, Died 1945, aged 65 years in Surrey NE.

SKEWES GERTRUDE MARY
Born 1891, Plymouth. Married James E. Axon in Plymouth, 1916.

SKEWES GERTRUDE OLIVE
Lived at 9 Coombe Road, Allenby Gardens, Hindmarsh, South Australia in 1959 with Ralph Skewes and Stanley Victor Skewes.

SKEWES GILBERT JAMES
Chart 12. Son of William John and Nora Skewes. Mother's maiden name Thomas. Born 29 April 1937. Married Kathleen Joyce Dennis at Helston Register Office 21 September 1957. Children: Janet M., Sandra, John C., David, Peter and Carole M. Lives at Trelimminey, St Martin, Helston.

SKUES GILLIAN
Chart 8. Daughter of Sydney Thomas Skues. Mother's maiden name Parnell. Born 1954, Hackney, London. Married Michael J. Cameron, Nuneaton, 1979.

SKEWES GILLIAN ANN
Chart 12. Daughter of James Harry Skewes. Mother's maiden name Pearce. Born 1939, Truro. Lived at Woodlands, Mithian, St Agnes, Cornwall. Married Charles William Bone, 1957, Truro. After marriage lived at 1 Head Lane, Goonbell, St Agnes.

SKEWES GILLIAN MARY
Chart 50. Daughter of David Buick and Irene Margaret (née Murphy) Skewes. Born 12 April 1944, Ballarat, Victoria, Australia. Married Donald McOmish 6 November 1966, Ballarat. Issue: 1 son and 1 daughter. Now divorced. Lives at 29 Lyons Street, North Ballarat, 3350, Victoria, Australia. Primary school teacher.

SKEWES GILLIAN WENDY
Chart 2. Daughter of Eric William and Pamela (née Drummond) Skewes. Born 8 December 1955, Ringwood, Victoria, Australia. Married Brian Lawrence Leckey 3 November 1979.

SKUSE GLADYS
Daughter of Herbert Henry & Ada (née Cocks) Skuse. Born 1903. Married Harold Bailey. Issue: one daughter. Died 1973, aged 70 years.

SKEWES GLADYS
Chart 36. Daughter of Robert Northey and Sarah Agnes (née Connell) Skewes. Lives in Wellington, New South Wales, Australia.

SKUES GLADYS
Chart 3. Née Thompson. Married Arthur Skues, 1922. Child: George Ernest Skues (1924).

SKEWES GLADYS C.
Mother's maiden name Gurney. Born 1917, Truro. Married Lappin at St Thomas, Exeter, 1936.

SKEWES GLADYS E.
Daughter of Sidney Hope and Anna (née Hosking) Skewes. Born 19 November 1895. Lived in Montreal, Canada until 1899 when she moved with her family to New York.

SKEWES GLADYS JEAN E. E.
Lives at 22 Talbot Avenue, Canterbury, Victoria, Australia, 3103 with Richard Morley Skewes.

SKEWES GLADYS LOCK
Chart 36. Daughter of John Vivian and Gertrude Mary (née Lock) Skewes. Born 1 April 1908. Married George Harold Clark 15 July 1936. Issue: 1 son and 3 daughters. Lives in Strathalbyn, 5255, South Australia.

SKUES GLADYS MARGUERITA
Chart 9. Daughter of Thomas Henry J. and Gladys May (née Clemmans) Skues. Born 1926, Wandsworth, London. Married Edward J. Goulston, 1949, Wandsworth.

SKEWES GLADYS MARY
Chart 12. Wife of William Henry Skewes of Brea. Born 1895. Children: Vera, William Henry and Phyllis. Buried Tuckingmill Parish Church 31 October 1933, aged 38 years.

SKEWES GLADYS MARY
Chart 40. Daughter of William and Laura Skewes. Mother's maiden name Allen. Born 1929, Penzance. Married Peter Rosewarn, 1973, Penzance.

SKUES GLADYS MAY
Chart 9. Née Clemmans. Born 17 December 1902. Married Thomas Henry James Skues, 1926. Children: Gladys Marguerita (1926) and Roy Arthur Truscott (1928).

SKEWES GLADYS MAY
Chart 38. Daughter of Horace Henry and Agatha Blanche Skewes. Born 1 August 1911, Kadina, South Australia. Married 28 May 1938 to Harold Boundy.

SKEWS GLADYS VIOLET
Born 1895, Liskeard.

SKEWES GLEN DALE
Chart 11. Son of Thomas John and Laura B. Skewes. Born 27 February 1896, America. Served in U.S. Navy.

SKEWES GLEN WILSON
Doctor (PhD). Chart 14. Son of George Jessop and Ruth (née Viall) Skewes of Wisconsin, USA. Born 12 April 1941. Bachelor of Chemistry, Institute of Technology, University of Minnesota, 1964. PhD of Physical Chemistry, Washington University, St Louis, 1973. Married Patricia Faye Manthey (she born 16 November 1944) on 29 January 1965. She has a degree — Bachelor of Science, University of Missouri (St Louis Branch), 1961. Children: Jason Collier Skewes (1973) and Elizabeth Anne Skewes (1976).
Author of "Discrete Structure in the Spectrum of vapour phase sodium iodide." (Thesis, Washington Univ., St Louis, 1971).
Is now Programme Head of Biomedical Electronics at Western Wisconsin Technical Institute, La Cross, Wisconsin. Developed a microcomputer instruction for multiply-handicapped children. Partner in consulting firm Quality Design Consortium.

Glen Wilson Skewes aged 9 years

SKUES GLENDA BERYL
Daughter of William Ashdown and Edith Beryl (née Saul) Skues. Born 1 August 1962. Lives at 7 Cormack Road, Beacon Hill, New South Wales, Australia.

SKEWES GLENDA LORRAINE
Chart 38. Daughter of Eric Emil Ludwig and Mavis Irene (née Rowland) Walter. Born 29 January 1939. Married William Seymour Skewes, bootmaker, 12 June 1965. Children: Craig William Skewes (1969) and Bryon Anthony Skewes (1974). Lives at 15 Alawa Avenue, Modbury North, South Australia, 5091. Telephone number: Adelaide 263 0629.

SKEWES   GLENLEIGH BERTIE WILLIAM
Chart 36. Son of Henry John and Phoebe Marie (née Holdsworth) Skewes. Born 16 November 1912, Putney, Ryde, New South Wales, Australia. Worked in timber cutting business, also potato and hay harvesting. Served in army during Second World War. Trained as a medical orderly for twelve months at Royal Park Camp Hospital. Nursing corporal. Posted to Singapore in 1941 with 2/13th Australia General Hospital. Taken Prisoner-of-War and witnessed terrible famine and sickness in Thailand which killed many hundreds of men. He wrote a diary (part of which is reproduced in Appendix) in which he kept notes inscribed in diluted purple dye. This notebook was hidden from the enemy, but was damaged by the damp and mildew of the monsoon climate. At all times it was carried through the war at great risk, as severe punishment was meted out to the person with any such document found upon them. Glen had a simple love for his country and his family, faith in God, and a deep feeling for suffering humanity. He was released in November, 1945 and returned home to Australia to be with his wife Mary Evelyn Harriet (née Watkins) whom he married on 28 March 1936, and their sons Kenneth (1937) and Robert (1940). Soon after he arrived home he went down with pleurisy and malaria and was transferred to Melbourne Repatriation Hospital.
By July, 1947 Glen was able to work, albeit light work, but had to resign from his nursing job which he had enjoyed so much. He became a handyman and gardener at a teachers'college. He retired completely in 1973 and was put on a service pension.
Four more children were born to Glen and Evelyn, namely Ruth (1947), Bruce (1949), Stuart (1951) and Leigh (1953).
Lives at 141 Spencer Street, Sebastopol, 3356, Victoria, Australia.
Now in his spare time he enjoys a game of bowls and landscape painting. He regularly attends his local Methodist Church.

Diary of Glenleigh Bertie William Skewes during his days as a P-O-W in Thailand, 1941-1945

SKEWES   GLORIA JUNE
Chart 36. Daughter of Aubrey Rupert and Annie (née Townsend) Skewes. Born Uralla, New South Wales, Australia, 15 June 1923. Married Reginald Bullen. Issue: two daughters. Lives at 35 Uralla Street, Uralla, 2358, New South Wales, Australia.
SKEWES   GLORIA MADGE
Lives at 19 Cross Street, Fairfield, 4103, Queensland, Australia with Kenneth Skewes, floor sander.
SKEWES   GORDON
Born 1906, Penzance.
SKEWS   GORDON
Chart 41. Son of George and Minnie (née Addy) Skews. Born 1934, Barnsley, South Yorkshire. Died 1934, aged 0.
SKUSE   GORDON
Son of Tom and Muriel (née Goodhead) Skuse. Born 31 August 1937, Nottinghamshire. Married Janet Mellor at Hucknall Parish Church, Notts., 7 March 1959. Children: Dale (1961) and Linda (1964).
Became a collier at Newstead Colliery at the age of 15 years. Worked as a face fitter for 10 years, followed by a spell on general surface work. In 1978 he was promoted to Assistant Mechanical Engineer.
His family have worked for a total of 120 years at Newstead Colliery.
Lives at 30 Abbey Road, Newstead Village, Nottingham.
Telephone number: 0623 757335.
SKEWS   GORDON H. L.
Mother's maiden name Webber. Born 1924, Totnes, Devon.

SKEWES   GORDON WILLIAM
Chart 2. Son of William James and Laura Annie (née Davies) Skewes. Born 20 April 1900. Married Eileen Margaret Tritchler 4 August 1928, Australia. (She born 15 June 1900 — died 8 February 1971, aged 70 years.) Bank manager.
Children: Margaret Laura Skewes (1929) and William John Skewes (1934).
In 1959 lived at 18a Churchill Street, Surrey Hills, Victoria, Australia. Died 3 July 1961, aged 61 years.
SKEWES   GRACE
Married Nyclis Vybyst at Ludgvan 20 November 1575.
SKEWES   GRACE
Daughter of Richard and Jane Skewes. Bpt St Anthony in Meneage 21 October 1649.
SKEWES   GRACE
Daughter of John Skewes. Bpt St Keverne 24 October 1669.
SKEWAS   GRACE
of St Keverne. Married Thomas Rownson 28 August 1703 at Mawgan in Meneage.
SKEWS   GRACE
Born 1710. Pauper of Crowan. Buried St Hilary 24 July 1791, aged 81 years.
SKEWES   GRACE
Daughter of Richard & Rebecca. Bpt St Just in Penwith 7 May 1727.
SKEWES   GRACE
Born 1783. Died 1829, aged 46 years. Buried Chacewater 6 August 1829.
SKEWES   GRACE
Chart 18. Daughter of John and Ann Skewes. Bpt Kenwyn 5 March 1787.
SKEWIS   GRACE
Daughter of John and Mary Skewis. Bpt Gwennap 21 October 1788.
SKEWES   GRACE
Born 1789. Lived at Brill, Constantine. Buried Constantine 26 May 1826, aged 37 years.
SKEWIS   GRACE
Widow of Falmouth. Married Henry Dunstone at Towednack 2 May 1793.
SKEWS   GRACE
Chart 9. Daughter of James and Joanna Skews of Lower Sticker, St Ewe. Bpt St Ewe 5 November 1793. Married . . . . . Thoms.
SKEWIS   GRACE
Buried Gwennap 7 November 1796.
SKEWES   GRACE
Chart 19. Daughter of Alexander and Christian Skewes. Bpt Gwennap 12 March 1797. Married Alexander Teague at Gwennap 6 July 1822. Children called Skewes Teague.
SKEWES   GRACE
Born 1801. Lived at Jolly's Bottom, Chacewater. Died 1857. Buried Chacewater 16 November 1857, aged 56.
SKEWES   GRACE
Chart 2. Daughter of Henry and Grace Skewes of Bosawsack, Constantine. Bpt Constantine 23 July 1809. Married James SKEWES of Cury at Constantine 8 April 1834, in presence of Henry Skewes. Children: Eliza Grace.
SKEWES   GRACE
Daughter of John and Elizabeth (née Hendy) Skewes. Bpt Cury 24 July 1803.
SKEWES   GRACE
Chart 25. Second wife of Thomas Skewes. Born 1811. Married Thomas Skewes 22 August 1829, Falmouth. Died Falmouth 1871, aged 60 years.
SKUES   GRACE
Chart 3. Née Noy. Born 1801. Married Richard Skues (son of Richard and Ann Skues). Issue: one daughter Grace Noy Skues (1819). Died 8 April 1821, aged 20 years. Buried in Mawnan Churchyard in a table tomb alongside her daughter who died 26 December 1821, aged 2 years.
SKEWES   GRACE
Chart 36. Daughter of Henry and Grace Skewes of Constantine. Born 1809. Married James Skewes of Cury at Cury 8 April 1834. One daughter Eliza Grace (1846). By 1871 had moved from Cury to Sethnoe and was listed as mother-in-law to Jacob Rowe. James Skewes died 19 October 1856, aged 59 years. Grace died at Sethnoe, Breage, 24 September 1892, aged 83 years.
SKEWES   GRACE
Chart 32. Née Ford. Married Richard Skewes at Kenwyn 10 October 1803. Lived at Whitehall, Kenwyn. Later moved to Gwennap. Children: Richard, John, James Henry and James Marley.
SKEWIS   GRACE
Born 1826. Died Ulverston, 1890, aged 64 years.
SKEWES   GRACE
Chart 10. Née Harris. Born 1808, Penryn. Married Peter Skewes, farmer of Kerley, Kea, 16 October 1830. Children: Richard, Mary, John, Thomas, Peter, Grace and Maria. In 1871 Census Returns was living at Baldhu, Truro — a widow. Died at the residence of her son-in-

law John Coad of Penstraze, Chacewater, 27 February 1896, aged 88 years. Buried in Baldhu Churchyard 1 March 1896.

SKEWIS   GRACE
Born 1807 Camborne. Died 1847. Buried Camborne 11 April 1847, aged 40 years.

SKEWS   GRACE
Chart 10. Daughter of Peter and Grace Skews of Kea, miner. Bpt Chacewater 31 July 1831. Lived at Kerley, Kea. Buried Chacewater 31 March 1840, aged 10 years.

SKEWES   GRACE
Married Samuel Hendy at Cury 27 December 1831.

SKEWES   GRACE
Chart 22. Daughter of William and Christian Skewes. Bpt St Keverne 29 June 1834.

SKEWES   GRACE
Chart 50. Daughter of Thomas and Jane Skewes. Born 1836. Buried Chacewater 9 November 1848, aged 12 years.

SKEWES   GRACE
Daughter of John and Ann Skewes of Kea, miner. Bpt Kenwyn 20 August 1843.

SKEWES   GRACE
Chart 24. Married Francis Skewes of Illogan Highway, blacksmith. Children: Richard Ernest, Jane Rogers and John.

SKEWES   GRACE
Died 1840, Truro.

SKEWES   GRACE
Chart 2. Born 1841 Sithney. Daughter of William and Elizabeth Skewes of Bolitho, Crowan. In 1861 Census Returns was listed as a housemaid at Bolitho.

SKEWES   GRACE
Daughter of James Richards; miner. Widow of Chacewater (25) married James Harry of Chacewater, miner at Kenwyn Parish Church 4 July 1842. She was formerly married to Thomas Skewes.

SKUES   GRACE
Daughter of John and Ann Skues. Bpt Kenwyn 20 August 1843 with her two sisters Emma and Ellen and brother John.

SKEWS   GRACE
Born 1844. Daughter of Peter and Elizabeth Skewes of Kea. Born 16 September 1844. Bpt 5 January 1845 at Primitive Methodist Perranwell Circuit.

SKEWES   GRACE
Chart 10. Daughter of Peter and Grace Skewes of Kerley, Kea. Born 1845. In 1861 Census Returns was living at Kerley, Kea; in 1871 Census Returns was living at Baldhu. Married Stephen Davey late of Real del Monte, Mexico 29 June 1874 at Baldhu Church.

SKEWES   GRACE
Chart 33. Daughter of William and Susan (née Oates) Skewes, miner. Born 1847. Married Thomas Colenso (22), son of Michael Colenso, harness maker, at St George's, Truro on 3 October 1864.

SKEWES   GRACE
Died Truro, 1848.

SKEWS   GRACE
Died Neath, 1849.

SKEWES   GRACE
Chart 36. Daughter of William and Christian Skewes. Bpt St Keverne 29 June 1834. Married 15 November 1855 to Samuel Phillips Veal, innkeeper (at Mawnan Parish Church). He was son of James Veal of Helford Passage. Wedding took place in presence of James Skewes.

SKEWES   GRACE
Died 1857, Truro.

SKEWES   GRACE
Married 1873 in Helston.

SKEWES   GRACE
Born 1878, Neath.

SKEWES   GRACE
Born 1894, Missouri, USA. Lived in Mississippi, USA, 1900.

SKEWES   GRACE
Lived at Barncoose Terrace, Illogan, 1897-1906.

SKEWIS   GRACE ANNE
Born 1861, Redruth. Married 1884, Redruth.

SKEWES   GRACE ELIZABETH
Chart 10. Born 12 October 1883, Truro. Daughter of John and Catherine (née Williams) Skewes. Emigrated to Mexico, 1891, via Vera Cruz with her parents. Lived in Real del Monte, Mexico. Married John Rabling. Issue: six children. Died 1968, aged 85 years.

SKEWES   GRACE ELIZABETH
Chart 30. Born 1894. Daughter of William Browne Skewes, house-painter of St Dominic Street, Truro. Married Edward Charles Moses (26), Sergeant in 2nd DCLI of Mark Road, Truro, son of James Moses, labourer, at St George's, Truro, 29 June 1918.

SKUES   GRACE JOAN
Born 1908. Married 1938 to William G. Goodwin at Stoke Newington, London.

SKEWIS   GRACE MARIA M.

Born 1882, Ulverston.

SKUES   GRACE NOYE
Chart 3. Only child of Richard and Grace Skues of Helston. Born October 1819. Bpt Helston 28 December 1819. Died at Trenarth, the seat of Henry Noye, December 1821, aged 2 years and 2 months of water on the chest. Buried in Mawnan churchyard in a table tomb alongside her mother.
"Around the tenants of this sacred tomb,
Connubial and parental love combine,
In sadly pleasing cares to mourn the doom,
Of joys scarce blown are blighted by decline.
Lov'd lost lamented such the brief events
That marked the history of their swift career,
Yet while fond memory their worth presents
Affection pours the unveiling tear.
No sooner known that lov'd scarce lov'd ere lost
But oh how long shall lamentation dwell,
On bless departed hopes for ever crossed,
And virtues which angelic tongues might tell.
The Bough and Fruit pale Deaths untimely spoil,
Together laid here wait the happy day.
When rais'd and planted in a brighter soil,
Their leaf shall bloom and never know decay."

SKEWIS   GRACE RABLING
Chart 2. Daughter of Francis Harry and Annie Skewis. Born 7 May 1899, America. Married Arthur Mohr 2 June 1920. Issue: Three sons and two daughters. Lives at 12442 Grandee Drive, San Diego, California, 92128. (1980).

SKUES   GRACE RICHARDS
Chart 3. Daughter of Richard and Ann Skues. Born 8 July 1799. Bpt Helston 10 June 1801. Married William Radford, a Wesleyan minister in Ashburton, Devon, 24 August 1824 (at Helston Parish Church). He was ordained 1803 and was Wesleyan Minister at Liskeard and Camelford 1830-1833. He died June 1844, aged 65 years. Grace died in Bristol 1868, aged 69 years. No children.

SKEWES   GRACE RICHARDS
Daughter of Thomas and Jane Skewes, miner of Kea. Born 10 September 1836. Bpt 5 March 1837 at Truro Wesleyan Chapel.

SKEWES   GRACE THERESA
Chart 10. Daughter of Thomas and Grace Skewes of Jolly's Bottom, Chacewater; miner. Bpt Chacewater 16 January 1839. Buried Chacewater 9 May 1843, aged 4 years.

SKEWES   GRAEME DOUGLAS
Chart 36. Son of Douglas William and Elsie May (née Smith) Skewes. Born 19 July 1942. Married Rosalie Campbell 25 April 1964. Children: Julie Ann (1964), Peter Charles and Paul—twins (1967). Lives at 424 Chapman Road, Geraldton, 6530, Western Australia. Police officer.

SKEWES   GRAEME TREVOR
Lives at 2/105 Petra Avenue, Tamworth, 2340, New South Wales, Australia with Elizabeth Ruth Skewes. Welder.

SKEWES   GRAHAM
Chart 36. Son of Francis James and Valerie (née Foster) Skewes. Born Watsons Creek, via Bendemeer, New South Wales, Australia. Married.

SKEWES   GRAHAM HENRY
Chart 2. Son of Archibald William and Gwendoline (née Jones) Skewes. Born 27 August 1942. Married Dorothy Cheryl Fitzclarence at Maffra, Victoria, Australia. Children: Katrina Louise (1972) and Jacqueline Ann (1974). Lives at 15 Crossen Street, Echuca, 3625, Victoria, Australia. Teacher.

SKEWIS   GRAHAM M.B.T.
Born 1933, Camalchie, Scotland. Married McDermott in Bridgeton, Scotland 1953. Married McColligan in Glasgow, 1970.

SKEWES   GRANT
Chart 26. Son of Wallace R. Skewes of Connecticut, United States of America.

SKEWES   GRANT
Chart 24. Adopted son of Alan and Shirley (née Rutherford) Skewes. Born 4 October 1973. Lives in Christchurch, New Zealand.

SKEWES   GRANT PHILIP
Chart 26. Son of Edward James and Harriet A. (née Rockwell) Skewes. Born 4 June 1903. Died 1979, Connecticut, USA, aged 76 years.

SKEWES   GRAYSON PAUL
Chart 38. Son of Geoffrey Garfield and Donna Louise (née Bridge) Skewes. Born 30 December 1972, South Australia. Lives at 28 York Street, Cauldfield South, Victoria, Australia, 3162.

SKEWES   GREGORY
Chart 36. Illegitimate son of Norma Kathleen Skewes. Born 22 December 1950, New South Wales, Australia. When Norma married James Battis he assumed the name Gregory Battis. After her death he reverted to the name Skewes in 1975 and now lives in New Zealand.

SKEWES   GREGORY ARCHER
Chart 36. Son of Geoffrey and Dorothy May (née Chapman) Skewes. Born 3 January 1952. Married Janette Mary Robinson (she born 25 September 1953), 1 May 1976. Issue: One daughter Wendy Jane (1979). Lives in Queensland, Australia.

SKEWES   GREGORY DAVID
Son of David Leslie and Irma Margaret (née Green) Skewes. Born 14 October 1956. Lives at Flat 7, 12 Vine Street, Blackburn, 3130, Victoria, Australia with Craig Leslie Skewes, clerk. Teacher.

SKEWES   GREGORY JOHN
Lives at 68 Rowan Street, Manilla, 2346, New South Wales, Australia.

SKEWES   GREGORY KENNETH
Lives at 40 David Street, Tamworth, 2340, New South Wales, Australia with Kerrilyn Skewes. Welder.

SKEWIS   GRETTA J.
Chart 50. Daughter of Alfred and Edith Alice Skewis. Mother's maiden name Hughes. Born 1934. Lived at 13 Dartmouth Gardens, Milford Haven, Pembrokeshire.

SKEWES   GUILLERMO
Chart 10. Son of Nazario and Dolores (née Riofrio) Skewes. Born 30 January 1909, Real del Monte, Mexico. Married Herminia Rosati 24 December 1939, Mexico City (Evangelist Church). Children: Guillermo (1942) and Herminia (1940). He attended school in Real del Monte and Pachuca. Speaks no English. Left school at age of 13 years and joined La Rica Mine, Real del Monte, first as an assistant carpenter (also his hobby) for one year and as a warehouse clerk for two years. He worked for 23 years as administrator in the Mine Office 1925-1948.
He can remember that his parents kept horses, rabbits, sheep, dogs, cats and cows in Real del Monte. Prior to the motor car becoming popular, the recognised way of transport was by horse. However, one could travel to Mexico City by train from both Real del Monte and Pachuca.
Lives at Alejandro, Malaspina No 56, Mexico City.

SKEWES   GUILLERMO
Chart 10. Mexican. Son of Guillermo and Herminia Skewes. Born 8 August 1942, Real del Monte, Mexico. Married Teresa Bonnet 13 June 1970 at St Patrick's Church, Mexico City. Lives at Puerto Real No 28, Colonia Condesa, Mexico, DF 11.
Children: Guillermo Federico (1970), Eduardo Gustavo (1972) and Ricardo Rafael (1974).

Guillermo Skewes of Mexico holding an oil painting of his grandfather John Skewes

SKEWES   GUILLERMO FEDERICO
Chart 10. Son of Guillermo and Teresa (née Bonnet) Skewes. Born 15 December 1970, Mexico City. Lives at Puerto Real No 28, Colonia Condesa, Mexico, DF 11.

SKEWES   GWEN
Chart 36. Daughter of William Wilfred John and Annie (née Borgas) Skewes. Born 1909. Married John Brown. Issue: 1 son and 1 daughter. Lives at Geraldton, Western Australia.

SKEWES   GWENDA ELIZABETH
Chart 36. Daughter of Cuthbert George and Violet (née Ferris) Skewes. Born 6 October 1928. Married Herbert S. Jones in Armidale, Australia, 10 January 1949. Issue: 5 daughters. Now dead.

SKEWES   GWENDOLINE
Chart 30. Born 1884, St Thomas, Exeter. Spinster. Lived at 80 Wellington Road, St Thomas, Exeter. Only daughter of John Beer and Bessie (née Whether) Skewes. Died 22 March 1928 at Royal Cornwall and Exeter Hospital. Buried in Exwick cemetery 28 March 1928.

SKUES   GWENDOLINE
Chart 5. Born 1903. Daughter of John Charles Skues of Redruth.

SKEWES   GWENDOLINE
Lived at 4 Kynance Terrace, Landewednack, Lizard, in 1969.

SKEWES   GWENDOLINE
Chart 2. Née Jones. Married Archibald William Skewes 7 December 1940, Sunshine, Victoria, Australia. Children: Graham Henry (1942), Barbara Ann (1947), Helen Elizabeth (1949) and Robert William (1951). Lives at 34a Kerford Street, Essendon North, 3041, Victoria, Australia.

SKEWS   GWENDOLINE D.
Chart 17. Daughter of David George and Doris Adelaide (née Parrott) Skews. Born 30 April 1948. Lived at 60 Valentines Way, Dagenham, Essex. Married Reginald Cooper at St Peter's and St Paul's Church, Dagenham Village 1 March 1969.

SKEWES   GWENDOLINE MARIE ANNIE
Daughter of Wilfred J. and Anna Louisa (née Borgas) Skewes. Married John William Waldron Brown in South Australia. Issue: 1 son and 1 daughter.

SKEWES   GWENDOLINE EUPHEMIA
Lived at 21 Gainsborough Street, Ferryden Park, South Australia, 1959, with Allan Skewes and Kenneth Mervaine Skewes.
Now lives at 13 Cuncliffe Street, Port Hughes, 5558, South Australia.

SKEWES   GWENDOLINE JOYCE
Lives at 79 Payten Street, Kogarah, 2217, New South Wales, Australia with Arthur Vivian Skewes, boilerman. Accountant.

SKEWES   GWENDRA MARGARET
Lives at 12 Akarana Road, Lilydale, 3140, Victoria, Australia with Neville Herbert Skewes, manager.

SKEWES   GWENDRA MIRIAM
Lives at Kinnersley Avenue, Mount Clear, Victoria, Australia, 3350 with Michael John Skewes.

SKEWES   GWENDRA PEARL
Lives at 45 Glenhuntley Street, Woodville, 5011, South Australia with Ralph Edward Skewes, David John Skewes and Steven Melville Skewes.

SKEWES   GWENETH
Chart 36. Née Adams. Married Benjamin Samuel Skewes, 22 September 1945. Children: Warren Benjamin, Daryl, Dianne Gweneth and Marilyn Pearl. Lives at Glenelg, Watsons Creek, via Bendemeer, 2352, New South Wales, Australia.

SKEWES   GWENYTH ELIZABETH
Lives at 101 Wilburtree Street, Tamworth, 2340, with Stanley Bruce Skewes. Clerk.

SKEWES   GWENLLIAN F.
Chart 50. Daughter of George Skewes. Mother's maiden name Phelps. Born 1919, Pontypridd. Died 1919, aged 0.

SKEWES   GWYN MARTIN
Chart 36. Son of Trevor John and Bonney (née Kite) Skewes. Born 19 June 1968. Lives c/o P.O. Box 96, Stirling, 5152, South Australia.

SKEWES   GYTHA EVELEEN MORNA
Chart 36. Daughter of William Hicks and Elizabeth (née McLeod) Skewes. Born 1889, Australia. Lived at 88 French Street, Joondanna, Western Australia. Spinster. Died 1968, aged 79 years.

H

SKEWES H.
Mine agent. Lived at Tuckingmill, 1856.

SKEWIS   HANK
Living at 1836 Humboldt, Sebastopol, Sonoma, United States of America, 1980. Telephone number (707) 526 1185.

SKEWS   HANNAH
Born 1720. Married William Skews of St Gluvias. Children: Mary, Henry, William, Catherine and Richard. Buried 16 February 1777, aged 57 years at St Gluvias.

SKEWS   HANNAH
Daughter of William and Hannah Skews. Bpt St Gluvias 1 April 1746.
SKEWES   HANNAH
of Penzance. Married Charles Coleman of Penzance at St Gluvias 2
November 1762.
SKUES   HANNAH
Born 1801. Died Wheatenhurst 1897, aged 96 years.
SKEWES   HANNAH
Chart 36. Daughter of John and Loveday Skewes. Bpt Cury 4 July 1824.
Listed in 1851 Census Returns living at home with her widowed father at
Nantithet, Cury.
SKEWIS   HANNAH
Married 1852, Helston district.
SKEWES   HANNAH
Chart 36. Daughter of William and Priscilla Skewes. Born 1855, St
Erth. Worker in a tin mine in 1871 Census Returns.
SKUES   HANNAH
Born 1874. Died Colchester, Essex, 1940, aged 66 years.
SKEWIS   HANNAH BARCLAY SNEDDON
Born 1922, Blackridge, Scotland. Married John Critchley, 1942,
Shettleston, Scotland.
SKEWES   HANNAH LOUISE
Née Gurney. Born 1822. Married James Skewes, 15 February 1909 at
Baptist Chapel, Truro. Child: Cardine Skewes who married Lappin.
Died 25 February 1956 at Oak Cottage, Downley, High Wycombe.
Formerly of Devoran, Cornwall.
SKEWES   HANNIBAL
Chart 14. Son of Henry and Grace (née Lugg) Skewes, school master.
Born St Martin, Cornwall. Bpt Helston 8 November 1838. In 1851
Census Returns was living at Laddervean, St Keverne with his parents
and sisters Jane and Sarah Ann and brother Samuel Henry.
Emigrated to United States of America and sailed from Falmouth in
Charles Chalmer on 17 April 1958 for Yorkville, Wisconsin, via
Quebec, Montreal, Hamilton, Windsor, Detroit, Chicago and Union
Grove. He arrived at Yorkville 25 May 1858. Married Eliza Phillips (she
born 1841) 15 June 1865. Became a teacher in an eighth grade school
room. For many years was superintendent of Yorkville Methodist
Sunday School. Children: Edith Grace, Edward Henry, Manley
Thomas, Clinton Hannibal and Lillie Ann. Died 27 April 1912, aged 74
years.
SKEWES   HANNIBAL
Chart 14. Son of Anthony and Christian Skewes of Tresodden, Ruan
Major, farmer. Born 1854. Bpt Ruan Major 1 April 1855. Married
Frances Ann. . . . . . 1890, Helston. She died 16 July 1931, aged 76 years.
Lived at Chybarles, Ruan Major. Died 12 April 1928, aged 73 years.
SKEWES   HAROLD
Chart 50. Son of Thomas and Sarah Ann (née Lord) Skewes. Born 1890.
Australia. Killed in World War I — 6 April 1918 — aged 38 years.
SKEWES   HAROLD
Chart 25. Son of Edward and Eliza Skewes. Born 17 April 1892 at 54
Princess Street, Broughton, Manchester. Lived at 117 Yew Tree Road,
Manchester 14. Married Agnes Lally at All Saints Register Office,
Chorlton on Medlock, 1912. Children: Doris Mary (1914), Lily (1916),
Joseph Frederick (1918), John Harold (1919), Edna May (1923),
Barbara (1930). Died 20 May 1968, aged 76 years.
SKEWS   HAROLD
Lived at 9 President Street, Kalgoortie, Victoria, Australia in 1959.
SKEWES   HAROLD A.
Son of Sidney Hope and Anna (née Hosking) Skewes. Born Montreal,
Canada February 1897. Moved to New York, 1900.
SKEWES   HAROLD COURTIS
Chart 18. Son of John Courtis Skewes. Born 1893. Died 1893, Windsor,
aged 0.
SKEWES   HAROLD EDWIN
Chart 38. Son of Richard and Mary Jane (née Reynolds) Skewes. Born
21 May 1891 at Moonta, South Australia. Married Fanny Rita
Galliford, 1 March 1913. Lives at Haywood Rest Home, Caltowie,
South Australia, 5490.
SKUES   HAROLD FREDERICK CLAUDE
Chart 8. Son of George Henry Skues. Born 1882, Westminster. Married
Margaret Kuhlmire (21), daughter of Charles Henry Kuhlmire, tailor,
of 74 Haberdasher Street, East Road, Christchurch, Hoxton, London, 6
September 1903 at the Parish Church, Hoxton, in presence of Walter
Edward Skues.
Silversmith at 4 Citizens Buildings, City Road, Hoxton. Died 1950, aged
68 years.
SKEWES   HAROLD GEORGE
Lives at 27 Barkl Avenue, Padstow, Ravensby, 2211, New South Wales,
Australia with Barbara May Skewes. Driver.
SKEWES   HAROLD GRENVILLE
Son of Harold William and Alma Bernice (née Walker) Skewes. Born 23
March 1932, Australia. Married Constance Shirley Andrews. Children:
Peter (1960), Jennifer (1961) and David (1968). Lives at 5 Holmfield
Court, Warragul, 3820, Victoria, Australia. Manager of Gippsland and
Northern Company, stock agents. Also an auctioneer.

*Harry Stanley Skewes with his wife Beatrice Annie and
son Arthur*

SKEWES   HAROLD HERSCHELL
Son of William and Elizabeth Alberta Mary Jessop. Born 24 July 1905,
Challenge, Houghton, Michigan, USA. Married Gladys J. Batty 15
March 1935 at St George's, Utah. Children: Harold Herschell Jnr
(1936), Douglas George (1941), Joseph Sylvester (1945) and Sylvia Jane
(1949).
SKEWES   HAROLD HERSCHELL Jnr.
Son of Harold Herschell and Gladys (née Batty) Skewes. Born 30
November 1936, Tazewell, Virginia. Married Helen Diane Wendall 30
January 1960.
SKEWES   HAROLD JOHN
Chart 36. Son of Robert Northey Skewes of Dunedoo, New South
Wales, Australia.
SKEWES   HAROLD MELVILLE
Chart 38. Son of Horace Henry and Agatha Blanche Skewes. Born 24
June 1923, Broken Hill, New South Wales, Australia. Died 3 June 1924,
aged 1 year.
SKUES   HAROLD SEARLE
Born 1888. Was a corporal with Oxfordshire and Buckinghamshire
Light Infantry and killed in action in 1916.
SKEWES   HAROLD WARREN
Lived at Wangadary Street, Wangaratta, Victoria, Australia in 1959
with Lilian Joan Skewes. Orchardist. Now lives at Oxley, 3678.
SKEWES   HAROLD WILLIAM
Mother's name Eva Skewes. Born 10 April 1901. Married Alma Bernice
Walker at Warragul, Australia. Children: Patricia (1931), Harold
Grenville (1932) and Judith (1946). Auctioneer. Died 1946, aged 45
years. Lived at 103 Victoria Street, Warragul, Victoria, Australia.
SKEWES   HARRIET
Chart 10. Née Francis. Born 1819. Married John Skewes 29 September
1836, Kea. Children: Philippa, John Henry and Matthew. Lived at
Kerley, Kea. Buried Baldhu 5 October 1899, aged 80 years.
SKEWES   HARRIET
Chart 28. Daughter of Richard and Mary Skewes of Nancevellan
Common, Kea. Bpt Kea 12 January 1823.
SKEWES   HARRIET
Chart 11. Née Hodge. Born 1823, Landewednack. Married Henry
Skewes at Cury 24 June 1845. Moved to Landewednack after marriage.
Henry was a wheelwright — she a hotel keeper (Three Tuns). Children:
James Henry, John, William, Mary Ann Mander and Thomas Henry.
Died 1888, aged 65 years.
SKUES   HARRIET
Born 1838. Died 1907, Lambeth, aged 69 years.
SKEWES   HARRIET
Married Philemon Betty, 16 May 1842 at Madron.

SKEWS HARRIET
Born 1848. Died Gravesend, 1908, aged 60 years.

SKEWS HARRIET
Married 1851, Neath.

SKEWIS HARRIET
Chart 49. Wife of William Skewis of Totnes. Born 1853. Children: Elizabeth Ann (1876), William Henry (1877), George (1879), Jane (1881) and Harriet (1883). Died Totnes, 1921, aged 68 years.

SKEWIS HARRIET
Chart 2. Daughter of Edward and Kittie Skewis of Shullsburg, Wisconsin, USA. Born 1859.

SKEWS HARRIET
Born 1866, Liskeard. Died 1868, aged 1 year.

SKEWS HARRIET
Born 1876, Neath.

SKEWS HARRIET
Married 1881, Bethnal Green.

SKEWIS HARRIET
Chart 49. Born 1883, Totnes. Daughter of William and Harriet Skewis. Died 1884, aged 0.

SKEWS HARRIET ANN
Born 1861. Died Liskeard 1920, aged 59 years.

SKEWES HARRIET JANE
Born 1872, Helston. Died 1873, aged 1 year.

SKEWS HARRIET MARY
Born 1860, Marylebone, London.

SKEWES HARRY
Born Redruth January, 1866. Emigrated to New York 1887. Married Mary..... 1888 in New York. Children: Edgar (1890), Mattie (1893), Leonard (1896) and Viola (1897). In 1900 lived at North Hempstead, New York.

SKEWS HARRY
Chart 15. Son of Peter and Elizabeth Skews of Pensilva, Liskeard, miner. Bpt St Ive 19 January 1871.

SKEWS HARRY
Chart 15. Son of John and Isabella Skews of Altarnun. Bpt Altarnun Parish Church 23 October 1873.

SKEWES HARRY
Born 1898. See HENRY SKEWES born 1898.

SKEWS HARRY
Chart 15. Son of Samuel Gregory and Harriet Ann Skews of Pensilva. Bpt St Ive 21 April 1903. (Born 10 January 1900.) Died 1973, aged 73 years in Plymouth.

SKUES HARRY
Chart 8. Son of Walter Edward Skues. Mother's maiden name Bond. Born 1915, Shoreditch. Died 1915, aged 0.

SKEWES HARRY
Chart 50. Son of Stephen James and Ethel (née Pollard) Skewes. Born 12 February 1916. Attended East End and Trewirgie schools, Redruth, and later undertook professional training (for social work) at the University of Liverpool and the London School of Economics.
Left Redruth 1940, after spending his early working days in the clothing trade, and as a result of being a conscientious objector during the 1939-1945 war, joined the Friends' Ambulance Unit and engaged in relief work in London, the Middle East and Greece.
Harry Skewes was engaged in professional social work in London, involved in child care, prison welfare and with the aged and handicapped, before assuming administrative roles in two Social Services Departments.
He married Josephine Rousse-Short in Southwark on 16 March 1974. Whilst in London he had a lengthy association in a voluntary capacity with the Bede House Association.
Returned to Cornwall in 1976 on partial retirement and spent the last five years in hospital social work.
Lives at "Boskewys", Burthallan Lane, St Ives, Cornwall, TR26 3AA. Tel no: 0736 797896.

SKEWS HARRY
Chart 15. Son of Harry and Hilda (née Jane) Skews. Born 4 October 1917, Pensilva, Liskeard, Cornwall. As a boy raced pigeons with his father. Won a trophy in 1927. With his four brothers played football for Pensilva who were junior champions for the seasons 1951/1952 and 1952/1953.
Self-employed mason.
During the Second World War saw service in Scotland, North Africa, Italy and Austria between 1941 and 1946. Was demobbed in July, 1946 with rank of Company Sergeant Major (Royal Engineers).
Married Jean Jamieson Adam at Logie Church, Stirling, Scotland 26 April 1943. One son: Derek Thomas Skews (1951).
Was secretary of Pensilva Football Club 1974-1975. Chairman of Pensilva Village Hall since 1976. Is a Parish Councillor for St Ive. Vice Chairman from May 1979.
Lives at Mount View, Quarry Road, Pensilva, Liskeard, Cornwall. Tel no: 0579 62733.

SKEWES HARRY
Chart 38. Son of Horace Henry and Agatha Blanche Skewes. Born 16 July 1918, Broken Hill, South Australia. Died 16 July 1918, infant.

SKEWES HARRY
Illegitimate son of Edith Skewes, domestic servant. Born at Goldsithney, Perranuthnoe, Penzance, 5 December 1922. Lived at 2 South Terrace, Penzance.
Was a boatswain with Isles of Scilly Steamship Company for 21 years aboard *Scillonian* and *Queen of the Isles*. He had the annual task of painting, scraping, polishing and cleaning the 515 ton *Queen of the Isles*.
In January 1969 Harry Skewes said "The ship has to be checked from bow to stern. Every piece of equipment from the lifeboats to the winches must be in perfect order."
He was well-known and popular with island visitors and residents. He was a bachelor, and had no close relatives other than a half-sister Mrs Iris Harvey. Harry Skewes was admitted to St Mary's Hospital 28 May 1975 and died there three days later, aged 53 years.
It was believed he joined the Royal Navy as a boy seaman, and later served with the Steamship Company, taking his radio officers' certificate.
He was interred in St Mary's Churchyard 3 June 1975. The church was packed with mourners when the funeral was held. Members of the islands R.A.O.B. Lodge were bearers.

SKEWS HARRY
Lived at Golla, Callestick, Perranzabuloe in 1932 with Maude Mary, James Henry and Lilian Skewes.

SKEWS HARRY
Chart 31. Mother's maiden name Jane. Born 1942, Liskeard.

SKEWES HARRY
Chart 50. Son of Jack and Betony Skewes. Born 10 May 1949. Lived at 6 Cardigan Street, Stockton, Now South Wales, 2295, Australia. Died 17 January 1966, aged 16 years.

SKEWES HARRY BLAIN
Chart 2. Son of Arthur Wayne and Lorene (née Parker) Skewes of Texas, USA. Born 25 April 1935 at Pampa, Texas. Married Elizabeth Ann Laycock, 29 March 1959 at Baytown, Texas, USA. Children: Ellen Kay (1961) and Carol Ann (1964).

SKEWS HARRY HAROLD
Lives at 9 President Street, Kalgoorlie, 6430, Western Australia. Labourer.

SKEWES HARRY JAMES
Lived on Farm 1765, Whitton, Leeton, New South Wales, Australia in 1959 with Margaret Jane Skewes. Labourer.

SKEWES HARRY OSWALD
Chart 12. Son of James Henry & Mary Jane Skewes of Central America, carpenter. Born December 1865. Bpt Cury 24 October 1867. Married Emily Ann Taylor, 1892. Lived at Moor Street, Camborne 1923 and later College Row, Camborne. Emily Ann Taylor was daughter of George Taylor of Rose Cottages, Camborne. Marriage took place 12 November 1892. Tinsmith and plumber. Was a member of "B" Company Volunteers (forerunner of the Territorial Army), volunteer member of the Fire Brigade, a member of the Loyal Basset Lodge of Oddfellows, a bell ringer at Camborne Church; helped produce one of the first steam motor cars in Britain; with J.S.V. Bickford invented the forerunner of the Primus Stove and sold patent to Sweden. Represented Camborne Rugby Club on the county selection committee; also represented Cornwall on the national selection committee. Children: James Henry Oswald, Doris Muriel, George Hennessy, Jack Pattison and Veronica Mary. Died at St Michael's Hospital, Hayle 18 September 1940, aged 74 years. Emily Ann died October 1940, aged 69 years.

SKEWES HARRY STANLEY
Chart 12. Son of John Wesley Skewes of Roseville, Mawgan, Cornwall. Born 23 December 1893. Was a master market gardener. Twice married: 1) to Beatrice Annie Rosevear (29) of Mawgan Cross, Mawgan, daughter of W. Rosevear, labourer at Helston Methodist Church 12 January 1921. One son William Arthur Skewes, schoolmaster. 2) Rose May Hockin (53), spinster, Ministry of Mines clerk of 6 Holgrove Road, Bromley, Kent and daughter of Thomas Hockin, deceased, draper at Helston Methodist Church 9 February 1946, in presence of William Arthur Skewes.
Was a postman for sixteen years. Lived at Garras, Mawgan in Meneage. Died 21 August 1950 at Helston and District Cottage Hospital, aged 57 years.

SKEWS HARVEY
Chart 6. Son of William and Alice J. Skews of Mineral Point, Wisconsin, USA. Born 19 July 1883. Died 7 September 1898, aged 15 years.

SKEWES HARVEY HILTON
Chart 36. Son of Cuthbert George and Violet (née Ferris) Skewes. Born 4 July 1927, Uralla, New South Wales, Australia. Married Jean Francis, 27 November 1951. Issue: three daughters. Now divorced. Lives at 1/Lot, 51 O'Donnell Drive, Figtree, New South Wales, 2525, Australia.

SKEWS HARVEY THOMAS
Chart 6. Son of John and Clara Jeanette (née Babcock) Skews. Born 25 April 1904, Mineral Point, Wisconsin, USA. Married Bernice Shackley 1 September 1932 at Freepoint, Illinois, USA. Children: Marilyn (1933), Shirley (1935) and Dena (1942).

Harvey Thomas Skews

Carpenter. Built his own house at 220N Iowa, Mineral Point, Wisconsin, 53565, USA — current address.

SKEWS HAYLEY LISA
Chart 10. Daughter of Peter B. Skews. Mother's maiden name Blight. Born 1970, St Austell.

SKUCE HAZEL
Daughter of Stewart Tennyson and Gertrude (née Roe) Skuce. Born 1922, Australia.

SKEWS HAZEL CATHERINE
Lived at 5 Paget Street, Oakleigh, Victoria, Australia in 1959. Clerk. Now lives at 6/892 Burke Road, Canterbury, 3126, Victoria, Australia.

SKEWS HAZEL NETTA
Lives at 94 Wingara Avenue, Keilor East, 3033, Victoria, Australia.

SKEWS HEATHER J.
Mother's maiden name King. Born 1959, Thurrock. Daughter of William Skews.

SKEWES HEATHER LEONE
Lived at Carnie Station, Blackall, Kennedy, Queensland, Australia in 1959 with John Locke Skewes, Station Bailiff. Now lives at Duthie Park, via Blackall with John Locke Skewes, Janette Lydia Skewes and Peter William Skewes.

SKEWES HEATHER MARIAN
Lives at 4 Morris Street, Kidman Park, 5025, South Australia with Robert James Skewes, teacher.

SKEWES HECTOR
Chart 10. Mexican. Son of Salvador and Carmen (Ramirez) Skewes. Born 11 May 1956, Mexico. Married Georgina Cardoso. Son: Eric Skewes (1974).

SKEWES HEDLEY JAMES
Born 1878, Redruth. Died 1878, aged 0.

SKUSE HEIDI
Daughter of Peter Robin and Frances (née Mace Hardyman) Skuse. Born 3 November 1979. Lives at 46 Beverley Road, Whytleafe, CR3 ODX, Surrey.

SKEWIS HELEN
Born 1839. Died 1900, Dennistoun, Scotland, aged 61 years.

SKEWIS HELEN
Born 1872, Glasgow. Had an illegitimate son William Benson Skewis at Camalchie, 1898. Married 1900, at Camalchie, Scotland.

SKEWIS HELEN
Born 1869. Died Shettleston, Scotland, 1924, aged 55 years.

SKEWIS HELEN
Chart 50. Illegitimate daughter of James Skewis (iron turner) and Helen Jamieson. Born at 263 Caledonia Road, Glasgow, 23 February 1872. James lived at 130 Garngad Road, Glasgow.

SKUES HELEN
Daughter of John and Margaret Ferrier, formerly Webster. Born 1807. Married Thomas Skues, seaman and merchant sailor. In 1851 Census Returns was a widow, aged 46 years, born Foffash Craig, Scotland, living at Virginia Street, East Aberdeen. Daughters: Violetta who married Howe and Margaret born 1826 (unmarried in 1851), who became a cotton spinner. Helen had a grandson John Booth (born 1847). She died at 3 Robertson Street, Dundee, 27 January 1874, aged 67 years. Pauper.

SKEWES HELEN
Daughter of Robert Nisbett. Born 1863. Married William Henry Skewes 1882. Australia. Issue: 2 sons and 3 daughters. Died 16 November 1909, aged 46 years. Buried Port Pirie Cemetery, South Australia.

SKEWS HELEN
Chart 41. Née Ackroyd. Married David Skews, 1964 in Staincross, Barnsley. Child: Emma Jane (1975). Lives at 11 Woodlands View, Wombwell, Barnsley, South Yorkshire. Tel No: Barnsley 753530.

SKEWIS HELEN
Lives at 17 Rhyde Street, Toowoomba, 4350, Queensland, Australia, with Wilfred Roy Skewis.

SKEWIS HELEN ANDREW
Born 1900. Died 1970, Airdrie, Scotland, aged 70 years.

SKEWES HELEN ANN
Chart 14. Daughter of Charles Skewes of America. Married Clarence Sorenson.

SKEWES HELEN BEATRICE
Chart 14. Daughter of Manley and Eva Skewes of America. Died 1915.

SKEWS HELEN BELINDA
Chart 11. Daughter of Thomas John and Laura B. Skewes of America. Born 16 August 1892.

SKEWS HELEN DOROTHY
Chart 17. Daughter of Brian A.E. Skews. Mother's maiden name Newby. Born 1969, Enfield.

SKEWES HELEN ELIZABETH
Chart 2. Daughter of Archibald William and Gwendoline (née Jones) Skewes. Born 4 September 1949, Victoria, Australia. Married John Ormond Butler at North Essendon. Children: 2 daughters and 1 son. Lives at 4 Allawah Court, South Vermont, 3133, Victoria, Australia.

SKEWES HELEN ELIZABETH
Chart 36. Daughter of Geoffrey and Dorothy May (née Chapman) Skewes. Born 24 March 1960. Lives at 35 Jean Street, Grange, 4051, Queensland, Australia.

SKEWS HELEN GALE
Lives at 8 Leham Avenue, Oakleigh South, 3167, Victoria, Australia with Richard Anthony Skews, engineer. Scientist.

SKEWES HELEN H.
Widow of Richard J. Skewes of Seattle, Washington, USA. In 1970 lived at 2328 Delamere Drive East, Seattle, Washington, United States of America.

SKEWES HELEN JOYCE
Chart 38. Daughter of Cyril George and Dorothy Melva (née James) Skewes. Born 25 October 1949, South Australia. Married 1) Kim Polgreen 1966. Issue: 1 daughter. Divorced 1972. 2) John Williams at Port Pirie 22 November 1973. Issue: 2 daughters.

SKUSE HELEN KATHLEEN
Daughter of Eric Albert and Winifred Kathleen (née Palmer) Skuse. Born 20 August 1947, Cheam, Surrey. Emigrated with parents to Victoria, Australia, 1959. Lives at North Fitzroy, Melbourne, Australia.

SKEWES HELEN MARGARET
Lives at Ouyen Highway, Underbool, 3509, Victoria, Australia with James Calvin Skewes. Teacher.

SKEWES HELEN MARGARET
Chart 50. Daughter of David Buick and Irene Margarert (née Murphy) Skewes. Born 14 November 1942, Adelaide, South Australia. Married Robert J. Thomas 13 December 1968, Ballarat, Victoria, Australia. Issue: 3 sons. Lives at 197 Colham Road, Kew, Melbourne, 3101, Victoria, Australia.

SKUES HELEN MARY
Born 24 December 1946. Died 1973, aged 27 years, Dover, Kent.

SKEWES HELEN NANCY
Chart 2. Daughter of William Henry and Clara Bertha (née Ahlvers) Skews. Born 9 January 1939, United States of America. Married James Roberts. Issue: 1 son and 4 daughters.

SKEWES HELEN R.
Wife of James M. Skewes of Northern Traffic Service, 8040 39th Avenue NE, Seattle, Washington, USA.

SKEWES HELEN ROBERTA
Chart 14. Née Horr. Born 10 January 1931. Married Arthur Russell Skewes, D.V.M., 30 June 1951.
Children: Russell Frank, Martha Rene, Melinda Irene, Rodrick Arthur and Roberta Glee. Lives at 157 Swigert Avenue, Lexington, Kentucky, 40505, United States of America.

SKEWIS HELEN THOMASINE
Born 1871. Married William Bawden Skewis in Tavistock, 1886 (who died 14 June 1935). After his death returned to West Cornwall and lived

at 4 Regence Terrace, Penzance. Died 13 April 1939, aged 68 years.

SKEWES HENRIETTA
Born 1826. Lived at Newham Street, Kenwyn. Buried Kenwyn 20 July 1827, aged 9 months.

SKEWES HENRIETTA
Chart 30. Bpt Kea 5 November 1826. Daughter of Thomas and Jane Skewes, mason (then living in St Clement). Dressmaker. Married William Henry Crewes of Kenwyn Street; blacksmith (son of James Crewes, shoemaker) at Kenwyn Parish Church 17 December 1851 in presence of Philippa Jane Skewes and Thomas Skewes.

SKEWES HENRIETTA
Chart 33. Daughter of Daniel & Elizabeth Skewes. Born 1863, Newton Abbot. Married in 1886, Totnes, Devon.

SKEWES HENRIETTA
Chart 30. Daughter of William and Blanche Skewes; painter of St Dominic Street, Truro. Born 11 September 1890. Bpt St Paul's 5 August 1891. Married Frederick James West (33) of Devon, carpenter, son of David West, carpenter, at St George's, Truro 31 December 1921 in presence of Marion Skewes and William Skewes.

SKUES HENRIETTA
Lived at 37 Vale Street, St Kilda, Melbourne, Victoria, Australia in 1931.

SKEWES HENRIETTA CATALINA
Chart 10. Daughter of Captain John Thompson Richards. Born 31 December 1889. Married Rev. Herbert John Skewes, St Paul's Church, Chacewater. Child: Ernestine Mary (1911). Lived at Salem House, Chacewater (1922) and later at Crowan Vicarage. Died 2 April 1942, aged 52 years.

SKEWES HENRIETTA MARIA
Born 1854, Truro. Buried St Mary's, Truro 17 February 1857, aged 2 years.

SKEWES HENRIETTA MARIA
Chart 30. Daughter of John Beer and Mary Brown Skewes; cabinet maker of Kenwyn Street, Truro. Born 1860 at St Clement. Married in West Ham, 1884.

SCUES HENRY
Chart 2. Son of William and Margaret Scues. Bpt Camborne 21 July 1672. Married Mary .... 9 April 1705. Children: Henry, Margaret, Mary, John and William. Died 21 February 1744, aged 72 years.

SCUES HENRY
Chart 2. Son of Henry and Mary Scues. Bpt Camborne 2 June 1707. Children: James, Henry, John, Margaret, William and Absalom.

SKUES HENRY
Son of Richard Skues. Bpt Kenwyn 14 January 1716.

SKEWES HENRY
Chart 14. Married Judith Walters at Constantine Parish Church 28 October 1718. Children: Anne, Edward, Thomas, Anthony, George and Henry (twins), Jane and Judith.

SKEWES HENRY
Chart 14. Twin to George Skewes. Son of Henry and Judith Skewes. Bpt Cury 6 September 1727. Buried Cury 5 April 1729, aged 1½ years.

SKEWES HENRY
Buried Cury 26 October 1733.

SKEWES HENRY
Married Constance Paul at Crowan 9 July 1737.

SKEWIS HENRY
Chart 2. Son of Henry Skewis. Bpt Camborne 24 June 1739. Was a yeoman at Killivoase. Died 7 February 1814, aged 75 years. W(CRO) proved 17 May 1814.

SKEWES HENRY
of Kea. Married Margery Behenna of Kea at Kenwyn 20 December 1740.

SKEWES HENRY
Chart 14. Born 1749. Farmer of Tresodden, Ruan Major. Twice married 1) .... 2) Jane Retallack around 1800. Children: Anthony, Samuel, Edward, Henry, Thomas, Jane, Margaret, John, Mary and Eleanor. Died November 1831 after a long lingering illness, aged 82 years. W(CRO) proved 19 December 1831. Effects under £200.

SKEWS HENRY
Son of Henry Skews. Bpt Kea 8 July 1749. Was parish clerk of Kea Church upwards of 40 years. Died 18 February 1833, aged 84 years.

SKEWES HENRY
Son of William and Hannah Skewes of St Gluvias. Bpt St Gluvias 28 October 1750. Buried St Gluvias 20 March 1774, aged 24 years.

SCUIS HENRY
Chart 2. Son of William and Mary Scuis. Bpt Camborne 12 April 1752.

SKEWES HENRY
Chart 35. Married Elizabeth ...... Lived in Cury. Child: Welmot Skewes.

SKEWES HENRY
Son of Edward and Margaret Skewes. Bpt Cury 2 December 1753.

SKEWIS HENRY
Chart 25. Son of Thomas and Esther Skewis. Bpt St Keverne 19 December 1758. Died 28 December 1758; infant.

SKEWIS HENRY
Buried Cury 25 January 1760.

SKEWES HENRY
Born 1762. Lived at Penponds, Camborne. Buried Camborne 20 December 1837, aged 75 years.

SKEWIS HENRY
Chart 25. Son of Thomas and Esther Skewis. Bpt St Keverne 1 January 1764.

SCUES HENRY
Chart 2. Son of James and Charity Scues. Bpt 5 May 1765, Camborne Parish Church.

SKEWES HENRY
Son of Henry Skewes. Bpt Camborne 8 April 1772. Born 1771. Yeoman at Gwinear. Married Margaret Phillips 11 August 1792, Gwinear. Lived at Roseworthy, Gwinear. At least five children including Mary (1794), Elizabeth (1792), Stephen (1798) and Lavinia. One daughter married in Camborne to Edward Tippett. Latterly lived in Camborne. Died at the house of Edward Tippett October 1849, aged 78 years.

SKEWES HENRY
Died Camborne 2 May 1774.

SKEWES HENRY
Buried Camborne 18 May 1776.

SKEWES HENRRY
Chart 28. Married Mary Jolly at Kenwyn 4 November 1776. Children: Henry (1784) and Richard (1786).

SKEWES HENRY
Chart 2. Son of Richard and Alice Skewes. Bpt Camborne 21 June 1778. Married Grace Tremayne at Constantine Parish Church 9 March 1806. Lived at Bosawsack, Constantine. Children: Mary, William, Grace, Alice, Elizabeth, Henry, Josiah, Fanny, Caroline and Eliza. Died 3 June 1844, aged 66 years. Will CRO, 1844. Effects under £200. Buried Constantine 5 June.

SKEWES HENRY
Son of Henry Skewes. Bpt Kea 8 July 1779.

SKEWES HENRY
Chart 25. Son of Thomas and Eleanor Skewes. Bpt St Keverne 15 June 1777. Buried St Keverne 28 December 1777; infant.

SKUES HENRY
Born 1780. Bpt Camborne 21 October 1781. Buried Camborne 19 May 1824, aged 44 years. Lived at Carlean, Camborne.

SKEWES HENRY
Chart 2. Son of John and Philippa Skewis. Bpt Camborne 21 October 1781.

SKEWES HENRY
Chart 28. Son of Henry and Mary Skewes. Bpt Kenwyn 15 August 1784.

SKEWES HENRY
Married Jane Pascoe at St Keverne 1 January 1787. She died 26 December 1792.

SKEWES HENRY
Died 17 June 1791, aged 77 years. Buried in Old Kea Churchyard.

SKUES HENRY
Son of Absalom and Elizabeth Skues. Bpt Crowan 7 August 1791. (Born 18 June 1791.)

SKEWES HENRY
Chart 30. Married Catherine Wasley of Kea at Kenwyn Parish Church 22 May 1793. Children: Mary Jolly, Ebenezer John, Thomas and Henry.

SKEWES HENRY
of St Keverne. Married Jane ....
Children: Margaret (1793) and Edward (1795).

SKEWES HENRY
Chart 14. Son of Henry and Jane Skewes. Born 23 October 1801. Bpt Ruan Major 27 December 1801. Married Grace Lugg at Ruan Major Church 28 July 1829 in presence of Edward Skewes. Was clerk to Sir R.R. Vyvyan's Stewards Office, Trelowarren. Later became a school master. Children: Edward, Jane L., James Lugg, Margaret Ann, Sarah, Samuel Henry and Hannibal.
Died 16 February 1878, aged 76 years.

SKEWES HENRY
Married Ann Blamey at Gwennap 7 July 1801.

SKEWES HENRY
Chart 30. Son of Henry and Catherine Skewes. Bpt Kea 14 November 1802. Buried Kenwyn 22 October 1826, aged 24 years.

SKEWES HENRY
Born 1803. Buried Gwennap 2 November 1869, aged 66 years.

SKEWES HENRY
Married Grace Tremayne by special licence 9 March 1806 at Constantine.

SKEWES HENRY
Son of Absalom and Elizabeth Skewes. Buried Camborne 14 October 1808.

SKEWES HENRY
Chart 36. Bpt Cury 24 May 1812. Son of William and Alice Skewes of Treloskan, Cury. Died Nantithet, Cury 29 November 1850, aged 38 years.

Henry Skewes, 1827-1908

SKUES　HENRY
Chart 2. Son of William and Mary Skewis. Bpt Camborne 31 October 1812. Married Grace Martin 2 June 1832 at Camborne Parish Church in presence of Mary Skewes. Lived at Penponds. Was a mine captain. In 1851 Census Returns refers to his wife as Hannah — 1861 Anna. A member of the Wesleyan Society for 50 years and President of the Wall Band of Hope for 23 years. Children: William Henry, Richard Martin, Elizabeth, Stephen, Philip, Samuel, Mary, Henry, Edward, Sarah Ann and Annie. Died 11 October 1881 in Gwinear, aged 69 years. A trusted servant of Messrs Vivians for 40 years.

SKEWES　HENRY
Illegitimate son of Blanch Skewes of Treloskan, Cury. Bpt Cury 4 April 1817.

SKEWES　HENRY
Chart 2. Son of Henry and Grace Skewes of Bosawsack, Constantine. Born 10 October 1818. Called "Harry". Bpt Constantine 5 December 1818. Married Avis Bath, daughter of Malachi Bath (she born 8 February 1824; died 1865, Bodmin) at St Stithians, Redruth 26 July 1845. Lived at Angarrack, Phillack. Was a farmer and later police officer. Children: Josiah (1847), William Henry (1846), James (1849) and Alfred (1852). Died 4 April 1852, aged 34 years, at Angarrack. Buried in Gwinear.

SKEWES　HENRY
Chart 12. Son of James and Elizabeth Skewes of Cury; labourer. Bpt Cury 5 July 1818. Married Harriet Hodge, 24 June 1845 at Cury. Was a carpenter and wheelwright. Harriet was a hotel keeper of "the Three Tuns Hotel", Landewednack. Children: James Henry, John, William, Mary Ann Mander and Thomas Henry.

SKEWIS　HENRY
Chart 2. Son of John and Philippa Skewes. Bpt Camborne 21 October Parish Church 27 November 1819. Copper miner. Married Elizabeth Bennetts at Breage Parish Church 15 September 1847. Lived at Beacon Hill, Camborne in 1861. Moved to Brenton's Cottages, Calstock in 1860's. Moved to Luxborough, West Somerset from 1867 and lived there until 1883. Became mine captain of Brendon Hills iron ore mine and built the engine house in 1880. When this closed he became manager of West Somerset Mineral Railway until he retired. He died of a heart attack in October, 1889 at Watchet, Somerset, aged 69 years. Child: Edwin (1853).
His wife Elizabeth (born 1820) died 1887, aged 67 years.

SKEWIS　HENRY
Born 1819. Died 1866, aged 47 years in Helston district.

SKEWES　HENRY
Chart 36. Son of William and Christian Skewes. Born 1827. Married Ann Gribble at Mawnan Parish Church 24 December 1850, in presence of Grace Skewes. She was daughter of William Gribble. Henry Skewes was a gold miner who went out to Ballarat, Australia where Ann died 16 May 1863, aged 36 years.
Children: Mary, Jack and William.
Married again (wife's name Barbara). Children included Simon (1864). Died 1908, aged 81 years. Buried in Watcham Cemetery, Victoria, Australia alongside his second wife (she died 1905).

SKEWES　HENRY
Married Ann Aunger at Gwennap 7 September 1828.

SKEWIS　HENRY
Chart 2. Son of Edward and Mary Skewes. Born 17 September 1831. Bpt Camborne Wesleyan/Methodist Chapel, 24 November 1833. Emigrated to Wisconsin, USA. Married Mary ..... Died 25 February 1859, aged 28 years. Mary died 16 October 1860, aged 26 years. Buried in Shullsburg Cemetery.

SKUES　HENRY
Son of Stephen and Margaret Skues. Bpt Camborne 26 November 1831.

SKEWES　HENRY
Innkeeper. In April 1832 John Williams was charged with stealing five shillings from Henry Skewes. He was found guilty and given six months imprisonment and hard labour.

SKEWES　HENRY
Chart 14. Son of John and Jane Skewes. Bpt Grade 30 June 1834. Emigrated to Wisconsin, USA, travelling out from England to Panama to San Francisco on 19 April 1851, eventually arriving at Yorkville, Wisconsin. Served with "G" Company, 2nd Wisconsin Cavalry as a sergeant during American Civil War. Twice married. 1) Nellie Matthews. Child: Edwin and 2) K. Oehls. Children: George Stanley and Lila.

SKEWIS　HENRY
Son of James and Ann Skewis of Kenwyn. Bpt St Mary's Truro 8 March 1835. Shoemaker.

SKEWES　HENRY
Son of James and Nancy Skewes of Kenwyn, shoemaker. Bpt St Mary's, Truro, 10 January 1836.
Copper miner. Emigrated to Australia aboard *Isle of Thanet*, which arrived in Port Adelaide, 6 July 1854.

SKEWES　HENRY
of Penzance. Married Miss Courtis at St Hilary 10 August 1838.

SKEWIS　HENRY
Chart 36. Born 1841. Bpt St Hilary 16 January 1842. Son of Henry and Ann (née Gribble) Skewes, lead miner. Later moved to St Pinnock, and by 1862 had emigrated to Australia with his parents. Died 1908?

SKEWES　HENRY
Chart 2. Son of James Skewes, farmer. Married Ann Bawden, dressmaker of Pengiggan, daughter of William Bawden, mine agent at Camborne Parish Church 27 October 1842. Henry, who was a miner, had a brother William who married Peggy Bawden (sister) at Camborne Parish Church 29 March 1847.

SKEWES　HENRY
Died 1844, Falmouth.

SKEWIS　HENRY
Married 1845, Redruth.

SKEWES　HENRY
Chart 14. Son of Anthony and Christian Skewes, farmer. Bpt Ruan Major 31 May 1845. In 1871 was living at Tresodden, Ruan Major.

SKEWES　HENRY
of the New Inn, Truro. His wife Margaret Skewes died 8 December 1847, aged 78 years.

SKEWES　HENRY
Chart 36. Born 1848. Lived in Camborne. Died 21 February 1922, aged 74 years.

SKEWIS　HENRY
Born 1849, Redruth.

SKEWIS　HENRY
Married 1849, Redruth.

SKUES　HENRY
Chart 2. Son of Henry and Grace Skues. Born 1849. Became Rev. and Pastor of Evanston Rocky Mountains, Utah Territory, USA. Married Martha M. Welborn of Carlton Institute, Missouri, 26 August 1875.

SKEWES　HENRY
Born 1854, Helston.

SKEWES　HENRY
Died 1856, Helston.

SKEWES　HENRY
Chart 36. Son of Edward and Julia Skewes of Cury. Born 31 January 1857. Bpt Cury 5 March 1857. Lived at Bonython House, Cury. In 1871 Census Returns living with his parents and family at Nantithet. Died 12 September 1926, aged 69 years. Buried in Cury Churchyard.

SKEWIS　HENRY
Born 1858, Penzance.

SKEWIS　HENRY
Chart 10. Son of Digory and Fanny Skewes of Trevenner, Marazion. Born 25 January 1867. Married Elizabeth Richards 28 April 1891. Emigrated to USA (Martinez, California) with his wife and brother John Joseph (who married Elizabeth Richards's sister, Catherine Mary). Children: John Henry and Frederick Charles. Died 18 June 1945, aged

Henry and Elizabeth Skewes of Hamilton, Ontario, Canada

78 years. Elizabeth died 22 March 1947.

SKEWES   HENRY
Chart 2. Born 1868. Farmer at Mabe. Twice married. 1) Ada Eliza Courage, daughter of William James Courage, farmer at Constantine 16 September 1896 (she died 28 February 1919, aged 47 years). 2) Maude Annie Matthews in Falmouth, 1922. Lived at Packsaddle, Mabe. One son Lional James. Retired to 1 Penmere Terrace, Falmouth where he died 26 November 1939, aged 71 years. Buried Falmouth Cemetery. Cousins H. Knowles and H. Bone.

SKEWS   HENRY
Chart 15. Son of John and Isabella Skews of Trewint, Altarnun. Bpt Altarnun 18 April 1870. Died 1871, aged 1 year.

SKEWES   HENRY
Lived at 4810 Morris, Morris County, USA. Left a will in America, 1870.

SKUES   HENRY
Married 1871 in Cricklade.

SKEWS   HENRY
Born 1872 Liskeard. Died 1872, aged 0.

SKEWS   HENRY
Cattle dealer living in Kooringa, South Australia in 1872. Later became a farmer at Booboorowie, South Australia.

SKEWES   HENRY
Chart 36. Son of William and Priscilla Skewes of Carnarthen, Illogan, Born 1872. Bpt Illogan Parish Church 25 September 1872. Married Elizabeth Johanna Ham (she born 1874) at Redruth Register Office 25 November 1893. Henry was a tin miner. Children: Edward and William Henry.

SKEWES   HENRY
Chart 50. Son of Samuel and Mary (née Sanders) Skewes. Born 19 August 1873, Helston. Married Emily Moyle, 1897, Redruth. Emigrated to South Africa. One son: Stanley (1899). Died 29 September 1902, aged 29 years. Emily died 22 January 1954.

SKEWES   HENRY
Born 1873, Helston.

SKEWES   HENRY
Married 1876, Redruth.

SKEWES   HENRY
Chart 2. Son of Josiah and Janet Muir (née McPhee) Skewes. Born 19 February 1884, Bowenvale, Victoria, Australia. Married Annie May Cross (she born 4 May 1886). Children: Henry Josiah (1910), Annie Ellen (1912), Archibald William (1916), Leila Mavis (1918) and Ronald George (1920).

SKEWIS   HENRY
Lived at Lamin, Gwinear 1885/1886.

SKEWES   HENRY
Lived at Adelaide Street, Camborne, 1885/1906.

SKEWES   HENRY
Chart 2. Mexican. Son of Henry and Hortencia (née Castillo) Skewes. Born Real del Monte, Mexico 17 June 1973. Died 24 June 1973, aged 7 days.

SKEWS   HENRY
Married 1897, Holyhead.

SKEWES   HENRY
Chart 25. Son of Frederick and Alice (née Taylor) Skewes. Born 1898, Salford. Married Sarah Ellen Barrett (26), daughter of Harry Barrett, electrician, of 5 Queens Court, Orange Street, Halifax at St James Church, Halifax, 14 May 1921. Child: Edna (1922). Died 1957, aged 59 years in Halifax.

SKUSE   HENRY
Son of Herbert Henry and Ada (née Cocks) Skuse. Born 1907. Married Margery Bishop. Issue: one daughter Anne (1935). Died 1936, aged 29 years.

SKUES   HENRY
Confectioner at 24 Oakley Street, Lambeth, SE London. Listed in 1908 London Street Directory.

SKEWS   HENRY
Lived at Derby Crescent, Caulfield, East Victoria, Australia in 1913. Railway guard.

SKEWES   HENRY
Married Maud A. Matthews, Falmouth, 1922.

SKEWES   HENRY
Mexican. Chart 10. Son of Salvador and Carmen (née Ramirez) Skewes. Born 6 December 1940. Married Lourdes Escudero. Children: Carolo (1973), Eva (1975) and Joseph (1979). Lives in Real del Monte, Mexico.

SKEWS   HENRY BLEWETT
Son of William and Nancy Skewes. Bpt St Ewe 18 November 1810. Labourer at Levaston Downs, St Ewe. Bachelor. Died 1 January 1847, aged 37 years. A(SH) £44.

SKEWES   HENRY CHARLES
Son of James and Ann Skewes of St Mary's, Truro. Bpt St Mary's 24 November 1843. Buried Kenwyn 3 February 1844.

SKUES   HENRY ERNEST
Born 1873, Lambeth. Died 1947, aged 74 years in Lambeth.

SKEWES   HENRY ERNEST
Chart 2. Son of William Henry and Catherine (née Collins, née Tregoning) Skewes. Born 3 March 1875, Australia. Married Annie Emily Hayes (she born 19 November 1882 — died 8 November 1971) 19 August 1905. Children: Linda Mary (1906) and Herbert Ernest (1910). Died 10 September 1970, aged 95 years.

SKEWES   HENRY ERNEST
Born 1903, Falmouth. Died 1904, aged 0.

SKEWES   HENRY ERNEST
Lived at 61 Hawkestone Street, Cottersloe, Victoria, Australia in 1959 with Annie Emily Skewes. He was a tailor.

SKEWS   HENRY FREDERICK
Born 4 January 1898. Married Gosnell in Southwark, 1922. Died Lambeth 1976, aged 78 years.

SKEWS   HENRY GEORGE
Born 1840, Bloomsbury, London. Emigrated to USA in 1852. Butcher. Married Kate ..... of Pennsylvania in 1876. Four children (including George S. Skews, 1878). Two had died by 1900. Lived in Sioux City, Woodbury County, Iowa, USA in 1900.

SKEWS   HENRY GEORGE
Chart 17. Son of Henry James Skews. Mother's maiden name Hilliard. Born 6 January 1911. Awarded Imperial Service Medal on retirement in 1967 from Post Office, London. Married Queenie Holgate in Maldon, 1933. Child: Jean Q. (1934). Lives at 107 Bulstrode Road, Hounslow, Middlesex.

SKEWS   HENRY JAMES
Chart 17. Son of Richard Nathaniel Edward and Sarah (née Harding) Skews. Born 23 February 1880 at 10 Granby Street, Bethnal Green. Lived at 39 Shakespeare Road, Walthamstow, London E 17. Married Elizabeth Hilliard 1910, Bethnal Green. She died 1919, aged 30 years. Married Morgan, West Ham, 1920. Died 14 November 1944, aged 64 years in Walthamstow.

SKUES   HENRY JAMES
Chart 2. Twin to Juliana Skues. Son of Absalom and Jane Skues. Bpt Camborne 16 July 1831.

SKEWIS   HENRY JAMES
Chart 2. Son of Henry and Grace Skewis of Penponds; miner. Born 1845. Bpt Camborne 27 November 1845. Buried Camborne 1 December 1845, aged 4 weeks.

SKEWES   HENRY JOHN
Born 1872, Pancras. Died 1902, aged 30 years.

SKEWES   HENRY JOHN
Chart 36. Son of William and Annie (née Taylor) Skewes. Born 1878 Watchem, Victoria, Australia. Married Phoebe Marie Holdsworth 1904. Children: Henry Tom Holdsworth, Owen Eric Edward, Alma Phoebe and Glenleigh Bertie William. Died 30 March 1949, aged 71 years. Phoebe Marie died 31 December 1938, aged 63 years.

Henry John Skewes (1878-1949)

SKEWES HENRY JOSIAH
Chart 2. Son of Henry and Annie May (née Cross) Skewes. Born 23 June 1910. Lived at 5 Dalgety Street, Preston, Victoria, Australia in 1959 with Elsie Miriam Skewes. Civil servant. Died 1974, aged 64 years.

SKEWES HENRY NISBETT
Son of William Henry and Helen (née Nisbett) Skewes. Born Port Pirie, South Australia. Died 9 August 1954. Buried in Port Pirie.

SKEWES HENRY OSWALD
Lived at College Street, Camborne, 1897; Moor Street, Camborne 1906-1922. In 1932 living with Veronica May, Doris Muriel and George at 4 Centenary Street, Camborne.

SKEWIS HENRY PERCY
Born 1877, Wellington, Somerset.

SKEWIS HENRY R.
Born 1859, Wisconsin, USA. Lived in Mineral Point in 1870.

SKEWES HENRY R.
Mother's maiden name Revell. Born 1919. Marylebone, London.

SKEWES HENRY RALPH
Lived at 103 Greenhill Road, Toorak Gardens, Rose Park, South Australia in 1959 with Alice Jean Skewes. He was a manager.
Now lives at 5 Mariner Street, London Park, 5065, South Australia.

SKEWES HENRY ROBERT
Lived at 104 Railway Street, Merewether, New South Wales, Australia in 1959 with Rachel Lydia Skewes. Now lives at 38 Golding Avenue, Belmont North, 2280, New South Wales, Australia. Formerly a millwright — now a conductor.

SKEWES HENRY SNOWDEN
Son of Leslie Henry Irving and Edith Ann (née White) Skewes. Born 1 April 1926. Married Marjorie Joyce Munro 19 April 1949 at Yarrawonga, Victoria, Australia. Children: Ian Geoffrey (1950), Peter Snowden (1953), Bruce Alexander (1956), Ann Margaret (1959) and Andrew Philip (1962). Lives at 58 Tom Street, Yarrawonga, 3730, Victoria, Australia.

SKEWES HENRY THOMAS
Born July, 1923, South Australia. Died 11 August 1923, aged 3 weeks. Buried Hindmarsh Cemetery, South Australia.

SKEWES HENRY TOM HOLDSWORTH
Chart 36. Son of Henry John and Phoebe Marie (née Holdsworth) Skewes. Born 28 March 1907, Victoria, Australia. Married Isabel Curtis, 1938, Ballarat, Australia. Children: Lorraine (1940), Neil Holdsworth (1943) and Kaye (1947). Railway employee. Died 21 November 1978, aged 71 years.

SKEWES HERBERT
Chart 30. Son of Thomas and Mary Skewes of Parkvedras Terrace, Truro. Born 1865, Truro. Ironmonger. In 1871 Census Returns was living at Edward Street, Truro with his parents and sisters, Mary Ann Peters Skewes, Elizabeth J. and Florence.
Married Emilia Richmond Morgan at Newton Abbot Congregational Church 24 December 1893. She was daughter of Thomas Morgan, farmer and lived at 50 Daniell Street, Kenwyn. Herbert lived at 16 Prospect Terrace, Newton Abbot, Devon. Ironmonger.

SKEWIS HERBERT
Son of John and Caroline (née Beckerleg) Skewis. Born 1881, Ulverston.

SKEWES HERBERT
Chart 2. Son of Henry Ernest and Annie Emily (née Hayes) Skewes. Born 22 April 1910. Married Edna Cuthertson 27 April 1939 (she born 22 October 1910). Children: John Herbert (1940), and Patricia (1948). Civil servant.
Lives at 171 Middleton Road, Albany, 6330, Western Australia.

SKEWES HERBERT
Lived at 109 Maltravers Road, Ivanhoe, Victoria. Australia in 1959 with Violet May Skewes. He was a gas employee.

SKEWS HERBERT
Lived at 125a Park Street, Abbotsford, Victoria, Australia in 1959 with Ethel May Skewes. He was a factory worker.

SKUSE HERBERT HENRY
Third son of Daniel Skuse. Born 4 February 1874. Wraysbury, Bucks. Lived in Brixton and later Streatham, London. Married Ada Mary Cocks, 1901. Children: Gladys (1903), Percy (1905) and Henry (1907). Signalman and later station manager, London Underground. Died Epsom, Surrey 7 March 1959, aged 85 years.

SKEWES HERBERT JAMES
Chart 10. Son of Herbert Tregonning and Florence Martha Skewes. Born 7 May 1930, at Hamilton, Ontario, Canada. Married Patricia Helen Drysdale 8 October 1949 in Canada. Children: Kim (1955) and Jamie (1958). Lives at 132 Ridge Street, Hamilton, Ontario, Canada. A keen "do it yourself" man. Belongs to a square dance team. Professional job — stationary engineer.

SKEWS HERBERT JAMES S.
Born 1905, Bethnal Green. Died 1906, aged 0.

SKEWES HERBERT JOHN Rev.
Chart 10. Son of Capt Richard Skewes of Mexico; mine captain. Born 1885. Bpt at Chacewater 11 March 1887. Lived in Mexico as a young lad. Married by special licence to Henrietta Catalina Richards, youngest daughter of the late Capt. John Thompson Richards,

M.I.M.E., 25 April 1908 at St Paul's, Chacewater. Lived at Salem House, Chacewater in 1922. Moved to Crowan Vicarage in 1932. Daughter Ernestine Mary Skewes. Was Vicar of Crowan from 1926-1954. Henrietta died 1942, aged 52 years. At the age of 35 Herbert John was accepted for Holy Orders and trained at St Augustine's College. Ordained deacon, 1921; priest in Truro, 1922. First curacy was at St Day from 1921 to 1923 and the next three years he spent as curate at Egloshayle, Wadebridge. Became Vicar of Crowan, 1926.

During his incumbency he was responsible for the carrying out of a number of notable additions and improvements to the church including the addition of two bells added to the tower increasing the number to eight; and electric light was installed in the church. He was responsible for the raising of a large sum of money for the renovation and overhaul of the pipe organ which was completed at the same time as his retirement.

Although a staunch churchman and parish priest, he maintained friendly relations with his Methodist parishioners, and often took part in services in their church. His parishioners totalled some 2,000, and he was keen on educational advancement and was for many years manager of Crowan, Breage and Germoe group of provided schools. He was also chairman of Crowan Nursing Association. In his younger days he was an active member of the old Praze Fair Show Committee. During the Second World War he acted as chaplain to troops stationed at Clowance.

He died 11 October 1958 at 10 Trewirgie Road, Redruth, aged 73 years, and was buried in Crowan Churchyard.

SKEWES HERBERT TREGONNING
Chart 10. Son of John Joseph Skewes of Marazion, Cornwall. Born 29 August 1898 at Philadelphia, Pa., United States of America. Later moved to Hamilton, Ontario, Canada. Married Florence Martha Stephens 22 September 1924, at Victoria Harbour, Ontario. (She born 4 October 1901.) Was manufacturer of jewellery in Hamilton, Ontario for 54 years. During First World War served with 1st Canadian Machine Gun Battalion 1915-1918 in France.
Children: Ethel Catherine (1925), Olive Edith (1927), Herbert James (1930), Marion Martha (1933) and William Charles (1936). Lives at 8515 Dickenson Road, Mount Hope, Ontario, Canada, LOR IWO.

Herbert Tregonning Skewes

SKUES HERBERT V.
Chart 8. Mother's maiden name Harris. Born 1917, Shoreditch, London.

SKUES HERBERT W.
Chart 7. Son of Francis Albert Skues. Mother's maiden name Jeffery. Born 1915, Dartford, Kent. Died 1918, aged 3 years.

SKEWES HERMINIA
Chart 10. Mexican. Née Rosati. Born 20 January 1905. Married Guillermo Skewes 24 December 1939 at Evangelist Church, Mexico City. Children: Herminia (1940) and Guillermo (1942). Lives at Alejandro, Malapsina No 56, Mexico City.

SKEWES HERMINIA
Chart 10. Mexican. Daughter of Guillermo and Herminia (née Rosati) Skewes. Born 24 December 1940, Real del Monte, Mexico. Married Rafael Sainz in Mexico City 16 August 1963. Issue: two sons and one daughter.
Lives in Mexico City.

SKEWES HESTER
Married Philip Eller at Falmouth 12 April 1777.

SKEWES HESTER ANN
Chart 36. Eldest daughter of James and Frances Skewes of Mawnansmith. Born 1846. Bpt Mawnan Parish Church 5 July 1846. In 1871 Census Returns was living at home with her family, then aged 24 years. Died, spinster 9 October 1893, aged 46 years.

SKEWES HESTER JESSIE
Lives at 56 Sisely Avenue, Wangaratta, Victoria, 3677, Australia with Stanley Ogilvy Skewes. She is a clothing inspector; he a clerk.

SKEWES HETTY CATALINA
See SKEWES HENRIETTA CATALINA

SKEWES HETTY LOUISE
Chart 10. Born 29 October 1895 at Marazion, Cornwall. Bpt Marazion 20 December 1895. Daughter of Richard and Frenetta (née Littleton) Skewes. Emigrated to America with her parents, 1906. Married William Hugh Cobourne 18 August 1915 at Hamilton, Ontario. Issue: three daughters and one son. (He died 16 July 1944.) She married Kenneth Davies 22 May 1954 at Arthur Street United Church, Toronto, Canada. Now lives at 8 Redwood Avenue, Toronto, Ontario, Canada. Tel. No: (406) 466 4789.

SKEWES HILARY
Chart 50. Daughter of David Garland and Lorelle (née Davey) Skewes. Born 23 November 1970, Melbourne, Australia. Now lives at 27 Riverside Grove, Chiswick, London W4 3Q1.

SKEWS HILDA
Chart 15. Née Jane. Born 1901, Liskeard. Married Harry Skews about 1917. Children: Beatrice Melba Irene (1920), Harry (1917), Courtenay John Gregory (1922), Joseph Herbert Martyn (1923), Wilfred Gerald (1925), Frederick Thomas (1926), Stanley George (1929) and Albert Peter (1932). Died January 1966, aged 65 years.

SKEWES HILDA
Lived at Carnarthen Moor, Carn Brea, Illogan in 1932 with James Skewes.

SKEWS HILDA BLANCHE
Born 1907, Devonport. Married Wilson in Devonport, 1932.

SKEWS HILDA JANE
Born 1893, Helston. Married Carter in Helston, 1923.

SKEWES HILDA LAURA WILLIAMS
Chart 10. Daughter of John and Catherine (née Williams) Skewes of Chacewater and Mexico. Born 12 October 1882. Bpt Chacewater 26 November 1882. Emigrated to Mexico with her family at the age of 9. Lived in Real del Monte, Mexico. Married Frederick James Pratt. Issue: 11 children. Died 29 June 1962, aged 80 years.

SKEWS HILDA MARGARET
Lives at 32 Frome Avenue, Frankston, 3199, Victoria, Australia with Edmond John Skews and Brendan Ashley Jay Skews.

SKEWES HILDA MAUD
Chart 36. Daughter of James and Edith Louise (née Richards) Skewes. Born 1901. Married Albert Carter, 19 March 1932 at Illogan Church by Rev. H. Oxland. Celebrated Silver Wedding on 14 March 1957; then living at Penhallack, Carn Brea, Redruth. Issue: 1 son.

SKEWS HILDA R.
Living at Pentamar Flats, Plymouth, 1976.

SKEWES HOBSON
Chart 50, Eldest son of Thomas and Sarah Ann (née Lord) Skewes. Lived in Australia.

SKEWES HONOR
Daughter of Edward and Mary Skewes. Buried Helston 11 February 1764.

SKEWS HONOR
of Penryn. Married James Pursell of Penryn at St Gluvias 21 January 1788.

SKEWES HONOR
Buried Camborne 24 June 1791. Pauper.

SKEWES HONOR
Bpt Sancreed 12 September 1797.

SKEWES HONOR
Chart 2. Daughter of Edward and Mary Skewes. Bpt Wesleyan/Methodist Chapel, Camborne, 28 July 1829 (born 28 May 1829). In 1841 Census Returns was listed as "dressing ore".

SKUES HONORA H.
Married 1866, Marlborough. There are a large number of SKUSE entered in Somerset House for Marlborough. Probably a misspelling.

SKUES HONORA HARRIET
Born 1842, Malmsbury. Married 1846.

SKEWES HOPE
Chart 36. Daughter of William Wilfred John and Annie (née Borgas) Skewes. Born 1913. Married Bob Armstead. Issue: 3 sons and 1 daughter. Died 1978, aged 65 years.

SKEWES HORACE
Chart 12. Son of William John and Edith Mary Skewes. Mother's maiden name Truran. Born 18 June 1913 at Carnkie, Redruth. Married Iris Verbina Jose 12 July 1939 at Camborne North Parade Chapel. Lived at 6 Roskear Road, Camborne, until 1956 when they moved to 49 Dolcoath Road, Camborne. Present address. Child: Carl (1940).

SKEWES HORACE HENRY
Chart 38. Son of Richard and Mary Jane (née Reynolds) Skewes. Born 15 May 1886, Moonta, South Australia. Married Agatha Blanche Johns 31 August 1907. Children: Richard Horace Henry, Frank Horace, Violet Blanche, Gladys May, Clarice Olive, Dorothy Alice, Eva Lorraine, Harry, Laurel Jean, Muriel Melbanear, Horatio Gerald and Harold Melville. Died 7 January 1925, aged 39 years.

SKEWES HORACE RAYMOND
Lived at 205 Springvale Road, Mitcham, Victoria, Australia in 1959 with Mary Miriam Skewes. Industrial chemist. Now lives at 9 Chelsea Street, Brighton, 3186, Victoria, Australia.

SKUSE HORACE SIDNEY
Son of Sidney and Nellie Skuse. Born 1899. Married Ada Lilian Tomsett. Children: Barbara (1928) and Michael (1931). Lives in Cheam, Surrey.

SKEWES HORATIO GERALD
Chart 38. Son of Horace Henry and Agatha Blanche Skewes. Born 8 April 1922 at Broken Hill, New South Wales, Australia. Twin to Muriel Melbanear Skewes. Married Phyllis Manetta Bowden 22 November 1947. One son Jeffrey William Skewes (1948). Having left school at the age of 15 he worked on sheep properties. Served in the Army 1941-1945. Worked for South Mine (Zinc and Lead) for 23 years until the closure of the mine in 1972. Now works as a shift worker on wards in Broken Hill Hospital. Bred and showed Fox Terrier dogs. Has an Australian terrier as a pet.
Lives at 236 O'Farrell Street, Broken Hill West, 2880, New South Wales, Australia.

SKEWES HOWARD
Chart 36. Son of Samuel H. and and Mary (née Thomas) Skewes. Born in Yorkville, Wisconsin, USA, 1877.

SKEWES HOWARD
Chart 18. Son of Samuel Dawe Skewes. Born 1871. Farmer. Married 1907, Bristol. Lived at Old Rectory, Gidleigh, Devon and later Berry Down Farm, Gidleigh, Chagford, Devon. Died at Melvin Nursing Home, Newton Abbot 11 May 1945, aged 75 years. No children. W(SH) £6084.

SKEWES HOWARD G.
Teller, Merchant Bank at 814 Irolo, Los Angeles, 1910.

Howard Hoyt Skewes

SKEWES   HOWARD HOYT
Chart 14. Son of George and Ruth (née Hoyt) Skewes. Born 25 May 1878, Racine, Wisconsin, USA. Married Myrtilla Perrin 24 December 1924 in Los Angeles. No children. Clerk living at 1327 Allesandro, Los Angeles, 1910. Clerk at General Hospital, 1063 W 80th, Los Angeles in 1939.

SKEWES   HUBERT MERVYN
Chart 36. Son of William Hicks and Elizabeth (née McLeod) Skewes. Born 1891, South Australia.
Bachelor. Moved to Western Australia and lived in Kelmscott. Died 1930, aged 39 years.

SKEWIS   HUGH MacDONALD
Born Shettleston, Scotland 1939. Married Isabella McManus Hutchison in Provan, Scotland, 1961.

SKUES   HUGH WILLIAM
Born 1910. Called up during 2nd World War and was a gunner (1708505) with 2nd Battalion The Dorsetshire Regiment (54th Foot). Killed in Mandalay 15 March 1945, aged 35 years.

SKEWES   HUMBERTO
Chart 10. Mexican. Son of Elisa Skewes, single person. Born 8 October 1926, Real del Monte, Mexico. Married Laura Borja 16 December 1955. Children: Jose Humberto (1959) and Dora Maria (1957). Lives in Pachuca, Mexico.

SKEWES   HUMFREY
Son of Katherin Skewes, single woman. Bpt Gerrans 20 November 1574. Married Mary Evans at Gerrans 3 November 1612. Children: John (1616), Florence (1618), and Doriter (died 1619). Buried Gerrans 5 November 1641, aged 67 years.

SKEWES   HUMFREY
Chart 2. Married Christian Farmer 23 October 1637 at Camborne Parish Church. Children: William, George and Remfre.

I

SKEWES   IAN
Chart 12. Son of Carl and Elizabeth (née Clackworthy) Skewes. Born 27 July, 1966, Redruth.

SKEWES   IAN
Chart 26. Son of Frank Anson and Mary (née Wier) Skewes. Born September 1972, Florida, United States of America.

SKEWIS   IAN
Born 1949 College Park, Glasgow, Scotland. Married June Allison Gillies, 1969, Dumbarton, Scotland.

SKEWIS   IAN
Born 1970, Dumbarton.

SKEWES   IAN
Chart 36. Son of William and Margery (née Moran) Skewes. Born Watson's Creek, Bendemeer, New South Wales, Australia. Married. One son Benjamin.

SKEWES   IAN CHARLES
Chart 36. Son of Geoffrey and Dorothy May (née Chapman) Skewes. Born 6 September 1953. Married Marianne Holm 30 August 1980 (she born 26 January 1956). Lived at 41 Coonan Street, Indooroopilly, 4068, Queensland, Australia until 1980, but now lives in Denmark.

SKEWES   IAN DOUGLAS
Lives at 2 Miller Street, Kidman Park, 5025, South Australia with Douglas Skewes and Lorna May Skewes. Carpenter.

SKEWES   IAN GEOFFREY
Son of Henry Snowden and Marjorie Joyce (née Munro) Skewes. Born 27 November 1950. Married Debra Kay Ginger, January 1975. Child: Ian Guy Skewes (1980). Lives at 20 Deakin Street, Hampton, 3188, Victoria, Australia.

SKEWES   IAN GEOFFREY
Lives at 33 Austral Road, Kalgoorlie, 6430, Western Australia. Fitter.

SKEWES   IAN GUY
Son of Ian Geoffrey and Debra Kay (née Ginger) Skewes. Born November 1980. Lives at 20 Deakin Street, Hampton, 3188, Victoria, Australia.

SKEWIS   IAN JAMES
Son of Jim Skewis of Toronto, Canada. Born 1976.

SKUES   IAN KEITH
Chart 8. Mother's maiden name Cox. Son of Sydney V. Skues. Born 1953, Brentwood, Essex.

SKEWES   IAN ROBERT MORRISON
Chart 18. Son of John Edgar and Amy (née Morrison) Skewes. Born 8 May 1927. House prefect at All Hallow's (Rousden) School, 1944; Rugby Football XV, 1943; Hockey XI 1942-1944. Triple colour. Proceeded to Royal West of England Academy of Art to study architecture. Served in Royal Artillery and later in the Honourable Artillery Company.
Married Pamela Brienna Brampton, 8 August 1952 at St Alban's Parish Church, Westbury Park, Bristol. No children. Divorced 1971. Married

Elfreda Grimes in Kensington, 1973.

SKEWES   IAN THOMAS
Son of Douglas Westmore and Lorna Jean (née Farquhar) Skewes. Born 28 December 1951. Twin to Lynette Mary Skewes. Married Charmaine Burles. Children: Penny (1974) and Jason (1978). Lives at Clyde Road, Clyde, 3978, Victoria, Australia.

SKEWES   IDA FLORENCE
Chart 50. Daughter of John and Mary Jane (née Cole) Skewes. Born 1890, New South Wales, Australia. Married with 6 children.

SKEWES   IDA MARY
Chart 48. Née Corbett. Born 24 September 1902. Second wife of William Frederick Charles Skewes whom she married in Doncaster, 1950. Lived at 24 Cecil Court, 73 Eaton Rise, London W5. Died 2 April 1971, aged 69 years.

SKEWES   IDA OLIVE
Chart 36. Daughter of Samuel Sidney and Sarah (née Pennall) Skewes. Born 1902. Married her first cousin William Skewes, August 1922. Children: Leslie Kevin, Earl, Eric, Brian, Lorna Meg, Donald Lloyd, Dorothy Dawn, Janice and Jennifer. Lived at 88 Rawson Avenue, Tamworth, 2340, New South Wales, Australia. Died 15 September 1980, aged 78 years.

SKEWES   IDE
Married Garret Sampson at St Clement, Truro, 19 July 1616.

SKEWES   IESTYN
Chart 50. Child of George Skewes. Mother's maiden name Phelps. Born 1922, Pontypridd, Wales.

SKEWES   ILMA ELIZABETH
Chart 50. Née Dodd. Born 30 August 1910. Married Thomas Grenville Skewes 2 July 1938, Melbourne, Victoria, Australia. Children: Geoffrey Grenville Skewes (1939), Celia Elizabeth (1943) and Therese Jean (1944). Lives at 3/9 Rowell Avenue, Camberwell, 3124, Victoria, Australia.

SKEWES   ILMA MURIEL
Lived at 103 Villiers Street, New Farm, Brisbane, Queensland, Australia in 1959 with Inez Olive Skewes. Typist.

SKEWES   INEZ OLIVE
Lives at 103 Villiers Street, New Farm, Brisbane, Queensland, 4005, Australia. Typist.

SKEWS   IRENE
Chart 41. Daughter of Frederick and Frances (née Smith) Skews. Born 1915, Houghton. Died 1915, aged 0.

SKEWIS   IRENE
Chart 50. Born 1926, Hull. Married James Airns Skewis, 1945, Aldershot. Children: Michael Ian (1947), James (1948), David (1950). Sadie (1953), Elizabeth (1955) and Philip E. (1957). Died 17 October 1968, aged 42 years.

SKEWES   IRENE
Chart 12. Mother's maiden name Woolcock. Born 1948. Married Fred Keast, Truro, 1969. No children.

SKEWIS   IRENE ANN
Chart 50. Daughter of John Brown and Margaret Forrest Skewis. Born 3 March 1956, Dundee, Scotland. Lives at 19 Trent Street, RAAF Base, Forest Hill, Wagga Wagga, New South Wales, 2651, Australia.

SKEWES   IRENE ELIZABETH
Chart 14. Née Olson. Born Chicago, Illinois 11 January 1889. Daughter of Charles Oscar and Emma (née Anderson) Olson. Married Arthur Edwin Skewes 25 October 1919 at Yorkville, Wisconsin, USA. One son: Arthur Russell Skewes (1922). Lives at 157 Swigert Avenue, Kentucky, 40505, United States of America.

Irene Olson Skewes

SKEWES IRENE KAYE
Chart 38. Daughter of Malcolm and Irene Myrtle (née Miller) Shammall. Born 25 May 1947. Married Brian Wayne Skewes 6 January 1968, Enfield Methodist Church, South Australia. Child: Rebecca Jade (1980). Lives at 18 Launceston Avenue, Banksia Park, 5091, South Australia.

SKEWS IRENE M.
Chart 17. Daughter of Ernest W. Skews. Mother's maiden name Falconer. Born 1939. Married Andrews in Waltham Forest, 1969.

SKEWES IRENE MARGARET
Chart 50. Née Murphy. Married David Buick Skewes, 28 February 1942. Lived at 1518 Sturt Street, Ballarat, Victoria. Australia in 1959. Later lived at Windarra, 213 Sim Street, Ballarat, 3350, Victoria, Australia. Children: Helen Margaret (1942), Gillian Mary (1944), David Garland (1946), Margaret Alison (1949) and Christine Ann (1952). Died 22 August 1976.

SKEWES IRENE MARY
Chart 36. Daughter of William Vere and Annie Rebecca (née Strain). Skewes. Born Tamworth, New South Wales 28 May 1927. Married Frederick Gordon White. Issue: 3 daughters and 1 son. Lives at 16 Belmore Street, West Tamworth, 2340, New South Wales, Australia.

SKEWES IRENE MAUD
Lived at 24 Pacific Highway, Greenwich, Woll-Stonecroft, New South Wales, Australia in 1959 with Lawrence and Lawrence Thomas Skewes. Now lives at 29 Oxley Street, Naremburn, 2065, New South Wales, Australia.

SKEWES IRMA MARGARET
Lived at 35 Macnally Street, Yarrawonga, Victoria, Australia in 1959 with David Leslie Skewes.

SKEWS IRIS
Lives at 65 Boundary Road, Newcombe, 3219, Victoria, Australia.

SKEWS IRIS D.
Chart 17. Daughter of David George and Emily (née Lampey) Skews. Born 29 May 1933. Married Derek Houchell at St John's, Gorsebrook Road, Dagenham, Essex 14 June 1952. Issue: three children.

SKEWES IRIS M.
Chart 12. Daughter of Thomas Henry and Annie (née Jory) Skewes. Born 1916, Redruth. Married Prisk in Redruth, 1939.

SKEWES IRIS VERBINA
Chart 12. Née Jose. Married Horace Skewes, 12 July 1939 at Camborne North Parade Chapel. Lived at Roskear Road, Camborne until 1968 when they moved to 49 Dolcoath Road, Camborne. One son: Carl (1940).

SKEWES IRLENE
Chart 37. Daughter of John Skewes of Australia.

SKEWES IRMA MARGARET
Née Green. Married David Leslie Skewes, 10 October 1952. Children: Gregory David (1956), Craig Leslie (1959) and Susan Margaret (1964). Lives at 35 Macnally Street, Yarrawonga, 3730, Victoria, Australia.

SKUES ISAAC
Born 1866, Chester-le-Street, Durham.

SKEWES ISAAC
Chart 10. Mexican. Illegitimate son of Blasa Skewes. Born 20 January 1905, Real del Monte, Mexico.

SKEWES ISAATT
Married Hercules Niclas at Truro St Mary, 18 September 1654.

SKEWES ISABEL
Chart 10. Née Bray. Married Peter Skewes in Real del Monte, Mexico. Children: Richard Henry (1871), George Harris (1875), John (1878), Lilian Beatrice (1884) and Belita (1897). Died at Nourse Mines, Johannesburg, South Africa about 1918.

SKEWIS ISABEL
Chart 2. Daughter of Francis Harry and Annie Skewis. Born 13 October 1893, America. Died 1 December 1898, aged 5 years.

SKEWES ISABEL
Chart 10. Daughter of Juan and Fransisca (née Meneses) Skewes. Born 20 November 1913, Real del Monte, Mexico. Died 20 November 1913, aged 10 hours.

SKEWIES ISABEL ANDERSON
Born 1918, Hillhead, Scotland. Married Stuart, 1947, Hamilton, Scotland.

SKEWES ISABELLA
Daughter of John and Mary Skewes. Chart 3. Bpt Helston 27 May 1781.

SKUES ISABELLA
Born 1824. Died St Giles 1908, aged 84 years.

SKUES ISABELLA
Died 1847, Penzance.

SKUES ISABELLA
Born 1851. Daughter of George Gilbert and Isabella Skues. Bpt St Luke, Westminster 8 February 1852. Married 1870, St James.

SKEWS ISABELLA
Born 1897, Plympton. Died 1900, aged 3 years.

SKEWS ISABELLA
Born 1923. Mother's maiden name Consitine. Died Scotland 1977, aged 54 years.

SKEWES ISABELLA
Lived at 33 Graham Avenue, Wangaratta, Victoria, Australia in 1959.

SKEWES ISABELLA MAUD
Chart 36. Daughter of Samuel Sidney and Sarah (née Pennall) Skewes. Born 12 August 1887, New South Wales, Australia. Married George Berry. Issue: 6 daughters and 1 son. Lived in Tamworth, New South Wales. Died 28 August 1972, aged 85 years.

SKEWES ISABELLA REYNOLDS
Born 1949, Redruth.

SKEWES ISELA
Chart 2. Mexican. Daughter of Aaron and Maria Teresa (née Navarrete) Skewes. Born Pachuca 6 June 1970. Twin to Miriam Skewes.

SKEWES IVAN HERBERT
Lived at 73 Ashburton Road, Glen Iris, Victoria, Australia, 1959 with Ethel Ivy Skewes. He was a bus driver.

SKEWES IVY JEAN SELINA
Daughter of Thomas Herbert and Catherine Ann Elizabeth (née Harvey) Skewes. Born 20 December 1913. Lives in Victoria, Australia.

SKUES IVY MARGUERITA
Chart 9. Born 18 January 1909, Southwark, London. Mother's maiden name Clorinda Emma Guidotti. Married Alfred C. White in Camberwell, 1933.

SKUES IVY MAUD
Chart 8. Daughter of Harold Frederick Claude Skues. Born 1909, Edmonton. Married Albert W. Dawson, 1930, Edmonton, North London.

SKUSE IZOTE
Married Christine Harden, 1648, Ottery St Mary, Devon.

Wedding of Isabella Maud Skewes to George Berry, Australia

J

SKEWES J.
Farmer living at Treloskan, Cury, 1856.

SKEWES J.
Farmer living in Cargenwen, Crowan, 1856.

SKEWES J.
Beer retailer living in Chacewater in 1856.

SKEWES J.
Farmer living at Roscroggan, Illogan, 1856.

SKEWIS J.
Shopkeeper in Mawnan, Falmouth, 1856.

SKEWIS J.
Farmer living at Mawnan, Falmouth, 1856.

SKEWES J.
Working at 41 Old Town Street, Plymouth, 1904/5.

SKEWS J.
Living at 26 Portland Square, Plymouth 1906/7.

SKEWES J.
Living at 4 Connaught Avenue, Plymouth 1920/21.

SKEWS J.
Publican of The General Wolfe, Bodmin Road, St Austell, 1856.

SKEWES JACK
Chart 36. Son of Simon Skewes, Born 15 September 1893, Australia. Married. Lived in Malvern, Victoria. Died November, 1949, aged 56

years.

SKEWES JACK
Chart 50. Born 30 March 1899. Married Victoria Florence Francis and lived in Carrington, New South Wales, Australia. Now lives at 131 Douglas Street, Stockton, New South Wales, 2295, Australia. Children: Jack (1927) and Leo William (1927).

SKUES JACK Rev.
Chart 3. Son of Ernest and Clara (née Roberts) Skues. Born 27 May 1911 at Barnsley, South Yorkshire. Attended St James School, Blackburn 1916-1920; St Mary's, Stockport, 1920-1925; Stockport Technical College (evenings) 1927-1930. In Barnsley lived at The Poplars, Gawbor Road; Blackburn — 9 Eldon Road and 42 Langham Road; Stockport — 196 Turncroft Lane, 20 Derby Road, Heaton Moor, 4 Peel Moat Road, Heaton Moor and 4 Ashburn Grove, Heaton Norris.
His first job was as an apprentice in baking and confectionery in Stockport, commencing 17 June 1925.
He married Lily Bruckshaw, daughter of John Henry and Lily (née Singleton) Bruckshaw, 26 December 1935. Children: Joy Christine (1937), Jennifer (1939) and Patricia Mary (1943).
In 2nd World War he served with Royal Army Service Corps 1943-1945 in Belgium, France, Holland and Germany.
Served as a lay preacher in Methodist Church from 1930 to 1967, holding every office within the local church (non ministerial).
Jack trained as a baker/confectioner/patisserie chef and caterer. Studied hygiene and public health, degree A.R.I.P.H. & H. Ran a guest house in Blackpool 1963-1967. For 38 years was a local preacher in three circuits in Lancashire & Cheshire 1929-1967.
Emigrated to Canada 28 January 1967. Took six art courses with Queen's University, Kingston, Ontario, 1968-1972. Ministerial training at Pine Hill Divinity Hall, Halifax, Nova Scotia, Canada, 1968-1972 and St Andrew's University, Saskatoon, Saskatchewan, 1972-1973. His first appointment was with United Church of Canada, Harrington Harbour, Eastern Quebec. His entry into the ministry as a minister took place on 17 October 1973 at Valleyfield United Church, Quebec. It was at Valleyfield Jack recalls an amusing story: "When a minister at Valleyfield, I was the Dame in a pantomime. On dress rehearsal night I was just going onto the stage when a message arrived to say a man was waiting to see me in the vestry.
"I arrived there and asked 'Whom do you wish to see?'
"'The minister please', came the reply.
"'I'll go and get him for you', I answered. I waited in the corridor for a couple of minutes then went back into the vestry saying 'Here is the Minister. What can I do for you?'"
The United Church of Canada was formed in June, 1925 by the amalgamation of the Methodist, Presbyterian and Congregational Churches, and is the largest Protestant Church in Canada.
Jack Skues retired in 1977 and now lives at P.O. Box 41, Albright Gardens, Beamsville, Ontario, Canada. His hobbies are swimming, shuffleboard, carpentry, poetry, gardening and writing.

Jack Skues

SKEWES JACK
Chart 50. Son of Richard James and Amy (née Post) Skewes. Born 29 December 1927, North Sydney, Australia. Married Shirley Beryl Callaghan 3 March 1951, Gladesville. Divorced 2 March 1977. Children: Dennis Paul (1951), John Gregory (1953), Michael Bruce (1953), Bryan Patrick (1955) and Kim Narelle (1957).
Lives at 120 Smart Street, Fairfield, 2165, New South Wales, Australia.

SKEWES JACK
Chart 50. Son of Jack and Victoria Florence (née Francis) Skewes. Born 22 March 1927, Wickham, New South Wales, Australia. Married Betony Irene Roach, 1 February 1947. Children: Alan, Harry, Julie and Donna May. Lived at 71 Howard Street, Carrington, New South Wales and later 6 Cardigan Street, Stockton, 2295, New South Wales, Australia. Died 2 May 1979, aged 52 years.

SKEWES JACK
Chart 12. Son of William John and Nora Skewes. Mother's maiden name Thomas. Born 1 September 1951. Died 9 October 1966, aged 15 years in a tractor accident. He was killed outright when travelling on the machine driven by Kenneth Henson when it overturned after crashing through a hedge on a steep hill at Parc-an-Fox, Tregarne, St Keverne. Jack was the second youngest of a family of nine, and had recently left school and was working part time for the owner of the tractor, Leslie Hugg of Halwyn Farm, who witnessed the accident. He was buried in St Keverne Churchyard 13 October 1966. Kenneth Henson, who was also killed in the accident, was buried at St Keverne on the same day.

SKEWIS JACK
Married Roberston in Surrey Mid East, 1974.

SKEWES JACK PATTISON
Chart 12. Son of Harry Oswald and Emily Ann Skewes. Born 1904, Redruth. Died 1904, aged 0.

SKEWES JACK PATTERSON OSWALD
Chart 12. Son of James Henry Oswald and Jessie Victoria (née Cockram) Skewes of 7 Moor Street, Camborne. Born 10 May 1923. Attended Roskear Boys School 1931-1934. Admitted to Redruth County School August, 1934. Left school 26 July 1940. Bachelor. Lives at 12 Atlantic Terrace, Camborne. Tel. Number 0209 712422.

SKEWES JACK ROE
Chart 36. Son of William Roe and Evelyn Dorothy Skewes. Born 12 September 1919, Adelaide, South Australia. Married Dorothy May Burn, 1942. Lived at 178 North Terrace, Adelaide in 1959. Caretaker. Children: Trevor John (1944), Timothy Lester (1948), Christopher Allen (1954) and Peter Nathaniel (1955). Now lives at 16 Alawara Road, Ingle Farm, South Australia 5098.

SKUES JACK SYDNEY
Chart 5. Son of Samuel Francis and Florence Rachael (née Rosenburg) Skues. Born 31 August 1916, Victoria, Australia. Married Doris Hope, daughter of Victor Ernest and Christina (née Bedwell) Hope 10 August 1940.
Children: Margaret Lorraine (1941) and John Barry (1945). Director and Manager of Dane Taylor Steel Company, Melbourne since 1935. Hobbies: horse racing, gardening and golf. Has visited United Kingdom, Europe, Asia, Hong Kong, Japan and United States of America.
Lives at 202 Were Street, East Brighton, 3187, Victoria, Australia.

Doris & Jack Skues of Melbourne, Australia

SKEWES JACKELINE
Chart 10. Mexican. Daughter of Henry and Lourdes (née Escudero) Skewes. Born 26 June 1966. Lived in Real del Monte, Mexico.

SKEWES JACKIE
Lives at 146 Maplewood Avenue, Hamilton, Ontario, Canada.

SKEWIS JACQUELINE
Born 1975, Dundee East, Scotland.

SKEWES JACQUELYNN ANN
Chart 26. Daughter of Frank Anson and June Beverley (née Spaulding) Skewes. Born 13 March 1953, New London, Connecticut, USA. Married Kenneth Sorenson 12 August 1971. Issue: one son and one daughter. Lives at Box 788, Centerville, Utah, 84104, United States of America. Tel. Number (801) 292 8157.

SKEWES JACQUELINE ANN
Chart 2. Daughter of Graham Henry and Dorothy Cheryl (née Fitzclarence) Skewes. Born 27 February 1974, Victoria, Australia. Lives at 15 Crossen Street, Echuca, 3625, Victoria, Australia.

SKEWES JAMES
Son of John Skewes. Bpt Gerrans 26 August 1573.

SKEWIS JAMES
Married Agnes Ellis at Camborne 21 April 1589.

SKEWES JAMES
Married Tamson Tonkin at St Just in Roseland 28 January 1607. Mentioned in Cornwall Protestation Returns, 1642.

SKEWS JAMES
Buried St Just in Roseland 28 February 1644.

SKEWES JAMES
Chart 36. Married Sarah . . . . Children: Jane, Elizabeth, William, James, Sarah, Mary, Blanch, John and Edward.

SCUES JAMES
Son of Peter Scues. Bpt Otterton, Devon 10 Sept 1700.

SKEWES JAMES
Chart 36. Son of James and Sarah Skewes. Bpt Cury 7 November 1711.

SCUES JAMES
Chart 2. Son of Henry Scues; pauper. Bpt Camborne 14 January 1739. Married Charity Ellis 10 April 1763 (she died 3 July 1787). Children: James, Constance, William and James (twins).

SKEWES JAMES
Buried at Cury 7 February 1741.

SKEWES JAMES
Son of Elizabeth Skewes. Bpt Mawgan in Meneage 19 July 1741.

SKEWES JAMES
Chart 36. Son of John and Mary (née George) Skewes. Bpt Cury 12 April 1748. Married Anne Richards at Mawgan in Meneage 19 October 1773. Children: Anne (1773), Mary (1774), James (1777), Sarah (1779), Elizabeth (1782), James (1785), Jane (1791) and James (1797). Lived at Treloskan, Cury. Died 11 June 1817, aged 69 years.

SKEWS JAMES
Chart 9. Son of Philip and Mary Skews. Bpt St. Ewe 6 July 1760. Married Joanna Truscott 4 November 1792 at St Ewe. Children: Grace, Ann, Joanna, James, Jane, Philip, Elizabeth, William Truscott, Mary Ann, Thomas Truscott and Thomas.
Buried St Ewe 8 July 1838, aged 78 years. Joanna died 1864, aged 90 years.

SKEWES JAMES
Buried Mawgan in Meneage 10 May 1762.

SKEUS JAMES
Chart 2. Son of Roben (Robart) Skeus. Bpt Camborne 12 September 1762; tinner. Married Elizabeth Handcock 1 November 1789. Children: James and Mary Ann.

SCUES JAMES
Chart 2. Son of James and Charity Scues. Bpt privately 7 June 1763; publicly 12 June 1763. Died 12 January 1772, aged 9 years.

SKEWES JAMES
Chart 29. Son of John and Alice Skewes of Kea. Bpt Kenywn 12 May 1767.

SKEWES JAMES
Born 1773, Gwennap. Buried Gwennap 11 June 1829, aged 56 years.

SKEWES JAMES
Son of Joseph and Elizabeth Skewes. Bpt 22 June 1777, Mawgan-in-Meneage.

SKEWES JAMES
Chart 36. Son of James and Anne Skewes. Bpt Mawgan in Meneage 29 June 1777.

SCUES JAMES
Chart 2. Twin to William Scues. Son of James and Charity Scues. Bpt Camborne 19 December 1779 when each were five years old.

SKEWES JAMES
Chart 36. Son of James and Ann Skewes. Bpt Cury 13 May 1785. Buried Cury 16 December 1785.

SKEWES JAMES
Chart 12. Illegitimate son of Mary Dorten. Bpt Cury 13 August 1786. Married Elizabeth Tremayne at Cury Parish Church 25 July 1808. Children James (1809), Mary (1811), William (1813), John (1815),

Elizabeth (1817), Henry (1818), Ann (1820), Josiah (1824), Loveday (1824) and Thomas (1826). Farmed at Gilly, Cury in 1841 Census Returns. Died at Skewes Gate, Cury 8 October 1845, aged 56 years.

SKEWES JAMES
Chart 2. Son of James and Elizabeth Skewes. Bpt Camborne 22 August 1790. Farmer at Killivoase. Buried Camborne 15 March 1875, aged 85 years.

SKEWES JAMES
Chart 36. Son of James and Ann Skewes. Born 1793. Bpt Cury 2 April 1797. Married Simonette Barnett, 5 October 1824, Cury. Children: James (1825), Nancy (1826), William (1828), Nancy (1831), Alice (1834), John (1836), Edward (1838), Elizabeth Jane (1840), Blanch (1845), Mary (1846) and Ellen Willcocks (1849). Lived at Piece, Illogan. Buried Illogan 19 October 1871, aged 78 years.

SKEWES JAMES
Chart 2. Son of Absalom and Elizabeth Skewes. Bpt Camborne 7 June 1795. Married Joanna Rule 8 April 1817. Children: Absalom, John Rule and Nanny. Emigrated to Wisconsin, USA. Buried in Shullsburg Cemetery, United States of America.

SKEWES JAMES
Chart 36. Son of John and Mary Skewes. Bpt Cury 20 August 1797. Farmer at Treloskan, Cury. Married Grace SKEWES of Constantine (daughter of Henry and Grace Skewes) 8 April 1834. Child: Eliza Grace Skewes (1846). Died 19 October 1856, aged 58 years. Buried in Cury Churchyard 22 October 1856. Had a brother Edward Skewes, sister Ann Freeman; nephew John Skewes, son of brother William Skewes.

SKEWES JAMES
Born 1797. Died 1870, aged 73 years in Medway.

SKEWES JAMES
Chart 29. Son of Richard and Roseanna Skewes. Bpt Kenwyn 9 September 1798.

SKEWES JAMES
Buried 4 March 1799 at Kea.

SKUES JAMES
Married Susannah Thomas at Wendron 21 September 1799.

SKEWS JAMES
Chart 9. Son of James and Joanna Skews of Lower Sticker, St Ewe. Bpt St Ewe 21 May 1802. Lime burner. Married Elizabeth . . . . of Pirran, St Austell. In 1851, 1861 and 1871 Census Returns lived at 125 Back Row, Charlestown, St Austell. Died 1875, St Austell, aged 73 years.

SKEWES JAMES
Son of Henry and Catherine Skewes. Bpt Kea 15 June 1805. Buried Kenywn 8 February 1849, aged 44 years.

SKEWES JAMES
Buried Camborne 10 June 1804.

SKEWIS JAMES
Chart 50. Born 1805. Roll turner. Married Mary Ann Griffiths 25 July 1825, Llanover, Monmouthshire. Went north to Scotland and married Elizabeth Gemmell and Helen Jamieson.
Convicted of bigamy in the Sheriffdom of Lanark 31 December 1869. (Register of Corrected Entries, vol 111, page 27; entry 644.2 "bigamy.")

SKEWIS JAMES
Son of James and Elizabeth Skewis. Bpt Cury 8 October 1809.

SKEWES JAMES
Tinner. Married Jane Richards, widow at Camborne Parish Church 16 March 1812.

SKEWES JAMES
Son of James and Ann Skewes. Bpt Camborne 26 December 1812. Lived at William Street, Camborne. Buried Camborne 19 October 1879, aged 66 years.

SKEWES JAMES
Born 1814. Married Margaret . . . . . 1814. Died Goldsithney, Perranuthnoe, Penzance, 1886, aged 72 years.

SKUSE JAMES
of Trowbridge, Wiltshire. Married Elizabeth Richards, 1815, Awre, Gloucestershire.

SKEWES JAMES
Chart 36. Son of William and Christian (née Lugg) Skewes. Farmer at Mawnan. Born 24 June 1815 in Ruan Minor. Married Frances Kempthorne of Mawnan at Mawnan Parish Church 2 October 1845. Farmed at Rosemullion, Mawnan. Children: Hester Ann, Frances Maria, Edward, William Henry, Emily Kempthorne, James Lugg, Alma Jane, Mary, Kate and Ellen. Died 30 July 1899, aged 84 years. Was parish clerk at Mawnan for 50 years.

SKUES JAMES
Chart 2. Son of James and Joanna Skues of Killivoase, Camborne. Bpt Camborne privately 8 May 1818 and publicly 9 May 1818. Married Sally Sems, daughter of Samuel Sems, miner, at Camborne Parish Church 25 January 1844. Child: Joanna. In 1851 Census Returns lived at Pendarves Row, Camborne with Emily (5), Stephen (3) and Mary J. (1). James was a copper miner.

SKEWES JAMES
Chart 33. Son of John and Grace Skewes of Hugus, Kea; miner. Bpt Kenwyn 1 July 1821. Bachelor. In 1871 Census Returns was a boarder at Calenick Street, Truro; labourer.

SKEWS JAMES
Chart 50. Son of Richard Skews of Chacewater, miner. Born 1822. Married Harriet Curno, daughter of John Curno, miner of Chacewater at Kenwyn, 19 June 1844. Moved to Neath, South Wales. Children: Mary (1846) and Richard (1848).
Died 1849, aged 27 years. Harriet married again in Neath, 1851.

SKEWS JAMES
Born 1823, Kenwyn. Bachelor. In 1871 Census Returns resided at Killiwerris as a lodger. Later went to Truro Union House. Buried Baldhu July 1877, aged 54 years.

SKEWIS JAMES
Born 1823. Son of James Skewis, farmer of Cury. Married Eleanor Harris (32), daughter of James Harris, labourer 9 January 1848 at Cury Parish Church.

SKEWES JAMES
Chart 36. Son of James and Simonette (née Barnet) Skewes. Bpt Cury 30 January 1825. Missing from Census Returns after 1841 when he was listed as aged 16 years.

SKEWIS JAMES
Chart 2. Son of Edward (miner) and Mary Skewis of Camborne. Born 10 February 1825. Bpt Redruth Wesleyan Circuit Church 19 March 1825.
Copper miner. Lived at Vyvyan's Row, Camborne. Left Camborne for the United States of America in the spring of 1846 and was very impressed with the country. He returned to Cornwall for a short while before the family emigrated. They left Camborne and travelled by rail to Liverpool and thence to New Orleans by ship *Mary Ward*. James eventually moved to Shullsburg where his father bought a house. In 1850 there was a big rush to the gold fields of California and James joined the queue. His travels then took him to Mexico and a little later by sea to Australia and to the town of Bendigo where gold had been discovered. He earned enough money to secure a passage on the ship *Anglesey*, bound for Penzance.
James had been away from England for six years and in the spring of 1855 he revisited Cornwall. He announced his engagement to Jane Thomas Rabling. They married later that year and departed for Shullsburg, USA. They bought a farm with 70 acres of ground. This was sold in 1861 and in March of that year they moved to Mexico. James landed a job working underground at a mine in Pachuca and was later promoted to look after the company's stamp and to receive ore brought from the mines to be stamped. The Skewis family stayed in Mexico for seven years and in 1868 they returned to the United States to Inwood close by the Milwaukee railroad.
The Skewis family comprised Anita (1856), William James (1858), Francis Harry (1860), Edward John (1865), George Absalom (1867), Charles Samuel (1869), Jennie Rabling (1872) and Elmer Arthur (1877). He was a Freemason with Amicilia Lodge, No.25, F. & A.M., Wisconsin, USA.
In 1870 his real estate was valued at $2300 and his personal estate $4000. He died 11 May 1911 and was buried at Inwood, Iowa. His wife Jane died 18 May 1908, aged 74 years. For the complete story of James Skewis see Chapter 9 of *Cornish Heritage*.

SKEWIS JAMES
Natural son of Ann Skewis of Ruan Major. Bpt Cury 7 May 1826.

SKEWES JAMES
Married Charity Vial at Gwennap 17 December 1827. Son: James Skewes (1831). Lived at Carvanner, Gwennap. Miner.

SKEWIS JAMES
Chart 36. Son of William and Christian Skewis of Tregarne; farmer. Bpt St Keverne 1 July 1827.

SKEWES JAMES
Chart 11. Carpenter of Trelowarren Street. In 1841 Census Returns living at College Row, Camborne. Married Alice Hocking. Children: Mary (1838) and Thomas John (1846). Emigrated to USA?

SKEWES JAMES
Son of James and Charity Skewes; miner of Carvannel. Bpt Gwennap 25 December 1831.

SKEWES JAMES
Was principal witness in a murder case heard in Launceston 28 March 1832. Full story in Appendix "Press Cuttings", *Cornish Heritage*.

SKEWES JAMES
Born 1834, England. In 1870 was a farm labourer at Yorkville, Wisconsin, USA. Wife's name Jane. Real estate valued at $4000. Personal estate $1000.

SKUSE JAMES
Married Amy Robins, 1834, Newington Bagpath, Gloucester.

SKUES JAMES
Chart 8. Born 26 December 1838 at 43 Upper Cornwall Street, St George's East, London. Son of William Henry and Sarah (née Young), coal whipper. Bpt St George's East 12 July 1840.

SKEWIS JAMES
Died 1838, Merthyr Tydfil.

SKEWES JAMES
Married 1839, Falmouth.

SKUES JAMES

Married Grace Skues of Brill, Constantine at Constantine, April 1834. In presence of Henry Skewes.

SKEWES JAMES
Son of Henry and Ann Skewes of Penstrathal; miner. Bpt Gwennap at the age of 6 on 22 April 1841.

SKEWIS JAMES
Son of James and Margaret Skewis. Bpt St Erth 21 November 1841.

SKEWES JAMES
Chart 2. Son of William and Elizabeth Skewes of Bolitho, Crowan. Born 1842 in Sithney. Died 1904 in Battle, Sussex, aged 62 years.

SKEWIS JAMES
Chart 50. Born 1842, Merthyr Tydfil, Wales. Father English. Mother Welsh. Emigrated to Pennsylvania, USA, 1862. Married 1876. Wife's name Georgia from Connecticut, USA. Children included: Joseph R. (1881), Alfred (1884), Everson (1888) and Ralph (1899). There were nine children in all, seven of whom had survived by 1900. Lived at 7 Hutson, Allegheny City, Pennsylvania, USA in 1900. Roll turner.

SKUES JAMES
Died 1842, St George's East, London.

SKUES JAMES
Married 1845, Marlborough.

SKEWES JAMES
Born 1846, England. Farm labourer in Yorkville, Wisconsin, USA, 1870.

SKEWIS JAMES
Married 1848, Helston.

SKEWES JAMES
Chart 2. Son of Henry & Avis (née Bath) Skewes. Born 27 February 1849, Redruth. Died 12 May 1852, Stithians, aged 3 years.

SKEWS JAMES
Died 1849, Neath, South Wales.

SKEWES JAMES
Lived in Mamakati, New York, 1850.

SKEWES JAMES
Chart 36. Son of Edward and Julia Skewes of Cury (skoemaker). Born 1850, Cury. Married Susan Thomas (20) of Cury and daughter of Francis Thomas, labourer. In 1871 Census Returns living at Carthvean, Wendron and listed as a bachelor and agricultural labourer. Died 7 February 1877, aged 27 years.

SKEWS JAMES
Born 1851. Died 1915, aged 63 years in Dartford.

SKEWES JAMES
Born 1852. Died 1866, aged 14 years in Redruth.

SKEWS JAMES
Born 1852, North Aylesford.

SKEWSE JAMES
Died 1852, Greenwich.

SKUES JAMES
Born 1854, Medway.

SKEWES JAMES
Died 1855, Redruth.

SKEWES JAMES
Chart 36. Son of William and Elizabeth (née Northey) Skewes. Born 23 November 1856, Australia. Killed in an accident 17 January 1881, aged 25 years.

SKEWES JAMES
Chart 2. Son of Josiah and Fanny Skewes of Bosawsack, Constantine. Born 1857. Married Mary Ellen . . . . . Lived at 29 Cecil Street, Plymouth and later 5 Mutley Park Villas, Plymouth. Died at the Cattle Market, Yealmpton, Devonshire 24 September 1917, aged 60 years. His wife died at 51a Cranley Road, Westcliffe on Sea, Essex 14 May 1939.

SKEWES JAMES
Married 1858, Redruth.

SKEWES JAMES
Born 1861. Lived at Carnarthen, Illogan, Redruth. Died 1874, aged 13 years. Buried Illogan 20 August 1874.

SKEWIES JAMES
Born 1861. Died Hamilton, Scotland, 1921, aged 60 years.

SKUES JAMES
Chart 5. Son of John Penrose and Elizabeth Skues. Born 1862. Died 1864, aged 2 years. Buried Redruth Parish Churchyard 8 May 1864.

SKEWIS JAMES
Born 13 June 1863. Died 28 October 1948, Shullsburg, Wisconsin, USA, aged 85 years.

SKEWES JAMES
Chart 24. Born 1863. Son of William and Priscilla Skewes of Carnkie.

SKUES JAMES
Born 1866. Died 1914, aged 48 years, Lambeth.

SKEWES JAMES
Born 1866, Kea. Nephew of Susan Skewes, widow of Tippet's Backlet, Truro (St Mary's, Truro — 1871 Census Returns).

SKEWIS JAMES

Married 1868, Highchurch, Glasgow.
SKEWES JAMES
Married 1869, Helston.
SKEWES JAMES
Married 1869, Redruth.
SKEWIS JAMES
Chart 50. Son of Joseph and Marion (née Hamilton) Skewis, iron roller. Born 23 November 1870 at 102 William Street, Glasgow. Iron roller. Emigrated to Pennsylvania, 1880. Married Mollie . . . . . 1896. Children included: Joseph H. (1899). Lived at 12 Division Street, Lawrence, Pennsylvania, USA in 1900. His brother Joseph also resided there.
SKEWIS JAMES
Chart 2. Son of Frank and Daisy Skewis of America.
SKEWES JAMES
Married 1873, Helston.
SKEWES JAMES
Married 1875, Helston.
SKEWIS JAMES
Chart 36. Son of John and Eliza Jane (née Mitchell) Skewes. Born 1876, Redruth. Married Edith Louise Richards, Illogan Parish Church, 1900. Children: Hilda Maud (1901) and Arthur (1905). Lived at Bosleake Row, Illogan. Died between 1950 and 1960.
SKEWS JAMES
Married 1876, Farnham.
SKEWIES JAMES
Born 1876. Died Bothwell, Scotland, 1948, aged 72 years.
SKEWES JAMES
Born 1877. Died Redruth, 1939, aged 62 years.
SKEWES JAMES
Born 1883, Penzance.
SKEWES JAMES
Married 1883, Penzance.
SKEWES JAMES
Chart 36. Son of William and Hannah (née Gale) Skewes. Born 21 July 1883. Married Stella Margaret Farrell 26 April 1922. Children: Francis James (1922), Clarice Margaret (1925), Shirley Yvonne (1927), Barbara Hannah (1928), William (1930), Peter Michael (1931) and Judith Rosemary (1935). Known as "Scissors", for when things annoyed him, he would not use rude words but just say "Oh scissors!" Lived at Watson's Creek, via Bendemeer, New South Wales, Australia. Served in the Great War in the 7th Light Horse Regiment, ANZAC, 1914-1918, Gallipoli, Turkey. Died 7 April 1977, aged 93 years.

James Skewes (1883-1977)

SKEWIES JAMES
Married Catherine Lare, 13 June 1884, Hamilton, Scotland.
SKEWIES JAMES
Lived at Bolitho, Crowan 1885/1886.
SKEWIES JAMES
Son of James and Catherine (née Lare) Skewies, coal miner. Born 19 April 1885 at 84 Darngaber Row, Hamilton, Scotland.
SKEWIS JAMES
Chart 50. Son of William and Elizabeth. (née Shaw) Skewis, hammerman. Born 9 Gateside Street, Glasgow on 3 February 1887. Structural steel inspector. Went out to America in 1910. He returned to Scotland shortly after and married Helen Ann McRae, daughter of John and Agnes McRae of 12 St Mungo Street, Glasgow, at St Giles Presbyterian Church, Glasgow, 11 March 1912 and emigrated to Canada in 1913. He became foreman of Dominion Bridge Company and resided in Islington, Toronto, Canada. Son: William J. Skewis.
SKUES JAMES
Greengrocer. Lived at 77 Webber Street, Blackfriars Road, London SE. (1888).
SKEWES JAMES
Married 1889, Penzance.
SKEWES JAMES
Pork butcher at 29 Cecil Street, Plymouth 1890.
SKEWES JAMES
Proprietor of Henry H. Whipple (provision dealer) of 40 Old Town Street, Plymouth (1895).
SKEWIS JAMES
Chart 50. Son of Joseph Richard and Martha (née McIlroy) Skewis, iron worker. Born 18 April 1898 at 17 Quarry Road, Coatbridge, Scotland. Died Glasgow, 1966, aged 68 years.
SKEWES JAMES
Married 1899, Redruth.
SKEWIS JAMES
Married 1900, Redruth.
SKEWES JAMES
Lived at Bosleake, Illogan 1906/1922 with Edith Skewes.
SKEWES JAMES
Lived at Treskillard, Illogan, 1906.
SKEWIES JAMES
Married 1907, Hamilton, Scotland
SKEWES JAMES
Son of Captain Richard Skewes of Mexico. Married Hannah Louise Gurney of 2 Clarence Street, Penzance at Baptist Chapel, Truro, 15 February 1909. Lived at Carnon Crease, Perranwell.
SKEWIS JAMES
Born 1911, Hamilton, Scotland.
SKEWIS JAMES
Born 1912, St Rollox, Scotland.
SKEWIS JAMES
Born 1918, New Monkland, Scotland.
SKEWES JAMES
Chart 50. Born 1919, Redruth. Son of Stephen and Ethel (née Pollard) Skewes. Lived at Trefusis Terrace, Redruth. Attended Redruth East End School. Admitted 2 June 1924 and left 1 April 1926. Died 1940, aged 21 years.
SKEWES JAMES
Lived at Carnarthen Moor, Carn Brea, Illogan in 1932 with Hilda Skewes.
SKEWIS JAMES
Chart 50. Son of James Airns and Irene (née Fox) Skewis. Born 7 April 1948, Hull. Married Smart, in Hull, 1975. Child: Anna Maria (1975).
SKEWIS JAMES
Chart 10. Son of Richard and Evelyn Skewes of Ontario, Canada. Born 16 August 1952, Canada.
SKEWIS JAMES
Son of William J. Skewis of Toronto, Canada. In 1967 was a student living at 12 Glenrose Avenue, Toronto. Two years later he was a data processing engineer with IBM until 1970 when he had moved to 205, 80 Coe Hill Drive, Toronto. From 1976 to present day he lives at 53 Stubbswood Square South, Toronto. Tel. No: (416) 291 3910. Married with two children: Donald James Skewis (1974) and Ian James Skewis (1976).
SKEWIS JAMES
Married Rode, 1969 in Holderness.
SKEWES JAMES A.
Married Elsie M. Cooke, 1918 in Bristol.
SKEWES JAMES A.
Chart 12. Son of John H. and Eva (née Keast) Skewes. Born 1950, Truro. Married Wendy J. Hooper, 1970. Children: Sally Jean (1971) and Sarah Jane (1974).
SKEWIS JAMES AIRNS
Chart 50. Born February 1925, Airdrie, Scotland. Married Irene Fox in New Monkland, Scotland, 1945 (she died 1968). Children: Michael Ian (1947), James (1948), David (1950), Sadie (1953), Elizabeth (1955) and

Philip E. (1957). Married Beatrice M. Fox (also known as Beatrice M. Wilson) in Hull, 1970. Now lives in Grimsby.

SKUES   JAMES ALBERT
Chart 5. Son of Joseph Pearn Skues. Born 1907, Redruth.

SKUES   JAMES ALBERT
Chart 6. Son of John Charles Skues. Born 1907, Redruth.

SKEWIS   JAMES ALDERTON
Chart 2. Son of Francis James and Lucretia Skewis of America. Born 1924. Died 1926.

SKEWS   JAMES ARTHUR
Chart 17. Son of George Alfred and Lucy Skews. Born 26 October 1885. Married 1910, Stepney, London. Children: Margaret (1911), Alfred S.A. (1914), Richard N.E. (1916), Alice and John — twins — (1919) and Eileen (1920). Died in Southend, Essex, 1970, aged 85 years.

SKEWES   JAMES ARTHUR
Born 1890, Redruth. Died 1891, aged 0.

SKEWIS   JAMES BROWN
Chart 50. Son of John Clempson and Ann (née Brown) Skewis. Born 1931, St Andrew, Dundee, Scotland. Bus driver in Dundee until 1962 when he emigrated to Australia with his wife (née Margaret Forest- married 1953, Dalmeny, Scotland) and two children Irene Ann (1956) and John James (1957). Joined Royal Australian Air Force in medical department and was assistant in charge of operations at Richmond Hospital. Later served with medical units in Vietnam and was given a citation for outstanding conduct. He has since served in New South Wales, Victoria, and Western Australia. Is now a flight sergeant. Lives at 19 Trent Street, RAAF Base, Forest Hill, Wagga Wagga, New South Wales, 2651, Australia.

SKEWES   JAMES BUCKINGHAM
Chart 14. Son of James Henry and Grace Skewes. Born 12 February 1928, Milwaukee, Wisconsin, USA. Married Hilda Catherine McLean 4 August 1956. No children. Editor and publisher of *Meridian Star* in Mississippi. Lives at 3432 18th Street, Meridian, Mississippi, 39301, USA.

SKEWES   JAMES CALVIN
Lives at Ouyen Highway, Underbool, 3509, Victoria, Australia with Helen Margaret Skewes. Teacher.

SKEWES   JAMES CHARLES
Chart 38. Son of Charles Percival and Nancy Merle (née Ham) Skewes. Born 14 August 1950. Married Sandra Goodwin 7 February 1976, Broken Hill, New South Wales, Australia. One son: Christopher James Skewes (1979). Lives at 111 Dick Street, Deniliquin, 2710, New South Wales, Australia. Welfare officer with New South Wales Government.

SKEWIS   JAMES CLEMPSON
Born 1961, Dundee East, Scotland.

SKUES   JAMES D.
Served with the Royal Norfolk Regiment and was killed in action in 1943.

SKEWES   JAMES EDWARD
Born 12 March 1887, USA. Married Wilma Bacon 31 December (year not known). Children: Byron James and Harriet.

SKEWIS   JAMES EDWARD
Chart 2. Son of Edward John and Franc Skewis. Born 8 August 1908, America. Married Alice B. Frazier (who later married Brown). Lived at 2414 North Union Street, Tacoma, Washington. Killed in 2nd World War in 1944.

SKEWS   JAMES EDWARD
Born 1882, Gravesend, Kent. Married Allridge in Bromley, Kent, 1914.

SKEWES   JAMES EDWARD
Chart 36. Son of Robert Northey Skewes. Lived at 4 Netherby Street, Wahroonga, Normanhurst, New South Wales, Australia in 1959 with Agnes Veronica Skewes. Children: James Edward Skewes and Anthony Joseph Skewes. Now lives at 27 Eastern Valley Way, Northbridge, 2063, New South Wales, Australia. Postal officer.

SKEWES   JAMES ELDRED
Chart 2. Son of Josiah and Minnie Skewes of 212 Ballards Lane, Finchley, London. Born 1904. Married Kate Schwersee in Hampstead, 1933. Lives at 419 Watford Way, London NW 4. Tel No: 01 203 2347. Optician. Shop 240 Earl's Court Road, London SW 5. Tel No: 01 370 4912. No children.

SKEWES   JAMES FEARGUS O'CONNOR
Chart 11. Born 1842. Son of James and Alice Skewes. Bpt Camborne 9 March 1842. Married 1868, Bristol. Died Truro 1908, aged 66 years.

SKUES   JAMES FREDERICK
Chart 5. Son of Lewis and Eliza (née Pearn) Skues, mason of St Catherines Street, Fowey. Born 19 March 1879. Bpt Fowey Parish Church 29 June 1879. Married Ada Tregonning (she died 1945, aged 60 years) in Redruth, 1905. Mason. Children: Ada May, James Frederick, Phyllis, Lewis and Ernest. Lived at 16 Trefusis Terrace, Redruth from 1923 to his death in 1941, aged 61 years.

SKUES   JAMES FREDERICK
Chart 5. Son of James Frederick and Ada (née Tregonning) Skues. Born 1909. Lived at 16 Trefusis Terrace, Redruth. Died 1969, aged 59 years.

SKUES   JAMES FREDERICK M.
Chart 5. Son of John Charles Skues. Born 1904, Redruth.

SKEWIES   JAMES FYFE
Born 1921, Hamilton, Scotland. Married Dykes in Belshall, Scotland, 1950. Married Margaret Stokhoe, in Canongate, 1966.

SKEWES   JAMES HANLEY
Chart 32. Son of Richard and Grace Skewes, formerly of Kenwyn. Bpt Gwennap 23 July 1817. Buried Gwennap 27 December, aged 9 months.

SKEWES   JAMES HARRIS
Son of James and Eleanor Skewes of Treskillard, Illogan; labourer. Born 1853. Bpt Illogan Parish Church 20 July 1853.

SKEWES   JAMES HARRY
Chart 12. Son of James Henry Skewes and Maud (née Richards). Born 1907, Truro. Twice married: 1) Doris Pearce, 1934 who died Truro 1942, aged 32. 2) Florrie Woolcock, 1943 who died July 1977, aged 64 years. Children: First marriage Gillian A. Second marriage Dawn and Irene. Lived at Woodlands, Mithian St Agnes. Died 17 July 1978, aged 70 years. Buried 20 July 1978 at St Agnes Cemetery.

SKEWES   JAMES HENRY
Chart 12. Born Cury 1 November 1840. Son of John and Julianna Skewes of Gilly, Cury. In 1861 Census Returns he was a carpenter at Trelowarren Street, Camborne. Married Mary Jane Eudey, daughter of Edward Eudey at Camborne Parish Church, 5 March 1865, in presence of Mary Skewes. Child: Harry Oswald Skewes (1865). Went abroad to Nicaragua, Central America where he became foreman carpenter of the Chontales Mines. On 24 May, 1868 he was invited by the doctor of the company to go with him on a visit to a patient who lived some 20 miles away. Not having been out of the mines for some months he agreed to go with the doctor. On their way back they called at the company's farm, where they found one of the underground agents Captain James White, and a miner, both of whom had been drinking rather a lot. Refusing the invitation to drink, Skewes and the doctor rode home accompanied by Capt White and his companion. The latter became weary and soon lagged behind the rest of the party. Skewes pointed out the danger of the man's being left to take care of himself in such a locality. It was then that White became angry, rode up to Skewes, struck him a severe blow with his fist. Skewes, a fine stalwart of a man, then aged 36, soon got the best of the encounter, knocking White down three times. White became so antagonistic that he drew out his revolver and with an oath placed it at Skewes' head and fired.
Skewes was killed and the doctor raised the alarm as soon as was possible, and the body was removed to the mines for interment. White was placed in prison.
James Henry Skewes was universally liked and respected at the mines, by natives as well as English. He was a steady, inoffensive man, besides being a most useful servant of the company. White was sentenced to be hanged.

SKEWES   JAMES HENRY
Chart 12. Born 1848. Son of Henry and Harriet (née Hodge) Skewes of Landewednack, St Keverne. Lived at Three Tuns Hotel, Landewednack in 1861 Census Returns. In 1871 Census Returns lived with his wife Elizabeth (born Landewednack 1847) and daughter Ann (1870).

SKEWES   JAMES HENRY
Chart 2. Born 1857, Shullsburg, Wisconsin, USA. Married Juana Brito. Lived at 129 Abasolo Street, Pachuca, Mexico. Children: Luis Enrique (1907), Fransisco (1905) and Zeferino Severo Skewes (1899). Died 9 December 1915, aged 58 years. Wife died 25 July 1947.

James Henry Skewes (1857-1915)

SKEWES JAMES HENRY
Married 1869, Helston.

SKEWES JAMES HENRY
Chart 12. Born 1872. Bpt Cury 4 November 1872. Nickname "Sunny". Son of John and Thirza Skewes of Chypons; labourer. Lived at Tresodden. Married Maud Mary Richards of Trevelgan Farm, Gweek in 1898 (she died 1946, aged 70 years). Children: Sydney Arthur, Mabel, Elizabeth Mary, Bertram, William Frank, Renee, Lilla, Maud, Janie, John H. and James Harry.
He was a great horse lover; spent 37 years farming in the Perranporth district and up to 1960 was a familiar figure travelling by pony and trap, his favourite form of transport. Every year he rode to Helston Flora Day. He died 12 January 1965, aged 92 years. The funeral service was held at Bolingey Methodist Church on Saturday 16 January.

SKEWS JAMES HENRY
Born 1876, Gravesend, Kent.

SKEWES JAMES HENRY
Born 1886, Helston.

SKEWES JAMES HENRY
Chart 14. Son of William John and Prudence Jane (née Mundy) Skewes. Born 2 February 1886, Helston. He emigrated with his parents from Cornwall to the United States of America in 1891. Educated at Milwaukee State College. Later a reporter for *Milwaukee Journal* and *Milwaukee Daily News, The Kansas City Star* and *Racine Daily News*. Married Grace Buckingham, daughter of Edward Buckingham (she born 1 January 1892), 24 February 1914. Issue: one son, James Buckingham Skewes (1928).
James Henry Skewes became editor of *Racine Journal News* in 1912 and editor of *Meridian Star* from 1922. In 1935 was awarded a trophy for "untiring and unselfish work as President of the Meridian Chamber of Commerce for six years."
In 1925 the Meridian Kiwanis Club awarded him a silver loving cup as "Meridian's most worthwhile citizen".
In 1938 the Exchange Club gave him a cup with the inscription "Citizen Number One, 1938."
He received various awards for community service. James Henry Skewes was a Freemason (Shriner) Elk KP. Lived at 1703 23rd Avenue, Meridian, Mississippi, 39301, USA. Died Mississippi 6 May 1958, aged

James Henry Skewes (1886-1958)

72 years.

SKEWS JAMES HENRY
Chart 15. Son of Edmund and Maria Skews of Pensilva, Liskeard. Bpt St Ive 22 August 1894. Died Birmingham 1946, aged 53 years.

SKEWES JAMES HENRY
Chart 36. Son of George and Mary (née Dowling) Skewes. Born 30 May 1905, Rocky River, Uralla, New South Wales, Australia. Married Elsie Snow, 1930. Children: George Alton and Douglas James. Died 26 July 1969, aged 64 years at Quirindi, Tamworth.

SKEWES JAMES HENRY
Chart 12. Born 21 July 1907. See JAMES HARRY SKEWES.

SKEWES JAMES HENRY OSWALD
Chart 12. Son of Harry Oswald and Emily Ann Skewes. Born 1894. Married Jessie Victoria Cockram in Axbridge in 1920. Lived at 7 Moor Street, Camborne and later Centenary Street, Camborne and Trecarne, 12 Atlantic Terrace, Camborne. Child: Jack Pat Oswald (1923). In the First World War he served as an engineer artificer in the Royal Navy and later he was an officer in the Merchant Navy. Before returning to Camborne he was employed by Parnell Aircraft Company in Bristol and the Westland Aircraft Company at Yeovil. He then became a toolmaker with Holman Brothers Number 3 works where he was employed for over 30 years.
He was a member of Camborne British Legion and was associated with Centenary Methodist Church. His father Harry Oswald had been a well-known Rugby player.
Died 27 March 1954, aged 59 years.

SKEWS JAMES JOHN
Born 1872, Neath.

SKEWIS JAMES L.
District Manager, *Tacoma News Tribune,* Tacoma, Washington State, USA in 1976. Resided at Olympia.

SKEWES JAMES LEONARD
Born 24 March 1950. Son of Leonard and Virginia (née Sterler) Skewes. Lives at 304 Elm Street, Marshall, Minnesota, 56528, United States of America. Tel no: (507) 532 6231.

SKEWES JAMES LEONARD
Lives at 24 First Avenue, Glengowrie, 5044, South Australia.

SKEWES JAMES LEONARD
Lives at Sacks Lane, Victoria Estate, 4850, Queensland, Australia.

SKEWES JAMES LESLIE
Lives at 90 Invermore Street, Mount Gravatt, 4122, Queensland, Australia with Joan Hanna Skewes. Manager.

SKEWES JAMES LUGG
Chart 22. Son of William and Christian Skewes, labourer. Bpt 25 June 1815, Ruan Major.

SKEWES JAMES LUGG
Chart 14. Son of Henry and Grace Skewes of Hendra, Ruan Major, schoolmaster. Bpt Ruan Major 20 July 1834. Emigrated to Yorkville, Racine County, Wisconsin, USA, 1842 with his uncle Samuel Skewes and lived at Grovean Farm. Farmer. Married Jane Phillips. No children of their own, but adopted four — Morley, Silas, Lottie and Earl. Moved to Atlanta, Nebraska, USA. Died 1904.

SKEWES JAMES LUGG
Chart 36. Born 1855. Bpt Mawnan, 7 October 1855. Son of James and Frances Skewes of Mawnan. Buried 20 May 1856, aged 8 months.

SKEWES JAMES LUGG
Chart 36. Son of James and Frances Skewes of Mawnan Smith. Born 1859. Bpt Mawnan 16 January 1859. Died at sea aboard vessel *Webfoot,* 1875, aged 17 years.

SKEWES JAMES MARLEY
Chart 32. Son of Richard and Grace Skewes; miner of Kenwyn. Bpt Gwennap 6 June 1824.

SKEWES JAMES MARTIN
B.A. Chart 11. Son of Thomas John and Eunice (née Martin) Skewes. Born 15 December 1914. Married Helen Ruth Robbins (she was born 21 April 1918) 29 September 1941. B.A. in E & B, 1939. Then lived at 4210 Brooklyn, Seattle, Washington. Now works at Coastal Company, Pier 16, Seattle, Washington 98134, USA. Children: Victoria Jane (1940), Sara Jo (1943), James Martin (1951) and Janet Sue (1953).
Freemason with Constellation Lodge, No 266 F & A.M., Seattle, Washington. USA. Lives at 8040, 39th Ave NE, Seattle, Washington, 98115.

SKEWES JAMES MARTIN II
Chart 11. Son of James Martin and Helen Ruth (née Robbins) Skewes. Born 26 September 1951 in Seattle, Washington, USA. Married Susan Countryman 26 July 1977 in Tacoma, Washington, USA.

SKEWS JAMES M.S.
Born 1882. Died Wycombe 1966, aged 84 years.

SKEWIS JAMES O'NEIL
Born 1959, Bridgeton, Scotland.

SKEWES JAMES ROBERT
Born 21 December 1914. Son of William and Alberta Mary Jessop Skewes at Superior, Houghton, Michigan, USA. Married Elizabeth Yaniskauis.

SKEWES   JAMES ROBERT
Lived at 13 Longueville Road, Lane Cove, New South Wales, Australia
in 1959 with Dorothy Jessie Skewes.
SKEWES   JAMES ROBERT
Chart 36. Son of Samuel Sidney and Sarah (née Pennall) Skewes. Born
22 July 1897. Married Pearl Isabel Chapman. Died 13 January 1973,
aged 75 years.
SKEWES   JAMES ROBERTS
Born 1850, Helston.
SKEWES   JAMES WILLIAM
Son of Byron James and Margaret Cecilia (née Morrison) Skewes. Born
10 March 1949. Married Christine Anne Gallagher 23 June 1973, New
York. Children: Ryan James Skewes (1974) and Kerry Ann Skewes
(1975). Lives at 169 Westwood Drive, Brentwood, New York, 11717,
USA.
Previous address: 126 Toronto Avenue, Massapequa, New York. Tel
No: (516) 231 4994.
SKEWES   JAMES WILLIAM
Lives at 17 Gaskin Avenue, Flinders Park, 5025, South Australia.
SKEWES   JAMES WILLIAM
Chart 36. Son of Percy and Mary (née Farrell) Skewes. Born 3 March
1916. Married Pauline Beatrice Seymour, 18 November 1939.
Children: Elaine Mary (1940), Noel James (1941) and Yvonne (1945).
Tin dredger. Lives at Lower Watson's Creek, Bendemeer, 2352, New
South Wales, Australia.
SKEWES   JAMESON
Son of Henry Skewes, builder of Camborne. Married Miss Evans,
daughter of Mr Evans, general builder; at Hayle, 17 March 1899.
SKEWES   JAMIE
Chart 10. Son of Herbert James and Patricia Helen (née Drysdale)
Skewes. Born Hamilton, Ontario, Canada 19 April 1958. Laboratory
technician. Lives at 132 Ridge, Hamilton, Ontario, Canada.
SKEWIS   JAN
Born 1968, Inverness, Scotland.
SKEWES   JAN MAREE
Chart 36. Née Mellor. Married Philip Stephen Skewes 28 February
1975. Lives at Flat 4, 75 Paradise Island, Surfers Paradise Island, Gold
Coast, Queensland, 4217, Australia.

*Steam engine presented to Watsons Creek School, New
South Wales, Australia by James William Skewes in
1972*

SKEWES   JANE
Daughter of Thomas Skewes. Married William Hayne at Gerrans 3
October 1563.
SCOOSE   JANE
Married Thomas Hore at Menheniot 18 September 1587.
SCOOSE   JANE
Buried Menheniot 16 May 1604.
SKEWES   JANE
Daughter of Thomas Skewes. Bpt Exeter St Mary Major 27 June 1607.
SKEWES   JANE
Chart 36. Daughter of James and Sarah Skewes. Bpt Cury 24 March
1705. Married John James of Mullion at Cury 3 June 1727.
SKUES   JANE
Chart 4. Daughter of William and Jane Skues. Bpt Redruth 5 April
1684. Married John William 5 February 1708.
SKEWES   JANE
Born 1722. Lived in Illogan. Died 5 May 1822, aged 100 years.
SKEWIS   JANE
Chart 3. Née Coombe. Married at Kenwyn Parish Church 16 December
1722 to Richard Skewis, tinner. Children: Stephen, John, Mary,
William, Richard and Jenefar. Died 23 June 1782.
SKEWES   JANE
Died Camborne 29 October 1722.
SKEWES   JANE
Daughter of Edward and Jane Skewes. Bpt Mevagissey 24 June 1724.
SKEWS   JANE
Wife of Richard Skews. Buried Kea 12 July 1730.
SKEWES   JANE
Chart 14. Daughter of Henry and Judith Skewes of Cury. Bpt Cury 25
July 1731.
SKEWES   JANE
Daughter of Joseph and Jone Skewes. Bpt Gunwalloe 2 November 1736.
SKEWS   JANE
Daughter of Henry Skews of Kea. Bpt 29 March 1752 at Kenwyn.
SKEWES   JANE
Chart 2. Daughter of Robert Skewes. Bpt Camborne 30 May 1756.
SKEWIS   JANE
Married John Banfield, labourer at Mawgan in Meneage 12 February
1760.
SKEWIS   JANE
Chart 25. Daughter of Thomas and Esther Skewis. Bpt St Keverne 16
November 1760.

SKEWES JANE
Chart 14. Née Retallack. Born 1768 St Antony. Married Henry Skewes (by licence) at St Keverne 15 August 1793, in presence of John Skewes. Lived at Tresodden, Ruan Major.
Children: Margaret, Edward, Jane, Henry, John, Thomas, Anthony, Samuel and Mary. Died 1853, Helston district, aged 85 years.

SKUES JANE
Married Richard Harris at St Mary's Truro, 1771.

SKEWES JANE
Chart 3. Daughter of John and Mary Skues. Born 1772, Helston. Died 20 January 1783, aged 11 years.

SKEWES JANE
Chart 2. Born 1777. Née Angove. Married John Skewes 8 February 1799. Buried Camborne, 30 March 1821, aged 44 years.

SKEWS JANE
Married Andrew Mitchell of Paul 18 November 1787 at Falmouth.

SKEWIS JANE
Daughter of Richard and Jane Skewis. Bpt Kenwyn 27 July 1788.

SKEWES JANE
Born 1790. Lived at Vyvyan's Row, Camborne. Died 1878, aged 88 years. Buried Camborne 4 November 1878.

SKEWES JANE
Daughter of James and Ann Skewes. Bpt 26 June 1791, Cury.

SKEWES JANE
Wife of Henry Skewes. Buried St Keverne 26 November 1792.

SKEWIS JANE
Chart 14. Daughter of Henry and Jane Skewis. Bpt 2 July 1797 at St Keverne. Married James Lugg at St Keverne 16 July 1822. Issue: 5 sons and 4 daughters. Died 1853.

SKEWES JANE
Chart 30. Née Beer formerly of St Teath. Born 1799. Married Thomas Skewes at Kenwyn Parish Church 12 February 1824. Lived at Daniel Street, Truro. Children: Mary Ann, Henrietta, John Beer, Philippa Jane and Thomas. Died 19 September 1889, aged 90 years.

SCKEWS JANE
Born 1754. Buried Kenwyn 7 July 1809, aged 55 years.

SKEWS JANE
Chart 9. Daughter of James and Joanna Skews of Lower Sticker. Bpt St Ewe 28 April 1805.

SKEWES JANE
Born 1806. Lived at Nantithet, Cury. Buried Cury 4 February 1886, aged 80 years.

SKUES JANE
Daughter of William and Jane Skues. Bpt Mylor 24 April 1808.

SKEWES JANE
Married John Carthew of Illogan at Kenwyn 8 May 1815. In presence of Peter Skewes.

SKEWES JANE
Chart 28. Daughter of Richard and Mary Skewes of Nancevellan Common, Kea. Bpt Kea 14 May 1815. Married James Goldsworthy of Bissoe 26 December 1839 at Kea. Witnesses: Tamson Skewes & Ann Skewes.

SKEWES JANE
Chart 2. Daughter of John and Jane Skewis. Bpt Camborne 31 May 1821. John was a widower by the time of the christening.

SKUES JANE
Illegitimate daughter of Maria Skues of Hugus. Bpt Kenwyn 17 February 1822.

SKEWES JANE
Married James Lugg at Ruan Major 16 July 1822.

SKEWES JANE
Daughter of Matthew and Mary Skewes (née Jeffrey); miner of Chacewater, Kenwyn. Born 4 December 1824. Bpt Truro Wesleyan Chapel 14 March 1837.

SKEWES JANE
Daughter of Matthew Skewes, miner. Lived at Chacewater. Born 1825. Married Joseph Davey; mason, son of Thomas Davey, mason at Kenwyn Church 21 December 1850. In presence of Matthew Skewes.

SKEWES JANE
Married Richard Edwards at St Blazey 19 January 1826.

SKEWES JANE
Born 1827. Died Redruth 1903, aged 76 years.

SKEWES JANE
Chart 18. Born 1828, Bere Alston, Devon. Married Samuel Dawe Skewes at the Independent Chapel, Tavistock, Devon 1 April 1856. Lived at Pepper Street, Beer Ferris. Children: Mary Anna Courtis (1858), Jane (1859), Alice Kate (1862), Howard (1871), Florence Rosalie (1868) and Arthur Dawe (1873). Died 24 April 1881, aged 54 years. Buried in Bere Alston.

SKEWES JANE
of Nangiles. Born 1830. Spinster. Died 9 July 1894, aged 64 years. Buried Baldhu 15 July 1894.

SKUES JANE
Chart 3. Daughter of William and Mary Skues. Married Henry Pascoe

17 July 1831 in Helston.

SKEWES JANE
Daughter of Henry and Grace Skewes; schoolmaster. Born 1832. Bpt Helston 5 December 1832. Milliner in 1861 Census Returns.

SKEWES JANE
Daughter of Peter and Ann Skews of Gwennap. Bpt Kea 9 July 1833.

SKEWES JANE
Married William Simons, sojourner at Camborne Parish Church 19 January 1837.

SKEWES JANE
Chart 10. Daughter of Peter and Elizabeth Skewes. Bpt Kea 8 October 1837.
Married William Francis Wasley, smith of Baldhu, son of Samuel Wasley, miner, at Baldhu Church 10 April 1862.

SKEWES JANE
Died 1838, Redruth.

SKEWS JANE
Born 1839. Died St Columb 1913, aged 74 years.

SKEWES JANE
Born 1840, Helston.

SKEWIS JANE
Chart 44. Daughter of Thomas and Elizabeth Skewis. Born 1841, Abergavenny. Died 1841, aged 0.

SKEWS JANE
Died 1841, Truro.

SKEWES JANE
Died 1842, Redruth.

SKEWIS JANE
Chart 44. Daughter of James and Elizabeth Skewis. Born 1843, Abergavenny. Married 1864.

SKEWIS JANE
Daughter of John Skewis of Illogan; farmer. Married Henry Jenkin, miner at Illogan 13 October 1842. Henry was son of James Jenkin, farmer of Illogan Downs.

SKEWES JANE
Died 1845, Helston.

SKEWS JANE
Born 1847. Died Dartford, 1923, aged 74 years.

SKEWES JANE
Chart 25. Née Jameson. Born 1847. Married William John Skewes at Lower Broughton Church, Salford 14 August 1881. Children: William (1883), Frederick (1885), Jessie (1887) and Louisa (1889). Emigrated to Australia with Jessie and Louisa aboard vessel Cuzco which sailed from London and arrived in Sydney 5 June 1892. Buried 1 February 1917 at Grace Cemetery, Sydney, aged 70 years.

SKEWES JANE
Married 1853, Helston.

SKEWES JANE
Married 1853, Truro.

SKEWS JANE
Died 1856, St Austell.

SKEWS JANE
Born 1857. Lived at 2 Arwenack Avenue, Falmouth. Widow. Died 27 March 1929, aged 72 years at 19 Poplar Road, Merton, Surrey.

SKEWES JANE
Chart 18. Daughter of Samuel Dawe and Jane (née Courtis) Skewes of Pepper Street, Bere Alston, Devon. Born 1859. Married ...... Wright. Died in 1950's. One daughter, Winifred, who married Dr David Beaston in 1921.

SKEWS JANE
Chart 50. Born 1866, Redruth. Daughter of William and Jane (née Bullock) Skews, of Lower Penponds, Camborne.

SKEWS JANE
Born 1866, Redruth.

SKUES JANE
Chart 5. Daughter of John Penrose and Sally (née Tubb) Skues. Born 1845 (?). Married Henry Sobay at Illogan Highway, Association Chapel 27 January 1864. In 1861 Census Returns was listed as a dressmaker then aged 16 years.

SKEWES JANE
Born 1870, Helston.

SKUES JANE
Married 1871, Chippenham.

SKEWES JANE
Chart 49. Daughter of William and Harriet Skewes. Born 1881, Totnes. Died 1901, aged 19 years.

SKEWES JANE
Chart 14. Daughter of Charles J. and Loretta Skewes of America.

SKEWES JANE
Married 1888, Plymouth.

SKEWS JANE
Born 24 March 1893. Died Barnsley, South Yorkshire 1978, aged 85 years.

SKEWES JANE
Married 1894, Redruth.
SKEWS JANE
Married 1928 to Braidwood, West Derby.
SKEWS JANE
Mother's maiden name Cadmore. Born 1957, Worcester.
SKEWES JANE
Lived at Kangaroo Road, Oakleigh, Victoria, Australia in 1913 with John Ogilvie Skewes, painter. By 1959 had moved to 17 Dover Street, Clayton, Oakleigh East, Victoria, Australia.
SKEWES JANE
Chart 25. Daughter of Frank Robert and Anne (née Taylor) Skewes. Born 15 June 1961, Wilmslow, Cheshire. Lives at 21 Capesthorne Road, Wilmslow, Cheshire SK9 6LU.
SKEWS JANE
Chart 41. Mother's maiden name Margaret Skews. Born 1963, Sheffield, South Yorkshire.
SKEWS JANE
Married Lockwood, Waveney, Suffolk, 1977.
SKEWIS JANE BAWDEN
Born 1848. Lived at Pengiggan Moor, Camborne. Buried Camborne 4 July 1852, aged 4 years.
SKEWES JANE FRANCES
Married 1862, Liskeard.
SKEWS JANE GRACE
Born 1841. Died 1907, Redruth, aged 66 years.
SKUES JANE JEFFREY
Daughter of John and Avis (née Jeffrey) Skues. Bpt Cury 1 August 1824. John and Avis were married 4 March 1824.
SKUES JANE LOUISE
Chart 8. Daughter of Terence F. Skues. Mother's maiden name Jean Moore. Born 1970, Newham.
SKEWES JANE LUGG
Chart 14. Daughter of Henry and Grace Skewes; innkeeper. Bpt Helston 5 December 1832. Married Edward Smith.
SKEWS JANE M.
Chart 10. Daughter of Martin Rex Skews. Mother's maiden name Miriam Martin. Born 1949, Eton. Married Collins in St Pancras, 1970.
SKEWES JANE MITCHELL
Born 1885, Helston. Died 1885, aged 0.
SKEWES JANE PIPER
Chart 2. Daughter of Absalom and Jane Skewes. Bpt Camborne 7 April 1811.
SKEWIS JANE RABLING
Chart 2. Daughter of Edward John and Franc Skewis. Born 14 November 1905. Married Louis Thorness 10 March 1929. Divorced 1946. Issue: 2 daughters. Lives at Box 170, Borrego Springs, California, 92084, USA (1980).
SKEWS JANE ROGERS
Chart 36. Daughter of Francis and Grace Skews of Illogan Highway, blacksmith. Born 1870. Bpt Illogan Parish Church 24 February 1874.
SKEWIS JANE O'NEIL
Born 1953, Camalchie, Scotland.
SKEWS JANE T.
Chart 2. Née Rabling. Born 1834. Married James Skewis, in Camborne 1855. Emigrated to the United States of America (Shullsburg, Wisconsin). Children: Anita (1856), William James (1858), Francis Harry (1860), Edward John (1865), George Absalom (1867), Charles Samuel (1869), Jennie Rabling (1872) and Elmer Arthur (1877). Died 18 May 1908, aged 74 years. Buried in Inwood Cemetery, Iowa.
SKEWIS JANE T.
Chart 2. Née Osborne. Born 9 March 1828. Married Absalom Skewis in Camborne and emigrated to Shullsburg, Wisconsin, 1849. Children: Mary Ellen (1851), Emily Jane (1854), Elizabeth Adeline (1857), John Rule (1858) and Bennett Osborne (1862). Died 10 November 1866, aged 39 years. Buried in Shullsburg Cemetery, USA.
SKEWES JANE TREWEEK
Chart 19. Daughter of John and Jennifer Skewes. Bpt 5 June 1822, Gwennap. Married Edward Penna, of St Day, farmer at Gwennap 2 January 1843.
SKEWIS JANE TUBB
Born 1844, Redruth.
SKEWES JANELLE
Chart 36. Née Heyward. Married David Michael Skewes, 10 June 1978. Son Simon David (1980). Lives in New South Wales, Australia.
SKEWES JANELLE ANNE
Chart 36. Daughter of Leslie Kevin and Jill Cecilia (née Pullman) Skewes. Born 2 February 1951. Lives at Caroline Street, Bendemeer, 2352, New South Wales, Australia.
SKEWES JANET
Buried 23 April 1590, Wendron.
SKEWES JANET
Lives at 1 Eva Street, Morphett Vale, 5162, South Australia with Peter Nathaniel Skewes, butcher.

SKEWS JANET AUDREY
Chart 41. Daughter of William John and Mary (née Rump) Skews, of 44 Elemore Lane, Easington Lane, Hetton-le-Hole, County Durham. Born 28 April 1928. Married Gordon Brown 21 June 1952, Durham. Issue: 1 daughter. Lives at 8 Swaledale Close, Moorsley, Hetton-le-Hole, County Durham. Telephone number: 0783 265117.
SKEWES JANET BARBARA
Chart 36. Daughter of Brian Lock and Barbara Jessie (née McKinley) Skewes. Born 2 March 1957. Lives at Areyonga, via Alice Springs, 5751, Northern Territory, Australia.
SKEWS JANET G.
Chart 6. Daughter of William Alexander and Gale (née Julson) Skews. Born 12 April 1951. Single. Lives in Hollandale, Wisconsin, USA.
SKEWIS JANET GRACE
Born 1931, Shettleston, Scotland. Married William Law in Camalchie, Scotland, 1952.
SKEWIS JANET HOUGHTON
Chart 2. Daughter of Francis Henry Skewis II and Mary Jane Skewis. Born 9 July 1953, America. Married Barry Conklin 14 June 1975.
SKUSE JANET LESLEY
Known as "Rusty". Née Field. Born 20 December 1943, Shipley, Yorkshire. Educated at Manor House School, Ferndown, Dorset and St Cuthbergers Convent Boarding School for Girls, Wimborne, Dorset. Married William Harold Bernard Skuse, son of Leslie Walter Harold Skuse, 5 July 1976.
She is recognised as Britain's most tattooed lady. 85% of her body has been tattooed by her husband in 12 years. "He always had designs on her."
Appeared with her husband on Southern Television production "Second Skin" on 11 April 1980.

Janet Lesley 'Rusty' Skuse

Lives at Park View, Hawley Road, Hawley, near Camberley, Surrey.

SKEWES JANET MAY
Chart 12. Daughter of Gilbert J. and Kathleen Skewes. Mother's maiden name Dennis. Born 9 March 1958. Lives at Trelimminey, St Martin, Helston.

SKEWES JANET MUIR
Chart 2. Née McPhee. Married Josiah Skewes, Helston, 1881. Emigrated to Australia. Children: Henry, Josiah, Archibald, Laura, Agnes, Avis and Olive. Lived at 7 Grant Street, Ballarat, Victoria, Australia in 1912. Died 1924, Victoria, Australia.

SKEWES JANET SUE
Chart 11. Daughter of James Martin and Helen Ruth Skewes. Born 21 November 1953, USA.

SKEWES JANETTE LYDIA
Chart 36. Daughter of John Locke and Heather Leonne (née McKenzie) Skewes. Born 15 July 1955. Lived at Duthie Park, via Blackall, 4723, Queensland, Australia. Married Rodney George, dentist at Bunderberg, Australia, 5 May 1980.

SKEWES JANETTE MARY
Chart 36. Née Robinson. Born 25 September 1953. Married Gregory Archer Skewes 1 May 1976. Issue: One daughter Wendy Jane (1979). Lives in Queensland, Australia.

SKEWES JANICE
Chart 36. Daughter of William and Ida Olive (née SKEWES). Twin to Jennifer Skewes. Born 14 November 1942, New South Wales, Australia. Married Richard Farrell, 24 April 1964. Issue: 2 sons and 1 daughter. Lives in New South Wales, Australia.

SKEWES JANICE ELIZABETH
Lives at 205 Victoria Street, Ballarat, Victoria, Australia, 3350 with John Michael Skewes.

SKEWIS JANICE FLORENCE
Lives at 14 Heeny Street, Chilla, 4413, Queensland, Australia with Dudley Walter Kent Skewis, sawmill hand.

SKEWES JANICE KATHLEEN
Chart 36. Née Egan. Married Ronald Edgar Skewes 7 March 1959. Children: Anthony Wayne (1960) and Craig Stephen (1964). Lives at Mallee-Brae, Goolwa, 5214, South Australia.

SKEWS JANICE LYLA
Lives at 4 Green Valley Crescent, Hampton Park, 3976, Victoria, Australia with Ronald Skews, butcher.

SKEWS JANIE
Married 1896, Bedminster.

SKEWES JANIE
Born 1874. Lived at 52 Trevethan Road, Falmouth. Widow. Died 30 August 1960, aged 86 years.

SKEWES JANIE
Married 1894, Redruth.

SKEWES JANIE
Chart 12. Daughter of James Henry and Maud Skewes. Born 1915. Died 1930 in Redruth, aged 15 years of pyorrhoea — disease of the gums.

SKEWES JANIS PATRICIA
Lives at 205 Victoria Street, Ballarat, Victoria, 3350, Australia with David Eric Skewes.

SKEWS JAQUELINE A.
Chart 10. Daughter of Thomas H. Skews. Mother's maiden name Harris. Born 1949, St Austell. Married Truman, St Austell, 1975

SKEWES JASON
Chart 36. Son of Timothy Lester and Lynette Skewes of Australia. Born 9 May 1970.

SKUSE JASON
Son of Dean and Margaret (née Barnes) Skuse. Born 21 August 1971. Lives at 26 Fraser Street, Newstead Village, Nottingham.

SKEWES JASON COLLIER
Chart 14. Son of Glen Wilson and Patricia (née Manthey) Skewes. Born 9 July 1973, Wisconsin, USA. Lives at 918 South Ninth Street, La Crosse, Wisconsin, 54061, USA.

SKEWES JASON GARY
Chart 36. Son of Gary Earle and Jennifer Joy (née Matthews) Skewes. Born 6 September 1971, Tamworth, New South Wales, Australia.

SKEWS JASON MARK
Mother's maiden name SKEWS. Born 1971, Truro.

SKEWES JASON MAXWELL
Chart 36. Son of Maxwell Charles and Cheryl (née Sprowle) Skewes. Born 31 August 1971. Lives at 12 Julia Place, Moree, 2400, New South Wales, Australia.

SKEWES JASON PETER
Mother's maiden name Wathing. Born 1972, Truro.

SKEWES JEAN
Lived at Railway Street, Scarborough, New South Wales, Australia in 1959 with Harvey Hilton Skewes, fuelman.

SKEWS JEAN
Chart 15. Née Fishleigh. Married Stanley George Skews, 1958, St Germans. Children: Maureen J. Skews (1959) and David J. Skews (1960). Lives in Pensilva, Liskeard.

SKUSE JEAN
of Sydney, Australia. In April, 1981 she said that women translators should be used to remove sexist slants when a new version of the Bible is prepared. As secretary of the Australian Council of Churches she said that some modern versions of the Bible had been translated by men, who were victims of "their own sexisms and times", and the result was the translations were unnecessarily sexist. The revised standard English Bible was among these. Miss Skues said that some passages, which should refer to the "children of God", had been translated as the "sons of God". This could make women feel excluded.

SKUES JEAN D.
Married David C. Boothman in Gloucester, 1954.

SKEWES JEAN E.
Lives at Pengilly Avenue, Apollo Bay, Victoria, Australia. Member of the Latter Day Saints. Interested in family history of Skewes from Helston 1826-1919.

SKEWES JEAN GLADYS
Lives at 6 Hillcrest Road, Kewdale, 6105, Western Australia with Douglas William Skewes, sub-foreman. Nurse.

SKEWS JEAN JAMIESON
Chart 15. Née Adam. Born 18 October 1922, Scotland. Married Harry Skews at Logie Church, Stirling, Scotland 26 April 1943. Child: Derek Thomas Skews (1951). Lives at Mount View, Quarry Road, Pensilva, Liskeard, Cornwall. Tel no: 0579 62733.

SKUES JEAN MARGARET
Chart 8. Daughter of Ernest John and Jennie (née Franklin) Skues. Born 30 March 1935, Finsbury, London. Married Ernest J. Davies 24 March 1956, in Hackney. Issue: 2 sons and 1 daughter.

SKEWS JEAN Q.
Chart 17. Daughter of Henry George and Queenie (née Holgate) Skews. Born 1934, Lexden. Married Hodges in Ealing, 1955. Issue: two sons and two daughters.

SKEWES JEANETTE CYNTHIA
Chart 36. Daughter of Edward Keith and Masie (née Lawson) Skewes. Born 26 August 1942, Guildford, Western Australia. Married Kay. Issue: 1 daughter. Lives at 36 Rae Road, Safety Bay, Western Australia 6169.

SKEWES JEANNE R.
Was a member of the U.S. State Department. Was shot to death near Saigon 7 March 1948 and was the first American civilian to be killed in Indochina fighting since VJ Day. She was 32 and lived in Evanston, Illinois. Jeanne was a librarian in Saigon for the U.S. Information Service and was a wartime employee of the office of War and Information in San Francisco. Her name before marriage was Workman and her parents lived in Phoenix Arizona.

SKEWIS JEAN S.O.
Married Dobson, 1973, Kettering.

SKEWES JECOLIAH
Chart 24. Née Uren. Daughter of William Uren, miner. Born 1840. Married Edward Skewes at Lannarth Parish Church 27 April 1861. Formerly of Cury, Edward was a railway employee. In 1871 Census Returns they lived at Lanner, Gwennap with their children: Edward J., William and Eliza J. Died 1875, aged 35 years. Buried Gwennap 3 August 1875.

SKEWES JEFFRIE
Chart 14. Son of Edgar and Beulah Skewes of America.

SKUES JEFFREY
Chart 7. Son of Francis Harry Skues. Mother's maiden name Henson. Born 1948, Dartford, Kent.

SKEWES JEFFREY KEITH
Chart 12. Son of George and Joyce (née Hawken) Skewes. Born 1 December 1950. Lives at "Rosskeith", 140 Agar Road, Illogan Highway, Redruth.

SKEWES JEFFREY LIONAL
Chart 12. Son of William John and Norà (née Thomas) Skewes. Born 5 November 1946, Tregidden, St Martin. Married Angela Caddy at St Keverne Church 23 April 1973. Labourer in building trade. No children. Lives at Restormal, Nancmullion Road, Mullion, Helston, Cornwall. Tel No: Mullion 240143.

SKEWES JEFFREY WILLIAM
Chart 38. Son of Horatio Gerald and Phyllis Manetta (née Bowden) Skewes. Born 20 August 1948. Married Mary Jane Gilles, 31 January 1970. Children: Jodie Ann (1971) and Michael John (1979). Lives at 358 Brookfield Avenue, Broken Hill, 2705, New South Wales, Australia.

SKEWES JEMIMA
Chart 6. Daughter of Peter and Mary Skewes of the Poorhouse, Kenwyn; miner. Bpt Kenwyn 22 October 1826. Married 1841, Truro.

SKEWIS JENEFAR
Chart 3. Daughter of Richard and Jane Skewis. Born 18 October 1730. Married James Gritton 19 July 1753 at Helston Parish Church.

SKEWES JENEFER
Daughter of John and Ann Skewes; miner of Hugus. Bpt Kea 12 May 1811. Married at Kenwyn to James Rowe (28) of Hugus, miner, son of James Rowe, miner, 11 January 1844.

SKEWES JENIFER

Daughter of Peter and Grace Skewes; milliner. Bpt Kea 24 December 1820.

SKEWES   JENNEFAR
Chart 18. Daughter of William and Ann Skewes. Bpt Kenwyn 18 June 1809.

SKEWES   JENNEFAR
of Kea. Married John Bastian of Kea at Kenwyn 27 January 1798.

SKEWIS   JENNEFER
Daughter of Peter and Peggy Skewis. Bpt Kenwyn 12 July 1795.

SKEWES   JENNENE RHONDA
Lives at 119 Thornside Road, Thornlands, Queensland, 4158, Australia with Vernon John Skewes, concreter.

SKEWS   JENNIE
Chart 41. Daughter of Fred and Ellen Boynton. Born 5 October 1919. Married Roy Skews 4 November 1939 at Christ Church, Harrogate. Children: David (1943) and Margaret (1945). Lives at 47 Wood Walk, Wombwell, Barnsley, South Yorkshire. Tel. no: Barnsley 755946.

SKUES   JENNIE E.
Chart 8. Born 1915. Married Ernest John Skues, 16 February 1935, Shoreditch, London.
Divorced 1961. Married Alfred T. Chandler, 1961, Hackney. Died September 1979, aged 64 years.

SKEWIS   JENNIE RABLING
Chart 2. Daughter of James and Jane Skewis. Born 1 December 1872, America. Died October, 1963, aged 91 years. Spinster.

SKUES JENNIFER
Chart 3. Daughter of Jack and Lily (née Bruckshaw) Skues. Born 6 October 1939, Cheshire. Educated at Far Lodge High School (1950-1953) and Collegiate High School, Blackpool (1953-1955). Married John Rothwell Reeves at Chapel Street Methodist Church, Blackpool, 20 June 1959. Emigrated to Canada, 1965. Issue: three daughters.
Lives at 4940 Fabien, Pierrefonds, Quebec, H8Z 2N6, Canada. Tel No: (514) 626 7625.

Jennifer Skues

SKEWES   JENNIFER
Lives at Old Warburton Road, Warburton, 3799, Victoria, Australia. Teacher.

SKEWES   JENNIFER
Chart 36. Daughter of William and Ida Olive (née SKEWES) Skewes. Twin to Janice Skewes. Born 14 November 1942, Watson's Creek, Bendemeer, New South Wales, Australia. Married Rex Burgess, 8 February 1964. Issue: 1 son and 1 daughter.

SKEWES   JENNIFER ANN
Lives at 28 Leawarra Crescent, Doncaster, Victoria, Australia, 3109 with Catherine Patricia Skewes.

SKEWES   JENNIFER ANN
Lives at 151 Avalon Beach, 2107, New South Wales, Australia with Lionel Skewes.

SKUES   JENNIFER ANNE
Daughter of William Ashdown and Edith Beryl (née Saul) Skues. Born 10 January 1965. Lives at 7, Cormack Road, Beacon Hill, New South Wales, 2100, Australia.

SKEWES   JENNIFER JOY
Chart 36. Née Matthews. Married Gary Earl Skewes, 27 February 1971, New South Wales, Australia. Children: Jason Gary (1971) and Adam David (1973).

SKEWES   JENNIFER MARGARET
Lives at 37 Vincent Street, Glen Iris, 3145, Victoria, Australia.

SKEWES   JENNIFER MARGARET
Lives at 29 Drake Street, Torrens, Canberra, 2607, Australia with Alison Boyd Skewes and David Thomas Skewes.

SKEWES   JENNIFER R.
Lives at Lisfreda, Croft Mitchell, Troon, Camborne with John C. Skewes.

SKEWES   JENNINE MARY
Chart 26. Daughter of Frank Anson and June Beverley (née Spaulding) Skewes. Born 17 June 1962, Connecticut, USA. Lives in East Lyme, Connecticut, USA.

SKEWIS   JENNY
Daughter of Thomas and Ann Skewis. Bpt Kenwyn 7 October 1776.

SKUSE JEREMY
Son of Michael and Mary (née Armstrong) Skuse. Born 1958.

SKUES   JEREMY DEREK
Chart 5. Son of Derek Peter and Deborah Jessie (née McMillan) Skues. Born 8 March 1972. Lives at 467 Thurgoona Street, Albany, 2640, New South Wales, Australia.

SCOOSE   JESPER
Son of John Scoose. Bpt Menheniot 2 February 1565.

SKEWES   JESSIE
Married 1868, Bedwellty.

SKEWIS   JESSIE
Born 1860. Died 1941, aged 81 years in Springburn, Scotland.

SKUES   JESSIE
Married 1879, Pontypridd.

SKEWIS   JESSIE
Married 1880, Old Monkland, Scotland.

SKEWS   JESSIE
Born 1882, Abergavenny.

SKEWES   JESSIE
Born 1882. Died 1882, aged 0 in Truro.

SKEWES   JESSIE
Chart 25. Daughter of William and Jane (née Jameson) Skewes. Born 1877, Manchester. Assisted emigrant to Australia with her mother and sister Louisa (3) on vessel *Cuzco* from London which arrived in Sydney, 5 June 1892.

SKEWES   JESSIE
Chart 14. Daughter of George and Ruth (née Hoyt) Skewes. Born 1874, Yorkville, Wisconsin, USA.

SKEWES   JESSIE C.
Book-keeper with Fona Machinery Co., 1327 Allesandra, Los Angeles, California, USA in 1939.

SKEWES   JESSIE M.
Married 1933 to Hunt in Chepstow.

SKEWES   JESSIE MARGARETTA
Born 1890, Redruth.

SKUES   JESSIE PEPITA
Chart 5. Daughter of Derek Peter and Deborah Jessie (née McMillan)' Skues. Born 12 September 1974. Lives at 467 Thurgoona Street, Albany, 2640, New South Wales, Australia.

SKEWES   JESSIE VICTORIA
Chart 12. Née Cockram. Born 1893. Married James Henry Oswald Skewes in Axbridge, 1920. Lived at Moor Street, Camborne; later Centenary Street and 12 Atlantic Terrace, Camborne. Child: Jack Patterson Oswald (1923). Died 13 October 1977, aged 80 years.

SKEWES   JILL
Chart 36. Daughter of William Vere and Annie Rebecca (née Strain) Skewes. Born 8 December 1933, Tamworth, New South Wales, Australia. Married Kevin Carmichael at St Joseph's Catholic Church, West Tamworth, 24 March 1951. Issue: 2 sons and 4 daughter. Livest at 43 Bradman Street, Charlestown, 2290, Newcastle, New South Wales, Australia.

SKEWES   JILL ALEXANDER
Chart 40. Daughter of Matthew Henry and Ann Skewes. Mother's maiden name Morgan. Born 8 December 1952. Lived at Trewince Farm, St Martin, Helston. Married William G.A. Jenkin, 1977, Kerrier.

SKEWES   JILL CECILIA
Chart 36. Née Pullman. Married Leslie Kevin Skewes. Children: Marie Colleen, Bede Kevin, Lesley, Kerrie, Janelle Anne, Mark, Nigel, Ranae and Peter Michael
Lives at Caroline Street, Bendemeer, 2352, New South Wales, Australia.

SKEWES   JILL KATHRYN
Chart 25. Daughter of Joseph Frederick and Doreen (née Issac) Skewes. Born 10 July 1970. Lives at 12 Walnut Walk, Stretford, Manchester.

SKEWES   JILLIAN FAY
Chart 36. Daughter of Earle William and Edna Fay (née Chad) Skewes. Born 28 October 1959. Lives at 520 Peel Street, Tamworth, 2340, Australia, with Sharon Gae Skewes and Suzanne Lynda Skewes. Shop assistant.

SKEWES   JOAN
Wife of Keverne Skewes. Buried St Keverne 24 April 1671.

SKUES   JOAN
Chart 19. Daughter of Thomas Skues. Bpt Gwennap 3 September 1676. Married Anthony Michel 27 November 1701 at Gwennap.

SKEWS   JOAN
Married John Mills at St Martin, Exeter, Devon, 1638.

SKEWES   JONE
Daughter of Charles and Jone Skewes. Bpt Ottery St Mary, Devon 2 June 1639.

SKEWS   JOAN
Buried Gwennap 8 June 1680.

SKUES   JONE
Chart 2, Illegitimate daughter of Ann Skues. Bpt Camborne 23 June 1695. Died 3 June 1697, aged 2 years.

SKEWS   JOAN
Daughter of William Skews. Bpt Gwennap 23 April 1698.

SKUES   JOAN
Chart 4. Daughter of William and Jane Skues. Bpt 25 April 1698, Redruth Parish Church. Married John Cauldwell 2 January 1718, Redruth.

SKEWES   JOAN
Chart 19. Daughter of Thomas and Margaret Skewes. Bpt Gwennap 27 September 1715. Married John Gregory 14 August 1735.

SKEWES   JOAN
of Truro. Married William Walkham of St Clement 14 September 1724 at Feock Parish Church.

SKEWIS   JOAN
Married Richard Traplyn at Mawgan in Meneage 6 November 1755.

SKEWIS   JONE
Buried Gunwalloe 23 July 1757.

SKEWES   JOAN
Daughter of William and Ann Skewes. Bpt Gwennap 12 June 1756.

SKEWES   JOAN
Daughter of Joseph and Philippa Skewes. Bpt Mawgan in Meneage 8 April 1760. Married James Meager, tinner at St Breage 9 September 1793.

SKEWES   JOAN
Married William Tregonning at Gwennap 23 May 1779.

SKEWES   JOAN
Chart 42. Daughter of Richard James and Amy (née Post) Skewes. Born 17 November 1933, North Sydney, Australia, Married Kevin John Morrison, 15 November 1952. Issue: one son.

SKEWS   JOAN
Mother's maiden name Eddy. Born 1935, East Stonehouse, Devon.

SKEWES   JOAN BENTLEY
Chart 36. Daughter of William Vere and Annie Rebecca (née Strain) Skewes. Born 23 May 1931, Tamworth, New South Wales, Australia. Married Aubrey Alderton, 1952. Issue: 3 sons. Lives at Mandowa, Warria, via Tamworth, New South Wales, Australia.

SKEWIS   JOAN CALLISON
Chart 2. Daughter of Francis Henry and Mary Jane Skewis. Born 8 December 1954, America.

SKUES   JOAN DORETTE
Chart 9. Née Causton. Born 26 June 1928. Married Roy Arthur Truscott Skues 21 March 1953, Ilford, Essex. Children: Barry Russell (1954) and John Michael (1959). Lives at 7 Rylands Road, Bybrook, Ashford, Kent. Telephone number 0233 23057.

SKEWES   JOAN HANNA
Lives at 90 Invermore Street, Mount Gravatt, 4122, Queensland, Australia with James Leslie Skewes, manager.

SKEWS   JOAN L.
Mother's maiden name Dyer. Born 1926, Stepney.

SKEWS   JOAN L.D.
Chart 17. Daughter of David George Skews and Emily (née Lampey). Born 16 October 1930, Romford, Essex. Died February, 1932 aged 1 year.

SKUES   JOAN M.
Chart 7. Née Hawkins. Married Edwin Thomas Skues, 1940, Dartford, Kent. Lived at 54 Lansbury Crescent, Dartford. (He died 1974, aged 63 years in Cuckfield, Sussex.) Children: Edwin Michael (1942) and Christine Evelyn (1945).

SKUES   JOAN MACKENZIE
Chart 3. Twin to Sheila Mackenzie Skues. Daughter of Charles Ayre Mackenzie and Elizabeth (née Gaute) Skues. Born 1904. Spinster. Lived at 20 Copers Cope Road, Beckenham, Kent. Spent a number of years in

India. Returned to England and became very depressed and in 1954 entered hospital voluntarily. Was discharged 8 January 1957. She was blind in her left eye.
On 13 January 1957 she was found dead on a railway line at Bickley Station, Kent. At an inquest it was learned that Joan Mackenzie Skues had previously opened carriage doors on the wrong side and only at the last minute realised her mistake. An open verdict was recorded by the jury. Witnesses said she had been extremely religious.
Her body had been found at 11am by a porter. A handbag had been recovered some distance back from the edge of the platform, there were very few people about and no one saw the accident. A police inspector said he found in Miss Skues's handbag a ticket from Holborn Viaduct to Bickley stamped 13 January.

SKEWES   JOAN MORVA
Lived at Lot 17, Thompson Road, Geelong North, Victoria, Australia in 1959 with William Thomas Skewes.
Now lives at 543 Thompson Road, Norlane, 3214, Victoria, Australia with William Thomas Skewes and Julie Marion Skewes.

SKEWS   JOAN PATRICIA
Lives at 24 Waloe Avenue, Wagga Wagga, 2650, New South Wales, Australia.

SKEWES   JOANNA
Chart 9. Née Truscott. Born 1774. Married James Skews at St Ewe 4 November 1792. Lived at Lower Sticker. Children: Grace, Ann, James, Jane, Philip, Elizabeth, William Truscott, Mary Ann, Thomas Truscott and Thomas. Died 1864, aged 90 years.

SKEWES   JOANNA ROBIN
Chart 50. Daughter of Geoffrey Grenville and Ruth Lois (née Philp) Skewes. Born 15 July 1971, Victoria, Australia. Lives at 33 Howard Street, Warrnambool, 3280, Victoria, Australia.

SKEWS   JOANNA
Chart 9. Daughter of James and Joanna (née Truscott) Skews of Lower Sticker. Bpt 15 January 1797. Married John Toms, St Ewe 1 July 1820.

SKEWES   JOANNA
Chart 19. Daughter of Alexander and Christian Skewes. Bpt 5 July 1803. Married Ambrose Bray at Gwennap 27 October 1832. Children: Walter Skewes Bray and George Skewes Bray.

SKEWES   JOANNA
Born 1843. Died 1844. Buried Camborne 18 January 1844, aged 3 months.

SKEWES   JOANNA
Daughter of Richard and Joanna (née Wasley) Skewes of Kea. Born 18 October 1843. Bpt at Primitive Methodist Chapel — Perranwell Circuit — 7 March 1844. Emigrated with her parents to Melbourne, Australia arriving at Port Phillip on 22 March 1849.

SKEWS   JOANNA
Born 1877, Liskeard.

SKEWES   JOANNE KAY
Chart 38. Daughter of Albert John and Kathleen Mavis (née Clark) Skewes. Born 28 June 1964. Lives at Government Road, Bute, South Australia, 5560.

SKEWES   JODI ANN
Chart 38. Daughter of Jeffrey William and Mary Jane (née Gilles) Skewes. Born 20 January 1971. Lives at 358 Brookfield Avenue, Broken Hill, 2705, New South Wales, Australia.

SKEWES   JODI LYNNE
Chart 36. Daughter of Bruce Skewes. Born 5 October 1972, Victoria, Australia.

SKEWS   JODI VICTORIA
Mother's maiden name Blight. Born 1979, St Austell.

SKEWES   JOHAN
Illegitimate daughter of Elnor Skewes. Bpt Gerrans 24 September 1581.

SKEWES   JOHANE
Daughter of Thomas Skewes. Bpt Exeter St Mary Major 5 March 1611.

SKEWIS   JOHANNA
Born 1790. Died 1844. Buried Camborne 7 August 1844, aged 54 years.

SKEWES   JOHANNA
Chart 2. Daughter of James and Sally Skewes of Pendarves Field; miner. Born 1844. Bpt 4 January 1845. Camborne.

SKEWIS   JOHANNA
Born 1844, Redruth. Died 1845.

SKEWES   JOANNA MARY
Chart 12. Daughter of Maurice and Mary J. Skewes. Mother's maiden name Payne. Born 1969, Penzance.

SKEWS   JOANNA TRUSCOTT
Chart 20. Daughter of Philip and Sally Skews of Horrabridge, Buckland Monachorum, Tavistock. Born 1840. Married 1857.

SKEWES   JOHANNE
Chart 36. Daughter of Neville Percy and Helen (née O'Lockland) Skewes. Born 17 June 1949, Australia. Married William Asa Townsend, 13 January 1970. Issue: four children.

SKEWYS   JOHANNES
of Helston Borough. Member of Parliament for the town 1331. Chart 1.

SKEWYS   JOHN de

Chart 1. Commissioner of Peace. Living 1343. Married daughter of tasse Bennalleck. Had a son, Matthew **Skewys** who married Mary, daughter of Andrew Ferners of Trelowarren.

SKEWYS JOHN
Chart 1. Lord of Skewys 1386. Son of Matthew Skewys and Mary (née Ferners). Married Margaret Trevery. Son: Matthew Skewys.
MP. For Helston Borough 1397-1398.

SKEWYS JOHN
Chart 1. Lord of Skewys. Son of Matthew and Margaret Skewys. Married Joan Tomyowe. Son: John Skewys, legal adviser to Cardinal Wolsey. Licence to celebrate 1437.

SKEWYS JOHN
Chart 1. Lord of Skewys. Son of John Skewys and Joan (née Tomyowe). Born 1467 at Skewys, Cury. Bred a lawyer, becoming confidential servant of the all powerful Cardinal Wolsey, and a Counsellor-at-Law. He was admitted to Lincoln's Inn Fields 12 February 1487.
Became a Governor of Lincoln's Inn 1505. He was educated at Exeter College, Oxford. In 1514 he had the pleasure of wearing his hat in the King's (Henry VIII) presence. In June 1529 he was appointed a member of the commission to adjudicate on cases in Chancery committed to them by Cardinal Wolsey.
John Skewys was the owner of much property in Cornwall including the Manor of Polroda in St Tudy; Skewys in Cury; and the lease of the Tolls in Tin in Tewington, Tywarnhaile and Helston. He was placed on Commission for the county of Cornwall in 1510, 1511, 1514 and 1515 and was on Commission for Middlesex in 1528, 1531, 1537 and 1539. In July, 1518 and July, 1521 he was appointed one of the Commissioners for the Duchy of Cornwall. In 1521 he served as High Sheriff for the Duchy.
John Skewys was author of *Brevyat of a Chronicle*, made by Matthew Paris of the *Conquests of Duke William of Normandy*. He wrote a treatise *De Bellor Trojano* and a history *Chronicorum Epitome*. He was credited by Bishop Bale with *Abbreviations Chronicorum*. And he was the author of the *Black Book of Merthen*, which was a complete survey of the Reskymer Estate in Latin.
John Skewys married Katherine Tretherff, daughter of John Tretherff. He had no children of his own; his sister was married to John Denzell of Denzall, near St Columb, Serjeant-at-Law, another Cornish landowner who, like himself, had become a well-known lawyer. The Denzells had no son, but several daughters and it was arranged that one of these, Alice, should marry William Reskymer, John Skewys's youngest stepson and that John should settle seven manors in Cornwall upon them and their children. This took place in 1538.
Skewys's eldest stepson was called John Reskymer. John Skewys died 23 May 1544, aged 77 years. He was buried at St John's, Clerkenwell, London next to his wife Katherine. There was an elaborate funeral and masses for his soul.
For full story of John Skewys see Chapter Six of *Cornish Heritage* which also includes a copy of his will.

SKEWYS JOHN
Was Charity Priest mentioned in the Court Rolls of the Manor of St Columb Major 1448 and 1450.

SCOOSE JOHN
Married Jane Piper at Menheniot 18 June 1562.

SKEWES JOHN
Son of Oliver Skewes. Bpt 24 December 1575, Perranzabuloe.

SKEWES JOHN
Married Maud Penperth at Gerrans 23 November 1572.

SCOOSE JOHN
Buried Menheniot 20 April 1580.

SKEWES JOHN
Buried Gerrans 6 August 1582.

SKEWES JOHN
Son of Humfry Skewes. Bpt Gerrans 8 September 1616.

SKEWES JOHN
Son of James Skewes. Bpt St Just in Roseland 23 November 1617.

SKEWES JOHN
Married Ann Harwood at St Keverne 15 November 1624.

SKEWES JOHN
Married Margaret Cheran at St Keverne 20 April 1632.

SKEWSE JOHN
Married Mary Crooke 2 January 1636, St Gregory by St Paul, London.

SKEWIS JOHN
Buried St Just in Roseland 1 March 1639.

SKEWES JOHN
Son of John and Margaret Skewes. Bpt St Keverne 12 May 1640.

SKEWES JOHN
Mentioned in Cornwall Protestation Returns for Gerrans, 1642.

SKEWES JOHN
Mentioned in Cornwall Protestation Returns for Gorran, 1642.

SKEWES JOHN
Mentioned in Cornwall Protestation Returns for St Anthony in Meneage, 1642.

SKEWES JOHN
Mentioned in Cornwall Protestation Returns for St Keverne, 1642.

SKEWES JOHN

Son of Richard and Jane Skewes. Bpt St Keverne 5 June 1642.

SKEWES JOHN
Son of John Skews. Bpt Gerrans 1 Sept 1650.

SKUES JOHN
Married Pasco Tomkins at Portsmouth, Hants, 1665.

SKEWES JOHN
Married Mary Cornelius 15 April 1667 at St Keverne.

SKEWS JOHN
Chart 13. Married Elizabeth Whitford 23 November 1674. Children: John (1675) and William (1677).

SKEWS JOHN
Chart 13. Son of John and Elizabeth Skews. Bpt Mevagissey 23 June 1675.

SKUSE JOHN
Married Ann Jeffries 1686 at Southwark, London.

SKUSE JOHN
Married Alice Pill, 1698 in Salisbury.

SKEWIS JOHN
Married Mary ...... at Madron with Penzance 31 October 1690.

SKEWES JOHN
Son of William Skewes. Bpt Gwennap 25 April 1703.

SKEWES JOHN
Chart 19. Son of Thomas Skewes, junior; tinner. Bpt Gwennap 12 August 1704.

SKUES JOHN
Son of Richard Skues. Bpt Kenwyn May 1716.

SKEWES JOHN
Married Catherine Nicholas at St Buryan 13 November 1716. Children: John, Richard, William, Michael, Catherine and Robert.

SKEWS JOHN
Son of John and Catherine Skews. Bpt St Buryan 7 July 1717.

SCUIS JOHN
Chart 2. Son of Henry and Mary Scuis. Bpt 23 November 1717, Camborne. Died 19 October 1720, aged 3 years.

SCUIS JOHN
Chart 2. Son of Henry and Mary Scuis. Bpt Camborne 3 September 1721. Died 2 May 1743, aged 22 years. Bachelor.

SKEWES JOHN
Chart 36. Son of John and Mary Skewes. Bpt Cury. Mentioned in his father's will.

SKEWES JOHN
Chart 36. Son of James and Sarah Skewes. Bpt Cury 25 March 1722. Married Mary George 12 September 1747, Cury. Children: James, Sarah, John, Edward, Margery, Elizabeth, William and Richard.

SKEWES JOHN
Buried St Ewe 26 February 1734.

SKEWS JOHN
Marriage licence granted at Exeter 22 August 1734 to marry Elizabeth Symons of Penzance. Marriage took place at Madron with Penzance 25 August 1734.

SCUIS JOHN
Chart 2. Son of William and Mary Scuis. Bpt 20 November 1737, Camborne. Children: William and John. Died 26 April 1813, aged 77 years.

SKEWES JOHN
Chart 19. Son of Thomas and Elizabeth Skewes. Bpt Gwennap 11 October 1740. Married Mary Tregonning 18 September 1769 at Gwennap. Children: Richard, Elizabeth, Mary and William. Died 18 May 1811, agd 71 years.

SKEWES JOHN
Married Mary Webb of Kea at Gwennap 8 November 1740.

SKEWS JOHN
,Son of John Skews. Bpt Madron 4 January 1741.

SKEWIS JOHN
Chart 2. Son of Henry Skewis. Bpt Camborne 7 March 1741. Yeoman. Married Philippa King 1 November 1767. Children: William and Mary (twins), Sarah, John, Catherine, Stephen, Henry, Philippa and Richard. Died 26 May 1816, aged 75 years. Philippa died 15 August 1815.

SKUES JOHN
Chart 3. Son of Richard and Jane Skues. Born 8 June 1744. Married Mary Hockin 28 March 1769. Borough Mason of Helston. Children: Ann, William, Elizabeth, John, Isobella, Jane, Richard, Charles and Joseph. Died 20 September 1801, aged 57 years.

SKEWES JOHN
Son of Edward and Margaret (née Rogers) who were married in Sithney 13 May 1743. Bpt Cury 23 September 1744.

SKEWES JOHN
Buried Cury 26 November 1744.

SKEWS JOHN
Son of Philip & Anne Skews. Bpt St Ewe 19 May 1746.

SKEWS JOHN
Son of Martin Skews of Kea. Bpt Kenwyn 6 June 1747. Buried Kea 23 August 1749.

SKEWIS JOHN

Son of Edward and Margaret Skewis. Bpt Cury 7 June 1749. Buried Cury 5 November 1811, aged 62.

SKEWS JOHN
Son of Martin Skews of Kea. Bpt Kenwyn 28 April 1750.

SKEWES JOHN
Chart 36. Son of John and Mary Skewes. Bpt Cury 24 March 1753. Married Mary Williams at Cury 3 January 1778. Lived at Treloskan, Cury. Children: Edward, Mary, Blanch S., William, James, Anne and John. Died 14 December 1825, aged 72 years.

SKEWES JOHN
Buried Gwennap 3 May 1754.

SKEWS JOHN
Son of Peter Skews. Bpt Kea 25 January 1757.

SKEWES JOHN
Son of John and Philippa Skewes. Bpt Mawgan in Meneage 21 March 1757.

SKEWES JOHN
Chart 29. Married Alice John, lic., at Perranarworthal 23 June 1759. Children: Mary, Maria, John, Richard, James, Alice, Lucey and Elizabeth. Died at Kea 25 April 1781.

SKEWES JOHN
Chart 29. Son of John and Alice Skewes. Bpt Kea 9 August 1763.

SKEWES JOHN
Chart 18. Son of Thomas Skewes. Bpt 5 October 1766, Kenwyn. Lived at Kerley, Kea. Miner. Married Anne Stephens at Kenwyn 8 November 1787. Children: Grace and Maria. Died 7 July 1833. Buried Kea 9 July 1833, aged 67 years.

SKEWES JOHN
Chart 10. Son of Martin and Mary Skewes of Kea. Bpt Kenwyn 17 April 1767.

SKEWS JOHN
Buried St Ewe 3 June 1769.

SKEWES JOHN
Buried Gwennap 8 July 1770.

SKEWES JOHN
Married Mary Dennis at Kenwyn 23 February 1771.

SCUIS JOHN
Chart 2. Son of John Scuis. Bpt Camborne 29 December 1771.

SKEWES JOHN
Chart 19. One son: William Skewes. Buried Gwennap 2 June 1772.

SKEWES JOHN
Son of John Skewes. Bpt Helston 7 November 1773.

SKEWIS JOHN
Buried Camborne 7 May 1774.

SKEWIS JOHN
Chart 2. Son of John and Philippa Skewis. Bpt privately 15 March 1775; publicly 9 April 1775. Husbandman in Illogan. Married Jane Angove 8 February 1800. Child: Jane. Died 1840. Buried Camborne 29 January 1840, aged 64 years. Jane died 30 March 1821, aged 44 years.

SKEWIS JOHN
Chart 39. Son of John and Mary Skewis. Bpt Cury 17 May 1775.

SKEWES JOHN
Married Mary Mitchell at Gwennap 17 June 1776.

SKEWES JOHN
Chart 36. Son of John and Mary Skewes. Bpt Cury 17 May 1778. Married Loveday Hendy at Maker, 9 July 1810. Lived at Nantithet, Cury. Children: John (1810), Edward (1814), Samuel (1815), Ann Hendy (1817), Mary (1820), William (1822) and Hannah (1824). Buried Cury 21 October 1852, aged 75 years. Loveday was buried 12 August 1830, aged 39 years.

SKEWES JOHN
Buried Mawgan in Meneage 6 July, 1777.

SKEWES JOHN
Son of John and Mary Skewes. Bpt Gwennap 12 October 1777.

SKEWS JOHN
Son of Martin Skews. Bpt Kea 23 August 1779.

SKUES JOHN
Chart 3. Bpt Helston 1780. Son of John and Mary P. Skues.

SKEWS JOHN
Son of John and Ann Skews. Bpt Endell Street, Holborn, London 18 October 1781.

SKEWIS JOHN
Buried Gwennap 22 April 1789.

SKEWES JOHN
Buried Cury 1 June 1789.

SKEWS JOHN
Son of John & Ann Skews. Bpt Kenwyn 4 October 1789.

SKEWES JOHN
Chart 19. Wife: Mary Skewes. Lived in Gwennap.

SKEWES JOHN
Married Eleanor Philips at Kea 7 March 1791.

SKEWES JOHN
Son of William and Ann Skewes. Bpt Gunwalloe 6 November 1791.

SKEWES JOHN
Born 1791. Wife's name Ann (same age). Daughter Mary Skewes a scholar in 1851 Census Returns, born in Camborne. Lived at Miners Row, Redruth. Died March 1855, aged 64 years.

SKEWES JOHN
Buried Kea 5 January 1792.

SKEWES JOHN
Buried Gunwalloe 1 March 1792.

SKEWES JOHN
Chart 2. Twin to Ann Skewes. Son of Absalom and Elizabeth Skewes. Bpt Camborne 21 May 1793. Miner. Married Ann Simmons 18 February 1822. Children Ann, Mary and John.

SKEWES JOHN
Born 1794. Lived at Nantithet, Cury. Buried Cury 22 July 1858, aged 64 years.

SKEWES JOHN
Chart 10. Son of Digory and Elizabeth Skewes. Bpt Kenwyn 6 October 1794.

SKEWIS JOHN
Chart 29. Son of Richard and Roseanna Skewis. Bpt Kenwyn 15 May 1796.

SKUES JOHN
Son of Peter & Ann Skues. Bpt St Agnes 7 December 1797.

SKEWES JOHN
Son of William and Ann Skewes. Bpt Gunwalloe 4 March 1798.

SKEWES JOHN
Chart 36. Son of William and Alice Skewes. Bpt Cury 4 July 1798.

SKEWIS JOHN
Was a private with Camborne Volunteers 1798-1800, He was discharged on 16 March 1800.

SKEWS JOHN
Son of James and Joanna (née Truscott) Skews. Bpt St Ewe 21 January 1799. Buried St Ewe 14 October 1830, aged 31 years.

SKEWES JOHN
Born 1799. Died 1869, Plymouth, aged 70 years.

SKEWES JOHN
Married Ann Dinnis 21 December 1799 at Kea.

SKEWES JOHN
Married Elizabeth Hendy at Cury 23 September 1800.

SKEWES JOHN
Chart 18. Son of Thomas and Mary Skewes. Bpt Kenwyn 10 May 1801.

SKEWES JOHN
Buried Kea 30 October 1801.

SKEWS JOHN
Son of William & Nancy Skews. Bpt St Ewe 27 Nov 1802.

SKEWES JOHN
Born 1803. Lived in Killiwerris, Chacewater. Buried Chacewater 19 January 1862, aged 59 years.

SKEWS JOHN
Chart 23. Born 1803, St Austell. Worked at The General Wolfe Inn, St Austell. Children: William, Edwin and Mary. Died 4 September 1858, aged 55 years. W (CRO) £100.

SKEWES JOHN
Chart 14. Son of Henry and Jane Skewes of Tresodden, Ruan Major. Bpt Ruan Major 27 May 1804. (Born 30 January 1804.) Twin to Eleanor Skewes. Married Mary Jane Boulden at Grade Parish Church 18 June 1833. Lived at Chybarles, Ruan Major. Emigrated to Wisconsin, USA in 1850's. Was elected Treasurer of Yorkville Township in 1858. Children: Henry (1834), Thomas Boulden (1836), Edwin (1838), Betsy (1840) and George (1842).

SKEWES JOHN
Chart 19. Son of Richard and Mary Skewes. Bpt Gwennap 28 August 1804. Lived at Little Carharrack, Gwennap. Married Ann .... of Carharrack. Died 10 March 1884, aged 80 years. Buried in Old Ground, Gwennap Churchyard with headstone.

SKEWS JOHN
Buried 4 September 1805, Mylor.

SKEWES JOHN
of Gwennap. Sent articles on mathematics to *The Ladies Diary*, London, 1807, et seq.

SKEWES JOHN
Listed as occupier of a house in Meneage Street, Helston for the year 1809.

SKEWES JOHN
Chart 10. Son of John and Ann Skewes. Bpt Kenwyn 4 June 1809.

SKEWES JOHN
Chart 19. Yeoman. Married Jenifer Treweek of Redruth 24 November 1810 at Gwennap. Children: John, Jane Treweek, Mary Ann and Caroline Treweek. Died 1 July 1839. W(CRO) £600.

SKEWES JOHN
Chart 36. Son of John and Loveday Skewes of Nantithet. Bpt privately Cury 2 December 1810. Publicly 23 February 1812.

SKEWES JOHN
Buried Kea 22 May 1811.

SKEWES JOHN
Chart 19. Son of John and Jennifer Skewes. Bpt Gwennap 6 December 1812.

SKEWES JOHN
Born 1812, Cury. Son of John Skewes, husbandman. Wheelwright/carpenter. Married Martha Harris, daughter of Christopher Harris, farmer at Sithney 8 January 1845. In 1871 Census Returns living at Trannack, Sithney with his wife Martha. Died 1886, aged 74 years.

SKEWES JOHN
Chart 32. Son of Richard and Grace Skewes; miner of Whitehall, Gwennap, formerly of Kenwyn. Bpt Gwennap 17 May 1814.

SKUES JOHN
Born 1814. Son of Joseph Penrose Skues, mason. Married .... Married again 7 May 1859 at Parish Church, Ludgvan to Elizabeth Osborne. John lived in Redruth. Elizabeth was daughter of N. Osborne, veterinary surgeon of Ludgvan, Penzance. She was 33 years old — spinster. Emigrated to Australia around 1860.

SKEWES JOHN
Chart 10. Son of Richard and Agnes Skewes of Chacewater, miner. Born 1815. Bpt Kenwyn 7 May 1815. Married Harriet Francis 29 September 1836; witness Matthew Skewes. Married at Kea. Children: Philippa, John Henry and Matthew.

SKEWES JOHN
Chart 12. Son of James and Elizabeth Skewes of Cury. Bpt Cury 23 April 1815. Farmer at Chypons, Cury, 1861. Married Juliana Hendy 3 January 1837. Lived at Gilly Lane, 1841; Trewolla, 1851. Children: Juliana Hendy, James Henry, Elizabeth Mary and John. Buried Cury 20 June 1860, aged 46 years.

SKEWES JOHN
Born 1815, Redruth. Died Redruth 1890, aged 75 years.

SKEWES JOHN
Chart 19. Son of John and Jennifer Skewes of Shilstones, miner. Bpt Gwennap 22 March 1816.

SKEWES JOHN
Chart 36. Son of William and Christian Skewes. Bpt Ruan Major 29 December 1816. Buried St Keverne 5 February 1830, aged 13 years.

SKUCE JOHN
Quartermaster with 3rd Regiment of the Foot Guards (Second Battalion). Served in the Battle of Waterloo. He left the regiment in May, 1819.

SKEWS JOHN
Born 1817. Bricklayer. Children include: William (1833). Died 1901, Fulham, aged 84 years.

SKEWIS JOHN
Chart 36. Son of John and Jane Skewis. Bpt Illogan, 22 June 1816.

SKEWES JOHN
of Kea. Married ANN SKEWES of Kenwyn (by licence) at Kenwyn 2 September 1818.

SKEWS JOHN
of Chacewater. Married Miss NANCY SKEWS of Twelveheads, 9 September 1818.

SKEWES JOHN
of Ruan Major. Born 1818. Died 1895. Buried Cury 15 December 1895.

SKEWES JOHN
Chart 33. Married Elizabeth Jeffrey of Kenwyn at Kea 10 November 1819.

SKEWES JOHN
Chart 33. Bpt Kea 1 July 1821. Married Grace Bray at Kea, 18 November 1820 in presence of Richard Skewes. Son: James Skewes. Lived at Hugus, Kea.

SKEWS JOHN
Inhabitant of Illogan. Lent his name to "The Declaration" which approved the conduct of the High Sheriff of Cornwall in refusing to call a county meeting to consider the propriety of petitioning the House of Commons for the insertion of the Queen's name in a liturgy. March 1821.

SKEWES JOHN
A freeholder and inhabitant of Meneage. Lent his name to "The Declaration" which approved the conduct of the High Sheriff of Cornwall in refusing to call a county meeting to consider the propriety of petitioning the House of Commons for the insertion of the Queen's name in a liturgy. March 1821.

SKUES JOHN
Married Margery Jenkin at Kenwyn 14 March 1822. Children include: Matthew (1843).

SKEWS JOHN
Chart 10. Son of Digory and Sophia Skewes, miner. (Sophia was daughter of Joseph and Sarah Jordan.) Born 24 June 1823. Bpt Truro Wesleyan Chapel, 28 March 1837. Married Julianna Ley, daughter of Samuel Ley, carpenter, at the Register Office, Liskeard, 18 October 1850. Miner at St Cleer.

SKEWS JOHN
Chart 15. Born 1823, Altarnun. Married Isabella Gregory (born 1829) at Altarnun 26 March 1848. Children: Elizabeth Jane, John Gregory,

Samuel Gregory, John William, Alfred, Emma, Amos, Thomas, Charles, Mary, Henry and David. In 1871 Census Returns living at Trewint, Altarnun. Died 1881, aged 59 years.

SKEWES JOHN
Married Avis Jeffrey at Cury 4 March 1824.

SKEWES JOHN
Chart 39. Married Mary ..... Children: John, William, Mary, Blanch, Ann, Edward and James. Died 1824. Will dated 1824. Witnesses Henry Skewes, Henry Skewes Junior and Margaret Skewes.

SKEWES JOHN
Son of John & Margery Skewes. Bpt Phillack 26 June 1825.

SKUES JOHN
Chart 2. Son of John and Ann Skues of Park-en-Bowen. Bpt Camborne 31 January 1826. Died 5 February 1826, aged 6 weeks.

SKEWES JOHN
Chart 19. Son of Richard and Mary Skewes. Bpt Gwennap 28 August 1804. Married Ann Davey at Gwennap 30 July 1826, Children: Mary (1827), John (1829), Thomas (1832), Alexander (1834), Simon Davey (1838), Simon Davey (1845), Richard (1840) and Elizabeth Emma (1848). Lived at Little Carharrack. Died 13 March 1884, aged 80 years.

SKEWIS JOHN
Born 1828. Buried Crowan 6 January 1876, aged 48 years.

SKEWES JOHN
Son of John and Avis Skewes of Gilly, Cury, labourer. Bpt Cury 26 October 1828.

SKUES JOHN
Chart 2. Son of John and Ann Skues. Bpt Camborne privately 10 January 1828. Died 17 January 1828, aged 10 weeks.

SKEWES JOHN
Chart 19. Son of John and Ann Skewes, miner of Carharrack. Bpt Gwennap 29 October 1829.

SKUES JOHN
Married Mary Ann Stoddan at Kenwyn 12 July 1830.

SKEWES JOHN
Born 1831. Son of John Skewes, miner of Chacewater. Married Mary Ann Sandoe (21) 27 February 1851 at Kenwyn Parish Church. Mary Ann was daughter of William Sandoe, miner. Witness to the marriage was John Skewes.

SKEUCE JOHN
Married Elizabeth James, 1831, Winterbourne, Gloucester.

SKEWES JOHN
Born 1832. Buried Chacewater 13 February 1839, aged 7 years.

SKEWES JOHN
Son of John and Ann Skewes of Kea, miner. Bpt Kenwyn 15 August 1832.

SKEWES JOHN
Chart 36. Son of William and Christian Skewes. Bpt St Keverne 3 April 1836.

SKEWES JOHN
Chart 36. Son of James and Simonette (née Barnet) Skewes. Bpt Cury 22 May 1836. Later became a copper miner. Married Eliza Jane Mitchell Semmens, daughter of John Semmens, farmer of Bolennowe, Camborne at St John's, Camborne 19 March 1862. Children: James, John Henry, Edith, Richard Charles, Kate, Arthur, Mary and Annie. Died 1908, aged 70 years.

SKEWES JOHN
of St Hilary. Married Juliana Hendy at Cury Parish Church 3 January 1837.

SKUES JOHN
Son of Richard Skues, miner. Lived at Shallow Adit, Redruth. Married Mary Barnfield at Redruth Parish Church 31 December 1837. Miner.

SKEWES JOHN
Chart 10. Son of Peter and Grace (née Harris) Skewes of Kerley, Kea, miner. Born 21 August 1838. Bpt Chacewater 17 January 1839. Copper and tin miner. Went to Mexico and worked in Rosario Mine, Pachuca. Married Luisa Garcia about 1866. Children: Blasa, Nazario, Tomas, Maria, Juan, Federico and Pedro. Returned to Cornwall and whilst still married to Luisa he married Catherine Williams, daughter of Michael Williams, grocer of Chacewater at St Paul's, Chacewater 4 January 1880. Lived at Elder Cottage, Chacewater and later Ivy Cottage, Chacewater. Issue: John Herbert (1881), Hilda Laura (1882), Katie Beatrice (1883) and Thomas Edgar (1886). His wife Catherine died 12 April 1889, aged 34 years. John returned to Mexico with his children (two of whom had died in the meantime). He called upon his first wife Luisa and sought permission for his English children to live alongside his Mexican children, but this was not granted. Descendants of both his wives' children live on to this day in Real del Monte, Mexico and the United States of America. John died in a mine accident at Pachuca 29 November 1903, aged 65 years. His death certificate relates: "Juan Skewes died at Rosario Mine, Pachuca 10.00am on 29 November 1903 from pneumonia." He is buried in the English Cemetery at Real del Monte. On his headstone we read: "Should not the judge of all earth do right."

SKEWES JOHN
Chart 5. Son of John Penrose and Sally Skewes. Born 1838. Lived at

John Skewes (1839-1903) of Cornwall & Mexico with his daughter Hilda Laura Skewes

Hodders Row, Redruth. Bpt Redruth 2 February 1840. Died 1908, aged 70 years in Redruth.

SKEWES JOHN
Chart 36. Son of Edward and Martha Skewes of Nantithet (shoemaker). Bpt Cury 10 April 1838. Became a policeman (PC 73) in 1864, by which time he was married with two children. Resigned from police force in 1865. Lived at Nantithet.
Emigrated to Australia on board *Trevelyan* which sailed from Plymouth in December, 1865 and arrived at Port Adelaide 21 March 1866. Travelled with his wife Susan and children William Hicks and John Henry.

SKEWES JOHN
Born 1839. Son of John and Ann Skewes of Kea. Bpt Kenwyn 20 August 1843. Miner.

SKEWES JOHN
Chart 10. Son of Peter and Grace Skewes of Kerley, Kea, miner. Bpt Chacewater 17 January 1839 (born 21 August 1838). Copper and tin miner.

SKEWES JOHN
Died Truro, 1839.

SKUES JOHN
Died St George's, Hanover Square, London, 1839.

SKEWS JOHN
Died Greenwich, 1839.

SKEWES JOHN
Son of John and Ann Skewes, miner and yeoman of Penance. Bpt Gwennap 16 December 1840.

SKEWIS JOHN
Died 1840, Redruth.

SKEWES JOHN
Born December 1841, Redruth. Emigrated to USA 1864. Married and a widower by 1900. Lived in Nevada township, United States of America. Superintendent of a gold mine.

SKEWES JOHN
Was brought before magistrates at St Austell on 7 September 1841

accused of allowing spirits to be consumed on his premises. John was a retail brewer of Carthew.
Mr Elias Martin of St Austell gave a dinner party to the numerous persons employed in his clay works on 24 August using the rooms of John Skewes' house. Following the dinner Mr Martin gave each person a glass of spirits; a bowl of punch was also made. Skewes had not knowingly permitted the spirit to be consumed, and the bench dismissed the case.

SKUES JOHN
Son of John and Ann Skues of Kea, miner. Bpt Kenwyn 20 August 1843 along with his three sisters, Ellen, Emma and Grace.

SKEWES JOHN
Son of John Skewes, farmer of Gwennap. Married Ann Lanyon, daughter of Simon Lanyon, farmer at St Clement, Truro 28 January 1843.

SKEWIS JOHN
Married 1845, Helston.

SKEWES JOHN
Son of John Skewes, engineer of Foundry Row, Redruth. Married Caroline Ripper of Blight's Row, Redruth, daughter of William Ripper, miner 19 April 1845, in presence of Thomas Jenkin Skewes, at Redruth Parish Church.

SKEWES JOHN
Chart 33. Son of Martin and Ann (née Hocking) Skewes. Bpt Chacewater 10 October 1845.

SKEWES JOHN
Chart 2. Born 6 February 1846. Youngest son of William and Elizabeth Skewes of Bolitho, Crowan. Educated Crowan and Oxford University. B.A. 1873. M.A. 1876. Ordained 1874. Church of All Soul's, Manchester 1875-1882. Sailed for Australia for the benefit of his health 21 October 1882. Was presented with £225 by his parishioners before his departure. Married 1883. Died Sandhurst, Australia 1 October 1884.

SKEWS JOHN
Married 1847, East London.

SKEWS JOHN
Married 1848, Launceston.

SKEWES JOHN
Chart 12. Son of John and Juliana Skewes, labourer. Bpt Cury 4 November 1849 at Cury. Married Thirza Thomas (19), daughter of Francis Thomas, labourer at Cury 17 April 1872. Interesting to note that John could not sign his name on the Marriage Certificate. By 1872 most people could at least write their own name. Labourer. Children: James Henry (1872), Julia Annie (1873), Elizabeth Mary (1877) Ellen Jane (bpt 1877), Susan (1883), Bessie (1882), Thirza (1887), John (1884), Lilly Emma (1872) and Grace (1888). Died 7 April 1922, aged 71 years. Buried in Cury Churchyard. Thirza died 11 February 1941, aged 87 years.

SKEWS JOHN
Married 1849, Launceston.

SKEWES JOHN
Won prize from Cornwall Agricultural Association for bringing up the largest family in a parish without any parochial relief. John, of Kea, won £5 for bringing up 15 children. June 1849.

SKEWIS JOHN
Born 1849. Died St Andrew, Dundee, 1927, aged 78 years.

SKEWES JOHN
Born 1851, Redruth.

SKEWES JOHN
Chart 12. Son of Henry and Harriet (née Hodge) Skewes of Landewednack, St Keverne formerly of Cury. Born 27 January 1851. Married Louisa ..... about 1870. John worked as a farmer at Chyponds, Cury; Skewes, Cury; Polglase, Cury; Chybarles and Tresodden, Ruan Major and Halwyn, St Keverne. He lived at The Three Tuns Hotel, Landewednack, 1861. His mother was a hotel keeper and father a carpenter employing one boy. Children: Louisa (1870) and Mary (1871).

SKEWES JOHN
Born 1851. Died 1907, Truro, aged 56 years.

SKEWES JOHN
Born 1851. Died 1913, Yarmouth, aged 62 years.

SKEWIS JOHN
Born 1852, Liskeard.

SKEWS JOHN
Died 1852, Liskeard.

SKEWES JOHN
Born 1853, Redruth.

SKEWES JOHN
Married 1853, Helston.

SKEWES JOHN
Chart 10. Son of William and Mary Skews. Born 1854, Illogan.

SKEWS JOHN
Married 1854, Plymouth.

SKEWES JOHN
Chart 10. Son of William and Mary Skews. Married 1854 Redruth. Copper and tin miner.

SKEWIS JOHN
Born 1854/1855. Son of John Skewis, miner. Married Caroline Beckerleg (24) at Register Office, Ulverston, Lancaster 3 July 1880. Caroline was daughter of James Beckerleg, miner. John Skewis lived in Queen Street, Dalton, Ulverston. Children: Herbert (1881), Grace Maria M. (1882), John James (1884) & William Stratheway (1891).

SKEWS JOHN
Chart 6. Son of Thomas and Mary Ann (née Hooper) Skews. Born 21 January 1855, Egloshayle, Bodmin. Emigrated with parents to Mineral Point, Wisconsin, USA. Stonemason, farmer and carpenter. Married Clara Jeanette Babcock (she born 1860, died 1950) at Waldwick, 11 May 1882. Children: Shirley (1899), William Alexander (1903) and Harvey Thomas (1904). Buried on his 64th wedding anniversary 11 May 1945, aged 90 years.

SKEWES JOHN
Chart 30. Born 1856 at St Clement, Truro. Son of John Beer and Mary Brown Skewes, compositor.

SKEWS JOHN
Born 1856, St Cleer. Copper and tin miner. In 1871 Census Returns was living at Common Moor, St Cleer, Liskeard.

SKEWES JOHN
Chart 50. Born 1858, Sofala, New South Wales, Australia. Married Mary Jane Cole 1 January 1884. Children: Rachel Jane (1885), Cyril Thomas (1889), Ida Florence (1890), Pearl (1891), Angelina Mary (1893), Bertie Cole (1894), Elizabeth Frances (1897) and Jack (1899).

SKEWIS JOHN
Born 1858 Shullsburg, Wisconsin, USA. In 1880 was a farm hand in Yorkville. His parents came from England.

SKEWES JOHN
Died 1858, Truro.

SKEWS JOHN
Born 1859, Penzance. Died 1859, aged 0.

SKEWES JOHN
Married 1861, Helston.

John Skews (1855-1945)

Son of John Skewes, farmer. Married Elizabeth Jane Hill, daughter of William Hill at Constantine, 3 April 1862. Farmer.

SKEWES JOHN
Chart 36. Son of William and Elizabeth (née Northey) Skewes. Born 1 April 1862, Australia. Died May 1894, aged 32 years.

SKEWS JOHN
Died 1862, Liskeard.

SKEWES JOHN
Born 1863, Truro.

SKEWES JOHN
Chart 15. Son of Peter Skewes, miner. Born 1864, Truro. Married Annie Gartrell, daughter of Walter Gartrell, cordwainer of Callington, at Register Office, Liskeard, 6 October 1890. Lived at Bowling Green, Kelly Bray, Cornwall. Emigrated to USA, 1891.

SKEWS JOHN
Chart 23. Born 1864. Married Bertha .... Children: William Hedley (1898), Gertrude Alberta (1896) and Mabel Millicent (1902). Lived at Coxbarrow, St Austell. Died 18 February 1936, aged 72 years.

SKEWS JOHN
Married 1866, Kensington, London.

SKEWES JOHN
Married 1869, Helston.

SKEWES JOHN
Born 1869, Falmouth. In 1871 Census Returns living at Goldmartin House, Mawnan and listed as grandson to head of household Ann Kempthorne, widow, aged 61. His mother was Mary E. Skewes, widow, aged 30 years.

SKEWES JOHN
Born 1871. Died 1871, aged 0, Redruth.

SKEWES JOHN
Chart 36. Born 1872. Died 1880. Buried Illogan, 26 June 1880, aged 8 years.

SKUES JOHN
Born August 1872, New York of English parents. In 1900 lived at Southern Boulevard, Bronx Borough, New York. Blacksmith.

SKEWS JOHN
Married 1872, Helston.

SKEWES JOHN
Chart 10. Son of Matthew Henry and Mary Jane Skewes of Illogan Highway, blacksmith. Bpt Illogan 24 February 1874. Married Sarah Greenslade, 22, daughter of Charles Greenslade master mariner of Portreath 16 June 1898 at Illogan Parish Church. In presence of William Skewes. Lived at 5 Cauldfield Place, Redruth; formerly Plain-an-Gwarry, Redruth (1922). Children: Minnie (1900), Percival (1902) and Matthew John (1910). Died 3 May 1929, aged 54 years. Sarah died 1966, Penstraze, aged 90 years.

SKEWIS JOHN
Chart 50. Son of Joseph Skewis, iron foreman and Marion Hamilton. Born 2 April 1875 at 18 Calder Street, Cathcart Road, Govanhill, Glasgow.

SKEWES JOHN
Born 1878, Bedwellty. Died 1878, aged 0.

SKEWES JOHN
Born 1878, Redruth. Emigrated to New York and was admitted 27 January 1901.

SKEWES JOHN
Chart 10. Son of Peter and Elizabeth Skewes. Born Chacewater 25 December 1877. Bpt Chacewater 19 September 1878. Went to live in South Africa prior to the Boer War. He returned to England for a while, but when the war in South Africa finished he returned to Johannesburg. Worked for the Nourse Mines as a fitter and turner for 53 years. In his youth he had done some amateur boxing and sang in the church choir. He had no hobbies but enjoyed watching horse racing and soccer. Married Lilian May Maynard. Children: Richard John (1916), Dennis Milner (1918) and Rex Owen (1923). Freemason.
Died 9 February 1961, aged 83 years.
Lilian May died 15 February 1978, aged 82 years.

SKEWS JOHN
Married 1880, Plymouth.

SKEWES JOHN
Married 1880, Truro.

SKEWIS JOHN
Married 1880, Ulverston.

SKEWES JOHN
Married 1882, Chorlton, Manchester.

SKEWIS JOHN
Born 1884, New Monkland, Scotland.

SKEWES JOHN
Chart 12. Son of John and Thirza Skewes. Born 4 May 1884 at Penhale, Ruan Minor. Married "Cissie" (Susan Jane) Gilbert of Redanick in 1907 at Helston Register Office. Children: Samuel Percy, Constance Jane, William John and Oswald. Cissie died 1951, aged 63 years. Buried in Mawgan Churchyard. John died October 1975, aged 91 years.

SKEWIS JOHN
Lived at Bolenowe Crofts, Camborne 1885/1886.

SKEWES JOHN
Lived at Cargenwen, Crowan, 1885/1886.

SKEWES JOHN
Born 1889. Lived at Goldsithney. Died 11 January 1890.

SKEWES JOHN
Chart 47. Gold miner. Married Emma Goldsworthy in Liskeard, 1890. Children: Samuel John (1893) and Rose Pearl (1915). Lived at Kelly Bray, Callington, Cornwall. Died in California, USA 16 September 1898.

SKEWIS JOHN
Chart 50. Son of William and Elizabeth (née Shaw) Skewis, fruit storeman. Born at 25 Market Street, Glasgow on 31 May 1896. Died Glasgow 1896, aged 0.

SKEWS JOHN
Chart 15. Son of John Gregory & Annie (née Gartrell) Skews of Callington. Born 9 February 1894. Married May Louisa Mallet, Liskeard Parish Church, 1918. (She died 1937.) Children: Morley David John (1919), Constance Margaret (1920) and Marion Rhoda (1923). Lived at 1 Friendship Place, Pound Street, Liskeard; Bay Tree Hill, Liskeard and 31 Mutley Plain, Plymouth. Master baker and confectioner. Married Evelyn M. Cox at the Register Office, Plymouth November 1940. Lives at 68 Glen Park Avenue, Plymouth, Devon.

SKEWIS JOHN
Lived at Condurrow, Camborne 1897/1906.

SKEWES JOHN
Married 1907, Helston.

SKEWIS JOHN
Chart 33. Son of William Richard Skewis. Born 1907. Died 1909. Totnes, Devon, aged 2 years.

SKEWS JOHN
Chart 17. Son of James Arthur Skews. Mother's maiden name Jarvis. Born 1919, Stepney. Died 1919, aged 0.

SKEWS JOHN
Lived at 7 Swithy Road, Plymouth 1935/1939.

SKEWS JOHN
Chart 41. Son of Thomas Ernest and Lily (née Brayford) Skews. Born 1948. Bachelor. Lives at 67 Wood Walk, Wombwell, Barnsley, South Yorkshire. Tel No: Barnsley 755053.

SKEWES JOHN
Lived at 25 Queen Street, Ballarat East, Victoria, Australia in 1959 with Margaret Ellen Skewes. Engine driver.

SKEWS JOHN
Lived at 19 Brooks Street, Wonthaggi, Victoria, Australia, in 1959 with Lynette Skews.

SKEWES JOHN
Chart 12. Son of Oswald and Celia (née Holbrook) Skewes. Born 1963, Redruth. Lives at Trezemper Farm, Goonhilly Downs, Mawgan, Helston. Telephone number: 0326 22607.

SKEWES JOHN
Lived at 8 Burbage Road, Manchester 23 in 1971.

SKEWES JOHN
Married Rita Easton in Nottingham, 1971.

SKEWES JOHN A.
Born 1931. Married Shirley ..... Children: Mike, Gail, Rod, Pam, Kaylene, Judy and Sally. Lived at 337 Richard Street, Ballarat, Victoria, 3350, Australia. Died following an accident 25 May 1977, aged 46 years. Buried in Ballarat New Cemetery, Australia.

SKEWES JOHN ALBERT
Lived at 10 Stawell Street, Warrenheip, Victoria, Australia in 1959 with Frances Anita Skewes and Shirley Skewes. Sawmill employee.

SKUES JOHN ANTHONY Rev. M.A.
Chart 3. Son of Rev. Eric and Lily (née Brearley) Skues. Born 23 January 1930 at Tsinan-Fu, Shantung, China. Was schooled at home in China 1935-1940; St Giles, Tsingtao, 1941; Cathedral School, Shanghai, 1942; Lungwha Internment Camp, Shanghai 1943-1945; Hurstpierpoint College, Sussex 1946-1949.
Queen's College, Cambridge. B.A. 1952. M.A. 1956. Whilst at university was Cambridge Hockey Blue, 1952. Played for Yorkshire 1952 and 1953 and was Captain 1954-1955. Played for Gloucestershire 1958-1959 and 1959-1960. For Eastern Counties 1952. Northern Counties 1953 and 1954. Western Counties 1958-1960. Final England trial possibilities 1953.
Married Rosemary M. Bamber, October 1956 at Holy Trinity Church, North Malvern, Worcester. Children: Bridget Mary (1959) and Judith Ann (1957). Rosemary was killed in a car accident, 1960.
John married Teresa R. Cockerell at St Mary's, Lambeth, Southwark, London, November 1963. Child: Jonathan Paul (1965).
Religious career: College of Resurrection, Mirfield, 1952; Deacon, 1955, Lincolnshire. Priest Grimsby for Canterbury, 1956. Curate of Boston 1955-1958; Stroud 1958-1959; Cirencester with Watermoor 1959-1962. Chaplain to the Forces (Church of England) Reserve of Officers from 10 February 1960.
Hospital chaplain to St Thomas's, London 1962-1969. In August, 1969 John moved to Coventry and became full time chaplain to Walsgrave Hospital, and a public preacher.
Current address: 8 Shirley Road, Walsgrave, Coventry. Telephone number: 0203 614193.

SKEWES JOHN ANTHONY
Chart 12. Son of Dennis I.J. Skewes of Porthallow. Mother's maiden name Letcher. Born 1967, Penzance.

SKEWS JOHN ANTHONY
Mother's maiden name SKEWS. Born 1969, St Austell.

SKEWES JOHN ARTHUR
Chart 36. Son of Colin Arthur and Joyce Eva (née Brockley) Skewes. Born 3 November 1952. Bachelor. Lives at 4 Parkhouse Avenue, Seaton, 5023, South Australia.

SKUES JOHN BARRY
Chart 5. Son of Jack Sydney and Doris (née Hope) Skues. Born 19 February 1945, Melbourne, Australia. Married Suzanne Emery 12 April 1980.
Assistant Manager of Walton's Store, Taree, 2430, New South Wales, Australia. Lives in Northern Wingham, New South Wales.

SKEWES JOHN BEER
Chart 30. Son of Thomas and Jane Skewes; cabinet maker of Daniell Street, Truro. Born 20 May 1830. Bpt Kea 25 August 1830. Married Mary Brown Windon (daughter of James Windon, shipwright of Padstow) living at Kenwyn Street, Truro on 3 December 1849 at Kenwyn Parish Church. Addresses during marriage: Paul's Row, St Clement; Kenwyn Street, Truro (1871 Census Returns), Pydar Street, Truro and Fairmantle Street, Truro. Children: Elizabeth Jane, John Beer, William B., Henrietta Maria, Thomas James, Philippa Mary, Richard Henry & Frederick. Died 25 April 1899, aged 68 years.

SKEWES JOHN BEER
Chart 30. Born 1856. Son of John Beer and Mary Brown Skewes of Kenwyn Street, Truro.
Compositor with *Royal Cornwall Gazette*. Married Bessie Whether, daughter of Thomas Whether, St Austell Street, Truro at St George's, Hannover Square, London 8 May 1880. Moved back to the West Country in 1884 to Exeter and lived at Westgate Coffee Tavern, Edmund Street until 1916. Then moved to 8 Waterloo Road, Exeter. Finally to 80 Wellington Road, St Thomas, Exeter in 1926.

In Devon he was a compositor with Chudleigh's, Printers. Children: Ernest John (1881), Gwendoline (1884) and Frederick Henry (1891). Died 1941, aged 84 years.

SKEWIS JOHN BENNETT
Chart 2. Son of Benjamin Peters and Amelia Skewis. Married Leila Jones. No issue. Lived in America.

SKUES JOHN BENNETT
Son of William and Jane Skues. Bpt Mylor 3 July 1803. Buried 24 March 1805, aged 2 years.

SKEWES   JOHN BILLING
Chart 2. Son of William and Sarah (née Billing) Skewes. Born 16 May 1849. Emigrated to the United States in 1867. Quartz miner. He spent two years in Massachusetts, after which time he went to Nevada. He was based at Grass Valley, California where he married Sarah Ellen Martland (she died 1893, Bodie, California). Issue: one son, John Billing Skewes, Junior (1881).
In 1895 John married Elizabeth Floyd. They moved to south eastern Utah, in the Big Indian territory of San Juan County shortly after staying in the Blue Mountains for two years.
In 1897 he was associated with C.E. Loose and Reed Smoot and bought the Big Indian Mining Property which was valued at $200,000.00 (£100,000). John owned a quarter of the stock in the company. On 23 December 1909 he was kicked in the chest by a horse and died two days later, on Christmas morning 25 December 1909, at his home in Big Indian. He was buried at Moab, Utah, 27 December 1909, aged 56 years.

SKEWES   JOHN BILLING II
Chart 2. Son of John Billing and Sarah Ellen (née Martland) Skewes. Born 16 May 1881, Marysville, California, USA.
Married Lydia Ann Taylor, 3 June 1907.
Children: Elaine Madoline, Arthur Wayne, John Billing III, Madge Ruth and Erma Deone.
Freemason with Orient Lodge No 15 F and A M, Green River, Utah. Originally a miner and later peace officer. Was County Sheriff for 22 years.
Died from a fall from a tree in Moab, Utah, 21 February 1952, aged 70 years.

SKEWES   JOHN BILLING III BSc.
Chart 2. Son of John Billing II and Lydia (née Taylor) Skewes. Born 15 June 1913, Moab, Utah, USA. Married Veda Poulson, 10 September 1938. She died 12 April 1942, Salt Lake City.
Served in U.S. Naval Construction Battalion in 2nd World War from 1942 to 1945.
Married Mary Josephine Armington 28 February 1948. Children: John Billing IV (1942), Charles Armington (1949), Robert Joseph and Mary Ann (twins) 1950, Nancy Lynn (1955) and William Taylor (1961).
Bachelor of Science, University of Utah, 1938. Administratively responsible for construction of all major Utah highways from 1955 to 1978. Retired in 1978.
Freemason with Bonneville Lodge No 31 F and A M, Utah (Worshipful Master 1979) and Orient Lodge, No 15, Green River, Utah.
Lives at 133 West 1800 South, Bountiful, Utah, 84010, United States of America. Telephone number: (801) 295 1813.

John Billing Skewes III

SKEWES   JOHN BILLING IV
Chart 2. Son of John Billing III and Veda (née Poulson) Skewes. Born 30 March 1942, Salt Lake City, Utah, USA. Married Delores Davis 5 September 1969, Las Vegas, Nevada, USA. Children: John Billing V (1972) and Robert Curtis (1977).
Contractor. Partner in earth moving firm Skewes and Hamilton. Lives at Duchesne, Utah, United States of America.

SKEWES   JOHN BILLING V
Chart 2. Son of John Billing IV and Delores (née Davis) Skewes. Born 30 March 1972, Duchesne, Utah, USA.

SKUES   JOHN C.
Chart 9. Mother's maiden name Bremer. Born 1926, Camberwell.

SKEWES   JOHN C.
Lives at Lisfreda, Croft Mitchell, Troon, Camborne, Cornwall with Jennifer R. Skewes.

SKEWIS   JOHN C.
Married Patricia M. Eady in Corby, Northants, 1976.

SKUES   JOHN CHARLES
Chart 5. Son of Lewis and Eliza (née Pearn) Skues. Bpt Fowey 26 May 1881. Mason. Married Margaret Ellen Banfield (24), daughter of William John Banfield, shoemaker; at Redruth Parish Church 19 April 1902, in presence of John Frederick Skues. Children: John Charles (1902), Florence Lilian (1906), Gwendoline (1903), James Frederick M. (1904), Joseph Charles (1906) and James Albert (1907).

SKEWES   JOHN CHARLES
Chart 12. Son of Gilbert J. and Kathleen Skewes. Mother's maiden name Dennis. Born 9 September 1959, Kerrier.

SKUES JOHN CHARLES R.
Chart 5. Son of John Charles Skues. Born 1902, Redruth.

SKEWIS   JOHN CLEMPSON
Chart 50. Son of Joseph Richard and Martha McIlroy Skewis. Born 7 November 1903, Aitchison Street, Airdrie, Scotland. Married Ann Brown 22 September 1924. Children: John Clempson (1925), James Brown (1931), Joseph Richard (1928) and Annie (1935). He emigrated to Australia at the age of 75 years.
Joined merchant navy as a youngster. At the outbreak of the Second World War joined the army and served in the Middle East, and after demobilisation went back into the merchant navy. Now lives at 19 Trent Street, RAAF Base, Forest Hill, Wagga Wagga, New South Wales, 2651, Australia.

SKEWIS   JOHN CLEMPSON
Chart 50. Son of John Clempson and Ann (née Brown) Skewis. Born 25 July 1925, Scotland. Married Catherine Strachan in Arbroath, 1948. Died 1955, aged 30 years in Dundee East.

SKEWIS   JOHN CLEMPSON
Chart 50. Son of Joseph Richard Skewis. Born 1927, New Monkland, Airdrie, Scotland. Married Jane Sheppard O'Neil at Camalchie, Glasgow, 1952. Children: Jane O'Neil (1953), John Clempson (1956), James O'Neil (1959) and George O'Neil (1961).

SKEWIS   JOHN CLEMPSON
Chart 50. Son of John Clempson and Jane Sheppard (née O'Neil) Skewis. Born 1956 Bridgeton, Scotland.

SKEWES   JOHN COURTIS
Chart 18. Son of Samuel Dawe and Jane (née Courtis) Skewes. Born 10 January 1864, Bere Alston, Devon. Married 1892 in Exeter to Ann . . . . . . Children: Harold Courtis, Arthur Courtis and Edgar. Helped establish Skewes Brothers of Plymouth. Later moved to "Newcombes", Crediton, Devon.
There he carried out the many and varied duties of public bodies to which he was connected.
He was a member of the Crediton Urban District Council of which he had been Chairman. He was a member of Crediton Joint Cemetery Board; the Guardians Committee; a member of the Crediton Committee for Higher Education; a Governor of Crediton Parish Church; a Governor of the High School and Queen Elizabeth Grammar School; a manager of Crediton Hayward's Schools and a member of Crediton United Charities Trustees. John Courtis Skewes took an active interest in the Crediton Fat Stock Show of which he was President for several years. He was President of the Crediton Cricket Club; Bowling Club; Boys Club and Golf Club. He also took an interest in the local rugby and association football clubs and the local nursing association.
His concern for the welfare of the public was shown when he was instrumental in the forming of the Crediton Housing Association to which the many houses called "Courtis Gardens" bear testimony.
He died 13 May 1936, aged 72 years. The funeral service took place at Crediton Parish Church and the vicar Rev. J.A. Durling said: "We are mourning the death of John Courtis Skewes, a governor of this church. He had been in failing health for a long time, but with characteristic courage he continued to play his part in the many activities to which he had devoted himself.
"Since he came to live in Crediton some 15 years ago no man could have been more conscientious in the discharge of his duties and it was always a pleasure to serve on any of the committees which he was associated with. His religion was simple and undemonstrative, but it went very deep. To him Christianity was essentially a practical affair; hence his keenness and energy in the cause of better housing in which matter he was an

enthusiastic leader. His place in the parish and town of Crediton will be difficult to fill."

His house and grounds "Newcombes" went up for auction. It comprised: Freehold residential estate. Fine Georgian residence with colonnade verandah, beautifully timbered grounds, carriage drive, lodge, prolific fruit and vegetable gardens, glass houses, two modern built cottages, farmery and valuable accommodation land — 18 acres. Auction date was June, 1936.

The property was purchased by the Area Health Authority and the house demolished in 1978. New buildings have been erected on the ground including a dental centre and a school for physically handicapped.

SKEWES   JOHN DAVID
Chart 36. Son of Samuel Edgar and Erlestoun Minneta (née Mudge) Skewes. Born 18 September 1937. Married Beryl May Johnson 25 February 1961. Children: Robyn May (1962). Mark Andrew (1964) and Philip John (1966). Lives at Ackland Hill Road, Cherry Gardens, 5157, South Australia. Missionary.

SKEWES   JOHN DAVID PERCIVAL
Lived at Christmas Hills, Eltham, Victoria, Australia in 1959. He was a wood carter.

SKEWES   JOHN EDGAR
Chart 18. Son of John Courtis and Ann Skewes. Born 1895, Windsor. Married Amy Morrison in Chelsea, 1924. Children: Arthur J. (1925), Ian Robert Morrison (1927) and Jill Thirza A. (1934). Lived at South View, Stockton Hill, Dawlish followed by St Ives, Teignmouth and Lustleigh (Devon) before moving to South Africa in 1958.

SKEWES   JOHN EDWARD
Chart 25. Son of Edward and Eliza (née Maddocks) Skewes. Born 19 September 1886 at 50 Corporation Street, Chorlton, Manchester. Married Rachel Cardwell Gleave (she died 1966) in Chorlton, 1914. Served in First World War in France and was badly injured. Lost his right leg. Later became a civil servant with H.M. Stationery Office, London. During the Second World War was responsible for providing maps of Europe to the military commanders and politicians.

After retirement moved south to 25 Surrey Road, Bournemouth and later 17 Mornish Road, Branksome Park. Poole, Dorset. No children. Died 8 January 1971, aged 88 years.

SKEWES   JOHN EDWARD
Chart 36. Son of John Henry and Annie Skewes. Lived in Australia. Children: Robin and Dorothy.

SKEWS   JOHN EDWIN
Chart 50. Born 28 March 1863, Killigrew Street, Falmouth, Cornwall. Son of William and Jane (née Bullock) Skews. Married Eliza Wells, 1896 at Highworth. He was a coach finisher. Later moved to 6 Horsall Street,

John Edwin Skews (1863-1947)

Swindon, Wiltshire. Children: Lilie (1903) and Albert Edward (1904). Died 11 March 1947, aged 83 years.

SKEWES   JOHN FREDERICK
Born 1852, Helston. Son of Francis and Juliana Skewes. Bpt Cury November 1852.

SKEWS   JOHN GEORGE
Chart 23. Son of George William and Caroline (née Nottage) Skews. Born 20 September 1897, at 14 Busk Street, Haggerstone, Shoreditch, London. Wood last maker. Married Mabel Cooper White in 1920 (she died 27 December 1963, aged 68 years). Children: Mabel I. (1921) and John G.P. (1923). Lived at 109 Centre Parade, Kettering in 1960's. Now lives at 28 South Street, Crowland, Peterborough. Telephone number: 0733 210352. Married Mills, 1969, Peterborough.

SKUES   JOHN GILBERT
Chart 8. Born 12 January 1865 at 77 Berwick Street, Soho, London. Son of George and Mary Sophia Skues. Bpt 26 March 1865 at Old Church, St Pancras. Married Elizabeth ...... (who died 4 December 1946, aged 83 years). Lived at 24 Tintern Road, Wood Green, London. Died 3 May 1935, aged 71 years.

SKEWIS   JOHN GLEN
Born 1951 St Andrews, Scotland.

SKEWS   JOHN GREGORY
Born 1848, Launceston. Died 1848, aged 0.

SKEWS   JOHN GREGORY
Chart 15. Born 1853. Son of John and Isabella (née Gregory) Skews of Altarnun, Launceston. Bpt Altarnun 15 September 1853. Died 1853, aged 2 months.

SKEWS   JOHN GREGORY
Born 1855, Launceston. Died 1855, aged 0.

SKEWS   JOHN GREGORY
Chart 15. Son of Peter and Elizabeth (née Gregory) Skews, of Woolston, Callington. Born 1860, Liskeard. Married Annie Gartrell, daughter of Walter Gartrell, cordwainer of Valentine Row, Callington at Register Office, Liskeard 16 October 1890. Children: John (1894), Clarence (1896), Winifred Mary (1898), Edith Jane (1901) and Fernley Walter (1907). Lived in Valentine Row, Callington. Died 1932 aged 72 years.

SKEWES   JOHN GREGORY
Chart 50. Son of Jack and Shirley Beryl (née Callaghan) Skewes. Born 6 June 1953, North Ryde, Australia. Serving with Royal Australian Air Force. Lives at 158 Pittwater Road, Gladesville, 2111, New South Wales, Australia.

SKEWS   JOHN G.P.
Chart 23. Son of John George and Mabel Cooper (née White) Skews. Born 1923, Kettering. Married Dorothy Boyland, 1946, Peterborough. Children: Stephen J. (1950), David A.H (1952), Christopher (1954) and Gerald N. (1957). Previous address: 109 Centre Parade, Kettering. Present address: 5 Lime Tree Avenue, Peterborough. Tel No: 0733 62073.

SKEWS   JOHN H.
Married Lundell, 1939 in Edmonton. Issue: daughter, Judith M. (1945).

SKEWS   JOHN H.
Married Duff, 1952 in Birmingham.

SKEWS   JOHN HAROLD
Chart 25. Son of Harry and Agnes Skewes of 117 Yew Tree Road, Manchester. Mother's maiden name Lally. Born October 1919, Chorlton. Married Sheila Winifred Wynne, 30 January 1941 at St Malachy, Manchester. Children: Kevin P. (1942), Diane M. (1944) and Martin (1953).

SKEWES   JOHN HENRY
Son of John and Anne Skewes of Chacewater, miner. Bpt Kenwyn 29 June 1828. Murderer in Nevada?

SKEWES   JOHN HENRY
of Chacewood. Buried Chacewater 31 March 1829, aged 2 years.

SKEWES   JOHN HENRY
Chart 10. Son of John and Harriet Skews. Born Kea 1847. Bpt Chacewater 8 August 1847. Listed as aged 3 in 1851 Census Returns; aged 14 in 1861 Census Returns.

SKEWES   JOHN HENRY
Born 1854, Helston.

SKEWES   JOHN HENRY
Chart 36. Son of John and Susan Skewes of Pool, police officer. Born 31 May 1864. Bpt Illogan Parish Church 11 December 1864. Emigrated to Australia aboard vessel *Trevelyan* which left Plymouth in December, 1865 and arrived at Port Adelaide 21 March 1866.

Married Annie Shillabeer 16 December 1884, South Australia. Children: William Roe Skewes (1895), Melvina Skewes, Olive Mabel Skewes and John Edward Skewes.

Died 13 February 1946, aged 81 years.

SKEWES   JOHN HENRY
Chart 10. Born 1877, Redruth. Married Eliza Jane Bartle, 1896, Redruth. One daughter Doris.

Died 1940, aged 61 years in Redruth. Eliza Jane died 1959, aged 77 years. John Henry was a miner, and in his youth worked in California.

SKEWS   JOHN HENRY
Born 1880. Married Eva Mary ..... Lived at Wallaford Venn Crescent,

Plymouth. Died 13 September 1946, aged 66 years.

SKEWES JOHN HENRY
of 415a Hill Street, Laguna Beach, California, United States of
America. Tailor. Died 18 February 1959 at Hoag Memorial Hospital,
Newport Beach, California, USA. A(SH) £1324.

SKEWS JOHN HENRY
Chart 15. Son of Amos Skews. Born 1890 Stoke Devonport. Married
Amy Emma ..... 1918, Devonport. Lived at 4 Shenstone Gardens,
Honicknowle, Plymouth. Died 7 August 1954, aged 63 years.

SKEWES JOHN HENRY
Chart 10. Son of Henry Skewes of Ashton, Helston, Cornwall. Born 8
October 1892 at Philadelphia, Pa, U.S.A. Musician. Bachelor.

SKEWES JOHN HENRY
Married 1904, Helston.

SKEWS JOHN HENRY
Married 1906, Totnes.

SKEWES JOHN HENRY
Chart 12. Son of John and Edith Skewes of Carnkie, miner. Born 18 July
1910. Bpt 22 September 1910, at Wesleyan/Methodist Circuit,
Camborne/Redruth. Known as "Froggie" or "The Frog King." Married
Evelyn May Cork, 1930, Redruth. Children: Margarette Jean (1935)
and Dorothy Marina (1939), both now married.
John was later divorced and married Florence Blenes in 1949. The
marriage only lasted five weeks. A son, Carlton B. Skewes, was born
1950. He again married, this time to Hilda Martha Trenear on 22
March 1956 at the Register Office, Redruth.
John would describe himself as "accident prone" — he broke his leg in
1920 and received multiple fractures in both legs on 16 March 1928
when he was hospitalised in Redruth for six months. He had been
travelling home in his horse and cart when part of a hillside collapsed
and buried him. In 1943 he suffered from tuberculosis and in 1977
from phlebitis.
In earlier days he had offered his services for the Royal Air Force at the
outbreak of the 2nd World War, but was turned down on medical
grounds. He worked for the Bristol Aircraft Corporation at Filton in
1939, but returned to Cornwall and became a bus driver in Falmouth
(1940-1942).
After yet another illness John began his own haulage business
incorporating building and demolition which employed 25 men
throughout Cornwall. This he successfully ran for 30 years from 1943.
During this time he did much voluntary work for the West Cornwall
Hospital Management and tarmacked church paths in parishes
including Hayle, Budock and Mabe for which he refused to accept
money. His firm sank wells, built houses and demolished churches and
chapels including a Falmouth Chapel and Church at Lostwithiel, all of
which had become unsafe. Likewise St Mary's Church, Portreath. John
Skewes has always been interested in frogs from a child. For him it was a
hobby, albeit profitable. He sent frogs all over the country from
Redruth station for 45 years. He became one of British Rail's most
regular exporters. These frogs were sent to hospitals and universities for
medical research.
It was whilst collecting frogs that he experienced one or two "ups and
downs." On a cold, foggy winter night at a deserted quarry he slipped
and fell into cold, dark freezing water, but was fortunately rescued.
Over the years he has handled many millions of frogs.
Just prior to the 2nd World War he also took an interest in snails and sold
them to London restaurants for eight (old) pence per dozen.
A sign outside his house in Camborne reads:
"Suppliers of pigeons to Her Majesty The Queen." He has been
interested both as a pigeon fancier and breeder since 1915, and over the
years has collected many cups and awards. He has been sending pigeons
to the Queen since 1952 and his name is familiar with the Loft Manager
at Sandringham. He has sent pigeons all over Britain and to the
Continent as well as the Phillippines, the Channel Islands and the
United States of America.
John Skewes has appeared on both radio and television talking about his
fascinating hobbies and interests. Addresses since marriage: Dundance
Lane (1930-1957), Pool, Redruth; Barncoose Terrace (1976-1977); 7
Chariot Road, Illogan (1977); 22 Bullers Terrace, Redruth (1978) and
10 Rose Cottages, Camborne (from 1 December 1978).
Telephone number: 0209 712571.

SKEWS JOHN HENRY
Born 30 November 1928. Married Duff, 1952, Birmingham. Issue:
David J. Skews (1965). Died Walsall, 1976, aged 48 years.

SKEWES JOHN HENRY
Lived at Four Lanes, Illogan, 1932 with Eliza Jane Skewes and Doris
Skewes.

SKEWES JOHN HERBERT
Chart 10. Son of John and Catherine (née Williams) Skewes. Born 17
August 1881. Bpt Chacewater 29 September 1881. Emigrated to
Mexico with his family in 1891 via Vera Cruz and settled in Real del
Monte, Mexico. Married Beatrice Pratt 25 September 1905 in Mexico
City. Child: Oswald Herbert Skewes (1909). Silver mining engineer with
United States Mining and Refining Company. Author of mining articles
in Mexico (see Appendix). Died 23 July 1957, Florida, USA. Buried in
Sanford, Florida. Beatrice died 18 April 1971, Sanford, Florida, USA.

SKEWES JOHN HERBERT

John 'Froggie' Skewes

Chart 2. Son of Herbert Ernest and Edna (née Cuthbertson) Skewes.
Born 18 October 1940, Australia. Married Thelma Jean Ettridge 21
March 1964. Children: Lisa Catherine (1965) and Gary Leonard
(1967). Thelma Jean was born 24 October 1941. Now lives at Lot/85
Eclipse Drive, Albany, 6330, Western Australia. Representative.

John Herbert Skewes (1881-1957)

SKEWS   JOHN HILARY
Chart 41. Son of William John and Mary (née Rump) Skews. Born 22 May 1933, Durham North. Married Annette Lennox, 23 June 1962, Durham North. No children. Lives at 14 Chepstow Road, Bury St Edmonds, Suffolk. Telephone number: 0284 63564.

SKEWS   JOHN HOOPER
Son of Thomas Skews. Bpt Egloshayle, 5 June 1853.

SKEWES   JOHN HORNBY
F.I.S.T.M., M.B.I.M., M. Ins. M. Chart 48. Son of William Frederick Charles and Dorothy Marion (née Hornby) Skewes. Born 8 November 1933, Doncaster, South Yorkshire. Attended Kimbolton Grammar School, Cambridge, 1944-1951. Married Madge Freeman, daughter of George Frederick Freeman of Sunnycroft Farm, Melton Brand, near Doncaster, farmer, at St James' Church, Doncaster 12 February 1955. Children: Linda Marion (1955) and Karen Elizabeth (1958). Began his career as a newspaper reporter. National Service with Royal Army Pay Corps, including overseas service in Kenya 1952-1953. Later entered musical instruments industry as a representative for Hohner.
In 1965 started his own musical instrument wholesale company aided by his wife Madge. Now is major shareholder in John Hornby Skewes & Co. Ltd operating from Salem House, Main Street, Garforth, Leeds of which he is also managing director. The company employs a staff of over 60. The offices were originally two Methodist churches, a police station and a cinema. A new block was added in 1971. The company exhibits in many countries around the world including the annual Frankfurt International Spring Fair.
John Hornby Skewes and Company Ltd represents manufacturers from various countries of the world and imports from the United States of America, Mexico, Communist China, Japan, Spain, Italy, East and West Germany, Sweden, Austria and Switzerland.
John Hornby Skewes is a member of the Institute of Commercial and Technical Representatives and Commercial Travellers Association.
He has been President of the Garforth Musical Society since 1970.
He is a past President of the Association of Musical Instrument Industries.
Is a member of the British Institute of Management and a member of the Institute of Marketing.
He is a member of the British Society of Russian Philately.
The company is a member of the Electronic Organ Distributors Association. From 1978 they sponsored an Eko Organ Rally Car.
John Hornby Skewes' hobby is golf.
Telephone numbers: Office 0532 865381. Home: 0532 862440. Home address: 5 Station Fields, Garforth, Leeds, LS25 1PX.

John Hornby Skewes

SKUES   JOHN HOSKIN
Chart 2. Son of Stephen and Margaret Skues of Treswithian, Camborne. Bpt Camborne 25 September 1824. Married 20 September 1846 to Nanny Provis, spinster, daughter of Alexander Provis, miner of Treswithian at Redruth Parish Church. Emigrated to USA. Lived in California in 1900.

SKEWES   JOHN HOWARD
Chart 12. Son of James Henry and Maud (née Richards) Skewes. Born 1918, Helston. Married Eva S. Keast in Truro, 1950. One son: James A. (1950).

SKEWIS   JOHN JACK
Born 1880, Old Monkland, Scotland. Died Old Monkland, aged 0.

SKEWES   JOHN JAMES
Born 1843. Died 1903, Brentford, Middlesex, aged 60 years.

SKEWES   JOHN JAMES
Married 1874, Plymouth. In Plymouth Street Directory 1885 he was living at 2 Union Street, Plymouth. Still there in 1890 and listed as a beer retailer. Had moved by 1893. In 1906/1907 Plymouth Street Directory was at 40 Old Town Street, Plymouth.

SKEWIS   JOHN JAMES
Born 1884, Ulverston. Son of John and Caroline (née Beckerleg) Skewis.

SKEWIS   JOHN JAMES
Chart 50. Son of James Brown and Margaret Forrest Skewis. Born 4 April 1957, Dundee, Scotland. Lives at 19 Trent Street, RAAF Base, Forest Hill, Wagga Wagga, New South Wales, 2651, Australia.

SKEWIS   JOHN JAMIESON
Chart 50. Born 1906, Blackfriars, Glasgow, Scotland. Married Margaret Middlemas Jack, 1933, Cadder, Scotland. Children: William Iain (1936) and Margaret Munro (1940).

SKEWIS   JOHN JAMES SQUIRES
Born 1843, Falmouth.

SKUES   JOHN JOSEPH G.
Born 1926. Married Iris M.A. Davies in Woolwich in 1955. Children: Teresa (Davies), Anthony (1956), Paul (1956) twins; and Martin (1958).

SKEWES   JOHN KEMPTHORNE
Chart 36. Son of Edward and Mary Ellen (née Kempthorne) Skewes of Mawnan; blacksmith. Born 1870. Was the first "Skewes" in the London Telephone Directory (1902-1903). Milliner, draper and outfitter of 31 Broadway, Wimbledon. Freemason and founder member of Wimbledon Lodge. He retired at the early age of 40. After retirement interested himself in property dealing. He was on holiday in Cornwall just prior to the outbreak of war in 1939, and decided to make his home there.
However, he was fatally injured in a car accident when his vehicle was in collision with a large motor lorry belonging to Messrs H & G Simonds of Tamar Brewery, Plymouth. He was accompanied in the car by Miss Violet Coad, hairdresser of Coinagehall Street, Helston, aged 31 years who was killed outright, His chauffeur George Bye was seriously injured.
In Cornwall John lived at Parc Vro, Mawgan-in-Meneage: in London at the Averdale Hotel, 10 Lancaster Gate, London W.2.
He died in the Prince of Wales Hospital, Plymouth 23 November 1939, aged 70 years. Bachelor.

SKEWES   JOHN LESLIE
Lives at 8 Douglas Street, Townsville, 4810, Queensland, Australia with Gaye Lorraine Skewes. Mechanic.

SKUES   JOHN LESLIE
Chart 5. Son of Leigh Harold and Ethel Maude (née Poynton) Skues. Born 6 December 1945. Lives at 10 Acland Close, Mulgrave, Melbourne, 3170, Australia.

SKEWES   JOHN LOCKE
Chart 36. Son of Archer William and Elsie May (née Handley) Skewes. Born 18 April 1921. Married Heather Leonne McKenzie, 3 September 1953. Children: Janette Lydia (1955), Elizabeth Margaret (1961) and Peter William (1959). Lives at Duthie Park, via Blackall, 4723, Queensland, Australia.

SKEWES   JOHN MARTIN
Chart 12. Son of William Henry Skewes. Born 9 July 1903, Missouri, USA. Changed his name to James Patterson.

SKUES   JOHN MICHAEL
Chart 9. Son of Roy Arthur Skues. Mother's maiden name Joan D. Causton. Born 28 December 1958, Ashford, Kent. Lives at 7 Rylands Road, Bybrook, Ashford, Kent.

SKEWS   JOHN MICHAEL
Chart 41. Son of Desmond Skews. Mother's maiden name Lunn. Born 1966, Staincross.

SKEWES   JOHN MICHAEL
Chart 36. Son of Owen Eric Edward and Stella Tabitha (née Harris) Skewes. Born 2 August 1949, Ballarat, Australia. Married Janice Elizabeth Miles, 13 November 1971, All Saints Church, Ballarat. Children: Danielle Elizabeth (1973), Nathan John (1974) and Linda Jane (1976). Technician with BTV6 Television in Ballarat. Lives at 702 Neil Street, Ballarat, 3350, Victoria, Australia.

SKEWES   JOHN OGILVIE
Lived at Kangaroo Road, Oakleigh, Victoria, Australia in 1913 with Jane Skewes. Painter.

John Leslie Skues

SKEWES JOHN OSBURN
Chart 12. Son of William John and Nora (née Thomas) Skewes. Born 7 June 1945. Married Pat Williams 6 June 1970 at Mawgan Church.
SKUES JOHN PENROSE
Chart 5. Son of Joseph and Elizabeth Skues, soldier. Bpt Redruth Parish Church 5 December 1813. Mason. Twice married.
1) Sally Tubb, 16 July 1837. She died 24 March 1853, aged 42 years.
2) Elizabeth Osborne, daughter of Nabotti Osborne, veterinary surgeon of Ludgvan in Penzance, 7 May 1859 at Ludgvan Parish Church.
Lived at Hodders Row, Redruth (1871 Census Returns). Children: Charles Penrose, Lewis Tubb, Sarah, Elizabeth, Jane, Joseph Penrose and James. Died 10 May 1896, aged 74 years.
SKUES JOHN PHILIP WILLIAM
Chart 9. Born 28 March 1891 at 14 Oakley Street, Waterloo, Lambeth. Son of Philip Henry and Florence Emma (née Guidotti) Skues. Married Florence M. Bremer in Camberwell, London, 1915 (she died 1955, aged 56 years). He married Rhoda Dawson, 1956, Woolwich. Worked at the Post Office and was presented with Imperial Service Medal in 1950. Children: Cyril Albert J. (1917), Philip Ernest (1922), John Joseph G. (1926), Audrey F. (1928) and Derek A. (1933). Died 1977, aged 86 years.
SKEWES JOHN R.
Married Trenear, 1956, Redruth.
SKEWES JOHN RAYMOND
Chart 50. Son of Leo William and Betty (née Thompson) Skewes. Born 3 August 1947. Lives at Colonial Inn, Hume Highway, Berrima, 2577, New South Wales, Australia.
SKEWES JOHN REGINALD
Lived on Farm 1425, Leeton, New South Wales, Australia in 1959 with Athol Henry Skewes and Nora Louise Skewes. Labourer.
SKEWES JOHN REGINALD
Lives at 62 Harris Road, Elliminyt, 3249, Victoria, Australia with Meredith Fae Skewes. Accountant.
SKUES JOHN RICHARD
Chart 3. Son of George and Mary Gibbs Skues. Born 26 May 1839. Died 1846, aged 7 years.
SKEWES JOHN RICHARD
Chart 37. Son of Richard John Skewes. Born December 1888. Married ...... Green, 1917 (?) in Sydney, Australia. Was a woolclasser at Nyngan, New South Wales. Children; K.M. Skewes and Donald Richard Skewes.

SKEWES JOHN RICHARD
Chart 10. Son of Richard Herbert and Alice Skewes. Born 24 September 1944, Ontario, Canada.
SKEWES JOHN RICHARD
Chart 50. Son of Bertie Cole and Doris Skewes. Lives at 54 Henry Street, Tighes Hill, 2297, New South Wales, Australia. Seaman. Married.No children.
SKEWES JOHN ROGER
Chart 12. Son of William Arthur Raymond and Mavis Emily Skewes. Mother's maiden name Rogers. Born 17 June 1959. Bachelor. Lives at Seagulls Cry, Cadgwith, The Lizard, Cornwall.
SKUES JOHN RULE
Chart 2. Son of James and Joanna Skues. Bpt Camborne 1 December 1827. Died Liskeard 1852, aged 25 years (?).
SKEWS JOHN RULE
Son of John and Mary Ann Skews, miner of Kenwyn. Bpt Gwennap 22 May 1831. Emigrated to USA. Married Isabella Jane Spensley. Son: Ronald James Skews who was born in Mineral Point, Wisconsin, USA.
SKEWIS JOHN SAMUEL
Chart 2. Son of Henry and Grace Skewis of Penponds, miner. Born 1845. Bpt Camborne 27 November 1845.
SKEWIS JOHN THOMAS
Illegitimate son of Jane Skewis of Nantithet, Cury. Bpt Cury 18 June 1826.
SKEWES JOHN THOMAS
Chart 40. Son of Richard and Caroline (née Laity) Skewes of Perran Downs, miner. Born 1862. Bpt 22 February 1863. Died 21 September 1863, aged 10 months.
SKEWES JOHN TREVOR
Chart 12. Son of William Frank and Annie Doris Skewes. Mother's maiden name Williams. Born 1935, Truro. Lived at Chybarles Farm, Ruan Major, Helston in 1969. Bachelor. Now lives at 30 Glebe Place, Ruan Minor, Helston, Cornwall.
SKEWES JOHN TROWNSON
Born 1867, Helston.
SKEWES JOHN VIVIAN
Chart 36. Son of Samuel and Mary Ann (née Waters) Skewes. Born 30 August 1876. Twice married. 1) Gertrude Mary Lock, 2 April 1902 and 2) Flora Wakefield, 2 December 1929. Children: Samuel Edgar (1903) and Gladys Lock (1908). Lived at 15 Gillan Street, Norman Park, Butimba, Queensland, Australia. Died 20 November 1961, aged 85 years.
SKEWES JOHN W.
Captain. Son of Captain Henry Skewes, formerly of Gwinear. Born 1848, Canada. Lived at Algoma, Ontario, Canada. Died at Zacatecas, Mexico on 2 April 1894, aged 46 years.
SKEWS JOHN WALTER
Chart 15. Son of Fernley Walter and Susan (née Wilcocks) Skews. Born 9 December 1938, Plymouth. Served 25 years in the REME until 1978 when he retired as Warrant Officer First Class. Silver Jubilee Medal, 1977. Married Margaret Joan Hill, 1964, St Germans. Runs West End Cafe, Callington, Cornwall. Lives at 2 Urban Terrace, Callington, Cornwall. Telephone number: 05793 2789. No children.
SKUES JOHN WALKER WILLIAMS
Born 1864, St James, London. Died 1864, aged 0.
SKEWES JOHN WALLACE
Lived at 130 Cowper Street, Yarraville, Victoria, Australia in 1959 with Lilian de Leon Skewes. Fitter and turner.
SKEWES JOHN WESLEY
Chart 12. Illegitimate son of Alice Ann Skewes, dressmaker of Cury. Born 1860. Bpt Cury 27 July 1860. Married 1886. Children: Ella (1886), Harry Stanley (1893) and William (1900). Lived at Nantithet, Cury and after marriage at Garras, Mawgan in Meneage. Died 3 February 1951, aged 89 years at Mount View Hospital, Madron.
SKEWES JOHN WILLIAM
Chart 6. Son of Peter and Mary Skewes of the Poor House, Kenwyn. Bpt Kenwyn 24 December 1826.
SKEWS JOHN WILLIAM
Born 8 March 1825, Redruth. Married 1) 1845 and 2) 1854. By second marriage had emigrated to South Australia. Children included Samuel Richard Skewes (1856). Wife's name on second marriage — Susanna May. Lived in Burra, South Australia. Died 1881, Burra, aged 56 years.
SKEWES JOHN WILLIAM
Born 1846, Redruth.
SKEWS JOHN WILLIAM
Chart 15. Son of John and Isabella (née Gregory) Skews of Trewint, Altarnun.
Born 15 September 1859. Bpt Altarnuun 16 March 1860. Emigrated to Napier, Hawkes Bay, New Zealand about 1880. Many of his descendants still live in New Zealand. Dora Skews writing from New Zealand in December, 1981 says that many of the present day Skews' have Cornish characteristics.
SKUES JOHN WILLIAM
Born 1878, Lambeth. Died 1880, aged 2 years.

Jonathan Braddon Skewes

John Wesley Skewes on the Hayle Towans, Cornwall, 1939

SKEWES   JOHN WILLIAM
Chart 10. Son of Thomas George Skewes of Marazion. Born 19 December 1880. Bpt Marazion 20 February 1881. Emigrated to USA with his parents 1896. Married Lillian Robbins 22 November 1905. Children: Arthur George and Ruth Lillian. Died 18 January 1961, aged 81 years at Ishpemming, Michigan, USA. Wife Lillian died 6 July 1943.

SKEWES   JOHN WILLIAM
Chart 50. Son of Cyril Thomas and Annie Mary (née Leathan) Skewes. Born New South Wales, Australia. Wife's name: Joyce Maxine. Children: Robert John, Paul Mervyn, Peter, Carmel and Kerrie. Lived at 11 Griffiths Street, Mayfield, New South Wales, Australia, in 1959. Now lives at 2 Marine Drive, Bardouroka, 2315, New South Wales, Australia.

SKEWES   JOHN WILLIAM
Lives at 160 Mansfield Street, Thornbury, 3071, Victoria, Australia with Shirley Margaret Skewes. Teacher.

SKEWS   JOHN WILLIAM HENRY
Born 1854. Married 1877 to Elizabeth Sarah .... (she born 1858). In 1890 Plymouth Street Directory lived at 16 King Gardens. Boatswain in Royal Navy (Lieutenant). In 1895 lived at 4 Eddystone Terrace, Plymouth. Died 26 January 1913 at 10 Hazelwood Terrace, Peverell, Plymouth, aged 58 years. Elizabeth Sarah died 4 July 1934, aged 76 years.

SKEWIS   JOHN WOODLEY WAINE
Born 20 August 1874. Illegitimate son of Mary Skewis of Crockaton, Ashburton, Newton Abbot, Devon. Died 1897, aged 25 years.

SKEWES   JONATHAN BRADDON
Chart 10. Son of Richard and Frenetta (née Littleton) Skewes of Marazion. Born 2 February 1898. Bpt Marazion 11 March 1898. Emigrated to Canada in 1905 with his parents and family. Served in First World War with 19th Battalion Canadian Infantry (1915-1918). Saw action in France and was wounded in Mones 10 November 1918. Two years previous he had been "blown up" in Lilles, France. After the war he ran a general contracting business and remained in business for 45 years. His son Bert now runs the operation. Married May Evelyn Gallagher 16 June 1920 (she died November 1978, aged 81 years). Children: Evelyn June (1922), Richard Herbert (1924), Norine Violet Margaret (1925) and Aileen Mary (1927). His hobbies include fishing, gardening and reading. Lives at 67 Limeridge Road West, Hamilton, Ontario, L9C 2T9, Canada.

SKEWS   JONATHAN MICHAEL
Mother's maiden name Perry. Son of Paul J. Skews. Born 1976, Stoke on Trent.

SKUES   JONATHAN PAUL
Chart 3. Son of Rev. John Anthony and Teresa Skues. Mother's maiden name Cockerell. Born 23 February 1965. Lives at 8 Shirley Road, Walsgrave, Coventry. Tel number 0203 614193.

SKEWES   JONATHAN ROSS
Chart 12. Son of George and Joyce (née Hawken) Skewes. Born 9 April 1957. Lives at "Rosskeith", 140 Agar Road, Illogan Highway, Redruth.

SKEWES   JORGE
See GEORGE H. SKEWES (Mexico)

SKEWS   JORGE ENRIQUE
Chart 2. Son of Luis Enrique Skewes. Born 7 September 1954, Mexico.

SKEWS   JOSE HUMBERTO
Chart 10. Son of Humberto and Laura (née Borja) Skewes. Born 1 December 1959, Pachuca, Mexico.

SCEWES   JOSEPH
Son of Henry and Elizabeth Scewes. Bpt Mullion 30 January 1686.

SKEWES   JOSEPH
Son of Joseph and Jone Skewes. Bpt Gunwalloe 20 March 1733.

SKEWES   JOSEPH
Married Jane Corien 5 August 1738.

SKEWISH   JOSEPH
Illegitimate son of Margery Skewish. Bpt Paul 8 November 1747.

SKEWIS   JOSEPH
Buried Gunwalloe 20 July 1751.

SKUES   JOSEPH
Son of Moses and Mary Skues. Bpt Mylor 23 August 1752.

SKEWES   JOSEPH
of Mawgan. Married Philippa Martin 8 June 1756 at St Martin in Meneage.

SKEWES   JOSEPH
Son of Joseph and Philippa Skewes. Bpt Mawgan in Meneage 8 August 1758.

SKEWES JOSEPH
Married Elizabeth Pearce at Mawgan in Meneage 14 January 1772.
SKEWES JOSEPH
Chart 3. Son of John and Mary Skewes. Bpt Helston 15 July 1787.
SKUES JOSEPH
Buried Mawgan in Meneage 18 May 1798.
SKUES JOSEPH
Private with Breage Volunteers 1798-1801. He quit the Volunteers on
25 April 1801.
SKEWES JOSEPH
Son of William and Ann Skewes. Bpt Gunwalloe 14 July 1799.
SKEWES JOSEPH
Buried Gunwalloe 31 October 1799.
SKUES JOSEPH
Son of William and Ann Skues of Mullion.
Bpt 29 November 1801.
SKEWES JOSEPH
Buried Mullion 1 November 1804.
SKEWES JOSEPH
Illegitimate son of Blanch Skewes. Bpt St Keverne 24 March 1811.
SKEWES JOSEPH
Son of Robert Skewes. Bpt 1 February 1811, Bedwellty.
SKUES JOSEPH
Chart 5. Sojourner, soldier and later mason. Married Elizabeth Penrose
at Redruth Parish Church 9 February 1813. Children: John Penrose and
Mary.
SKEWES JOSEPH
Chart 10. Son of Digory and Sophia Skewes. Born 3 April 1825. Bpt
Truro Wesleyan Chapel 28 March 1837. Married Elizabeth .... of
Kenwyn in Liskeard, 1849. Daughter Eliza (1850). Lived at Dobwalls,
Liskeard (1851 Census Returns).
SKEWIS JOSEPH
Chart 50. Son of James and Mary Ann (née Griffiths) Skewis. Born 17
September 1837, Aberdare, Merthyr Tydfil, Wales. Died 1844,
Merthyr Tydfil, aged 7 years.
SKEWIS JOSEPH
Born 1838, Redruth.
SKUES JOSEPH
Illegitimate son of Elizabeth Skues of Treloskan. Bpt Cury 14 April
1837.
SKEWES JOSEPH
Chart 2. Son of William and Elizabeth Skewes. Born 1837, Constantine.
Farm labourer. Married 1864, Helston.
SKEWIS JOSEPH
Chart 44. Son of Thomas and Elizabeth Skewis. Born 1846,
Abergavenny.
SKEWIS JOSEPH
Chart 50. Son of James Skewis, iron roller and Mary Ann Griffiths. Born
1847, Scotland. Married 11 February 1870 at East Campbell Street Free
Church, Glasgow to Marion Hamilton, daughter of John and Elizabeth
Hamilton (née Russell). Children: James (1870), Elizabeth Russell
(1873), John (1875) and Joseph (1878).
SKUES JOSEPH
Born 1848. Died 1917, in Eton, aged 69 years.
SKEWS JOSEPH
Chart 36. Son of Henry and Ann Skewes (lead miner) of East
Taphouse, St Pinnock, Liskeard. Born 1850. Bpt St Pinnock Parish
Church 7 April 1852. Brother: Henry. Sisters: Blanch, Maria and
Sarah Ann. Emigrated with his parents to Ballarat, Australia.
SKEWES JOSEPH
Died 1851, Abergavenny.
SKEWS JOSEPH
Died 1861, Liskeard.
SKUES JOSEPH
Married 1875, Chippenham, Wiltshire.
SKEWIS JOSEPH
Chart 50. Son of Joseph Skewis, iron turner and Marion Hamilton. Born
3 February 1878 at 18 Calder Street, Govanhill, Glasgow, Scotland.
Emigrated to Pennsylvania, USA in 1880. Lived with his brother James
in 1900 at 12 Division Street, Lawrence, Pennsylvania, USA. Roll
turner.
SKEWS JOSEPH
Chart 41. Son of Thomas Skews. Born 1901, Barnsley, South Yorkshire.
Married Nellie Randerson at Ardley Parish Church 18 April 1921.
Children: George (1921), Eric (1923), Baron S. (1924) and Arthur S.
(1926). Nellie died 1926, aged 26 years. Joseph married Alice Lumb
1928, Barnsley. Children: Rita (1929), Desmond (1930), Raymond
(1931), Brenda (1932) and Brian J. (1946). Died 1963, aged 61 in
Barkston Ash.
SKEWES JOSEPH
Chart 10. Mexican. Son of Henry and Lourdes (née Escudero) Skewes.
Born 1 January 1979. Lives in Real del Monte, Mexico.
SKUES JOSEPH CHARLES
Chart 5. Son of Joseph Pearn Skues. Born 1906, Redruth. Emigrated to

Australia with his parents. In 1912 lived at Barclay Place, Bendigo,
Victoria with Ettie Skues and Charles Joseph Skues. Died 2 December
1946. Buried in Bendigo Cemetery, Victoria, Australia.
SKEWES JOSEPH FREDERICK
Chart 25. Son of Harold and Agnes (née Lally) Skewes. Born 20 July
1918 at 6 Curry Street, Ardwick, Manchester. Married Doreen Isaac at
Edge Lane Methodist Church, Stretford 5 July 1958. Children: Allison
Elizabeth (1960), Melanie Anne (1961) and Jill Kathryn (1970). Lives at
12 Walnut Walk, Stretford, Manchester, M32 9AQ. Tel No: 061 865
5748.
SKEWES JOSEPH HENRY The Rev.
M.A. Chart 17. Son of William and Elizabeth Skewes of Constantine,
farmer. Born 29 April 1837. Bpt at Methodist Chapel, Falmouth 9
June 1837. Married, 1866 in Leeds. Children: Bessie Maud and
Sidney Hope. Lived at Fitzclarence Street, Liverpool. Wesleyan min-
ister 1862. Left the connexion 1875 and entered Church of England,
1876. Author of *A Complete Digest of the Polity of Methodism* (London — Elliot Stock, 1869); *Pulpit Palladium of Christendom* (London S.W. Partridge, 1891); *A Complete and Classifed Index of the
Journals of Rev John Wesley* (London, Elliot Stock, 1874); and *Sir
John Franklin — the Secret Discovery of His Fate* (London, Bembrose and Sons, 1889).
Three times before his ordination to the full work of the ministry, Joseph
Henry Skewes was taken from his regular work to superintend three
extensive county circuits. It was in this capacity that he had a wide area
for personal and close observation as to the knowledge of the working of
Methodism possessed by large numbers of people in rural districts. In his
book *A Complete Digest of the Polity of Methodism* each subject is
arranged in alphabetical order. On publication Skewes said: "I have no
wish to parade this, my maiden effort, before the public as a paragon of
perfection." Died 18 March 1898, aged 61 years.
SKEWS JOSEPH HERBERT MARTYN
Chart 15. Son of Harry and Hilda (née Jane) Skews, of Albert Cottages,
Pensilva, Liskeard. Born 11 August 1923. Bpt St Ive 5 September 1923.
Died 1925, aged 2 years.
SKEWES JOSEPH JOHN
Chart 10. Son of Digory and Fanny (née Tregonning) Skewes. Born 2
March 1865. Married Catherine Mary Richards of Gurma, Ashton,
Helston. Emigrated to Hamilton, Ontario, Canada, 1906. Served with
the Royal Navy in the Pacific for 9 years and later became an engineer in
Philadelphia, Pa at the docks, supervising traffic. Died 14 February
1931, aged 66 years in Hamilton, Ontario. Children: William Joseph
Skewes (1895) and Herbert Tregonning Skewes (1898).
SKEWES JOSEPH JOHN
Chart 10. Son of Richard and Frenetta Skewes of Marazion. Bpt
Marazion 23 February 1890 (born 5 December 1889). Died during First
World War aged about 25 years.
SKEWES JOSEPH JOHN
Married 1892, Lambeth.
SKEWS JOSEPH JORDAN
Born 1827. Died 1879 in Liskeard, aged 52 years.
SKEWES JOSEPH MARK
Lived at 57 Burlington Street, Crows Nest, New South Wales, Australia
in 1959 with Amy Skewes. He was a plumber.
SKUES JOSEPH PEARN
Chart 5. Son of Lewis and Eliza (née Pearn) Skues. Born 12 April 1887.
Attended Redruth East End School. Admitted 8 May 1892. Lived in
Fore Street, Redruth. Married 1906, Redruth. Emigrated to USA.
Lived at 2567 Wgdbl, Detroit, Michigan, USA.
SKUES JOSEPH PENROSE
Chart 5. Son of John Penrose Skues. Born about 1839. As a boy he was
apprenticed to a cabinet maker in Wales. After serving his time he
received his diploma. Emigrated to Australia in 1850's to the gold fields
of Chewton, approx 75 miles from Melbourne, where he married.
Children: John, Samuel, Charles, Frederick Henry and Bessie. Later
went to Bendigo where he built a home and workshop and started in
business as a builder and contractor.
SKEWIS JOSEPH R.
Junior (wife Edith G.) Worked at Cigars, 117W 9th Lobby, Los Angeles
in 1939. Private residence: 1423 Magnolia Avenue, Los Angeles, USA.
SKEWIS JOSEPH RICHARD
Chart 50. Son of James and Mary Ann (née Griffiths) Skewis. Born
January 1846, Tynemouth. Worked in the steel mills in Glasgow,
Scotland. He was offered work by Andrew Carnegie who was opening
new steel mills in Pennsylvania, USA. The large Skewis family
emigrated about 1880. Married to Marion Hamilton, daughter of John
Hamilton and Elizabeth (née Russell) at East Campbell Street Free
Church, Glasgow 11 February 1870, he went to America as a foreman in
the mill at Homestead Steel Works.
Unfortunately due to a disagreement with the way in which Carnegie
handled the Homestead strike, Joseph Richard Skewis left his job. He
visited his brother in Melbourne, Australia possibly to investigate job
opportunities over there, but returned to the USA to join his family.
Children included: John Hamilton, Joseph, James, Charles, William,
Amelia and Marion (Mae).
Joseph Richard Skewis was a proud man, with a deep sense of fairness.

He was strict in raising his sons, but fair in his punishment with them, as he was with his men at the mill.

He encouraged his children to study and offered the opportunity of college education to each who requested it.

Died 24 April 1915, aged 59 years.

SKEWIS   JOSEPH RICHARD
Chart 50. Son of Thomas and Sarah (née Nurse) Skewis, roll turner. Born 1868, Scotland. Lived at 5 Deeds Street, Airdrie. Married Martha McIlroy, domestic servant, aged 17 years of 40 Kidman Street, Coatbridge, Scotland, daughter of James and Mary (née Climson) McIlroy of 5 Quarry Road, Coatbridge in 1886.
Children: Mary (1888), William (1889) and James (1898). Died New Monkland, Scotland, 1951, aged 83 years.

SKEWIS   JOSEPH RICHARD
Born 1900, Coatbridge, Scotland. Died Townhead, Glasgow, 1951, aged 51 years.

SKEWIS   JOSEPH RICHARD
Born 1918, Shotts, Scotland.

SKEWIS   JOSEPH RICHARD
Born 1919, New Monkland, Scotland. Died 1925, aged 5 years.

SKEWIS   JOSEPH RICHARD
Married 1922, New Monkland, Scotland.

SKEWIS   JOSEPH RICHARD
Born 1923, New Monkland, Scotland.

SKEWIS   JOSEPH RICHARD
Born 1923, East Greenock. Son of Joseph Richard Skewis, iron puddler and Graham MacDonald Skewis (née Thompson).
Married and divorced. Lorry driver.
Lived at 165 Stamford Street, Glasgow.
Married Martha McIlroy Skewis (45), ward maid, spinster of 87 Govanhill Street, Glasgow; daughter of Thomas Skewis, iron puddler and Agnes Forbes Skewis (née Grant), in Glasgow on 18 July 1967.

SKEWIS   JOSEPH RICHARD
Born 1928 St Andrew, Scotland. Died Broughty Ferry, 1964, aged 36 years.

SKEWIS   JOSEPH RICHARD
Born 3 September 1930. Died 1978, Kettering, Northants, aged 48 years.

SKEWIS   JOSEPH RICHARD
Born 1931, New Monkland, Scotland.

SKEWIS   JOSEPH RICHARD
Married Isabella Bennett, 1944, Maryhill, Scotland.

SKEWIS   JOSEPH RICHARD
Married Annie Collins, 1949 St Andrew, Dundee, Scotland.

SKEWIS   JOSEPH RICHARD
Born 1951, St Andrew, Scotland.

SKEWIS   JOSEPH RICHARD
Married Carol Bruce Kilpatrick in Glasgow, 1962.

SKEWIS   JOSEPH RICHARD
Born 1964, Glasgow North.

SKEWIS   JOSEPH RICHARD
Married Carol Doig in Dundee East, 1974.

SKEWES   JOSEPH SYLVESTER
Born 21 January 1945 at May Beary, MacDowell, West Virginia. Son of Harold Herschell and Gladys Jane (née Batty) Skewes.

SKEWES   JOSEPH T.
Born 1843, Yorkville. Served with H Company, 22nd Infantry during American Civil War. Enlisted 15 August 1862. Wounded at Resaca. Absent-sick at muster out of regiment 15 November 1865.

SKEWES   JOSEPH V.
Born 1866, Gwinear. Father was a miner who worked in California. Mother called Elizabeth. In 1871 Census was living with his mother and sister Grace and brothers Richard, John and Harry at Carnell Green, Gwinear.

SKEWES   JOSIAH
Chart 2. Son of Henry & Grace Skewes of Bosawsack, Constantine. Bpt 6 August 1820, Constantine. Farmer of 100 acres employing 3 men and 2 boys. Married Fanny Bone, eldest daughter of James Bone of Penzance, 12 October 1852 at Wesleyan Chapel, Falmouth. Did jury service in Cornwall 1859/1860. Died 2 June 1878, aged 58 years.Wife Fanny died 18 June 1895, aged 68 years. Both buried in Constantine Churchyard alongside their five infant children.

SKEWES   JOSIAH
Chart 12. Son of James and Elizabeth Skewes, labourer. Bpt Cury 30 June 1824. Married Elizabeth Polglase of Sithney at Sithney 28 July 1846. Moved to Wendron (St Elvan) after marriage. Child: Eliza Ann Skewes. Elizabeth Polglase (28) was daughter of George Polglase, miner. In 1871 Census Returns living at Carthvean, Wendron. Died 1894, aged 69 years. Was an agricultural labourer.

SKEWES   JOSIAH
Chart 2. Son of Henry and Avis (née Bath) Skewes. Born 3 September 1847. Travelled out to Australia as steerage passenger aboard *True Briton* which sailed from Plymouth 28 September 1867 and arrived at Melbourne December 1867. Returned to England and married Janet Muir McPhee in Helston, 1881. Children: Henry, Josiah, Archibald,

Laura, Agnes, Avis and Olive. Lived at 7 Grant Street, Ballarat, Victoria in 1912. Died Melbourne 10 June 1919, aged 71 years.

SKUS   JOSIAH
Son of John and Elizabeth Skus. Bpt St Ewe 25 September 1853.

SKEWES   JOSIAH
Chart 2. Son of Josiah and Fanny Skewes. Born 1865, Falmouth. Married 1903 to Minnie ..... in Hampstead (she died 1937). Lived at 212 Ballards Lane, Finchley, London. Son: James Eldred Skewes, optician. Died 16 September, 1948, aged 83 years.

SKEWES   JOSIAH
Chart 2. Son of Josiah and Janet Muir (née McPhee) Skewes. Born Ballarat, Victoria, Australia. Married Mary Jane Padfield. Children: Linda, Millicent and William.

SKEWES   JOSIE McLEOD
Chart 36. Daughter of Bruce and Judith Rosemary (née Taylor) Skewes. Born 30 April 1974, Australia.

SKEWES   JOY
Lives at Adelaide River, 5783, Northern Territory, Australia with Thomas John Skewes.

SKUES   JOY CHRISTINE
Chart 3. Daughter of Jack and Lily (née Bruckshaw) Skues. Born 14 June 1937, Stockport, Cheshire. Married Donald Cooper in Blackpool, 15 June 1957 at Chapel Street Methodist Church. Issue: one daughter and three sons.
Lives at 5 Bransome Avenue, Preswich, Manchester M25 2AG. Telephone number 061 773 5240.

Joy Christine Cooper (née Skues) with her uncle Richard Skues, 1981

SKUCE   JOYCE
Daughter of Stewart Tennyson and Gertrude (née Roe) Skuce. Born 1920, Australia. Married Caldwell. Issue four children and nine grandchildren. Lives at 7 White Street, Henley Beach, South Australia, 5022.

SKUES   JOYCE
Chart 3. Daughter of Eric and Lily (née Brearley) Skues. Born 28 December 1925, Tsinanfu, Shantung, China. Returned to Britain in 1945. For many years Deputy Matron, St Thomas' Hospital, London. Now Divisional Nursing Officer, St Thomas'. Lives at "Juxon", Lollards Tower Chambers, Lambeth Palace Road, London S.E.1. Telephone number: 01 928 9292 Ext. 2572.

SKEWS   JOYCE
Chart 41. Née Morrell. Born 26 April 1926, Sunderland. Married William Clifford Skews 18 June 1949. Issue: One son Kevin Robert (1953). Lived at New Bottle, Houghton-le-Spring. Died 1977, aged 51 years.

SKEWES   JOYCE
Chart 12. Née Hawken. Married George Skewes at Camborne Parish Church 13 December 1948. Lived at 12 Lower Pumpfield Row, Pool, Redruth, in 1949. Children: Jeffrey Keith Skewes (1950) and Jonathan Ross (1957). Present address: "Rosskeith", 140 Agar Road, Illogan Highway, Redruth.

SKEWES JOYCE
Lived at 172 Burns Bay Road, Lane Cove, New South Wales, Australia in 1959 with Richard Skewes, storeman.
Now lives at 37 Mermaid Drive, Bateau Bay, 2261, New South Wales, Australia.

SKEWES JOYCE EVA
Chart 36. Née Boundy. Married Colin Arthur Skewes 24 June 1950, South Australia. Children: John Arthur (1952) and Julie Lorraine (1954). Lives at 4 Parkhouse Avenue, Seaton, 5023, South Australia.

SKEWES JOYCE M.
Married Whitburn in Truro, 1939.

SKEWES JOYCE MABEL
Chart 37. Née Everingham. Born 21 January 1919. Married Keith Matthew Skewes 25 November 1944, New South Wales, Australia. Children: Philip Matthew (1945), Vernon John (1947), Roger Keith (1950) and Elizabeth Ann (1956). In 1959 lived at Government Road, Mount Kurringai, Hornsby, New South Wales. Present address: Harwood Avenue, Mount Kurringai, 2080, New South Wales, Australia.

SKEWES JOYCE MARGARET
Lived at 178 York Street, Warrenheip, Victoria, Australia in 1959 with Edward Ernest Skewes. Now lives at 24 Pico Avenue, Point Ponsdale, 3225, Victoria, Australia.

SKEWES JOYCE MAXINE
Chart 50. Wife of John William Skewes. Children: Robert John, Paul Mervyn, Peter, Carmel and Kerrie. Lives at 2 Marine Drive, Bardouroka, 2315, New South Wales, Australia.

SKEWES JUAN
Chart 10. Mexican. Son of John and Luisa (née Garcia) Skewes. Born 1872, Real del Monte, Mexico. Appears to have been married to three ladies at a similar time 1) Fransisca Meneses 2) Maria Mendoza and 3) Paula Polica.
Children from first wife: Juan (1891), Justo (1896), Elizabeth, Lorenzo, Edward, Ricardo (1902), Elisa (1900), Dora and Isabel (1913). Wife number two: Salvador (1907), Eva, Fernando, and Blasa (1906). No children from wife number three. However he was father to another daughter, Celia, whose mother was Sereto Castro, aged 50. Died in Real del Monte from silicotuberculosis, 19 February 1939, aged 72 years.

SKEWES JUAN
Chart 10. Mexican. Son of Juan and Fransisca (née Meneses) Skewes. Born 1891, Real del Monte. Married Maria de Jesus Ortego. Children: Carmen and Leonor. Died 23 November 1918, aged 27 years. Buried in Real del Monte, Mexico.

SKEWES JUAN
Chart 10. Mexican. Son of Salvador and Carmen (née Ramirez) Skewes. Born 24 November 1933, Real del Monte, Mexico. Married Leonor Munoz. Children: Juan (1957), Elisa (1958), Ariel (1959), Fred (1961), Abril (1965) and Dora Maria (1968).

SKEWES JUAN
Chart 10. Son of Juan and Leonor (née Munoz) Skewes. Born 12 March 1947, Real del Monte, Mexico.

SKEWES JUANA
Chart 2. Daughter of Luis Enrique Skewes. Born Mexico 19 March 1941.

SKEWIS JUANA BRITO
Chart 2. Wife of James Henry Skewis. Died Pachuca, Mexico 25 July 1947.

SKEWES JUDITH
Chart 38. Née Walters. Married Henry Skewes at Constantine 28 October 1718. Children: Anne, Thomas, Anthony, George, Henry, Jane and Judith.

SKEWES JUDITH
Chart 14. Daughter of Henry and Judith Skewes of Cury. Bpt Cury 26 March 1733.

SKEWIS JUDITH
Chart 25. Daughter of Thomas and Esther Skewis. Bpt St Keverne 24 November 1754. Married John Mildren, 11 August 1783, St Keverne in presence of Thomas Skewes.

SKEWIS JUDITH
Married Thomas Harry at Helston, 1762.

SKEWIS JUDITH
Daughter of Anthony and Eleanor Skewis of Cury. Bpt Gunwalloe 6 May 1764. Buried Mawgan in Meneage 21 October 1769, aged 5 years.

SKEWES JUDITH
Daughter of Harold William and Alma Bernice (née Walker) Skewes. Born 1964. Warragul, Victoria, Australia. Married R. Gilbert. Issue: 1 son and 1 daughter. Lives in Australia.

SKEWES JUDETH
Buried Cury 26 November 1764.

SKUES JUDITH ANN
Chart 3. Daughter of Rev John Anthony and Rosemary Skues. Mother's maiden name Bamber. Born 5 August 1957, Boston, Lincs. Lives at 8 Shirley Road, Walsgrave, Coventry. Tel no: 0203 614193.

SKEWES JUDITH ANN
Lives at 19 Thompson Street, Woonona, 2517, New South Wales,

Australia with Cyril James Skewes, driver.

SKEWS JUDITH ANN
Lives at 207 Seacombe Road, South Brighton, 5048, South Australia.

SKEWES JUDITH ELAINE
Lived at Kingston, Uralla, New South Wales, Australia in 1959 with Malcolm Robert Skewes, station hand.

SKEWES JUDITH M.
Daughter of John H. Skewes. Mother's maiden name Lundell. Born 1945, Edmonton, London. Married Lane in Edmonton, 1963.

SKEWES JUDITH MAY
Lives at 12 Grevillia Road, Chester Hill, 2162, New South Wales, Australia with Leonard James Skewes and Barbara Helen Skewes.

SKEWES JUDITH ROSEMARY
Chart 36. Daughter of James and Stella Margaret (née Farrell) Skewes. Born 21 July 1935, Bendemeer, New South Wales, Australia. Married James Flitcroft. Issue: 1 son and 1 daughter (adopted).

SKEWES JUDITH ROSEMARY
Chart 36. Née Taylor. Married Bruce Skewes 10 February 1973. Children: Josie McLeod, Libby McLeod and Alexander McLeod. Lives at 21 Ridge Street, Tamworth, 2340, New South Wales, Australia.

SKEWES JULIA
Chart 36. Born 1825 at the Lizard. Wife of Edward Skewes of Poleskan, Cury, shoemaker. Children: Thomas, Henry, Annie, Bessie, Edith, Laura, Edward and Julia Anna. Died 13 August 1910, aged 85 years. Buried in Cury Churchyard.

SKEWES JULIA
Daughter of Thomas & Grace (née Trezize) Skewes. Bpt Chacewater 9 October 1831.

SKEWS JULIA
Daughter of Peter and Ann Skews of Gwennap. Bpt Kea 9 July 1833.

SKEWES JULIA
of Camborne. Married Richard Bullock 1 December 1854, Redruth.

SKEWES JULIA
Died 1860, Helston.

SKEWES JULIA
Died 1865, Redruth.

SKEWES JULIA ANNIE
Chart 12. Daughter of John and Thirza Skewes. Born 1873. Married William Stevens, 1897, Helston. Lived in Chacewater. Issue: two sons and two daughters. Died in 1960's, aged about 70 years.

SKEWES JULIA HANNAH
Married 1894, Helston.

SKEWS JULIA RUTH
Lives at 9 Harding Street, Ascot Vale, Victoria, 3032, Australia in 1959 with Reginald Thomas Skews, fitter.

SKEWES JULIENA
Daughter of Peter and Margaret Skewes. Bpt Kenwyn 28 April 1799.

SKUES JULIANA
Married Thomas Davey at Kenwyn 2 June 1819.

SKUES JULIANA
Twin to Henry James Skues. Daughter of Absalom and Jane Skues. Bpt Camborne 16 July 1831.

SKEWES JULIANA
Married 1866, Helston.

SKEWES JULIANA
Chart 36. Born 1868, Cury. Daughter of Edward and Julia Skewes of Nantithet. Bpt Cury 20 June 1869. In 1871 Census Returns living with brothers Thomas, Henry and Edward and sisters Annie, Bessie, Edith and Laura.

SKEWES JULIANNA HENDY
Chart 12. Daughter of John and Julianna Skewes of Cury. Bpt Cury 16 July 1837. Illegitimate son: Frederick Trezize Skewes.

SKEWES JULIE
Chart 24. Daughter of Jack and Betony Skewes of Stockton, New South Wales, Australia. Born 30 November 1954. Married David Woodward, 1972. Issue: 2 daughters.

SKEWES JULIE ANN
Chart 36. Daughter of Graeme Douglas and Rosalie (née Campbell) Skewes. Born 31 October 1964, Western Australia.

SKEWES JULIE ANN
Mother's maiden name Lissemore. Born 1975, Southend, Essex.

SKEWES JULIE LORRAINE
Chart 36. Daughter of Colin Arthur and Joyce Eva (née Boundy) Skewes. Born 28 March 1954. Lives at 4 Parkhouse Avenue, Seaton, 5023, South Australia.

SKEWES JULIE MARION
Lives at 543 Thompson Road, Norlane, 3140, Victoria, Australia with Joan Morva Skewes and William Thomas Skewes.

SKEWES JULIO
Chart 10. Mexican. Son of Alfredo and Letricia (née Bello) Skewes. Born Mexico City 9 June 1974.

SKEWES JULYA
Married 1851, Truro.

SKEWES JUNE

Chart 12. Née Letcher. Married Dennis Ivor John Skewes, 1964, Redruth. Children: John Anthony (1967) and Richard Andrew (1971). Lives at Rose Glen, Porthallow, St Keverne, Helston, Cornwall. Telephone number 0326 6214.

SKEWES JUNE PATRICIA
Daughter of William and Elizabeth Alberta Jessop Skewes. Born 12 June 1918, Superior, Houghton, Michigan, USA. Married Victor H. Dennis.

SKEWES JUNE ROSEMARY
Lived at 2/94 Lagoon Street, Narrabeen, New South Wales, Australia in 1959. Now lives at 35 Whale Beach Road, Avalon Beach, 2107, New South Wales, Australia.

SKEWES JUSTO
Chart 10. Mexican. Son of Juan and Fransisca (née Meneses) Skewes. Born 28 February 1896. Died 28 February 1896 aged 1 hour in Real del Monte, Mexico.

K

SKEWIS KAREN
Born 1962, Springburn, Scotland.

SKEWIS KAREN
Born 1977, Dundee East, Scotland.

SKEWES KAREN COLLEEN
Chart 10. Daughter of Robert Arthur and Lilian (née Foster) Skewes. Born 15 May 1962. Lives at Box 335, Waterdown, Ontario, Canada.

SKEWS KAREN D.
Chart 11. Daughter of Stanley Skews. Mother's maiden name Soady. Born 1962, St Austell.

SKEWES KAREN ELIZABETH
Chart 48. Daughter of John Hornby and Madge (née Freeman) Skewes. Born 3 July 1958, Leeds, West Yorkshire. Married Roy Malcolm, 1981 at Pontefract Register Office. Lives in West Yorkshire.

SKEWS KAREN EMMA
Chart 17. Daughter of Terence W. Skews. Mother's maiden name Walters. Born 1977, Swansea.

SKEWIS KAREN JAYNE
Chart 50. Daughter of David Skewis. Mother's maiden name Bratton. Born 1968, Holderness.

SKEWES KAREN MARIE
Chart 2. Daughter of William M. and Laverne Helen (née Getty) Skewes. Born 13 April 1967, Minnesota, USA.

SKEWIES KAREN WILSON
Born 1961, Bellshill, Scotland.

SKEWES KATE
Chart 36. Daughter of James and Frances Skewes of Mawnan. Born 1863. Bpt Mawnan 13 September 1863. In 1871 Census Returns living at Mawnansmith with her parents and sisters Hester Ann, Frances, Minnie and Ellen and brother James Lugg.
Married John Chaffe Harman, innkeeper of Falmouth at Mawnan Church 13 December 1888.

SKEWES KATE
Married 1898, Redruth.

SKEWES KATE ELIZABETH
Chart 38. Daughter of Thomas Edgar Skewes. Born 15 June 1979. Lives at 246 Chloride Street, Broken Hill, New South Wales, Australia.

SKEWES KATHARINE
Daughter of John and Katharine Skewes. Bpt St Buryan 18 June 1724.

SKEWS KATHERINE
Daughter of Martin Skews. Buried Kea 16 May 1742.

SKUES KATHERINE
Daughter of Digory Skues. Bpt Kenwyn 3 February 1760.

SKEWES KATHERINE
of Illogan. Born 1813. Buried Camborne 25 September 1822, aged 9 years.

SKEWES KATHERINE
Chart 12. Son of Carl and Doreen Skewes of Camborne. Mother's maiden name Berryman. Born 12 June 1971.

SKEWIS KATHERINE J.
Lived at 509 NE, Tacoma, Washington in 1911 with Bennett Osborne Skewis, Martha Skewis, Martha K. Skewis and Shirley M. Skewis.

SKUES KATHERINE PEPITA
Chart 5. Daughter of Major Harry and Violet Turner Shaw, OBE. Born 12 January 1917. Married Kenneth Frederick Skues, 1 August 1942, All Saints Church, Melbourne, Australia. Children: Derek Peter (1945) and Diana Katherine (1947). Lives at 407 Beach Road, Beaumaris, 3193, Victoria, Australia.

SKEWES KATHLEEN
of St Buryan. Married Simon Blagdon at Sancreed 21 August 1734.

SKEWS KATHLEEN
Born 1873. Died 1928, Gravesend, Kent aged 55 years.

SKEWS KATHLEEN
Chart 41. Daughter of Thomas and Jane (née Renshaw) Skews. Born 26 July 1915, Barnsley, South Yorkshire. Married Gilbert Cooke in Staincross, June, 1940.

SKEWES KATHLEEN
Chart 38. Daughter of Charles Leslie and Ellen Jane (née Ritter) Skewes. Born 24 July 1921. Married Jack Deed 12 May 1945. Issue: 1 son and 1 daughter. Lives at 20 Myall, Murray Bridge, Adelaide, 5253, South Australia.

SKEWES KATHLEEN JOYCE
Chart 12. Née Dennis. Married Gilbert James Skewes at Helston Register Office 21 September 1957. Children: Janet M., John C., Sandra, David, Peter and Carole M. Lives at Trelimminey, St Martin, Helston.

SKEWES KATHLEEN LILLIAN
Lives at 4 West Avenue, Cammery, 2062, New South Wales, Australia with Ann Marie Skewes and Leonard Francis Skewes, printer.

SKEWES KATHLEEN MARGUERITE
Lived at 46 Banksia Street, Heidelberg, Victoria, Australia in 1959 with William Josiah Skewes, accountant. Now lives at 2/131 Ivanhoe Parade, Ivanhoe, 3079, Victoria, Australia.

SKEWES KATHLEEN MAVIS
Chart 38. Née Clark. Married Albert John Skewes, 7 March 1964. Children: Joanne Kay (1964), Kym John (1965) and Ricky Wayne (1971). Lives at Government Road, Bute, South Australia, 5560.

SKEWES KATHLEEN MURIEL
Chart 48. Daughter of William (Verdayne) and Elizabeth (née Marsh) Skewes. Born 31 December 1913, Croydon, Surrey. Joined ATS (which later became WRAC) in 1940 (Sergeant). Later became head receptionist at Eccleston Hotel, Victoria, London. Subsequently took up jobbing gardening and housekeeping. Beneficiary under the Will of her mother (1965).

SKEWES KATHLEEN P.H.
Chart 17. Mother's maiden name Smith. Born 1916, Brentford, Middlesex. Married Painter in Hammersmith, 1938.

SKEWES KATHRYN MARY
Chart 36. Daughter of Brian Lock and Barbara Jessie (née McKinlay) Skewes. Born 30 September 1963. Lives at Currency Creek, 5251, South Australia.

SKEWES KATHY
Chart 2. Daughter of David Neal and Patricia Skewes. Born 1966, Missouri, USA.

SKEWS KATHY JANE
Chart 41. Son of Trevor Skews. Mother's maiden name Guirey. Born 1979 Barnsley, South Yorkshire.

SKEWES KATIE
Chart 36. Née Ford. Married Walter Nicholas Skewes at St John's Church, Treslothan, Redruth 16 April 1913. Children: Cecil (1916), Doreen M. (1915) and Leslie (1920). Lived at 51 Pendarves Street, Beacon, Camborne, 1932 and later at 42a, Fore Street, Beacon, Camborne.

SKEWES KATIE BEATRICE
Chart 10. Daughter of Captain John and Catherine Skewes of Chacewater. Born 2 January 1885. Bpt Chacewater 24 January 1886. Died at Ivy Cottage, Chacewater 15 August 1886, aged 1½ years.

SKEWES KATRINA LOUISE
Chart 2. Daughter of Graham Henry and Dorothy Cheryl (née Fitzclarence) Skewes. Born 23 April 1972, Australia. Lives at 15 Crossen Street, Echuca, 3625, Victoria, Australia.

SKEWES KATY LEE
Chart 2. Daughter of Charles Armington & Cindy Skewes. Born 2 February 1980, Bountiful, Utah, USA.

SKUSE KAY
Company Leader of St Leonard's Guide Company, Bournemouth. Presented with Long Service Medal for 18 years service in 1980.

SKEWES KAYE
Chart 36. Daughter of Henry Tom Holdsworth and Maude Isabel (née Curtis) Skewes. Born 1947, Ballarat, Victoria, Australia.

SKEWES KAY ELIZABETH
Chart 36. Daughter of Douglas Arthur and Coleen Marie (née McKenzie) Skewes. Born 28 October 1957. Police officer. Married Kelvin Michael Crowe, 5 February 1979. Lives in Queensland, Australia.

SKEWES KAYLENE DAPHNE
Chart 42. Née Bourke. Mrd Dennis Paul Skewes, 6 December 1970 in Wagga Wagga, Australia. Children: Tracey Lee (1971), Terry Paul (1972) and Bradley John (1975). Lives at 25 McKay Street, Nowra Hill, 2540, New South Wales, Australia.

SKEWES KEEFE MITCHELL
Mother's maiden name Skewes. Born 1967, Paddington.

SKUES KEITH
See RICHARD KEITH SKUES.

SKUSE KEITH
Son of Cyril Edwin Charles Skuse. Mother's maiden name Trundell. Born 1941, Surrey Mid East. Married 1963 in Sodbury.

SKUSE KEITH
Lives at 33 Burraneer Drive, Keysborough, 3173, Victoria, Australia with Catherine Elizabeth Skuse.

SKEWES KEITH MATTHEW

Chart 37. Son of John Richard and Ivy Elizabeth (née Green) Skewes. Born 16 September 1917, Naremburn, New South Wales, Australia. Married Joyce Mabel Everingham (she born 21 January 1919), 25 November 1944. Children: Philip Matthew (1945), Vernon John (1947), Roger Keith (1950) and Elizabeth Ann (1956). Panel beater at Wahroonga, New South Wales. Enjoys building houses. Keen sailor. Helped his son build a 36 foot steel yacht. Competed in sailing races in Sydney Harbour. Lives at 22 Harwood Avenue, Mount Kurrangai, Australia, 2080.

SKEWES   KEITH RAYMOND
Lived at 13 Fraser Avenue, Carrum, Victoria, Australia in 1959. Building supervisor.

SKEWES   KEITH WILLIAM
Lives at The Willows, Halls Creek, 2346, New South Wales, Australia.

SKEWES   KELLY
Chart 36. Daughter of Danny and Jacqueline (née Fairall) Skewes. Born 24 July 1980, New South Wales, Australia.

SKEWES   KENNETH
Chart 36. Son of Glenleigh Bertie William and Mary Evelyn Harriet (née Watkins) Skewes. Born 10 May 1937. Bachelor. Lives at 141 Spencer Street, Sebastopol, 3356, Victoria, Australia.

SKEWES   KENNETH
Lives at 19 Cross Street, Fairfield, 4103, Queensland, Australia with Gloria Madge Skewes. Floor sander.

SKEWS   KENNETH D.
Chart 41. Son of Samuel and Mary (née Parden) Skews. Born 1933 Barnsley, South Yorkshire. Married Lord in Staincliffe, 1957. Children: Beverley J. and Nigel S.
Went out to South Africa and was involved in a car crash about 1970 which killed his wife and two children. He married again and now lives at 20 Soliter Road, Kirstenhof, Cape Town, South Africa.

SKEWIS   KENNETH D
Lived at San Jose State College, 475 Northern Road, San Jose, California, USA in 1960.

SKEWS   KENNETH F.
Chart 14. Son of George Edwin and Emma Skewes. Born 16 August 1911, America. Died in a farm accident 31 October 1918, aged 7 years.

SKUES   KENNETH FREDERICK

Kenneth Frederick Skues

O.B.E. D.D.Sc. Chart 5. Son of Frederick Henry and Ellen (née Hosking) Skues. Born 17 March 1905, Bendigo, Australia. Education: Bendigo High School; Queens College, University of Melbourne 1923-1927 B.D.Sc (1927), D.D.Sc (1932). Dentist. Private practice in Collins Street, Melbourne 1930-1981. Enlisted in army as dental officer with Australia Imperial Forces. Served from January 1942 to February 1946 in Borneo & New Guinea. Captain.
Married Katherine Pepita Shaw 1 August 1942, All Saints Church, Melbourne. Children: Derek Peter (1942) and Diana Katherine (1947). Principal Dental Officer, Repatriation Headquarters, Melbourne from 1956 to 1965; Chairman of Graduate Union, University of Melbourne 1967 and 1968. Vice President, Royal Dental Hospital, Melbourne 1966-1972; President 1972-1973; Senior Dental Surgeon, Royal Melbourne Hospital 1950-1965; Consulting Dentist, Royal Melbourne Hospital since 1965.
Author of *Development of Dental Enamel in Marsupials* published in Australia 1932.
Recreations: golf and tennis. Clubs: Melbourne Naval and Military; Royal Melbourne Golf Club; Melbourne Club.
Lives at 407 Beach Road, Beaumaris, 3193, Victoria, Australia. Telephone no: Melbourne 991 995.

SKEWS   KENNETH HAROLD
Lives at 23 Valentine Street, Morawa, 6623, Western Australia with Catherine Elizabeth Skews.

SKEWES   KENNETH LINDSAY
Lives at Bell Street, Balmoral, 3407, Victoria, Australia with Marilyn Ann Skewes. Policeman.

SKEWES   KENNETH McLEOD
Chart 36. Son of Charles Harold Vivian and Maude Emiline (née Lamphee) Skewes. Born 9 July 1924, Brookton, Western Australia. Married Gloria Cockburn, 25 April 1946, St Matthew's Church, Guildford, West Australia.

SKEWES   KENNETH MERVAINE
Lived at 21 Gainsborough Street, Ferryden, South Australia in 1959 (fitter) with Gwendoline Euphemia and Allan Skewes. Now lives at 14 Wexcombe Street, Elizabethville, 5112, South Australia.

SKEWS   KENNETH PAUL
Lives at 2/2 Daphne Street, Mount Isa, 4825, Queensland, Australia with Lynette Anne Skews.

SKUES   KENNETH PETER
Chart 8. Son of Arthur E.W. and Winnie (née Jackson) Skues. Born 25 November 1948, London. Emigrated to New Zealand in 1973. Bachelor. Works at Guardian Royal Exchange Insurance Company in Auckland. Lives at Flat 2, 75 Arawa Street, New Lynn, Auckland, New Zealand. Tel No: Auckland 874 809.

SKEWES   KENNETH RICHARD
Chart 50. Son of Richard James and Amy (née Post) Skewes. Born 8 June 1925, North Sydney. Died 25 April 1979, aged 53 years.

SKEWES   KENNETH ROY
Chart 12. Son of Roy and Violet (née Trengove) Skewes. Born 1938, Redruth. Married his sister in law. Lives at Dolcoath Road, Camborne.

SKEWES   KENNETH WILLIAM
Son of Frederick Thomas and Rose (née Trudgeon) Skewes of Michigan, USA. Born 14 August 1917.

SKEWS   KENNETH WILLIAM WEIRING
Chart 15. Son of Edith Jane Skews, single lady of Callington, Cornwall. Born 8 June 1923. As a young boy of 5 suffered from polio for six months.
Attended school in Callington. Later moved to Plymouth and worked for London Furnishing Company until the beginning of the Second World War. He returned to Callington and joined Seymour Cabinet Works as a cabinet maker from 1941 to January 1947.
Kenneth then went back to Plymouth and worked for Selfridges in the Barbican making garden furniture from 1947 to 1951. He spent 25 years with Plymouth Dockyard until he retired in 1976. He married Enid Pascoe at the Congregational Church, Liskeard 24 November 1951. They have an adopted son Stephen Kenneth (1959). Lives at 11 Bodgara Way, Liskeard, Cornwall.

SKEWES   KERRIE MARGARET
Chart 36. Daughter of Robert Keith and Shirley Cicely (née Jacobs) Skewes. Born 9 May 1960. Lives at Laurel Street, Kootingal, 2352, New South Wales, Australia.

SKEWES   KERRILYN LEE
Lives at 40 David Street, Tamworth, 2340, New South Wales, Australia with Gregory Kenneth Skewes, welder.

SKEWES   KERRY ANN
Daughter of James William and Christine Ann Skewes (née Gallagher). Born 9 June 1975, New York, USA. Lives at 169 Westwood Drive, Brentwood, New York, 11717, USA.

SKEWES   KERRY GAIL
Chart 36. Daughter of Pat and George Dobbyn of Navigator, Victoria, Australia. Born 7 August 1952, Ballarat. Married Leigh Skewes 10 May 1975. Children: Adam (1976) and Nathan (1980). Lives at 5 Woolway Court, Delacombe, Victoria, 3356, Australia.

SKEWES   KERRY NARELLE
Chart 36. Daughter of Leslie Kevin and Jill Cecilia (née Pullman)

Skewes. Born Watsons Creek, 17 March 1955. Lives at Caroline Street, Bendemeer, 2352, New South Wales, Australia.

SKEWES   KERWYN JAMES
Lived at Williamstown, South Australia in 1959. Farmer.

SKEWES   KEVERNE
Married Joanna Nicholas at St Keverne 11 September 1654. Children include John (1669) and Samuel (1665).

SKEWES   KEVIN
Chart 12. Son of William Arthur and Gwendoline (née Bray) Skewes. Born 1956. Twin to Paul Skewes. Died 1956, aged 0.

SKEWS   KEVIN
Mother's maiden name Skews. Born 1966, Sheffield.

SKEWS   KEVIN
Chart 41. Son of Paul Skews. Mother's maiden name Taylor. Born 1979 Barnsley, South Yorkshire.

SKUES   KEVIN RICHARD
Lived at 5 Leslie Street, Payenham, St Peter, Australia in 1959. TV engineer.

SKEWES   KEVIN PETER
Chart 25. Son of John H. and Sheila Winifred (née Wynne) Skewes. Born 1942, Bucklow, NE Cheshire.

SKUES   KEVIN RICHARD
Chart 5. Son of Leigh Harold Skues. Born Melbourne, Australia. Married Margaret Lynette Malley. Son: Wayne Richard (1957). Now divorced. Lives at 61 Fifth Avenue, Chelsea Heights, 3196, Victoria, Australia.

SKEWES   KEVIN RICHARD
Chart 10. Son of Richard Albert and Ann Marie (née Millar) Skewes. Born 5 September 1964, Hamilton, Ontario, Canada. Lives at 1207 Royal York, Islington, Toronto, Canada.

SKEWS   KEVIN ROBERT
Chart 41. Son of William Clifford and Joyce (née Morrell) Skews. Born 18 April 1953, Sunderland. Area manager in charge of stores for National Coal Board, Team Valley, Gateshead.

SKUES   KEVIN WILLIAM
Son of William Ashdown and Edith Beryl (née Saul) Skues. Born 20 December 1960. Lives at 7 Cormack Road, Beacon Hill 2100, New South Wales, Australia.

SKEWES   KIM
Chart 10. Daughter of Herbert James and Patricia (née Drysdale) Skewes. Born 26 April 1955 at Hamilton, Ontario, Canada. Died 1 July 1973, aged 18 years.

SKEWES   KIM NARELLE
Lives at 4 Murrumbong Road, Summerland Point, 2259, New South Wales, Australia.

SKEWES   KIM NARELLE
Chart 50. Daughter of Jack and Shirley Beryl (née Callaghan) Skewes. Born 5 October 1957, Darlinghurst, New South Wales, Australia. Married Ronald Spiteri, 10 May 1973. Issue: one daughter. Divorced 5 October 1977. Married Garry Robertson. Issue: one daughter.

SKEWS   KIRTLEY
Chart 41. Son of William John and Mary (née Rump) Skews. Born 3 November 1923, Houghton. Married Nancy Tubmen, M.A., at St Michael's and All Angels, Houghton-le-Spring, 24 October 1959. No children. Lived at 29 Wordsworth Avenue East, Houghton-le-Spring, Durham. **Engineer. Died 6 November 1979, aged 56 years in Bangladesh.**

SKEWS   KIRTLEY ROLAND
Chart 41. Son of Roland Gerald and Linda (née Greaves) Skews. Born 19 July 1965 British Military Hospital Aldershot.

SKEWIS   KITTY M.
Chart 2. Wife of Edward Skewis of Shullsburg, Wisconsin, USA. Born 16 May 1831. Issue: 6 children. Died 3 September 1911, aged 80 years. Buried in Shullsburg Cemetery, USA.

SKEWES   KYM JOHN
Chart 38. Son of Albert John and Kathleen Mavis (née Clark) Skewes. Born 12 August 1965. Lives at Government Road, Bute, South Australia, 5560.

L

SKEWES   L.
Shopkeeper at Ruan Minor, Helston, 1856.

SKEWES   L.
Miss. Publican of the Golden Lion, Calenick Street, Truro, 1856.

SKEWES   LA MAR
Chart 14. Son of Duane William and May (née Farrington) Skewes. Born 10 January 1903, America. Married Mildred Schwartz. Lived in Minnesota. No children. Died 1971, aged 68 years.

SKEWES   LARRY
Chart 10. Son of Ernest William and Gladys Skewes of Ontario, Canada.

SKEWES   LAURA

SKEWES   LAURA
Chart 2. Only daughter of Josiah and Fanny Skewes of Bosawsack. Born 1854. In 1871 Census Returns listed as living at Bosawsack with her parents and brothers James, Josiah and Henry. A very pretty girl. Married Edwin Tregaskis of Hicks Mill, Gwennap in March 1882 at Constantine, in presence of James Skewes.

SKEWES   LAURA
Chart 36. Daughter of Edward and Julia Skewes of Cury; shoemaker. Born 1864. Bpt Cury 27 August 1865. In 1871 Census Returns listed as living at Nantithet, Cury with her sisters Annie, Bessie, Julia Anna and Edith and brothers Thomas, Henry and Edward. Married William Tippett Tripp (29) at Helston Parish Church 26 September 1882.

SKEWS   LAURA
Born 1880, Truro. Died 1882, aged 2 years. Buried St Mary's, Truro 27 April 1882.

SKEWIS   LAURA
Chart 50. Née Waters. Born 1890. Married Samuel Skewis in Haverfordwest, 1913. Lived at Redbraes, 2 Hayston Avenue, Milford Haven, Pembrokeshire. Children: Mildred E. (1914) and Samuel Leslie (1920). Died 31 May 1957, aged 67 years at Withybush Hospital, Haverfordwest.

SKEWES   LAURA
Chart 10. Daughter of Richard and Frenetta (née Littleton) Skewes. Born 29 November 1892, Marazion. Bpt Marazion 22 January 1892. Emigrated to America with her parents and family. Married Robert Cecil Johnston 19 July 1910 in Toronto, Canada. Issue: one daughter.

SKEWES   LAURA
Married 1896, West Ham.

SKEWES   LAURA A.
Born 1866, Helston.

SKEWES   LAURA ANNE
Lived at Beaver Street, Malvern East, Australia in 1913 with William James Skewes.

SKEWES   LAURA ANNIE
Chart 48. Daughter of William Verdayne Skewes and Elizabeth Biddle. Born 1901. Married James Danvers, 1926 in Lincoln. Issue: 3 daughters. Died November 1977, aged 76 years.

SKEWES   LAURA FLORENCE
Chart 36. Daughter of Simon Skewes of Malvern, Victoria, Australia. Born Australia 5 June 1889. Married with six children.

SKEWES   LAURA H.
Born February, 1872, New York. English father; Scottish mother. In 1900 was a nurse at King's County Hospital, New York.

SKEWES   LAURA HUNT
Born 1871, Truro.

SKEWES   LAURA MARY
Born 1873, Helston.

SKEWES   LAUREL JEAN
Chart 38. Daughter of Horace Henry and Agatha Blanche Skewes. Born 6 July 1919, Broken Hill, New South Wales, Australia. Married 26 March 1938 to Ronald William Stevenson.

SKEWES   LAUREL MARIE
Lived at 27 Stanley Avenue, Blair Athol, Kilburn, South Australia in 1959 with William Henry Skewes. Present address.

SKEWES   LAURENCE JOHN
Lives at Farm/404 Dalbata Road, Leeton, 2705, New South Wales, Australia with Garry Reginald Skewes, Pearl Louisa Skewes and Reginald Lionel Skewes.

SKUES   LAURENCE PENROSE
Chart 5. Son of Frederick Henry and Ellen (née Hosking) Skues. Born 19 March 1907, Australia. Dentist. Married Bae Lucy Crawford, who had a son by a previous marriage. Australian Army Dental Corps (Dental Surgeon). Lieutenant 29 September 1933; Captain 18 September 1936; Major 6 January 1943. Lives at Boongala, Rosehill Road, Lower Plenty, 3093, Victoria, Australia.

SKEWES   LAVINIA
Born 1806. 5th daughter of Henry and Margaret Skewes, formerly of Roseworthy, Gwinear. Died of typhoid fever at Richmond Hill, Truro 10 July 1868, aged 61 years. She was bpt 21 December 1806 at Camborne Parish Church. Spinster. Buried at Kenwyn 12 July 1868.

SKEWES   LAVINIA
Born 1835, Chacewater. Buried Chacewater 15 April 1846, aged 11 years.

SKUES   LAVINIA
Born 1837, Truro.

SKEWES   LAVINIA
Daughter of John and Ann Skewes of Killiwerris, Kea. Born 1844. In 1861 Census Returns was a house assistant.

SKEWES   LAVINIA
Died 1846, Truro.

SKEWS   LAVINIA
Died 1851, Launceston.

SKEWES   LAVINIA
Died 1852, St Columb.

SKEWES LAVINIA
Born January 1852, New York. Married Skewes approx 1873. Issue: 8 children. Three died young. Those living: Gertrude G. (1874), Rosa L. (1877), Fred L. (1881) and twins Blanche and Bertha (1883). Was a widow by 1900 living in New York. Dressmaker.

SKEWES LAVINIA
Born 1853, Truro.

SKEWES LAVINIA
Died 1853, Truro.

SKEWES LAVINIA
Daughter of John and Ann Skewes of Seveock, miner. Bpt Baldhu 4 June 1854 with her brother William Skewes.

SKEWIS LAVINIA
Chart 2. Daughter of William and Peggy Skewis of America. Married John Bullock, mining engineer of Mexico at Camborne Parish Church 31 December 1857. Lived in America. Issue: 2 sons and 1 daughter.

SKEWIS LAVINIA
Chart 33. Née Shute. Married William Richard Skewis, 1898, Totnes, Devon. Children: Olive May (1900), Fearnley John (1902), Ronald (1904), John (1907), Vida (1908), Ellie (1909), Clarence James (1911) and Dorothy M. (1912). Buried 1 November 1949 at Buckfastleigh, Devon.

SKEWES LAWRENCE
Chart 41. Daughter of Frederick Crago and Ruth (née Thompson) Skews. Born 1940, Durham North. Married Brown in Durham North, 1966. Daughter: Ashley Jane (1968).

SKEWES LAWRENCE
Lived at 24 Pacific Highway, Greenwich, Woll-Stonecroft, New South Wales, Australia in 1959 with Irene Maud and Lawrence Thomas Skewes.

SKEWIS LAWRENCE CHARLES
Chart 2. Son of Charles Edward and Sharon Skewis. Born 26 March 1960, America.

SKEWES LAWRENCE THOMAS
Lived at 24 Pacific Highway, Greenwich, Woll-Stonecroft, New South Wales, Australia in 1959 with Lawrence and Irene Maud Skewes. Now lives at 29 Oxley Street, Naremburn, 2065, New South Wales, Australia.

SKEWES LEANNE MARGARET
Lives at 53 Elgin Avenue, Christies Beach, 5165, South Australia with Dawn Florence Skewes and Terence Allan Skewes.

SKEWES LEANNE MAY
Chart 38. Daughter of Albert Murray and Olive May (née Brand) Skewes. Married Donald Henry Ahmann 25 February 1978. Issue: 2 sons. Lives in South Australia.

SKEWES LEIGH
Chart 36. Son of Glenleigh Bertie William and Mary Evelyn Harriet (née Watkins) Skewes. Born 4 January 1953. Married Kerry Gail Dobbyn, 10 May 1975. Children: Adam (1976) and Nathan (1980). Ward assistant at Psychiatric Hospital, Ballarat, Victoria. Lives at 5 Woolway Court, Delacombe, 3356, Victoria, Australia.

SKUES LEIGH HAROLD
Chart 5. Son of Oliver Harold and Ruby Skues. Born April 1911, Bendigo, Victoria, Australia. Twice married. 1) A.F. Galway and 2) Ethel Maude Poynton. Children — from first marriage Kevin Richard and from second marriage Mervyn Leigh (1943), John Leslie (1945) and Beverley Jean (1953). Painter. Lives at 73 Wattle Drive, Doveton, 3177, Victoria, Australia.

SKEWES LEILA MAVIS
Chart 2. Daughter of Henry and Annie May (née Cross) Skewes. Born 30 December 1918. Lives at 2/84 Claremont Avenue, Malvern, 3144, Victoria, Australia. Clerk.

SKEWIS LELAND
Chart 2. Offspring of Percy Vernon Skewis.

SKEWES LENA MARY
Chart 38. Née Hass. Married Ernest John Skewes, 30 November 1940. Children: Albert John (1941) and Peter William (1946). Lives at 8 West Terrace, Wallaroo Mines, 5554, South Australia.

SKEWES LENITA KAYE
Lives at 30 Tara Kan Avenue, Enfield, South Australia.

SKEWES LENORE
Chart 36. Daughter of Cyrus Lyle and Alice (née Welbourne) Skewes. Born 26 January 1951. Married Neil Ditton. No children. Lives in Trangie, New South Wales, Australia.

SKEWES LEO WILLIAM
Chart 50. Son of Jack and Victoria Florence (née Frances) Skewes. Born 6 August 1925. Married Betty Thompson 10 October 1946. Children: John Raymond, Leone Frances, Christine Joy, Catherine Ann and Vicki Louise. Lives at 7 Nerong Road, Lambton, 2299, New South Wales, Australia. Boilermaker.

SKEWES LEON DONALD
Lived at 66 Sussex Street, North Adelaide, South Australia in 1959. Shoemaker. Now lives at 43 Fletcher Road, Elizabethville, 5112, South Australia with Evelyn Mary Skewes and Stanley Crawford Skewes.

SKEWES LEONARD

Chart 37. Daughter of Richard John Skewes of Australia.

SKEWS LEONARD
Son of Clara Skews. Born Colorado, USA, August 1883. His mother had married a Skews in 1882 and emigrated to USA the following year. She then married Richard Eddy in 1885 and had a further five children.

SKEWES LEONARD
Son of Harry and Mary Skewes. Born December 1896, New York. In 1900 was living at North Hempstead, Nassau, New York, USA.

SKUES LEONARD
Chart 8. Son of John Gilbert Skues. Born 8 May 1905. Married Mary E. Woodyer in Pancras, London, 1929. One offspring, Gene (1930).

SKEWES LEONARD
Born 15 May 1919, Michigan, USA. Son of Frederick Thomas and Rose (née Trudgeon) Skewes. Married Virginia Sterler in Marshall, Minnesota, 1941. Lives at 304 Elm Street, Marshall, Minnesota, 56528, USA. Children: James Leonard Skewes (1950) and Barbara Jo Skewes (1953). Tel No: (507) 532 6231.

SKEWES LEONARD
Chart 40. Son of William and Elizabeth M. (née Roberts) Skewes. Born 1919, Penzance. Died 1919, aged 0.

SKEWES LEONARD FRANCIS
Lived at 4 West Avenue, Cammery, New South Wales, Australia in 1959 with Ann Marie Skewes and Kathleen Lillian Skewes. He was a painter.

SKEWES LEONARD JAMES
Lives at 12 Grevillia Street, Chester Hill, 2162, New South Wales, Australia with Barbara Helen Skewes and Judith May Skewes. Linotype operator.

SKEWES LEONARD JOSEPH
Lived at 51a Wycombe Road, Neutral Bay, New South Wales, Australia in 1959.

SKEWES LEONARD RICHARD
Chart 36. Son of Samuel Sidney and Sarah (née Pennall) Skewes. Born 29 August 1899. Married Mercy Davis. Children: Richard and Moya. Lived at Watsons Creek, via Bendemeer, New South Wales, Australia. Died 3 February 1980, aged 80 years.

SKEWES LEONIE FRANCES
Chart 24. Daughter of Leo William and Betty (née Thompson) Skewes. Born 2 September 1948, New South Wales, Australia.

SKEWES LEONIE JANE
Chart 36. Daughter of Robert Skewes. Born 17 September 1969, Victoria, Australia.

SKEWES LEONOR
Chart 10. Mexican. Daughter of Juan and Maria de Jesus (née Ortega) Skewes. Born 1919. Spinster. Died 18 November 1940, aged 21 years in Real del Monte, Mexico.

SKEWES LESLEY CHERYL
Chart 36. Daughter of Leslie Kevin and Jill Cecilia (née Pullman) Skewes. Born 5 February 1952, Watsons Creek, via Bendemeer, New South Wales, Australia.

SKEWIS LESLIE
Born 1909, Tonbridge, Kent.

SKEWS LESLIE
Chart 42. Son of Frederick and Frances (née Smith) Skews. Born 1916, Houghton. Married Mabel Wakefield, 1940, Durham North. Lives at The Avenue, Hetton-le-Hole, Tyne and Wear, One son: Leslie (1940).

SKEWES LESLIE
Chart 36. Son of Walter Nicholas Skewes. Mother's maiden name Katie Ford. Born 1920. Wrestler. Married Lilian Body in Kerrier, 1941. Lives at 44 Weeth Lane, Camborne. One son: Maxwell (1942). Tel. no: 0209 714629.

SKEWS LESLIE
Chart 41. Son of Leslie and Mabel (née Wakefield) Skews. Born 1940, Durham North. Lives at The Avenue, Hetton-le-Hole, Tyne and Wear.

SKEWES LESLIE HENRY IRVING
Son of Henry and Eliza Ann Florence (née Snowden) Skewes. Born 9 July 1894. Married Edith Ann White, 21 April 1925. Children: Henry Snowden Skewes, Dulcie Margaret Skewes and David Leslie Skewes. Lived at 43 Tom Street, Yarrawonga, Victoria, Australia. Died 21 October 1976, aged 81 years.

SKUES LESLIE JAMES
Chart 7. Son of Francis Albert Skues. Mother's maiden name Jeffery. Born 18 August 1913. Bachelor. Lived at 119 Great Queen Street, Dartford, Kent. Died 1970, Dartford, aged 57 years.

SKEWES LESLIE JOHN
Chart 36. Son of Samuel Sidney and Sarah (née Pennall) Skewes. Born 18 November 1891. Lived at Watsons Creek, Bendemeer, New South Wales, Australia. Labourer. Died 3 December 1969, aged 78 years. Buried in Methodist section of Bendemeer Cemetery.

SKEWES LESLIE KEVIN
Chart 36. Son of William and Ida Oliva (née Skewes) Skewes. Married Jill Cecilia Pullman. Children: Maria Gladys, Bede Kevin, Lesley, Kerrie, Janelle, Mark, Nigel and Ranae.
Lives at Caroline Street, Bendemeer 2352, Bendemeer, New South

Wales, Australia.

SKEWES   LESLIE RICHARD SAMUEL
Lived at 79 McCarthur Street, Pyrmont, New South Wales, Australia in 1959 with Marjorie Joy Skewes. Fireman. Now lives at 3/277 Balmain Road, Leichhardt, 2040, New South Wales, Australia.

SKUSE   LESLIE WALTER HAROLD
Born 17 March 1903 at Kings Down, Bristol. Married Amadine Butler. Son: William Harold Bernard Skuse. Died 14 June 1974, aged 71 years.

SKEWES   LESLEY CHERYL
Lives at 1/5 Loftus Street, Ashfield, 2131, New South Wales, Australia.

SKEWES   LETICIA
Chart 10. Mexican. Daughter of Alfredo and Leticia (née Bello) Skewes. Born 26 November 1976, Mexico City.

SKEWES   LEWIS
Chart 5. Born 1842. Son of John Skewes. Stonemason. Lived at St Mewan. Married Eliza Pearn (23), daughter of Joseph Pearn of Fowey, shoemaker at Fowey Church 21 January 1877. Children: Edith Jane, James Frederick, Charles John and Joseph Pearn.

SKEWIS   LEWIS
Lived at Bellvue, Redruth, 1906.

SKUES   LEWIS
Chart 5. Son of James Frederick Skues. Mother's maiden name Tregonning. Born 12 July 1912, Redruth. Attended Redruth East End School 1 October 1917 to 31 July 1919, after which he went to a "special school". Lived at 90 Tresaddern Road, Redruth, 1968.

SKEWES   LEWIS LLEWELLYN
Born 24 July 1885, Redruth. Attended Redruth East End School. Admitted 1 April 1889. Lived at Roaches Row, Redruth.

SKEWS   LEWIS P.
Married Cadmore in Birmingham, 1947.

SKUES   LEWIS TUBB
Chart 5. Son of John Penrose and Sally (née Tubb) Skues. Bpt Redruth Parish Church 2 February 1840. Died in Redruth 1908, aged 68 years.

SKEWES   LIBBY McLEOD
Chart 36. Daughter of Bruce and Judith Rosemary (née Taylor) Skewes. Born 30 August 1975, Tamworth, New South Wales, Australia.

SKEWES   LILA
Chart 14. Daughter of Henry Skewes of Wisconsin, USA. Mother's maiden name K. Oehls. Married Rich. Issue: 2 sons and 2 daughters.

SKEWES   LILAH
Chart 38. Daughter of Stanley Victor and Gertrude Olive (née Trimper) Skewes. Born 1910. Married William Sawtell. Issue: 1 son and 2 daughters. Died 1974, aged 64 years.

SKEWS   LILIAN
Chart 23. Daughter of William and Jane (née Bullock) Skews. Born 1873, Camborne. Died 1884, Highworth, aged 11 years.

SKEWES   LILLIAN
Born 1883. Lived at 85 Gilbert Street, Adelaide, South Australia. Died 14 September 1945, aged 63 years. Buried Adelaide Public Cemetery.

SKEWES   LILIAN
Chart 10. Née Robbins. Born 2 November 1883. Married John William Skewes, formerly of Marazion. Children: Arthur George and Ruth Lilian. Died in Michigan, 6 July 1943.

SKEWES   LILIAN
Born 24 August 1894, Redruth. Daughter of Lewis Skewes of Clarence Villas, Redruth. Attended Redruth East End School from 3 September 1900 to 28 February 1902. "A delicate pupil."

SKEWES   LILIAN
Chart 12. Youngest daughter of John Wesley Skewes. Born 1900, Helston. Became a school teacher. Married William Cecil Ivey, 1925, Helston. On her marriage she was a pillar of strength in the introduction and expansion of the coal business which she and her husband operated after the First World War. Later she acquired the village general store and Post Office in Nancegollan and was appointed Post Mistress. She took an active interest in the local Methodist Church and affiliated herself with the Sithney Women's Institute, of which she was a founder member. Lived at Pengarth, Nancegollan. Died 1979, aged 79 years. Buried in Helston Cemetery.

SKEWS   LILIAN
Chart 23. Daughter of John Edwin and Eliza (née Wells) Skews. Born 10 December 1902. Married Gardener in Swindon, 1928.

SKEWES   LILIAN
Chart 36. Née Body. Married Leslie Skewes 1941 in Kerrier. One son: Maxwell (1942). Lives at 44 Weeth Lane, Redruth. Previous address (1949) 15 Newton Road, Troon, Camborne.

SKEWES   LILIAN
Lived at Lower Condurrow, Camborne, 1949 with William Skewes.

SKEWES   LILIAN
Married Hucalak, 1965 in Halifax, Yorkshire.

SKEWES   LILIAN BEATRICE
Chart 10. Daughter of Peter and Elizabeth Skewes, mine agent, formerly of Kea, working in Real del Monte, Mexico. Born 18 July 1884. Bpt Chacewater 11 March 1887. Married Arthur J. Everington at Kimberley in Johannesburg, South Africa 14 December 1906. Issue: 1

son and 1 daughter. Died 1961, aged 77 years.

SKEWES   LILIAN BEATRICE
Chart 36. Born 25 July 1894, Australia. Married William Clibborn 19 February 1919. Issue: 6 sons and 2 daughters. Died 29 October 1946, aged 52 years.

SKEWES   LILIAN FRENETTA
Chart 10. Daughter of Richard Henry and Mary Elizabeth (née Doughty) Skewes. Born 26 April 1920, Hamilton, Ontario, Canada. Educated at Barton Township School 1926-1935. Worked as a salesgirl in Eaton's Store, Hamilton from 1944-1952. Married Eugene Alvin Woodworth 26 July 1952. Lives at 786 Ashley Avenue, Burlington, Ontario, Canada. Tel No: (416) 634 6565.

SKEWES   LILIAN G.
Married John Stevens, 1923, Helston.

SKEWES   LILIAN GLADYS
Chart 12. Daughter of William Frank and Doris Skewes. Mother's maiden name Williams. Born 1929. Married Sidney Edward Johnson, an evacuee, 1952, Kerrier. Issue: two sons.

SKEWES   LILIAN GREENLAW
Born 1891, Helston.

SKEWS   LILIAN L.
Chart 15. Daughter of Frederick C. Skews. Mother's maiden name Charles. Born 1925, Hackney, London. Died 1925, aged 0.

SKEWS   LILIAN de LEON
Lives at 130 Cowper Street, Yarraville, 3011, Victoria, Australia.

SKEWES   LILIAN LINDA MAY
Daughter of Richard Henry Skewes. Born 13 March 1892. Spinster. Lived at Ivy Court, Perran Downs, Rosudgeon, Penzance. Died 22 May 1952, aged 60 years at St Michael's Hospital, Hayle.

SKEWES   LILLIAN JOAN
Lives at Oxley, 3678, Victoria, Australia. Storekeeper.

SKEWIS   LILIAN M.
Wife of Ronald Skewis. Born 1909. Married 1934. Maiden name Wyatt. Child: Eileen M. (1941). Died Totnes 1965, aged 56 years.

SKEWS   LILIAN MARGARET
Born 1887, Bethnal Green. Died 1887, aged 0.

SKEWES   LILIAN MAUD
Married 1909, Abergavenny.

SKEWES   LILIAN MAUD
Daughter of William Henry (moulder) and Alarina Skewes. Born 8 February 1888. Bpt Tuckingmill 16 May 1888. Lived at Edward Street, Tuckingmill.

SKEWES   LILIAN MAY
Born 20 February 1893. Spinster. Died Bodmin 1976, aged 83 years.

SKEWES   LILIAN MAY
Chart 10. Née Maynard. Born 19 November 1895. Married John Skews. Lived in South Africa. Children: Richard John (1916), Dennis Milner (1918) and Rex Owen (1923). Died 15 February 1978, aged 82 years.

SKEWS   LILIAN MAY
Born 1900. Married Stanley Wells, in Devonport, 1926.

SKEWES   LILIAN MAY
Chart 36. Born 1901, Redruth. Married William John Bray, 1922 in Redruth.

SKEWES   LILIAN MAY
Lived at Condurrow Farm, Beacon in 1932 with William John Skewes.

SKEWES   LILIAN JOAN
Lived at Wangadary Street, Wangaratta, Victoria, Australia in 1959 with Harold Warren Skewes, orchardist.

SKEWS   LILIAN ROSE
Lived at 11 Acland Street, St Kilda West, Victoria, Australia in 1959. Proprietress.

SKEWES   LILIAN S.
Mother's maiden name Lilian Ellen Melinda Foster. Born 1943 Hastings. Died in Hastings 1943, aged 0.

SKEWES   LILIE
Born 1892, Helston.

SKEWES   LILLA
Chart 12. Daughter of James Henry Skewes. Born 1910, Helston. Married Lawrence Cleave, 1934. Issue: 2 daughters and 1 sons. When single lived at Golla, Callestick, Perranzabuloe. Died approx. 1968.

SKEWES   LILLA EMMA
Chart 12. Daughter of John and Thirza Skewes. Bpt Cury 4 November 1872. Married John Williams, 1921. Issue: 1 son and 1 daughter. Lived at St. Keverne. Died approx. 1963.

SKEWES   LILLIAS BETTY
Lives at 60 Ridgeway Avenue, Southport, 4215, Queensland, Australia.

SKEWS   LILLIE
Chart 50. Daughter of John Edwin and Eliza Skews. Born 1903, Swindon. Married Gardener in Swindon, 1928.

SKEWES   LILLIE ANN
Chart 14. Daughter of Hannibal and Eliza (née Phillips) Skewes. Born 14 December 1881, Yorkville, Wisconsin, USA. Married Derek West, farmer, 1 September 1910. Issue: 2 sons and 1 daughter. Died 1920,

aged 39 years.

SKEWES   LILY
Born 1867. Died 31 December 1918 at Bendigo, Australia, aged 51 years. Was wife of George H. Skewes.

SKEWES   LILY
Chart 33. Daughter of Susan Skewes, single woman and laundress of Truro. Bpt St Mary's Truro 20 September 1880. Buried St Mary's, Truro 29 July 1882, aged 3 years.

SKUES   LILY
Chart 3. Née Brearley. Born 1894. Married Rev. Eric Skues in Halifax, 1924. Children: John Anthony (1930) and Joyce (1925). Died 1958, aged 64 years.

SKUES   LILY
Chart 3. Daughter of John Henry and Lily (née Singleton) Bruckshaw. Born 17 August 1912. Married Jack Skues 26 December 1935. Children: Joy Christine (1937), Jennifer (1939) and Patricia Mary (1943). Lives in Canada. Box 41, Albright Gardens, Beamsville, Ontario, Canada, LOR IBO.

SKEWES   LILY
Chart 25. Daughter of Harold and Agnes (née Lally) Skewes. Born 26 June 1916, Chorlton, Manchester. Married John Taylor in Manchester, 1937.

SKEWS   LILY
Chart 41. Twin daughter of Frederick and Frances Skews. Born 1920, Houghton. Died 1921, aged 1 year.

SKEWS   LILY
Married Searle, 1932 in Islington, London.

SKEWES   LILY
Chart 18. Wife of Howard Skewes whom she married in 1907 in Bristol. Lived at The Old Rectory, Gidleigh, Devon. No children. Died 24 May 1938 at Southmead Hospital, Bristol.

SKEWES   LILY
Lived at 8 Scowbuds, Tuckingmill, Camborne in 1968 with Alfred J. Skewes.

SKUES   LILY MARIE
Chart 8. Daughter of Walter Edward Skues. Born 1903, Shoreditch. Died 1906, aged 3 years.

SKEWS   LILY R.
Chart 41. Née Brayford. Wife of Thomas E. Skews of Barnsley, South Yorkshire. Married 1942, Staincross. Children: John (1948) and Catherine (1954). Lives at 67 Woodwalk, Wombwell, Barnsley. Tel no: Barnsley 755053.

SKEWES   LINDA
Chart 50. Daughter of Thomas and Sarah Ann (née Lord) Skewes. Born 1886, Australia. Died 16 April 1887, aged 6 months.

SKEWIS   LINDA
Chart 2. Daughter of Mason and Clara Skewis. Born 21 July 1941, USA. Married David Miller. Issue: 1 son.

SKEWS   LINDA
Chart 41. Daughter of Thomas and Linda (née Cockburn) Greaves. Born 29 September 1942, Tyne and Wear. Married Roland Gerald Skews, 15 August 1964, St Nicholas Parish Church, Hetton-le-Hole. Children: Kirtley Roland (1965) and Stephen John (1966). Lives at St Nicholas House, Hetton-le-Hole, Tyne and Wear.

SKEWS   LINDA
Chart 15. Née McManamon. Daughter of Thomas and Rosemary McManamon. Born 18 August 1953. Married Derek Thomas Skews, St James Church, Glasgow, 17 August 1974. Children: Michele Rosemary (1970) and Alistair Derek (1976). Lives at 4 Moonsfield, Calington, Cornwall.

SKEWIS   LINDA
Chart 50. Daughter of David and Bridie (née Maher) Skewis. Born 26 March 1962. Lives at 9 Drumry Place, Glasgow 15, Scotland. Telephone number: 041 944 1426.

SKUSE LINDA
Daughter of Gordon and Janet (née Mellor) Skuse. Born 3 June 1964. Lives at 30 Abbey Road, Newstead Village, Nottingham.

SKEWES   LINDA ANN
Chart 2. Daughter of Arthur Wayne and Lorene (née Parker) Skewes of Pampa, Texas. Born 18 November 1940, Pampa, Texas. Married David Earl Holt, 3 June 1961, Stillwater, Oklahoma, United States of America.

SKEWIS   LINDA ANN
Chart 50. Daughter of Joseph Richard and Annie (née Collins) Skewis. Born 1951, Dundee, Scotland. Married 1973 to James Craig in Dundee.

SKEWS   LINDA J.
Chart 10. Daughter of Stanley and Mavis (née Soady) Skews. Born 1948, St Austell. Married to Westley in St Austell, 1968.

SKEWES   LINDA JANE
Chart 36. Daughter of John Michael and Janice Elizabeth (née Miles) Skewes. Born 19 July 1976. Lives at 702 Neil Street, Ballarat, 3350, Victoria, Australia.

SKEWES   LINDA L.
Mother's maiden name Williams. Born 1952, Redruth.

SKEWES   LINDA LAURA
Chart 2. Daughter of William James and Laurie Annie (née Davies) Skewes. Born 21 October 1907, Australia. Married Charles Alsop 25 January 1935. No children. Died 25 June 1966, aged 58 years.

SKEWES   LINDA MARGARET
Chart 36. Daughter of Simon Skewes. Born 1 April 1895, Australia. Spinster. Died Oakleigh, Victoria, Australia, 1974, aged 79 years.

SKEWES   LINDA MARION
Chart 48. Daughter of John Hornby and Madge Irene (née Freeman) Skewes. Born 22 November 1955, Leeds, West Yorkshire. Married David Christopher Walmsley, 3 July 1976, Leeds.

SKEWES   LINDA MARY CATHERINE
Chart 2. Daughter of Henry Ernest and Annie Emily (née Hayes) Skewes. Born 1 July 1906, Australia. Married John Edwin Lindsay, 4 August 1934. Issue: 3 daughters. One daughter is Joan Goerling who lives at "Acuna", 10 Paterson Road, Pinjarra, 6208, Western Australia.

SKEWES   LINDA ROSEMARY
Chart 48. Daughter of Cyril William and Marie (née Ambrose) Skewes. Born 7 May 1947. B.A. Cambridge University 1968. M.A. 1972. Married John Rowntree Fussey in Cambridge July, 1970. Issue: 2 sons.

SKEWES   LINDA ROSEMARY
Chart 46. Daughter of Ernest Lloyd and Doris Irene Patricia (née Penhaligon) Skewes of 30 Boskyvor Road, Truro, formerly of 68 Chapel Hill, Truro. Born 8 May 1964. Bpt St George's, Truro 20 June 1954. Married John Dunn at Kenwyn Parish Church 20 October 1973. Issue: one daughter, Tara.

SKEWES   LINTON
Chart 14. Offspring of Edgar and Beulah Skewes of America.

SKEWES   LIONAL
Married Jones in Aled, 1964.

SKEWES   LIONAL
Lived at 23 Tamar Street, Sutherland, New South Wales, Australia in 1959 with Eileen Skewes. He was a labourer.

SKEWES   LIONEL
Lived at 10 Brook Street, Crows Nest, New South Wales, Australia in 1959 with Ruby Gertrude Skewes and Thomas Lionel Skewes.

SKEWES   LIONEL
Lives at 151 Avalon Parade, Avalon Beach, 2107, New South Wales, Australia.

SKEWES   LIONEL
Lives at 19 Freeman Road, Heathcote, 2233, New South Wales, Australia. Gardener.

SKEWES   LIONAL JAMES
Chart 2. Born 1897. Married Olive May Symons in Redruth, 1935. Lived at Packsaddle, Mabe; later Trenowerth Vean, Mabe and 3 Corpascus Cottages, Mabe, Penryn. After serving in the First World War he was employed by Messrs Rowe and Knowles of Falmouth. He farmed for many years at Trenowerth Vean. He was a member of Mabe Parish Council. Died 23 February 1965 at Miners Hospital, aged 67 years.

SKUSE   LISA
Daughter of Dean and Margaret (née Barnes) Skuse. Born 3 September 1967. Lives at 26 Fraser Street, Newstead Village, Nottingham.

SKEWES   LISA CATHERINE
Chart 2. Daughter of John Herbert and Thelma Jean (née Ettridge) Skewes. Born 11 November 1965, Australia. Lives at Lot/85 Eclipse Drive, Albany, 6330, Western Australia.

SKEWS   LISA JAYNE
Chart 10. Daughter of Michael J. Skews. Born 1974. Mother's maiden name Clifft. Born in Truro.

SKUES   LIZABETH
Daughter of William and Margaret Skues. Born 25 Janaury 1893. Lived in New South Wales, Australia.

SKEWS   LIZZIE
Born 1897, Plymouth. Died 1897, aged 0.

SKEWES   LIZZIE MARION
Born 1873. Widow of 2 Victoria Terrace, Newquay. Died 21 January 1935, aged 62 years.

SKEWES   LIZZIE MARION
Chart 30. Daughter of William Brown Skewes, housepainter. Born 1898. Married William John Vercoe (23), plumber of St Paul's, Truro at St George's, Truro, February 1926, in presence of William Skewes.

SKEWES   LOIS ADA
Chart 36. Daughter of Aubrey Rupert and Annie (née Townsend) Skewes. Born 19 June 1932, Uralla, New South Wales, Australia. Married Clarence Barnden. Issue: 3 sons. Lives at Kentucky Station, Kentucky, Uralla, 2354, New South Wales, Australia.

SKEWS   LOIS VIOLET
Lived at 141 Hare Street, Kalgoortie, Victoria, Australia in 1959 with Donald Ian Skews, railway employee.

SKEWES   LORENZO
Chart 10. Mexican. Son of Juan and Fransisca (née Meneses) Skewes. Born 15 August 1909, Real del Monte. Died 30 August 1909, aged 15 days.

SKEWES   LORNA AGNES
Chart 36. Daughter of Robert Northey and Sarah Agnes (née Connell) Skewes.
Now lives at 12 Tweed Street, Brunswick Heads, 2483, New South Wales, Australia.

SKEWES   LORNA ELAINE
Lived at Arthur Street, Naracoorte, South Australia in 1959.

SKEWES   LORNA JEAN
Née Farquhar. Married Douglas Westmore Skewes, 28 February 1948 at Wangaratta, Victoria, Australia. Children: Gary Douglas (1949) and Ian Thomas and Lynette Mary — twins — (1951). Lives at 13, Barton Drive, Mount Elizabeth, 3930, Victoria, Australia.

SKEWES   LORNA MAY
Lives at 2 Miller Street, Kidman Park, 5025, South Australia with Douglas Skewes, mechanic and Ian Douglas Skewes, carpenter.

SKEWES   LORNA MEG
Chart 36. Daughter of William and Ida Oliva (née Skewes) Skewes. Lived at Beulah, Watsons Creek, Bendemeer, New South Wales, Australia in 1959. Married John Morgan 7 May 1959. Issue: 2 sons

SKEWES   LORRAINE
Chart 36. Daughter of Henry Tom Holdsworth and Maud Isabel (née Curtis) Skewes. Born 1940, Australia.

SKEWES   LORRAINE
Chart 10. Daughter of Ernest William and Gladys Skewes of Ontario, Canada.

SKEWIS   LORRAINE MAHER
Chart 50. Daughter of David and Bridie (née Maher) Skewis. Born 23 July 1972.
Lives at 9 Drumry Place, Glasgow 15, Scotland. Telephone number 041 944 1426.

SKEWES   LOTTIE
Chart 14. Adopted daughter of James Lugg and Jane Skewes. Married with issue. Lives in America.

SKEWES   LOTTIE DOREEN
Chart 15. Second wife of Thomas Henry Skewes. Married 1964, Redruth. Lives at 10 Loscombe Road, Four Lanes, Redruth.

SKEWIS   LOUANN ANITA
Chart 2. Daughter of Charles Elmer and Leotice Skewis of America. Born 3 July 1945.

SKEWES   LOUISA
Born 1846. Wife of John Skewes of Lizard Town. Children: Ada L. and Mary. Died 1911, aged 65 years.

SKEWS   LOUISA
Married 1861, Gravesend.

SKEWS   LOUISA
Born 1878, North Aylesford.

SKEWES   LOUISA
Chart 25. Daughter of William and Jane (née Jameson) Skewes. Born 1889, Manchester. Emigrated to Australia with her mother and sister Jessie (5) aboard vessel Cuzco from London arriving Sydney 5 June 1892.

SKEWS   LOUISA
Chart 41. Daughter of Thomas and Ada (née Sheldon) Skews. Born 1891. Married James F. Briggs in Barnsley, 1912. Issue: 2 sons and 1 daughter.

SKEWS   LOUISA
Married 1898 in Bromley.

SKEWES   LOUISA JANE
Born 1838, Falmouth.

SKEWES   LOUISA JANE
Born 1838. Died Lambeth, aged 63 in 1901.

SKEWES   LOUISA JANE
Born 1867. Lived at 2 College Street, Camborne and later 70 College Street, Camborne. Died 1936, aged 69 years. Buried Camborne 16 March 1936.

SKEWES   LOUISA JANE
Daughter of William Henry and Alarina Skewes. Born 20 February 1885. Bpt 6 August 1885 at Tuckingmill Parish Church.

SKEWES   LOUISA JANE
Chart 25. Daughter of Charles and Elizabeth Skewes, shoemaker. Born 1870. In 1871 Census Returns living at Brook Street, Falmouth. Moved north with her parents in 1870's. Married 1900 in Chorlton.

SKEWES   LOUISA JANE
Married 1907, Hereford.

SKEWES   LOVEDAY
Daughter of William and Avise Skewes. Bpt Gunwalloe 22 May 1726. Mrd George Jewil 25 May 1746, Gunwalloe.

SKEWES   LOVEDAY
Chart 36. Née Hendy. Wife of John Skewes. Born 1791. Lived at Nantithet, Cury. Children: John, Edward, Samuel, Ann Hendy, Mary, William and Hannah. Buried Cury 12 August 1830, aged 39 years.

SKEWES   LOVEDAY
Daughter of John and Elizabeth Skewes. Bpt Cury 7 December 1806. Mrd Thomas Cock, 19 September 1835, Breage.

SKEWES   LOVEDAY
Chart 12. Daughter of James and Elizabeth Skewes of Cury. Bpt Cury 25 April 1824. Died Cury 10 January 1826, aged 2 years.

SKEWES   LOVEDAY
Chart 14. Née Mundy. Born 1809, Ruan Minor. Married Thomas Skewes at Ruan Minor 14 December 1831. In 1871 Census Returns living at Churchtown, Ruan Minor. (At Grade in 1841, 1851 and 1861.) No children. Died 21 February 1890, aged 81 years. Thomas died 22 January 1869, aged 63 years.

SKEWES   LOVEDAY HENDY
Chart 36. Daughter of Edward Skewes of Nantithet, Cury, shoemaker. Born 1841. Married John Penrose Crowl, son of John Crowl, gardener, 27 November 1864 at Cury. John was a pattern-maker, Loveday a house servant. (1861 Census Returns.)

SKUES   LOVELIA
Born 1844, Lambeth. Died 1844, Lambeth aged 0.

SKEWS   LOVINA
Died 1845, St Germans.

SKEWS   LUCCRETIA
Born 1798. Married to Philip Skews, farmer of 8 acres at St Ewe. Lived at Little Lavalsa in 1851 Census Returns. Died 1868, aged 70 years.

SKEWES   LUCILLE REED
Chart 14. Daughter of Manley and Eva (née Reed) Skewes. Born Yorkville, Wisconsin, USA.

SKUES   LUCY
Chart 3. Née Pickard. Born 1837. Married Richard Skues at Halifax Parish Church 9 July 1859. Lived at 10 Norfolk Place, Halifax. Children: William, Florence, Ernest, Frederick Gordon and Richard James.
In her younger days she used to bake bread for herself. When the Luddites marched on Halifax she fed them as they looked starved. The Luddites saw the introduction of machinery during the industrial revolution as a threat to their livelihood and sought to destroy it.
There were Luddite riots in Nottinghamshire, Lancashire and Yorkshire, and many rioters were hanged.
Died 2 January 1911, aged 74 years.

SKEWS   LUCY
Died 1848, St Giles, London.

SKUES   LUCY
Chart 3. Daughter of Richard James and Eleanor Skues. Born 27 September 1898 at Princess Street, Sowerby Bridge. Schooled at Bolton Brow, Sowerby Bridge (Primary); Hough Shaw, Moorfield Street, Savile Park; Parkinson Lane Junior School; Clare Road Secondary School.
Joined Skues' Cafe in Princess Street, Halifax with her younger sister Evelyn, both working for their aunt Florence Mary Skues who was proprietor. Lucy and Evelyn took over their own confectioner's shop at 66 King Cross Street, Halifax in early 1950's. Remained there until retirement in 1962. Moved to 11 Bell Hall Terrace, Savile Park, Halifax in 1962. Died 4 September 1980, aged 81 years. Following a service at St Jude's Church, Savile Park, Halifax where she was a regular attender, was interred alongside her grandparents in All Saints Cemetery, Salterhebble, Halifax. Graveside service was conducted by her brother Rev Eric Skues.

SKEWS   LUCY CAROLINE
Chart 54. Née Moore, formerly Bernard. Born 1846. Married George Alfred Skews, 1870, Strand, London. Children: Alfred David Richard

Lucy Skues (1898-1980)

(1871) and George Francis W. (1872). Died Bethnal Green 1904, aged 58 years.

SKUES   LUCY DOROTHY
Born 1901 in Shoreditch, London. Married 1922 to Albert W. Dawson. Issue: 1 son and 1 daughter.

SKEWS   LUCY ELIZABETH
Born 1874, Islington, London. Died 1894, aged 18 years.

SKUES   LUCY ELIZABETH
Chart 8. Daughter of Walter Edward Skues. Born Bethnal Green 1895. Married Howard G. Williams, 1928, Bethnal Green.

SKUES LUCY SOPHIA
Chart 8. Daughter of George and Mary Sophia Skues. Born July 1862 at 77 Berwick Street, Soho, London. Bpt 28 September, Old Church, St Pancras. Married Redinger, 1888, St James, London and lived at 31 Gaisford Street, Camden Town, London.

SKEWES   LUIS BRITO
Mexican. Died 27 August 1974. Buried in Pachuca Cemetery, Mexico. "In Memory, from his wife and sons. Father, this grave keeps your body; God keeps your soul and we keep your memory."

SKEWES   LUIS ENRIQUE
Chart 2. Son of Enrique and Juana (née Brito) Skewes. Born 21 June 1907, Pachuca, Mexico. Bpt 9 July 1907. Married. Children: Silvia (1943), Aaron (1937), Juana (1941), Yolande and Jorge Enrique (1954). Died 23 August 1974, aged 67 years.

SKEWES   LUISA
Chart 10. Née Garcia. Married John Skewes in Real del Monte, Mexico. Children: Blasa, Nazario, Tomas, Maria, Juan, Federico and Pedro.

SKEWES   LUISA
Chart 10. Mexican. Daughter of Nazario and Piedad (née Lozano) Skewes. Born 18 April 1895, Rel del Monte, Mexico. Married Manuel Bezies. Issue: 2 daughters and 2 sons. Died 16 January 1979, aged 83 years.

SKEWES   LULU
Chart 14. Daughter of Samuel and Betsy (née Philips) Skewes. Born 1878, Wisconsin, USA. Died from diphtheria 1881, aged 3 years.

SKEWES   LULU
Chart 11. Daughter of Thomas John and Laura B. Skewes. Born 2 May 1881, America.

SKEWS   LUTHER
In 1967 was living at 414 4th Avenue, Seattle, Washington, USA.

SKEWIS   LYDIA
Chart 2. Daughter of Edward and Catherine Skewis of America. Married Emporia Kansas. Issue: 3 daughters.

SKEWES   LYMAN HANNIBAL
Chart 14. Son of Edward Henry and Helen (née Gilmore) Skewes. Born 1904, Yorkville, Wisconsin, USA. Married Lilian Bertke 12 July 1926. Lived in Yorkville. Issue: Edgar Harold Skewes (1928). Died 1974, aged 70 years.

SKEWES   LYNDA SUZANNE
Chart 36. Daughter of Earle William and Edna Fay (née Chad) Skewes. Born 3 November 1956. Married David Bennett 9 September 1978. No children.

SKEWIS   LYNETTE
Chart 2. Daughter of Frank and Daisy Skewis of United States of America.

SKEWES   LYNETTE
Lived at 19 Brooks Street, Wonthaggi, Victoria, Australia in 1959 with John Skewes.

SKEWES   LYNETTE
Lives at 8 Epping Street, Malvern East, 3145, Victoria, Australia with David John Skewes.

SKEWS   LYNETTE
Lives at 39 Amiel Street, Springvale, 3171, Victoria, Australia with Daryl Andrew Skews, salesman.

SKEWES   LYNETTE AMELIA
Lives at 23 Tantara Street, Ingle Farm, South Australia, 5098.

SKEWS   LYNETTE ANNE
Lives at 2/2 Daphne Street, Mount Isa, Queensland, 4825, Australia with Kenneth Paul Skews.

SKEWS   LYNETTE GAIL
Chart 10. Daughter of Rex Owen and Jean Lilian (née Van Rensburg) Skewes. Born 29 December 1947, Transvaal, South Africa. Married Peter Best.

SKEWES   LYNETTE MARGARET
Chart 36. Daughter of Colin Archer and Flora Heather (née McKenzie) Skewes. Born 17 August 1950, Australia. Married Warren Robert Crowther, dentist, 4 August 1973. Issue: 1 son. Lives in Australia.

SKEWES   LYNETTE MARY
Daughter of Douglas Westmore and Lorna Jean (née Farquhar) Skewes. Born 28 December 1951. Twin to Ian Thomas Skewes. Married Kevin Cowe, 9 July 1976. Issue: one son. Lives in Victoria, Australia.

SKEWS   LYNETTE MARY
Chart 36. Née Smith. Born 20 October 1948. Married Gary William Skewes 25 November 1966. Children: Donna Ann (1968), Teasha

Maree (1970), Marc William (1973) and Clint Edward (1974). Lives at 9 Surrey Road, Wilson, 6107, Western Australia.

SKEWS   LYNN
Chart 41. Daughter of Eric Skews. Mother's name Rasburn. Born 1950, Staincross. Married Atkinson, 1969, Staincross.

SKEWS   LYNN
Chart 41. Daughter of George David and Olwynne (née Thirwell) Skews. Born 1959 Sunderland. Married Arkley, 1977, Sunderland. Now divorced.

SKEWES   LYNN MARIE
Chart 14. Adopted daughter of Richard Edwin and Victoria (née Lohman) Skewes of America. Born 26 January 1960. Lives at Short Street, Faribault, Minnesota, 55021, United States of America.

M

SKEWES   M.
Beer retailer living at Chacewater, 1856.

SKEWES   M.
Living at h50 Clearview Heights, (York) Apartment 20, Toronto, Canada — 1977.

SKEWES   M.A.
Milliner and dressmaker living at St Day, Redruth, 1856.

SKEWS   MABEL
Born 1886, Redruth. Died 1886, aged 0.

SKEWS   MABEL
Chart 41. Daughter of Thomas and Ada (née Sheldon) Skews. Born 1893, Barnsley, South Yorkshire. Married Arthur Hunt, 1917. Issue: 2 sons and 3 daughters.

SKEWES   MABEL
Chart 14. Daughter of Samuel Skewes of America. Married Glen Francher in America.

SKEWES   MABEL
Chart 12. Born 1900. Married Charlie Rogers, 1923, Helston. Issue: 3 daughters and 2 sons. Died approx. 1955.

SKEWS   MABEL
Chart 41. Daughter of Thomas Skews. Mother's maiden name Bradley. Born 1917, Barnsley.

SKEWS   MABEL
Chart 41. Daughter of Frederick and Frances Skews. Mother's maiden name Smith. Twin to Lily Skews. Born 1920, Houghton. Died 1922, aged 1 year.

SKEWES   MABEL
Lived at Growangerup, Katanning, Victoria, Australia, in 1959.

SKEWS   MABEL COOPER
Chart 23. Née White. Born 1895. Married John George Skews, wood last maker, 1920. Children: Mabel I. (1921) and John G.P. (1923). Lived at 109 Centre Parade, Kettering, Northants. Died 27 December 1963, aged 68 years at Victoria Hospital, Lewes, Sussex.

SKEWES   MABEL G.
Chart 11. Daughter of Thomas John and Laura B. Skewes. Born 6 September 1883, America.

SKEWS   MABEL I.
Chart 17. Daughter of John George and Mabel Skews. Mother's maiden name Mabel Cooper White. Born 1921, Kettering. Lived at 109 Centre Parade, Kettering, Northants. Married Footer, 1943, Kettering.

SKEWS   MABEL J.
Chart 10. Daughter of Peter and Maude Mary Skews. Mother's maiden name Rickard. Born 1921, St Austell. Married Lander, 1951, St Austell.

SKEWES   MABEL JANE
Born 1886, Redruth.

SKEWES   MABEL JANE
Chart 10. Daughter of Richard Henry Skewes of Marazion, Cornwall. Born 31 December 1915. Attended Barton Township School, Hamilton, Ontario, Canada leaving at the age of 14. Worked with her father from age of 14 selling produce at Hamilton Market until 1939. Married Robert Oliver Bryant 2 September 1939 at Brantford, Ontario, Canada. Issue: 3 sons and 1 daughter. Now lives at 237 West 33rd Street, Hamilton, Ontario, Canada. Tel no: (416) 383 7130.

SKEWS   MABEL MILLICENT
Chart 23. Daughter of John and Bertha Skews. Born 1902, St Austell. Married Rosevear, 1935, St Austell.

SKEWES   MADELINE
Lives at 78 Taylor Street, Woy Woy, 2256, New South Wales, Australia with Douglas James Skewes, engraver.

SKEWES   MADGE
Chart 48. Née Freeman. Daughter of George Frederick Freeman of Sunnycroft Farm, Melton Brand, near Doncaster. Married John Hornby Skewes at St James' Church, Doncaster 12 February 1955. Children: Linda Marion (1955) and Karen Elizabeth (1958). Lives at 5 Station Fields, Garforth, Leeds LS25 IPX. Telephone number: 0532 862440.

SKUES MADGE IRENE
Chart 7. Née Meades. Born 3 November 1893. Married Edward Alfred Skues in Tonbridge, Kent, 1920. Children: Eric Edward Alfred (1922), Betty Irene (1924) and Roydon Thomas (1929). Died 1971, aged 78 years.

SKEWES MADGE RUTH
Chart 2. Daughter of John Billing Skewes II and Lydia. Born 26 November 1915, Moab, Utah, USA. Married Verd E. Duncan, 2 February 1934.

SKEWES MAGDALENA
Chart 10. Mexican. Daughter of Pedro and Severa (née Martinez) Skewes. Born 24 August 1910. Spinster. Lives in Mexico City.

SKEWES MAGDALENA
Chart 10. Mexican. Daughter of Franklin and Margarita (née Sanchez) Skewes. Born 22 June 1972. Lives in Real del Monte.

SKEWS MAGGIE
Born November 1873. Lived in Jefferson, Missouri, USA in 1900. Married. No children. Born in England. Father born in Ireland. Mother born in England. Emigrated in 1885. Seamstress.

SKEWES MAGGIE ISABELLA SIMPSON
Born 1886. Married William R. Skewes 1918, South Shields. Lived at 11 Station Road, County Durham. No children. Died 16 November 1948, aged 62 years.

SKEWES MAISIE
Chart 36. Née Lawson. Born 13 January 1918. Married Edward Keith Skewes 7 February 1942. Children: Jeanette C. (1942), Norman J.H. (1943), Ronald E. (1944), Gary W. (1949), Robert A. (1950) and Bruce P. (1953). Lives at 28 Perkins Road, Melville, 6156, Western Australia.

SKEWIS MALCOLM GEOFFREY
Lives at 8 Gormleys Road, Chilla, 4413, Queensland, Australia with Geoffrey Wilfred Skewis and Valma Aileen Skewis.

SKEWES MALCOLM ROBERT
Chart 36. Son of James Robert and Pearl Isabel (née Chapman) Skewes. Born 27 July 1931. Married Judith Elaine Godley 7 May 1955. Children: Monica Elaine and Gavin. Died 24 January 1963, aged 31 years.

SKEWES MANDY LOUISE
Lives at 8 Cassia Court, Wantirna, 3152, Victoria, Australia with Gay Yvonne Skewes. Student.

SKEWES MANLEY THOMAS
Chart 14. Son of Hannibal and Eliza Skewes. Born 12 October 1873, Wisconsin, USA. Married Eva Grove Reed in Yorkville, Wisconsin, USA 6 June 1900. Children: Marjorie Grace, Dorothy, Lucille, Helen Beatrice and Phyllis. He was a St Paul railroad telegrapher.

SKEWES MARC WILLIAM
Chart 36. Son of Gary William and Lynette Mary (née Smith) Skewes. Born 31 March 1973. Lives at 9 Surrey Road, Wilson, 6107, Western Australia.

SKEWES MARGARET
Widow. Buried St Anthony in Meneage 26 May 1656.

SKUES MARGARET
Chart 10. Daughter of Digory Skues. Bpt Kenwyn 3 January 1705.

SKEWS MARGARET
Daughter of Richard and Margaret Skews. Bpt Paul 14 December 1707.

SKEWES MARGARET
Chart 19. Daughter of Thomas and Margaret Skewes. Bpt Gwennap 26 March 1709.

SCUES MARGARET
Chart 2. Daughter of Henry and Mary Scues. Bpt 6 May 1710, Camborne.

SKEUES MARGARET
Married Isaac Crusielieur at Paul 27 April 1726.

SKEWES MARGARET
Married Henery Michel at Crowan 28 September 1734.

SKEWES MARGARET
Spinster of Ludgvan. Buried St Hilary 27 January 1735.

SKEWES MARGARET
Buried Gwennap 23 December 1738.

SKEWIS MARGARET
Chart 2. Daughter of Henry Skewis. Bpt 17 June 1744, Camborne.

SKEWES MARGARET
Chart 19. Daughter of Thomas and Elizabeth Skewes. Bpt Gwennap 13 May 1749. Spinster. Died 25 November 1816, aged 67 years.

SKUES MARGARET
Born 1752. Buried Camborne 31 December 1823, aged 71 years.

SKEWES MARGARET
Buried Gwennap 28 April 1753.

SKEWES MARGARET
Buried in Kenwyn Churchyard. Born 1769 she died 17 August 1847, aged 78 years. Wife of Henry Skewes. Also buried there was MARY SKEWES (daughter) who died 25 March 1868, aged 73 years and LAVINIA SKEWES (daughter) who died 10 July 1868, aged 61 years.

SKEWES MARGARET
Widow. Buried Kea 8 April 1784.

SKEWES MARGARET

SKEWES MARGARET
Chart 14. Née Rogers. Married Edward Skewes at Sithney 13 May 1743. G. (1920) and Iestyn J. (1922). Born 1897. Died 1922, aged 25 years in Pontypridd.

SKEWIS MARGARET
Married 1902, Haverfordwest.

SKEWIS MARGARET
Born 1906. Died Galashiels, Scotland, 1973, aged 67 years.
Buried Mawgan in Meneage 15 May 1786.

SKEWIS MARGARET
Chart 14. Daughter of Henry and Jane Skewes. Bpt St Keverne 26 December 1793. Died 14 May 1798, aged 4½ years. Buried St Keverne Churchyard.

SKEWES MARGARET
Married John Harris 22 June 1794 at St Keverne, by licence; in presence of Edward Skewes.

SKEWES MARGARET
Chart 2. Daughter of Absalom and Elizabeth Skewes. Bpt Camborne 8 February 1798. Married Joseph Rosevear 29 April 1826, St Austell. Issue: 2 sons and 2 daughters.

SKEWES MARGARET
Chart 19. Daughter of Alexander and Christian Skewes. Bpt Gwennap 29 November 1798. Married Ambrose Bray, widower who was originally married to Joanna Skewes. Married at Gwennap 8 October 1837.

SKEWES MARGARET
Chart 14. Daughter of Henry and Jane Skewes of Ruan Major. Bpt Ruan Major 7 July 1799. Married John Harris at St Keverne 10 December 1833. Died 1834. No issue.

SKEWES MARGARET
Chart 2. Illegitimate daughter of Constance Skewes. Bpt Camborne 29 July 1799. Died 6 February 1801, aged 1½ years.

SKEWES MARGARET
Daughter of Henry and Margaret Skewes. Bpt Camborne 24 October 1801.

SKEWES MARGARET
Daughter of Henry and Margaret Skewes of Mylor. Buried 15 April 1823, aged 22 years.

SKUES MARGARET
Born 1803. Née Hoskin. Married 29 July 1824 to Stephen Skues, husbandman. Died of scarlet fever 30 August 1836, aged 33 years. Children: John Hoskin (1824), William (1826), Elizabeth (1829) and Henry (1831).

SKEWES MARGARET
Married Matthew Wasley at Kea 17 October 1805.

SKEWES MARGARET
(Widow) Married John Tregaskis at Gwennap 21 March 1811.

SKEWES MARGARET
Born 1817 St Just. Married James Skewes of Perran-uthnoe — Goldsithney. Children: James, Elizabeth, Anne, Sarah and Thomas H. Died 1 July, 1884, aged 67 years.

SKUES MARGARET
Daughter of Thomas and Helen (née Ferrier) Skues, seaman. Born 1826. In 1851 Census Returns was listed as living at Virginia Street, East Aberdeen, aged 25 years. Cotton spinner.

SKUES MARGARET
Chart 3. Daughter of Christopher Ayre, clerk to Parliament and Acting Colonial Secretary of St John's, Newfoundland. Born 1836. Married William Mackenzie Skues, 2 October 1857 in Newfoundland. Children: George Edward Mackenzie, Mary Isabella, Margaret Caroline, Gertrude Eliza, Fred William, Minnie Mackenzie, Elsie and Charles Ayre Mackenzie. Died 5 June 1890, aged 54 years, Christchurch, Hampshire.

SKUES MARGARET
Chart 3. Née Oliver. Born 1836. Married William James Gordon Skues at St Andrew's Parish Church, Plymouth 22 May 1858. Died 1882, aged 46 years.

SKEWES MARGARET
Chart 14. Daughter of Samuel and Catherine (née Lugg) Skewes. Born 3 July 1848, Yorkville, Wisconsin, USA. Spinster who lived with her parents at Grovean Farm, Ives Grove, Yorkville. Died 26 January 1893, aged 45 years.

SKEWES MARGARET
Listed in 1862 Plymouth Street Directory as living at 3 Clarence Cottages, Stonehouse, Plymouth. Had gone by 1864.

SKEWS MARGARET
Chart 15. Daughter of William Simmonds. Born 1865. Married Alfred Skews at Christ Church, St Olave, London, 15 February 1885. Children: Elizabeth Martha (1888), Alfred William (1890), William George (1893), Emily Anne (1895), Henry Frederick (1897), George Thomas (1899) and Martha Margaret (1901). Her husband Alfred died 1902. Margaret married again in 1921, to Easom in Southwark.

SKEWES MARGARET
Born 1875, Missouri. Lived in Mississippi 1900. Married William H. Skewes 1894, Missouri, USA. Children: Grace V. (1895), Margaret J.(1896) and William H. (1899).

SKEWS   MARGARET
Born 28 January 1889. Died 1970. aged 81 years in Southend, Essex.
SKEWES   MARGARET
Born 1895 (March), Missouri. Lived in Mississippi, USA, 1900.
SKEWES   MARGARET
Chart 50. Née Phelps. Married George Skewes at St David's Chapel, Pontypridd, Glamorgan, 23 November 1918. Lived at 1 Aely Cryn, Panleygraigeven, Pontypridd. Children: Gwenllian F. (1919), Thomas G. (1920) and Iestyn J. (1922). Born 1897. Died 1922, aged 25 years in Pontypridd.
SKEWIS   MARGARET
Married 1902 Haverfordwest.
SKEWIS   MARGARET
Born 1906. Died Galashields, Scotland, 1973, aged 67 years.
SKEWS   MARGARET
Chart 17. Daughter of James Arthur Skews. Mother's maiden name Jarvis. Born 1912, St George's East, London. Died 1914, aged 2 years.
SKUES   MARGARET
Married John Drew, 1915, Redruth.
SKEWIS   MARGARET
Born 1924, New Monkland, Scotland. Died New Monkland, 1924, aged 0.
SKEWS   MARGARET
Chart 41. Daughter of Roy and Jennie (née Boynton) Skews. Born 1945 Wortley, South Yorkshire. Married William Barry Lawson, in Staincross, 1967. Now lives in Wingerworth. One daughter, Jane (1963).
SKEWES   MARGARET ALISON
Chart 50. Daughter of David Buick and Irene Margaret (née Murphy) Skewes. Born 15 July 1949, Ballarat, Victoria, Australia. Spinster. Lives in Milan, Italy.
SKEWES   MARGARET ANN
Born 1834. Died Penzance 1887, aged 53 years.
SKEWES   MARGARET ANN
Chart 14. Daughter of Henry and Grace Skewes, innkeeper. Bpt Helston 22 February 1837. In 1861 Census Returns was listed as a milliner.
SKEWES   MARGARET ANN
Married 1858, Mile End, London.
SKEWES   MARGARET ANN
Lives at 58 Tom Street, Yarrawonga, 3730, Victoria, Australia with Marjorie Joyce Skewes and Henry Snowden Skewes, grocer.
SKEWES   MARGARET ANN
Student at La Trobe University, Bundoora, 3083, Victoria, Australia.
SKEWS   MARGARET B.
Chart 15. Daughter of Henry Frederick Skews. Mother's maiden name Gosnell. Born 1923, Southwark, London. Married Hirst, 1945, Camberwell.
SKEWIES   MARGARET BELL
Born 1887. Died Hamilton, Scotland 1914, aged 27 years.
SKEWES   MARGARET BETTY
Chart 12. Née Coward. Née Healey. Daughter of James Russell and Betsey Healey. Married Anthony Ronald Skewes 23 August 1969 at Helston Register Office. One daughter Ruth by previous marriage who married in 1978.
Formerly school teacher at St Keverne. Wrote song "The Mohegan" (see page 302). Retired from teaching in 1980. Now runs an antique shop in Mullion.
Lives at Kittiwake, Churchtown, Mullion, Helston, Cornwall. Telephone number: 0326 240727.
SKUES   MARGARET CAROLINE MACKENZIE
Chart 3. Daughter of William Mackenzie and Margaret (née Ayre) Skues. Born 16 February 1861 at 36 School Hill, Aberdeen, Scotland. Died 1888, aged 27 years at Camberwell, London.
SKEWES   MARGARET CECELIA
Née Morrison. Married Byron James Skewes. Children: James William, Edward Nelson, William Byron, Margaret Gail and Beatrice Donna. Lives at 126 Toronto Avenue, Massapequa, New York, United States of America.
SKUES   MARGARET E.
Born 1884. Died 1961, aged 87 years, in Wood Green, London.
SKUES   MARGARET ELAINE
Chart 3. Only daughter of Richard and Doris Eileen (née Hughes) Skues. Born 18 January 1947, Cheshire. Attended Park Road Primary School, Timperley, Cheshire and Wellington Road Secondary Modern School, Altrincham, Cheshire. She was a regular attender of St Alban's Parish Church, Broadheath. After leaving school she became a florist, first at a shop in Sale, Cheshire then moving to Southport, Lancashire where she lived at 27 Chambers Road, Southport, Lancashire. Her Cheshire address had been "Richleen", 21 Buckingham Grove, Timperley.
Margaret celebrated her 21st birthday in January, 1968. Two months later she was a passenger in a car being driven through Halsall, Southport which was involved in a crash. She sustained multiple injuries and died on 11 March 1968. The funeral service took place at St

Margaret Elaine Skues (1947-1968)

Alban's Parish Church, Broadheath followed by cremation at Altrincham Crematorium.
SKEWES   MARGARET ELLEN
Lived at 25 Queen Street, Ballarat East, Australia with John Skewes, engine driver in 1912.
SKUES   MARGARET ENGLISH
Chart 5. Lived at 97 Wills Street, Bendigo, Victoria, Australia in 1913.
SKEWIS   MARGARET FORREST
Née Forrest. Married James Brown Skewis, 1953, Dalmery, Scotland. Children: Irene Ann (1956) and John James (1957). Now lives at 19 Trent Street, RAAF Base, Forest Hill, Wagga Wagga, New South Wales, Australia.
SKEWES   MARGARET GAIL
Daughter of Byron James and Margaret Cecilia (née Morrison) Skewes. Born 2 September 1951, New York, USA. Married Paul Berenger 26 September 1975. No children.
SKEWES   MARGARET H.
Chart 14. Daughter of Henry and Grace Skewes of Ruan Major. Born 1837.
SKEWES   MARGARET H.
Chart 12. Mother's maiden name Trengrove. Born 1950, Truro. Died 1950, aged 0.
SKEWS   MARGARET ISOBEL
Lives at 5/203 Brighton Road, Elwood, 3182, Victoria, Australia with Alan Claude Skews. Labourer.
SKEWIS   MARGARET J.
Née Cameron. Married 1928 to Wass in Brighton.
SKEWES   MARGARET JANE
Born 1887, Barnet, London.
SKEWES   MARGARET JANET
Chart 37. Née Williams. Married Vernon John Skewes 26 February 1977 in Australia. Lives at 7 Beatrice Close, Berowra Heights, Australia 2080. One son: David Lance (1979).
SKEWS   MARGARET JOAN
Chart 15. Née Hill. Married John Walter Skews 1964. No children. Runs "West End Cafe", Callington, Cornwall. Lives at 2 Urban Terrace, Callington. Tel No: 05793 2789.
SKEWIS   MARGARET JOSEPHINE
Chart 2. Daughter of Charles Samuel and Myrtle Skewis. Born 31 January 1905, America. Married Rose Rufus (she born 1905, died 1975). Issue: three sons.
SKEWES   MARGARET JOYCE
Lives at 17 Willie Street, Werris Creek, 2341, New South Wales, Australia with Geoffrey John Skewes, miller.
SKEWES   MARGARET JUNE
Lives at 7 Teak Street, Leeton, 2705, New South Wales, Australia.
SKEWES   MARGARET LAURA
Chart 2. Daughter of Gordon William and Eileen Margaret (née Tritchler) Skewes. Born 24 July 1929. Married William Goodman Sprott. Issue: 2 sons and 2 daughters.
SKUES   MARGARET LORRAINE
Chart 5. Daughter of Jack Sydney and Doris (née Hope) Skues. Born 26 July 1941, Melbourne, Australia. Worked as a hostess for Qantas Airlines. Lived in Maida Vale, London (1960-1963). Married Chris Robertson, 15 May 1969. Issue: 1 son and 1 daughter. Lives at Maida Vale, Sydney, Australia.

SKUES MARGARET LYNETTE
Chart 5. Née Malley. Born 26 July 1941, Australia. Married Kevin Richard Skues. One son: Wayne Richard Skues (1957). Now divorced. Lives at Flat 2, 16 Gordon Avenue, Elwood, 3184, Victoria, Australia. Clerk.

SKEWS MARGARET M.
Born 1865. Died 1937, aged 72 years in Southwark, London.

SKEWIS MARGARET MAIR
Born 1890. Died 1945, Hamilton, Scotland, aged 55 years.

SKUES MARGARET MELVILLE
Daughter of William and Margaret Skues, Born 14 November 1888. Lived in New South Wales, Australia.

SKEWIS MARGARET MUNRO
BSc., PhD. Chart 50. Daughter of John Jameson and Margaret Middlemas (née Jack) Skewis. Born 1940, Pollock, Scotland. Married Patrick William Penney, BSc., MSc., Glasgow, Scotland, 1964. Issue: one son and one daughter.

SKUES MARGARET PAMELA
Chart 3. Daughter of Ernest and Doris (née Gamble) Skues. Mother's maiden named Marsh. Born 7 August 1924, Epsom, Surrey. Married 1945 to Maximillian J. Pawlack of Canada. Lives in Canada.

SKEWES MARGARET ROSE
Lived at 11 Fifth Street, Elizabeth Grove, Gawler, South Australia in 1959 with Thomas Stanley Skewes.

SKEWES MARGARET ROSE
Lives at 32 Yanda Street, Warramanga, 2607, Canberra, Australia.

SKEWES MARGARET ROSE
Lives at 393 Murray Road, Preston, 3072, Victoria, Australia with Clive Raymond Skewes, minister.

SKEWES MARGARET ROSEMARY
Chart 46. Daughter of William Douglas and Gladys Maud Skewes of Carclew Cottages, Truro, Chief Petty Officer, Royal Navy. Mother's maiden name Little. Born 6 December 1944. Bpt St John's, Truro 9 February 1945. Married Stanley Pitt, 14 March 1968, Kenwyn Parish Church.

SKEWIS MARGARET S.
Married McKay, 1943, Hamilton, Scotland.

SKEWES MARGERETTE JEAN
Chart 12. Daughter of John Henry (Froggie) and Evelyn May Skewes. Mother's maiden name Cork. Born 1935, Redruth. Married Pearson, 1956, in Willesden.

SKEWES MARGERY
Chart 10. Née Spargo. Born 1733, Kea. Married Digory Skewes of Kea at Kenwyn 27 December 1756. Children: Margery, Mary, Matthew, Digory, Catherine and Peter. Died 1 December 1807, aged 74 years.

SKEWES MARGERY
Born 1743, Kea. Buried Kea 14 July, 1820, aged 77 years.

SKEWS MARGERY
Daughter of Henry Skews. Bpt Kea 24 February 1746.

SKEWES MARGERY
Chart 36. Daughter of John and Mary Skewes. Bpt Cury 4 March 1759. Married John White at Cury 4 June 1783.

SKEUS MARGERY
Chart 2. Daughter of Roben (Robart) Skeus. Bpt Camborne privately 21 November 1760; publicly 30 March 1761. Died 16 April 1761; infant.

SKEWES MARGERY
Chart 10. Daughter of Digory and Margery Skewes. Bpt Kenwyn 13 April 1771. Died 5 July 1772, Kea.

SKEWES MARGERY
Daughter of Henry Skewes. Bpt Kea 24 February 1776.

SKEWES MARGERY
Chart 10. Daughter of Digory and Margery Skewes. Bpt 31 May 1777 at Kenwyn.

SKEWES MARGERY
Buried in Camborne 16 November 1777.

SKEWES MARGERY
Daughter of Digory Skewes. Buried Kea 8 September 1779.

SKEWES MARGERY
Chart 30. Daughter of Digory and Elizabeth Skewes. Bpt Kea 8 October 1781. Married Wasley.

SKEWES MARGERY
Buried Kea 5 May 1797.

SKEWES MARGERY CATHERINE
Lives at Stoddart Street, Manilla, 2346, New South Wales, Australia with William Edward Skewes.

SKEWS MARGERY MARY
Chart 23. Née Henly. Born 12 March 1915. Married Albert Edward Skews 21 May 1952. Swindon, Wiltshire. No children. Lives at 52 South View Avenue, Swindon. Tel. no: 0793 29884.

SKEWIS MARIA
Chart 29. Daughter of John and Alice Skewis of Kea. Bpt Kenwyn 1 June 1761.

SKEWIS MARIA
Daughter of John and Mary Skewis. Bpt Helston 21 January 1770.

SKEWES MARIA
Chart 18. Daughter of John and Ann Skewes. Bpt Kenwyn 2 September 1791.

SKUES MARIA
Daughter of James & Ann Skues. Bpt Mawgan in Meneage, 2 November 1974.

SKEWES MARIA
Buried Cury 14 November 1794.

SKEWES MARIA
Daughter of Peter and Margaret Skewes. Bpt Kenwyn 11 June 1797.

SKEWES MARIA
Chart 10. Daughter of Digory and Elizabeth Skewes. Bpt Kea 5 April 1801.

SKEWES MARIA
Chart 29. Daughter of Richard and Roseanna Skewes. Bpt Kenwyn 6 February 1803.

SKEWIS MARIA
Chart 2. Illegitimate daughter of Constance Skewis. Bpt Camborne 24 November 1800. Married William Shearman, miner, 8 May 1819 at Camborne.

SKEWES MARIA
Married Richard Hooper 17 October 1818, St Agnes.

SKEWES MARIA
Married William Jones at Kea 23 November 1823.

SKEWES MARIA
Chart 10. Daughter of Matthew and Mary Skewes of Kenwyn, miner. Bpt Chacewater 15 August 1828. Buried Chacewater 31 March 1829, aged 2 years.

SKEWES MARIA
Married William Wasley at Kea, 15 February 1834.

SKEWES MARIA
Born 1837. Married Rev Joseph Henry Skewes, 1866, in Leeds. Children: Bessie Maud and Sidney Hope. Lived at Fitzclarence Place, Liverpool. Died 29 January 1890, aged 53 years.

SKEWES MARIA
Chart 10. Youngest daughter of Peter and Grace Skewes of Kerley, Kea, farmer. Born 1847. Bpt Chacewater 11 January 1855. Married 19 September 1876 at Baldhu to John Letcher, miner, son of James Letcher, farmer of Penstraze, by licence.

SKEWES MARIA
Chart 36. Daughter of Henry and Ann Skewes of East Taphouse, St Pinnock, Liskeard, formerly of St Hilary. Born 1848. Bpt Cury 4 November 1849. Brothers — Henry and Joseph. Sisters — Blanche and Sarah Ann. By 1862 had emigrated to Ballarat, Australia with her parents and family.

SKEWES MARIA
Daughter of James and Nancy Skewes of Piece, Illogan, miner. Born 1862. Bpt Illogan 23 July 1862.

SKUES MARIA
Chart 27. Daughter of William and Mary Skues. Born 1867, Bath.

SKEWS MARIA
Chart 15. Born 1868. Married Edmund Skews 1892, Plymouth. Lived at 123 King Street, Plymouth. Died Plymouth 1955, aged 87 years.

SKEWES MARIA
Chart 10. Mexican. Daughter of John and Luisa (née Garcia) Skewes. Born 1871, Real del Monte, Mexico. Spinster. Lived in Real del Monte. Died 12 November 1963, aged 92 years. Buried in English Cemetery, Real del Monte, Mexico.

SKEWES MARIA
Married December 1873, Helston district.

SKEWES MARIA
Chart 49. Born 8 August 1879. Married George Skewes, in Totnes, 1905. Lived at 75 South Milton Street, Plymouth. Died Plymouth 1976, aged 97 years.

SKEWES MARIA
Married 1884, Redruth.

SKEWS MARIA
Chart 10. Daughter of Nigel G. Skews. Mother's maiden name Walls. Born 1968, Falmouth.

SKEWES MARIA ABRIL
Chart 10. Mexican. Daughter of Salvador and Carmen (Ramirez) Skewes. Born 5 May 1935, Real del Monte, Mexico. Married Inocencio Hernandez. Died 15 December 1962, aged 27 years.

SKEWES MARIA GLADYS
Chart 36. Daughter of Leslie Kevin and Jill Cecilia (née Pullman) Skewes. Born 31 July 1950, Bendemeer, New South Wales. Lives at Caroline Street, Bendemeer, 2352, New South Wales, Australia.

SKEWES MARIANNE
Married James Rablin, 11 October 1834, Camborne.

SKEWS MARIANNE
Died 1849, Launceston.

SKEWES MARIE
Married William Tamlyn at Kenwyn 12 November 1785.

SKEWES MARIE

Married William Shearman, miner at Camborne 8 May 1819.

SKEWES   MARIE LESLEY
Mother's maiden name Hall. Born 1972, Truro.

SKEWIS   MARIENNE
Chart 2. Daughter of Edward George and Margaret Johnson Skewis.
Born 7 October 1934 in America. In 1957 worked as a clerk in the
Prudential Insurance Company, Tacoma, Washington, USA. Married
Victor Brown 13 June 1959. Issue: 1 son and 1 daughter.

SKEWS   MARILYN
Chart 6. Daughter of Harvey Thomas and Bernice (née Shackley) Skews
of Mineral Point, Wisconsin, USA. Born 11 April 1933. Married Leslie
Benson, 1950. Issue: 3 sons and 2 daughters. Now divorced. Lives at
Cobb, Wisconsin, USA.

SKEWS   MARILYN ANN
Lives at Bell Street, Balmoral, 3407, Victoria, Australia. Nursing sister.

SKEWES   MARILYN PEARL
Chart 36. Daughter of Benjamin Samuel and Gweneth (née Adams)
Skewes. Born 17 February 1952. Married John Keen 6 May 1972,
Tamworth Methodist Church, New South Wales, Australia. Issue: 1 son
and 1 daughter.

SKEWS   MARILYN VICKI
Lives at 23 River Terrace, Surfers Paradise, 4217, Queensland,
Australia. Waitress.

SKEWES   MARION
Married 1907, Barnstaple.

SKEWS   MARION
Chart 15. Daughter of Clarence and Ethel (née Duke) Skews. Born 1938
St Germans. Lived at 25 Valentines Row, Callington, Cornwall.

SKEWS   MARION
Mother's maiden name SKEWS. Born 1939, Redruth.

SKEWS   MARION
Chart 41. Married George Skews, Barnsley, 1944. Maiden name
Littledyke. Child: Sandra (1946). Lives at 1 Wharfe Street, Barnsley.
Tel No: Barnsley 41664.

SKUSE   MARION
of 8 Exley Bank, Salterhebble, Halifax. Changed her name to Stewart
13 January 1945.

SKEWES   MARION JOYCE
Daughter of William John and Rose Skewes. Mother's maiden name
Drew. Born 2 April 1921, Truro. Bpt St John's Truro 19 July 1921.

SKEWES   MARION MARTHA
Chart 10. Daughter of Herbert Tregonning and Florence Martha
Skewes. Born 13 January 1933 at Hamilton, Ontario, Canada. Married
Douglas Lloyd King 16 July 1955. No children.

SKEWS   MARION RHODA
Chart 15. Daughter of John and May Louisa (née Mallet) Skews of 1
Friends Pound Street, Liskeard. Born 27 March 1924. Bpt 4 May 1924
at Liskeard Wesleyan/Methodist Church. Married Pollard in
Plymouth, August 1946. Issue: two sons. Lives in Plymstock, Devon.

SKEWES   MARJORIE
Chart 36. Daughter of Robert Northey and Sarah Agnes (née Connell)
Skewes. Born New South Wales, Australia.

SKEWIS   MARJORIE CONSTANCE
Chart 34. Née Crook. Born 13 September 1904. Married George Skewis
26 January 1937. Lived at 31 Farncombe Road, Tunbridge Wells,
Kent. Died 17 June 1979, aged 74 years. No children.

SKEWS   MARJORIE E.
Chart 17. Daughter of Robert Albert Skews. Mother's maiden name
Waite. Born 1925, Poplar, London.

SKEWIS   MARJORIE ELIZABETH M.
Born 27 March 1920. Died Peterborough, 1976, aged 56 years.

SKEWES   MARJORIE GRACE
Chart 14. Daughter of Manley and Eva Skewes. Born 1901, Yorkville,
Wisconsin, USA.

SKEWES   MARJORIE GRACE
Daughter of Samuel Richard Skewes and Sarah Elizabeth Downton.
Married S.K. Johnson at 6 Kent Street, Lindisfarne, Australia, 30 June
1904.

SKEWES   MARJORIE JOY
Lived at 79 McCarthur Street, Pyrmont, New South Wales, Australia in
1959 with Leslie Richard Samuel Skewes, fireman. Now lives at 3/277
Balmain Road, Leichhardt, 2040, New South Wales, Australia.

SKEWES   MARJORIE JOYCE
Née Munro. Married Henry Snowden Skewes, 19 April 1949,
Yarrawonga. Children: Ian Geoffrey (1950), Peter Snowden (1953),
Bruce Alexander (1956), Ann Margaret (1959) and Andrew Philip
(1962). Lives at 58 Tom Street, Yarrawonga, 3730, Victoria, Australia.

SKEWES   MARJORIE LORRAINE
Lives at 9 Trudgeon Street, Shepperton, 3630, Victoria, Australia.
Teacher.

SKEWIS   MARK
Chart 34. Son of Trevor and Linda (née Hanslip) Skewis. Born 1965,
Canterbury. Lives at 24b Old Park Road, Canterbury, Kent. Tel
number 0227 51672.

SKUES   MARK
Born 1853, Malmsbury.

SKUES   MARK ALASTAIR
Chart 3. Son of George Ernest and Joyce (née Littlewood) Skues. Born
17 February 1957, Rugby, Warwickshire.

SKEWES   MARK ALEXANDER JOSEPH
Chart 10. Son of Richard Albert and Ann Marie (née Millar) Skewes.
Born 24 June 1963, Halifax, Nova Scotia, Canada. Lives at 1207 Royal
York, Islington, Toronto, Canada.

SKEWES   MARK ANDREW
Chart 36. Son of John David and Beryl May (née Johnson) Skewes. Born
3 March 1964. Lives at Ackland Hill Road, Cherry Gardens, 5157,
South Australia.

SKEWES   MARK ANTHONY
Chart 36. Son of Leslie Kevin and Jill Cecilia (née Pullman) Skewes.
Born 8 April 1960, Bendemeer, New South Wales. Lives at Caroline
Street, Bendemeer, 2352, New South Wales, Australia.

SKEWES   MARK ANTHONY
Chart 36. Son of Peter Michael and Marie (née Blair) Skewes. Born 18
November 1965 Watsons Creek, Bendemeer, 2352, New South Wales,
Australia.

SKEWES   MARK CHRISTOPHER
Chart 12. Son of Christopher John and Hazel (née Williams) Skewes of
Helston. Born 30 April 1978. Lives at 7 Lady Street, Helston.

SKEWES   MARK E.
Lives at 1052 Ibis Road, Jacksonville, Florida, USA (1980). Tel. number
(904) 725 8436.

SKEWS   MARK H.V.
Chart 15. Son of Albert Edward Victor and Daphne (née Lowe) Skews.
Born 1962, Plymouth. Lives at 25 Acklington Place, Ernesettle,
Plymouth, Devon.

SKEWES   MARSHA
Boarder at Carlton College, Missouri. Born 1843, Missouri, USA.

SKEWES   MARTHA
of Nantithet, Cury. Born 1817. Wife of Edward Skewes, shoemaker.
Children: John, Loveday Hendy and Martha Elizabeth. Died 17
September 1843, aged 26 years.

SKEWES   MARTHA
Born 1817, Sithney. Wife of John Skewes, carpenter. Lived at Sithney
(Tregoose) in 1871 Census Returns. Buried Sithney 31 December 1891,
aged 74 years.

SKEWIS   MARTHA
Chart 2. Daughter of Bennett Osborne and Martha Skewis of America.

SKEWES   MARTHA
Married John Fennell of Cullompton, Devon at Kenwyn 8 May 1823, by
licence.

SKEWS   MARTHA
Died 1864, Kensington.

SKEWIS   MARTHA
Born 1871. Died 1948, New Monkland, Scotland, aged 77 years.

SKEWS   MARTHA
Born 1875. Died Hackney, London, 1908, aged 33 years.

SKEWES   MARTHA
Chart 2. Daughter of Aaron and Maria Teresa (née Navarrete) Skewes
of Pachuca, Mexico. Born Pachuca 2 April 1962.

SKEWES   MARTHA
Chart 10. Mexican. Daughter of Pedro and Severa (née Martinez)
Skewes. Born 27 September 1908. Married. Issue: two daughters. Lived
in Mexico City. Died 7 February 1957, aged 48 years.

SKEWIS   MARTHA BARCLAY
Born 1888. Daughter of Richard and Margaret Stark. Married Joseph
Richard Skewis 31 December 1913 at 9 Broompark Terrace, Glasgow.
Died 1914, New Monkland, Scotland, aged 26 years.

SKEWES   MARTHA ELIZABETH
Chart 36. Daughter of Edward and Julia Skewes of Nantithet, Cury,
shoemaker. Born 1842. Married Charles Courtis 27 November 1864 at
Cury.

SKEWES   MARTHA JANE
Lived at 4 Toorak Avenue, Victoria, Australia in 1959.

SKEWIS   MARTHA K.
Chart 2. Daughter of Bennett Osborne and Martha M. (née Morton)
Skewis. Lived at 509 NE., Tacoma, Washington in 1911.

SKEWIS   MARTHA M.
Chart 2. Née Morton. Married Bennett Osborne Skewis. Children:
Catherine, Martha K. and Shirley. Lived in Tacoma, Washington,
USA.

SKEWS   MARTHA MARGARET
Chart 15. Daughter of Alfred and Margaret (née Simmonds) Skews.
Born 1901, St Olave, London.

SKEWIS   MARTHA McILROY
Daughter of James McIlroy and Mary (née Climson) McIlroy. Born
1869. Domestic servant. Married Joseph Richard Skewis 1886 at 40
Kidman Street, Coatbridge. Children: Mary (1888), William (1889),
Annie (1891), Thomas (1893) and James (1898).

SKEWIS   MARTHA McILROY

Chart 50. Daughter of Joseph Richard and Martha (née McIlroy) Skewis. Born 1901, New Monkland, Scotland. Married Jolly, 1923, New Monkland. Lives at Flat 1, St Hilda's House, Borough Road, Darlington, County Durham.

SKEWIS MARTHA McILROY
Born 1921, New Monkland, Scotland. Daughter of Thomas and Agnes Forbes (née Grant) Skewis. Married Joseph Richard Skewis (44) divorcee on 18 July 1967 in Glasgow. She was a ward maid, spinster and lived at 87 Govanhill Street, Glasgow.

SKEWIS MARTHA McILROY
Born 1925, New Monkland, Scotland. Married James Richard Todd, 1949, Camalchie, Scotland.

SKEWES MARTHA RENE
Chart 14. Daughter of Arthur Russell and Helen Roberta (née Horr) Skewes. Born 12 December 1952, Racine, Wisconsin, USA. Graduated from Bryan Station Senior High School, Lexington, Kentucky, in 1970. She attended Indiana University for one year and received a Bachelor of Science degree in Home Economics from the University of Kentucky, 1974. She received a Master of Science degree in Home Economics from the University of Kentucky in 1975, after attending summer school in Europe on a fashion design study tour sponsored by the University of Kentucky. Both her undergraduate and graduate majors were in textiles, clothing and merchandising.
Among her professional experiences are a graduate teaching assistantship at the University of Kentucky. She is a member of the American Home Economics Association.
Wrote "Survey of Retrieval Systems for Historical Costumes", 1975. Thesis, University of Kentucky for Master of Science Degree in Home Economics. Married William D. Heminger 4 September 1976.

SKEWIS MARTHA STARK
Born 1888. Daughter of William Barclay and Martha (née Stark) Barclay. Married William Skewis, widower, on 28 April 1916, at 25 Victoria Street, Harthill, Scotland. Died Bridgeton, Scotland, 1962, aged 74 years.

SKEWIS MARTHA STARK BARCLAY
Chart 50. Born 1919, Shotts East, Scotland. Married Alexander Bell, 1937, Camalchie, Scotland. Married Thomas Laurie, 1979, Kirkcaldy, Scotland.

SKUES MARTIN
Chart 10. Son of Digory Skues. Bpt Kenwyn 25 May 1701.

SKUES MARTIN
Married Mary Coad, Kenwyn 15 June 1729.

SKEWES MARTIN
Chart 10. Son of Martin and Mary Skewes. Bpt St Enoder 5 September 1731.

SKEWES MARTIN
Married Mary Polkinhorne at Kenwyn 16 February 1760, in presence of Martin Skewes. Children: Elizabeth (1762), Martin (1764), John (1767), Thomas (1770), Elizabeth (1774) and Peter (1777).

SKEWES MARTIN
Chart 10. Son of Martin and Mary Skewes. Born 1763. Bpt Kenwyn 14 July 1764. Married Elizabeth May at St Clement 4 June 1786. Buried St Mary's, Truro 13 November 1829, aged 66 years.
Elizabeth was buried St Mary's, Truro 8 April 1834, aged 69 years.

SKEWES MARTIN
Buried Kea 17 March 1764.

SKEWES MARTIN
Son of Martin Skewes of Kea. Bpt Kenwyn 14 July 1764.

SKEWES MARTIN
Chart 22. Married Ann Hocking at Kea, 22 September 1836. Children: Martin (1837), Thomas (1839) and John (1845).

SKEWES MARTIN
Chart 22. Son of Martin and Ann Skewes of Kerley, Kea; miner. Bpt Chacewater 26 March 1837.

SKEWS MARTIN
Son of Richard Skews, mine agent. Widower. Remarried Elizabeth Bennetts, daughter of Thomas Bennetts, farmer of Redruth at Chacewater 12 March 1851.

SKEWS MARTIN
Chart 10. Son of William and Mary Skews. Born 1862, Redruth. In 1871 Census Returns living at Illogan Highway with his parents and brothers Matthew Henry, John and Edwin and sisters Sarah and Emma.

SKEWS MARTIN
Chart 10. Son of .... and Mary Jane Skews. Born 1886, Redruth. Married Ethel Jane Nancarrow, 1915, Redruth. Lived at 12 Bellvue, Redruth 1923 and in 1929 moved to 3 Bellvue. Son: Martin Rex (1919). Died 1942, aged 56 years. Ethel Jane, born 1890, died 1963, aged 70 in Croydon.

SKEWES MARTIN
Chart 25. Son of John Harold and Sheila Winifred Skewes. Mother's maiden name Wynne. Born 10 December 1953, Manchester.

SKUES MARTIN
Chart 9. Son of John Joseph G. Skues. Mother's maiden name Iris Davies, formerly Whincop. Born 1958, Woolwich.

SKEWS MARTIN C.

Chart 10. Son of Stanley and Mavis (née Soady) Skews. Born 1958 St Austell. Married Angela Daniels, St Austell, 1976. Child: Michelle Deborah (1977).

SKEWS MARTYN R.
Chart 15. Son of Albert Edward Victor Skews. Mother's maiden name Daphne B. Lowe. Born 1959, Plymouth. Lives at 25 Acklington Place, Plymouth. Married Susan A. Hodge, 1980, Plymouth.

SKEWS MARTIN REX
Chart 10. Son of Martin and Ethel Jane Skews. Born 1919, Falmouth. Married Miriam Martin, youngest daughter of Charles Martin of 43 Langton Road, Plymouth at Pike's Hill Church, Falmouth 21 February 1940. He was then a private in the army and was married in military uniform. Children: Nigel R. (1946), Michael R. (1948) and Jane M. (1949). Lived for a while in Eton/Croydon area. Now lives at 14 Kernick Road, Penryn. Tel No: 0326 72419.

SKEWES MARTIN RICHARD
Lives at 3/277 Balmain Road, Leichhardt, 2040, New South Wales, Australia with Leslie Richard Samuel Skewes and Marjorie Joy Skewes.

SKEWES MARTINEZ MAGDALENA
Lives at Apicultura 227ZP2, Mexico City. Telephone number (905) 789 9808.

SCOOSE MARY
Daughter of John Scoose. Bpt Menheniot 18 February 1571.

SKEWES MARY
Married John Babbe at Gerrans 5 November 1582.

SKEWS MARY
Née Evans. Married Humfry Skewes at Gerrans 3 November 1612. Died 2 June 1651.

SKEWS MARY
Married Thomas Jack, alias Peerse at St Just in Roseland 14 July 1640.

SKUES MARY
Married William Bastone at Ottery St Mary, 1648.

SKEWES MARY
Married Gedeon Harrie at St Keverne 12 January 1659.

SKEWES MARY
Married Ambrose John 2 February 1659.

SKEWES MARY
Married John Freeman at Kenwyn 30 April 1685.

SKEWS MARY
Married Thomas Beech at Wheathampstead, Herts, 1693.

SKUES MARY
Chart 4. Daughter of William and Jane Skues. Bpt 2 June 1689. Married John Angove 20 May 1710.

SKEWES MARY
Married Charles Betty at Cury 26 December 1693.

SKEWS MARY
Daughter of John Skewes. Bpt Madron 16 June 1695.

SCUIS MARY
Daughter of Thomas and Philippa Scuis. Bpt Wendron Parish Church 22 February 1701. Married James Williams at Wendron Parish Church 5 January 1722.

SKEWS MARY
Chart 19. Daughter of John Skewes of Gwennap. Married Tregaskis, Gwennap.

SKEWS MARY
Daughter of William Skews. Buried Gwennap 1 April 1707.

SKEWES MARY
of Madron. Married Tobias Richards at St Levan, 19 February 1708.

SKEWS MARY
Daughter of William Skews. Bpt Gwennap 24 May 1708.

SKUES MARY
Widow. Buried St Keverne 22 May 1709.

SCUES MARY
Chart 2. Daughter of Henry and Mary Scues. Bpt Camborne February 1715. Died 12 October 1730, aged 15 years.

SKEWES MARY
Chart 36. Daughter of James and Sarah Skewes. Bpt Cury 2 March 1717.

SKUES MARY
Married Walter Staple at Kenwyn 1724.

SKEWS MARY
Daughter of Edward and Ann Skews. Bpt St Ewe 21 January 1728.

SKEWES MARY
Daughter of Edward and Ann Skewes. Bpt Cury 3 November 1728.

SKEWIS MARY
Chart 3. Daughter of Richard and Jane Skewis. Born 15 May 1733. Died 8 September 1737, aged 4 years.

SKUES MARY
Chart 3. Née Hitchen. Born 1737. Married William Skues (son of Richard and Jane Skewis) at Gwennap 3 January 1765. Children: Richard, William, Elizabeth, Mary and Stephen. Buried Helston 22 October 1809, aged 72 years.

SKEWIS MARY
Chart 3. Daughter of Richard and Jane Skewis. Born 23 May 1738.

Married Ralph Harvey in Helston, 26 December 1757.
SKEWIS   MARY
Married Thomas Bastard at Crowan 1 April 1737.
SKEWS   MARY
Daughter of Martin Skews. Bpt Kenwyn 24 February 1740.
SCUIS   MARY
Chart 2. Daughter of William and Mary Scuis. Bpt Camborne 25 April 1742. Married Stephen Rowe at Camborne 9 September 1764.
SKEWS   MARY
Daughter of Henry Skews. Bpt Kenwyn 19 December 1743.
SKUES   MARY
Chart 3. Née Hoskin. Born 1746. Married John Skues, Borough Mason of Helston and son of Richard and Jane Skewis at Helston Parish Church 28 March 1769. Children: Ann, William, Elizabeth, John, Isobella, Jane, Richard, Charles and Joseph. Died 20 August 1799, aged 63 years.
SKEWES   MARY
Chart 36. Née George. Married John Skewes at Cury, 12 September 1747.
SCUIS   MARY
Chart 2. Née Temby. Wife of William Scuis. Married 15 July 1735. Died 22 September 1781.
SKEWS   MARY
Wife of Martin Skews. Buried Kea 22 February 1751.
SKEWIS   MARY
Chart 25. Daughter of Thomas and Esther Skewis. Bpt St Keverne 26 January 1752.
SKEWIS   MARY
Daughter of Robert Skewis. Bpt Camborne 30 May 1756.
SKEWES   MARY
Born 1756. Wife of John Skewes of Treloskan, Cury. Died 3 October 1842, aged 86 years.
SKEWIS   MARY
Chart 2. Daughter of Robert Skewis. Bpt Camborne 2 February 1754. Died 30 May 1761, aged 7 years.
SKEWES   MARY
Born 1759. Daughter of William and Hannah Skewes of St Gluvias. Bpt St Gluvias 17 April 1759. Buried St Gluvias 5 April 1761, aged 2 years.
SKEWES   MARY
Daughter of John and Alice Skewes. Bpt 18 September 1759, Perranarworthal.
SKEWES   MARY
Married Ferninando Behenna at Kea 18 October 1759.
SKUES   MARY
Daughter of Martin Skues. Bpt Kenwyn 2 April 1760.
SKUES   MARY
Chart 3. Née Richards. Born 1764. Married Richard Skues 4 December 1793 at Helston Parish Church. Children: Richard, George, Grace Richards, Mary, William, Edward and Ann. Died 8 February 1847, aged 83 years at Durnford Street, East Stonehouse.
SKEWES   MARY
Chart 10. Daughter of Digory and Margery Skewes. Bpt Kenwyn 24 August 1765. A Mary Skewes married a John Blacklet at Kenwyn 1789.
SKEWES   MARY
Chart 2. Daughter of Richard and Alice Skewes. Bpt Camborne 22 February 1767. Died 28 November 1770, aged 3½ years.
SKEWES   MARY
Buried Cury 23 March 1767.
SKEWIS   MARY
Chart 2. Twin to William Skewis and daughter of John and Philippa Skewis. Bpt privately 20 October 1768. Publicly 13 November 1768. Married William Smythram of Breage at Camborne 2 June 1793 in presence of Henry Skewes.
SKEWES   MARY
Chart 18. Daughter of Thomas Skewes. Bpt Kenwyn 28 October 1770.
SKEWIS   MARY
Chart 2. Daughter of Richard and Alice Skewis. Bpt Camborne 9 December 1770. Married William Thomas 18 October 1791 at Camborne Parish Church.
SKEWES   MARY
Buried Gwennap 22 December 1770.
SKEWES   MARY
Daughter of Richard Skewes. Bpt Kenwyn 25 March 1771.
SKEWES   MARY
Daughter of Richard Skewes. Buried Kenwyn 9 January 1773.
SKEWES   MARY
Buried Gwennap 19 July 1773.
SKEWES   MARY
Daughter of William and Mary Skewes. Bpt Helston 7 January 1774.
SKEWES   MARY
Wife of Richard Skewes. Buried Kenwyn 26 January 1774.
SKEWS   MARY
Married William Coad at St Stephens in Brannel, 6 February 1774.
SKEWES   MARY
Daughter of James and Anne Skewes. Bpt Mawgan in Meneage 10

September 1774.
SKEWES   MARY
Married William Jennings of Crowan at Cury 8 April 1777.
SKEWES   MARY
Married James Auery of St Agnes 19 July 1778, Kenwyn.
SKEWES   MARY
Married Thomas Shepherd at Kea 3 February 1781.
SKEWES   MARY
Daughter of John and Mary Skewes. Bpt Gwennap 18 March 1781.
SKEWES   MARY
Married Thomas Dale at Mawgan in Meneage 31 October 1782.
SKUES   MARY
Chart 3. Born 1783. Wife of William Skues of Helston, carpenter. Sister in law to Ann Skues. Died same day as her sister in law 5 February 1838, aged 55 years.
SKEWES   MARY
Daughter of John and Mary Skewes. Bpt Cury 15 August 1784.
SKEWES   MARY
Buried Cury 25 December 1784.
SKEWS   MARY
Chart 28. Born 1785. Wife of Richard Skews of Kea Churchtown; parish clerk. Died 3 October 1854, aged 69 years.
SKEWES   MARY
Chart 36. Daughter of John and Mary Skewes of Cury. Bpt 21 May 1786.
SKEWES   MARY
Daughter of John and Mary Skewes. Bpt Gwennap 15 October 1786.
SKEWES   MARY
Buried Kenwyn 27 April 1787.
SKEWES   MARY
Born 1789. Died Newton Abbot 1868, aged 79 years.
SKEWES   MARY
of Kea. Married John Blackler of Kea at Kenwyn 28 March 1789.
SKEWIS   MARY
Daughter of Richard and Jane Skewis. Bpt privately 1 August 1792, Kenwyn.
SKEWIS   MARY
Chart 2. Née Pearce. Born 17 December 1793. Married Edward Skewis 3 March 1817, Camborne. Emigrated to Wisconsin, USA. Children: Mary, Edward, Ann, Catherine, James, Eliza, Honor, Henry, Caroline and William. Died June 1858, aged 41 years. Buried in Shullsburg Cemetery, Wisconsin, USA.
SKEWES   MARY
Married Henry Williams at Cury 1 October 1793.
SKEWES   MARY
Second daughter of Henry and Margaret Skewes. Bpt Gwinear 14 October 1794. Died 25 March 1868 of jaundice, aged 73 years. Buried in Kenwyn churchyard with her parents and sister Lavinia. Spinster. Buried 29 March 1868.
SKEWES   MARY
Buried Kenwyn 1 May 1795.
SKEWES   MARY
Chart 36. Daughter of William and Alice Skewes of Treloskan, Cury. Bpt Cury 10 July 1796.
SKEWES   MARY
Chart 10. Née Jeffrey. Born 1797. Married Matthew Skewes of Chacewater, miner at Kea 22 June 1819. Children: Elizabeth and Mary. Died 17 November 1882 at Kerley, Kea, aged 85 years. Brd Chacewater.
SKEWES   MARY
Chart 18. Daughter of William and Ann Skewes. Bpt Kenwyn 22 April 1798.
SKEWES   MARY
Chart 10. Daughter of Digory and Elizabeth Skewes. Bpt Kea 26 August 1798.
SKEWES   MARY
Chart 18. Daughter of Thomas and Mary Skewes. Bpt Kenwyn 26 May 1799.
SKEWS   MARY
of Kerley, Kea. Born 1799. Buried Baldhu 18 September 1867, aged 68 years.
SKEWES   MARY
Chart 36. Née Williams. Born 1756. Married John Skewes at Cury 3 January 1778. Children: Edward, Mary, Blanch S., William, James, Anne and John. Died 3 October 1842, aged 86 years.
SKEWES   MARY
Born 1767. Lived at Wheal Busy. Died 1853, aged 86 years. Buried Chacewater 24 March 1853.
SKUES   MARY
Chart 3. Daughter of Richard and Ann Skues. Born 29 December 1800. Bpt Helston 24 March 1801. Married Richard Rodd, solicitor of East Stonehouse. Died 29 February 1848, aged 48 years. Issue.
SKEWS   MARY
Born 1800. Died Truro 1864, aged 64 years. Buried Kenwyn 8

December 1864.

SKEWES MARY
Chart 29. Daughter of Richard and Roseanna Skewes. Bpt Kenwyn 9 March 1800.

SKEWES MARY
Buried Cury 21 April 1801.

SKUES MARY
Chart 3. Daughter of William and Mary Skues of Helston. Married William Michell, merchant at Truro 3 May 1802 at Helston Parish Church. Lived at Compigney, Kenwyn. Children: Mary Michell and William Michell.
Died 20 April 1811, after an illness of seven years. Michell later remarried Elizabeth Cornish Vincent of Kenwyn.

SKEWES MARY
Buried Cury 16 October 1802.

SKEWES MARY
Born 1803. Buried Camborne 23 February 1826, aged 23 years.

SKEWIS MARY
Daughter of John and Jane Skewis. Bpt Illogan 23 October 1803.

SKEWES MARY
Buried Gwennap 24 June 1804.

SKEWES MARY
Buried Kea 12 February 1805.

SKEWES MARY
From Grade. Born 1806. Buried St Keverne 21 July 1846, aged 40 years.

SKEWES MARY
Chart 2. Daughter of Henry and Grace Skewes of Bosawsack, Constantine. Bpt Constantine 6 July 1806. Married Stephen Eddy 29 March 1828.

SKEWES MARY
Chart 28. Née Ninis. Married Richard Skewes at Kea Church 25 April 1807, who was a labourer of Nancevellan Common, Kea.
Children: Patience, Peggy, Jane, Ann Eynes, Elizabeth, Harriet and Thomasine.

SKEWES MARY
Buried Gwennap 1 February 1808.

SKEWES MARY
Married Richard Tregaskis at Gwennap 14 January 1809, in presence of Alexander Skewes.

SKUES MARY
Daughter of William and Jane Skues. Bpt Mylor 26 October 1806.

SKEWES MARY
Daughter of William & Elizabeth Skewes. Bpt Camborne 25 June 1808.

SKEWS MARY
Chart 9. Daughter of William and Nancy Skews of Nansladron, St Ewe, yeoman. Bpt St Ewe 17 January 1813. Married Joseph Truscott, labourer, son of John Truscott, farmer at St Ewe 10 April 1839, in presence of Philip Skews.

SKEWES MARY
Chart 14. Daughter of Henry and Jane Skewes, farmer. Bpt Ruan Major 9 October 1814. Married Josiah Boulden of St Keverne at Ruan Major 12 January 1837, in presence of Anthony Skewes and Samuel Skewes. Emigrated to Wisconsin, USA. Issue: 4 sons and 6 daughters.

SKEWES MARY
Chart 28. Daughter of Richard and Mary Skewes, parish clerk at Kea. Bpt Kea 23 April 1810. Married Thomas Triganowan 31 December 1831 at Kea. Named in father's will.

SKEWES MARY
Buried Kea 12 June 1810.

SKEWES MARY
Married Richard Dudley at Cury 5 November 1810.

SKEWES MARY
Born 1811. Died Redruth 1877, aged 66 years.

SKEWES MARY
Chart 12. Daughter of James and Elizabeth Skewes of Cury. Bpt Cury 11 April 1811.

SKEWES MARY
Buried Gwennap 27 November 1811.

SKEWES MARY
Born 1812. Buried Cury 26 July 1855, aged 43 years.

SKEWES MARY
Chart 19. Daughter of Alexander and Christian Skewes. Bpt Gwennap 10 June 1812. Lived at Lanner House, Gwennap. Spinster. Died 10 December 1877, aged 66 years. Buried Gwennap 14 December 1877.

SKUES MARY
Chart 5. Daughter of Joseph and Elizabeth Skues; soldier. Bpt Redruth Parish Church 18 June 1815. Married William Penrose, 19 May 1839.

SKEWS MARY
Chart 10. Née Dennis. Born 1816. Wife of William Skews, tailor. Children: William Richard Francis Dennis, Thomas Albert Jeffrey, Mary Agnes Elizabeth Dennis, Teresa Hermina Amelia, Matthew Henry, John Edwin, Sarah and Martin. Buried Illogan 7 November 1865, aged 49 years. William then remarried Jane Thomas 29

September 1866.

SKUES MARY
Chart 2. Daughter of Edward and Mary Skues. Born 16 February 1818. In 1841 Census Returns worked in a fuse factory. Married John Chappel. Emigrated to America, 1849. Died 4 February 1884 at Mineral Point, Wisconsin.

SKUES MARY
Married Joseph Repper at Mawgan in Meneage 1 January 1817.

SKEWES MARY
of Kea. Born 1820. Buried Kenwyn 5 June 1825, aged 5 years.

SKEWES MARY
Chart 36. Daughter of John and Loveday Skewes of Nantithet, Cury. Bpt Cury 17 February 1820.

SKEWES MARY
of Kea. Married Richard Tonkin at Kenwyn 5 March 1820, in presence of Henry Skewes.

SKEWES MARY
Married Thomas Piercey at Cury 24 April 1821.

SKEWES MARY
Chart 22. First wife of Edward Skewes of Mawnan. Born 1821. Died 25 February 1867, aged 46 years. Edward later remarried Mary Ellen Kempthorne in June 1867.

SKUES MARY
Chart 10. Daughter of Thomas and Grace Skues. Bpt Kenwyn 1 July 1821.

SKEWES MARY
Chart 26. Daughter of Matthew and Mary Skewes of Kea. Bpt Kenwyn 5 May 1822.

SKUES MARY
Married Jacob Michell at Kenwyn 14 March 1822, in presence of Eleanor Skues.

SKEWES MARY
Chart 2. Daughter of John and Ann Skewes. Bpt 7 March 1824, Camborne. Died 23 September 1825, aged 20 months.

SKEWES MARY
Chart 33. Bpt Kenwyn 6 June 1824. Daughter of William and Mary Skewes of Kea. Married Thomas Trevethan, son of Henry Trevethan, miner; at Chacewater 3 March 1842 in presence of William Skewes.

SKEWES MARY
Chart 36. Daughter of William and Christian Skewes, farmer. Bpt Ruan Major 28 June 1824.

SKEWES MARY
Chart 19. Daughter of John and Ann Skewes, miner of Carharrack, Gwennap. Bpt Gwennap 14 April 1827. Buried Gwennap 14 November 1842, aged 16 years.

SKEWES MARY
Married Stephen Eddy 29 March 1828, Constantine.

SKEWES MARY
Daughter of James and Charity Skewes, miner of Gwennap. Bpt Gwennap 26 January 1829.

SKEWES MARY
Born 1830. Buried Camborne 25 November 1834, aged 4½ years.

SKUES MARY
Married Robert Rabey at Kenwyn 14 August 1830.

SKUES MARY
Married Richard Skues (widower) at Kenwyn Church 17 November 1831.

SKEWES MARY
Born 1832. Died Truro 1914, aged 82 years.

SKEWES MARY
Daughter of Thomas and Loveday Skewes. Bpt Ruan Minor 17 February 1833.

SKUES MARY
Chart 2. Daughter of John and Ann Skewes. Bpt Camborne 18 April 1833.

SKEWES MARY
of Chacewater. Born 1833. Buried 22 March 1861, Chacewater, aged 28 years.

SKEWS MARY
Daughter of Peter and Ann Skews of Gwennap. Bpt Kea 9 July 1833.

SKEWES MARY
Chart 10. Daughter of Digory and Sophia Skewes. Born 24 August 1833. Bpt Truro Wesleyan Chapel 28 March 1837. Living with her parents at Dobwalls, Liskeard (1851 Census Returns) and also with her brothers Matthew and Samuel.

SKEWIS MARY
Born 1834. Married Edward Skewis. Lived in Shullsburg, Wisconsin, USA. Died 16 October 1860, aged 26 years. Buried in Shullsburg.

SKEWES MARY
Chart 14. Daughter of Anthony and Christian Skewes, of Chybarles, Ruan Major. Bpt Ruan Major 5 April 1835. Married James Nicholls of Treleague, Ruan Minor at Ruan Major 15 April 1868.

SKUES MARY
Chart 2. Daughter of James and Joanna Skues. Bpt Camborne 16 May

1835.

SKEWES   MARY
Married Thomas Martin, miner at Camborne 5 November 1835 in presence of Henry Skewes.

SKEWES   MARY
Chart 12. Married William Skewes 3 November 1834. Children: Elizabeth Mary (1835), Alice Ann (1837), Emily (1840), Eliza (1844) and William James (1850). Lived at Cury.

SKEWES   MARY
Daughter of John Skewes and Ann Hammett. Bpt 19 March 1837, Bible Christian Church, Falmouth.

SKEWES   MARY
Chart 10. Daughter of Peter and Grace Skewes, of Kerley, Kea. Bpt Chacewater 21 February 1837. Dressmaker. Married Alfred Williams, farmer, son of Solomon Williams, miner, at Baldhu, 8 August 1865.

SKEWES   MARY
Married 1837, Falmouth.

SKEWES   MARY
Chart 44. Daughter of James and Elizabeth Skewes of Tredeger, Abergavenny. Born 1838. Married 1856, Abergavenny.

SKEWES   MARY
Born 1838. Died Redruth 1913, aged 75 years.

SKEWES   MARY
Born 1839, Redruth.

SKEWIS   MARY
Born 1839, Totnes. Widow. Late of Newquay. Died at the Post Office, Totnes 4 February 1912, aged 73 years.

SKEWES   MARY
Married 1839, St Austell.

SKEWES   MARY
Born 1840, Redruth.

SKEWES   MARY
Chart 31. Daughter of John and Jane Skews. Bpt St Austell 5 April 1840. Died 1840 St Austell.

SKEWES   MARY
Chart 31. Daughter of John and Jane Skews. Bpt St Austell 12 September 1842. Married Thomas Hancock, son of William Hancock, accountant on 16 July 1861 at Parish Church, St Austell.

SKEWES   MARY
Chart 50. Daughter of Thomas and Jane Skewes of Kerley, Kea. Bpt Chacewater 17 January 1841. Emigrated with parents to Australia in 1850's.

SKEWES   MARY
Chart 36. Daughter of James and Simonette Skewes of Cury. Born 1842. Bpt Cury 12 September 1842.

SKEWES   MARY
Daughter of Peter and Elizabeth Skewes of Kea. Born 30 April 1842. Bpt Primitive Methodist Chapel, Perranwell Circuit, 7 March 1844.

SKEWES   MARY
Died 1842, Redruth.

SKEWES   MARY
Chart 10. Daughter of Peter and Elizabeth Skewes of Hugus, Kea. Born 1843.

SKEWES   MARY
Married William Tripconey at Budock 29 April 1843.

SKEWES   MARY
Buried Mullion 17 July 1843, aged 11 years.

SKEWES   MARY
Widow, aged 29 years. Daughter of Richard Bamphyle, miner. Married William Mitchell, 35, widower and carpenter of St Day, Gwennap, 23 November 1843.

SKUES   MARY
Chart 2. Daughter of Henry and Grace Skues. Born 1844, Camborne. Milliner.

SKEWES   MARY
Married William Scoble at Kenwyn, October 1844.

SKEWES   MARY
Died 1844, Helston.

SKEWES   MARY
Daughter of James Skewes of Piece, Illogan, husbandman. Born 1846. Married William Carter at Illogan Parish Church 27 April 1874. William Carter was son of James Carter, miner.

SKEWES   MARY
Chart 36. Daughter of James and Simonette Skewes. Born 1846, Cury. Was a visitor to a private house near Three Tuns Hotel in 1861 Census Returns. In 1871 Census Returns was a tin dresser living at Treskillard, Cury with her widowed father then 77 and sister Ellen, aged 22 years.

SKEWS   MARY
Born 1846, Neath.

SKEWES   MARY
Chart 10. Née Stripp. Born 16 April 1848. Married Richard Skewes at St Austell 25 January 1872 by licence. Emigrated to Mexico. Issue 3 sons and 2 daughters. Was an exemplary Christian woman and always acted in every good work, which she generally regarded more as a pleasure

than a duty. In the years she resided in the Mexican community she won the esteem and deep respect of everyone. There appeared to be in her an embodiment of those sterling traits of character which constitute a noble type of womanhood. Died at Pachuca, Mexico of pulmonia on 12 May 1896, aged 48 years. Buried in English cemetery, Real del Monte, Mexico. "Wash me and I shall be whiter than the driven snow."

SKEWIS   MARY
Married 1849, Falmouth.

SKEWES   MARY
Chart 50. Née Sanders. Daughter of John Sanders, agricultural labourer. Born 1 January 1851. Married Samuel Skewes at Helston Register Office, 17 March 1870. Children: Jane (1870), William (1871), Esther (1874), Clara (1877), Myra (1883), Mary Margaret (1882), Henry (1873) & Stephen (1880). Died St Columb 1919, aged 68 years.

SKEWES   MARY
Bpt Neath, Glamorgan 26 December 1852. Daughter of James and Harriet Skews.

SKEWIS   MARY
Born 1852, Redruth.

SKEWES   MARY
Born 1855. Died Tavistock 1908, aged 53 years.

SKEWIS   MARY
Married 1856, Helston.

SKEWES   MARY
Married 1857, Redruth.

SKEWES   MARY
Chart 36. Daughter of William and Priscilla Skewes. Born 1858, Illogan.

SKEWS   MARY
Died 1858, Stepney, London.

SKEWES   MARY
Born 1860, Redruth.

SKEWES   MARY
Died 1860, Redruth.

SKEWES   MARY
Chart 36. Daughter of James and Frances Skewes of Mawnansmith. Born 1860. Bpt Mawnan 28 October 1860. Spinster. Died 20 February 1946, aged 85 years.

Mary Skewes (1860-1946)

SKEWS   MARY
Born 1860, Penzance.

SKEWES   MARY
Daughter of John Skewes, farmer of Killiwerris. Married George Warner, son of John Warner of Killiwerris, smith, at Chacewater 24 April 1860.

SKEWIS   MARY
Chart 2. Daughter of Edward and Kittie Skewis of Shullsburg, Wisconsin, USA. Born 1861.

SKEWES   MARY
Chart 36. Daughter of Henry and Ann (née Gribble) Skewes. Born Victoria, Australia, 1861. Died 10 April 1865, aged 4 years. Buried Ballarat Old Cemetery, Victoria, Australia.

SKUES   MARY
Chart 8. Daughter of George Gilbert and Isabella Skues. Bpt St Jude, Southwark 5 May 1862.

SKEWES   MARY
Died 1861, Truro.

SKEWS   MARY
Died 1861, Penzance.

SKEWS   MARY
Married William Hubber at Cubert 13 April 1862.

SKEWES   MARY
Born 1863, Redruth.

SKEWS   MARY
Died 1863, Plymouth.

SKEWIS   MARY
Married 1864, Redruth.

SKEWES   MARY
Wife of Harry Skewes of New York. Born October, 1867, England. Married 1888, New York. Children: Edgar (1890), Mattie (1893), Leonard (1891) and Viola (1897). Three other children died young.

SKEWS   MARY
Chart 15. Daughter of John and Isabella (née Gregory) Skews. Bpt Altarnun 5 September 1868. Died 1 Octboer 1868, aged 10 weeks.

SKEWIS   MARY
Married 1869, Kensington, London.

SKEWES   MARY
Chart 14. Daughter of Samuel J.and Betsy (née Phillips) Skewes. Born 17 February 1872, Ives Grove, Racine County, Wisconsin, USA. Died from diphtheria 1881, aged 9 years.

SKEWES   MARY
Born 1873, Redruth.

SKEWES   MARY
Born 1874, Redruth. Died 1874, aged 0.

SKEWS   MARY
Born 1874, Neath.

SKEWES   MARY
Chart 36. Daughter of John Skewes, railway guard of Higher Condurrow. Born 1875. Married 27 November 1897 to Samuel House (23) son of Nicholas House, engine driver, at Tuckingmill Parish Church in the presence of John Skewes and Kate Skewes.

SKEUSE   MARY
Born 1877, Ireland. Lived at 446 West 58th Street, Manhattan, New York, USA in 1900 with her brother-in-law Andrew Patchell.

SKEWIS   MARY
Married Lawry from Ashburton in 1877 in Newton Abbot district. Issue: 3 sons and 2 daughters.

SKEWES   MARY
Born 1884, Helston.

SKEWES   MARY
Chart 10. Daughter of Thomas George and Jane (née Mitchell) Skewes. Born 9 July 1887, Marazion. Emigrated with her parents to Marquette, Michigan, USA, 1896. Spinster.

SKEWIS   MARY
Daughter of Joseph Richard Skewis, iron turner foreman and Martha (née McIlroy). Born 16 October 1888 at Rochsollock, Scotland. Married 1908.

SKEWIS   MARY
Born 1889. Died New Monkland, 1935, aged 46 years.

SKEWIS   MARY
Born 1888, Airdrie, Scotland.

SKEWS   MARY
Born 1897, Bethnal Green. Died 1897, aged 0.

SKEWES   MARY
Living at Buller Terrace, Redruth, 1906.

SKEWES   MARY
Married James B.H. Pedler, 1914, Falmouth.

SKEWES   MARY
Chart 14. Daughter of Earl Skewes. Married Bert Robey in America.

SKEWES   MARY
Chart 14. Daughter of Mortier Boulden and Mildred Skewes. Born 1 September 1939, America. Married Otis N. Fisher 27 February 1965. Issue: two children.

SKEWES   MARY
Chart 14. Daughter of Samuel and Betsy Skewes. Born in America and died there of diphtheria, aged 10 years.

SKEWES   MARY
Chart 37. Daughter of Richard John Skewes of Australia.

SKEWS   MARY
Married Tapson, 1924, St Columb.

SKEWIS   MARY
B.M. 1924 (Teacher). Address: Longview, Washington, United States of America.

SKEWS   MARY
Married Luxton, 1929, Redruth.

SKEWES   MARY
Clerk at Porter Furniture Company, Box 394, Racine, Wisconsin, USA. (1941).

SKEWES   MARY
Married Faust, 1944, Stockport, Cheshire.

SKEWES   MARY
Chart 36. Daughter of Neville Percy and Helen (née O'Lockland) Skewes. Born 25 July 1960, Australia.

SKEWS   MARY
Married Fallan, 1976, Waltham Forest.

SKEWS   MARY A.
Born 1830, England. Wife of Thomas Skews, mining labourer. Living in Wisconsin, USA 1870 — at Mineral Point. Children: John and William.

SKEWS   MARY A.
Born 1866. Died 1932, Houghton, aged 66 years.

SKEWES   MARY A.
Born 1874. Died 1950, Salford, aged 76 years.

SKEWS   MARY A.
Born 1880. Died 1918, Strood, aged 38 years.

SKEWES   MARY A.
Mother's maiden name Boyd. Born 1915, Fulham. Married Wright, 1939, Battersea.

SKEWES   MARY AGNES
Daughter of John Skewes, miner. Born 1837, Gwennap. Married Edward Odgers (21), miner of Trevarth at Gwennap 28 July 1859, in presence of Mary Ann Skewes. She was a dressmaker.

SKEWS   MARY AGNES
Born 1845, Truro.

SKEWES   MARY AGNES
Born 1870, Helston. Married 1902, Helston.

SKEWIS   MARY AGNES ELIZABETH
Died 1844, Redruth.

SKEWS   MARY AGNES ELIZABETH DENNIS
Chart 10. Born 1844, Kenwyn. Daughter of William and Mary Skews (blacksmith). Was a mine girl until her marriage in 1868.

SKEWIS   MARY ALBERTA
Chart 2. Daughter of Francis Harry and Annie Skewis. Born 13 August 1901, America. Married Irwin Skinner 11 June 1933. Issue: one son.

SKEWES   MARY ALFREDA
M.B., B.S. Chart 50. Daughter of Thomas Garland and Marion Edith Alfreda (née Wilson) Skewes. Born 17 April 1899, Ballarat, Victoria, Australia. Graduated from University of Melbourne 1924. First woman resident doctor of Ballarat Base Hospital. Went overseas in 1926. Returned to Ballarat and married William Raymond Dudley Griffiths, F.R.C.S. (Ed)., F.R.A.C.S., M.R.C.O.G., 20 December 1928. Issue: 3 sons and 1 daughter. Private practice at 710 Sturt Street, Ballarat. Lives at 1729 Sturt Street, Ballarat, 3350, Victoria, Australia.

Mary Alfreda Griffiths (née Skewes) with her brother David Buick Skewes in Ballarat, Australia, 1981

SKEWES   MARY ANN
Chart 2. Daughter of James and Elizabeth Skewes. Bpt Camborne 15
January 1792. Married Richard Rogers (husbandman) 24 September
1818 at Camborne in presence of James Skewes.
SKEWES   MARY ANN
Chart 2. Daughter of Absalom and Jane Skewes. Bpt 12 December
1812, Camborne. Married James Rablin, miner 11 October 1834.
SKEWS   MARY ANN
Chart 9. Daughter of James and Joanna Skews of Lower Sticker. Bpt St
Ewe 7 March 1813.
SKEWES   MARY ANN
Daughter of David Roberts of Kea, miner. Born 1817. Married Jeffery.
On 16 May 1868 as a widow married Richard Skewes (49), widower. At
the time of her marriage to Richard Skewes she lived at Three Burrows,
Kenwyn. Later lived at Truro Union House. Died 1887, aged 70 years.
Buried Kenwyn 5 May 1887.
SKEWES   MARY ANN
Daughter of John and Jennifer Skewes, miner of Poldice. Bpt Gwennap
30 March 1819.
SKEWS   MARY ANN
Born 1820. Died 1897, aged 77 years, Fulham, London.
SKEWES   MARY ANN
Chart 30. Daughter of Thomas and Jane Skewes of Daniell Street,
Truro, mason of St Clement. Bpt Kea 5 December 1824. Married John
Mills (26), son of Philip Mills, lawyer of Truro at Kenwyn Parish Church
30 April 1853, in presence of Thomas Skewes. Lived at Daniell Street,
Truro (1851 Census Returns) with his parents and sisters Henrietta and
Philippa and brother Thomas.
SKEWS   MARY ANN
Born 1831. Died 1904, Redruth, aged 73 years.
SKUES   MARY ANN
Chart 8. Daughter of William Henry and Sarah Skues. Bpt St Dunstan,
Stepney 4 July 1831.
SKEWES   MARY ANN
Born 1832. Lived at Baldhu. Died 23 August 1850, aged 18 years at
Kea.
SKEWS   MARY ANN
Born 1833. Daughter of William Allen, coach builder of 7 Johnson
Street, Westminster. Married William Skews at the Parish Church of St
John the Evangelist, Westminster 1 October 1854. He was a mariner
and died 1907.
Child: Thomas Prouse Skews (1855).
SKEWES   MARY ANN
Illegitimate daughter of Jane Skewes of Hugus, Kea. Bpt Kea 6 October
1834.
SKEWES   MARY ANN
Daughter of Thomas James, butcher of Kerley, Kea. Born 1831,
Kenwyn. Married Richard Skewes at Kea Parish Church 15 May 1851.
Moved to Carharrack, Gwennap. Children: John, Mary and Fanny
Jane. In 1861 Census Returns living at Simmons Street, Gwennap and
was a dressmaker and milliner. In 1871 Census Returns had become
widowed and was living at Carharrack as a domestic. Buried Gwennap
25 October 1904, aged 73 years.
SKUES   MARY ANN
Chart 3. Daughter of Richard Skues, surgeon. Married William Edward
Cornelius, son of William Cornelius, master mariner at St Andrew's
Church, Plymouth, 20 December 1842. Issue: one daughter.
SKEWES   MARY ANN
Died 1845, Tavistock, Devon.
SKEWES   MARY ANN
Chart 36. Née Waters. Born 9 September 1846. Married Samuel
Skewes, 16 June 1870. Children: Fanny Elizabeth (1873), Elsie Mary
(1875), John Vivian (1876) and Rosa Lilian (1879). Lived in
Queensland, Australia. Died 29 April 1936, aged 89 years.
SKEWES   MARY ANN
Born 1850, Truro.
SKEWES   MARY ANN
Born 1850. Buried Crowan 29 December 1881, aged 31 years.
SKUES   MARY ANN
Married 1852, Shoreditch.
SKEWIS   MARY ANN
Born 1859, Redruth.
SKEWES   MARY ANN
Born 1860, Redruth.
SKEWIS   MARY ANN
Died 1860, Redruth.
SKEWS   MARY ANN
Married 1862, Falmouth.
SKEWS   MARY ANN
Born 1866. Married William John Skews, coal miner, 1894 in
Sunderland. Lived at Elemore Lane, Houghton-le-Spring. Children:
Mary Ann (1895) and William John (1898). Died 1932, aged 66 years.
SKUES   MARY ANN
Married 1867, Medway.

SKEWIS   MARY ANN
Died 1868, Glasgow, aged 63 years.
SKEWES   MARY ANN
Chart 18. Wife of Daniel Hodge Skewes. Born 1797, Beer Ferris, Devon.
Lived at 26 Pepper Street, Beer Ferris, Tavistock in 1851 Census
Returns. Daughter: Mary Ann Lipson born 1838, married 1863. After
Mary Ann died Daniel Hodge remarried in 1863 and also died the same
year.
SKEWES   MARY ANN
Married 1871, Plymouth.
SKEWS   MARY ANN
Married 1872, Kensington.
SKEWIS   MARY ANN
Chart 2. Daughter of William and Martha Skewis. Born 29 June 1872,
America. Married Leslie Foote. Issue: 2 daughters. Died 11 February
1934, aged 61 years.
SKEWES   MARY ANN
Married 1873, St Thomas.
SKEWS   MARY ANN
Born 1878, Liskeard.
SKEWS   MARY ANN
Born 1886, Stepney.
SKEWS   MARY ANN
Chart 41. Daughter of William John and Mary Ann (née Whysall)
Skews. Born 30 June 1895, Houghton. Married John James Cooper.
Issue: 1 son and 1 daughter. Later divorced. Married Richard Usher in
Watford, 1946. Lives at 88 Sandringham Avenue, Watford, Herts.
SKEWS   MARY ANN
Married 1905, Witham.
SKEWES   MARY ANN
Chart 2. Twin to Robert Joseph Skewes. Daughter of John Billing and
Mary Jo (née Armington) Skewes. Born 24 December 1950 in Richfield,
Utah, USA. Business and accountancy degree, University of Utah,
1978. Internal auditor with Ford Motor Company. Lived at 6051 North
Wildwood, Westland, Michigan, 48185, USA until 1980. Married
Michael Evans in Santa Ana, California, USA, January, 1981.
SKEWS   MARY ANN BROWN
Married 10 March 1828 at Old Charlton, St Luke, Kent.
SKEWES   MARY ANNA COURTIS
Chart 18. Eldest daughter of Samuel Dawe Skewes of Bere Alston,
Devon. Born 1855. Emigrated to Australia at an early age and died in
Brisbane, 5 February 1881, aged 22 years. Buried with her parents at
Bere Alston.
SKEWS   MARY ANN E.
Born 1870, Portsea. Died 1871, aged 0.
SKEWES   MARY ANN LIPSON
Daughter of Daniel Hodge and Mary A. Skewes. Born 1838. Lived at 26
Pepper Street, Beer Ferris, Bere Alston, Tavistock, Devon (1851 Census
Returns). Married 1863, Tavistock.
SKEWES   MARY ANN MANDER
Chart 12. Daughter of Henry and Harriet Skewes. Born 1854 in Cury.
Later moved to Landewednack, Lizard. Married 1876, Plymouth. Was
a witness to the wedding of her cousin Elizabeth Mary Skewes who
married at Mawgan Church 25 July 1871.
SKEWS   MARY ANN PERREN
Born 1864, Plymouth. Married 1887, Plymouth.
SKEWES   MARY ANN PETERS
Chart 30. Daughter of Thomas and Mary Skewes of Edward Street,
Truro. Born 1863. In 1871 Census Returns living with her parents at
Edward Street, Truro and also sisters Elizabeth J. and Florence and
brother Herbert. Married 1891, Truro.
SKEWIS   MARY ANN SMITH
Born 1918, New Monkland. Died 1918, New Monkland, aged 0.
SKEWIS   MARY BELL
Born 1953, College, Glasgow. Married Patrick Queen Noble, 1959 in
Dennistoun, Scotland.
SKUES   MARY BENNETT
Born 1821. Died 1869, aged 48 in Westbury. A Mary Bennett Skues,
daughter of Charles and Ann Skues (tailor) of Helston was born 15
December 1817 and christened at Wesleyan Chapel, Helston 4 January
1818.
SKEWES   MARY CAMPBELL
Born 1887, Penzance.
SKEWES   MARY E.
Born 1842, Brentford. Died 1925, aged 83 years.
SKEWES   MARY ELEANOR
Chart 26. Daughter of Robert Ernest and Elaine Helen (née Albanese)
Skewes of London, Connecticut, USA. Born 8 February 1959.
SKEWES   MARY ELIZA
Chart 12. Daughter of Frederick Tresize Skewes. Born 1886, Redruth.
Married 1909 to Sleeman in Redruth. Died in 1950's.
SKUES   MARY ELIZABETH
Chart 3. Born 1829. Née Malcolm. Married Frederick Mackenzie Skues,
Deputy Surgeon General. Children: Frederick Mackenzie, Edward,

Mary and Margaret Mackenzie. Died 1903, aged 74 years in Lewisham.

SKEWES MARY ELIZABETH
Chart 36. Daughter of George and Mary (née Dowling) Skewes. Born 22 March 1910, Uralla, New South Wales, Australia. Married Clarence Joseph Nelson. Issue: 3 daughters and 1 son. Lives at 3 Queen Street, Uralla, New South Wales, 2358, Australia.

SKEWES MARY ELIZABETH
Chart 18. Daughter of Arthur Dawe and Eva Skewes. Born 2 March 1911. Married David Polkinhorne, 4 June 1934, Plymouth. Issue: 1 daughter. Lives at 9 Grove Hill Crescent, Falmouth.

SKEWS MARY ELIZABETH
Lived at Highbury East, South Australia, in 1959 with Albert James Skewes, miner.

SKEWIS MARY ELLEN
Chart 2. Daughter of Absalom and Jane Skewis. Born August 1851, America. Married George Ladd. Issue: 6 children.

SKEWS MARY ELLEN
Married 1852, East Stonehouse.

SKEWES MARY ELLEN
Chart 17. Born 1856. Married James Skewes of Bosawsack, Constantine. Moved to 29 Cecil Street, Plymouth and later 5 Mutley Park Villas, Plymouth. Died 14 May 1939, aged 83 years at 51a Cranley Road, Westcliffe on Sea, Essex. Buried at Efford Cemetery, Rochford, Essex. James Skewes died at the Cattle Market, Yealmpton, Devonshire 24 September 1917, aged 60 years.

SKEWES MARY ELLEN
Born 1861, Newton Abbot. Married 1888, Newton Abbot.

SKEWES MARY ELLEN
Born 1864. Died 1884, aged 20 years in Redruth.

SKEWES MARY ELLEN
Born 1872, Redruth. Died 1872, aged 0.

SKEWES MARY ELLEN
Born 1879, Redruth.

SKUES MARY ELLEN
Daughter of William & Margaret Skues, Born 18 April 1897. Lived in New South Wales, Australia.

SKUES MARY EMILY
Born 1839, Truro.

SKEWES MARY EMILY
Married 1859. Redruth.

SKEWIS MARY EMMA
Chart 43. Daughter of Edwin and Louisa (née Day) Skewis, iron turner. Born 9 April 1876 at 33 Newhall Road, Brightside, Sheffield, South Yorkshire.

SKEWES MARY ETTA
Chart 10. Daughter of Jackson and Fanny (née McGlothlin) Robbins. Born 21 January 1904, California, USA. Married George Owen Skewes, 14 December 1927, California, USA. No children. Member of Escondido First Methodist Church. Member and past president of the J.B. Clark Post 149. Member of American Legion Auxiliary. Lives at 130 West 10th Avenue, Escondido, California, 92025, USA. Telephone number: (714) 745 4637.

SKUES MARY EVA LYDIA RANDOLPH MACDONALD
Chart 5. Daughter of Vivian William Skues. Born 24 April 1948 in Calcutta, India. Lives at 34 Maysenger Road, Mahwah, New Jersey, 07430, United States of America.

SKEWES MARY EVELYN HARRIET
Lived at Eyre Street, Buninyong, Sebastopol, Victoria, Australia, in 1959 and 141 Spencer Street, Sebastopol, Victoria 3356, Australia in 1980.

SKEWES MARY FANNY SOPHIA
Chart 19. Daughter of Thomas Lean Skewes. Born 1853. Died Wareham, Dorset, 1879, aged 26 years.

SKEWES MARY FLETCHER
Married 1888, Derby.

SKUES MARY GARRETT
Born 1849, St James. Married 1867, St James.

SKUES MARY GIBBS
Chart 3. Née Mackenzie. Born 1796. Married Lieut. George Skues, R.N., son of Richard and Ann Skues, 25 March 1827. Children: William Mackenzie, Richard Alexander, John Richard, Fred Mackenzie, Edward Walker, Gertrude, Eliza and Georgina Mary. Died 1881, aged 85 years.

SKEWS MARY GRACE
Born 1857, Liskeard. Married Lewis, 1880, in Liskeard. Mary was a granddaughter of Ann Cock of Green Lane, Liskeard.

SKEWS MARY HANNAH WEIGHTMAN
Chart 41. Née Rump. Born 29 November 1896. Married William John Skews of 44 Elemore Lane, Easington Lane, Hetton-le-Hole, County Durham, 21 June 1919 at Hetton-le-Hole Wesleyan Chapel. Children: Muriel (1920), Kirtley (1923), William Clifford (1925), Janet Audrey (1928), George David (1931), John Hilary (1933) and Roland Gerald (1938). William John Skews died 29 January 1955, aged 56 years. She married John Robert Blench, 16 September 1961 at St Nicholas Church, Hetton-le-Hole. Died 1 July 1979, aged 83 years.

SKUES MARY ISABELLA MACKENZIE
Chart 3. Daughter of Brigade Surgeon William Mackenzie and Margaret Skues. Born Newfoundland January 1860. Spinster. Lived at 14 Moreton Road, South Croydon. Died 14 April 1947 at Warlingham Park Hospital, Surrey, aged 87 years.

SKEWES MARY J.
Chart 12. Née Payne. Married Maurice Skewes, 1966. Children: Joanna Mary (1969) and Anthony John (1970). Lives at Laflouder, Mullion, Helston.

SKEWIS MARY JANE
Born 1864. Lived in Fore Street, Marazion. Died 1922. Buried Marazion 17 November 1922, aged 58 years.

SKEWS MARY JANE
Chart 30. Née Peters, daughter of John Peters, master mariner. Born 1835, Truro. Married Thomas Skewes at St George's, Truro 28 April 1860. In 1871 Census Returns living at Edward Street, Truro. Children: Mary Ann Peters, Herbert, Elizabeth and Florence. Died 24 April 1908 at 6 Richmond Hill, Truro, aged 73 years. Buried St Mary's, Truro 28 April 1908.

SKEWES MARY JANE
Chart 19. Daughter of Collan and Ann Skewes, miner of Lanner, Gwennap. Bpt Gwennap 17 December 1840.

SKEWES MARY JANE
Chart 12. Daughter of Edward Eudey, labourer of College Row, Camborne. Born 1842. Married James Henry Skewes, 5 March 1865 at Camborne Parish Church. Son: Harry Oswald (1865). James Henry Skewes was murdered in Central America shortly after marriage. Mary Jane then married James Gilbert, widower, son of Philip Gilbert, labourer of Camborne on 14 December 1871.

SKEWES MARY JANE
Born 1847, Redruth.

SKEWS MARY JANE
Chart 26. Née Nettle. Born 1850. Married Matthew Henry Skews at Redruth 17 August 1873. Children: John (1874), Matthew (1876) and Martin (1886). Died 1929, aged 79 years.

SKEWIS MARY JANE
Born 1855. Died Coatbridge, Scotland 1907, aged 52 years.

SKEWES MARY JANE
Chart 38. Née Reynolds, of Cornwall. Born 1857. Married Richard Skewes at Moonta, South Australia 6 April 1882. Children: Richard James, Edgar William, Albert Victor, Horace Henry, Stanley Victor, Albert Milton, Harold Edwin, Sydney Howard, Clarice Arcadia, Charles Leslie, George Percy, Ernest Seymour. Died 25 November 1926, Adelaide, South Australia. Buried in West Terrace Cemetery, Adelaide.

SKEWIS MARY JANE
Born 1858, Redruth.

SKEWES MARY JANE
Daughter of James and Margaret Skewes of Goldsithney; groom. Born 17 December 1863. Bpt 28 May 1865 at Perranuthnoe Parish Church.

SKEWES MARY JANE
Married 1863, Redruth.

SKEWS MARY JANE
Born 1868, Liskeard.

SKEWS MARY JANE
Chart 41. Born 1871, Guisborough.

SKEWES MARY JANE
Chart 12. Daughter of William James Skewes, labourer of Mawgan in Meneage. Born 1871. Married William Thomas Rowe (24), grocer of Mawgan and son of William Hocking Rowe, labourer at Mawgan in Meneage Church 2 November 1893, in presence of William Skewes.

SKEWIS MARY JANE
Married 1873, Old Monkland, Scotland.

SKEWS MARY JANE
Born 1876, Redruth.

SKEWS MARY JANE
Born 8 January 1880, Mineral Point, Wisconsin, USA. Died 15 February 1928. Buried in Jackson Cemetery, Mineral Point.

SKEWES MARY JANE
Married 1882, Redruth.

SKEWES MARY JANE
Married 1888, St Austell.

SKEWS MARY JANE
Married 1892, Redruth.

SKEWS MARY JANE
Married 1898, Redruth.

SKEWES MARY JANE
Chart 38. Née Gilles. Married Jeffrey William Skewes 31 January 1970. Children: Jodie Ann (1971) and Michael John (1979). Lives at 358 Brookfield Avenue, Broken Hill, 2705, New South Wales, Australia.

SKEWES MARY JOLLY
Chart 30. Daughter of Henry and Catherine Skewes. Born 27 February 1794. Bpt Kea 17 August 1794. Married Thomas Gilbert at Kenwyn Parish Church 3 July 1825; in presence of Thomas Skewes.

SKEWS   MARY K.
Mother's maiden name Eva Mary Barrett. Born 1917, Plymouth. Married Todd in Gloucester, 1948.

SKEWIS   MARY LANGMEAD
Chart 33. Daughter of Robert Northcott, farmer. Born 1839. Married Trebilcock and later made a widow. Married Daniel Skewis at Register Office, St Thomas, 19 June 1877. Died at the Post Office, Totnes, Devon, 4 February 1912, aged 73 years.

SKEWES   MARY LEAN
Daughter of Colin and Ann Skewes. Bpt 13 September 1824, Mold, Flint.

SKEWIS   MARY LEHR
Born 7 October 1876, Shullsburg, Wisconsin, USA. Married to Clarence G. Skewis. Died 7 May 1971, aged 94 years. Buried in Shullsburg Cemetery.

SKEWS   MARY LILIAN
Born 1891, Bethnal Green. Married Sutton in Poplar, London, 1913.

SKEWS   MARY LOUISA
Born 1889. Married Theodore Thomas, 1915, in Preston.

SKEWS   MARY LOUISA T.
Born 1878, East Stonehouse. Married in Brentford in 1900.

SKEWIS   MARY LUCINDA
Chart 2. Daughter of Francis Harry and Mary Jane Skewis. Born 28 December 1951, America. Married Michael D. Jergenssen 18 June 1977.

SKEWES   MARY MARGARET
Chart 50. Born 12 December 1882. Lived at 1 Channel View Terrace, Redruth. Married Alfred Thomas Bird (24), butcher of 2 Lansdowne Terrace, Newquay, son of Sydney Bird, engine driver, at Redruth Methodist Church 11 April 1914.

SKEWES   MARY MARGERY
Chart 36. Daughter of Richard Charles and Ada Jane (née Collins) Skewes. Married James Henry Nile, 1940, Redruth. Lives at 14 Pendarves Road, Camborne.

SKEWES   MARY MAUDE
Lives at 47 Scrivenor Street, O'Connor, 2601, Tasmania, Australia. Storekeeper.

SKEWES   MARY MILDRED
Chart 36. Née Rooney. Married Reginald John Skewes, compositor. Children: Coral Skewes, Valda Skewes, Shirley Skewes and Noel Skewes. Lives at 41 North Street, Tamworth, 2340, New South Wales, Australia.

SKEWES   MARY MILLAR
Lives at O'Connor Street, Uranquinty, 2650, New South Wales, Australia with Andrew John Skewes, technician.

SKEWES   MARY MIRIAM
Lived at 205 Springvale Road, Mitcham, Victoria, Australia in 1959 with Horace Raymond Skewes. Now lives at 9 Chelsea Street, Brighton, 3186, Victoria, Australia.

SKEWIES   MARY MURRAY B.
Born 1921. Died Carluke, Scotland, 1963, aged 42 years.

SKEWES   MARY ODGERS
Chart 11. Daughter of James and Alice (née Hocking) Skewes of Camborne. Born 1839. Bpt Camborne 10 April 1839.

SKEWES   MARY P.
Worked at Health Foods, 8109 South Vermont Avenue, Los Angeles, USA in 1939.

SKEWES   MARY S.
Born 1864. Died Kerrier 1948, aged 84 years.

SKEWIS   MARY SAMPSON
Born 1838, Penzance.

SKUES   MARY SOPHIA
Chart 8. Born 1843. Née Birch. Married George Henry Skues at St Pancras Church 13 April 1862. Children: Lucy Sophia, John Gilbert, George Henry, Walter Edward, Harold Frederick Claude, Alexander James and Evelyn Rose. Died 1909, aged 66 years, Edmonton.

SKUES   MARY THERESA
Chart 3. Born 1860. Spinster. Daughter of Fred Mackenzie and Mary Skues. Lived at 16 Riggindale Road, Streatham, London, Died at 4 Gravel Walk, Cullompton, Devon 4 May 1944, aged 83 years.

SKEWES   MARY TREZIZE
Born 1866, Helston. Died 1866, aged 0.

SKEWES   MARY VERONICA
Chart 12. Daughter of Harry Oswald and Emily Ann Skewes of 17 Moor Street, Camborne. Bpt Camborne 25 November 1899. Married William Henry Cockram (56), widower, station master of Congresbury, son of Henry Cockram, carrier at Camborne 19 July 1938.

SKEWS   MARY WILKINS
Born 1851, Truro.

SKEWS   MARY WILLIAMS
Chart 6. Daughter of Peter and Mary Skewes of Kea, miner. Bpt Kea 19 February 1827. Married 1844, Truro.

SKEWIS   MASON
Chart 2. Son of Raymond and Lottie Skewis. Born 31 January 1912, United States of America. Married Clara Long. Children: Linda and Donna.

SKEWES   MATILDA
Daughter of Henry and Margaret Skewes. Bpt Camborne 7 May 1809.

SKEWS   MATILDA
Daughter of Joseph Skews of Tremar Combe, Liskeard. Born 1872. Married Edward Stephens of Silver Plume, Colorado in Denver 18 May 1899.

SKEWES   MATILDA
Daughter of Henry Skewes, farmer, deceased. Married at Camborne Parish Church 3 August 1874 to Robert Goodfellow, of Mylor, widower and farmer, son of Charles Goodfellow, farmer, deceased.

SKEWES   MATILDA
Chart 34. Born 1880. Married Alfred John Skewes. Lived at: Pengelly's Row, Illogan (1922), Mayne's Row, Tuckingmill (1932), Bartles Row, Tuckingmill (1949) and 99 Pendarves Street, Tuckingmill. Children: Alfred John, Sylvia Doreen, Matilda Joan and Edward Morley. Was a member of Tuckingmill Wesleyan Church and of its Women's Bright Hour. Died 24 April 1958, aged 78 years at Barncoose Hospital, Redruth. Funeral service conducted by her grandson, Rev A.J. Vincent.

SKUES   MATILDA JANE
Married 1876, Chippenham

SKEWES   MATILDA JOAN
Chart 36. Youngest daughter of Alfred John and Matilda Skewes of Bartles Row, Tuckingmill. Mother's maiden name Hill. Born 1918, Redruth. Married A.C. James Ernest Polkinghorne at Tuckingmill Methodist Church 3 August 1940. She was given away by her brother Alfred John Skewes of Mullion, Helston.

SKEWS   MATILDA SARAH
Born 1879, Bethnal Green. Married 1912 to Rolph in Bethnal Green.

SKEWYS   MATTHEUS
M.P. for Helston Borough 1407.

SKEWYS   MATTHEW
Chart 1. Son of John Skewys. Lord of Skewys, St Wenn, 1386 and Cury. Married Mary, daughter of Andrew Ferners of Trelowarren. Son: Matthew Skewys. Grandson John Skewys; great grandson John Skewys, lawyer. Matthew witnessed a charter dated at Merthen on 12 May 1398.

SKEWYS   MATTHEW
Chart 1. Son of John and Fortesse Skewys. Married Mary, sister of John Heleman. Son: John Skewys.

SKEWYS   MATTHEW
Chart 1. Son of John and Mary Skewys. Married Margaret Trevery (Trener). Son: John Skewys, who married Johan, daughter of Richard Tomyowe and had a son John Skewys who married Katherine, daughter of John Trethurffe and widow of John Reskymer, but died without issue. Family crest: Gul, a Chevron Or between three quivvers Or (*Memorandums in Heraldry*, 1740. Kept at Penzance Library). MP for Borough of Helston, 1407.

SKEWES   MATTHEW
Chart 10. Son of Digory and Margery Skewes. Bpt Kenwyn 9 January 1774. Buried at Chacewater 28 March 1838, aged 66 years.

SKEWES   MATTHEW
Chart 10. Son of Digory Skewes. Bpt Kea 22 March 1796. Born 1796. Married Mary Jeffrey at Kea 22 June 1819. Was originally a miner, later an innkeeper at The Royal Oak, Chacewater. Children: Elizabeth, Mary and Matthew. Died 27 September 1856, aged 60. Buried Chacewater 28 September 1856. Mary died 17 November 1882; buried Chacewater 20 November 1882, aged 84 years.

SKEWS   MATTHEW
Married at St Mary's Whitechapel, Stepney 27 January 1828.

SKEWS   MATTHEW
Born 1829, Chacewater. Buried Chacewater 20 November 1831, aged 2 years.

SKEWES   MATTHEW
Chart 10. Son of Digory and Sophia Skewes. Born 24 June 1827. Bpt Truro Wesleyan Chapel 28 March 1837. Lived at Dobwalls, Liskeard with his parents (1851 Census Returns) and also sister Mary and brother Samuel.

SKEWS   MATTHEW
Chart 41. Son of Peter Skews, miner. Born 1831. Miner. Married Mary Hattam (19) at Kenwyn Parish Church 4 December 1852. Mary was daughter of John Hattam of Chacewater. She died March 1861, aged 28 years. Matthew married Betsy Tresider at St Breock, Wadebridge, 13 July 1861. She was daughter of John Tresider, labourer of Wadebridge. Children: William John (1862), Matthew (1864) and Thomas (1867).

SKEWES   MATTHEW
Died 1838, Truro.

SKEWES   MATTHEW
Son of John and Margery (née Jenkin) Skewes. Born 14 April 1843, Foundry Row, Redruth. Died 1898, aged 55 years.

SKEWES   MATTHEW
Died 1843, Redruth.

SKEWES   MATTHEW
Born Cornwall. Emigrated to South Australia. Married Selina Ann Annear. Children: Thomas Henry, Oswald, Matthew, Kenneth, Jack, William, Ada, Clara, Lillian and Selina.

SKEWES MATTHEW
Only son of Matthew Skewes of Chacewater. Married Anna Maria Nettle daughter of late Mr Nettle of Redruth at Oporto, Portugal 15 September 1855. Worked at Polhol Mines. A son born 24 July 1856.

SKEWES MATTHEW
Married 1856, Liskeard.

SKEWS MATTHEW
Died 1857, Liskeard

SKEWS MATTHEW
Chart 41. Born 26 June 1858. Son of John and Juliana (née Ley) Skews, copper miner of St Cleer, Liskeard. In 1871 Census Returns lived at Common Moor, St Cleer. Later moved north to Durham and lived at 17 Best View Terrace, Chester Road, Shiney Row, Houghton le Spring, County Durham. Miner. Married 1911 in Durham to Amelia . . . . . Died 17 December 1934, aged 76 years.

SKEWS MATTHEW
Born 1861. Lived in Grass Valley, California, USA in 1870.

SKEWS MATTHEW
Chart 41. Son of Matthew and Betsy (née Tresider) Skews of St Allen, miner. Born 1864. Bpt 6 December 1864 at Bible Christian Chapel, St Allen Lane. Died Truro, 1873, aged 8 years.

SKEWS MATTHEW
Born 1875, Liskeard.

SKEWS MATTHEW
Chart 10. Born 1876. Son of Matthew Skews, miner of Illogan. Married Elizabeth Roberts, 10 December 1898. Elizabeth was daughter of William Edward Roberts, carter. Marriage was at Illogan Parish Church in the presence of Elizabeth Skews.

SKEWS MATTHEW
Born 1878, Easington.

SKEWS MATTHEW
Married 1895, Redruth.

SKEWES MATTHEW
Living at Rose Row, Redruth 1897/1906.

SKEWS MATTHEW
Living at Carnarthen Street, Camborne, 1897.

SKEWS MATTHEW
Living at Illogan Highway, 1906.

SKEWES MATTHEW
Lived at Stanhope Street, Malvern East, Australia in 1913 with Alice Edith Skewes. Warehouseman.

SKEWS MATTHEW
Married Taylor in Sunderland, 1920.

SKEWES MATTHEW CHARLES
Chart 36. Son of Donald Lloyd and Elizabeth Blair (née Fisher) Skewes. Born 8 November 1973, Tamworth, New South Wales, Australia.

SKEWES MATTHEW CHARLES
Chart 2. Son of Charles Armington and Cindy Skewes. Born 7 October 1976, Bountiful, Utah, United States of America.

SKEWES MATTHEW HENRY
Son of Richard and Agnes Skewes of Kea. Bpt Kenwyn 21 May 1826. Miner.

SKEWS MATTHEW HENRY
Chart 10. Born 1850. Son of William and Mary Skews of Illogan Downs. Miner. Married Mary Jane Nettle (22), daughter of Edward Nettle, miner of Blights Row, Redruth, 17 August 1873. In 1871 Census Returns he was living with his parents at Illogan Highway, also brothers John, Edwin and Martin and sisters Sarah and Emma. After marriage lived at 3 Bellvue, Redruth. Children: John (1874), Matthew (1876) and Martin (1886). Died 1921, aged 70 years. Mary Jane (born 1850) died 27 March 1929, aged 79 years.

SKEWS MATTHEW HENRY
Born 1882, Redruth. Died 1956, aged 74 years in Durham North.

SKEWES MATTHEW HENRY
Chart 40. Son of William and Laura Skewes. Mother's maiden name Allen. Born 16 September 1923 at Perranuthnoe. Married Ann Morgan in Eltham, London, 11 October 1945. Children: Carol (1946), Susan Barbara (1949), Jill Alexandra (1953) and William Clive (1954). Lives at Trewince, St Martin, Helston. Tel No: 0326 23304.

SKEWES MATTHEW HERBERT
Lives at 8 Claire Street, Bentleigh, 3204, Victoria, Australia with Amelia Madeline Skewes and Neville Herbert Skewes. Salesman.

SKEWES MATTHEW JAMES
Mother's maiden name Thomas. Born 1979, Penzance.

SKEWS MATTHEW JOHN
Chart 10. Second son of John and Sarah Skews of 5 Canfield Place, Plain-an-Gwarry, Redruth; master bootmaker. Born 7 August 1910. Bpt 26 October 1910, Wesleyan/Methodist Circuit, Redruth. Attended Trewirgie School, Redruth and later Redruth County School from 19 September 1923. Married Kathleen Thomas, 6th daughter of the late Mr & Mrs J. Thomas of Union Street, Camborne at St George's Methodist Church, Truro 16 December 1933. No children.

SKEWS MATTHEW LEE
Married 1878, Redruth.

SKEWS MATTHEW THOMAS
Son of Matthew and Eliza Ann of Illogan Highway; miner. Born 1899. Bpt Camborne 10 September 1899.

SKEWES MATTHEW VERE
Chart 36. Son of Robert Skewes. Born 22 January 1970, New South Wales, Australia.

SKEWS MATTHEW WARNE
Chart 10. Son of John and Harriet Skews of Kerley, Kea; miner. Born 1851. Bpt Chacewater 11 January 1855.

SKEWS MATTIE
Daughter of Harry and Mary Skewes of North Hempstead, Nassau, New York, USA. Born May 1893, New York.

SKEWS MAUD
Chart 15. Daughter of Amos Skews. Born 1898, Stoke Devonport. Married Browne, 1934.

SKEWS MAUD
Born 1907, Strood, Kent. Died 1917, aged 9 years.

SKEWES MAUD
Chart 12. Daughter of James Henry and Maud Mary Skewes. Born 1911, Helston. Married Alfred Phillips. Issue: one son. Lived in Perranporth. Now dead.

SKEWS MAUD ANN
Born 1872. Lived at 1 Penmere Hill, Falmouth. Died 8 April 1943, aged 71 years.

SKEWS MAUD ANNIE
Lived at Packsaddle, Mabe with Henry and Lional James Skewes in 1922 and 1932.

SKUES MAUD C.
Born 1879. Died Honiton, Devon, 1938, aged 59 years.

SKUES MAUD CHARLOTTE
Born 1877, Eton.

SKUES MAUD EVELYN
Chart 8. Daughter of Walter Edward Skues. Born 1909, Shoreditch. Married Ernest T. Wackett, 1938, Romford, Essex.

SKEWS MAUD EVELYN
Lives at 15 Gillan Street, Norman Park, 4170, Queensland, Australia with John Vivian Skewes.

SKEWES MAUD ISOBEL
Chart 36. Née Curtis. Married Henry Tom Holdsworth Skewes. Children: Lorraine, Neil Holdsworth and Kay. Lived at 100 York Street, Warrenheip, Victoria, Australia in 1959. Now lives at 422 York Street, Ballarat, 3350, Victoria, Australia.

SKEWS MAUD JANE
Daughter of William and Jane (née Northey). Skewes. Born 19 July 1877 at Houghton, Michigan, USA. Married Fred J. Hamill. Died 1964, aged 87 years.

SKEWS MAUD MARY
Chart 10. Born 1881. Married Peter Skews, 1901. Children: Peter (1906), Violet Irene (1913), Charles R. (1916), Thomas Henry (1919), Mabel J. (1921) and Stanley (1924). Died 1962, St Austell, aged 81 years.

SKEWES MAUD MARY
Chart 12. Daughter of Captain Richard and Maria (née Stripp) Skewes of Real del Monte, Mexico. Born January 1884. Died 26 September 1884, aged 8 months. Buried in the English Cemetery, Real del Monte, Mexico.

SKEWES MAUD MARY
Chart 12. Married James Henry Skewes, 1898. Children: Arthur, Mabel, Elizabeth Mary, Bertram, William Frank, Olive Irene, Lilia, Maud, Janie, John H. and James Harry. Lived at Golla, Callestick, Perranzabuloe. Died 1946, aged 70 years.

SKEWIS MAUD RAY
Born 1886, Islington, London.

SKEWES MAUREEN
Chart 12. Daughter of Thomas Henry Skewes. Mother's maiden name Jory. Born 1937, Redruth. Married 1958 to Thomas in Redruth.

SKEWS MAUREEN J.
Chart 15. Daughter of Stanley Gregory Skews. Mother's maiden name Fishleigh. Born 1959, Liskeard.

SKEWES MAURICE
Chart 12. Son of William John and Bessie Skewes. Mother's maiden name Curnow. Born 1933, Helston. Married Mary J. Payne, 1966. Lives at Laflouder, Mullion, Helston. Children: Joanna Mary (1969) and Anthony John (1970).

SKEWES MAVIS E.
Lived at Wellfield House, Cadgwith, Helston in 1969 with Arthur R. Skewes.

SKEWES MAX
Chart 36. Son of William Vere and Annie Rebecca (née Strain) Skewes. Born 3 July 1942. Bachelor. Lives at 16 Hyman Street, Tamworth, 2350, New South Wales, Australia. Printer.

SKEWES MAXWELL
Chart 36. Son of Leslie Skewes, wrestler. Mother's maiden name Lilian Body. Born 1942. Married 1966, in Penzance to Jennifer J. Wills. Child: Fiona (1969).

Mervyn Leigh Skues

SKEWES MAXWELL CHARLES
Chart 36. Son of Percy and Muriel (née Norris) Skewes. Born 1 June 1947. Married Cheryl Anne Sproule, 13 January 1968. Children: Jason Maxwell (1971) and Tania Maree (1968). Lives at 12 Julia Place, Moree, 2400, New South Wales, Australia.

SKEWES MAY
Chart 36. Daughter of Robert Northey and Sarah (née Connell) Skewes. Born New South Wales, Australia.

SKEWES MAY DOROTHY
Chart 36. Daughter of Archer William and Elsie May (née Handley) Skewes. Born 1 July 1937. Clerk/typist at Queensland University, Brisbane. Lives at 355 Swann Road, St Lucia, 4067, Queensland, Australia.

SKEWS MAY LOUISA
Chart 15. Née Mallet. Born 1892. Married John Skews at Liskeard Parish Church 1918. Children: Morley D.J. (1919), Constance M. (1920) and Marion Rhoda (1923). Died 26 June 1937, aged 44 years.

SKEWES MAY MARGARET
Daughter of Samuel Skewes of Ford's Row, Redruth. Born 24 June 1882, Redruth. Attended Redruth East End School; admitted 20 July 1885.

SKEWES MELANIE ANNE
Chart 25. Daughter of Joseph Frederick and Doreen (née Isaac) Skewes. Born 2 July 1961. Lives at 12 Walnut Walk, Stretford, Manchester M32 9AQ. Telephone number: 061 865 5748.

SKEWES MELINDA
Chart 10. Daughter of Ronald Lanier and Patricia (née Fountain) Skewes of USA. Born 29 February 1972, Manassas, Virginia, 22110, Virginia, USA.

SKEWES MELINDA IRENE
Chart 14. Daughter of Arthur Russell and Helen Roberta (née Horr) Skewes. Born 25 October 1955, Racine, Wisconsin, USA. Educated at Bryan Station, Lexington, Kentucky and Transylvania University, Lexington. Graduated with B.A. in Physical Education, 1978. Married Gregory H. Martelli 17 June 1978 at Lexington First United Methodist Church, Lexington, Kentucky, 40505. Now lives at 309 Tulane Drive, Lexington, Kentucky, 40502.

SKEWS MELVIN
Mother's maiden name Thompson. Born 1952, Durham North. Married Snowden, 1973. Daughter: Rachel Anne (1980).

Maxwell Charles Skewes and his family of New South Wales, Australia

SKEWS MERCY
Married Milton, 1901.

SKEWES MERCY
Chart 36. Née Davis, Married Leonard Richard Skewes, New South Wales, Australia.

SKEWES MERIDITH FAE
Lives at 62 Harris Road, Elliminyt, 3249, Victoria, Australia with John Reginald Skewes, accountant,

SKEWIS MERRIL
Chart 2. Daughter of John Rule and Jane Skewis of United States of America.

SKEWES MERRIL JOY
Chart 36. Daughter of Percy and Muriel (née Norris) Skewes. Born 11 July 1955. Lives at 40 Mahony Avenue, Tamworth, 2340, New South Wales, Australia. Stenographer. Spinster.

SKUES MERVYN LEIGH
Chart 5. Son of Leigh Harold and Ethel Maude (née Poynton) Skues. Born 27 May 1944, Melbourne, Australia. Twice married. 1) Eileen Bell 10 December 1966. One daughter, Nicole Elizabeth (1971). Divorced 1977. 2) Sylvia Marie Buttie, 1 September 1979. One son, Jason Leigh Christopher (1980). Lives at 5 Viridis Place, Endeavour Hills, Melbourne, 3802, Australia.

SKEWES MERVYN ROY
Chart 36. Son of Charles Harold Vivian and Emiline (née Lamphee) Skewes. Born 12 October 1919, Cometvale, Western Australia. Married Evelyn Neilson at Kalgoorlie Methodist Church, 1944. Child: Wayne (1945). Died 1945, aged 26 years.

SKEWES MERVYN WAYNE
Lives at 3184 Bonney Avenue, Clay, 4011, Queensland, Australia.

SKEWES MERYLE KAY
Chart 36. Daughter of Douglas William and Elsie May (née Smith) Skewes. Born 21 August 1945. Western Australia. Married Duncan MacKellar 24 September 1967. Issue: one daughter.

SKEWES MICHAEL
Son of John and Catherine Skewes. Bpt 23 March 1722. Buried St Buryan 28 June 1722, infant.

SKUSE MICHAEL
Son of Horace Sydney and Ada (née Tomsett) Skuse. Born 1931. Married Mary Armstrong 1957. Issue: one son, Jeremy Skuse.

SKEWS MICHAEL
Mother's maiden name Skews. Born 1951, Birmingham

SKEWES MICHAEL
Chart 2. Son of David Neal and Patricia Skewes. Born 1961, Missouri, United States of America.

SKEWES MICHAEL BRUCE
Chart 42. Lives c/o 724 Squadron, R.A.N.A.S. Nowra Hill, 2540, New South Wales, Australia. Son of Jack and Shirley Beryl (née Callaghan) Skewes. Born 6 June 1953. Married Dianne Dickson, 24 November 1973, Fairfield, Australia. Children: Micheale (1974), Derek (1976) and Paul (1979).

SKEWIS MICHAEL C.
Born 1962, Dundee East, Scotland.

SKEWS MICHAEL D.
Chart 17. Son of William Albert and Jean (née Leach) Skews. Born 15 June 1957, Bury.

SKUES MICHAEL DAVID E.
Chart 7. Son of Roydon Thomas Skues. Mother's maiden name Valerie Cooke. Born 6 October 1972, Sussex. Lives at 16 Lower Drive, Seaford, Sussex. Telephone no: 0323 894436.

SKEWES MICHAEL DOUGLAS
Son of Douglas George Skewes. Born 12 November 1964, Burbank, Los Angeles, California, USA.

SKEWIS MICHAEL IAN
Chart 50. Mother's maiden name Irene Fox. Son of James Airns Skewis. Born 5 April 1947, Hull. Married Audrey Humphries (she born 10 June 1948) in Hull 10 December 1966. Children: Andrea Dawn (1966) and Richard Darren (1969). Lives at 3 Woodhall Street, Stoneferry Road, Hull.
Served with Royal Air Force Regiment (1965-1970) including three years in Cyprus (1967-1970). Now a tool setter in Hull. Telephone number: 0482 217770.

SKEWES MICHAEL J.
Mother's maiden name Williams. Born 1949, Redruth.

SKEWS MICHAEL J.
Chart 10. Mother's maiden name Soady. Born 1950, St Austell. Married Clifft in St Austell, 1974. Children: Lisa Jayne (1974) and Daniel Richard (1977).

SKEWES MICHAEL JAMES
Lives at 41 Exeter Road, Wahroonga, 2078, NSW, Australia.

SKEWES MICHAEL JAMES
Chart 2. Son of Eric William and Pamela (née Drummond) Skewes. Born 22 June 1957, Ringwood, Victoria, Australia. Now lives at Lot 9, Cambridge Road, Mooralbark, Victoria, 3356, Australia. Pottery artist.

SKEWES MICHAEL JAMES
Mother's maiden name Williams. Born 1972, Redruth.

SKEWES MICHAEL JAMES
Son of Edward Nelson Skewes. Born 25 May 1977, New York, USA.

SKEWES MICHAEL JAMES
Chart 36. Son of James Edward and Agnes Veronica Skewes. Born 4 October 1936, Sydney, Australia. Married Millie van Naerssen 4 January 1964. Children: Monique Therese (1965) and David Michael (1968). Lives at 27 Cricklewood Drive, Templestone, 3107, Victoria, Australia.

SKEWES MICHAEL JAMES PATRICK
Chart 10. Son of Richard Albert and Ann Marie (née Millar) Skewes. Born 8 January 1967, Hamilton, Ontario, Canada. Lives at 1207 Royal York, Islington, Toronto, Canada.

SKEWES MICHAEL JESS
Chart 14. Son of Charles J. and Loretta Jean (née Swanson) Skewes. Born 1952, Wisconsin, USA. Married Debra Erickson. Later divorced. Married Kris Simpson at Bethania Lutheran Church.

SKEWES MICHAEL JOHN
Chart 38. Son of Jeffrey William and Mary Jane (née Gilles) Skewes. Born 3 September 1979. Lives at 358 Brookfield Avenue, Broken Hill, 2705, New South Wales, Australia.

SKEWES MICHAEL JOHN
Lives at Kinnersley Avenue, Doncaster, Victoria, 3356, Australia.

SKEWES MICHAEL LEIGH
Chart 36. Son of Robert Keith and Shirley Cicely (née Jacobs) Skewes. Born 19 October 1957. Lives at Laurel Street, Kootingal, 2352, New South Wales, Australia.

SKEWS MICHAEL R.
Chart 10. Son of Martin Rex and Miriam (née Martin) Skews. Born 1948, Eton.

SKEWES MICHAEL THOMAS
Chart 10. Son of Richard Herbert and Alice Skewes of Ontario, Canada. Born 26 May 1946. Married Mary ..... Children: Andrea Alice (1977) and Aaron Michael (1979).

SKEWES MICHEALE
Chart 50. Daughter of Michael Bruce and Dianne (née Dickson) Skewes. Born 17 April 1974, Fairfield, Australia. Now lives c/o 724 Squadron, R.A.N.A.S, Nowra Hill, 2540, New South Wales, Australia.

SKEWIS MICHELLE
Born 1967, Glasgow, Scotland.

SKEWES MICHELLE CLAIR
Chart 12. Daughter of Christopher John and Hazel (née Williams) Skewes. Born 26 June 1980. Twin to David John Skewes. Lives at 23 St John's Terrace, Helston. Tel no: 03265 2064.

SKEWS MICHELLE DEBORAH
Chart 10. Daughter of Martin C. and Angela (née Daniels) Skews. Born 1977, St Austell.

SKEWS MICHELLE JAYNE
Chart 10. Daughter of Peter B. Skews. Mother's maiden name Blight. Born 1967, St Austell.

SKEWES MICHELLE LOUISE
Chart 36. Daughter of Noel James and Veronica Elaine (née Cooper) Skewes. Born 27 November 1971. Lives at "Bantry", Watson's Creek, via Bendemeer, 2352, New South Wales, Australia.

SKEWS MICHELE ROSEMARY
Chart 15. Daughter of Derek Thomas and Linda (née McManamon)

Skews. Born Glasgow Royal National Hospital 28 September 1970. Lives at 4 Moonsfield, Callington, Cornwall.

SKEWIS MILDRED E.
Chart 50. Daughter of Samuel and Laura Skewis. Mother's maiden name Waters. Born 1914, Haverfordwest. Married Hawkins in Haverfordwest, 1940.

SKEWIS MILDRED E.
Married Morrow in Wellington, 1947.

SKEWES MILLICENT M.
Married Phillips in Truro, 1941.

SKEWES MINNIE
Born 1868. Married Josiah Skewes in Hampstead, 1903. Lived at 212 Ballards Lane, Finchley, London. Issue: one son James Eldred (1904). Died 14 January 1937, aged 69 years.

SKEWES MINNIE
Daughter of Richard and Elizabeth Ann Skewes of Carharrack, Gwennap; miner who worked in Mexico. Born 13 March 1867, Gwennap. Bpt Primitive Methodist; Perranwell Circuit 5 January 1845. Lived at Croft Row, Gwennap. Married Rooke Collins at St Andrew's Church, Redruth 19 August 1887.

SKEWES MINNIE
Born 1869. Née Blewett. Married Richard Skewes 23 May 1908 at the United Methodist Church, Redruth. Richard had previously been married to Bessie Eddy. Lived at 1 Ford's Row, Redruth. Died 19 August 1963, aged 94 years at Barncoose Hospital, Redruth. A (SH) £147. Buried in St Day Cemetery, Redruth.

SKEWS MINNIE
Chart 36. Born 1879. Married Richard Skewes, 1906. Lived at 36 Adelaide Road, Redruth. Died 8 November 1965, aged 86 years at Barncoose Hospital, Redruth.

SKEWS MINNIE
Born 17 July 1884. Died 1971, aged 87 years in Birmingham.

SKEWS MINNIE
Chart 41. Daughter of Thomas and Ada (née Sheldon) Skews. Born 1889, Barnsley, South Yorkshire. Married 1911 to Harry Harper. Issue: 3 sons and 2 daughters.

SKEWS MINNIE
Married 1896, Bromley, Kent.

SKUES MINNIE MACKENZIE
M.A. Chart 3. Born 27 December 1870 at Sliema, Malta. Daughter of William Mackenzie and Margaret Ayre Skues. Private tuition at Haberdashers Aske's Girls School, Hatcham (latterly as a pupil teacher); Newnham 1892-1895; Drapers Scholar, 1893; Oxford Educational Diploma 1905 MA (TCD); Assistant Mistress at Pendleton High School, 1895-1897; St Leonard's School, St Andrews, 1897-1899; Bradford Girls Grammar School 1899-1904; Headmistress of Newark High School 1905-1916; Headmistress of Rugby High School 1919-1926; Assistant Mistress in temporary posts 1918-1919; at Queen's College, Barbados, 1926-1929.
She proceeded to a degree in the University of Dublin from the University of Cambridge (1906) MA.
After retirement lived at 20 Copers Cope Road, Beckenham, Kent. Later moved to Yew Tree House, Stafford Street, Market Drayton, Shropshire. Died 21 June 1962, aged 91 years.

SKEWS MINNIE SARAH
Born 1876, Gravesend, Kent.

SKEWES MIRIAM
Chart 2. Mexican. Daughter of Aaron and Maria (née Navarrete) Skewes. Born Pachuca, Mexico 6 June 1970. Twin to Isela Skewes.

SKUES MIRIAM M.
Chart 9. Daughter of Philip Ernest Skues. Mother's maiden name Pinto. Born 1937, Southwark.

SKEWIS MOIRA E.
Married in Beverley to May, 1975.

SKEWIS MOLLIE
Chart 50. Born Pennsylvania, USA 12 February 1874. Married James Skewis, 1896. Child: Joseph H. (1899). In 1900 lived at 12, Division Street, Lawrence, Pennsylvania, USA.

SKEWES MONA DAVIE
Born 1906, Penzance. Married Mayrick, 1935, Penzance.

SKEWES MONA JOYCE
Chart 38. Daughter of Charles Leslie and Ellen Jane (née Ritter) Skewes. Born 16 May 1920. Married Kenneth Frank Brown, 16 January 1943. Issue: 3 daughters and 2 sons. Lives at 36, Clement Street, Plympton Park, Adelaide, 5038, South Australia.

SKEWES MONICA DORIS
Lived at Prince Street, Grange, Enoggera, Queensland, Australia in 1959 with Edwin Charles Skewes.

SKEWS MONICA E.
Mother's maiden name Parsons. Born 1931, Cannock. Married Phillips in Birmingham, 1950.

SKEWS MONICA O.
Mother's maiden name Skews. Born 1938, Totnes. Married Goring in Chesterfield, 1960.

SKEWES MONIQUE THERESE

Chart 36. Daughter of Michael James and Millie (née van Naerssen) Skewes. Born Victoria, Australia 21 November 1965.

SKEWES MORLEY
Chart 14. Adopted son of James Lugg and Jane Skewes of America. Married with issue.

SKEWS MORLEY DAVID JOHN
Chart 15. Son of John and May Louisa (née Mallet) Skews, of 1 Friends Place, Pound Street, Liskeard. Born 18 May 1919. Bpt Liskeard Wesleyan/Methodist Church 9 July 1919. Died 1927.

SKUES MORRIS
Born 1848. Son of George Skues, engine driver. Married 15 November 1877 at Register Office, Doncaster, South Yorkshire to Harriett Wardell, (22) daughter of Abraham Wardell, miner. Lived at Princess Street, Doncaster.

Mortier Boulden and Gladys Skewes

SKEWES MORTIER BOULDEN
Chart 14. Son of George Edwin & Emma (née Hagerdorn) Skewes. Born 6 November 1909, Luverne, Minnesota, USA. BA., University of Minnesota, 1930. LLb (Bachelor of Laws), 1932. Married Mildred Gladys Pettes, 28 December 1935. Children: Mary (1939) and William Frederick (1945). Admitted to Minnesota Bar 1932. General practice law, Luverne 1934 to date. Municipal Judge, Luverne 1935-1939. County Attorney 1939-1959. Director Northwestern State Bank of Luverne (Vice President 1958-1978); Secretary/Director A.R. Wood Manufacturing Company; Norwood Products Company, Luverne; Fire Apparatus Company; Siouxland Broadcasting Inc; Luverne Farm Store; Northco Ventilating Company.
Member of Board of Governors of the Minnesota State Bar Association for 15 years. Member of Governor's Committee on Mental Health. Past member of the Southwestern Minnesota Mental Health Centre; Treasurer of the Board of Directors, Independent School District 671, Luverne 1959-1972.
Secretary and member of board of North Central University Centre, Sioux Falls; Board of Directors Maplewood Cemetery Association; past President of Luverne Library Board; Board of Regents Augustana College, Sioux Falls, 1975 to date, and also Secretary.
Member of Minnesota County Attorneys Association (Past President), Minnesota Bar Association (Board of Governors, past council member and chairman Real Estate Division).
Office: A. Skewes Building, Luverne, Minnesota, MN 56156. Tel No: (507) 283 2115.
Augustana Fellows, Cen Coad, Sigma, Nu. Republican. Methodist. Freemason (Shriner) Ben Franklin Lodge No 114, F & AM, Luverne, Rotarian (Past President). Clubs: Luverne Country; Cardinal; University of Minnesota.
Home address: 601 N.E. Park, Luverne, Minnesota, 56156, United States of America. Tel. No: (507) 283 8644.

SKUSE MOSES
Sojourner. Married Mary Thomas at St Gluvias 26 December 1751.

SKUES MOSES
Married 1885, Bristol.

SKEWS MURIEL
Chart 41. Daughter of Thomas and Jane (née Renshaw) Skews. Born 26 September 1917, Wombwell, Barnsley, South Yorkshire. Married Walter Thewlis, 1 January 1941. Issue: one son and one daughter. Lives at 11a Wooler Avenue, Wombwell.

SKEWS MURIEL
Chart 41. Daughter of William John and Mary (née Rump) Skews. Born 1920, Houghton. Died 1924, aged 3 years 10 months.

SKEWES MURIEL
Chart 12. Daughter of William John and Edith Mary (née Truran)

Skewes. Born 19 June 1925. Lived at 1 Penhallick, Carn Brea, Illogan, 1949. Married Roy Bodilly, 31 March 1956. No issue.

SKEWES MURIEL
Lived at Maitland Street, Currabubula, Quirindi, New South Wales, Australia in 1959. Now lives at 40 Mahony Avenue, Tamworth, 2340, New South Wales, Australia with Merril Joy Skewes.

SKEWS MURIEL A.
Chart 15. Daughter of John Henry Skews. Mother's maiden name Gallacher. Born 1921 Devonport. Lives at 20 Saunders Walk, Plymouth, Devon.

SKEWES MURIEL EDITH
Née Garnham. Married Ainslie Herbert Skewes 19 July 1941. Son Brian Ainslie (1948). Lives at 12 Scammell Court, Mount Waverley, 3149, Victoria, Australia.

SKUES MURIEL M.
Chart 3. Daughter of Vincent and Eva Skues. Mother's maiden name Rowland. Born 1926. Married Jack Hesketh in Chorley, 1947. Issue: one son.

SKEWES MURIEL MAY
Lived at Murrah Street, Bermagui South, Cobargo, New South Wales, Australia in 1959.

SKEWES MURIEL MELBANEAR
Chart 38. Daughter of Horace Henry and Agatha Blanche Skewes. Born 8 April 1922 at Broken Hill, Australia. Twin to Horatio Skewes. Married Walter Eustace Best 26 October 1946.
Issue: 1 son and 3 daughters. Lives at 30 Morgan Street, Broken Hill, 2880, New South Wales, Australia.

SKEWES MYRA
Chart 50. Daughter of Samuel and Mary (née Sanders) Skewes. Born 1883, Redruth. Died 1884, infant.

SKEWIS MYRL LEONE
Chart 2. Daughter of Benjamin Peters and Amelia Skewis of America. Twice married: 1) Daniels. 2) Bilow—issue: one son and one daughter.

SKEWIS MYRTLE
Chart 2. Née Howe. Born May, 1869, Illinois, USA. Married Charles Samuel Skewis, 23 October, 1895, USA. Children: Dorothy Delphine (1900), Margaret Josephine (1905) and Elizabeth Marion (1908). Lived in Lyon County, Iowa, USA. Died 21 December 1954, aged 85 years.

SKEWES MYRTLE EMMA
Chart 38. Née Marks. Born 1891. Married Albert Milton Skewes 11 February 1911. Lived at 41 Digby Street, Kadina, South Australia in 1959 with Frank Skewes. Died 15 September 1966, aged 75 years. Buried Kadina Cemetery, South Australia.

N

SKEWS NANCY
Chart 20. Née Blewitt of Withiel. Born 1770. Married William Skews of St Ewe 13 August 1796, Withiel Church. Children: Ann, Elizabeth and Mary. Lived at Nansladron, St Ewe. Died 14 August 1842, aged 72 years.

SKEWS NANCY
of Twelveheads. Married JOHN SKEWS of Chacewater 9 September 1818.

SKEWES NANCY
Chart 36. Daughter of James and Simonette Skewes of Cury. Bpt Cury 10 December 1826. Died young.

SKEWES NANCY
Chart 36. Daughter of James and Simonette Skewes. Bpt Cury 14 August 1831.

SKEWS NANCY
Died 1859, Truro.

SKEWS NANCY
Died 1861, Plymouth.

SKEWS NANCY
Wife of Ralph Skews, butcher with Furi and Company, 2141 Mason, San Francisco, United States of America, in 1961.

SKEWES NANCY
Chart 2. Daughter of Aaron and Maria (née Navarrete) Skewes. Born Pachuca, Mexico 22 January 1968.

SKEWIS NANCY E.
Lived at 279 North Commercial Street, Salem, Oregon, United States of America, 1940.

SKEWES NANCY LYNN
Chart 2. Daughter of John Billing and Mary Jo (née Armington) Skewes. Born 20 August 1955, Salt Lake City, Utah, USA. Lives at 1235E 500S, Salt Lake City, Utah, USA.

SKEWES NANCY MERLE
Chart 38. Née Ham. Married Charles Percival Skewes 23 July 1948, Broken Hill, Australia. Children: James Charles (1950), Thomas Edgar (1954) and Francine Jean (1956).
Lives at 246 Chloride Street, Broken Hill, 2705, New South Wales, Australia.

SKEWES NANNY

Daughter of John and Elizabeth (daughter of Thomas and Elizabeth Jeffrey) Skewes, miner of Kenwyn. Born 7 October 1825. Bpt Truro Wesleyan Chapel 19 March 1837.

SKUES   NANNY
Chart 2. Daughter of James and Joanna Skues. Bpt Camborne 20 April 1833. Emigrated to America 1849.

SKEWIS   NANNY
Born 1846, Redruth.

SKEWES   NANNY
Married 1846, St Germans.

SKEWES   NANNY
Born 1852, Redruth.

SKEWES   NATHAN CARL
Chart 36. Son of Leigh and Kerry Gail (née Dobbyn) Skewes. Born 27 November 1980, Ballarat, Australia. Lives at 5 Woolway Court, Delacombe, 3356, Victoria, Australia.

SKEWES   NATHAN JOHN
Chart 36. Son of John Michael and Janice Elizabeth (née Miles) Skewes. Born 21 August 1974, Ballarat, Australia. Lives at 702 Neil Street, Ballarat, 3350, Victoria, Australia

SKEWES   NATHAN MARTIN
Mother's maiden name Daniels. Born 1979, St Austell.

SKEWS   NATHANIEL EDWARD RICHARD
Chart 17. Son of Richard Nathaniel Edward Skews. Born 27 April 1874 at 223 Bethnal Green Road. London. Mother's maiden name Sarah Harding. Father was a french polisher. Married, 1909, West Ham to Hilliard. Children: Ernest W. (1911).
Died 1916, Epsom, aged 42 years.

SKEWS   NATHANIEL R.H.
Born 1902, Bethnal Green. Died 1926, aged 24 years in Weymouth, Dorset.

SKEWES   NAZARIO
Chart 10. Mexican. Son of John and Luisa (née Garcia) Skewes. Born Real del Monte, 28 July 1867. Broke his spine at an early age and never fully recovered. Married Piedad Lozano 5 May 1895. Eleven months later she died. One daughter, Luisa (1896). Married Dolores Riofrio, 1902. Children: Rodolfo (1902), Piedad (1904), Angelica (1907), Alfredo (1911), Cristina (1913), Eloisa (1915), Elvira (1918), Elmina (1922) and Guillermo (1909). Died 14 February 1922, from congestion of the lungs. Buried in English Cemetery, Real del Monte, Mexico.

SKEWES   NEIL DAVID
Chart 38. Son of Norman and Ruth Melva (née Ellis) Skewes. Born 24 October 1951. Lives at 271 Hancock Road, Banksia Park, 5091, South Australia. Police officer.

SKEWIS   NEIL CRAIG
Born 1954 Dundee East, Scotland.

SKEWES   NEIL HOLDSWORTH
Chart 36. Son of Henry Tom Holdsworth and Maud Isabel (née Curtis) Skewes. Born 1943. Married and divorced. Issue: 2 sons. Lives at 320 York Street, Ballarat, 3350, Victoria, Australia.

SKEWES   NELLIE
Born 1884. Wife of William Hedley Skewes, commercial traveller. Lived at 61 East End, Redruth. Previous address (1922): Dopp's Terrace, Redruth. Died 7 December 1938, aged 54 years.

SKEWS   NELLIE
Born 1894, Bethnal Green. Married George T. Waite in Bethnal Green, 1918.

SKUES   NELLIE
Chart 7. Née Jeffrey. Married Francis Albert Skues, 23 November 1907, Dartford, Kent. Children: Edwin Thomas, Herbert, Leslie James, Raymond J., Bernard E., Enid Elizabeth and Francis Henry.

SKEWS   NELLIE
Chart 41. Née Randerson. Born 1900. Married Joseph Skews at Ardley Parish Church 18 April 1921. Child: Colin (1926).
Died 1926, aged 26 years in Barnsley, South Yorkshire.

SKEWS   NELLIE
Married Thomas C. Meredith, 1915, Aston.

SKEWES   NELLIE MONICA
Lived at 65 McMinn Street, Port Darwin, Australia in 1959 with Brian Samuel Skewes, labourer. Now lives at Humpty Doo Road, Humpty Doo, via Darwin, 5791, Australia with Neville Percival Skewes, publican and Patrick John Skewes, manager.

SKEWES   NELLY
Born 1910, Salford. Died 1910, aged 0.

SKEWS   NELSON
Born 1892, Dartford, Kent. Killed in action in the First World War, 1919. Was a private soldier with R.W.K.R.

SKEWES   NEVILLE HERBERT
Lives at 12 Akarana Road, Lilydale, 3140, Victoria, Australia with Gwenda Margaret Skewes. Manager.

SKEWES   NEVILLE JOHN
Chart 36. Son of Brian Lock and Barbara Jessie (née McKinlay) Skewes. Born 28 February 1962. Lives at Currency Creek, Victor Harbour, 5251, South Australia.

SKEWES   NEVILLE PERCIVAL
Chart 36. Son of Percy and Mary (née Farrell) Skewes. Born 11 June 1921, Watsons Creek, via Bendemeer, New South Wales, Australia. Married Helen O'Lockland, 15 February 1947. Children: Peter (1947), Johanne (1949), Patrick (1952), Danny (1959), Mary (1960) and Cecilia (1962). Lives at Humpty Doo Road, via Darwin, 5791, Australia.

SKUIS   NICHOLAS
Son of Skuis. Bpt Redruth 4 July 1594.

SKEWS   NICHOLAS
Chart 41. Son of Baron S. Skews. Mother's maiden name Barson. Born 1957, Halifax, Yorkshire.

SKEWES   NICHOLAS CHARLES
Chart 36. Son of Robert Skewes. Born 10 March 1970, Australia.

SKEWES   NICHOLAS MARK
Chart 12. Son of Ronald and Natalia Eve (née Curtis) Skewes. Born 1 July 1961, Redruth. Works in the drying and cleaning department of English China Clay, St Austell. Lives at 25 Southborne Road, St Austell, PL25 4PV, Cornwall. Telephone number 0726 3171.

SKEWES   NICOLA
Chart 12. Daughter of William Arthur Raymond and Mavis Emily (née Rogers) Skewes. Born 2 November 1956. Lived at Seagulls Cry, Cadgwith, Lizard. Married Jose, 1978.

SKEWIS   NICOLA
Born 1972, Glasgow, Scotland.

SKEWS   NICOLA JANE
Chart 17. Daughter of Christopher R. Skews. Mother's maiden name Kempson. Born 1975, Sudbury, Suffolk.

SKEWS   NICOLA LOUISE
Chart 10. Daughter of Stanley and Mavis (née Soady) Skews. Born 1966 Plymouth.

SKEWES   NICOLE LOUISE
Chart 36. Daughter of Geoffrey John and Margaret (née Shanley) Skewes. Born 31 August 1974. Lives at 17 Wilkie Street, Werris Creek, 2341, New South Wales, Australia.

SKEWS   NIGEL
Chart 15. Son of Peter and Mary (née Sylvester) Skews. Born 1960, Liskeard.

SKEWS   NIGEL G.
Chart 10. Son of Martin Rex Skews. Mother's maiden name Martin. Born 1946, Redruth. Married Pamela Edith Walls, 1967, Falmouth. Child: Maria (1968). Lived at 14 Kernick Road, Penryn, Falmouth. Divorced 1975. Now lives on his own at 72 Conway Road, Falmouth.

SKEWS   NIGEL S.
Chart 41. Son of Kenneth D. Skews. Mother's maiden name Lord. Born 1961, Worth Valley. Killed in a car crash with his mother and sister Beverley in South Africa about 1970.

SKEWES   NIGEL STEPHEN WILLIAM
Chart 36. Son of Leslie Kevin and Jill Cecilia (née Pullman) Skewes. Born 12 January 1964 Watsons Creek, via Bendemeer, New South Wales, Australia.

NEVILLE P. SKEWES
LICENSED DEALER IN LIQUOR

RECEPTION

Skewes of Watsons Creek, Australia. Left to right: Debbie, Dean and Michelle with their parents Noel and Veronica Skewes, 1981

SKEWIS NINA
Chart 2. Daughter of John Rule and Jane Skewis. Born 4 August 1894, America. Married Otto Haynes. Issue: 2 sons and 1 daughter. Died 3 June 1970.

SKUES NINA MAY
Chart 8. Daughter of John Gilbert and Elizabeth Skues. Born 1901, Edmonton. Married William J. Hale in Edmonton, London 1927.

SKUES NOAH JAMES
Chart 7. Son of Thomas and Elizabeth (née Harris) Skues of 44 Lowndes Square, Chelsea. Born 12 November 1877. Married 1907, Southwark. Married again in 1917 to Hannah Manning. Died 1926, aged 49 years in Greenwich.

SKEWIS NOEL ERNEST
Lives at 90 Mapleton Road, Nambour, 4560, Queensland, Australia with Carol Ann Skewis. Milk vendor.

SKEWES NOEL JAMES
Chart 36. Son of James William and Beatrice Pauline (née Seymour) Skewes. Born 24 September 1941, New South Wales, Australia. Married Veronica Elaine Cooper, 11 August 1962 at Tamworth, New South Wales. Children: Dean Anthony (1963), Debbie Gay (1964) and Michelle Louise (1971). Lives at Bantry, Watsons Creek, via Bendemeer, 2352, New South Wales, Australia. Tin miner until 1978. Now mines rhodonite. Also a sheep farmer.

SKEWES NOEL JOHN
Chart 36. Son of Reginald John and Mary Mildred (née Rooney) Skewes. Born 26 December 1939, Australia. Married Shirley Ann Smith 11 November 1961. Children: Terry, Mark and Annette. Lives at 35 Drummond Road, Oxley Vale, 2340, New South Wales, Australia. Printer.

SKEWES NORA
Chart 12. Née Thomas. Married William John Skewes at Helston Register Office 5 July 1933. Children: Anthony Ronald (1933), Barbara Joan (1934), Gilbert James (1937), Rosalie Susan (1940), John Osborn (1945), Jeffrey Lional (1946), Paul (1948), Jack (1951) and Sally (1955). Lived at 78 Wheal Rose, Porthlevan, Helston, Cornwall. Died 22 July 1981.

SKEWES NORA LOUISE
Lived at Farm 1425, Leeton, New South Wales, Australia in 1959 with Athol Henry Skewes and John Reginald Skewes. Now lives at 50 Railway Avenue, Leeton, 2705, New South Wales, Australia.

SKUES NORAH E.
Chart 7. Née Henson. Married Francis Henry Skues, 1946, Dartford, Kent. (He died 1950, aged 40 years.) Child: Jeffrey Skues (1947). Lived at 46 Barnham Road, Dartford, Kent. She married Wilfred J. King. 1968 in Bexley, Kent.

SKEWES NORINE VIOLET
Chart 10. Daughter of Jonathan Braddon Skewes. Born 20 September 1925 at Hamilton, Ontario, Canada. Married Fred Gravefell 27 September 1947. Issue: 3 daughters.

SKEWES NORMA KATHLEEN
Chart 36. Daughter of Percy and Mary (née Farrell) Skewes. Born 28 April 1926, Watsons Creek, Bendemeer, New South Wales, Australia. Prior to marriage to James Battis gave birth to a son, Gregory (1950).

Issue: 4 sons and 3 daughters. Died 19 July 1975, aged 49 years.

SKEWES NORMA MAY
Chart 38. Daughter of Charles Leslie and Ellen Jane (née Ritter) Skewes. Born 15 May 1925, Adelaide, South Australia. Married Norman Hancock, 1944. Issue: 1 son and 1 daughter. Died in childbirth 22 April 1958, aged 32 years.

SKEWES NORMAN
Born 1893, Redruth. Died 1893, aged 0.

Norman Skewes

SKEWES   NORMAN
Born 1904, Redruth. Died 1907, aged 3 years.
SKEWES   NORMAN
Was a clerk in Kenosha County, Wisconsin, USA in 1941.
SKEWES   NORMAN
Chart 38. Son of Stanley Victor and Gertrude Olive (née Trimper) Skewes. Born 13 February 1917. Married Ruth Melva Ellis, 13 May 1944, Adelaide, South Australia. Children: Brian Wayne (1947) and Neil David (1951). Served with Australian Imperial Forces in Borneo 1941-1945. Worked as a paint sprayer with British Tube Mills, Kilburn, Australia for 37 years. Retired in 1978. Lives at 15 Deakin Street, Blair Athol, 5084, South Australia.
SKEWES   NORMAN DAVID
Chart 10. Son of Richard Herbert and Alice Skewes of Hamilton, Ontario, Canada. Born 5 April 1950. Married Linda ..... 19 June 1972. Children: Tara Diane (1974) and David Regan (1975).
SKEWES   NORMAN JOHN
Lives at 1/8 Moore Street, Coogie, 2034, New South Wales, Australia. Student.
SKEWES   NORMAN JOHN HAROLD
Chart 36. Son of Edward Keith and Maisie (née Lawson) Skewes. Born 3 August 1943, Western Australia. Married Patricia Beatrice King, 9 December 1967. Divorced 1973. Trucker.
SKEWES   NORMAN WILLIAM
Lived at Poplar Grove, Murrembeena, Victoria, Australia in 1913 with Ethel Maud Skewes.
SKEWES   NORMAN WILLIAM
Lived at 12 Donald Street, Panama, New South Wales, Australia in 1959 with Eva Skewes.

O

SKEWES   OLIVE CAROLINE
Lived at 56 Russell Terrace, Kilkenny, Woodville, South Australia in 1959 with Sydney Rownton Skewes.
SKEWS   OLIVE D.
Mother's maiden name Dyer. Born 1929, Bethnal Green. Married Thomas B. Wilkinson, 1946 in Don Valley, South Yorkshire.
SKEWES   OLIVE EDITH
Chart 10. Daughter of Herbert Tregonning and Florence Martha Skewes. Born 27 November 1927 at Hamilton, Ontario, Canada. Married Conrad Hannah 2 June 1951. Issue: one adopted girl.
SKUES   OLIVE EMILY
Chart 8. Daughter of Walter Edward Skues. Born 10 November 1910, Shoreditch. Married Herbert C. Sharpe, 1938, Shoreditch. Issue: one son and two daughters.
SKEWES   OLIVE GYTHA
Chart 36. Daughter of Charles Harold Vivian and Maud Emiline (née Lamphee) Skewes. Born 8 January 1916, Southern Cross, Western Australia. Married Scott Absalom 1939. One daughter. Died 1945, Wagin, Western Australia, aged 23 years.
SKEWES   OLIVE IRENE
Chart 12. Daughter of James Henry and Maud Mary Skewes. Born 1905, Helston. Married James Lawrence, 1947, Kerrier. No children. Died in the 1960's.
SKEWES   OLIVE JACOBSON
Chart 14. Married Edwin M. Skewes, adopted son of William M. and Mary Skewes of Wisconsin, USA, at Yorkville Methodist Church 5 October 1946. No children.
SKEWIS   OLIVE MAY
Chart 33. Daughter of William Richard Skewis. Born 1900. Went into service with a family who later moved from Devon to London. Married Harry Brewer, 1931 in London. He was a coach driver at London's Heathrow Airport. Issue: 2 daughters. Died 1938, aged 38 years.
SKEWES   OLIVE MAY
Chart 2. Born 1903. Married Lional James Skewes, 1935. Lived at Trenowerth Vean Farm, Mabe, Falmouth. A native of Penryn, she was Superintendent of Trenowerth Methodist Sunday School and up to 1959 was secretary of Mabe Women's Institute. Buried at Mabe Church June 1960, aged 57 years. No children.
SKEWES   OLIVE MAY
Chart 38. Née Brand. Married Albert Murray Skewes. Children: Edward Skewes and Leanne May Skewes. Lives at 2 William Street, Croydon, 5008, South Australia.
SKUES   OLIVER HAROLD
Chart 5. Son of Charles Skues of Australia. Served in Second World War. Lived at 12 Chalmers Street, Bentleigh North, Victoria, Australia in 1959 with Ruby Skues. Children: Peggy, Leigh Harold and Norma.
SKEWS   OLWYNNE
Chart 41. Daughter of George David and Olwynne (née Thirwell) Skews. Born 1966 Sunderland.
SKEWES   OMAR
Chart 10. Mexican. Son of Salvador and Carmen (née Ramirez) Skewes. Born 27 January 1948, Real del Monte, Mexico.

Olive May Skewis

SKEWES   ORELIA
Born 1854, Truro.
SKEWES   OSCAR
Lives at Carlos Antunez 2420A, Santiago, Chile, South America.
SKEWES   OSWALD
Chart 10. Son of Oswald Herbert and Hesba Eugenia (née Touchstone) Skewes. Born 6 January 1948. Married Alice Obenchain 13 September 1968. One son, Brett Lanier Skewes (1974). Lives at 10,001 Moore Drive, Manassas, Virginia, 22110, USA.
SKEWES   OSWALD C.
Chart 12. Son of John and Cissie Skewes, farmer. Mother's maiden name Gilbert. Born 13 September 1915. Farmer of Higher Relouas. Married Celia Holbrook of Higher Relouas, Mawgan 27 September 1958 at Mawgan Parish Church. Children: Susan (1959) and John (1963). Ran the Goonhilly Downs Filling Station, The Lizard until 1970. Now lives at Trezemper Farm, Goonhilly Downs, Mawgan, Helston. Tel. no: Mawgan 607.
SKEWES   OSWALD HERBERT
Chart 10. Son of John Herbert and Beatrice (née Pratt) Skewes. Born 14 November 1909 at Gaffney, Cherokee County, South Carolina, USA. Educated at the University of South Carolina. Became a teacher in high school, Longwood, Florida. Entered powerhouse construction field in 1941 building electrical generating stations throughout the United States, as well as Calcutta, India and Hawaii. Retired in 1975.
Married Hesba Eugenia Touchstone, 25 March 1933 at Sanford, Seminole County, Florida. Children: Ronald Lanier (1936), Sandra Elizabeth

Oswald Herbert Skewes

(1940) and Oswald junior (1948).
Lives at Route 2, Box 366, Nokesville, Virginia, 22123, United States of America.

SKEWES   OSWALD PERCY
Chart 36. Son of Samuel Sidney and Sarah (née Pennall) Skewes. Born 1907, Tamworth, New South Wales, Australia. Married Emily Mann. No children. Died 8 April 1967, aged 60 years. Buried in Sydney, New South Wales, Australia.

SKEWES   OWEN ERIC EDWARD
Chart 36. Son of Henry John and Phoebe Marie (née Holdsworth) Skewes. Born 23 July 1914, Victoria, Australia. Married Stella Tabitha Harris, 26 March 1938. Children: David Eric (1943), Geoffrey Ian (1947), John Michael (1949) and Philip (1949). Lives at 44 Dytes Parade, Ballarat, 3350, Victoria, Australia.

P

SKEWES   P.F.
Served under the Australian Government with Royal Navy as Paymaster Commander 30 June 1940. Seniority until July 1946 then name disappears from "Navy List."

SKEWES   PAMELA
Chart 2. Née Drummond. Born 11 April 1929. Married Eric William Skewes 13 August 1953. Children: Gillian Wendy (1955), Michael James (1957) and Peter William (1957). Lives at Lot/422 Galoola Drive, Nelson Bay, 2315, New South Wales, Australia.

SKEWES   PAMELA
Lives at 18 Morton Parade, Rankin Park, 2287, New South Wales, Australia with Robert John Skewes.

SKEWES   PAMELA
Chart 2. Daughter of David Neal and Patricia Skewes of Missouri, USA. Born 1958.

SKEWS   PAMELA EDITH
Chart 10. Daughter of Henry Arthur and Primrose Serena Walls. Born 25 December 1945. Married Nigel G.Skews, 1967, Falmouth. Child: Maria (1968). Divorced 1975. Married Alan J. Webb, 1979, Falmouth. Lives at 9 Railway Cottages, Arwenack, Falmouth.

SKEWES   PAMELA BRIENNE
Chart 18. Daughter of Neville and Elsie Brampton. Educated at Clifton High School and Bristol University.
Married Ian Robert Morrison Skewes 8 August 1952 at St Alban's Parish Church, Westbury Park, Bristol. No children. Divorced 1971. Now lives in Richmond, Surrey.

SKEWS   PAMELA E.L.
Née Searle. Married Andrew J. Skews, 1974, St Germans. In 1977 Voters List lived at 19 Fairfield Estate, St Germans, Bodmin. Tel No: 05033 557.

SKEWS   PAMELA J.
Chart 10. Daughter of Stanley Skews. Mother's maiden name Soady. Born 1951, St Austell. Married, 1970, St Austell.

SKEWES   PAMELA J.
Chart 12. Daughter of Bertram and Elizabeth Skewes. Mother's maiden name Prowse. Born 1932, Truro. Married Frank Roberts, Truro, 1953. Issue: one son.

SKEWES   PAMELA LYNN
Chart 36. Née Kusmanvich. Married Ronald Edward Skewes, 4 June 1966. Lives at 84 Darley Circle, Bull Creek, 6153, Western Australia.

SKEWES   PAMELA MARGARET
Lives at 9 Cottel Street, Port Pirie, 5540, South Australia with Kevin John Skewes, director.

SKEWES   PATIENCE
Daughter of Henry Skewes. Bpt Kea 30 May 1762. Buried Kea 26 September 1763.

SKEWES   PATIENCE
Chart 28. Daughter of Richard and Mary Skewes of Nancevellan Common, Kea. Bpt Kea 18 October 1807. Married Michael Kent at Kea, 20 June 1829.

SKEWES   PATRICIA
Daughter of Harold William and Alma Bernice (née Walker) Skewes. Born 1931, Warragul, Victoria, Australia. Married Sid Seymour, 9 October 1958. Lives in Australia.

SKEWS   PATRICIA
Chart 17. Daughter of Frederick and Eileen Skews. Mother's maiden name Joyce. Born 8 September 1937, Pancras.

SKEWS   PATRICIA
Chart 17. Daughter of Arthur S. Skews. Mother's maiden name Stroud. Born 1944, Wrexham.

SKEWES   PATRICIA
Chart 2. Daughter of Herbert and Edna (née Cuthbertson) Skewes. Born 14 October 1948. Married John Arthur Pickett, 21 September 1968. Issue: 3 daughters.

SKEWS   PATRICIA
Married Webb, 1964, Devon Central.

SKEWES   PATRICIA

Lives at 42 Etwell Street East, Victoria Park, 6101, Western Australia.

SKEWES   PATRICIA ANNE
Chart 46. Daughter of Ernest Lloyd and Doris Irene Patricia Skewes of 68 Chapel Hill, Truro, Mother's maiden name Penhaligon. Born 28 April 1947. Bpt St George's Truro 7 June 1947. Married Jeffrey Purkiss 4 May 1968. Godparents: William Skewes and Gladys Skewes.

SKEWS   PATRICIA E.
Chart 17. Daughter of Edwin Arthur Skews. Mother's maiden name Lewis. Born 1950, New Forest.

SKEWS   PATRICIA E.
Married Dale, 1958, Hammersmith, London.

SKEWS   PATRICIA HELEN
Chart 10. Née Drysale. Married Herbert James Skewes 8 October 1949, Hamilton, Ontario, Canada. Children: Kim (1955) and Jamie (1958). Lives in Hamilton, Ontario.

SKUES   PATRICIA MARY
Chart 3. Daughter of Jack and Lily (née Bruckshaw) Skues. Born 15 January 1943, Stockport, Cheshire. Emigrated to Canada 13 April 1966. Works for Miracle Mart, Dollard Des Ormeaux (since 1966) and is in charge of children's, men's and boy's wear departments. A keen swimmer, enjoys art and reading. Was made an elder of St Genevieve United Church of Canada 27 May 1979 and is a member of the church choir.
Lives at Apartment 303A, 11706 Pierrefonds Boulevard, Pierrefonds, Quebec H9A 2X2. Telephone number: (514) 683 7860.

SKEWES   PATRICIA MARY
Lives at 19 Wolgarra Street, Salisbury, 5108, South Australia with Geoffrey Robin Skewes, motor mechanic.

SKEWES   PATRICK
Chart 36. Son of Neville Percy and Helen (née O'Lockland) Skewes. Born 7 January 1952, Australia.

SKEWES   PATRICK
Chart 36. Son of Anthony Joseph and Bronwyn (née Gapp) Skewes. Born 5 May 1975, New South Wales, Australia.

SKEWES   PATRICK JOHN
Lives at Humpty Doo Road, Humpty Doo, via Darwin, 5791, Australia with Nellie Monica Skewes, storekeeper and Neville Percival Skewes, publican.

SKEWES   PATTY
Chart 10. Daughter of Richard and Evelyn Skewes. Born 1 August 1948, Ontario, Canada.

SKEWES   PAUL
Chart 12. Son of William John and Nora Skewes. Mother's maiden name Thomas. Born 2 May 1948, Kerrier.

SKEWES   PAUL
Son of William Arthur Skewes. Mother's maiden name Gwendoline Bray. Born 1956, Redruth. Died 1956, aged 0. Twin of Kevin Skewes.

SKUES   PAUL
Chart 9. Twin to Anthony Skues. Mother's maiden name Davies, formerly Whincop. Son of John Joseph G. Skues. Born 1956, Woolwich. Married Elaine A. Hanlon in Greenwich, 1979.

SKEWS   PAUL
Chart 41. Son of Eric Skews. Mother's maiden name Rasburn. Born 1956, Staincross. Married Taylor in Barnsley, South Yorkshire, 1977.

SKEWES   PAUL
Mother's maiden name Williams. Born 1957, Redruth.

SKEWES   PAUL
Chart 36. Son of Graeme Douglas and Rosalie (née Campbell) Skewes. Born 10 May 1967, Western Australia.

SKEWES   PAUL
Chart 42. Son of Michael Bruce and Dianne (née Dickson) Skewes. Born 14 November 1979, Nowra. Lives c/o 725 Squadron, R.A.N.A.S., Nowra Hill, 2540, New South Wales, Australia.

SKEWES   PAUL ANDREW
Chart 12. Son of William John and Wendy (née Williams) Skewes. Born 26 April 1964, Helston. Lives at 27 Beacon Parc, Helston. Telephone number: 03265 4722.

SKEWES   PAUL DAVID
Mother's maiden name Easton. Born 1978, Nottingham.

SKEWIS   PAUL DAVID
Chart 50. Son of David and Patricia (née Gibson) Skewis. Born 1979, Hull.

SKEWES   PAUL FEARGUS
Chart 11. Son of Thomas John and Laura B. Skewes. Born 6 April 1901, America. Served in the United States Navy.

SKEWS   PAUL JAMES
Born 1951. Adopted child. Married Perry in Stoke on Trent, 1975. Child: Jonathan Michael (1976).

SKEWES   PAUL MERVYN
Chart 24. Son of John William and Joyce Maxine Skewes. Born New South Wales, Australia. Lives at 8 Lentara Street, Bardouroka, 2315, Australia with Sandra Gae Skewes.

SKEWIS   PAUL WILLIAM
Born 1975, Dundee East, Scotland.

SKUES PAULA MARIE
Chart 9. Daughter of Raymond Anthony and Elizabeth (née Collie) Skues. Born 1968, Surrey Mid East.

SKEWES PAULINE ELIZABETH
Lives at 2/62 Mountain Road, Austinmeer, 2514, New South Wales, Australia.

SKEWES PEARL
Chart 37. Daughter of Richard John Skewes of Ballarat, Victoria, Australia.

SKEWES PEARL
Chart 24. Daughter of John and Mary Jane (née Cole) Skewes. Born 1891, New South Wales, Australia. Married with 7 children.

SKEWES PEARL ISOBEL
Chart 36. Née Chapman. Born 7 April 1902. Married James Robert Skewes, New South Wales, Australia. Died 11 November 1951, aged 49 years.

SKEWES PEARL LOUISA
Lived at Farm 427, Whitton, Leeton, New South Wales, Australia in 1959 with Reginald Lionel Skewes. Cannery employee. Now lives at Farm/404 Dalbata Road, Leeton, 2705, New South Wales, Australia, with Reginald Lionel Skewes, Laurence John Skewes and Garry Reginald Skewes.

SKEWES PEARL MILDRED
Lived at 51a Wycombe Road, Neutral Bay, New South Wales, Australia in 1959 with Leonard Joseph Skewes.

SKEWES PEDRO
Chart 10. Son of John and Luisa (née Garcia) Skewes of Real del Monte. Born 1868. Married Severa Martinez. Children: Martha (1908) and Magdalena (1910). Died 1929, Mexico City.

SKEWES PEGGY
Married Thomas Roberts of Kea at Kenwyn 30 December 1802.

SKEWES PEGGY
Chart 28. Daughter of Richard and Mary Skewes of Nancevellan Common, Kea. Bpt Kea 5 April 1812. Married Thomas Chygwidden at Kea 24 December 1832.

SKEWIS PEGGY
Born 1823. Died 1909, aged 86 years in Tavistock.

SKEWES PEGGY
Lived at Meningie, South Australia, 1959.

SKEWES PEGGY
Chart 2. Née Smith. Born Australia. Married Ronald George Skewes 2 March 1945, Toowoomba, Queensland, Australia. Children: Robyn Kaye (1947) and Sandra Ann (1951). Lives at 10 Windermere Avenue, West Lakes, South Australia, 5021.

SKEWES PEGGY M.
Married Trenear, 1960, Redruth.

SKEWES PEITA DIANE
Chart 36. Daughter of Percy and Muriel (née Norris) Skewes. Born 8 May 1952, New South Wales, Australia. Married Ken Lewis 8 February 1975. Issue: 1 son and 1 daughter.

SKEWES PENELOPE
Chart 40. Daughter of William Roger Skewes. Mother's maiden name Richards. Born 1963, Penzance.

SKEWS PERCIVAL
Chart 10. Son of John and Sarah Skews of Truro, shoemaker. Bpt Bible Christian Chapel, Truro, 2 November 1902.

SKUES PERCIVAL WALTER
Chart 8. Son of Walter Edward and Atlanta Emily (née Bond) Skues. Born 1893. Drowned at sea January 1917. Was a lance corporal with London R.B. (19th W).

SKUSE PERCY HERBERT
Son of Herbert Henry and Ada (née Cocks) Skuse. Born 23 July 1905, London. Married Brenda Holman, 1935. Issue: one son, Peter Robin (1943). Served in RAF during Second World War. Optician's assistant and later booking clerk, London Transport.

SKEWES PERCY JOHN
Chart 36. Son of William and Hannah Jane (née Gale) Skewes. Born 1 September 1889. Married Mary Farrrell. Children: James William (1916), Beryl (1917), Thomas John (1919), Neville Percy (1921), Robert Keith (1923), Norma Kathleen (1926). Mary died 2 March 1936. Percy then married Muriel Norris 29 April 1943. Children: Anne (1943), Robin (1945), Maxwell Charles (1946), Geoffrey John (1949), Wendy (1951), Peita (1952) and Meryl (1955).
Lived at Watsons Creek, Bendemeer, 2352, New South Wales, Australia. Died 13 June 1955, aged 65 years.

SKEWS PERCY LOUIS
Born 1878, Dartford, Kent. Married in Strood, 1905.

SKEWIS PERCY VERNON
Chart 2. Son of Benjamin Peters and Amelia Skewis. Lived in Rotenai, Idaho, United States of America. Children: Edwin and Leland.

SKEWS PERCY VICTOR
Born 1904. Died 1923, aged 18 years in Maidstone.

SKEWES PERLA CAROLINA
Chart 10. Mexican. Daughter of Salvador and Carmen (née Ramirez)

Skewes. Born 9 January 1952, Real del Monte, Mexico. Died 7 July 1967, aged 17 years following an accident where she was hit in the stomach.

SKUES PETER
Chart 2. Illegitimate son of Ann Skues. Bpt Camborne 29 June 1693. Died Camborne 21 September 1693 — infant.

SKUES PETER
Son of Richard Skues. Bpt Kenwyn 17 July 1718.

SKEWES PETER
Married Margaret Newton of St Columb Minor at Kea 11 June 1750.

SKEWS PETER
Son of Martin Skews of Kea. Buried Kea 26 April 1752.

SKEWES PETER
Son of Martin Skews of Kea. Bpt Kenwyn 31 January 1752.

SKEWES PETER
of Blackwater. Born 1763. Buried Chacewater 11 July 1830, aged 67 years.

SKEWES PETER
Chart 10. Son of Digory and Margery Skewes. Bpt Kenwyn 14 May 1763. Buried Kea 5 July 1763; infant.

SKEWES PETER
Son of Thomas Skewes. Bpt Kenwyn 29 January 1764.

SKEWES PETER
Chart 10. Son of Digory and Margery Skewes. Bpt Kenwyn 21 August 1768. A Peter Skewes married Ann Crase at Kenwyn 10 September 1791. A Peter Skewes married Peggy Moyle at Kenwyn 7 January 1792.

SKEWES PETER
Buried Kea 15 October 1768.

SKEWES PETER
Chart 10. Son of Martin and Mary Skewes. Bpt Kea 3 August 1777.

SKEWES PETER
Son of Henry and Mary Skews. Bpt Kenwyn 20 August 1780.

SKEWES PETER
Chart 6. Born 1789. Lived at Charles Street, Truro. Married Mary Williams at Kenwyn 21 September 1817. Son: Thomas (1827). Buried Kenwyn 28 December 1864, aged 75 years.

SKEWES PETER
Married Ann Crase at Kenwyn 10 September 1791.

SKEWES PETER
Married Peggy Moyle by licence at Kenwyn 7 January 1792.

SKEWES PETER
Son of Henry Skewes of Kea. Buried Kenwyn 5 August 1793.

SKEWIS PETER
Son of Peter and Mary Skewis. Bpt Gwennap 3 January 1794.

SKEWES PETER
Buried Kea 1 October 1798.

SKEWIS PETER
Son of Peter and Ann Skewis. Bpt Kenwyn 9 May 1796.

SKEWES PETER
Buried Kea 11 September 1802.

SKEWES PETER
Chart 10. Son of Digory and Elizabeth Skewes. Bpt Kenwyn 19 June 1803. Married Elizabeth . . . of Kea. In 1851 Census Returns living at Hugus with his wife and children Elizabeth, Peter, Mary, Grace, Ellen and Emily. Buried Kea 26 May 1865, aged 61 years. Lived at Hugus, Kea.

SKEWES PETER
Son of John and Ann Skewes. Bpt Kenwyn 24 June 1804.

SKEWS PETER
Chart 10. Born 1803. Lived at Kerley, Kea. Farmer of 12 acres. Married Grace Harris of Penryn at Kea 16 October 1830, in presence of Mary Skewes. Children: Richard, Mary, John, Thomas, Peter, Grace and Maria. Buried Baldhu, 21 June 1867, aged 64 years.

SKEWES PETER
Born 1813. Lived at Blackwater. Buried Kenwyn 22 April 1825.

SKEWES PETER
Chart 22. Son of Peter and Ann Skewes of St Agnes; miner. Bpt Kenwyn 24 April 1814.

SKEWES PETER
of St Agnes. Buried Kenwyn 24 April 1814, aged 18 years.

SKEWES PETER
Chart 6. Son of Peter and Mary Skewes of the Poor House, Kenwyn, miner. Bpt Kenwyn 22 November 1826.

SKEWS PETER
Chart 15. Son of Peter Skews. Born 1832, Launceston. Married Elizabeth Gregory, daughter of Samuel Gregory, miner at Altarnun, 26 October 1855. Lived at St Ive. Children: Fanny Gregory, William Henry, John Gregory, Edmund and Samuel Gregory. Later became blind through a mine accident.

SKUES PETER
Born 1838, Patrington.

SKEWS PETER
Born 1838. Died 1912, aged 84 years in Liskeard.

SKEWS   PETER
Chart 10. Son of Peter and Elizabeth (née Scoble) Skews of Hugus, Kea, miner. Born 1840. Bpt Kea 19 March 1840. Had sisters Elizabeth, Mary, Grace, Ellen and Emily. In 1851 Census Returns was living at Hugus. Married Elizabeth Jane Youren in Truro, 1862. Children: William (1869) and Peter (1874). Iron miner. Died 1925, aged 85 years in St Austell.

SKEWES   PETER
Chart 10. Born 1842. Son of Peter and Grace Skewes of Kerley, Kea. In 1861 Census Returns was a copper and tin miner. Married at Mineral del Monte, Mexico to Elizabeth Bray, formerly of Lanner, Gwennap. Children: Richard Henry (1871), George Harris (1875), John (1878), Lillian Beatrice (1884) and Belita (1897). Died 21 May 1891, aged 48 years after a short illness in Mineral del Monte. Buried in English Cemetery, Real del Monte, Mexico.

SKEWS   PETER
Born 1866, Truro. Died 1867 aged 1 year in Liskeard.

SKEWS   PETER
Chart 10. Son of Peter and Elizabeth Skews, ironmonger. Mother's maiden name Youren. Born 2 April 1874 at Boscoppa Downs, St Austell. Married 1901 to Maud Mary Rickard. Lived at 1 Council Houses, Ruddle Moor, St Austell. Children: Violet Irene, Charles R., Thomas H., Mabel J. & Stanley. Died 1949, aged 75 years in St Austell.

SKEWES   PETER
Chart 10. Son of Richard Henry and Louie (née Pratt). Born 24 December 1894. Died 1 January 1895, aged 10 days. Buried in the English Cemetery, Real del Monte, Mexico.

SKEWS   PETER
Chart 10. Son of Peter and Maud Mary (née Rickard) Skews. Born 1906. Died 1929, St Austell, aged 23 years.

SKEWES   PETER
Chart 36. Son of Neville Percy and Helen (née O'Lockland) Skewes. Born 20 December 1947, Australia.

SKEWES   PETER
Chart 12. Son of Gilbert James and Kathleen Skewes. Born 13 December 1962, Kerrier.

SKEWES   PETER
Chart 12. Son of Carl and Elizabeth Skewes. Mother's maiden name Clackworthy. Born 1969, Redruth.

SKEWES   PETER
Lived at 510, 220 Lake Promenade, Toronto, Canada (1970-1973). Television technician, working at Six Point TV and Radio Services.

SKEWES   PETER
Chart 24. Son of John William and Joyce Maxine Skewes. Born New South Wales, Australia. Lives at Lot/2 Marine Drive, Bardouroka, 2315, New South Wales, Australia.

SKEWES   PETER ANDREW
Lives at 58 Clifford Street, Warragul, 3820, Victoria, Australia with Harold Grenville Skewes and Constance Shirley Skewes.

SKEWS   PETER B.
Chart 10. Son of Thomas H. Skews. Mother's maiden name Harris. Born 1945. Married Blight, 1967, St Austell. Children: Michelle Jayne (1967) and Hayley Lisa (1970).

SKEWES   PETER CHARLES
Chart 36. Son of Graeme Douglas and Rosalie (née Campbell) Skewes. Born 10 May 1967. Twin to Paul Skewes. Lives in Western Australia.

SKEWES   PETER EDWARD
Chart 36. Son of Douglas William and Jean Gladys (née Lovell) Skewes. Born 15 April 1970. Lives at 6 Hillcrest Road, Kewdale, 6105, Western Australia.

SKEWES   PETER MARSDEN
Chart 12. Son of William Frank and Annie Doris Skewes. Mother's maiden name Williams. Born 10 July 1941. Bachelor. Lived at Chybarles, Ruan Major, Helston (1969). Current address: 30 Glebe Place, Ruan Minor, Helston.

SKEWES   PETER MICHAEL
Chart 36. Son of James and Stella Margaret (née Farrell) Skewes. Born 6 June 1931. Married Marie Blair. Children: Scott Raymond (1962) and Mark Antony (1965). Lives at Caroline Street, Bendemeer, 2352, New South Wales, Australia.

SKEWES   PETER NATHANIEL
Chart 36. Son of Jack Roe and Dorothy May Skewes. Born 1955. Married Janet Luscott, 1974. Son: Robert (1975). Lives at 1 Eva Street, Morphett Vale, 5162, South Australia. Butcher.

SKEWES   PETER NEIL
Chart 12. Son of William John and Wendy (née Williams) Skewes. Born 26 October 1951, Helston. Lives at 27 Beacon Parc, Helston. Mason. Led the Helston Furry Dance (7.00am and 5.00pm) on 7th May, 1977 together with his sister Carole.

SKUES   PETER PERCIVAL
Chart 8. Son of Walter Edward and Violet (née Merton) Skues. Born 1934. Lives at 38 The Parade, Walton-on-Naze, Essex.

SKUES   PETER ROBIN
Son of Percy Herbert and Brenda (née Holman) Skuse. Born 26 August 1943 (3.15am). Educated Bonnerville School, Clapham; Battersea

Grammar School; University of London Goldsmith's College; BSc., BA.; diploma in science. Fellow of Zoological Society of London; Member of Institute of Biology. Teacher — Fainhildes School, Croydon 1965-1971; Bishop Thomas Grant School, Streatham, London 1971-1972. Now Head of Sciences (since 1973) and Computer Studies at the Chelsea School, London. Peter did part time work as a catering assistant with J. Lyons and Co 1963-1969; also locum pathologist in London hospitals 1967-1968. He married Frances Mace-Hardyman 22 December 1971. Children: Trudi (1973), Robin Toby (1974) and Heidi (1979). Lives at 46 Beverley Road, Whyteleafe, Surrey CR3 ODX. Telephone number: 01 660 0183.

SKEWES   PETER SNOWDEN
Son of Henry Snowden and Marjorie Joyce (née Munro) Skewes. Born 7 January 1953, Yarrawonga, Victoria, Australia. Married Marg D'Shanessy, December 1980. Lives at 8a Ferry Street, West Kogarah, 2217, New South Wales, Australia.

SKEWES   PETER WILLIAM
Chart 36. Son of John Locke and Heather Leonne (née McKenzie) Skewes. Born 18 August 1958. Lives at Duthie Park, via Blackall, 4732, Queensland, Australia. Solicitor at Blackall.

SKEWES   PETER WILLIAM
Chart 38. Son of Ernest Richard and Lena Mary (née Hass) Skewes. Born 2 August 1946. Married Carol Ann Wright, 26 January 1968. Son: Craig Richard (1972). Killed in a car crash in Sydney, Australia on 3 May 1972, aged 26 years.

SKEWES   PETER WILLIAM
Chart 2. Son of Eric William and Pamela (née Drummond) Skewes. Born 7 June 1971, Ringwood, Victoria, Australia. Lives at Corlette, Port Stevens, New South Wales, Australia.

SCOOSE   PETERNESS
Daughter of John Scoose. Bpt Menheniot 28 June 1577. Married Christopher Hicks at Menheniot 26 November 1604.

SCUIS   PETERNESS
Bpt Camborne 1619.

SKEWS   PHILIP
Son of John Skews. Bpt St Gerrans 10 July 1653.

SKEWS   PHILIP
Chart 13. Son of John Skews. Bpt Mevagissey 1 July 1683.

SKEWS   PHILIP
Chart 9. Married Ann Webb at Philleigh 7 May 1743. Lived at St Ewe. Children: Elizabeth (1746), Edward (1749), Elizabeth (1751) and Philip (1753).

SKEWS   PHILIP
Son of Philip and Ann Skews. Bpt St Ewe 10 June 1753.

SKEWS   PHILIP
Chart 9. Son of William and Nancy Skews. Bpt St Ewe 22 October 1797. Farmer. Married Lucretia Smith of St Mewan at St Stephen in Brannel 9 May 1837. Lived at Sticker, St Mewan. In the 1871 Census Returns was listed as a farmer of 8 acres. Died 1872, aged 75 years.

SKEWS   PHILIP
Chart 9. Son of James and Joanna Skews of Lower Sticker. Bpt St Ewe 24 May 1806. Married Sally . . . of Buckland Monachorum, Devon. Lived at Horrabridge, Tavistock, Devon. Copper miner. Child: Joanna Truscott (1840). Emigrated to Victoria, Australia by 1865.

SKUES   PHILIP
Chart 2. Son of Henry and Grace Skues. Born 1842.

SKEWES   PHILIP
Married 1861, Redruth.

SKEWES   PHILIP
Chart 36. Son of Owen Eric Edward and Stella Tabitha (née Harris) Skewes. Born 29 December 1954, Ballarat, Victoria, Australia. Married Jan Maree Mellor 28 February 1975. Lives at Flat 4, 75 Paradise Island, Gold Coast, Queensland, Australia.

SKEWES   PHILIP
Chart 36. Son of Francis James and Valerie (née Foster) Skewes. Born Watsons Creek, Bendemeer, New South Wales, Australia. Married 10 January 1981.

SKEWES   PHILIP
Chart 26. Son of Grant Phillip Skewes of Connecticut, United States of America.

SKEWES   PHILIP
Lives at 2751 Lansdowne Drive, Jacksonville, Florida, USA. Telephone number: (904) 744 6294.

SKEWS   PHILIP ADRIAN
Chart 17. Son of Roger D. Skews. Mother's maiden name Binnersley. Born 1975, Macclesfield, Cheshire.

SKEWIS   PHILIP E.
Chart 50. Son of James Airns and Irene (née Fox) Skewis. Born 24 September 1957, Hull.

SKUES   PHILIP ERNEST
Chart 9. Born 24 December 1899. Married Carmelo Pinto, 1922, St Saviour, London. Lived at 16 Ruxley Close, Ewell, Surrey. Children: Clorinda A., Raymond Anthony, Miriam M., and Sandra J. Died 27 December 1966, aged 68 years at Cuddington Hospital, Cheam.

SKUES   PHILIP ERNEST
Chart 9. Son of John Philip W. Skues. Mother's maiden name Florence M. Bremer. Born 1922, Camberwell, London. Married Constance L. Lucchesi, 1949. Children: Alan J. (1952) and Clive P. (1960). Lives at 42 Lynmere Road, Welling, Kent. Tel No: 01 303 2978.

SKUES   PHILIP ERNEST
Fishmonger of 79 Rodney Road, London SE 17. London Street Directory, 1930.

SKEWES   PHILIP GRAHAM
Chart 38. Son of Garfield Sydney and Doris Margaret (née Sandford) Skewes. Born 5 October 1949. Bachelor. Formerly a master hairdresser, but now owns his own restaurant in Surrey Hills, Sydney, Australia. Lives at Flat 14, 24 Ocean Street, Bondi, 2026, New South Wales, Australia.

SKUES   PHILIP HENRY
Chart 9. Born 9 September 1867 at 6 William Street, Lower Marsh, Lambeth. Son of William and Harriet (née Ash) Skues. Married 1890 to Clorinda Emma . . . a widow. Worked with Post Office. Children: John Philip W., Albert Edward, Thomas Henry James, Arthur Leonard Peter, Philip Ernest, Clorinda Doris and Ivy Margurette. Died 1930, aged 63 years. Clorinda Emma died 1949, aged 78 years.

SKEWES   PHILIP JAMES
Chart 2. Born 1841. Son of Henry and Grace Skewes of Penponds, miner. Bpt Camborne 13 November 1841.

SKEWES   PHILIP JOHN
Chart 36. Son of John David and Beryl May (née Johnson) Skewes. Born 19 April 1966. Lives at Ackland Hill Road, Cherry Gardens, 5157, South Australia.

SKEWES   PHILIP LITTLETON
Chart 10. Son of Richard Skewes of Marazion. Born 14 May 1908, Hamilton, Ontario, Canada.

SKEWES   PHILIP MATTHEW
Chart 37. Son of Keith Matthew Skewes. Born 19 October 1945, Australia.

SKEWES   PHILIP MICHAEL
Lives at Memana, 7255, Tasmania, Australia.

SKEWES   PHILIP RANDOLPH
Lived at 28 Anderson Road, Auburn, Victoria, Australia in 1959 with Annie Dorothea and Dorothea Alison Skewes. Clerk.

SKEWES   PHILIPPA
Married Henry Pascoe at Wendron Parish Church 30 January 1720.

SKEWES   PHILIPPA
Chart 2. Née King. Born 1741. Married John Skewes, yeoman 1 November 1767, Camborne. Died 15 August 1815, aged 74 years.

SKEWES   PHILIPPA
Buried St Keverne 10 September 1739.

SKEWS   PHILIPPA
Daughter of John Skews. Bpt Gerrans 10 July 1653.

SKEWES   PHILIPPA
Buried Gwennap 28 November 1742.

SCUIS   PHILIPPA
Née Angove. Married Thomas Scuis at Wendron 23 May 1692. Buried Wendron 25 December 1742.

SKEWS   PHILIPPA
Born 1748. Buried St Ewe 16 April 1828, aged 80 years.

SKEWES   PHILIPPA
Married William Skinner at Gwennap 12 June 1763.

SKEWES   PHILIPPA
Wife of Joseph Skewes. Buried Mawgan in Meneage 18 March 1768.

SKEWES   PHILIPPA
Chart 2. Daughter of John and Philippa Skewes. Bpt 30 March 1783, Camborne. Married John Phillips, yeoman of Gwithian, 14 November 1802 in presence of John Skewes.

SKEWES   PHILIPPA
Daughter of Thomas and Thomasine Skewes of Kea. Bpt Kenwyn 6 February 1774.

SKEWIS   PHILIPPA
Daughter of William and Ann Skewis of Gunwalloe. Bpt Mullion 4 March 1804. Buried 15 March 1804, infant.

SKEWES   PHILIPPA
Daughter of Henry and Margaret Skewes. Born 1804. Bpt Camborne 10 June 1804. Died 1838. Buried Camborne 16 October 1838, aged 34 years.

SKEWES   PHILIPPA
Born 1805. Spinster. Lived at Cargenwen, Crowan (1871 Census Returns). Had a brother John Skewes and a daughter Mary Ann (illegitimate). Buried Crowan 14 August 1883, aged 78 years.

SKUES   PHILIPPA
Buried St Mary's Truro 23 June 1806.

SKEWS   PHILIPPA
Born 1821. Lived at Kerley, Kea. Buried Chacewater 24 November 1833, aged 12 years.

SKEWS   PHILIPPA
Chart 10. Daughter of Richard and Agnes Skews of Kerley, Kea. Bpt Kea 31 August 1823.

SKEWS   PHILIPPA
Chart 10. Daughter of John and Harriet Skews of Kerley, Kea. Bpt Chacewater 9 July 1837. Married John Symons, miner of Baldhu, son of Richard Symons, miner 19 August 1858, Baldhu Church. Issue: 2 daughters by 1871.

SKEWES   PHILIPPA
Born 1841, Falmouth. Died 1841, aged 0.

SKEWES   PHILIPPA JANE
Chart 30. Daughter of Thomas and Jane Skewes of Daniell Street, Kenwyn. Bpt Kea 22 April 1832. Married Richard Henry Philips (son of Richard Philips, cordwainer) of St George's, carpenter at St George's Truro 29 August 1864, in presence of John Skewes.

SKEWIES   PHILIPPA M.
Born 1965, Bothwell, Scotland.

SKEWES   PHILIPPA MARY
Chart 30. Daughter of John Beer and Mary Brown Skewes. Born 1866. Lived at Kenwyn Street, Truro, 1871. (Census returns.) Married 1894, Redruth.

SKEWES   PHOEBE MARIE
Chart 36. Née Holdsworth. Born 1875. Married Henry John Skewes, 1904, Victoria, Australia. Children: Henry Tom Holdsworth, Owen Eric Edward, Phoebe Marie and Glenleigh Bertie William. Died 31 December 1938, aged 63 years. Buried in Ballarat Old Cemetery, Victoria, Australia.

SKEWS   PHYLLIS
Daughter of Richard and Margery Skews. Bpt Paul, 11 November 1736.

SKEWS   PHYLLIS
Daughter of John Skews. Bpt Penzance 17 July 1739.

SKEWS   PHYLLIS
of Penzance. Married Martin Hoskin at Madron with Penzance 5 January 1771.

SKEWIS   PHYLLIS
Daughter of John and Jane Skewis. Bpt Illogan 5 January 1806.

SKUES   PHYLLIS
Chart 5. Daughter of James Frederick & Ada (née Tregonning) Skues. Born 25 February 1908, Redruth. Attended Redruth East End School from 2 September 1912 to 12 April 1915. Married Joel James Waters, 1934, tin miner of Illogan, son of William John Waters, deceased, tin smelter; at Redruth Methodist Church 1 September 1934. Lived at 16 Trefusis Terrace, Redruth until marriage.

SKEWES   PHYLLIS
Chart 38. Daughter of Stanley Victor and Gertrude Olive (née Trimper) Skewes. Born 1909. Married Charles Calman. Issue: 1 daughter. Lives in South Australia.

SKEWES   PHYLLIS
Chart 36. Daughter of William Henry and Gladys (née Harris) Skewes. Born 1918, Redruth. Lived at Brea. Married Richard Williams, 1936.

SKEWS   PHYLLIS
Chart 14. Daughter of Manley and Eva (née Reed) Skewes of United States of America. Born Yorkville, Wisconsin, USA 1919. Married Daniel Fry. Issue: 2 sons and 2 daughters.

SKEWES   PHYLLIS JANE
Chart 12. Daughter of Henry and Mary Capel. Born 24 February 1910. Married George Hennessy Skewes at Treslothan Parish Church 27 April 1946. No children. Lived at 53 Tehidy Road, Camborne, Cornwall. Died 20 March 1982, aged 72 years.

SKEWES   PHYLLIS JEAN
Chart 36. Daughter of William Roe and Evelyn Dorothy Skewes. Born 10 November 1923. Married Frederick William O'Connell 5 April 1947. No children.

SKEWES   PHYLLIS MANETTA
Lives at 326 O'Farrell Street, Broken Hill, 2880, New South Wales, Australia.

SKEWES   PHYLLIS MARIAN
Lived at 26 Inmarna Avenue, Caringbar, New South Wales, Australia, in 1959 with Donald Richard Skewes.

SKEWES   PIEDAD
Chart 10. Mexican. Daughter of Nazario and Piedad (née Lozano) Skewes. Born 13 April 1904, Real del Monte, Mexico. Married an Englishman — Trevera. Issue: two sons. Died 9 November 1961, aged 57 years.

SKEWES   PRISCILLA
Chart 36. Née Mill. Daughter of William Mill, miner. Born 1831, Illogan. Married William Skewes at Illogan Parish Church 10 July 1853. Lived at Carnkie and later Higher Treskillard and Carnarthen. Children: Elizabeth Ellen, Ann Amelia, Henry, William, James, Hannah, Mary and Edward. Died 1874, aged 43. Buried Illogan 2 February 1874.

SKEWES   PRISCILLA
Daughter of William and Jane Skewes of Treskillard, farmer. Bpt 20 February 1884, Camborne/Redruth Wesleyan-Methodist Circuit.

SKEWES   PRISCILLA
Chart 36. Daughter of William Henry and Beatrice Skewes of Brea. Born 1938, Kerrier. (Née Reynolds.)

SKEWES PRISCILLA
Lived at Fernside, Carn Lane, Carnkie, Redruth, 1968, with Annie M. Skewes.

SKEUES PRUDENCE
Chart 2. Bpt Camborne 18 July 1675. Died 19 December 1723, aged 48 years.

R

SKEWS RACHEL ANNE
Daughter of Melvyn Skews, Mother's maiden name Snowden. Born 1980, South Glamorgan, Wales.

SKEWES RACHEL CARDWELL
Chart 25. Born 1889. Married John Edward Skewes, civil servant in Chorlton, Manchester, 1914. Maiden name Gleave. Lived at 25 Surrey Road, Bournemouth. Died at St Leonard's Hospital, Ringwood, Hants 1 November 1966, aged 77 years.

SKEWES RACHEL JANE
Chart 24. Daughter of John and Mary Jane (née Cole) Skewes. Born 1885, New South Wales, Australia. Married with two children.

SKEWES RACHEL LYDIA
Lived at 104 Railway Street, Mereweather, New South Wales, Australia in 1959 with Henry Robert Skewes, millwright. Now lives at 38 Golding Avenue, Belmont North, 2280, New South Wales, Australia.

SKEWES RALPH
Chart 10. Son of Ernest William and Gladys Skewes of Ontario, Canada.

SKEWS RALPH
Butcher with Furi and Company; 2141 Mason, San Francisco, USA (1961). Wife's name Nancy Skews.

SKEWES RALPH
Chart 38. Son of Stanley Victor and Gertrude Olive (née Trimper) Skewes. Born 1919. Married Elma SKUCE (she died 1977). No family. Lives at 27 Main Street, Beverley, 5009, South Australia. Detailer.

SKEWES RALPH EDWARD
Lives at 45 Glenhuntley Street, Woodville, 5011, South Australia with Gwendra Pearl Skewes, David John Skewes and Steven Melville Skewes. Turner at South Australian Railways, Islington machine shop. Well-known model-maker of trains who has contributed to Railways Institute arts and crafts exhibitions.

SKEWES RALPH TREGONNING
Chart 10. Son of Richard Skewes. Born 24 April 1910, Hamilton, Ontario, Canada.

SKEWS RANAE
Chart 36. Daughter of Leslie Kevin and Jill Cecilia (née Pullman) Skewes. Born Watsons Creek, Bendemeer, New South Wales, Australia.

SKEWS RAY SAMUEL
Chart 38. Son of Sydney Howard and Cordelia (née Blight) Skewes. Born 26 June 1926, Adelaide, South Australia. Married Betty Joy Sloan, 28 August 1948 at St Aiden's Church of England, Payneham, Adelaide. Children: Sandra (1950) and Barry John (1959). Timber worker in Adelaide. Lives at 31 Browning Street, Barton Vale, Clearview, 5086, South Australia.

Ray Samuel Skewes

SKEWIS RAYMOND
Chart 2. Son of John Rule and Jane Skewis. Born 7 February 1887. Married Lottie Ruby in America. Children: Mason, Shirley, Charlotte and Donald Earl and Dale (twins).

SKEWS RAYMOND
Chart 41. Son of Joseph Skews. Born 1931. Mother's maiden name Alice Lumb. Died aged 0 in Barnsley.

SKEWES RAYMOND ALLEN G.
Lived at 5 Corella Street, Doncaster, Victoria, 3108, Australia in 1980.

SKUES RAYMOND ANTHONY
Chart 9. Son of Philip Ernest Skues. Mother's maiden name Camela Pinto. Born 1929, Southwark. Married Elizabeth I. Collie, 1960, Surrey Mid East. Child: Paula Marie (1968). Deputy chief engineering inspector.

SKUES RAYMOND J.
Chart 7. Son of Francis Albert Skues. Mother's maiden name Jeffery. Born 1922, Dartford. Bachelor.

SKEWES RAYMOND KENWYN
Lived at Koornang Road, Murrembeena, Henty, Victoria, Australia in 1913 with Ada Mary Skewes.

SKEWES RAYMOND V.
Mother's maiden name Williams. Born 1951, Redruth. Married Cynthia Hall, 1972.

SKEWES RAYMOND VERNON
Mother's maiden name Williams. Born 1972, Redruth.

SKEWES REBECCA
Chart 50. Née Mitchell. Born 1805, Breage. Married William Skewes in Constantine 23 March 1828. Children: Ann and William. Died 18 June 1898.

SKEWES REBECCA
Daughter of Richard and Rebecca Skewes. Bpt Sancreed 1 February 1731.

SKEWIS REBECCA
Buried 28 January 1761, Sancreed.

SKEWES REBECCA
Born 1801. Lived at Rayle Stamps, Redruth. Buried Illogan 15 February 1868, aged 67 years.

SKEWS REBECCA
Born 1859. Died 1892, aged 33 years in Easington.

SKEWES REBECCA ANNIE
Chart 46. Born 1870. Daughter of William Skewes, labourer. Lived at Prince Street, Falmouth. Married William James Pascoe, son of Thomas Pascoe, gardener of Mawnan at Bible Christian Chapel, Falmouth, 24 January 1892. Prior to marriage had an illegitimate son, Charles Skewes. Died 19 February 1927, aged 57 years.

SKEWES REBECCA JADE
Chart 38. Daughter of Brian Wayne and Irene Kaye (née Shammall) Skewes. Born 20 December 1980. Lives at 18 Launceston Avenue, Banksia Park, Adelaide, 5091, South Australia.

SKEWS REBECCA MARIE
Chart 17. Daughter of Stephen J. Skews. Mother's maiden name Claridge. Born 1977, Peterborough.

SKEWES REBECCA PHYLLIS
Chart 40. Daughter of Colin Skewes. Mother's maiden name Jordan. Born 1976, St Austell.

SKUES REGINALD
Chart 5. Son of Charles Skues of Australia. Served in both world wars. Died shortly after 2nd World War.

SKUES REGINALD A.
Married Elsie J.D. Quede, 1919, St George's, Hannover Square, London.

SKUES REGINALD ADRIAN
Chart 5. Artist. Lived at 94 Wellington Street, St Kilda, Melbourne, Victoria, Australia in 1931.

SKUSE REGINALD ALLEN
B.A. Son of Robert Skuse. Born 25 January 1938, Ilford, Essex. Educated Leyton High School; King's College, Cambridge. Basketball captain 1959-1961. B.A. 1961. Married Christine Margaret Judd, 1958. Address: 24 St Leonards Road, East Sheen, Barnes, London, SW 14.

SKEWS REGINALD E.
Chart 15. Son of Albert Edward Skews. Mother's maiden name Weston. Born 1932, East Stonehouse. Died 1941, aged 8 years in Plymouth.

SKEWES REGINALD E.
Son of Edward Skewes. Born approx. 1927, Detroit, Michigan, USA. Wife: Loretta Marie. One daughter, Mary (1964). Lives 1173 Yorkshire Road, Grosse Point Park, Detroit, Michigan, 48230, USA. Telephone number: Detroit 882 3194.

SKEWS REGINALD ERNEST
Born 1902 Devonport. Died 1924, aged 21 years in Devonport.

SKEWES REGINALD JOHN
Chart 36. Son of George and Mary (née Dowling) Skewes. Born 12 October 1907. Married Mary Mildred Rooney, 24 July 1926 at Armidale Methodist Church. Children: Coryl Isabel, Valda Kathleen, Shirley Eva and Noel John. Spent his life in the printing trade. For many years was

production manager of the *Northern Daily Leader,* Tamworth, New South Wales, Australia Retired in 1972. Is interested in charitable organisations. Enjoys a game of bowls. Lives at 41 North Street, Tamworth, 2340, New South Wales, Australia.

SKEWES   REGINALD LIONEL
Lived at Farm 427, Whitton, Leeton, New South Wales, Australia in 1959 with Pearl Louisa Skewes. Now lives at Farm/404 Dalbata Road, Leeton, 2705, New South Wales, Australia with Pearl Louisa Skewes, Garry Reginald Skewes and Laurence John Skewes.

SKUES   REGINALD PENROSE
Chart 5. Son of Charles Penrose Skues. Born 6 December 1885. Married Elsie Eadon, daughter of Arthur and Mary Eadon of Sheffield at St Mary's Church, Walkley, Sheffield, 6 June 1919. No children. Lived at Trebron, The Downs, West Looe, Cornwall. Died 23 April 1966, aged 80 years.

SKEWS   REGINALD THOMAS
Lives at 9 Harding Street, Ascot Vale, 3032. Victoria, Australia with Julia Ruth Skewes.

SCEWIES   REMFRE
Chart 2. Son of Humfrey Scewies. Mentioned in Cornwall Protestation Returns, 1642. Died 25 January 1686, Camborne.

SCUES   REMFERY
Chart 2. Son of Robert Scues. Bpt Camborne 4 July 1696. Married 26 February 1722 to Mary (Margery) Bryant. Children: Roben and Renfery.

SKEWES   REMFERY
Chart 2. Son of Remfery Skewes. Bpt Camborne 26 December 1727. Died 8 January 1743, aged 16 years.

SKEWES   RENE JANE
Chart 36. Daughter of Leslie Kevin and Jill Cecilia (née Pullman) Skewes. Born 28 December 1971, Bendemeer, 2352, New South Wales, Australia.

SKEWS   RENEE
Chart 42. Daughter of Frederick Crago and Ruth (née Thompson) Skews. Born 1936, Houghton. Married Hackett, 1961, Durham East.

SKEWES   REX OWEN
Chart 10. Son of John and Lilian May (née Maynard) Skewes. Born 5 June 1923. Married Jean Lilian Van Rensburg, 17 October 1944. Children: Lynette Gail (1947) and Cynthia Elaine (1954). Lives at Blyvooruitzicht Gold Mining Company, Blyvooruitzicht, Transvaal, South Africa.

SKEWS   RHODA ELEANOR G.
Lived at 21 Maud Street, Bentleigh North, Victoria, Australia in 1959 with Claude Skews.

SKUES   RHODA SARAH
Chart 9. Née Dawson. Born 25 October 1893. Second wife of John Skues of Eltham. Died 1973, aged 80.

SKEWES   RICARDO
Chart 10. Mexican. Son of Juan and Fransisca (née Meneses) Skewes. Born 23 March 1902. Died 20 December 1966, aged 64 years in Pachuca, Mexico.

SKEWES   RICARDO
Residing at PLZ Conquista 609, Valparaiso, Chile, South America in 1971/1972.

SKEWES   RICARDO RAFAEL
Chart 10. Mexican. Born 21 October 1974, Mexico City. Son of Guillermo and Teresa (née Bonnet) Skewes. Lives at Calle Puerto Real No 28, Colonia Condesa, Mexico DF 11.

SKEWES   RICHARD
Son of Sandry Skewes. Buried Ludgvan 20 March 1570.

SKEWES   RICHARD
Son of Thomas Skewes. Bpt Exeter St Mary's 23 July 1620.

SKEWES   RICHARD
Son of Richard Skewes. Bpt Mullion 32 December 1631.

SKEWES   RICHARD
Son of John and Margaret Skewes. Bpt St Keverne 18 November 1636.

SKEWES   RICHARD
Son of Richard and Jane Skewes. Bpt St Keverne 12 December 1636.

SKEWES   RICHARD
Mentioned in Cornwall Protestation Returns, 1642, Gwennap.

SKEWES   RICHARD
Mentioned in Cornwall Protestation Returns, 1642, Mullion.

SKEWES   RICHARD
Mentioned in Cornwall Protestation Returns, 1642, St Keverne.

SKEWES   RICHARD
Son of Keverne Skewes. Bpt St Keverne 11 April 1668.

SKEUIS   RICHARD
Married Bridgett Williams at Gwennap 23 June 1675.

SCUES   RICHARD
Chart 2. Son of Robert Scues. Bpt Camborne 8 April 1685. Died 20 February 1721, aged 36 years. Buried in Camborne Church.

SKEWS   RICHARD
Married Margaret Tregewe at Paul 2 January 1700. Children included Richard (1704) & Margaret (1707).

SKEWYS   RICHARD
Son of Richard and Margaret Skewys. Bpt Paul 14 January 1704.

SKEWES   RICHARD
Married Mary James 12 November 1710 at Kea.

SKEWES   RICHARD
Son of Richard Skews. Buried Kea 19 October 1712.

SKUES   RICHARD
Son of Digory Skues. Bpt Kenwyn December 1714.

SKEWES   RICHARD
Son of John and Catherine Skews. Bpt 15 March 1718, St Buryan.

SKEWES   RICHARD
Chart 19. Son of Thomas and Margaret Skewes. Bpt Gwennap 3 May 1718.

SKEWIS   RICHARD
Chart 3. Tinner at Helston. Married at Kenwyn Parish Church 16 December 1722 to Jane Coombe. Children: Stephen (1743), Jenefar (1730), Richard, Mary (1733), William (1735), Mary (1738), Stephen (1747) and John. Died 23 December 1755.

SKEWES   RICHARD
Married Rebecca Boltenal of Sennan at Gwennap 6 September 1723.

SKEWS   RICHARD
Son of Richard Skews. Bpt Kea 18 October 1724.

SKEWES   RICHARD
Son of Richard Skewes. Buried Sancreed 20 October 1733.

SKEWES   RICHARD
Married Margery Warren 25 February 1734 at Paul.

SKUES   RICHARD
Chart 3. Son of John and Mary P. Skues. Bpt Helston 24 October 1734.

SKUES   RICHARD
Chart 10. Son of Degory Skues. Married Ann Polgreen at St Clement 15 December 1737. Died 2 March 1741.

SKEWIS   RICHARD
Chart 2. Son of William and Mary Skewis. Bpt Camborne 21 October 1739. Married Alice Knucky 17 November 1765 at Camborne Parish Church. Children: Mary, William, Richard, Alice, Henry and Elizabeth. Died Constantine and buried 1 August 1808, aged 68 years.

SKEWIS   RICHARD
Son of Richard Skewis. Buried Helston 3 February 1741.

SKEWS   RICHARD
Son of Thomas and Elizabeth Skews. Bpt Gwennap 14 May 1743.

SKEWS   RICHARD
Son of Martin Skews. Bpt Kenwyn 8 April 1744.

SKEWES   RICHARD
Son of John and Elizabeth Skewes. Bpt Gwennap 9 June 1745.

SKEWES   RICHARD
Son of William and Hannah Skewes of St Gluvias. Bpt St Gluvias 9 May 1753.

SKEWIS   RICHARD
Chart 3. Son of Richard and Jane Skewis of Helston, Mentioned in his father's will in 1755.

SKEWES   RICHARD
Son of Peter Skewes. Bpt Kea 25 September 1762.

SKEWES   RICHARD
Son of Peter Skews. Buried Kea 8 March 1765.

SKEWES   RICHARD
Chart 29. Son of John and Alice Skewes of Hugus. Bpt Kea 9 December 1765. Married Roseannah Anthony at Kenwyn 18 February 1793. Children: Alice (1793), John (1796), James (1798), Mary (1800), Maria (1803) and Betsy (1803). Buried Kenwyn 14 August 1823, aged 57 years. Rose (born 1766) died Kenwyn 12 March 1843, aged 77 years.

SKEWES   RICHARD
Buried Gwennap 15 June 1766.

SKUES   RICHARD
Chart 3. Son of William and Mary Skues. Born 1767. Bpt 28 September 1767. Married Ann Richards of Truthall, 4 December 1793 at Helston Parish Church. Children: Richard, George, Grace Richards, Mary, William, Edward and Ann. Borough surgeon. Was also a surgeon in Cornwall Meneage Loyal Yeomanry 1803-1807. Died 17 November 1811, aged 45 years. He had a gamekeeper's certificate for the Manor of Penventon 1802-1808. His wife Ann died in Durnsford Street, East Stonehouse, Plymouth 8 February 1847, aged 83 years.

SKEWS   RICHARD
Buried Kea 10 December 1767.

SKEWES   RICHARD
Chart 36. Son of John and Mary Skewes. Bpt Cury 15 June 1768.

SKEWES   RICHARD
Buried Gwennap 6 June 1769.

SKEWES   RICHARD
Married Mary Teague at Kenwyn 20 October 1770.

SKEWES   RICHARD
Son of John and Mary Skewes. Bpt Gwennap 11 June 1771.

SKEWIS   RICHARD
Chart 2. Son of Richard and Alice Skewes. Bpt Camborne 9 May 1773. Died 26 October 1785, aged 12 years.

SKEWES RICHARD
Son of John and Mary Skewes. Bpt Gwennap 11 March 1774.

SKEWES RICHARD
Married Frances Toy 11 April 1774, at Budock.

SKEWES RICHARD
Son of John and Mary Skewes. Bpt Gwennap 16 July 1779.

SKEWES RICHARD
Buried Gwennap 5 December 1779.

SKEWS RICHARD
Chart 10. Son of Digory Skews Junior and Elizabeth (née Wasley). Born 1783. Bpt Kea 22 June 1783. Married Agnes Jeffrey 4 April 1806 at Kea. Mine agent. Children: John, William, Richard, Philippa, Sarah, Matthew and Thomas. Died 1867, aged 84 years.

SKEWES RICHARD
Born 1784. Buried 28 March 1837 at Chacewater, aged 53 years. Lived at Salem.

SKEWES RICHARD
of Kerley, Kea. Son of Richard and Jane Skewes. Bpt Kenwyn 10 October 1784. Buried Baldhu 28 July 1867, aged 84.

SKUES RICHARD
Chart 3. Son of John and Mary Skues. Bpt Helston 24 October 1784. Died 21 December 1794, aged 11 years.

SKEWES RICHARD
Chart 2. Son of John and Philippa Skewes. Bpt 10 April 1785, Camborne. Died 9 August 1816, aged 31 years.

SKEWES RICHARD
Chart 28. Son of Henry and Mary Skewes. Born 1786. Bpt Kenwyn 20 August 1786. Married Mary Ninis at Kea Church 25 August 1811. Was a labourer at Nancevellan Common, Kea, and later Parish Clerk of Kea for upwards of 20 years. Children: Patience, Mary, Peggy, Jane, Ann Enyes, Elizabeth, Harriet and Thomasine. Died 3 October 1854, aged 68 years. His wife Mary died same day (3 October 1854), aged 69 years.

SKEWES RICHARD
Buried Kenwyn 26 January 1794.

SKUES RICHARD
Chart 3. Son of Richard and Ann Skues. Bpt Helston 4 December 1794. Twice married: 1) Grace Noy with issue Grace Noy Skues (1819). Wife died 8 April 1821. 2). . . . . .Children: Ellen, William James Gordon, Richard and Mary Ann. Freemason with Druids Chapter of Love and Liberality No 79 of Royal Arch. Exalted 27 May 1816. Also Knights Templar; Exalted 2 June 1817.

SKEWES RICHARD
Chart 10. Son of Thomas Skewes of Kea. Buried Kenwyn 11 March 1795.

SKEWIS RICHARD
Chart 10. Son of Thomas and Mary Skewis. Bpt Kenwyn 1 May 1795.

SKUES RICHARD
Chart 3. Captain with First Helston Volunteers, 3 September 1798.

SKUES RICHARD
A private soldier with Germoe Volunteers 1790's.

SKEWES RICHARD
Married Mary Lean of Perranarworthal 24 June 1798. Richard was from Gwennap.

SKEWES RICHARD
Chart 19. Son of Alexander and Christian Skewes. Bpt Gwennap 23 September 1800. Died 13 July 1827, aged 27 years, at Carharrack, Gwennap.

SKEWES RICHARD
Chart 32. Miner. Married Grace Ford at Kenwyn 10 October 1803. Lived at Whitehall, Kenwyn. Later moved to Gwennap. Children: Richard, John, James Hanley and James Marley.

SKEWES RICHARD
Chart 18. Son of Thomas and Mary Skewes of Kea. Bpt Kea 24 May 1807.

SKEWES RICHARD
Chart 19. Son of Thomas and Elizabeth Skewes. Moved to Shillingford, Devon. Died 1807.

SKEWES RICHARD
Chart 32. Son of Richard and Grace Skewes. Bpt Kenwyn 4 June 1809.

SKEWES RICHARD
Buried Gwennap 19 December 1809.

SKEWES RICHARD
Chart 19. Son of John Skewes. Married Mary . . . . Children: Collan, Elizabeth, John and Thomas.

SKUES RICHARD
of Helston and later Devonport. Changed his name to Scott by Royal Authority 12 March 1827. Married to Susannah Maria Martha Scott, daughter of John Scott of Saltash, principal officer in His Majesty's Dockyard at Devonport. Royal concession and declaration registered in the College of Arms. He had previously been deputy steward of H.M. Coinage in Cornwall and Devon and succeeded his grandfather William Skues in February 1817. *British Imperial Calendar*, page 97 (British Museum and Guildhall Library, London) listed him as deputy steward

of The Coinages (Officers of the Duchy of Cornwall) until 1827 after which time his name disappears. Freemason.

SKEWES RICHARD
Chart 10. Son of Digory and Sophia (née Jordan) Skewes. Born 1816. Married Johanna Wasley of Kerley, Kea, 3 September 1840 at Kea Parish Church. Emigrated to Australia in 1849 aboard *Osprey* and arrived at Port Phillip, Melbourne on 22 March 1849. He was described as a labourer from Plymouth. Religion: Wesleyan. Both he, his wife and eldest daughter could read and write. The family returned to England on a visit and went back to Australia with a Jane Skewes (widow), aged 46 years. Their family then comprised: Elizabeth J. (15), Johanna (11), Richard (10), Emilia (6), Sarah (4) and Emiley (1). They left Liverpool on 2 August 1857 and arrived in Melbourne November 1857.

SKEWES RICHARD
Illegitimate son of Ann Skewes. Bpt Kenwyn 22 August 1819. On one of his marriage certificates he is also listed as son of Charles Skewes, blacksmith. Farmer and later blacksmith at Kenwyn. Twice married. 1) Elizabeth Ann Skewes (28), daughter of John Skewes, farmer of Chacewater at Register Office, Truro, 18 February 1858. Lived at Penstraze, 1861. Elizabeth Ann died 1866, aged 37 years. Children: Richard and Daniel. Married 2) Mary Ann Jeffery, widow (51), daughter of David Roberts, miner, at the Register Office, Truro, 16 May 1868. Died 8 February 1873, aged 54 years.
There is a possibility that Richard Skewes was in fact married three times, as his marriage certificate to Elizabeth Ann Skewes refers to him as "widower."

SKEWES RICHARD
Son of William Skewes, miner. Born 1819, Truro. Carpenter and innkeeper of Pentrase, Kea. Married Elizabeth Rouse (20) of London, but lived at Charles Street, Truro, daughter of Charles Rouse, labourer, at Kenwyn 4 March 1852.

SKEWES RICHARD
Born 1820. Lived in Illogan. Buried Camborne 1 May 1821, aged 6 months.

SKEWES RICHARD
Chart 36. Son of William and Alice Skewes of Treloskan, Cury. Bpt 5 October 1820.

SKEWES RICHARD
Chart 40. Born 1821. Married Caroline Laity. Children: Richard (1847), Emma Laity (1854), Esther Jane (1854) and William Henry (1858). Died 1877, aged 56 years, Marazion district.

SKEWES RICHARD
Chart 10. Son of Richard and Agnes Skewes, mine agent. Bpt Kenwyn 5 May 1822. Copper miner, and later cordwainer. Married Mary Ann James, daughter of Thomas James, butcher of Kerley, Kea at the Parish Church, Kea 15 May 1851. Children: John, Mary and Fanny Jane. Died before 1871. Mary Ann died at Gwennap 25 October 1904, aged 73 years.

SKEWES RICHARD
Chart 19, Son of Collan and Ann Skewes. Born 1824. Bpt Mold, Flint 18 November 1827. Died 8 December 1867, aged 43 years in Wareham, Dorset. Buried in his mother's grave in Gwennap Churchyard.

SKUES RICHARD
Cornet. Listed as serving in Cornwall Hussars, 1825.

SKUES RICHARD
Widower. Married Mary SKUES at Kenwyn Parish Church 17 November 1831.

SKEWS RICHARD
Son of Peter and Ann Skews of Gwennap. Bpt Kea 9 July 1833.

SKUES RICHARD
Chart 3. Son of Richard Skues, surgeon. Born November 1833, Plymouth. Married Lucy Pickard, daughter of Samuel Pickard, saddler at Halifax Parish Church, 9 July 1859 in presence of Ellen Skues. Overseer at *Halifax Courier* newspaper.
He had travelled to Halifax from Plymouth in May 1853, four months after the *Courier* had commenced. He remained in its employ until March 1890. From the outset obstacles were put in the way of him, as his employers in Plymouth were desirous of retaining his services in the south. Instead of being present for the first edition of the Halifax paper on 8 January 1853 he did not arrive until Easter. His manager told him he was going to an uncivilised part of the country, that they were barbarous in Yorkshire and that he would be starved to death.
In later years he recalled his first impressions of Halifax ". . . . . a wretched hole, with but a dozen or so lampposts about, and those only lit in winter. Many shops were lighted with candles or lamps." In those early days the *Courier* had a struggle for its existence, and at one time funds were so short that Richard Skues could not receive the full amount of his wages. He went back to Plymouth, but after six weeks his arrears were sent on, and he returned to Halifax. He often told with pride that apart from those six weeks he never missed being present at the publication of every issue during his 37 years association with the *Courier*.
For a period of 40 years he never had a day in bed through illness, the long record being broken when he was 74 years of age.
Richard Skues was made manager of the composing and publishing departments in 1856. Later he became collector and advertisement

canvasser, and for a long time reported theatres and concerts. On his retirement from the paper he was presented with a marble clock and side ornaments: "Presented to Mr Richard Skues by the proprietors and employees of the Halifax Courier on his retirement after 37 years service. March 18, 1890."

The black clock had been supplied by Mr G. Davies, of the Old Market. The timepiece had bronze pillars and figures of chaste design. The side ornaments were in the form of a canopy, supported by bronze Corinthian pillars, each having beneath it a graceful mythical object. The *Courier* employees were entertained to tea at the Exchange Restaurant at the beginning of April, 1890 by Frederick Gordon Skues and we are told that "everyone from the oldest man to the junior apprentice was present. Early in the proceedings the presentation was made in singularly appropriate and generous tones in a speech by Mr W. Pickles. Richard Skues suitably and feelingly acknowledged the spontaneous and unanimous exhibition of respect and admiration on the part of those with whom he had been so long and agreeably connected. Mr Walter Potherton, chief reporter of the *Courier*, proposed the health of an old friend and colleague who had arranged to accompany Messrs Skues, thus severing relations that never for a moment had been dimmed by a single word that either could have wished to recall. The toast was honoured amid every manifestation of enthusiasm."

Gravestone of Richard Skues (1836-1916) at Salterhebble, Halifax, Yorkshire. Also buried there: his wife Lucy and granddaughter Lucy

Richard Skues took over as proprietor and editor of *Halifax Free Press,* a weekly which did not have a long existence. It was published, price ½ penny, from 18 Barum Top, Halifax, by Frederick Gordon Skues.

The first edition appeared on 26 March 1890 and ceased publication in 1894 following a libel action which went heavily against the newspaper. Richard Skues then commenced a cafe business. The addresses where he lived during his Halifax days were: 13 New Bond Street (1866), 3 Heath Mount, Savile Park (1890), 41 Moorfield Villas, Savile Park (1905), Oriental Cafe, 4 Princess Street, Halifax (1905) and 10 Norfolk Place (1916). Children: Frederick Gordon (1860), Richard James (1863), Charles Pickard (1864), William (1866), Ernest (1868) and Florence Mary (1875).

Skues was a stern, military type gentleman with no liking for children. He did not have a great sense of humour. He was stocky, but not tall, and always well dressed. A lifetime Liberal.

Died 3 April 1916, aged 83 years. Interred at All Saints Cemetery, Salterhebble, Halifax, alongside his wife Lucy. "Grant them O Lord Eternal Rest and Let Light Perpetual Shine Upon Them."

SKEWES   RICHARD
Chart 10. Son of Peter & Grace (née Harris). Born 1833. Bpt Kea 9 July 1833. Worked in Mexico for much of his life. Married Mary Stripp of St

Austell, by licence 25 January 1872. Children: 3 sons and 2 daughters.
Mine captain who worked at Rosario Mine, Pachuca, Mexico. Was also
manager of the Santa Gertrudis Mine, Pachuca. Died 12 October 1907,
aged 75 years at The Willows, Penstraze, Chacewater at the house of his
son-in-law, Mr John Coad. Buried Baldhu 15 October 1907. His wife
Mary (Maria) died in Mexico 12 May 1896, aged 48 years and is buried
in the English Cemetery, Real del Monte.

SKEWES   RICHARD
Chart 14. Son of Edward and Mary Skewes of Rosenithon, farmer. Bpt
St Keverne 19 April 1838.

SKEWES   RICHARD
Chart 19. Son of John and Anne (née Davey) Skewes, coal agent. Born
18 October 1840 at Penance, Gwennap. Bpt Gwennap 16 December
1840. Engineman.
Married Elizabeth Ann Magor, daughter of Samuel Magor, miner at
Register Office, Redruth, 13 June 1866, in presence of Alexander
Skewes. Emigrated to Fresno, California, USA together with his brother
William Skewes. Issue: 2 children (both alive in 1900). Was a fruit
grower in Fresno owning a freehold farm.

SKEWES   RICHARD
Chart 40. Son of Richard and Caroline (née Laity), miner. Born 5
August 1847, Germovean, Breage. Married Susannah (Susan) Donald
at Perranuthnoe Parish Church 27 August 1870. (She died 1937, aged
89 years.) Lived at Perran Downs. Was a miner, later fish salesman and
farmer. Children: Susan Annie, William, Lilian Linda and Richard
Henry. Died 24 April 1924, aged 76 years.

SKEWS   RICHARD
Son of James and Harriet (née Curno) Skews. Born 8 July 1848, Neath at
Miles End Row, Lantwit. Bpt Neath, Glamorgan 26 December 1852.
Married 1870, Neath. Children: James John (1872), Mary (1874),
Harriet (1876), Grace (1878), Richard (1882), Thomas (1880) and
Absalom (1884).

SKEWES   RICHARD
Chart 50. Son of Thomas and Jane Skewes, lead miner of St Allen,
Truro. Born 1848. In 1851 Census Returns was living at St Allen with his
parents and brothers Thomas and Samuel and sisters Elizabeth Jane,
Mary and Emily. Emigrated to Victoria, Australia with his parents
aboard *David G. Fleming* from Liverpool (2 August 1857) arriving
Melbourne November 1857. Also travelled with Richard and Joanna
Skewes and family.

SKEWES   RICHARD
Chart 38. Son of Richard and Joanna (née Wasley) Skewes. Born 1846,
Kea. Emigrated with his parents to Australia aboard *Osprey* arriving
at Port Phillip, Melbourne, 22 March 1849.

SKEWES   RICHARD
Chart 38. Born Cornwall. Emigrated to Australia in 1850's. Carpenter.
Married Elizabeth Stephens. Son Richard Skewes.

SKEWES   RICHARD
Son of Richard Skewes, farmer and carpenter. Born 1858. Married 1)
Bessie Eddy (21), daughter of Jacob Eddy, gardener, at Parish Church,
Mithian 2 April 1884. Divorced. 2) Minnie Blewett, daughter of John
Blewett, farm labourer at the United Methodist Church, Redruth, 23
May 1908. Lived at Beacon, Camborne. Mine engine driver. Died
Redruth, 1925, aged 67 years.

SKEWES   RICHARD
Born 1860. Son of John and Grace Skewes of Crowan. In 1871 Census
Returns living at Horse Downs, Crowan with his parents, brother John
H. and sister Annie J. Buried Crowan 4 January 1885, aged 25 years.

SKEWES   RICHARD.
Chart 38. Son of Richard & Elizabeth (née Stephens) Skewes. Born 1
March 1861 at Burra, South Australia. Married 6 April 1882 to Mary
Jane Reynolds of Cornwall at Moonta, South Australia. Children:
Richard James, Edgar William, Albert Victor, Horace Henry, Stanley
Victor, Albert Milton, Harold Edwin, Sydney Howard, Clarice
Arcadia, Charles Leslie, George Percy and Ernest Seymour. Died 19
January 1930, Adelaide, South Australia, aged 69 years. Buried in West
Terrace Cemetery, Adelaide.

SKEWES   RICHARD
Born 1863, Redruth. Son of Philip Skewes of Treslothan, miner.
Married Louisa Jane Tellam (19) of College Row, daughter of Francis
Tellam, miner 31 August 1884 at Camborne.

SKEWES   RICHARD
Chart 10. Son of Digory and Fanny (née Tregonning) Skewes. Born 8
September 1863, Marazion. Lived at Trevenner, Marazion. Married
Frenetta Littleton (who died 15 September 1899)..... 1886. Became a
market gardener at 3 Rose Cottages, Well Lane, Falmouth.
Married Henrietta Littleton (daughter of Jonathan Littleton, market
gardener, and sister of his first wife), domestic servant of 3 Stratton
Terrace, Falmouth at Register Office, Falmouth 8 February 1902.
In Cornwall Richard worked for T.F. Hoskins Seed House and Gardens.
Emigrated to Canada and Hamilton, Ontario in 1905. Children:
Gertrude, Richard Henry, John Joseph, Laura, Ernest, Hettie Louise,
Jonathan Braddon, Agnes Corona, Philip Littleton, Ralph Tregonning
and Alfred. Died 14 September 1925, aged 62 years.

SKEWS   RICHARD
Born 1864, Liskeard. Lived at Tremar Coombe. Emigrated to USA and

Richard Skewes (1861-1930)

married Emma Thomas of Tremar Coombe, Liskeard at Boulder City,
Colorado, USA, 29 November 1895.

SKEWES   RICHARD
Married 1866, Redruth.

SKEWES   RICHARD
Son of Peter Skewes of River Cottage, Chacewater. Bpt Chacewater 1
May 1874.

SKEWS   RICHARD
Born 1882, Neath. Son of Richard Skews.

SKEWES   RICHARD
Married 1902, Falmouth.

SKUES   RICHARD
Chart 3. Son of Ernest and Clara (née Roberts) Skues. Born 22 May
1904, Hanwell, Middlesex. Education: Bents Private School,
Barnsley; King James Grammar School, Almondbury, Huddersfield
and Blackburn Grammar School, Lancashire. In his teens he lived with
his parents at Derby Cottage, Derby Road, Heaton Moor; Peel Moat
Road, Heaton Moor and Ashburn Grove, Heaton Norris, Stockport,
Cheshire.
He was apprenticed to William Swann, architects and surveyors of St
Petersgate, Stockport. He left after nine months by which time he had
taken a great interest in furniture and admits modestly he had a flair for
salesmanship. He took a job as a junior salesman with Henry's Store,
Market Street, Manchester. By this time he was showing a talent for
cricket, which he practised in his spare time. He had been a good
sportsman at school, playing cricket, football, tennis and snooker. He
was offered a trial by Lancashire County Cricket Club as a member of
Sir Edwin Stockton's XI (he was then President of Lancashire County
Cricket Club) and whilst playing opposite Sir Julien Cahn's XI was
offered a position at Nottingham Furnishing Headquarters, known as
Jays and Campbells. Sir Julien was the owner of the then multiple
furnishing combine, the largest in the country. He had his own cricket
ground.
As well as playing cricket Richard Skues also wrote about the game for
the *Stockport Advertiser* (1927-1930) as well as the *Stockport Express*
and *Cheshire Echo*. In 1933 his journalistic flair was shown in
Furnishing World where he wrote a number of articles on the subject of
furnishing.
He commenced playing cricket at the age of nine. Ten years later he
played against Altrincham, who selected three county players. He was
then a member of Sir Edwin Stockton's XI specialising as a fast bowler
and taking a 23 yard run to the wicket. His best bowling analysis was
eight wickets for five runs, including a hat trick. He batted at number
seven. In 1928 he wrote the career of Lancashire cricketer Charles

Hallows through the *Stockport Express* and helped to raise funds for Hallows' Benefit. That year Hallows was one of the few cricketers to reach 1000 runs in May. Richard Skues received many letters of praise from top names in the cricketing world, including Neville Cardus, Walter Hammond and J.T. Tyldsley, for helping to raise a considerable amount of money towards Hallows' Benefit.

In 1936 he bought his own shop "R. SKUES, House Furnishers" at Lower Hillgate, Stockport, Cheshire, as well as a large warehouse in Waterloo Road, Stockport. The following year he was taken seriously ill with quinsy, and admitted to Stepping Hill Nursing Home, Stockport. He almost died, but was helped to recovery by a beautiful nurse, Doris Eileen Hughes. They married after an engagement of six months, on 5 March 1938 at Frodsham Parish Church, Cheshire. Children: Richard Keith (1939), Margaret Elaine (1947) and Christopher Raymond (1949).

During the 2nd World War Richard Skues was put in charge of the allocation of materials used in the production of the wings for Lancaster bombers at Metropolitan Vickers at Trafford Park, Manchester. He was also made a fire warden.

After the war he joined New Day Furnishing Stores as manager of their Northwich (Cheshire) branch where he remained for five years before being promoted to area supervisor. After two years he was again promoted — to buyer.

Richard Skues retired from business early following the tragic death of his daughter Margaret Elaine in a car crash in March 1968.

The Skues family had lived at "Richleen", 21 Buckingham Grove, Timperley, Cheshire. In 1969 they moved to Parkstone, Poole, Dorset. Doris Eileen Skues (daughter of John Frederick and Elizabeth (née Franklin) Hughes was born 8 March 1913. She died peacefully at Poole General Hospital 28 March 1974, aged 61 years.

Three years later Richard Skues moved to his present address at 26 Pine Park Mansions, Wilderton Road, Branksome Park, Poole. Tel No 0202 760786.

His only surviving son (Christopher Raymond died 1950), Richard Keith, is Programme Director of Radio Hallam, in Sheffield, South Yorkshire. Richard Skues spends much of his spare time writing, especially prose. He likes reading, and is also very involved in voluntary work and helping the blind. He is a sidesman at St Luke's Parish Church, Parkstone.

Wedding of Richard Skues to Doris Eileen Hughes at Frodsham, Cheshire, March 1938

SKEWS   RICHARD
Chart 10. Son of Peter and Maude Mary Skews. Born 1908, St Austell. Died St Austell, 1930, aged 23 years.

SKEWES   RICHARD
Chart 10. Son of Ernest and Marjorie Jane (née Coomber) Skewes of Marazion. Born 5 August 1919, Hamilton, Ontario, Canada. Married Evelyn Broach. Children: Richard (1943), Patsy (1948) and James (1952). Lives at 147 Glassco Avenue, North, Hamilton, Ontario. Production manager at Westinghouse.

SKEWES   RICHARD
Lived at Unity, St Day, Gwennap, 1922 with Minnie Skewes.

SKEWES   RICHARD
Chart 38. Married in England. Lived at 172 Burns Bay Road, Lane Cove, New South Wales, Australia in 1959 with Joyce Skewes. Storeman. Son: Daniel. Died 10 October 1978, Adelaide, South Australia.

SKEWIS   RICHARD
Mother's maiden name Lyons. Born 1968, Kettering.

SKEWES   RICHARD ALBERT
Chart 10. Son of Richard and Evelyn (née Broach) Skewes. Born 21 October 1942, Hamilton, Ontario, Canada. Married Anne Marie Millar (she born 20 November 1938) at St Michael's Cathedral, Toronto 28 April 1962. Children: Mark Alexander Joseph (1963), Kevin Richard (1964), Tamara (1965) and Michael James Patrick (1967).

SKUES   RICHARD ALEXANDER
Chart 3. Son of George and Mary Gibbs Skues. Born 12 April 1838. Ensign in 3rd West India Regiment 6 July 1855. Became a lieutenant in 69th (South Lincolnshire) Regiment of the Foot 1858-1873. Retired and went to live in America as Sheriff of Denver, Colorado.

SKEWES   RICHARD ANDREW
Chart 12. Son of Dennis I.J. and June (née Letcher) Skewes. Born 1971, Truro.

SKUES   RICHARD ANTONY
Chart 3. MSc., B.A. Son of George and Joyce Skues. Mother's maiden name Littlewood. Born 23 December 1953. Married Nicola Claire Johns at Carwen 29 May 1978.

SKEWS   RICHARD ALEXANDER
Lives at 8 Lehem Avenue, Oakleigh South, 3167, Victoria, Australia with Helen Gale Skews. Engineer.

SKEWES   RICHARD CHARLES
Born 1878, Redruth. Died 1878, aged 0.

SKEWES   RICHARD CHARLES
Chart 36. Son of John and Eliza Jane (née Semmens) Skewes. Born 12 March 1880, Troon Moor. Married Ada Jane Collins, 1907, Redruth, (Ada Jane born 1882; died 1976, aged 94 years.) Child: Mary Margery (1907). Lived at 10 Condurrow Road, Beacon, Redruth. Died 1930, aged 50 years.

SKEWES   RICHARD CHARLES
Born 1883, Redruth. Died 1883, aged 0.

SKEWS   RICHARD CHARLES
Born 15 January 1898, Bethnal Green. Lived at 11 Morpeth Street, Bethnal Green (1922). Died 1969, aged 71 years.

SKEWES   RICHARD CHARLES
Born 1906, Redruth. Lived at Maynes Row, Tuckingmill. Died 1906, aged 9 months. Buried Tuckingmill Parish Church 11 December 1906.

SKEWIS   RICHARD DARREN
Chart 50. Son of Michael Ian and Audrey (née Humphrey) Skewis of Hull. Born 23 July 1969, Cyprus. Lives at 3 Woodhall Street, Stoneferry Road, Hull. Tel. no: 0482 217770.

SKEWS   RICHARD E.
Lives at 73 James Street, Gillingham, Kent. Tel. no: 0634 572102.

SKEWIS   RICHARD EDWARD
Chart 2. Son of Edward George and Margaret Skewis. Born 16 January 1937, United States of America. Married Deanne Wilson. Lives at 4605 178th Avenue East, Sumner, Washington State, 98390. Children: Elizabeth Marie, Richard Edward, Eric Edward and Amy Eileen.

SKEWES   RICHARD EDWARD
Chart 2. Son of Richard Edward and Deanne (née Wilson) Skewis. Born 26 May 1964, Washington State, USA.

SKEWES   RICHARD EDWIN
Chart 14. Son of George Jessop and Ruth (née Viall) Skewes. Born 31 May 1937. Bachelor of Science, State University of St Cloud, 1959; Masters' Degree in Education, State University, St Cloud. PhD, University of Iowa, 1974, in Music Education. Married Victoria Lohman Holey (she born 15 April 1939; Bachelor of Science, State University of St Cloud, 1970), 12 July 1963. Adopted children: Lynn Marie Holey Skewes (1960) and Charles George Holey Skewes (1962). Divorced 1977. Married Peggy Pierce Twa (she born 4 August 1943; Bachelor of Science, State University of Mankato, Minneapolis, 1975), 5 June 1977. She already had one daughter, Teri Twa (born 14 December 1963). Lives at Faribault, Minnesota, United States of America.

SKEWS   RICHARD ERNEST
Chart 36. Son of Francis and Grace Skews of Illogan Highway. Born 1874. Bpt Illogan 24 February 1874. Married 1906, Redruth. Was living

at 18 Adelaide Road, Redruth (1922) with Minnie Skewes. By 1949 had moved to 36 Adelaide Road, Redruth. Died 1956, aged 81 years in Redruth.

SKEWES   RICHARD GARFIELD
Chart 10. Son of Thomas George Skewes of Marazion. Born 6 September 1900 at Ishpeming, Marquette, Michigan, USA. Married Marion Lenzie 14 February 1925.

SKEWES   RICHARD H.
Married Minnie Revell in Marylebone, 1919. Child: Henry R. (1919), Marylebone.

SKEWES   RICHARD HENRY
Chart 10. Son of Peter and Elizabeth (née Bray) Skewes. Born 1871, Chacewater, Cornwall. Bpt Chacewater 1 May 1874. First went to South Africa for a short while then to Mexico. Miner. Married Louie Pratt, daughter of John Pratt of Real del Monte, Mexico on 25 December 1893 at Mineral del Monte. Two sons: Peter (1894) and George Owen (1897). Lived at San Vicente Mine, Real del Monte. Became mine agent. He was involved in an accident on 1 March 1899 when he sustained injuries to his head after his horse shied at a telegraph post and then threw him with such force that he died four days later. Two doctors tried to save his life, but all efforts proved unavailing. Buried in English Cemetery, Real del Monte, 4 March 1899, aged 28 years. On tombstone is Masonic emblem and "Why do we mourne departing friends or shake at death's alarm. 'Tis but the voice that Jesus sends to call them to his arms." Louie married William Honey, 1899. Born in 1870, she died in Vancouver, British Columbia, 1945, aged 75 years.

SKEWES   RICHARD HENRY
Chart 30. Son of John Beer and Mary Brown Skewes. Born 1871 at Kenwyn Street, Truro. Married 1909 in Kensington. Died Battersea, 1936, aged 65 years.

SKEWES   RICHARD HENRY
Chart 40. Born 1874, Penzance. Married 1909 at Methodist Chapel, Chynhale, Sithney to . . . . Lived at Perran Downs, Marazion and later (1956) at Bolenna, Fore Street, Marazion. Child: Elsie (1910). Was involved in a number of police cases accused of being drunk. Latest on 12 July 1924 when he was found guilty of "being drunk in charge of a horse." . . . . and fined £1. Died July 1959, aged 85 years.

SKEWES   RICHARD HENRY
Chart 10. Son of Richard Skewes of Marazion. Born 1888, Penzance. Emigrated to Canada with his parents in 1905. Married Elizabeth Doughty 28 February 1914. Worked in a lime kiln at Gallagher Brothers. Later purchased 7 acres of land in Ryckman's Corner. Grew garden produce and raised pigs. With the help of his two daughters Mabel and Lillian he attended Hamilton, Ontario, market for 12 years, specialising in cauliflowers. He retired and sold the property in 1965. His wife Mary Elizabeth died 13 December 1965. Children: Lillian Frenetta (1920) and Mabel Jane (1915). He married again — to Charlotte Brown. She died 1977. Richard Henry died 23 March 1976, aged 89 years.

SKEWES   RICHARD HERBERT
Chart 10. Son of Jonathan Braddon Skewes. Born 2 February 1924 at Hamilton, Ontario, Canada. Married Alice Harriet Roberts 18 September 1943, in Canada.

SKEWES   RICHARD HORACE HENRY
Chart 38. Son of Horace Henry and Agatha Blanche Skewes. Born 30 January 1908, Kadina, South Australia. Died 8 April 1908; infant.

SKEWES   RICHARD J.
Manager of R.J. Skewes Furnishing Store, 211 Broadway East, Seattle, Washington, USA. Wife's name Helen H. Lived at 2328 Delmare Drive East, Seattle, Washington. Had died by 1967.

SKUES   RICHARD JAMES
Chart 3. Son of Richard and Lucy (née Pickard) Skues. Born 14 July 1862, Halifax. Became friendly with Eleanor Chorley whom he met socially when she was a barmaid at the Sportsman Inn, Halifax. They married at Trinity Church, Kendal, 1897. Worked as a die maker at Eglin and Company, Halifax. As a youth he had wanted to go into the Navy, but was stopped by his mother who thought he might drown! Lived at Trinity Place; 4 Princess Street, Halifax; Princess Street, Sowerby Bridge; Willow Cottage, Rochdale Road, Halifax; 10 Norfolk Place, Halifax; Peel House, Luddenden; Beech Road, Sowerby Bridge; 31 York Crescent, Rochdale Road, Halifax and 5 Kingston Drive, Halifax. Children: Lucy (1898), Eric (1899), Frederick (1900) and Evelyn (1902). Died May, 1948, aged 85 years.

SKEWES   RICHARD JAMES
Chart 38. Son of Richard and Mary Jane (née Reynolds) Skewes. Born 17 December 1882, Moonta, South Australia. Married Cecilia Andrew, 20 Sepember 1902. Died 28 December 1947, aged 65 years.

SKEWES   RICHARD JAMES
Chart 42. Son of Thomas and Annie (née McDowell) Skewes. Born 2 January 1898, Narrabri, Australia. Married Amy Post 20 August 1924, North Sydney. Children: Kenneth Richard (1925), Jack (1927), Joan (1933) and Valerie (1930). Died 21 January 1955, aged 57 years.

SKEWES   RICHARD JOHN
Born 1885, St Columb.

SKEWES   RICHARD JOHN
Chart 37. Born Ballarat, Victoria, Australia. Coach builder. Children:

Richard James Skues (1862-1948)

Pearl, Mary, John Richard, Irlene and Leonard.

SKEWES   RICHARD JOHN
Chart 10. Son of John and Lilian May (née Maynard) Skewes. Born 18 June 1916, Cleveland, Johannesburg, South Africa. Married Edna Thelma Manson, at St Mary's Cathedral, Johannesburg, 3 April 1940. Children: Delyse Merle (1943) and Beverley Karen (1947). Former new business manager of the Prudential Assurance Company Ltd, Johannesburg where he worked for 38 years. Hobbies include landscape painting and he is a bird fancier. Enjoys cricket, squash, soccer and tennis. Lives at 14 8th Avenue, Edenvale, Transvaal, South Africa.

SKEWES   RICHARD JOHN
Chart 40. Mother's maiden name Moon. Born 1943 Penzance. Son of Willie Skewes. Married Leonie P. Hall, 1965, Penzance. Children: Richard Terry (1972) and Edward Simon (1974). Lives at Three Jolly Tinners, St Hilary, Cornwall.

SKEWES   RICHARD JOHN
Chart 2. Son of William John and Barbara McKay (née Carroll) Skewes. Born 6 August 1970, Australia.

SKEWS   RICHARD JOHN
Chart 17. Son of Robert W. Skews. Mother's maiden name Agates.

SKUES   RICHARD KEITH
Chart 3. Son of Richard and Doris Eileen (née Hughes) Skues. Born 4 March 1939, Timperley Lodge, Cheshire. Bpt Frodsham Parish Church 2 July 1939. Education: Park Road Primary School, Timperley; Wellington Road Secondary Modern School, Timperley and County Grammar School, Altrincham. Member of St Alban's Choir and Amateur Dramatic Group and regularly appeared in their productions. Leader of St Alban's Youth Group 1954-1958. Editor of *Youth Fellowship Times* (1956-1958). National service, Royal Air Force (1958-1960), 229 OCU Chivenor, North Devon, followed by an attachment to British Forces Network, Cologne. Civilian commission as Announcer, British Forces Broadcasting Service: Kuwait, 1961; Kenya 1961-1964. Whilst in East Africa he and an RAF team successfully climbed to the summit of Mount Kilimanjaro (19,340 ft), Africa's highest mountain, in October, 1962 and the following year reached the summit of Mount Kenya (17,058 ft). Wrote articles for *East African Standard*; edited a features page for *Sunday Post* and compiled a pop page each week for *Daily Nation*. His radio shows "Skueball Speshall" and "Skues Me" collected awards two years running. When Kenya gained its independence in 1963 Forces Radio was closed down and he was posted to Aden early in 1964. Returned to England after three months and joined Radio Caroline as a disc jockey 1964-1965; Radio Luxembourg 1966 and Radio London (1966-1967). Was chosen as a member of the original team of announcers to launch Radio One 1967 and remained with the BBC until 1974 during which he broadcast regularly on Radios One and Two as well as appearing on

television. Shows included "Saturday Club", "What's New, "Breakfast Show", "Roundabout", "Sunday with Skues", "Housewives' Choice", "Album Time", "Radio One Club" and "Night Ride" (radio) and "Juke Box Jury", "Top of the Pops", "Wembley Festival of Stars", "Pop the Question", "Rough with the Smooth", "The Kenneth Williams Show", "The Ronnie Corbett Show", "Late Night Line Up", "Pop Quest" and "Calendar" (television). Appointed Vice President of National Association of Youth Clubs (Patron — H.M. Queen Mother) in 1972 and is actively involved in voluntary work up and down the country. In his spare time ("what spare time?" he quips) he enjoys writing and to his credit are *A Short History of Heanton Punchardon, North Devon*, 1958; *Pop Went the Pirates*, 1967; *Radio Onederland*, 1968; and *History of the Skues Family*, 1970 — revised 1979; *Cornish Heritage*, 1982; as well as many articles in magazines and newspapers. He is a Lord's Taverner; member of the Stars Organisation For Spastics; has written sleeve notes for LP records; has appeared in the award winning film "Sunday Bloody Sunday"; been the voice behind many television and radio commercials and film documentaries; has represented Great Britain as a disc jockey in South Africa (1971) and at different times been presented to the Queen Mother, Prince Charles, the Duke of Edinburgh, Princess Alexandra and Princess Alice.

He is a member of the Society of Genealogists; a council officer of Sheffield Association of Youth Clubs. Appointed Programme Director of Radio Hallam (South Yorkshire) in May 1974 and the following year became a full board member. In 1977 he won the National "Hit Pickers" Award. In 1978 and 1979 he compered the National Radio Awards in London. Pilot member of Aircraft Owners & Pilots Association. Always keen on travelling, he reels off countries he has visited or lived in: America, East Africa, North Africa, South Africa, Belgium, Holland, France, Germany, Austria, Canada, the Arctic, Swaziland, Aden, Persian Gulf, Kuwait, Malta, Spain, Cyprus, Mexico, Bahamas, Hong Kong, Australia & New Zealand. He relates: "It is quite an impressive list of countries, but I am just as happy visiting the county in which the Skues family had their beginnings — Cornwall, England". Current address: 11 Windsor Court, Hill Turrets Close, Ecclesall, Sheffield 11, South Yorkshire. Tel No: 0742 71188.

Richard Keith Skues, aged 18 months in 1940

SKEWES   RICHARD LALY
Son of Richard and Caroline Skewes of St Neot, miner. Bpt Cury 19 March 1848.

SKEWES   RICHARD LORY
Chart 14. Son of Edward and Mary Skewes, farmer. Born 1838. Bpt St Keverne 19 April 1838. In 1851 Census Returns lived at Carne and was employed at home. Died at Kugger, Grade 4 July 1862, aged 23 years.

SKUES   RICHARD MARTIN
Chart 2. Son of Henry and Grace Skues. Bpt Camborne 20 September 1834. Copper miner. Lived at Berrispiper, Camborne. Listed in 1841 and 1851 Census Returns. Died Gwinear 12 December 1852, aged 19 years.

SKEWES   RICHARD MORLEY
Lived at 22 Talbot Avenue, Canterbury, Victoria, Australia in 1959 with Gladys Jeanee Skewes. Clerk.

SKEWS   RICHARD N.E.
Chart 17. Son of James Arthur Skews. Mother's maiden name Jarvis. Born 1916, St George's East, London. Married Stonebridge in Lewisham, 1939.

SKEWS   RICHARD NATHANIEL EDWARD
Chart 17. Son of George and Charlotte (née Dane) Skews of Canal Cottages, Milton, Gravesend, Kent. Printer. Married Sarah Harding, 1873, Islington (she died 1936, aged 83 years). Lived at 5 Usk Street, London E2 in 1922. Children: Nathaniel Edward R. (1874) and Henry James (1880). Died 1932, Bethnal Green, aged 88 years.

SKEWES   RICHARD SAMUEL
Lives at 174 Mont Albert Road, Canterbury, 3126, Victoria, Australia. Bank officer.

SKEWES   RICHARD STEVENSON
2nd Lieutenant, Marine Corps, US Navy, 1959. Born 11 November 1935.

SKEWS   RICHARD T.
Mother's maiden name King. Born 1963, Rochford, Essex.

SKEWES   RICHARD TERRY
Chart 40. Son of Richard John and Leonie (née Hall) Skewes. Born 1972, Truro.

SKEWES   RICHARD W.
Lives at 87 Union Avenue, Lynbrook, Nassau, Manhattan, New York, USA. Tel no: (516) 593 4229.

SKEWES   RICKY WAYNE
Chart 38. Son of Albert John and Kathleen Mavis (née Clark) Skewes.

Born 17 March 1971. Lives at Government Road, Bute, South Australia, 5560.

SKEWES RINA MARY
Chart 19. Born 24 March 1891 at Elm House Academy, Dorset. Married Sidney Arthur Angold in Christchurch, Hants, 1912.

SKEWS RITA
Chart 41. Daughter of Joseph and Alice (née Lumb) Skews. Born 1929, Barnsley, South Yorkshire. Died 1929, aged 0.

SKEWES RITA OLIVE
Lived at Farm 109, Petersham Road, Leeton, New South Wales, Australia in 1959. Now lives at 24 Cudgerie Avenue, Leeton, 2705, New South Wales, Australia.

SKEWES ROBARD
Died Camborne 9 March 1721.

SCEWES ROBART
Chart 2. Son of Remfre Scewes. Bpt Camborne 26 March 1653. Children: Remfery, Richard and Elizabeth. Died 20 January 1717, aged 65 years. Buried in Camborne Church.

SKEUES ROBART
Chart 2. Son of Remfery Skeues. Bpt Camborne 8 April 1726. Children: Ann, Margery, James and Mary. Died 27 June 1776, aged 49 years.

SKEWES ROBERT
Mentioned in Cornwall Protestation Returns, 1642, Gwennap.

SKUES ROBERT
Buried Gwennap 3 December 1675.

SKUES ROBERT
Married Jane Mitchell at Wendron 17 February 1682.

SKEWES ROBERT
Son of William Skewes. Bpt Gwennap 18 August 1695.

SKEWES ROBERT
Son of John and Catherine Skewes. Bpt St Buryan 15 July 1727. Buried St Buryan 20 July 1793, aged 66 years.

SKEWES ROBERT
of Camborne. Married Jane Sandys at Helston Parish Church, 9 November 1751.

SKEWIS ROBERT
Son of Robert Skewis. Bpt Camborne privately 15 August 1752. Publicly 24 September 1752. Buried 13 November 1823, aged 75 years, in Camborne.

SKEWES ROBERT
Buried Camborne 27 June 1776.

SKEWES ROBERT
Born 1829. Appeared in court accused of stealing money on 6 May 1859 at East Looe. Found guilty and given 12 months hard labour. He had been pursuing a career of crime said the judge and had appeared in court six times previously. Full report *Cornish Heritage* — Appendix — Press Cuttings — *Royal Cornwall Gazette* 8 July 1859.

SKEWIS ROBERT
Chart 44. Son of Thomas and Elizabeth Skewis. Born 1845, Abergavenny. Died 1845, aged 0.

SKEWIS ROBERT
Son of James and Elizabeth Skewis. Born 1846, Abergavenny. Died 1855, aged 9 years.

SKEWIS ROBERT
Chart 2. Son of Arthur Lawrence and Elizabeth Skewis. Married several times. No children. Lives in San Jose, America.

SKEWIS ROBERT
Died Glasgow, Scotland, 1864.

SKEWES ROBERT
Son of William and Elizabeth Alberta Mary (née Jessop) Skewes. Born 4 May 1908, Challenge, Houghton, Michigan, USA. Died 9 September 1908.

SKEWIS ROBERT
Born 1952, Shettleston, Scotland. Died 1952, aged 0.

SKEWES ROBERT
Chart 36. Son of Glenleigh Bertie William and Mary Evelyn Harriet (née Watkins) Skewes. Born 16 April 1940, Victoria, Australia. Married Marjorie Lorraine Hartwick, 18 December 1965, Geelong, Victoria. Children: Deborah Leanne (1967), Leonie Jane (1969) and Andrea Louise (1974). Lives at 9 Trudgen Street, Shepparton, 3630, Victoria, Australia. School teacher.

SKEWES ROBERT
Lived at 174 Mont Albert Road, Canterbury, Victoria, Australia in 1959 with Annie Phillips Skewes. Teacher.

SKEWES ROBERT
Chart 36. Son of Peter Nathaniel and Janet Skewes. Born 26 July 1975. Lives at 16 Alawara Road, Ingle Farm, South Australia, 5098.

SKEWES ROBERT
Chart 36. Son of William Vere and Annie Rebecca (née Strain) Skewes. Born 9 June 1939, Tamworth, New South Wales, Australia. Married Thea Taylor in Tamworth. Children: Benjamin, Nicholas, Sally and Matthew Vere. Lives at 32 Anchor Road, Tamworth, 2340, New South Wales, Australia.

SKEWES ROBERT ALAN

Robert Skewes

Chart 36. Son of Edward Keith and Maisie (née Lawson) Skewes. Born 24 March 1950, Western Australia. Died 28 March 1950, aged 4 days.

SKEWS ROBERT ALBERT
Chart 17. Son of Richard Nathaniel Edward and Sarah (née Harding) Skews. Born 1887, Bethnal Green. Married Charlotte L. Waite, 1918, Bethnal Green. Children: Ellen M. (1919) and Marjorie E. (1925). Died 1951, aged 63 years.

SKEWES ROBERT ARTHUR
Chart 10. Son of Ernest and Jane (née Coomber) Skewes of Marazion and Canada. Born Hamilton, Ontario, Canada 24 September 1922. Married Lilian Foster 20 March 1943, Hendon, London. (She born 1 June 1923.)

SKEWES ROBERT BILLING
Chart 2. Son of William and Sarah Billing Skewes. Born 1861, Camborne. He emigrated with his parents to America about 1875. He was one of the pioneers in the undertaking business in Salt Lake City, Utah being associated with his father during the earlier years of his life, and later with his brothers. In 1903 he went to Park City, Utah and engaged in mining for a short time. Whilst there he did heroic service at the time of the Daly-West explosion in rescuing miners in that disaster and in caring for the mangled bodies of those who had been killed. During the last few years of his life he worked for Eber W. Hall of Salt Lake City and in 1907 took charge of a branch department of the business in Bingham Canyon, Utah. He died on the evening of Friday, 8 May 1908 at his place of business of "gastritis of the stomach." He had been a sufferer from the disease for some time, but was apparently in good health until about 24 hours before his death. The funeral service was held at Bingham Canyon on Sunday, 10 May 1908 and he was interred in Mount Olivet Cemetery, Salt Lake City, Utah. He was aged 47 years and a bachelor.

SKEWIS ROBERT BLYTH
Born 1902, Blackfriars, Scotland. Died 1926, aged 24 years in Possilpark, Glasgow.

SKUES ROBERT BRUCE
Son of William and Margaret Skues. Born 18 May 1889. Lived in New South Wales, Australia.

SKEWES ROBERT CURTIS
Chart 2. Son of John Billing IV and Dolores (née Davis) Skewes. Born 16 May 1977, Utah, USA.

SKEWIS ROBERT DON
Chart 2. Son of Donald Earl and Shirley Skewis. Born 14 December 1951, USA.

SKEWES ROBERT ERNEST
Chart 26. Son of Frank Edward and Eleanor May (née Darrow) Skewes. Born 13 January 1924, Manchester, Connecticut, USA. Married Elaine Helen Albanese (she born 16 October 1923) in New London,

Connecticut, USA, 11 January 1947. Children: Robert Leonard (1951), Edward Anthony (1955), David Darrow (1956) and Mary Eleanor (1959).

SKUCE ROBERT FREDERICK
Son of William Thomas Skuce. Born 12 October 1846, Australia. Married Emma Taylor 13 May 1868. One son Stewart Tennyson Skuce (1888). Died 1912, aged 66 years.

SKEWS ROBERT G.
Worked as a mailer with *Seattle Times* in 1967 and lived at Lake Stevens, Seattle, Washington, USA.

SKEWS ROBERT HENRY
Born 1824. Died Birmingham, 1894, aged 70 years.

SKEWS ROBERT HENRY
Married 1853, Plymouth.

SKEWES ROBERT HENRY
Chart 2. Son of William M. and Laverne (née Getty) Skewes. Born 8 September 1965, Minnesota, United States of America.

SKEWES ROBERT J.
Married Mary J. Nairne, 1968, Bexley, Kent.

SKEWIS ROBERT JAMES
Chart 2. Son of Robert and Ruth Skewis. Born 3 April 1951 in United States of America.

SKEWES ROBERT JAMES
Lives at 4 Morris Street, Kidman Park, 5025, South Australia with Heather Marian Skewes. Teacher.

SKEWES ROBERT JOHN
Son of William Henry and Helen (née Nisbett) Skewes. Born 13 December 1889. Lived at 110 Ellen Street, Port Pirie, South Australia in 1959 with Amy Skewes and Thomas Nisbett Skewes. Assistant. Died 15 November 1926, aged 36 years. Buried in Port Pirie, South Australia.

SKEWES ROBERT JOHN
Lives at 18 Morton Parade, Rankin Park, 2287, New South Wales, Australia with Pamela Skewes. Control officer.

SKEWES ROBERT JOSEPH
Chart 2. Son of John Billing and Mary Jo (née Armington) Skewes of Salt Lake City, Utah. Born 24 December 1950, Richfield, Utah. Twin to Mary Ann Skewes. Killed in action, Vietnam 30 March 1971, aged 21 years.

SKEWES ROBERT KEITH
Chart 36. Son of Percy and Mary (née Farrell) Skewes. Born 28 November 1923, Watsons Creek, Bendemeer, New South Wales, Australia. Married Shirley Cicely Jacobs. Children: Kerrie Margaret (1960), Michael Leigh (1957) and David (1963). Lives at Laurel Street, Kootingal, 2352, New South Wales, Australia. Manager.

SKEWIS ROBERT L.
Chart 2. Son of Arthur Lawrence and Elizabeth (née Ballard) Skewis. Wife's name Alice E. Electrician. Lives at 1263 Farrington Drive, San Jose, California, USA.

SKEWES ROBERT LEONARD
Chart 26. Son of Robert Ernest and Elaine Helen (née Albanese) Skewes. Born 8 November 1951 New London, Connecticut, USA. Married Diane Irene Wilkinson (she born 8 July 1955) on 20 December 1975. Coastguard.

SKEWIS ROBERT MERN
Chart 2. Son of Elmer Arthur & Maude Skewis. Born 25 February 1917. Married Ruth McKenny at Emmetsburg, Iowa, 2 July 1950. Children: Bettie Anne (1959), Robert James (1951) and Charles Arthur (1955). Lives at 2701 5th Street, Emmetsburg, Iowa, USA.

SKEWES ROBERT MONTAGUE
Consular birth about 1880, in Caldera, Chile.

SKEWES ROBERT MORGAN
Born 1875 Bedwellty. Died 1875, aged 0.

SKEWES ROBERT NORTHEY
Chart 36. Son of William and Elizabeth (née Northey) Skewes. Born 1 April 1867, New South Wales, Australia. Married Sarah Agnes Connell, 27 June 1894. Moved to Tingha, New South Wales, where he owned his own tin mine. Moved to Sydney about 1916 and lived there for some years before going to Uralla, New South Wales, where he prospected for gold at Rocky River. Children: James Edward, Harold John, Gladys, May, Lorna Agnes, Marjorie and Edna Mavis. Died 10 October 1931, aged 64 years. Interred in Uralla Methodist Cemetery, Australia.

SKEWS ROBERT W.
Chart 17. Son of Ernest W. Skews. Mother's maiden name Falconer. Born 1941, Essex SW. Married Agates 1967, Islington. Son Robert John (1972).

SKEWS ROBERT W.
Mother's maiden name King. Born 1957, Thurrock. Married Pauline Goddard in Thurrock, 1979.

SKEWES ROBERT WILLIAM
Chart 2. Son of Archibald William & Gwendoline (née Jones) Skewes. Born 3 October 1951, Victoria, Australia. Married Wendy Andrew at Rosedale, Victoria. Child: Zoe Naomi (1981). Lives at Willung Road, Rosedale, 3847, Victoria, Australia. Clerk.

SKEWES ROBERTA ANN
Chart 10. Daughter of Robert and Lilian Skewes. Born 29 September 1953, Ontario, Canada. Married Richard James Calderbank, 4 October 1975, Grace Anglican Church, Waterdown, Ontario, Canada. Lives at 473 Springbank Crescent, Burlington, Ontario, L7T 2U8, Canada.

SKEWES ROBERTA GLEE
Chart 14. Daughter of Arthur Russell and Helen (née Horr) Skewes. Born 14 July 1964, USA. Lives in Lexington, Kentucky, USA.

SKEWES ROBIN
Chart 36. Son of John Edward Skewes. Lives at 9 Beryl Street, Woodville West, 5011, South Australia with Enid Merle Skewes. Driver.

SKEWES ROBIN FAY
Chart 36. Daughter of Percy and Muriel (née Norris) Skewes. Born 30 August 1945, Australia. Spinster. Lives at 40 Mahony Avenue, Tamworth, 2340, New South Wales, Australia. Nurse.

SKUSE ROBIN TOBY
Son of Peter Robin and Frances (née Mace-Hardyman) Skuse. Born 29 September 1974. Lives at 46 Beverley Road, Whyteleafe, Surrey CR3 0DX.

SKEWES ROBYN ADELE
Lives at 106 High Street, Coffs Harbour, 2450, New South Wales, Australia with Roylance Geoffrey Skewes, mechanic.

SKEWES ROBYN KAYE
Chart 2. Daughter of Ronald George and Peggy (née Smith) Skewes. Born 11 June 1947, South Australia. Married Malcolm Jenkins 12 October 1968.

SKEWES ROBYN MAY
Chart 36. Daughter of John David and Beryl May (née Johnson) Skewes. Born 17 August 1962. Lives at Ackland Hill Road, Cherry Gardens, 5157, South Australia.

SKUSE RODERICK
Son of Trevor and Jean (née Wheatley) Skuse. Born 14 November 1956. Lives at 5 Abbey Road, Newstead Village, Nottingham.

SKEWES RODNEY CRAIG
Lives at 337 Richard Street, Ballarat, 3350, Victoria, Australia with Shirley Skewes.

SKEWES RODOLFO
Chart 10. Mexican. Son of Nazario and Dolores (née Riofrio) Skewes. Born 19 December 1902, Real del Monte, Mexico. Died 14 May 1903, aged 6 months.

SKEWES RODRICK ARTHUR
Son of Arthur Russell and Helen (née Horr) Skewes. Born 31 March 1961, USA. Lives in Lexington, Kentucky.

SKEWS ROGER D.
Chart 17. Son of Edwin Arthur Skews. Mother's maiden name Lewis. Born 1946, Reading. Married Binnersley in Shrewsbury, 1970. Son: Philip Adrian (1977).

SKEWES ROGER KEITH
Chart 37. Son of Keith Matthew Skewes. Born 4 April 1950, Australia. Lives at 22 Harwood Avenue, Mount Kurrangai, 2080, New South Wales, Australia.

SKEWES ROGER T.
Chart 12. Son of Arthur R. and Mavis (née Rogers) Skewes. Born 1961, Redruth.

SKEWS ROLAND GERALD
Chart 41. Son of William John and Mary (née Rump) Skews. Born 28 March 1938, Durham North. Educated at Houghton Grammar School, Tyne and Wear until 1954. First job as a clerk in Martin's Bank, Houghton-le-Spring for two years. National service in Army (1956-1958). Served with 1st Battalion Parachute Regiment in Cyprus. Demobbed in 1958 and joined National Coal Board in the costings and wages department in South Hetton.
Re-enlisted into the Army in 1961. Joined the Parachute Brigade and served in Bahrain, Sharjah, Cyprus, Europe, Norway, United States of America, Malta and Gibraltar.
Decorated with four sets of parachute wings: Britain — 8 jumps including 2 night descents (1956), France — 4 jumps (1962), Germany — 6 jumps (1976) and America — 15 jumps (1977).
Became a member of the crack Special Air Service. For security reasons he cannot comment in detail as to his activities. He served in the SAS in the Sultanate of Muscat and Oman where, in summer, temperatures reach 112 degrees Fahrenheit and in winter go to below freezing point. The sultans have relied on British soldiers for their security and to safeguard the transportation of crude oil through the Hormuz Peninsula. Iraqi-trained guerilla teams had started work among the primitive tribesmen. Across the border in Aden and South Yemen left-wing Arab nationalists had been engaged in terrorist activities against the British since 1963. The war in Oman lasted 6 years from 1970 to 1976 — a war which the SAS won, although they had lost 12 men dead. "To me the SAS (motto: "Who Dares Wins") gave me the opportunity of secret warfare, high adventure and an opportunity of helping to defend western society." Roland Skews has over 100 parachute jumps to his credit and has been on active service with the SAS training in Singapore and Borneo in jungle warfare. He has had five full tours of Northern Ireland with 2nd Battalion Parachute Regiment and worked with

HRH Prince Charles congratulates W.O.2. Roland Gerald Skews (2nd Parachute Brigade) and presents him with Long Service Medal in Berlin, 1979

Regimental Intelligence. Warrant Officer 2nd Class since 1976. Medals: United Nations (1964), Cyprus (1965), Northern Ireland (1971) and Long Service (1979).
Married Linda Greaves, 15 August 1964 at St Nicholas Parish Church, Hetton-le-Hole, Tyne and Wear.
Children: Kirtley Roland (1965) and Stephen John (1966).
Now serving with Royal Army Pay Corps.

SKEWES ROMAN
Chart 10. Mexican. Son of Franklin and Margarita (née Sanchez) Skewes. Born 16 January 1966, Real del Monte, Mexico.

SKEWIS RONALD
Chart 33. Son of William Richard and Lavinia (née Shute) Skewis. Born 9 November 1904 in Buckfastleigh, Devon. Married Lilian Margaret Wyatt (she born 24 January 1909) at the Parish Church, Totnes, Devon on 4 August 1934. Child: Eileen May Skewis (1941). Builder's labourer for 18 years, then loaned under government scheme during World War Two to Reeves Timber and Builder's Merchants. Became a skilled wood machinist. Semi retired at the age of 65 and then became a cleaner in a garage storeroom offices. Finally retired at the age of 70 years.
Hobbies included gardening, photography and reading. Was a member of the Devon County Fire Brigade through the war until retirement. He was also a member of the Devon and Cornwall Special Constabulary and remained with them until retirement.
His first wife Lilian died in 1965 aged 56 years. He married again to Vera Margaret Tape (widow) at the Parish Church, Totnes, 29 March 1969. Lived at 20 Paige Adams Road, Totnes. Died 22 June 1981, aged 76 years.

SKUSE RONALD
Born 1910. Lived at Baden Hill, Gloucester all his life. After leaving school he worked for the Humphries family of plumbers and decorators for 25 years, after which he decided upon a career in farming. Amongst his other interests were the Baden Hill Coal Company, and the delivery of Sunday newspapers to the Thornbury area, a business he inherited from his father.
He was a keen sportsman, and was a regular member of the Rock's team in the years before the war. He was also a Parish Councillor for 12 years from 1952 to 1964 during which time Baden Hill and Stidcott received mains water and electricity. Ronald Skuse married in 1952. Died 19 October 1980 at Crossham Hospital, Gloucester, aged 70 years. He had previously lived at Baden Hill Farm, Tytherington and was well known in the area.

SKEWES RONALD
Chart 12. Son of William John and Bessie (née Curnow) Skewes. Born 13 November 1929, Mullion, Helston. Attended Mullion Council School. National service with Royal Artillery from 1949 to 1951.
Married Natalia Eve Curtis, daughter of Mr and Mrs Jack Curtis of 5 Falmouth Road, Redruth; at St Andrew's Church, Redruth, 19 June 1954. Children: Diana Rose (1958) and Nicholas Mark (1961).
Manager of menswear shop in St Austell.
Is a Sub Divisional Officer (Inspector) with Special Constabulary, Cornwall.
Member of Cornwall Police Choir. Lives at 25 Southbourne Road, St. Austell, PL25 4PU, Cornwall. Tel no: 0726 3171.

SKEWS RONALD
Lives at 4 Green Valley Crescent, Hampton Park, 3976, Victoria, Australia with Janice Lyla Skews. Butcher.

SKEWS RONALD
Served in World War II in Egypt and Italy and in New Zealand at the Central Districts School at Trentham. Presented with efficiency medal on Anzac Day having completed 12 years of continuous efficient service in the army. He later trained as a carpenter and is now foreman of a New Zealand building firm in Palmerston North.

SKEWES RONALD EDGAR
Chart 36. Son of Samuel Edgar and Erlestoun Minetta (née Mudge) Skewes. Born 31 August 1834. Married Janice Kathleen Egan 7 March 1959. Children: Anthony Wayne (1960) and Craig Stephen (1964). Lives at Mallee-Brae, Goolwa, 5215, South Australia.

SKEWES RONALD EDWARD
Chart 36. Son of Edward Keith and Maisie (née Lawson) Skewes. Born 26 August 1944, Western Australia. Married Pamela Lynn Kuzmanvich, 4 June 1966. Lives at 84 Darley Circle, Bull Creek, 6153, Western Australia. Contractor.

SKEWES RONALD GEORGE
Chart 2. Son of Henry and Annie May (née Cross) Skewes. Born 3 June 1922, Australia. Commissioned into Australian military forces 14 February 1944. Lieutenant, Australian Electrical and Mechanical Engineers. Diploma Electrical Engineering. Diploma Mechanical Engineering. Married Peggy Smith 2 March 1945, Toowoomba, Queensland, Australia. Children: Robyn Kaye (1947) and Sandra Ann (1951). Now retired. Lives at 10 Windermere Avenue, West Lakes, South Australia, 5021.

SKEWIS RONALD JAMES
Chart 2. Son of Donald Earl and Shirley Skewis. Born 21 July 1949, United States of America. Married Sally M. Sweitzer.

SKEWES RONALD JAMES
Chart 36. Son of James Robert and Pearl Isabel (née Chapman) Skewes. Born 20 March 1925. Bachelor. Lived at Wy Wurrie, Watsons Creek,

Ronald George Skewes

Bendemeer, New South Wales, Australia in 1959. Carpenter. Now lives at Bendemeer Hotel, Bendemeer, 2352, New South Wales, Australia.

SKEWES RONALD LANIER
Chart 10. Son of Oswald Herbert and Hesba (née Touchstone) Skewes. Born 3 October 1936, Virginia, USA. Married Patricia Fountain 16 October 1961. Children: Stephen (1964), Deborah (1968) and Melinda (1972). Lives at 10210 Neid Lane, Nokesville, Virginia, USA 22123.

SKEWES RONALD LEONARD
Lived at 66 King Street, Port Pirie, South Australia in 1959 with Christina Thirza Skewes. Engineer. Current address.

SKEWES RONALD LESLIE
Lived at Asquith Street, Austinmer, New South Wales, Australia in 1959 with Dulcie Skewes. Wharf labourer.

SKEWES RONALD OSWALD
Lived at 13 Maitland Street, Malvern, Victoria, Australia in 1959. Now lives at 33 Graduate Crescent, Mulgrave, 3170, Victoria, Australia, with Agnes Rice Skewes. Panel beater.

SKEWES RONALD RICHARD
Lives at 3/51 Mitchell Street, Bondi Beach, 2026, New South Wales, Australia.

SKEWES ROSA LILLIAN
Chart 36. Daughter of Samuel and Mary Ann (née Waters) Skewes. Born 16 January 1879. Married Samuel Wright Bonnar, 28 December 1909. No children. Lived in Queensland, Australia. Died 7 June 1959, aged 80 years.

SKEWES ROSA M.
Born 1887. Died Dover, Kent 1965, aged 78 years.

SKEWES ROSA MARES
Widow of Skewes. Died Mexico and buried in Pachuca Cemetery 23 March 1977. "In Memory from her sons and grandsons."

SKEWES ROSA MARIA
Daughter of Rev J.H. Skewes, Wesleyan minister. Born 5 September 1872. Died St Agnes 19 April 1873, aged 7 months.

SKEWES ROSALIE ANNE
Chart 36. Daughter of Geoffrey and Dorothy May (née Chapman) Skewes. Born 9 May 1956. Married Gregory John Jeffesen 30 April 1977. Lives in Queensland, Australia.

SKEWES ROSALIE DAWN
Chart 36. Née Campbell. Married Graeme Douglas Skewes, police officer, 25 April 1964. Children: Julie Ann (1964) and Peter Charles and Paul Douglas — twins (1967). Lives at 424 Chapman Road, Geraldton 6530, Western Australia.

SKEWES ROSALIE SUSAN
Chart 12. Daughter of William John and Nora (née Thomas) Skewes. Born 12 December 1940. Married Claude Peters 16 May 1959. Issue: one son and one daughter. Marriage was at St Keverne Parish Church.

SKEWES   ROSAMUND EMILY
See Emily Rosamund.
SKEWES   ROSCOE
Chart 10. Mexican. Son of Salvador and Carmen (née Ramirez) Skewes.
Born 19 February 1937, Real del Monte, Mexico. Married Sofia Silva.
SKEWES   ROSE
Born 1766, Née Anthony. Married Richard Skewes 18 February 1793,
Kenwyn. Lived at Hugus, Kea. Children: Alice (1793), John (1796),
James (1798), Mary (1800), Maria (1803) and Betsy (1803). Buried
Kenwyn 12 March 1843, aged 77 years.
SKEWES   ROSE
Born 1890. Died 1949, Truro, aged 59 years.
SKEWES   ROSE PEARL
Chart 47. Born 1895, Launceston. Had a brother Samuel John Skewes.
SKEWES   ROSE PEARL
Chart 47. Daughter of Samuel John Skewes. Born 1926, Launceston.
Mother's maiden name Whiting. Married Tancock, 1955, in
Launceston.
SKEWS   ROSE SELINA
Born 1880, North Aylesford, Kent.
SKEWES   ROSEMARY
Chart 12. Daughter of Thomas Henry Skewes. Born 1931, Redruth.
Mother's maiden name Jory. Married Thomas, 1951, Redruth.
SKEWES   ROSEMARY
Lived at 65 Rutherglen Avenue, Valley View, South Australia, 5093 in
1979.
SKUES   ROSEMARY M.
Chart 3. Née Bamber. Born 1931. Married Rev. John Skues, 1956.
Children: Judith Ann (1957) and Bridget Mary (1959). Killed in car
crash 1960, aged 29 years.
SKEWES   ROSENA
Born 1889, Easington. Died 1889, aged 0.
SKEWES   ROSETTA
Born 1834. Died 1867, aged 33 years in Kensington.
SKUES   ROSINA
Chart 27. Born 1863, Bath. Daughter of William and Mary Skues. Died
1864, aged 0.
SKEWES   ROSINA
Daughter of Edwin and Elizabeth Skewes of Broad Lane, Illogan;
boilersmith. Born 27 September 1878. Bpt 18 November 1878 on
Wesleyan/Methodist Circuit, Camborne/Redruth. Married 1903,
Redruth.
SKEWS   ROSINA
Married 1908, Southampton.
SKEWES   ROSS
Chart 36. Son of Sidney Samuel and Ella (née O'Toole) Skewes. Died
aged about 7 years in Australia.
SKEWS   ROY
Chart 41. Son of Thomas and Jane (née Renshaw). Born 22 September
1913, Barnsley, South Yorkshire. Attended Hemingfield Church of
England School until aged 14 years (1927). Married Jennie Boynton 4
November 1939 in Harrogate, Yorkshire.
Worked for Wood Brothers Glass Works, Hoyle Mill, Barnsley until
1956 when he entered the coal industry. Became an underground
official at Elsecar Main Colliery in 1962. Retired in 1978. Member of
Wombwell Senior Citizens Choir. Hobbies and pastimes: gardening and
motoring. Children: David (1943) and Margaret (1945). Lives at 47
Wood Walk, Wombwell, Barnsley, South Yorkshire. Telephone
number: 0226 755946.
SKEWES   ROY
Chart 12. Son of William John and Edith Skewes. Mother's maiden
name Truran. Born 15 July 1916, Redruth. Married Violet Trengove,
1938. One son: Kenneth Roy (1938). Died 1942, aged 25 years.
SKEWES   ROY
Chart 36. Son of William and Edith (née Howarth) Skewes. Born 15
April 1918. Lived at Watsons Creek, via Bendemeer, New South Wales,
Australia.
SKUES   ROY ARTHUR TRUSCOTT
Chart 9. Son of Thomas Henry James and Gladys (née Clemmans)
Skues. Born 8 June 1928, Wandsworth. National Service with R.A.O.C.
Married Joan Dorette Causton 21 March 1953, Ilford, Essex. Children:
Barry Russell (1954) and John Michael (1959). Lives at 7 Rylands Road,
Bybrook, Ashford, Kent. Tel no: 0233 23057.
SKEWES   ROY EDWARD
Lived at 60 Adrian Street, Palmyra, Melville, Victoria, Australia in
1959 with Doris Skewes. Painter.
SKEWES   ROYLANCE GEOFFREY
Lives at 106 High Street, Coffs Harbour, 2450, New South Wales,
Australia with Robyn Adele Skewes.
SKUES   ROYDON THOMAS
Chart 7. Son of Edward Alfred and Madge Irene (née Meades) Skues.
Born 16 June 1929 Tonbridge, Kent. Married Valerie Cooke, 25
October 1969, St Mary's Church, Hampden Park, Eastbourne.
National service with Royal Air Force. Children: Carolyn Louise (1971)

and Michael David (1972). Lives at 16 Lower Drive, Seaford, Sussex.
Tel no: 0323 894436.
SKUES   RUBY
Lived at 12 Chalmers Street, Bentleigh North, Victoria, Australia in
1959 with Oliver Harold Skues, mechanic.
SKEWES   RUBY
Chart 24. Daughter of Cyril Thomas and Annie Mary (née Leathan)
Skewes. Born New South Wales, Australia. Married with one child.
SKEWES   RUBY GERTRUDE
Lived at 10 Brook Street, Crows Nest, New South Wales, Australia in
1959 with Lional and Thomas Lional Skewes.
SKEWS   RUBY IRENE
Born 1905, Devonport. Married Blewett, 1933, Devonport.
SKEWES   RUBY MAUDE
Chart 38. Daughter of Albert Samuel and Charlotte (née Gilmore)
Smith. Married Sydney Howard Skewes 5 October 1929, South
Australia. Daughter: Delma (1932). Lives at 11 Colley Street, North
Adelaide, 5006, South Australia.
SKEWIS   RUSSELL
Chart 2. Son of Edgar Skewis. Born 31 January 1912, United States of
America.
SKEWES   RUSSELL
Chart 26. Son of Wallace R. Skewes of Connecticut, United States of
America.
SKEWES   RUSSELL FRANK
Chart 14. Son of Arthur Russell and Helen Roberta (née Horr) Skewes.
Born 11 November 1959, USA. Farmer. Lives at Grovean, Ives Grove,
Racine County, Wisconsin, USA which has been in the Skewes family
possession for 140 years.
SKUES   RUSSELL THOMAS
Chart 9. Son of Barry Russell and Gillian Ann (née Epps) Skues. Born 7
January 1980.
Lives at The Hollies, Bromley Green Road, Ruckinge, near Ashford,
Kent.
SKUSE   RUSTY
See SKUSE JANET LESLEY.
SKEWES   RUTH
Chart 14. Née Bottomley. Daughter of Edwin and Martha Bottomley.
Born Huddersfield, Yorkshire 16 February 1832. Emigrated with her
parents to southeastern Wisconsin in 1842.
She suffered from typhoid fever in 1850.
In about 1852 Ruth went to work for Samuel and Catherine Skewes at
Grovean Farm, Ives Grove, Racine as a home help. Catherine was not
well, and there were four children, a teenage nephew, and others from
time to time who were temporarily part of the "farm."
When Catherine died in 1854, Ruth stayed on as housekeeper. The
children, aged 6, 8, 10 and 12, were already fond of her. Ruth married
Samuel Skewes in 1857 and Grovean Farm remained her home until she
died at the age of 61. Samuel and Ruth had four children: Edwin
Bottomley (1858), Emma (1860), Eleanor Jessop (1864) and Thomas
Henry (1869). Millie Squire, daughter of Mary Bottomley Burns,
remembers Ruth:
"She was a worker, made butter and visited Racine every week. She had
her work planned for each day of the week. Even the meals were the
same for Monday each week, and so on. She loved flowers and music and
was very ambitious for her children to have an education, and learn
music especially. She had a kindly personality and was rather quiet and
not much of a talker."
Ruth's granddaughter Alice Ruth Skewes Ford has some kindly words to
say about her:
"Among the heirlooms which remind me of Grandmother Ruth, besides
the furniture — the walnut sofa and cane seated chairs, the cherry and
walnut bureaus — are the luster-ware teapot, a Chinese bowl, and the
sterling silver 'Ruth' tea spoons which her four children gave her. But
more precious than any material possession are the indefinable but
creative contributions of her life to mine, transmitted through her
children: the high value placed on things of the spirit, the search for
knowledge, a willingness to work, loyalty and self-giving, and a love of
music. She gave me her name, too — a name to live up to."
SKEWES   RUTH
Chart 25. Née Hacking. Born 19 August 1903. Married Arthur George
Skewes in Manchester, 1927. Lived at 6 Blacksbrook Avenue, Paignton,
Devon. Child: Frank Robert Skewes (1927). Died 1972, aged 69 years.
SKEWES   RUTH
Chart 26. Daughter of Grant Phillip Skewes. Born Connecticut, United
States of America.
SKEWES   RUTH
Chart 36. Daughter of Glenleigh Bertie William and Mary Evelyn
Harriet (née Watkins) Skewes. Born 17 April 1947. Married Noel
Deutscher 23 December 1967. Issue: two children. Lives at 12 Stawell
Street, Ballarat, 3350, Victoria, Australia.
SKEWES   RUTH C.
Chart 14. Née Hoyt. Born 1848, Wisconsin, USA. Parents came from
Vermont, USA. Married George Skewes in Yorkville, Wisconsin, USA.
Children: Jessie (1874) and Howard Hoyt (1878). Later moved to the

Ruth Skewes (1903-1972)

West Coast and in 1910 (as a widow) lived at 1327 Allesandro, Los Angeles, USA.

SKEWIS   RUTH G.
Wife of Donald G. Skewis. Lived at 1755 Dolores, San Francisco, USA in 1951. Typist who worked at the American Trust Company.

SKEWIS   RUTH GENEVIEVE
Chart 2. Daughter of Francis Harry and Annie Skewis. Born 5 February 1904, United States of America. Died September 1924, aged 20 years.

SKEWES   RUTH LILIAN
Chart 10. Daughter of John William and Lilian (née Robbins) Skewes. Born 6 October 1914 at Ishpemming, Michigan, United States of America. Twice married. 1) Albert Carlton, 10 August 1933 — issue: two children. 2) Lester Bray, 5 December 1942. Issue: one child.

SKEWES   RUTH LOIS
Chart 15. Née Philp. Married Geoffrey Grenville Skewes, 13 June 1964. Children: Joanna Robin (1971) and Claudine Elizabeth (1973). Lives at 33 Howard Street, Warrambool, 3280, Victoria, Australia.

SKEWES   RUTH MELVA
Chart 38. Daughter of Alfred Louis and Pearl Garrett. Born 10 February 1921. Married Norman Skewes 13 May 1944 in South Australia. Children: Brian Wayne (1947) and Neil David (1951). Lives at 15 Deakin Street, Blair Athol, 5084, South Australia.

SKEWES   RUTH VIALL
Chart 14. Daughter of Frank and Sylvia (née Wyman) Viall. Born 12 November 1911, Wisconsin, USA. Married Professor George Jessop Skewes 22 August 1934 at Wesley Memorial Chapel, Madison, Wisconsin, USA. Graduated with Bachelor of Science degree from University of Wisconsin, 1934.
Children: Alice Eve (1935), Richard Edwin (1937) and Glen Wilson (1941).
George Jessop Skewes (born 1900) died 1964, aged 64 years. Parish visitor for St Cloud Methodist Church. Lives at 430 South East Riverside Drive, St Cloud, Minnesota 56301, United States of America.

SKEWES   RYAN JAMES
Son of James William and Christine Ann (née Gallagher) Skewes. Born 10 January 1974, New York, USA. Lives at 169 Westwood Drive, Brentwood, New York, 11717, United States of America.

S

SKEWIS   SADIE A.
Chart 50. Daughter of James Airns and Irene (née Fox) Skewis. Born 12 July 1953, Hull. Married Ducker in Hull, 1971.

SKUES   SALLY
Chart 5. Née Tubb. Born 1811. Married John Penrose Skues at Redruth Parish Church 16 July 1837. Died 24 March 1853, aged 42 years.

Children: Joseph Penrose, John, Jane, Sarah, Lewis Tubb and Charles Penrose.

SKEWES   SALLY
Chart 12. Daughter of William John and Nora Skewes. Mother's maiden name Thomas. Born 23 July 1955. Married Howard Marsh 23 August 1975 at St Keverne Parish Church. Now living in Cape Town, South Africa.

SKEWES   SALLY ALEXANDER
Chart 36. Daughter of Robert Skewes. Born 18 January 1975, New South Wales, Australia.

SKEWS   SALLY J.
Mother's maiden name Berryman. Born 1938, Brentford, Middlesex. Married Pettet, 1962, South Middlesex.

SKEWES   SALLY JEAN
Chart 12. Daughter of James A. and Wendy (née Hooper) Skewes. Born 1971, Truro.

SKEWES   SALVADOR
Chart 10. Mexican. Son of Juan and Maria (née Mendosa) Skewes. Born 24 June 1907, Real del Monte, Mexico. Married Carmen Ramirez approx 1932. Children: Juan (1933), Maria Abril (1935), Roscoe (1937), Henry (1940), Franklin (1945), Franz (1953), Omar (1948), Perla Carolina (1952), Carolo Federico (1950), Hector (1956) and Victoria (1958). He was also the father of another child, Theodora (1955) — mother Antonia Casanas. Lives in Real del Monte, Mexico.

SKEWS   SAMUEL
Son of Keverne Skewes. Bpt St Keverne 13 June 1665.

SKEWS   SAMUEL
Married Ann Quick at Madron with Penzance 26 December 1719.

SKEWES   SAMUEL
Born 1798. Carrier from Redruth. Died at Six Bells Inn, St Columb 28 November 1887, aged 89 years.

SKEWES   SAMUEL
Chart 14. Son of Henry and Jane (née Retallack) Skewes. Born 10 July 1811. Bpt Ruan Major 8 September 1811. Farmer. Lived at Tresodden, Ruan Major. He had five brothers and five sisters. Next door to Tresodden Farm was Hendra Farm owned by the Lugg family. Three of the Skewes brothers, Henry, Anthony and Samuel, married Lugg sisters Grace, Christian (Kitty) and Catherine; and two of the Skewes sisters, Jane and Eleanor married Lugg brothers, James and William. Samuel married Catherine Lugg, daughter of James Lugg at Ruan Major 2 March 1841. They emigrated to the United States of America in the autumn of 1842 (they sailed from Falmouth harbour in the barque *The Cornwall*, 13 August 1842) together with their infant son Samuel and eight year-old nephew James L. Skewes, son of Henry and Grace Skewes.
James L. Skewes was the oldest of Henry's six children. He worked for his uncle Samuel Skewes until he was 21, when he received 80 acres of land and a stipulated sum of money. Samuel was the "port of entry" for other nephews, including Henry's second son, Hannibal, who settled at Yorkville, and Anthony's son William John.
Samuel Skewes had a great love for trees. He named his farm "Grovean", meaning "small grove", and purchased land from the government for $1.25 an acre. He was responsible for planting many trees including willows, maple, Lombardy poplar, apple, pear, ash, linden, Scotch pine and 700 evergreens. His first farm was affectionately known as "the mud house", which had a coating of white plaster. Three more children were born to Samuel and Catherine: George (1844), Sarah (1846) and Margaret (1848). Catherine Skewes died 25 August 1854. Samuel married his housekeeper Ruth Bottomley, second daughter of Edwin and Martha Bottomley, originally from Huddersfield, Yorkshire, but who were living in the English Settlement, Racine. They married in 1857 and four children were born to them: Edwin Bottomley (1858), Emma (1860), Eleanor Jessop (1864) and Thomas Henry (1869). Samuel Skewes kept a methodical list of events and happenings in his diaries — everything from farm activities and transactions, family and church events, condition of livestock, state of crops and his personal finances.
The "mud house" was later replaced by a more modern building built by Samuel. His family built farms close by. Samuel Junior lived across the road; Thomas Henry moved to "Chybarles" (house across the lea) and George and Emma moved into homes of their own. In 1870 Samuel's personal estate was valued at $3500 — his real estate at $15,000.

Within a nine-month period in 1893, Samuel lost his daughter Margaret, his daughter Eleanor and his wife Ruth.
From that time until his death in 1898 he lived with his son Edwin's family, enjoying his grandchildren and the home place he had come to love. Echoes of his Cornish heritage were in the place names — Grovean, Chybarles, the paddock, the well field, the barn close, the Folly, and the south meadow.
Grovean is still in the family today, owned by Arthur Russell Skewes of Lexington, Kentucky and managed by Arthur's son Frank Russell Skewes.
Samuel Skewes died 18 November 1898, aged 87 years.

SKEWES   SAMUEL
of Kenwyn. Born 1812. Buried Chacewater 20 November 1831, aged 19 years.

SKEWES SAMUEL
Chart 33. Son of William and Mary Skewes of Kea, miner. Bpt Chacewater 12 October 1828. Married Susannah Tapper (20), daughter of Thomas Tapper of Ashburton, Devon; at the Register Office, Newton Abbot, Devon, 17 July 1847.
Children: Mary, Samuel, William and Daniel. Died Newton Abbot, 1887, aged 65 years.

SKEWES SAMUEL
Born 1836. Buried Chacewater 21 February 1837, aged 1 year.

SKEWS SAMUEL
Son of John and Ann Hemmett Skews. Bpt Bible Christian Circuit, Falmouth 19 March 1837.

SKEWES SAMUEL
Chart 36. Son of William and Christian (née Lugg) Skewes. Born 23 January 1839. Bpt Mawnan, 10 March 1839. Farm labourer. Married Mary Ann Thomas, daughter of Thomas Thomas, farm labourer of Cross Lanes, Cury, Helston Register Office 6 November 1862. No reference to their deaths. Possible emigration.

SKEWS SAMUEL
Born 1838, Truro.

SKEWES SAMUEL
Chart 50. Son of Thomas and Jane Skewes of Seveoke, miner. Born 1839, Truro. Emigrated with his parents to Australia in the 1850's.

SKEWIS SAMUEL
Chart 44. Son of Thomas and Elizabeth (née Moyle) Skewis, iron turner of Tredegar Parish, Bedwellty, Monmouth. Born 10 March 1840. Later moved north to Manchester. Married Ann Whitehead (she born December, 1838), of 17 Hastings Street, Chorlton, Manchester, daughter of Thomas Whitehead, mechanic; at Parish Church of St Saviour, Chorlton, Manchester, 12 November 1864. Lived at Hastings Street, Chorlton. No children. Emigrated to New Jersey, USA in 1880.

SKEWES SAMUEL
Chart 14. Son of Samuel and Catherine (née Lugg) Skewes. Born 9 February 1842 at Tresodden, Ruan Major. Bpt Ruan Major 27 March 1842.
Emigrated with his parents to Wisconsin, USA in August, 1842. Farmer. Married Betsy Phillips, having attended Racine High School in his school days. Children: William George (1868), Eva Katherine (1869), Mary (1872), Clifford (1873), Lulu (1878) and Ellen (1883).
Was a highly respected citizen of Ives Grove, Racine County. Very active in both church and Sunday school. Lived at Sunnyside, Ives Grove. In 1870 his personal estate was valued at $800 and real estate at $2300. His wife Betsy died 1910. Samuel died 14 December 1902, aged 60 years.

SKEWES SAMUEL
Chart 36. Base son of Ann Hendy Skewes. Born 1842. Baptised Cury 29 June 1842. His mother died due to a surplus of blood in the head when he was only six years old. He was initially cared for by his grandfather and later aunt and uncle at Nantithet, Cury.
In 1865 he emigrated to Australia with his cousins John and Susan Skewes of Nantithet on the ship *Trevelyan* which left Plymouth on 15 December 1865 and arrived in Port Adelaide, South Australia on 21 March 1866. He had previously set out aboard the *Amoor*, but this vessel was wrecked in Plymouth Sound.
After engaging in the shoe trade in Adelaide he resided at Blumberg, Lobethal and Gawler successively and eventually moved to Millicent as a shoemaker, retiring in 1907.
Whilst carrying on commercial pursuits he acquired the estate known as "Nantithet", named after his birthplace. This comprised 580 acres and in addition he owned other good grazing country amounting to 4000 acres in all; and followed the career as a grazier and agriculturist with excellent results.
As a businessman he was thoroughly respected and trusted. He proved the cross-bred type of sheep to be best suited to the district, and ran a flock of 4000 on the estate, which also carried a considerable herd of cattle.
He was Chairman of the directors of the Millicent Cheese Factory for eight years; trustee, manager and secretary of the Millicent Public Sheep Dipping Company Limited from its inception in 1890. Committee member of the Institute and also held office of treasurer for a period. Was one of the leading members of the Methodist church for a period which spanned in excess of 30 years.
Appointed trustee of Millicent Methodist Church in 1880 and held office of Circuit Steward for over 20 years. On 20 February 1908 he had the honour of laying the foundation stone of a new portion of the church building, and on this occasion was made recipient of a handsome silver trowel and ivory handle in recognition of his many valuable services in connection with the denomination.
Married Mary Ann Waters (she born 9 September 1846, and daughter of Thomas Alexander Waters of Sandy Creek, near Gawler and formerly of Wiltshire, England), 16 June 1870. Children: William (1872-1884), Fanny Elizabeth (1873), Elsie May (1875), John Vivian (1876), Rosa Lillian (1879) and Samuel Jarvis (1884-1901). The strong influence of his character was largely due to his outstanding personality which was daily nourished with prayer.
Died 3 June 1908, aged 65 years.

SKUES SAMUEL
Chart 2. Son of Henry and Grace Skues. Born 1845, Camborne.

Samuel Skewes (1842-1908)

SKEWES SAMUEL
Chart 14. Son of Anthony and Christian (née Lugg) Skewes of Tresodden, Ruan Major. Born 1847. Bpt Ruan Major 26 December 1847. Farmer of 145 acres. In 1871 Census Returns was living with his parents and sisters Ann and Catherine and brothers Henry, William John, Hannibal and George.
Emigrated to Racine, Wisconsin, USA. Married (wife's name Mary). Children: Earl and Charles J. (twins) and Mabel.

SKEWES SAMUEL
Married 1847, Newton Abbot, Devon.

SKEWES SAMUEL
Born 1851, Truro.

SKEWS SAMUEL
Born 1852 at St Cleer, copper and tin miner. Was son-in-law to John and Juliana Mildern of St Cleer, Liskeard. Lived with the above, then aged 18 years, in the 1871 Census Returns.

SKEWES SAMUEL
Chart 33. Son of William and Susan Skewes of Kerley, Kea, miner. Bpt Chacewater 2 January 1855.

SKEWES SAMUEL
Chart 10. Born 18 April 1860, Liskeard. Son of Digory and Fanny (née Tregonning) Skewes of Marazion. Married Clara Trevena, 1885. Children: Annie (1886) and William Trevena (1890).

SKEWS SAMUEL
Married 1865, Redruth.

SKEWES SAMUEL
Married 1872, Liskeard.

SKEWES SAMUEL
Lived at Fords Row, Redruth 1885/1886.

SKEWIS SAMUEL
Chart 50. Born 1887. Married Laura Waters, 1913, Haverfordwest. Lived at Redbraes, Hayston Avenue, Milford Haven, Pembrokeshire. Fish packer. Children: Mildred E. (1914) and Samuel Leslie (1920). Died 8 March 1958, aged 71 years in Haverfordwest.

SKEWES SAMUEL
Chart 10. Born 1895. Died Penzance 1926, aged 33 years.

SKEWES SAMUEL DAWE
Chart 18. Son of Daniel Skewes, mine agent. Born 1833, St Austell. Grocer and druggist. Twice married. 1) Jane Courtis 1 April 1856 at the Independent Chapel, Tavistock, Devon. Children: Mary Anna Courtis (1858), Jane (1859), John Courtis (1864), Alice Kate (1862), Ellen M. (1866), Florence Rosalie (1868), Howard (1871) and Arthur Dawe (1873).
Jane (née Courtis) Skewes died 24 April 1881, aged 54 years. Samuel married Emma Staplin (41), widow and daughter of William

Nantithet, South Australia, 1938

Blatchford, farmer at the Register Office, Newton Abbot, 6 September 1888. Children: Ernest (1888) and Edith (1889). Emma Skewes died 2 February 1922, aged 75 years. Samuel owned two freehold houses in Fore Street, Bere Alston, Devon and two houses in Bedford Street (1874). Lived at Pepper Street, Beer Ferris, Bere Alston, Tavistock. Died 15 August 1903, aged 71 years.

SKEWES   SAMUEL EDGAR
Chart 36. Son of John Vivian and Gertrude Mary (née Lock) Skewes. Born 11 April 1903. Married Erlestoun Minneta Mudge 25 February 1931. Children: Brian Lock (1932), Ronald Edgar (1934) and John David (1937). Lives at Charles Street, Port Elliot, 5214, South Australia. Farmer.

SKEWES   SAMUEL FRANCIS
Chart 36. Son of Francis and Grace Skewes. Born 1868, Illogan. In 1871 Census Returns was living with his parents and brother William and sister Jane R. at Illogan Highway. Lived at Barncoose Terrace, Illogan, 1922. Went to South Africa 1922 and died there at 39a South Street, Boksburg, Transvaal, South Africa, 17 October 1922, aged 54 years. Buried in Boksburg Cemetery.

SKUES   SAMUEL FRANCIS
Chart 5. Son of Joseph Penrose Skues of Redruth, builder, who emigrated to Australia about 1860. Born 26 April 1877, Victoria, Australia. Lived at 70 Tennyson Street, Elwood, Victoria, Australia with Florence Rachel Skues in 1959. Sales manager for McRobertson's Pty Limited. Child: Jack Sydney Skues (1916). Died 26 October 1959, aged 83 years.

SKEWS   SAMUEL GREGORY
Chart 15. Son of John and Isabella (née Gregory) Skews. Born 1856, Trewint, Altarnun. Bpt Altarnun 20 October 1856. In 1871 Census Returns was a stable boy at Knighton, Altarnun, aged 15 years.

SKEWS   SAMUEL GREGORY
Chart 15. Son of Peter and Elizabeth (née Gregory) Skews. Bpt St Ive 29 September 1869. Married 1899, Liskeard. Died 1938, aged 68 years in Liskeard.

SKEWES   SAMUEL GRENVILLE STOWE
Chart 50. Born Australia. Married Cecelia Elizabeth Oaten, 9 April 1903. Child: Thomas Grenville Skewes (1904). Died in the 'flu epidemic, January 1919, aged 45 years.

SKEWES   SAMUEL H.
Chart 36. Son of John and Loveday Skewes of Nantithet, Cury. Bpt Cury 27 August 1815. Married Mary Thomas (30) at Mawgan in Meneage Church 12 April 1842, in the presence of John Skewes. He was a carpenter.
Emigrated to Wisconsin, USA in 1842 via Milwaukee. Arrived in Yorkville 9 November 1842. In Milwaukee he had worked for a Mr Church, builder and contractor. He followed a similar trade in Yorkville for 15 years until 1857 and then engaged in farming.
Was appointed agent and trustee of the Union Grove Land Company for the sale of land owned by them. Later was engaged in the agricultural machinery business.
Samuel Skewes was one of the first settlers to Yorkville. When he arrived there was only a shanty 16 feet square in the whole village, which shanty stood as a relic of old times until 12 April 1879, when it burned down with several other stores and dwellings.
Mary Skewes died May 1865, and is buried in Yorkville.
He married again in Lyons, Iowa in December 1873, to Carolina Goldsworthy, a resident of Yorkville. She died 29 December 1876, and is buried in Yorkville. There are two children: Ella and Howard.

SKEWIS   SAMUEL HENRY
Chart 14. Son of Henry and Grace Skewis of Churchtown, St Keverne, schoolmaster. Bpt St Keverne 25 May 1845. Died 21 July 1877, aged 32 years.

SKEWS   SAMUEL JOHN
Born 1873, Liskeard. Died 1873, aged 0.

SKEWES   SAMUEL JOHN
Chart 47. Son of John and Emma (née Goldsworthy) Skewes, gold miner. Born 26 March 1893. Married Charlotte Whiting, 1915, Bodmin. Lived at the Railway Hotel, Kelly Bray (since demolished), Callington. Died 16 October 1954, aged 61 years. Children: Winifred A. (1915) and Rose Pearl (1926).

SKEWS   SAMUEL JOHN
Born 1899, Devonport. Died 1899, aged 0.

SKEWES   SAMUEL JOHN
Born 1903, Redruth. Lived at Condurrow Croft. Died 1904, aged 14 months. Buried Tuckingmill, 23 April 1904.

SKEWES   SAMUEL LAITY
Chart 50. Illegitimate son of Elizabeth Skewes of Nantithet, Cury. Born 10 August 1847. Bpt Cury 4 April 1852.
Married at Helston Register Office 7 March 1870 to Mary Sanders (20), domestic servant at Skewes, Cury, daughter of John Sanders. Samuel was an agricultural servant at Skewes, Cury at the time of his wedding. Children: Jane Skewes (1870), William Skewes (1871), Esther (1874), Clara Skewes (1877), Myra Skewes (1883), Wilfred Skewes (1885), Stephen James (1880), Harry (1873), Mary Margaret (1882).
Died 30 November 1887, aged 39 years.
Mary Skewes born 1 January 1851. Died 28 November 1919, aged 68 years.

SKEWIS   SAMUEL LESLIE
Chart 50. Son of Samuel and Laura Skewis. Mother's maiden name Laura Waters. Born 9 March 1920, Haverfordwest. Married Holdsworth, 1949, Chatham. Lived at 9 Beartsead Close, Gillingham, Kent. No children. Died 13 March 1971, aged 51 years. Profession: Engine fitter.

SKEWES   SAMUEL PERCY
Chart 12. Son of John and Cissie Skewes. Born 9 October 1909. Married Hilda Tremayne from Cury, 1940 at Methodist Chapel, Chynhale, Sithney. Child: Constance.

SKEWES   SAMUEL RICHARD
Son of John William and Susannah (née May) Skewes. Born 27 June 1856, Burra, South Australia. Married 1 January 1886 to Sarah Elizabeth Downton. Children included: Marjorie Grace Skewes. Died 3 July 1924, Lower Mitcham, aged 68 years. Buried in Mitcham Cemetery, South Australia.

SKEWES   SAMUEL SIDNEY
Chart 36. Son of William and Elizabeth (née Northey) Skewes. Born 28 February 1859, New South Wales, Australia. Married Sarah Pennall. Children: William (1886), Isabella Maud (1887), Ethel Eva (1889), Leslie John (1891), Elsie Beryl (1893), Sidney Samuel (1895), James Robert (1897), Leonard Richard (1899), Ida Olive (1902), Caroline (1902), Oswald Percy (1907) and Thelma Irene (1910). Lived at Watsons Creek, Bendemeer, New South Wales, Australia. Died 12 July 1951, aged 92 years. Buried in Methodist section of Bendemeer Cemetery.

SKEWES   SAMUEL THOMAS WILLIAM
Lives at Halls Creek, Manilla, 2346, New South Wales, Australia with Georgina May Skewes. Labourer.

Samuel Sidney and Sarah Skewes of Australia, 1885

SKEWES   SAMUEL TRUEN
Chart 18. Son of William and Ann Skewes. Bpt Kea 6 October 1811.

SKUES   SAMUEL WILLIAM
Born 1905, Chippenham, Wiltshire. Died 1909, aged 4 years.

SKEWS   SANDRA
Chart 41. Daughter of George Skews. Mother's maiden name Littledike. Born 1946, Sheffield, South Yorkshire. Married Cordingly in Bradford, 1965.

SKEWS   SANDRA
Mother's maiden name Batchelor. Born 1946, St Austell. Married Philip N.E. King, 1974, St Austell.

SKEWES   SANDRA
Chart 12. Daughter of Gilbert J. and Kathleen (née Dennis) Skewes. Born 28 August 1960, Redruth. Married Carl P. Davies, 1979, Kerrier.

SKEWS   SANDRA
Married Brown, 1967, Birmingham.

SKEWIS   SANDRA
Mother's maiden name Lyons. Born 1974, Kettering.

SKEWES   SANDRA
Chart 38. Née Goodwin. Married James Charles Skewes 7 February 1976, Broken Hill, New South Wales, Australia, 2880. Son: Christopher James (1979).

SKEWES   SANDRA
Née Wooton, Married Gary Douglas Skewes, printer. Children: Andrew (1973), Scott (1974), Paul (1976) and Kristy (1978). Lives at 11 Jillian Street, Cranbourne, 3977, Victoria, Australia.

SKEWES   SANDRA ANN
Chart 2. Daughter of Ronald George and Peggy (née Smith) Skewes. Born 16 April 1951 South Australia. Married Graham Lyons 24 April 1973.

SKEWES   SANDRA ELIZABETH
Chart 10. Daughter of Oswald Herbert and Hesba Eugenia (née Touchstone) Skewes. Born 15 December 1940. Married Kenneth Richardson 15 April 1961. Issue: one son and two daughters. Lives at 1431 East 1st, Mesa, Arizona, 85203, United States of America.

SKEWES   SANDRA GAE
Lives at 8 Lentara Street, Bardouroka, 2315, New South Wales, Australia.

SKUES   SANDRA J.
Chart 9. Daughter of Philip Ernest Skues. Mother's maiden name Pinto. Born 1944, Surrey Mid'East.

SKEWES   SANDRA JEAN
Lives at 1 Macquarie Street, Coonamble, 2829, New South Wales, Australia with James Charles Skewes, welfare officer. Waitress.

SKEWES   SANDRA LAUREL
Chart 38. Daughter of Ray Samuel and Betty Joy (née Sloan) Skewes. Born 1950. Lived at 31 Browning Street, Barton Vale, Clearview, 5086, South Australia. Died 26 January 1968, aged 17 years.

SKEWES   SANDRY
Buried Ludgvan 20 December 1598. Wife's name Enour. Children included Richard and Frances.

SKEWS   SARAH
Married Charles Betty in Cury, 1687.

SKEWES   SARAH
Chart 36. Wife of James Skewes. Children: Jane, Elizabeth, William, James, Sarah, Mary, Blanch, John and Edward.

SKEWES   SARAH
Chart 36. Daughter of James and Sarah Skewes. Bpt Cury 27 December 1713.

SKEWES   SARAH
Daughter of Edward and Ann Skews. Bpt St Ewe 26 June 1731. Married John Warrick at St Ewe 11 April 1757.

SKEWES   SARAH
Buried Cury 8 April 1738.

SCUIS   SARAH
Chart 2. Daughter of William and Mary Scuis. Bpt Camborne 8 February 1747.

SKEWES   SARAH
Chart 36. Daughter of John and Mary Skewes. Bpt Cury 4 March 1751. Married John Piercey of St Keverne at Cury 11 February 1777.

SKUSE SARAH
Married Richard Lobb at St Just in Penwith 28 August 1757.

SKEWS   SARAH
Chart 9. Daughter of Philip and Mary Skews. Bpt St Ewe 12 August 1764. Married John Sweet at St Ewe 19 December 1790.

SKEWES   SARAH
Buried Cury 5 February 1771.

SKEWIS   SARAH
Chart 2. Daughter of John and Philippa Skewis. Bpt 10 October 1773, Camborne. Married Isaac Jenkin according to her father's will, but to Gabriel Blewitt, 2 July 1796 in Camborne Parish Register.

SKEWES   SARAH
Daughter of James and Ann Skewes. Bpt Mawgan in Meneage 21 November 1779.

SKEWES   SARAH
Born 1795. Died Helston 1877, aged 82 years.

SKEWES   SARAH
Married William Anthony of St Keverne, widower 25 January 1797 at Mylor, in presence of William Skewes.

SKEWES   SARAH
Married Thomas Triggs, private in the Royal Cornwall Militia 12 December 1804 at Cury.

SKEWES   SARAH
Chart 36, Daughter of William and Alice Skewes of Treloskan, Cury. Bpt 9 June 1805.

SKEWES   SARAH
Born 1809. Wife of John Skewes, miner of 8 Higher Street, Plymouth (St Charles the Martyr District). Died 20 October 1847, aged 38 years of apoplexy, Plymouth.

SKUES   SARAH
Daughter of William and Mary Skues. Bpt Helston 22 January 1824.

SKEWES   SARAH
Chart 10. Daughter of Richard and Agnes Skewes, mine agent of Kea. Bpt Kenwyn 29 March 1825. Married William Pollard, miner of Chacewater, son of William Pollard, miner, 11 March 1852, Baldhu Church.

SKEWIS   SARAH
Married John Triggs at Cury 23 October 1872.

SKUES   SARAH
Born 1836. Died 1909, Medway, aged 73 years.

SKEWS   SARAH
Married 1843, Plymouth.

SKEWES   SARAH
Chart 14. Daughter of Samuel and Catherine Skewes of Wisconsin, America. Born 2 May 1846. Died 29 July 1858, aged 12 years. Lived at Grovean, Ives Grove.

SKEWS   SARAH
Born 1851. Buried Illogan, 2 November 1852, aged 1 year.

SKEWS   SARAH
Born 1852, Redruth.

SKEWIS   SARAH
Born 1852, Cricklewood.

SKEWS   SARAH
Married 1852, Truro.

SKUES   SARAH
Chart 5. Daughter of John Penrose and Sally (née Tubb) Skues. Born 1853, Redruth. Died 1853.

SKEWS   SARAH
Chart 17. Née Harding. Born 1853. Married Richard Nathaniel Edward Skews, 1873, Islington. Lived at 4 Parmiter House, Parmiter Street, London E2 in 1922 and the following year had moved to 5 Usk Street, London E2. Children: Nathaniel Edward (1874) and James Henry (1880). Died 1936, aged 83 years in Bethnal Green.

SKEWES   SARAH
Born 1854, Redruth.

SKUES   SARAH
Married 1856, Stepney.

SKEWES   SARAH
Chart 10. Daughter of William and Mary Skews. Born 26 August 1859, Illogan. In 1871 Census Returns she was living at Illogan Highway with her father who had remarried a Jane .... and with her brothers and sisters Matthew Henry, John, Edwin, Martin and Emma, all born in Illogan. Married John Jones in Ivercargill, New Zealand, 1 October 1879. He was a bullock driver. Lived at Invercargill and later Stewart Island. She disappeared in the 1890's, believed to have run away with a sea captain, but later returned to Stewart Island.

SKEWIS   SARAH
Born 1863, Chorlton.

SKUES   SARAH
Married 1863, Dursley.

SKEWES   SARAH
Chart 36. Née Pennall. Born 1868, Australia. Married Samuel Sidney Skewes. Children: William (1886), Isabella Maud (1887), Ethel Eva (1889), Leslie John (1891), Elsie Beryl (1893), Sidney Samuel (1895),

James Robert (1897), Leonard Richard (1899), Ida Olive (1902), Caroline (1902), Oswald Percy (1907) and Thelma Irene (1910). Died 14 June 1955, aged 87 years. Buried in Methodist section of Bendemeer Cemetery, New South Wales, Australia.

SKEWES   SARAH
Chart 26. Née Greenslade. Born 1876. Married John Skewes. shoemaker at Illogan Parish Church 1898. Lived at 5 Cauldfield Place, Plain-an-Gwarry. Children: Minnie (1900), Percival (1902) and Matthew John (1910). Died 1966 in Penzance District, aged 90 years. John died 3 May 1929, aged 54 years.

SKEWS   SARAH
Born 1876. Lived at 65 St John Street, Copperhouse, Hayle. Died 24 October 1966, aged 90 years.

SKEWIS   SARAH
Married 1876, Old Monkland, Scotland.

SKEWES   SARAH
Married 1877, Penzance.

SKEWES   SARAH
Married 1887, Redruth.

SKEWES   SARAH
Born 1891, Penzance.

SKEWIS   SARAH
Born 1896, Coatbridge, Scotland. Died Coatbridge 1900, aged 4 years.

SKEWS   SARAH
Chart 41. Married George William Skews in Easington 1889. He died 1907, aged 38 years. She married again in 1911 at Easington.

SKEWES   SARAH
Married Edward Symons, 1915, Penzance.

SKUES   SARAH A.
Born 1833. Died 1915, Grimsby, aged 82 years.

SKEWES   SARAH A.
Born 1892. Died 1960, aged 68 years in Manchester.

SKEWES   SARAH AGNES
Chart 36. Née Connell. Born 3 August 1866, New South Wales, Australia. Married Robert Northey Skewes, 27 June 1894. Children: James Edward, Harold John, Gladys, May, Lorna Agnes, Marjorie and Edna Mavis. Died 19 September 1960, aged 94 years.

SKEWIS   SARAH ANN
Bpt Tredegar Iron Works, English Wesleyan 9 February 1834. Daughter of John and Elizabeth Skewis.

SKEWES   SARAH ANN
Chart 14. Daughter of Henry and Grace Skewes of Ruan Major. Born 1841. Bpt Mawgan in Meneage Church 13 June 1841.

SKEWES   SARAH ANN
Chart 36. Daughter of Henry and Ann Skewes of St Hilary. Born 1844. Bpt St Hilary 14 January 1844. Later moved to St Pinnock. Her father was a lead miner. By 1862 had emigrated with her parents to Ballarat, Australia.

SKEWES   SARAH ANN
Born 1845, Redruth.

SKEWS   SARAH ANN
Born 1847, North Aylesford.

SKEWES   SARAH ANN
Died 1850, Helston.

SKEWES   SARAH ANN
Born 1852, Penzance. Daughter of James and Margaret Skewes. Bpt Perranuthnoe, 6 March 1853.

SKEWS   SARAH ANNE
Chart 2. Born 1856, Gwinear. Daughter of Henry and Grace Skews. Lived at Rewlya Lane, Gwinear. In 1871 Census Returns parents were listed as Henry and Hannah Skewes.

SKEWS   SARAH ANN
Born 1860, Plymouth.

SKEWES   SARAH ANN
Chart 11. Daughter of James Henry and Elizabeth Skewes of the Lizard. Born 1870, Landewednack. Father was a carpenter.

SKEWES   SARAH ANN
Married 1887, Redruth.

SKEWS   SARAH ANN
Married 1889, Dartford.

SKEWES   SARAH ANN
Married 1892, Helston.

SKEWES   SARAH ANNIE
Chart 12. Daughter of Frederick Tresize Skewes. Born 1889. Married ..... Jeffrey, 1914, Redruth. Died in the 1950's.

SKUES   SARAH A.M.
Born 1883. Died 1914, aged 31 years in Lewisham.

SKEWIS   SARAH BELL
Born 1924, West Greenock, Scotland. Died West Greenock, 1924 aged 0.

SKEWIS   SARAH BLACK
Born 1938 College, Glasgow, Scotland. Married Charles O'Neil Gillan, 1959, Bridgeton.

SKEWS   SARAH E.
Born 1884. Died 1960, aged 76 years in Bournemouth.
SKEWS   SARAH E.
Born 1838. Died 1915, aged 77 years in Portsmouth.
SKEWES   SARAH ELIZABETH
Née Downton. Born 21 March 1864, Macclesfield, South Australia.
Married Samuel Richard Skewes (his second wife) on 1 January 1886.
Children included Marjorie Grace. Died 20 April 1944, aged 80 years at
Woodville, South Australia. Buried in Mitcham Cemetery, South
Australia.
SKEWES   SARAH E.E.
Chart 17. Mother's maiden name Smith. Born 1914, Brentford.
Married Marker in Hammersmith, 1937.
SKEWS   SARAH FRANCES
Born 1858, Blean.
SKEWES   SARAH JANE
Born 1865, Redruth.
SKEWES   SARAH JANE
Chart 12. Daughter of James A. and Wendy (née Hooper) Skewes. Born
1974, Truro.
SKEWES   SARA JO
Chart 11. Daughter of James Martin and Helen Ruth Skewes. Born 7
March 1943, America.
SKEWES   SARAH MARIE
Chart 14. Daughter of Charles and Loretta Skewes of America.
SKUES   SARAH MINNIE ELLEN
Chart 8. Daughter of William George and Alice Florence Porter. Born
23 March 1911, Clerkenwell, London. Married Ernest John Skues, 30
May 1961. Lives at 13 Blundell Road, Edgware, Middlesex. Telephone
number: 01 959 0582.
SKEWIS   SARAH NURSE
Born 1920, Shotts East, Scotland. Married James Blair Redmond in
Shettleston, Scotland 1949.
SKEWIS   SAVINA STARK
Chart 50. Daughter of John Hamilton and Bina Stark Skewis. Born 22
August 1906, Addison, Pennsylvania, USA.
Formerly Dean of Women at the University of Pittsburgh, Penns-
ylvania. Spinster. Lives at 154 North Bellfield Avenue, Pittsburgh,
Pennsylvania, 15213, USA.
SKEWES   SCOTT RAYMOND
Chart 36. Son of Peter Michael and Marie (née Blair) Skewes. Born 3
April 1962, Watsons Creek, Bendemeer, New South Wales, Australia.
SKEWES   SEDWELL
Died Camborne 11 July 1713.
SKEWS   SELINA
Chart 10. Daughter of Thomas and Grace Skews of Chacewater. Bpt
Chacewater 11 April 1830. Buried Chacewater 26 December 1843, aged
15 years.
SKEWES   SELINA ANN
Lived at Taylor Street, Oakleigh, Murembeena, Victoria, Australia in
1913.
SKEWS   SELINA G.
Born 1842. Died 1866, aged 24 years in Tavistock.
SKEWES   SENERETTA ELIZABETH
Born 1878, Helston. Married Mitchell, 1920, Helston.
SKEWS   SHARON
Chart 41. Daughter of Desmond Skews. Mother's maiden name Lunn.
Born 1958, Barnsley, South Yorkshire. Married Knowles 1977,
Barnsley.
SKEWES   SHARON
Lives at 23 Troy Terrace, Daglish, 6008, Western Australia. Shop
assistant.
SKEWES   SHARON GAE
Chart 36. Daughter of Earl William and Jillian Fay (née Chad) Skewes.
Born 22 August 1958. Lives at 520 Peel Street, Tamworth, 2340, New
South Wales, Australia.
SKEWIS   SHARON NANCY
Born 1966, Dundee East, Scotland.
SKEWS SHAUN MICHAEL
Son of Thomas H. and Dorothy (née Gould) Skews. Born 1980, Brad-
ford, West Yorkshire.
SKEWES   SHEILA M.
Married William J. Skewes in St Austell, 1973. Maiden name — Pope.
SKUES   SHEILA MACKENZIE
Chart 3. Twin to Joan Mackenzie Skues. Daughter of Charles Ayre
Mackenzie and Elizabeth Skues. Born 1904. Spinster.
SKEWES   SHERYL MARGARET
Lives at 160 Mansfield Street, Thornbury, 3071, Victoria, Australia
with John William Skewes. Teacher.
SKEWIS   SHIRLEY
Chart 2. Daughter of Bennett Osborne and Martha Skewis of America.
SKEWIS   SHIRLEY
Chart 2. Daughter of Raymond and Lottie Skewis. Born 20 October
1913, America. Married Ray Macfarland.

SKEWES   SHIRLEY
Chart 10. Daughter of Ernest Skewes of Marazion. Born 5 November
1925 at Hamilton, Ontario, Canada. Married Leslie Robinson. Issue: 1
son & 1 daughter.
SKEWS   SHIRLEY
Chart 6. Daughter of John and Clara Jeanette (née Babcock) Skews of
Mineral Point, Wisconsin, USA. Born 26 February 1899. Married
Joseph Ley. Lives at 510 South Union, Dodgeville, Wisconsin, USA.
SKUCE SHIRLEY
Daughter of Stewart Tennyson and Gertrude (née Roe) Skuce. Born
1924, Australia. Married 1944. Issue: 3 children and 3 grandchildren.
SKEWS   SHIRLEY
Chart 6. Daughter of Harvey Thomas and Bernice (née Shackley)
Skews. Born 25 June 1935, Mineral Point, Wisconsin, USA. Married
Bob Blank 14 September 1973. No children. Lives at Madison,
Wisconsin, USA.
SKEWES   SHIRLEY A.
Chart 36. Daughter of Cecil and Dolores (née Millett) Skewes. Born
1939, Redruth. Married Rumden in Redruth, 1958.
SKEWES   SHIRLEY ANN
Lives at 35 Drummond Road, Oxlyvale, 2340, New South Wales,
Australia withn Noel John Skewes, printer.
SKEWES   SHIRLEY BERYL
Chart 42. Née Callaghan. Married Jack Skewes, March 1951. Children:
Dennis Paul (1951), John Gregory (1953), Michael Bruce (1953), Bryan
Patrick (1955) and Kim Narelle (1957). Divorced 2 March 1977. Lives
at 120 Smart Street, Fairfield, 2165, New South Wales, Australia.
SKUES   SHIRLEY C.J.
Chart 8. Mother's maiden name Brassett. Born 1941, Islington,
London. Married James E.T. Everton in St Pancras, 1965.
SKEWES   SHIRLEY CICELY
Lived at Willoh Station, Brewarrina, New South Wales, Australia in
1959 with Robert Keith Skewes, manager. Now lives at Laurel Street,
Kootingal, 2352, New South Wales, Australia with Robert Keith
Skewes, Kerrie Margaret Skewes and Michael Leigh Skewes.
SKEWES   SHIRLEY DOREEN
Lives at 5 Prince James Avenue, Coffs Harbour, 2450, New South
Wales, Australia.
SKEWES   SHIRLEY E.
Married James, 1970, Redruth.
SKEWES   SHIRLEY EVA
Chart 36. Daughter of Reginald John and Mary Mildred (née Rooney)
Skewes. Born 24 November 1931, New South Wales, Australia. Married
Dudley Pankhurst, 6 January 1954. Issue: 4 children.
SKEWES   SHIRLEY JANE
Chart 24. Daughter of Alan and Shirley (née Rutherford) Skewes. Born
15 January 1975. Lives in Christchurch, Hampshire.
SKEWIS   SHIRLEY MARTIN
B.A. Chart 2. Daughter of Bennett Osborne and Martha (née Morten)
Skewis. Lived at 509, NE Tacoma, Washington State in 1911.
Bachelor of Arts, University of Washington. 1919.
SKEWES   SHIRLEY YVONNE
Chart 36. Daughter of James and Stella Margaret (née Farrell) Skewes.
Born about 1926, Watsons Creek, Bendemeer, New South Wales,
Australia. Married Edward Peak. Issue: 2 sons.
SKEWES   SIDNEY ARTHUR
Chart 12. Son of James Henry Skewes of Halwyn Farm, St Keverne. Born
12 February 1901. Married Violet Rashleigh 24 February 1926 at
Helston United Methodist Church. Violet (22) was a spinster of
Porthallow and daughter of Cyril Blour, stonemason. Former teacher at
St Keverne School. See Cornish Heritage Appendix, page 605 for his
story as a teacher. Child: Dennis I.J. Died 13 December 1973, aged 72
years.
SKEWES   SIDNEY HOPE
Only son of Rev. Joseph Henry Skewes. Born November, 1870. Married
in Montreal, Canada, by licence, to Annie Bowden Hosking, second
daughter of Edward Hosking, farmer of Burhos, Helston, 1894.
Children: Gladys E. (1895), Harold A. (1897) and Arthur H. (1899).
Lived at 218 Princess Arthur Street, Montreal, Canada. Emigrated to
New York 1900. Bookkeeper.
SKEWES   SIDNEY SAMUEL
Chart 36. Son of Samuel Sidney and Sarah (née Pennall) Skewes. Born
1902, New South Wales, Australia. Married Ella O'Toole. Children:
Ross, Betty and Peggy. Died 23 April 1948, aged 46 years. Buried in his
parents' grave in the Methodist section of Bendemeer Cemetery, New
South Wales, Australia.
SKUES   SIDNEY ST JOHN
Chart 8. Son of John Gilbert and Elizabeth Skues. Born 1890,
Edmonton. Died 1899, aged 9 years from rheumatic fever.
SKUCE   SIDNEY STEWART
Son of Stewart Tennyson and Gertrude (née Roe) Skuce. Born 4 August
1918, Australia. Married 23 April 1941. Issue: two children and five
grandchildren.
SKEWS   SIDWELL
Née Millard. Married Thomas Skews at Gwennap, 1 July 1665. Buried

Gwennap 18 August 1678.

SKEWS SIDWELL
Married Henry Rogers of Illogan, tinner at Gwennap, 28 April 1705.

SKEWES SILAS HARRY
Chart 14. Adopted son of James Lugg and Jane (née Phillips) Skewes. Born 1867. Died of diphtheria, 1881, aged 14 years.

SKEWES SILVIA
Chart 2. Mexican. Daughter of Luis Enrique Skewes of Pachuca, Mexico. Born 16 December 1943. Lives in Pachuca.

SKEWES SIMON
Chart 36. Son of Henry Skewes. Born 1864, Victoria, Australia. Children: Laura (1889), Jack (1893). Linda Margaret (1895) and Ella Barbara (1897). Secretary of Watchem Race Club when it was formed in 1893. Died April 1932, aged 68 years. Buried in Watchem Cemetery, Victoria, Australia.

SKEWES SIMON DAVEY
Chart 19. Son of John and Anne Skewes, miner of Penance, Gwennap. Bpt 25 December 1838, Gwennap. Buried 30 October 1842, Gwennap, aged 6 years. Died of scarlet fever.

SKEWES SIMON DAVEY
Chart 19. Son of John and Anne Skewes of Penance, Gwennap. Born June 1845. Bpt Lanner Wesleyan Methodist Chapel.

SKEWES SIMON DAVID
Chart 36. Son of David Michael and Janelle (née Heyward) Skewes. Born 20 March 1980. Lives in New South Wales, Australia.

SKEWES SIMON WILLIAM
Chart 36. Son of Donald Lloyd and Elizabeth Blair (née Fisher) Skewes. Born 19 September 1975, Tamworth, New South Wales, Australia.

SKEWES SIMONETTE
Chart 36. Née Barnet. Born 1799. Married James Skewes of Cury at Cury 5 October 1824. Children: James, Àlice, Ann, John, Edward, Nancy, Elizabeth, Jane, Mary, Blanche, William and Ellen Willcocks. Lived at Gilly Lane and Treloskan, Cury and later Treskillard, Illogan. Died 1866, aged 67 years.

SKEWES SIRREL ARTHUR
Chart 24. Son of Cyril Thomas and Annie Mary (née Leathan) Skewes. Lives at Boat Harbour Road, Boat Harbour, 2301, New South Wales, Australia with Edna Phyllis Skewes. No children. Bricklayer.

SKEWS SONIA
Mother's maiden name Batchelor. Born 1959, St Austell.

SKEWES SOPHIA
Chart 10. Daughter of Digory and Sophia Skewes. Born 24 June 1831. Bpt Truro Wesleyan Chapel 28 March 1837.

SKEWS SOPHIA
Married 1851, Liskeard.

SKEWES SOPHIA
Died 1864, Liskeard.

SKEWS STANLEY
Chart 17. Born 22 April 1919, West Ham. Son of Henry James and Elizabeth (née Hilliard) Skews. Married Marjorie Hardcastle 13 May 1944 at St Andrews Church, Drypool, Hull. Children: Wendy Lynne Skews (1946) and Barbara Kathleen Skews (1953). Lives at 161 James Reckitt Avenue, Hull. Tel no: 0482 798492.

SKEWES STANLEY
Professor. Son of Henry and Emily (née Moyle) Skewes. Born 29 June 1899, Transvaal, South Africa. Educated at South African College School. Later University of Cape Town 1920. Admitted to King's College, Cambridge 10 October 1923. B.A. 1925, MA 1929, PhD 1938. Became Lecturer in Mathematics at University of Cape Town. Married Florence Rothkugel, 1926 and lived at Chetwynd, Links Drive, Pinelands, Cape Town. Married Ena Allen, 1935, Cambridge. Children: Stephen and Margaret. Lives at 9 Firdale Road, Newlands, Cape Town, South Africa.

SKEWS STANLEY
Chart 10. Son of Peter and Maude Mary Skews. Mother's maiden name Rickard. Born 1924, St Austell. Married Mavis Soady, 1947. Children: Wendy A. (1947), Linda J. (1948), Michael J. (1950), David P. (1953), Andrew P. (1956), Trudy M. (1957), Martin C. (1958), Karen D. (1962) and Nicola Louise (1966).

SKEWES STANLEY BRUCE
Lives at 101 Wilburtree Street, Tamworth, 2340, New South Wales, Australia with Gwenyth Elizabeth Skewes.

SKEWES STANLEY CRAWFORD
Chart 38. Son of Stanley Victor and Gertrude Olive (née Trimper) Skewes. Born 1912. Known as "Tom." Married Evelyn Mary Lysacht. Issue: 3 daughters and 2 sons. Lives at 43 Fletcher Road, Elizabethville, 5112, South Australia.

SKEWES STANLEY GEORGE
Chart 15. Son of Harry and Hilda Skews of Albert Cottages, Pensilva, Liskeard. Born 21 May 1929. Mother's maiden name Jane. Bpt St Ive 21 August 1929. Married Jean Fishleigh, 1958, St Germans. Children: Maureen J. (1959) and David J. (1960).

SKEWES STANLEY OGILVY
Lives at 56 Sisely Avenue, Wangaratta, 3677, Victoria, Australia with Hester Jessie Skewes. Cost clerk.

SKEWS STANLEY R.E.
Mother's maiden name Dyer. Born 1922, Poplar.

SKEWS STANLEY RICHARD
Lived at 306 Dorcas Street, South Melbourne, Australia in 1959 with Daphne Grace Skews. Accountant.
Now lives at 268 Wade Avenue, Mildura, 3500, Victoria, Australia. Teacher.

SKEWES STANLEY VICTOR
Chart 38. Son of Richard and Mary Jane (née Reynolds) Skewes. Born 18 July 1887, Moonta, South Australia. Married Gertrude Olive Trimper, 7 May 1908. In 1959 lived at 9 Coombe Road, Allenby Gardens, Hindmarsh, South Australia. Died 8 June 1960, aged 73 years.

SKEWES STELLA TABITHA
Lived at 209 Victoria Street, Ballarat, Victoria, Australia in 1959 with Owen Eric Skewes, metal machinist. Current address: 44 Dytes Parade, Ballarat, Victoria, Australia, 3350.

SKEWES STELLA MARGARET
Chart 36. Née Farrell. Born 13 Augsut 1902. Married James Skewes, 26 April 1922. Children: Francis James (1922), Clarice Margaret (1925), Shirley Yvonne (1926), Barbara Hannah (1928), William E. (1930), Peter Michael (1931) and Judith Rosemary (1935). Lived at Bantry, Watsons Creek, Bendemeer, New South Wales, Australia. Died 16 July 1978, aged 75 years. Buried in Bendemeer Cemetery, New South Wales, Australia.

SKEWES STELLA VICTORIA MAY
Lived at 9 Edward Street, Essondon West, Victoria, Australia in 1959. Teacher.

SKEWES STEPHEN
Son of John Skewes. Bpt Gerrans 21 January 1580.

SCUES STEPHEN
Son of Stephen and Christian Scues. Bpt St Just in Roseland 3 January 1612.

SKEWES STEVEN
Son of Olyver Skewes. Bpt Perranzabuloe 18 Oct 1573.

SKEWES STEPHEN
Son of John Skewes. Bpt Gerrans 21 January 1580.
Married Christian Jenkin at St Just in Roseland 11 June 1605. Children: Christopher (1609), Stephen (1612) and Ann (1615).

SKEWES STEPHEN
Buried St Just in Roseland 2 May 1622.

SKEWS STEPHEN
Married Blanch Penrose 15 January 1638 at St Just in Roseland. Son: Abigail (1639).

SKEWS STEPHEN
Mentioned in Cornwall Protestation Returns, 1642, St Just in Roseland.

SKEWS STEPHEN
Married Sarah Wilkeson at Southwark, London, 1650.

SKUES STEPHEN
Buried Perranarworthal 4 March 1684.

SKUES STEPHEN
Chart 4. Son of William and Jane Skues, Bpt 5 December 1686, Redruth. Married Frances Lydgy 4 March 1716 (she died 16 October 1717). Church warden at Redruth 1727. Married Jane Lydgy 9 December 1727 (who died 20 February 1761). Died 17 January 1752.

SKUES STEPHEN
Buried Redruth 28 April 1693.

SKEWES STEPHEN
Son of Richard and Margery Skewes. Bpt Paul 19 April 1735.

SKEWIS STEPHEN
Chart 3. Son of Richard and Jane Skewis. Born 11 April 1743, Helston. Died 22 May 1743, infant.

SKEWIS STEPHEN
Chart 2. Son of William and Mary Skewis. Bpt Camborne 20 January 1744. Lived at Park Colly, Camborne. Died 29 September 1823, aged 80 years.

SKEWIS STEPHEN
Chart 3. Son of Richard and Jane Skewis. Born 16 August 1747, Helston. Died 21 August 1747 — infant.

SKUES STEPHEN
Chart 3. Son of William and Mary Skues. Bpt 10 August 1778, Helston. Died 10 May 1781, aged 2½ years.

SKEWIS STEPHEN
Chart 2. Son of John and Philippa Skewis. Bpt 26 December 1778. Died 15 April 1799, aged 21 years in Camborne.

SKEWES STEPHEN
Son of Henry and Margaret Skewes. Bpt Gwinear 4 February 1798.

SKEWES STEPHEN
Son of John and Jenefar Skewes. Bpt Camborne 31 August 1800. Died 1 January 1826, aged 26 years.

SKUES STEPHEN
Chart 2. Son of William and Mary Skues. Bpt Camborne 26 December 1803. Married Margaret Hoskin 29 July 1824 (she died 30 August 1836, aged 33 years of scarlet fever). Stephen, a husbandman, married Elizabeth Provis at Camborne Church 2 April 1837. Children: John

Hoskin, William, Elizabeth and Henry.

SKUES STEPHEN
Chart 2. Son of James and Joanna Skues. Bpt Camborne 21 August 1830. Lived at Killivoase. Died 20 July 1834, aged 4 years.

SKEWES STEPHEN
Married Susannah Woodman, 12 March 1831, Budock.

SKUES STEPHEN
Chart 2. Son of Henry and Grace Skues. Born 1838, Camborne. Bpt Camborne 18 August 1838. Miner.

SKEWS STEPHEN
Died 1858, Liskeard.

SKEWES STEPHEN
Died 1859, Falmouth.

SKEWES STEPHEN
Chart 50. Son of Stanley and Ena (née Allen) Skewes of Cape Town, South Africa.
Lives at 61 Burnside Way, Longbridge, Birmingham, B31 4J2. Telephone number 021 477 3914.

SKEWES STEPHEN
Chart 36. Son of Francis James and Valerie (née Foster) Skewes. Born Watsons Creek, Bendemeer, New South Wales, Australia.

SKEWIS STEPHEN
Chart 50. Son of David Jamieson Wilson and Bridie (née Maher) Skewis. Born 17 March 1963. Lives at 9 Drumry Place, Glasgow 15, Scotland. Telephone number: 041 944 1426.

SKEWES STEPHEN
Chart 10. Son of Ronald Lanier and Patricia (née Fountain) Skewes. Born 3 July 1964, Manassas, Virginia, 22110, United States of America.

SKEWES STEPHEN ANTHONY
Lives at Thornby, via St George, 4393, Queensland, Australia. Station hand.

SKEWS STEPHEN J.
Chart 17. Son of John G.P. and Dorothy (née Boyland) Skews. Born 1950, Peterborough. Married Claridge, 1975, Peterborough. Children: Thaddeus John (1975) and Rebecca Marie (1977).

SKEWES STEPHEN JAMES
Chart 50. Son of Samuel and Mary (née Sanders) Skewes, carter of Ford's Row, Redruth. Born 28 July 1880, Ford's Row. Became a gold miner and moved to 2 Bullers Terrace, Redruth. Married Ethel Pollard (29) of Trefusis Terrace, Redruth, daughter of Nathaniel Pollard, miner, at Redruth Methodist Church 8 June 1911. Children: Harry (1915) and James (1919).

SKUES STEPHEN JOHN
Chart 8. Son of Sydney Thomas and Lilian (née Parnell) Skues. Born 4 August 1950, Hackney, London. Married Susan Wosket, 9 October 1976, St Andrews Church, Islington, London. Works at a menswear shop, Oxford Street, London. Lives at 55b Compton Road, London N 21. Tel No: 01 360 9567.

SKEWS STEPHEN JOHN
Born 1848, Redruth.

SKEWS STEPHEN JOHN
Chart 41. Son of Roland Gerald and Linda (née Greaves) Skews. Born 3 November 1966, Aldershot, Hampshire.

SKEWES STEPHEN MELVILLE
Lives at 45 Glenhuntley Street, Woodville South, 5011 South Australia with Gwendra Pearl Skewes, David John Skewes and Ralph Edward Skewes.

SKEWS STEPHEN TREVOR
Chart 41. Son of Trevor and Kathleen (née Guirey) Skews. Born 1977, Barnsley, South Yorkshire.

SKEWES STEVEN ALAN
Chart 2. Son of William M. and Laverne Helen (née Getty) Skewes. Born 23 September 1960, Minnesota, United States of America.

SKUES STEVEN BRUCE
Son of William Ashdown and Edith Beryl (née Saul) Skues. Born 28 January 1969. Lives at 7 Cormack Road, Beacon Hill, New South Wales, 2100, Australia.

SKUCE STEWART TENNYSON
Born 13 October 1886, Wallaroo, South Australia. Married Gertrude Roe 30 August 1916. Children: Sidney Stewart (1918), Joyce (1920), Hazel (1922), Shirley (1924) and Fay (1926), Died 3 June 1961, aged 73 years.

SKEWES STUART
Chart 36. Son of Glenleigh Bertie William and Mary Evelyn Harriet (née Watkins) Skewes. Born 21 April 1951. Lives at 141 Spencer Street, Sebastopol, 3356, Victoria, Australia.
Married Liesje Maria Artz, 21 March 1981 at Ballarat, Victoria, Australia at St Alipus Catholic Church. Lives at Nuns Road, Snake Valley, 3351, Victoria, Australia.

SKUES STUART JONATHAN
Mother's maiden name Wiener. Born 1980, Thanet.

SKEWES SUSAN
Born 1807. Wife of Stephen Skewes of Penryn. Died 7 May 1865, aged 58 years.

SKEWES SUSAN

Born 1823. Lived at Centenary Row, Redruth. Died 1887, aged 64 years. Buried Camborne 4 October 1887.

SKEWES SUSAN
Chart 33. Daughter of John Oates. Born 1820, Kenwyn. Married William Skewes at Chacewater, 24 December 1840. Children: Mary (1841), William (1843), Susan (1845), Grace (1847), Elizabeth (1850), Samuel (1853) and Amelia (1855). Husband had died by 1871. In Census Returns for 1871 living in Tippets Backlet, St Mary's, Truro. Died 1876, aged 55 years.

SKEWIS SUSAN
Chart 33. Née Tapper. Born 1825. Married Samuel Skewis 17 July 1847. Lived at Ashburton, Devon. Children: Mary (1852), Samuel (1859), William (1862) and Daniel (1865). Died Newton Abbot, 1893, aged 68 years.

SKEWES SUSAN
Born 1838, Redruth.

SKEWES SUSAN
Chart 33. Daughter of William and Susan (née Oates) Skewes. Born 1845. Laundress of Tippets Backlet, Truro. Single lady who had illegitimate child — Lily (1880). Buried St Mary's, Truro, 5 April 1900, aged 55 years.

SKEWES SUSAN
Born 1850. Died 1902, aged 52 years in Helston.

SKEWES SUSAN
of White Cross, Cury. Born 1856. Buried 31 October 1880, aged 24 years in Cury.

SKEWES SUSAN
Married 1857, Redruth.

SKEWES SUSAN
Chart 12. Born 1879. Daughter of John and Thirza Skewes. Bpt Cury 18 January 1883. Married in Midhurst, Sussex and died there in 1950's.

SKEWES SUSAN
Mother's maiden name Richards. Born 1915, Helston.

SKEWS SUSAN
Mother's maiden name Batchelor. Born 1952, St Austell. Married Guy in St Austell, 1971.

SKEWES SUSAN
Chart 12. Mother's maiden name Holbrook. Born 7 July 1959. Daughter of Oswald and Celia Skewes.

SKEWES SUSAN
Chart 12. Daughter of Carl and Elizabeth Skewes. Mother's maiden name Clackworthy. Born 22 March 1968. Lives at 33 Roskear Road, Camborne.

SKEWES SUSAN ANN
Born 1859, Redruth.

SKEWES SUSAN ANNIE
Chart 40. Daughter of Richard and Susan Skewes of Perran Downs. Born 1871. Bpt 28 May 1871 (Whit Sunday) at Perranuthnoe Parish Church. Married Thomas E. Floyd, 1900. Died 8 October 1929, aged 58 years.

SKEWES SUSAN BARBARA
Chart 40. Daughter of Matthew Harry Skewes. Mother's maiden name Morgan. Born 25 June 1949. Married Mark A.C. Dowland, 24 April 1974 in Penzance.

SKEWES SUSAN GLENYS
Chart 38. Née Schramm. Married Edward Kent Skewes 20 February 1971. Children: Verity Kate (1974) and Carmen Victoria (1977). Lives: c/o Ungarra Post Office, 5610, South Australia.

SKEWES SUSAN JANE
Daughter of Edward and Mary Skewes. Bpt Grade 25 March 1845.

SKEWES SUSAN JANE
Died 1845, Helston.

SKEWES SUSAN JANE
Married 1858, Redruth.

SKEWES SUSAN JANE
Died 1861, Helston.

SKEWS SUSAN JANE
Daughter of Peter Skews, miner of St Mary's, Truro. Married, by licence, at St Clement to John Onear, son of Frederick Onear, watch maker, 25 March 1862.

SKEWIS SUSAN JANE
Born 1871, Penzance.

SKEWES SUSAN JANE
Chart 12. "Cissie". Née Gilbert. Married John Skewes at Helston Register Office 1907. Children: Samuel Percy, Constance Jane, William John and Oswald. Died 1951, aged 63 years. Husband John died October 1975, aged 91 years. Both buried in Mawgan churchyard.

SKEWES SUSAN MARGARET
Daughter of David Leslie and Irma Margaret (née Green) Skewes. Born 10 March 1964. Lives at 35a McNally Street, Yarrawonga, 3730, Victoria, Australia.

SKEWES SUSAN PATRICIA
Lives at 8 Leeworthy Street, Victor Harbour, 5211, South Australia with Andrew Cuthbert Skewes, principal.

SKEWES   SUSAN S.
Married Boyson, 1944, St Germans.

SKEWES   SUSANNA
Born 1768. Buried Gwennap 6 April 1848, aged 80 years.

SKEWES   SUSANNAH
Daughter of Richard and Jane Skewes. Bpt Gwennap 3 Oct 1782.

SKEWES   SUSANNAH
Daughter of Richard Skewes (pauper). Buried Kenwyn 25 February 1793.

SKEWES   SUSANNAH
Daughter of Richard & Grace Skewes. Bpt St Agnes 20 May 1804.

SKEWES   SUSANNAH
Daughter of James and Susannah Skewes. Bpt Gwennap 6 June 1808.

SKUES   SUSANNAH
Married William Harris at Kenwyn 2 August 1823.

SKEWES   SUSANNAH
Married William Jeffery at Kenwyn 18 February 1826.

SKEWES   SUSANNAH
Married Samuel Henwood at St Blazey 5 February 1829.

SKEWES   SUSANNAH
Née May. Born 1833, Australia. Second wife of John William Skewes. Married 1854. Children included Samuel Richard Skewes (1856). Died 30 June 1915 at Yatala East, aged 82 years.

SKEWES   SUSANNAH
Chart 14. Daughter of Edward and Mary Skewes. Born 1841, Grade.

SKEWES   SUSANNAH
Daughter of James Skewes, miner of Lanner. Married Thomas Mills of Tryulla 9 April 1846, Gwennap.

SKEWES   SUSANNAH
Born 1848. Née Donald. Daughter of Stephen Donald, farmer. Married Richard Skewes, miner, at Perranuthnoe 27 August 1870. Children: Susan Annie (1871), William (1889), Lilian Linda (1892) and Richard Henry (1873). Lived at Perran Downs, Perranuthnoe. Died 1937, aged 89 years.

SKEWES   SUSANNAH
Daughter of Francis and Julia Skewes of Churchtown, Cury; labourer. Bpt Cury 23 March, 1856.

SKEWES   SUSANNAH JANE
Born 1846, Helston.

SKEWES   SUSANNAH MOYLE
Daughter of Peter and Peggy Skewes. Bpt Kenwyn 28 June 1801.

SKEWES   SUZANNE LYNDA
Chart 36. Daughter of Earl William and Fay (née Chad) Skewes. Born 28 October 1959. Lived at 520 Peel Street, Tamworth, 2340, New South Wales, Australia. Married David John Bennett, 9 September 1978.

SKUSE   SYDNEY
Son of Daniel and Louise (née Clouder) Skuse. Born 1870. Married Nellie Cox. Children: Horace Sydney (1899) and Constance (1901). Died 1912, aged 42 years.

SKEWES   SYDNEY HOWARD
Chart 38. Son of Richard and Mary Jane (née Reynolds) Skewes. Born 18 October 1893, Moonta, South Australia. Miner until Wallaroo Mines closed and then he moved to Adelaide where he became a tram conductor. Twice married:
1) Cordelia Blight (she died 10 September 1928, aged 33 years). Children: Blanche (1916), Elva (1917), Valda (1919), Garfield Sydney (1922) and Ray Samuel (1926).
2) Ruby Maude Smith, 5 October 1929 at the Church of Christ, Adelaide. Child: Delma (1935).
Grand Master of Loyal Orange Lodge of Adelaide South in the 1950's. Lived at 11 Colley Street, North Adelaide. Died 8 June 1964, aged 71 years. Buried in Adelaide West Terrace Cemetery.

SKEWES   SYDNEY JAMES
Born 1875, Helston. Died 1876, aged 1 year.

SKEWES   SYDNEY ROWNTON
Chart 38. Known as "Tom". Lives at 56 Russell Terrace, Kilkenny, Woodville, South Australia with Olive Caroline Skewes. Wheelwright.

SKUES   SYDNEY THOMAS
Chart 8. Son of Walter Edward Skues. Mother's maiden name Harris. Born 1921, Shoreditch. Married Lilian M. Parnell, 1948. Children: Stephen J. (1950), Gillian (1954) and Andrew J. (1956).

SKUES   SYDNEY VICTOR
Chart 8. Son of Victor Claude Skues. Mother's maiden name Ingey. Born 1925, Edmonton, London. Married Jean E. Cox, 1949. Brentwood, Essex. Children: Ian Keith (1953), Andrew P. (1955) and David A. (1958).

SKEWES   SYDONIA
Born 1895, Salford. Married Wilson, 1921.

SKEWS   SYLVIA
Chart 15. Née Arnold. Married Courtenay John Gregory Skews, 1950, St Germans. One son: Andrew J. Skews (1950).

SKEWES   SYLVIA A.
Married Mahon, 1974, Truro.

SKEWIS   SYLVIA ANN

Chart 2. Daughter of Francis James and Lucretia (née Callinson) Skewis of America. Born 6 April 1920. Married Harvey Ronne. Issue: 3 daughters and 1 son. Lives in Salem, Oregon, USA.

SKEWES   SYLVIA DOREEN
Chart 36. Daughter of Alfred John and Matilda (née Hill) Skewes of Tuckingmill. Born 4 August 1916. Bpt with her sisters and brother at Tuckingmill Parish Church 12 September 1917. Married John Joseph Tredinnick, 1937.

SKUES   SYLVIA G.
Chart 8. Daughter of Charles Gilbert and Elsie (née Wyatt) Skues. Born 1929, Edmonton, London. Married Richard C. Slater, Edmonton, 1951.

SKEWES   SYLVIA JANE
Daughter of Harold Herschell and Gladys Jane (née Batty) Skewes. Born 4 January 1949, Maybeary, MacDowell, West Virginia, USA.

T

SKEWES   T.
Builder living in Daniel Street, Truro, 1856.

SKEWES   T.
Grocer living in Daniel Street, Truro, 1856.

SKEWIS   TAMARA
Chart 2. Daughter of Charles Edward and Sharon Skewis. Born 13 January 1964, America.

SKEWES   TAMARA
Chart 10. Daughter of Richard Albert and Ann Marie (née Millar) Skewes. Born 15 November 1965, Hamilton, Ontario, Canada. Lives at 1207 Royal York, Islington, Toronto, Canada.

SKEWS   TAMSON
Married James Skews at St Just in Roseland, 28 January 1607. Buried St Just in Roseland 8 August 1644.

SKEWES   TAMSYN
Daughter of John and Sarah Skewes. Born 2 April 1637, St Anthony in Meneage. Bpt 7 April 1637.

SKEWES   TANIA JANE
Chart 36. Daughter of Donald Lloyd and Elizabeth Blair (née Fisher) Skewes. Born 2 February 1967, Tamworth, New South Wales, Australia.

SKEWES   TANIA MAREE
Chart 36. Daughter of Maxwell Charles and Cheryl (née Sprowle) Skewes. Born 31 May 1968. Lives at 12 Julia Place, Moree, 2400, New South Wales, Australia.

SKEWES   TARA DIANE
Chart 10. Daughter of Norman David and Linda Skewes of Hamilton, Ontario, Canada. Born 2 May 1974.

SKEWES   TEASHA MAREE
Chart 36. Daughter of Gary William and Lynette Mary (née Smith) Skewes. Born 5 November 1970. Lives at 9 Surrey Road, Wilson, 6107, Western Australia.

SKEWES   TEODORO
Chart 10. Mexican. Son of Franklin and Margarita (née Sanchez) Skewes. Born Real del Monte, Mexico, 19 September 1968.

SKEWES   TERENCE ALLAN
Lived at 74 Daly Street, Kuualta Park, Plympton, Australia in 1959 with Dawn Florence Skewes. Tool maker. Now lives at 53 Elgin Avenue, Christies Beach, 5165, South Australia.

SKUES   TERENCE F.
Chart 8. Son of Alfred Edgar Skues. Mother's maiden name Brassett. Born 1947, Islington. Married Jean F. Moore in Barking, Essex, 1968. Children: Jane Louise (1970), Claire (1971) and Terence James (1973).

SKUES   TERENCE JAMES
Chart 8. Son of Terence F. Skues. Mother's maiden name Jean Moore. Born 1973, Barking, Essex.

SKEWS   TERENCE W.
Chart 17. Mother's maiden name Leach. Born 9 February 1950, Bury. Married Valerie Walters at Upper Lougher, Swansea, 1973. Daughter Karen Emma born 1977, Swansea.

SKEWES   TERRI
Chart 24. Adopted daughter of Alan and Shirley (née Rutherford) Skewes. Born 26 September 1972. Lives in Christchurch, New Zealand.

SKEWES   TERRI ANN GREEN
Chart 11. Daughter of Thomas John and Elgin Louise Bean Skewes. Born 25 December 1943, United States of America.

SKEWES   TERRY GRAHAM
Lives at 8 Emma Street, Athol Park, 5012, South Australia. Sheet metal worker.

SKEWES   TERRY PAUL
Chart 42. Son of Dennis Paul and Kayleen Daphne (née Bourke) Skewes. Born 15 September 1972, Fairfield, New South Wales, Australia. Now lives at 25 McKay Street, Nowra Hill, 2540, New South Wales, Australia.

SKUES   TERRY STEVEN

Mother's maiden name Skues. Born 1973, Chelmsford, Essex.

SKEWS THADDEUS JOHN
Chart 17. Son of Stephen J. Skews. Mother's maiden name Claridge. Born 1975, Peterborough.

SKEWES THEA ALEXANDRA
Lives at 32 Anchor Road, Tamworth, 2340, New South Wales, Australia with Robert Skewes, printer.

SKEWES THELMA IRENE
Chart 36. Daughter of Samuel Sidney and Sarah (née Pennall) Skewes. Born 1910. Married Mark Fisher in Tamworth, New South Wales, Australia. Issue: 3 sons. Died 5 September 1967, aged 57 years.

SKEWES THELMA JEAN
Lives at Lot/85 Eclipse Drive, Albany, 6330, Western Australia with John Herbert Skewes.

SKUES THELMA MILDRED
Chart 8. Née Howard. Married Christopher Herbert Victor Skues at Thames Ditton Parish Church, 27 June 1970. Lives at Sylcombe Hunt Lodge, Petersfield Road, Ropley, Hampshire. Telephone number 096277 3463.

SKEWES THEODORA
of Ruan Minor. Born 1889. Buried Cury 12 January 1890, aged 6 weeks.

SKEWES THEODORA
Chart 10. Mexican. Daughter of Salvador and Antonia (née Casanas) Skewes. Born 11 November 1955. Died 18 December 1955, aged 5 weeks.

SKUES THERESA
Chart 3. Née Kaye. Born 1905. Married Frederick Skues at St Paul's Church, Halifax 11 April 1929. No children. Lived at 14 Second Avenue, Manor Drive, Halifax. Died 12 July 1980, aged 75 years.

SKEWS THERESA HERMINNA AMELIA
Chart 10. Born 1848, Camborne. Daughter of William and Mary Skews. Lived at Illogan Highway. Married 1874.

SKEWS THERESA JANE
Chart 17. Daughter of Brian A.E. Skews. Mother's maiden name Newby. Born 1973, Enfield, Middlesex.

SKEWES THERESE JEAN
Chart 50. Daughter of Thomas Grenville and Ilma Elizabeth (née Dodd) Skewes. Born 7 June 1944, Victoria, Australia. Married John Kaufman 19 December 1967. Issue: Three children.

SKEWES THIRZA
Daughter of Francis and Julia Skewes of Churchtown, Cury; labourer. Bpt Cury 16 April 1854.

SKEWES THIRZA
Chart 12. Born 1854. Wife of John Skewes who died 7 April 1922. Children: James Henry, Julia Annie, Elizabeth Mary, Ellen Janie, Susan, Bessie, Thirza, John, Grace and Lily Emma. Died 11 February 1941, aged 87 years at Chyrean, St Keverne.

SKEWES THIRZA
Chart 12. Born 1887. Daughter of John and Thirza Skewes of Penhale, labourer. Bpt Cury 13 January 1887. Married 1907, in Helston to William Thomas. Died approx 1960.

SKEWES THIRZA A.J.
Chart 18. Daughter of John Edgar Skewes. Mother's maiden name Morrison. Born 1934, Bristol. Emigrated with her parents to South Africa. Now married with issue.

SKEWES THOMAS
Was assessed in 1523 on £10 for property he owned in Cury. He paid ten shillings.

SKEWES THOMAS
Bpt St Enoder 9 August 1574. Son of Thomas Skewes.

SKEWES THOMAS
Buried Gerrans 7 April 1580.

SKEWES THOMAS
Chart 19. Married Sidwell Millard at Gwennap 1 July 1665. Children: Blanche, John (1676) and Thomas.

SCUES THOMAS
Chart 2. Son of William and Margaret Scues. Bpt Camborne 21 October 1665. Died 21 December 1666, aged 1 year.

SKEWES THOMAS
Chart 19. Son of Thomas Skewes. Buried Gwennap 7 March 1668.

SKUES THOMAS
Chart 19. Son of Thomas Skues. Bpt Gwennap 19 May 1673. Married Margaret Richards 7 December 1702 at Gwennap. Owned property at Chinhale and Carharrack, Gwennap. See *Cornish Heritage* — Appendix for Deeds. Children: Blanche, John, Richard, William, Thomas, Margaret and Joan. Will proved 11 February 1735. W(CRO).

SKUES THOMAS
Son of Henry and Elizabeth Skues. Bpt Cury 21 September 1684.

SKEWES THOMAS
Listed as a commissioned sea officer, 1685. Lieutenant, Royal Navy.

SCUIS THOMAS
Married Philippa Angove at Wendron 23 May 1692. Children included Mary (1701) and Elizabeth (1695).

SKEWS THOMAS

Married Margaret Richards, Gwennap, 7 December 1702.

SKEWES THOMAS
Buried 12 July 1696, Cury.

SKEWES THOMAS
Son of Thomas Skewes. Bpt 31 July 1614, Exeter St Mary Major.

SKEWS THOMAS
Son of Thomas Skews. Bpt Gwennap 16 January 1711.

SKEWS THOMAS
Chart 19. Son of Thomas Skews. Bpt Gwennap 6 January 1711. Buried Gwennap 7 January 1711.

SKUES THOMAS
Son of Richard Skues. Bpt Kenwyn 18 September 1711.

SKEWES THOMAS
Chart 19. Son of Thomas and Margaret Skewes. Bpt Gwennap 16 December 1712. Married 29 April 1738 to Elizabeth Webb in Gwennap. Children: Alexander, Margaret, William, Thomas, John, Richard, Elizabeth. Died 29 August 1763.

SKEWES THOMAS
Married Mary Retallack at St Martin in Meneage 22 August 1713.

SKEWES THOMAS
Buried Cury 11 March 1715.

SKEWES THOMAS
Chart 14. Son of Henry and Judeth Skewes. Bpt Cury 14 February 1722.

SKEWES THOMAS
Son of John and Elizabeth Skewes. Bpt Sancreed 4 January 1736.

SKEWES THOMAS
Chart 19. Son of Thomas and Elizabeth Skewes. Bpt Gwennap 10 March 1738. Miner. A Methodist. Bachelor? Died 8 December 1816, aged 78 years. W(CRO).

SKEWES THOMAS
Chart 19. Son of William Skewes of Gwennap.

SKEWES THOMAS
Chart 25. Married Esther James at St Keverne 23 October 1746, in presence of Thomas Skewes. Children: Esther (1747), Thomas (1749), Mary (1752), Judith (1754), Henry (1758), June (1760), Henry (1764) and Ann (1766).

SKEWES THOMAS
Chart 25. Born 1749. Bpt St Keverne 15 October 1774. Children: Charles Gilles, Thomas, Elizabeth, Esther, Thomas Henry and Eleanor. Died 12 January 1808, aged 58 years.
Son of Thomas and Esther Skewes. Married Eleanor Giles at St Keverne 29 October 1774.

SKEWES THOMAS
of Kea. Married Jane Crossman of Kea at Kenwyn 29 December 1759, in presence of Mary Skewes.

SKEWES THOMAS
Son of William and Hannah Skewes. Bpt St Gluvias, 31 August 1760.

SKEWES THOMAS
Son of Thomas Skewes. Bpt Kenwyn 31 March 1762.

SKEWES THOMAS
Son of John and Mary Skewes. Bpt Gwennap 26 December 1769.

SCKEWS THOMAS
Born 1769. Buried Kenwyn 23 May 1811, aged 42 years.

SKEWES THOMAS
Chart 10. Son of Martin Skewes of Kea. Bpt Kenwyn 11 August 1770. Married Mary Turner at Kea 7 March 1791.

SKEWES THOMAS
Chart 25. Son of Thomas and Eleanor Skewes. Buried St Keverne 28 December 1777.

SKEWES THOMAS
Chart 18. Son of Thomas and Thomasine Skewes of Kea. Bpt Kenwyn 8 August 1778. Married Mary Tippet of Kea at Kenwyn 6 January 1798. Children: Thomas, Richard, Mary, John, William and Ann.

SKEWES THOMAS Jnr
Buried Kea 24 July 1779.

SKEWES THOMAS Snr
Buried Kea 15 August 1780.

SKEWES THOMAS
Chart 25. Son of Thomas and Eleanor Skewes. Born 13 October 1780. Bpt Falmouth 12 November 1780. Died 24 November 1782, aged 2 years.

SKEWES THOMAS
Chart 10. Son of Digory and Elizabeth Skewes. Bpt Kenwyn 11 September 1785.

SKEWES THOMAS
Chart 25. Son of Thomas and Eleanor Skewes. Born 15 April 1790. Bpt Falmouth 24 April 1790. Married ....(she died 9 June 1824). He remarried Grace Pollard of Constantine 22 August 1829. Children: Benjamin Hellings, Thomas Henry (first marriage) and Charles (second marriage). In 1871 Census Returns was living at Retreat, Falmouth; 1861, living at Porham Street, Falmouth; and 1851, living at Jubilee Court, Falmouth. Died 1871 in Manchester, aged 81 years.

SKEWES THOMAS
Chart 10. Born 1792, Kea. Son of Thomas and Mary Skewes. Bpt

Kenwyn 25 December 1792. Lived at Jolly's Bottom, Kea. Married Grace Trezize 13 July 1820, Kenwyn in presence of Thomas Skewes. Children: Mary (1821), Eleanor (1823), Thomas (1825), Elizabeth Trezize (1827), Selina (1830), Julia (1831), Emma Jane (1834), Emily (1836), Grace Theresa (1839), Walter Trezize (1842) and William Trezize (1844). In 1871 Census Returns was a widower living at Chacewater and was listed as a farmer of seven acres. Died 15 March 1875, aged 83 years. Buried at Chacewater 18 March 1875.

SKUSE   THOMAS
Married Hester Butt, Minety, Gloucester, 1796.

SKEWES   THOMAS
Chart 30. Son of Henry and Catherine Skewes. Bpt Kea 31 March 1799. Married Jane Beer (of St Teath) at Kenwyn Parish Church 12 February 1824 in presence of Mary Jolly Skewes. Was a mason who lived at Daniell Street, Truro — later a grocer. Jane died 19 September 1889. Children: Mary Ann, Henrietta, John Beer, Philippa and Thomas. Died 16 July 1868, aged 69 years, after a long illness.

SKEWES   THOMAS
Buried Gwennap 16 April 1800.

SKEWES   THOMAS
Buried Kenwyn 5 September 1806.

SKEWES   THOMAS
Chart 14. Son of Henry and Jane Skewes. Bpt Ruan Major 1 July 1806. Labourer. Married Loveday Mundy at Ruan Major 14 December 1831 in presence of Edward Skewes. Died 22 January 1869, aged 63 years at Ruan Major. Loveday died 1890, aged 81 years.

SKEWES   THOMAS
Buried Kea 12 May 1808.

SKEWES   THOMAS
Chart 50. Son of Richard and Jane Skewes. Bpt Kenwyn 30 September 1810. Married JANE SKEWES at Kea, 11 June 1832. Children: Elizabeth Jane (1833), Thomas (1835), Grace (1837), Samuel (1839), Mary (1841), Emily (1844) and Richard (1848). Miner. Emigrated to Australia aboard *John and Lucy* which left Liverpool 9 June 1854 and arrived in Port Phillip, Melbourne, September 1854.

SKEWIS   THOMAS
Born 1813. Died West Derby 1883, aged 70 years.

SKUCE   THOMAS
Born Crawley, Sussex, 1814. Emigrated to South Australia. Died Adelaide, South Australia 2 May 1861, aged 47 years.

SKEWS   THOMAS
Chart 9. Son of James and Joanna Skews of Lower Sticker. Bpt St Ewe 17 February 1817. Buried 7 November 1847, aged 30 years.

SKEWS   THOMAS
Chart 6. Born 1828. Married Mary Ann Hooper. Children included: John (1855) and William (1856). Lived in Mineral Point, Wisconsin, USA in 1870. Was gassed in the Linden Mine Disaster, Mineral Point and died 11 September 1874, aged 46 years 10 months and 3 days.

SKEWES   THOMAS
Born 1824. Buried Chacewater 29 September 1829, aged 5 years.

SKEWES   THOMAS
Born 1824. Son of Peter and Elizabeth Skewes of the Poorhouse, Kenwyn. Bpt 22 November 1826. Buried Kenwyn 19 February 1827, aged 3 years.

SKEWES   THOMAS
Chart 10. Son of Thomas and Grace Skewes of Kea, miner. Bpt Kenwyn 10 July 1825. Bured Chacewater 29 September 1829, aged 5 years.

SKEWES   THOMAS
Chart 12. Bpt Cury 2 April 1826. Son of James and Elizabeth Skewes of Cury. Agricultural servant at Gilly, Cury in 1841 Census Returns.

SKEWES   THOMAS
Son of Thomas and Elizabeth Skewes. Bpt Kenwyn 22 November 1826.

SKUSE   THOMAS
Married Diana Cordy, 1826, Westleigh, Gloucester.

SKEWES   THOMAS
Chart 6. Son of Peter and Mary Skewes (Mary, daughter of John and Elizabeth Williams), miner of Kenwyn. Born 8 December 1827. Bpt Truro Wesleyan Chapel 28 March 1837.

SKEWIS   THOMAS
Born 1828. Died 1915, Coatbridge, Scotland, aged 67 years.

SKEWES   THOMAS
Born 1829. Died Plymouth 1889, aged 60 years.

SKEWES   THOMAS
Chart 10. Son of Richard and Agnes Skewes of Kerley, Kea; mine agent. Bpt Chacewater 7 October 1830. Buried Chacewater 21 November 1830, aged 1 year.

SKEWIS   THOMAS
Son of John and Ann Skewis, miner of Crophendy, Gwennap. Bpt Gwennap 24 October 1832. Buried Gwennap 16 November 1842, aged 10 years.

SKUES   THOMAS
Chart 28. Married Grace...Children: Mary and Eleanor. Lived at Kea.

SKEWES   THOMAS
Chart 30. Son of Thomas & Jane Skewes, builder. Born 1834. Bpt Kea 6 April 1834. Innkeeper and ironmonger. Married Mary Jane Peters,

daughter of John Peters, master mariner, at St George's, Truro 28 April 1860, in presence of Thomas Skewes and Philippa Jane Skewes. Children: Mary Ann Peters, Herbert, Elizabeth J. and Florence. In 1871 Census Returns was living at Edward Street, Truro; later at Parkvedras Terrace, Truro. Died 26 January 1894, aged 59 years. Buried St Mary's, Truro 30 January 1894.

SKEWES   THOMAS
Chart 50. Son of Thomas and Jane Skewes of Seveoke, miner. Bpt Chacewater 21 June 1835. Emigrated to Australia aboard *Fairlie*, which sailed from Plymouth 20 February 1856 arriving Melbourne 4 June 1856.
Married Sarah Ann Lord. Children: Hobson, Maud, Cecilia, Harold, Linda, Thomas Garland, Elvina, Stella, Samuel Grenville Stowe, Addie and Sarah. Died 13 November 1908, aged 73 years.

SKEWES   THOMAS
Was a witness to the wedding of William Pengelly and Peggy Bray at Ruan Major, 22 February 1837.

SKEWES   THOMAS
Son of Peter and Mary (née Williams) Skewes. Bpt Truro St Mary 28 March 1837.

SKEWS   THOMAS
Born 1837. Wife's name Catherine. Lived at Northcote and Maldon, Victoria, Australia. Died 24 May 1908 at 9 Sterling Street, Kew, Melbourne, aged 69 years.

SKEWES   THOMAS
Married Grace Richards at Kenwyn 24 January 1838.

SKEWES   THOMAS
Chart 19. Son of Richard and Mary Skewes. Lived at Gwennap. Died 3 March 1838.

SKEWS   THOMAS
Chart 31. Son of John and Jane Skews. Born 6 December 1836. Bpt St Austell 1 April 1838.

SKEWES   THOMAS
Chart 22. Son of Martin and Ann (née Hocking) Skewes. Bpt Chacewater 9 June 1839.

SKEWES   THOMAS
Chart 10. Son of Peter and Grace Skewes of Kerley, Kea. Born 1840. Was a miner in Mineral del Monte, Mexico where he died 6 January 1874, aged 33 years. Buried in the English Cemetery, Real del Monte.

SKEWES   THOMAS
Son of William Skewes, baker. Married Elizabeth Jenkins, daughter of Charles Jenkins, tailor at Swansea Parish Church, Glamorgan, 31 March 1842. Lived at The Strand, Swansea.

SKUSE   THOMAS
Died 1842, Malmsbury, Wiltshire.

SKUSE   THOMAS
Son of Thomas Skuse of Malmsbury, Wiltshire. Born 1849. Emigrated to Australia in 1866, aged 17 years. Married 1867 to Mary Ann Curtis, South Australia. Issue: 5 sons and 4 daughters. Died Adelaide 6 April 1918, aged 69 years.

SKEWES   THOMAS
Married 1849, St Columb.

SKEWES   THOMAS
Born 1851 Redruth. Buried St Mary's, Truro, 5 February 1857, aged 5 years.

SKEWIS   THOMAS
Died 1851, Abergavenny.

SKUES   THOMAS
Chart 7. Son of John Skues of South Street, St George's, Hannover Square, London. Born 1853. Labourer. Married 6 September 1874 to Elizabeth Harris, daughter of John Harris, labourer of Brenchley, Kent, at St George's, Hannover Square.
Lived at 33 North Street, Chelsea and later (1889) moved to Kent. Children: Noah James, Edward Alfred, Blanche Louise, Ada Alice, Florence Emily and Francis Albert.
Died 30 October 1908, aged 55 years in General Hospital, Tunbridge Wells, Kent.
His wife died 1925, aged 72 years in Cuckfield, Sussex.

SKUSE   THOMAS
Son of Thomas and Elizabeth (née Grimes) Skuse of Jubilee Buildings, Ashley, Bristol. Born 1 January 1854.

SKUSE   THOMAS
Son of Henry and Elizabeth (née Hallier) of 11 Sards Rents, St John's, St Olave, London. Born 11 April 1854.

SKEWES   THOMAS
Born 1856. Died Preston 1895, aged 39 years.

SKEWES   THOMAS
Married 1855, Plymouth.

SKEWS   THOMAS
Chart 15. Son of John and Isabella Skews of Trewint, Altarnun. Born 1866. Died 16 March 1866.

SKEWS   THOMAS
Chart 41. Son of Matthew and Betsy (née Tresider) Skews. Born 1867. Bpt St Allen Lane Bible Christian Chapel, Cornwall, 1 April 1867. Married Ada Sheldon, 1886, Ecclesall, Sheffield, South Yorkshire.

Thomas and Elizabeth Skues

Children: Thomas (1886), Minnie (1889), Louisa (1891), Betsy (1892), Mabel (1893), Ernest (1895), George (1897), Olive (1900), Joseph (1901), Samuel (1903) and Edgar (1905). Coal ripper.
Died 1911, aged 43 years in Barnsley, South Yorkshire.
Ada married John Michael Dolan in 1913.

SKEWS   THOMAS
Born 1872, Liskeard. Died 1872, aged 8 months in Liskeard. Buried Charlestown 16 November 1872.

SKEWS   THOMAS
Chart 6. Son of William and Alice J. Skews of Mineral Point, Wisconsin, USA. Died 1882 — an infant.

SKEWS   THOMAS
Chart 41. Son of Thomas and Ada (née Sheldon) Skews. Born 29 June 1886 at 15 Wentworth Street, Nether Hallam, Sheffield, South Yorkshire.
Married Jane Renshaw 25 September 1911, Barnsley, South Yorkshire. Trammer in Wombwell Main Colliery. Lived at 27 Lundhill Road, Wombwell, South Yorkshire.
Children: Ada Ivy (1911), Roy (1913), Kathleen (1915), Mabel (1917) and Thomas Ernest (1919). Well-known organist and choirmaster at Broomhill Chapel, South Yorkshire for nearly 20 years. Due to ill health in 1951 it was the first time in 35 years that he did not conduct anniversary singing in Lundhill Chapel, Wombwell.
A native of Sheffield, Thomas Skews was brought to Wombwell as a baby. He first lived at Jump and later at Lundhill and Wombwell Main. He was a member of Barnsley and Wombwell Operatic Societies, and as a youth he was a keen physical culturist.
He spent all his working life at Wombwell Main and Cortonwood collieries.
Died 21 July 1952 at the Royal Hospital, Sheffield, aged 66 years. Buried in Hemingfield Cemetery.

SKEWE   THOMAS
Chart 10. Son of Thomas George and Jane Skewes. Born 7 May 1889, Marazion. Died 1894, aged 5 years.

SKEWIS   THOMAS
Born 1893, Airdrie, Scotland. Married 1917, New Monkland, Scotland. Died 1931, aged 38 years, New Monkland.

SKEWIS   THOMAS
Born 1963, Dennistoun, Scotland.

SKEWES   THOMAS ALBERT JEFFERY
Chart 10. Son of William and Mary Skewes, blacksmith. Born 1841, Kenwyn. Miner. Married Charlotte Chigwyn (24) of Pool, and daughter of William Chigwyn, horse dealer; at Illogan Parish Church 19 October 1865. Lived at Kerley, Kea.

SKEWES   THOMAS BOULDEN
Chart 14. Son of John and Jane (née Boulden) Skewes. Bpt Grade 18 May 1836. Emigrated to Racine, Wisconsin, USA, May 1850. During the Civil War served in the US Navy under the name Thomas Cleveland. He married, and lived under that name ever after. Children: Edwin, Frank and Bessie.

SKEWES   THOMAS EDGAR
Chart 10. Son of John and Catherine Skewes of Ivy Cottage, Chacewater. Born 5 April 1886. Died 8 March 1887 at Ivy Cottage, aged 11 months.

SKEWES   THOMAS EDGAR
Chart 38. Son of Charles Percival and Nancy Merle (née Ham) Skewes. Born 15 October 1954. Lives at 246 Chloride Street, Broken Hill, 2705, New South Wales, Australia. Married Valerie Ann Pearson, 30 September 1978, Adelaide, South Australia. Daughter: Kate Elizabeth Skewes (1979).

SKEWES   THOMAS EDWARD
Born 1869, Lambeth. Married 1900. Died 1946, at Pancras, London, aged 76 years.

SKEWS   THOMAS ERNEST
Chart 41. Son of Thomas and Jane (née Renshaw) Skews, coal miner. Born 5 August 1919 at 3 Fitzwilliam Street, Hemingfield, Barnsley, South Yorkshire. Married Lily R. Brayford, 1942, Staincross. Children: John (1948) and Catherine (1954).
Lives at 67 Wood Walk, Wombwell, South Yorkshire, Telephone number: 0226 755053.

SKEWES   THOMAS G.
Chart 50. Son of George and Margaret (?) Skewes. Mother's maiden name Phelps. Born 1920, Pontypridd. Died 1925, aged 4 years.

SKEWES   THOMAS GARLAND
Chart 50. Son of Thomas and Sarah Ann (née Lord) Skewes of Australia. Born 15 September 1873, Victoria, Australia. Lived in Ballarat. Chemist at 1102 Main Street, Ballarat, Victoria, Australia. Married Marion Edith Alfreda Wilson, 13 October 1897. Children: Mary Alfreda (1899) and David Buick (1910). Died 1 May 1945, aged 72 years.

SKEWES   THOMAS GEORGE
Chart 10. Son of Digory and Fanny (née Tregonning) Skewes of Marazion. Born 15 March 1857. Bpt Marazion Parish Church 1 July 1857. Married Jane Mitchell of Marazion 5 March 1880. Miner of iron ore. Emigrated to the United States of America 1891. Jane followed with the family in 1896. Children: John William Skewes, Amelia Skewes,

Thomas Henry Skewes (1869-1939)

Mary Skewes, Thomas Skewes and Richard Garfield Skewes. Died June 1932, aged 75 years in Marquette, Michigan, USA. Jane died August 1922.

SKEWS   THOMAS GEORGE
Born 1865, Liskeard.

SKUES   THOMAS GEORGE
Chart 8. Son of George Henry Skues. Born 1894, Paddington. Mercantile clerk. Married Lilian Sophia Ivy Taylor in Hampstead, 1931. Lived at 47 Ashford Road, Cricklewood, London, NW2. Died 12 January 1964, aged 70 years at Neasden Hospital, London NW 10.

SKEWS   THOMAS GEORGE A.
Born 1893, Bethnal Green. Died 1894, aged 1 year.

SKUES   THOMAS GILBERT
Born 1857, St James. Died 1857, aged 0.

SKEWES   THOMAS GRENVILLE
Chart 50. Son of Doctor Samuel Grenville Stowe and Cecelia Elizabeth (née Oaten) Skewes. Born 9 November 1904. Married Ilma Elizabeth Dodd 30 August 1910, Melbourne, Victoria, Australia. Pharmacist. Lived at 51 Dorrington Avenue, Darling, Victoria, Australia. Children: Geoffrey Grenville (1939), Celia Elizabeth (1943) and Therese Jean (1944). Died 16 November 1975, aged 71 years.

SKEWS   THOMAS H.
Son of William and A.J. Skews of Mineral Point, Wisconsin, USA. Born 1878. Died 25 March 1879, aged 11 months and 15 days.

SKEWS   THOMAS H.
Married Dorothy H. Gould, 1977, Evesham.

SKEWIS   THOMAS HAROLD
Chart 43. Son of Edwin and Louisa (née Day) Skewis, engineer. Born 27 February 1886 at 2 George Street, Brightside, Sheffield, South Yorkshire.

SKEWES   THOMAS HENRY
Chart 25. Son of Thomas and Eleanor Skewes. Born 25 February 1824. Bpt Falmouth 9 June 1824.

SKEWES   THOMAS HENRY
Chart 12. Born 1856, Landewednack. Son of Henry and Harriet Skewes of Landewednack, The Lizard. Died 12 April 1904, at Rose Cottage, The Lizard.

SKEWES   THOMAS HENRY
Son of Thomas and Margaret Skewes, horse breaker. Born 1857. Bpt Perranuthnoe 25 December 1857. In 1871 Census Returns (then 15) he was a servant to John Verrant. Married Clarinda Ralph (she born 1858) at Perranuthnoe Parish Church, 19 February 1881. Children: Walter (1881) and Annie (1882). Died 1938.

SKEWES   THOMAS HENRY
Chart 14. Son of Samuel and Ruth (née Bottomley) Skewes of Wisconsin, USA. Born 29 January 1869, America. Married Floy C. Hale, 23 June 1930 at Yorkville, Wisconsin, USA. Floy was daughter of Hiram and Melinda (née Gilbert) Hale. Died 8 December 1939, aged 70 years. Insurance agent.

SKEWES   THOMAS HENRY
of The Lizard. Married 11 January 1881 to Jane Weatherly of The Lizard, daughter of the late William Weatherly at Falmouth.

Thomas Henry James Skues (1894-1971)

SKEWES   THOMAS HENRY
Chart 12. Son of John Skewes (?) Born 1893, Redruth. Married Annie
Maud Jory 1915 (she died 1962, aged 68 years). In 1922 lived at Redruth
Coombe; 1932 Higher Carnkie, Illogan and 1949 Four Lanes, Redruth.
Children: Iris M. (1916), Enid (1920), George (1921), Veronica J.
(1930), Rosemary (1931) and Maureen (1937). He married Lottie
Doreen Williams, 1964, Redruth. Died 1971, aged 77 years.

SKEWS   THOMAS HENRY
Chart 10. Son of Peter and Maude Mary Skewes.
Mother's maiden name Richard. Born 1919, St Austell. Married
Constance Patricia Harris, 1943, in St Austell. (She died 1975, aged 52
years.) Children: Peter B. (1945), Jacqueline A. (1949) and Barry J.
(1955).

SKUES   THOMAS HENRY JAMES
Chart 9. Born 21 June 1894, St Mary, Newington. Married Gladys May
Clemmens, 1926. Children: Roy Arthur Truscott (1928) and Gladys
Marguerita (1926). Lived at 172 Bybrook Road, Kennington, Ashford,
Kent. Died 23 August 1971, aged 77 years.

SKEWES   THOMAS HERBERT
Born 3 March 1882, Quora, South Australia. Married Catherine Ann
Elizabeth Harvey, 8 August 1911.
Children: Ainslie Herbert (1912) and Ivy Jean Selina (1913). Lived in
Victoria, Australia. Died 19 July 1959, aged 76 years.

SKEWES   THOMAS J.
Lived at B6-1729 Boylston Ave, Seattle, Washington, USA, 1912.
Wife's name Eunice J. Skewes.

SKUSE   THOMAS J.
Was Assistant Controller of Customs at the Port of New York. Lived at
337 Senator Street, Brooklyn with his wife Anna M. Skuse. He died
suddenly of a heart attack whilst he was in his office — Room 219 of the
Custom House — 6 June 1934. Aged 65 years. He had been connected
with the Customs Service in New York for 46 years. He passed through
the civil service grades to that of Controller, the highest in that office.

SKEWES   THOMAS JAMES
Eldest son of John Skewes of Truro; cabinet maker. Born 1852, Truro.
Died 1857, aged 5 years.

SKEWES   THOMAS JAMES
Chart 30. Son of John Beer and Mary Brown Skewes. Born 1863, Truro.
Married in St Columb, 1894. Was a painter and decorator in Newquay.
Did jury service in 1913 and 1919. Was a member of Newquay Odd
Fellows. He had a brother, J. Skewes, a sister-in-law, Mrs Treblicock; a
niece, Mrs Curnoe and another sister-in-law Mrs Rhodda. In 1871
Census Returns was living at Kenwyn Street, Truro with his parents and
sisters Henrietta Maria & Philippa Mary & brothers John Brown,
William Brown and Richard Henry.

SKUES   THOMAS JENKIN
Son of John and Margery Skues of Chacewater; miner. Bpt Kenwyn 18
May 1823. Later moved to Redruth. Married 1846 in Bristol.

SKEWES   THOMAS JOHN
Chart 11. Son of James and Alice (née Hocking) Skewes. Born 16
January 1846. Lived with his parents (carpenter) at Trelowarren Street,
Camborne and later emigrated to America. Children: Thomas John II,
Clyde, Paul, Glenn, Lulu and Helen. Grandson Thomas John Skewes
III.

SKEWES   THOMAS JOHN
Chart 26. Born Cornwall. Emigrated to the United States of America.

Married Louisa Brooks. Issue: son Edward James Skewes (1867).

SKEWES   THOMAS JOHN
Born 1854. Son of Matthew and Mary (née Hattam) Skewes, miner of
Chacewater. Born 25 October 1854.

SKEWS   THOMAS JOHN
Died 1856, Liskeard.

SKEWES   THOMAS JOHN
Born 1861, Truro. Buried St Mary's Truro 5 January 1862, aged 1 year.

SKEWES   THOMAS JOHN
Chart 11. Son of Thomas John and Laura B. (née Gest) Skewes. Born 27
March 1885, Ohio, USA. Married Eunice Martin 28 June 1911, Seattle,
Washington, USA. Warrant officer in US Navy, World War I. Lived at
5710 Admiral Way, Seattle (1907) and later B6-1929 Boylston Avenue,
Seattle, Washington, USA. Children: Thomas John II (1913) and James
Martin (1914). Died 1960, aged 75 years.

SKEWES   THOMAS JOHN II
BSc. Chart 11. Son of Thomas John and Eunice (née Martin) Skewes.
Born 28 September 1913, Seattle, Washington, USA. Married Elgin
Louise Bean (born 23 December 1913), 20 August 1938. Captain, US
Navy 1936-1969. Freemason with Constellation Lodge No 266, Seattle,
Washington, USA. Master, 1955.
President of Alexander Gow Maritime.
Children: Thomas John III (1942) and Terri Ann (1943). Lives at 5227
South West Andover, Seattle, Washington, Seattle 98116, USA.

SKEWES   THOMAS JOHN III
Chart 11. Son of Thomas John II and Elgin Louise (née Bean) Skewes.
Born 6 May 1942, Seattle, Washington. Married Virginia Ann Day, 18
January 1962, Seattle, Washington. Lives at Bashon Island, Seattle.
Children: Thomas John IV (1962) and Charles Andrew (1964).

SKEWES   THOMAS JOHN IV
Chart 11. Son of Thomas John III and Virginia Ann (née Day) Skewes.
Born 24 August 1962, Seattle, Washington, USA.

SKEWES   THOMAS JOHN
Chart 36. Son of Percy and Mary (née Farrell) Skewes. Born 8 May 1919,
Watsons Creek, Bendemeer, New South Wales, Australia.
Married Joy Quaile.
Lives at Adelaide River, 5783, Northern Territory, Australia.
Storeman.

SKEWES   THOMAS LEAN
Chart 19. Son of Collan and Ann Skewes, mine captain. Born 1827. Bpt
Mold, Flint 18 November 1827. Married Anna Maria Mary Young (23),
daughter of Charles Young, gentleman 13 July 1852 at the Parish
Church, Plumstead, London. (She died 1879, aged 50 years.)
Remarried 1890 to Elizabeth Ann .... of Barnstaple. Retired school
master of 31 Elm Grove, Bideford; formerly of Wareham, Dorset and
Redruth. Children: Mary Fanny Sophia, Annie, Charles Collan,
Alexander Richard, Emily and Albert Henry.
Before marriage he lived at Shalters Hill, Wareham in 1885/1886
Voters List. In Wareham he ran gentleman's boarding school, Elm
House, which was later taken over by his son Albert Henry (1859
Directory). In 1874/1875 Dorset Directory he was listed as Alderman
Skewes living at Elm House Scholastic Academy. He had been a
Councilman in 1871. Died 17 February 1903, aged 75 years.

SKEWS   THOMAS LESLIE
Lived at 58 St James Road, Heidelberg, Victoria, Australia in 1959 with
Alice May Skewes. Bricklayer.

SKEWES   THOMAS LIONAL
Lived at 10 Brook Street, Crows Nest, New South Wales in 1959 with
Lional Skewes and Ruby Gertrude Skewes. Labourer.

SKUES   THOMAS MACKENZIE
Chart 3. Son of William Mackenzie Skues, deceased; Deputy Surgeon
General. Born 1870.
Merchant of 35 Westmorland Road, Bayswater. Married Augusta
Kretschmann, aged 28 of 14 Turyford Mansions, Marylebone Street,
London; daughter of Ernest Kretschmann, deceased, farmer at the
Register Office, St Marylebone 7 June 1915. He was a widower — she a
spinster.
Married in the presence of Prince Albert of Ashanti. Child: Frederick
Mackenzie Skues.

SKEWES   THOMAS NISBETT
Lived at 110 Ellen Street, Port Pirie, South Australia in 1959 with Amy
Skewes and Robert John Skewes. Chemist. Current address: 6 William
Street, Port Pirie, South Australia, 5540.

SKEWS   THOMAS PROUSE
Born 25 October 1855, Plymouth. Son of William and Mary Ann (née
Allen) Skews of 17 Stillman Street, Plymouth, merchant seaman.

SKEWS   THOMAS PROUSE P.
Born 1894. Died Preston 1895, infant.

SKEWES   THOMAS STANLEY
Lived at 11 Fifth Street, Elizabeth Grove, South Australia in 1959 with
Margaret Rose Skewes. Clerk.

SKEWS   THOMAS TRUSCOTT
Chart 9. Son of James and Joanna Skews of Lower Sticker, St Ewe. Bpt
23 August 1815, St Ewe. Buried St Ewe 29 August 1815 — infant.

SKEWS   THOMAS W.
Lives at 153 E 57 Street, Manhattan, New York. Tel no: (516) 755 3822.

SKEWES   THOMAS WESTMORE
Son of Harold Skewes. Born 23 May 1898. Mrd Isobel Summerville 31 December 1921. Children: Douglas Westmore (1922) and Warren (1923). Lived in Victoria, Australia.

SKEWES   THOMAS WILLIAM
Married Sabina Roose, 16 January 1838 at St Nicholas, Liverpool.

SKEWES   THOMAS WILLIAM
Chart 36. Son of Edward and Julia Skewes of Cury. Born 1852. Joined Cornwall Constabulary 9 December 1872. PC 157. Height 5' 9½". Long visage; dark complexion; light brown eyes; dark brown hair; no particular marks; spare figure; profession before joining the force — shoemaker. Can read and write. Single, but married Eliza Emma Bray of Stithians 15 September 1874. Child: William Hedley Skewes (1879). Resided in Cury. Served in Penzance District from 1 May 1873: Truro, 26 January 1884: Bodmin 8 May 1895 and Launceston from 31 October 1899.
He was promoted to 2nd class PC 29 July 1877. Promoted to 1st Class PC 28 December 1890. Promoted to Sergeant 6 May 1895. Resigned from police force under medical certificate 30 September 1900. Superannuation £51 14 2d.
His wife died 1928, aged 78 years. Lived at Carnmarth Cove, Gwennap (1922) and Trevarth Road, Gwennap 1932.
Died 23 December 1943, aged 91 years.

SKEWES   THOMAS WILLIAM
Born 1858, Truro.

SKEWIS   THOMASINE
Buried Gwennap 21 March 1797.

SKEWES   THOMASINE
Chart 28. Daughter of Richard and Mary Skewes of Nancevellan Common, Kea. Bpt Kea 22 May 1825. Married Thomas Williams at Kea, excise man of Truro, 14 August 1843, in presence of Harriet Skewes.

SKEWES   THOMAZIN
Married Edward Sanders at St Anthony in Meneage 3 November 1662.

SKEWES   TIMOTHY DONALD
Chart 36. Son of Donald Lloyd and Elizabeth Blair (née Fisher) Skewes. Born Tamworth, New South Wales, Australia, 17 July 1961.

SKEWES   TIMOTHY LESTER
Chart 36. Son of Jack Roe and Dorothy May (née Burn) Skewes. Married Lynette Amelia Swain 1969. Children: Jason (1970) and Daniel (1974). Lives at 23 Tantara Street, Ingle Farm, South Australia, 5098.

SKEWS   TINA P.
Daughter of Brian A.A. Skews. Mother's maiden name Alldis. Born 1959, Dartford, Kent.

SKEWES   TOBIAS
Married Elizabeth Davy at St Just in Penwith 16 April 1754.

SKEWS   TOM
Chart 23. Son of William and Jane (née Bullock) Skews. Born 1878. Died Highworth, 1897, aged 19 years.

SKEWES   TOM
Born 1887, Penzance.

Una Irene Skewes

SKUSE   TOM
Born 25 November 1902, Keynsham, Bristol.
Married Muriel Goodhead (she born 11 May 1906 — died 1966, aged 60 years) at St Thomas' Church, Kirkby in Ashfield, Nottingham, 25 December 1926. Children: Trevor (1934), Gordon (1937) and Dean (1945). Miner. Moved north to Nottingham at the age of 17. Became an operator on the control panel of the Remotely Operated Longwall Face (ROLF) machine. Had brothers Frank, Don and Jim and sisters Jesse, Doris, Helene and Laura. Died 1970, aged 68 years.

SKEWES   TOMAS
Chart 10. Mexican. Son of John and Luisa (née Garcia) Skewes. Born Real del Monte 1870. Married Maria Herrera. No children. Died 4 April 1964, aged 94 years. Buried in English Cemetery, Real del Monte, Mexico.

SKEWES   TONI JENNIFER
Lives at 7 Mary Street, Boonah, 4310, Queensland, Australia with Eric Lawrence Skewes and Evelynne Roseina Skewes. Dental assistant.

SKEWES   TONY
Mother's maiden name Williams. Born 1964, Redruth.

SKEWES   TRACEY LEE
Chart 42. Daughter of Dennis Paul and Kayleen Daphne (née Bourke) Skewes. Born 31 March 1971. Lives at 25 McKay Street, Nowra Hill, 2540, New South Wales, Australia.

SKUSE   TREVOR
Son of Tom and Muriel (née Goodhead) Skuse. Born 6 January 1934. Married Jean Wheatley 20 August 1955. Children: Roderick, Beverley and Geoffrey. Seam chargeman at Newstead Colliery, Nottingham. Lives at 5 Abbey Road, Newstead Village, Nottingham.

SKEWIS   TREVOR
Chart 34. Son of Frank Skewis. Mother's maiden name Kate Baker. Born 11 February 1942 at 9 Poulders Ave., Sandwich, Kent. Married Linda Hanslip, 1965, Canterbury. One son Mark (1965). Lives at 24b Old Park Road, Canterbury, Kent. Tel no: 0227 51672.

SKEWS   TREVOR
Chart 41. Son of Eric Skews. Mother's maiden name Rasburn. Born 1953 Staincross. Married Kathleen Guirey, 1972, Staincross. Son: Stephen Trevor (1977).

SKEWES   TREVOR ALLEN
Lives at 14 Wexcombe Street, Elizabethville, 5112, South Australia with Kenneth Mervaine Skewes and Elva Beryl Skewes.

SKEWES   TREVOR JOHN
Chart 36. Son of Jack Roe and Dorothy May (née Burn) Skewes. Born 20 December 1944. B.A. Adelaide University. Married Bonney Maule Kite at St Cuthbert's Church, Prospect, South Australia. Children: Cherylyn Kay (1964) and Gwyn Martin (1968).
Teacher at Birchwood High School (Senior Master, Geography), Stirling, South Australia. Address: c/o P.O. Box 96, Stirling, 5152, South Australia.

SKUSE   TRUDI
Daughter of Peter Robin and Frances (née Mace-Hardyman) Skuse. Born 2 April 1973. Lives at 46 Beverley Road, Whyteleafe, Surrey CR3 ODX.

SKEWS   TRUDY M.
Chart 10. Daughter of Stanley and Mavis (née Soady) Skews. Born 1957, Redruth. Married Stephens in Redruth, 1974.

U

SKEWES   UNA IRENE
Chart 36. Daughter of George and Mary (née Dowling) Skewes. Born 22 April 1900, Uralla, New South Wales, Australia. Married Herbert Couchman 29 December 1934. No children. Lives at 131 Wingham Court, Wingham, New South Wales, Australia, 2429.

SKEWES   URSELA
Married James Thomas of St Martin at Cury 27 December 1714.

SKEWES   URSULA
Daughter of Richard Skewes. Bpt Kea 12 July 1730.

V

SKEWES   VALDA
Chart 38. Daughter of Sydney Howard and Cordelia (née Blight) Skewes. Born 15 November 1919, Wallaroo Mines, South Australia. Married Ronald Sydney Dinham, 23 February 1945, Holy Trinity Church, Adelaide. Issue: 1 son and 1 daughter. Lives at 14 Ragless Avenue, Enfield, South Australia, 5085.

SKEWES   VALDA KATHLEEN
Chart 36. Daughter of Reginald John and Mary Mildred (née Rooney) Skewes. Born 13 February 1929, New South Wales, Australia. Married Kevin Whitton, 9 February 1946. Issue: 2 sons & 2 daughters.

SKUES   VALERIE
Chart 7. Daughter of Cyril Herbert and Alice (née French) Cooke. Born 9 June 1936. Married Roydon Thomas Skues 25 October 1969 at St Mary's

Valerie Ruth Skuse

Church, Hampden Park, Eastbourne, Sussex. Children: Carolyn Louise (1971) and Michael David (1972). Lives at 16 Lower Drive, Seaford, Sussex. Telephone number: 0323 894436.

SKEWES   VALERIE
Chart 42. Daughter of Richard James and Amy (née Post) Skewes. Born 3 September 1950, North Sydney, Australia. Married Charles Edward Smith 28 March 1953. Issue: one son. Lives in Australia.

SKEWS   VALERIE
Lives at Lot/36 Hardy Road, Glen Forrest, 6071, Western Australia.

SKEWES   VALERIE ANN
Chart 38. Née Pearson. Married Thomas Edgar Skewes 30 September 1978, Adelaide, South Australia. Daughter: Kate Elizabeth (1979).

SKEWS   VALERIE B.
Chart 17. Daughter of Frederick and Eileen (née Joyce) Skews. Born 30 March 1944, Hammersmith. Married O'Brien, 1964 in Hammersmith.

SKUSE   VALERIE RUTH
Daughter of Leonard Kitchener and Winifred (née Murphy) Skuse. Born 21 December 1949, Australia. Married Bernardus Johannes Vette, 29 May 1971, Salisbury Methodist Church, South Australia. Issue: 2 sons. Lives at 9 Leitrim Street, Salisbury Downs, South Australia, 5108.

SKEWIS   VALMA AILEEN
Lives at 8 Gormleys Road, Chilla, 4413, Queensland, Australia with Geoffrey Wilfred Skewis and Malcolm Geoffrey Skewis.

SKEWES   VALMA BERNICE
Lived at Meldron, Uralla, New South Wales, Australia in 1959.

SKEWIS   VARA
Chart 2. Daughter of William James and Mattie Skewis. Born 10 September 1888, United States of America. Married Hans Peterson. Issue: five children. Died 28 January 1951, aged 63 years.

SKEWES   VARELA CLARA
Lives at T-Avenida 11 No 178ZP 13, Mexico. Telephone number: (905) 532 5293.

SKEWES   VEDA POULSON
Chart 2. Née Poulson. Born 1913, USA. Married John Billing Skewes III, 10 September 1938, Utah, USA. Child: John Billing IV (1942). Died Salt Lake City, 12 April 1942, aged 29 years.

SKEWES   VEMBA MERRIELL
Chart 36. Daughter of Aubrey Rupert and Annie (née Townsend) Skewes. Born 3 November 1928, Uralla, New South Wales, Australia. Married Alex James Melville 15 March 1950. Issue: one son and one daughter. Lives at 13 Kulang Street, Old Bar, 2430, New South Wales, Australia.

SKEWES   VERA
Chart 36. Daughter of William Henry and Gladys Skewes. Mother's maiden name Harris. Born 1919. Married 1937 to Frederick Risden in Penzance. He was killed in a mine disaster at Tuckingmill approx 1960. She remarried Bray of Brea.

SKEWES   VERA
Chart 10. Daughter of Ernest Skewes of Marazion. Born 13 February 1921 at Hamilton, Ontario, Canada. Married Patrick McGuire. Issue 3 sons & 3 daughters.

SKUES   VERA JOAN
Chart 3. Daughter of Vincent and Eva (née Rowland) Skues. Born 1924, Blackburn. Died 1945, aged 21 years.

SKEWES   VERA LOUISE'
Lived at 67 Monitor Road, Merrylands, New South Wales, Australia in 1959.

SKEWES   VERITY KATE
Chart 38. Daughter of Edward Kent and Susan Glenys (née Schramm) Skewes. Born 27 July 1977. Lives: c/o Ungarra Post Office, 5610, South Australia.

SKEWES   VERNA JOY
Chart 36. Daughter of Cuthbert George and Violet (née Ferris) Skewes. Born 30 August 1934. Lives at 93 O'Dell Street, Armidale, 2350, New South Wales, Australia. Unmarried.

SKEWES   VERNON JOHN
Chart 37. Son of Keith Matthew Skewes of Australia. Born 27 August 1947. Married Margaret Janet Williams 26 February 1977. Child: David Lance (1979). Lives at 7 Beatrice Close, Berowra Heights, Australia, 2080.

SKEWES   VERNON JOHN
Lives at 119 Thornside Road, Thornlands, 4158, Queensland, Australia with Jennene Rhonda Skewes. Concreter.

SKEWES   VERONICA DAWN
Lived at 101 Normandy Street, Inglewood, Marylands, Victoria, Australia in 1959 with William Keith Skewes, radio mechanic.

SKEWES   VERONICA J.
Chart 12. Daughter of Thomas Henry and Annie Maud (née Jory) Skewes. Born 1930, Redruth. Married Hawkin in Redruth, 1957.

SKEWES   VERONICA ELAINE
Chart 36. Née Cooper. Born 8 February 1946. Married Noel James Skewes 11 August 1962, Tamworth, Australia. Children: Dean Anthony (1963), Debbie Gae (1964) and Michelle Louise (1971). Lives at "Bantry", Watsons Creek, Bendemeer, 2352, New South Wales, Australia.

SKEWES   VERONICA MARY
Chart 12. Daughter of Harry Oswald and Emily Ann Skewes. Born 1899. Lived at 4 Centenary Street, Camborne in 1932 with Doris Muriel, George and Henry Oswald and Emily Ann Skewes. Married William Cockram at Camborne Parish Church 1938. No children.

SKEWES   VICKI LOUISE
Chart 24. Daughter of Leo William and Betty (née Thompson) Skewes. Born 5 March 1957. Lives at 2/11 William Street, Lambton, 2229, New South Wales, Australia with her sister Catherine Anne Skewes.

SKUES   VICTOR CLAUDE
Chart 8. Son of John Gilbert Skues. Born 6 April 1893. Married Annie Maria Ingrey, 1924. (She died 23 September 1975, aged 80 years.) Decorator. Lived at 228 Point Clear Road, St Osyth, Clacton, Essex. Son: Sydney Victor Skues. Grandchildren: Ian Keith, Andrew P. and David. Died 16 May 1975, aged 82 years.

SKEWS   VICTOR GEORGE
Born 1894. Lived at 39 Peppercroft, Gravesend, Kent. Died 3 November 1951, aged 57 years in Chatham.

SKEWIS   VICTORIA
Chart 2. Daughter of Francis Harry and Annie Skewis. Born 26 May 1897, America. Died 2 December 1898, aged 1½ years.

SKEWES   VICTORIA
Chart 10. Mexican. Daughter of Salvador and Carmen (née Ramirez) Skewes. Born 22 January 1958. Lives in Mexico.

Vincent and Eva Skues

SKEWS   VICTORIA ANN
Chart 15. Daughter of Andrew J. and Pamela L. (née Searle) Skews.
Born 1975, Plymouth. Lives at 19 Fairfield Estate, St Germans,
Plymouth.
SKEWES   VICTORIA CLARE
Chart 40. Daughter of Donald James and Annie (née Thomas) Skewes.
Born 1977, Truro.
SKEWES   VICTORIA JANE
Chart 11. Daughter of James Martin and Helen Ruth Skewes. Born 21
August 1940, America.
SKEWIS   VIDA
Chart 33. Daughter of William Richard and Lavinia (née Shute) Skewis.
Born 1908, Totnes. Died 1910, aged 2½ years.
SKUES   VINCENT
Chart 3. Son of Ernest and Clara (née Roberts) Skues. Born 7 May 1899,
Nottingham. Married Evelyn Rowland 22 December 1922. Lived at
"Vinclyn", Dawson Lane, Whittle-le-Woods, Chorley, Lancs.
Children: Donald (1929), Vera Joan (1924) and Muriel (1926).
Died 18 July 1970, aged 71 years.
SKEWES   VIOLET
Chart 12. Née Rashleigh. Born 14 July 1903. Married Arthur Skewes 24
February 1926. Lived at Rose Glen, Porthallow, St Keverne. Died 1972,
aged 69 years.
SKEWES   VIOLET
Chart 10. Daughter of William Joseph and Mabel Alice (née Johnson)
Skewes. Born 11 June 1919, Hamilton, Ontario, Canada. Married
George Wellington Tuck, 27 December 1941 at Grassies, Ontario,
Canada. Issue: three daughters.
SKEWES   VIOLET
Lived at 3 Laity Road, Troon, Camborne, 1949.
SKEWES   VIOLET
Chart 36. Née Ferris. Married Cuthbert George Skewes. Children:
Hilton Harvey, Gwenda Elizabeth and Verna Joy. Lived at Mann Street,
West Armidale, New South Wales, Australia. Died 7 May 1964.
SKEWES   VIOLET ADELAIDE
Lives at 9 Clyde Street, Glen Iris, 3146, Victoria, Australia with Frank
Bullivant Skewes.
SKEWS   VIOLET ALICE
Born 1908, Bethnal Green. Died 1908, aged 0.
SKEWES   VIOLET BLANCHE
Chart 38. Daughter of Horace Henry and Agatha Blanche (née Johns)
Skewes. Born 13 June 1910, Kadina, Australia. Married Robert George
Renton 9 March 1929 in Walhalla, Australia. Issue: 1 son and 1
daughter. Married Keith South 17 April 1976 (he died 28 February
1978). Lives at 168 William Street, Broken Hill, 2880, New South
Wales, Australia.
SKEWES   VIOLET GWENDOLINE D.
Born 1900, Penzance.
SKEWS   VIOLET IRENE
Chart 10. Eldest daughter of P. Skews of 1 Council Houses,
Ruddlesmoor, St Austell. Mother's maiden name Rickard. Born 1913.
Married Arthur Henwood Pearce at Greensplatt Methodist Church, 11
April 1942.
SKEWES   VIOLET M.
Lived at 46 Laity Road, Troon, Camborne, 1968, with Kenneth Roy
Skewes.
SKEWES   VIOLET MAY
Chart 10. Daughter of William Trevena and Edith (née Jenkin) Skewes,
farmer. Born 8 January 1918. Bpt 14 April 1918 at White Cross
Wesleyan/Methodist Church. Lived at Gonew, Lelant, Penzance.
Married Thomas Francis Trezise (30), farmer of Kerris Farm, Paul, son
of Richard Thomas Trezise, deceased; at Ludgvan 12 April 1941, in
presence of William Trevena Skewes.
SKEWES   VIOLET MAY
Lived at 109 Maltravers Road, Ivanhoe, Victoria, Australia in 1959 with
Herbert Skewes.
SKEWES   VIOLET V.
Born 1901. Died Plymouth 1941, aged 40 years.
SKUES   VIOLETTA
Daughter of Helen and Thomas Skues, seaman of Aberdeen, Scotland.
Married Howe in Dundee, 1861.
SKEWES   VIRGINIA
Chart 26. Daughter of Grant Phillip Skewes, of Connecticut, USA.
SKEWES   VIRGINIA
Chart 36. Daughter of Cyrus Lyle and Alice (née Welbourne) Skewes.
Born Armidale, New South Wales, Australia 29 March 1953. Married
Eric Taylor in Uralla. Issue: 2 children. Lives in Uralla, New South
Wales, Australia.
SKEWES   VIVIAN
Chart 2. Son of William Henry and Clara Bertha (née Ahlvers) Skewes
of Charlton, Missouri, USA. Born 24 November 1931. Married James
Luesley. Issue: 5 sons and 2 daughters.
SKUES VIVIAN WILLIAM
Chart 5. Son of William John and Eva (née Garvey) Skues. Born 1912,
Watford. Married Marie Helen Margaret Randolph MacDonald, 1946.

Child: Mary Eva Lydia Randolph MacDonald Skues (1948), born in
Calcutta, India. Lives at 34 Maysngr Road, Mawwah, New Jersey, USA.
Tel no: (201) 529 3262.
SKEWES   VIVIEN DAWN
Lives at 195 Coode Street, Bedford, 6052, Western Australia, with
William Wilfred Keith Skewes, radio technician.
SKEWES   VODANOVIC CRISTIAN
Lives at Arqto El Arcangel, Santiago, Chile, South America.

W

SKEWES   W.
Farmer living at Bolitho, Crowan, 1856.
SKEWES   W.
Mine agent living at Mitchell, Grampound, 1856.
SKEWES   WALLACE R.
Chart 26. Son of Edward James and Harriet A. (née Rockwell) Skewes.
Born 25 November 1894, Connecticut, USA. Married. Two sons: Grant
and Russell.
SKEWES   WALTER
Mentioned in Cornwall Protestation Returns, 1642, St Keverne.
SKEWES   WALTER
Born 1839. Lived at St Agnes but emigrated to New Zealand where he
died March 1865, aged 26 years.
SKEWES   WALTER
Born 1863, Truro.
SKEWS   WALTER
Lived at 316 Douglas, San Francisco, USA in 1917. Gardener. Wife's
name Bertha C. Skews.
SKEWIS   WALTER BLYTH
Chart 50. Born 1902, Blackfriars, Scotland. Mother's maiden name
Munro. Married Thompson, 19 July 1926, at Shettleston, Scotland.
Children: Walter Blyth (1926), Janet Grace (1931), Graham M.B.T.
(1933), William (1936), Sarah Black (1943) and Mary Bell (1943).
Died 1975, aged 73 years.
SKEWIS   WALTER BLYTH
Chart 50. Son of Walter Blyth Skewis. Born 1926, Shettleston, Scotland.
Married Margaret Wilson, 1949. Children: Ian (1949), Brian (1951),
Robert (1952) and Linda (1958).
Married Charlotte Ann Riddell, 1968, Glasgow. Children: Anne (1969)
and Nicola (1972).
SKUES   WALTER CECIL
Son of William & Margaret Skues. Born 7 October 1903, Australia.
SKUES   WALTER EDWARD
Chart 8. Son of George Henry Skues. Born 4 January 1873 at 6 Little
Chapel Street, Soho, London. Married 23 April 1893, Westminster to
Atlanta Emily Bond. Children: Walter Edward (1894), Percival Walter
(1893), Elizabeth (1895), Atlanta Violet (1896), Florence Ruby (1904),
Maud Evelyn (1909), Olive Emily (1910), Ernest John (1912) and Alfred
Edgar (1914). His wife died 1915 aged 43 years.
Walter Edward then married Florence E. Bundy, 1916, Islington,
London. Children: Christopher Herbert Victor (1917), Arthur E.W.
(1919), Sydney Thomas (1921) and Elsie F.A. (1924), He ran a
chandler's shop at 88 Shaftsbury Street, Hoxton, North London.
Died 1958, aged 85 years.
SKUES   WALTER EDWARD
Chart 8. Son of Walter Edward Skues. Born 1894. Married Violet
Merton, 1928. Lived at 6 Newgate Street, Walton on Naze, Essex. Died
6 September 1968, aged 74 years.
SKEWES   WALTER GEORGE
Son of William and Elizabeth Alberta Mary (née Jessop) Skewes. Born
18 May 1904, Adventure Mine, Houghton, Michigan, USA.
SKEWES   WALTER JAMES
Born 1888. Died Redruth 1958, aged 69 years.
SKEWES   WALTER NICHOLAS
Chart 36. Son of Edward James Skewes, coal fitter. Born 1889. Married
Katie Ford, daughter of Albert Ford, builder, 16 April 1913 at St John's
Church, Treslothan, Redruth.
Lived at Pendarves Street, Beacon 1922; 51 Pendarves Street, Beacon
1932 and 42a Fore Street, Beacon, 1949. Children: Cecil (1916), Albert
J. (1913) and Leslie (1920). Supposedly died 1971, aged 82 years, but no
reference to his death in General Registry, 1971 or 1972.
SKEWS   WALTER TRESIZE
Born 1841. Bpt Chacewater 15 May 1842. Son of Thomas and Grace
Skews of Jolly's Bottom, Kea, miner. Married, Truro, 1861.
SKEWES   WARREN BENJAMIN
Chart 36. Son of Benjamin Samuel and Gweneth (née Adams) Skewes.
Born 22 February 1950, Tamworth, New South Wales, Australia.
Sheep shearer in Watsons Creek, Bendemeer until 1976. In October
1977 built and entered a competition car which came third in one class
and was one of thirty vehicles from the seventy six starters to finish. Over
600 man hours went into the production of the vehicle "Skewesbuilt." It
featured a 1200cc Volkswagen engine coupled to a Kombi transmission
system. The wheelbase was extended to 120 inches with the axles and
shock absorbers remounted to give the vehicle a 10½ inch wheel base.

Warren went in for breeding quarter horses in 1969 shortly after he began work at Eddie Wilson's New Frontier Stud, where he remained for nine months learning as much as he could about the breeding world. He then went back to shearing before getting married to Barbara Kaye Stephen on 11 November 1972. Now he owns 17 horses and has won numerous exhibits and ribbons.

In his spare time he is the local agent for Vacationer annexes — is also marketing a self-designed "thief proof" horse trailer-caravan hitch lock and a new type of horse rug, which he adapted from an American design. These "rugs" fit the horse like a body shirt and feature a cutaway tail section with cross-over girths which pull the rug in around the body, thus reducing heat loss. They comprise 50% polyester and 50% cotton. When he is not breeding and/or showing horses or selling caravan hitch locks, annexes and horse rugs he is vice-president of the New England Quarter Horse Association.

Lives at George Street, Moonbi, 2352, New South Wales, Australia. No children.

SKEWES   WAYNE NEVILLE
Lives at 1/4 Peel Street, Prospect, South Australia, 5082.

Warren Benjamin Skewes riding 'Del Mingo' at Bendemeer, Australia, 1969

SKUES   WAYNE RICHARD
Chart 5. Son of Kevin Richard and Margaret Lynette (née Malley) Skues. Born April 1957. Lives in Melbourne, Victoria, Australia.
SKEWES   WELMET
Chart 35. Daughter of Henry and Elizabeth Skewes. Bpt Cury 26 December 1694. Married Peter Fabyn of Mawgan at Cury, 12 November 1726.
SKEWIS   WELMET
Married Christopher Harris at Cury, 12 April 1740.
SKEWES   WENDY
Chart 2. Née Andrew. Married Robert William Skewes at Rosedale, Victoria, Australia. Child: Zoe Naomi (1981). Lives at Willung Road, Rosedale, Victoria, 3847, Australia.
SKEWS   WENDY A.
Chart 10. Daughter of Stanley and Mavis (née Soady) Skews. Born 1947, Redruth. Married Sturtridge, 1966, St Austell.
SKEWES   WENDY GERALDINE
Chart 10. Daughter of Robert and Lilian (née Foster) Skewes. Born 16 December 1948, Hamilton, Ontario, Canada. Married Jack William Bonner, 2 May 1970 at Grace Anglican Church, Waterdown. Issue: 2 daughters.
SKEWES   WENDY JANE
Chart 36. Daughter of Gregory Archer and Janette Mary (née Robinson) Skewes. Born 28 August 1979. Lives in Queensland, Australia.
SKEWES   WENDY JEAN
Chart 36. Daughter of Percy and Muriel (née Norris) Skewes. Born 10 April 1951, New South Wales, Australia. Married Paul Maher, 6 May 1972. Issue: 2 sons and 1 daughter.
SKEWS   WENDY LYNNE
Chart 17. Daughter of Stanley and Marjorie (née Hardcastle) Skews. Born 27 January 1946, Hull. Married Trevor Harry Coulman in Hull, 20 March 1965. Issue: 2 sons and 2 daughters.
SKEWES   WENDY VIOLET
Chart 12. Daughter of George Sowden and Mabel Williams. Born 24 September 1928, Helston, Cornwall. Married William John Skewes at Mullion Church 12 September 1946. Children: Carol Wendy (1947), Christopher John (1949), Peter Neil (1950) and Paul Andrew (1957). Lives at 27 Beacon Parc, Helston. Tel no: 03265 4722.
SKEWS   WESLEY
Lived at 7500 Renton Avenue South, Apartment 11, Seattle, Washington, USA in 1967. Wife's name Esther.
SKEWES   WILFRED
Born 7 March 1885, Redruth. Lived at Shute Row, Redruth. Attended Redruth East End School — admitted 14 April 1888.
SKEWES   WILFRED
Married 1905, Falmouth.
SKEWS   WILFRED GERALD
Chart 15. Son of Harry and Hilda (née Jane) Skews of Albert Cottages, Pensilva, Liskeard. Born 15 June 1925. Bpt St Ive 5 August 1925.
SKEWES   WILFRED HAWKINS
Married 1908, Totnes, Devon.
SKEWES   WILFRED J.
Born South Australia. Married Anna Louisa Borgas. Children: Keith, Gwendoline, Marie Annie, Dorothea Hope. Died 1960.
SKEWIS WILFRED ROY
Born 1908, Tonbridge, Kent.
SKEWIS   WILFRED ROY
Lived at Gormleys Road, Chinchilla, Marona, Queensland, Australia in 1959 with Helena Skewis and Dudley Walter Kent Skewis. Now lives at 17 Rhyde Street, Toowoomba, 4350, Queensland, Australia.
SKEWES   WILIAM
Son of John Skewes. Bpt Gerrans 11 March 1577.
SKEWES   WILLIAM
Buried Wendron 8 February 1585.
SKEWES   WILLIAM
Son of William Skewes. Bpt Tiverton 24 December 1630.
SCUES   WILLIAM
Chart 2. Married Margaret Thomas 24 September 1664, Camborne Parish Church. Children: Anne, Thomas, Henry and Prudence. Died 13 February 1715.
SKEWS   WILLIAM
Chart 13. Son of John and Elizabeth (née Whitford) Skews. Bpt St Ewe 21 October 1677.
SKUES   WILLIAM
Chart 4. Married Jane John 23 September 1680. Children: William, Jane, Stephen, Mary, Joan and Ann. Lived in Redruth.
SKUES   WILLIAM
Chart 4. Son of William and Jane Skues. Bpt 9 October 1681. According to the will of his brother Stephen, William had a son called Stephen.
SKEWES   WILLIAM
Chart 35. Son of Edward and Elizabeth Skewes. Bpt Cury 13 July 1690.
SKEWES   WILLIAM
Son of William Skewes. Bpt Gwennap 13 November 1692.

SCUES   WILLIAM
Son of Ann Scues. Bpt Madron 13 January 1703.
SCUIS   WILLIAM
Chart 2. Son of Henry and Mary Scuis. Bpt 1 November 1705 Camborne Parish Church. Married Mary Temby 15 July 1735. Lived at Treslothan. Children: William, Mary, John, Sarah, Richard, Stephen and Henry. Died 24 June 1788, aged 85 years.
SKEWS   WILLIAM
Chart 36. Son of James and Sarah Skewes. Bpt Cury 22 January 1709. Died Cury 20 June 1713, aged 4½ years.
SKEWES   WILLIAM
Buried Gwennap 22 April 1714.
SKEWS   WILLIAM
Chart 36. Son of James and Sarah Skewes. Bpt Cury 13 May 1716.
SKEWS   WILLIAM
Married Avise Rowe at Gunwalloe 24 June 1718. Children: Edward (1721) and Loveday (1726). Avise died 10 October 1757.
SKUES   WILLIAM
Son of William Skues by Bennett his wife. Bpt 28 June 1719 at St Paul's, Covent Garden, London.
SKEWS   WILLIAM
Son of John and Catherine Skews. Bpt St Buryan 12 March 1720. Married Hannah Dayworth, widow at St Gluvias 30 January 1744.
SKEWS   WILLIAM
Buried Gwennap 27 July 1721.
SKEWS   WILLIAM
Chart 19. Son of Thomas and Margaret Skewes. Bpt Gwennap 6 October 1722.
SKEWES   WILLIAM
Son of Richard and Rebecca Skewes. Bpt St Just in Penwith 1 November 1725.
SKUES   WILLIAM
Chart 3. Son of Richard and Jane Skues. Born 28 October 1735. Married Mary Hitchin of St Dum, Cornwall at Gwennap 3 January 1765. Was Secretary of the Tinners Association, Helston in 1788. Worked for the office of the Tin Coinage for Cornwall and Devon under the Duke of Cornwall upwards of 50 years. He was succeeded in his office by his grandson Richard Skues. Children: Richard, William, Elizabeth, Mary and Stephen. Died 26 February 1817, aged 81 years.
SKEWIS   WILLIAM
Chart 2. Son of William and Mary Skewis. Bpt Camborne 21 February 1735. Died 9 December 1807, aged 72 years.
SKEWES   WILLIAM
Buried Cury 4 February 1737.
SKEWIS   WILLIAM
Buried Sancreed 7 January 1742.
SKEWES   WILLIAM
Son of John and Mary Skewes. Bpt Gwennap privately 10 September 1743.
SKEWES   WILLIAM
Chart 19. Son of Thomas and Elizabeth Skewes, miner. Bpt Gwennap 9 February 1744. Had died by 1814.
SKEWES   WILLIAM
Born 1745. Buried Gwennap 2 July 1824, aged 79 years.
SKEWES   WILLIAM
Chart 2. Son of Henry Skewis. Bpt privately 4 August 1747. Publicly 16 August 1747. Married Elizabeth ..... Died 8 October 1770, aged 23 years.
SKEWS   WILLIAM
Son of William and Hannah Skews of St Gluvias. Bpt St Gluvias 24 April 1748. Buried St Gluvias 12 January 1772, aged 24 years.
SKEWES   WILLIAM
Married Ann Bawdan at Gwennap 18 August 1753.
SKEWS   WILLIAM
Chart 9. Bpt St Ewe 24 August 1755. Son of Philip and Mary Skews. Married Nancy Blewett at Withiel Church 13 August 1796. Children: Ann, Elizabeth and Mary. Died 14 August 1842, aged 72 years (Nancy). William died 23 April 1840, aged 84 years. W (CRO). Lived at Nansladron, St Ewe.
SKEWES   WILLIAM
Son of Joseph and Philippa Skewes. Bpt Mawgan in Meneage 28 December 1762.
SKEWES   WILLIAM
Born 1765. Buried Kea 21 December 1815, aged 50 years.
SKEWES   WILLIAM
Son of Joseph and Philippa Skewes. Bpt Mawgan in Meneage 5 May 1765.
SKEWES   WILLIAM
Born 1766. Lived at Trethowan Downs. Buried Constantine 6 March 1846, aged 80 years.
SKEWES   WILLIAM
Chart 36. Son of John and Mary Skewes. Bpt Cury 15 June 1766. Lived at White Cross, Cury. Buried Cury 7 February 1849, aged 82 years. Died at White Cross of general decay.

SKEWIS   WILLIAM
Chart 2. Son of John Skewis. Bpt Camborne privately 19 August 1768.
Died Camborne 20 August 1768.

SKEWIS   WILLIAM
Chart 2. Son of Richard and Alice Skewis. Bpt Camborne 6 November
1768. According to the will of Stephen Skewis, William had two sons,
Henry and Stephen

SKEWIS   WILLIAM
Chart 2. Twin to Mary Skewis. Son of John and Philippa Skewis. Bpt
Camborne privately 20 October 1768; normally 13 November 1768.
Married Elizabeth ..... Children: Stephen, William, Betsy and Henry.
Lived at Treswithian. Died 17 December 1824, aged 56 years.

SKEWES   WILLIAM
Chart 18. Son of Thomas Skewes of Kea. Bpt Kenwyn 11 February 1769.
Yeoman. Married Ann Trewan 6 October 1793 at Kea. Died 21
December 1815, aged 50 years. Children: William (1794), Ann (1796),
Mary (1798), Eleanor (1805), Daniel (1807), Jennifer (1809) Jane,
Samuel Trewan (1811), John and Elizabeth (1814).

SKEWES   WILLIAM
Born 1769. Lived at Penryn. Buried Constantine 13 October 1813, aged
44 years.

SKUES   WILLIAM
Chart 3. Son of William and Mary Skues of Helston. Bpt Helston 3
February 1771. Buried Helston 23 August 1771.

SCEWES   WILLIAM
Married Ann Lee 22 November 1773, Higham near Gravesend, Kent.

SKEWIS   WILLIAM
of Glebe Cottage. Born 1774. Buried Camborne 22 October 1845, aged
71 years.

SKUES   WILLIAM
Chart 3. Son of William and Mary Skues. Bpt Helston 24 March 1776.
Was an ensign in the Volunteer Corps of the Borough (1st Helston)
under Captain Richard Skues. He was promoted to lieutenant 3
September 1798. Died one year later after a year's illness. Died 21
August 1800, aged 23 years.

SKUES   WILLIAM
Chart 3. Son of John and Mary Skues. Bpt Helston 22 December 1776.
Child: Jane Skues, who married Henry Pascoe in 1831. Her children
called Skues Pascoe. Died 24 November, 1842, aged 66 years.

SKEWES   WILLIAM
Chart 2. Twin to James Skewes. Son of James and Charity Skewes.Bpt
Camborne 19 December 1779, when each were five years old.

SKEWIS   WILLIAM
Buried Gwennap 25 December 1784.

SKURCE   WILLIAM
Buried at Constantine 19 November 1785.

SKEWES   WILLIAM
Chart 2. Son of Absalom and Elizabeth Skewes. Bpt Camborne 7
November 1786. Died 14 October 1808, aged 22 years.

SKEWES   WILLIAM
Born 1786. Buried Camborne 27 April 1844, aged 58 years.

SKEWES   WILLIAM
Buried 18 May 1788 at Cury.

SKEWES   WILLIAM
Chart 39. Son of John and Mary Skewes of Cury. Bpt Cury 1 March
1789.

SKEWS   WILLIAM
Born 1789. Corporal. He received medals for battles in Salamanga and
Vittoria serving with 5th Foot Regiment. Medal presentation, 1847.
Died 22 September 1863 at Northfleet, Kent of "natural decay", aged 74
years.

SKEWES   WILLIAM
Buried Cury 13 March 1790.

SKEWES   WILLIAM
Married Ann Williams at Gunwalloe 10 July 1791.

SKEWS   WILLIAM
Illegitimate son of Ann Skews. Born 9 August 1793. Bpt by charity 11
August 1793 at St Mary's, Truro.

SKEWES   WILLIAM
Chart 36. Son of John and Mary Skewes. Bpt Cury 6 March 1794.
Married Christian Lugg at Ruan Major 28 March 1815. Farmer at Little
Insight Farm, Mabe 1851-1861. Children: James (1815), John (1816),
Edward (1819), Elizabeth (1821), Ann (1825), Henry (1827), James
(1827), William (1829), Christian (1832), Grace (1834), John (1836) and
Samuel (1838). Buried at Mawnan Church 14 August 1861, aged 66
years. Christian buried 14 November 1864, aged 70 years.

SKUCE   WILLIAM
Served with Royal Navy. Awarded medal on 1 June 1794 for his part in
Lord Howe's victory with the capture of six sail of the line and one sunk
in defeat of the French fleet. Served on board Defence. Also awarded
medal for Copenhagen (1801) and Battle of the Nile (1798).

SKEWES   WILLIAM
Chart 18. Son of William and Ann Skewes. Bpt Kea 7 June 1794.

SKEWES   WILLIAM
Chart 45. Married ALICE SKEWES of Falmouth at Falmouth 26
September 1794. Children: Alice, Mary, John, Ann, William, Sarah,
Elizabeth, Edward, Henry and Richard. Lived at Treloskan, Cury.
Farmer. Wife Alice died Cury 17 January 1831, aged 54 years.

SKEWES   WILLIAM
Son of William and Ann Skewes. Bpt Gunwalloe 28 December 1794.
Buried Gunwalloe 19 March 1795.

SKEWES   WILLIAM
Chart 2. Illegitimate son of Constance Skewes. Bpt Camborne 31 May
1795.

SKEWES   WILLIAM
Son of William and Ann Skewes. Bpt Gunwalloe 6 November 1796.

SKEWES   WILLIAM
Born 1796. Lived at Churchtown, Constantine. Buried Constantine 11
November 1861, aged 65 years.

SKEWES   WILLIAM
Drummer with Volunteer Corps of Helston 1797-1798.

SKEWIS   WILLIAM
Private with Camborne Volunteers 1798-1799. His spelling changed to
Skewes in Muster Rolls 1799. He was discharged on 27 December 1799.

SKUES   WILLIAM
Private with First Helston Volunteers and was on duty four times in
February 1800 at Penryn where he helped to guard 102 French
prisoners.

SKEWES   WILLIAM
Son of John and Temperence Skewes. Bpt Kea 29 November 1801.

SKUES   WILLIAM
Sojourner. Married Jane John 10 June 1802 at Mylor. Children included
John Bennett, Elizabeth, Mary, Jane, Ann and William John. Married
in presence of Elizabeth Skues.

SKUES   WILLIAM
Chart 3. Son of Richard and Ann Skues. Born 10 January 1802. Died 17
February 1802 — infant.

SKEWES   WILLIAM
Chart 36. Son of William and Alice Skewes of Treloskan, Cury. Bpt
Cury 28 February 1802.

SKEWES   WILLIAM
Miner. Married Ann Ellis at Camborne Parish Church, 28 November
1802.

SKEWES   WILLIAM
Married Elizabeth Thomas at Crowan 1803.

SKEWES   WILLIAM
Chart 18. Son of Thomas and Mary Skewes. Bpt Kenwyn 9 April 1803.

SKEWES   WILLIAM
Chart 36. Son of William and Alice Skewes of Treloskan, Cury. Bpt
Cury 22 May 1803. Buried Cury 30 June 1804, aged 1 year.

SKUES   WILLIAM
Chart 3. Son of Richard and Ann Skues. Born 6 February 1804. Bpt 26
December 1804. Died 16 May 1805 — infant.

SKEWES   WILLIAM
Chart 50. Born 1805 at Gunwalloe. Married Rebecca Mitchell at
Constantine Church 23 March 1828. Lived at Churchtown,
Constantine. Children: Ann and William.

SKEWIS   WILLIAM
Married Margaret Edwards at Gwennap 6 July 1805.

SKEWIS   WILLIAM
Chart 2. Son of William and Elizabeth Skewis. Bpt Camborne 9
February 1806. Married Eliza Vivian, widow, by licence, 7 February
1830.

SKEWES   WILLIAM
Chart 2. Son of Henry and Grace Skewes of Bosawsack, Constantine.
Bpt 29 November 1807, Constantine. Married Elizabeth Glasson,
daughter of Joseph and Bathsheba Glasson. (Elizabeth was born at
Truthall, Sithney 20 March 1808.)
Children: Joseph, Christian, Grace, James, John and Elizabeth. Moved
from Constantine to Budock to Sithney to Crowan and lived and farmed
at Bolitho, Crowan. Died Bolitho 23 December 1886, aged 79 years. His
wife died 9 April 1882, aged 74 years.

SKEWES   WILLIAM
Chart 36. Son of William and Alice Skewes. Bpt Cury 21 April 1808.
Emigrated to Australia 1853. Married Elizabeth Northey on 4 August
1856 at 24 Lower Fort Street, Sydney, New South Wales, Australia
according to the rites of the Presbyterian Church and the ceremony was
conducted by Alexander Salmon.
Children: James (1856), William (1858), Samuel (1859), Elizabeth Ann
(1860), John (1862), Frances Charlotte (1864), Robert Northey (1867),
Emily Susan (1869), George (1871), Amy Elizabeth (1873), Caroline
Mary (1876) and Alice Beatrice (1878).
Moved to Rocky River Gold Field, Uralla in its boom days, arriving by
horse and dray on 17 March 1857. They took up residence at what is now
known as Horse and Fowls Gully and later selected land in the
immediate locality on a property called Elm Grove where the family
resided until William's death in 1887, aged 78 years.

SKEWIS WILLIAM
Son of William and Alice Skewis. Bpt Cury 21 April 1808.

SKEWES WILLIAM
Chart 19. Son of Alexander and Christian Skewes. Bpt Gwennap 13 August 1808.

SKEWES WILLIAM
Buried Gwennap 29 November 1808.

SKEWES WILLIAM
Chart 12. Born 1809, Nantithet, Cury. Bpt Cury 29 July 1813. Married MARY SKEWES at .... 3 November 1834. Was a widower by 1861. Children: Elizabeth Mary, Alice Ann, Emily, Eliza and William James. In 1871 Census was living at Nantithet with his daughter Alice Ann and grandsons John Wesley Skewes and Arthur Wesley Skewes. Died 22 July 1877, aged 68 years. He was an agricultural labourer.

SKEWES WILLIAM
Chart 19. Son of John Skewes of Gwennap. Son: Thomas Skewes. Died 13 March 1810.

SKUES WILLIAM
Son of James and Joanna Skues. Bpt St Ewe 4 August 1811. Died Lambeth 1876, aged 64 years.

SKEWES WILLIAM
Born 1816, Cury. Son of James Skewes, labourer. Agricultural labourer and grocer. Married Amelia Odgers (23) of Mawgan in Meneage at Mawgan Church 7 October 1841, in presence of Henry Skewes and Josiah Skewes. In 1861 Census Returns was living at Degibua, Wendron with Amelia; in 1871 Census Returns was living at Manley, Wendron with Amelia. Died 1889, aged 72 years.

SKEWES WILLIAM
of Chenhale. Buried Gwennap 5 February 1813, aged 1 year.

SKEWS WILLIAM
Chart 10. Son of Richard and Agnes Skews. Bpt Kea 2 August 1818. Tailor, later blacksmith. Married Mary Dennis of Chacewater 4 June 1839 at Kea. She was born 1816 and died 1865, aged 49 years and buried Illogan 7 November 1865. William remarried Jane Thomas 27 September 1866. Children: William Richard Francis Dennis, Thomas Albert Jeffrey, Mary Agnes Elizabeth Dennis, Theresa Hermina Amelia, Matthew Henry, John, Edwin, Sarah, Martin and Emma. Died 1886, aged 69 years.

SKEWES WILLIAM
Chart 33. Son of William and Mary Skewes of Blackwater, miner. Bpt Kenwyn 8 October 1820. Lived at Jolly's Bottom, Chacewater. Married Susan Oates of Jolly's Bottom at Chacewater 24 December 1840. She was daughter of John Oates, miner. Children: Mary (1841), William (1843), Susan (1845), Grace (1847), Elizabeth (1850), Samuel (1853) and Amelia (1855).

SKEWES WILLIAM
Chart 2. Son of James and Joanna Skewes. Born 1821. Bpt Camborne 7 October 1821. Married Peggy Bawden of Vyvyan's Row, Camborne, daughter of William Bawden, mine agent at Camborne Parish Church 29 March 1847, in the presence of Henry Skewis. Copper miner. Emigrated to USA. Children: Lavinia and William.

SKEWES WILLIAM
Married Mary Staplis 27 October 1821 at Helston Parish Church.

SKEWIS WILLIAM
Born 1822, Camborne. Was secretary of Roskear Mining Company, Camborne between 1862 and 1867 and owned 4000 shares out of a total company holding of 6000.
Was brought before the Stannaries Court in Truro in May, 1866 for owing money for purchase of shares. A writ was issued seeking £300 back payment but he failed to pay. The company was "wound up" on 27 April 1871.
Was chief principal agent for South Roskear Tin and Copper Mine, Camborne 1872-1876. Was brought before the Stannaries Court in 1876 for payment of £79 11 6d. A third time he was brought before the Courts in August 1876 for allowing adventurers to damage land in Calstock at Drake Walls Mines where Skewis was principal agent from 1873 to 1876.
He was manager of the following mines in Devon and Cornwall: Exmouth, Christow (1858-1860); North Exmouth, Christow (1860-1861); Crelake, Tavistock (1861-1870); Lydford Consols, Lydford (1861-1862); Kit Hill, Callington (1862-1870); Gunnislake Clitters (1863-1883); New Birch Tor and Vitifer (1864-1871); West Maria and Fortescue, Lamerton (1864-1877); New East Birch Tor, North Bovey and Manaton (1865-1868); Great Devon and Bedford, Tavistock (1866); Colcharton, Tavistock (1868); Victoria, Ashburton (1868); King's Oven and Water Hill, North Bovey (1869-1870); East Kit Hill, Stoke Climsland (1870); South Kit Hill, Stoke Climsland (1870-1872); Hawkmoor, Gunnislake (1870); Wheal Arthur, Calstock (1872-1873); New Victoria, Ashburton (1870-1871); White Works, Princetown (1869-1870); Dunsley Wheal Phoenix, Linkinhorn (1872-1875); Slimford Tin Waste Dressing Company (1873); Trebartha Lemarne, North Hill (1881-1884); Sortridge, Whitchurch (1881-1883); Collacombe, Lamerton (1883-1884); Old Gunnislake (1880-1883) and East Wheal Rose, Newlyn East (1881-1885).
In 1880 Voters List described as a landowner in Calstock, East Cornwall and Tavistock, Devon. Owned 5 acres, 3 poles and 17 perches at an annual rent of £34.
Was a member of the Mining Association and Institute of Cornwall 1886 to 1888, paying an annual subscription of 10/6d.
In 1883 lived at Langstone, North Brentor, Bridestow. Died 1893, aged 71 years.

SKEWES WILLIAM
Chart 36. Son of John and Loveday Skews of Nantithet, Cury. Bpt Cury 17 March 1822.

SKEWES WILLIAM
Chart 33. Married Cordelia Pollard at Kea, 9 December 1822.

SKEWES WILLIAM
Born 1823. Buried Chacewater 28 May 1836, aged 13 years.

SKEWES WILLIAM
Born 1823. Married Ann Prideaux Trezise (37), widow of Goldsithney, 11 February 1854 at Perranuthnoe Parish Church. Daughter: Ann from previous marriage (born 1846). Emigrated to Australia aboard ship *Geelong* which sailed from Plymouth in May 1854 and arrived at Port Phillip, Melbourne 11 August 1854. Engaged by Mr Prowlett of Brighton at the rate of £80 per annum including rations for a period of three months as an agricultural labourer.

SKUES WILLIAM
Chart 2. Son of Absalom and Jane Skues of Little Pendarves, miner. Bpt Camborne 5 June 1824.

SKUES WILLIAM
Chart 2. Son of Stephen and Margaret Skues. Bpt Camborne 8 July 1826. Married Sarah Billing, daughter of John Billing, mine agent of Treswithian, Camborne at St Agnes. 26 December 1849. (Sarah, born 1831, died in Idaho, USA, 1915.) Lived at Treswithian during childhood, and Roskear Fields during early marriage. Emigrated to the United States of America in 1871. Spelling changed to Skewes on arrival in USA. Was an undertaker. Children: John Billing, Emily Louisa, William H., Robert Billing and Charles Henry. In Cornwall William had been a mine agent. Died Salt Lake City, Utah 19 November 1891, aged 65 years. Buried in Mount Olivet Cemetery, Salt Lake City.

SKEWES WILLIAM
Married Rebecca Mitchell 23 March 1828 at Constantine.

SKEWES WILLIAM
Chart 36. Son of James and Simonette Skewes, farmer. Bpt 25 December 1828, Cury. Miner of Carnkie. Married Priscilla Mill, daughter of William Mill, miner, at Illogan Parish Church 10 July 1853. Lived at Carnkie and later Higher Treskillard. Later became a farmer and moved to Carnarthen. Children: Elizabeth, Ellen, Ann, Amelia and Henry. Priscilla (born 1829) died 2 February 1874, aged 43 years.

SKEWES WILLIAM
Chart 22. Son of William and Christian Skewes. Born 1829. Bpt St Keverne 28 August 1829. Married 5 December 1850 to Jane Kempthorne, daughter of James Kempthorne, farmer at Mawnan Parish Church, in the presence of Henry Skewes.

SKEWES WILLIAM
Son of Henry and Ann Skewes, miner of Rough Street, Gwennap. Bpt Gwennap 24 April 1829.

SKEWES WILLIAM
Married Sarah Hodge at Cury, 6 July 1833.

SKEWS WILLIAM
Born 1833. Son of John Skews, bricklayer. In 1854 lived at 7 Johnson Street, Westminster. Mariner. Married Mary Ann Allen 1 October 1854, daughter of William Allen, coach builder at the Parish Church of St John the Evangelist, Westminster. Died 1867, Westminster, aged 34 years. She married again in 1872, Kensington.

SKEWES WILLIAM
Chart 2. Son of Edward and Mary Skewes. Born 9 December 1834. Bpt Wesleyan/Methodist Chapel, Camborne 13 March 1835. Emigrated to USA, 1849. Went missing in 1853. Never seen again. Bachelor.

SKUES WILLIAM
of Constantine. Married Elizabeth Glasson at Wendron Parish Church 11 November 1834.

SKEWES WILLIAM
Chart 50. Son of William and Rebecca Skewes, labourer. Bpt Constantine 6 April 1834. Lived at Trethowan Downs. Died 1889, aged 54 years.

SKEWES WILLIAM
Son of John Skewes, miner of Carharrack, Gwennap. Born 1834. Married Eliza Jose (23) of White Stile, Gwennap 26 July 1856 at Gwennap in presence of William Skewes.
Child: William John (1861).

SKEWES WILLIAM
Born 1834. Died Redruth 1911, aged 77 years.

SKEWES WILLIAM
Son of John and Jane Skews. Bpt St Austell 4 October 1835.

SKEWES WILLIAM
Son of William and Elizabeth Skewes of Constantine, famer. Bpt Methodist Chapel, Falmouth, 22 January 1836 (born 2 December 1835).

SKUES WILLIAM
Carpenter. His wife Mary died in February 1838, aged 55 years in Helston.

SKEWES   WILLIAM
Son of James and Ann Skewes. Bpt Truro 25 July 1838. Lived in John
Street, Kenwyn. Buried Kenwyn 23 September 1838, aged 10 weeks.
SKEWS   WILLIAM
Chart 23. Born 1838, St Austell. Married Jane Bullock, approx 1862.
Children: John Edwin (1863), Jane (1866), Annie (1868), Lilian (1870)
and Tom (1878). Died 1896, aged 58 years in Strood, Kent.
SKEWES   WILLIAM
Born 1840. Died St Columb 1914, aged 74 years.
SKUES   WILLIAM
Chart 27. Son of Isaac Skues of Victoria Cottage, Bath, plasterer.
Married Mary Francis (21) of Victoria Cottage, daughter of John
Francis, tea dealer; at the Parish Church of Trinity, Bath, 9 December
1860. Labourer. Children; Emma (1861); Rosina (1863) — Amelia
(1863) twins; Emma (1866); Maria (1867) and Alice (1871).
SKEWS   WILLIAM
Born 1842, Truro.
SKUES   WILLIAM
Chart 9. Son of William and Lovelia (née Noakes) Skues. Born 22
November 1842, Tonbridge, Kent. Died 1887, aged 45 years in
Tonbridge.
SKEWES   WILLIAM
Chart 33. Son of William and Susan (née Oates) Skewes. Born 1843.
Buried Chacewater, 22 July 1864, aged 21 years.
SKEWIS   WILLIAM
Died 1844, Redruth.
SKEWS   WILLIAM
Son of William Skews, carpenter. Labourer. Married Louisa Ann Johns
of Willow Street, Plymouth at St Andrew's Parish Church, Plymouth,
26 September 1845.
SKEWES   WILLIAM
Born 28 September 1847. Son of William Skewes. Married Jane
Northey, daughter of Josiah Northey of Baldhu, miner at St Michael's
Church, Baldhu, 30 September 1864. Emigrated to Michigan, USA
about 1867. Children: Elizabeth Ann (1865), Emily (1871), William
(1873), James (1875) and Maud (Maria) Jane (1877).
Died 19 December 1916 at Tecumseh, Houghton, Michigan, USA.
SKEWES   WILLIAM
Son of William and Lovelia Skewes. Bpt St Mewan 28 May 1848.
SKEWES   WILLIAM
Died 1848, Helston.
SKEWES   WILLIAM
Died 1848, Stoke Devonport.
SKEWS   WILLIAM
Son of John Skews, seaman of 41 George Street, East Stonehouse,
Plymouth. Born 5 May 1851. Died 12 May 1851, aged 7 days.
SKUES   WILLIAM
Born 8 June 1851. Married Margaret, who was known as "Abby" as she
came from Aberdeen, Scotland. Lived in Australia. Children: Margaret
Melville (1888), Robert Bruce (1889), Lisabeth (1893), Colin Campbell
(1895), Mary Ellen (1897) & Walter Cecil (1903). Was employed with
New South Wales Railways.
SKEWES   WILLIAM
Chart 36. Son of Henry and Ann (née Gribble) Skewes. Born 1852,
Victoria, Australia. Married Annie Taylor. Lived in Ballarat,
Bunninyong and Eureka, Australia. Children: Ernest, Henry John,
Bertie and Minnie. Died 8 November 1931, aged 79 years.
SKEWES   WILLIAM
Chart 49. Born 1853. Son of John Skewes. Miner. Married Harriet
Lidstone, daughter of William Lidstone, labourer of Buckfastleigh,
Devon; at the Parish Church, Buckfastleigh 12 September 1875.
Children: Elizabeth Ann (1876), William Henry (1877), George (1879),
Jane (1881) and Harriet (1883). Died Totnes, 1921, aged 67 years.
Harriet died Totnes 1921, aged 68 years.
SKEWES   WILLIAM
Chart 12. Son of Henry and Harriet Skewes of Landewednack. Born
1853, Lizard. In 1871 Census Returns was aged 18, a carpenter, and
boarder at the home of Sampson Hill on The Lizard. Spent much of his
life in Chile. Married Clorinda Salcedo. Children: William Henry and
Robert Montague. Returned to Cornwall a few years prior to his death
on 2 October 1930, aged 77 years and settled at Channel Views, The
Lizard. In his will he refers to his son as Guillermo Enrique (William
Henry).
SKEWES   WILLIAM
Chart 10. Son of Digory and Fanny (née Tregonning) Skewes. Born 29
March 1854, Marazion. Bpt Marazion Parish Church 29 September
1854.
SKEWS   WILLIAM
Married 1854, Westminster.
SKEWS   WILLIAM
Died 1854, Plymouth.
SKEWES   WILLIAM
Chart 2. Son of William & Sarah (née Billing) Skewes. Born 1856,
Illogan. Died 18 November 1891, aged 35 years. Buried in Mount Olivet
Cemetery, Salt Lake City, Utah.

SKEWS   WILLIAM
Born 1856, Lewisham.
SKEWS   WILLIAM
Chart 6. Son of Thomas and Mary A. Skews. Born 2 December 1856,
Cornwall. Carpenter. Emigrated to Mineral Point, Wisconsin, USA
with his parents in 1866. Married Alice J. .... (she born 31 July 1861 —
died 4 July 1896). Died 13 May 1925, aged 70 years. Children: Harvey
(1883) and Thomas (1882).
SKEWS   WILLIAM
Died 1856, Redruth.
SKEWES   WILLIAM
Chart 36. Born 22 January 1858, Australia. Son of William and
Elizabeth (née Northey) Skewes. Married Hannah Jane Gale. Children:
James, Amy, William, Percy and Lily.
Moved from Uralla, New South Wales to Watsons Creek about 1870.
Tin miner. Died 23 August 1943, aged 87 years.
SKEWS   WILLIAM
Born 1859. Died Liskeard 1943, aged 84 years.
SKEWES   WILLIAM
Born 1859. Died 6 October 1900, aged 41 years. Buried in St Thomas
Churchyard, North Sydney, Australia.
SKEWES   WILLIAM
Died 1860, Bideford.
SKEWES   WILLIAM
Chart 36. Born 1861, Camborne. Son of William and Priscilla (née Mill)
Skewes of Illogan, agricultural labourer. Aged 10 in 1871 Census
Returns living at Carnarton, Illogan with his brothers and sisters James,
Eliza, Hannah, Mary and Edward. Died 1891, aged 30 years.
SKEWES   WILLIAM
Born 1861, Newton Abbot.
SKEWES   WILLIAM
of Lannarth, Gwennap. Born 1862. Buried Illogan 1 December 1862,
aged 6 months.
SKEWES   WILLIAM
Chart 36. Son of Edward and Jecoliah Skewes of Lanner, Gwennap.
Born 1864. In 1871 Census Returns living at Gwennap, then aged 7, a
scholar, with his mother and father and brother Edward J. (10) and
sister Eliza J. (2 months). Father was a railway labourer. Died 1902, aged
37 years. Twice married.
SKEWIS   WILLIAM
Died 1864, Redruth.
SKEWS   WILLIAM
Married 1865, Portsea.
SKEWES   WILLIAM
of The Highway, Illogan. Married Jane Thomas of Redruth 15
September 1865 at Redruth.
SKUES   WILLIAM
Chart 3. Son of Richard and Lucy Skues. Born 1866, Halifax. Died
1890, aged 24 years.
SKEWS   WILLIAM
of Hugus, Kea. Born 1866. Buried Kea 12 October 1867, aged 1 year.
SKEWIS   WILLIAM
Born 1866, Scotland. Son of James Skewis, iron turner and Helen (née
Jamieson) Skewis. Married Elizabeth Shaw (24), of 5 Nuneaton Street,
Glasgow, daughter of Martin Shaw, shoemaker and Ann (née McLean)
Shaw; 22 October 1884 at Broad Street, Glasgow. Children included:
James (1887), George (1891) and John (1896).
Elizabeth died 1896, aged 33 years.
William married Ellen Blythe, yarn twister (26), daughter of James and
Agnes Blyth at 104 Armdale Street, Glasgow 17 June 1898. Children:
Walter Blyth (1902) and Robert Blyth (1904).
Died Dennistoun, Scotland, 1916, aged 50 years.
SKEWES   WILLIAM
Born 1868. Lived at 10 Golf Villas, Falmouth. Died 1932 — 12 August,
aged 64 years. Married to Janie ......
SKEWIS   WILLIAM
Chart 2. Son of William and Peggy (née Bawden) Skewis. Married
Martha Waters (she born 24 July 1844). Daughter: Carolyn Skewis
(1876). Lived in America. Died 1881. Martha married William Liddell
1884, and died July 1926.
SKEWS   WILLIAM
Chart 10. Son of Peter and Elizabeth Jane (née Youren) Skews; lead
miner. Born 13 September 1869 at Pengover, Menheniot. Later lived at
Coxbarrow, Carthew, St Austell. Died 1904, aged 34 years in St Austell.
SKEWES   WILLIAM
Son of William and Jane (née Northey) Skewes. Born 22 February 1873
at Humboldt, Michigan, USA. Married Elizabeth Alberta Mary Jessop 7
March 1899. (She born 4 April 1878 at Boston, Ontario — died 18 June
1954, aged 76 years.) Children: William Jessop (1900), Alberta (1902),
Walter George (1904), Harold Herschell (1905), Dorothy Dainty (1906),
Robert (1908), James Robert (1914) and June Patricia (1918).
Died 20 July 1939 at Hancock, Houghton, Michigan, USA, aged 67
years.
SKEWES   WILLIAM
Married 1874, Redruth.

SKEWES WILLIAM
Married 1875, Totnes.
SKEWES WILLIAM
Chart 48. Illegitimate son of Amelia Skewes of Truro Union Workhouse.
Born 27 December 1875. Began his life as a butcher's errand boy,
pushing a barrow filled with meat through the streets of Truro. He had a
sense of purpose and dignity and decided this was not the life for him, so
he went to work for a shoemaker; shortly afterwards another change of
job, this time working for a bookbinder. It was whilst in Truro he took a
great interest in photography and his fourth job saw him working for
E.I. Ellery, "Photographer in the Newest Style, enlargements of every
description finished in oil, water colour or monochrome."
His days at the Ellery studio at 32 River Street, Truro made a lasting
impression upon him, and William lived as one of the family for several
years, learning the photographic trade in the days when a photographer
had to make his own plates and sensitised paper.
At the age of 16 he saw an advertisement for a photographer in Jersey,
and sailed from Falmouth to take up the appointment. It was a rough
crossing and he was very ill, having smoked his first ever cigar en route.
On arrival he discovered the job was for a promenade photography
business and he told the proprietor he was not prepared to "walk up and
down touting for business." But he found suitable employment and
stayed in Jersey for the summer season and returned to Cornwall to take
up work with Major and Parker in Falmouth until 1894. William
travelled north to Wigan, Lancashire and was employed by Crippin &
Co. of Spring Bank, Pemberton. Their testimonial when he left in
March 1896, after working there for a year read: "He is strictly honest
and straightforward and will do his best to push business. We shall at all
times be glad to hear of his success."
London was the next city where William worked and in 1897 was
employed by Henry Seagrave in Plumstead. Thence to Pembroke Dock
(1898) to work for S.J. Allen. It was about this time he met a Mrs Biddle
with whom he eloped to Gretna Green. He was unaware, initially, that
her husband was still alive, and being rather naive felt that he was
committed to staying with her, although he quickly realised that he had
made a serious mistake. Two children were born out of this partnership:
William Frederick Charles (1899) and Laura Anne (1902). For a while
William worked in Dundee, but returned to Pemberton, Wigan in 1902
to work for Pemberton Photographic Company at Spring Bank.
The following year he went to Cork, Eire for a year, after which he set up
his own business in Park Crescent, Wigan.
He was initiated into Makerfield Lodge No 2155, Leigh on 20 February
1906 — "A Photo artist, aged 30, of Wigan". He was a member of Peace
Chapter of Royal Arch Masons (exalted 18 January 1907). Advanced to
degree of Mark Master Mason 13 February 1907 with Rose and Thistle
Lodge No 1581, Wigan. He was a Royal Ark Mariner with Mount
Ararat Lodge, Wigan (2 November 1907) and a member of the Knight
of the Red Cross of Constantine, St George's Council No 4 (27 January
1908). He was a founder member of Norbury Lodge No 4046.
Sometime about 1906 he met Elizabeth Marsh in a country public house
called "Martland Mill Inn." Documents retained by his daughter
Elizabeth Mary Skewes relate:
'The proprietor had two charming daughters. One of the girls was called
Ellen, known by her family as Nellie, and the other was Elizabeth
(Lizzie). In those gracious Edwardian days, drawing room
accomplishments were de rigueur, and Nellie had heard Mr Skewes (as
he was known to his friends) sing, and she went behind the scenes to
fetch her young sister to play the piano. But Elizabeth had never played
an accompaniment for a singer before and was unwilling to make a fool
of herself. However, she was persuaded because the singer had no music,
so he had to sing whatever was available and on this basis she felt perhaps
they were starting more or less level. The song he sang was "Star of My
Soul", a rather prophetic Edwardian ballad, and although Elizabeth
agreed Mr Skewes had a beautiful voice, she was unimpressed. "He's
soft", she said with down-to-earth northern candour.'
However, Mr Skewes persuaded Elizabeth to travel to London and they
married at Hackney Register Office on 22 September 1910. William
gave his address as: Kenilworth Hotel, Great Russell Street, London.
Elizabeth, who was daughter of James Marsh, licensed victualler, was
staying with friends at 20 Brooksby Walk, Homerton, London before
the wedding.
On his wedding certificate William is listed as son of William Frederick
Skewes, deceased, master cabinet maker. However, records at St
Catherine's House, London give no birth, marriage or death of such a
person.
William and Elizabeth spent a month's blissful honeymoon at Westcliffe
on Sea, Essex and returned to the London area where William
purchased a photographic business with living accommodation at 62
George Street, Croydon. This was in 1910, and he remained in business
there until the 1920's, but in 1913 built two semi-detached houses in
Bisenden Road, Croydon and lived in one of these for nearly ten years.
Three children were born to William and Elizabeth: Cyril William
Skewes (1912), Kathleen Muriel Skewes (1913) and Elizabeth Mary
Skewes (1926).
The family moved house again on New Year's Day, 1922 to 49
Addiscombe Road, East Croydon.
William continued his photographic business at Tranquil Vale,

William Verdayne Skewes (1875-1957)

Blackheath in premises which were formerly a bank which he bought for
£100. These he transformed into a studio and sold the business as a
going concern several years later, for a considerable profit.
Later he opened a business in Croydon High Street, but took an early
retirement from the world of photography to specialise in selling and
letting property.
William, who adopted the name "Verdayne", died 9 January 1957, aged
81 years. Elizabeth died 17 February 1965, aged 82 years.
SKEWS WILLIAM
Born 1877, Redruth.
SKEWIS WILLIAM
Chart 2. Son of William and Martha Skewis. Born 19 October 1878. A
wanderer! Lived in America. Died 10 April 1906, aged 28 years.
SKEWES WILLIAM
Married 1883, Redruth.
SKEWES WILLIAM
Chart 36. Son of William Hicks and Elizabeth (née McLeod) Skewes.
Born 1883, South Australia.
SKEWES WILLIAM
Chart 25. Son of William and Jane (née Jameson) Skewes. Born 1883,
Salford. Died 1883, aged 0.
SKEWES WILLIAM
Married 1884, Redruth.
SKEWES WILLIAM
Born 1885. Lived at Primrose Hill, Perranuthnoe. Died 1886. Buried
Perranuthnoe 19 April 1886, aged 14 months.
SKEWES WILLIAM
Born 1885. Lived at Nancegollan. Buried Cury 5 January 1886, aged 6
months.
SKEWES WILLIAM
Lived at Treloweth, Illogan 1885/1886.
SKEWES WILLIAM
Married 1885, Redruth.
SKEWIS WILLIAM
Married 1886, Newton Abbot.
SKEWIS WILLIAM
Married 1886, Calton, Scotland.

William Skewes (1887-1968)

SKEWES   WILLIAM
Chart 36. Son of Samuel Sidney and Sarah (née Pennall) Skewes. Born 13 April 1886. Married Edith Howarth, 1907, New South Wales, Australia. Lived at Watsons Creek, New South Wales. Children: May (1908), Eva (1910), Dulcie (1912), William (1915), Roy (1918), Daphne (1921), Frank (1925). Died 2 August 1963, aged 77 years. Buried in Methodist section of Bendemeer Cemetery.
SKEWIS   WILLIAM
Born 1887, Newton Abbot.
SKEWES   WILLIAM
Chart 36. Son of William and Hannah (née Gale) Skewes. Born 1887. Married his first cousin IDA OLIVE SKEWES, August 1922. Children: Leslie Kevin, Earle William, Eric, Brian, Lorna, Meg, Donald Lloyd, Dorothy Dawn, Janice and Jennifer. Lived at Watsons Creek, via Bendemeer, New South Wales, Australia. Died 5 June 1968, aged 81 years.
SKEWES   WILLIAM
Chart 40. Son of Richard and Susan (née Donald) Skewes, fish dealer. Born 17 June 1889, Perranuthnoe. Farmer at Chiverton, Rosudgeon. Twice married.
1) Elizabeth M. Roberts in 1910. She died 1921, aged 32 years.
2) Laura Allen of Prussia Cove, St Hilary, daughter of Henry Allen, fisherman at Perranuthnoe Parish Church 1 October 1921, in presence of Richard Henry Skewes. Children from first marriage: William Richard and Leonard. Children from second marriage: Dorothy, Mary, Donald, Willie (stepson) and Matthew Henry. Died 5 October 1937, aged 48 years.
SKEWIS   WILLIAM
Chart 50. Son of Joseph Richard Skewis, steam hammer driver and Martha (née McIlroy) Skewis. Born 25 December 1889, Coatbridge, Scotland. Coal miner. Lived at 18 Connor Street, Airdrie, Scotland. Married Martha Barclay Stark (25), farm servant, daughter of Richard Stark, coal miner and Margaret Stark (née Hendrie) at 9 Broompark Terrace, Glasgow, Scotland, 31 December 1913. She died 1914, aged 26 years. He married again 28 April 1916 at 25 Victoria Street, Harthill, Scotland to Martha Stark Barclay (28), daughter of William Barclay, coal miner and Martha Barclay (née Stark).
SKEWIS   WILLIAM
Died 18 November 1891.
SKEWIS   WILLIAM
Lived at Treskillard, Illogan, 1897/1906.
SKEWES   WILLIAM
Born 1894, Redruth. Died 1895, aged 1 year.
SKEWS   WILLIAM
Married 1895, St Austell.
SKEWES   WILLIAM

Lived at 23 High Street, Ballarat, Australia 1906/1912 with Jane Skewes. Carter.
SKEWIS   WILLIAM
Born 1901. Died Glasgow, 1971, aged 70 years.
SKUSE   WILLIAM
Rev., B.A. at Trinity College Dublin, 1909. Deacon, 1910. Priest, 1911. Limerick county of Kenmare with Templence and Tuosist 1910/1912. Ematris with Rockcorry 1912/1915. Dingle with Ventry 1915/1916. Chaplain of Villiershewn and Curate of Cappoquin 1916/1919. Incumbent of Kilflynn with Ratoo 1922/1932. Incumbent of Grean with Caherconlish 1932/1955. Diocese Curate of Cash and Emly 1951/1956. Address (1973): Woodcoate, Roundhill, Bandon, County Cork, Eire.
SKEWES   WILLIAM
Married 1910, Hackney.
SKEWS   WILLIAM
Lived in Scotsburn, Ballarat, Victoria, Australia in 1912 with Annie Skews. Engine driver.
SKEWIS   WILLIAM
Son of James Skewis. Born 1 March 1913, Toronto, Canada. Married 24 May 1941. Children: James (1943) and Florence Sandra (1948). Is director of Ontario Natural Gas Association. Lives at 4196 Dunvegan Road, Burlington, Ontario, Canada L7L 1P8.
SKEWIS   WILLIAM
Born 1913, Dennistoun, Scotland.
SKEWES   WILLIAM
Chart 36. Son of William and Edith (née Howarth) Skewes. Born 31 May 1915. Lived at Watsons Creek, via Bendemeer, New South Wales, Australia.
SKEWS   WILLIAM
Married Susan Childs in Bethnal Green, 1915. Children: Elsie (1917), Doris (1920), William A. (1920) and Eileen (1927).
SKEWES   WILLIAM
Married Janie Gosling 1916, Falmouth.
SKEWIS   WILLIAM
Married 1916, Shotts East, Scotland.
SKEWIS   WILLIAM
Shopkeeper with Hart Battery Company.
Resided at 790 Crawford, Toronto, Canada in 1927. By 1939 he was a clerk with Page-Hersey Tubes living at the same address. He was missing in the 1940/1941 directories, but was back again in 1942 and had moved to 22 Douglas Drive. By 1946 he was a service engineer with Page-Hersey Tubes, but was living at 12 Glenrose Avenue. By 1963 he had moved again, this time to 52 Delhi, North York, Toronto and had been promoted to district manager.
SKEWS   WILLIAM
Mother's maiden name Jarvis. Born 1928, Romford, Essex. Married King, 1953.
SKEWIS   WILLIAM
Born 1936, Camalchie, Scotland.
SKEWIS   WILLIAM
Married Mitchell, 1937, Cadder, Scotland.
SKEWES   WILLIAM
Lived at Trevarth Vean, Lanner, Redruth, 1949, with Emma Skewes.
SKEWES   WILLIAM
Lived at Lower Condurrow, Camborne with Lilian Skewes, 1949.
SKEWS   WILLIAM
Chart 6. Son of William Alexander and Gale (née Julson) Skews. Born 9 November 1949. Married Fay Keist. Lives in Wisconsin, USA.
SKEWIS   WILLIAM
Married Rachel Creek Lyons in Cadder East, Scotland, 1960. No children.
SKEWES   WILLIAM
Lived at Tregarne, St Keverne, 1969 with Nora Skewes.,
SKEWIS   WILLIAM A.
Chart 2. Son of Arthur Lawrence and Elizabeth (née Ballard) Skewis. Born 7 June 1911.
SKEWS   WILLIAM A.
Daughter of William and Susan (née Childs) Skews. Born Hackney, London 1920. Died 1920, aged 0.
SKEWS   WILLIAM ALBERT
Chart 17. Son of David George and Emily (née Lampey) Skews. Born 11 November 1928. Married Jean Leach, 1949 at the Register Office, Severn Kings, Ilford, Essex. Children: Terence W. (1950) and Michael D. (1957).
SKEWES   WILLIAM ALEXANDER
Son of Thomas and Elizabeth Skewes. Born 1854. Bpt St Mary, Swansea, Glamorgan 9 July 1854.
SKEWS   WILLIAM ALEXANDER
Chart 6. Son of John and Clara Jeanette (née Babcock) Skews. Born 1903, Mineral Point, Wisconsin, USA. Married Gale Julson, who died when their first daughter was born. He married again — Wilma Buttfuss — 12 April 1949. Children: Gale (1927), William (1949) and Janet G. (1951).

Lives in Hollandale, Wisconsin, USA.

SKEWES WILLIAM ARTHUR
Born 1882, Redruth.

William Arthur Skewes

SKEWES WILLIAM ARTHUR
Chart 12. Son of Harry Stanley and Beatrice A. (née Rosevear) Skewes of Roseville, Garras, Helston. Born 14 April 1924.
Joined army at Bury St Edmunds, Suffolk, 17 December 1942. After training in Royal Artillery as a signaller/wireless operator, he joined the 128th Field Battery, Royal Artillery (part of 51st Highland Division) in Normandy on D Day plus one, and was with them throughout the European Campaign. He returned to the Royal Artillery Depot, Woolwich in mid 1945 and remained there on the administrative staff until he was demobilised in May, 1947.
From November 1947 to June 1949 Arthur Skewes held a temporary teaching place at St Keverne, Cornwall. He became a student at Burderop Park College, Swindon, Wiltshire in July 1949 and 14 months later became assistant teacher at Trewirgie School, Redruth.
In January 1958 he moved to Wellington, Somerset and became assistant teacher at Courtfields Secondary Modern School where he specialised in Religious Education and Music. He remained there until April 1961 when he moved to Marlborough in Wiltshire, becoming head of Oare Church of England (Controlled) Primary School.
In April 1965 Arthur Skewes became head of St James Church of England (Aided) School, Isle of Grain, Rochester, Kent.
He married Gwendoline Bray at Treleigh Church, Redruth on 31 December 1954. Twins Kevin and Paul were born in 1956 but died at birth. Arthur Skewes is warden of St James Church, Grain and organist. Assistant secretary to Strood Deanery Synod from 1970 to 1978. Was deanery representative to Diocesan Synod and Rochester Diocesan Board of Education from 1970 to 1978.
From 1972 to 1974 he was district councillor with Strood Rural District Council, which merged with others to become Medway Borough Council in 1974.
He had been Chairman of Medway Towns' Schools Music Association since 1978 and a member of committee since 1972. Layreader since 1975. In this spare time Arthur Skewes enjoys listening to music.
He is a Freemason with Hoo St. Werburgh Lodge No 4829; Royal Arch Mason with St Peter's Chapter No 4193; Mark Master Mason with Trinity Lodge No 1379; also associated with the Mariners' Lodge. Member of Holy Trinity Preceptory No 391 of Knights Templar and Knights of Malta. Member of Gravesend Chapter of Rose-Crois of

Heredown No 677. Member of Royal Order of Scotland and Provincial Grand Lodge of Kent.
Address: School House, Isle of Grain, Rochester, Kent. Telephone number 0634 270471.

SKEWES WILLIAM ARTHUR RAYMOND
Chart 12. Son of William Frank and Annie Doris Skewes. Mother's maiden name Williams. Born 25 March 1931. Lived at Chybarles, Ruan Major during childhood. Married Mavis Emily Rogers at Ruan Minor Parish Church 10 December 1955. Children: John Roger (1959) and Nicola (1956). Lives at "Seagulls Cry", Cadgwith, Helston.

SKEWES WILLIAM ASHDOWN
Son of William Thomas and Vera Louise (née Ashdown) Skues. Born 26 April 1924 Forest Lodge, Australia. Married Edith Saul, 14 November 1959, St. Anne's Church, Ryde, New South Wales. Children: Kevin William (1960), Glenda Beryl (1962), Jennifer Anne (1965) and Steven Bruce (1969). Lives at 7 Cormack Road, Beacon Hill, 2100, New South Wales, Australia. Mechanic.

SKEWIS WILLIAM B.
Married Solomon in Sheppey, 1912.

SKEWIS WILLIAM BAWDEN
Born 1855. Married 1886 in Tavistock to Helen Thomasine ..... Although born in Redruth lived at Myrtle Cottage, Brighton Ladock. Appeared in 1880 voters list for Calstock, East Cornwall as Copyhold House and Land in Tavistock. Died 14 June 1935. Helen Thomasine died 13 April 1939, aged 68 years.

SKEWIS WILLIAM BENSON
Born 26 September 1898, Camalchie, Scotland. Illegitimate son of Helen Skewis, steamborn weaver.

SKEWES WILLIAM BROWN
Chart 30. Son of John Beer and Mary Skewes. Born 1857, Truro. In 1871 Census Returns living at Kenwyn Street, Truro with his parents and sisters Henrietta Maria, Philippa Mary and brothers John Brown, Thomas John and Richard Henry. Died 1941, aged 84 years in Exeter.

SKEWES WILLIAM BYRON
Son of Byron James and Margaret Cecilia (née Morrison) Skewes. Born 29 July 1963. Lives in New York.

SKEWES WILLIAM CHARLES
Chart 10. Son of Herbert Tregonning and Florence Martha Skewes. Born 4 February 1936 at Hamilton, Ontario, Canada. Bachelor.

SKEWS WILLIAM CLIFFORD
Chart 41. Son of William John and Mary (née Rump) Skews. Born 22 July 1925, Houghton. Married Joyce Morrell 18 June 1949 in Durham North.
One son: Kevin Robert (1953). Cashier for National Coal Board.

SKEWES WILLIAM CLIVE
Chart 40. Son of Matthew Henry and Ann Skewes. Mother's maiden name Morgan. Born 2 March 1954, Penzance.

SKEWES WILLIAM CYRIL MARSH
Chart 48. Son of William (Verdayne) and Elizabeth (née Marsh) Skewes, of 49 Addiscombe Road, Croydon, Surrey. Born 4 January 1912. District manager of Halifax Building Society. Married Marie Florence Ambrose 22 April 1939, Croydon. Children: Anne Marie (1944) and Linda Rosemary (1947). Hobbies: woodwork, photography, gardening, cookery, golf and oil painting. Lives at 9 Croft Rise, Menston, West Yorkshire. Tel no: 0943 73051.

SKEWS WILLIAM DAVID
Born 30 March 1907. Married Winifred Honor Groves, 1934, Hackney. Lived at 1 Holm Oak Cottages, East Preston, Sussex. Died 7 July 1970, aged 63 years in Worthing.

SKEWES WILLIAM DOUGLAS
Chart 46. Son of Charles and Bessie (née Teague) Skewes, of 76 Chapel Hill, Truro. Born 28 November 1914. Attended St George's School, Truro. Joined Royal Navy and served during Second World War (chief petty officer). Married Gladys Maud Little, June 1939 at St Clements, Truro. Children: William John (1943) and Margaret Rosemary (1944). Lived at Carclew Cottages, Truro.

SKEWES WILLIAM EDWARD
Chart 36. Son of James and Stella Margaret (née Farrell) Skewes. Born 6 June 1931. Married Margery Catherine Moran. Children: Ian and Amanda. Lives at Stoddart Street, Manila, 2346, New South Wales, Australia.

SKEWES WILLIAM ERNEST
Born 1874, Helston. Died 1876, aged 1 year.

SKEWES WILLIAM FRANCIS
Born 1885, Helston.

SKEWES WILLIAM FRANK
Chart 12. Son of James Henry and Maude Mary (née Richards) Skewes. Born 14 December 1903. Farmer. Married Annie Doris Williams of St Keverne 27 September 1927 at Helston Wesleyan/Methodist Church, Meneage Street, Helston. Lived at Chybarles, Ruan Major 1944-1970. Previous address: Lovely Vale, Mithian, St Agnes (1927-1934) and Lower Tregidden, St Martin (1934-1944). Children: Lilian Gladys (1929), William Arthur Raymond (1931), John Trevor (1935) and Peter Marsden (1941).
Now lives at 30 Glebe Place, Ruan Minor, Helston.

William Frank Skewes

SKEWES   WILLIAM FREDERICK
Chart 25. Born 1894, Chorlton, Manchester.

William Frederick Skewes (1894-1944)

SKEWES   WILLIAM FREDERICK
Chart 14. Son of Mortier Boulden and Mildred Gladys (née Pettes) Skewes of Luverne, Minnesota, USA. Born 13 February 1945. Solicitor with Kelly, Stansfield & O'Donnell, 990 Public Service Company Building, 550 15th Street, Denver, Colorado 80202, USA. Married Kathleen Audrey Hogan of Naperville, 24 June 1978 at Aspen, Colorado, USA.

SKEWES   WILLIAM FREDERICK CHARLES
Chart 48. Son of William (Verdayne) and Elizabeth (née Biddle; née Kilner). Born 15 September 1899 at Pemberton, Wigan. Married Dorothy Marion Hornby in Doncaster 4 April 1929.
Children: Barbara Ann (1931) and John Hornby (1933). Electrician with a shop at 28 South Parade, Doncaster. Past President of Doncaster Chamber of Trades 1939-1941.
After death of his wife in 1947 he married Ida Mary Corbett, 1950, Doncaster. She died 2 April 1971, aged 68 years.
Private address: 9 St Augustine's Road, Bessecar, Doncaster.
Died at Western Hospital, Springwell Lane, Doncaster, 29 November 1953, aged 54 years.

SKEWES   WILLIAM G.
Lives at Greenview Manor, Apartment 4, Bluefield, Virginia 24605, USA. Graduated from Virginia Technical College, Blacksburg, Virginia. His great grandfather emigrated from Cornwall to the mines of Michigan — Upper Peninsular.

SKEWES   WILLIAM GEORGE
Doctor. Chart 14. Son of Samuel J. and Betsy (née Phillips) Skewes. Born 21 January 1868, Ives Grove, Racine County, USA. As a boy he enjoyed farm and carpentry work. He graduated in Dentistry from the Milwaukee Medical College, now Marquette University, in 1898. He located in Mukwonago, but illness forced his retirement after 10 years of practice.
In 1917 he received an appointment as rural mail carrier out of Waukesha where he lived until his death. He retired as a mail carrier in 1933. As his health improved he became active in the Congregational Church, acting as deacon for 31 years.
Doctor Skewes was a Freemason with Blue Lodge (Master in 1932) and a member of Chapter, Council and Commandery.
In 1901 he married Kate Thomas, who died in 1923. He married Winifred Hale in 1927. No children. He visited England in 1925 and travelled to all the states in America except one.
Died 20 December 1953, aged 85 years at 703 Lincoln Avenue, Waukesha, Milwaukee.
He was interred in Mound Cemetery, Racine.

SKEW   WILLIAM GEORGE
Born 1875, Lymington.

SKUES   WILLIAM GEORGE
Born 1880, Eton. Died 1881, aged 1 year.

SKEWS   WILLIAM GEORGE
Born 1893. Died 1909, St Olave, aged 16 years.

SKEWES   WILLIAM GEORGE
Chart 36. Son of William Vere and Annie Rebecca (née Strain) Skewes. Born 24 May 1929, Tamworth, New South Wales. Married Eunice Howard, May 1953, Tamworth. Child: Anne. Lives at Burleigh Heads News Agency, Gold Coast, 4220, Queensland, Australia. Newsagent.

SKEWS   WILLIAM GEORGE ALFRED.
Son of William and Emily (née Homan) Skews. Born 29 July 1894 at 28 Mace Street, Bethnal Green, London. Died 1970, Hackney, London, aged 76 years.

SKEWIS   WILLIAM H.
Chart 2. Son of Edward and Kittie Skewis. Born 15 January 1865, Shullsburg, Wisconsin, USA. Died 25 July 1934, aged 69 years.

SKEWES   WILLIAM H.
Born August 1969, Missouri. Lived in Mississippi, 1900.

SKEWES   WILLIAM H.
Died 9 October 1892, Salt Lake City, Utah, USA.

SKEWES   WILLIAM H.
Son of William H. and Margaret Skewes. Born May 1899, Missouri. Lived in Mississippi, 1900.

SKEWES   WILLIAM H.
Married Pollard, 1945, Redruth.

SKEWES   WILLIAM H.
Married Hill, 1952, Kerrier.

SKEWES   WILLIAM H.
Lives at 819 San Gabriel, Las Vegas, Nevada, USA. Tel No: (702) 564 1629.

SKUSE   WILLIAM HAROLD BERNARD
Son of Leslie Walter Harold Skuse. Born 24 November 1932 at Bath. Married Janet Lesley (Rusty) Field 5 July 1976. Tattooist. Lives at Park View, Hawley Road, Hawley, near Camberley, Surrey. He successfully tattooed his wife over a period of 12 years. Rusty is Britain's most tattooed lady.

SKEWES   WILLIAM HEDLEY
Chart 36. Son of Thomas William and Eliza Emma (née Bray) Skewes, police sergeant. Born 17 June 1879, Penzance. Commercial traveller/draper/Inland Revenue clerk. Lived at Dopp's Terrace,

Above left: *Photograph taken in 1903 by William Verdayne Skewes of his daughter Laura, and son William Frederick.* Above right: *William Frederick Skewes of Doncaster, South Yorkshire (1899-1953).* Below: *The electrical shop owned by William Frederick Skewes in Doncaster. Photograph taken 1935*

Above: *Ellen Street, Port Pirie, South Australia. Skewes chemist shop on right, Australian bullock wagon in centre*

Below: *Handsome Gothic shops designed and built by William Henry Skewes in 1897 in Port Pirie, South Australia*

Redruth, 1922 with Nellie Skewes whom he married in Shoreditch, London, 1907. She died 7 December 1939. Married Emma Pollard (52), widow and daughter of John Rosevear, farm labourer of Lanner Moor, Redruth at the Register Office, Redruth, 25 July 1945.
Was a member of Lanner Cricket Club. A trustee and trust treasurer of Lanner Moor Methodist Church. Was a Freemason with Druids Lodge, Redruth.
Died 9 November 1964 at Barncoose Hospital, Redruth. Buried in St Days Road Cemetery, Redruth.

SKEWS   WILLIAM HEDLEY
Chart 23. Born 17 June 1898. Son of John and Bertha Skews. Lived at Oak View, Coxbarrow, Cathew, St Austell. Died 26 March 1973, aged 75 years in St Austell.

SKEWES   WILLIAM HENRY
Born 1806. Lived at Bolitho Farm, Crowan. Died 1886, aged 79 years.

SKUES   WILLIAM HENRY
Chart 8. Born 1808. Lived at 3 Bath Terrace, St Paul's, Middlesex. Married Sarah Young. Children: George Henry, William Henry and James. Died of cholera, 3 August 1854, aged 46 years. Was a coal whipper.

SKEWS   WILLIAM HENRY
Son of Stephen and Susannah Skews. Bpt Budock 26 November 1831.

SKUES   WILLIAM HENRY
Chart 2. Son of Henry and Grace Skues. Bpt Camborne 16 February 1833. Copper miner. Emigrated to Missouri, USA. Married Lavinia Johnese (French). Son: William Henry (1899).

SKEWES   WILLIAM HENRY
Born 1838. Illegitimate son of Jane Skewes of Nantithet, Cury. Bpt Cury 16 December 1838.

SKUES   WILLIAM HENRY
Chart 8. Born 11 April 1846. Son of William Henry and Sarah (née Young) Skues of 44 Devonshire Street, St Paul's District of St George's East, London.

SKEWES   WILLIAM HENRY
Chart 2. Son of Henry and Avis (née Bath) Skewes. Born 29 May 1846, Redruth. Emigrated to Australia aboard ship *Great Britain* which left Liverpool in July 1864 and arrived at Port Phillip, Melbourne, September 1864. Also on board were a Jos. Collins and his wife Catherine. It would appear she was widowed shortly after their arrival in Australia for she married William Henry Skewes on 30 September 1869. Her maiden name was Tregoning. Children: William James (1870), Ada (1872), Henry Ernest (1875), Albert Joseph (1879), Cerceda Emily (1881) and Elizabeth Lucinda (1887). Died 10 October 1918, aged 72 years. Catherine (born 8 January 1840) died 31 May 1932, aged 92 years.

SKEWES   WILLIAM HENRY
Born 1846 Redruth. Emigrated to Australia with his mother in 1853. His father, one of the former proprietors of the Burra Mine, had arrived some 18 months earlier. Received his scholastic training at Burra Grammar School and on leaving school was apprenticed to Mr Parker, chemist of Gawler, who afterwards became his brother-in-law.
At the age of 21 he entered employment of Messrs G.N. and W.H. Birks at the Wallaroo branch of their business, which he later managed for several years. Severing his connection with this firm, he joined the staff of Messrs A.M. Bickford and Sons of Adelaide and he represented this house as traveller for seven years.
In 1877 he moved to Port Pirie and purchased the business of Mr Richard Gell.
He was a man of sterling integrity, energetic and with a thorough knowledge of his profession. He made rapid progress, and in the year 1897 built the handsome Gothic shops in Ellen Street, Port Pirie, one of which he fitted up in the best style for his own business. He took considerable interest in local public affairs and at one time represented North Ward in the Town Council.
He was a prominent member of the Congregational Church, and a member of the Masonic Fraternity.
He married Helen Nisbett, daughter of Robert Nisbett of Mitcham in 1882. Children: 2 sons — Robert John and Henry Nisbett — and 3 daughters.
Died 4 August 1901, aged 66 years.

SKEWES   WILLIAM HENRY
Died 1849, St George's East, London.

SKEWES   WILLIAM HENRY
Chart 36. Son of James and Frances Skewes, parish clerk of Mawnan Church. Born 1851. Bpt Mawnan 27 April 1851. Died 27 October 1869, aged 18 years.

SKEWES   WILLIAM HENRY
Chart 2. Son of Edward and Catherine Skewis. Born 1853. Died 1858 of cholera, aged 5 years.

SKEWS   WILLIAM HENRY
Chart 40. Son of Richard and Caroline (née Laity) Skewes. Bpt St Hilary August 1858.

SKEWS   WILLIAM HENRY
Chart 15. Born 1858. Son of Peter and Elizabeth (née Gregory) Skews of Pensilva, Liskeard. Bpt Altarnun 1 November 1858. No reference to his death in Britain. Possible emigration.

SKEWES   WILLIAM HENRY
of Gilly Lane, Cury. Died 14 January 1858, aged 18 years.

SKEWES   WILLIAM HENRY
Chart 10. Born 1863, Camborne. Grandson of James (62) and Mary (63) Mitchell. Son of William Trezize and Maria Skewes, miner of Camborne. Bpt Chacewater 27 December 1863.

SKEWS   WILLIAM HENRY
Born 1865, Redruth.

SKEWES   WILLIAM HENRY
Chart 49. Son of William and Harriet Skewes. Born 1877, Totnes. Died 1901, aged 24 years in Totnes.

SKEWES   WILLIAM HENRY
Chart 12. Son of William and Clorinda (née Salcedo) Skewes. Born 10 March 1880, Caldera district of Chile, South America.

SKEWIS   WILLIAM HENRY
Born 1884, Newton Abbot. Died 1884, aged 0.

SKEWES   WILLIAM HENRY
Married 1884, Redruth.

SKEWS   WILLIAM HENRY
Born 1885, Redruth. Died 1886, aged 1 year.

SKEWS   WILLIAM HENRY
Born 1885, Helston. Died 1886, aged 1 year.

SKEWIS   WILLIAM HENRY
Born 1889, Hendon. Died 1889, aged 0 years.

SKEWES   WILLIAM HENRY
Chart 36. Son of Henry and Elizabeth Johanna (née Ham) Skewes, tin miner. Born 30 May 1894, Condurrow, Camborne. At least twice married. 1) Gladys Harris, 1917. She died 1933, aged 38 years. 2) Beatrice Reynolds, 1936, who died in a car crash in 1951, aged 54 years. Lived at Brea, Illogan in 1922 and 1932 with Gladys. A native of Condurrow, he farmed at Brea, Kehelland and Mullion. He was a prominent figure at Cornish shows as a successful exhibitor of Jersey cattle and he was known for entries at horticultural shows as well. Children: Vera (1919), William Henry (1921), Phyllis (1918) and Priscilla (1938). Died 19 April 1956 at St Michael's Hospital, Hayle, aged 61 years. However confusion in his will, 1956 as he left his estate to Annie May Skewes, widow. £1500. An Annie May Pollard married a William Henry Skewes in Redruth, 1945. Could this be two separate William Henry Skeweses?

SKEWES   WILLIAM HENRY
Chart 2. Son of William Henry Skewes. Born 26 May 1899, Charlton, Missouri, USA. Married Clara Bertha Ahlvers 30 June 1923. Children: William M., Alan, David, Neal, Vivian and Helen Nancy.

SKEWES   WILLIAM HENRY
Chart 2. Son of William H. Skewes. Died about 1904 in a hunting accident in the United States of America. Children: William Henry, Margaret Grace, Edith and John Martin.

SKEWES   WILLIAM HENRY
Chart 36. Son of William Henry and Gladys (née Harris) Skewes of Brea. Born 1921, Redruth. Joined Royal Air Force. Flight sergeant No 1384994 with 190 Squadron. Killed in World War II in Arnhem.

SKEWES   WILLIAM HENRY
Lived at 27 Stanley Avenue, Blair Athol, Kilburn, South Australia in 1959 with Laurel Marie Skewes. Welder. Current address.

SKEWS   WILLIAM HENRY
Lived at 4 Bonleigh Avenue, Elsternwick, Victoria, Australia in 1959 with Gay Yvonne Skews. Process worker.

SKEWS   WILLIAM HENRY
Lives at 6/56 Fitzgerald Road, Essendon, 3040, Victoria, Australia. Taxi driver.

SKEWS   WILLIAM HENRY PERREN
Born 1858, Plymouth. Died 1875, aged 17 years in Plymouth.

SKEWES   WILLIAM HENRY HERBERT
Born 1887. Son of Richard and Louisa Jane Skewes of College Row, miner. Bpt Camborne 11 May 1887. Buried 23 April, 1888 aged 14 months.

SKEWES   WILLIAM HICKS
Chart 36. Born 1861, Helston. Son of John Henry and Susan Skewes of Cury, cordwainer. Bpt Cury 15 May 1861. Emigrated to Australia with his parents before 1871. Ran a hardware shop in Adelaide, South Australia. Married Elizabeth McLeod at York Peninsula, South Australia. Children: William (1883), Charles Harold Vivian (1885), Winifred (1887), Gytha Eveleen Morna (1889) and Hubert E. Mervyn (1891).
Became an orchardist at Relmsworth, Western Australia. Died 1938, aged 77 years.

SKEWS   WILLIAM HOOLIER
Born 1853, Bodmin. Died 1854. Death referred to William Hooper Skews.

SKEWIS   WILLIAM IAIN
BSc., PhD., MCIT. Chart 50. Son of John Jamieson and Margaret (née Middlemass) Skewis. Born 1 May 1936. Married Jessie Frame Weir at Dollar, Scotland, 1963. Children: Jan (1968) and Alan (1971).
Educated at Hamilton Academy and Glasgow University. PhD thesis

published as "Highlands and Islands" (1962).
British Rail (1961-1963); Transport Holding Company (1963-1966); Highlands and Islands Development Board as Head of Transport and Tourism and then Director of Industrial Development and Marketing (1966-1972). In 1973 was appointed first director of Yorkshire and Humberside Development association.
Since 1977 has been chief executive. Development Board for Rural Wales.

SKEWS   WILLIAM J.
Born 1866. Regimental birth with 52nd Regiment Aldershot. Died 1866, aged 0 in Farnham.

SKEWES   WILLIAM J.
Born 1892. Died Redruth 1963, aged 71 years.

SKEWIS   WILLIAM J.
Was a helper with Dominion Bridge Company Ltd and lived at 46 Chambers Avenue, Toronto, Canada (1921). By 1926 he had moved to Toronto Hydro, but lived at the same address.
He died about 1949. In 1951 Toronto Street Directory his wife Lillian was listed until 1960 when her surname disappeared.

SKEWES   WILLIAM JAMES
Chart 12. Born 1850. Son of William and Mary Skewes of Cury. Moved to Mawgan in Meneage. Married Susan ..... of Wendron, 1869. Children: Mary Jane (1871) and Ethel May (1883). Died 1926, aged 76 years.

SKEWIS   WILLIAM JAMES
Born 1857, Crowan. Buried Crowan 27 December 1860, aged 4 years.

SKEWIS   WILLIAM JAMES
Chart 2. Son of James and Jane Skewis. Born 27 February 1858. Married Mattie Maclean 14 May 1884. Daughter: Vara Skewis. Died May 1955, aged 97 years. Lived in Shullsburg, Wisconsin, USA.

SKEWES   WILLIAM JAMES
Born 1861, Redruth.

SKEWES   WILLIAM JAMES
Chart 2. Son of William Henry and Catherine (née Collins, née Tregoning) Skewes. Born 14 July 1870, Ballarat, Victoria, Australia. Attended Ballarat and Clunes State Schools. Assistant Town Clerk of Clunes Municipality 1888. Entered state service in 1889. Married Laura Annie Davies (she born 27 March 1870) on 15 April 1895. Children: Clarence George (1897), Gordon William (1900) and Linda Laura (1907). Had a distinguished career in Government service including: President of Clifton Hills Branch of Australian Natives Association (1900); Secretary to Royal Commission on the Shops and Factories Acts; Secretary to the Queensland Gun Accident Board; Secretary to the Neglected Children's Conference; Private Secretary to each successive Minister of Education from 1890-1900; Amanuensis to Lord Brassey; Secretary to Royal Commission on Technical Education.
Was appointed to membership of the Commonwealth Public Service Board, as a member under Sir Brudinell White and finally became Chairman of the Board until he retired.
Lived at three addresses in Malvern, but retired to Grandview Road, Glen Iris, Victoria, Australia. Died 13 July 1954, aged 84 years. Laura Annie died 25 February 1932, aged 61 years.

SKEWES   WILLIAM JAMES
Born 1885, Redruth. Died 1886, aged 6 months.

SKUES   WILLIAM JAMES GORDON
Chart 3. Son of Richard Skues, surgeon of 4 Ham Street, Plymouth. Born 1837. Customs House Officer of 30 Clarence Place, Plymouth. Married Margaret Oliver, aged 23 years of Catherine Street, Plymouth, daughter of John Oliver, butcher, at St Andrew's Parish Church 22 May 1858. Died 1892, aged 55 years. Margaret died 1882, aged 46 years.

SKEWIS   WILLIAM JAMIESON
Born 1888 Camalchie, Glasgow.

SKEWES   WILLIAM JESSOP
Son of William and Elizabeth Alberta Mary (née Jessop) Skewes. Born 31 January 1900 at Keararge, Houghton, Michigan, USA. Married Ann Gardner.

SKUES   WILLIAM JOHN
Son of William and Jane Skues of Flushing, Falmouth. Bpt Mylor November 1815. Buried Mylor 27 May 1817, aged 18 months.

SKEWIS   WILLIAM JOHN
Chart 14. Son of Anthony and Christian (née Lugg) Skewes, of Ruan Major. Born 17 December 1849. Bpt Ruan Major 2 June 1850. Listed in 1871 Census Returns as a farmer's assistant. Lived with his parents and sisters Ann and Catherine and brothers Henry, Samuel, Hannibal and George. Emigrated to Wisconsin, USA.
Lived at Yorkville, Racine County, USA. Married Prudence Mundy. Children: Catherine Mary, William M., James Henry. Connected with Grange Avenue Methodist Church, Racine.
Died October 1913, aged 63 years.

SKEWES   WILLIAM JOHN
Chart 25. Son of Charles and Elizabeth Skewes. Born 1860. Listed in 1861 Census Returns as living at Smithwick Hill, Falmouth. In 1871 Census Returns (then aged 11) he was an errand boy for a grocer and lived with his parents and sister Louisa J. and brothers Charles, George and Edward at Brook Street, Falmouth. Married Jane Jameson (34) at Lower Broughton, Manchester on 14 August 1881. Children: William

(1883), Frederick (1885). Although descendants indicate William John Skewes died in Manchester in 1898 (at Churchill Street, Chorlton on Medlock), the General Register Office in London does not hold any death certificate. However, from Australia there is a tombstone in St Thomas' Cemetery, Sydney, saying: "William Skewes, late of Manchester, England, died 6 October 1900, aged 41 years."

SKEWES   WILLIAM JOHN
Son of William and Elizabeth (née Jose) Skewes of Trevarth, Gwennap, copper miner. Born 23 September 1861. Bpt Gwennap 20 July 1862.

SKEWES   WILLIAM JOHN
Chart 41. Son of Matthew and Betsy (née Tresider) Skews, lead miner. Born 5 April 1862, Padstow. Coal miner who moved north to County Durham. Twice married: 1) Rebecca Crago (she born 1859 — died 1892, aged 33 years). Children: Matthew, Clara, Frederick, Edward and Edith Jane.
2) Mary Ann Whysall, formerly Kirtly, 1894, Sunderland. Children: Mary Ann (1895) and William John (1898). Lived at 44 Elemore Lane, Easington Lane, Hetton-le-Hole, County Durham. Died 21 November 1935, aged 73 years.

Mary Ann & William John Skews of County Durham

SKEWES   WILLIAM JOHN
Born 1869. Son of William James and Susan Skewes of Cury, labourer. Bpt Cury 8 November 1869. Died 1870, aged 1 year.

SKUES   WILLIAM JOHN
Chart 5. Born 2 February 1880. Son of Charles Penrose Skues. Married Eva Garvey in Amersham, Bucks, 1911 (she died 3 July 1966, Truro, aged 77 years). Child: Vivian William, who lives in America. Lived at Fern Cottage, Fore Street, Probus. Died March 1976, aged 96 years.

SKEWES   WILLIAM JOHN
Married 1881, Helston.

SKEWES   WILLIAM JOHN
Born 1888. Died Redruth 1961, aged 73 years

SKEWS   WILLIAM JOHN
Born 1890, Easington. Died 1890, aged 0.

SKEWES   WILLIAM JOHN
Chart 12. Born 1891. Married Edith Mary Truran (born 1891, died 1956, aged 65 years), 1910, Redruth. Lived Carnmarth North, 1922; Carnarthen Farm, Brea Adit, 1932. He lived away from home for much of his married life. Children: John Henry (Froggie), Horace, Roy, Muriel and Doriel. Died at 28 Albany Road, Redruth 8 October 1949, aged 58 years.

SKEWES   WILLIAM JOHN
Born 1893. Son of William John Skewes, painter of Calenick Street, Truro. Married Rose Drew of 24 Charles Street, Truro (father not known) at St John's , Truro 17 February 1921. Lived at Daniell Square, Truro. Children: Marion Joyce (1921) and Cereta Betty (1924).

SKEWS   WILLIAM JOHN
Married 1894, Sunderland.

SKEWS   WILLIAM JOHN
Chart 41. Son of William John and Mary Ann (née Whysall, formerly Kirtley) Skews. Born 23 May 1898, Elemore Lane, Hetton-le-Hole. Educated at local village school. Married Mary Hannah Weightman Rump, 21 June at Hetton-le-Hole Wesleyan Chapel. Children: Muriel (1920), Kirtley (1923), William Clifford (1925), Janet Audrey (1928), George David (1931), John Hilary (1933) and Roland Gerald (1938). Land sale agent for Coal Board. Diocesan lay reader for 30 years. Died 29 January 1955 in Durham North, aged 56 years.

SKEWES   WILLIAM JOHN
Chart 12. Born 21 October 1900. Illegitimate son of Ellen Janie Skewes of Cury. Married Bessie Curnow 10 December 1925 at Landewednack Church, most southerly church in Great Britain. Farmer and later postman.
Children; William John, Ronnie and Maurice. Lived at 42 Redannick Estate, Mullion, Helston. Died 12 June 1977, aged 77 years.

SKEWS   WILLIAM JOHN
Chart 10. Son of Peter and Maude Mary Skews. Born 1903, St Austell. Died St Austell 1927, aged 24 years.

SKEWES   WILLIAM JOHN
Chart 12. Son of John and Cissie (née Gilbert) Skewes. Born 21 September 1911 at Ledra Mill, Ruan Minor. Married Nora Thomas of Manaccan 5 July 1933 at Helston Register Office. Children: Anthony Ronald (1933), Barbara Joan (1934), Gilbert James (1937), Rosalie Susan (1940), John Osburn (1945), Jeffrey Lional (1946), Paul (1948), Jack (1951) and Sally (1955).
He was a farmer at Tregarne, St Keverne for 25 years. Retired 1976. Lives at 78 Wheal Rose, Porthlevan, Helston, Tel No: 03265 62344.

SKEWES   WILLIAM JOHN
Lived at Condurrow, Camborne, 1922 and at Condurrow Farm, Camborne, 1932 with Lillian May Skewes.

SKEWES   WILLIAM JOHN
Chart 12. Son of William John and Bessie (née Curnow) Skewes. Born 4 October 1927, Mullion. Married Wendy Violet Williams at Mullion Church 12 September 1946. Children: Carol Wendy (1947), Christopher John (1948), Peter Neil (1951) and Paul Andrew (1964). Carpet fitter. Lives at 27 Beacon Parc, Helston. Tel no: 03265 4722.

SKEWES   WILLIAM JOHN
Chart 2. Son of Gordon William and Eileen Margaret (née Tritchler) Skewes. Born 12 June 1934, Australia. Married Barbara Mackay Carroll 7 April 1962. Children: Andrew William (1964), Debra Christine (1965) and Richard John (1970).

SKEWES   WILLIAM JOHN
Chart 46. Son of William Douglas and Gladys Maud (née Little) Skewes of Carclew Cottages, Truro. Born 26 July 1943. Bpt St John's, Truro, 3 September 1943. Married Watkins, Truro, 1968. Later divorced. Married Sheila Mary Pope of Newquay 8 June 1973. Lives at 22 Chapel Close, Crantock, Newquay.

SKEWES   WILLIAM JOHN
Lived at 256 Camberwell Road, Camberwell, Victoria, Australia in 1959. Chemist.

SKEWES   WILLIAM JOHN
Lives at 40 Kitchener Street, Broadmeadows, 3047, Victoria, Australia with Barbara Joyce Skewes, dressmaker. Driver.

SKEWES   WILLIAM JOHN P.
Born 1977, Truro. Mother's maiden name Hall.

SKEWES   WILLIAM JOSEPH
Chart 10. Son of John Joseph Skewes of Marazion. Born 29 August 1895, Philadelphia, Pa, USA. Moved to Hamilton, Ontario, Canada. Married Mabel Alice Johnson 26 April 1916. Died 11 February 1920. His wife died 20 February 1920. Child: Violet (1919).

SKEWES   WILLIAM JOSIAH
Lived at 46 Banksia Street, Heidelberg, Victoria, Australia in 1959 with Kathleen Marguerite Skewes. Accountant.

SKEWES   WILLIAM KEITH
Lived at 101 Normandy Street, Inglewood, Marylands, Australia in 1959 with Veronica Dawn Skewes. Radio mechanic.

SKEWES   WILLIAM L.
Born 1866, Truro.

SKEWES   WILLIAM M.
Chart 14. Son of William John and Prudence (née Mundy) Skewes. Born in Racine County, Wisconsin, USA. Married Mary Reamussen. One son, Edwin Skewes.

SKUES   WILLIAM MACKENZIE
Chart 3. M.D., M.B. Son of Lieutenant George and Mary Gibbs (née Mackenzie) Skues, Royal Marines. Born 15 March 1828, Aberdeen. Bpt St Nicholas Church, Aberdeen, 15 April 1828.
Surgeon. Licentiate Royal College of Surgeons (Edinburgh), 1852; M.B. Maris College, Aberdeen 1853; M.D. 1860.
Married Margaret Ayre, daughter of Christopher Ayre, clerk to Parliament, St John's, Newfoundland on 2 October 1857 in Newfoundland.
Assistant Surgeon to Forces 29 July 1853; Royal Newfoundland Company 2 November 1855; Staff 21 September 1860; Surgeon to Forces 8 July 1862 — Army Medical Department — Surgeon Major, 109th Regiment of Foot 28 June 1864. Staff 23 July 1870. Retired 2 December 1881 with rank of Brigade Surgeon.
Children; George Edward Mackenzie, Mary Isabella, Margaret Caroline, Gertrude, Fred William, Minnie Mackenzie, Elsie and Charles Ayre Mackenzie.
Wife Margaret lived at 4 Alfred Road, St John's Wood, London in 1868 Street Directory. Died 18 June 1892 in Nunhead, Surrey, aged 64 years.
Wife Margaret died 5 June 1890, aged 54 years.

SKEWES   WILLIAM MARTIN
Chart 2. Son of William Henry and Clara Bertha (née Ahlvers) Skewes. Born 10 July 1928, St Louis, Missouri, USA. Married Laverne Helen Getty, 27 June 1959. Children: Steven Alan (1960), Robert Henry (1965) and Karen Marie (1967). Lives at 3105 Texas Avenue South, Minneapolis, Minnesota, 55426, USA.

SKEWES   WILLIAM MUNDY
Chart 10. Born 1884, Helston.

SKEWES   WILLIAM PERCIVAL
Lived at 46 Brighton Road, Glenelg, South Australia in 1959 with Daisy Skewes.

SKEWES   WILLIAM QUARME
Received his warrant from the Admiralty Office in London on 20 April 1810.

SKEWES   WILLIAM R.
Born 1893, South Shields. Married Maggie I.S. Wills, South Shields, 1918. No children. Died 1925, aged 32 years.

SKEWES   WILLIAM RAYMOND
Chart 14. Son of Charles J. and Loretta Jean (née Swanson) Skewes. Lives in Wisconsin, USA.

SKEWIS   WILLIAM RICHARD
Chart 33. Son of Daniel and Elizabeth Jane (née Willcott) Skewis; miner of Bell Mount, Ashburton, Devon. Born 9 August 1872. Married Lavinia Shute, daughter of James Shute, wheelwright, 24 December 1898 at Buckfastleigh, Devon. Children: Olive May (1900), Fearnley John (1902), Ronald (1904), John (1907), Vida (1908), Ettie (1909), Clarence James (1911) and Dorothy M. (1912).
Gardener and groom for two doctors who were in partnership. Visited and worked in America on three occasions.
Buried 4 May 1957 at Buckfastleigh, Devon, aged 84 years.

William John Skewes with two of his sons Jeffrey Lional (left) and Anthony Ronald (right), 1979

SKEWES   WILLIAM RICHARD
Born 1891, Redruth. Bpt Camborne 17 January 1892. Son of Richard and Louisa Jane Skewes of College Row, Camborne, miner.

SKEWES   WILLIAM RICHARD
Chart 40. Stepson of William and Laura Skewes. Mother's maiden name Roberts. Born 1913, Penzance. Married Thelma Moon, 1936, in Penzance. Farmer and market gardener. Children: William Roger (1938), Colin and Elizabeth Ann — twins (1947) and Richard John (1943). Freemason with Cornubian Lodge 450 since 1945. Lives at Trebarvah Farm, Perranuthnoe, Penzance. Tel No: 0736 710430.

SKEWS   WILLIAM RICHARD FRANCIS DENNIS
Chart 10. Son of William and Mary Skews. Born 1840, Kenwyn. Blacksmith and tailor. Bpt Chacewater 27 September 1840. Married Jane .... 1864, Redruth. Lived at Penrlos House, St Columb. Children: Mary and Beatrice. Died 5 January 1914, aged 74 years. Jane died 1913, aged 73 years at St Columb.

SKEWES   WILLIAM ROE
Chart 36. Son of John Henry and Annie (née Shillabeer) Skewes. Born 5 June 1895. Children: Jack Roe Skewes (1919), Phyllis Jean (1923) and Colin Arthur Skewes (1927). Lived at 47 Harvey Street, Woodville Park, South Australia. Wife's name Evelyn Dorothy. Died 7 July 1967, aged 72 years.

SKEWES   WILLIAM ROGER
Chart 40. Son of William Richard Skewes. Mother's maiden name Moon. Born 1938, Penzance. Married ... Richards, Penzance, 1959. Market gardener. Lives at Chiverton Way, Rosudgeon, Penzance. Tel No Germoe 3344.

SKEWIS   WILLIAM S.
Mother's maiden name Lyons. Born 1964, Kettering, Northants.

SKEWES   WILLIAM SEYMOUR
Chart 38. Son of Ernest Seymour and Eleanor May (née Stapleton) Skewes. Born 27 November 1925 at Rosewater, Adelaide, South Australia. Married Glenda Lorraine Walter 12 June 1965. Children: Craig William (1969) and Bryon Anthony (1974).
Bootmaker since 1940. Member of Orchid Club of Thebarton, Adelaide. Lives at 15 Alawa Avenue, Modbury North, Adelaide, 5092, South Australia.

SKEWIS   WILLIAM STARK
Chart 50. Son of William Skewis, coal miner and Martha Barclay (née Stark) Skewis. Born 6.40am 10 October 1913 at 33 Flower Hill, Airdrie, Scotland. Died Dennistoun, 1933 aged 19 years.

SKEWIS   WILLIAM STRATHEWAY
Born 1891, Ulverston.

SKUISE WILLIAM S.H.
Married 1911, Lambeth, London.

SKEWES   WILLIAM TAYLOR
Chart 2. Son of John Billing and Mary Jo (née Armington) Skewes. Born 5 April 1961, Salt Lake City, Utah, USA. Lives at 133 W 1800 South, Bountiful, Salt Lake City, Utah, USA, 84010.

SKUS   WILLIAM THOMAS
Son of Thomas and Ann Skus. Bpt St Ewe 27 March 1836.

SKUCE   WILLIAM THOMAS
Born 10 October 1813, Crawley, Sussex. Emigrated to Australia on *Tam O'Shanter,* arriving in Adelaide 26 November 1836. Married 31 July 1838. Issue: Four sons and one daughter. Died South Australia 2 May 1861, aged 48 years.

SKEWS   WILLIAM THOMAS
Chart 17. Born 5 February 1877 at 8 Marian Street, Hackney Road, Bethnal Green, London. Son of George and Lucy Skews, wood turner. Lived at 29 Gales Gardens, Bethnal Green. Wood turner. Married Emily Homan and moved to 51 Sale Street, London E.2. Child: David George (1899). Died 10 December 1943, aged 66 years in Bethnal Green Hospital.

SKEWES   WILLIAM THOMAS
Lived at 33 Guthrie Street, Brunswick South, Victoria, Australia in 1959 with Hazel Netta Skewes. Carrier.

SKUES   WILLIAM THOMAS
Son of William and Margaret Skues. Born 21 April 1891. Married Vera Louise Ashdown, 1919. Child: William Ashdown Skues (1924).

SKEWES   WILLIAM THOMAS
Lived at Lot 17, Thompson Road, Geelong North, Victoria, Australia in 1959 with Joan Morva Skewes. Engineer.
Now lives at 543 Thompson Road, Norlane, 3214, Victoria, Australia with Joan Morva Skewes and Julie Marion Skewes.

SKEWES   WILLIAM TREZIZE
Chart 10. Son of Thomas and Grace Skewes of Redruth, farmer and miner. Born 1844. Bpt Chacewater 6 October 1844. Married Maria Mitchell, daughter of James Mitchell, miner 28 June 1862. Lived at Carnkie, Illogan, 1906. Children: William Henry (1863) and Alfred (1865).

SKEWES   WILLIAM TREVENA
Chart 10. Son of Samuel and Clara (née Trevena) Skewes. Born 11 June 1890. Bpt 2 September 1890. Married Edith Jenkin, 1915. Daughter: Violet May (1918). Lived at Mount Carne Farm, Nancladra, Ludgvan, Penzance. Died 14 September 1953, aged 63 years at St Michael's Hospital, Hayle.

SKUES   WILLIAM TRUSCOTT
Chart 9. Son of James and Joanna Skues of Lower Sticker, St Ewe. Born 1812. Married Lelia Little, daughter of John Little, miner of St Ewe at the Register Office, St Austell 6 September 1840. Carpenter who made window frames for the Houses of Parliament and helped put the facing on Big Ben. Children: William, Charles John, Thomas, James and Philip Henry. Died 21 February 1876, aged 64 years.

SKEWES   WILLIAM VERDAYNE
See William born 1875.

SKEWES   WILLIAM VERE
Chart 36. Son of George and Mary (née Dowling) Skewes. Born 7 June 1902, Rocky River, Uralla, New South Wales, Australia. Married Annie Rebecca Strain, 24 August 1926. Children: Irene Mary, Joan Bentley, Jill, Robert, Max, Bruce and William George. Lived at Gympie, Queensland, Australia. Died 24 August 1947, Tamworth, New South Wales, Australia, aged 45 years.

William Seymour Skewes

William Vere Skewes

SKEWES WILLIAM WHITE
Born 1871, Helston. Son of W. Skewes. Died at Ford's Row, Redruth 22 April 1890, aged 17 years.

SKEWES WILLIAM WILFRED JOHN
Chart 36. Son of William Hicks and Elizabeth (née McLeod) Skewes. Born 1883, Yorke Peninsula, South Australia. Moved to Western Australia at the turn of the century where his father managed a store in Narrogin.
His first love was music and later in life turned to it to earn a living, setting up a music shop in Bunbury. He married Annie Borgas of Narrogin in 1908. Children: Gwen (1909), Hope (1913) and William Wilfred Keith (1919).
Became Mayor of Bunbury 1925/1926. An energetic and civic-minded leader.
He continued his interest in civic affairs as a councillor at Subiaco. He spent periods of time in Perth and Albany before eventually settling in Narrogin, where he married Dorothy Small in 1944, following the death of his first wife in 1941. Child: David (1945).
Member of Toc H. President of Native Welfare Committee of Western Australia. Secretary of the Baptist Men's Association.
Died in Narrogin Hospital, 19 November 1959, aged 76 years. Buried in the Baptist portion of the Narrogin cemetery.

SKEWES WILLIAM WILFRED KEITH
Chart 36. Son of William Wilfred John and Annie (née Borgas) Skewes. Born 3 February 1919, Leaderville, Western Australia. Married Veronica Dawn Bellis. No children. Radio technician. Lives at 195 Coode Street, Bedford, 6052, Western Australia. Telephone number: Perth 271 4969.

Keith Skues meets Keith Skewes in Perth, Western Australia, 1981

SKEWIS WILLIAMINA AGNES
Chart 50. Daughter of William and Ellen (née Blyth) Skewis. Born 1910, Dennistoun, Scotland. Married McKechnie, 1936, Pancras, London. Lives at 183 Petershill Drive, Flat 16/2, Balornock, Glasgow.

SKEWES WILMET
Son of Thomas and Mary Skewes. Bpt St Martin in Meneage 14 October 1716.

SKEWES WILLMOTE
Daughter of Richard Skewes. Bpt St Keverne 16 March 1633. Married Thomas Oliver 30 December 1661 at St Keverne Parish Church.

SKEWES WILSON
Lives at 87 Union Avenue, Lynbrook, Nassau, Manhattan, New York, USA. Tel No: (516) 593 4229. Also at 51 Ebway, Roslyn, Nassau, Manhattan, New York, USA. Tel no: (516) MAI 7947.

SKEWES WILSON E.
Lives at 87 Union Avenue, Lynbrook, Nassau, Manhattan, New York, USA. Tel No: (516) LY9 2275.

SKEWES WINIFRED
Chart 36. Daughter of William Hicks and Elizabeth (née McLeod) Skewes. Born Australia 1887. Married George Robson. Issue: 3 sons. Died 1975, aged 88 years.

SKEWS WINIFRED
Married Lawry, 1937, St Germans.

SKEWES WINIFRED A.
Chart 47. Son of Samuel John and Charlotte Skewes. Mother's maiden name Whiting. Born 1915, Bodmin.

SKUES WINIFRED C.
Née Kethro. Wife of Christopher Herbert Victor Skues whom she married in 1941. Child: Carol C.A. Skues (1942). She later married Reginald H. Morgan, 1952 in Bristol.

SKEWES WINIFRED JEAN
Chart 18. Daughter of Arthur Dawe and Eva Skewes. Mother's maiden name Vallantine. Born 1920, Plympton. Married Van Doran in Los Angeles, 1953. Issue: three children.

SKEWIS WINIFRED KATE
Chart 34. Née Baker. Married Frank Skewis 6 December 1930 at Greenhythe, Kent. Children: Barbara M. (1931) and Trevor (1942). Frank died 1949. Winifred Kate remarried Worgan, 1949 at Bridge.

SKEWS WINIFRED MARY
Chart 15. Daughter of John Gregory and Annie (née Gartrell) Skews. Born 1898, Liskeard. Married John Kelly in Plymouth, 1931. Issue: 2 daughters and 1 son.

SKUES WINIFRED ROSE
Chart 8. Née Seebright. Born 1865. Married George Henry Skues at Paddington, 1888. Children: Winifred Rose (1893) and Thomas George (1894). Died 23 February 1924 at Park Hospital, Acton Lane, Middlesex, aged 59 years.

SKUES WINIFRED ROSE
Chart 8. Daughter of George Henry Skues. Born 1893, Pancras. Married Ralph C. Cary in Newton Abbot, 1919. Lives at "Louville", 31 Cecilia Road, Paignton, Devon.

SKUES WINIFRED VIOLET
Born 1884, Westminster. Died 1885, aged 1 year.

SKEWES WINNIE
Chart 10. Daughter of John and Sarah Skewes of Kenwyn, shoemaker. Born 1899. Bpt 27 February 1900 at Bible Christian Chapel, Truro. Married 1924, Oliver at Truro.

Y

SKEWES YOLANDE
Chart 2. Daughter of Luis Enrique Skewes. Born Mexico. Died when only 5 years old.

SKEWES YVONNE
Chart 36. Daughter of James William and Pauline Beatrice (née Seymour) Skewes. Born 14 June 1945, Watsons Creek, Bendemeer, New South Wales, Australia.

SKEWS YVONNE M.
Mother's maiden name Parsons. Born 1934, Birmingham. Married Chapman in Birmingham, 1954.

SKEWES YVONNE MARIE
Lives at 8 Maysbury Avenue, Elsternwick, 3185, Victoria, Australia with Brian Lawrence Skewes, TV mechanic. Typist.

Z

SKEWIS ZEVERINO SEVERO
Chart 2. Son of James Enrique and Juana (née Brito) Skewis. Born 27 August 1899.

SKEWES ZOE NAOMI
Chart 2. Daughter of Robert William and Wendy (née Andrew) Skewes. Born 29 January 1981. Lives at Willung Road, Rosedale, Victoria, 3847, Australia.

SKEWS ZOWIE
Chart 15. Daughter of Andrew J and Pamela L. (née Searle) Skews. Born 1976. Lives at 19 Fairfield Estate, St Germans, Plymouth. Tel No: 05033 557.

SKEWIS ZQUIN JAMES B.
Chart 50. Son of David Skewis. Mother's maiden name Bratton. Born 1974, Hull.

Double Barrelled SKEWES'

SKEWES-BENNEY
Clara Skewes Benney (21) of Mill Lane, Helston, daughter of Thomas Benney, farmer, married Ernest Opie (32), farmer of East End, Stithians, son of Thomas Opie, deceased, grocer at Helston Methodist Church 16 December 1910.

SKEWES-BRAY, CHRISTIANA ALEXANDRINA
of Lanner House, Gwennap. Born 1858. Buried Gwennap 18 December 1923, aged 65 years.

SKEWES-BRAY, GEORGE
Solicitor from Redruth. Appeared in a court case claiming £923 from John Mitchell Phillips. Skewes-Bray won the case *(West Briton — 16 June 1898).*

SKEWES-COX, (Male)
Mother's maiden name Struban. Born 1920, Farnsham.

SKEWES-COX, B.
Author of *Peace in the Lexicon of U.S. Foreign Policy Decision Makers,* Washington, 1965. Typewritten.

SKEWES-COX, ELIZABETH D.
Wife of Martin V. Skewes-Cox, personnel manager, Balfour Guthrie & Co., 2203 Divisadero, San Francisco, USA, in 1971.

SKEWES-COX, EVELYN MARY
Fourth child and only daughter of Sir Thomas Skewes-Cox. Born 1885. Married 23 September 1905 to Captain Eric Mosley Mayne, A.P.D.: at Richmond, Surrey.

SKEWES-COX, FLORENCE LILIAN
Born 12 November 1894. Died Waveney, 1978, aged 84 years.

SKEWES-COX, JESSIE
Only daughter of the late Edward Warne of London. Born 1862. Married Thomas Skewes-Cox, solicitor and JP in 1882. He was later Alderman and Mayor of Richmond (1892). She lived at Laburnham Cottage, Petersham, Surrey. Died 18 May 1930, aged 68 years.

SKEWES-COX, JULIAN H.L.
Mother's maiden name Macmullan. Born 1953, Marylebone. Died 1954, aged 1 year in St Albans.

SKEWES-COX, MARGARET
Born 1887, Richmond South. Died 1887, aged 0.

SKEWES-COX, MARTIN V.
Personnel manager, Balfour Guthrie and Company, 2203 Divisadero, San Francisco, USA in 1961. Wife's name: Elizabeth D. Skewes-Cox.

SKEWES-COX, MILES L.D.
Lieut. Colonel. Born 1920. Married Gillian Macmullen, 1948. Daughter: Nicola. Lieutenant colonel in Royal Army Pay Corps. Lived at 62 Hyde Vale, London, SE 10. Gillian died 4 November 1976 after a sudden illness.
In 1976 he moved to Uphill House, Ponsworthy, Ashburton, Devon. Telephone number: 03643 386. Married Hirsch at Westminster, 1978. Was founder and chairman of the Dartmoor Badger Protection League in 1979 which had over 10,000 members.
Found unconscious with head injuries at his home in Uphill House on 19 December 1979 and died on Boxing Day in Torbay Hospital. He did not regain consciousness.

SKEWES-COX PAMELA S.
Married Trotton, 1942, Westminster.

SKEWES-COX, ROBIN W.
President, David Ward Company, 2465 Washington, San Francisco in 1961. Wife's name Sylvia F. Skewes-Cox.

SKEWES-COX, ST JOHN
Third son of Sir Thomas and Jessie (née Warne) Skewes-Cox. Born 3 July 1893.

SKEWES-COX, SUSETTE P.
Mother's maiden name Struben. Born 1916, Newton Abbot, Devon. Lived at 411 Nell Gwynne House, Sloane Avenue, London SW 3.

SKEWES-COX, SYLVIA F.
Wife of Robin W. Skewes-Cox, President, David Ward Company, 2465 Washington, San Francisco, USA in 1961.

SKEWES-COX, Sir THOMAS
Born 6 February 1849, son of William Nicholas Cox of Richmond, Surrey. Assumed the prefix Skewes in 1874. Married Jessie Warne, only daughter of Edward Warne of London (she died 1930, aged 68 years). He was a JP, Alderman and in 1892 Mayor of Richmond. Was County Alderman for Surrey. Chairman of Isleworth Brewery. Member of the Thames Conservancy Board. Conservative MP for Kingston Division 1895-1906. Chairman of Richmond Horticultural Society. Director of Richmond Royal Horse Show. Children: Three sons and one daughter. Member of Carlton Club and Badminton Club. Was created a knight, 1905. Professional job — solicitor at 8 Lancaster Place, Strand, London WC. Lived at The Manor House, Petersham, Surrey. Died 15 November 1912, aged 63 years.

SKEWES-COX, THOMAS EDMUND
Son of Sir Thomas and Jessie (née Warne) Skewes-Cox. Born 5 January 1884, Richmond South. Married Florence Lilian Struben of Spitchwick Manor, Ashburton, Devon, daughter of Frederick Struben, 22 August

1914.
Major in East Lancs Regiment. Children: (male — 1920) and Susette P. (1916). Died at Providence Cottage, South Green, Southwold, Suffolk 26 March 1971, aged 86 years. Requiem Mass at Roman Catholic Church, Southwold, 30 March at 2.30pm which was followed by private cremation.

SKEWES-COX, VERNON
Second son of Sir Thomas and Jessie (née Warne) Skewes-Cox. Born 24 August 1885, Richmond South. Emigrated to the United States of America in 1937. Was deputy manager, Balfour Guthrie and Company, 2020 Broadway, San Francisco, USA.

SKEWIS-FARR, MARGARET
Buried Gwithian 3 July 1902.

SKEWES-HEARD, PHILIPPA
Born 1853. Lived at 59 Enys Road, Camborne. Buried Camborne 25 March 1947, aged 94 years.

SKEWES-LUGG, HENRY
Son of James Lugg, labourer. Married Eleanor Carlyon, of St Martin, daughter of John Carlyon, schoolmaster of St Martin 2 January 1859. Henry was born 1833.

SKEWES-MARTIN, RICHARD
Born 1830. Buried Helston 24 November 1897, aged 67 years.

SKUES-PASCOE, ELIZABETH
Born 1838. Buried Helston 12 January 1837, aged 1 year.

SKUES-PASCOE, HENRY
Born 1840, Helston. Buried 12 April 1840; infant.

SKEWES-PHILLIPS, BERTRAM
Farm labourer. Born 1915. Son of John Skewes Phillips, labourer. Married Christiana Laity (25) of 67 North Roskear Road, Tuckingmill, daughter of William Thomas Laity, deceased, at Tuckingmill Parish Church 26 December 1940.

SKEWES-ROWE, WILLIAM THOMAS
Born 1895, Son of William Thomas Rowe, gardener, deceased of Trelowarren, Mawgan, Helston. Married Sarah Jane Cooke (born 1895) daughter of William Thomas Cooke, builder of Rosevear, Mawgan at Helston Methodist Church 17 January 1917.

SKEWES-SAUNDERS, THOMAS
Lived in Mexico. His wife August Edith Gertrude died 22 August 1905 at Compania Minerata de Penoles, Mapami, Estado de Durango, Mexico, aged 28 years.

SKEWES-TEAGUE, RICHARD
Born 1829. Lived at Illogan Highway, Redruth, 1885-1897. Buried Gwennap 1 June 1905, aged 76 years.

SKEWES-WASLEY, WILLIAM
Born 1878. Son of William Wasley, farmer, deceased. Lived at Boscolla, Kenwyn. Married Lavinia Jane Hore (28), daughter of William Hore, market gardener at Kenwyn Parish Church 20 April 1905.

APPENDIX

CORNWALL FEET OF FINES 1195-1461

(Edited by J.H. Rowe, Devon & Cornwall Record Society, 1914) Feet of Fines are records of lawsuits. A fine may be described briefly as being in substance a conveyance of land, and in form a compromise of an action at law. Feet of Fines is the name given to the terms agreed upon and registered in court after a friendly suit whereby in early terms an interest in free land was conveyed from party to party.

Reference: (5) At Westminster, on the actave of the Purification of the Blessed Mary, in the first year of King John (9 February 1200).

Before Geoffrey, son of Peter, William de Warenne, Richard de Her (iet), Simon de Pateshill, Osbert, son of Herevey, John de G(eslinges), justices and other barons of our lord the King there present. Between Hugh le Macun, plaintiff by Hugh, his son, in his place, and WILLIAM DE ESCHES (SKEWES), tenant, by Peter, son of of Ernold in his place; as to a messuage in Bomine (Bodmin). William acknowledges the messuage to the right of Hugh. For this, Hugh granted the messuage to William and his heirs to hold of him and his heirs for ever by the service of 2½ pence yearly for all service, to be rendered at Easter. For this William gave Hugh 50 shillings sterling.

Ref: 28 April 1214
ODO DE SKEWIOT (SKEWES) holds Walebravuse and Lameinwal Manors.

Ref: 445 A.D. 1315
At Westminster, on the morrow of St Martin, 9 Edward II (12 November, 1315).
Before William de Bereford, Lambert de Trikyngham, John de Benstede, Henry le Scrop, William Inge and John Bacun, Justices and others.
Between John de Kelennen and Gilda his wife, claimants and John de Bosvurgh (Vicar of Paul, 1317), Chaplain, deforciant; as to 2 Messuages and a Moiety of one acre of land in Kelennen and Gonelgy. Plea of Covenant was summoned. John de Kelennen acknowledged the tenement to be the right of John de Bosvuragh as by gift of John de Kelennen. For this John de Bosvuragh granted them to John de Kelennen and Gilda, and gave them up the Court. To have and to hold to John de Kelennen and Gilda during their lives of the Chief Lords of that fee by the services which belong to those tenements.
After their deaths the tenements shall revert in their entirety to NICHOLAS de SKEWYS (SKEWES in Crowan or SKEWS in Cury) and MARGERY his wife and his heirs by her. To hold of the Chief Lords of that fee by the services which belong to those tenements for ever.
Should Nicholas die without heir of his body by Margaret then after the deaths of both Nicholas and Margaret the tenements shall revert in their entirety to JOHN de SKEWYS Junior and the heirs of his body. To hold as aforesaid for ever. Should he die without heir of his body then the tenements shall revert in their entirety to the right heirs of the aforesaid John de Kelennen. To hold as aforesaid for ever.

LAY SUBSIDY ROLLS

In the Lay Subsidy Roll for 1327 for the parish of St Wenn JOHNE SKEU (JOHN SKEWYS) of Helston and Wendron paid two shillings.
JOHNA SKEWYS (JOHN SKEWYS) of the parish Cury was taxed 6 pence.
In the Lay Subsidy Roll for 1523 for the parish of Kenwyn JOHNE SKEWKEK (JOHN SKEWYS) in a partnership owned goods valued at £5. Tax paid was 2/6d.

From THOMAS CHIVERTON's "BOOK OF OBITS."

JOHN de SKEWYS of St Crewyb (Crowan) had a daughter and heir DEONISE (DIONYSIA) who married Henry Serle of SKEWIS, Crowan. She died 4 July 1349.

CALENDAR OF FINE ROLLS 1272 - 1471

The FINE ROLLS take their name from the enrolment of them of Fines or payments made for Writs, Grants, Licences, Pardons and exemptions of various kinds.

These Rolls are presented in 14 Volumes from 1272 to 1471 and are retained at the Public Record Office in London.

The following are references to the Skewes family.

8 February 1350 Westminster:	**Membrane 48** Order to Amaury Fitz Waryn, escheator in the county of Devon — pursuant to an inquisition made by him shewing that William de Botreaux held in chief by Knight service on the day of his death, as of the right of Isabel his wife, the Manor of Dupeford in demesne, with the hundred of Stanburgh, and that he held no other lands in demesne in the said county, either of the King or of any other lord, because sometime before his death he demised the manors of Molland with its woods, mills and other appurtances, and with the hundred of Molland, to Robert de Ford, Thomas Gova, John Proutz, JOHN de SKEWYS and John de Chageford, clerk, for their lives, and the manors of Stokeleigh

Englisch to Thomas, his son, for life, the said manors of Molland and Stokeleigh being held by divers service of other lords — to retain in the King's hand until further order the manor of Dupeford with the hundred of Stanburgh and to meddle no further the manors of Molland and Stokeleigh, or the hundred of Molland, delivering any issues he has taken therefrom to those whom they belong.

14 April, 1399
Westminster:

Membrane 26
Order to the escheator in the county of Cornwall to take into the King's hand and keep safely until further order the lands whereof ISABEL SKEWYS of Cornwall, was seized in demesne as of fee on the day of her death, and to make inquisition touching her lands and heir.

25 October, 1397
Westminster:

Membrane 25
Commitment to William Tregos by mainprise of John Rosemeryn, JOHN SKUYS and William Kaelwe all of the county of Cornwall — of the keeping of Divers lands in the towns of Rippery, Bodmyn, Kanalisy, Pengwennawoles, Pengwennawartha, Ruthdour, Trelyver and Tregamur, late of William Eyr, which are in the King's hand by reason of an outlawry promulgated against William, to hold the same from Michaelmas last for as long as the land shall remain in the King's hand for the above cause, rendering the extent thereof yearly by equal portions at the Easter and Michaelmas Exchequers, or whatever may be agreed upon between him and the treasurer; with clause touching maintenance of buildings and support of charges.
By Bill of the Treasurer.

8 November, 1455
Westminster:

Membrane 24
Order of the escheator in the county of Cornwall. Pursuant to an inquisition taken before him showing that John Petyt, esquire, on the day of his death held no lands in the said county of the king-in-chief as of the Crown, and in demesne or in Service, but held in his demesne as of fee tail a messuage, two Cornish acres of land and a Mill in Melynsy, two messuages and two Cornish acres of land in Carveynek Woles, a messuage and two Cornish acres of land in SKYWYJEK and the manors of Trelanmur & Eglesros and the messuages, mills, land, meadow and pasture in Melynsy, Carveynek Woles and SKYWYJEK.

HISTORICAL MANUSCRIPTS COMMISSION
Hastings I (series 78), pages 284, 285 and 310

20 July, 1349
Grant by William de Botreaux to Robert de Forde, Thomas Gona, JOHN de SKEWYS, John Proutz and John de Chakeford for their lives and that of the survivor, of the annual rent of 200 Pounds out of his manors of Penheale (Penhel in Egloskerry), Biscovey (Boswythgy in Par), Tywarnhayle (Trewarneyl in Perranzabuloe), Trevethoe (Trevethou in Uny Lelant), Uny Leland (Lavanta) and Trewathnant, countie Cornwall. Witnesses: Henry de la Pomeroy, Lord of Berry, knight; Robert Crues, knight; Henry de la Pomeroy, junior, knight.........etc.
Monday, St Margaret the Virgin, 23 Edward III.
Endorsed — "A grant of a rent of the Lord Botreaux."

4 July, 1369
Appointment by William de Botreaux, knight of James Gerveys, JOHN SKEWYS, John Lordman, William Wollegh, Richard Spore and others, his attorneys for delivering to Master Stephen de Penpel, dean of Wells, Henry Percehay, Walter de Clopton, John Tremayne, Walter Hethenham, parson of the church of Pucklechurch, Peter Grogob, parson of the church of Landewednak, John de Chageford, parson of the church of North Cadbury and Henry Nanfan, seisin of the vills of Uny Lelant (Lavanta) and Boscastle (Botreauxcastel) and all the Manors mentioned in the above deed of 1349, together with the Manors of Botelet (Botylet in Lanreath), Crackington (Crackhampton in St Gennys), Worthyvale in Minster and Lugans, countie Cornwall; the Manors of Langford in Ugborough and Molland Botreaux countie Devon and the Manor of Babington, countie Somerset.
4 July, 43 Edward III
Exceedingly fine little Seal of Arms — a griffin Segreant. Sigi .... De Botriaux (Catalogue of Seals in British Museum, Volume II No 7647)

20 October, 1532 and 22 June, 1533
Ten Deeds, six of the former date and four of the latter, being grants by George Earl of Huntingdon to feoffees (Reginald Pole, dean of Exeter, Sir Geoffrey Pole, knight, Sir Richard Lyster, knight, Chief Baron of the Exchequer, Edward Montague, JOHN SKEWYS, Richard Beaumont and others) in pursuance of various covenants and agreements for marriage (i.e. that of Francis Lord Hastings with Katherine, daughter of Henry Lord Montague) contained in indentures of 20 June, 24 Henry VIII, made between him and Margaret, Countess of Salisbury and Henry Lord Montague, her son and heir, of all the below mentioned Manors, etc, to hold, after the death (in the case of all save the Wiltshire and Devon premises) of Sir Samuel Sacheverell, knight, to the uses specified in the same indentures.

The premises were:
Co. Somerset; Manors of Maperton, Clopton, Halton, Hatherleigh, Holbrook, Wootton Courtney, Aller, Aller Moor, Kilmersdon and Walton.
Co. Devon; Manors of Plymtree, Sutton in Widworthy, Coldewell, Dupford, Langford in Ugborough, South Pool, Harleston, Wyke Cobham, Wolmeston.
Co. Cornwall; Manors of Uny Lelant (Lavanta), Boscastle (Botreaux Castell), Worthyvale in Minster, Penheale in Egloskerry, Botlet (Bodelett in Lanreath) with the Hundred of Worthyvale.
Co. Wilts; The Manors of Britford, Bramshaw, Somerford Mawdettes.
Co. Bucks; Manors of Stoke Poges, Eyton, New Windsor, Cippenham, Burnham, Fulmer, Beachendon, Ludgershall, Ilmer and Chadesley
Co. Oxford; Manor of Henley on Thomas.
20 October, 24 Henry VIII.
Signed. G. Hunttyngdon.

HASTINGS MANUSCRIPTS

The collection of documents, relating to the most part to the historic family of Hastings and its connections, which was preserved until the 1920's at the Manor House, Ashby de la Zouch.
Page 180. 12 Wells II
1 October, 1504 Manuscripts of the Dean & Chapter of Wells
Grant to JOHN SKEWYS, Gent, of a pension of 20 shillings in like form.

CORNISH MANUSCRIPTS Volume VII Being a Calender of Deeds formerly among the Buller records at Antony and given to Charles Henderson in 1920 by Lieut General Sie Reginald Pole Carew.

14 September, 1447
Thursday before the exaltation of the Cross 26 Henry VI MARINA relict of JOHN SKYWES enfectts Ralph Joran of all her lands in SKYWES, TRESCEWYN and Trerangwyth and all her goods and chattels — to hold to him and Enora his daughter and the issue between them Ralph and Enora his wife will allow Marina — meat, drink and lodging — at the direction of John Penrosmethele, John Luddre, RICHARD SKYWES and John Trerys.
Witnesses: W. Gurlyn, RICHARD SKYWES and John Treris.

TESTAMENTA VETUSTA being Illustration from Wills by Nicholas Harris Nicholas, pages 494, 495.

EDWARD EARL OF DEVON

EDWARD COURTENAY, knight, Earl of Devon, 27 May 1 Henry VIII (1509). My body to be buried in the Chapel of Tiverton, near the grave of my wife, and I bequeath lands to the yearly value of four pounds to found a chauntry in the said chapel. And I appoint John Smith, Doctor of Physick and Canon of St. Paul's, in London, and JOHN SKEWYS, that hath married my sisters daughter, supervisors of my Will. Proved 11 July, 1509.

CALENDAR OF CLOSE ROLLS 1307-1509

The Close Rolls of the 14th and 15th centuries contain entries of the most varied character, illustrating the history of every branch of public administration, judicial, civil, ecclesiastical, naval and military. They also contain copies of a vast number of deeds, agreements and awards concerning the private persons, which were exhibited in Chancery for enrolment.

EDWARD III 1330-1333   **Membrane 5d**
October 9th 1331   Writ for payment for his expenses for attending Parliament at 2 shillings a day.
Westminster: John SKEWYS, burgess of Hellston, for 46 shillings.

20 RICHARD II Part II   **Membrane 30d**
18 July 1396   To the Sheriff of Devon. Writ of supersedeas, by mainprise of John Tregoys, JOHN
Westminster: SKEWYS, Eurinos Boneithon and Robert Syreston of Cornwall, in favour of John
                             Shireston at suit to Master Hugh Hickerlynge, William Eyrmyn, Thomas Barton
                             and John Lugans, clerks, William Hankeforde and John Copleston, executors of
                             Thomas de Brantyngham, late Bishop of Exeter for render of £17 13 4d.

21 RICHARD II Part II   **Membrane 5d**
20 May 1398   Memorandum of a mainprise under a pain of 100 Marks, made in Chancery 19 May
Westminster: this year by John Syreston, Henry Gerveys, Eurinos Boneithon and JOHN SKEWYS
                             of Cornwall for John Rosmeryn, that he shall do or procure no hurt or harm to
                             William Cullynge.

HENRY IV 1399-1402   **Membrane 12d**
7 February 1400   To the Sheriff of Cornwall. Writ of supersedeas, by mainprise of JOHN SKEWYS,
Westminster: Pascoe Polreden, Hamelin Cavell and John Gay Bossoghan of Cornwall, in favour of
                             John Tecta, clerk, whom the King ordered the Sheriff to attach upon an information
                             that by colour of a papal provision he accepted the vicarage of St Gorom in
                             Cornwall, in the diocese of Exeter, and in the court christian sued divers processes
                             within the realm and elsewhere, and procured that John Quynterell chaplain,
                             vicarage thereof, should be set to answer touching the possession of same, and that
                             other things should be done in contempt of the King and of the vicar's hunt,
                             contrary of the statutes.

HENRY IV 1399-1402 20 June 1401 Westminster	**Membrane 14d** Thomas Colyn, JOHN SKEWYS, Ralph Cardrewe and John Penrose of Methele, in the county of Cornwall to Henry, Prince of Wales. Recognisance for £24 to be levied in Cornwall.
HENRY IV 1403-1413 24 February 1413 Westminster:	**Membrane 5d** To the Sheriff of Hertford. Writ of supersedeas in favour of Thomas Symonde, John Custance, William Somersweyn, all of Berlee, Peter de Bury, William Starlynge of Berlee, William Bregge of Northampstede, and by order of mainprise of William Ketnyche of Hertfordshire, James Berlee of London and MATTHEW SKEWES of Cornwall to set them free, if taken at suit of Henry Wyne for trespass.
HENRY V 1419-1422 2 July 1420 Westminster:	**Membrane 14d** John Arlyn chaplain to John Tretheake, esquire, and to the heirs of his body, with remainder to William Tretheake and to the heirs of his body, with remainder to Odo Tretheake, and to the heirs of his body, with remainder to Joan, sister to Odo, and to the heirs of her body. Charter indented of feoffment of all messuages, lands etc in Tretheake, Karellowe, Helwyn, Arlyn, Rescoll, Carnowe and Tregaer, with the corn mill of Tretheake, which the said chaplain had by feoffment of John Tretheake. Witnesses: JOHN SKEWYS, William Brette and others. Dated: Tretheake 11 July 8 Henry V. Memorandum of acknowledgement 11 July 8 Henry V.
HENRY V 1419-1422 2 July 1420 Westminster:	**Membrane 14d** Memorandum of a mainprise under a pain of £40 made in Chancery 30 June this year by Henry Trevenour, JOHN SKEWYS, Thomas Tregome, each of Cornwall, "gentilmen", and John Seys of London "sadeler", for William Bodrugan, knight, that he shall do or procure no hurt or harm to Thomas Roberde of London "taillour", or any of the people.
HENRY V 1419-1422 5 July 1420 Westminster:	**Membrane 13d** John Waley's chaplain to Henry Trevenour, son and heir of Thomas Dewy of Trewytheneke by Truro, and to the heirs of his body with remainder to John Trethaeke, esquire and to the heirs of his body, with remainder to William Trethaeke and to the heirs of his body, with remainder to Odo Trethaeke and to the heirs of his body with the remainder to John Bailey etc. Charter of feoffment indented of all the messuages, lands etc in Trewtheneke, Tresempell, Nanssoke, Truruburgh etc which the grantor had by feoffment of the said Henry. Witnesses: JOHN SKEWYS, William Brette and others. Dated Trewytheneke 11 July 8 Henry V. Memorandum of acknowledgement 11 July 8 Henry V.
HENRY V 1419-1422 5 July 1420 Westminster	**Membrane 13d** John Trethaeke, esquire to John Arlyn chaplain, his heirs and assigns. Charter with warranty of all of the grantors, messuages, lands etc in Trethaeke, Karellowe, Helwyn, Penmene, Melyntrukke, etc with a corn mill on Trethaeke. Witnesses: JOHN SKEWYS, William Brette and others. Dated: Trethaeke 1 July 8 Henry V. Memorandum of acknowledgement 12 July 8 Henry V.
HENRY V 1429-1435 13 February 1430 Westminster:	**Membrane 17d** John Arundell, knight to Thomas Arundell, John Herle, knight, Thomas Harry, clerk and John Tresithney and to the heirs of the body of Thomas Arundell. Charter tripartite indented of the manors of Talsferne, Prispynneke, Soor Pengwenna and of all his messuages, lands, rents, services, reversions and knight's fees of all his several tenants in Trevranov, Penrynburgh, Skywysbyhan (LITTLE SKEWYS, ST WENN) and Skewys moer (GREAT SKEWYS, ST WENN), in the county of Cornwall, rendering, maintaining and finding within two years after the death of the grantor of the rents, issues, and profits of the premises five chaplains and one honest clerk to serve them, one to be named warden of the other four, to be chosen by the grantees and by the heirs of the body of Thomas Arundell etc etc.
HENRY VII 1500-1509 1501	**Membrane 27d** John Powlet of Gotehurst, esquire to Oliver, Bishop of Bath and Wells, Reynold Brey, knight, Elizabeth Cosyn, widow, William, dean of Wells, Robert Cosyn, Thomas Beaumont, provost of Wells Cathedral, Thomas Tomyowe, doctor of laws, John Pykeman, archdeacon of Bath, JOHN SKEWES and John Baron, their heirs and assigns. Release and quit claim with warranty of Gotehurst manor with 40 messuages, 500 acres of land, 200 acres of meadow, 500 acres of pasture, 500 acres

of wood, 40 acres of heath, 40 acres of moor, and two shillings rent in Gotehurst, Stokegursey, Monketon Abbatis, Glastonbury and Roreford in the county of Somerset, the adwoson of Gotehurst church, a messuage in Wells, now inhabited by John Pomeroy and an orchard on le Pole in Wells.
Dated 10 October 17 Henry VII.

HENRY VII 1500-1509
1502

Membrane 16d
Henry and Laurence Aylmere to Richard Merland, Edward Chesman, Edward Thornborowe and Richard Colnett, gentlemen, their heirs and assigns. Charter with warranty confirming gift of all their lands and tenements in the parish of St. Andrew the Apostle in Holborne without Temple Bar, in the county of Middlesex, or elsewhere; appointment of John Franke and William Bounde as attorneys to convey seisin.
Dated 4 January 17 Henry VII.
Witnesses: JOHN SKEWES, Thomas Meryng and others.

HENRY VII 1500-1509
1504

Membrane 21d
Edmund Carewe, John Speke, Amyas Paulet, knights, William Carent and John More of Colompton, esquires, JOHN SKEWYS and John Pole to Giles, Lord Daubeney, Henry his son and heir apparant and the heirs male of Giles body. Writing quadripartite indented confirming livery of the manors of South Peret in the county of Dorset, and North Peret and Pepilpen, in the county of Somerset with advowsons etc wherewith John Byconell, knight enfeoffed them together with the said Giles, William Hody, chief baron of the Exchequer and others now deceased for the fulfillment of his last will, to the uses and with the remainders there specified. (Calendar of Inquisitions Post Mortem, Henry VII, No 683). Appointment of Robert More, esquire and Richard Harvey as attorneys to convey seisin.
Dated 22 November, 20 Henry VII.

HENRY VII 1500-1509
1504

Membrane 21d
Memorandum of acknowledgement by SKEWYS and Pole on 4 February in Chancery and by the others on 3 January before Thomas Abbot of Forde by virtue of a writ of "dedimus Potestatem."

HENRY VII 1500-1509
1509

Membrane 17d
Hervey Talgarrek to JOHN SKEWYS, James Erysy, Richard Penros and Odo Geoff and their heirs and assigns. Charter of gift with warranty, to the use of John and his heirs of all his messuages and lands in Talgarrek, Redruyth, and elsewhere in Cornwall; appointment of William Tretherff and John Robyn as attorneys to convey seisin. Witnesses: John Arundell, knight, Richard Code, esquire, Peter Seyntaubyn and others.
Dated London 8 February, 24 Henry VII.
Memorandum of acknowledgement 12 February, 24 Henry VII.

SURREY FINES 1509-1558
1522
No 113.

Richard Page, Esq., Thomas Denys, knight and JOHN SKEWYS, Esq., (plaintiffs). Nicholas Partriche and Marion, his wife (deforciant).
12 messuages, 200 acres of land, 300 acres of pasture, 40 acres of meadow, 100 acres of wood, 60 acres of heath and 40/-d rent in Walton on Thames and West Mowsley. £200 Warranty omitted. Form A. October of St Martin. 286/15.

CALENDAR OF PATENT ROLLS
Henry V
12 February, 1420

Grant by mainprise of William Bryt and JOHN SKEWYS, both of the county of Cornwall to William Bodrugan "Chivaler", of the marriages of Joan and Margaret, daughters and heiresses of John Seyntaubyn, esquire, tenant in chief by knight service, without disparagement, paying 200 marks to the King, viz. 100 marks within a month of Easter next, and 100 marks at Michaelmas following, and finding a competent maintenance for the heiresses during minority.
By bill of William Kynwolmerssh, deputy treasurer. 14 February 1420.

17 Henry VII Part 2.
21 February, 1502
Westminster

Membrane 16 (21)
Licence for Ciles Daubeney of Daubeney, knight, William Hody, knight, chief Baron of the Exchequer, Edmund Carew, John Speke, Amias Paulet, William Sayntmaure, knights, William Carent, John More of Cullumpton, esquire, JOHN SKEWYS, John Pole and John Stoune, to grant in mortmain the abovementioned manors, advowson and lands, being of yearly value of £52 to the said abbot of St Mary's, Glastonbury.

18 Henry VII Part 2.
12 July, 1503
Westminster

Membrane 1 (30)d
Commission to William Seyntmaure, knight and JOHN SKEWYS to enquire by juries of the counties of Southampton, Wiltshire, Somerset and Dorset of concealed lands in these counties.

18 Henry VII Part 2.
17 July, 1503
Westminster

Membrane 4 (27)d
Commission to William Seyntmaure, knight and JOHN SKEWYS to enquire of concealed lands in Southampton, Wiltshire, Somerset and Dorset.

21 Henry VII Part 1.
25 August, 1506
Westminster

Membrane 4 (33)d
Commission to John Burgchier of Fitzwarren, knight, William Hody, knight, Robert Drury, knight, Hugh Lutterell, knight, Edmund Gorge, knight, Nicholas Wadham, knight, Humphrey Harvey, JOHN SKEWIS, John Brent, James Daubeney, Edward Wadham, William Mallet and Alexander Buller for coast of the sea and of the marsh and streams of fresh water descending to the Severn and thence to the high sea within the county of Somerset, to wit, from Theolwell in the parish of Wedmore to Clyuer and thence to Were, and from Were to Redcliffe, thence to Axwater, thence to the Severn; and the fresh waters descending from Assllecote to Sapwyke, thence to Cadecote through Edyngton, Chelton, Cosyngton, Wullavyngton and other hamlets in Hunspill, thence to Highbrigge and thence to the Severn; also from Radclyff to Brenedowne, thence to Brene, thence to Berghes, and from Berghes to Burnham and thence to Highbrigge aforesaid.

23 Henry VII Part 2
12 July, 1508
Westminster

Membranes 29, 30 and 31.
Pardon to Richard Willoughby, Lord of Broke, John Mowne of Halle, esquire, Peter Bevyll of Gwerneck, esquire, John Godolghan of Godolghan, esquire, James Erysy of Erysy, gentilman, John Bevyll of Marghasyowe the younger, gentilman, Thomas Tregoos of Penpoll, gentilman , JOHN SKEWYS of Merthyn, gentilman, Thomas Treunwith of Treunwith, gentilman (and 32 other names) all of whom have not introduced the names of new possessors of tin-works newly bounded with the names of the works at the next stannary court after the said bounding — tinners or buyers of black and white tin changing the marks — tinners, buyers, blowers or fabricators of false tin or hard tin as well with the letter "h" as without; for all offences against the stannary statutes made by the king and his projenitors or predecessors or by his first born son, Arthur, Prince of Wales, Duke of Cornwall, Earl of Chester and his council, and statutes against unjust measuring of black or weighing of white tin and other offences with regard to tin which have been issued by any other authority. Also pardon for offences against the statutes of liveries, measures, etc. And grant that if these letters are insufficient in law shall be issued at the suit of individuals without further warrant. With mandate to William, Archbishop of Canterbury and other chancellors and keepers of the great seal to issue this pardon to any other tinners nominated by the Mayor and commonalty of Truro and Lostwithiel under their common seals. Also grant to the said tinners, of this privilege, to wit, that the statutes made by the King and Arthur shall be annulled and henceforth no statutes should by made by the King or Prince of Wales, Duke of Cornwall, affecting their interests without the concurrence of twenty four men chosen from the four stannaries of Cornwall, to wit, by the Mayor and council, of the borough of Truro, six men of the stannary of Tywarneheyle by the Mayor and council of the borough of Lostwithiel, six of the stannary of Blakemour, by the Mayor and council of the borough of Launceston, six of the stannary of Fowymour by the Mayor and council of the borough of Helston in Kerrier; six of the stannary of Penwith and Kerrier.
Also exemption of the said tinners from all customs on exported tin except such as other denizen merchants have been accustomed to pay in the ports of London and Southampton. And further grant that the pardons hereby granted shall be authorised by the authority of the King's next parliament and all the King's grants and annullings of the laws annulled as aforesaid shall be confirmed by the said parliament; also that customers and searchers shall exact no higher weighing fee from tin for export than that appointed by statute. (At this point the membrane is worn away and mutilated.)

Elizabeth
4 March 1562
Membrane 23

Licence for £3 15 2d in the hanaper, for Gerard Lowther to alienate the tithes of corn, hay and lambs of Bampton, Bonby Grange, Knype, SKEWES, and elsewhere in Bampton, county Westmorland now in the tenure of Lowther, late of the monastery of Shap, county Westmorland to Richard Cliborne and Edmund Clyborne.

DOCUMENTS RELATING TO JOHN SKEWYS (1467-1544)

From Charles Henderson Collection of Manuscripts Volume 3, pages 5-7 kept at Royal Institution of Cornwall, Truro.

William Reskymer one of your (maties) Valett Chambre-whereas one JOHN SKEWYS, Esquire in consideration that your orator should take his wyffe on Alys daughter of John Densselle deceased cosyn and one of the heyres apparant of the said John Skewys granted to your orator and to Alys and the heyres of their bodies all his lands in Polrode, SKEWYS, Boland, Skawen, Tredrym, Fentonvedna .... and in default of issue remainder to dyvers psons by deed 6 July A° — Henry VIII and your orator was in seizin with Alys but the said John Skewys wythout any cause hath entered the premises and sued your orator and forged leases etc.

The answer of JOHN SKEWYS: He says William Reskymer may spend yerely beyond fyftye pounds and also on Mari moden of the said Alys now wyfe to the said William and full exucutrix of the tenement of one John Densell had by the dethe of the said John Densell her late husband 1000 marks with goods and plate and denies that the said John Skewys yr consideration that William should marry the said Alis and without that then was any such grounde which shoulde move the said John Skewys such things to consider for the said William hath by the same Alys 40 marks of lande yerly and William hath not fully £10 of his owne land yerly and he says he by his deed long after the maryge gave the lands to William and Alys heires of their body at a rent and if the rent was unpayed John Skewys should lawfully re-enter and the rent was unpayed three years so he re-entered. A° 34, Henry VIII.

Laurence Courtenay, Esquyer (30) says John Skewys gave the lands to William Reskymer and Alys at a rent of £24 with the re-enter clause and re-entered for non-payment and he (deponent) was at Skewis is house yr servant John is lane by Smythfelde the 29 October A° 34, Henry VIII. Whereas the said William Reskymer was sutor to Skewys and desyned him to be his good fader and Skewes demanded "whye so Sir as I drepceyne ye have re-entered unto yor lands agen that ye gave me and that ye aremynded to put me from the same contrary to the dede that you made to me and my wyff, wherefore I pity you to make me v my wyff theroff better assurance" and Skewes answered "If the assurance that have made you be not good already ye shall have noe oder assurance of me then ye have for ye have broken your covenants and have put me in the lawe full unkyndley and ungently to my grete costs and therefore ye have deserved no kyndness of me."

Reskymer desired him "I pity you to be so good fader to me to give me the on half and to Mr Courteny thod' halff." "Noe Sir, not so I wyll gyve my lands to hym that doeth moost for me" and wyll be ruler of the same as long as he lived and so Reskymer departed this communication being on 29 October last then beying present the said Laurence Courteny, Will'am Perys, William Trubody, Thomas Horseman and Sir Richard Page, Chaplain to the said Skewis and Rose Woolman, sirvant to Skewis, and afterwards made on Tomeowe stuard to the Lady Anne Clyve on 3 December following to be sutor for him to the said Skewes and Tomeyowe hadde lyke aunswere and more he sayth not.

THOMAS BLEWETT (67) was steward to John Skewys of his manors of Polrode, Scawen and Bulland als est Draynes.

THOMAS JOHN (60) sayeth that John Skews ordeyned him to be his rent gatherer of all his manors and lands called Skewys, Fentenwena, Sullegena, Seynt Crede and Tredryme in the west parts of the countie and that on Thomas Botalek of Seynt Juste phshe in Penwith beyng tenant to Skewes in a place called Botalleck did not attorne etc.

Examynacons on behalf of William Reskymer 27 December A° Henry VIII.

JOHN TRELAWNY, Esq., (36) says about Lent A° 30 this deponent was present at the manor of Skewys when Warren Bennett, then servant to John Skewys said that his master had geryn by his dede to William Reskymer and Alys his wyff all his manors of Skewys, Polrode, Skawen, Bulland, Fentonvenna, Tredrym, Selena and Seynt Crede in tail.

Note: Alice Reskymer died 14 January, 6 Elizabeth. The above all taken from "Court of Requests", Public Record Office, London.

JOHN SKEWYS appeared in name in various Wills.
In that of William St Maur, knight, 3 September, 1503 who said in his Will:
"I bequeath all my wering gere and garments to my bedfelowe JOHN SKEWYS and also 40 marks in money."

In the Will of .....
Elizabeth Byconyll, 30 June, 1504. Her first husband was John St Maur who was father of Sir William St Maur. In the Will she said:
"To JOHN SKEWIS, a bason and a ewer of silver and £10."

In the Will of .....
Thomas Tomyowe, 30 September, 1517.
"To my nephew JOHN SKEWYS one standing cup and gilt with its cover with my arms impressed on top."

LETTERS AND PAPERS, FOREIGN AND DOMESTIC, OF THE REIGN OF HENRY VIII

List of persons receiving the King's general pardon (Proclamation) "that whereas the late King granted a general pardon of all offences before 10 April last, the King now grants a more ample pardon for all things except debt."

Pardon Roll 438 (4) m 6 Year 1509-1510

JOHN SKEWYS of SKEWYS, Cornwall and London, gentleman (one of the executors of William Sayntmaure, knight, deceased and of Lady Elizabeth Byconyll, widow and executrix of John Byconyll, knight, and one of the guardians of John, son and heir of John Mohun, esq) and Katherine his wife, late wife of John Reskymer, esq., deceased. 12 May 1509.

Grants: September, 1509. g190 (22)
JOHN SKEWYS, Lease for 20 years of the tolls on Tin in Tewington, Tywarnaill and Helston in Kerryar, in Cornwall, at the annual rent of £15.
P.S. Pat 1 Henry VIII p.l. m20 (506)

Grants: May, 1514 g 2964 (61)
JOHN SKEWYS. Exemption from serving on juries etc., or being made a Knight or burgess of Parliament, or the Justice of the Peace etc., with the privilege of keeping his hat on in the presence of the King. Westminster, 22 May 6 Henry VIII.

Expenses: 10 Henry VIII (1518), 152 (viii)
Expenses for Henry Courtenay, Earl of Devon to Mr SKEWYS £6 13 4d for 26 yards of black velvet for a gown and frock at 10 shillings a yard.

Sheriff Role: 12 Henry VIII (6 November, 1520) 1042
Cornwall: John Chamond, JOHN SKUSE and William Lowthe.

Wolsey's Colleges: 16 Henry VIII (7 January 1525) 1001
Suppression of St Fridewide's, Oxford, Lincs diocese, and other monastries. Commission to John Aleyn, clerk, JOHN SKEWSE and John Seyntclere, for the conversion of the above house into a secular college, and appropriation of its revenues to the use of the same, considering that the funds for the support of teachers are becoming daily less sufficient, and in danger of being extinguished, also for translation of the inmates to other houses. Pat. 16 Henry VIII, p.2. m.10d.

Wolsey's College, Oxford 17 Henry VIII (29 October 1525) 1728
Indenture between Sir William Cascoyne, treasurer of Wolsey's household and John Higden, dean of his college, dated 29 October 17 Henry VIII, witnessing the delivery to the latter of certain evidences belonging to the above college. Attested by John, bishop of Lincoln, Robert Carter, JOHN SKEWYS, Thomas Cromwell and Thomas Canner, in the presence of William Burbanke.

London district and commissioners 16 Henry VIII (6 November 1542) 430
From Temple Bar to Charing Cross, county of Middlesex — Thomas Hennedge, Richard Paige and Mr SCEWS.

FROM "*HISTORY OF HELSTON*", by H. Spencer Toy, page 129.
A list of Members of Parliament for Helston was compiled by Lawrence from 1298-1885. The official returns of Members of Parliament (1878) give JOHN SKEWYS in Parliament in September 1331. Skewys is not entered by Lawrence, nor does his name appear in Parliamentary Writs, but his claim to insertion is supported by a Writ (Calendar of Close Rolls, 1331 (413),) for the payment of 46 shillings to him for expenses in attending Parliament at 2 shillings a day

The following list is taken from Official Returns to the House of Commons and contains M.P.'s for Helston before the grant of the charter of Queen Elizabeth in 1585.

King Edward III	1331	September	JOHN SKEWYS
King Richard II	1397	September	JOHN SKYWYS
King Henry IV	1407	October	MATTHEW SKEWYS

SYLLABUS of the Documents Relating to England and other Kingdoms contained in the Collection known as "RYMER's FOEDERA" (1873).

1525, 7 January Commission to John Aleyn, JOHN SKEWSE, and John Seyinclere
                 for the Monastry of St. Fridewood's.
                 Westminster O. xiv 32. H. vi. p ii 15

CALENDAR OF INQUISITIONS POST MORTEM
Upon the announcement of the death of any person reputed to hold land directly of the King, a Writ was prepared in the Chancery and sent under the Great Seal to the escheators of those counties where the deceased's land was situated requiring them to certify to the King, upon the oath of a jury to be empanelled by the Sheriff, touching certain matters specified in the Writ. The reply known as the Inquisition was sent to the Chancery, sewn on to the Writ, and the name of the person delivering it and the date of its receipt were noted by the receiving clerk. Upon the receipt of the Inquisition in the Chancery a copy was sent to the Exchequer.

VOLUME 7, page 276
Ref: 385 **Otto de Bodrigan**
Cornwall Writ of certioram de feodis. 23 March, 6 Edward III (1332).
        SKEWYS — an eleventh part of a knight's fee held by JOHN de SKEWYS by suit of Court; a fifteenth part of a fee held by John de Polhorman.

VOLUME 9, page 164
Ref: 164 **William de Botreaux**
Devon   Writ 16 August 23 Edward III (1349 — the year of the Black Death in England).
        Inquisition taken at Exeter, Tuesday after St Lucy, 23 Edward III

Dupeford — the Manor with the Hundred of Stanburgh, held of the King in Chief as of the right of Isabel his wife with knight's service. He held no other lands in the county as of fee, because long before he died he demised the Manor of Molland, with its woods, mills, etc and the Hundred of Molland to Robert de Ford, Thomas Goua, John Proutz, JOHN de SKEWYS and John de Chageford, clerk for their lives. To hold of him and his heirs by service of a grain of corn yearly; which Manor the said William held of Sir Roger de Mortuo Mari by knight's service. And long before he died he demised the Manor of Stokkelegh Englysh, which he held of William de Chaumbernon in Socage to Thomas de Botreaux, his son, for his life by service of a grain of corn yearly, with remainder to the said Robert de Ford, Thomas Goua, John Proutz, JOHN de SKEWYS and John de Chageford, clerk for their lives by the same service

VOLUME 2, pages 683, 743, 810 and 834

Ref: 683 **John Byconell, knight**

Dorset Writ of Mandamus 8 March: Inquisition 20 June, 19 Henry VII (1504)

Long before his death he was seised of the under mentioned Manor etc in Fee and, being so seised, by charter enfeoffed Giles Daubeney de Daubeney, knight, William Hody, knight, Chief Baron of the Exchequer, Edmund Carewe, Knight, John Speke, knight, Amyas Paulet, knight, William Sayntmaur, esquire, William Carent, esquire, John More, esquire, JOHN SKEWYS, John Pole and John Stone thereof, to the use of himself and his heirs, and the performance of his last will.

They were seised thereof accordingly in the fee to the use aforesaid. And afterwards 15 August, 16 Henry VII he made his last will, viz, that after his death his feoffees should demise the manor of South Perot (Dorset) to Elizabeth Biconyll, his wife, for her life, and that she during her life from the issues and profits thereof shall find yearly five scholars in the University of Oxford in Divinity to the intent of the said scholars shall instruct the people therein; that after he decease the manor should remain to the said William Sayntmaur for his life, he finding two scholars as above; that after his decease the manor should remain to the said Giles and Henry his son of the terms of their lives in survivorship. with the remainder to the said William Sayntmaur and the heirs male of his body issuing.

Ref: 743 **William Saintmaur, knight**

Dorset Writ of diem clausit missing — Inquisition 18 March, 19 Henry VII (1504)

Thomas Wode, serjeant-at-law, John Biconyll, knight, and Piers Eggecombe, knight, by the name of Piers Eggecombe, long before the taking of this Inquisition viz. in Hilary term, 4 Henry VII at the special request of one Thomas de Sancto Mauro, knight, recovered the undermentioned manors against Henry, late Earl of Northumberland, by writ of right, as by exemplification of the said record under the King's seal more fully appears; by virtue of which recovery they were seised thereof in fee to the use of the said Thomas de Sancto Mauro, knight, died, whereupon the said Thomas Wode and others were seised of the premises to the use of the said William Saintmaur, knight, named in the writ, as cousin and heir of the said Thomas, viz. son of John Saintmaur, son of the said Thomas Saintmaur, and to the use of his heirs. The survivor of them, the said Piers, is still seised thereof in fee, to the use aforesaid. By his testament and last will, 3 September, 19 Henry VII, under his seal, the same Wiliam Sayntmaur willed that Dame Elizabeth Biconyll, his mother, as one of his executors, should have and take all the issues and profits of the premises, for the payment of his debts and legacies, and after their payment should have the said issues, etc for the term of her life. If she died before they were paid, he willed that Margaret, his wife, and JOHN SKEWYS, other executors with the said Elizabeth, should take the said issues etc. until his said debts etc. were paid, and, after his debts and legacies were paid and his will performed, and after the death of the said Elizabeth, that the said Piers, his heirs and assigns should be seised of the premises, to the use of his right heirs.

(He died 5 September, 19 Henry VII, seised of the under mentioned land and advowson in fee. Joan Sayntmaur, aged 2 and more, is his daughter and heir — reference no 715)

Dorset — Manor of Ramsham, worth £12, held of the King, as of Dover Castle, by fealty and 20 shillings for all service.

Manor of Childefrome, worth £7, held of Hugh Lutrell, as of Dunster Castle, by fealty and 12 pence rent for all service.

Manor of Wraxhale, worth £9, held of the King, as of the Lonor of Clare, by fealty, for all service.

Manor of Maperton, worth £10, held of the heirs of Humphrey de Redhorn, service unknown.

Ref: 834 **Elizabeth Byconyll, widow**

Dorset Writ 5 July, 19 Henry VII (1504). Inquisition 29 January, 20 Henry VII.

John Biconyll, knight, deceased, late her husband, by charter indented, long before her decease, enfeoffed Giles Daubny, knight, Lord Daubney, William Hody, knight, Chief Baron of the Exchequer, Edward Carew, John Speke, and Amyas Pawlet, knights, William Carent and John More of Colompton, esquires, JOHN SKEWYS and John Pole with others since deceased of 'inter alia' the under mentioned manor and advowson of South Perot, for the performance of his last will.

By his last will the said John directed that his said feoffes, after his death, should permit the said Elizabeth to have the said manor etc 'inter alia' for the term of her life, and after her decease they should remain to William Seyntmaure, knight, now deceased for the term of his life, with remainder to Giles Daubney, knight, Lord Daubney and Henry Daubney, son and heir apparant to the said Giles, for the term of their lives in survivorship with remainder to the said William Seyntmaure, and the heirs male of his body issuing.

The said William Seyntmaure died without heir male of his body begotten and afterwards the said William Hody by his charter released to the said Giles, Lord Daubney and others his co-feoffes, all his estate for the performance of his last will of the said John.

Ref: 810 **William Seyntmaure, knight**
Somerset Inquisition 20 June, 20 Henry VII (1505)
He was seised in fee of the under-mentioned manors, and enfeoffed thereof Roger Holland and JOHN SCUYS, to hold to them and their heirs to the use of himself and the heirs of his body, and in default of such issue to the use of his right heirs.
He died on 5 September, 19 Henry VII whereupon the said feoffees were seised of the premises in fee to the use of Joan Sayntmaure (his daughter and heir) and the heirs of her body, and in default of such issue to the use of her right heirs.
Somerset — Manor of Durston, worth £9, held of Henry, Earl of Northumberland, services unknown.
Manor of Mighelchirche, worth £4, held of the King, as his Duchy of Lancaster, by a twentieth part of a knight's fee.

CALENDAR OF STATE PAPERS Pages 261, 468 and 544
From   **STEPHEN SKEWES** to Admiralty Committee
Date   23 July, 1649. "The Satisfaction", Chesterwater.
We have been attending on the Army in Inverlochy, at the back side of Scotland and when refitted and victualed for six months, are to return there. We generally carry from 130-140 men, but they are continually coming and going, choosing rather to loose a little time than to serve long. I hope the Captain will tell you our proceedings.

From   **STEPHEN SKEWES** to Admiralty Committee
Date   30 March, 1654. "The Satisfaction", Pembroke. Skewes complains of his purser and steward, Philip Weedon of Greenwich, who not only insufficiently supplied the ship with provisions, but deserted, whereby he was put to much inconvenience in his voyage to Dublin. They ordered a recruit at Kinsale, but were forced into Milford, where Richard Browne supplied bread and beer. Awaits further orders. References Vol 80, page 145.

From   **STEPHEN SKEWES** to Navy Committee
Date   17 August, 1654. "The Satisfaction", Liverpool Water.
Philip Weedon left the ship at Portsmouth, eight months since. Another purser put in by General Fleetwood; resigned the place in Skewes' favour through illness, and held it for some time, but now Weedon has returned to take charge by their instructions. He has no warrant, and they may be ignorant of his former absence. Asks orders. Does not desire the place for profit, being already provided for by them, but for the good of the service in which he has lost one of his hands. References Volume 87, page 8.

CLAIM FOR EXPENSES—PARLIAMENTARY WRITS VOL. 1. EDWARD III
Helston—16 July, 1331
No original writ for the County of Cornwall produced.
Writ de Expensis for JOHANNES SKEWYS only for 46 shillings for 23 days for attendance at Parliament, coming and returning, at the rate of 2 shillings each per diem. Tested at Westminster 9 October, 5 Edward III (Rot. C.l. 5 Edward III, p 2. m6d).

DEVON MUSTER ROLL for 1569 (A.J. HOWARD & T.L. STOATE, 1977)
JOHN SKEWES senior in the Hundred of East Bridleigh, village of Coleton Rawlighe.
In each village men were either Archers, Harqbusiers, Pikemen or Billmen. Skewes was a Billman.

EXETER MARRIAGE LICENCES 1600-1837
August 22	1734	JOHN SKEWES of Gwennap and Elizabeth Symons of Penzance.
November 2	1743	ANN SKEWES of St Clement, widow and John Williams of Gwennap, tinner.
11 July	1826	JOHN SKEWES of Gwennap and Ann Davy of Gwennap.
October 26	1832	JOANNA SKEWES of Gwennap and Ambrose Bray of Gwennap.

CORNWALL PROTESTATION RETURNS (T.L. Stoate, 1974)
This book, which became available early in 1975, is invaluable to the genealogist. It gives a list of the inhabitants of the parish above the age of 18 who freely and willingly (in the presence of a Minister, Constables, Churchwardens and Overseers) took this Protestation as the Minister, Constables etc did formerly before the justices.
The Protestation Returns owe their existence to the unrest which prevailed in Parliament during the passage of the bill for the Attainder of the Earl of Strafford in 1641. The House of Commons had passed the bill on 21 April and the House of Lords gave it a second reading on 27 April.
The House of Commons learned on 28 April that a plan had been made for rescuing Strafford, and rumours were current of various plots to persuade the King to use the Army to overawe Parliament and thus release Strafford. An unsuccessful attempt made the King to occupy the Tower of London, caused rioting near the Houses of Parliament and his speech in the House of Lords on 1 May against the execution of Strafford also produced great alarm.
A committee of ten members was appointed on 3 May to draw up a form of Prostestation, and it was ordered that no members should stir out of the House without leave, nor speak to the messengers. The Protestation was agreed upon and all members were ordered to sign it. On the following day 4 May the Protestation was agreed to by the House of Lords and all Protestant Peers signed it.

On 6 May a Bill was introduced in the House of Commons imposing the obligation of signing the Protestation on all Englishmen. It provided that those who refused to sign were held to be incapable of holding office. The following January the Protestation itself was printed. In the Cornwall Returns some 30,000 names appear and they represent about 97% of all adult males living in the county. It is the most important piece of evidence for giving the size of population between the Poll Tax of 1377 and the first Census of 1801.

The signing of the Protestation took place in Cornwall in the early part of 1642. The Returns were then sent back to Parliament with all speed asked for by the Speaker.

These are the names of the SKEWES family that appear:

Cury Parish	EDWARD SKEWES
Gwennap Parish	COLLAN SKEWES
	ROBERT SKEWES
	ROBERT SKEWES) two separate entries
	RICHARD SKEWES
Mullion Parish	RICHARD SKEWES
Perranaworthal Parish	ARTHUR SKEWES
St Anthony in Meneage Parish	JOHN SKEWES
St Keverne Parish	RICHARD SKEWES
	WALTER SKEWES
	JOHN SKEWES
Gorran Parish	JOHN SKEWES
Camborne Parish	RENFRE SKEWES
Gerrans Parish	JOHN SKEWES
St Just in Roseland Parish	STEPHEN SKEWES
	JAMES SKEWES

LEASES and DEEDS relating to various Lands and Property in Cornwall

(All Leases and Deeds retained at the County Record Office, Truro.) Series WH and DDEN.

CARHARRACK-VEOR, GWENNAP. SKEWES' TENEMENT

This tenement was in existence in 1692. On 3rd March that year John Haweis of Killiow, gent., issued a lease to Richard Nicheolls of Gwennap, tinner. SKEWES tenement comprised a dwelling house in Carharrack Veor with barn belongings and half the stable, quarter part of mowhay and townplace, with liberty to make fuel and soil. There was also an orchard and garden behind the dwelling house, meadow before the door of the house, meadow behind mowhay, with other fields, also common with stamping mill called Carharrack Mill and water, and leats, whole property supposed to be a fourth part of Carharrack-Veor.

Dated 28 April, 1705
99 year lease (life of Lessee's wife MARGARET SKEWES). Rent 14/4d. John Haweis of Killiow, gent to THOMAS SKEWES junior of Gwennap, tinner.
Consideration: £25 0 0d
Property: Chinhale, alias Carharrack Veor with stamping mill.

Dated 29 July, 1727
99 year lease (lessee's son THOMAS SKEWES). Rent 14/4d.
Reg Haweis of Killiow, Esq, to THOMAS SKEWES of Gwennap, tinner.
Consideration: £26 1 0d
Property: Tenement called Chinhale, alias Carharrack Veor with stamping mill built there.

Dated 11 April, 1741
99 year lease (lessee, and THOMAS and JOHN, son of lessee's brother THOMAS SKEWES of Gwennap). Rent 7/-d.
John Hearle of Penryn to RICHARD SKEWES of Gwennap, tinner.
Consideration: £60.
Property: SKEWES' Tenement. Dwelling house in Carharrack Veor with orchard behind with quarter part of mowhay and all Tremaines old walls, with garden plot and quarter part of townplace; also fields with liberty to fetch water from the well through Well Close, and to water cattle there, but not to stay longer than necessary.

Dated 3 February, 1770
Deed. John Enys, Esq, to THOMAS SKEWES of Killiwerris, Kea. Part of a house and three acres of ground in Killiwerris. THOMAS SKEWES of Kea, tinner, aged 32 years or thereabouts. ANN his wife, aged 31 years, or thereabouts; THOMAS their son, aged 7 or thereabouts. THOMAS SKEWES to pay yearly rent of two shillings. Survey conducted by Thomas Enys 12 September, 1778 on lands in Killiwerris. Part of the commons were tenanted by THOMAS SKEWES and ANN his wife and THOMAS their son. A note added in rough writing that Mrs SKEWES died 22 November, 1783.

Dated 1 July, 1791
99 year lease (lessee COLLAN SKEWES). Rent 7/-d.
Francis Rodd of Trebartha Hall, and Sam Wallis of Upper Seymour Street, London to JOHN SKEWES of Gwennap, tinner.

Consideration £26 5 0d.

Property: Tenement known as SKEWES' Tenement comprising Dwelling House in Carharrack Veor with orchard behind with quarter part of mowhay with garden plot and quarter part of townplace; also fields with liberty to fetch water from the well through Well Close, and to water cattle, but not to stay longer than necessary.

Lease dated 28 October, 1794

John Enys to THOMAS SKEWES. By this date both parties had died. THOMAS SKEWES junior was 32, JOHN SKEWES, his brother 28 and WILLIAM SKEWES his brother 25.

Lease dated 24 June, 1795

Lease between John Enys of Enys of one part and PETER SKEWES of Killiwerris, Kea, tinner of the other. PETER SKEWES was 25 years. Reference was also made to his brother MATTHEW SKEWES, aged 20 years. Peter to pay annual rent of £16.

Survey of the Subsiting Lives on Mr Enys, one fourth part in the Barton of Killiwerris. Made in 1795 by Thomas Warren.

Tiddy's Tenement:	originally PETER SKEWES (aged 25) but now crossed out. Likewise MATTHEW SKEWES (20).
Magors Tenement:	originally Samuel Truren, but crossed out and inserted with WILLIAM SKEWES. MARY SKEWES (2) crossed out. THOMAS SKEWES, aged 1 remained. Note in ink added MARY SKEWES died about three years since, which was also crossed out.
Harris Tenement:	JOHN SKEWES aged 1 and WILLIAM SKEWES aged 11.
SKEWES' Tenement:	THOMAS SKEWES (32) deleted. THOMAS SKEWES died in 1806. Inserted with MARY SKEWES, also JOHN SKEWES (28) and WILLIAM SKEWES (25).

Lease dated 5 October, 1738

99 year lease (lessee, and brother RICHARD SKEWES). Rent 1/-d John Hearle of Penryn, Esq., to JOHN SKEWES of Gwennap, tinner.

Consideration: £8 3 4d

Property: One third part of dwelling house, two gardens and three fields (about 2½ acres) in Raby's Premises, St Day, Gwennap, late occupied by John Raby, part of Tresaddern and Croft Hendy.

Dated 14 December, 1769

99 year lease (lessee's daughter JOAN SKEWES). Rent 4/-d.

Mary Hearle of Penryn, widow and Thomas Hearle, rector of St. Michael Penkivel, clerk, to WILLIAM SKEWES of Gwennap, tinner.

Consideration: £7 10 0d.

Property: Ar Carharrack comprising dwelling house and field formerly called The Outer Croft (about three acres) and called Bowles Tenement.

Dated 1 September, 1802

99 year lease (lessee's daughter GRACE SKEWES). Rent 14/4d.

Francis Rodd of Trebartha Hall, Esq., Betty Wallis of Devonshire Street, Middlesex to ALEXANDER SKEWES, of Gwennap, yeoman.

Consideration. Sundry damages likely to be done to premises by working of Carharrack Mine.

Property: Tenement called Chinhale, alias Carharrack Veor, except stamping mill late occupied by JOHN SKEWES.

Dated 2 January, 1804.

99 year lease (lessee's children MARGARET and RICHARD SKEWES, and Francis, son of Francis Tuckfield of Gwennap). Rent 10/-d.

Francis Rodd, Esq., of Trebartha Hall and Betty Wallis of Devonshire Street, Middlesex to ALEXANDER SKEWES, miner.

Consideration: 10/-d

Property: At Carharrack Common. Lessor's part of piece of ground, part of Carharrack Common, lately enclosed, now occupied by ALEXANDER SKEWES.

Date 1 September, 1807.

99 year lease (lessee, wife ANN SKEWES and JAMES SKEWES junior, son of JAMES SKEWES and nephew of lessee). Rent 7/-d. (also counterpart). Francis Rodd, Esq., of Trebartha Hall, and Henry Hawkins Tremayne of Heligan, clerk, to HENRY SKEWES of Gwennap, yeoman.

Consideration: £21.

Property: Carharrack Downs and Moor. Tenement on Carharrack Downs being cottage and three acres of land late occupied by John May, then John Francis, then John Barrett.

A survey of the lives on Mr Enys one quarter part of Barton of Killiwerris made in 1881 by Thomas Warren. Unlike previous survey there are no alterations.

Tenement	Tenants in 1811	Subsisting Lives	Age in 1811
Tiddy's Tenement	James Truran	MATTHEW SKEWES	36
Magor's Tenement	WILLIAM SKEWES	Samuel Truran	40
	WILLIAM SKEWES	THOMAS SKEWES	19
Stephen's Tenement	MARY SKEWES	THOMAS SKEWES	18
	MARY SKEWES	JOHN SKEWES	10
	MARY SKEWES	WILLIAM SKEWES	17

SKEWES's Tenement   THOMAS SKEWES   JOHN SKEWES   45
                     THOMAS SKEWES   WILLIAM SKEWES   42

A later survey in 1816 (many alterations and very bad writing) listed MATTHEW SKEWES (20), THOMAS SKEWES (1), THOMAS SKEWES (9) and JOHN SKEWES (1).

RENT BOOK FOR KILLIWERRIS 1791-1792
Fields in Killiwerris   PETER SKEWES paid yearly rent of £1 0 0d
SKEWES Tenement   THOMAS SKEWES paid yearly rent of £2 0 0d but owed 16/-d in arrears.

RENT BOOK FOR KILLIWERRIS 1794-1795
Fields in Killiwerris   PETER SKEWES paid yearly rent of £1 0 0d
SKEWES Tenement   THOMAS SKEWES paid yearly rent of £2 0 0d
                         paid his arrears as well.

RENT BOOKS FOR KILLIWERRIS 1796-1801
Teedy Tenement   PETER SKEWES paid yearly rent of 2/6d
SKEWES Tenement   THOMAS SKEWES paid yearly rent of 2/6d

RENT BOOKS FOR KILLIWERRIS 1802-1805
Teedy Tenement   PETER SKEWES paid yearly rent of 2/6d
Stevens Tenement   THOMAS SKEWES paid yearly rent of 2/6d
SKEWES Tenement   THOMAS SKEWES paid yearly rent of 2/6d

RENT BOOKS FOR KILLIWERRIS 1806-1807
Magors Tenement   WILLIAM SKEWES paid a yearly rent of 2/6d
Stevens Tenement   MARY SKEWS paid a yearly rent of 2/6d
SKEWES Tenement   MARY SKEWS paid a yearly rent of 2/6d

RENT BOOKS FOR KILLIWERRIS 1808-1815
Magors Tenement   WILLIAM SKEWES paid a yearly rent of 2/6d
Stevens Tenement   MARY SKEWS paid a yearly rent of 2/6d
SKEWES Tenement   THOMAS SKEWS paid a yearly rent of 2/6d

RENT BOOK FOR KILLIWERRIS 1816-1817
Magors Tenement   ANN SKEWS paid a yearly rent of 2/6d
                         (WILLIAM SKEWS died in 1816)
Stevens Tenement   MARY SKEWS paid a yearly rent of 2/6d
SKEWES Tenement   THOMAS SKEWS paid a yearly rent of 2/6d

RENT BOOK FOR KILLIWERRIS 1818-1819
Magors Tenement   ANN SKEWS paid a yearly rent of 2/6d
Stevens Tenement   MARY SKEWS paid a yearly rent of 2/6d
SKEWES Tenement   Daniel Hodges paid a yearly rent of 2/6d

QUARTERLY MEETINGS OF THE SOCIETY OF FRIENDS (QUAKERS) 1609-1837

SKEWES SAMUEL DAWE   Born 16 March 1823 at Holmbush, St Austell, son of Daniel and Anna Skewes of Holmbush, blacksmith.

SKEWES ANNA   Buried 25 March 1832 at Trenangeeves. Wife of Daniel Skewes, engine man of St Austell. Lived in St Austell. Died 23 March 1832, aged 32 years.

SKEWES WILLIAM HENRY Died 24 June 1836, aged 6 months. Died at Pool, Illogan. Son of John Skewes. Buried Redruth 26 June 1836. He was not a member of the Society of Friends.

RECORDS OF THE REDRUTH UNION WORKHOUSE
Death on 13 March 1856, aged 62 years ANN SKEWES

CAMBORNE WESLEYAN INSTITUTE (1858)
At a meeting of the Camborne Wesleyan Institute held on 17 August 1858 Captain HENRY SKEWES seconded a motion (proposed by Dr George Smith, LLD., President).
HENRY SKEWES was on the committee in 1860 through to 1866. The object of the Institute was to promote the attainment of Biblical, Religious and General Knowledge, in direct accordance with the established Theology, Principals and Polity of the Methodist Connexion.

From the book "EARLY METHODISM IN CAMBORNE WESLEY CHAPEL 1828-1958" by J.E. Odgers (1959)
Appointed class leader in 1837 was EDWARD SKEWES.
The Wesley Sunday School, opposite the School of Mines in Camborne, in 1862 comprised 510 scholars with 92 teachers. The Superintendent was Captain SKEWES.

LAND TAX ASSESSMENTS FOR THE YEAR 1809 (Retained at County Record Office, Truro, Cornwall).

Camborne   Tenement   Carlean Wollas

| | Proprietor | Lord De Dunstanville |
| | Occupier | JOHN SKEWES |

	Tenement	Carlean Wartha
	Proprietor	Gregor and Harris
	Occupier	jOHN SKEWES

Cury	Tenement	Higher Treloskan
	Proprietor	Thomas Grylls, Esq.
	Occupier	JOHN SKEWES

St Ewe	Tenement	SKEWS
	Proprietor	John Rashleigh, Esq.
	Occupier	PHILIP WILLIAM SKEWS
	Date of contract	14 February 1800
	Contractor	John Rashleigh

Gwennap	Tenement	Chigenter
	Proprietor	Captain Trelawney
	Occupier	WILLIAM SKEWES

Helston	Tenement	Meneage Street, Helston
	Proprietor	Mr SKEWIS
	Occupier	Chopell and others

	Tenement	Meneage Street, Helston
	Proprietor	John Rogers
	Occupier	JOHN SKEWIS
	Stock & Trade	RICHARD SKUES

St Keverne	Tenement	Kenewas (part of)
	Proprietor	Rev Sir Carew Vyvyan
	Occupier	JOHN SKEWIS

	Tenement	Trelan
	Proprietor	Sir Michael Knowell
	Occupier	HENRY SKEWIS

	Tenement	Kenewas (part of)
	Proprietor	JOHN SKEWIS
	Occupier	Himself

	Tenement	Trelan and Gwenter
	Proprietor	James Murrish
	Occupier	HENRY SKEWIS

Kenwyn	Tenement	Basone Common
	Proprietor	Viscount Falmouth
	Occupier	RICHARD SKEWES

Ruan Major	Tenement	Tresodden (part of)
	Proprietor	Heirs of George Hunt, Esq.
	Occupier	HENRY SKEWES

	Tenement	Chybarlis
	Proprietor	Heirs of George Hunt, Esq.
	Occupier	HENRY SKEWES
	Contract for both	
	properties signed	24 December 1799
	Contractor	Miss Hunt.

TITHE APPORTIONMENT FOR TOWNS AND VILLAGES IN CORNWALL (1841-1843)

MAWNAN — Rosemullion

Landowners:	William Laity and John Laity
Occupier:	WILLIAM SKUES
Total contents of land:	85 acres 1 Rood 10 Perches
Total rent:	£18 10 0d

CURY   — Gilly

Landowner:	William Dale
Occupiers:	JAMES and EDWARD SKEWES
Total contents of land and cottages 14A 1R 39P	
Rent to vicar:	£1 4 0d
Rent to impropriator Richard Gerverys Grills	
	£1 17 0d

— Gilly

Landowners:	EDWARD and JAMES SKEWES
Occupiers:	EDWARD and JAMES SKEWES

Total contents of land and cottages and
orchards: 3A 1R 36P
Rent to vicar   9/6d
Rent to impropriator Richard Gerverys Grills
                      £— 14 0d

Poleskan   Landowner: JOHN SKEWIS
                      Occupier: JOHN SKEWIS
                      Total contents of cottage & garden 1R 30P
                      Rent to vicar   1/6d
                      Rent to impropriator Richard Gerverys Grills 1/6d

Treloskan   Landowner: JAMES SKEWES with Glynn Grills
                      Occupier: JAMES SKEWES
                      Total contents of fields & crofts 21A 1R 16P
                      Payable to vicar £1 5 6d
                      Payable to impropriator Richard Gerverys Grills
                      £2 6 0d

Treloskan   Landowner: WILLIAM SKEWIS
                      Occupier: WILLIAM SKEWIS
                      Total contents of cottages, fields and crofts
                                     26A 3R 3P
                      Payable to vicar £2 3 6d
                      Payable to impropriator Richard Gerverys Grills
                      £5 0 0d

Treloskan   Landowner: WILLIAM SKEWIS
                      Occupier: WILLIAM SKEWIS
                      Total contents of crofts & fields 6A 0R 36P
                      Payable to vicar 9/6d
                      Payable to impropriator Richard Gerverys Grills
                      14/-d

Treloskan   Landowners: EDWARD & JAMES SKEWIS
                      Occupiers: EDWARD & JAMES SKEWIS
                      Total content of fields & gardens 35A 1R 35P
                      Payable to vicar £3 4 0d
                      Payable to impropriator Richard Gerverys Grills
                      £7 0 0d

Treloskan   Landowners: EDWARD & JAMES SKEWIS
                      Occupiers: EDWARD & JAMES SKEWIS
                      Total content of homestead and common 1A 2R 18P
                      No rent payable

GWENNAP   Landowner: Peggy Whitter
                      Occupier: JOHN SKEWES
                      Total contents of land: 1 rood 25 perches
                      Payable to vicar: 2/2d
                      Payable to impropriator: 1/4d

GWENNAP   Landowner: Betty Stephens
                      Occupier: JOHN SKEWES
                      Total contents of land: 1 acre 3 roods
                      Payable to vicar: 8/8d
                      Payable to impropriator: 5/4d

GWENNAP   Landowner: Betty Stephens
                      Occupier: JOHN SKEWES
                      Total contents of land: 5 acres 24 perches
                      Payable to vicar: 10/6d
                      Payable to impropriator 6/6d.

GWENNAP   Landowner: Betty Stephens
                      Occupier   JOHN SKEWES
                      Total contents of land: 8 acres 28 perches
                      Payable to vicar: £1 0 7d
                      Payable to impropriator: 10/8d

GWENNAP   Landowner: Betty Stephens
                      Occupier: JOHN SKEWES

Total contents of land: 2 acres 1 rood
Payable to vicar: 5/8d
Payable to impropriator: 3/4d

GWENNAP   Landowner   Betty Stephens
                   Occupier   George Jones
                   Lessee: ALEXANDER SKEWES who leased cottage court and land. He also leased to Andrew Paul land and cottages at Carharrack comprising 3 acres 3 roods 17 perches; to John Davey a cottage and court 3 acres 21 perches; John Benbow, a cottage and court at Carharrack 2 roods 18 perches and to John Evoker-Fox, Esq., a coalyard at Carharrack 30 perches.

Total contents of land: 2 acres 1 rood 38 perches.
Payable to vicar: 5/8d
Payable to impropriator: 3/4d

GWENNAP   Landowner: Peggy Whitter
                   Occupier: JOHN SKEWES
                   Lessee: JOHN SKEWES for land, field, cottage and court.

Total contents of land: 1 rood 25 perches
Payable to vicar 2/2d
Payable to impropriator: 1/4d

ST DAY   Landowner: Betty Stephens
                   Occupier: JOHN SKEWES
                   Lessee: JOHN SKEWES for three arable fields at Carharrack.

Total contents of land: 1 acre 3 roods
Payable to vicar: 11/10d
Payable to impropriator 7/4d

ST DAY   Landowner: Betty Stephens
                   Occupier: JOHN SKEWES
                   Lessee: JOHN SKEWES for fields, cottage, court and watering place.

Total contents of land: 8 acres 28 perches
Payable to vicar: £1 0 7d
Payable to impropriator: 10/8d

ST DAY   Landowner: Betty Stephens
                   Occupier: JOHN SKEWES
                   Lessee: JOHN SKEWES on three arable fields.

Total contents of land: 2 acres 1 roods
Payable to vicar: 5/8d
Payable to impropriator: 3/4d

ST DAY   Landowner: Betty Stephens
                   Occupier: JOHN SKEWES
                   Lessee: JOHN SKEWES on six arable fields, croft and waste.

Total contents of land: 5 acres 24 perches
Payable to vicar: 10/6d
Payable to impropriator: 6/6d

GWENNAP   Landowner: Lord Clinton
                   Occupier: Frances Uren
                   Lessee: ALEXANDER SKEWES on garden, house, court and fields in Penance, Gwennap.

Total contents of land: 4 acres 2 roods 22 perches
Payable to vicar: 12/6d
Payable to impropriator: 8/6d

GWENNAP   Landowner: Lord Clinton
                   Occupier: John SKEWES
                   Lessee: Simon Davey on house, court, six arable fields and cottage.

Total contents of land: 4 acres 3 roods 12 perches
Payable to vicar: 13/-d
Payable to impropriator: 8/6d

GWENNAP   Landowner: Major Polwhele
                   Occupier: HENRY SKEWES
                   Lessee: Jane Williams on cottage, court, croft, close and five arable fields in Lannarth Common.

Total contents of land: 8 acres 3 roods 10 perches
Payable to vicar: 6/10d
Payable to impropriator: 4/4d

GWENNAP

Landowner: Rev James Blencowe
Occupier: JAMES SKEWES
Lessee: JAMES SKEWES on cottage, court, six arable fields and croft at Penstruthal, Gwennap.
Total contents of land: 5 acres 3 roods 24 perches
Payable to vicar: 6/6d
Payable to impropriator: 4/-d

CONSTANTINE:

Landowner: Rev John Rogers
Occupier: HENRY SKEWES
Total contents of land: 127 acres 2 roods 25 perches
Payable to vicar: £9 12 8d
Payable to impropriator: £9 0 9d

ILLOGAN

Landowner: Lady Bassett
Occupier: JOHN SKEWES
Total contents of land: 16 acres 5 roods 24 perches
Payable to vicar: £7 12 3d
Payable to impropriator: 12/9d

ILLOGAN

Landowner: Lady Bassett
Occupier: William Sincock
Lessee: JOHN SKEWES on land in Illogan
Total contents of land: 1 acre 2 roods 30 perches
Payable to vicar: 6/-d
Payable to impropriator: —

ILLOGAN

Landowner: Lady Bassett
Occupier: JOHN SKEWES
Total contents of land: 31 acres 2 roods 14 perches
Payable to vicar: £5 8 0d
Payable to impropriator: —

KENWYN

Landowner: Earl of Falmouth
Occupier: MATTHEW SKEWES
Total contents of land: 2 roods 24 perches
Payable to vicar: —
Payable to impropriatior: —

KENWYN

Landowner: Earl of Falmouth
Occupier: ROSE SKEWES
Total contents of land: 1 acre 1 rood 6 perches
Payable to vicar: 2/4d
Payable to impropriator: 2/5d

KENWYN

Landowner: Earl of Falmouth
Occupier: JOHN SKEWES
Total contents of land: 1 acre 32 perches
Payable to vicar: 2/2d
Payable to impropriator: 2/10d

KENWYN

Landowner: Earl of Falmouth
Occupier: JOHN SKEWES
Total contents of land: 1 acre 2 roods 12 perches
Payable to vicar: 2/5d
Payable to impropriator: 1/8d

KEA Seveock

Landowner: Earl of Falmouth
Occupier: JOHN SKEWES
Total contents of land: 12 acres 3 roods 7 perches
Payable to vicar: 12/1d
Payable to impropriator: £1 6 0d

KEA Cusveoth

Landowner: Earl of Falmouth
Occupier: RICHARD SKEWES
Lessee: RICHARD SKEWES
Total contents of land: 5 acres 3 roods 16 perches
Payable to vicar: 3/7d
Payable to impropriator: 3/3d

KEA Kerley

Landowner: Earl of Falmouth
Occupier: PETER SKEWES
Lessee: PETER SKEWES

Total contents of land: 4 acres 26 perches
Payable to vicar: 3/5d
Payable to impropriator: 6/9d

KEA Kerley
Landowner: Earl of Falmouth
Occupier: PETER SKEWES
Lessee: PETER SKEWES
Total contents of land: 7 acres 2 roods 25 perches
Payable to vicar: 5/5d
Payable to impropriator: 10/3d

KEA Nansauallan
Landowner: Earl of Falmouth
Occupier: RICHARD SKEWES
Lessee: Josiah Wasley
Total contents of land: 1 acre 1 rood 19 perches
Payable to vicar: 1/4d
Payable to impropriator: 2/6d

KEA Hugus Common
Landowner: Earl of Falmouth
Occupier: PETER SKEWES
Lessee: PETER SKEWES
Total contents of land: 2 acres 2 roods 12 perches
Payable to vicar: 1/4d
Payable to impropriator: 2/6d

KEA Nansauallan
Landowner: Earl of Falmouth
Occupier: RICHARD SKEWES
Lessee: RICHARD SKEWES
Total contents of land: 9 acres 2 roods 33 perches
Payable to vicar: 7/7d
Payable to impropriator: 6/4d

KEA Killiwerris
Landowner: Lord Clinton
Occupier: THOMAS SKEWES
Lessee: THOMAS SKEWES
Total contents of land: 19 acres 1 rood 15 perches
Payable to vicar: 6/-d
Payable to impropriator: 10/3d

KEA Killiwerris
Landowner: Lord Clinton
Occupier: THOMAS SKEWES
Lessee: George Pollard
Total contents of land: 3 acres 2 roods 14 perches
Payable to vicar: 1/5d
Payable to impropriator: 2/6d

CAMBORNE
Landowner: JAMES SKEWES
Occupier: William Sincock
Total contents of land: 7 perches
Payable to vicar: —
Payable to impropriator: —

CAMBORNE
Landowner: JAMES SKEWES
Occupier: JAMES SKEWES
Total contents of land: 31 acres 1 rood 37 perches
Payable to vicar: £6 16 3d
Payable to impropriator: —

CAMBORNE Red River Moor
Landowner: JAMES SKEWES
Occupier: William Sincock
Total contents of land: 3 acres 1 rood 10 perches
Payable to vicar: 8/6d
Payable to impropriator: —

CAMBORNE Killivoase
Landowner: JAMES SKEWES
Occupier: JAMES SKEWES
Total contents of land: 3 acres 1 rood 10 perches
Payable to vicar: 8/6d
Payable to impropriator: —

ST EWE Polgooth
Landowner: JOHN SKUES
Occupier: JOHN SKUES

Total contents of land: 18 acres 34 perches
Payable to vicar: £1 10 0d
Payable to impropriator: —

ST EWE Penstraze   Landowner: ANN SKUES
                    Occupier: Jacob Warne
                    Total contents of land: 3 acres 31 perches
                    Payable to vicar: 2/-d
                    Payable to impropriator: —

KILLIWERRIS LANDS RECEIPT PAPERS 1790-1840

First entry 1794

30 October, 1794	PETER SKEWES	paid £1 0 0d
23 November, 1795	PETER SKEWES	paid £1 0 0d
21 November, 1796	PETER SKEWES	paid 2/6d
	THOMAS SKEWES	paid 5/-d
23 October, 1797	PETER SKEWES	paid 2/6
	THOMAS SKEWES	paid 5/-d
9 August, 1798	PETER SKEWES	paid 2/6d
	THOMAS SKEWES	paid 5/-d
10 August, 1799	PETER SKEWES	paid 2/6d
	THOMAS SKEWES	paid 5/-d
23 October, 1800	PETER SKEWES	paid 2/6d
	THOMAS SKEWES	paid 2/6d
22 October, 1801	PETER SKEWES	paid 2/6d
	THOMAS SKEWES	paid 2/6d
5 October, 1802	PETER SKEWES	paid 2/6d
	THOMAS SKEWES	paid 2/6d
7 February, 1804	PETER SKEWES	paid 2/6d
	THOMAS SKEWES	paid 5/-d
22 October, 1804	THOMAS SKEWES	paid 5/-d
20 November, 1805	THOMAS SKEWES	paid 5/-d
27 November, 1806	THOMAS SKEWES	paid 2/6d
	MARY SKEWES	paid 2/6d
29 October, 1807	THOMAS SKEWES	paid 2/6d
	WILLIAM SKEWES	paid 2/6d
27 October, 1808	THOMAS SKEWES	paid 2/6d
	WILLIAM SKEWES	paid 2/6d

1809-1813 No SKEWES entries

10 November, 1814	WILLIAM SKEWES, THOMAS SKEWES & MARY SKEWES	each paid 2/6d
30 November, 1815	WILLIAM SKEWES, THOMAS SKEWES & MARY SKEWES	each paid 2/6d
25 November, 1816	WILLIAM SKEWES, THOMAS SKEWES & MARY SKEWES	each paid 2/6d
25 August, 1817	WILLIAM SKEWES, THOMAS SKEWES & MARY SKEWES	each paid 2/6d
31 August, 1818	WILLIAM SKEWES and MARY SKEWES	each paid 2/6d
9 August, 1819	WILLIAM SKEWES and MARY SKEWES	each paid 2/6d
19 June, 1820	WILLIAM SKEWES and MARY SKEWES	each paid 2/6d
2 July, 1821	WILLIAM SKEWES and MARY SKEWES	each paid 2/6d
5 August, 1822	MARY SKEWES paid 2/6d	WILLIAM SKEWES paid 2/6d
8 September, 1823	MARY SKEWES paid 2/6d	WILLIAM SKEWES paid 2/6d
21 September, 1824	MARY SKEWES paid 2/6d	WILLIAM SKEWES paid 2/6d
8 August, 1825	MARY SKEWES paid 2/6d	WILLIAM SKEWES paid 2/6d
14 July, 1826	MARY SKEWES paid 2/6d	WILLIAM SKEWES paid 2/6d
11 June, 1827	MARY SKEWES paid 2/6d	WILLIAM SKEWES paid 2/6d
28 July, 1828	MARY SKEWES paid 2/6d	WILLIAM SKEWES paid 2/6d
19 June, 1829	THOMAS SKEWES and MARY SKEWES	each paid 2/6d
27 May, 1830	THOMAS SKEWES and MARY SKEWES	each paid 2/6d
11 July, 1831	THOMAS SKEWES and MARY SKEWES	each paid 2/6d
25 June, 1832	THOMAS SKEWES and MARY SKEWES	each paid 2/6d
1 July, 1833	THOMAS SKEWES and MARY SKEWES	each paid 2/6d
23 June, 1834	THOMAS SKEWES and MARY SKEWES	each paid 2/6d
6 July, 1835	THOMAS SKEWES and MARY SKEWES	each paid 2/6d
20 June, 1836	THOMAS SKEWES and MARY SKEWES	each paid 2/6d
26 June, 1837	THOMAS SKEWES and MARY SKEWES	each paid 2/6d
23 July, 1838	THOMAS SKEWES and MARY SKEWES	each paid 2/6d
2 September, 1839	THOMAS SKEWES and MARY SKEWES	each paid 2/6d
11 May, 1840	THOMAS SKEWES and MARY SKEWES	each paid 2/6d

TRADE DIRECTORY FOR CORNWALL, 1844
CAMBORNE: ANN SKEWES, Shopkeeper.
REDRUTH: MATTHEW SKEWES, Retailer of beer, Chacewater.
TRURO: THOMAS SKEWES, Kenwyn Street. Tavern called "New Inn."

TRADE DIRECTORY FOR CORNWALL, 1847
REDRUTH: MARTIN SKEWES, Victualler, Britannia Inn, Chacewater.
REDRUTH: MATTHEW SKEWES, Beer Retailer, Chacewater.
ST. AUSTELL:JOHN SKEWS, Victualler "Death of General Wolfe", St Austell.
TRURO: HENRY SKEWES, Victualler, "New Inn", Kenwyn Street.
TRURO: THOMAS SKEWES, Shopkeeper, Daniell Street, Truro.

POSTAL DIRECTORY FOR DEVON AND CORNWALL (Harrison) for the year 1862

CROWAN	SKEWES	JAMES	Farmer
	SKEWES	WILLIAM	Farmer
TRURO	SKEWES	THOMAS	Grocer of Daniell Street
MAWNAN	SKEWIS	EDWARD	Blacksmith
	SKEWIS	JAMES	Coal Merchant and Farmer
CONSTANTINE	SKEWES	JOSIAH	Farmer
CURY	SKEWES	EDWARD	Farmer
	SKEWES	Mrs	Farmer
LIZARD TOWN	SKEWES	HENRY	Wheelwright, carpenter andd lodging house keeper
MAWGAN-IN-MENEAGE	SKEWES	HENRY	Schoolmaster
RUAN MAJOR	SKEWES	ANTHONY	Farmer
RUAN MINOR	SKEWES	LOVEDAY	Shopkeeper
ST DAY	SKEWES	Mrs M.A.	Dressmaker
ILLOGAN	SKEWIS	JOHN	Farmer at Roscroggan
GWINEAR	SKEWES	HENRY	Mine Agent
BEER ALSTON	SKEWES	DANIEL	Grocer and Mine Agent
	SKEWES	SAMUEL	Druggist and tea dealer

COURT BOOKS-QUARTER SESSIONS 1831-1836 (County Record Office, Truro) General Quarter Sessions at Truro 3 April 1832.
Upon the Appeal of HENRY SKEWIS against an assessment for the necessary relief of the poor and for other purposes in the several Acts of Parliament mentioned relating to the poor in the Parish of Constantine in the said county made and assessed 23 day of February last by James Mayn and Henry Harvey, Churchwardens and Thomas Boaden and Jonathan Stephens, Overseers being third rate at nine pence in the pound for the present year and upon hearing what could be alleged it is ordered by this court that the said appeal be continued over to the next General Quarter Sessions of the Peace to be holden for this county.

QUARTER SESSIONS AT BODMIN 1836-1845
Midsummer Session, Bodmin 30 June 1841
BENJAMIN SKEWES, late of the parish of Budock in this county, labourer was at this Sessions indicted and tried for that he, on the 22nd day of April last, with force and arms at the parish aforesaid three pounds weight of copper to the value of sixpence and three pounds of weight of metal to the value of another sixpence, the property of James Bell and then and these being fixed to a covered shed of the said James Bell there situate feloniously did steal, take and carry away against the form of the Statute and acquitted by the Country.

Bodmin, 1 December 1844
Elizabeth Dunstone late of the parish of Kea in this county, spinster and John Dunstone, late of the same place, labourer, were at this Sessions indicted and tried for feloniously stealing 24 pounds weight of potatoes to the value of two shillings — the property of JOHN SKEWS — and acquitted by this Country.

BIBLIOTHECA CORNUBIENSIS by George Clement Boase & William P. Courteney
A catalogue of writings, both manuscript and printed, of Cornishmen, and of works relating to the county of Cornwall, with biographical memoranda and copious literary references. (1874)
SKUES RICHARD; deputy steward of H.M. Coinage in Cornwall and Devon; took the surname of Scott instead of that of Skues by Royal Licence and Authority 12 March, 1827. Married Susannah Marie Martha Scott, daughter of John Scott of Saltash, Principal Officer of H.M. Dockyard, Devonport.
SKEWES, Rev JOSEPH HENRY M.A. (Son of William SKEWES, born Constantine 4 November, 1807; married Elizabeth daughter of Joseph and Bathsheba Glasson. She was born Truthall, Sithney 20 March, 1808); born Constantine 29 April, 1837. Wesleyan Minister 1862. Left the connection 1875 and entered Church of England 1876. A Complete and Classified Index (to suit all editions) of the Journals of the Rev. John Wesley, M.A. by the Rev. J.H. SKEWES. London, Elliot stock, 1872. pp64 price one shilling.
SKEWES EDWARD — miner — c.f. Rep. of Miners' Association of C & D. 1876, p4. The Gwinear Mining District; an essay. Rep. RCP. Soc. 1875, p32.

CAREW's SURVEY OF CORNWALL, published 1811   Re: JOHN SKUISH (SKEWYS)
Born said Doctor Fuller in Cornwall, probably at SKEWES in Cury, where a family of that name then resided. He was a man of much experience and general learning. He was, saith Bale, de Script Brit cent 9, number 19, "A Councilius to Cardinal Wolsey whereby I collect him learned of the laws, and of his counsel."
This Skuish wrote a Chronicle, being collected out of many several authors. I have some presumption to conclude him inclined of the Protestant reformation. He flourished Anno Domini 1530. Thus far Fuller, Bishop Nicholson saith "He was Cardinal Wolsey's menial servant, and he is reported to have compiled a notable Epitome of our Chronicles, about the year 1530, but I am not able to direct the reader where to meet with it."
For my part I am tempted from the sameness of the the name and subject, viz, "An Epitome of Chronicles", to believe that these two John Skewish's maybe reslolved into one and the same person, notwithstanding the difference of the times they are severally. said to have lived in, but am not able to guess which is in the right to that, though I incline to Mr Carew, or at least, that the last was not a writer, though mentioned as such.

DIRECTORY FOR DORSET — 1859
WAREHAM
Insurance clerk for Emperor Insurance T.T. SKEWES
Gentleman's Boarding School, Elm House — THOMAS LEAN SKEWES

DIRECTORY FOR DORSET — 1874-1885 inc
THOMAS LEAN SKEWES was listed as an Alderman living at Elm House, North Street, Wareham (In 1871 Directory he was a Councilman). He had moved on from an Alderman, but still living at Elm House Scholastic Acadamy (1890 Directory).
From 1903-1939 (at least) ALBERT EDWARD SKEWES was an Elective Auditor for Wareham Corporation. He is listed in the directories (1907 — 1939) as living at Elm House, North Street, Wareham, Boarding School for young gentlemen. In the 1900 Wareham Pictorial Guide there is an advertisement for the school:

> ELM HOUSE, WAREHAM
> BOY'S BOARDING AND DAY SCHOOL
>
> A good modern education is guaranteed.
> Established upwards of 60 years.
> Pupils prepared for Public Examinations.
> Terms most moderate. Principal Mr A.E. SKEWES. M.R.C.P

DRAKE WALLS MINE, CALSTOCK, EAST CORNWALL
A very ancient tin mine, situate near Gunnislake, on the right bank of the River Tamar in East Cornwall.
The position of the mineral deposit is marked by a great excavation and a long run of broken ground resulting from the working away of the back of the lode and of a series of subordinate branches which have been wrought as a stockwork from time immemorial. A length of about 400 fathoms has thus been thoroughly worked away to a depth of 80 fathoms.

(Observations of the West of England Mining Region. J.H. Collins
(William Brendon and Son, Plymouth, 1912 page 77)
The mine has many times been abandoned and restarted.
From 1853 to 1860 tin ore tons 2064 value £137,368.
1861-1870 1673 tons value £111,451
1871-1880. 911 tons value £53,451
1881-1890 441 tons value £23,088

The engine shaft was sunk to a depth of 190 fathoms.
Captain WILLIAM SKEWIS was the principal Agent of Adventurers who worked lands in the parish of Calstock, part of the Manor of Calstock.
Very considerable damage had been caused by the adventurers to the lands, tenements, waters and water courses. The damage was of a continuing nature. The adventurers were accused of polluting streams of pure drinking water which belonged to Reginald Buller Edgecumbe Gill. The streams ran to the farm house rendering it unfit for drinking and thereby causing the owner great expense and inconvenience as he had to obtain other waters for the use of his tenants and for cattle. Damage was estimated at £83 18 6d. Mr Gill had made frequent applications to SKEWIS for compensation and gave him full particulars of the damage done. Gill lived at Ward House, Beer Ferris, Devon.
SKEWIS was ordered to appear before the Court at Princes Hall, Truro, 21 February 1876 at 10.30am. The case lasted three days. It was adjourned until 8 August 1876 at 11.00am.
Six witnesses were called for Gill who were two yeomen, three land surveyors and one banker.
SKEWIS was found to be in fault and ordered to pay £42 11 6d for damage done to Gill's lands and was ordered to pay within four days, and also to pay the costs incurred in the case which totalled £51 15 3d. That also to be paid within four days.
Amongst the Solicitors charges was 3/6d for a letter sent to Captain Skewis on 29 December 1875 and attending Skewis' house, seeing him with the claim on 4 January 1876 — 6/8d.

LIST OF ARREARS IN THE MATTER OF THE COMPANIES ACT 1862 — WEST DRAKE WALLS MINING COMPANY.

WILLIAM SKEWIS, Mine Captain of Tavistock in his own right owned 100 shares. A call for 1/-d per share (£5) was made on 11 February. And a further call of 2/-d was made on 13 May 1873. (£10.00) 1873

On 15 July 1875 Skewis paid by cheque £45 on a call of 9/-d per share.

ROSKEAR MINE CAMBORNE Formerly Wheal Chance. A very ancient mine "Yielded large quantities of copper ore about 50 years ago" (Pryce — Mineralogia Cornubiensis, 1778). In 1770 Richard Trevethick received a grant of the settlement from Sir Francis Bassett and erected an engine there in 1777.

ROSKEAR MINING COMPANY

WILLIAM SKEWIS of Crelake, near Tavistock was the Secretary or Purser and kept the books of the said mine and that the principal place of business of the said Company was on the Mine. The Company was divided into 6000 shares. William Skewis owned 4000 shares.
A petition was filed 26 May 1866 which sought to wind up the Company in the Court of the Vice Warden of the Stannaries.
William Skewis was served on 19 May 1866. The hearing was set for 28 May 1866 at Princes Hall, Truro.
It was agreed that the Mine would be sold at 12 noon 22 June 1866. "For Sale about 140 tons of tin stuff and a variety of articles and effects in general use in the Mine." The sale of items brought £52 11. 0d. Capt William Skewis bought a Horse Whim for £2 15 0 and a Pully Stand and Shieves, shaft tackle and pulleys for £1 15 0 and a whim chain for £4 13 0d., as well as Iron Ladders from West Ladder Road shaft for 15/-d

16 persons had claims against the Company for £219, including Edward Skewes who was allowed £24.

A call of 1/6d per share was called on all shareholders 22 November 1867. William Skewis was due to pay £300 on 25 November but he did not pay up, so a writ was issued by the Lord Warden of the Stannaries 13 December 1867 to pay £300 plus 11/8d for the writ. William Monk, Bailiff confirmed that William Skewis paid the debt on 4 January 1868.
The Company was wound up 27 April 1871. It had been in operation since September 1863.
(Roskear Cash Book, General Papers. County Record Office, Truro)

WARD v SKEWIS
COURT OF THE VICE-WARDEN OF THE STANNARIES
STANNARIES OF CORNWALL
SOUTH ROSKEAR TIN AND COPPER MINE

Between Frank Ward, Plaintiff and WILLIAM SKEWIS, Defendant

18 August 1877. WILLIAM SKEWIS received a Summons on 2 June 1877 at Langstone, Devon.
"To the Adventurers and others interested in the mine called South Roskear Tin and Copper Mine.
Notice is hereby given that a Petition was on 2 June instant filed in the Vice-Wardens Court by Mary Anne Ward, John Caddock Chowen and Frank Ward against WILLIAM SKEWIS the Principal Agent of the above mine, for payment of the sum of £79 11 6d due from the adventurers, and for the sale of the ores, machinery, materials and effects, in default of payment. Dated 2nd day of June 1877. J.G. Chilcott, Agent for Edward Chilcott, Tavistock, Plaintiffs Solicitor.
The £79 11 6d being £76 14 6d for goods and materials purchased by the Roskear Tin and Copper Mine at Bottle Hill Mine sale on 18 July 1876 and £2 17 0d for interest thereon.
The Court costs amounted to £7 8 4d making a total of £86 19 0d and on receipt of that amount of money being received the petition would be withdrawn. An amount was paid 12 June 1877, but a letter from Captain James Hosking asked for more time to pay the costs. Further letters were sent on June 28th 1877, 6 July, 10 July and 21 July. He did not pay up so he was summoned to appear in Court.

INDEX OF POLICE CONVICTIONS FOR THE COUNTY OF CORNWALL QUARTER SESSIONS
1865-1880, retained at the COUNTY RECORD OFFICE, TRURO.

Sessions	Name	Offence	Conviction date
Easter	JAMES SKEWES	Allowing cows to stray on the highway	29 March 1865
Epiphany	SAMUEL SKEWES	and Matthew Palmer for felony	24 Oct 1865
Easter	JAMES SKEWES	Allowing four bullocks to stray on highway	25 Feb 1868
Midsummer	JOHN SKEWES	Allowing a horse to stray on highway	2 May 1868
Michaelmas	JAMES SKEWES	Unjust weights	27 Sept 1871
Epiphany	JAMES SKEWES	Cattle straying	25 Oct 1872
Michaelmas	ELIZABETH SKEWES	Drunk	10 Sept 1872
Epiphany	JAMES SKEWES	Vagrancy	6 Nov 1872
Michaelmas	JOHN SKEWES	Cattle straying	24 May 1873
Easter	ELIZABETH ANN SKEWES	Drunk	31 March 1874
Midsummer	JOHN SKEWES	Cruelty to animals	23 May 1874
Epiphany	PETER SKEWES	Offence against Mines Act	4 Nov 1874
Midsummer	JOSEPH SKEWES	Donkey straying	4 April 1872
Michaelmas	JAMES SKEWES	Bullocks straying	28 March 1877
Michaelmas	JOHN SKEWES	Furious driving	23 Aug 1877
Easter	WILLIAM SKEWIS	and Moses Bawden. Keeping unfenced shafts	3 Jan 1878

Michaelmas WILLIAM SKEWIS	Offence against Metalliferous Mines Act	5 Sept 1878
Michaelmas JAMES SKEWES	Cows straying	31 July 1878
Epiphany BENJAMIN SKEWES	Keeping dog without licence	27 Nov 1878
Epiphany WILLIAM SKEWIS	Keeping unfenced shafts	5 Dec 1878
Midsummer JAMES SKEWES	Bullock straying	26 May 1879

QUARTER SESSIONS 1898-1900

Christmast, West Penwith RICHARD SKEWES Bullocks straying	6 Dec 1899	
Midsummer, West Penwith RICHARD SKEWES No light on vehicle	6 June 1900	
Michaelmas, West Penwith RICHARD HENRY SKEWES Riding furiously	1 Aug 1900	
Michaelmas, Helston RICHARD SKEWES Drunk whilst in charge	22 Sept 1900	

COLLECTANEA CORNUBIENSA.... George Clement Boase, Truro, 1890

SKEWES   FAMILY cf. Macleans History of Trigg Minor iii 385-387; C.S. Gilberts Cornwall i. 129, ii 265, 613, 642

SKEWES   JOHN of Gwennap. Sent articles on mathematics to the Ladies Diary. London, 1807, et seq.

SKEWES   Rev JOHN, youngest son of WILLIAM SKEWES of Bolitho, Crowan. Born 6 February, 1846. Educ. Crowan. Of Univ. of Oxford. B.A. 1873; M.A. 1876. Ordained 1874. C of All Souls, Manchester 1875-1882. Sailed for Australia for the benefit of his health 21 October, 1882. Was presented with £225 by his parishioners before his departure. Married September, 1883. Died Sandhurst, Australia 1 October, 1884.

SKEWES   ALEXANDER of Gwennap was named with R. Bain to be receivers of Williams, Foster and Company. The Times, 2 August 1862, p. 13. Col 5; West Briton 8 August, 1862, p6.

SKEWES   JAMES of Cury. John Symons born 6 March, 1680. Of Ruan Minor and Sidbury. Died 9 March, 1736. Married i) HANNAH SKEWES only child of JAMES SKEWES of Cury. Issue one son John Symons. He married ii) 1719, Ann, daughter of W. Dommett of Shute, Devon. Issue two children: William Symons and Ann Symons

SKEWES   MARY of Helston. William Michell, fourth child of R & E Michell of Calenick, 1776. With his brother Robert was a merchant at Truro. Resided at Comprigney, Kenwyn. Died Perranporth 5 February, 1845. Buried Kenwyn. Monument in Church. Cf. Bibl Cornub. 355. Married i) 1802, MARY SKEWES of Helston. She died Truro 20 April, 1811. Issue: Mary Michell and William Michell. William Michell remarried ii) Elizabeth Cornish Vincent of Liskes in Kenwyn. Issue: Elizabeth Michell.

SKUES   RICHARD. Surgeon. Died Helston 17 November, 1811, aged 45 years.

SKUES   RICHARD of Helston. Wife died Falmouth 8 April, 1821.

SKEWES. Appointment of H. de Montfort to take the assise arraigned by ALAN de SKIWERS and ANNORA his wife, against MATTHEW de SKIWERS and DODUS de SKIWERS touching a tenement in SKEWES.
Patent Rolls. III Edward; i 1275. Forty fourth Rep. Dep. Keeper of Records 1883, page 239.

From "THE PARLIAMENTARY HISTORY OF CORNWALL", by W.P. Courtney (1889)

A JOHN SKEWES sat for the Borough of Helston in 1331 (possibly he was the ancestor of the JOHN SKEWES who, two generations later, lived in Wolsey's household and acted as his deputy when the Cardinal officiated as Lord Chancellor), and the name, after the lapse of many generations, is still common in the parishes around Helston.

From "TUDOR CORNWALL", A.L. ROWSE

Of Cornish Members of Henry's last Parliament we only know William Trewynnard, member for Helston in 1542, for he gave his name to a leading case concerning the privilege of a member from arrest for debt. He was imprisoned for a debt of £75 to JOHN SKEWES and released by the Sheriff Richard Chamond on receipt of a Writ of Privilege from the King.
(Hastell — Precedents in the House of Commons (i) 59-65)

RETURN OF OWNERS OF LAND IN GREAT BRITAIN (1873)

		Acres	Poles	Perches
CORNWALL	SKEWES, EDWARD of Cury. Extent of Land	—	8	23
	Gross estimated rental £13			
	SKEWES, GRACE of Breage. Extent of Land	3	1	6
	Gross estimated rental £16			
	SKEWES, JAMES of Mawnan. Extent of Land	32	1	23
	Gross estimated rental £66			
DEVON	SKEWIS, WILLIAM of Tavistock. Extent of Land	5	3	17
	Gross estimated rental £34			

TIN DEPOSITS OF THE WORLD by Sydney Fawns (1905)

Makes reference to an article by EDWARD SKEWES in the Engineering and Mining Journal, 19 September, 1903

THE MINING ASSOCIATION & INSTITUTE OF CORNWALL — List of Members, Annual Subscribers and Associates, 1st January 1886 to 1 January 1888 inc

Members include W. SKEWES of Tavistock, Devon. Subscription 10/6d

Successful candidates at the May examination, 1889 R. SKEWIS of Redruth.

UNITED METHODIST CHAPEL, REDRUTH. LIST OF MEMBERS (1886-1921)

1886 JANE SKEWES of Fords Row, Redruth was on trial in Thomas Trounson's class on Wednesdays at 7.15pm. She became a full member by 1887, but was missing from the registers from then on.

1887	MARY SKEWES	Full member
	ELIZABETH SKEWES	Full member
1900	AMELIA SKEWES	On trial
	MAGGIE SKEWES	On trial
	MARY SKEWES	Full member
1905	ELIZABETH SKEWES	Full member-unattached
	MAGGIE SKEWES	Full member
1908	MAGGIE SKEWES	Removed
	MARY SKEWES	Full member
1911	ETHEL SKEWES	Full member
	MARY SKEWES	Full member
1916	ETHEL SKEWES	Full member
1918	ETHEL SKEWES	Full member
1921	ETHEL SKEWES	Trefusis Terrace

(Registers retained at the County Record Office, Truro)

METHODISM IN CURY To celebrate Diamond Jubilee of the Church 1799-1950
In 1887, the year of Queen Victoria's Jubilee, Mr James Lawrence records that the Wesleyan Society included the SKEWES of Nantithet.

On Good Friday, 1891 the completed Wesleyan Chapel building was open for public worship. Included in the 15 trustees was HENRY SKEWES.

HENRY SKEWES also became Superintendent of the Wesley Methodist Sunday School.

The Superintendents of the United Methodist Sunday School included WESLEY SKEWES and William Hendy of SKEWES, Cury.

GWENNAP CHURCHYARD GRAVESTONES and BURIAL PLACES 1884-1912
From a notebook retained at the County Record Office, Truro.
1884 SKEWES JOHN 13 March Old ground Headstone
1888 SKEWES ANN of Little Carharrack Old ground Aged 81 years.

HISTORICAL SURVEY OF THE COUNTY OF CORNWALL by C.S. GILBERT
London, 1820.

OFFICERS of the DUCHY of CORNWALL for the year 1819
Vice Warden: John Vivian, Esq. His secretary John Edwards, Esq.
Deputies to the surveyor-general and auditor: Robert Gray, Esq., & Robert Abbot, Esq.
Deputy receiver-general: Charles Carpenter.
Steward of the Stannary Courts: J. James, Esq.
Steward of the Coinages: RICHARD SKUES, Esq.
Supervisors of Tin in Cornwall and Devon: B. Hearne, RICHARD SKUES, Nicholas Middlecoat and John Roe.

JURORS LIST FOR CORNWALL 1859/1860
Constantine Josiah Skewes, farmer of Bosawsack.
Gwennap Alexander Skewes, agent of Trevarth, Gwennap.
Gwennap James Skewes, farmer of Carvannell.
RUAN MAJOR Anthony Skewes, farmer of Tresodden.
CROWAN William Skewes of Bolitho, farmer.
KEA John Skewes, farmer of Killiwerris, Kea.
TRURO Thomas Skewes, mason of Daniell Street, Truro.

DEEDS BROUGHT FROM ST ANTHONY TO FALMOUTH 31 JULY 1920 (translated by Charles Henderson) and retained at the Royal Institution of Cornwall, Truro.

Bundle 5 (Press 29/30)
Thursday before the exaltation of the Cross 26 Henry VI. (14 September 1441). MARINA relict of JOHN SKYWES enfeoffs Ralph Joran of all her lands in SKYWES, TRESCREWYN and Treranguyth and all her goods and chattels and to hold to him and Enora his wife and the issue between them. Ralph and Enora will allow Marina meat, drink and lodging.
At the discretion of John Penros Methele, Jho Luddre, RIC SKYWES and John Trevys.
Witnesses: W. Gurlyn, RIC SKYWES, John Trevis.

The above letters have been copied exactly from the original letters and include (in some cases) spelling mistakes and grammatical errors.

ADMISSION REGISTERS TO CORNISH SCHOOLS
CROWAN GIRLS 1856-1874
SKEWIS MARY ANN aged 9 years. Lived at Cargenwin, Crowan. Was admitted on 14 July 1856. Father's occupation — small farmer. Previous instruction in education was at this school. She was readmitted on October 12th 1857. She could not write.

REDRUTH EAST END PRIMARY SCHOOL (1885-1945)
SKEWS MAGGIE
Daughter of Samuel Skews of Fords Row. Born 24 June 1882. Date of admission 20 July 1885.
SKEWS CHARLES
Son of William Skews of Roaches Row, Redruth. Both 6 September 1881. Admitted 23 March 1885. Left 19 July 1886 for the New School.
SKEWS CHARLIE
Son of James Skewes of Roaches Row, Redruth. Born 26 March 1882. Admitted 1 March 1886. Left 19 July 1886 for the New School.
SKEWS MATTHEW
Son of Matthew Skews of Roaches Row, Redruth. Born 25 March 1883. Admitted 12 April 1886.
SKEWS BESSIE
Daughter of John Skews of Roaches Row, Redruth. Born 16 July 1882. Admitted 2 May 1886. Left 19 July 1886 for the New School.
SKEWS MAGGIE
Daughter of John Skews of St Day Road, Redruth. Born 21 April 1883. Admitted 31 May 1886.
SKEWS BESSIE
Daughter of C. Skews of Roaches Row, Redruth. Born 18 February 1883. Admitted 1 March 1887.
SKEWS MAGGIE
Daughter of J. Skews of Shute Row, Redruth. Born 19 June 1883. Admitted 14 March 1887.
SKEWS CHARLES
Son of W. Skews of Blights Row, Redruth. Born 12 June 1883. Admitted 10 August 1887.
SKEWS WILFRED
Son of S. (?) Skews of Shute Row. Born 7 March 1885. Admitted 14 April 1888.
SKEWS LOUIS
Son of S. (?) Skews of Roaches Row, Redruth. Born 24 July 1885. Admitted 1 April 1889.
SKEWES LILLIE
Daughter of J. Skewes of East End, Redruth. Born 4 January 1885. Admitted 15 April 1890.
SKEWES JOSEPH
Son of W. Skewes of Fore Street, Redruth. Born 12 April 1887. Admitted 8 May 1892.
SKEWES CLARA
Daughter of W. Skewes of Bellevue, Redruth. Born 16 February 1889. Admitted 24 April 1893.
SKEWES LILY
Daughter of Lewis Skewes of Clarence Villas, Redruth. Born 24 July 1894. Admitted 3 September 1900. Left school 28 February 1902. "A delicate pupil."
SKEWES DORIS
Daughter of E.A. Skewes of East End, Redruth. Born 6 September 1900. Admitted 23 April 1906. Left 1 April 1908.
SKEWES MAY
Lived at St Day Road, East End, Redruth. Born 28 May 1904. Admitted 9 March 1909. Left 1 April 1912.
SKEWES LILY
Lived at East End, Redruth. Born 3 June 1906. Admitted 13 June 1910. Left 1 April 1913.
SKEWES PHYLLIS
Daughter of Fred Skewes. Born 25 February 1908. Admitted 2 September 1912. Left 12 April 1915.
SKEWES J. FREDERICK
Son of Fred Skewes of Trefusis Terrace, Redruth. Born 28 June 1909. Admitted 14 July 1913. Left 1 April 1917.
SKUES LEWIS
Son of James Frederick Skues of Trefusis Terrace, Redruth. Born 12 July 1912. Admitted 1 October 1917. Left 31 July 1919 to go to a special school.
SKEWES HARRY
Son of Stephen James Skewes of Trefusis Terrace, Redruth. Born 12 February 1916. Admitted 14 February 1921. Left 9 April 1923.
SKEWES JAMES
Son of Stephen James Skewes of Trefusis Terrace, Redruth. Born 26 June 1919. Admitted 2 June 1924. Left 1 April 1926.

REDRUTH COUNTY SCHOOL 1895-1950
SKEWS   MATTHEW
Son of John Skews of 5 Canfield Place, Plain-an-Gwarry, Redruth; master bootmaker. Born 7 August 1910. Admitted 19 September 1923. Previous school Trewirgie School, Redruth.
SKEWES   JACK PATTISON OSWALD
Son of James Henry Oswald Skewes of 7 Moor Street, Camborne. Born 10 May 1923. Father was a fitter and turner. Admitted 14 September 1934. Previous school Roskear Boys School 1931-August 1934. Left school 26 July 1940.

ST GEORGE's SCHOOL, TRURO 1885-1922
SKEWES   CHARLES
Son of Mrs Skewes of Tippetts Backlet. Born 19 March 1881. Date of admission .31 January 1888. Previously attended St Mary's Truro.
SKEWES   MARION
Daughter of William Skewes of 1 John Street, Truro. Born 4 April 1897. Admitted 11 January 1904. Left school January 1906.

SKEWES   WILLIAM
Son of Mrs C. Skewes of 76 Chapel Hill, Truro. Born 28 November 1913. Admitted 3 June 1918. Left to go to Plymouth May 1920.
Readmitted 3 April 1922. Left for Baldhu 3 April 1925.
SKEWES   JOHN
Son of H. Skewes of 9 St Dominic Street, Truro. Born 31 May 1910. Admitted 15 October 1917.

REGISTER OF POLICE FOR THE COUNTY OF CORNWALL (1857-1920)
Retained at the County Record Office, Truro.

SKEWES   JOHN P.C. 73.
Aged 25 years. Height 5' 11¾". Long visage. Pale complexion. Dark grey eyes. Dark brown hair. No particular marks. Good figure. Born in Cury. Trade: Shoemaker. Can read and write. Married with two children; Lived at Nantithet, Cury. Last employed by his father Edward Skewes in Nantithet. Declaration taken 27 September 1864. Declaration — "I do declare that I will well and truly serve our Sovereign Lady The Queen in the office of Constable for the county of Cornwall without favour or affection, malice or ill will, and that I will, to the best of my power, casue the Peace to be kept and preserved, and prevent all offences against the persons and properties of Her Majesty's Subjects; and that while I continue to hold the said office, I will, to the best of my skill and knowledge, discharge all the duties thereof faithfully, according to law."
Date of appointment 6 August 1864. Attached to Penzance District 30 September 1864. Resigned from the force 27 October 1865. Character good. Conduct good. Abilities moderate.
SKEWES   THOMAS WILLIAM
P.C. 157. Aged 21 years. 5'9½". Long visage. Dark complexion. Light brown eyes. Dark brown hair. No particular marks. Spare figure. Born Cury. Trade: shoemaker. Can read and write. Single but married 15 September 1874 to Eliza Bray of Stithians. No children: Resided in Cury. Employed by his father Edward Skewes formerly in Cury.
Dated 10 December 1872. Date of appointment 9 December 1872. Promoted to second class P.C. 29 July 1877.

Promoted to first class P.C. 28 December 1890. Promoted to Sergeant 6 May 1895.
1 May 1873 Penzance.
26 January 1884 Truro.
8 May 1895 Bodmin.
31 October 1899 Launceston.
Resigned from the force under Medical Certificate 30 September 1900. Superannuation £51 14 2d.
Died on 23rd December 1943, aged 91 years.

From the book "Devonshire Regiment", by Lt. Col. O.G.W. White (1948)
Gunner HUGH WILLIAM SKUES (1708505), aged 35 served with 54 Brigade, 2nd Battalion The Devonshire Regiment. He and his colleagues were on the advance to Mandalay fighting the Japanese in 1945. They were advancing 14 miles from Sinde to Kadozeik "a right hook across country which varied from wood to rock to open paddy ending up in tall jungle grass."

"At 08.30 on 15th March, 1945 B and C Companies ran smack into enemy positions about half a mile west of the village of Kadozeik.The country around the village was thickly cultivated with banana plantations." It was here that Gunner Skues and a dozen colleagues were killed in action 'on the road to Mandalay' just four days short of reaching their destination.

SCHOOLS ROUNDABOUT — Memeries of St Keverne, Traboe and Porthallow
Schools 1877-1977.

Articles written by past and present teachers and pupils.

THE OLD SCHOOL SPEAKS by M.B. SKEWES, Teacher

Where are they now, the children I recall?
Gone from the village, grown so fine and tall,
Johnnie who laughed, and only longed to play.
And Willie, little Willie, who dreamed the days away.

Where are they now, the children I once knew?
Grown soon to manhood, how their young years flew!
Jimmie who toiled, whose thoughts would never stray,
And Willie, little Willie, who dreamed the days away.

Johnnie marched out to fight the Boers. He lies
In sun parched earth, far from Cornish skies;
And Jimmie met his Maker on a Flanders Hill,
And Willie lies in the Atlantic, dreaming still.

DENNIS IVOR JOHN SKEWES:

I can remember carrying a gas mask to school and the beach barricaded with barbed wire. The wall at the top of the beach was much bigger then. One day the boys were fishing from the rocks, when a German aeroplane came over. The plane was low enough for the German Crosses to be seen easily. This is the plane that went on to bomb Coverack. Mr Dyer, teacher and voluntary warden, came running along the beach blowing on his whistle and shouting to the boys to lay flat.
On another occasion shrapnel was found lodged in the school roof.

ARTHUR SKEWES, former Teacher:

School Camp. Circa 1950. This was a new venture indeed. During the summer holidays a number of the old pupils were going for a week's camp at Maker. Plans were made and pennies saved. The journey itself involved several changes en route — but was I suspect easier to make by public transport then than it might be today — nearly 30 years later. The morning was bright and fair and no doubt there was much excitement in St Keverne Square and many attentive ears listening for the bus coming up from Laddenvean. Then followed an hour's bus journey to Helston station and a change to the train which took the party to Gwinear Road. Here excitement mounted again, for we were to join the Cornish Riviera train for Plymouth and we found several who had never actually seen it, travelled on it, or indeed, been further from home in Truro.
The journey proved enjoyable and in due course the train pulled in at Plymouth station, and we all made our way to join another bus. This gave many of our youngsters their first view of the centre of Plymouth, still only partially rebuilt after wartime ravages. I can easily remember one young lady, who shall remain anonymous, viewing the lobelia and geraniums growing on the central reservation and exclaiming "Id'n it 'ansum up 'ere, they even got flower gardens on the pavement."
However, in due time we boarded the ferry to Millbrook and once more by bus we journeyed to the camp gate. At the camp there was a comfortable dormitory accommodation and a resident catering staff who provided us with well cooked meals. The week was one of brilliant sunshine and considerable time was spent on the beach and in the water.
Friendships were soon struck up with staff and children from other schools visiting the site. It was soon discovered that the quickest way to travel to Plymouth was by launch along the coast. One excursion, I know, was made to the Hoe swimming pool, the fountain of which provided fun.
Another trip was made to Plymouth in the latter part of the week, for shopping for presents to bring home and that, too was a success, if only for affording an opportunity to ride on Dingles escalator. All too quickly the week came to an end and we all returned home, feeling we all had a thoroughly first rate holiday.

Tristan Knight, a young pupil, talks of a member of staff:
"Mrs SKEWES teaches class 2. She plays the guitar like my daddy. She has short light hair, and she wears glasses. She drives a red sports car and goes home for supper."

ANDREW SKEWES, another young pupil, talks of another member of staff:
"Mrs Retallack used to help us make things. She helps Mrs Lugg with the younger ones."

HISTORY OF MEXICO'S RICHEST SILVER MINES by J.H. SKEWES

One of the largest and most important silver-mining camps in the Republic of Mexico, and probably in the world, is in Pachuca, the capital of the State of Hidalgo, which is situated about 60 miles northeast of Mexico City at an altitude of 8,000 feet above sea level and has a population of 50,000. Pachuca is a Castillian corruption of the Toltec word Pachuacan — meaning "near a gulch", the name given the city by its Toltec founders. The Spaniards afterwards renamed it Pachuca. It is a typical mining-camp town surrounded by high mountains of the Sierra de Pachuca range, which is dotted with scores of stone monuments marking the corners of mining claims. These now barren mountains, so some of the older inhabitants claim, were once thickly wooded — the trees that grew there having been cut for mining purposes and for fuel.

The history of the camp is very interesting, as it is one of the oldest Spanish settlements in the country. Silver ore was first discovered in 1534 in what is today the little mining town of Real Del Monte, which lies at an elevation of 9,000 feet slightly to the northeast and about five miles from Pachuca, and numbers 10,000 people. This community is very picturesque and, like Pachuca, is encircled by mountains that are, however, covered with dense forests. One of these mountains, El Zumate, rises to a height of 11,000 feet and is said to be the loftiest peak in the state of Hidalgo.

With reference to the discovery of the precious ore in Real Del Monte, the story is told that a party of Spaniards, exploring the country, happened to camp one night near the site of the old Dolores shaft and built their camp fire on an outcropping of the Santa Brigida vein.

Imagine their surprise next morning, when they saw molten silver running from the rocks beneath the fire. Be that as it may, the fact remains that subsequent mining operations proved this vein to be a big producer and exceptionally rich in places — some of the workings extending up to "grass roots." Later, the Spaniards discovered ore in Pachuca; and the Xacal and Rosario mines in that district were exploited by them for many years, as were also the Santa Brigida and Vizcaina veins in Real del Monte. In 1557, Friar Bartolome de Medina invented, at Pachuca, the patio process for amalgamating silver ores, and this was used in the region for nearly three and a half centuries after its discovery.

In 1739 a Spaniard, named Pedro Romero de Terreros, acquired ownership of the mines for a comparatively small sum of money; and, being energetic and enterprising, he worked them on a large scale. Fortune favoured him, for soon afterwards rich ore was found in both the Pachuca and Real del Monte mines. Torreros became fabulously wealthy and made large loans and presents to the King of Spain, by whom he was knighted and given the title of Conde de Regla. It was Terreros who established the national pawnshop in Mexico City, where a bronze bust of the founder may today be seen atop one of the arches decorating this building. Several other interesting buildings erected by his orders are still standing. These include the Casas Coloradas, in Pachuca, now used for government offices, and the Casa del Conde and the Casa Grande in Real del Monte. The first was supposed to have been the residence of the Conde de Regla and, until partly destroyed by fire a few years ago, served as a boarding house for employees of one of the local mining companies. The Casa Grande is the home of the company's general superintendent of mines.

It is recorded that during the time Terreros worked the mines they produced ore to the value of more than 10,000,000 pesos notwithstanding the rather crude methods they employed and the difficulties they encountered. As the mines got deeper, large quantities of water hindered operations because the flow could not be handled for want of adequate pumping equipment. An effort was made to lower the water by using horse *malacates*, or whims, to hoist the water out in buckets made from bullock hides and operating continuously in seventeen different shafts. The Moran Adit in the creek bed near the old Moran Mine, about a mile to the east and approximately 558 feet below Real del Monte, was started at this time in an attempt to unwater the workings. But all these measures proved to be of no avail, for a sudden increase in the flow inundated the mines with the result that operations were practically suspended near the end of the seventeenth century. The Moran Adit was later advanced by other companies and, ultimately, had a length, including its several branches, of 6.2 miles.

History records that Baron Alexander von Humboldt visited the mines of Pachuca and Real del Monte in 1803; and his memoirs give an account of the great riches in the flooded mines.

In 1842 the John Taylor Company was formed in London, England, to work the mines, and several hundred Cornish miners with their families were sent out to Pachuca. Some of their descendants may still be found there. Cornish steam pumps and hoists were also shipped from England by way of Vera Cruz — the laborious task of getting them to the properties may well be imagined when it is realised that all this heavy machinery was dragged up the steep grades from Vera Cruz. The company built a good road from Pachuca to Real del Monte. It was blasted out of the solid rock of the mountainside, and then represented something of an undertaking and engineering achievement. It is in use today, and is kept in repair by the present operators — being considered one of the best mountain roads in the country.

The first three Cornish pumps in Real del Monte were installed at the Terreros, San Cayetano and Dolores shafts. As soon as they were running and the steam hoists were ready for service, the shafts were carried down to the 984-foot level and the drainage tunnel started just above the river bed near the town of Omitlan and about three miles to the east of Real del Monte. The tunnel, including branches, is 7½ miles long; and its outlet is approximately 1,000 feet below the point at which the water enters.

The task of driving this tunnel and of sinking the shafts was at that time a laborious one, as all drilling was done with hand steel, black powder was employed for blasting and inflowing water hampered progress. Still, under the circumstances, good work was done; and the Aviadero Tunnel, as it was named, and some of its shafts are in use today.

The English company found the mines in a ruinous and deplorable condition; but after solving the drainage problem and unwatering the workings both in Pachuca and Real del Monte, it was able to put them on a producing basis. Several of the shafts in the Real del Monte district were sunk to the 1,312-foot level or, as it was called, the Taylor level. Today, this is the main haulage level for the mines in that district.

The company also built a well-equipped machine shop at Real del Monte, and this was operated under supervision of experienced mechanics brought from England. Besides the machine shop, the surface plant included a foundry, a blacksmith shop, and a pattern-making department. Pumps, hoists, and other machinery from the mines and mills in Real del Monte and Pachuca were repaired in these shops, which were used until 1914 when most of the equipment was moved to a larger and more modern plant at Pachuca. This plant is being run by the present mine owners.

Notwithstanding the fact that the mines produced a large tonnage of silver ore during the years they were in the possession of the John Taylor Company, the cost of getting out the ore was also very high. The purchase of large quantities of machinery, and its transportation, installing and operating, involved such heavy expenditures that the company was forced to go into liquidation after working the properties for 24 years — sustaining a loss of 10,000,000 pesos.

In 1850, the properties were sold to a local concern which, soon afterwards, opened up the famous bonanza at the Rosario Mine in Pachuca. This was a fabulously rich strike. In a year or so it yielded 30,000 tons of ore worth 10,000,000 pesos; and the finds of specimens rich in native silver were common. The high-grade ore was bagged at the mines in canvas sacks for shipment. The Rosario is one of the oldest mines in the camp, and, up to 1926, was a steady producer. In its early days this mine was drained by a Cornish pump at the San Nicolas shaft. This was the first pump of its kind to be installed at Pachuca. Later the San Juan and the San Pedro shafts were sunk, and each was equipped with a larger pump of the same type.

Rich ore bodies wer next discovered in Real del Monte in the Santa Brigida vein at the Dolores Mine, also in the Santa Ines vein at the Dificultad and Carretera mines. Smaller but equally rich veins were opened up at the Resquicio, Cabrera and Dolores mines.

As the workings increased in depth, more powerful pumping equipment was provided. The old pump at the Terreros shaft was dismantled and the pump house converted into a fort for the housing of hundreds of convicts who were hired for a small sum of money from the government to labour in the mines. The company maintained a force of 200 armed guards, mostly cavalrymen, to watch the prisoners and escort the silver bullion on its way from the mines to Mexico City and to Vera Cruz as well as the payrolls en route to the mines and the mills. As an added protection against brigands, the bullion and the silver pesos were put in large, iron-strong boxes which were bolted to the wagons carrying them. These wagons were mule drawn, and some of them may still be seen on the streets of Real del Monte.

Often the guards were called upon to fight the bands of robbers in protecting company property, and to go into action in preserving order in the camp. They were a fine body of men — well mounted, lavishly uniformed in silver braided trousers, coats and hats, and splendidly equipped with silver ornamented saddles and other trappings. Señor Mello, who was the director of the company in 1885, was very proud of these men, and on occasion commanded them himself when going in pursuit of marauders. Señor Mello was of distinguished Spanish extraction; and it is told of him that he made frequent visits to the mines at night, disguised himself, rewarding the industrious with the gift of a small gold coin and punishing the slumbering with dismissal.

Up to that time, working conditions in the mines were very poor. Little attention was paid to hygiene, to adequate ventilation, and to accident prevention. Few steam hoists were in use. Horse *malacates* and bullock hides did most of the work of hoisting the ore and the waste and of lowering materials. Few of the shafts were provided with skips; and cages were not introduced until some time afterwards. Most of the ore was packed to the shaft stations on men's backs and, in some of the smaller mines, even up to the surface by way of ladders. Wages were very low, a *barretero* or driller got from 75 centavos to one peso per day, and a *peon* received from 37 to 50 centavos per day, working 10-hour shifts. Then the lowest grade of ore handled contained around 800 grams of silver to the metric ton, hence the vast amount of pay ore and fills left in the mine and on the dumps. These were exploited by other companies formed subsequently to operate the mines in the Pachuca and Real del Monte districts.

All these companies used the patio process for treating ore. The Real del Monte Company treated most of the ore from their Pachuca mines in this way at Loreto; the San Rafael Company, at the Bartolome de Medina Mill; the Guadalupe Fresnillo Company at the Purisima Grande; the El Bordo y Anexas Company, at the Purisima Chica; the Maravillas y Anexas, at the Progreso and San Francisco Mills; the Santa Gertrudis Company, at Guadalupe; and later, the La Blanca and Santa Ana mines at the La Luz Mill. Hundreds of horses and mules were needed in these mills to operate the *arrastres* or stone mills that crushed the ore, and to tread, in the *patios*, the ore mixed with quicksilver, sulphate of copper, salt, and water to form a thick slime.

It was a pitiful sight to see these poor creatures, their hoofs and fetlocks green from the copper sulphate. Various mechanical appliances were invented as a substitute for the animals in mixing the slimes, but none of these was satisfactory. The patio process was not only a costly but also an inefficient one — the silver recovery amounting to about 75%. Besides, the loss in quicksilver was great. Small fortunes in silver have been found in recent years in old patios and nearby creek bottoms. At Pachuca, all the tailings were emptied into the creek that runs through the town; and these have since been recovered and treated at a profit by the cyanide process.

Large quantities of salt were required for this work, the Real del Monte Company alone using several thousand tons of it annually in the patios. Most of it was obtained from the states of Campeche and San Luis Potosi; but, later on, a plant was installed on the outskirts of Mexico for the recovery of salt from the lakes of Texoco.

The ore from the Real del Monte mines and that from the workings in Pachuca were treated in the early days of the districts in a number of mills or *haciendas de beneficio*. These mills were operated at different periods, and were variously situated close to the creek running below the town of Real del Monte. They all made use of the water flowing thence from the outlet of the Aviadero drainage tunnel.

The first of these mills, of small capacity, was not long in use. It was located at San Juan Guerrero, where a chimney shaft was sunk by the Taylor Company for ventilating the Aviadero Tunnel. Today, this is the site of a big cyanide-process plant which was erected in 1905 for treating the ores from the Real del Monte district. The plant has a capacity of about 1,300 tons daily. At the outlet of the drainage tunnel was a mill that was abandoned many years before the mines were sold to their present owners. Another, which was in operation until 1905, was just on the outskirts of the village of Omitlán. A fourth, at Velasco and about a mile from Omitlán, was formerly one of the most important of the old mills. There was located the country residence of the director of the Taylor Company. His house and garden are still standing; but the plant was shut down some time before the property was taken over by the people now running it. Still another *hacienda*, called Penafiel, lies a little to the east of Valesco. This was also closed down years ago. Six miles from Valesco were two adjoining mills, the San Antonio and the San Miguel. With the exception of the San Antonio Mill, where the manganese silver ores were treated by roasting, all the others used the patio process.

The last in this list of *haciendas* is at Regla, in a gorge which is one of the scenic points of interest in the state of Hidalgo. There may be seen the famous Basalt Columns of Regla, also known as the Giant's Causeway of America, which stand close to 200 feet high. This mill was in operation until 1905. The transportation of ores from the Pachuca to the Real del Monte districts was done by mule teams and pack mules, some owned by the company and others by local freighters. In its heyday, when these scattered plants were working to capacity, the region roundabouts was a thriving one, and many small communities grew up around the mills. Some of these are now deserted and in ruin.

Although the Pachuca and the Real del Monte districts are in close proximity, there is a considerable difference in their vein systems. While the majority of those in Pachuca run east and west, the veins in Real del Monte run north and south. The Vizcaina vein which extends east and west through both districts might be termed the Mother Lode. It has yielded large returns, especially in Pachuca. On this vein are the El Bordo, Santa Ana, San Rafael and Carmelia mines, all of which have been and still are big producers.

In the Real del Monte district the ore taken from the Vizcaina vein occurred in pockets, some to which were extremely rich; but none of this ore was found to be as continuous as that from the same vein in Pachuca. This state of affairs has, at different times, given rise to argument anent the question whether or not it is one and the same vein — some authorities contending that what is known in Real del Monte as the Vizcaina vein is only a fault mineralised along its contacts with the north and south veins.

The early Spanish owners did not seem to recognise the importance of the north and south veins in Real del Monte for, with the exception of the Santa Brigida vein, very little work was done on them. The same thing applies to the Taylor Company. Not until the property came into the hands of the present company were the veins uncovered and extensively exploited. These included the Santa Ines vein which extended from the Dificultad to the Carretera Mine, a matter of a little more than three-fifths of a mile. It yielded large tonnages of rich ore, and was considered one of the bonanzas of the camp. The ore was extracted through the Dificultad and San Ignacio shafts — the separate mines being operated up to 1925. There still is a big reserve of low-grade ore in these workings. Plans are now afoot to mine it.

Considerable difficulty was experienced in mining the Santa Ines vein because of seepage, the incoming water reaching a flow of 1,600 gallons a minute. This was handled by two Cornish pumps, one at the Dolores and the other at the Acosta shafts. The pump at the last-named shaft was afterwards moved to the San Pedro shaft in Pachuca for the purpose of unwatering of the Rosario Mine.

In 1880, a big steam pump, then one of the largest in the world, was brought from Germany and installed at the Dificultad shaft. It was a cumbersome piece of machinery, and did not give very satisfactory results. It developed 900hp., and had a capacity of close on 2,000 gallons per minute. The huge pumphouse of cut limestone, with its brick chimney 100 feet high, is still one of the landmarks in Real del Monte. The cost of the pump — including freight, installation and the pump house — is said to have been 1,000,000 pesos. Charges for its upkeep and operation were very high. Its seven tubular steam boilers consumed about 40 tons of coal every 24 hours. The plant was later dismantled, as were also all the Cornish pumps, and replaced with more modern centrifugal, electric pumps.

To encourage ore production, there was in vogue at that time in almost all the mines a system of compensation called *partido*, under which contractors were permitted to retain in payment for their work one-eighth of the ore broken down by their men. These contractors were supplied with sacks and rope for bagging the ore; and each used a different marker to distinguish his sacks from those of his fellow contractors. These markers were sewed to the sacks, and usually consisted of a piece of fibre string not infrequently ingeniously made to form a cross, ring, lizard, or other distinctive object.

This method of payment involved much assorting of the ore, which was done in large patios or yards. As the bags were brought to the surface they were placed, according to their markers, in separate piles, from which each contractor's eighth was taken once a week and stacked for inspection. Friday nights were busy ones at these yards, for then it was that everything was made ready for the company's buyer who made the circuit of the several mines every Saturday morning to purchase back the ore allotted to the contractors — the price being based upon an average assay previously made of the ore. However, the contractors were free to sell to the local buyers in town, if they so preferred. Some of these dealers — who had their own treating plants — did a thriving business, as they also bought ore that was stolen from the mines. After the sacks had been thus handled many times they were emptied, and the ore broken to a convenient size, washed, sorted into three grades, and again resacked for shipment to the mills.

Then there were the *parados por la casa* — men who worked in pairs, assisted by a *peon*, breaking down ore and cleaning up sections of the veins neglected by the contractors. For this the company paid each man one peso per day, while the *peon* got 50 centavos for his labours. Another practice was that of allowing men to go down into the mines on Sundays and holidays, receiving in payment for their toil one-eighth of all the ore they could produce and sack. This privilege, however, was not accorded only to the miners. As a matter of fact much favouritism was shown by those in charge; shifters, boss timbermen, pumpmen, and even workers generally otherwise occupied were given preference, while merchants were granted the opportunity of hiring men to mine for them on those days.

Such methods, obviously, were in many ways detrimental to the interests of the operating company as well as to the workers themselves. If not closely watched, the miners worked only the richest ore bodies, and did so in a manner that invited danger. Hence the many accidents that occurred and for which scant compensation was made. Ore was left on the walls, many pillars of good ore were buried, and large quantities of pay rock were left in the fills, and was proved subsequently by companies using modern methods of production.

British people then outnumbered the foreigners in the camp; and to Englishmen is due credit for much of the pioneer mining done there. Aside from what the Taylor Company achieved, others of that nationality formed lesser companies, did a lot of prospecting, and discovered several of the veins now being worked. In the Real del Monte district these small-scale operations exploited the Santa Elena, Almoloya, San Esteban, Peregrinos, San José de Garcia, Cabrera, La Reina and numerous other claims. In the Pachuca district they opened up the Santa Gertrudis Mine which, later, turned out to be one of the richest and largest properties in the camp. It was due to the influence and efforts of Captain Frank Rule, one of the most influential Englishmen of the colony, that the Santa Gertrudis became famous. He also organised the companies which developed the Maravillas, Santa Ana and La Blanca mines — all big producers. Local concerns started the El Bordo and San Rafael mines which, likewise, are among the big producers of the camp today.

In 1898, at the Camelia Mine, operated by the Real del Monte Company in the Pachuca district, an enormous stream of water was suddenly encountered in an east drift on the 952-foot level, inundating it as well as most of the lower levels in many of the other mines in the neighbourhood. At that time the Camelia had no pumping equipment; and the pumps at the other properties in the affected area were inadequate and could not begin to cope with so great and unexpected a volume of water. Consequently, ore production in some of the mines was paralysed and in others very much reduced for more than a year until additional pumping units could be placed in service. The Real del Monte Company installed two electric pumps in the Camelia Mine; the San Rafael Company increased the number of its pumps — the new ones being larger in size than those already in use; and the Maravillas Company put up a Cornish pump at the El Carmen Mine. By combining forces, the several operators in the field were finally able to get the water under control, once again, to restore normal working conditions.

In 1899, the Real del Monte Company, in conjunction with the San Rafael Company, began the driving of the Girault Tunnel, which was named after Edmundo Girault who conceived the idea of connecting the Loreto Mill with the Camelia and San Rafael mines. The tunnel had a length of 6,095 feet, and took two years to complete — all the driving being done with hand steels. This piece of work has proved of great benefit not only to the mining companies who initiated it but also to other properties traversed by the tunnel, as it improved their ventilation and saved time in getting the men in and out of the mines. The Camelia Mine uses it for transporting its ores and that from certain other properties leased by it to the Loreto Mill, and also for hauling supplies to the underground workings. The tunnel has likewise been instrumental in reducing the pumping head in the Camelia and San Rafael mines about 558 and 722 feet respectively.

In 1906, after thorough examination and sampling, the entire holdings of the Real del Monte y Pachuca Mining Company were sold to the United States Smelting, Refining and Mining Company. This marked a new epoch in the camp, for since that time it has undergone a complete change. Both mines and mills have been put on a thoroughly modern basis for quantity production; working conditions have been improved; and the scale of wages raised — in fact, the whole community has benefited through the transaction. All steam pumps and hoists have gradually been discarded and replaced by modern electric machinery; and pneumatic drills are now used instead of hand steels.

Programmes calling for extensive exploratory and development work have been put into effect in the Pachuca, Real del Monte and El Chico districts. Several rich veins have been uncovered; and some new shafts have been sunk and old ones carried to greater depths.

In 1914 the famous Purisima vein was cut in the Real del Monte district after continuing the Guardaraya crosscut from the Dificultad Mine for a distance of about 230 feet to the west on the 1,312-foot level. This vein proved to be a bonanza and, undoubtedly, one of the most productive ever found in the camp. It was then said to be one of the longest-known silver fissure ore bodies in the world. Its total continuous length was in excess of two-thirds of a mile, and the pay values were found to extend from a depth of 492 feet to the 2,264-foot level. For developing this ore body, a shaft was sunk from the surface to the 1,312-foot level. It was timbered with steel sets, at an average speed of 33 feet weekly, and equipped with an electric hoist and compressor plant. It has since been carried down to the 2,132.5-foot level.

Other rich veins opened up in the Real del Monte district by the United States Smelting, Refining and Mining Company are the La Rica and the Dios te Guie, which have been made accessible by a shaft that was sunk on the La Rica property. This shaft is also steel timbered; it is 1,968.5 feet deep; and is provided with two electric hoists. Exploratory crosscuts on the 1,312-foot level from the Dolores and the La Rica mines revealed that the north-south veins continued beyond the Vizcaina east-west fracture; and in this area were opened up the Santa Margarita and the Sr. San Jose mines. Another important discovery made in recent years was the Dos Carlos vein system located by the Santa Gertrudis Company by cutting crosscuts from the old Santa Gertrudis working.

The Acosta shaft is now the main hoistway for the Real del Monte district, having replaced the San Ignacio shaft which had been used for that purpose since 1910. The Acosta shaft is equipped with crushers underground and with an electric hoist at the surface. The hoist has a maximum speed of 1,400 feet per minute, and is driven by a 500-hp motor. Self-dumping skips, with a capacity of 5.5 tons, are used for hoisting the ore.

From there an aerial tramway carries it to the Guerrero Mill, about 1½ miles distant. On the site of the old *hacienda* now stands a modern cyanide-process plant that has a capacity of about 1,300 tons daily. Water for use in the mill is pumped from the Aviadero Tunnel through the chimney shaft, which has been reconditioned and provided with electric pumps that run automatically. The Escobar and Cabrera mines, which produced small tonnages for a long while, have been worked out; but an electric pumping plant is still maintained at Cabrera for keeping the water out of some of the nearby mines.

Most of the properties in the Real del Monte district which have at different times been in the hands of small local companies have been taken over by the United States Smelting, Refining and Mining Company, the only organistaion operating there at present. The total output of the district is about 2,200 tons a day.

In the Pachuca district, the old Loreto Mill, which was equipped to use the patio process, has been remodelled and now treats approximately 2,750 tons of ore daily by the cyanide process. The Santa Ana group of mines in the same region and the Arevalo mines in El Chico were purchased by the company, and aerial tramways constructed for transporting the ore to the Loreto Mill. The Santa Ana mines have been connected underground with the San Juan shaft, which adjoins the Loreto Mill. The ore from these workings is carried to the shaft by electric haulage and is also hoisted electrically to the mill storage bins.

When underground connections now being driven from the Fortuna or 886-foot level in the San Juan Mine in Pachuca and from the 1,805-foot level in the La Rica Mine in Real del Monte are completed, then all the ore from those districts will thus be hauled and hoisted electrically to the Loreto Mill. The Guerrero Mill will then be done away with. To this end, the Loreto Mill is being enlarged to take care of the total tonnage from all the company's mines, which is in excess of 110,000 tons monthly.

Another important operator in Pachuca is the Santa Gertrudis Company. This company, which came to the field in 1909 and purchased several properties from local concerns, is exploiting the El Bordo, Santo Tomás and Santa Gertrudis group of mines, as well as the Dos Carlos properties — an entirely new discovery that is yielding rich returns. All the ore from the Santa Gertrudis Company's mines is treated at a large and up-to-date mill using the cyanide process.

Other operators in the Pachuca district are the San Rafael Company, with a large group of mines and a mill two miles north of the town, and the Guadalupe Fresmillo Company which is developing a small group of mines about a mile east of Pachuca and treating the ore in the Purisima Grande Mill. The San Rafael Company's properties have produced well for years and are still producing steadily.

At the present time the total monthly output of all the silver mines in Pachuca, Real del Monte and El Chico districts is something like 220,000 tons, yielding approximately 90 tons of silver and 1,070 troy pounds of gold. And to keep all the underground workings in the field in proper condition, the pumps are required to handle around 10,000 gallons of water every minute. Electric power is supplied to the district by the Mexican Light and Power Company from three of its plants at Regla, Cuandó and Necaxa, the last-named furnishing most of the current needed.

Published in "Compressed Air Magazine" (February, 1930) and printed in London, New York and Paris.

Richard Henry Skewes, born in Cornwall in 1871, who went to Mexico as a youth. He spent some time there as a miner, and died of injuries sustained when he was thrown from his horse in 1899

THREE YEARS AS A PRISONER-of-WAR OF THE JAPANESE IMPERIAL ARMY

On 15 February 1941 Singapore fell to the Japanese. The big guns of the British Naval Base had fixed emplacements, pointing out to sea and so were no help when the Japanese approached Singapore from the Malayan interior. The cost of building the base was put at £11,000,000. An Allied squadron was wiped out in the Battle of the Java Sea in February, 1941 and on 13 March the Japanese landed in the Solomon Islands threatening the vital route to Australia.

Mandalay fell to the Japanese on 2 May and they completed their conquest of Burma.

But eventually the West won. The first atom bomb was dropped on Hiroshima on 6 August 1945 and three days later another destroyed most of Nagasaki, the second coming less then 24 hours after Russia declared war upon Japan. Japanese forces in South East Asia surrendered to the British on 12 September, 1945.

The Second World War, which had gone on for six long years, cost many lives, especially civilians. It was estimated that 54.8 million civilians had been killed in a war which involved 57 nations. Military deaths in South East Asia were: Japanese 1.5 million; British 398,000 and Australian 29,935.[1]

By November, 1942 Australian forces had been augmented by unhardened British soldiers from Changi, Singapore and Dutch troops from Java. Before the end of 1942 almost 10,000 prisoners-of-war began to clear the jungle, heaping dirt by the basketful on embankments and chiselling through hillsides at the Burmese end of the railroad. A like number of captives, mostly British, worked in Thailand at the other end of the envisaged line.

Dedicated doctors and orderlies worked with little sleep to do some good, but they had no medicines, and Japanese medical inspectors refused consistently to make any available. Boiled water, salt and soda were the main drugs at hand, and men who suffered from tropical ulcers, dysentery and malaria needed at least one more important pharmaceutical — hope! This the doctors and orderlies could not dispense and they had to watch thousands of young men die of a combination of minor ailments, which could have easily been cured by food, rest and sanitation. The railroad of death employed 331,000 men — 61,000 Allied P-O-W's and roughly 270,000 natives. Of these 61,000 Allied P-O-W's, 20.6% or 12,568 had died. Broken down by country they were: 6318 British, 2815 Australian, 2490 Dutch, 356 Americans and 589 whose nationality was never identified. In laying down their lives they had constructed a 250-mile railroad which was abandoned after the war, and given back to the wilderness. They had built nine miles of bridges and moved 150 million cubic feet of earth. They left one dead body for every thirteen feet of track. If Japan had lifted a finger of her managerial genius, the idiotic waste of life could have been avoided and the railroad built more quickly, cheaply and lastingly. As handled by Imperial Headquarters the project had only one virtue; it was a way of killing prisoners that would be justified to the Prime Minister Hideki Tojo and other responsible officials in the Tokyo Government.

Tojo was brought to justice after the war and hanged on 22 December, 1948.[2]

One Australian who witnessed many of the deaths during the building of the railroad from Burma to Thailand was VX Private GLENLEIGH BERTIE WILLIAM SKEWES from Victoria. He was attached to the 2/13th Australian General Hospital in Singapore. He was taken prisoner in 1942 and for three years kept a diary, written on small notebook pages, being inscribed in diluted purple dye, due to the total absence of proper writing materials.

This diary was kept hidden from the enemy at all times, and became damaged by the damp and mildew of the monsoon climate. It was carried through the war at great risk, for if one was found concealing such material, severe punishment was administered to the person with any such document found upon them.

Glenleigh Skewes describes himself as an ordinary Australian with a love for his country and family. He had faith in God and during his days of imprisonment a deep feeling for suffering humanity. He arrived in Singapore on 15 September, 1941 just five months prior to being taken prisoner by the Japanese.

My first impression of the Gateway to the East was of a harbour scattered with natives' boats, gangs of them unloading boats, and native fruit-sellers in their canoes trying to sell to us even before we disembarked.

Our first job on landing was to change our Australian money into currency of the Malay Federated States. Then we were loaded into trucks and taken to our barracks at St Patrick's College, Katong, four miles out of Singapore where we were to remain for two months. It was at Katong that we first saw a funeral file past. This was of differing customs, as well as different standards of living. Many undertakers do not use their truck for the one purpose. The hearse we saw was really a 30cwt or two-ton truck converted into a hearse for the funeral. Afterwards, the versatile undertaker would back his vehicle into his shed and, with ropes and pulleys employed, would pull the canopy with its plumes up to the rafters. When there were no funerals the truck would be used as a licenced carrier. Later on, as a P-O-W, I saw a Malayan funeral when the vehicle used as a hearse was a side-car attached to a bicycle.

About the middle of November Glenleigh Skewes moved with his unit to a vacated mental hospital at Tampoi in the state of Johore, Malaya, just a few miles from Singapore Island.

He was taken Prisoner-Of-War by the Japanese on 15 February 1942 and spent 14 months at Changi Prison. On Thursday, 21 April 1943 he, and about 600 fellow P-O-W's were moved.

Here we had to turn out at 6 o'clock in the morning in darkness and everyone's belongings were thrown in a heap on the ground and we jumped down and only had a few minutes to sort out our gear.

There were no latrines on the train. Every so often it would stop and if one wanted to see to one's "personal needs" the Japs made it very difficult as they threw stones at our P-O-W's to hurry them up.

---

[1]*People's Chronology*, James Trager, London 1979, p. 984
[2]*Japanese Imperial Conspiracy*, David Bergamini, London, 1971, pp 966-971

Five days later they arrived by train at Bampong in steel rice trucks.

When we got outside this station, we were told we had to carry all our kit, I suppose about 80 lbs weight on our backs for about nine miles and march. Will I ever forget it! The sweat just streamed down my face and my heart pounded as we marched down those dusty streets under this strain. Shops were beginning to open in the early morning and the Thailanders stood and watched in amazement. We had practically no sleep and no food whatsoever for over thirty-six hours, so one can imagine what state our bodies and minds were in. However, after travelling for some time, I never saw a more welcome sight as the long column of men ahead turned into a camp. Here we were given a breakfast which consisted of rice and grass stew. We were told we had many marches ahead of us of approximately 15 miles each night.

This is where I had to part with my kitbag and all the treasured things I had gathered during the past fourteen months, especially my big medical book of doctors' lectures which I had written up and studied and which described experiences of various diseases, their symptoms, characteristics, and the latest treatment of same. But we were told that, on account of the long march ahead, we would be able to carry only a pack on our back with a change of clothing in it and as few necessary articles as possible. Our kitbags were to be brought on later by motor truck, but we never saw our personal belongings again. We were to march for a whole month. It was a terrible never-to-be-forgotten march through the jungle of Thailand, 196 miles, after fourteen months of malnutrition. Dear God, only those who went through it know just what those hellish conditions were!

These fifteen mile marches were through the thickest and most unhealthy jungle in the world. He would march through thorns, spikes and prickles and being bitten on the ears and nose by sand flies,"midges", often falling into thick mud. There were thunderstorms on most nights followed by torrential rain. Glenleigh Skewes had developed a septic foot which he had to nurse through days and nights of agony clambering through swamps, ridges and gullies. On 13 May 1943 the soldiers were 21 days out of Changi Prison, still marching 15 miles each night, often close to tigers and other wild beasts of the jungle.

I feel that my body calls out for food and nourishment for nerves and stamina, which I cannot get. Rice can never sustain the vital foods of value which we had before taken prisoner, and therefore the suffering men are in no state to be forced to do these laborious marches by night, when we should be sleeping. Life under certain circumstances can be very hard, especially when, through fate, one falls into enemy hands. God, please give me food and strength to bear up and see it through.
Today I was able to sell my nickel Eversharp pencil and with the 50 cents I bought some duck eggs to help sustain life. I cooked two for dinner, and it made me feel a new creature. There is wonderful life-giving food in an egg or two.
Marvellous answer to prayer yesterday. I prayed in solitude in the wild bush and in a few hours Christ came to my aid in a wonderful way ..... pencil ..... watch ..... money ..... Good Japanese guards last night!
Saturday, 15 May, 1943: We set off for our next camp at 6.30 pm without sleep. My shoulders ached under the pack, especially when on stiff climbs.
A kindly Japanese guard sawed a bamboo section off for me to carry my water in a section about 1ft by 4 inches wide. I was thankful for this thoughtful deed.
We have been, and still are, amidst tall mountains — the highest I have ever seen. Sheer rock in places, hundreds of feet high. The bamboo in the jungle is very tall, anything from 40 to 90 feet high, and thousands and thousands of acres of it .... endless miles of bamboo jungle.
The journey through the night was shorter than usual and at 1 a.m. we stopped for three quarters of an hour when the Japanese gave us a drink of hot water and we lay down for a while. But on account of my clothes being wringing wet with sweat as usual, I caught a chill in my stomach with pains which turned to diarrhoea. I had no blanket, so lay on a piece of canvas with a cape over me and was soon shivering from my own sweat and the heavy dew of the night. Later, when I could stand it no longer, I forced my tired self to shift along the road to where the head of the column was sleeping and there was a fire to keep away tigers. Here I was able to dry my clothes and at last get about one hour's sleep. We marched off at first dawn and arrived at Kinsayo Camp at 7.40 am. This is a big construction camp where thousands of P-O-W's work for the Nippon Master, clearing big trees of the jungle for a railway line .... on rice! There have been many die here in this area.
The Japs give you no peace at all. When you try to sleep they pull at you, wake you up several times. My septic foot still hurts, but I must carry on.

Glenleigh arrived at his eventual destination on 25 May 1943.

It was a big camp where construction was under way for a railway viaduct. We got into a hut, twelve to a bay, and slept as we had not for weeks — thankful for a roof over our heads. There are natives here. When they get sick they go out a few yards from the others and lie in the wet and cold until death! I saw it myself, two dying the first night we got here. Later, they were taken into the bush to die, then, when they were dead, were hardly covered with soil. Dear God above, this is terrible. I also saw a woman skeleton staggering back to the native camp with a stick, from the place in the bush where she had been taken to die. She must have recovered sufficient strength and was endeavouring to fight death. It was a tragic sight and a deplorable state of affairs.

The Japanese guards put Glenleigh Skewes to navvying and helping to build a road from the camp to Burma. He worked in bare feet because he had no socks, but very sore feet.

Tuesday, 1 June, 1943: Hell, Hell and Hell again! Rain, rain, rain and more rain. You have to work in it regardless of the state of your clothing. I often have wet pants all day, and no shirt. Then, when you return, you sleep with sick all around you, bad smells, bad breaths, coughing, flies, mosquitoes and death! I say this is Hell — hellish misery that those outside know nothing of.

In June, 1943 Glenleigh reported that in one English camp some 800 British P-O-W's died whilst trying to erect one timber bridge and they were buried on a rise near the bridge named Songkrai (meaning River Camp). He saw many soldiers looking like "skeletons" suffering from dysentery and malaria.

Monday 12 July, 1943.
It was with sadness that a few of us attended the funeral of Sgt Jock Taylor, who died from tropical ulcers, malaria, dysentery and pneumonia, but who had fought tenaciously to live.
I was asked by Lieut. Hughes if I could carry the casket, which I did with great willingness out of my respect for Jock. The ashes were still warm from cremation as I carried them in a round casket made from bamboo about 1ft 6 inches in length. We climbed up the side of a big hill to the small cemetery where there are now about 20 graves. I will always remember poor Jock and his patience. Only two days before he died, he invited me over to Western Australia to see him after the war, and he would show us around. Poor soul.

The camp was under the command of Colonel Banno of the Imperial Japanese Army, who tried on a number of occasions to have the Australian P-O-W's returned to Malaya. In the First World War Colonel Banno had been on the side of the British and helped "escort" many of our ships to Europe and elsewhere. But here his orders were to ensure that a railway was put through the dense jungle and over gorges and great rivers — a project that Britain had abandoned in the 1930's because of the loss of lives it would involve through cholera, malaria and dysentery. So the Japanese authorities insisted on the railway being built no matter how many lives it cost among the Prisoners-of-War.

15 August, 1943.
I have been a Prisoner-of-War for eighteen months and we have had a thousand deaths in "F" Force in three months. We have just undergone a big Japanese search before dark. We had to get outside, patients included, and sit by our gear whilst the Japs went through it. Many knives were taken. I managed to hide this diary. It was a pathetic scene — patients and all sitting on the ground with their few worldly possessions scattered around them.
Monday, 30 August, 1943.
I had a heavy day today. As well as nursing 9 pneumonia cases, I had to look after Sgt Appleby. Just as I would try to do something for my pneumonia cases, I would have to rush to clean him up — as well as his bed — for he would just let the diarrhoea go in his bed of groundsheet, also some on patients next to him. He is now delirious again. What messes I have to clean up today! There are no conveniences, but a few leaves and some water. Sgt Appleby has had typhus, malaria, cholera and malaria again. Now I believe he has beriberi and acute diarrhoea — all these diseases in about 2½ months. As well, he has a large sore on his back, near the base of his spine, as big as a saucer.

Sgt Appleby died on 1 September, 1943. Glenleigh Skewes, although spending much of his time helping others, also suffered various diseases and complaints including an ulcerated mouth, beriberi, malaria and pains in the ankles, legs and kidneys, as well as diphtheria and infected scabies.
By September, 1943 Australia had lost 1,300 men of "F" Force in four months. There were some 800 patients in camp who were hospitalised. Glenleigh Skewes fought on maintaining a cool outlook on life and never panicking. Day and night he and his colleagues would be bitten by bugs and various kinds of lice. Often, for days at a time, he was given quinine by the Medical Officer to help ward off the malaria.

Saturday, 18 September, 1943.
The men are toiling night and day with three to four hours sleep per 24 hours so as to finish the Great Nippon Railway through the jungle of Thailand. Thousands of British and Australian prisoners have died in this White Man's Grave and, at the cost of these lives, the Japanese will boast of what they did for Thailand during the war. The railway will be complete from Burma to Thailand within a week.
Tuesday, 21 September, 1943.
I am still working like a slave and getting only 3½ hours sleep out of 24. Feel washed out, but must carry on. At night a couple of mates and I had to take soiled clothing of dysentery patients down to the river and wash clean before we could go off duty and have some sleep. We complained after a number of days to the sergeant in charge and he got three orderlies to do this job after they had dispensed the rice for breakfast. There has been torrential rain lately and it has made life very difficult. I got wet during the night shift and had nothing to change into — having only my shorts and remainder of my shirt which is torn and worn almost in half — nothing to keep my back warm. Result: bad cold and severe lumbago in my back and pains in legs, but cannot get off work to rest or apply packs.
19 men were buried yesterday. Because of the heavy rain, wood was hard to get and would not burn for cremations. Some only half-cremated were buried in one big grave. Many Englishmen died over the weekend. The Jap guards are afraid of half-burned bodies, which is remarkable, considering all their cruelty and harshness. Lord, God, may we soon be moved. I'm done!'

As each day dawned more and more soldiers died. By 11 October, 1943 no less than 245 men had died in the camp in just over four months, bringing the total to 2400 out of the 7000 who marched from Banpong. By early November Glenleigh Skewes had been told that he would be moved away from the camp to Singapore within a few days. But there were the inevitable delays. He spent his 31st birthday in the camp, which he described as "the most terrible of Hell's places." But on Friday, 26 November, 1943 he left Kami Songkrai on his journey by train south to

Kanchanaburi.

We left at 3.30 p.m. and all the sick — heavy sick, approximately 120 lying down bed patients — were lined up along the road a few feet from the railway line. The engine and trucks slowed up, stopped, and all hands got to the stretchers and gear. We travelled to Neichki where we were given a breakfast of rice with two spoons of sugar. What a treat that was!

At 10 a.m. on the morning of 27 November we pushed off for the south. That trip was a nightmare. We had 25 men in our truck, including three stretcher cases (amputees) and men suffering from terrible tropical ulcers, some almost the size of saucers, and the usual diarrhoea cases and one acute dysentery. Five men died in our truck alone — two amputation cases which I had been nursing, and two Englishmen and one Australian by "cardiac beriberi and encephalitis." Patients had to lie right against the corpse for hours. The smell was almost unbearable. Two days and nights lapsed before the Japanese guards would allow the body to be removed from the rail truck to be buried near a rail-stop.

I spent a great deal of time forever putting out flames which started on patients' clothing caused by the fact that the Japanese only used wood in their locomotive engines, and we were in an open truck. The sparks flew back and often landed on our clothes.

In all the train journey took the painful time of 5 days and 4 nights to cover 200 miles. We went to a hospital in Kanchanaburi which was run by the Australian Army Medical Corps and the Royal Army Medical Corps. It was a rough hospital — not much better in many ways to the one we were at in the jungle — but the huts were weather-proof from rain. We were put in wards of approximately 100 to a ward. I was suffering from infected scabies and diarrhoea and, to some extent, exhaustion. Here at the hospital the padre conducted three funeral services per day. I have seen 18 bodies taken away for burial in one day. 15,000 men died at Kanchanaburi, including natives. The estimated death toll among all who were put to work on the construction and maintenance of that cursed railway line from Middle Thailand to Burma — English, Australian, Javanese, and Dutch P-O-W's, plus Tamils, Indians, Chinese and Burmese was 100,000 lives lost. One life for each sleeper!

Glenleigh Skewes only remained at Kanchanaburi for a fortnight. He then continued his journey to Malaya thence to the island of Singapore. The journey took 4½ days and 4½ nights.

We arrived at Singapore and travelled to Changi by road. On arrival at the Garden and Wood area at Changi, we walked across a padang of long turf, green and soft. At the other end we were shown into new adaf huts erected by P-O-W's of Changi for the return of "F" Force. We repeated to ourselves and to one another, "Brand new huts for us! And electric lighting as well!" We could scarcely believe our eyes after the verminous, reeking huts of the north which could not be called huts at all.

The following day we were told of showers, and again could not repress our joys at the sight of so much water and its exhilarating effect upon our bodies — and the washing of clothes. We felt like children allowed out to play.

The scenery of green pasture and picturesque tiled-roofed cottages and flats was new and fascinating to our eyes.....But we were timid and now many, or most, suffering from reaction. We felt not the men who left this place only seven months before. As the many folks of Changi said, "The men of 'F' Force who returned walked about with a haunted look — even as frightened creatures." I resumed work on Ward 188b.

Glenleigh Skewes did not keep a diary for every day he was away from Changi upcountry. But when he returned to Changi in 1944 he did list further experiences suffered during the seven months nightmare in the jungle of Thailand.

The greatest sin of all on the part of our captors, the Imperial Japanese Army, was not allowing in Red Cross ships. These would have brought us our proper food and medical supplies. Had they been allowed, thousands upon thousands of lives would have been saved. Now, as the days of another year pass, I hope and pray that the remainder of us all shall see release before the close of this year 1944. But I can only hope and pray — as do those loved ones far away — for the dawning of the day when the yoke which is not easy shall be lifted from us.

But another year passed before Glenleigh Skewes was released when the Japanese surrendered to the British in Singapore in September, 1945. It was then that soldiers discovered piled up in the big sheds on the wharves five years supply of tinned meat and vegetables. All this could have easily been sent on to the P-O-W's, but it was sent to Japan to feed the civilian population.

On release Glenleigh Skewes weighed 7 stone 4lbs and boasted a waist measurement of 19½ inches!

He arrived home in Australia in November, 1945 and soon went down with pleurisy and another bout of malaria. He was taken to Melbourne Repatriation Hospital, transferred to a convalescent home in Ballarat, and then returned to Melbourne. It was two years later before he could resume his normal work. Even then he was only allowed light work, so had to resign his nursing job. He became a gardener, but at the age of 61 years he suffered back trouble and retired when he was put on a service pension.

A SLICE OF CORNWALL — WITH SAFFRON CAKE AND ALL
By KEITH SKUES (West Briton, 30 August 1979)

A Cornish pasty, saffron cake, clotted cream and a glass of mead may be nothing unusual in Helston, Camborne or Penzance, but one does not expect to find such luxuries 4000 miles from Cornwall.

Yet in Mineral Point, Wisconsin, America, the Cornish atmosphere is alive and well. This small town with a population of 2000 was the centre to which Cornish miners flocked in the mid-1800's, when the tin mining depression took its toll.

The quiet, good natured Cornishmen and women formed a distinctive group in the south-west rough and tough mining country. The men were skilled in their hard rock mining, and were able to mine areas more extensively than before. They brought with them expert knowledge of how to build stone cottages reminiscent of their homes back in England, and these were the first permanent residences in Mineral Point.

JAMES THE FIRST

The Cornish gave new life to lead production. They took over shallow diggings that the Americans had abandoned and blasted through hard rock to the hidden mineral below. There was a saying that when a Cornishman "cousin Jack" quit a mine, all lead was gone.

It is recognised that the first Cornishman to come direct to Mineral Point was Edward James, who arrived in 1830. Within seven years he became Marshal of the Territory.

By 1835 a number of Cornishmen were living in Mineral Point, including Thomas Prisk, John Tregaskis, James Glanville, Joseph Stephens and James Nancarrow. There were 6000 Cornishmen in south-western Wisconsin by 1850, and half of the population of Mineral Point came from Camborne, Redruth and Helston.

THE MINERS' REFUGE

One is still very much aware of the influence the Cornish have had on this town. Today there is a Pendarvis complex, with a group of restored Cornish mine houses on Shake-Rag Street which are a tribute to the miners who built them. One cottage is called Trelawney — another Polperro.

Shake-Rag Street has a fascinating name, and is derived from the Cornish wives who would shake rags from their doorways to signal the men in the nearby mines that it was time to eat.

Also at Mineral Point there is a Gundry House, a limestone home built in 1868 by Joseph Gundry, who came to Wisconsin from Cornwall in 1845. He started a dry goods store and clothing business which was said to be the finest store in the region in its time.

Another Cornish miner whose name lives on is John Gray. His 16-room Victorian mansion is still an elegant home today.

In nearby cemeteries we read Cornish names: James H. Polglase 1850-1931; William C. Hoskin, 1836-1922; Joseph Treweek, 1877-1968; John Trevillian, 1841-1911; William Penhallegon, 1857-1931; Henry Ivey, 1833-1909 and John Skews, 1855-1945.

One feels very much at home when visiting the Walker House, an old railroad hotel which offers a variety of Cornish delicacies, including a pasty, Mawgan meat balls (seasoned ground beef in sour cream, sherry, mushroom sauce, over rice) and Cornish bread pudding served with caramel sauce and clotted cream.

FIGGYHOBBIN

In addition one can have saffron cakes, Cornish mead and figgyhobbin (Cornish pastry filled with brown sugar and raisins). A pasty costs £3. 50p; Cornish bread pudding £1 and a small glass of mead 75p.

The Cornish heritage is unmistakeable in Mineral Point even today. A glance through the local telephone directory for 1979 yields such names as Ivey, Rowe, Polglase, Polkinghorne, Pengilly, Penhallegon, Trehearn, Symons, Tonkin, Skews, Treloar, Treweek, Tripp, Spargo, Liddicoat, Pascoe, Vivian and Williams.

Mineral Point — once the metropolis of the lead mining region of Wisconsin — is now the centre of historic preservation, and more than a warm welcome awaits any visitor from Cornwall.

Two visitors from Cornwall recently "discovered" the group of restored Cornish miners' homes at Mineral Point.

They were Mrs Audrey Stephens, of Mount Hawke, who went to the U.S. to see her brother, 75-year-old Mr William Jones, who left Mount Hawke to emigrate when he was 19. He lives at Wauwastosa, Milwaukee. With Mrs Stephens was a friend, Mr E.J. Allen of Truro.

A TWENTIETH CENTURY PSALM by RUTH SKEWES FORD of KENTUCKY, USA

O God, our Creator, Thou has placed us in a world of beauty and wonder; all things bear the imprint of Thy hand.

If we take the telescope and search the farthest reaches of space, we find Thy law written in the star dust. If we take the microscope and seek to discover the structure of the atom, even there we find Thy moving presence.

The crocus knoweth its own colouring, and the wild plum its time of blossoming. The humming bird and the seagull find their proper food, and the baby wren leaveth its nest on confident wings. The grain of wheat sendeth up a tender shoot, and the sun and the rain and the warm earth nourish it, so that it cometh in its perfect cycle to the golden harvest.

How dull of comprehension are we, and how slow to think Thy thoughts after Thee! Let not the beauty of the pattern escape us, nor fear and doubt darken our days.

If we plant truth in our hearts, shall it not bring forth justice? And if we cherish love and compassion, shall they not flower into Christlikeness?

Therefore will I choose beauty and goodness; I will trust and await the harvest. For Thou art the Creator of star and seed; Thou art the God of steadfastness and truth.

TEMPUS FUGIT by BERNARD SKUSE of TIDEFORD, CORNWALL

"Tempus fugit", how time flies
And though 'tis old it never dies,
And though it swiftly flies away,
It is a part of every day.
So soon our precious time is gone
As ends a melody or song.
Time once done is gone and past
Nor comes again — the die is cast.
Future time we cannot see
Kindly so that may well be.
On past or future dwell not long
Lest you find the present gone.
Time flies on silent fleeting wings
In haste we notice not these things.
"Tempus Fugit", how time flies
In those words life's story lies.

EMIGRANTS WHO ARRIVED AT PORT PHILLIP, MELBOURNE, AUSTRALIA 1839-1896

RICHARD SKEWS, aged 33 years, labourer from Plymouth arrived aboard "Osprey", 22 March 1849, together with his wife JOHANNA (30), from Kea, Cornwall, and their children ELIZABETH (7) from Kea, JOHANNA (5) from Kea and RICHARD (3) from Kea. All were Wesleyans. Assisted passengers.

RICHARD SKEWS arrived aboard "Mount Stuart Elphonstone", July 1852. Unassisted passenger.

MARTIN SKEWS (37) arrived aboard "Agnes Blaikie", July, 1853 together with his wife ELIZABETH (32) and children MARTIN (13), THOMAS (12), ELIZABETH (8) and JOHN (6). Also on board were JOHN SKEWS (47), miner and SAMUEL SKEWS (18), miner. Sailed from Bristol 21 February 1853. Unassisted passengers.

CHRISTINA SKEWES left Plymouth on 11 January 1854 aboard "Merchantman" and arrived Melbourne 20 April 1854. She was a domestic servant from Cornwall. Church of England. Aged 22 years. Engaged by Edward Cotton of Richmond at the rate of £27 per year (including rations) for a period of one month. Assisted passenger.

ANN SKEWES (36), WILLIAM SKEWES (31) and ANN SKEWES (8) from Cornwall; agricultural labourer, sailed from Plymouth May, 1854 and arrived aboard "Geelong", 11 August 1854. Engaged by Mr Prowlett of Brighton 17 August 1854 at the rate of £80 per annum for a period of three months including rations. Assisted passengers.

THOMAS SKEIWS (45), miner sailed from Liverpool 9 June 1854 and arrived aboard "John and Lucy" September 1854. Unassisted passenger.

JOHN SKEWS (25), miner sailed from Liverpool 11 August 1854 and arrived aboard "Delgany" December 1854. Unassisted passenger.

ELIZABETH SKEWES (21) sailed from Plymouth 5 September 1854 and arrived aboard "Phoebe Dunbar" 25 December 1854. Church of England. Came from Cornwall. Engaged by Mr Bushby at Lower Lonsdale Street, Melbourne at the rate of £20 per annum including rations for a period of three months. Unassisted passenger.

JOHN SKEWS (15) miner sailed from Liverpool 20 November 1855 and arrived aboard "Mermaid" February 1856. Unassisted passenger.

THOMAS SKEWES (26), labourer from Cornwall sailed from Plymouth 20 February 1856 aboard "Fairlie" and arrived 4 June 1856. Unassisted passenger.

RICHARD SKEWS (24), miner sailed from Liverpool 7 August 1856 aboard "South Carolina" and arrived December 1856. Unassisted passenger.

ELIZABETH SKEWES (57), widow from Cornwall sailed from Liverpool 22 August 1857 and arrived aboard "Ebba Brahe" 8 December 1857. Church of England. Engaged by her daughter to go to Ballarat, Victoria.

PHILIP SKEWS (31) labourer from Cornwall and his wife SARAH SKEWES (28) sailed from Liverpool 28 May 1857 and arrived aboard "Ben Nevis" August 1857. Unassisted passengers.
RICHARD SKUES (42), farmer from Cornwall sailed from Liverpool on 2 August 1857 aboard "David G. Fleming" and arrived November 1857. He travelled with his wife JOHANNA (38) and children ELIZABETH J. (15), JOHANNA (11), RICHARD (10), EMELIA (6), SARAH (4) and EMILY (1); together with JANE SKUES (46) widow.
    Also on board the "David G. Fleming" were THOMAS SKUES (23), miner; SAMUEL SKUES (19), MARY SKUES (15), EMILY SKUES (11) and RICHARD SKUES (9). Unassisted passengers.
JOSEPH SKEWES (30) miner from Cornwall sailed from Plymouth on 15 March 1858 and arrived aboard "Agincourt" June 1858. Unassisted passenger.

JOHN SKEWS (20) miner sailed from Liverpool 20 August 1858 and arrived aboard "White Star" November 1858. Unassisted passenger.

MATTHEW SKEWES (52), farmer; HANNAH SKEWES (30), widow and THOMAS SKEWES (1) sailed from Liverpool 7 January 1858 aboard "Royal Charter" and arrived March 1858. Unassisted passengers.

JOHN SKEWES (26), farm labourer and ELIZABETH SKEWES (24) sailed from Plymouth 12 April 1862 aboard "Wellesley" and arrived July 1862. Unassisted passengers.

JOSIAH SKEWES (20), gentleman sailed from Plymouth 28 September 1867 on board "True Briton" and arrived December 1876. Steerage passenger.

JOSEPH SKEWES (29), agricultural labourer; JANE SKEWES (32) and JOHN SKEWES (2) sailed from Plymouth June 1870 aboard "Colonial Empire" and arrived September 1870. Unassisted passengers.

WILLIAM HENRY SKEWES (21) agricultural labourer sailed from Liverpool July 1868 aboard "S.S. Great Britain" and arrived September 1868. Unassisted passenger.

EMIGRANTS WHO ARRIVED AT SYDNEY, AUSTRALIA 1880-1896
Arrived Sydney 5 June 1892 on vessel "Cuzco" from London JANE SKEWES (44), Church of England, JESSIE SKEWES (5) and LOUISA SKEWES(3).

EMIGRANTS WHO ARRIVED AT PORT ADELAIDE, SOUTH AUSTRALIA 1846-1886
HENRY SKEWES (25), labourer from Cornwall. Married, Wife 21 (or 24 — bad writing); WILLIAM SKEWES (24), labourer from Cornwall. Married. Wife 21; HENRY SKEWES (23). Married; ANN SKEWES (24). Married; WILLIAM SKEWES (21). Married; JANE SKEWES (21). Married; SARAH SKEWES (32). Single. All sailed from Plymouth on 9 January 1851 and arrived aboard "Wanderer" 22 May 1851. On board 156 souls comprising 66 adults (male) and 62 (female); 12 male children, 13 female children and 3 infants.

HENRY SKEWES (19), copper miner from Cornwall arrived on board "lsle of Thanet" 6 July 1854.

SAMUEL SKEWES, assisted passenger, aged 22 years; single left Liverpool on 17 November 1862 and arrived on board "Morning Star" 15 February 1863. "Conduct on board — generally good."

MARY SKEWES (21), single left Plymouth 31 May 1865 on board "Cornwallis". Arrived 27 August 1865. "Good conduct during voyage."

JOHN SKEWES (27), SUSAN SKEWES (30), WILLIAM H. SKEWES (4) and JOHN H. SKEWES (1) left Plymouth on 15 December 1865 on board "Trevelyan." Arrived 21 March 1866. There were 423 passengers on board including: THOMAS SKUSE (17) agricultural labourer and WILLIAM SKUSE (18), agricultural labourer. Also SAMUEL SKEWES (23) gardener.

MARY SKEWES (20), cook left Plymouth on 23 January 1866 on board "Atlanta " and arrived 15 April 1866.

LIST OF EMIGRANT LABOURERS APPLYING FOR FREE PASSAGE TO AUSTRALIA 1836-1841
Compiled by Professor Douglas Pike held from records at the Public Record Office, London. Ref: CO 386, pieces 149, 150 and 151.

MARY SKEWES   dairymaid of Blackwater, St Agnes, aged 16 years
WILLIAM SKEWES   engineer of Blackwater,   St Agnes, aged 38 years. Married.
                       Wife aged 39 years.
WILLIAM SKEWES   miner of Blackwater,   St Agnes, aged 18 years.

(All emigrated 13 April 1840)

All information relating to emigrants was obtained from archives offices in Melbourne, Sydney and Adelaide and the writer is grateful to all concerned for allowing the information to be published.

THE MACKENZIE GENEALOGY

Lieutenant GEORGE SKUES, Royal Marines, born Helston 3 March 1797; married MARY GIBBS MACKENZIE at St Paul's Chapel, Aberdeen, Scotland, 25 March 1827.

Mary Gibbs Mackenzie was daughter of Alexander Mackenzie of Breda who married Maria Rebecca, daughter of Colonel William Humberston Mackenzie of Conan's Bay (father of last Lord Seaforth).

Alexander of Breda was the 5th son of James III of Highfield who married Mary, daughter of Rorie Mackenzie of Applecross.

James III was the 2nd son of John II of Highfield who married Margaret, daughter of James M'lean, Bailie, Inverness.

John II was first son of Thomas I of Highfield who married Agnes, daughter of Murdock Matheson of Balmacara.

Thomas I was 2nd son of John I of Ord who married Isobel, daughter of Alex Cuthbert of Drakies. Obtained Charters from Seaforth in 1607 and 1637. Died before 1652. He witnessed the burning of Gilchrist Church in 1602.

John I was 1st son (2nd marriage) of Thomas of Keanlochuichart, after of Ord, and Annabella, daughter of Murdoch Mackenzie of Fairburn. She later married Alexander Mackenzie I of Coul.

Thomas of Keanlochuichart was the 2nd son of Kenneth I of Gilchrest or Kilchrest who married Helen, daughter of Robert Loval of Balumbie, Forfar, 1539.

Kenneth I was the 5th son of Sir Kenneth 'A' Blair and ancestor of Suddie Inverlael Ord, Highfield etc., who married Lady Margaret, daughter of John, Earl of Ross. He married for the second time to Agnes, daughter of Hugh, Lord Frazer of Loval. Children legitimatised by Papal Bull of Alexander VI. Sir Kenneth died 1492.

Sir Kenneth was son of Alexander "Ionraic" (upright) who married first to Anna, daughter of Macdougall of Dunollich and then to Margaret, daughter of Macdougall of Morar. Alexander died 1488.

Alexander was son of Murdoch "Na Drochaid" (of the bridge) who married Finguala, daughter of Macleod of Harris. She died 1410.

Murdoch was son of Murdoch "Dubh" who married Isabel, daughter of Murdoch Macauley of Lochbroom. She died 1375.

Murdoch was son of Kenneth Mackenzie "Na Sroine" (of the nose) who married Finguala, daughter of Torquil Macleod II of the Lews.

Kenneth was put to death by the Earl of Ross in 1346. He was son of Kenneth or, by some manuscripts, Murdoch Mackenneth who married Margaret, daughter of David, 11th Earl of Athol, by Joan Comyn.

Kenneth (or Murdoch Mackenneth) was son of Kenneth who married Morba, daughter of Alexander MacDougall of Lorne. She died 1304.

Kenneth was son of Colin or Cailean, the "Gerald" of tradition, or of early Celtic or Irish derivation. He married a daughter of Kenneth Macmahon of Lochalsh.

Colin Mackenzie is the founder of this branch of the Mackenzie family. Of interest: The wife of Kenneth (Murdoch Mackenneth) was descended from King John of England via Richard Fitzroy, Countess Isabel de Dover, John de Strathbolgie and David, 11th Earl of Athol, on her paternal side. On her maternal side she was descended from David I, King of Scotland, via Prince Henry of Scotland; David, Earl of Huntingdon; Margaret, Countess of Galloway; King John Balliol and John de Comyn, the Red, who was killed by Bruce, 1306.[3]

TRANSCRIPT OF FAMILY BIBLE IN POSSESSION OF CHARLES AYRE MACKENZIE SKUES, 1958.[4]

RECORD OF DESCENT COMPILED FROM OLD FAMILY BIBLE, REGISTERS AND OTHER MEMORANDA IN POSSESSION OF Lieutenant GEORGE SKUES, Royal Marines, 3 MARCH 1862. COPY OF ENTRIES MADE IN HIS OWN HAND ON FLY LEAF OF HIS OWN FAMILY BIBLE by BRIGADE SURGEON WILLIAM MACKENZIE SKUES, M.D.

FIRST GENERATION OF WHICH THERE IS A RECORD

WILLIAM SKUES Receiver of the Rents of the Duchy of Cornwall under the Prince of Wales was born about 1733. He married May Hitchen of St Day by whom he had issue:
(1) RICHARD, eldest son of the above. Born 1767. Married Ann Richards, daughter of John Richards of Truthall and had issue.
(2) WILLIAM. Died without issue, aged 21 years.
(3) ELIZABETH. Married Rev. Byron of the Wesleyans and had issue, a son and two daughters. The son died without issue. The older daughter is at present alive and the wife of the Rev. Benjamin Andrews. They have no issue.
(4) MARY. Married William Mitchell, merchant of Truro and had issue.

The RICHARDS FAMILY

JOHN RICHARDS, Esq of Truthall, Cornwall succeeded his father and grandfather in the Estate. Born 1720. He married May of Sethna in the parish of Breage in Cornwall about the year 1756. He died about the year 1768 and his widow about 1794. They had issue:
(1) ANN. Born 1763. Married RICHARD SKUES, son of WILLIAM SKUES and died 8 February 1847 and left issue.
(2) GRACE. Born about 1764 and married Rev. Thomas Robinson, vicar of St Hilary about 1802 who died 3 April 1814. She died 24 September 1846 without issue.
(3) MARGARET. Born 11 January 1766. Died a spinster 15 May 1852.

---

[3]Mackenzie genealogy compiled from various documents retained at the Society of Genealogists, London.
[4]This transcript was sent to the author by C.A.M. Skues two months prior to his death in 1958. He says "It is in very faint ink and pencil and very small writing so that neither I nor my sister Minnie can read it by daylight." This transcript has been copied as sent by C.A.M. Skues.

SECOND GENERATION SKUES

RICHARD SKUES. Born 1767. Married ann Richards, daughter of John Richards of Truthall, Cornwall and had issue. They were married in Helston Church by Rev. R.G. Grylls on 4 December 1793. He died 17 November 1811. She died 8 February 1847 in Plymouth.

(1) RICHARD, son of the above. Born 5 October 1794. Baptised 4 September following. Was twice married but left no issue.

(2) EDWARD, son of the above. Born 14 September 1795. Died 11 October following.

(3) GEORGE, son of the above. Born 3 March 1797. Baptised 5 October following. Married Mary Gibbs Mackenzie, daughter of Sir Alexander Mackenzie of Breda, Aberdeenshire by Rebecca his wife, sister of Lord Seaforth and had issue. George Skues died at Upper Holloway, Middlesex on 9 January 1872 and was buried in churchyard at Aberdeen. His widow died at Ealing and was buried in same vault.

(4) GRACE RICHARDS, daughter of the above. Born 8 July 1799. Baptised Helston 10 June 1801. Married William Radford, Wesleyan preacher who left her a widow without issue. She died at Bristol 4 July 1862.

(5) MARY, daughter of the above. Born 29 December 1800. Baptised 10 March 1801. Married Richard Rodd, solicitor of Stonehouse in December 1826. Died 29 February 1848 and had issue.

(6) WILLIAM. Born 10 January 1802 and died 14 February the year following.

(7) WILLIAM. Born 6 February 1804. Died 19 May 1805.

(8) ANN. Born 29 January 1807. Baptised 26 February following and died 1 May 1817.

THIRD GENERATION SKUES

GEORGE SKUES. Son of Richard Skues, surgeon of Helston, Cornwall. Born 3 March 1797. Entered the Royal Marines as Second Lieutenant, 25 October 1813. Placed on half pay January 1815. Married at Aberdeen in St Paul's Chapel, Gallowgate by Rev. Charles Gardener to Mary Gibbs Mackenzie, daughter of Alexander Mackenzie, Esq., of Breda by his wife Maria Gibbs Mackenzie sister of Francis Lord Seaforth on 25 March 1827 and had issue.

(1) WILLIAM MACKENZIE. Born 15 March 1828. Staff Surgeon M.D. 29 July 1853. Later Brigade Surgeon. Married Margaret Ayre and had issue.

(2) EDWARD WALKER. Born 17 July 1830. Staff Surgeon 1860. Died with no issue.

(3) GERTRUDE ELIZA MACKENZIE. Born 16 February 1832. Died 16 February 1835.

(4) FREDERICK MACKENZIE. Born 21 October 1833. Staff Surgeon 28 February 1855. Married and had issue — two sons and two daughters all of whom died single.

(5) ELIZA MACKENZIE. Born 6 June 1837. Died 1858.

(6) RICHARD ALEXANDER. Born 12 April 1838. Ensign 3rd West India Regiment 6 July 1855. Retired and went to South America and took up mining engineering. Later became Sheriff of Denver, Colorado. Died unmarried.

(7) JOHN RICHARDS. Born 26 May 1839. Died in 1846.

(8) GEORGINA MARY. Born 31 October 1840. Died a spinster about the end of the 19th century.[5]

Record sleeve of an old 78 rpm gramophone record as distributed in 1940 by William Frederick Charles Skewes of King Street, Thorne, near Doncaster, Yorkshire

---

[5]Some of these dates do not coincide with dates given in parish registers in Cornwall.

PRESS CUTTINGS
1800-1980

PRESS CUTTINGS
LG London Gazette
RCG Royal Cornwall Gazette
WB West Briton
RCG 8 May 1802
Monday were married Mr Michell of Calenick near Truro to Miss SKUES of Helston.

RCG 18 September 1802
"List of Certificates issued on Deputations or Appointments of Gamekeepers, within the county of Cornwall from the 1st day of July 1802 to the 1st day of September following, inclusive.
Gamekeeper — RICHARD SKUES, Gent.
Manor   — Penventon
Deputed by   — The Duke of Leeds"

LG 2 July 1803
To be Lieutenant Loyal Meneage Volunteers RICHARD SKUES, Gent.

RCG 10 September 1803
"List of Certificates issued on Deputations or Appointments of Gamekeepers, within the county of Cornwall from the 1st day of July 1803 to the 3rd day of September following, inclusive.
Gamekeeper — RICHARD SKUES, Gent.
Manor   — Penventon
Deputed by   —Duke of Leeds"

LG 10 November 1803
RICHARD SKUES, Lieutenant to read RICHARD SKUES, Gent to be Captain.

LG 29 November 1803
Meneage Loyal Volunteers Infantry RICHARD SKUES, Gent to be Surgeon.

RCG 13 September 1806
"List of Certificates issued on Deputations or Appointments of Gamekeepers, within the county of Cornwall from the 1st day of July 1806 to the 4th day of September following, inclusive.
Gamekeeper — RICHARD SKUES, Gent.
Manor   — Helston in Kirrier
Deputed by   —John Rogers, Esq."

RCG 12 September 1807
"List of Certificates issued on Deputations or Appointments of Gamekeepers, within the county of Cornwall from the 1st day of July 1807 to the 7th September following, inclusive.
Gamekeeper — RICHARD SKUES, Gent
Manor '   — Helston in Kirrier
Deputed by   —John Penrose, Esq."

RCG 10 September 1808
"List of Certificates issued on Deputations or Appointments of Gamekeepers, within the county of Cornwall from the 1st day of July 1808 to the 8th September following, inclusive.
RICHARD SKUES (Helston residence) Rate of duty £3 3 0d."

RCG 21 October 1810; 7 July 1810; 14 July 1810 and 21 July 1810.
PROTEST OF THE MINERS OF CORNWALL
We, the Miners of Cornwall, having seen the Plan, said to be proposed by Mr Edward Budd, schoolmaster of Truro, and acknowledged by him, for establishing a second newspaper in this county to be called "West Briton" or "Miner's Journal" which we think likely to implicate us in what he calls in his Prospectus "Discussion of public measures and judgement on the conduct of public men", and conceiving it probable that we may be exhibited to the Nation and the Government by this unauthorised use of our name, as men who participate in approve of his principals. WE DO SOLEMNLY PROTEST against this unwarrantable assumption, and declare that we are determined peaceably and firmly to support the King, the Laws and the Constitution of our Country. The signatures of various Lords and Adventurers include: ALEXANDER SKEWES and WILLIAM SKUES.
The paper inserted list of Lords and Adventurers and Agents and Managers of Mines, but the signed protest included five sixths of all miners in the county.

GENTLEMAN's MAGAZINE, 1817

A Cornish newspaper relates the following praiseworthy example of persevering industry, and of the benefit of attaching small pieces of ground to cottages.

"PETER SKEWES resides at Blackwater, in the parish of St Agnes: he holds a small tenement consisting of about an acre and three quarters of land, the soil of which is naturally sterile. This is divided into two nearly equal plots. One of these he plants with potatoes, the other he tills to wheat, and so on alternatively, every year one of his little fields producing potatoes, and the other, wheat. By proper attention in the cultivation, he has, on average, 80 Cornish bushels of potatoes, and 9 of wheat, each season.

He keeps two donkeys which graze on the neighbouring common during the summer, and are partly fed with the straw of his wheat in the winter. With these he carries coal etc. for his neighbours, and collects manures for his ground. The refuse, potatoes etc. enable him to feed a pig, which, with fish purchased in the season, affords all that is required for food, in addition to the produce of his fields and little garden.

In this way Peter Skewes passed the last seven years, and supported a wife and family, now consisting of six children, not only without parish aid, but with a degree of comfort and the independence of which there are not many examples in his situation in life — he never wants the means of satisfying any demands that are made upon him whether for parochial assessment or for supplying the wants of his family."

At the Cornwall Lent Assizes on Wednesday 28 March 1832, there was the trial of Peter Matthews for murder of Grace Andrew of the village of Calenick, near Truro. A witness was JAMES SKEWES.

RCG 31 March 1832.

"I am the son of Henry SKEWES who lived in Fairmantle Street, Truro. I am a cordwainer. My father was parish clerk of Kea. The prisoner lodged with my father. Before and on 20 January he slept with me. Before he came to live with my father he lived with his sister at Calenick. The prisoner was not then in constant work. He told me he was in debt to a Mr Barrett — a tailor. He paid two shillings a week for lodgings.

I never heard him say he was in arrears for lodgings, but heard him speak of his want for money. About a fortnight before the murder he complained to me about his want for money. He said he must have money, and he would have money and he'd be damned if he would not have money. He used those words more than once, but that one in particular.

About a fortnight before the murder, I remember his being in bed with me; he then said he must have money and he would have money and he'd be damned if he would not have money. He said he thought he could tell where he could get money. I asked him where and he said Calenick. I said Calenick? Where there — Mr Matthew? He replied 'Mr Mitchell's. No! William Andrews.'

I answered Mr Andrews, how should he have any money? He again replied and said 'I know he has got some money, or spoons or something.' He then said he would go and take out a pane of glass. He would put his hand in and open the window, and go in and open the back door. 'They will hear me, to be sure. I'll be carrying my lathing hammer. I'll soon do their business for them.'

I said do you mean it and he said 'Yes'. The prisoner asked me to go, but I said I wouldn't go for the world. About a week after this time I had another conversation with him. He said 'Where do you think I was last night?' I said I didn't know. He replied 'Calenick. I was forth to William Andrews' window and saw the old man and woman sitting down by the fire. I trembled like a rush. I had my lathing hammer in my pocket too.' This conversation took place a week before the murder. On the same day of the murder I awoke about daybreak. He usually got up at the same time as I did, but this morning he got up before me. I said how are you going to get up so soon. He said 'What use is it to stay here, I can't sleep.'

He was not at this time in work. The prisoner then got up and went downstairs. I heard him say to my father there was a pretty job done down at Calenick, that Grace Andrew was murdered and it was said she was killed with a flat polled instrument something like a hammer. I jumped out of bed (I had never heard that report before) and went downstairs, but the prisoner was gone out. I met him that day in Tabernacle Street and said Peter is this your job done down at Calenick. He said 'No — what do you think?' I said what have you got there, and pointed to his waistcoat. I observed some red spots upon his waistcoat which was a light summer one. He swore and said 'Don't be such a da...d fool. Do you think that if I had done it the blood would fly up like that?'

The spots were just on his breast. We then parted. I charged him with the murder often afterwards, but he always denied it. I remember that on one occasion when denying it he said 'How do you think I could do it? If I had done it how should I not have any money?'

I said he had some, but he had hid it at Newham or somewhere. I remember one occasion his telling me that he came into my father's house the night of the murder at half past nine. I said he did not come in at half past nine for it was after ten that I went to bed, and he was not then in the house."

Cross examined JAMES SKEWES said:

"I have lived for many years at Truro and had carried on the business of cordwainer for some time. I had never known the Andrews. I first knew the prisoner at Calenick. He was not in steady work. He worked occasionally with Battershall. I wanted money. I did not know how to get in my bills and I used to say so, often to my mother. I do not ever recollect saying to the prisoner that I wanted money — he might have been present when I said it to my mother. About six weeks after the murder I went to a Magistrate voluntarily. £100 had been offered for a discovery of the murderer. I knew of the reward a fortnight after the murder.

I usually went to bed between nine and ten, but cannot say the precise time of any other evening. I had not been to sleep the night the prisoner came to bed on the night of the murder. I heard him come into the bed, but there was no light. In the morning he dressed as usual and went downstairs.

The prisoner had been out some time before I heard him conversing with my father on his return, when he said old Grace Andrew has been murdered. He continued to sleep with me for a month until after the murder.

It was shortly after that Ellis, the Bow Street Officer, came down to investigate the matter. He talked to me about him, but I did not mention anything of what I am now saying. I never told Ellis that I could clear the prisoner, who was soon after discharged. I believe the reward was offered after Ellis came down.

I mentioned my suspicions to my brother the day after the murder; it was in consequence of some conversation with him that I withheld the information of the hour of his going to bed."

Cross examined by the Judge JAMES SKEWES said:

"He told me his sister owed him £12. The reason I did not accuse him at first was because I wanted to sift him, not being sure. I was afraid of my life all the time I slept with him, but I wanted to be certain before I brought him into trouble."

CATHERINE SKEWES, Mary Gilbert her daughter, THOMAS SKEWES a mason, and several other witnesses were cross examined as to conversations that had taken place with the prisoner about the time of, and after the murder, but nothing of a particular nature was elicited.

The prisoner on being called on for his defence, said he knew nothing of the murder. Mr Crowther, who gratuitously undertook his defence in Court, called no witnesses.

The Judge summing up the evidence, did not appear to consider the evidence of James Skewes entitled much attention.

In conclusion he clearly stated the Law on the subject, and thought that the suspicions entertained did not warrant the Jury to find the prisoner guilty.

The Jury consulted for a few minutes and returned a verdict of "Not Guilty." The trial lasted from 8 o'clock in the morning until half past five in the afternoon.

RCG 26 July 1839
SERIOUS ACCIDENT
On Monday (22 July) as Mr SKEWES of Cury was returning from Helston Fair, he was thrown from his horse against the wheel of a cart, and fractured his skull. But slight hopes are entertained of his recovery.

The Australian; 3 November 1840
ENGLISHMAN CHARGED WITH MURDER
Before His Honour The Chief Justice. The jury being put into the box and sworn — THOMAS SKEWES was placed at the bar and charged with the wilful murder of John Parry at Sydney, on the 11th August last, by stabbing him in the upper part of the left side of the belly with a knife. The prisoner pleaded not guilty. Mr Purifoy appeared as council for the prisoner.

William Savage called and examined — I am Chief Officer of the brig "Ullswater" of London, Atkin Gibson, master; she arrived on the 4th August and was lying at Moore's Wharf, in Darling Harbour. The prisoner was Second Officer. On 11th August last, at about 8 o'clock in the evening I retired to rest. I heard a disturbance in the forepart of the ship. I dressed myself and went forward and found the prisoner rather in liquor, and quarrelling with some seamen. I requested him to go below, but he would not. He followed me to the quarter deck and said he would do for me before morning. In half an hour afterwards I was awakened by the cries of "murder!" I came on deck and found the prisoner struggling in the hands of two men who were endeavouring to confine him. They took the knife from him and put him in irons and handed him over to the police. I then went forward and saw the deceased Parry, a seaman who joined us at Marseilles, lying on the main hatchway with a wound in his belly. The wound was cut with an old case knife ground to the joint. I sent for the doctor to dress his wounds. The deceased was then taken to the hospital. Prisoner was aware the seaman was wounded for I heard him say he had killed one man he was certain. This was after I had given him in charge of the constable.

Cross-examined: I came up from London as Chief Officer. We arrived in Marseilles in March. Both the prisoner and deceased joined us at Marseilles. I had often heard the prisoner and deceased quarrelling about many things. The vessel was moored about 20 feet from the shore. The vessel had been in port for about seven days. The prisoner lived in the forecastle. I observed the stains of blood on the knife when it was given to me. I examined it a few minutes before I gave it to the constable. The blood was then dry.

William George called — I am an apprentice on the brig "Ullswater" and remember the 11th August. I got Parry his supper and cut up some tobacco, and got the lamp down on the deck and was going to light my pipe. In the meantime Skewes came down and said: "What is that light doing there?" I said I was going to light my pipe. He said: "You had better get it out of that."

I said I would when I had lighted my pipe. He said "None of your cheek." I said "That is no cheek." He then commenced beating me. I shouted for assistance and Parry ran towards me saying "What's the matter Bill?" I saw the prisoner going towards him with a knife and I heard Parry say " I am stabbed." I ran ashore to the police station and reported the circumstances. I saw Parry's wound and his entrails hanging out of his left groin. I left him at the hospital.

Cross-examined: I am an Englishman belonging to Bristol. The prisoner, deceased and I lodged at the same house in Marseilles. It was the duty of the prisoner to see that everything was right when lying in the wharf. The First Officer was in bed.

James Fitzgerald called — I am District Constable of Sydney. I went on board the "Ullswater" on the night of 11th August with the last witness and another seaman. I saw a man lying on the deck covered over and bleeding very much. The prisoner was tied with his hands behind him — he was roaring — I think he was in liquor at the time. The prisoner said he had killed the man and that he meant it for four or five more if he could only get his hands loose and he was willing to suffer for the man he had killed. He told me he had a wife in England.

Cross-examined: I told the prisoner on his way to the watch house that it was a very bad job for him and that he would sure to be hanged for killing the man. He said he did not care.

Henry Graham called — I am one of the Colonial Assistant Surgeons. I remember Parry complaining of great pains and I understood he had been stabbed. He died at 7 o'clock the following evening. He died of inflamation. I made a post-mortem examination. The wound was about five inches deep in the abdomen. Nothing could have saved the man's life.

Captain Gibson of the "Ullswater" for the defence, proved that the prisoner was a man of quiet disposition, and not quarrelsome and the deceased quite the reverse.

His Honour summed up and laid down the law of manslaughter and murder. The jury retired and brought in a verdict of manslaughter.

Skewes was sentenced to transportation for 14 years. (See also page 663.)

Other articles in Royal Cornwall Gazette 1810-1850 are reproduced in Chapter 3 "Records Records Records."

RCG 17 October 1851
Marriage at the Register Office, Helston on Saturday last of Mr FRANCIS THOMAS SKEWES of Cury to Miss Julia Thomas of Mullion.

RCG 19 December 1851
Death at Drakewell's Mines, on Saturday last, of ANN, infant daughter of Captain HENRY SKEWIS, aged 3 years.

RCG 26 December 1851
Marriage at Kenwyn, on Wednesday last, Mr W. Crewes, coachsmith to Miss HENRIETTA SKEWES, both of Truro.

RCG 12 March 1852
Marriage at Kenwyn, on 4th instant, Mr RICHARD SKEWES, innkeeper of Penstrase, in the parish of Kea, to Miss Elizabeth Rouse of London.

RCG 9 April 1852 (two entries)
Birth at Angarrack, in the parish of Phillack, on Monday last, the wife of Mr HENRY SKEWES, police officer, of a son.

Death at Angarrack, in the parish of Phillack, on Sunday last, Mr HENRY SKEWES, police officer, aged 34 years.

RCG 21 May 1852
Birth at Truro, on Tuesday last, the wife of Mr JOHN SKEWES, cabinet maker, of a son.

RCG 15 October 1852
Marriage at the Wesleyan Chapel, Falmouth, on Tuesday last, Mr JOSIAH SKEWES of Constantine, to Fanny, eldest daughter of Mr James Bone of Penance, in the parish of Budock.

RCG 17 December 1852
Death at Gwinear, on Sunday last, of Mr R.M. SKEWES, aged 19 years.

RCG 1 April 1853
Death at Redruth on 24 March the wife of JOHN SKEWES, aged 42 years.

RCG 6 May 1853
Marriage at Kenwyn, on Saturday last, Mr John Mills to Miss MARY ANN SKEWES, both of Truro.

RCG 20 May 1853
Birth at Redruth the wife of Mr THOMAS SKEWES, of a son.

RCG 8 July 1853
Death at Redruth on the 27 June, the infant daughter of JOHN SKEWS.

RCG 22 July 1853
Birth at Bosawsack in the parish of Constantine, on Friday last, the wife of JOSIAH SKEWES, of a daughter since dead.

RCG 29 September 1854
Birth at Realwa, in the parish of Gwinear, on the 15th instant, the wife of Captain HENRY SKEWES, of a daughter.

RCG 3 November 1854
Birth at Chacewater, on the 25th October, the wife of Mr SKEWS, of a son.

RCG 8 December 1854
Marriage at Camborne, on Saturday last, of Mr Richard Bullock to Miss JULIA SKEWES, both of Camborne.

RCG 2 March 1855
Death at Redruth of Mr JOHN SKEWES, aged 64 years.

RCG 7 May 1855
WRECK OF THE BARQUE "JOHN"
The wreck of the Barque "John" (468 tons) on the Manacles Rocks on 3 May 1855 resulted in a loss of 196 lives. The ship was bound from Plymouth to Quebec with emigrants. There were 268 passengers and a crew of 19. The Master was Edward Rawle.
On board was JOHN SKEWES, shoemaker of Falmouth, aged 25 years who was a steerage passenger. He was one of the persons saved.
BENJAMIN SKEWES of Falmouth, shoemaker, was also a passenger on board. About three quarters of an hour after the tide began to rise, he got on the poop, which was then crowded with passengers, and he saw several washed off, principally children. He was on the poop for about half-an-hour when, the sea breaking over, he went up the mizzen rigging. There were so many there he could get no higher, he was carried off by the sea, but caught hold of a raft or something else, and after ten minutes got into the main rigging, where he remained until he was taken off. He did not see the captain, mates or crew assist the passengers. He thought the captain had been drinking; he was smelling of liquor; but he could not swear he was the worse for liquor.
RCG 18 May 1855.
An enquiry took place in May 1855 when a verdict of manslaughter was brought against Captain Rawle. The disaster was due to criminal incompetence of the master and crew. The captain was later given a prison sentence, as were a number of St Keverne men, who were found guilty of looting from the dead as they lay on the beach.

RCG 5 October 1855
Death at Tuckingmill on 25th September, Mrs ELIZABETH SKEWIS, aged 58 years.

RCG 9 November 1855
Marriage at Oporto, Portugal, on the 15th September last, MATTHEW SKEWES, only son of MATTHEW SKEWES of Chacewater, to Anna Maria, daughter of the late Mr Nettle of Redruth.

RCG 4 April 1856
Marriage at the Independent Chapel, Tavistock, on Tuesday last, Mr S.D. SKEWES of Beer Alston to Miss Jane Courtis of the same place.

RCG 27 June 1856
Birth at Gwinear last week to the wife of Captain SKEWIS, of a son.

RCG 15 August 1856
Birth at Polhol Mines, near Oporto, Portugal, on the 24th July, the wife of MATTHEW SKEWES, junior, of a son.

RCG 3 October 1856
Death at Chacewater, on Friday last, suddenly, much respected Mr MATTHEW SKEWES, of the Royal Oak, aged 60 years.

RCG 31 October 1856
Death at Treloskan, in the parish of Cury, on the 19th instant, Mr JAMES SKEWES, aged 59 years.

RCG 30 January 1857
Death on Tuesday last, the eldest son of Mr JOHN SKEWES of Truro, cabinet-maker, aged 5 years.

RCG 13 February 1857
Birth at Nantithet, Cury, on Saturday, the wife of Mr EDWARD SKEWES, of a son.

South Australian Register; 20 March 1857
MARRIAGE:
On Monday 9 March, Joseph Parker, chemist of Kooringa, son of Richard Parker, Esq., married MARY SKEWES, second daughter of JOHN SKEWES of Liwchyr, at the residence of the bride's father.

RCG 3 July 1857
Marriage at St Paul's Chacewater, on 25 June, by the Reverend G.L. Church, Mr Joel Wasley to Miss EMMA JANE SKEWES, both of Chacewater.

RCG 28 August 1857
Death at Ruan Major, on 25th August, EDWARD, son of Mr ANTHONY SKEWES of Tresodden, aged 4 years.

RCG 8 January 1858
Marriage at Camborne, on Thursday 31st December, Mr John Bullock to Miss LAVINIA SKEWES.

RCG 16 July 1858
Francis Richards, farmer at TRESKEWES FARM, married Jane Boulden Roberts at St Keverne on 13th July.

RCG 20 August 1858
Marriage at Baldhu, on 19th August, by Rev. John Symonds, Mr John Symonds of Chacewater to Miss PHILIPPA SKEWS of Baldhu.

RCG 10 September 1858
Death at St Austell, on Saturday last, after a lingering illness, Mr JOHN SKEWS, late of the General Wolfe Inn, aged 55 years.

RCG 26 November 1858
Birth at St Day, on Friday 19th instant, Mrs SKEWES, the wife of Mr R. SKEWES of Ballarat Diggings, Australia, of a daughter.

RCG 10 December 1858
Death at SKEWES, Cury, on Thursday 2nd instant, Mr Thomas James, yeoman, aged 72 years.

RCG 22 April 1859
Death of the infant son of Mr MATTHEW SKEWS at St Ives on the 12th instant.

RCG 14 May 1858
COURT CASE AT TRURO
Michael Williams, M.P. v Henry Lean Whiting of Penryn.
This was a case to recover possession of a mill, land and premises in Veryan.
Defendant held under a lease for a term of years, but there was a clause in the lease to determine it on the rent being more than half a year in arrear, and insufficient goods on the premises on which to levy a distress.
Mr Robert for plaintiff called Mr ALEXANDER SKEWES, who proved that there was as much as a year and a half's rent in arrear, amounting to £72, the yearly rent being £48. The High Bailiff Mr Drew gave evidence that when he went to the premises recently to distrain for only a few shillings, he could not find sufficient to meet that amount. His Honour gave judgement for the plaintiff, and ordered possession to be given by the defendant in a month. This was the first case under the section of the Act which had occurred in this court.

RCG 21 May 1858
SERIOUS ACCIDENT
In the afternoon of Thusday last week, Mr Matthew Thomas, a cattle dealer of Truro, accompanied by his brother Mr Richard Thomas of Troon, Camborne and Mr SKEWES, farmer at St Erme, was returning to Truro from Summercourt fair in a dog-cart, Mr Matthew Thomas driving. On reaching the top of Killiserth Hill, the horse taking the bit in his teeth, bolted off at a rapid pace, keeping the near side of the road, and free from almost any control by the driver.
On reaching the turnpike gate, the near wheel of the dog-cart struck against the gate post with great violence; and all three in the vehicle were thrown out, and all received injuries more or less severe. Mr Matthew Thomas was thrown forward a distance of about 12 feet, pitching on his forehead on the road near the hedge; he was stunned and senseless for some hours, but by Monday was enabled to attend business.
Mr Richard Thomas pitched on his shoulder and received considerable injury by the spraining of the tendons and by the bruises on the arm. He still remains under medical care.
The most seriously injured of the party was Mr Skewes who was thrown between the bars of the turnpike gate, thus breaking a leg, and fracturing the knee of the other leg. He was first conveyed to his home at St Erme, and thence, in a spring cart, kindly lent for the purpose by E. Collins, Esq., of Truthan, to the Cornwall Infirmary at Truro, where the broken leg was set, and he still remains under medical care with hope of recovery.

RCG 18 June 1858
Kerrier Agricultural Show was held at Heston on 15 June 1858. The prize for the best sow went to Mr JOHN SKEWES.

RCG 23 July 1858
At the Kerrier Ploughing Match on 14 July 1858 the second prize for round combing went to JOHN SKEWES of Sithney.

RCG 30 July 1858
At the St Day Show Fair held on 27 July 1858 the prize for the best sow went to JOHN SKEWES of Sithney.

RCG 8 July 1859
12 MONTHS HARD LABOUR FOR ROBERT SKEWES
Trial of ROBERT SKEWES (30), paper hanger; Mary Williams (39), hawker and Robert Drew (39), french polisher.
The charge was that the defendants stole 14 sovereigns and three shillings, the property of Richard Searle, farmer, at East Looe on 6 May 1859. All three pleaded "not guilty."
Mr Bishop conducted the Prosecution and Mr Brian of Plymouth, the Defence.
Richard Searle, the Prosecutor stated that he was at Looe Fair on 6 May, with money in his pocket. At five or six o'clock he paid some money to a saddler at Looe, and in the evening at about 9 o'clock he was at the Swan Inn, East Looe; he was quite sober and drank nothing at the inn. Whilst there he satisfied himself that his money was safe in his pocket — £14 in sovereigns and half sovereigns, and about a pound's worth of silver. After remaining in the inn a short time, he was coming out when Williams tapped him on the shoulder and attempted familiarities with him. He resisted and told her to go away. She clasped him around the waist and then made off.
Before she proceeded far Mr Searle, going over the bridge, found that his waistcoat was torn, his purse abroad and his money gone.
Robert Snell, a shipwright's apprentice: At about 10 o'clock he saw the three men and woman talking together and walking in the direction of the bridge. They went onto Bridge End and while they were on the bridge, Snell (who appears to have been active in watching the prisoners) overheard one of the men say to the woman "If you don't tell where it is, I'll kick you." The third man then went away. And Drew, Skewes and the woman Williams went over the bridge to West Looe, where the fair was being held, and here, by means of the fair lights, Snell saw the faces of the two men, as they were together.

Snell, having communicated with the policeman Pappin went into the Jolly Sailor Inn, and the two male prisoners came in there shortly afterwards, and they were soon followed in there by Pappin. Evidence as to the prisoners being together at the fair was also given by Catherine Rundell, after which Police Sergeant Pappin was examined. It appeared that, after having received a communication from Snell, during three quarters of an hour, he lost sight of the prisoners for only two minutes. This interval being when they were on the bridge and when, it was suggested, they might possibly have got rid of a portion, or the whole, of the stolen property.

Immediately after that Pappin got onto the bridge, and saw the two men lying in a ditch. He got over the hedge into a ditch and put his hands on them. They pretended to be fast asleep, one of them, SKEWES, snoring and Drew said he was resting a bit and pretended to be drunk. Pappin, with aid, afterwards took them into custody and searched them.

On one of the men he found £2 10 in gold, and twenty-three shillings in silver.

The men pretended to have no knowledge of each other, or of the woman, while she professed to know nothing of the men.

Police Inspector William Thomas from Plymouth proved that Skewes and the woman Williams had long lived together in Stonehouse Lane, Plymouth, and he had frequently seen them together.

The Jury at 4 o'clock retired for consultation and in about half an hour returned a verdict of "Guilty" against the prisoners.

ROBERT SKEWES was imprisoned at the House of Correction, Bodmin and given 12 months hard labour. The Chairman said it had come to the knowledge of the Court, though fortunately for the prisoner it was not charged against him at his trial, that he had been six times previously convicted, and during the past six or seven years he had been pursuing a career of crime.

SKEWES on receiving his sentence, impudently and laughingly explained "Long life to your Honour and thank you!"

Thomas Drew was given nine months hard labour and Mary Williams twelve months hard labour.

RCG 28 September 1860
Birth at Truro, on Sunday last, the wife of Mr JOHN SKEWES, cabinet-maker, of a daughter.

RCG 21 December 1860
Birth at St Ives, the wife of Mr MATTHEW SKEWES, of a daughter.

RCG 8 February 1861
Death at Camborne on the 1st instant, Mrs ANN SKEWES, aged 83 years.

RCG 27 December 1861
Marriage on 23rd instant at Redruth of Mr Joseph Gribble of Redruth to Miss ALICE SKEWES of Illogan.

RCG 24 January 1862
Death at Killiwerris, Chacewater, on 17th instant, Mr JOHN SKEWES, aged 60 years.

RCG 21 March 1862
Marriage at Treslothan, on 17th instant, by the Rev. G.T. Bull, Mr JOHN SKEWES to Miss Elizabeth Jane Semmons.

RCG 18 April 1862
Marriage at Baldhu on the 10th instant by the Rev. G.L. Church, Mr William Francis Wasley to Miss JANE SKEWS of Hugus.

RCG 4 July 1862
Birth at Redruth, the wife of Mr JOHN SKUES, of a son.

RCG 18 July 1862
Death at Kugger in the parish of Grade on 4 July, Mr RICHARD SKEWES, aged 23 years.

RCG 17 April 1863
Marriage at the Wesley Chapel, Redruth on the 11th instant Mr R. Dunn to Miss SKEWES, both of Carharrack.

RCG 26 June 1863
Mr ALEXANDER SKEWES, deceased
Pursuant to the Act to Parliament of the 22nd and 23rd Victoria, Chapter 35, entitled "An Act to further amend the Laws of Property and to relieve Trustees", Notice is hereby given that all Creditors and other persons having claim on or against the Estate of ALEXANDER SKEWES, late of Gwennap Moors, in the parish of Gwennap, in the county of Cornwall (who died on 12 December, 1862, and whose Will was duly proved by RICHARD SKEWES MARTYN, of Helston, in the said county, grocer, and RICHARD SKEWES TEAGUE, of Redruth Highway, in the said county, grocer, the Executors therein named, in the District Registry of Her Majesty's Court of Probate for the county of Cornwall, at Bodmin, on 5th February, 1863) are hereby required to send in the particulars of their claims and demands upon the Estate of the said Deceased, to the said Executors, or to Messrs Smith and Roberts, their Solicitors on or before 6 August, 1863, or in default thereof the said Executors will proceed to administer the Estate and distribute the Assets of the said Deceased among the parties entitled thereto, having regards to the claims and demands only of which they shall then have notice, and the said Executors will not be liable for the assets or any part thereof so distributed to any person of whose claim they shall not then have had notice, and all persons indebted to the estate of the said ALEXANDER SKEWES are hereby required to pay the

amount of their respective debts to the said Executors, or to the said Messrs Smith and Roberts forthwith, who are hereby authorised to receive the same.
Dated this 24th day of June, 1863.
        Smith and Roberts,
        Truro, Solicitors for the said Executors.

RCG 7 August 1863
Death at Ballarat, Australia, on 16th May, the wife of Mr HENRY SKEWES, formerly of Mawnan, Cornwall, aged 36 years.

RCG 29 January 1864
Marriage on the 27th instant at the Association Chapel, Redruth, by the Rev. W. Jones, Mr Henry Sobey of Illogan Highway to Miss JANE SKUES of Redruth.

RCG 3 June 1864
Birth at Nantithet, Cury, the wife of Mr EDWARD SKEWES, of a daughter.

RCG 7 October 1864
Marriage at Baldhu, 30 September, by the Rev. John Symonds, Mr WILLIAM SKEWES to Miss Jane Northey of Seveock.

RCG 10 March 1865
Marriage at Camborne Parish Church, 5 March by Rev.W.P. Chappel, Mr JAMES H. SKEWES, of Cury, to Mary Jane, daughter of Mr Edward Eudey of Camborne.

RCG 24 March 1865
Death at New Zealand of fever Mr WALTER SKEWES, formerly of St Agnes, aged 26 years.

RCG 12 May 1865
Death at Penryn 7 May of SUSAN, widow of the late Mr STEPHEN SKEWES, in her 58th year.

RCG 9 June 1865
JOHN SKEWES of Cury was fined 6d with 7/6d costs at Helston County Petty Sessions for allowing two horses to stray onto the highway.

RCG 9 November 1865
Death at The Highway, Illogan, 5 November, the wife of Mr WILLIAM SKEWES, aged 40 years.

RCG 27 September 1866
Marriage at Redruth, 15 September, Mr W. SKEWES of The Highway, Illogan, to Miss Jane Thomas of Redruth.

RCG 26 March 1868
Death at Richmond Hill, Truro, 25 March of jaundice, MARY, second daughter of the late Mr HENRY SKEWES, yeoman, formerly of Roseworthy, Gwinear.

RCG 7 May 1868
Birth at Edward Street, Truro, 3 May, the wife of Mr THOMAS SKEWES, Junior, of a daughter.

RCG 16 July 1868
Death at Richmond Hill, Truro, 10 July of typhoid fever, LAVINIA, fifth daughter of the late Mr HENRY SKEWES, yeoman, formerly of Roseworthy, Gwinear.

RCG 23 July 1868
Death at Daniell Street, Truro, 16 July, after a long illness, Mr THOMAS SKEWES, aged 76 years.

RCG 30 July 1868
Marriage at St Paul's Church, Chacewater, 24 July, by the Rev. G.L. Church, Mr R. Trice of Beer Alston, Devon to EMMA, second daughter of the late Mr JOHN SKEWES of Killiwerris, in the former parish.

RCG 6 November 1869
Death at Redruth, 29 October, Mr HENRY SKEWES, aged 66 years.

RCG 22 December 1869
GREAT SKEWES, St Wenn was from where Mr John Lander (eldest son of Mr Christopher Lander) originated. On 18th December he married Susan Little of Tregolls, St Wenn at the Wesleyan Chapel, St Columb.

RCG 8 January 1870
Birth at Edward Street, Truro, 3 January, the wife of Mr T. SKEWES, of a daughter.

RCG 23 July 1870
Marriage at Real Del Monte, Mexico, 25 May, Mr PETER SKEWES, the youngest son of the late Mr PETER SKEWES, farmer of Kerley, to Elizabeth, third daughter of Mr William Bray of Lanner.

RCG 25 February 1871
Birth at Kenwyn Street, Truro, 22 February, the wife of Mr JOHN SKEWES, cabinet-maker, of a son.

RCG 25 March 1871
Birth at The Vicarage, St Agnes, 15 March, the wife of the Rev. J.H. SKEWES, of a daughter.

RCG 3 February 1872
Marriage at St Austell, 25 January, by licence, Mr RICHARD SKEWES of Kerley, late of Mexico, to Miss E. Stripp of St Austell.

RCG 14 September 1872
Birth at St Agnes, 5 September, the wife of Rev. J.H. SKEWES, M.A. of a daughter.

RCG 26 April 1873
Death at St Agnes, 19 April, ROSA MARIA, youngest daughter of Rev. J.H. SKEWES, Wesleyan minister.

RCG 17 January 1874
Death at Mineral Del Monte, Mexico, 6 January, Mr THOMAS SKEWES, late of Kerley, Kea, after 4 days of illness, aged 33 years.

RCG 6 June 1874
Birth at Pydar Street, Truro, 30 May, the wife of Mr JOHN SKEWES, cabinet-maker, of a son.

RCG 4 July 1874
Marriage at Baldhu Church, 29 June, by Rev. John Symonds, Mr Stephen Davey late of Real del Monte, Mexico, to GRACE, daughter of the late Mr PETER SKEWES, farmer of Kerley.

RCG 15 August 1874
Marriage at Camborne Parish Church, 3 August, by the Rev. W.T. Keeling, Mr R.G. Goodfellow of Mylor to Miss MATILDA SKEWES of Camborne.

RCG 12 September 1874
Marriage at St Paul's Church, Truro, 10 September, by Rev. A.H. Cummings, Mr T. Lambshead of London, formerly of Truro, to ANNIE, eldest daughter of the late Mr JOHN SKEWES of Trevella Farm.

Mining Journal 21 November 1874
Letter to the Editor: What is Electricity?
I can hardly reconcile the statement of Mr R.J. Crickmer in the supplement of last week's journal that they are mistaken who think that water consists of hydrogen and oxygen with the hitherto acknowledged and easily demonstrable fact, as shown by Professor Frankland in the "Mining Journal" of the 14th instant, and by every tyro in chemistry, both by analysis and synthesis, that pure water consists exclusively of hydrogen and oxygen in the ratio of two of hydrogen to one of oxygen. One cannot but admire the frankness and willingness of Mr Crickmer to demonstrate his theory by experiment and which very many of your readers will impatiently wait for in your next issue. EDWARD SKEWES.

Virginia City and Territorial Enterprise, USA 20 December 1874
MAN SHOT AND INSTANTLY KILLED ON THE DIVIDE
Last night at about 11 o'clock, at the Washington House, on the Divide two miners — JOHN SKEWES and Alfred Rule — had some words over a game of cards, when Skewes drew his revolver and shot Rule through the head, killing him almost instantly. There being no Officer on the Divide, someone came down town for a policeman. Officers Jackson and Merrow went out to the scene of the killing where Skewes was found and gave himself up without difficulty. He was brought down town and lodged in the County Jail, where he now remains.
As the history of the affair is related to us, the killing appears to have been done with very little provocation. The men were in the bar-room of the Washington House playing a game of cards when they had a dispute about the count; one saying it was "five points" made, and the other that it was "six points." Finally they became excited about the matter, when Rule called Skewes a liar. Skewes told him he must take that back. Rule said he would "take nothing back." Skewes then drew his six-shooter and said "If you don't take it back, I'll kill you." Rule declared that he would not take back what he had said, when Skewes fired on him. The bullet struck Rule just back of the left ear, passing into the head and producing an almost instant death.

Alfred Rule, the man who was killed, was a young man of 27 years. He has a brother in the city who arrived here from the East about two months since. It is said that both men were sober at the time of the shooting and nobody present had the least idea that the little war of words was going to end in anything serious, or that the men would come to blows.
The affair caused much excitement up on the Divide among the friends of the parties.

RCG 13 March 1875
Death at Pydar Street, Truro, 7 March, FREDERICK, infant son of JOHN and MARY SKEWES, aged 9 months.

RCG 10 April 1875
Birth at River Cottage, Chacewater, 29 March, the wife of Captain P. SKEWIS, of a son.

Virginia City and Territorial Enterprise, USA 20 May 1875
STATE OF NEVADA versus J.H. SKEWES.
The defendant is indicted for murder.
The case has once been tried, the jury failing to agree. The amount of bail was reduced from $10,000 to $6,000.
The defendant being unable to furnish bail in that amount was remanded for confinement in the county jail.

(The trial was set for 1st November 1875, but newspapers covering this period are not held at the Library of Congress or Newspaper Library.)

RCG 25 September 1875
Marriage at Farmington, Missouri, United States of America, 26 August, by the Rev J. Wesley Johnson, Rev. HENRY SKEWES, pastor of Evanston, Rocky Mountains, Conference, Utah Territory, but formerly of Gwinear, to Miss Martha M. Welborn of Carlton Institute. Missouri.

RCG 8 January 1876
Birth at Pool, Illogan, 29 December 1875, the wife of THOMAS SKEWS, of a son, since dead.

RCG 22 January 1876
Birth at the Police Station, Redruth, 11th January, the wife of Mr T.W. SKEWES of the County Constabulary, of a daughter.

RCG 23 September 1876
Marriage at Baldhu, 19th September (by licence) by the Rev. John Symonds, John, son of the late James Letcher of Penstraze to MARIA, youngest daughter of the late Mr PETER SKEWES, of Baldhu.

RCG 10 February 1877
Death at Gilley Street, Redruth, 7th February, Mr JAMES SKEWES, aged 26 years.

RCG 18 May 1877
Death at Lanner House, Gwennap, 12 May, ELIZABETH SKEWES, spinster, aged 66 years — much respected.

RCG 4 January 1878
Birth at Symonds Terrace, Redruth, 25 December, the wife of Captain P. SKEWES, of a son.

RCG 7 June 1878
Death at Bosawsack, Constantine, 2 June, Mr JOSIAH SKEWES, aged 58 years.

RCG 23 May 1879
Marriage of FRANCES MARIA SKEWES, second daughter of JAMES SKEWES, farmer of Mawnan to Arthur Liddicoat of Falmouth, by Rev. W. Rogers at St Michael's Church, Mawnan, 15 May.

RCG 30 May 1879
Birth at Kerley, Chacewater, 26 May, the wife of Mr RICHARD SKEWES, a daughter, stillborn.

RCG 22 August 1879
Marriage at Kenwyn Church, Truro,17 August, by Rev. J. Andrews Reeve, Mr J.H. Flynn to Miss E.J. SKEWES, both of Truro.

RCG 28 November 1879
Death at Wareham, Dorset, 18 November, MARY FANNY SOPHIA, eldest daughter of THOMAS LEAN SKEWES, Esq., late of Lanner, Gwennap, aged 26 years.

RCG 14 May 1880
Marriage at St George's, Hannover Square, London, 8 May, JOHN BROWNE SKEWES, compositor (formerly of the Royal Cornwall Gazette, Truro), to Bessie, second daughter of Mr Thomas Whether, St Austell Street, Truro.

RCG 21 January 1881
Marriage at Falmouth, 11 January, Mr THOMAS HENRY SKEWES to Jane, eldest daughter of the late Mr William Weatherly, both of The Lizard.

RCG 15 April 1881
Birth at Fowey, the wife of Mr LEWIS SKEWES, builder, late of Redruth, of a son.

RCG 29 April 1881
Birth at Mineral del Monte, Mexico, the wife of Mr RICHARD SKEWES (late of Chacewater) of a daughter.

RCG 19 August 1881
Birth at Elder Cottage, Chacewater, 17 August, the wife of Captain JOHN SKEWES, of a son.

RCG 14 October 1881
Death at Gwinear, 11 October, Captain HENRY SKEWES, a trusted servant of Messrs Vivian for 40 years, a member of the Wesleyan Society for half a century, and the President of the Wall Band of Hope for 23 years, aged 69 years.

RCG 10 March 1882
Marriage at Constantine Church, 2nd March, by Rev. F. R. Hole, Edwin, only son of the late Mr Edward Tregaskis, of Hicks Mill, Gwennap, to LAURA, only daughter of the late Mr JOSIAH SKEWES of Constantine.

RCG 14 April 1882
Death at Bolitho, Crowan, 9 April, ELIZABETH, wife of WILLIAM SKEWES, aged 74 years. She was a member of the Wesleyan Society for 54 years. Highly respected.

RCG 21 April 1882
Birth at The Lizard 3 April, the wife of Mr L.H. SKEWES, of a daughter.

RCG 19 May 1882
Birth at Mineral Del Monte, Mexico, 26 March, the wife of Captain RICHARD SKEWES, of a son.

RCG 24 November 1882
Death at Kerley, Kea, 17 November, MARY, relinct of Mr MATTHEW SKEWES, late of Chacewater, aged 85 years.

RCG 15 December 1882
Marriage at the Parish Church, Mawnan, 9 December by Rev.W. Rogers, Reuben Cobeldick of Mawgan-in-Pydar to EMILY KEMPTHORNE, third daughter of JAMES SKEWES of Mawnan.

RCG 19 October 1883
Birth at Elder Cottage, Chacewater, 12 October, the wife of Captain JOHN SKEWES, of a daughter.

RCG 14 March 1884
Death at Little Carharrack, 10 March, Mr JOHN SKEWES, for a great many years clerk under Messrs Williams and Co., aged 80 years.

RCG 27 June 1884
Marriage at The Cathedral, Truro, 20 June, CHARLES SKEWES, baker to Ellen Hawkins, both of Truro.

RCG 5 September 1884
Birth at Mineral del Monte, Mexico, 18 July, the wife of Captain PETER SKEWES, of a daughter.

RCG 24 October 1884
Death at Mineral del Monte, Mexico, 26 September, MARY MAUD only child of Captain RICHARD SKEWES, aged 6 months.

RCG 28 November 1884
Death in Australia of the Rev. JOHN SKEWES, for seven years Incumbent of All Souls, Manchester (youngest son of Mr WILLIAM SKEWIS, of Bolitho, Crowan).

RCG 9 January 1885
Birth at Elder Cottage, Chacewater, 2 January, the wife of Captain JOHN SKEWES, of a daughter.

RCG 23 January 1885
Death at Mineral del Monte, Mexico, 10 December, GEORGE HARRIS, second son of Captain PETER SKEWES, aged 10 years.

RCG 20 February 1885
Death at Ivy Court, Perranuthnoe, 16 February, EMMA, infant daughter of Mr RICHARD SKEWES, aged 1 year.

RCG 21 August 1885
Birth at The Lizard, 12 August, the wife of Mr T.H. SKEWES, of a son.

RCG 28 August 1885
Birth at Chacewater 21 August, the wife of Captain RICHARD SKEWES, late of Mexico, of a son.

RCG 9 April 1886
Birth at Ivy Cottage, Chacewater, 5 April, the wife of Captain JOHN SKEWES, of a son.

RCG 6 August 1886
Birth at Marazion, 24 July, the wife of Mr S. SKEWIS, of a daughter.

RCG 20 August 1886
Death at Ivy Cottage, Chacewater, 15 August, KATIE BEATRICE, youngest daughter of Captain JOHN SKEWES, aged 1 year 8 months.

RCG 31 December 1886
Death at Bolitho Farm, Crowan, 23 December, Mr WILLIAM SKEWES, aged 79 years.

RCG 18 February 1887
Death at Truro, 11 February, ANN, relinct of Mr JAMES SKEWES, aged 77 years.

RCG 11 March 1887
Death at Ivy Cottage, Chacewater, 8 March, THOMAS EDGAR, infant son of Captain JOHN SKEWES, aged 11 months.

RCG 19 August 1887
Marriage at St Andrew's Church, Redruth by Rev. John Stona, Mr Rooke Collins of Liverpool to Miss MINNIE SKEWES of Redruth.

RCG 23 September 1887
Death at Madron 10 September MARGARET ANN, wife of JAMES SKEWES, aged 58 years.

RCG 9 December 1887
Death at Six Bells Inn, St Columb, 28 November, Mr SAMUEL SKEWES, carrier of Redruth, aged 89 years.

RCG 20 December 1888
Marriage at Mawnan, 13 December, Mr J.C. Harman of Falmouth to KATE, fifth daughter of Mr JAMES SKEWES of Mawnan.

RCG 18 April 1889
Death at Ivy Cottage, Chacewater, 12 April the dearly beloved wife of JOHN SKEWES of Pachuca, Mexico, aged 34 years.

RCG 26 September 1889
Death at Daniell Street, Truro, 19 September, JANE, relinct of JOHN SKEWES, aged 90 years.

RCG 24 April 1890
Marriage at the Parish Church, Mawnan, 22 April, by Rev. E.J.Hardy, John Sadler of Derby to ELLEN (NELLIE) SKEWES of Mawnan.

RCG 1 May 1890
Death at Ford's Row, Redruth, 22 April, WILLIAM, son of the late Mr W. SKEWES, aged 17 years.

RCG 21 August 1890
Birth at Ponsanooth, 12 August, the wife of Mr WILLIAM HENRY SKEWES, of a daughter.

RCG 21 August 1890
Marriage at Kenwyn Church, Truro, 18 August by Rev.G.H. Walpole, William Thomas, eldest son of Mr W. Tonkyn, butcher, Victoria Place, to FLORENCE CECILIA, youngest daughter of Mr THOMAS SKEWES of Parkvedras Terrace, Truro.

RCG 18 June 1891
Death at Real Del Monte, Mexico, 21 May, after a short illness, Captain PETER SKEWES, formerly of Redruth and Chacewater, aged 48 years.

Northern Argus, South Australia; 4 December 1891
FATAL ACCIDENT
A fatal accident occurred on the Hill Town Road, about three miles north west of Claire, between 5 and 6 o'clock on the evening of the 30th November whereby Mrs E. A. SKEWES, an old resident of Hill Town, lost her life. She was returning home in a one-horse trap when the horse shied, and the wheel coming into contact with a stump, the trap was overturned and the deceased was thrown out. Doctor Smith of Claire visited the scene of the disaster, and pronounced life extinct, the neck being broken. She was a married woman, although not living with her husband.

RCG 4 February 1892
Marriage at Falmouth 24 January Mr William J. Pascoe of Mawnan to Miss R.A. SKEWES of Falmouth.

RCG 17 March 1892
Birth at 1 Ivy Court, Perranuthnoe, 13 March, the wife of Mr RICHARD SKEWES, of a daughter.

RCG 9 June 1892
Marriage at the Methodist Connection Chapel, Truro, 7 June by Rev. P. Baker assisted by Rev. J. S. Paige, Joseph Stephens Argall, ironmonger, Plymouth to JANIE, second daughter of Mr T. SKEWES of Parkvedras Terrace, Truro.

RCG 16 June 1892
Birth at SKEWES' HOTEL, The Lizard to Mrs Jolly, wife of the proprietor, of a daughter.

RCG 21 July 1892
Birth at Middle Rosewin Row, Truro, 16 July, the wife of WILLIAM SKEWES, painter, of a son.

RCG 29 September 1892
Death at Sethnoe, Breage, 24 September, GRACE, widow of the late Mr JAMES SKEWES, aged 83 years.

RCG 15 June 1893
Marriage at Montreal, Canada, by licence 27 May, SIDNEY HOPE, formerly of Burhos, near Helston, only son of Rev. JOSEPH H. SKEWES of Liverpool to Annie Bowden, second daughter of Mr Edward Hosking, farmer of Burhos, near Helston.

RCG 12 October 1893
Death at Mawnan, Falmouth 9 October, HESTER, the beloved eldest daughter of JAMES and FRANCES SKEWES, aged 46 years.

RCG 1 February 1894
Death in London, 26 January, THOMAS SKEWES of Parkvedras Terrace, Truro, aged 59 years.

RCG 3 May 1894
Death at Zacatecas, Mexico 2 April, Captain J.W. SKEWES of Algoma, Ontario, Canada, son of the late Captain HENRY SKEWES of Gwinear, aged 46 years.

RCG 20 June 1895
Death at Bosawsack, Constantine 18 June, FANNY, relinct of Mr JOSIAH SKEWES, aged 68 years.

RCG 19 December 1895
Birth at 218 Princess Arthur Street, Montreal, Canada, 19 November the wife of Mr S.H. SKEWES, of a daughter.

RCG 9 January 1896
Marriage at Boulder City, Colorado, USA 29 November 1895, RICHARD SKEWES, formerly of Tremar Coombe, near Liskeard, to Emma Thomas, also of Tremar.

RCG 27 February 1896
Death at Choon, Kenwyn, 27 February, ANN BUCKLAND SKEWES, aged 85 years. Funeral on Monday leaving the house at 10.00am for St Mary's Burial Ground, Truro. No cards.

RCG 5 March 1896
Death at the residence of her son-in-law Mr John Coad, Penstraze, Chacewater, 27 February, Mrs GRACE SKEWES, aged 89 years.

RCG 21 May 1896
Death at Redruth 10 May JOHN PENROSE SKEWES, aged 81 years.

RCG 18 March 1897
Birth at Real Del Monte, Mexico 4 February, the wife of Captain DICK SKEWES, of a son.

RCG 3 June 1897
Death at St Clement's Terrace, Truro, JIMMY SKEWES, aged 14 years.

RCG 26 August 1897
Birth at Marazion, 15 August the wife of Mr HENRY SKEWES, of a son.

RCG 13 January 1898
Death at Camborne, 3 January, ANN wife of Mr MATTHEW SKEWES, aged 49 years.

RCG 16 June 1898
The name GEORGE SKEWES BRAY, a solicitor from Redruth, appears in a case claiming £923 from John Mitchell Phillips. Skewes Bray won the case.

RCG 23 June 1898
Marriage at Illogan, 16 June, JOHN son of MATTHEW SKEWES, of Redruth to Miss Sarah Greenslade, daughter of Captain C. Greenslade of Portreath.

RCG 23 March 1899
Marriage at Hayle, 17 March, Mr JAMESON SKEWES, son of Mr HENRY SKEWES, builder of Camborne, to Miss Evans, daughter of Mr Evans, general builder.

RCG 30 March 1899
Death at Pachuca, Mexico, from injuries sustained by being thrown from a horse, Mr RICHARD SKEWES of Redruth, aged 28 years.

RCG 27 April 1899
Death at 13 Fairmantle Street, Truro, 25 April, JOHN BEER SKEWES, aged 68 years.

RCG 18 May 1899
Marriage at Denver, Colorado, 18 May, Edward Stephens of Silver Plume, Colorado, to MATILDA SKEWES, daughter of the late JOSEPH SKEWES of Tremar Coombe, Liskeard.

RCG 21 September 1899
Death at West End, Marazion, 15 September, FRENETTA SKEWIS, wife of Mr RICHARD SKEWIS, aged 31 years.

RCG 28 September 1899
Death at Cross Common, The Lizard, 23 September, BARRY SKEWES, son of Mr T. SKEWES, aged 12 years.

RCG 2 November 1899
Birth at East End, Goldsithney, 20 October, the wife of Mr T.H. SKEWES, of a daughter.

RCG 5 March 1903
Death at Bideford, Devon, 17 February, THOMAS LEAN SKEWES, late of Wareham, Dorset, and also formerly of Lanner, Redruth, aged 75 years.

RCG 23 July 1903
Birth at Packsaddle, Mabe, 13 July the wife of Mr H. SKEWES, of a son.

RCG 8 October 1903
Death at Carnhell, near Camborne, 4 October KATHERINE SKEWES, the wife of E. Sowell, blacksmith, Carnhell.

RCG 21 April 1904
Death at Rose Cottage, The Lizard 12 April of THOMAS HENRY SKEWES, aged 48 years.

RCG 21 September 1905
Death at the Hospital of the Compania Minera de Penpoles, Mapami Estado de Durango, Mexico, 22 August, Edith Gertrude Saunders, wife of THOMAS SKEWES SAUNDERS, aged 28 years.

RCG 18 January 1906
Marriage at Johannesburg, South Africa, 14 December, LILIAN BEATRICE SKEWES, daughter of the late Captain PETER SKEWES, of Real Del Monte, Mexico, to Arthur J. Everington of Kimberley.

RCG 16 May 1907
Death at Mawnan, Falmouth, 10 May FRANCES SKEWES, aged 82 years.

RCG 17 October 1907
DEATH OF CAPTAIN RICHARD SKEWES
Captain RICHARD SKEWES (late of Rosario Mine, Pachuca, Mexico) who has been seriously ill for some weeks at the residence of his son-in-law Mr John Coad of the Willows, Penstraze, died on Sunday morning at the age of 75 years.
Deceased, who was widely known and respected, was born at Kerley, Chacewater, and was much interested in mining matters, having spent the major part of his life in foreign mining fields. He had latterly been identified with the mining industry in Mexico where he had held some lucrative appointments, including that of manager of the Santa Gertrudis Mine for many years, and formerly under the Real del Monte Mining Company, and had a large amount of capital invested in mines there.
His wife predeceased him many years since in Mexico, and he leaves one son to mourn his loss.
The funeral took place on Tuesday afternoon at St Michael's, Baldhu. The cortège was met at the church by the vicar (Rev. Garth Whitley) and the Rev. J. Gilbert (vicar of St Paul's, Chacewater), both ministers taking part in the service in the church and at the graveside. The coffin was of polished oak. The interment was in a brick grave. There were twelve mourning coaches. The chief mourners were Mr H.J. SKEWES (son) and Mr John Coad (brother-in-law) and his sister Mariah. Deceased leaves two nieces and one nephew in Mexico, Captain J.H. SKEWES, manager of Barron Mine, Pachuca; Mrs John Rabling of Guanajuato and Mrs F.J. Pratt of Real del Monte.

Northern Echo 17 December 1907
FATAL SEQUEL: HORDEN MAN's DEATH AFTER A FIGHT. ALLEGED COMBAT ON THE SANDS AT DENE HOLME.

A man, GEORGE SKEWS, of 3 Seventh Street, Horden, died yesterday. It is alleged that he and another man quarrelled on Saturday night and that yesterday they met on the sands at Dene Holme and fought for nearly an hour and a half. Both were in an exhausted condition and in the last round fell to the ground.
On his return home Skews became seriously ill and died as stated.

Northern Echo 19 December 1907
FIGHT ON BEACH ENDS IN A HORDEN MINER's DEATH
MANSLAUGHTER — VERDICT AGAINST HIS OPPONENT

Coroner Cadle held an inquest at the Primitive Methodist Chapel, Horden Colliery, near Seaham Harbour yesterday on GEORGE SKEWS, aged 38 years, miner of Seventh Street, Horden, who died on Monday after a fight on the beach at Dene Holme on Sunday.
Supt. Thompson of the Durham County Police was present as was also John Richards, the man with whom the deceased fought. The latter was assisted into the room by two men and walked as though in a weak condition.

SARAH SKEWS, widow of the deceased, gave evidence of identification but knew nothing of the affair, excepting that her husband went out at 1.30pm on Sunday to meet a man and was brought home about 4.30pm bleeding from the face. He was put to bed, and a doctor sent for, but he died the next morning about 9.00 am.
Dr Muir of Horden described the results of the post mortem examination. There were large bruises on the jaw of the deceased, also collar-bone, arms, lips, face and ears. There was a large clot of blood between the surface of the brain and the internal lining of the skull caused by a rupture of a fairly large vein. There was a fracture about 1¾ inches long running along that part of the base of the skull just above the right ear.
Continuing witness said he was called to see the deceased on Sunday night at 8.15pm and found him unconscious. Next morning at 9.06am he died. Death was due to compression of the brain caused by the hemorrhage, and due to a fracture of the skull.

CAUSED BY A BLOW
By the Coroner: The fracture was caused by a blow on the jaw. It was most improbable that this blow could be caused by a fall to the ground. The blow could have been caused by a man's fist.
Thomas Purvis, miner of Eden Street, Horden deposed that on Sunday about 12.30pm he was told by Richards in the club at Horden that he and the deceased had quarrelled the previous night on the way back from Deaf Hill and that they were going to fight it out on the beach. Richards had had a drink, but he was not under the influence of drink.
The witness went to the beach and saw the fight begin. Richards stripped to his singlet and Skews stripped to his top shirt, but afterwards stripped bare to the waist.
There was no time arranged for the number of rounds or the duration of the encounter. A man named Johnson was referee.

The fight lasted about an hour and a half, and both men were badly punished and both fell down at the finish in an exhausted state. The men shook hands before they left the sands. Skews gave up the fight. The witness helped to pick up Richards. Skews walked away with a man on each side of him.

Thomas George Salmon was next called and admitted that he was the stakeholder. After being cautioned by the Coroner he elected to give evidence and said he was 21 years of age and a clerk. He was in the club on Sunday afternoon and saw Richards and the deceased there.

"ANYTIME YOU LIKE"

Richards said something to Skews which he could not hear and the latter replied "any time you like." Richards replied "your time is my time." Skews laid down a sovereign on the counter and Richards put down another saying to the witness "You take hold of that Tot and be on the beach at 3.00pm."

On the beach Richards asked witness to be referee, but he declined and Johnson eventually became referee. At the end of the fight a man named Walters on behalf of Skews said "we will chuck it." The witness gave Richards the two sovereigns. Both men were severely punished. There were about 60 people present. William Richards, brother of John Richards also spoke to witnessing the fight. He heard a man named Howard try to persuade Skews to stop, but he refused.

Ralph Waters deposed to trying without success to get the men not to fight. Skews seemed more eager to fight than Richards. At the ninth round Richards was down and by about 3 minutes the witness said to William Richards "The fight will be over now." However, the latter replied "No, no, no, there is no time fixed." After about 30 rounds the men fell down together.

The witness and a man named Auld picked up Skews, put his clothes on and helped him home. He was bleeding from the eye and nose, and his lips were very much swollen.

Ralph Auld spoke to the two men quarrelling while on his way back from Deaf Hill to Horden on Saturday night. On Sunday Skews told him they were going to have a fight on the beach. The witness was present at the fight and tried to dissuade the men from their purpose, but they both refused. The fight lasted an hour and a half and about 30 rounds were fought. As far as he could see it was a fair fight.

A FAIR FIGHT

Other spectators of the fight gave evidence & said as far as they could see it was a fair fight.

Robert Johnson, miner, the referee next gave evidence. He said he consented in order to see fair play, but he could not say who asked him.

The Coroner summed up and after receiving the evidence suggested to the jury that they should return a verdict of manslaughter. The jury retired but the foreman shortly returned and said they could not agree. The Coroner again addressed the jury and advised them that they would not be justified in returning any other verdict but manslaughter.

Eventually the jury returned a verdict of manslaughter and John Richards was committed for trial at the Assizes.

Northern Echo 21 December 1907
SPECIAL POLICE COURT AT CASTLE EDEN
John Richards was committed for trial at the next Assizes.

Durham County Advertiser 27 December 1907
THE FATAL FIGHT AT HORDEN: PRISONER COMMITTED FOR TRIAL
On Friday at a special sitting of the Castle Eden Police Court — before Mr William Armstrong — John Richards (34), miner, was charged with the manslaughter of GEORGE SKEWS (38), miner, also of Horden, in connexion with the fatal fight on the sea beach at Dene Holm on Sunday the 15th December.

Mr W. Watts Moses prosecuted and Mr A. Geipel defended.

The prisoner sat on a seat behind the solicitors' table. His arms were bandagd, but he looked much better than he did at the inquest held before Mr Coroner Cadle on Wednesday, when a verdict of manslaughter was recorded against Richards.

In opening the case Mr Moses said the story was a most shocking one, and he thought his Worship would have no difficulty in saying that Richards should be committed for trial.

The men undoubtedly agreed to fight and, perhaps, the deceased was just as keen as the prisoner. They fought for an hour and a half or more, until both were practically exhausted and fell on their knees absolutely worn out. They were got home. Deceased was put to bed and died the next morning from a fractured skull.

Mr Armstrong:	Who was practically responsible for the fight?
Mr Moses:	There was a referee appointed.
Mr Armstrong:	I think that is a matter which should be taken up.
Mr Moses:	It is a matter for further consideration.
Supt Thompson:	It will be taken up.
Mr Moses:	A man held the watch and called time, and there were other men present, I understand, with water and clothes, to attend to each of the contestants.

Thomas Purvis, a spectator, described the fight, and in answer to the magistrate, said that as near as he could say, the longest rest between the rounds was about two minutes.

Ralph Walters, one of the men who assisted deceased home, spoke of endeavouring both before and during the fight to get the deceased to give up, but without success.

At the ninth round prisoner was knocked out,and lay on the ground three minutes. Witness spoke to William Richards (prisoner's brother), and said "The fight will be over now."

William Richards replied "No, no, Ralph, there was no time fixed." They fought about 30 rounds, as far as he could say. When the deceased was taken home, the only complaint that he made was that he was tired. As far as he could tell there were 30 to 40 men and boys present.

By the magistrate: Deceased seemed more keen to fight to the end than the prisoner.

Arthur Deakin spoke of the quarrel between the two men on Saturday night, while coming home from a football match at Deaf Hill.

Dr Muir gave evidence of attending deceased, and also of the result of the post-mortem examination, showing that death was due to a fractured skull.

Thomas George Salmon, the stakeholder, detailed the laying down of £1 a side by the two men. It was intimated to the witness that he need not say anything to incriminate himself, after which he proceeded with the story of the fight. The combat came to an end when Ralph Waters said "We will chuck it up", meaning deceased. Witness paid the stake money to Richards.

By the magistrate: Two other men saw the money put down.

Sergeant Robinson gave evidence of arrest and the charge to which the prisoner made no reply.

Country Advertiser 28 February 1908

MANSLAUGHTER CHARGE

John Richards, 34, miner of Horden who was indicted for the manslaughter of GEORGE SKEWS, miner, also of Horden on 16 December.

William Richards, Thomas Purvis, Robert Johnson, Ralph Waters and Ralph Auld, miners and Thomas George Salmon, clerk were indicted for notoriously assembling with other persons to disturb the public peace and also with assaulting GEORGE SKEWS on 15 December. All the accused pleaded "guilty." Mr Simey prosecuting: Mr Short defending.

Mr Simey: A number of men had been to a football match and were returning home in a brake. Richards and Skews had a quarrel.

Nothing more occurred that day, but they met again the next day.

The quarrel was over a decision of the referees. On Sunday morning the quarrel was to a certain extent renewed.

Lordship:	I understand Skews to have died from a specific fracture and not from exhaustion.
Simey:	It might have been sustained in the fall.
Lordship:	I understand from the Doctor's evidence this is not so.
Simey:	The general opinion was that the fight was fair, but hard, and Richards was as severely handled as Skews. However, the police were forced to take notice and bring the case before the courts to make it known that such things were illegal.
Mr Short:	The prisoners were all respectable, hard working men and, like most pitmen, they had a strong love of sport and a contest which was fair, however severe it might be. None had been in trouble before — they regarded it as a fair fight — nothing from which a man could not recover. Both men shook hands at the end of the fight. I believe the quarrel was to do with their work, but that the fight was more in the nature of a contest, to see who was the better man. The whole incident had shocked them and had acted as a scare and deterrent to the whole district. They had already taken steps to provide for the widow and children. The colliery had agreed to stop part of their wages. The men all realised it was dangerous and illegal.

His Lordship then expressed concern that leniency would result in hero worship. Police Sergeant Robinson doubted that.

Lordship: I am pleased about the widow's consideration. I cannot help feeling that it is far more satisfactory that quarrels, which I suppose must occur as long as men are men, should be fought out fairly without weapons, and not kept as a matter for revenge; and still more satisfactory that they should not be fought out, as was the case with some foreigners, with deadly weapons.

I am deciding not to send you to prison but am directing you to enter into your own recognizances to come up for judgement when called upon. If you do not provide for the family and were found brawling you would appear and take punishment for the offence to which you have pleaded guilty. I do not know who is the more guilty — the witnesses or the participants. I am warning you all not to allow any one of you to make a triumph as men who had got the better of the law.

The prisoners then entered into their recognizances and were allowed to go.

RCG 23 January 1908

Marriage at Redruth, 11 January, Miss AMELIA SKEWES to Mr T. Harry, both of Redruth.

RCG 30 April 1908

Marriage at St Paul's, Chacewater (by special licence). By Reverend J. Gilbert, HERBERT J. SKEWES, only son of the late Captain RICHARD SKEWES and the late Mrs SKEWES of Pachuca, Mexico, to Henrietta C. Richards, youngest daughter of the late Captain J. Thompson Richards, M.I.M.E. and Mrs Richards of Salem House, Scorrier.

The Leader, Victoria, Austalia; 30 May 1908

Death: SKEWS

On 24 May 1908 at 9 Sterling Street, Kew, Melbourne, Australia, THOMAS SKEWS the beloved husband of the late CATHERINE SKEWS, late of Northcoat and Maldon, in his 70th year.

RCG 21 January 1909

Death at Carnon Crease, Perranwell, 16 January, CAROLINE, wife of BENJAMIN H.SKEWES, aged 79 years.

RCG 18 February 1909

Marriage at Baptist Chapel, Truro, 15 February, Mr JAMES SKEWES, of Carnon Crease, Perranwell, to Miss Hannah Louise Gurney of 2 Clarence Street, Penzance.

The Chronicle, Adelaide, South Australia; 27 November 1909
Death at Port Pirie, 17 November 1909, Mrs W.H. SKEWES who died at her Ellen Street residence. The deceased was an active member of various charitable institutions, and was highly esteemed. Two sons and three daughters are left. The late Mr SKEWES started business in Port Pirie as a chemist over 30 years ago.

RCG 3 February 1910
Death at The Lizard, 30 January, ELIZABETH, wife of the late JAMES HENRY SKEWES, aged 61 years.

RCG 22 June 1911
Birth at Salem House, Scorrier, 13 June, the wife of HERBERT JOHN SKEWES, of a daughter.

RCG 15 June 1911
At the Constantine Show held on 13 June, in the section for Horses, J. SKEWES from Ruan Major came first.

RCG 7 September 1911
Cricket March: Truro Second XI versus Truro Press at Tremorvah on 31 August. For the Press side W. SKEWES scored 0 and 24 in first and second innings. In the second innings he was the highest scorer of his side. However, the Press lost the match.

Salford Chronicle and Telephone 30 December 1911
CHARLES SKEWES died 27 December 1911, and was interred at Weaste Cemetery. Mr Skewes, who was 74 years of age, lived at 20 Garden Street, Salford.

RCG 15 February 1912
Death at High Street Post Office, Totnes, 4 February, MARY LANGMEAD SKEWIS, late of Newquay, aged 73 years.

RCG 27 February 1913
Death at Bissoe, 24 February, BENJAMIN H. SKEWES, aged 87 years.

RCG 24 April 1913
Marriage at St John's Church, Treslothan, 16 April, Mr WALTER SKEWES to Miss Katie Ford, both of Beacon.

RCG 14 August 1913
CORNISH BANQUET IN SOUTH AFRICA:
The eighth Annual Dinner of the Cornish Association of South Africa was held at The Carlton Hotel, Johannesburg on Friday 13 June. Over 300 enthusiasts from the old country attended. Among the guests were Mr J. SKEWES, Goldsithney and Mr J.S. SKEWES, Illogan Highway.

RCG 8 February 1917
Death at St Dominic Street, Truro, 29 January, BLANCHE, wife of WILLIAM SKEWES, aged 55 years.

RCG 15 August 1923
Death of Mr T.J. SKEWES of Newquay:
Residents of Newquay heard with great regret on Thursday evening (8th August) of the death of Mr T.J. SKEWES, after a short illness. Deceased who had carried on the business of painter and decorator for several years, was greatly respected and much sympathy is extended to the widow.
The funeral took place on Saturday afternoon and was largely attended by members of the Newquay Bowling Club, Newquay Oddfellows, and tradesmen of the town. The Rev. Hon. J. Yarde-Buller (vicar) officiated both at the church and the graveside. Brother James Vivian, P.P.G.M. read the Oddfellows' service.
The principal mourners were Mr J. SKEWES (brother), Mrs Trebilcock (sister-in-law), Mrs W. SKEWES (brother's wife), Mrs Curnoe (niece) and Mrs Rhodda (sister-in-law).

RCG 19 December 1923
Death at Lanner House, Gwennap, 14 December, Christiana Alexandria SKEWES BRAY, aged 75 years.

RCG 30 July 1924
HELSTON POLICE CASE:
RICHARD H. SKEWES of Perran Downs near Marazion did not appear to answer a summons for being drunk whilst in charge of a horse and wagon at Godolphin Road on 12 July.
Defendant, however, sent a letter in which he stated he could not appear in court on that day as it was his market day at Falmouth. He pleaded "guilty" and was very sorry that the offence had occurred. On his way back he would call at the Police Station and pay the fine.
The Mayor (Mr H. Toy) presiding over the case: "It is a very serious offence and we think the defendant ought to be here."
Inspector Lee said that the defendant had asked him to explain the reason for his absence.
The Mayor: "Was he drunk on the high road?"
Inspector Lee: "Yes."
The Mayor: "It is a very serious case."
Inspector Lee said that he told the defendant that it was a very serious offence. Although defendant was quiet when constable saw him, the police had a very serious complaint against him with regard to what happened a few miles further back. The defendant was going at such a speed that might have resulted in his being summoned for cruelty.
The Mayor said the Bench took the view that defendant should be present. He was charged with a serious offence, and the case would be adjourned until the next court for his appearance and attendance.

RCG 13 August 1924
CARTED HIM OFF: WHAT A BOTTLE OF WHISKY DID AT HELSTON
Helston Borough Magistrates sat on Saturday. The Mayor (Mr H. Toy) presided. RICHARD HENRY SKEWES, of Perran Downs, near Marazion pleaded "guilty" to being drunk whilst in charge of a horse and wagon on 12 July. P.C. Hill said he spoke to the defendant, and saw from his appearance that he was drunk. On being told that he was not in a fit state to be in charge of the animal, defendant replied that might be the case.
Inspector Lee proved three previous convictions against the defendant, two of which were for being drunk whilst in charge of a horse.
Defendant said he was not feeling very well, and as he had a lot of night work to do, he took a little bottle of whisky with him. One could not get anything to drink on the roads late at night.Before he got to Helston he took the bottle out and "put it down," and the liquor "carted him off a bit."
The Mayor: Don't you realise that it is a serious matter, especially at the present time, to be drunk whilst in charge of a horse and wagon? You have other people properly at your mercy!
Defendant said he was not accustomed to taking so much drink, and it upset him.
The Mayor: You have been before the Bench three times already and this is the fourth occasion.
Defendant: I drank it down clean. I did not have any water or anything with it.
The Mayor said the Bench wished to impress upon the defendant the seriousness of the offence, and considered that for his own safety, and for the safety of the public he should become a teetotaller. He would be fined £1.

Sydney Herald, Australia, 22 August 1927
DEATH AT URALLA
Mrs ELIZABETH SKEWES, one of the oldest residents of Uralla district has died at the age of 94 years. She was a native of Cornwall, England and with her late husband, came to the Rocky Diggings in Uralla in 1857, and had resided there ever since.
Four daughters and four sons of a family of twelve survive and there are 63 grandchildren and 95 great grandchildren and one child of the fifth generation.

Express and Echo, Exeter 24 March 1928
Death: On 22 March at the Royal Devon and Exeter Hospital GWENDOLINE (GWEN) SKEWES, beloved daughter of J. and B. SKEWES of 80 Wellington Road, St Thomas, Exeter. Funeral at Exwick Cemetery, Wednesday 28 March at 2.00pm.

RCG 26 September 1928
A member of the Truro Rangers Skittle Team was W. SKEWES.

RCG 10 October 1928
Marriage on 4 October at Helston, FRANK SKEWES, of Callestick to Annie Doris Williams of St Keverne.

RCG 18 December 1929
Death at SKEWIS, Nancegollan, Helston on 15 December, Alfred Rowe, husband of Alice Rowe, aged 70 years.

RCG 26 February 1930
Marriage on 22 February at Illogan Parish Church by Rev. Harry Oxland (Rector), ARTHUR SKEWES, of Carn Brea to Effie Winifred Peters of Pool. Mr JACK SKEWES, uncle of the bridegroom was best man. Sister of the bridegroom was HILDA SKEWES. After the wedding the couple left for Plymouth.

RCG 9 October 1930
Death: Mr. W. SKEWES of.The Lizard. The funeral took place at Landewednack Church on Sunday of Mr WILLIAM SKEWES, aged 77 years of Channel Views, The Lizard. Deceased who was a native of The Lizard spent the greater part of his life in Chile returning home a few years ago to settle in his native village. A large congregation filled the church.

RCG 5 November 1930
Marriage at St Keverne Wesleyan Church on 1 November, by Rev. F.Chenhalls Williams, MARY, third daughter of Mr and Mrs JOHN HENRY SKEWES of Golla Farm, Callestick to William Henry Eustice, of Me-Hall-Hill, St Keverne.

RCG 20 December 1933
Marriage on 16 December at St George's Methodist Church, Truro, by Rev. A. Ralph, MATTHEW JOHN SKEWS, second son of the late J. SKEWS of Redruth and Mrs SKEWS of Exton, Devon, to Kathleen Thomas, sixth daughter of the late Mr and Mrs J. Thomas of Union Street, Camborne.

Western Morning News 6 July 1934
ELIZABETH SARAH SKEWS died on 4 July at Coryton House, Ford Park Road, beloved wife of the late Lieutenant J.W.H. SKEWS, R.N., aged 76 years. Funeral, Saturday leaving the house at 10.15am. Service Mutley Methodist Church. Mourning optional.

The Times 16 May 1936
JOHN COURTIS SKEWES.
On 13 May 1936 at Newcombes, Crediton, Devon, JOHN COURTIS SKEWES. Cremation, Bristol (today Saturday) 12 noon. No flowers.

Crediton Chronicle 21 May 1936
A TOWN MOURNS: FUNERAL OF Mr J.C. SKEWES
It is with profound regret that we record the death of Mr JOHN COURTIS SKEWES, which took place at his residence on Wednesday, 13 May. His health had not been good for some time, but he continued to carry out the duties of the many public bodies with which he was connected. A week ago Mr Skewes was about, as usual, and his passing on Wednesday cast quite a gloom over the whole town. His sympathies were always with every deserving cause, and promoters of charitable causes found in him a true friend. He was always willing to allow the use of his beautiful grounds at "Newcombes" for such causes.
Amongst his many activities Mr Skewes was a valued member of the Crediton Urban District Council, of which body he had been Chairman. He was a member of Crediton Joint Cemetery Board, the Guardian's Committee, a member of the Crediton Committee for Higher Education, a Governor of Crediton Parish Church, a Governor of the High School and Queen Elizabeth Grammar School, a manager of Crediton Hayward's Schools and a member of Crediton United Charities Trustees.
Mr Skewes took an active interest in the Crediton Fat Stock Show of which he was President for several years. His whole-hearted interest in the Crediton Cricket Club and Bowling Club, Boys Club and Golf Club, in each of which he held office as President, were much appreciated. He also took an interest in the local rugby and association football clubs and the local nursing association.

His concern for the welfare of the public was shown when he was instrumental in the forming of the Crediton Housing Association to which the many houses called "Courtis Gardens" bear testimony. He will be sadly missed, and to Mrs Skewes and family the deepest sympathy is extended.
The funeral took place on Saturday when Mr Skewes was taken to Bristol for cremation.
Prior to the sermon on Sunday morning at Crediton Parish Church the following "In Memorium" from the vicar (the Rev. J.A. Durling, M.A.) took place. It was read to a large congregation:
"We are mourning the death of John Courtis Skewes, a governor of this church. He had been in failing health for a long time, but with the characteristic courage he continued to take his part in the many and varied activities to which he had devoted himself. Since he came to live in Crediton some 15 years ago, no man could have been more conscientious in the discharge of his duties and it was always a pleasure to serve on any committee which he was associated with.
His religion was simple and undemonstrative, but it went very deep. To him Christianity was essentially a practical affair; hence his keenness and energy in the cause of better housing in which matter he was an enthusiastic leader. His place in the parish and town of Crediton will be difficult to fill. Our deep sympathy is extended to Mrs Skewes in her bereavement."

Western Morning News 25 July 1936
Mr JOHN COURTIS SKEWES of Newcombes, Crediton, Devon, founder of the firm SKEWES BROTHERS, who died on 13 May, aged 72 years left estate of the gross value of £66,773, with net personality of £61,453 (Estate duty £10,474).
He left £250 and his household effects to his wife; 2500 shares in SKEWES BROTHERS to his son JOHN EDGAR SKEWES; and the residue of his property to his wife during widowhood; on her death or remarriage one fifth to his son John Edgar Skewes, absolutely, and the income from the remainder for life and the ultimate residue to his son's issue as he may appoint or failing appointment equally.
Note: Newcombes was auctioned in June, 1936. It comprised Freehold residential estate; fine Georgian Residence with Colonnade Verandah, beautifully timbered grounds, carriage drive, lodge, prolific fruit and vegetable gardens, glass houses, two modern built cottages, farmery, valuable accommodation land of 18 acres.
The property was demolished in 1975 and now the land is owned by the Devon Area Health Authority. On the original site there are now many old people's bungalows and there is a training school for the mentally handicapped, as well as a dental centre.

RCG 16 September 1936
Marriage on 12 September at Fore Street Methodist Church, Redruth, by Rev. J.A. Thompson, ADA MAY SKUES, elder daughter of Mr and Mrs F. SKUES of 16 Trefusis Terrace, Redruth to Leslie Pearce of Lanner Hill, Redruth.
The wedding took place at Fore Street Methodist Church on Saturday of Mr Leslie Pearce, son of the late Mr and Mrs John Pearce of Lanner Hill, Redruth and Miss ADA MAY SKUES of 16 Trefusis Terrace, Redruth. The Rev. J.A. Thompson officiated.
The bride wore a periwinkle blue silk marocain dress, with hat and silver shoes to match, and carried a bouquet of pink carnations and trailing fern. She was given away by her brother Mr FRED SKUES and was attended by Misses Flo and Mary Pearce (sisters of the bridegroom). Mr Sam Woodcock of Camborne was best man. A reception took place afterwards at Trefusis Terrace. Mr and Mrs Pearce will live at Carnside, Lanner Hill.

Western Morning News 26 May 1938
Death at Clifton, Bristol on 24 May, LILY SKEWES, the devoted wife of HOWARD SKEWES, of the Old Rectory, Gidleigh, Chagford, Devon.

Western Morning News 16 May 1939
Death at Westcliffe on Sea, Essex, MARY ELLEN, widow of the late JAMES SKEWES, Mannamead. Funeral at Efford Cemetery, Wednesday 3.00pm.

Falmouth Packet 1 December 1939
Death at 1 Penmere Terrace, Falmouth on 26 November of HENRY SKEWES, aged 71 years.

FORMER MABE FARMER

The funeral of Mr HENRY SKEWES of 1 Penmere Terrace took place at Falmouth Cemetery on Wednesday. Rev. N.F. Gibson officiated (Baptist Church). Deceased, who was 71 years of age, had retired from farming at Mabe. He leaves a widow and one son.

Family mourners were: the widow, Mr L.J. SKEWES, son; Messrs H.Knowles and H. Bone, cousins; and Mrs L.J. SKEWES, daughter-in-law.

Falmouth Packet 1 December 1939

SECOND VICTIM OF CAR CRASH: Mr J.K. SKEWES SUCCUMBS TO INJURIES

The car crash at Cartuther railway bridge near Liskeard on 17th November has claimed another victim with the death at the Prince of Wales' Hospital, Plymouth of JOHN KEMPTHORNE SKEWES, aged 70 years, late of Parc Vro, Mawgan-in-Meneage, and also of 10 Lancaster Gate, London.

At the inquest, which Doctor E.S. Toogood opened at Liskeard on Saturday, evidence of identification was given by Mr Gerald Beaumont Cottier of 24 Bedford Row, London, solicitor, practising at Lane and Cottier, a firm established in Plymouth from 1871 until fairly recently. Mr Cottier represented the relatives of Mr Skewes and the injured parties and the executor of Mr Skewes. The inquest was adjourned indefinitely.

Mr Skewes was a native of Cornwall. He set up a drapery business at Wimbledon, which he carried on for many years, retiring at the age of 40.

He was a prominent Freemason and Founder Member of Wimbledon Lodge. After retirement he interested himself in property dealing. He was on holiday in Cornwall prior to the outbreak of war, and decided to make his home there pending the continuation of hostilities.

He was accompanied in the car by Miss Violet Coad, hairdresser of 23 Coinagehall Street, Helston, aged 31 years, who was killed outright, and Mrs Mary Coad of Parc Vro, who is at present in the Prince of Wales' Hospital, Plymouth with serious injuries. The chauffeur, George Bye, is also in hospital and was stated on Sunday night to be a little better.

Mr Skewes' car was in collision with a large motor lorry belonging to Messrs H & G Simonds of Tamar Brewery, Plymouth.

Falmouth Packet 23 February 1940

MATRIMONY:

Wearing military uniform Private MARTIN REX SKEWS, only son of Mr and Mrs MARTIN SKEWS of 2 Lower Bell-vue, Redruth was married on Wednesday to Miss Miriam Martin, youngest daughter of Mr and Mrs Charles Martin of 43 Langton Road. The ceremony took place at Pike's Hill Church. The bride, one of the proprietresses of the Verman hairdressing salon, was given away by her father and wore a blue ensemble, with hat and shoes to tone. She also carried a bouquet of rose tulips and trailing fern.

The bride's gift to the bridegroom was a gold signet ring and that of the bridegroom to the bride an enamelled dressing set.

The reception was held at the home of the bride, after which the happy couple left for a tour of Cornwall.

Cornish Guardian 4 April 1940

LETTERS TO THE EDITOR: Mrs RESKYMER of ST TUDY

Sir, — Before her marriage Mrs Reskymer was Miss Alice Denzil, and resided at a place of that name in the parish of Mawgan in the neighbourhood of St Columb. "There is sufficient evidence", says the late Canon Taylor, "to show that the Bronze Age dwellers in our land worshipped the sun. A manuscript of the early part of the 12th century states that St Michael's Mount was distinguished and called in the language of the province Dinsol, a word which may well mean the Hill of the Sun, unless the second syllable be Sul, the name of a goddess who gave her name to Bath, Aquae Suli. A recent explanation identifies Dinsol with Denzil or Dinsol, a farm in the parish of Mawgan, a few miles from Padstow where St Cadoc, with whom the manuscript is concerned, had a chapel and well."At this place was seated the family of Denzil, of whom Thomas, in the time of the sixth Henry, had a son John, who married a Trenowth of Probus. John was the father of another John, who entered Lincoln's Inn and rose to be a serjeant-at-law, and dying in 1535 was buried in the church of St Giles in the Fields. Serjeant Denzil married a sister of John SKEWYS, and by her left two daughters Anne and Alice. Alice was married to William Reskymer and was the Mrs Reskymer mentioned above.

John Skewys (or Skuish), who now comes into the story, sprung from a wealthy landed family, settled at Skewys in the parish of Cury, and is famed for his translation of the chronicles of Matthew of Paris. Matthew, who died in 1259, gave interesting descriptions of his contemporaries and their doings, and if Skewys had done similar work for his generation, present day readers would learn how he, residing so far from the metropolis, became a lawyer, a serjeant, and a confidential servant and friend of the great Cardinal Wolsey, and presumably personally known to Henry, VIII, for he had the unusual privilege of wearing his hat in the presence of the king.

When Wolsey was Lord Chancellor, Skewys frequently acted as his Vice-Chancellor in the Court of Chancery. The last years of his life were disturbed by family disputes and litigation; he was apparently then living in London, for in his will he desired to be buried in the church of St John, Clerkenwell, next to his wife, Katherine, where a marble tomb was already prepared.

We now turn to John Reskymer, another wealthy Cornish landowner living in the western part of the country who, in 1498, married a lady more wealthy than himself, Elizabeth Holland, an illegitimate daughter of the Duke of Exeter. Elizabeth did not live long but left two young boys, John and William. John, the bereaved husband, took a second wife, Katherine Trethurffe of Trethurffe in Ladock, a family much in evidence at that time in Cornish history and one that pointed with pride to the fact that Katherine's mother, Elizabeth, was the sister of Edward Courtenay, Earl of Devon, and that consequently Katherine was a coheir of that unfortunate nobleman. On John Reskymer's death John Skewys married the widow and became guardian to the two boys, John and William

Reskymer.
As Serjeant Denzil and his wife (a sister of Skewys) had daughters and no sons Serjeant Skeyws promoted a marriage between his ward William Reskymer and his niece, Alice Denzil, promising to give them a bountiful endowment to celebrate the event. As already stated the wedding came off and then the newlywed pair found that the promises of Skewys were not fulfilled though the law courts were invoked and in the end the Reskymers obtained a verdict in their favour, and in due time the four daughters obtained possession of their parents' land.
This happened in 1570 when the youngest daughter came of age; there were four daughters, one of them never married, but that seems an insufficient reason for omitting her figure on the monument. These were the last legal descendants of the Reskymers.
William Reskymer, the father of these ladies, was at the Court of Henry VIII, as a gentleman of the chamber. At Hampton Court is a splendid portrait by Holbein of a handsome, bearded man, entitled "Reskimeer a Cornish Gent." This has usually been supposed to be John Reskymer, but, as his younger brother William lived at Court, the portrait is far more probably his.
7 March 1940.

LANJE.

RCG 7 August 1940
Marriage took place at Tuckingmill Wesleyan Methodist Church on 3rd August by the Rev.J.H. Dodrell, A.C. James Polkinghorne, younger son of Mr and Mrs R. Polkinghorne of Carnarthen Moor, Carn Brea, to Miss JOAN SKEWES, youngest daughter of Mr and Mrs A.SKEWES of Bartles Row, Tuckingmill.
The bride, who was given away by her brother, Mr A.J. SKEWES of Mullion, was attired in a white satin gown, with bridal veil, and orange blossoms, and carried a bouquet of dark red roses. The bridesmaids were Miss Noreen George and Miss Rosemary Vincent, nieces of the bride. Mr S.E. Polkinghorne, brother of the bridegroom was best man.

RCG 18 September 1940
Death at St Michael's Hospital, Hayle 15 September, HARRY OSWALD SKEWES, husband of EMILY ANN SKEWES.

DEATH OF A FORMER CAMBORNE FIREMAN
After an illness lasting several years, Mr HARRY OSWALD SKEWES of Centenary Street, Camborne, died on Sunday at St Michael's Hospital, Hayle. Before his retirement through ill-health, he worked as a plumber. He was an old member of "B" Company Volunteers, the Fire Brigade, the Loyal Bassett Lodge of Oddfellows, and bellringer at the parish church. For a long time he represented the Camborne Rugby Club on the County Selection Committee.
He is survived by an invalid widow, two daughters and a son.

RCG 23 October 1940
Death at Centenary Street, Camborne, EMILY ANN, widow of HARRY OSWALD SKEWES.

Cornish Echo, Falmouth and Penryn Times 30 January 1942
Obituary: We regret to record the death of an old and respected inhabitant in the person of Mr EDWARD SKEWES which occurred at his residence, Gold Martin, at the advanced age of 92 years. The deceased was a well-known farmer in the district.
The funeral took place on Tuesday afternoon at the Sanctuary Church when Rev.A.B. Gunstone officiated. The mourners were Messrs R. Cobbledick, E. Sadler, R. Salder, M. Liddicoat (nephews), Messrs G.S. Matthews, J.I. Kempthorne and C.K. Bishop (cousins). The tributes were inscribed as follows: In Loving Memory from his two sisters at West Close; In Loving Memory from sister Fanny and family; Captain Vyvyan; all at Trewen.

RCG 15 April 1942
Marriage on 11 April at Greensplatt Methodist Church, by Rev.E.C. Solomon, Arthur Henwood Pearce, St Columb, to VIOLET IRENE SKEWS, eldest daughter of Mr and Mrs P. SKEWS, 1 Council Houses, Ruddlemoor, St Austell.

Union Grove Sun, Wisconsin, USA 22 July 1942
PHILLIPS-SKEWES CENTENNIAL WELL ATTENDED JULY 11
Among the many English emigrants to Racine County in 1842 were the Cornish families of SAMUEL SKEWES senior and Jacob Lory, who were brothers-in-law, as their wives were the Lugg sisters.
A few years later came Thomas Phillips from the same section of England. There were four intermarriages between the Skewes and Lugg families and three between the Skewes and Phillips families. In the 1890's seventeen first cousins were the descendants of these early settlers of whom only six survive at the present time.
This year the descendants attended the Centennial Celebration of the coming of Samuel Skewes senior and Jacob Lory to this country. Fortunately Samuel Skewes senior had kept a diary from 1839 to 1869, from which a most vivid picture of the migration and settlement can be drawn. So valuable is this diary that the State Historical Society has made photostatic copies of every page of the six volumes. The original books were most carefully cherished by THOMAS H. SKEWES, youngest son of Samuel Skewes senior and at his death their protection and preservation were entrusted to Professor GEORGE J. SKEWES, his nephew of Mayville.
A perfect picnic day on Saturday, July 11, greeted the gathering this year at the Old Settlers Park, Union Grove. The oldest son of the oldest son of Samuel Skewes senior, Doctor WILLIAM G. SKEWES of Waukesha, presided, with the next oldest member of the Clan, EDWARD H. SKEWES, acting as secretary. During the business meeting, which followed an ample picnic dinner, presided over by Mrs WILLIAM M. SKEWES of Yorkville, greetings were read from absent members and friends.

The most distant came from HOWARD and JESSIE SKEWES of Los Angeles, California, whose father GEORGE SKEWES was once superintendent of Racine County Schools and later cashier in the Racine Manufacters' Bank. JAMES SKEWES, the editor, and GRACE, his wife, had sent besides their telegram, their 13 year-old son as their representative from Meridian. Greetings were sent by GEORGE and BOULDEN SKEWES of Luverne, Minnesota, and the son of GEORGE, MORTIER SKEWES, lawyer and district attorney of Luverne.

An intermission for the annual baseball game followed the business. The game was supervised by Wilfred Siewert and EDGAR SKEWES, great-great grandsons of Samuel Skewes' brother HENRY, who came to America soon after the Civil War.

Later in the afternoon nearly 80 persons gathered for the Centennial programme, which consisted of historical sketches and of music with drum majorette demonstrations under the leadership of Mr Dave McElroy. Professor GEORGE J. SKEWES of Mayville spoke from the early diaries about the original settlers in Racine County. EDWARD H. SKEWES represented the HANNIBAL SKEWES branch of the family with reminiscences of the seventeen cousins. Mrs Edith West DeMoulpied read prepared anecdotes of the West family, and concluded with a poem by the late Mrs Ellen Skewes Donald, based upon the black walnut trees planted by her grandfather Samuel Skewes senior, when past the age of 80 years.

The presiding officer, Dr W.G. SKEWES stated that the descendants of ANTHONY SKEWES and the Hay family would speak for themselves next year. Between programme items he made the Cornish country more real by frequent references to his visit at the old home in 1925.

Supper and final visiting completed a perfect day, during which interested groups of people had surrounded the exhibit tables, where were displayed genealogical charts; the large book of family pictures mounted by Mrs EDWARD H. SKEWES; and samples of handicraft and writing from various members of the Clan.

The Centennial stationery is headed with a picture of the beloved "Old Mud House" at Grovean Farm. It was a matter of regret that the Centennial exercises could not conveniently be held at Grovean, the farm near Ives' Grove, which had been in the possession of the Skewes family for a century. Many times during the day it was mentioned, together with the "Mud House" which sheltered the family from 1843 to 1874. Mention was made, too, of the groves of trees planted by Samuel Skewes senior.

Tradition has it that the name Grovean means "Little Grove." In summarising the close of a century, the Clan finds it has contributed to the new country many farmers with prosperous acres, an editor, railroad men, a dentist, a merchant, a professor and teachers, a soldier, a lawyer, a post office man, carpenters, surveyors, insurance men, nurses, librarians, book-keepers, a banker and school superintendent.

America has been a land of opportunity!

RCG 29 December 1943
Death at Grove View, Carharrack, 23 December, THOMAS WILLIAM SKEWES, ex-Sergeant Cornwall Constabulary, aged 91 years.

RCG 11 February 1948
Death on Saturday 7 February, at the residence of Mrs C.A. Maynard, at Barncoose Lane, Illogan Highway, ELIZABETH SKUES, aged 87 years.

The Times 12 August 1949
OBITUARY: G.E.M. SKUES, MASTER ANGLER
Mr G.E.M. SKUES, whose death on Tuesday at Beckenham, Kent a few days before his ninety-first birthday was by common consent the senior angler of his day.

George Edward Mackenzie Skues was the eldest son of W.M. Skues, a surgeon in the Army Medical Department, and was born on 13 August 1858. He was a scholar of Winchester, and was articled to James Powell, a solicitor, in 1879. Admitted in 1884, he became Powell's partner 11 years later, and on the latter's death in 1925 succeeded him as senior partner in the business, and so remained until his retirement from practice in 1940. But busy and successful though his practice was, he found another and at least equally absorbing interest in the life of the quiet chalk streams of Hampshire. This developed early and while still at school he stole many hours from his books, taking breathless runs to and from the river to learn the craft of which he became so consummate a master.

His predecessor, Halford, was one of the great fly-fishermen, who some 70 years ago set a new fashion of approach by perfecting the use of the floating fly as a definite technique and fly-fishermen all over the world went dry-fly crazy. For these dry-fly purists the whole aqueous insect world then lives only on the surface of the water, and those who caught large trout on the wet, sunk fly concealed the fact and were in danger of blackballing if found out! Thus, as Lord Balfour remarked in another fishing connection, the "odium theologicum"had a parallel in the "odium ichtylogicum." If the bitter feeling has to some extent died down and less jealousy subsists between the two schools, no little credit for the change is due to Mr Skues.

At some time in the nineties he developed the nymph fashion. The nymph is the life-form of most water-borne insects between the larval stage in the mud or gravel bottom and their water-borne and ephemeral existence as duns and spinners. Having discovered that the nymph was just as attractive to trout as the imago, and being an expert fly-dresser, Skues set himself to produce tiny nymphs, which were marvels of close imitation, and fished them sunk below the surface — with results that seemed wonderful to the older rule-of-thumb anglers. It was all so simple when there came a man who fished "with brains", and that discovery revolutionised trout fishing. Being the result of acute observation and logical reasoning, Skues' methods changed when conditions changed. While he "nymphed" greatly and successfully, he was also unquestionably a great master of the use of the dry-fly at the proper time, so that thanks to his writing all can fish with a new pleasure in the knowledge of what they are doing and why.

For much of his long life he contributed to numerous journals, and especially to "The Field", under various pseudonyms, and he was, of course, an old and honoured member of the Flyfishers' Club. His book "Minor Tactics of the Chalk Stream", published in 1910, and "The Way of a Trout with a Fly" (1921), are already classics, and his volumes of fugitive papers, "Sidelights, Sidelines and Reflections" (1932), are examples of his excellent style of writing, unspoilt by the usual fishing cliches, with pleasant hints of Horace and a pretty wit. His "Nymph Fishing For Chalk Stream Trout", published in 1939, is largely a re-statement of the discoveries he gave to the angling world in 1910 in order to combat the objections of the dry-fly purists and instruct those who damage the sport by indiscriminate use of the nymph downstream.

RCG 12 October 1949
Death on Saturday 8 October at 28 Albany Road, Redruth, WILLIAM JOHN SKEWES, aged 58 years.

RCG 23 August 1950
MAWGAN POSTMAN's DEATH IN HOSPITAL
A well-known resident of Mawgan-in-Meneage Mr HARRY STANLEY SKEWES, who has been a postman for nearly sixteen years, has died at Helston and District Cottage Hospital, aged 57 years. Son of JOHN WESLEY SKEWES, of Roseville, Mawgan he leaves one son and a father in his 90th year.

West Briton 24 January 1951
Death at Helston Cottage Hospital, after a car accident, BEATRICE MARY, beloved wife of W.H. SKEWES, Higher Carnbone Farm, Wendron, aged 48 years. She was daughter of Ellen and the late David Reynolds and sister of Hilda, Edward and Charles. Funeral (today) leaving the house at 2.15pm for Wendron Church.

WENDRON FARMER's WIFE DIED AFTER CAR ACCIDENT
Giving evidence at the inquest at Helston on Wednesday about a motoring accident in which his wife, Mrs BEATRICE MARY SKEWES, aged 48 years, was fatally injured, Mr WILLIAM HARRY SKEWES, farmer of Higher Carnbone Laity, Wendron, said "All of a sudden I felt the car shudder and it dived straight across the road."
The accident happened on Sunday evening, 21st January, near Sithney School, between Helston and Camborne. The car which Mr Skewes was driving, with his wife and daughter as passengers got out of control, and ran into a hedge.
Mrs Skewes died while an operation was being performed at Helston Cottage Hospital.
DENSE FOG
Mr Skewes told the Coroner that as there was a dense fog he decided to drive by way of Helston instead of Four Lanes. The fog lifted a little after he had passed through Helston.
His car was in perfect mechanical condition and he had been driving cars since 1918. The near-side front headlamp was burning well, and the other headlamp was dipped.
The car suddenly shuddered and dived across the road, his speed then being 25 to 30mph. He put on the brakes at once and when the car struck the hedge its speed could not have been 10mph.
Mr Skewes said he did not think either his wife or daughter were injured, but when they got out of their car witness saw blood running from the wife's forehead, while his daughter had cut her lip.
Witness and his family called at the home of Mr and Mrs E.V. Jenkin, where Mrs Jenkin rendered assistance to his wife and daughter. Doctor Patterson of Helston, who was called, advised his wife's removal to Helston Cottage Hospital where, she said, it would be necessary to insert a stitch in her forehead. At the hospital, however, his wife had a relapse.
Doctor J.P. Mitchell said that when she was admitted to hospital on Sunday evening Mrs Skewes, who was semi-conscious, had a wound on her forehead, and inside the skull. He and a specialist from Truro performed a decompression operation to relieve pressure on the brain. That was the only hope there was of saving her life, and even that was a fifty to one chance, which did not come off.
Mrs Skewes did not recover consciousness before she died.
P.C. Trewella said the road had a good surface.
Answering Mr W.F.B. Nott (Mr Skewes' solicitor), Mr George Johns, a mechanic of Saltash Motors, Helston who examined the car said he could not say where there was any defect in the mechanism of the car before the accident.
The Jury returned a verdict of "Accidental Death" and expressed their sympathy with Mr Skewes, whom they exonerated from all blame for the accident.

WB 18 October 1951
Golden Wedding: Gribble-SKEWES. On October 23rd 1901 at Wesley Church, Camborne by Rev. W. Spink, Tobias to CATHERINE ANN. Present address "Estrella", Chacewater, Truro.

Bournemouth Echo 17 May 1951
On 15 May at Elm House, Wareham, Dorset, ALBERT EDWARD SKEWES passed peacefully away, aged 89 years. Funeral: Lady St Mary's, Wareham, on Friday.

WB 19 August 1952
The death took place at Helston and District Cottage Hospital of Mr EDWARD SKEWES, aged 86 years, of Rinsey Lane, Ashton. Mr Skewes lived for many years at Bonython House and Nantithet, both in Cury Parish, but the past five years has resided in the parish of Breage. About six weeks ago he fell and was removed to hospital.
The funeral took place on Wednesday at Cury Methodist Church, where he attended for many years. As a tribute, the rostrum was draped in black and the organist Mr J.C. Boaden played selected hymns and music. The Rev. J. Stocks (Porthleven) who officiated, paid tribute to a "grand and good man" and a regular member of Ashton Methodist Church.

The mourners were W.H. SKEWES (Redruth), C. Tresize (Breage), M. and D. Moyle (Gweek), G. Moyle (Helston), J.H. Moyle (Carharrack), J. Allen (Carharrack), nephews. And Mesdames A. Blatchford, J. Allen, R. Thomas and Miss D. Tresize (nieces).

WB 16 April 1953

A DEAF MUTE: MAGISTRATES AT TRURO SEND HIM FOR TRIAL

ERNEST SKUES, a deaf mute of 16 Trefusis Terrace, Redruth was sent for trial at Penzance Sessions, on Saturday, when at Truro he was charged with breaking and entering the dwelling house of Harold Benjamin Pearce, tailor and outfitter of 8 Quay Street, Truro on 14 March, and stealing a shirt valued at £2 4 0d.

Through an interpreter Skues pleaded "guilty". He was remanded in custody and granted a legal aid certificate.

Supt. H.R.J. Bennetts said that Mr Pearce retired to bed just before midnight on Friday, 13 March, after securing the premises. The following morning at about 8.15 he went into the kitchen and found the window unlatched. He then went into the shop at the front of the premises and found a shirt collar lying on the floor. Going to a box which he knew contained the collar he found that a shirt and one collar was missing. The police were informed and enquiries were made by Sgt Boscumbe and P.C. Sandy. Outside the kitchen window was found a trowel which bore marks suggesting it had been placed between the sashes of the window.

Supt. Bennetts said that after some days it was learned that the accused was in Truro on the morning of the 14th March. On Sunday 29th March Skues was seen at Redruth Police Station and was brought back to Truro. Mentioning that the accused was both deaf and dumb but that he could read and write, Supt Bennetts said that various questions were written down and Skues replied to them in writing. In his answers Skues admitted stealing the shirt after gaining admittance to the premises by pushing the catch of the kitchen window with a trowel. He said he sold the shirt in Plymouth.

Saying that the shirt had not been recovered despite enquiries made in Plymouth, and from the dealer mentioned, Supt Bennetts stressed that there was no corroboration. The case rested on the evidence of Mr Pearce and the police and the admission made by the accused.

Sgt W.J. Buscombe said he arrested Skues at Redruth on 29 March. Next day he interviewed him at Truro Police Station. After he had cautioned the accused he wrote certain questions and Skues wrote down the answers, signing the answers as being true. His answers comprised an admission that he entered Mr Pearce's premises by opening the window fastener with a trowel at about 7.30am on 14 March and that later he sold the shirt in Plymouth.

WB 23 April 1953

At the funeral of a Methodist lay preacher Mr W.J.T. Stone, representing Loscombe Methodist Church was T. SKEWES.

WB 16 July 1953

A photograph of Mr W.J. SKEWES of Perranuthnoe who was the first Cornishman ever to attain international honours in clay pigeon shooting. He shot for England in the International Match at Stirling (Scotland). Mr Skewes scored 92 "kills" out 100.

WB 1 April 1954

SUDDEN DEATH: TOOLMAKER EMPLOYED AT HOLMAN WORKS

Mr JAMES HENRY OSWALD SKEWES, aged 59 years of Trecarne, Atlantic Terrace, Camborne, died suddenly on Saturday a few hours after finishing his usual day's work. Eldest son of the late Mr and Mrs H.O. SKEWES of Centenary Street, Camborne, Mr Skewes was a toolmaker with Holman Brothers, Number 3 Works having been employed by the firm for over 30 years.

In the First World War he served in the Royal Navy as an engineer artificer, and later he was an officer in the Merchant Navy. Before returning to Camborne Mr Skewes was employed by Parnell Aircraft Company in Bristol and the Westland Aircraft Company at Yeovil.

He was a member of the Camborne British Legion and was associated with the Centenary Methodist Church. His father had been a well-known Rugby player and his only brother GEORGE SKEWES takes the leading comedy roles in Redruth Amateur Operatic Society's productions. Mr Skewes leaves a widow, a son, Mr J.P.O. SKEWES, and is also survived by two sisters, Mesdames W. Cockram (Sandford) and R. Rogers (Camborne).

WB 24 June 1954

Wedding: SKEWES-Curtis

The wedding took place on Saturday at St Andrew's Church, Redruth by Rev. G.M. Russell officiating of Miss Natalia Eve Curtis, youngest daughter of the late Mr J. and Mrs E.R. Curtis of 5 Falmouth Road, Redruth and Mr RONALD SKEWES, second son of Mr and Mrs SKEWES of Trewoon, Mullion. Mr B. SKEWES (brother) was best man. Given away by her mother, the bride was attired in a full length gown of white silk crepe with an embroidered net bridal veil and a head dress of orange blossom. She carried red carnations. She was attended by the Misses Jill and Marie Watson and Vivienne Bowles (her nieces) and CAROL SKEWES (niece of the bridegroom).

Mr A. Richard (brother-in-law of the bride), Mr M. SKEWES (brother of the bridegroom) were ushers. After the reception at the Ambulance Hall, Redruth, the couple left for Torquay for their honeymoon. Among the many presents were gifts from the management and staffs of Jaquemands Ltd., Portreath and Messrs Bray and Sons, Helston, employers of the bride and bridegroom.

WB 21 October 1954

L. SKEWES was a mourner at the funeral of William Stanley Johns, aged 54 years, well-known farmer who lived at Carpisus Farm, Mabe.

WB 23 December 1954
A photograph of GEORGE SKEWES in Redruth Amateur Dramatic Society's Christmas pantomime "Red Riding Hood." He played Squire Graball. The following week the paper reported of Mr Skewes:
"The not so evil squire is played by GEORGE SKEWES, and he is one of the great successes of the show. As long as Redruth is going to put on pantomimes, the audience will want to see Mr Skewes for he is the type of comedian who cannot fail in this sort of thing, and he plays his part this year with never ebbing energy."

WB 13 October 1955
REDRUTH PILLION FATALLY INJURED
The pillion passenger of a motorcycle which collided with a stationary van at Mount Pleasant, Roche, on Monday evening was fatally injured. Mr ERNEST SKUES of 16 Trefusis Terrace, Redruth the pillion passenger died in the Royal Cornwall Infirmary in the early hours of the following morning. Mr Wilfred Ellis of Mount Pleasant Farm, Roche, who was standing near his stationary van when the collision occurred was taken to hospital with a fractured leg and other injuries. The driver of the motorcycle, Mr Raymond Pryor of Boscadjack Green, Sithney received slight injuries.

WB 20 October 1955
Deaths: Mr ERNEST SKUES
The funeral of Mr ERNEST SKUES, aged 32 of 90 Tresaddern Road, Redruth took place in St Day Cemetery, Redruth on Friday. Mr Skues who was deaf and dumb died in the Royal Cornwall Infirmary from injuries received in a road accident whilst he was a pillion passenger on a motorcycle ridden by Mr R. Pryor of Boscadjack Green, Sithney. The machine became involved at Mount Pleasant, Roche in a collision with a stationary van. For some time Mr Skues had been working in Plymouth. He was a member of an old Redruth family, being the son of the late Mr and Mrs Skues, formerly of Trefusis Road, Redruth.
The funeral service was conducted in the cemetery chapel by the Rev. S. Luke. Mourners and friends included Messrs J.F. and L. SKUES (brothers), J. Tregonning (uncle), J. Trevaskis (uncle), L. Pearce (brother-in-law) and J. Waters (brother-in-law).

WB 23 February 1956
Wedding: SKEWES-Laity
The wedding took place on 15 February at Gulval Church by Canon C.H. Buckley, Archie, son of Mrs A. and the late Z. Laity, Rosudgeon, to ELSIE, only daughter of Mr and Mrs R.H. SKEWES of Bolenna, Fore Street, Marazion.

WB 1 March 1956
Death: HANNAH LOUISA SKEWES
The death occurred on 25 February at Oak Cottage, Downley, High Wycombe of HANNAH LOUISA, aged 75 years, beloved wife of JAMES SKEWES formerly of Cornwall. "For ever with the Lord."
The death occurred on 25 February at Oak Cottage, Downley, High Wycombe of HANNAH SKEWES, dear mother of CAROLINE Lappin, Gloucester Road, Reading, formerly of Devoran.

WB 26 April 1956
WELL KNOWN FARMER: FUNERAL OF Mr W.H. SKEWES
The funeral took place in Redruth Parish Church on Monday of Mr WILLIAM HENRY SKEWES, aged 61 years of Fernside, Carn Lane, Carnkie, Redruth who died in St Michael's Hospital, Hayle. A native of Condurrow, Camborne, Mr Skewes had farmed at Brea, Kehelland and Mullion before moving to Carnkie.
For some years he was a prominent figure at Cornish shows as a successful exhibitor of Jersey cattle and he was also known for his entries at horticultural exhibitions. He is survived by his widow and daughters.
The funeral service was conducted by Rev. T.C. Sharp (assistant curate). Mourners included the widow, Mrs R. Williams and Miss P. SKEWES (daughters), Messrs R. Williams and J. Bray (sons-in-law), G. Mayne and E.W. Whitford (brother-in-law) and C.S. Reynolds (stepson). Floral tributes included those from friends at Carn Lane, South Carn Brea and friends and neighbours in Carnkie village.

WB 27 December 1956
REDRUTH AMATEUR DRAMATIC SOCIETY PRESENT "CINDERELLA."
A long write up mentions GEORGE SKEWES as follows:
"Humour is as natural as breath itself to George Skewes and in this show he leads comedy which is superbly handled by a sextet."

WB 14 March 1957
Silver Wedding: Carter-SKEWES
At Illogan Parish Church on 19 March 1932 (by Rev. H. Oxland), Albert to HILDA. Present address: Penhallack, Carn Brea, Redruth.

WB 11 April 1957
Births: SKEWES
At Redruth Hospital on 9 April to JOYCE (née Hawken) and GEORGE, God's gift of a son — JONATHAN ROSS SKEWES, a brother for GEOFFREY.

Weston Telegraph 6 June 1957
Deaths: SKEWIS
On 31 May suddenly LAURA, dearly beloved wife of Mr SAMUEL SKEWIS, mother of MILDRED and SAM. At rest.

DAUGHTER FLEW HOME FROM CYPRUS: DEATH OF Mrs LAURA SKEWIS
Only the day before she would have celebrated her 44th wedding anniversary Mrs LAURA SKEWIS, a well-known Milford Haven lady, passed away on Friday in her 68th year. That very day Mrs Skewis had been visiting in Milford Haven and upon her return home she was suddenly stricken and never recovered. She died at Withey Bush Hospital, Milford Haven.
Mrs Skewis whose home was at 2 Hayston Avenue, Hakin, was the mother of two children, Mr SAMUEL L. SKEWIS, who now lives at Tillingdon, Kent and Mrs M. Morrow whose husband is serving in the forces in Cyprus. Mrs Morrow flew home from that island as soon as she heard the sad news.
Mrs Skewis was born in Roberts Street and married in 1913 and has spent the whole of her life in the town. She had very few outside interests, but devoted her life to her husband and the bringing up of her children. They were a happy couple, Mr and Mrs Skewis, and many sympathise deeply with her husband in his irreparable loss. A younger sister, Mrs A. Evans now lives at Cardiff.
A large crowd of sympathisers attended the service of which the principal mourners were SAMUEL SKEWIS (husband), MILDRED Morrow (daughter), SAMUEL SKEWIS (son) and Mr and Mrs Frank Evans (sister and brother-in-law).

Altrincham & Bowdon Guardian and Sale & Stretford Guardian 14 June 1957
START CAUTIOUSLY YOUNG EDITORS TOLD
A warning against being over ambitious was given by KEITH SKUES of Timperley when he addressed members of Stretford Children's Theatre on editing a youth magazine. Keith is the editor of "Youth Fellowship Times."
"It is far better to commence publication with a one-page monthly issue and slowly increase in both size and circulation rather than present a six-page edition and slowly deteriorate", he said. The Children's Theatre hope to start their own newsletter in the near future.

WB 2 January 1958
Marriage: Bone-SKEWES
The marriage of Mr Charles Williams Bone to Miss JILLIAN ANN SKEWES only daughter of Mr J.H. SKEWES and the late Mrs D. SKEWES of Woodlands, Mithian, St Agnes took place quietly at St Agnes Methodist Church recently. The service was conducted by Rev. J.A.D. Ridholls. Given away by her father the bride wore a blue coat and white hat. Mr H. Lobb was best man.
The reception was held at 1 Head Lane, Goonbell, St Agnes. The bride has been a mother's help to Mrs Godfrey of Mithian. Mr and Mrs Bone will live at 1 Head Lane, Goonbell.

Weston Telegraph 13 March 1958
Death: SKEWIS
It is with deep regret that we record the death on Saturday of Mr Samuel SKEWIS of Red Braes, Hayston Avenue, Hakin. Aged 71 years, Mr Skewis had been ill for seven weeks, but his condition had deteriorated rapidly during the last week.
A native of Felixstowe, Mr Skewis had resided in Milford Haven for 50 years. He was exceptionally well-known in the town and on the dock, where he was employed by Messrs J.R. Redding for many years. Mr Skewis was also a popular member of the Waterloo Club, where his quiet humour and pleasant manner will be very much missed. Mr Skewis' wife passed away eight months ago and the loss had had an irreparable effect on him. Throughout his illness he had been devotedly nursed by his only daughter Mrs M. Morrow of Southampton. He passed away at his home.
He also leaves one son Mr SAMUEL SKEWES of Tillingdon, Kent, a sister Mrs F. Shrives of Pill, and one brother Mr ARTHUR SKEWIS now in Belgium, to whom deepest sympathy is extended at their sad loss.

Weston Telegraph 20 March 1958
Acknowledgements: SKEWIS
The son and daughter and family of the late Mr S. SKEWIS, 2 Hayston Avenue, Hakin wish to express grateful thanks to all those who sent messages of sympathy and floral tributes in their bereavement.

WB 1 May 1958
Death: Mrs M. SKEWES
The death occurred on Thursday in Barncoose Hospital, Redruth of Mrs MATILDA SKEWES, aged 78 years of 99 Pendarves Street, Tuckingmill, the wife of Mr A.J. SKEWES. Born at Illogan Highway, Mrs Skewes had lived at Tuckingmill most of her life. She was an old member of Tuckingmill Wesley Church and of its Women's Bright Hour. Deceased is survived by two sons and five daughters.
The funeral took place in Camborne Parish Church on Saturday (Rev. A.J. Vincent, curate of Camborne, and grandson of Mrs Skewes officiated). Mourners included Messrs A.J. SKEWES (also representing the widower), E.M. SKEWES, sons; Mrs E. Johnson (niece), Mesdames J. Lawry, A.J. Harvey, D. Vincent, J.J. Tredinnick and J.E. Polkinghorne (daughters); Messrs E. Harvey, B.D. Vincent, D.J. Vincent, R. Webster and W. Kemp (grandsons); Mesdames R. Webster and W. Kemp (granddaughters), Messrs J. Lawry, J. Harvey, D. Vincent, J. Tredinnick and J. Polkinghorne (sons-in-law), Mrs A.J. SKEWES (daughter-in-law), Mr and Mrs Colliver and Mrs E. Dunstan nephew and niece.

WB 16 October 1958
28 YEARS VICAR OF CROWAN — FUNERAL OF A WELL LOVED PRIEST
The death in a Redruth nursing home after a long period of ill health, of the Rev. HERBERT JOHN SKEWES, aged 73 years, of Gilmore, Crowan Churchtown, has removed a greatly-esteemed clergyman, the memory of whose faithful and devoted work in the parish of Crowan will long remain.

Born at Chacewater, Mr Skewes spent his boyhood and youth in Mexico, where his father was a mining engineer. At the age of 35 he was accepted as a candidate for Holy Orders and he trained at St Augustine's College. Mr Skewes was ordained deacon in 1921 and priest in 1922 in Diocese of Truro. His first curacy was at St Day from 1921 to 1923 and the next three years he spent as curate at Egloshayle, Wadebridge. In 1926 Mr Skewes became vicar of Crowan in succession to Canon A. Adams who had died as a result of a motorcycling accident.

Although affected by ill-health during the latter years, Mr Skewes retained the living until 1954, when he retired and settled a short distance from the church he loved and to which he had administered so faithfully for 28 years. During his incumbency Mr Skewes was responsible for the carrying out of a number of notable additions and improvements to the church. Through the generosity of Mr J. Carah Roberts and with funds for the second provided by a trust, two bells were added to the tower, increasing the number to eight.

Electric light was installed in the church with funds provided by the Misses Trevenen of HIGHER SKEWES. Mr Skewes was responsible for the raising of a large sum of money for the renovation and overhaul of the pipe organ, which was completed at about the same time as his retirement.

Although a staunch churchman and a faithful and devoted parish priest, Mr Skewes maintained friendly relations with his Methodist parishioners. From time to time leading Methodists took part in a special service at the Parish Church and Mr Skewes had visited Methodist churches in the area.

In his notes in Kerrier Deanery's monthly magazine he recorded happenings to, and the activities of, parishioners irrespective of religious denomination, thus showing the scope and range of his pastoral work and his great love for and interest in all the people of his wide and scattered parish of some 2000 residents.

Keenly interested in educational advancement, Mr Skewes was for many years a manager of Crowan, Breage and Germoe group of provided schools, and for a long time he was Chairman of the group. He was also Chairman of Crowan Nursing Association.

In his younger days he was an active member of the old Praze Fair Show Committee. During the last war he acted as chaplain to troops stationed at Clowance.

Mrs Skewes died in 1942 and Mr Skewes is survived by a daughter, Miss E.M. SKEWES, who resided with him, and who for many years has been on the civilian clerical staff of Cornwall Constabulary, doing duty at Redruth Police Station.

The coffin was on Sunday removed to Crowan Parish Church, where it was received by the vicar (Rev. J.E. Beckerlegge) who conducted a short service. Peals were rung.

Peals were again rung at the Parish Church yesterday before the funeral service, which was conducted by the vicar, assisted by Rev. H.H. Dixon, vicar of Manaccan with St Anthony, and rural dean of Kerrier. Psalms 23 and 130 were chanted and the choir also led the singing of hymns.

In his address Mr Beckerlegge paid tribute to the life and character of Mr Skewes who, he said, had rightly been described as a good man and a faithful and well-loved parish priest. They thanked God for his life, example and work in the parish.

During that period improvements and additions were made to the church, but far more important was the ministry Mr Skewes fulfilled among his parishioners. After retirement he retained the greatest interest in the parish. They would miss the presence of a good, kind-hearted friend.

Mourners were Miss E.M. SKEWES (daughter), Mr A.D. Richards (nephew), Mr and Mrs W.J. Phillips (brother-in-law) and (sister-in-law), Mr F.E. Hancock and Miss F. Ward (cousins).

(The paper then listed another 100 distinguished mourners.)

WB 26 February 1959
Death: ELIZA JANE SKEWES
The death occurred on Wednesday, 25 February, at 10 Sparnon Hill, Redruth of ELIZA JANE, aged 77, the beloved wife of the late Mr J. SKEWES and dearest mother of DORIS.
Funeral on Saturday leaving her home at Pencoys, Four Lanes for service in Pencoys Church at 4.00pm.

WB 5 March 1959
Death: Mrs E.J. SKEWES
Pencoys Church was almost filled on Saturday for the funeral of Mrs ELIZA JANE SKEWES, aged 77 years, of Pencoys, Four Lanes, who died at the home of her grandson Mr W.R. Peters at 10 Sparnon Hill, Redruth. Mrs Skewes was one of the oldest members of Forest Methodist Church having been associated with the society for about 30 years. Widow of Mr J. SKEWES, a miner who died some 19 years ago, Mrs Skewes is survived by her daughter Mrs D. Peters. The vicar, Rev. J.A. Griffiths officiated.
Mourners included Mrs D. Peters (daughter), Messrs T.C. Bartle (also representing brothers in the USA), J.H. Bartle, (Mrs J.H. Bartle, sister-in-law) and C. Bartle, brothers; Mr and Mrs S.J. Hocking (brother-in-law and sister); Mesdames E. Huthnance, A. Hocking and M. Miles (sisters), Mr A. SKEWES (nephew) and many more nephews and nieces.

WB 30 April 1959
DEATH OF NEW VICAR's GRANDFATHER
The death of Mr ALFRED JOHN SKEWES, aged 81 years, formerly of 99 Pendarves Street, Tuckingmill, occurred on Saturday at Kenwyn Vicarage, the residence of his grandson, Rev. J. Vincent, the newly instituted vicar of Kenwyn. It occurred only five days after moving into his new home. A native of Troon, Mr Skewes had been a moulder retiring in 1947. For about 30 years he lived in Detroit, USA and when he retired he returned home to Camborne.
His wife Mrs M. SKEWES died exactly a year ago. He leaves two sons Mr A.J. and E.M. SKEWES and five daughters Mesdames J. Lawry, D. Vincent, J. Harvey, J. Tredinnick and E. Polkinghorne as well as nine grandchildren and five great grandchildren.
The Rev. J. Vincent conducted the funeral service at Camborne Parish Church on Tuesday.

Evening Chronicle 4 September 1959

That young man with a rather unusual surname, and the itch for writing, Mr KEITH SKUES of Buckingham Grove, Timperley, has just completed a book.

He wanted to be a journalist when he left school, but couldn't get a newspaper job and went into an insurance broker's office. As an outlet for his writing energy he took over the journal "Youth Fellowship Times", worked it up with considerable success and then had to go into the Royal Air Force.

But he kept on writing, and having been curious about his family name, has returned his researches about it into a book — "The Family Tree." He is now with the RAF in Jever, Germany, studying radar and electronics, and hopes to get his pilot's licence in about six months.

Keith's father Mr RICHARD SKUES was a well-known cricketer in his day and played under Sir Julian Cahn and Sir Edwin Stockton. He is also related to the late G.E.M. SKUES, the well-known writer and broadcaster on fishing.

Evening News, Manchester 4 September 1959

WHAT's IN A NAME

When he was at school, masters and pupils alike used to ask KEITH SKUES of Buckingham Grove, Timperley, the origin of his unusual name. Eventually Keith himself was goaded into doing some research. Now 21, and nearing the end of his National Service with the RAF in Germany, he tells me he has completed a thick volume of typescript which traces his ancestors back to the 15th century and the Cornish village of Skewis.

His research took him to Manchester's Central Library, the British Museum and Cornwall, and he gained useful information from relatives in Australia.

Manchester's librarians were so interested that they had an impressive red and gold cover made for the book.

One of the earliest ancestors was John Skewys, born in 1467, a lawyer who became legal adviser to Cardinal Wolsey. Another was G.E.M. Skues, who lived in Kent and wrote books on fishing, broadcast regularly during the last war and died in 1949, aged 91 years.

South Western Times, Western Australia, 26 November 1959

FORMER BUNBURY MAYOR DIES

The former Mayor of Bunbury, Mr W.W.J. SKEWES died in Narrogin last week. Mr Skewes who served in the office of Mayor of the Municipality during 1925/1926 will be remembered as one of the district's most energetic and civic minded leaders. He conducted a music business in Victoria Street, and was always closely associated with the town's every progressive move.

Said former Mayor Fred Withers: "I was associated with the late Mr Skewes on numerous occasions including the work that was done on the Five-Mile Brook. At that time Mr Skewes, as Mayor, joined the voluntary workers who went out each weekend with horses and drays to put the cut through from South Bunbury. He was known as one of the town's most stalwart workers and never hesitated to peel off his coat and help in any voluntary work."

When he went to live in Narrogin, Mr Skewes took an active interest in civic affairs and held office of Mayor of that district. He died in Narrogin Hospital on the 19th November and was buried in the Baptist section of the Narrogin cemetery.

Narrogin Observer, Western Australia, 3 December 1959

FORMER MAYOR DIES: WILLIAM WILFRED JOHN SKEWES

During his lifetime, the late Wilfred Skewes resided in many towns in this state, and in all of these he was regarded as a good citizen, which indeed is a proud memory for anyone to leave behind. His death occurred at Narrogin Hospital on 19th November, aged 76 years. He was born at Yorke Peninsula, South Australia and came to West Australia at the turn of the century, when his father managed a store in Narrogin which stood on the site of what is now known as the A.M.P. Buildings. Wilf Skewes' first love was music and when he reached maturity he turned to it to earn a living, setting up a music shop in Bunbury, having married Annie Borgas of Narrogin in 1908. He was a man of keen intellect and always interested in public affairs. As a result he became a member of the Bunbury Municipal Council and eventually aspired to become its first citizen as Mayor.

He later continued his interest in civic affairs as a councillor at Subiaco. He spent periods of time in Perth and Albany before eventually settling in Narrogin, where he married Dorothy Small in 1944, following the death of his first wife in 1941.

The late Mr Skewes was always a staunch adherent of the Baptist faith, which church claimed a good deal of his energy and time. But he devoted himself to other organisations for the benefit of the community in particular the now defunct Toc H, and the first Native Welfare Committee to be formed in this state, of which he was President. Wilfred Skewes was Secretary of the Baptist Men's Association.

He was buried in the Baptist portion of the Narrogin cemetery on 21 November following a service in the Baptist church conducted by Mr Jeffries.

WB 9 June 1960

Death: Mrs L.J. SKEWES

The funeral took place at Mabe Parish Church on Saturday of Mrs OLIVE MAY SKEWES, aged 57 years, wife of Mr L.J. SKEWES. She died at her home Trenowerth Vean Farm, Mabe.

A native of Penryn, Mrs Skewes was a Superintendent of Trenowerth Methodist Sunday School and up to 1959 she was secretary of Mabe Women's Institute. Funeral service was conducted by Rev. J.E. Roberts. Mourners included widower, Mrs W. Martin (sister), Messrs W.H.A. and C. Symons (brothers), Mesdames K. Symons and J. Symons (nieces), Mesdames W.H. and C. Symons (sisters-in-law), Mr W. Martha (brother-in-law).

Among the floral tributes were those from Mabe Women's Institute and Trenowerth Methodist Church.

WB 16 February 1961

P. SKEWES was a mourner at Pencoys Church, Four Lanes for the funeral of Edwin John Brown, aged 88 years, on 11 February.

Evening Chronicle, 4 March 1961
HE'S 21 TODAY
Not many young men will be spending their 21st birthday by producing a radio show, but one who will do so is
KEITH SKUES, of Buckingham Grove, Timperley.
Always he has wanted to be a journalist — and still wants to — but that ambition is so far unfulfilled, although he
has kept on writing, and ran the "Youth Fellowship Times."
Now he is with the RAF in Germany, and recently secured a post with the British Forces Network. Already this
bright young man is finding his feet, and is regularly producing programmes for the troops.
And at 21, that's not bad going!

ALTRINCHAM & BOWDON GUARDIAN 4 March 1961
Founder and former editor of "Youth Fellowship Times", KEITH SKUES of 21 Buckingham Grove, Timperley,
did not let grass grow under his feet during two years National Service with the RAF.
Instead of relaxing into uniformed anonymity, he became interested in broadcasting and worked with the WVS
compering shows in northern Germany.
Keith, who celebrates his 21st birthday today, was invited last year to an audition at the British Forces Network
Headquarters in Cologne. He was accepted, and a month ago he began work with the network.
Already he is working on presentation, and produces several shows a week.
Friends who were hoping to see him when he returned home on demobilisation leave will have to postpone the
pleasure; he cancelled the trip to start straight away in his new job.

Evening Chronicle 4 July 1961
Bound for Nairobi, Kenya is a young man who has been making a name for himself with the British Forces
Network in Germany.
He is 22-year-old KEITH SKUES of Buckingham Grove, Timperley, a former Altrincham Grammar School boy
who for the past 18 months has been spinning discs, announcing, and reading the news to troops in Europe.
Keith has been accepted for a similar appointment lasting three years in East Africa.
After leaving school Keith took to producing plays and sketches for the Youth Fellowship at St Alban's Church,
Broadheath. While in the RAF for two years National Serivce he studied radio and telecommunications.
He became interested in radio as a career and worked with the WVS compering shows in northern Germany. Then
he went to BFN. The work is often hard — sometimes from 6.30am to 11.30am followed by an evening stint from
6.30pm until 11.30pm, but Keith enjoys it immensely.
As for Kenya ..... "Maybe I can interest the Mau Mau into having their top ten", he says. He has just donated a
book "The Family Tree" to Manchester Reference Library — bound in blue and gold — which took him a
number of years to compile.

Sunday Nation, Nairobi, Kenya 28 October 1962
KILIMANJARO CONQUERORS
The first Forces team to reach the top of Kilimanjaro without "losing" one of its members on the way up,
triumphantly hoisted a flag on the summit of Kibo at 06.02 hours on the morning of 23 October, having
climbed all through the night.
The 10-man RAF team consisted of eight RAF Eastleigh climbers led by Senior Technician Peter Smith and
two from Forces Broadcasting, Nairobi: Keith Skues and Paul Keeble.
The FBS men carried with them a portable tape-recorder, and from the recordings made in camp and
during the climb will be producing a feature programme for broadcast from FBS.
"It is a wonderful thing to look back on", said Keith Skues yesterday. "But I will never do it again." The party
estimated it walked a total of 80 miles during the climb, which took place from the southern side of the
mountain.
All but two of the party are married men, and the average age is 26.
(Author's note: "I have over 200 articles from East Africa, but modesty prevents me reproducing them all —
only the out of the ordinary stories.)

Weekly News, 23 February 1963
IT'S A GREAT WORLD: DISC JOCKEY's 96-HOUR MARATHON
Disc jockey KEITH SKUES of Timperley, Cheshire has just finished the four most hectic days of his career.
He and a team of announcers and disc jockeys put on a marathon record programme over the British
Forces Network in Kenya.
The show, to raise money for charity, ran a record 96 hours. But because of all the organisation, 23-year-old
Keith had no sleep for four days.
The disc jockey team raised more than £3250 from people in Kenya phoning the radio station asking for a
record and pledging an amount of cash. Donations varied from five shillings to fifty pounds, and more than
2000 requests were played.
During the broadcast Keith and a young actress were "kidnapped." They were lured outside the studio,
bundled into two cars and driven away. Other announcers told the radio audience what had happened.
Keith and the actress were released when a listener promised to pay the required "ransom."
Keith was a member of an RAF team which climbed Mount Kilimanjaro, Africa's highest mountain.
But after his marathon session he reckons disc jockeying is just as strenuous.

WB 14 February 1963
Death: SKEWS

On 29 January 1963 at Mayday Hospital, Croydon, ETHEL JANE SKEWS aged 73 formerly of Redruth, widow of MARTIN SKEWS, beloved mother of REX SKEWS. Cremated at Croydon 4 February. Interred at Treleigh Church 11 February. At rest.

Gravesend Reporter 22 March 1963
SKEWS, ALICE ELIZABETH passed away peacefully on 12 March at her new home 84 High Street, Swanscombe, Kent, aged 80 years.

WB 11 July 1963
Death: Mrs E. SKEWES, Redruth
The death occurred in Barncoose Hospital on Thursday of Mrs ETHEL SKEWES, aged 81 years of 27 Cardew Close, Redruth. Mrs SKEWES was the widow of Mr S.J. SKEWES for many years a member of the clerical staff at Redruth Brewery Company Ltd. A daughter of the late Mr and Mrs N. Pollard of Redruth she had a long association with Fore Street Methodist Church where before her marriage she was a teacher in the Sunday School and a chorister. Her elder son Mr HARRY SKEWES is senior welfare officer, H.M. Prison at Brixton, London. Her younger son Mr JAMES SKEWES died over 20 years ago.
The funeral of Mrs Skewes took place on Sunday in St Day Road Cemetery, Redruth, the Rev. S.E.A. Underhill officiating. Mourners were her son, Mr and Mrs N.K. Kitto, Mr K. Tippett, Mr and Mrs H. Rich, Miss J.E. Kitto, Mr and Mrs P. Rich, Mr S. and Mr and Mrs H. Paull, Mrs G. Hosking, Mr and Mrs F. Miles, Mr and Mrs A.E. Dumpleton and Mr F.S. Opie (nephews and nieces), and Mr A.T. Bird (brother-in-law).
Floral tributes included those from all her friends and neighbours and from the Bede House Settlement in Bermondsey with which Mr Skewes has had a long association.

Death: Mrs E. SKEWES
At Redruth 4 July, ETHEL (née Pollard) born 1881. Much loved but by none more than STEPHEN and JIMMY with whom she may now rest, and by HARRY, who with many others mourns her passing. Interred in St Day Road Cemetery, Redruth on Sunday 7 July.

WB 22 August 1963
Death: SKEWES
On 19 August at Barncoose Hospital, MINNIE SKEWES, aged 94 years, widow of RICHARD SKEWES. Funeral today (Thursday) at 2:30pm at St Day Road Cemetery.

Manchester Evening News 3 October 1963
GOING UP
It does not seem long since KEITH SKUES called to show me a school magazine he was editing. But now Keith, whose parents live in Buckingham Grove, Timperley, is 24, and he has just been accepted for a BBC senior producers' course in London.
He flies in on Sunday from Nairobi, where he is one of East Africa's top disc jockeys and producers. Last year his weekly variety show "Skueball Speshall" was voted the most popular programme of the year. When it was announced that his "Skues Me" programme would be rested after running in Kenya for many months, a petition with over 1,000 signatures was sent in to retain it.
On his "Kenya Hit Parade" he has had many personal guests including Cliff Richard, Helen Shapiro, Anne Shelton, Alma Cogan and Petula Clark.

Times of Swaziland 20 March 1964
As mentioned in The Times of Swaziland last week, Forces Broadcasting Service announcer KEITH SKUES was visiting Swaziland. He has now returned to Nairobi, Kenya.
Before leaving by air, Keith said that he had spent a very enjoyable few days. "I was overwhelmed by the hospitality everyone offered. I have never been to a place so friendly, so easy going and so perfectly charming." Whilst in Swaziland Keith did a few broadcasts for Radio Mbabane. Off the radio Keith Skues is quite a lad. Two weeks ago he and a few colleagues from FBS in Nairobi climbed to the summit of Mount Kenya. Two years ago he was on top of Mount Kilimanjaro, Africa's highest mountain.
Keith has written a book on the "History of the Skues Family." The name comes from Cornwall in England.
He started broadcasting with the British Forces Network in Germany, after which he went to the desert of Kuwait whilst the Iraqi crisis was on in 1961. From there he went to Kenya after a short time in Bahrain and Aden.
Last year he was with the BBC in London and is now back in Kenya to help organise the run down of the FBS Station, which is scheduled to close transmission in November, when the majority of British troops will have left Kenya.

WB 23 April 1964
CORNISH DISC JOCKEY
Disc jockeys who delve into history and climb mountains and direct films are rare. Such a person is a 25-year-old Cornishman, KEITH SKUES, who is an announcer with the British Forces Broadcasting Service in Kenya.
His programme "Skues Me" was voted the most popular programme of 1963 and he also introduces "Kenya Hit Parade", "Skueball Speshall", "Housewives Choice" and many more.
Last week Mr Skues climbed to the summit of Mount Kenya and in October, 1962, he was on top of Africa when he reached the summit of Mount Kilimanjaro (19,340ft), the sixth highest mountain in the world.
Over the Christmas period he and his fellow announcers worked non-stop night and day manning the FBS station in Nairobi raising £3,500 which they gave to the British and Kenya Wireless for the Blind funds. A month later Mr Skues found himself in the centre of activity with the uprisings in Zanzibar, Tanganyika, Uganda and Kenya. He has made a documentary film about Forces Broadcasting.

During the past few years he has been compiling "The History of the Skues Family", which goes back to the very early days in the Helston, Camborne and Redruth districts. He was hoping to visit Helston when he was home in Britain last October on a BBC course. But at the last minute he had to return to Kenya in time for Christmas.

Although he spends the greater part of his time on the radio, he appears regularly on Kenya television, and has his own "pop" page in one of Nairobi's daily newspapers. Next week he is off to Swaziland for a week, to be followed by a two-year tour in Aden.

WB 3 September 1964
Silver Wedding: Prisk-SKEWES
At Illogan Parish Church on 6 September 1939 by the late Rev. George Renner, Kenneth to IRIS. Present address: Golden Villa, Carnkie, Redruth.

Altrincham & Bowdon Guardian 3 October 1964
SKUES US
There was excitement in a certain house in Timperley when two MARGARET SKUESES met....... one was from England and the other from Australia. Meeting point was 21 Buckingham Grove, Timperley, and it all came about through the tracing of a "family tree".

For a number of years KEITH SKUES, now a disc jockey with Radio Caroline had been delving into the family history. His searches included writing to Australia to a Mr SAMUEL SKUES in 1956, and the letter was passed from father to son.

Then it passed from son to daughter. Last year Margaret Skues from Melbourne arrived in Britain to find Keith, but he was with the British Forces Network in Kenya.

It was only when he arrived back in England that the meeting took place and then it was further arranged for the family get together at Timperley.

Both Margarets — the English one is 17, and the Australian one 23 — have mothers with the same Christain name Doris, and the girls both keep budgies with the same names, Peter.

Another coincidence — when Keith was presenting a programme from Radio Caroline last week he received a letter from a PETER SKUES of Walton on Naze, Essex, asking if they were related!

Said Keith this week...... "And I thought our surname was unusual!"

Essex County Standard 30 October 1964
DISC JOCKEY HURT IN MISHAP IN SHIP
Radio Caroline disc jockey KEITH SKUES was detained in Myland Hospital, Colchester, with a cut head following an accident on board ship on October 21st.

Mr Skues, who is 25, was hit by a swinging door while the ship was riding heavy weather soon after broadcasting ended in the evening. He received a cut on his forehead, and though he was given first-aid treatment, the captain of the ship was not satisfied the next morning, and an emergency call was made to the Coastguard.

The tender which usually makes one visit a day to Radio Caroline was called out and made an emergency trip to the ship to carry Mr Skues ashore.

He was taken to Myland Hospital for treatment and detained. He was temporarily blinded in one eye when he knocked his head, but was released from hospital on Tuesday.

WB 12 November 1964
Deaths: SKEWES
On Monday 9 November at Barncoose Hospital WILLIAM HEDLEY SKEWES, aged 85 years of Trevarth Vean, Lanner beloved husband of AMY. Funeral today (Thursday) leaving the house at 2.00pm for service at Lanner Moor Chapel. Interment St Day Road Cemetery, Redruth. Friends please accept this (the only) intimation.

WB 19 November 1964
Death: W.H. SKEWES, Lanner
At Lanner Moor Methodist Church where he had been a trustee and trust treasurer for many years, the funeral service took place on Thursday of Mr W.H. SKEWES, aged 85, of Trevarth Vean, Lanner, a well-known draper. The Rev. A.A. Adams officiated. He referred to his lifetime of service to Methodism at Treruffehill, Redruth and the Moor Chapels.

Mourners included the widow, Messrs F.G. Gregory, J. & K. Jenkin (nephews), Mr J. Allen (brother-in-law), Mesdames F.S. Gregory, A.R. Stephens, J. & K. Jenkin and M. Griffiths (nieces), Mrs W. Johns, Mr J. Richards, Mr and Mrs R. Allen (cousins).

Representing Druids Lodge of Freemasons, Redruth were Messrs E.L. Smitherham (Worshipful Master), W. Hart, W. Bishop and T.E. Opie. Friends in church included representatives from Lanner Cricket Club and United Kingdom Travellers Alliance.

Floral tributes included those from Lanner Moor Methodist Chapel and Lanner Cricket Club.

WB 14 January 1965
Death: SKEWES
On 12 January, JAMES HENRY SKEWES, aged 92 years of Penwartha, Perranporth. Funeral service at Bolingey Methodist Church on Saturday 16 January at 2.30 pm.

WB 21 January 1965
PONY POWER WAS HIS FAVOURITE MODE OF LOCOMOTION
The funeral service for 92-year-old Mr JAMES HENRY SKEWES of Penwartha Manor Farm, Perranporth was held at Bolingey Methodist Church on Saturday, Rev. F.B.J. Quire officiating.

Mr Skewes, a great horse lover, spent 37 years farming in the Perranporth district, and up to the past few years he was a familiar figure travelling by pony and trap or jingle-his favourite form of transport. Every year he drove to Helston Flora Day.

Mourners included Messrs A., B., F., H., J. and J.D. SKEWES (sons), Mesdames J. Cleave and W. Eustice (daughters), Mr J. SKEWES (brother), Mesdames A., B., H., J. and J.D. SKEWES (daughters-in-law), T. SKEWES, D. Treweek, the Misses D. and I. SKEWES (grandchildren), Mesdames Cox, French, Pearce, G.SKEWES, Messrs G. SKEWES, Cox, French, PAT SKEWES (nieces and nephews).

(the paper then listed another 50 mourners)

WB 25 February 1965
Death: SKEWES
On Tuesday 23 February at Camborne/Redruth Hospital, LIONEL JAMES SKEWES, aged 67 years, husband of the late OLIVE MAY SKEWES. Service followed by cremation at Penmount 11.30am Saturday 27 February. No flowers. Will friends please meet at the crematorium.

WB 4 March 1965
FORMER MABE COUNCILLOR
The funeral of Mr LIONEL JAMES SKEWES, aged 67 years, of 3 Corpascus Cottages, Trenowerth, Mabe, took place at Penmount Crematorium on Saturday.
After serving in the First World War, Mr Skewes was employed by Messrs Rowe and Knowles of Falmouth.
He farmed for many years at Trenowerth Vean, Mabe but retired soon after the death of his wife. He was a former member of Mabe Parish Council. The Rev. J.R.G. Martin (Chacewater) officiated. Mourners included Mr J. SKEWES (London), Mr A.W. Courage, Mrs J. Knowles and Mrs G.F. Lee (cousins), Messrs and Mesdames W.H. and C. Symons (brothers-in-law and sisters-in-law) and Mr J.H. Symons (nephew).

Altrincham and Bowdon Guardian 6 March 1965
STAR PART
On Sunday Timperley disc jockey KEITH SKUES will visit ITV's studios in Birmingham and record "Thank Your Lucky Stars."
Keith appears as guest disc jockey of the week to give his views on three new records. Keith works aboard Radio Caroline South, anchored 17 miles from Harwich, off the East Anglian coast and yesterday celebrated his 26th birthday.
In August last year he joined the Caroline company as a disc jockey after being with the British Forces Network overseas. A former Altrincham Grammar School boy, he recently completed — and also directed — a film about Radio Caroline. Last month he appeared in a Pathe Pictorial film about the radio station due for release this month.
The TV programme will be shown nationally on 13th March.

Daily Mirror 9 June 1965
STUDENT PRINCE VISITS POP PIRATES
The Student Prince paid a surprise visit to the pirate radio ship Caroline yesterday.
Prince Richard of Gloucester, 20, went aboard the ship off the Essex coast with two chums from Cambridge University where he is studying architecture. They took cameras and notebooks and got first hand material for an article they are doing for the students' magazine "Granta."
The party arrived at Harwich in the Prince's car in time for a trip in Caroline's supply tender "Offshore."
Two of the Caroline's team of disc jockeys — KEITH SKUES and Bryan Vaughan — made the 17 mile trip with the Prince.
Usually Caroline dee-jays announce special visitors. But listeners did not get a hint that Prince Richard was on board. A Caroline spokesman said "There was a request that there should be no fuss."

Racine Journal Times, USA 26 August 1965
NEW COUNTY WAYSIDE GIFT FROM SKEWES FAMILY
Union Grove — A grove of black walnut trees, hand planted 70 years ago by the late SAMUEL SKEWES, provides shade for picnickers at one of Racine's newest wayside parks, SKEWES PARK, located at County Trunk Road "C" and 51st Drive in the town of Yorkville, about half a mile west of Ives Grove.
The four-acre park was given to Racine County by Doctor ARTHUR R. SKEWES, now of Lexington, Kentucky, a great-grandson of Samuel Skewes. Improvements made at Skewes Park by the county include fencing to enclose the park site, grading and installing a gravelled driveway that encircles a large stone, to which a historical plaque has been attached.
The story of the plaque is an abbreviated version of the Skewes family history, beginning with Samuel's arrival in the United States from England in 1842. It reads as follows:
"These black walnut trees grew from nuts planted in 1895 by Samuel Skewes, aged 84. Samuel Skewes was born on 10 July 1881, in Ruan Major, Cornwall, England. He emigrated to Wisconsin in 1842 with his wife Catherine Lugg Skewes and infant son Samuel, and an eight-year-old nephew, James L. Skewes. This farm land was purchased from the government and named 'Grovean' meaning small grove or woods.
Three more children were born to Samuel and Catherine; George, Sarah and Margaret. After the death of his wife Catherine, he married Ruth Bottomley of the English Settlement. Four children, Edwin, Emma, Eleanor and Thomas, were born of this marriage. Grovean Farm has been the home of Samuel Skewes (died 1898); his son Edwin Bottomley Skewes (1858-1913); his grandson Arthur Edwin Skewes (1891-1921) and his great grandson Doctor Arthur Russell Skewes.

"This wayside park is given to Racine County by members of the Skewes family in memory of Samuel Skewes and his descendants, to whom 'Grovean' has been home."

Visitors to Skewes Park may wonder whether the large stone on which the historical plaque is mounted came from "Grovean Farm." "No", says John Blum, Racine County Parks Superintent, and thereby hangs another tale. Blum said the county often provides stone markers for its parks. He doesn't know where the big stone at Old Settlers Park came from, but Blum conducted a personal search in farm rock piles all over the county until he found stones of the right size and shape for the plaques at Skewes Park and at Tabor Park.

The stone at Skewes Park was found on the Albert Kutzke farm in Kenosha County on the County Line Road. It weights over two tons and is sunk 18 inches into its concrete base.

County machines were used to lift the stone from the Kutzke farm and haul it to the Highway Department garage on South Green Bay Road. Here it was steam-cleaned and sand-blasted.

WB 7 October 1965
Wedding: SKEWES — Clackworthy
The vicar, Rev. J.D. Cox officiated at the wedding at Madron Church of Mr CARL SKEWES only son of Mr and Mrs H. SKEWES of 49 Dolcoath Avenue, Camborne and Miss Shirley Elizabeth Clackworthy, fourth daughter of Mr and Mrs E. Clackworthy of 19 Trelawny Estate, Madron. Given away by her father the bride wore a full length white brocade dress and carried white roses. Mr I. Toy was best man. After the reception for 36 guests in the Landithey Hall, the couple left for a honeymoon at Gwithian. The bride, a machine operator at Holman Brothers, received an electric kettle from her colleagues and the bridegroom a carpenter with South Crofty Limited, was given a china cabinet and fruit bowl. The couple will live at 2 Penventon, Four Lanes, Redruth.

WB 5 May 1966
Death: SKEWES
On 20 April at Downley, High Wycombe, JAMES MARTIN SKEWES, aged 86 years, formerly of Devoran, beloved father of CAROLINE Lappin of 45 Gloucester Road, Reading, Berkshire.

East Anglian Daily Times 9 September 1966
DISC JOCKEY "SATISFACTORY."
Disc jockey KEITH SKUES, 27 years old, from Radio London successfully underwent an appendix operation at Ipswich's Foxhall Hospital yesterday.
Several weeks ago he was taken to Ipswich and East Suffolk Hospital for medical observation and discharged to await yesterday's operation. His condition was described by a hospital spokesman today as "satisfactory."

WB 13 October 1966
CAME HERE TO LIVE: DIES IN TRACTOR TRAGEDY
A 38-year-old former engineer in the aircraft industry who came to live in Cornwall three months ago from Cheshire met his death on Sunday when driving a farm tractor down a steep field.
The tractor ran away and a 15-year-old farmer's son, who was also riding on the machine, was killed outright when it overturned after crashing through a gorse hedge to a lower field.
The tragdy occurred at Parc-an-Fox, Tregarne in St Keverne parish. The lad killed outright was JACK SKEWES, son of Mr and Mrs WILLIAM SKEWES of Tregarne Farm.
The engineer, Mr Kenneth Frederick Harrison, a married man with three children died from his injuries in the Royal Cornwall Hospital, Truro, later the same day.
The mid-Cornwall Coroner (Mr L.J. Carlyon, Truro) opened an inquest on both the deceased at Helston on Monday afternoon, and then adjourned the enquiry to a date to be fixed.
The boy, the second youngest of a family of nine children, had recently left school and was working part time for the owner of the tractor Mr Leslie Lugg of Halwyn Farm, Tregarne who was also present in the field when the accident occurred.
Funeral of both victims of the accident are taking place in St Keverne Parish Churchyard this afternoon.

WB 21 September 1967
Death: SKEWES
On Tuesday 19 September at the home of his sister at 77 Higher Fore Street, Redruth, EDWARD MORLEY SKEWES, aged 47 years, son of the late Mr and Mrs A.J.SKEWES of Bartle's Row, Tuckingmill. Funeral on Friday leaving the house at 10.30am for cremation at Penmount, Truro at 11.00am. Will friends please accept this the only intimation.

Melody Maker, 23 September 1967
KEITH SKUES
Ex Radio London DJ KEITH SKUES has landed one of the plum jobs in the new BBC Radio One set-up — the chair of Saturday Club, occupied for nine years by Brian Matthew.
Keith, aged 28, hosts the programme for at least 13 weeks, possibly for good. And he says the programme is to be completely revamped. "It is to be speeded up, and we have had the needle time increased to 65 minutes out of the two-hour show", he said over coffee in a Fleet Street restaurant.
Keith, a slim dark-haired veteran of broadcasting, began his broadcasting career in the time-honoured way of joining the British Forces Network whilst a National Serviceman.
He became a regular broadcaster and when his National Service time was up, he rejoined BFN as a civilian. He was posted to Nairobi, Kenya, and later worked for BFN in Aden.
Back in London he joined Radio Caroline and was with the station from August 1964 until December 1965. He left Caroline and freelanced, doing a three month series on Radio Luxembourg for CBS as well as personal appearances and club work.

He joined Radio London and stayed with the station until they went off the air.

With the BBC he has presented "Roundabout", "Swingalong", "Juke Box Jury" and "Late Night Line Up." In addition he has been doing a lot of work for the BBC's Overseas Service.

Skues is a dedicated broadcaster. "Once you have been bitten by the bug, it's impossible to get rid of it. But if I was told I would have to get out of radio, I'd like to become a journalist."

Keith has the radio experience to stay the course with the BBC.

WB 28 September 1967
ELECTRICITY WIREMAN
Cremation took place at Penmount on Friday of Mr EDWARD MORLEY SKEWES, aged 47 years, who died at the home of his brother-in-law and sister, Mr and Mrs J.H. Harvey, at 77 Higher Fore Street, Redruth. Rev. A.J. Vincent, vicar of Kenwyn, a cousin, officiated at the service. Mr Skewes formerly lived with his parents, the late Mr and Mrs A.J. Skewes at Tuckingmill. He was a wireman with the South West Electricity Board for 32 years.

Mourners included Messrs and Mesdames J. Tredinnick, N. Harvey, E. Polkinghorne and H. Vincent (brothers-in-law and sisters), Messrs J. Lawry (brother-in-law), S. Polkinghorne, E. Harvey, B. & D. Vincent, Messrs and Mesdames R. Webster and W. Kemp (nephews and nieces), Messrs D. Macphearson, R. Colliver, P.L. Rowe, W. Stone and Mrs M. Oliver (cousins).

Express and Echo, Exeter 8 March 1968
Death: ERNEST JOHN SKEWES
On 6 March ERNEST JOHN SKEWES, aged 87 years of 7 Courtenay Road, St Thomas, Exeter. Funeral service Monday 11 March, Exwick Cemetery Church, 11.00am. Cortège will leave from 80 Wellington Road, Exeter. Beloved husband of the late FLORENCE LUCY SKEWES and brother of FREDERICK SKEWES.

Altrincham & Bowdon Guardian 22 March 1968
Obituary: Miss M.E. SKUES
The funeral took place at Altrincham Crematorium on Monday, after a service at St Alban's Parish Church, Broadheath, of Miss MARGARET ELAINE SKUES, of 27 Chambers Road, Southport whose parents live at "Richleen", 21 Buckingham Grove, Timperley. The Rev. R.J. Mentern officiated at both the service and committal.

Margaret, who was 21 in January, died after a car in which she was travelling as a passenger was involved in an accident at Halsall, near Ormaskirk.

She was a regular attender of St Alban's Parish Church during her childhood. When she left in 1962 Margaret went in for floristry and later her job took her to Southport. She had been working and living in Southport for the past two years.

Margaret was the sister of BBC radio man KEITH SKUES and had been on his radio programme numerous times. An inquest was opened on Friday, but then adjourned until 19 April.

Chief mourners were: Mr and Mrs RICHARD SKUES (parents), KEITH (brother), Mrs F. Coulthurst (aunt), Mr and Mrs V. SKUES (uncle and aunt), Mr and Mrs G. Hughes (uncle and aunt), Mr and Mrs L. Hughes (uncle and aunt), Mrs G. Frayne (aunt), Mrs N. Glazebrook (aunt), Olive, Sylvia, Susan, Jennifer, John (cousins), Mr and Mrs Fawkes and Roy, Miss G. Pike, Miss O. Pike, Mr and Mrs Arnold and many close friends from Southport and St Alban's Church congregations.

Kettering Leader, 29 March 1968
DISC JOCKEY SPINS INTO TROUBLE
As Kettering disc jockey KEITH SKEWS spins the records at the Wednesday night discotheque at Kettering Athletic Club, he could be spinning big trouble for himself and the club.

Because 18-year-old Keith — real name Brian Wilmer — of 13 Burghley Street, Kettering — had adopted the same sounding name as BBC Radio One DJ, KEITH SKUES.

And Keith number one — the big man of the pops — is real mad. In fact he has even considered legal action. But that won't be necessary because local boy Brian is likely to change his disc going name .... on order of club entertainments secretary Mr Jimmy Walding.

Keith Skues' London manager Roger Easterby told the "Leader", "This is a very serious matter. I am personally very annoyed and Keith himself is terribly upset."

He said he could not believe the club had not been trying to cash in on the real Keith Skues' name "This was an obvious attempt to misrepresent the public", said Mr Easterby.

Brian launched the Wednesday night discos three weeks ago, and each night has been a bigger success. Whether this was due to his adopted name is not known. But the numbers have increased to more than 200.

Brian said he took the name on the advice of the club's entertainments committee.

The real Keith Skues is host of Radio One's "Saturday Club" and "What's New" and TV's "Top of the Pops".

Southport Visitor 1 June 1968
ON CARELESS DRIVING CHARGE
Charges under Section 3 of the Road Traffic Act alleging careless driving have been preferred against a young produce merchant who overtook a mini-car on a sharp bend and was involved in a head-on crash in which a girl died.

An Ormskirk inquest was told this yesterday when a jury returned a verdict of misadventure on Miss MARGARET ELAINE SKUES, aged 21, a florist of 27 Chambers Road, Southport.

South West Lancashire Coroner Mr R.A. Lloyd heard that an MG 1100 car, driven by William Church, aged 19 and a produce merchant of 88 Jacksmere Lane, Scarisbrick, overtook a mini-car on a bend in Gorsuch Lane, Scarisbrick at 11.00pm on 8 March.

Church's car collided head-on with a Singer Vogue car, driven by Mr Alan Baldwin, aged 21 and a driver, of 165 Carr Moss Lane, Halsall, who had Miss Skues as his passenger. The driver of the mini-car, apparently unaware of the accident, carried on.

The Coroner said an appeal had been made on the BBC to the driver of the mini-car to come forward, but without success.

Mr Baldwin said he was driving towards Southport, and due to patchy fog visibility was between 20 and 100 yards. He knew the road well and as he approached a sharp right-hand bend he looked across the fields and saw a pair of headlights coming towards him. He had almost reached the bend and the approaching car was almost level when suddenly another car came from behind it.

"The driver gave the impression that he had not seen me and was going to overtake the car in front, although there was no room to do so.

"As a result of this manoeuvre there was a head-on collision between my car and the car which had been overtaking", said Mr Baldwin.

Miss Susan Frances Johnson, aged 18, a civil servant of 66 Linaker Street, Southport, told the Coroner that she was driving towards Scarisbrick and there was a car in front. Suddenly she saw two sets of headlights coming towards her. There was a mini-car on the inside and the driver was switching his lights on and off. Miss Johnson said she slowed down and almost immediately the two vehicles collided in the centre of the road. The driver of the mini-car was apparently unaware of the accident and continued towards Halsall.

Police Constable Peter Ashton said Church was trapped in the driving seat of the MG 1100. There was debris on the offside of the road and glass from the windscreen of the Singer Vogue.

P.C. Graham Midgley said Miss Skues was lying on the front bench seat of the Singer Vogue saloon with extensive face injuries.

In a statement to police, made under caution, Church said he was driving towards Halsall. It was a bit misty and he was following another car. "I was following the car ahead at a reasonable distance and after that I do not remember anything except when I was trapped inside my car, and when my mother and father came to see me in hospital", read the statement.

Hendon Times, Kilburn Times, Willesdon and Brent Chronicle 21 June 1968
JAIL WRECKS A CABBY's PLAN TO WED
The day Terence Dunne received and used a Barclaycard belonging to Radio One disc jockey KEITH SKUES he wrecked his own wedding plans. After Dunne, a 33-year-old mini-cab driver of Richborough Road, Cricklewood, received the card, which had gone astray in the post to Mr Skues, he used it to obtain a gold chain bracelet, shoes worth 19 guineas, hosiery valued at £6 and items from various shops, a court heard on Friday.

Detective Duncan Macrae told Marlborough Street Magistrate Mr Edward Robey that Dunne planned to marry in August. But the magistrate jailed Dunne for nine months and told him "I'm afraid you won't be able to marry in August. You will have to postpone that."

Dunne pleaded guilty to receiving the Barclaycard, obtaining shoes, a gold chain bracelet, hosiery and other items by false pretences. He also admitted that he had similarly attempted to obtain four shirts worth £17 from Krantz Ltd of Regent Street.

He was said to have eleven convictions recorded against him, the last in 1960 when he went to prison for four years for warehouse-breaking. Dunne told the magistrate that when he last left jail he had been determined not to have anything more to do with crime.

He had let himself commit the offences only because his car had been smashed up. He had now sold the car and wished to make restitution to those who had lost by his activities.

The magistrate said that Dunne had a bad record, but he would refrain from sending him to the Sessions for sentence because there had been a big gap since the last conviction.

London Gazette 25 June 1968
The Queen has been graciously pleased to award the Imperial Service Medal to the following officer on retirement.
HENRY GEORGE SKEWS, Technical Officer, Post Office, London Telecommunications Region.

London Evening News 8 August 1968
DECREE FOR FIRE EATER
Mr FREDERICK MACKENZIE SKUES — "Prince Neekeyzolo, snake charmer and fire eater" has been granted a decree nisi in the London Divorce Court, because of adultery by his wife DOREEN with Mr Patrick Ernest Bushnell. The petition was not contested. Mr and Mrs Skues were married in Manchester in April 1948.

Evening Star, Ipswich 30 October 1968
IT'S ONEDERFULLY PUNNY
KEITH SKUES, the disc jockey Ipswich tends to regard as its very own, has just published a book.
Appropriately enough, it's all about Radio One. And appropriately enough, too, knowing Keith's funny sense of humour, it is called Radio Onederland".
He did have two other titles in mind, "From Ship to Shore", and my favourite "A Life on the Medium Wave". However, they were thrown overboard by "Auntie" as smacking too much of pirate days. Keith's connection with Ipswich dates from the days of the pop ships of course. Like many of the BBC DJ's Keith came ashore when the pirates were banned. He is now the resident compere of "Saturday Club" on Radio One.

When Radio Caroline was in full swing, Keith was a regular visitor to the town. He was so impressed with Ipswich that at one time he was thinking of living here. Now he has a flat in London. There is a reminder of Skuesdays more tangible than those happy memories. His appendix lurks in the bowels (pun!) of the Ipswich and East Suffolk Hospital — in a bottle! (Tony Bennett left his heart in San Francisco, but what do we get?)

His book was written in something like record time. It was on the book stalls only three months after the idea was put forward. The book, too, has local connections as it is published by the Lavenham Landmark Press. The general editor of Landmark Press is John Venmore-Rowland. He has written a handbook on Britain's pop pirates. One day when he was in London he saw a typescript of another book on the pirates written by Keith called "Pop Went the Pirates".

He was very impressed with it and asked to meet the DJ. When they finally managed a meeting — in a tea tent at a Brentwood Garden fete — he commissioned Keith to write a book about Radio One.

The book Keith has produced is absolutely jam-packed with facts and figures all clearly explained. There is an excellent section on the DJ's. The whole book, though informative, is written in a lively easy-to-read way ..... full of horrible puns he makes all the time.

Actually, I think he is very funny. It is a good combination of hard fact and entertainment.

Keith says he may see the reappearance of the notices that appeared on some doors at the BBC when he was running round collecting material: "Am busy. Keep out record pluggers and Keith Skues."

Seriously though, for all Radio One fans, this is a must. In paperback form this book costs 10 shillings and casebound it comes at 17/6d. Pat Jones.

WB 12 January 1969
ONE MAN, ONE BRUSH and a 500-TON SHIP
Doing a spot of decorating this weekend? Then spare a thought for Mr HARRY SKEWES. He is in the process of painting a whole ship — inside and out.

Mr Skewes is doing a one-man overhaul of the 515-ton "Queen of the Isles", laid up for the winter at Hayle. The ship, owned by the Isles of Scilly Steamship Company, is destined for charter work along the south coast next summer.

Ahead of Mr Skewes lies the mammoth annual task of painting, scraping, polishing and cleaning before the Queen is in more regal trim.

In the three weeks that the ship has been moored at Hayle, Mr Skewes, the 46-year-old bosun of the Queen, has made quite an impression. The sides have been painted, the lifeboat davits greased and checked and much of the superstructure has had a first coat of paint.

Mr Skewes explained "The ship has got to be checked from bow to stern. Every piece of equipment from the lifeboats to the winches must be in perfect working order."

Mr Skewes, who says he has long conversations with his paint brush to pass away the time, has not tried to work out how much paint he is going to use.

One of his most difficult tasks will be painting the main mast. "It's a long way to climb, and it will be a tough job. I am not really looking forward to it," he added.

That is just another item in Mr Skewes' long list of jobs to be done before the spring — but one thing he is sure of. When it comes to decorating his home at Penzance he is definitely not available.

WB 20 March 1969
COLLAPSED IN SHOP
The funeral took place on Wednesday of Mr JAMES FREDERICK SKUES aged 59 years of Ford House, Ford's Row, Redruth, who collapsed and died in a shop in Fore Street, Redruth, last week.

The Rev. Tom Saunders officiated at the service in a private chapel of rest.

Born at Redruth, Mr Skues was employed as a mason with a local building firm until he became ill.

He was a member of Redruth British Legion Club.

Mourners included L. SKUES (brother), A., B., D.J., and T. Pearce (nephews) and R.L. Pearce (brother-in-law). Floral tributes included those from Redruth British Legion and the Collins Arms.

WB 12 June 1969
Birth: SKEWES
On 6 June at Treliske Maternity Unit to JENNIFER and MAX, a daughter FIONA. Sincere thanks to staff and doctors.

Facts on File (New York) 9 October 1969
Weekly World Digest:
JUNE SKEWES (known professionally as June Collins), testified in an Army Club probe. A Senate investigation into alleged corruption in the operation of Non Commissioned Officers' clubs implicated two top Army figures — Sgt Major William Woolridge and retired Major General Carl Turner. Witness testified that between $5000 and $7000 week were stolen from slot machines alone at 24th Infantry Brigade Division in West Germany.

June Skewes, an Australian booking agent for entertainers in Vietnam service clubs testified on 9 October that the had to pay kick backs to sergeants who controlled the clubs and sometimes had to provide them with women. The agent said Woolridge was known as "one of the ringleaders in the kickback system."

Helston Packet 1 May 1970
RADIO D.J. PROMISES A FURRY DAY PROGRAMME
Radio disc jockey KEITH SKUES has just returned to London after a week's stay in Helston collecting information for the "History of the Skues Family", which he has been compiling for the last few years, and hopes to publish.

He said before leaving the town: Our family has been connected with Helston since 1700. **Perhaps** the two most famous members were WILLIAM SKUES, who was secretary of the Tinners' Association for more than 50 years and elected a Freeman of the Borough in 1786, and RICHARD SKUES, borough surgeon, also elected as a Freeman of the Borough — in 1804.

Mr Skues spent many hours searching through the archives in the County Record Office, Truro. He said "I also met a number of the SKEWES family,including BILL and WENDY SKEWES of Beacon Parc, Helston and BILL and BESSIE SKEWES of Redannack Estate, Mullion." The 31-year-old disc jockey gave a mention to many people in and around Helston in his Easter Monday pop programme on Radios 1 and 2, and has promised to do a feature on the Heslton Furry Dance on Sunday, 3 May, in his Breakfast Show.

Australian Dental Journal, August 1970
Doctor KENNETH SKUES
The announcement has been made of the retirement of Dr KENNETH SKUES, O.B.E. as Principal Dental Officer in the Department of Repatriation, a position he has held since 1956 and prior to that had been Senior Dental Officer, Victoria. Kenneth Skues has had a long association with the Royal Melbourne Dental Hospital and the Royal Melbourne Hospital and was sometime lecturer in Dental Pathology and Embryology and Examiner in Conservative Dentistry in the University of Melbourne.

WB 8 October 1970
Ruby Wedding: SKEWES — Prowse
On 7 October, 1930 at Bolingey Methodist Church by Rev.Francis G. Gray, BERTRAM SKEWES to Lily (née Prowse). Present address: Kai Ping, Goonvrea, St Agnes.

WB 24 December 1970
FARMER WEDS HOSPITAL WORKER
A member of Penhallows Snooker team, Mr JAMES ARTHUR SKEWES, only son of Mr and Mrs J. SKEWES of Manor Farm, Penwartha, Parranporth was married to Miss Wendy Jean Hooper, third daughter of Mr and Mrs S. Hooper of 5 River View, Tresillian, at Perranzabuloe Parish Church by Rev.F.P. Royle,vicar.
Given away by her father, the bride wore an empire style white full length gown and carried freesias and carnations. Mr Terry Hooper was best man.
After the reception for more than 50 guests at the Rosemundy Hotel, St Agnes, the couple left for a honeymoon touring Devon. The bride had been employed at Treliske Hospital, Truro. The groom is a farmer, and they will live at Manor Farm.

WB 14 January 1971
Death: SKEWES
On Monday 11 January at Barncoose Hospital, Redruth, EMMA (AMY) SKEWES, aged 77 years of Trevarth Vean, Lanner, widow of HEDLEY SKEWES. Funeral tomorrow (Friday) 15 January leaving the house at 1.55pm for service at Lanner Moor Chapel — interment at Lanner Churchyard.

WB 28 September 1972
WOMAN CRITICALLY ILL
A 61-year-old woman severely burned in a fire in a garage on Monday was still critically ill at the Royal Cornwall Hospital, Treliske, Truro, yesterday.
Miss ERNESTINE M. SKEWES of Gilmore House, Crowan, daughter of the former vicar of Crowan,was dragged clear by a neighbour, Mr Theodore Glasson. She was given first aid by Camborne firemen, who were called to put out the small fire.
Yesterday the cause was still being investigated. Specimens were taken from the garage and sent for forensic examination.
Miss Skewes, a former teacher, was a clerk at Redruth Police Station for 30 years. She retired earlier this year.

Camborne/Redruth Packet, 18 October 1972
GARAGE FIRE WAS MISADVENTURE
A lethal mixture of petrol fumes and air which built up in her garage may have caused the death of 61-year-old Miss ERNESTINE M. SKEWES, of Gilmore House, Crowan. A verdict of misadventure was recorded at the inquest at Camborne yesterday.
Miss Skewes, an arthritis sufferer who lived alone, was found in her garage on 25 September and died in Treliske Hospital, Truro on 8th October from third degree burns.
Miss Skewes, the daughter of a former Crowan clergyman, was a clerk at Redruth Police Station for 30 years until she retired in June because of her rheumatoid arthritis.
On the day of the fire she told her neighbour, farmer Mr Theodore Glasson, that she was going to clear out her garage.
He said he saw flames shooting from the roof and heard two explosions. He rescued Miss Skewes whose clothes were alight from the blaze.
"When I got back from fetching a blanket I found she had gone back into the garage and was sitting in the same position on a pile of wood", he told the inquest.
He said Miss Skewes' only words were "I was smoking ..... a can." Assistant Divisional Officer John Workman of Camborne Fire Station said there was a strong smell of petrol in the garage, but no container. He said the cause of the fire will always be supposition, but a pool of petrol could have formed on the floor of the garage over a period of time, and the vapours made an explosive mixture which ignited because of Miss Skewes' cigarette.

The Mid-Cornwall Coroner Mr Edward Carlyon said "There is no suggestion it was a fire deliberately started", and recorded a verdict of misadventure.

Later Mr Alec David Richards of Wareham, Dorset thanked Mr Glasson and Mr Johns for the part they played in helping his cousin, and to the firemen, police and hospital staff.

Dr Sidney John Hopkins, deputy county pathologist, said Miss Skewes had third degree burns over sixty per cent of her skin area. Mainly the burning was on the left side. Death, he said, was from toxaemia due to third degree burns.

WB 19 October 1972
MUFFLED PEALS AT CROWAN
Muffled peals were rung at Crowan Parish Church on Friday before the funeral service of Miss ERNESTINE MARY SKEWES, aged 61 years, of Gilmore, Crowan. Only child of the late Rev.H.J. and Mrs Skewes, formerly of Chacewater, she came to Crowan with her parents in 1925.

Educated at Truro High School, she trained as a teacher, but relinquished her training duties in order to look after her invalid mother and to assist her father in his duties as vicar of Crowan.

After her mother's death in 1942 she became a civilian clerk with Cornwall Constabulary at Camborne, and later Redruth. She retired in June after 30 years service.

At Crowan she directed the St Crewenna Players until they were disbanded.

The Rev.J.E. Beckerlegge, vicar, officiated at the funeral service, assisted by Canon R.O. Oatey, an old friend of Miss Skewes' family. Cremation was at Penmount.

Family mourners were Mr and Mrs A.D. Richards; Mrs Susan Wasley; Mr G. Richards; Mr J. Mills; Miss M. Goldsworthy and Mrs E. Lavin (cousins).

The Cornwall and Devon Police were represented by Divisional Commandant R.F. May and Assistant Commandant A.J. Dunstan. Also in the large congregation were uniformed sergeants and constables from Camborne and Redruth area, and many ex-police officers.

Morning Telegraph, Sheffield 7 September 1973
OUT TO BOOST JOBS AND WAGES
Dr IAIN SKEWIS became Yorkshire and Humberside's new industry getter yesterday. ..... and promptly announced he was out to get the region more jobs and higher wages.

Dr Skewis, a 37-year-old Scot, was named as the first director of the Yorkshire and Humberside Development Association, the top post with a salary of £9000 a year.

Dr Skewis plans to spend his first month on a factfinding tour of the region before he downs to plan a strategy of selling Yorkshire and Humberside to industrialists.

And he plans to do his selling on hard facts.

"I'm no believer in the wining and dining method of attracting industrialists. I'm going to give them the hard stuff — facts", he said yesterday.

Dr Skewis said the region needed more jobs and more better paid jobs. "A recent survey showed Yorkshire and Humberside bottom of the league table in wages for manual workers and manufacturers.

"Even in the area where there is full employment at the moment there is no reason for complacency", he said.

The new association — which had its origin at a Leeds conference a year ago — is being backed by all the big local authorities with the exception of Doncaster and Barnsley County Boroughs, and has a first year's budget of £42,000.

Government grants are hoped for later to boost the budget.

Doncaster is already linked to the association through the town's Development Council and both South Yorkshire towns are expected to become fully involved next year following local government reorganisation.

The chairman of the Association, Rotherham's Alderman Stan Crowther, pointed out yesterday that South Yorkshire was one of the problem areas of the region which Doctor Skewis will be tackling.

The association has already put in a bid for the proposed new factory of British Leyland and it was suggested yesterday that South Yorkshire could provide the right site and labour for this project.

Dr Skewis, who is planning a central planning centre at his Leeds base, sees the transport facilities and key "European" position of the region with its Humberside outlet to the Continent as two of the key selling points to industrialists.

Before taking up his present post Dr Skewis was managing director of the Cromarty Firth Development Company and before that director of industrial development and marketing with the Highland and Islands Development Board.

Manchester Evening News 25 October 1973
A NEW CAREER AT 62:
Former Cheshire baker and confectioner JACK SKUES has been ordained into the ministry of the United Church of Canada at Valleyfield, Quebec, at the age of 62.

Mr Skues was in business in Stockport for may years before moving to Blackpool with his wife Lily to take over a guest house. He was a Methodist local preacher both in Stockport and Blackpool.

Seven years ago they went out to join their daughters in Canada, where Mr Skues became a full time lay pastor at a mission station at Harrington Harbour, Labrador.

In the summer he and his wife did their parish visiting by specially built boat and in the winter they travelled around by motorised sledge.

Mr Skues took up the pastorate at Valleyfield three years ago and studied for the ministry by taking college courses in the summer.

His sister-in-law, Mrs M. Hardern of Blackpool, flew over to Canada for the ordination ceremony.

W.B. 20 December 1973
Mr and Mrs H. SKEWES of Mithian, St Agnes, wish all relatives and friends a Merry Christmas and a Happy New Year.

Bournemouth Echo 25 March 1974
Deaths: DORIS EILEEN SKUES of Bearwood, 19 De Redvers Road, Parkstone, peacefully at Poole Hospital on 23 March, 1974 aged 61 years, beloved wife of Richard and mother of Keith. Funeral service at St Luke's Church, Parkstone on Thursday, 28 March at 11.30am, followed by cremation at Bournemouth. Cut flowers only to H.J. Cole and Sons (Funeral Directors) 68/70 Lagland Street, Poole 4047.

The Times 25 March 1974
SKUES: On 23 March, peacefully at Poole General Hospital, aged 61 years, DORIS EILEEN, of Bearwood, 19 De Redvers Road, Parkstone, Poole, Dorset, beloved wife of RICHARD and mother of KEITH. Funeral service Thursday 28 March at 11.30am at St Luke's Parish Church, Parkstone, followed by cremation at Bournemouth Crematorium.

Daily Telegraph 25 March 1974.
SKUES: On 23 March, peacefully at Poole General Hospital, aged 61 years, DORIS EILEEN, of Bearwood, 19 De Redvers Road, Parkstone, Poole, Dorset, beloved wife of RICHARD and mother of KEITH. Funeral service Thursday 28 March at 11.30am at Luke's Parish Church, Parkstone, followed by cremation at Bournemouth Crematorium.

Bournemouth Evening Echo 20 April 1974
KEITH SKUES QUITS BBC
KEITH SKUES is leaving the BBC to become Head of Programmes for Radio Hallam, the commercial station which will serve the Sheffield and Rotherham areas.
Keith, whose father lives in Parkstone, was editor of the BBC's longest-running broadcast "The Story of Pop", which ran for six months and was heard by millions all over the world.
Radio Hallam hopes to go on air in October and Keith as Head of Programmes will become a director of the company which will run it. He commences on 1 May officially, although he has already attended several board meetings.
Keith will be responsible for engaging staff to serve throughout the broadcasting side, and will probably take over some of the broadcasting commitments himself.
He joined the BBC in July, 1967 and subsequently appeared in several well-known shows, perhaps the one for which he will be best remembered being Saturday Club.
Incidentally Keith will be on television in the near future when, in the BBC 1 comedy series "The Rough With the Smooth", he plays the part of — a radio announcer.
Keith's broadcasting career has taken him to many parts of the world — research for "The Story of Pop", for example took him to America and Elvis Presley.
In Kenya, two of his shows won awards from local papers, and whilst in East Africa he climbed both Mount Kilimanjaro and Mount Kenya.
Away from his many broadcasting commitments, Keith is an active worker for spastics and a vice president of the National Association of Youth Clubs.

The Scillonian, Winter, 1975
HARRY SKEWES, BOS'N OF "THE SCILLONIAN" DIES
Mr HARRY SKEWES, who has served the Isles of Scilly Steamship Company during the past 21 years aboard two Scillonians and The Queen of the Isles, died on 3 June at St Mary's Hospital, aged 52 years. During much of the time he was boatswain of the Scillonian and Queen of the Isles. He was well known and popular with visitors and Penzance and Island residents.
Mr Skewes was a single man, without close relations, but Old Town Church, St Mary's was filled with mourners paying their last respects when the funeral was held. The service was conducted by the Chaplain to the Isles (Rev. T. McCabe) and members of the Islands RAOB Lodge were bearers. A half-sister Mrs Iris Harvey travelled to the islands for the service.
During recent years Mr Skewes had a flat at No 2 South Terrace, Penzance, but in most respects The Scillonian was his real home, and for many years the vessel was his only address. He was admitted to St Mary's Hospital three days ago. Believed to have joined the Royal Navy as a boy seaman Mr Skewes began his career with the Steamship Company on board The Scillonian in 1954. During the years 1965-1970 when the company operated the Queen of the Isles, Mr Skewes served as Bos'n, taking his radio officer's certificate.

Helston Packet 15 December 1975
SURPRISE FAMILY PARTY
Mr and Mrs W.J. SKEWES, of Redannack Estate, Mullion were entertained to a surprise family party at St Mary's Hall, Helston to celebrate their golden wedding anniversary. Before her marriage 50 years ago Mrs Skewes was Miss Bessie Curnow, from Cury. Her husband William, smallholder and village postman, has spent his whole life in Mullion.
Mr and Mrs Skewes are members of Mullion Old Cornwall Society and Mrs Skewes also belongs to the Evergreen Club. A large decorated iced cake was cut for the party, which was attended by 50 guests.

WB 4 March 1976
PARISH CHURCH WEDDING FOR HELSTON BRIDE
A senior chemist assistant at Boots, Helston, Miss Hazel Jean Williams, was married at St Michael's Church, Helston, to Mr CHRISTOPHER JOHN SKEWES, son of Mr and Mrs W. SKEWES of 27 Beacon-parc, Helston. The Rev. J.E.M. Woollan (vicar) officiated. The bride, daughter of Mr and Mrs Frank Williams, of 3 West Close, Gwealdues, Helston was given away by her father, and wore a white gown with long train and full-length veil. She was attended by Miss Dinah Putman and two flower-girls, Natalie Reed and Sarah Treloar.
A reception for 45 guests was held at the Waterwheel Restaurant, Wendron Forge. The honeymoon is being spent touring.
The bridegroom is a welder at Porthleven Shipyard. They will reside at Lady Street, Helston.

West Australian, 11 September 1976
TWO DIE IN ACCIDENT
A former Matron of the Mount Barker Hospital, Mrs FRANCES SKEWES and her husband Mr ANGUS SKEWES, died after a traffic accident in Victoria yesterday.
Their car collided with a semi-trailer. They were returning from Melbourne to their home at Phillip Island.
Mrs Skewes was the first infant health sister in the Mount Barker district. She was particularly interested in the welfare of Aborigines and was instrumental in having traditional houses built on the reserve.
Although a resident of Victoria for several years, she made frequent visits to Mount Barker and continued to give a prize for the best garden on the reserve until the reserve was closed.

Western Morning News, 6 November 1976
Death: SKEWES-COX
On 4 November, peacefully at Uphill after a sudden illness, GILLIAN, darling wife of MILES and beloved mother of NICOLA. Cremation private. Memorial service later.

W.B. 16 December 1976
Death: SKEWES
On Tuesday 14 December at his home 7 Chegwyn Gardens, St Agnes, BERTRAM, aged 74 years, beloved husband of LILY, loving father of PAM and MARLENE and darling pappa of Nicholas, Adrian and Gary. Funeral service in St Agnes Methodist Church tomorrow at 2.30pm followed by interment in St Agnes Cemetery.

Helston Packet 17 June 1977
HIS OWN FLOWERS IN CHURCH
The funeral service took place at Mullion Church of Mr WILLIAM JOHN SKEWES of 42 Redannack Estate, Mullion. He was 76. Mr and Mrs Skewes celebrated their golden wedding anniversary two years ago.
Mr Skewes loved his garden, which became his main interest during his retirement.
Flowers from his garden decorated the church for the funeral service which was conducted by Rev. Alan J. Sadler.
Mr Skewes was a member of the St Mellans Park Playing Fields Committee.

WB 27 October 1977
Mrs. J.V. SKEWES
The funeral service took place at Centenary Methodist Church, Camborne of Mrs JESSIE VICTORIA SKEWES (80) of Trecarne, 12 Atlantic Terrace, Camborne. The Rev. D.W. Elworthy officiated. She had lived at Camborne since her marriage to Mr JAMES HENRY OSWALD SKEWES in 1921.

WB 10 November 1977
Births: SKEWES
OSSIE and PAT (née Williams) are happy to announce the safe arrival on October 29th 1977, of a daughter AMANDA ELIZABETH SKEWES. Grateful thanks to the staff at Treliske.

WB 20 July 1978
Death: SKEWES
On Monday 17 July at the home of his daughter and son-in-law Mr and Mrs M. Trevethan of Meadow Vean, Bolingey, JAMES HENRY SKEWES, aged 70 years of Woodlands, Mithian; husband of the late FLORENCE SKEWES and beloved father of JILL, DAWN and IRENE. Funeral today (Thursday). Service at Mithian Chapel at 2.00pm followed by interment in St Agnes Cemetery.
No flowers, but donations if desired for the heart research to the funeral director, J.H.D. White, Boscavene, Mount Hawke.

The Day, New London, Connecticut, USA 9 March 1979
New London: BROTHERS TO FACE EACH OTHER IN NATIONALS
It's called the pommel horse, and some consider it the most difficult even in gymnastics.
But the SKEWES brothers of Waterford — both nationally ranked — will try to make it look easy as they go against national competition, and each other, later this month.
ED SKEWES, the elder, is a senior at Springfield College and is ranked number one in the nation on the pommel horse among small and medium-sized colleges.
DAVE SKEWES, 22, a senior at the Coast Guard Academy, is ranked 11th.
Their parents are ROBERT and ELAINE SKEWES of 188 Rope Ferry Road in Waterford, and their inspiration was their brother ROBERT, a gymnast specialising in the horse, who graduated from the Academy in 1973.

Ed Skewes, in fact, was an all America gymnast twice at the Academy. He left the Academy a year ago and transferred to Springfield. Ed and Dave will go to the National Collegiate Athletic Association's Small College Championships 29th to 31st March, travelling almost half-way across the country to the University of Northern Iowa for a compulsory and an optional performance, each of which lasts about 40 seconds.

Dave Skewes, captain of the Academy gymnastics team, recalled that he and his brother Ed were pretty close in ability in their years at Waterford High School. But by his senior year, Ed began to excel at a faster rate. But Dave believes the gap has begun to close again. "This is the first time we will be competing against each other. Our parents are very loyal and they want both of us to do the best we can. They have never favoured either of us", added Dave.

Evening Echo, Bournemouth 15 March 1979
MARATHON FAMILY TREE QUEST NEARS COMPLETION
Former BBC newsreader KEITH SKUES, whose father RICHARD lives in Branksome Park, is off globe-trotting again — but for a very different reason than his previous excursions.
In 1971, he compered the first-ever discotheque held in a show in South Africa.
In 1973 he went to America to interview stars for his 26 one-hour Radio One documentaries "The Story of Pop", and only last year Keith, now Programme Director of Sheffield's Radio Hallam, parachuted into the frozen wilds of Labrador on an RAF survival course.
He later went back to the other side of Canada and twice to Northern Ireland.
Now he's off to Mexico and the United States to complete work on a mammoth project, tracing his family tree.
His father tells me that Skues is a Cornish name and comes from Helston.
Keith actually started research into his unusual surname while still at school. This developed into correspondence with people called Skues, Skewes, Skewis and Skews.
For the past ten years he has spent his annual holiday in Truro, making further enquiries into his family tree.
The work is now nearing completion after 25 years, and a copy is at the County Record Office, Truro and County Museum. His own side of the family he finished 10 years ago, but it's the almost impossible task of tracing every other branch world-wide since 1968 that has been occupying his time this past decade. Soon, he should be in a position to publish the complete work, comprising 16 chapters, incorporating 65 separate branches, including those living in Mexico, the States, Australia, New Zealand and South Africa.

Evening Advertiser, Swindon 28 March 1979
KINSMAN IN THE WILD WEST
I was interested to read about the group who intend to carry on the traditions of the old Wild West (AE 17 March). Talk of the West reminds me of a kinsman of mine, a real hero of many years ago. I possess an old faded picture showing some of the famous men of that period. The photograph was taken in Norfolk, Nebraska, USA. Depicted are Doc Carver, Idaho Bill, Diamond Dick, Pawnee Bill, Captain North and Deadwood Dick, my great-uncle. They are not a very distinguished group, but are dressed in the style of the day in their working clothes. They are wearing large stetson hats, drooping moustaches, and guns slung at the knee. Richard Bullock, my kinsman, was a Cornish tin miner, and when eventually work got slack, at the age of 26, he emigrated to America where he managed to get work in the gold mining business.
While working there, stage coaches running from the Black Hills to the settlements were robbed so regularly that the miners despaired of getting their shipments through.
Richard gave up his work and declared war on the highwaymen, becoming one of the Homestake Mining Company's bullion guards, and many were the tales of bravery he attracted.
One of the most notorious of his feats was the shooting of Lame Johnny, the most daring of bandits. Deadwood Dick was guarding a stage travelling over the old Cheyenne Road when Johnny stepped out to hold it up. It was Johnny's last job.
Richard lived to the ripe old age of 76 in spite of his many injuries and was buried in California ...... without his boots on. If anyone's interested they can visit the museum at Truro, where they have all the facts about Cornwall's greatest hero, although I'm afraid not many of the Cornish people have heard of him today.
ALBERT SKEWS, South View Road, Swindon.

Sheffield Chronicle 6 April 1979
SKEWES, SKUES? KEITH's OFF AFTER CLUES
What's in a name? An awful lot if Programme Director of Sheffield's Radio Hallam is anything to go by.
For KEITH SKUES, who in his Radio One days was no stranger to globe-trotting, is soon to travel outside the station's transmission area to do a little research. To Mexico, Canada and America to be precise. The much travelled boss of the commercial station is off to dig deep to find the roots of his family tree!
It's the culmination of a massive project which started 25 years ago. But even before that when Keith was at school he was actively looking into his family's past.
The name "Skues" has Cornish traditions and during Keith's schooldays he actually tracked down, and corresponded with, people with similar surnames: Skues, Skewes, Skewis and Skews.
Every year, when he gets a break from Hallam, Keith travels to Cornwall digging deeper.
His monster project is now almost complete and he will soon be able to publish the work which will include 65 separate branches of the family stretching all over the world.

Sheffield Chronicle 14 September 1979
THE SKELETONS IN KEITH SKUES' CUPBOARD
If you fancy digging up your family tree, beware — you never know what horrors you might unearth.
Just ask KEITH SKUES. He decided to go in search of his roots and ended up discovering all sorts of skeletons in the

family cupboard. "There's a place in Cornwall called Skewes, where seven murders happened in rapid succession. The bloke got hanged for his troubles, though."

He also discovered that one of his distant ancestors was a bigamist who had twelve children.

Radio Hallam's Programme Director took off four weeks earlier this year to track down his family's "Mexican Connection."

And then the American Connection...... and the Canadian Connection. Although the name hails from Cornwall, "every post brings news of other members of the family", he said. "The repercussions of the trip have been tremendous."

On his office wall is a detailed chart, which he mapped out himself. That gives only the smallest hint of the endless mine of information he has amassed. And now he's got to find the time to finish the book, "Cornish Heritage", which has been postponed until at least next April.

It's almost 30 years since Keith began to wonder where his odd sounding name came from. And the variations, such as Skewes, Skewis, Skews, Skuse and even Skuce, total a staggering 64 in all!

And there are as many branches of the family, too, he claims.

But why should a former disc jockey turned radio director go in for such an obscure and "obsessive" hobby?

"Because I need the change from my work. I adore my job, but the hours are long, and it is hectic and high-pressured on a busy commercial station."

Keith admits that the cost of his hobby can shoot sky-high. "I send out copies of my findings to everyone who has helped me — even those who live abroad."

Western Morning News 4 January 1980
COLONEL's DEATH: NO FOUL PLAY
Police have ruled out foul play in their probe into the death of 59-year-old Lt.-Col. MILES SKEWES-COX, founder and chairman of the Dartmoor Badger Protection League, who died in Torbay Hospital a week after being found injured at his moorland home.

A post-mortem examination by Home Office Dr Albert Hunt has shown that there were no suspicious circumstances surrounding the death on Boxing Day of the retired Army Pay Corps officer.

On 19 December Col. Skewes-Cox was found unconscious with head injuries in the bedroom at Uphill, Ponsworthy. The colonel did not regain consciousness.

Mr Alan Peach, Devon and Cornwall police press officer said yesterday, "We are satisfied that no other person was involved in the incident and that foul play is not suspected."

A Torquay inquest was opened and adjourned yesterday by Mr Henry Sykes-Balls, Torbay and South Devon Coroner.

Constable Fred Stuttaford said that the body was identified by 32-year-old Dr Peter Edwards, of Buckfastleigh health centre. The colonel had been a patient of Doctor Edwards for three years and he had last seen him alive on 10 December, when he was complaining of depression.

Col. Skewes-Cox formed the Badger Protection League six months ago, when the Ministry of Agriculture was poised to start a gassing operation on South Dartmoor.

He led many protests and his league, which now has 10,000 members, won its fight when the Minister for Agriculture, Mr Peter Walker, halted the operation and agreed to set up an inquiry.

Southern Evening Echo, 13 August 1980
DOWN BY THE RIVER, A PILGRIMAGE IN WELLIES
Non-fishing enthusiasts might not take a bright shine to the idea of spending their leisure day up to their wellies in water, and there are many wives bored and bordered along these flowing rivers of ours who think that a Bloody Butcher is rather more than simply a name for a special fly.

But the scene can be imagined out there on Saturday at Abbots Barton Fisheries near Winchester when certain devotees gathered for a piscean pontification on a special memorial that was duly unveiled, with full fishcal ceremony.

The occasion was one of those rare magic moments in the fishing calendar, the memorial dedicated to GEORGE EDWARD MACKENZIE SKUES who, though his name may not be exactly household, is indeed well known along these banks.

Mr Skues is something of a fishing legend and Saturday's solemnity was to mark the 31st anniversary of the death of the man who from 1883 fished the waters thereabouts.

A Skues Memorial Appeal had been launched and, according to the organisers — Roy Darlington of Bishop's Waltham among them — it was most gratifying to discover that so many fly-fishers did indeed appreciate the worth of that grand old gentleman whose fishy writings are a must for devotees.

Donations came flying in, you might say, but few were apparently prepared to put their admiration on paper in search for a suitable memorial inscription. Simply saying that people give pleasure isn't always enough.

But an inscription had to be found and the committee were prepared to undertake the formidable task of selecting the right words. The honour fell upon Dr Christopher Jarman who submitted three succinct lines:

"In Memory of George Edward Mackenzie Skues who fished these waters from 1883 to 1938. A man who had a way with a trout."

Jealousy guarding their preserves, the Appeal committee went on to urge members to regard the ceremony as a special occasion. Don't invite other guests they said. Shame!

But though fishermen are noted for their private protection of all that is dear to them, their leaders' practicality wasn't lost in another message to members (and, of course those who contributed to the fund) that since the memorial was to be placed in the water meadows it was very wise indeed to bring along a pair of wellingtons. It was one of those days which made non-fishers realise just what pull the sport has on so many different people.

Among the wellied throng was DJ Keith Skues who had more than one good reason for escaping for the day. He's a great nephew of George Edward Mackenzie Skues and has, in fact, just written a book on the Skues family. As one misty-eyed indulgent put it just a couple of days before the Big Day. "Tis all very 'ampshire and should be fun."

Who could doubt it — except, perhaps, some of the wives?

Hampshire Chronicle 15 August 1980
ABBOTS BARTON MEMORIAL TO G.E.M. SKUES
A name forever linked with the River Itchen at Winchester is that of GEORGE EDWARD MACKENZIE SKUES, one of the best loved and most prolific writers in the past century.

It was appropriate, therefore, that Saturday, August 9th, the 31st anniversary of his death, should have seen the unveiling of the Skues Memorial in the form of a stone seat set on the banks of his beloved stream at Abbots Barton, opposite the spot where his ashes were scattered on the eastern bank of the Itchen by William Mullins, his old friend and river keeper, in the winter of 1949.

Skues was a weekend fisherman, often escaping from his lawyer's practice on Friday afternoons in time to enjoy the evening rise at Winchester. He travelled down from London by train, lodging at No. 16, City Road, then a guest house and since used as a labour exchange and offices. Today the "Corner House", as the fishermen still call it, is up for sale.

Among Skues' books, so well known to all river trout fisherman are *The Way of a Trout with a Fly, Minor Tactics of the Chalk Streams, Sidelines, Sidelights and Reflections, Itchen Memories* and the latest collection of his works *The Way of a Man with a Trout,* compiled by Donald Overfield and published in 1977.

Skues fished the Abbots Barton for an incredible 56 seasons, during which time he introduced a number of fly patterns in use today, including the Orange Quill, Little Red Sedge, and a series of nymph dressings. He is best remembered as the man who in the face of bitter opposition, argued the case for the use of sub-surface flies, and developed his highly successful method of nymph fishing which is still practised on rivers throughout the world.

Many of today's angling personalities were present at the ceremony including Donald Overfield, John Goddard and Gordon Mackie, as were Mr Keith Skues (great nephew of G.E.M. Skues), Mrs Iris Whitfield, owner of the Abbots Barton estate, and Roy Darlington, lessee of the fishing, whose devotion and unceasing work during the past seven years has so vastly improved the quality of the sport there. A few who attended were ready for action in full fishing garb, complete with rod. The occasion was delightfully informal, as Skues himself would doubtless have wished. Donald Overfield reminded the gathering of the great traditions of Abbots Barton and the unique place which the fishing holds in the history of trout fishing. He stressed that thanks were due entirely to Roy Darlington for having brought the fishery back to something approaching its former glory and that the ceremony was the happy culmination of Roy's long-held dream to erect a permanent memorial to this grand old Itchen fisherman. Keith Skues unveiled the seat, revealing some of the family's history, and of the character of G.E.M., who strongly insisted upon the correct spelling and pronunciation of his name.

Roy Darlington gave a charming address and Mrs Whitfield told of the day when her family came to Abbots Barton quite unaware, as farmers, of the value of the water which was included in the property.

The ceremony was followed by a splendid buffet which the ladies had prepared in the marquee.

Anglers from many parts of the world had sent contributions to the memorial fund and offered suggestions for a suitable epitaph. That chosen, one of the simplest, was submitted by Doctor Christopher Jarman — "In Memory of G.E.M. Skues who fished these waters from 1883-1938. A man who had the way with a trout."

The Times, 21 August 1980
SKUES A GRAND MASTER OF HIS TIME
A London solicitor, short and baggy and slightly bald, with stubby fingers and a good sight left only in one eye, recently had a stone memorial unveiled for him on the banks of the River Itchen, just above Winchester, 31 years after his death.

GEORGE EDWARD MACKENZIE SKUES (1858-1949) had a practice in Essex Street, off the Strand, and to some was a fine and reliable though pedestrian lawyer; to others a rather grumpy old man who never married and who liked cats, a man unnoticed in a crowd, though with a fierce eye — only the one eye — when aroused, as he often was, attempting and failing to suffer fools gladly. He was though, essentially a kindly man, and often lonely and sad in his old age, but he had two qualities which have assured him a certain amount of immortality and a stone memorial and bronze plaque.

Skues was a great fly fisherman. How great is difficult to say, because there are no batting averages as a yardstick for greatness with a fly, but he was, shall we say, one of the grandmasters of his time, and with his one eye could probably see more than most anglers with two; but the reason, above all others why he is so much revered by so many is that he could write. His books, printed and reprinted, still sell, are still read now more for pleasure than instruction, because of their evocation of the sights and sounds and smells of the river. They are remarkable, not only for that, but also for the acute observation, that shines from every page, of the habits and the ways of trout. So great an impact do they make that fishermen from two continents, or possibly three, depending on geological definitions, travel very long ways on a pilgrimage to the waters where Skues fished from 1883 to 1938, where his ashes were scattered, and where the memorial now records his achievements as a fisherman who had a way with a trout — a play on words taken from the title of one of his books.

Adelaide Advertiser, Australia; 27 August 1980
SOLICITORS SUSPENDED BY FULL COURT
Two Naracoorte solicitors convicted of conspiracy charges in Victoria last year were yesterday suspended from practice by the South Australia Full Court.

The Law Society of South Australia has applied to have the names of EDWARD FOSTER SKEWES and Francis

Vyner-Smith struck off the rolls. The Full Court for the hearing consisted of Justice Mitchell, Justice Mohr and Justice Matheson.

By a majority of two to one, the court suspended the two solicitors until further order.

The court also referred the matter to the Master of the Supreme Court, who will conduct a hearing and make a report.

Skewes and Vyner-Smith were convicted of the conspiracy charges in the Victorian Supreme Court in June, 1979. When the full court hearing began on 14 August, Justice Mitchell said it was in the nature of a scandal that the application had taken more than a year to get to court.

Halifax Evening Courier, 9 September 1980
DEATHS: SKUES
On 4 September 1980 at Higgins Close, LUCY SKUES, of 11 Bell Hall Terrace, loved sister of EVELYN, ERIC and FRED. Service at St Jude's Church, Savile Park at 11 o'clock on Friday, followed by interment at All Saint's Cemetery.

Family flowers only, please, but donations in lieu to St Jude's Church, c/o Rev. M. Walker, St Jude's Vicarage, Savile Park, Halifax, would be appreciated.

*   *   *

The writer is most grateful to Dawn Troy of the Archives Authority of New South Wales, Sydney, Australia and Mary McRae, Principal Archivist of Archives Office of Tasmania, for information concerning THOMAS SKEWES, pages 622 and 623.

Single. Aged 25. Height 5'7". Complexion — fresh. Colour of hair — brown. Colour of eyes — grey. He was accused of murder but found guilty of manslaughter by a civil jury on 7th November 1840 and sentenced to be transported to Van Dieman's Land for a period of 14 years.

He was sent to Sydney Gaol, then located in George Street, and on 26th November 1840 was sent to Hyde Park Barracks "to be identified" then returned to the gaol. On 30th November 1840 he embarked on board the ship *Abercromby* to be conveyed to Van Dieman's Land.

On arrival in Van Dieman's Land more information was taken from Skewes. He was the son of Richard Skewes, spirit maker. He had five brothers — James, Peter, August, John and Noah — and two sisters, Susannah and Elizabeth. He had previously been living in Falmouth. Whilst in Van Dieman's Land he was given nine months' probation on 15th December 1840. On 2 January 1843 he was sent to Royal Engineers Department for being disobedient. Again a further time at the Royal Engineers Department (2 May 1843) for misconduct and improperly obtaining a letter and opening and returning a letter. He was kept to hard labour in chains at his trade for six months. Nowhere in the records does it list Skewes as being pardoned or given a ticket of leave. One can only assume he was freed by servitude, although there are no records as to his leaving Tasmania. Where he went after 1843 remains a mystery. After a convict was freed no record was kept.

References: Colonial Secretary. Copies of Letters to the Sheriff 31st August 1838-29th June 1840, AO NSW ref. 4/3901, reel 1064. Letter no. 40/198 dated 26th November 1840, page 346 and Letter no. 40/203 dated November 1840, page 349.
Colonial Secretary. Assignment lists of Convicted Sentenced to Transportation for colonial Offences and sent to Van Dieman's Land, 31st December 1832-24th November 1853 AO NSW ref. 4/4523 Reel 901.
Convict Records: 31/41/2840 and 16/1/p.152-153, Tasmania.

Right: *Signs which greet the visitor to the North Yorkshire village of Skewsby*

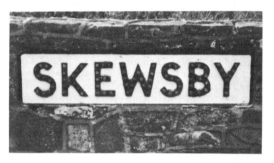

Below: *The racehorse Skewsby (ridden by P. Tuck), owned by Mr A. Phillips and trained by M. W. Easterby of Sheriff Hutton, winning the Healaugh Novice's Hurdle (Div. II) at Wetherby on 15 January 1980. Skewsby also had successful seasons in 1981 and 1982*

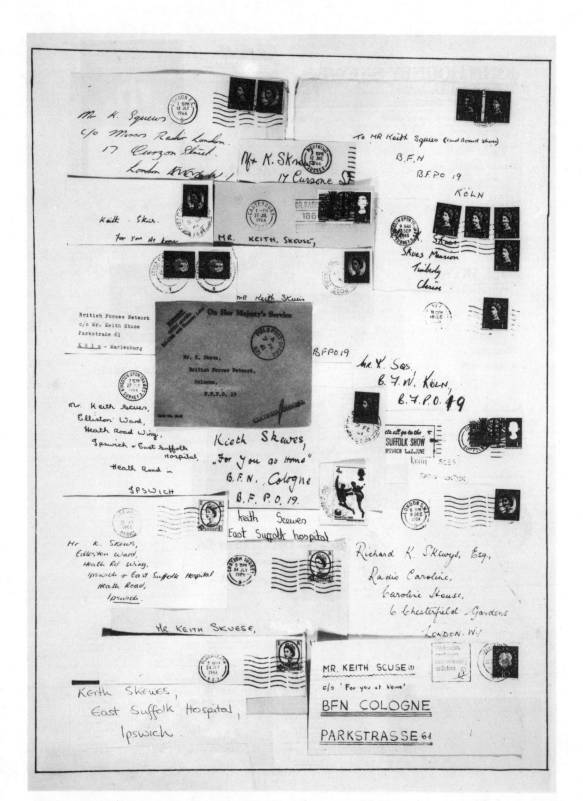

Various spellings of the author's name collected in the 1960's

Visiting cards & headed notepaper by different members of the Skewes/Skews/Skues Family

Richard Skues of
Helston, Cornwall   1756

June 9th 1819

Richard Skues of
Helston, Cornwall   1819

Richard Skues of
Branksome Park,
Poole, Dorset   1970

Richard Keith Skues
Sheffield, South
Yorkshire   1982

Index

N

Z